GW00862920

Bingham and Berrymans'
Motor Claims Cases

Bingham and Berrymans'
Motor Claims Cases

Tenth edition

Paul J Taylor LLB
Senior Partner, Berrymans

Timothy G Oliver BA (Law)
Partner, Berrymans

Michael Pether BA
Solicitor, Berrymans

With a chapter on legal aid by
David Lawton MA
Partner, Budd Martin Burrett

Butterworths
London, Dublin, Edinburgh
1994

United Kingdom	Butterworth & Co (Publishers) Ltd, Halsbury House, 35 Chancery Lane, London WC2A 1EL and 4 Hill Street, Edinburgh EH2 3JZ
Australia	Butterworths, Sydney, Melbourne, Brisbane, Adelaide, Perth, Canberra and Hobart
Canada	Butterworths Canada Ltd, Toronto and Vancouver
Ireland	Butterworth (Ireland) Ltd, Dublin
Malaysia	Malayan Law Journal Sdn Bhd, Kuala Lumpur
New Zealand	Butterworths of New Zealand Ltd, Wellington and Auckland
Puerto Rico	Butterworth of Puerto Rico, Inc, San Juan
Singapore	Butterworths Asia, Singapore
South Africa	Butterworths Publishers (Pty) Ltd, Durban
USA	Butterworth Legal Publishers, Carlsbad, California and Salem, New Hampshire

A CIP Catalogue record for this book is available from the British Library.

First published 1946

ISBN 0 406 02016 7

Printed and bound in Great Britain by Mackays of Chatham plc, Chatham, Kent

This edition is dedicated, with much respect, to John Arthur Taylor, the editor of the fourth to ninth editions, who died in January 1993

Preface

This, the tenth edition, brings the law up to date to October 1994. Unlike most earlier editions and supplements, there is no single reason for a new edition, but rather the need to bring the entire work up to date and under control. Although this is the first edition since the 1960s for which John Taylor was in no way responsible, the current editors have sought to reflect his views on the need to prune and reorganise, as well as introducing their own. Over 187 new cases have been added and 100 deleted. Many chapters have been completely reorganised; the key to this reorganisation is to be found in the detailed contents list.

The time when the law relating to motor claims was developing and expanding rapidly has passed, but this book still seeks to provide practical guidance and information to all practitioners involved with motor and personal injury insurance litigation, whether insurance claims handlers, loss adjusters, solicitors, barristers or even, on occasion, judges. It remains predominantly a case book but explanation and comment is provided by the editors on various topics to demonstrate both the current law and, where appropriate, its development over recent years. It is hoped that the reorganisation of this work will allow reference to particular subjects or cases to be both easier and quicker.

There have been few major developments in the law relating to liability, but the chapters dealing with damages have been expanded to cover provisional damages, structured settlements and the new Social Security provisions. Several cases demonstrate recent procedural changes (for example automatic directions and the early and compulsory exchange of witness statements) as well as the courts' encouragement of more open litigation—the 'cards on the table' approach.

The reluctance of the courts to accept more adventurous claims is covered by the inclusion of cases such as *Morris v Murray* and *Pitts v Hunt*, and the chapter dealing with the MIB Agreements has been fully updated with case summaries exploring the scope and application of the various Agreements.

We would like to thank our colleagues at Berrymans for their advice, encouragement and assistance in producing this new edition.

Paul Taylor
Timothy Oliver
Michael Pether

November 1994

Contents

Table of Statutes

References in this Table to *Statutes* are to Halsbury's Statutes of England (Fourth Edition) showing the volume and page at which the annotated text of an Act may be found.

Page references printed in **bold** type indicate where the section of an Act is set out in part or in full.

List of Cases

Page numbers printed in **bold** type indicate where case summaries may be found.

O

P

Q

R

CHAPTER 1

Negligence

1 LIABILITY FOR NEGLIGENCE

THE RULE

There are three elements to a cause of action for negligence: a duty to the person injured, a breach of that duty and foreseeability of loss.

There is a duty on the driver of a motor car to observe ordinary care or skill towards persons using the highway whom he could reasonably foresee as likely to be affected.

The concept of negligence has been developed over the course of the last century. There have been many attempts at a precise definition of negligence but in the words of Lord Atkin in *Donoghue v Stevenson* [1932] AC 562:

'To seek a complete logical definition of the general principle is probably to go beyond the function of the judge, for the more general the definition the more likely it is to omit essentials or to introduce non essentials.'

and per Lord Roskill in *Caparo Industries plc v Dickman* [1990] 1 All ER 568, HL:

'. . . There is no simple formula or touchstone to which recourse can be had in order to provide in every case a ready answer to the questions whether, given certain facts, the law will or will not impose liability for negligence or, in cases where such liability can be shown to exist, determine the extent of that liability. Phrases such as "foreseeability", "proximity", "neighbourhood", and "just and reasonable", "fairness", "voluntary exceptance of risk" or "voluntary assumption of responsibility" will be found used from time to time in the different cases. But, as your Lordships have said, such phrases are not precise definitions. At best they are but labels or phrases descriptive of the very different factual situations which can exist in particular cases and which must be carefully examined in each case before it can be pragmatically determined whether a duty of care exists and, if so, what is the scope and extent of that duty.'

Whether or not a duty of care exists depends so much on the particular circumstances of each individual case. Nevertheless, over the years the courts have given certain guidelines:

Blyth v Birmingham Water Works Co (1856) 11 Ex Ch 781, 25 LJ Ex 212, 4 WR 294:

'Negligence is the omission to do something which a reasonable man, guided upon those considerations which ordinarily regulate the conduct of human affairs, would do, or doing something which a prudent and reasonable man would not do.'

Donoghue v Stevenson [1932] AC 562, [1932] All ER Rep 1, 101 LJPC 119, 147 LT, 48 TLR 494, HL:

'The rule that you are to love your neighbour becomes, in law, you must not injure your neighbour; and the lawyer's question, who is my neighbour? receives a restricted reply. You must take reasonable care to avoid acts or omissions which you can reasonably foresee would be likely to injure your neighbour. Who, then, in law is my neighbour? The answer seems to be—persons who are so closely and directly affected by my act that I ought reasonably to have them in contemplation as being so affected when I am directing my mind to the acts or omissions which are called in question': per Lord Atkin.

Deyong v Shenburn [1946] KB 227, [1946] 1 All ER 226, 115 LJKB 262, 174 LT 129, 62 TLR 193, 90 Sol Jo 139, CA:

'It is not true to say that whenever a man finds himself in such a position that unless he does a certain act another person may suffer, or that if he does something and another person will suffer, then it is his duty in the one case to be careful to do the act and in the other case to be careful not to do the act. Any such preposition is much too wide. There has to be a breach of duty which the law recognises and to ascertain what the law recognises regard must be had to the decisions of the Courts': per du Parcq LJ.

Anglo-Saxon Petroleum Co v Admiralty Comrs [1947] KB 794, [1947] 2 All ER 465, [1948] LJR 153, 80 Ll L Rep 459, CA:

'The famous passage in Lord Atkin's opinion in *Donoghue v Stevenson* has been criticised as too wide: but not its essential principle, namely, that the duty of "diligence"—which word we use as correlative of "negligence"—is to be measured by such degree of skill and care as is requisite in the circumstances (which the actor knows or would know if he thought about it) for the purpose of safeguarding the interest of the potential plaintiff—the actor's "neighbour" in Lord Atkin's passage': per Scott LJ.

Nance v British Columbia Electric Rly Co Ltd [1951] AC 601, [1951] 2 All ER 448, [1951] 2 TLR 137, 95 Sol Jo 543, PC:

'In running down accidents, when two parties are so moving in relation to one another as to involve risk of collision, each owes to the other a duty to move with due care, and that is true whether they are both in control of vehicles, or both proceeding on foot, or whether one is on foot and the other controlling a moving vehicle. A pedestrian crossing the road owes a duty to the owner of a vehicle, eg if his rashness causes the vehicle to pull up so suddenly as to damage its mechanism, or as to result in following traffic running into it from behind, or in damage to the vehicle itself by contact with the pedestrian. When a man steps from a kerb into the roadway, he owes a duty to traffic which is approaching him with a risk of collision to exercise due care.'

Berrill v Road Haulage Executive [1952] 2 Lloyd's Rep 490:

'Paraphrasing the words of Lord Uthwatt in *London Passenger Transport Board v Upson* [1949] AC 155, [1949] 1 All ER 60, [1949] LJR 238, 65 TLR 9, 93 Sol Jo 40, HL, a driver is not bound to foresee every extremity of folly which occurs on the road. Equally he is certainly not entitled to drive upon the footing that other users of the road, either drivers or pedestrians, will exercise reasonable care. He is bound to anticipate any act which is reasonably foreseeable, which the experience of a road user teaches that people do, albeit negligently': per Slade J.

Note—See also *Nettleship v Weston*, p 59, below, on the duty of care of a driver.

Hughes v Lord Advocate [1963] AC 837, [1963] 1 All ER 705, [1963] 2 WLR 779, 107 Sol Jo 232, HL:

'In order to establish a coherent chain of causation it is not necessary that the precise details leading up to the accident should have been reasonably foreseeable: it is sufficient if the accident which occurred is of the type which should have been foreseeable by a reasonably careful person': per Lord Guest.

Yuen Kun-yeu v A-G of Hong Kong [1988] AC 175, [1987] 2 All ER 705:

'Foreseeability of harm does not of itself automatically lead to a duty of care. All the circumstances of the case, not only the foreseeability of harm, are to be taken into account in determining whether a duty of care arises. There needs to be sufficient close and direct relation between the parties to give rise to the duty of care': per Lord Keith.

D & F Estates Ltd v Church Comrs For England [1989] AC 177, [1988] 2 All ER 992, HL:

'No cause of action in tort arises in English law for the defective manufacture of an article which causes no injury other than injury to the defective article itself. If I buy a secondhand car to which there has been fitted a pneumatic tyre which, as a result of carelessness in manufacture, is dangerously defective and which bursts, causing injury to me or the car, no doubt the negligent manufacturer is liable in tort on the ordinary application of *Donaghue v Stevenson*. But if the tyre bursts without causing any injury other than to itself or if I discovered a defect before it bursts, I know of no principle upon which I can claim to recover from the manufacturer in tort the cost of making good the defect which, in practice, could only be the cost of supplying and fitting a new tyre. That would be, in effect, to attach to goods a non-contractual warranty of fitness which would follow the goods in whosoever hands they came. Such concept was suggested, obiter, by Lord Denning MR in Dutton's case, *Dutton v Bognor Regis United Building Co Ltd* but it was entirely unsupported by any authority and is, in my opinion, contrary to principle': per Lord Oliver.

Caparo Industries plc v Dickman [1990] 2 AC 605, [1990] 1 All ER 568, HL:

'What emerges is that, in addition to the foreseeability of damage, necessary ingredients in any situation giving rise to a duty of care are that there should exist between the party owing the duty and the parties to whom it is owed a relationship characterised by the law as one of "proximity" or "neighbourhood" and that the situation should be one in which the court considers it fair, just and reasonable that the law should impose a duty of a given scope on the one party for the benefit of the other': per Lord Bridge of Harwich.

Murphy v Brentwood District Council [1991] 1 AC 398, [1990] 2 All ER 908:

'It is preferable, in my view, that the law should develop novel categories of negligence incrementally and by analogy with established categories, rather than by a massive extension of prima facie duty of care restrained only by indefinable considerations with ought to negative, or to reduce or limit the scope of the duty or the class of persons to whom it is owed': per Brennan J in the Australian High Court case of *Sutherland Shire Council v Heyman* and approved of by the House of Lords.

CASES ON DUTY OF CARE

To whom a duty is owed

Muirhead v Industrial Tank Specialities

[1986] QB 507, [1985] 3 All ER 705, [1985] 3 WLR 993, 129 Sol Jo 855, CA
The plaintiff, a wholesale fishmonger, wanted to purchase lobsters in the summer and store them in tanks so he could sell them for higher prices at Christmas. The pump which kept the water in the tanks oxygenated continually failed. The plaintiff depended heavily on advice from the tank installers but neither knew of, nor had any contact with, the pump manufacturers. The judge held that there was sufficient reliance, in the circumstances, by the plaintiff on the manufacturers for a duty of care to be owed, and that the economic loss suffered, through loss of fish farm stock in stale uncirculated water, was reasonably foreseeable. The manufacturers appealed against this finding. He also held that the actual physical damage (ie the death of the lobsters) was unforeseeable. The plaintiff contended, on appeal, that this was wrong.
HELD, ON APPEAL: The manufacturers were not liable to the plaintiffs for economic loss. In the circumstances of this case there was no sufficient proximity or reliance by the plaintiff on the manufacturers to create a duty of care extending to liability for economic loss. But the physical damage (to the lobsters, as stock) was a foreseeable result of the pump motor failure and the manufacturers were liable for the cost of this and the consequential financial losses. *Junior Books Ltd v Veitchi Co Ltd* ([1983] 1 AC 520, [1982] 3 All ER 201, [1982] 3 WLR 477, 126 Sol Jo 538, HL) was very much a decision on its specific facts and represented only a very limited extension in principle.

Note—See also *Simaan General Contracting Co v Pilkington Glass Limited (No 2)* [1988] QB 758, [1988] 1 All ER 791, [1988] 2 WLR 761, 132 Sol Jo 463, CA.

Chaudhry v Prabhakar

[1988] 3 All ER 718, [1989] 1 WLR 29, 133 Sol Jo 82, CA
The plaintiff, who knew little about cars, asked a friend to find a car for her, which he agreed to do without payment. He found a car which a panel beater was offering for sale. The friend advised the plaintiff that the car was in very good condition, had not been involved in an accident, and that the vendor was a friend of his. In fact, the car had been involved in an accident, was unroadworthy, and he had never met the vendor before. The plaintiff brought an action against her friend as first defendant and the vendor as second defendant. The trial judge gave judgment against both defendants. The first defendant appealed.
HELD: The friend was a gratuitous agent of the plaintiff. The plaintiff had relied on the skill and judgment which he held himself out as possessing. The friend owed the plaintiff a duty of care in respect of the statements which he had made and on the evidence he was in breach of that duty, and was liable to her. Appeal dismissed.

Note—See also *Van Oppen v Clerk to the Bedford Charity Trustees* [1989] 1 All ER 273 when it was held that the school did not owe a duty to a pupil to obtain personal accident insurance or advise the pupils' parents to do so.

'The relationship of proximity which existed between the school and its pupils did not of itself give rise to a duty to insure or to protect the plaintiff's economic welfare. That was beyond what either party to the relationship contemplated': per Boreham J.

Eastman v South West Thames Regional Health Authority

(1991) RTR 389
The plaintiff was a passenger in the rear of an ambulance. She occupied a seat with no seat belt fitted. The driver braked non-negligently causing the plaintiff to be thrown from her seat and sustain injuries. The defendants accepted that they owed a duty to the plaintiff to take reasonable care for her safety in the ambulance. The plaintiff claimed that there had been a breach of this duty as the ambulanceman, the defendants' employee, had failed to advise the plaintiff to use a seat belt.
HELD: The defendants had discharged their duty as other seats with seat belts fitted were available and there was a sign in the rear of the ambulance advising the wearing of seat belts.

Burton v Islington Health Authority, de Martell v Merton and Sutton Health Authority

[1993] QB 204, [1992] 3 All ER 833, CA
The plaintiffs in these two actions had been injured *in-utero* during operations carried out on their mothers by the defendants' medical staff. As a consequence the plaintiffs were born with physical disabilities. The plaintiffs claimed that the defendant health authorities owed them a duty of care. The defendants argued that the damage was suffered by the plaintiffs whilst still *en ventre* and therefore they were not persons in the eyes of the English law. Thus, although subsequently born alive they could not sue.
HELD: The negligence of the defendants created a potential relationship between them and the plaintiffs which crystallised in the plaintiffs' birth. Thus, once born, the plaintiffs were clothed with the rights of action which they would have had if they were in existence at the date of the injury to the mothers.

Under the doctrine of *Donoghue v Stevenson* . . . an unborn child is within the foreseeable risk incurred by a negligent motorist (*S v Distillers Co (Bio Chemicals) Limited* [1969] 3 All ER 1412, [1970] 1 WLR 114: Per Fraser J).

Note—Actions arising after 22 July 1986 are subject to the Congenital Disabilities (Civil Liability) Act of 1976 which did not apply in this case.

Ancell v McDermott

[1993] 4 All ER 355, 137 Sol Jo LB 36, [1993] RTR 235
The police attended the scene of a road accident in which diesel fuel had been spilt. Two officers noted the spillage but left it to attend to the individuals involved in the accident. A car driven by one of the plaintiffs and in which the other plaintiff was a passenger later skidded on the diesel and collided with another vehicle as a result of which the plaintiffs suffered injury.

The question to be decided was whether individual police officers who, in the course of their employment, come across a potential hazard on the highway caused by a third party, owe a duty to individual members of the public who may subsequently be injured.

HELD: The extent of the duty owed depends on the precise circumstances such as the nature of the hazard, the extent of the danger and the likelihood of injury. In this instance the court did not consider that the officers' duty extended to the warning of an indeterminate number of third parties of an obvious hazard.

Cunningham v Reading Football Club Ltd

[1992] 1 PIQRP141 (Drake J)
The plaintiff was a police officer on duty at the defendants' football ground. The plaintiff was struck by a concrete missile thrown by some unruly fans. The plaintiff brought proceedings against the defendants on the basis that the defendants had taken insufficient steps to repair the ground and to exclude the hooligans.

HELD: The plaintiff's claim succeeded. Recent experience had shown that some fans would create trouble. It was foreseeable that these fans could break up part of the badly repaired terrace to use as missiles. The failure to make the match 'all ticket' was not negligent.

Foreseeability

THE RULE

Hay (or Bourhill) v Young

[1943] AC 92, [1942] 2 All ER 396, 111 LJPC 97, 167 LT 261, 86 Sol Jo 349, HL
A woman was at the front of a stationary tramcar on the offside loading a creel on to her back. A motor cyclist passed on the near side of the tramcar and collided with a car 45 to 50 feet ahead. The woman did not see the impact but merely heard the noise of the collision. She alleged shock caused by the noise of the collision. It was admitted that her terror did not involve any element of reasonable fear of immediate bodily injury to herself.

HELD: The motor cyclist owed no duty to the woman as he could not reasonably have foreseen the likelihood that she could be affected by his negligent act. She was outside the area of potential danger. The question was one of liability, not remoteness of damage. The mere accidental and unknown presence of a person upon the same street as, and somewhere within earshot of, the occurring of an accident in mid-carriageway, does not per se create any relationship of duty raising liability—some other and special element of immediacy is required.

Per Lord Wright: The breach of duty must be vis-à-vis the plaintiff. The plaintiff must sue for a wrong to herself. She cannot build on a wrong to somebody else. A blind or deaf man who crosses the traffic on a busy street cannot complain if he is run over by a careful driver who does not know of and could not be expected to observe and guard against the man's infirmity. These questions go to culpability, not compensation.

Per Lord Thankerton: The duty is to take such reasonable care as will avoid the risk of injury to such persons as he can reasonably foresee might be injured by failure to exercise such reasonable care.

Per Lord Macmillan: The duty to take care is the duty to avoid doing or omitting to do anything the doing or omitting to do which have as its reasonable and probable consequence injury to others, and the duty is owed to those to whom injury may reasonably and probably be anticipated if the duty is not observed.

Note—See also *McLoughlin v O'Brian*, p 401, below; *Smith v Littlewoods Organisation Ltd*, p 346, below; and *Hevican v Ruane* [1991] 3 All ER 65.

Alcock v Chief Constable of South Yorkshire Police

[1992] 1 AC 310, [1991] 4 All ER 907, [1991] 3 WLR 1057, HL

The plaintiffs were relatives and friends of football supporters injured or killed at the Hillsbrough Stadium disaster as a result of overcrowding in part of the stadium. The defendant was responsible for policing the football match. The plaintiffs were either present in another part of the stadium; outside the stadium; watching the football match live on television or later watched recorded television pictures. The plaintiffs claimed damages for psychiatric illness.

HELD: The plaintiffs' claims failed. They were either not within the class of persons to whom the defendant owed a duty or they were not sufficiently proximate to the accident in time and space.

Nolan L in the Court of Appeal expressed the view that: 'I would accept at once that no general definition is possible but I see no difficulty in principle in requiring a defendant to contemplate that the person physically injured or threatened by his negligence may have relatives or friends whose love for him is like that of a normal parent or spouse, and who in consequence may similarly be closely and directly affected by nervous shock . . . the identification of the particular individuals who come within that category, like that of parents and spouses themselves, could only be carried out *ex post facto*, and would depend on evidence of the "relationship" in a broad sense which gave rise to the love and affection. It is accepted that the proximity to the accident must be close both in time and space . . . in the circumstances of this case the simultaneous television broadcasts of what occurred cannot be equated with the "sight or hearing of the evidence or its immediate aftermath". Accordingly, shock sustained by reason of these broadcasts cannot found a claim.'

Farrugia v Great Western Rly Co

[1947] 2 All ER 565, CA

Defendants' lorry loaded with a large container attempted to drive under a low railway bridge. The container struck the bridge and was thrown off and injured the

plaintiff. The plaintiff had been on the lorry as a trespasser, had just got off and was running along the highway to get on it again.
HELD: The vehicle and load were a potential danger to anyone on the highway in the near neighbourhood, and defendants owed such person a duty whether there lawfully or unlawfully. The plaintiff was within the area of potential danger referred to in *Bourhill v Young* and might reasonably be expected to be injured. The plaintiff was lawfully on the highway; he was not trespassing on the defendants' vehicle. Judgment for plaintiff upheld.

Connelly v A and W Hemphill Ltd

[1949] WN 191, 93 Sol Jo 371, HL
A dock labourer and his mate were trucking goods unloaded from a ship into a shed. The truck was pushed alongside a stationary lorry from the rear to about halfway along the lorry and then turned away from the lorry. When turning the truck the plaintiff inadvertently placed his foot immediately in front of the rear wheel of the lorry. The lorry driver had started his engine, walked round the lorry, checked the load, ascertained that no one was near the rear wheels and then without warning drove forward slowly.

Plaintiff alleged failure to keep a proper look-out, starting from rest without warning and without ascertaining that it was safe. The Lord Ordinary found no negligence of the driver. The Second Division affirmed this decision.
HELD, ON APPEAL to the House of Lords: The plaintiff knew the lorry was ready to move off. The lorry driver was under no legal duty to give warning to the plaintiff that he was about to move off, which duty would only arise if he knew or ought reasonably to have known that danger to others might result. He neither knew nor ought reasonably to have known. Finding of no negligence upheld.

Setchell v Snowdon

[1974] RTR 389, CA
Snowdon and Ashton were acquainted with each other by being members of the same football team. Ashton asked Snowdon, who owned a car, to teach him to drive but Snowdon declined. When at a club together on the evening of that day Ashton asked Snowdon to lend him the key of his car, which was parked nearby, so that he could sit in it with a girl he had met. Ashton said expressly he did not want to drive the car. Snowdon lent him the key which was also the ignition key. When Ashton and the girl were in the car Ashton decided to drive it and, losing control, crashed it, severely injuring the girl. She sued Snowdon saying he should have realised Ashton might drive off in the car and was thereby negligent, knowing Ashton had not learned to drive. The judge accepted Snowdon's evidence that it never crossed his mind that Ashton would drive.
HELD: Snowdon was not liable. The test was: would a reasonable man in all the circumstances have realised that there was a real risk of Ashton driving the car? The answer was no; Snowdon had no reason to anticipate that Ashton would do something contrary to what he had promised and which would be in more than one respect a criminal offence.

Awad v Pillai

[1982] RTR 266, CA
Awad took his car to Pillai to be resprayed. The second defendant had taken her own car to him for the same purpose but it was not yet finished. Pillai lent her Awad's car

representing that it was his own and that it was insured for her driving. She had an accident due to her negligent driving and the car was a total loss. Awad sued her for the amount of his loss. She denied liability to him on the ground that as she did not know it was his car and believed Pillai had authority to say she was properly insured. Awad was not a person to whom she owed a duty of care: he was not her 'neighbour' within Lord Atkin's famous words in *Donoghue v Stevenson*.
HELD: This was not right. The first person who was closely and directly affected by the second defendant's negligent driving was the owner of the car, Awad. He was a person to whom she owed a duty of care, and she was liable to him for the damage.

Denton v United Omnibus Ltd

(1986) Times, 6 May, CA
The defendants garaged their buses in an open depot without doors or gates. Early one morning a thief drove one of the buses away and hit the plaintiff's parked car. The plaintiff claimed that even though this person was unidentified and unauthorised, the defendants were in breach of a duty of care to him because they had failed to secure their premises (despite previous incidents) and that this damage was foreseeable.
HELD: The defendants owed no duty of care to the plaintiff: there was no special relationship and the bus was taken unlawfully by an unauthorised person over whom they had no control. In any event, the defendants had not been negligent. *Perl (Exporters) Ltd v Camden London Borough Council* applied.

Topp v London Country Bus (South West) Ltd

[1993] 3 All ER 448, [1992] RTR 254
A public service mini bus was left unattended, unlocked and with the keys in the ignition. The bus was stolen and driven negligently causing the death of a cyclist.
HELD: No duty of care was owed by the bus operators to the cyclist for (i) there was no duty to prevent deliberate wrongdoings by a third party; (ii) it would be difficult to assess the degree of negligence based on the type of vehicle left and the period for which it was left unattended; and (iii) the likelihood of the vehicle being stolen, driven negligently and causing injury was low. An appeal to the Court of Appeal was dismissed.

BLIND PERSONS

Pritchard v Post Office

[1950] WN 310, 114 JP 370, 94 Sol Jo 404, CA
Post Office workmen opened a manhole in the pavement and placed the usual light wooden guard round the hole, which was adequate warning and protection to ordinary people. A woman totally blind walked along the pavement alone, collided with the guard which gave way and she fell in the hole.
HELD: Reasonable precautions had been taken for ordinary members of the public who could see. Post Office not liable.

Haley v London Electricity Board

[1965] AC 778, [1964] 3 All ER 185, [1964] 3 WLR 479, 129 JP 14, 108 Sol Jo 637, 63 LGR 1, HL.
The defendant's employees were searching for a cable in a trench dug along the pavement. They had put a punner-hammer in a sloping position across the pavement

to stop pedestrians walking along it and make them walk in the road. Any person with ordinary sight would see it and walk in the roadway. The plaintiff, who was blind, was walking alone on the pavement. His stick passed over the hammer, giving him no warning of the danger and he fell into the trench.
HELD: The duty owed by those who engage in operations on the pavement of a highway is to take reasonable care not to act in a way likely to endanger other persons who may reasonably be expected to walk along the pavement. That duty is owed to blind persons if the operators foresee or ought to have foreseen that blind persons may walk along the pavement and is in no way different from the duty owed to persons with sight, though the carrying out of the duty may involve extra precautions in the case of blind pedestrians. It is common to find blind persons walking along pavements in London. The punner-hammer was not an adequate protection because the handle was low at one end and a blind person's stick feeling for obstructions could pass over it. But elaborate or expensive precautions were not necessary. A light fence two feet high (such as the respondents normally used and which they would have used had not work been started before the fence arrived) across the end of the trench would have been adequate to discharge the respondent's duty of care to the appellant. The respondents were liable.

VOLUNTEER

Sherrard v British Gates Ltd

(1984) Times, 25 February (Kilner Brown J)
The plaintiff sustained injuries in an accident while helping the defendants to load and move logs with his tractor.
HELD: He was legally a volunteer and some duty of care was owed him by the defendants as a 'neighbour', namely, to ensure there was a safe system of working and not to expose the plaintiff to risk of injury. On the facts, the plaintiff being an expert tractor driver, there was no breach of duty because no reasonably foreseeable risk of injury.

CONTRIBUTORY NEGLIGENCE

In order to establish the defence of contributory negligence, the defendant must prove, first, that the plaintiff failed to take 'ordinary care for himself' or, in other words, such care as a reasonable man would take for his own safety, and, second, that his failure to take care was a contributory cause of the accident: Per du Parcq LJ in *Lewis v Denye* [1939] 1 KB 540, [1939] 1 All ER 310, 108 LJKB 217, 160 LT 224, 55 TLR 391, 83 Sol Jo 192, CA.

The failure to take care

A plea of contributory negligence should be treated as setting up want of care by the plaintiff for his own safety, whether in the circumstances of the accident the plaintiff owed a duty to the defendant or not.

The statement that, when negligence is alleged as the basis of an actionable wrong, a necessary ingredient in the conception is the existence of a duty owed by the defendants to the plaintiff to take due care, is, of course, indubitably correct. But when contributory negligence is set up as a defence, its existence does not depend on any duty owed by the injured party to the party sued, and all that is necessary to establish such a defence is to prove that the injured party did not in his own interest take reasonable care of himself, and contributed, by that want of care, to his own injury. Where a man was part author of his own injury, he could not call on the other party to compensate him in full: *Davies v Swan Motor Co* (p 176, below) followed: *Nance v British Columbia Electric Rly Co Ltd* [1951] AC 601, [1951] 2 All ER 448, [1951] 2 TLR 137, 93 Sol Jo 543, PC.

The test of contributory negligence in the case of a pedestrian is not whether he is under a duty of care towards the defendant, but whether he was acting as a reasonable man and with reasonable care: per Denning LJ in *Davies v Swan Motor Co*.

LAW REFORM (CONTRIBUTORY NEGLIGENCE) ACT 1945

1 Apportionment of liability in case of contributory negligence (1) Where any person suffers damage as the result partly of his own fault and partly of the fault of any other person or persons, a claim in respect of that damage shall not be defeated by reason of the fault of the person suffering the damage, but the damages recoverable in respect thereof shall be reduced to such extent as the court thinks just and equitable having regard to the claimant's share in the responsibility for the damage:

Provided that—

(a) this subsection shall not operate to defeat any defence arising under a contract;

(b) where any contract or enactment providing for the limitation of liability is applicable to the claim, the amount of damages recoverable by the claimant by virtue of this subsection shall not exceed the maximum limit so applicable.

(2) Where damages are recoverable by any person by virtue of the foregoing subsection subject to such reduction as is therein mentioned, the court shall find and record the total damages which would have been recoverable if the claimant had not been at fault.

(3) (*Repealed by the Civil Liability (Contribution) Act 1978, s 9(2).*)

(4) (*Replaced by the Fatal Accidents Act 1976, s 5: see note, below.*)

(5) Where, in any case to which subsection (1) of this section applies, one of the persons at fault avoids liability to any other such person or his personal representative by pleading the Limitation Act 1939, or any other enactment limiting the time within which proceedings may be taken, he shall not be entitled to recover any damages from that other person or representative by virtue of the said subsection.

(6) Where any case to which subsection (1) of this section applies is tried with a jury, the jury shall determine the total damages which would have been recoverable if the claimant had not been at fault and the extent to which those damages are to be reduced.

2 (*Replaced by the National Insurance (Industrial Injuries) Act 1946, s 89(1) and Sch 9.*)

3 Saving for Maritime Conventions Act 1911, and past cases (1) This Act shall not apply to any claim to which section one of the Maritime Conventions Act 1911 applies and that Act shall have effect as if this Act had not been passed.

(2) This Act shall not apply to any case where the acts or omissions giving rise to the claim occurred before the passing of this Act.

4 Interpretation The following expressions have the meanings hereby respectively assigned to them that is to say—

'court' means, in relation to any claim, the court or arbitrator by or before whom the claim falls to be determined;

'damage' includes loss of life and personal injury;

'dependant' means any person for whose benefit an action could be brought under the Fatal Accidents Acts 1846 to 1959;

'fault' means negligence, breach of statutory duty or other act or omission which gives rise to a liability in tort or would, apart from this Act, give rise to the defence of contributory negligence.

7 Short title and extent This Act may be cited as the Law Reform (Contributory Negligence) Act 1945.

Note—In respect of causes of action arising from deaths on or after 1 September 1976, s 1(4) of the 1945 Act had been replaced by the Fatal Accidents Act 1976, s 5, which is as follows:

'5 contributory negligence Where any person dies as the result partly of his own fault and partly of the fault of any other person or persons, and accordingly if an action were brought for the benefit of the estate under the Law Reform (Miscellaneous Provisions) Act 1934 the damages recoverable would be reduced under section 1(1) of the Law Reform (Contributory Negligence) Act 1945, any damages recoverable in an action brought for the benefit of the dependants of that person under this Act shall be reduced to a proportionate extent.'

As from the same date the definition of 'dependant' in s 4 of the 1945 Act was repealed and was replaced by the definition in the Fatal Accidents Act 1976, s 1(3). In respect of deaths after 1982 that definition was itself replaced by the definition in s 1(3) of the 1976 Act substituted by the Administration of Justice Act 1982, s 3. The words 'brought for the benefit of the dependants of that person' are to be omitted where the death occurred on or after 1 January 1983 (Administration of Justice Act 1982, s 4(2)).

The Consumer Protection Act 1987, s 6 now provides as follows:

(4) Where any damage is caused partly by a defect in a product and partly by the fault of the person suffering the damage, the Law Reform (Contributory Negligence) Act 1945 and section 5 of the Fatal Accidents Act 1976 shall have effect as if the defect were the fault of every person liable by virtue of this Part for the damage caused by the defect.
(5) In sub-s (4) above 'fault' has the same meaning as in the 1945 Act.

THE EFFECT OF THE LAW REFORM (CONTRIBUTORY NEGLIGENCE) ACT 1945

Note—Before the Law Reform (Contributory Negligence) Act 1945 a plaintiff who was guilty of contributory negligence could recover no damages at all. The courts, having to decide between all or nothing, developed rules of causation intended to ascertain the 'sole effective cause' of the damage in cases where common logic might have led to the conclusion that there were two or more effective causes. The 1945 Act (above), in providing for apportionment of damages where the plaintiff's injury was partly his own fault has, in practice, rendered the old cases and tests obsolete.

Per Denning LJ in *Davies v Swan Motor Co* (p 176, below): Speaking generally, the questions in road accidents are simply these: What faults were there which caused the damage? What are the proportions in which the damages should be apportioned having regard to the respective responsibilities of those in fault?

Questions of negligence and contributory negligence are pure questions of fact for the court, and the court finding of fact is binding if there is evidence to support it.

See also Chapter 4, pp 167 to 190.

Basildon District Council v J E Lesser (Properties) Ltd

[1985] QB 839, [1985] 1 All ER 20, [1984] 3 WLR 812, 128 Sol Jo 330, [1984] NLJR 330 (Judge Newey QC Official Referee)

On a clear and exact analysis of ss 1 and 4, the Law Reform (Contributory Negligence) Act 1945 does not apply to contracts.

The plaintiffs entered into a standard term contract with Lesser (who were system builders) for the construction of houses and maisonettes. The contract referred to drawings and specifications which had been prepared by or under the control of the plaintiffs' engineers or architects. Lesser subsequently assigned the benefit of the contract to the second defendants; then the third defendants (the holding company of Lesser and the second defendants) agreed to indemnify the plaintiffs against any breach of contract by them both. Defects developed in some of the houses and maisonettes caused, according to the plaintiffs, by foundation movement and inadequately supported cross walls. The plaintiffs sued the third defendants alleging breach of contract on the part of the second defendants. The third defendants alleged that the plaintiffs' architect and clerk of works were at fault and that they could plead contributory negligence in a contractual dispute; alternatively that, where a breach of contract involved a failure to take reasonable care, contributory negligence could be relied upon under the Law Reform (Contributory Negligence) Act 1945.
HELD: The 1945 Act only applied where the plaintiffs' cause of action related to an act or omission for which the defendants would be liable in tort even though they might also be liable in contract. The plaintiffs' claim was founded on the contract with the third defendants so the 1945 Act could not apply; the third defendants could not rely upon the defence of contributory negligence in answer to the local authority's claim for damages for breach of contract.
But contrast:

Forsikringsaktieselskapet Vesta v Butcher

[1989] AC 852, [1988] 2 All ER 43, [1988] 3 WLR 565, 132 Sol Jo 1181, [1988] 1 Lloyd's Rep 19, CA
The plaintiffs, Norwegian insurers, covered the owners of a fish farm against the loss of fish from any cause. They reinsured 90% of the risk through English brokers. The reinsurance policy included a warranty that a 24-hour watch had to be maintained on the site; failure to comply with this warranty would render the policy void. Although the warranty was then incorporated in the policy issued by the plaintiffs to the owners, the plaintiffs knew that it could not be observed and told the reinsurance brokers. These brokers undertook to discuss this matter with the underwriters but failed to do so. When a violent storm occurred, the fish farm suffered substantial damage. The plaintiffs met the claim but when they sought reimbursement the reinsurers refused to pay, depending on the breach of the warranty. The plaintiffs sued the reinsurers and the brokers claiming that if the reinsurers could successfully rely on the breach of warranty, the brokers were in breach of contract in failing to obtain valid and effective reinsurance and negligent in failing to inform the underwriters of the impossibility of providing a 24-hour watch. The brokers, in defending the action, alleged that the plaintiffs were guilty of contributory negligence in failing to ensure that the brokers told the reinsurers.
HELD: On the facts, reinsurers should indemnify insurers (so there was no loss). But the issue of contributory negligence by the plaintiffs was considered; where a defendant's liability arose from breach of a contractual provision which did not require or depend on negligence on his part the Law Reform (Contributory Negligence) Act 1945 would not permit a defence of contributory negligence but where the defendant's liability in contract was tantamount to liability in tort, regardless of the existence of a contract, the Act can apply and liability can be apportioned between plaintiff and defendant. Per Sir Roger Ormrod: 'The context of the 1945 Act, and the language of section 1, to my mind make it clear that the Act is concerned only with

tortious liability and the power to apportion only arises where a defendant is liable in tort and concurrent liability in contract, if any, is immaterial.' The narrow interpretation of the Act in *Marintrans (A B) v Comet Shipping Co Ltd* (below) was criticised by O'Connor LJ.

Note—An appeal to the House of Lords was dismissed: [1989] 1 All ER 402.

Marintrans (A B) v Comet Shipping Co Ltd, The Shinjitsu Maru No 5

[1985] Times, 19 March (Neill LJ)

A provision in a charterparty made the owners liable for bad stowage save to the extent they were able to show that the charterers had by some intervention caused the loss or damage. On the facts of the case the charterers were entitled to succeed in full unless the provisions of the 1945 Act entitled the owners to claim an apportionment.

HELD: The 1945 Act was not applicable. The opening words of s 1(1) of the Act were directed to tortious liabilities alone and were not apt to cover breaches of contractual duties of care, even if they were described as negligent breaches of contract.

Boothman v British Northrop

(1972) 13 K 112, CA

The plaintiff, injured in a factory accident, was held by the judge to have been negligent and his damages were reduced by 25%. On appeal counsel submitted that even if the plaintiff was negligent it was not 'just and equitable' on the facts to reduce the damages.

HELD: The words of the Law Reform (Contributory Negligence) Act 1945, s 1(1) do not entitle a court which has found a plaintiff guilty of contributory negligence to disregard that negligence and make no deduction in the damages on the ground that it would be 'just and equitable' not to do so.

Joliffe v Hay

1991 SLT 151

The plaintiff was driving a car in the vicinity of a junction, intending to turn right. He was hit by a car from behind attempting to overtake.

HELD: The plaintiff was 30% contributorily negligent as he had used his mirror only once having decided that the car behind would not pull out. The plaintiff had failed to exercise reasonable care.

100% CONTRIBUTORY NEGLIGENCE

Jayes v IMI (Kynoch) Ltd

[1985] ICR 155, [1984] LS Gaz R 3180, CA

The plaintiff, a production supervisor, was injured when he attempted to wipe grease off a moving belt with a rag. The rag was drawn in and his finger with it. He lost the end of his finger. He agreed that what he did was 'a crazy thing to do'. The judge assumed there was a breach of statutory duty by the employers under the Operation at Unfenced Machinery Regulations but held the plaintiff was entirely to blame.

HELD, ON APPEAL: There was no principle of law that where there was a breach of statutory duty there could not be an award of 100% contributory negligence. The judge was entitled to decide in the way he did.

Note—Now see *Pitts v Hunt*, p 51, below.

CONTRIBUTORY NEGLIGENCE NOT PLEADED

Fookes v Slaytor

[1979] 1 All ER 137, [1978] 1 WLR 1293, [1979] RTR 40, CA
The plaintiff, driving his car at night, collided with a stationary unlighted lorry and was injured. He sued the driver of the lorry in the county court. The driver filed no defence, did not attend on the trial and was not represented. The judge awarded damages to the plaintiff but reduced them by one-third on the ground that he was contributorily negligent.
HELD, ON APPEAL: The judge was not entitled to find contributory negligence against the plaintiff when it had not been pleaded. The damages should not have been reduced.

Other examples

CHILDREN

Gough v Thorne

[1966] 3 All ER 398, [1966] 1 WLR 1387, 110 Sol Jo 529, CA
Per Lord Denning MR: A very young child cannot be guilty of contributory negligence. An older child may be, but it depends on the circumstances. A judge should only find a child guilty of contributory negligence if he or she is of such an age as to be expected to take precautions for his or her own safety: and then he or she is only to be found guilty if blame should be attached to him or her. A child has not the road sense or the experience of his or her elders. He or she is not to be found guilty unless he or she is blameworthy.

Minter v D & H Contractors (Cambridge) Ltd

(1983) Times, 30 June (Tudor Evans J)
The plaintiff, aged nine, ran into a pile of hardcore when riding his bicycle and was injured. The hardcore had been negligently left in the roadway by the defendants.
HELD: The degree to which an infant plaintiff could be capable of contributory negligence was a question of fact in each case. The plaintiff, said in evidence to be 'a good rider', was not in the category of infants who were incapable of any contributory negligence. He was guilty of contributory negligence to the extent of 20%.

Morales v Eccleston

[1991] RTR 151, CA
The plaintiff, an 11 year old boy, was playing with a football along the pavement adjacent to a busy London road. The traffic was heavy but moving at 20–30 mph on both sides of the road. The weather was fine, the road was dry and the visibility was

good. The defendant was travelling at 20 mph on the opposite side of the road to which the plaintiff was walking. The plaintiff lost control of his football and, without looking in either direction, followed it across the first carriageway into the path of the defendant's vehicle. The plaintiff suffered serious injuries and sued the defendant. The trial judge held that the defendant was 80% to blame. The defendant appealed.
HELD: McCowan LJ: On the evidence presented to the trial judge the defendant could not have had much more than two seconds in which to see the plaintiff. Despite this there was some evidence upon which the judge could have arrived at the view that the defendant was not keeping a proper lookout. The plaintiff showed a reckless disregard for his own safety and must bear a higher proportion of blame for the accident than the defendant. Blame was apportioned at 25% to the defendant and 75% to the plaintiff.

Note—See also Chapter 2, pp 53 to 123.

CONTRIBUTORY NEGLIGENCE OF SERVANT

Thompson v Bundy

(1938) Times, 5 May
The plaintiff was a passenger in a car driven by her servant which collided with the defendant's car. The court found that the defendant's driver was negligent and the plaintiff's servant was also negligent and his negligence contributed to the accident. In those circumstances there was no doubt as to the law. It was quite plain that, although a passenger in a vehicle was not identified with the driver, a person responsible for the acts of the driver might be disabled from recovering damages from another person for negligence if the accident was contributed to by the negligence of the driver for whom the passenger in the vehicle was responsible. In this case the plaintiff was, so to speak, driving a car through her appointed agent for whose negligence she was in law responsible vis-à-vis third parties.

Note—Contributory negligence not being, since the 1945 Act, a complete defence to the recovery of damages, the plaintiff would now have had her damages reduced by an amount proportionate to her servant's share of the blame.

PLAINTIFF MOTOR CYCLIST NOT WEARING CRASH HELMET

Note—The Road Traffic Act 1962, s 41 (now the Road Traffic Act 1988, s 16(2)) empowering the Minister of Transport to make regulations requiring persons driving or riding on motor cycles to wear protective headgear was brought into force as from 1 October 1971 by the Road Traffic Act 1962 (Commencement No 7) Order 1971 (SI 1971/1335).

The wearing of helmets by riders of motor cycles, scooters and mopeds was made compulsory by the Motor Cycles (Wearing of Helmets) Regulations (SI 1973/180) which came into force on 1 June 1973. Paragraph 29 of the 1978 Highway Code says 'when on a motor cycle, scooter or moped you must wear a safety helmet of approved design.' A Sikh is excused from wearing a helmet while he is wearing a turban.

O'Connell v Jackson

[1972] 1 QB 270, [1971] 3 All ER 129, [1971] 3 WLR 463, 115 Sol Jo 742, CA
The plaintiff was riding his moped to work along a busy street when the defendant drove out in his car from a side street and collided with him. The plaintiff was thrown

off and struck his head violently on the roadway sustaining a severe fracture of the skull. He was not wearing a crash helmet: he had intended buying one but had not done so. There was evidence from three doctors that the injury would have been less serious had he been wearing one. The judge held the defendant solely to blame for the accident. He also found that if the plaintiff had been wearing a helmet it would have reduced the gravity of the head injuries but he declined to hold that the failure to wear one was contributory negligence.
HELD, ON THE DEFENDANTS' APPEAL: The Law Reform (Contributory Negligence) Act 1945 required damages to be reduced according to 'the claimant's share in the responsibility for the damage.' In *Jones v Livox Quarries* (p 177, below) Denning LJ had said a person was guilty of contributory negligence if he ought reasonably to have foreseen that if he did not act as a reasonably prudent man he might be hurt himself, and in his reckonings he must take into account the possibility of others being careless. Applying this test the plaintiff ought to have foreseen when travelling through a busy traffic area the possibility of an accident occurring even though he himself drove carefully and that he could well sustain greater hurt if he failed to wear a helmet. He knew as was clear from his own evidence, that it was a sensible practice to wear one. The plaintiff was partly to blame for the additional injury he sustained by not wearing a helmet and the reduction of damages should amount to 15% of the whole.

Note—See also 'Seat belts', p 181, below; *Capps v Miller*, p 186, below.

CONTRIBUTION BETWEEN TORTFEASORS

Note—When an injured party has suffered damage by the negligence of two or more persons, whether acting in concert or not, he may recover the whole of his damage from any one of them, or may sue all of them jointly in the same action. Formerly, joint wrongdoers or those severally liable for the same damage had no right of contribution or indemnity against each other. The rule was altered by the Law Reform (Married Women and Tortfeasors) Act 1935, s 6 of which enabled tortfeasors to recover contribution from any other tortfeasor who was, or would if sued have been, liable in respect of the same damage. This section of the 1935 Act was repealed and replaced with effect from 1 January 1979 by the Civil Liability (Contribution) Act 1978. Under this Act contribution may be claimed even if one or both of those concerned is liable to the plaintiff otherwise than in tort.

Civil Liability (Contribution) Act 1978

THE ACT

1 Entitlement to contribution (1) Subject to the following provisions of this section, any person liable in respect of any damage suffered by another person may recover contribution from any other person liable in respect of the same damage (whether jointly with him or otherwise).
(2) A person shall be entitled to recover contribution by virtue of subsection (1) above notwithstanding that he has ceased to be liable in respect of the damage in question since the time when the damage occurred, provided that he was so liable immediately before he made or was ordered or agreed to make the payment in respect of which the contribution is sought.
(3) A person shall be liable to make contribution by virtue of subsection (1) above notwithstanding that he has ceased to be liable in respect of the damage in question since the time when the damage occurred, unless he ceased to be liable by virtue of the expiry of a period of limitation or prescription which extinguished the right on which the claim against him in respect of the damage was based.

(4) A person who has made or agreed to make any payment in bona fide settlement or compromise of any claim made against him in respect of any damage (including a payment into court which has been accepted) shall be entitled to recover contribution in accordance with this section without regard to whether or not he himself is or ever was liable in respect of the damage, provided, however, that he would have been liable assuming that the factual basis of the claim against him could be established.
(5) A judgment in any action brought in any part of the United Kingdom by or on behalf of the person who suffered the damage in question against any person from whom contribution is sought under this section shall be conclusive in the proceedings for contribution as to any issue determined by that judgment in favour of the person from whom the contribution is sought.
(6) References in this section to a person's liability in respect of any damage are references to any such liability which has been or could be established in an action brought against him in England and Wales by or on behalf of the person who suffered the damage; but it is immaterial whether any issue arising in any such action was or would be determined (in accordance with the rules of private international law) by reference to the law of a country outside England and Wales.

Note—Subsection (3) gives statutory effect to the decision in *Hart v Hall and Pickles Ltd* (p 645, below) and preserves the effect of such cases as *George Wimpey & Co Ltd v British Overseas Airways Corpn* (p 532, below). Subsection (4) disposes of the difficulty met with by defendants who have settled a plaintiff's claim and seek contribution from another tortfeasor who was not a party to or bound by, the settlement, eg as in *Stott v West Yorks Road Car Co Ltd* (p 614, below). See also *Harper v Gray and Walker* [1985] 2 All ER 507, [1985] 1 WLR 1196.

Logan v Uttlesford District Council and Hammond

(1984) 134 NLJ 500 (Sheen J)
A third party who had ceased to be liable to the plaintiff by having settled the plaintiff's claim against him is not entitled to have a third party notice and statement of claim against him struck out. The Civil Liability (Contribution) Act 1978, s 1(3) relieves a person from liability to contribute only if he has ceased to be liable by effluxion of time. A settlement did not come within that proviso.

2 Assessment of contribution (1) Subject to subsection (3) below, in any proceedings for contribution under section 1 above the amount of the contribution recoverable from any person shall be such as may be found by the court to be just and equitable having regard to the extent of that person's responsibility for the damage in question.
(2) Subject to subsection (3) below, the court shall have power in any such proceedings to exempt any person from liability to make contribution, or to direct that the contribution to be recovered from any person shall amount to a complete indemnity.
(3) Where the amount of the damages which have or might have been awarded in respect of the damage in question in any action brought in England and Wales by or on behalf of the person who suffered it against the person from whom the contribution is sought was or would have been subject to—
(a) any limit imposed by or under any enactment or by any agreement made before the damage occurred;
(b) any reduction by virtue of section 1 of the Law Reform (Contributory Negligence) Act 1945 or section 5 of the Fatal Accidents Act 1976; or
(c) any corresponding limit or reduction under the law of a country outside England and Wales;
the person from whom the contribution is sought shall not by virtue of any contribution awarded under section 1 above be required to pay in respect of the damage a greater amount of those damages as limited or reduced.

Note—See above for the effect of ss 6(4) and 6(5) of the Consumer Protection Act 1987.

LIMITATION PERIOD

A tortfeasor who wishes to recover contribution from another tortfeasor who is liable for the same damage must bring the action for contribution within two years from the date on which the judgment or award was made against him or on which he admitted liability for the amount in respect of which he claimed contribution: Limitation Act 1980, s 10. See p 532, below.

Note—For contribution proceedings between tortfeasors already a party to the same action see *Kennett v Brown* [1988] 2 All ER 600 (p 529, below) and Chapter 14 generally.

Statutory duty: common law

Dooley v Cammell Laird & Co Ltd

[1951] 1 Lloyd's Rep 271 (Donovan J)
The plaintiff was a crane driver employed by shipbuilders, and the crane and plaintiff as driver were loaned to contractors working on the ship. The contractors supplied the sling and rope. The sling was unsuitable and the rope defective and the plaintiff was injured.

The contractors contended that as the liability of the shipbuilders was for breach of statutory duty and that of the contractors was breach of common law, they were not joint tortfeasors and there was no liability to contribute.

HELD: There was no authority for such a proposition, and it made no difference to contribute what was just and equitable.

Contrast with *McConkey v Amec* (1990) Times, 28 February, CA where an employer provided an incompetent employee and remained liable for his negligent acts.

Nature of the right to contribution

Ronex Properties Ltd v John Laing Construction Ltd

[1983] QB 398, [1982] 3 All ER 961, [1982] 3 WLR 875, 126 Sol Jo 727, CA
A building built for the plaintiffs in 1972 began to show defects in 1974. They issued a writ in 1978 against the builders and the architects. In 1979 the architects issued third-party proceedings against consulting engineers for indemnity or contribution under the Law Reform (Married Women and Tortfeasors) Act 1935, s 6 and at common law alleging breach of contract and/or negligence. The sole surviving partner of the firm of architects died in 1980: the plaintiffs obtained an order to carry on against his personal representatives. The third parties then applied to strike out the third-party notice on the ground that it disclosed no reasonable cause of action, since any right to recover contribution under the 1935 Act had been extinguished by the death of the architect. The third parties' argument was that the Law Reform (Miscellaneous Provisions) Act 1934, s 1 provided for the survival against the estate of a deceased person only of 'causes of action' and the architects had no cause of action until (which had not yet happened) they were found liable, or admitted liability,

to the plaintiffs; and that the maxim *actio personalis moritur cum persona* applied to destroy any right in the architects to claim contribution
HELD: It was no doubt right that no right to contribution arose under the 1935 Act unless the defendant was found liable to the plaintiff and that there was no subsisting cause of action in the architect at the time of his death which the 1934 Act could preserve, but it was not the case that the right to claim contribution died with him. It was a defined inchoate right and not a mere hope or expectation. The rule that a personal action dies with the person does not apply to that right, which passed to his personal representatives for the benefit of his estate under the law of succession.

Absence of person possibly liable

Maxfield v Llewellyn

[1961] 3 All ER 95, [1961] 1 WLR 1119, 105 Sol Jo 550, CA
The plaintiff's husband was killed when riding as a pillion passenger on a motor cycle. The motor cyclist was also killed. The plaintiff alleged that the accident was caused by the negligent parking of vehicle A and the negligent driving of vehicle B. She sued the owners and drivers of the two vehicles, but not the personal representatives of the motor cyclist, though there was evidence that he may have been travelling too fast. The Court having held the owners and drivers of both vehicles liable it was argued on behalf of the owners of vehicle A that the Law Reform (Married Women and Tortfeasors) Act 1935, s 6(2) did not empower the Court to apportion blame and order contribution as between the defendants when a person whose negligence may have contributed to the accident was not a party to the action.
HELD: The argument could not be supported. The duty of the Court was to apportion blame for the accident as between the defendants before the Court. The section would otherwise be unworkable. The Court must first consider whether the defendants were liable and then make such apportionment as may be 'just and equitable having regard to that person's responsibility for the damage'. That meant as between the defendants before the Court. The defendants could bring a separate action, if they thought it was worthwhile, asking for contribution against the personal representative of the motor cyclist.

Apportionment of blame

THE RULE

Note—The words in s 2(1) such as may be found by the court to be 'just and equitable having regard to the extent of that person's responsibility for the damage in question' present the same problem of interpretation as the words in the Law Reform (Contributory Negligence) Act 1945, s 1 (p 11, above) 'to such extent as the court thinks just and equitable having regard to the claimant's share in the responsibility for the damage'. Should proportions be assessed by reference to the extent to which the negligent acts of the parties caused the damage, or should the division depend on the relative blameworthiness of the parties? The conclusion to be drawn from the decided cases is that whilst causation is not to be ignored the degree of blameworthiness is the more important factor. The following cases include decisions on both Acts.

Croston v Vaughan

[1938] 1 KB 540 at 565, [1937] 4 All ER 249, CA
Per Scott LJ: In spite of the illogical details of the language of subsection (2) [of the 1935 Act, s 6] I think that the section should be read as giving the judge, on the evidence that he has heard, complete jurisdiction to assess the blame of each tortfeasor just as if he had held them liable as defendants to the plaintiff only for that portion of the blame.

Daniel v Rickett Cockerell & Co Ltd and Raymond

[1938] 2 KB 322, [1938] 2 All ER 631
Per Hilbery J: When I see the words ['just and equitable'] are coupled with 'having regard to the extent of that person's responsibility' I think the meaning of the subsection is that in exercising a judicial discretion in the matter I am intended to do that which I think is right between the parties, having regard, to what I think, on the true facts of the case, is the fair division of responsibility between them.

Note—The view taken by the same judge in *Collins v Hertfordshire County Council* ([1947] KB 598) that 'responsibility' had a causative connotation was considered and rejected by Hallett J in *Weaver v Commercial Process Co Ltd*.

Palser v Grinling

[1948] AC 291, [1948] 1 All ER 1 (Lord Simon)
The words 'have regard to' in the Law Reform (Contributory Negligence) Act 1945, s 1(1) call for the exercise of a broad judgment and any arithmetical conclusion is qualified by what is deemed to be fair and reasonable.

Note—See also *Newport Borough Council v Monmouthshire County Council* [1947] AC 520, [1947] 1 All ER 900, HL.

Davies v Swan Motor Co

[1949] 2 KB 291, [1949] 1 All ER 620, 65 TLR 278, CA
Per Denning LJ: While causation is the decisive factor in determining whether there should be a reduced amount payable to the plaintiff, nevertheless the amount of the reduction does not depend solely on the degree of causation. The amount of the reduction is such an amount as may be found by the court to be 'just and equitable' having regard to the claimant's 'share in the responsibility' for the damage. This involves a consideration, not only of the causative potency of a particular factor, but also of its blameworthiness. The fact of standing on the steps of the dust cart is just as potent a factor in causing damage, whether the person standing there be a servant acting negligently in the course of his employment or a boy in play or a youth doing it for a 'lark', but the degree of blameworthiness may be very different.

THE CASE LAW

Weaver v Commercial Process Co Ltd

(1947) 63 TLR 466 (Hallett J)
The second defendants supplied the first defendants with a jar of nitric acid which was cracked, and which broke when being handled by a young employee of the first defendants, injuring the plaintiff.

HELD: Both defendants were liable in damages, which were to be apportioned under s 6(2) of the 1935 Act. In *Collins*'s case Mr Justice Hilbery appeared to have come to the view that the contribution must be apportioned not according to the relative negligence, that is culpability, of the two tortfeasors but according to the relative effect of their acts in causing the damage. The same judge's decision in *Daniel*'s case (above) was preferable—to exercise a judicial discretion so as to do what is right between such parties having regard to what appears, on the facts, to be the fair division of the responsibility between them. By far the greater responsibility for the casualty should be laid on the shoulders of the second defendants. They were the suppliers of the cracked jar of nitric acid to the first defendants who were entitled to rely on them to supply a jar that was safe to handle. Apportionment 90% second defendants.

Cavanagh v London Transport Executive

(1956) 222 LT Jo 333, (1956) Times, 23 October (Devlin J)
The deceased was crossing the Strand, and stepped off a centre refuge behind a stationary taxi-cab, and was knocked down by a bus. The deceased neither saw nor heard the bus, but the driver braked and nearly avoided an accident.
HELD: If the sole test was 'causative potency' the assessment would be approximately an equal division of responsibility; if 'blameworthiness' were the only test, the driver's responsibility would be assessed at 20%. Giving effect to both tests, the defendant's contribution was one-third.

Brown v Thompson

[1968] 2 All ER 708, [1968] 1 WLR 1003, 112 Sol Jo 464, CA
Mrs Brown was injured when a car driven by her husband collided with the rear of the defendant's lorry. The accident occurred at about 3 am in winter on an unlighted road. The lorry had no lights and was without reflectors. Mr Brown did not see the lorry until just before the accident and was turning out to avoid it when he hit it. The judge apportioned liability 80% to the defendant and 20% to Mr Brown. The defendants appealed contending that 50% responsibility should be apportioned to Mr Brown.
HELD: Dismissing the appeal, regard must be had not only to the causative potency of the acts or omissions of each of the parties but to their relative blameworthiness (citing *The Miraflores* (below)). The act of driving in such a manner that the driver failed to turn out and ran into the back of a stationary vehicle was in a high degree potently causative of the injuries suffered by Mrs Brown. Equally it was potently causative of the collision that the lorry was left in the position it was without lights. But when one looked at the blameworthiness then it seemed plain that Mr Brown's fault was really quite small.

Note—See also *Baker v Willoughby*, p 110, below.

Gregory v Kelly

[1978] RTR 426 (Jones J)
The defendant was driving his mini car at a time when the footbrake was completely inoperative because part of the hydraulic system was missing. The plaintiff, a passenger in the defendant's car, knew the brakes did not work; furthermore he was not wearing the seat belt provided. The defendant, driving at about 40 mph on a narrow country road, was confronted, on rounding a bend, with a vehicle parked

partly on the roadway on his nearside. Being unable to brake he pulled out to overtake and crashed into a car coming in the opposite direction.
HELD: (1) The defendant's negligence was of a high order in driving too fast and in so driving when he knew he had no footbrake; (2) the plaintiff was negligent in not wearing a seat belt and additionally in travelling in the car as a passenger when he knew from the start it had no operative footbrake. In assessing the respective fault or blameworthiness of the two parties it would not be right to assess the percentages of negligence or contributory negligence separately and add them up. The matter must be looked at generally. Apportionment of blame 60% on the defendant, 40% on the plaintiff.

MORE THAN TWO PARTIES TO BLAME: PRINCIPLES OF ASSESSMENT

The Miraflores and The Abadesa

[1967] 1 AC 826, [1967] 1 All ER 672, [1967] 2 WLR 806, 111 Sol Jo 211, HL
The *Miraflores* and the *Abadesa* collided in the River Scheldt. The *George Livanes*, following the *Miraflores*, was presented with a difficulty and, failing to take action in time to avoid it, ran aground. In actions to determine liability for the damage caused to the vessels the judge first apportioned liability for the collision between the *Miraflores* and the *Abadesa* at one-third and two-thirds respectively. Then to ascertain liability for damage to the *George Livanes* due to grounding he treated the negligence of the other two vessels leading to the collision as one unit and the negligence of the *George Livanes* in running aground as the other. Finding the *George Livanes* one-half to blame for the grounding he awarded the owners one-half of their damages to be paid two thirds by the *Abadesa* and one-third by the *Miraflores*.
HELD, ON APPEAL: The 'unit approach' was wrong. In assessing degrees of fault blameworthiness as well as causation must be considered—it is necessary to weigh the fault of each negligent party against each of the others separately and not conjunctively: by putting the several acts of negligence of the *Abadesa* and the *Miraflores* into one characterless 'unit' the judge did not measure their respective blameworthiness against the blameworthiness of the *George Livanes*. The proportions of fault in the other two ships for the grounding of the *George Livanes* should be assessed at two-fifths to the *Abadesa* and one-fifth to the *Miraflores*.

Per Lord Pearce: The Law Reform (Contributory Negligence) Act 1945, s 1 does not give any support to the unit approach. Its intention was to allow the plaintiff, though negligent, to recover damages reduced to such an extent as the court thinks just and equitable, having regard to his share in the responsibility for the damage (s 1(1)). But that share can only be estimated by weighing his fault against that of the defendant or, if there are two defendants, against that of each defendant. It is true that apportionment as between the defendants comes theoretically at a later stage (under the Law Reform (Married Women and Tortfeasors) Act 1935). But as a matter of practice the whole matter is decided at one time and the Court weighs up the fault of *each* in assessing liability as between plaintiff and defendants themselves. And I see nothing in the 1945 Act to show that it intends the Court to treat the joint defendants as a unit whose joint blameworthiness could only, one presumes, be the aggregate blameworthiness of its differing components.

Fitzgerald v Lane

[1989] AC 328, [1988] 2 All ER 961, [1988] 3 WLR 356, 132 Sol Jo 1064, HL
The plaintiff, who was a trainee negotiator working for estate agents and surveyors, was walking to a house one mile away to meet a prospective purchaser. As he began crossing the road at a pelican crossing the light showed red for pedestrians and green for traffic. He was hit by the first defendant's car, thrown forward across the road and struck by the second defendant's car coming in the opposite direction. He sustained multiple injuries resulting in partial tetraplegia. The judge found all three parties equally to blame and entered judgment for the plaintiff against the defendants for two-thirds of the total damages. The Court of Appeal held that the plaintiff was entitled to only half the amount in a case where all three parties were held equally to blame. The plaintiff appealed.
HELD: The plaintiff was not entitled to judgment for more than 50% of this claim. Apportionment of liability in a case of contributory negligence between plaintiff and defendants must be kept separate from the apportionment of contribution between the defendants inter se. The decision is to be approached in two separate stages. Per Lord Ackner: 'What is being contrasted is the plaintiff's conduct on the one hand with the totality of the tortious conduct of the defendants on the other.'

CONTRIBUTION MAY BE 100%

Note—See s 2(2) of the Civil Liability (Contribution) Act 1978.

Whitby v Burt, Boulton and Hayward Ltd

[1947] KB 918, [1947] 2 All ER 324, [1947] LJR 1280, 177 LT 556, 111 JP 481, 63 TLR 458, 91 Sol Jo 517 (Denning J)
A workman was injured whilst employed by building contractors engaged on repairing a factory. The occupiers of the factory were held liable for failing to provide safe means of access under the Factories Act 1937, s 26; the employers were held liable for an unsafe system. The occupiers were granted indemnity against the employers. *Ryan v Fildes* (100% contribution) followed.

Appeal against apportionment

British Fame v MacGregor, The MacGregor

[1943] AC 197, [1943] 1 All ER 33, 112 LJP 6, 168 LT 193, 59 TLR 61, 86 Sol Jo 367, 74 LI L Rep 82, HL
The decision of the Court of Appeal in *The Testbank* [1942] P 75, [1942] 1 All ER 281, that the apportionment was open to the same right of appeal as any other conclusion of fact by the judge was overruled on the ground that the statement is too wide.

The House of Lords decided that the finding of the trial judge as to the degrees of blame to be attributed to two or more tortfeasors involves an individual choice or discretion and will not be interfered with on appeal save in very exceptional circumstances, eg if the trial judge has misapprehended a vital fact (per Viscount Simon LC), or there is some error in law or in fact in his judgment (*The Otranto* [1931] AC 194) or he has misinterpreted a rule of navigation (*The Peter Benoit* (1915) 84 LJP 87).

The apportionment of damages is unlike an ordinary finding of fact, and the rules applicable to one are not applicable to the other, but of proportion, of balance and relative emphasis, and of weighing different considerations. It involves an individual choice or discretion.

Ingram v United Automobile Service Ltd

[1943] KB 612, [1943] 2 All ER 71, CA

A lorry of the first defendants was left near a bend on an icy road in the black-out. A bus of the second defendants in passing ran into a bridge and a passenger was injured and sued both defendants. The trial judge found both defendants liable and apportioned two-thirds of the liability to the lorry owners and one-third to the bus owners.

HELD, ON APPEAL: The Court of Appeal should not interfere with the apportionment. The same rule applies as in collisions at sea: *British Fame v MacGregor* was applied.

Brown v Thompson

[1968] 2 All ER 708, [1968] 1 WLR 1003, 112 Sol Jo 464, CA

In a case where liability had been apportioned 80/20 it was argued on behalf of the appellant that where some blame had been attributed to a party by the trial judge the appellate court was at liberty to substitute its own opinion on the proportion.

HELD: This was quite wrong. The principle was, as Lord Wright said in *British Fame v MacGregor* (above) that it would require a very strong case to justify any review of or interference with the question of apportionment. There should be no interference with the judge's view where no error of principle is alleged and no misapprehension of the facts on the part of the judge is suggested.

Hardy v Walder

[1984] RTR 312, CA

The plaintiff, riding a motor cycle, overtook a car at 55 to 60 mph on a blind corner just before reaching a junction with a minor road on the left. The defendant, driving a car, came out of the minor road across dotted white lines without stopping; he looked both ways initially but was looking to his left as he entered the major road and the plaintiff crashed into the side of the car. The judge held the plaintiff two-thirds to blame: he appealed. It was argued on his behalf that the blind overtaking and the excessive speed were irrelevant since he was so near the car when it came out that a collision could not have been avoided whatever his speed.

HELD, DISMISSING THE APPEAL: It was impossible to say that the accident was caused otherwise than by the negligence of both parties. There was no reason to interfere with the judge's apportionment of blame.

Costs on apportionment

The Trivia

[1952] 1 Lloyd's Rep 548 (Wilmer J)

The procedure in Admiralty is different from the QBD where defendants can pay in. The principle in respect of costs is therefore different.

Note—Hence shipping cases are no guide to apportionment of costs in motor cases.

MacCarthy v Raylton Productions

[1951] WN 376, 95 Sol Jo 381, CA
Collision between two motor vehicles; the trial judge held plaintiff alone to blame. On appeal, the Court of Appeal held plaintiff two-thirds to blame and defendant one-third. Defendant contended costs should be apportioned in the same proportions.
HELD: Costs were in the discretion of the court. Where a case raised several distinct issues, it might be a proper exercise of discretion to apportion costs, but the practice is, costs follow the event. Here, all the facts had to be gone into, whether the claim was for the whole of the damages suffered or was limited to a part of them. Plaintiff awarded costs in Court of Appeal and below.

Note—The plaintiff is usually awarded the whole of his costs, even if he is held partly to blame, unless he has failed to recover more than the defendant had paid into court. It is the procedure of payment into court which is now the effective factor in determining the award of costs. See the following:

Waller v Levoi

(1968) 112 Sol Jo 865, Times, 16 October, CA
In a claim for damages arising from a road accident the county court judge found the plaintiff 80% to blame and the defendant 20% and awarded the plaintiff £24. He ordered him to pay four-fifths of the defendant's costs on Scale 3 and ordered the defendant to pay one-fifth of the plaintiff's costs on the same scale.
HELD, ON APPEAL: This order could not stand. There had been no payment into court or counterclaim nor any misconduct on the plaintiff's part. In these circumstances it was wrong to deprive a successful plaintiff of his costs or order him to pay the defendant's costs. The right order where a plaintiff was successful, even though guilty of contributory negligence, was that he should recover costs on the scale appropriate to the amount of damages awarded to him. The plaintiff had been awarded £24 and should have his costs of the action on Scale 2.

2 *RES IPSA LOQUITUR*

THE DOCTRINE

Purpose of doctrine

Scott v London and St Katherine Docks Co

(1865) 3 H & C 596, 34 LJ Ex 220, 13 LT 148, 11 Jur NS 204
Merchandise being lowered in a crane slipped out of its fastenings and fell upon the plaintiff.
HELD: That where the thing is shown to be under the management of the defendants or his servants, and the accident is such as in the ordinary course of things does not happen if those who have the management use proper care, it affords reasonable evidence, in the absence of explanation by the defendant, that the accident arose from want of care.

Cole v De Trafford (No 2)

[1918] 2 KB 523, 87 LJKB 1254, 119 LT 476, 62 Sol Jo 635, CA
The doctrine of *res ipsa loquitur* means that an accident may by its nature be more consistent with its being caused by negligence for which the defendant is responsible than by other causes, and that in such a case the mere fact of the accident is prima facie evidence of such negligence. In such a case the burden of proof is on the defendant to explain and to show that it occurred without fault on his part.

Woods v Duncan

[1946] AC 401, [1946] 1 All ER 420n, [1947] LJR 120, 174 LT 286, 62 TLR 283, HL
Per Viscount Simon: That principle only shifts the onus of proof, which is adequately met by showing that the defendant was not in fact negligent. He is not to be held liable because he cannot prove exactly how the accident happened.

Per Lord Simonds: To apply the principle is to do no more than shift the burden of proof. A prima facie case is assumed to be made out which throws upon the defendant the task of proving that he was not negligent. This does not mean that he must prove how and why the accident happened; it is sufficient if he satisfies the court that he personally was not negligent. It may well be that the court will be more easily satisfied of this fact if a plausible explanation which attributes the accident to some other cause is put forward on his behalf; but this is only a factor in the consideration of the probabilities. The accident may remain inexplicable, or at least no satisfactory explanation other than his negligence may be offered: yet, if the court is satisfied by his evidence that he was not negligent, the plaintiff's case must fail. The defendant can by an affirmative proof that he was not negligent discharge the burden that lies upon him without satisfying the court how otherwise the accident happened, and I think he has done so.

Turner v Mansfield Corpn

(1975) 119 Sol Jo 629, CA
The driver of a dustcart was injured when the tipping body of the dustcart inexplicably rose when the vehicle was being driven and struck a railway bridge.
HELD: Not a case of *res ipsa loquitur*. The vehicle was not under the control of the defendants but under the joint control of the plaintiff and defendants. *Res ipsa loquitur* was not a doctrine but a rule as to the weight of evidence from which negligence could be inferred.

Defendants' onus of proof

Barkway v South Wales Transport Co Ltd

[1950] AC 185, [1950] 1 All ER 392, 66 TLR 597, 94 Sol Jo 128, HL
Per Asquith LJ: The onus is on the defendants to show either a specific cause not connoting their negligence or that they used all reasonable care, it being insufficient merely to show that the accident could have happened without negligence on their part.

Note—For facts, see p 37, below.

Bennett v Chemical Construction (GB) Ltd

[1971] 3 All ER 822, [1971] 1 WLR 1571, 115 Sol Jo 550, CA
The plaintiff, a foreman steel erector, was supervising the installation of electrical control panels. One of the panels started to topple and the plaintiff rushed forward to steady it; as he was doing so another panel next to it fell on him, causing injuries. At the trial the plaintiff was unable to show what caused the panel to fall, nor could the defendants suggest any explanation for the accident. The judge said the panels could not have fallen unless their stability had been interfered with or unless there was some lack of care by the workmen working on the first panel. He accordingly held the defendants negligent.
HELD, ON APPEAL: On the evidence before him the judge could not have come to any other conclusion. It was a classic case of *res ipsa loquitur*. It was not necessary for that doctrine to be pleaded when it was proved that the accident could not have happened without negligence on the part of the defendants.

Aspin v Bretherton

See p 220, below.
If the defendants give an explanation consistent with negligence or no negligence, the onus of proof of negligence passes to the plaintiff.

The defendants are not required to prove exactly how the accident happened. It is sufficient for them to give an explanation which is consistent with no negligence.

Note—See also *Ludgate v Lovett*, p 30, below.

Swan v Salisbury Construction Co Ltd

[1966] 2 All ER 138, [1966] 1 WLR 204, 109 Sol Jo 195, PC
The plaintiff was employed by the defendants as a labourer on pile-driving, which was done by means of a crane. In the course of the work the crane toppled over and the plaintiff was injured. At the trial the judge accepted the evidence of another servant of the defendants' that the cause of the crane falling was that the ground gave way under one of the wheels of the crane and the wheel bolts sheared as a result of the jolt. The judge also found that having regard to the work which had already been done it was not reasonable to anticipate that the ground would give way or that extra precautions should have been taken against it. He gave judgment for the defendants.
HELD, ON APPEAL: There had been no failure on the part of the judge to apply the principles summarised in the phrase '*res ipsa loquitur*'. When once the plaintiff had proved he was injured by the collapse of the crane he was well on the way to proving his care—*res ipsa loquitur*. But the mere fact that the crane fell did not establish that the case must inevitably succeed: it was then for the defendants to show that they had not been negligent. The judge had decided on the evidence what caused the crane to fall over and that the defendants had taken reasonable care in positioning it. This was a conclusion of fact and not based on any error in law. Appeal dismissed.

Ng Chun Pui v Lee Chuen Tat

(1988) 132 Sol Jo 1244, [1988] RTR 298, PC
A coach in Hong Kong skidded, crossed the central reservation of a dual carriageway and collided with a light bus. The plaintiffs relied on the doctrine of *res ipsa loquitur*. The defendants called evidence to show that the accident occurred because an

untraced car cut into the fast lane some 6 feet ahead of the coach, causing the driver to brake and swerve.
HELD: The plaintiffs' claim failed; they had not proved negligence. The burden of proof remains with the plaintiff and it is misleading to talk of this shifting to the defendant if *res ipsa loquitur* is pleaded.

Worsley v Hollins

[1991] RTR 252, CA
The plaintiff was stationary in a line of traffic. The first defendant driving the second defendant's nine year old van, failed to stop and drove into the rear of the plaintiff's vehicle. The plaintiff brought proceedings against both defendants.

It was ruled by the judge that the maxim *res ipsa loquitur* applied and the defendants gave evidence first. The first defendant claimed that the van's brakes failed and it was established that an essential part was missing. When replaced the brakes operated correctly. This evidence was accepted and the judge found the driver had not been negligent.

The next question to be dealt with was whether the owner had taken reasonable care to have the van properly maintained. In his defence the second defendant produced a valid MOT certificate and a bill from a reputable firm of engineers for a 'full service' carried out some six weeks before the accident. Parts were charged at £13.64 and labour of £28.00. The judge found that on the basis of these charges a full safety check would not have been obtained and, therefore, the second defendant had run a very old vehicle without having it properly checked. The plaintiff succeeded against the second defendant. The second defendant appealed.
HELD: The production of a valid MOT certificate was not sufficient to discharge the second defendant's burden of proof. However, it was not correct of the judge to reject the second defendant's unchallenged evidence and conclude that on the basis of the amount charged the second defendant had not given instructions for a full service. Therefore the plaintiff's claim against the second defendant failed.

Defendant electing not to give evidence

Chapman v Copeland

(1966) 110 Sol Jo 569, Times, 7 May, CA
The plaintiff's husband was crossing the first lane of a dual carriageway on his moped when he was struck and killed by a car driven by the defendant. The evidence brought on behalf of the plaintiff was that her husband had waited for a time at the side of the road and had crossed 17 feet of the 24 feet wide lane when hit. A police officer gave evidence of marks on the road 184 feet long made by the car. The defendant by his counsel elected to give no evidence, maintaining that there was no evidence of negligence against him on behalf of the widow. The judge held the defendant wholly to blame.

An appeal was dismissed. In such a case as this the defendant was not under an obligation to give evidence, but if he chose not to do so he could not complain if on a narrow balance of probability the evidence justified the court in drawing the inference of negligence against him. On the slender evidence of the length of the brake marks the inference was sufficient for the court's purposes. On the question of contributory negligence it was for the defendant to prove it and again he had not done so.

Failure to discharge onus

Ludgate v Lovett

[1969] 2 All ER 1275, [1969] 1 WLR 1016, 113 Sol Jo 369, CA

The defendant hired a motor van from the plaintiff. It was in good condition with no mechanical defects. When the defendant was driving along a motorway at speed it suddenly swerved to right and left and turned over. The plaintiff sued for the damage done, pleading *res ipsa loquitur*. The county court judge accepted the defendant's evidence that he did not go to sleep or fail to pay attention and that he was not negligent. The judge suggested an explanation of the accident which was not supported by any evidence and dismissed the claim.

HELD, ON APPEAL: The plaintiff was entitled to succeed. In a *res ipsa loquitur* case it is open to the defendant to satisfy the court that he took all reasonable precautions and was not negligent even though he cannot explain why or how the accident happened. But in the present case the presumption of negligence from the facts of the accident was too strong to be overcome merely by the defendant's denial that he had done anything negligent. The judge had accepted the defendant's evidence of no negligence only by advancing an explanation of his own. As this was not acceptable it remained that the defendant had not discharged the onus placed upon him by the plea *res ipsa loquitur*.

McBride v Stitt

[1944] NI 7, CA

The plaintiff's daughter was killed by a lorry owned by one of the defendants and driven on the public road by the other defendant. At the trial of an action brought by the plaintiff claiming damages for the negligent driving of the lorry no eye-witness of the accident was called and the principal evidence consisted of certain statements made by the defendants to the effect that two little boys having run from behind a motor car travelling in the opposite direction, the driver of the lorry was obliged to swerve in order to avoid hitting them, and in doing so struck the plaintiff's daughter who was cycling from a side street on to the road on which the lorry was travelling. At the close of the plaintiff's case the trial judge held that the statements were not admissions of negligence, that they pointed to inevitable accident, and that the plaintiff had not discharged the onus of proof, and gave judgment for the defendants.

HELD: By the Court of Appeal that the plaintiff had established a prima facie case of negligence of which no satisfactory explanation had been given by the defendants; and that the statements of the defendants whether in favour of the plaintiff or the defendants were admissible in evidence in toto; and that there should be a new trial of the action.

VEHICLE COLLISIONS—INFERENCE OF NEGLIGENCE

Hummerstone v Leary

[1921] 2 KB 664, 90 LJKB 1148, 125 LT 669, Div Ct

A collision between two cars raises an inference of negligence and the onus is on the defendants.

Plaintiffs, who were injured in a collision between a motor lorry, in which they were passengers, and a motor car, brought an action in the county court claiming

damages, making the owners of both vehicles defendants. Plaintiffs' evidence appeared to make it probable that the driver of the car rather than the driver of the lorry was to blame, but they could do no more than state what they observed just before the collision occurred. Their evidence did not affirmatively or conclusively show that the driver of the lorry was not to blame. At the close of plaintiffs' case counsel for the owner of the lorry submitted that there was no evidence against him and the county court judge took this view and dismissed that defendant from the action. The case then proceeded against the other defendant, whose witnesses threw all the blame on the driver of the lorry, and the county court judge found that the driver of the car was not negligent, and accordingly entered judgment for the second defendant.
HELD: As a state of facts was proved by the plaintiffs from which the reasonable inference to be drawn was that, prima facie, one, if not both, of the defendants was negligent, the county court judge should not have dismissed the first defendant, the owner of the lorry, from the action at the close of the plaintiffs' case, but should have heard the case against both defendants before coming to a decision, and therefore, there must be a new trial.

Baker v Market Harborough Co-operative Society Ltd
Wallace v Richards (Leicester) Ltd

[1953] 1 WLR 1472, 97 Sol Jo 861, CA
A motor lorry and a motor van, in the hours of darkness, descending hills in opposite directions, met at the bottom. The two vehicles had collided whilst the offside front wheel of one or other, or perhaps both, was over the 'cat's eyes' which demarked the centre of the road. Both drivers were killed. The widow of each sued the employers of the other. One action was dismissed by Ormerod J on the ground that the plaintiff had failed to prove negligence. In the second, Sellers J differed from Ormerod J in the inference to be drawn from the same facts and held both drivers equally to blame. Appeals in both cases were taken together.
HELD: The inference was that both drivers were negligent in not keeping a proper look-out and hugging the centre of the road. In the absence of evidence that one was more to blame than the other, the blame should be apportioned equally. Assuming that one vehicle was over the centre line a few inches, and thus to blame, why did not the other pull in more to its nearside? The absence of any avoiding action makes that vehicle also to blame. It was not necessary to prove that the other vehicle was over the cat's eyes. It was sufficient to show that the defendant should have taken avoiding action.

Bray v Palmer

[1953] 2 All ER 1449, [1953] 1 WLR 1455, 97 Sol Jo 830, CA
A motor cyclist with a pillion passenger was proceeding on the main road from Gloucester to Bristol and a small motor car with passengers was proceeding in the opposite direction. The time was about midday on 6 August 1951. The road was approximately 26 feet wide. There was no other traffic. There was a pool of water on the car's nearside. The car turned to the off to avoid this pool. The motor cycle also turned to its off side and there was a collision in the middle of the road. Both vehicles were proceeding at a reasonable speed. The motor cyclist alleged that the car turned so far to its off that he had to turn to the off to avoid a collision. The judge decided that the accident was due either to the sole negligence of the car driver or the sole negligence of the motor cyclist and was not prepared to find both to blame. He was unable to decide which was the right story, and on the principle that the claimant must

prove his case he dismissed the claim of the motor cyclist and the counterclaim of the motor car driver.
HELD: The possibility of both to blame should not have been excluded. Until a judge has decided that an accident has happened in some particular way, he is not in a position to decide. New trial ordered.

Note—Distinguished in *Salt v Imperial Chemical Industries* (1958) Times, 1 February, CA.

Price v Price

(1954) Times, 12 February, CA
In March 1949, the plaintiff was a pillion passenger on a motor cycle driven by his son and was injured in a collision with a Wallasey Corporation omnibus. On 19 April 1950, Mr Justice Oliver dismissed an action by the plaintiff against the Corporation, finding the son alone to blame.

The father then brought an action against the son. Mr Justice Devlin dismissed the claim and gave judgment for the son.

In both actions the plaintiff had given evidence that the son was not to blame.
HELD, ON APPEAL: The plaintiff had only himself to blame for not suing both parties in the first action. Appeal dismissed.

France v Parkinson

[1954] 1 All ER 739, [1954] 1 WLR 581, 98 Sol Jo 214, CA
Two motor cars collided at crossroads of equal status. The driver of the plaintiff's car had hired the car under a false name and disappeared after the accident. The plaintiff's only evidence was that of a police officer from whose evidence it was reasonably plain that both cars were on the right side of their respective roads and they collided somewhere where the two crossroads met. He also gave evidence that the defendant said—'I was going along the road and we met in the middle.' The defendant called no evidence and the judge dismissed the plaintiff's claim.
HELD, ON APPEAL: Following *Baker*'s case, the balance of probabilities was in favour of both drivers having been negligent, particularly having regard to the place of collision and the statement to the police officer. There was a prima facie case against the defendant on which the court should have found him negligent in the absence of any evidence given by him. Appeal allowed.

Shiner v Webster

(1955) Times, 27 April
A motor cyclist was riding along a main road in broad daylight at 40 mph, and the rider of an auto-cycle was proceeding in the opposite direction and presumably was turning into a side road on his off side. A collision occurred and the auto-cyclist was killed and the motor cyclist suffered severe concussion and was unable to recollect anything about the accident. The only witness was the driver of a motor car following the auto-cyclist. This witness was certain that the deceased was intending to cross the road as he made a circular turn up to the middle of the road, showing that he was going to turn into the side road. It looked to him as though both acted as though the other was not on the road at all.

Finnemore J held there was not enough evidence to show whose negligence caused the accident and as in neither case had it been proved before him that there had been negligence, he gave judgment for the defendant in each of the two actions of the

deceased's administrator against the motor cyclist and of the motor cyclist against the administrator. The administrator appealed.
HELD: A court cannot say—we do not know whose fault it was and therefore there is no remedy for anyone. It was impossible to take the view that neither saw the other. The trial judge was wrong in thinking that it was not proved that either were negligent. There was evidence of negligence on the part of both. Appeal allowed and, by a majority, both held equally to blame.

W and M Wood (Haulage) Ltd v Redpath

[1967] 2 QB 520, [1966] 3 All ER 556, [1966] 3 WLR 526, 110 Sol Jo 673 (Ashworth J)
Shortly before midnight a lorry and a car collided on the Great North Road, there was no other traffic, visibility was clear and from the point of collision it was possible to see in both directions for 350 yards. The occupants of the car were killed and the lorry driver died later. There were no other witnesses. There was some police evidence as to marks on the road which was inconclusive.
HELD: It was not possible to say with confidence which of the vehicles was over the centre line. In these circumstances the case fell within the principle applied in *Baker v Market Harborough Co-op Society*. There was no cogent evidence suggesting that one driver was more to blame than the other and the drivers must be held equally to blame.

Davison v Leggett

(1969) 133 JP 552, 113 Sol Jo 409, CA
The plaintiff driving his van on a straight main road overtook a car. The defendant riding a motor cycle in the opposite direction also overtook a car. The van and motor cycle collided in the middle of the road. The judge said he could find no indication who began overtaking first and who was in the wrong: it was feasible that neither was negligent. He dismissed both claim and counterclaim.
HELD, ON APPEAL: Following *Baker v Market Harborough Co-op Society* (above) where one or both parties were to blame and the court could not decide which, the inference was that both were equally to blame. The principle was not confined to cases where both drivers were dead or could not remember.

Howard v Bemrose

[1973] RTR 32, CA
On a country road in the dark a motor cyclist and car collided at a bend. The car driver did not remember anything of the accident; the motor cyclist was killed. Marks and débris on the road and the final positions of the vehicles were the only evidence. The judge said that having examined all the facts and argument as put to the court he was unable to say whether or not (as had been argued) the car was on its offside of the road or not at the moment of impact. He therefore considered the right course to adopt was to apply the *Baker v Market Harborough Co-op* principle and hold the parties equally to blame. The motor cyclist's personal representative appealed.
HELD: The judge was entitled so to hold. What he was saying was that it was no more probable that the collision took place on the car driver's wrong side than that it took place in the centre of the road at the bend. As he was quite unable without independent evidence to say whether it was caused by the negligence of the motor cyclist rather than of the car driver he was right to divide the blame between them equally.

EVENTS IMPLYING NEGLIGENCE

Sudden stop or swerve

O'Hara v Central Scottish Motor Traction Co Ltd

1941 SC 363, 1941 SLT 202
Pulling up suddenly and violently is prima facie evidence of negligence (*Mars v Glasgow Corpn* 1940 SC 202, 1940 SLT 165) and so is a violent swerve.

Ballingall v Glasgow Corpn

1948 SC 160, 1948 SN 22, 1948 SLT 261, Scot
Sudden braking of a tramcar to avoid a collision with a motor van going in the opposite direction did not per se establish negligence of the driver. *Mars*'s case and *O'Hara*'s case distinguished.

Doonan v Scottish Motor Traction Co

1950 SC 136, 1950 SLT 100, Ct of Sess
The fact that a bus struck a fence after a swerve raised a presumption of the driver's negligence despite the explanation that the swerve was due to a child's sudden running across the road.

Note—In the above three cases the plaintiff was a passenger in the defendant's vehicle.

Ritchie's Car Hire Ltd v Bailey

(1958) 108 L Jo 348, Epsom CC (Gordon–Clarke J)
Defendant hired a car from plaintiffs on terms that he was liable for damage to the car unless he could show that such damage was not due to his act or default. He was driving in an empty suburban street about 36 feet wide at 4.40 am. He was neither tired nor sleepy, driving under 30 mph about a yard from the kerb when a cat suddenly ran out very near the car from the near side. He instinctively swerved and hit a kerb tree almost simultaneously. He had no time to apply his brakes. The plaintiff sued defendant for the damages to the car.
HELD: There might be a school of thought which said that a driver should subordinate the interests of animals to the safety of passengers, or even of a vehicle, but such a doctrine has never been expressed by Parliament or in the Highway Code. Nowhere was it stated that a driver was at fault in swerving to avoid an animal. The defendant had apparently no time for thought, but it could not be said that his action would have been a correct one had he had time to reflect on it, yet in the particular circumstances it could not also be said that what the defendant did was unreasonable. Judgment for defendant.

Gussman v Gratton-Storey

(1968) 112 Sol Jo 884, CA
The defendant was driving her car along a country road in daylight when a pheasant dashed out in front of the car. She instinctively braked hard and swerved to avoid it. The plaintiff who was driving close behind her ran into the back of her car. The county court judge in the plaintiff's claim for £62 damages said the defendant was negligent in braking and swerving for a pheasant when there was a car behind and gave judgment for the plaintiff.

HELD, ON APPEAL: As the amount was under £200 there was no appeal on fact and as the judge's view was a perfectly tenable one it could not be said there was no evidence on which he could so decide. Appeal dismissed.

Note—Contrast *Ritchie's Car Hire Ltd v Bailey*, above, and *Parkinson v Liverpool Corpn*, p 169, below.

Vehicles overlapping pavement

Ellor v Selfridge & Co Ltd

(1930) 46 TLR 236, 74 Sol Jo 140
Where a motor van gets on to a pavement intended for foot passengers and injures persons standing there, these facts, in the absence of explanation, constitute evidence of negligence.

McGowan v Stott

(1920) 99 LJKB 357, 143 LT 217, CA
Plaintiff was walking along a well defined footpath. Defendant's motor vehicle mounted the footpath and struck plaintiff. This was considered sufficient evidence of negligence.

Laurie v Raglan Building Co Ltd

[1942] 1 KB 152, [1941] 3 All ER 332, 111 LJKB 292, 166 LT 63, 86 Sol Jo 69, CA
Where a portion of the vehicle sweeps across the pavement, the facts raise a prima facie case of negligence just as much as where the wheels mount the pavement. It is a position where it has no right to be. No vehicle has a right so to manoeuvre itself that its tail or its radiator, or whatever it may be, projects over the pavement to the injury of pedestrians lawfully there.

Watson v Thomas S Whitney & Co Ltd

[1966] 1 All ER 122, [1966] 1 WLR 57, 130 JP 109, 110 Sol Jo 73, CA
Shortly after midnight the plaintiff was walking along the pavement about six inches from the edge and with the roadway on his left. The defendants' van turned in suddenly from the middle of the road to draw in alongside the pavement for a passenger to alight. In doing so it struck the plaintiff's left arm with the projecting handle of a door, causing him slight injury. The registrar of the Liverpool Court of Passage held the defendant's driver not to blame: he had difficulty in seeing the plaintiff whom he would not expect to be there.
HELD, ON APPEAL: The registrar was wrong. There was no blame to be attached to the plaintiff in walking close to the edge of the pavement. The pavement should give security to those who use it from vehicles using the road. There was clear liability on the driver where, as here, the vehicle overlapped the footpath.

Note—See also *Chapman v Post Office* p 113, below.

Car in shop window

Gayler and Pope Ltd v Davies

[1924] 2 KB 75, 93 LJKB 702, 131 LT 507, 40 TLR 591, 68 Sol Jo 685 (McCardie J)
When a pony and van (or a motor vehicle) wholly unattended dash into plaintiff's shop window adjoining a highway there is a prima facie case of negligence.

Car on hill

Martin v Stanborough

(1924) 41 TLR 1, 69 Sol Jo 104, CA
To leave a motor car unattended on a fairly steep slope in a public highway, with the brakes out of order and with only an easily removable block of wood to keep the car in position, so that the car could easily be started downhill by any mischievous person, constitutes evidence of negligence.

Car turning over

Halliwell v Venables

(1930) 99 LJKB 353, 143 LT 215, 74 Sol Jo 264, CA
The defendant was driving a fast small sports car. It was a dark night, dry; broad road; no other traffic, slight bend. The defendant said he was going at 35 mph, driving with one hand only on the wheel as was his usual practice. The car was found to have turned over, possibly twice, and bounced along the road. The passenger was thrown out on the right-hand side of the road and fatally injured. The car was found some way off the road on the left-hand side. On a submission by defendant's counsel in an action brought by the passenger's widow the judge held there was no case to go to the jury. HELD, ON APPEAL: There was evidence which should have been submitted to the jury. The mere happening of the accident, unexplained, may be and often is in itself evidence of negligence. The facts required explanation by the person driving the car; they constituted an accident which would not usually happen with proper driving. New trial ordered.

Note—See also *Hurlock v Inglis*, p 73, below.

Collided with stationary vehicle

Randall v Tarrant

[1955] 1 All ER 600, [1955] 1 WLR 255, 99 Sol Jo 184, CA
The plaintiff stopped his car in a lane which was a public highway but only led to a farm occupied by the defendant. The lane was about 15 feet wide. The car was 5 feet 6 inches wide and as close as possible to the near side. The plaintiff trespassed into an adjoining field of the defendant, and while he was there the defendant drove a tractor towing a baler which was 9 feet wide along the lane. On approaching the car, which the defendant thought was unattended, he slowed down. His servant was sitting at the back of the baler and shouted 'I think we can get through, guv'nor.' In attempting to pass, the baler struck the car and damaged it.

HELD: When there is a collision between a moving vehicle and a stationary vehicle which is plainly visible, the onus is on the driver of the moving vehicle to show that he has taken all reasonable care and the onus had not been discharged. The fact that the plaintiff was trespassing on the defendant's field at the time did not make the plaintiff a trespasser on the highway in respect of the car, or that he was committing a nuisance, and the defence based on trespass failed.

Tyre bursting

Barkway v South Wales Transport Co Ltd

[1950] AC 185, [1950] 1 All ER 392, 66 TLR 597, 94 Sol Jo 128, HL
A motor omnibus of the defendants was proceeding along the highway when the off front tyre burst. The omnibus then went to the off side of the road, mounted the pavement, crashed into some railings and fell on its side down an embankment. Four passengers were killed and others injured.

The burst was caused by an impact fracture of the cord of the outer tyre brought about by a blow more severe than in the ordinary course on the external surface of the tyre causing some of the plys to become fractured. The tyre which burst was periodically examined on the rim by an expert fitter of the defendants. He examined it on frequent dates during January and February 1943, the last occasion on 24 February, three days before the accident and on each occasion adjusted the pressure, and he tested the pressure on 20 February and 22 February. There was no evidence when the impact fracture was caused. No instructions were given to drivers to report an unusual and heavy blow on the tyre. There was no examination of the internal surface. A burst in this size of tyres is very rare. The tyre would go in for thorough examination at 25,000 miles. It had not been taken off for examination for nearly 18 months, during which time it had run about 21,750 miles.
HELD, ON APPEAL to the House of Lords:

Per Lord Porter: Adopting the language in *Scott v London and St Katherine Docks Co* (p 26, above), if the facts are sufficiently known, the question is whether on the established facts, negligence is to be inferred or not.

The decision in favour of the plaintiff depends on one or other of the grounds (1) whether there was negligence in the system of inspection, or (2) of any of the drivers in not reporting a blow severe enough to cause an impact fracture. The evidence established that a competent driver would recognise the difference between a blow heavy enough to endanger the strength of the tyre and a lesser concussion. If this be so, the fact that he would be unlikely to report it would still leave him negligent in not doing so, and for that negligence his employers must answer. In the second place, it was the duty of the respondents, who were fully aware of the possibility of an impact fracture, to instruct their employees as to the effect which a heavy blow may produce, and to impress upon them the necessity of reporting its incidence. An uninstructed driver might not know nor have experience of such a danger, and that difficulty would be surmounted if proper instructions were given. Such an incident is a rare event but the duty of a transport company is to take all reasonable precautions for the safety of their passengers and not to leave them in danger of a risk against which some precautions, at any rate, can be taken. Although the practice of inspection and overhaul of tyres was adequate in other respects, and was in accordance with the practice of companies carrying on a similar occupation, the respondents did not take all the requisite steps to protect their passengers from risk.

Per Lord Normand: The drivers themselves failed to report impacts which they ought to have reported, the respondents failed to instruct their drivers about impact fractures and to require them to report, and the tyre examiners ought to have been, but were not, informed. The defendants were liable.

Note—See also 'Latent Defect', p 214, below.

Elliott v Chiew

(1966) 110 Sol Jo 724, Times, 24 May, CA
The defendant was driving the plaintiff's car on the M1 motorway with the plaintiff as a passenger. When travelling at 70 to 80 mph the defendant felt a swaying of the car over the back wheels. It was corrected after a little distance but the defendant said at some point 'I can't hold the car'. After going all right for a few moments the car began to sway again: the defendant applied the brakes but the car went out of control over an embankment, seriously injuring the plaintiff. A police officer gave evidence that after the accident the rear offside tyre was flat. An expert gave evidence that the tyre had probably deflated gradually and that it should have been possible to bring the car under control. The judge found that the cause of the accident was in all probability a deflated tyre, that when the brakes were applied the car went out of control and that nothing which a reasonably competent driver could have done at that time could have prevented the accident. He dismissed the claim.
HELD, ON APPEAL: It was essentially a matter for the judge who heard the case and saw the witnesses. The principle of *res ipsa loquitur* enabled the plaintiff to get the case on its legs but at the end the judge had to ask himself: was the defendant negligent or not? It was a matter for regret that he had not referred to the expert's evidence but a judgment was not to be criticised because a judge did not refer to everything which no doubt had passed through his mind. Where there was this evidence from the driver and passengers from which the judge could conclude that the driver was not guilty of negligence the Court of Appeal should not interfere.

Independent wrongdoer

Ruoff v Long & Co

[1916] 1 KB 148, 85 LJKB 364, 114 LT 186, 32 TLR 82, 60 Sol Jo 323
The principle does not apply where the negligence is wholly that of an independent wrongdoer. A person lawfully leaving his property unattended on a highway must take reasonable means to prevent such mischief as he ought to contemplate as likely to arise from his use of the highway. He is not liable for damage caused by his property through such interference of a third person as he is not bound to anticipate.

Defendant's servants momentarily left stationary but unattended on a highway a steam motor lorry. In order to start the lorry it was necessary to withdraw a hand-pin from the gear lever and then to remove that and two other levers. Two soldiers seeing the lorry mounted it. One tried but failed to set it in motion. The other succeeded in starting it backwards, so that it ran into plaintiff's shop front and did damage, for which the action was brought.
HELD: (1) There was in the circumstances no evidence of negligence in leaving the lorry unattended. (2) Assuming that there was negligence, there was no evidence that it caused the damage.

Animals on highway

Note—See Chapter 8.

Inference of negligence rebutted

Knight v Fellick

[1977] RTR 316, CA
In the hours of darkness in an unlighted street the plaintiff, a street sweeper, was injured when knocked over by the defendant's car. The plaintiff remembered nothing of the accident. The defendant did not see the plaintiff before the impact. There was a brief written statement by a witness who had since died but otherwise no account at the trial from an eye witness. The judge concluded from the available evidence including the position of damage to the car that the defendant was not to blame.
HELD, ON APPEAL: The judge's conclusions on a balance of probabilities were justified. It was not a case to which the principles applied in such cases as *Baker v Market Harborough Co-operative* and *Davison v Leggett* (pp 31–33, above) were applicable. That line of cases related to collisions between two vehicles more or less in the centre of the road and were not to be extended beyond that ambit. The inference of negligence from the defendant not having seen the plaintiff before impact had, on the available evidence, been rebutted.

Note—See also *Morales v Eccleston*, 15, above.

3 CONDITIONS OF NO LIABILITY

INTRODUCTION

Accident: definition

Fenton v Thorley & Co Ltd

[1903] AC 443, 72 LJKB 787, 89 LT 314, HL
An unlooked-for mishap or an untoward event which is not expected or designed. Any unintended and unexpected occurrence which produces hurt or loss, or such hurt or loss apart from its cause especially if the cause is not known.

R v Morris

[1972] 1 All ER 384, [1972] 1 WLR 228, 136 JP 194, 116 Sol Jo 17, Div Ct
'Accident' in the present context [The Road Safety Act 1967, s 2(2)] means an unintended occurrence which has an adverse physical result.

Chief Constable of West Midlands Police v Billingham

[1979] 2 All ER 182, [1979] 1 WLR 747, 123 Sol Jo 98, [1979] RTR 446, QBD
It would not be right to treat the definition of 'accident' in *R v Morris* (above) as if it were written into the statute (now the Road Traffic Act 1972, s 8(2)). Where a man deliberately entered a police car, released the brake, steered it round a parked car and then let it run downhill and crash down an embankment 25 feet deep there was an 'accident' for the purposes of the section. The test was whether an ordinary man would say in the circumstances that an accident had occurred.

Note—Section 8(2) of the Road Traffic Act 1972 has been replaced by s 7(2) of the Road Traffic Act 1988.

Chief Constable of Staffordshire v Lees

[1981] RTR 506, QBD
The defendant deliberately drove his car through a locked gate, smashing it.
HELD: Applying *Chief Constable of West Midlands Police v Billingham* (above) an 'accident' could be said to have occurred within the meaning of the Road Traffic Act 1972, s 8 (2). It was relevant to note that among the meanings to be found in the Oxford English Dictionary is 'an unfortunate event, a mishap'.

Wind records

A report on weather conditions, temperatures and wind force at any time or place can be obtained from the Meteorological Office, London Road, Bracknell, Berks. Alternatively application may be made for reports on the weather to the London Weather Centre, 284–286 High Holborn, WC1, or the Manchester Weather Centre 56 Royal Exchange, Manchester, 2, or the Southampton Weather Centre, 160 High St, Below Bar, Southampton, Hants.

ACT OF GOD

Nugent v Smith

(1876) 1 CPD 423, 45 LJQB 697, 34 LT 827, 41 JP 4
A direct, violent, sudden and irresistible act of nature, which could not, by any reasonable care, have been foreseen or resisted.

Trent and Mersey Navigation Co v Wood

(1785) 4 Doug KB 287, 3 Esp 127
The act of God is natural necessity, as winds and storms, which arise from natural causes, and is distinct from inevitable accident.

Greenock Corpn v Caledonian Rly Co

[1917] AC 556, 86 LJPC 185, 117 LT 483, 81 JP 269, HL
Circumstances which no human foresight can provide against, and of which human prudence is not bound to recognise the possibility.

AGONY OF THE MOMENT AND ALTERNATIVE DANGER

Brandon v Osborne, Garrett & Co

[1924] 1 KB 548, 93 LJKB 304, 130 LT 670, 40 TLR 235, 68 Sol Jo 460 (Swift J)
Where a person or a third party is placed in danger by the wrongful act of the defendant, that person is not negligent if he exercises such care as may reasonably be expected of him in the difficult position in which he is so placed. He is not to blame if he does not do quite the right thing in the circumstances.

Note—See also *Tocci v Hankard*, p 70, below. 'Alternative danger' has a somewhat similar principle to 'agony of the moment'. See the cases of *Jones v Boyce* (p 167, below), *Adams v Lancashire and Yorkshire Railway Company* ((1869) LR 4 CP 739, 20 LT 850, 17 WR 884) and *Tocci v Hankard* (p 70, below).

INEVITABLE ACCIDENT

Note—See also 'Act of God', p 40, above.

In an unreported case where a wasp entered a car and settled on the driver's eye (*Gilson v Kidman* (28 October 1938, unreported), Mr Justice Lewis adopted the definition of inevitable accident of Sir James Colville in *The Marpesia* (1872) LR 4 PC 212. Nothing was done or omitted to be done which a person exercising ordinary care, caution and maritime skill, in the circumstances, either would not have done, or would not have left undone, as the case may be.

The judge held that the defence of inevitable accident had not been made out and gave a verdict for the plaintiff.

Per Lord Justice Fry (in *The Merchant Prince* [1892] P 179): The burden rests on the defendants to show inevitable accident. To sustain that, the defendants must do one of two things. They must either show what was the cause of the accident, and show that the result of that cause was inevitable; or they must show all the possible causes, one or other of which produced the effect, and must further show with regard to every one of these possible causes that the result could not have been avoided. Unless they do one or other of these two things, it does not appear to me that they have shown inevitable accident.

The principles were followed in *The Saint Angus* [1938] P 225.

McBride v Stitt

[1944] NI 7, CA (Andrews CJ)
'Inevitable accident' was defined by Dr Lushington in the Admiralty case of *The Virgil* (1843) 2 Wm Rob 201 in terms which have since received general acceptance—'that which the party charged with the offence could not possibly prevent by the exercise of ordinary care, caution and maritime skill'. Omitting the word 'maritime' the definition is as applicable to Courts of Common Law as to the Court of Admiralty.

Pleading inevitable accident

Rumbold v London County Council

(1909) 25 TLR 541, 53 Sol Jo 502, CA
Where in an action claiming damages for negligence the defence denies negligence, the defendant may give evidence that the accident was an inevitable accident. In such case the defence of inevitable accident need not be specifically pleaded.

Note—In view of an Irish decision, the above statement was formerly doubted, but it is accepted in the *Supreme Court Practice*, 1993, notes to Ord 18, rr 8 and 12. Nevertheless when inevitable accident is relied upon the invariable practice is to plead it.

INVOLUNTARY ACT

Driver overcome by illness/death

Ryan v Youngs

[1938] 1 All ER 522, 82 Sol Jo 233, CA
Driver died whilst driving lorry, which ran on and injured the plaintiff. Driver appeared to be in sound health but suffered from fatty degeneration of the heart. Medical examination would not have indicated any liability to sudden collapse.
HELD: (1) The man appeared to be in good health; medical examination would not have disclosed any defect; the defendant was under no obligation to have the driver medically examined; and the defendant was not negligent. (2) There was no defect in the lorry and it was not a nuisance. (3) The accident was due to an act of God.

Waugh v James K Allan Ltd

[1964] 2 Lloyd's Rep 1, 1964 SC (HL) 102, 1964 SLT 269
The driver of a lorry was suddenly disabled by an attack of coronary thrombosis which killed him. The lorry mounted the pavement and struck the appellant injuring him. Fifteen minutes before the accident the driver had been taken ill when loading the lorry but had recovered, at least partially, and had driven off. He had driven a quarter of a mile when the accident occurred. He had had gastric attacks from time to time in the past but had otherwise enjoyed good health.
HELD: A motor vehicle is potentially a dangerous and lethal instrument; there rests upon every driver of such a vehicle a serious duty owed to his fellow human beings not to drive the vehicle on a public highway if he has or should have any reasonable ground for thinking that, from illness or otherwise, his skill or judgment as a driver may have been impaired. Nevertheless, on the facts of this case, the driver was not negligent in taking the lorry out; he had no reason to suppose that his illness was not another gastric attack which, when it passed off, had left no serious disability. The respondents, his employers, were not liable.

Jones v Dennison

[1971] RTR 174, CA
The defendant was driving his car when it ran out of control on to the pavement, striking the plaintiff and injuring her. His defence to her claim for damages was that he had temporarily lost control due to a 'blackout', ie a loss of consciousness. His medical history included a coronary thrombosis six years earlier and a slight cerebral thrombosis. His doctor had not advised he should not drive. He had also had four short blackouts in the previous ten months but had been unaware of them: his wife knew of them but did not tell him of them until after the accident. In the court below the judge accepted the defendant's evidence that he did not know of the blackouts before the accident and held that he had discharged the burden of proof on him. His wife was not called to give evidence because of illness. On appeal it was argued that without the wife's evidence as to when, where and how the blackouts had taken place it was an undefended case.

HELD: The judge had properly directed himself that the real issue was whether the defendant ought to have realised from what had happened in the past that he ought not to have been driving. On the evidence of the defendant and his doctor there was no ground for saying he ought reasonably to have suspected that he was or might be subject to an attack such as he had. The onus was on the defendant and he had established his case. Appeal dismissed.

Driver overcome by sleep

Kay v Butterworth

(1945) 173 LT 191, 61 TLR 452, 89 Sol Jo 381
The driver of a motor car who had been working all night until 7.45 am at an aircraft factory, was driving a car at about 9 am and was overcome by sleep or drowsiness and ran into the rear of a party of soldiers marching in column in the same direction. The police prosecuted under the Road Traffic Act 1930, ss 11 and 12 (now the Road Traffic Act 1972, ss 2 and 3).
HELD, by Divisional Court, allowing appeal from justices: If a driver allows himself to drive while he is asleep, he is guilty of driving without due care and attention, because it is his business to keep awake; if drowsiness overtakes him whilst at the wheel, he should stop and wait until he shakes it off and is wide awake again. If a person through no fault of his own becomes unconscious while driving, eg by being struck by a stone, or being taken ill, he ought not to be held liable at criminal law. The respondent must have known that drowsiness was overtaking him.

Note—Sections 2 and 3 of the Road Traffic Act 1972 are replaced by ss 2 and 3 of the Road Traffic Act 1988 from 15 May 1989.

Henderson v Jones

(1955) 119 JP 304, 53 LGR 319, Div Ct
Defendant was charged with driving without due care and attention. She contended she was not 'driving' the car because she was admittedly asleep, she had no control over her actions.
HELD: Driving while asleep was at least driving without due care and attention. Being asleep was no excuse.

State of automatism

Watmore v Jenkins

[1962] 2 QB 572, [1962] 2 All ER 868, 126 JP 432, 106 Sol Jo 492, 60 LGR 325, Div Ct
The defendant was a diabetic. Whilst driving home in the evening he was seen at several points en route to be swerving about in the road and finally collided with a parked car. He remembered nothing of the last five miles of the journey. He had injected himself with a normal dose of insulin that morning but medical investigation showed that he was suffering from a hypoglycaemic episode due to the effects of recovery from a recent illness. The episode resulted from an excess of bodily and injected insulin. When the episode overtook him he was driving his car and continued to perform the functions of driving after a fashion until the accident happened. He was

charged with (1) driving a vehicle on a road whilst unfit to drive through drugs; (2) dangerous and careless driving. The charges were dismissed. On the first charge the justices held that the defendant's unfitness to drive was not directly due to the dose of insulin: on the other charges they held that the defendant had been driving in a state of automatism.
HELD: On case stated (1) the justices were entitled on the evidence to entertain a reasonable doubt whether the injected insulin was more than a predisposing or historical cause of the hypoglycaemic episode; (2) the justices had not defined 'a state of automatism'. The expression is no more than a catch phrase to connote the involuntary movement of the body or limbs of a person. It was not reasonable to conclude that the defendant's condition was such that throughout the five miles when he was 'driving after a fashion' the whole of such performance was involuntary or unconscious. There must be a conviction on the charge of dangerous driving.

Farrell v Stirling

[1978] Crim LR 696 (Sheriff Ct)
After a collision with another car the defendant continued to drive his car for a distance of four miles and collided with two other cars. His defence to a charge of careless driving was that he was diabetic and had been in a state of hypoglycaemia.
HELD: The test to determine whether he was 'driving' was whether at the material time he was in conscious control and whether his movements were voluntary. On the evidence he was convicted but given an absolute discharge.

Note—See also *Broome v Perkins* [1987] RTR 321 in which the defendant was charged with driving without due care and attention and relied upon a very similar defence. He was also convicted. Sections 87 and 170 of the Road Traffic Act 1972 have been replaced by ss 92 and 174 respectively of the Road Traffic Act 1988.

Roberts v Ramsbottom

[1980] 1 All ER 7, [1980] 1 WLR 823, 124 Sol Jo 313, [1980] RTR 261 (Neill J)
The defendant, a man of 73, was driving his car when it collided with a parked van. He continued on his journey and shortly afterwards collided with a stationary car, injuring the plaintiffs. He told the police 'I felt a bit queer before I ran into the van. I went away and felt all right. After that I felt a bit queer again and I hit the other car.' He was found on medical examination to have suffered a stroke just before starting his journey. The defendant had no previous symptoms or warning signs. After its onset his consciousness was impaired, but he was sufficiently in possession of his faculties to have some awareness of his surroundings and of traffic conditions and to make deliberate and voluntary though inefficient movements of hands and legs to manipulate the controls. He was not aware that he was unfit to drive.
HELD: In civil as well as in criminal matters (following *Watmore v Jenkins* (above)) a state of automatism means in law a complete loss of consciousness; a driver will escape liability only if his actions at the relevant time were wholly beyond his control. If he retained some control, albeit imperfect, he remains liable. The defendant was liable on this ground, and liable also in having continued to drive when he should have been aware of his unfitness.

Moses v Winder

[1981] RTR 37, QBD
The defendant drove his car into collision with another in circumstances justifying a

conviction for careless driving. He pleaded automatism, being a diabetic of 20 years' duration. He called no medical evidence.
HELD: (1) Cases must be exceedingly rare where a defence of automatism can succeed without medical evidence; (2) the defendant was well aware of the danger of his going into a coma. He felt he was about to have an attack and took sugar sweets to ward it off; he then drove off and the attack became worse. In those circumstances he failed to take those precautions which he should, both in his own interests and in the interests of public safety. The justices must convict.

Epilepsy

Balmer v Hayes

1950 SC 477, 1950 SLT 388, Ct of Sess, Scot
A motor omnibus collided with a motor lorry and a passenger in the motor omnibus was injured. She brought an action against the driver of the omnibus, who averred that immediately before the accident he suffered a temporary loss of consciousness owing to a fit of epilepsy. The pursuer replied averring that it was the driver's duty when applying for a driving licence to disclose that he suffered from lapses of consciousness which were likely to cause his driving to be a danger to the public.

The Road Traffic Act 1930, s 5(1) enacts that an applicant for a licence shall make a declaration as to whether or not he is suffering from any such disease or physical disability specified in the form or any other disease or physical disability which would be likely to cause his driving to be a source of danger to the public. Subsection (2) allows an application for a test except in prescribed cases. The Motor Vehicles (Driving Licences) Regulations 1947, reg 5 prescribes as an exception epilepsy, liability to sudden attacks of disabling giddiness or fainting.

Section 112(2) of the 1930 Act provides a penalty for false statement on application for a licence and for a false statement or withholding of material information on application for a certificate.

Note—The Road Traffic Act 1930, ss 5 and 112 have been replaced so far as they affect this case by the Road Traffic Act 1988, ss 92 and 173.

Green v Hills

(1969) 113 Sol Jo 385, Times, 22 April (James J)
The plaintiffs, man and wife, were injured when they were knocked off their moped by the defendant, a woman, who stepped off the kerb in a state of automatism after an attack of *petit mal*. She suffered from two different forms of epileptic attacks, major attacks of which she received warning and which occurred once or twice a year, and minor attacks which were more frequent and some of which were accompanied by periods of time when she was not conscious of what was going on or afterwards of what had gone on. She remembered going out on the afternoon of the accident and going into a shop but did not remember the accident. She had not been advised by her doctor not to go out alone. A neurologist said in evidence he did not think it reasonable to forbid a person such as the defendant from going into the street.
HELD: The defendant was not liable. She had first to satisfy the court on the balance of probabilities that she was in a state of automatism: on her own evidence she had discharged this burden. The issue was then whether it was reasonable for her to have gone out alone. Clearly there was some risk but one could not 'chain' an epileptic

person to his house. A reasonable person, knowing her life history, would be prepared to balance the risk of causing injury with the need to go out and live as normal a life as possible.

VOLENTI NON FIT INJURIA

The maxim

Note—A person who has expressly or impliedly assented to an act cannot claim for its consequences, but the principle is *volenti*, not *scienti*, that is, consent as distinct from mere knowledge.

Cutler v United Dairies (London) Ltd

[1933] 2 KB 297, 102 LJKB 663, 149 LT 436, CA
A man who, without being under any duty, went into a field to help to catch a runaway horse, was held to be a volunteer.

Haynes v Harwood

[1935] 1 KB 146, 104 LJKB 63, 152 LT 121, 51 TLR 100, 78 Sol Jo 801, CA
If the act of the plaintiff is pursuant to duty, or is a reasonable act to avoid injury to others, the principle does not apply. The plaintiff, a police constable, was on duty inside a police station in a street in which, at the material time, were a large number of people, including children. Seeing the defendants' runaway horses with a van attached coming down the street he rushed out and eventually stopped them, sustaining injuries in consequence, in respect of which he claimed damages.
HELD: (1) That on the evidence the defendant's servant was guilty of negligence in leaving the horses unattended in a busy street: (2) that as the defendants must or ought to have contemplated that someone might attempt to stop the horses in an endeavour to prevent injury to life and limb, and as the police were under a general duty to intervene to protect life and property, the act of, and injuries to, the plaintiff were the natural and probable consequences of the defendants' negligence: (3) that the maxim *volenti non fit injuria* did not apply to prevent the plaintiff recovering.

Note—Followed in *The Gusty and The Daniel M* [1940] P 159, 109 LJP 71, 164 LT 271, 56 TLR 785, 84 Sol Jo 454. Considered in *Smith v Littlewoods Organisation Ltd*, p 346, below.

Morgan v Aylen

[1942] 1 All ER 489 (Cassels J)
The plaintiff was escorting a child of three-and-a-half years, and when they reached a cross-road, the child was a little way in front of her and ran forward and began to cross the road. The defendant was riding a motor cycle along the road about 7 feet from the near side. He was about 7 yards from the corner when the child ran into the road and about 5 yards from the child. The plaintiff ran out to save the child. If the plaintiff had been alone, an attempt by her to cross the road in front of the defendant might have been negligent. Here the circumstances were different. The American rule is that the doctrine of the assumption of risk does not apply where the plaintiff has, under an exigency caused by the defendants' wrongful misconduct, consciously and deliberately faced a risk, even death, to rescue another from imminent danger of personal injury or death, whether the person endangered is one to whom he owes a

duty of protection, as a member of his family, or is a mere stranger to whom he owes no such special duty. What the plaintiff did here was, in the circumstances, natural and proper. The initial wrongful act was on the part of the defendant, who was approaching the cross-roads at too great a speed. The plaintiff saw the danger and ran out to save the child, which was a natural and proper thing to do, and there was no contributory negligence on her part. The defendant was in law solely responsible for the accident.

Note—See also 'Rescue cases', p 49, below.

White v Blackmore

[1972] 2 QB 651, [1972] 3 All ER 158, [1972] 3 WLR 296, 116 Sol Jo 547, CA
The defendants organised a race meeting for jalopy cars. The plaintiff's husband took his car and entered his name as a competitor. He brought his wife, child and mother-in-law to the meeting as spectators. He competed in a race but during the next race, in which he was not a competitor, he stood near a post to which safety ropes were fastened talking to his family. The ropes were faultily arranged and on being fouled by a car in that race, pulled out the post and caused the plaintiff's husband injuries from which he died. He had seen the notices around the track: 'Warning to the Public. Motor racing is dangerous. It is a condition of admission that all persons having connection with the promotion and/or organisation and/or conduct of the meeting are absolved from all liabilities arising out of accidents causing damage or personal injury (whether fatal or otherwise) howsoever caused to spectators or ticketholders.'
HELD: (1) The deceased was at the time of the accident a spectator not a competitor; (2) the defence of *volenti non fit injuria* was available only against one who had impliedly agreed, with full knowledge of the nature and extent of the risk, to incur it. It was not obvious to the deceased that he was standing in a particularly dangerous place and the defence of *volenti* did not apply; (3) the warning notice applied to the deceased as a spectator at the time of the accident and the action failed.

Latchford v Spedeworth International Ltd

(1983) 134 NLJ 36 (Hodgson J)
The plaintiff was a competitor at a 'hot rod' car racing stadium. He had often raced there and was aware of the danger presented to drivers by two concrete flower beds within the area of the race track. He was not aware until the evening of the accident of the organiser's practice of marking the edge of the track with small tyres. The organiser (the defendant company) knew that the practice was potentially hazardous and that larger tyres would have been safer. The plaintiff did not know this. During a race another competitor dislodged some of the tyres of which one jammed under the back axle of the plaintiff's car causing him to crash into one of the concrete flowerbeds. He was seriously injured.
HELD: The accident resulted from the defendant's negligence with regard to the tyres and as the plaintiff was unaware of that danger the defence of *volenti non fit injuria* could not avail in respect of it. The defendant had also pleaded that the plaintiff was on his own admission aware of the danger presented by the flowerbeds and had consented to run that risk. However, the defendant had failed to prove that the plaintiff actually had a full appreciation of the nature and extent of the risk. The plea of *volenti non fit injuria* thus failed entirely.

Winnik v Dick

1984 SC 48, 1984 SLT 185, Ct of Sess
The plaintiff accepted a lift from a friend who he knew was drunk. En route an accident occurred, injuring the plaintiff. The defendant driver pleaded *volenti non fit injuria.*
HELD: The maxim did not negative negligence: it merely absolved a party from the consequences of his negligence. In the present case the plaintiff had to be taken as having appreciated and consented to the defendant's lack of reasonable care. However, the Road Traffic Act 1972, s 148(3) expressly provided that the fact that a passenger had willingly accepted the risk that the driver may be negligent was not to be treated as negativing the driver's liability. The subsection excluded the operation of the maxim. The plaintiff was entitled to damages subject to 50% deduction for contributory negligence.

Note—Section 148(3) of the Road Traffic Act 1972 has been replaced by s 149 of the Road Traffic Act 1988 from 15 May 1989 (see p 190, below).

Cook v Cook

[1987] 41 SASR 1
A learner driver was involved in a collision: her passenger sustained personal injury, and sued the driver. At the time of the accident the passenger was aware that the learner had minimal experience—she had not yet passed the examination to obtain a learner's permit.
HELD: The passenger was fully aware of the driver's inexperience and had waived the right to legal remedy. *Volenti non fit injuria* applied. (Australian case.)

Drunken driver

Dann v Hamilton

[1939] 1 KB 509, [1939] 1 All ER 59, 83 Sol Jo 155 (Asquith J)
The plaintiff was injured while travelling as a non-paying passenger in a car driven by one H. Prior to the accident H had been drinking, and this had markedly affected his driving, which thereafter was fast and erratic. During a stop to let down a passenger, the plaintiff, who by then knew that H, while far from being dead drunk, was not sober, and that there was a certain danger in being a passenger in a car driven by him, had an opportunity of leaving the car, but elected to continue the journey. Shortly afterwards, the accident occurred, and it was contended for the defence that the maxim *volenti non fit injuria* applied.
HELD: The plaintiff was entitled to succeed. By voluntarily travelling in the car with knowledge that through drink H had materially reduced his capacity for driving safely, she did not impliedly consent to, or absolve H from liability for, any subsequent negligence on his part which might cause injury to the plaintiff.

Note—Comments on this decision in 55 LQR 184 and 65 LQR 20 and elsewhere suggested that even if the plea of '*volenti*' did not apply, there was a cast-iron defence on the ground of contributory negligence. Lord Asquith wrote (69 LQR 817) that contributory negligence was not pleaded and counsel for the defendant declined a suggestion from the judge that he should apply for leave to amend and add this plea. The Law Reform (Contributory Negligence) Act

1945 was still in the future. See also the Road Traffic Act 1972, s 148(3), p 190, below. See also 'Consent to Drunken Driving' 17 NLJ 1079.

In *Slater v Clay Cross Co Ltd* [1956] 2 QB 264, [1956] 2 All ER 625, [1956] 3 WLR 232, 100 Sol Jo 450, Denning LJ said of the judgment of Asquith J in *Dann v Hamilton* and of the note written by Lord Asquith. 'In so far as he decided that the doctrine of *volenti* did not apply, I think the decision was quite correct. In so far as he suggested that the plea of contributory negligence might have been available, I agree with him.' Parker and Birkett LJJ agreed.

See also *Dawrant v Nutt*, p 177, below.

Section 148(3) of the Road Traffic Act 1972 has been replaced by s 149 of the Road Traffic Act 1988 from 15 May 1989 (see p 190, below).

Morris v Murray

[1991] 2 QB 6, [1990] 3 ALL ER 801, [1991] 2 WLR 195, 134 Sol Jo 1300
The plaintiff and defendant, having been drinking in each others company for some time, decided to go on a joy ride in the defendant's light aeroplane. The plaintiff drove the defendant to the aerodrome, assisted in starting the engine and was generally anxious to commence the ride. The weather was bad. The local flying club had suspended flying. The defendant just managed to take off but a few minutes later the aeroplane crashed killing the defendant and seriously injuring the plaintiff. An autopsy of the defendant found that he had consumed the equivalent of 17 whiskies or three times the limit permitted for a car driver. The judge awarded the plaintiff damages with reduction of 20% for his contributory negligence. The defendant, through his estate, appealed.
HELD: The plaintiff's claim failed by virtue of the defence of *volenti non fit injuria*. The plaintiff knew that he was going on a flight, he knew the plane was to be flown by the defendant and he knew that the defendant had been drinking heavily that afternoon. The plaintiff co-operated fully in the joint activity and did all he could to assist it. By embarking on the flight with the defendant the plaintiff had implicitly waived his rights in the event of injury consequent upon the defendant's failure to fly with reasonable care.

Assistance was derived from the dictum of Asquith J in the case of *Dann v Hamilton* [1939] 1 KB 509, [1939] 1 All ER 59, and particularly at p 518 where Asquith J mentions the example of the case where:

'The drunkenness of the driver at the material time is so extreme and so glaring that to accept a lift from him was like engaging in an intrinsically and obvious dangerous occupation . . .'

Rescue cases

Baker v T E Hopkins & Son

[1959] 3 All ER 225, [1959] 1 WLR 966, 103 Sol Jo 812, CA
Defendants, builders and contractors, had arranged to clean out a well at a farm. Two workmen in defendants' employ went down the well and were overcome by poisonous gases. A doctor was summoned by telephone, and, though warned of the danger, went down the well to see what he could do for them. He was overcome and died.

The court held the defendants liable in negligence in respect of the deaths of the two workmen. Defendants contended that they owed no duty to the doctor; that his

conduct was unreasonable and amounted to a *novus actus interveniens*; and it was a case of *volenti non fit injuria*.
HELD, ON APPEAL: It was a natural and proper consequence of the defendants' negligence that someone would attempt to rescue, and the defendants should have foreseen that consequence; accordingly the defendants were in breach of duty towards the doctor (*Donoghue v Stevenson*).

It was not a case of *novus actus interveniens*. The act in question was the very kind of thing that was likely to happen as a result of the negligence.

The maxim *volenti non fit injuria* could not be successfully invoked as a defence by a person who had negligently placed others in a situation of such peril that it was foreseeable that someone would attempt their rescue. Appeal dismissed.

Videan v British Transport Commission

[1963] 2 QB 650, [1963] 2 All ER 860, [1963] 3 WLR 374, 107 Sol Jo 458, CA
Per Lord Denning: The right of the rescuer is an independent right, and is not derived from that of the victim. The victim may have been guilty of contributory negligence—or his right may be excluded by contractual stipulation—but still the rescuer can sue. Foreseeability is necessary, but not foreseeability of the particular emergency that arose. Suffice it that he ought reasonably to foresee that, if he did not take care, some emergency or other might arise, and that someone or other might be impelled to expose himself to danger in order to effect a rescue. Whoever comes to the rescue, the law should see that he does not suffer for it. It seems to me that, if a person by his fault creates a situation of peril, he must answer for it to any person who attempts to rescue the person who is in danger. He owes a duty to such a person above all others. The rescuer may act instinctively out of humanity or deliberately out of courage. But whichever it is, so long as it is not wanton interference, if the rescuer is killed or injured in the attempt, he can recover damages from the one whose fault has been the cause of it.

Harrison v British Railways Board

[1981] 3 All ER 679 (Boreham J)
The plaintiff was the guard on a passenger train. At a station en route he gave the ready-to-start signal to the driver and the train began to move. An off-duty member of the station staff, Howard, then attempted to board the train by seizing the handrail at the guard's door. The plaintiff saw him but failed to apply the emergency brake as he could and should have done. Instead he attempted to help Howard off his feet and he fell between the train and the platform, causing the plaintiff to fall down with him. The plaintiff was injured.
HELD: As an experienced railwayman, Howard was negligent in attempting to board the train when it was moving. Moreover he knew the plaintiff had seen him and would try to help him if he got into trouble. He should have foreseen that by intervening the plaintiff would probably endanger himself. A duty is owed to a rescuer if his intervention is reasonably foreseeable even if the defendant owes no duty to the person being rescued (*Videan v British Transport Commission* (above)). A duty must likewise be owed to a rescuer when the person being rescued is the person who created the peril. Howard was liable to the plaintiff; but he was himself guilty of contributory negligence to the extent of 20% in failing to apply the emergency brake and thus reduce the chance of injury to himself.

Note—See also *Chadwick v British Transport Commission*, p 401, below.

Non volenti

Clayards v Dethick and Davis

(1848) 12 QB 439
Commissioners of Sewers made a trench in the only outlet from some mews, leaving only a narrow passage on which they heaped sand and gravel. A cab proprietor, in order to get his horse out of the mews led it over the heaped up gravel, which gave way and the horse slipped into the trench, causing its death. He recovered damages on the principle that where the inconvenience is great and the risk is not so great that no sensible man would have incurred it, the principle of *volenti* does not apply.

Master and servant cases

Bowater v Rowley Regis Corpn

[1944] KB 476, [1944] 1 All ER 465, 113 LJKB 427, 170 LT 314, 60 TLR 356, CA
A workman complied after protest with a direction to take out a horse known to make attempts to run away. The horse ran away and he was injured.
HELD: The maxim did not prevent the workman from recovering damages from his employers. The defence hardly ever applies between master and servant.

EX TURPI CAUSA NON ORITUR ACTIO

(no action arises out of a base cause)

Pitts v Hunt

[1991] 1 QB 24, [1990] 3 All ER 344, 3 WLR 542, 134 Sol Jo 834, CA
The plaintiff was a pillion passenger on the first defendant's motorcycle. The plaintiff and the first defendant had been drinking together that evening. After the accident the first defendant's blood alcohol was twice the legal limit for driving. The plaintiff was aware that the first defendant was not even licensed to drive the motorcycle nor insured. The judge accepted evidence from witnesses that on the way home the first defendant, encouraged by the plaintiff, drove the motorcycle in a fast, haphazard manner deliberately intending to frighten members of the public. The motorcycle collided with the car driven by the second defendant. The first defendant was killed and the plaintiff seriously injured. The plaintiff brought an action for personal injuries against both defendants.

The judge at first instance dismissed the plaintiff's claim on the basis that:

(1) The maxim *ex turpi causa non oritur actio* applied for the plaintiff and the first defendant were engaged on a joint illegal enterprise.
(2) It would be against public policy for the plaintiff to succeed.
(3) The nature of the joint enterprise was such that it precluded the court from finding that the defendant owed any duty of care to the plaintiff.
(4) The plaintiff was 100% contributorily negligent.

The plaintiff appealed against the dismissal of the claim against the first defendant.
HELD: The plaintiff's claim failed. The judge's findings at (1), (2) and (3) were upheld. The application of the maxim *ex turpi causa* was not to be judged by the degree of moral turpitude or illegal character involved in the joint enterprise but whether the

conduct of the person claiming, the character of the enterprise and hazards involved made it impossible for the court to determine the appropriate standard of care because the joint illegal purpose had displaced the ordinary standard of care.

The judge's finding at (4) above was disapproved. A finding of 100% contributory negligence is logically unsupportable for the Law Reform (Contributory Negligence) Act 1945 operates on the premise that there is fault on the part of both parties which have caused the damage. Thus responsibility must be shared.

Note—The judge at first instance held that the plaintiff's claim would also have been defeated by the doctrine of *volenti non fit injuria* but for the operation of s 148(3) of the Road Traffic Act 1972. This provides that an 'agreement or understanding' between a driver and passenger of a motor vehicle has no effect so far as it purports to negative or restrict the drivers liability to the passenger. Section 148(3) of the Road Traffic Act 1972 has been replaced by s 149 of the Road Traffic Act 1988.

CHAPTER 2

Liability of the Driver

1 HIGHWAY CODE

INTRODUCTION

The Highway Code is issued with the authority of Parliament. The Road Traffic Act 1988, s 38(7) provides:

'A failure on the part of a person to observe a provision of the Highway Code shall not of itself render that person liable to criminal proceedings of any kind, but any such failure may in any proceedings (whether civil or criminal . . .) be relied upon by any party to the proceedings as tending to establish or to negative any liability which is in question in those proceedings.'

The current edition of the Highway Code was issued in January 1993. Paragraphs 1 to 27 relate to pedestrians and paras 28 to 154 to drivers, motorcyclists and cyclists. There are extra rules for cyclists in paras 187 to 211 and for those in charge of animals in paras 212 to 224. Motorway driving is dealt with in paras 155 to 186 and level crossings in paras 225 to 234.

The current edition of the Highway Code has a different format to its predecessor. The appearance is more attractive and as a consequence the booklet is more readable than before. Emphasis is placed on the fact that the code is essential reading for everyone—pedestrians, cyclists and horseriders, as well as motorists.

The fact that roads are becoming busier and busier is taken into account. For example, in the previous edition of the Highway Code pedestrians were told not to try to cross between parked cars. In the current edition pedestrians are advised to try and avoid crossing between parked cars. (Paras 7(a) and 23.)

KEEP TO THE LEFT

THE HIGHWAY ACT 1835, S 78

78 . . . if the driver of any waggon, cart or other carriage whatsoever . . . shall not keep his waggon, cart or carriage . . . on the left or nearside of the road . . . [he] shall, in addition to any civil action to which he may make himself liable . . . forfeit any sum not exceeding five pounds . . .

Nuttall v Pickering

[1913] 1 KB 14, 82 LJKB 36, 107 LT 852, Div Ct
A waggon was being driven so far beyond the centre of the road that when a motor car approached from behind the waggoner drew further to his offside and waved to

the motorist to overtake on his nearside, which he did. There were no other vehicles on the road.
HELD: The waggoner was not guilty of an offence under s 78 (above). No inconvenience was caused to the motorist, who was quite willing to pass on the nearside and did. When there is no other traffic on a road the driver of a vehicle is entitled to go on to any part of the road he wishes.

Phillips v Britannia Hygienic Laundry Co

[1923] 1 KB 539; affd [1923] 2 KB 832, 93 LJKB 5, 129 LT 777, 39 TLR 530, 68 Sol Jo 102, CA
Per McCardie J: So far as I know, it has not been held that a mere breach of [s 78] ipso facto gives a cause of action for damage. On the contrary, it has been held in cases of collision there is no such rule of the road as to make the left always the proper side . . . I think that in spite of s 78 a man may sometimes and without negligence keep on his right hand side, and, indeed, if by so doing he can avoid a collision, it is his duty to do so.

PLEADING

Wells v Weeks

[1965] 1 All ER 77, [1965] 1 WLR 45, 108 Sol Jo 1032 (Lawton J)
A statement of claim in an action arising from a road accident included in the particulars of negligence the words 'The plaintiff will also rely on s 74 of the Road Traffic Act 1960 (now s 38 of the Road Traffic Act 1988), and on all the provisions of the Highway Code applicable to the drivers of motor vehicles in so far as the same are applicable in the circumstances', said by counsel to be adapted from *Bullen & Leake* (11th edn) p 227. The judge said pleading in such an imprecise manner invited a request for further and better particulars and he was surprised no request had been made.

2 CAUSATION AND REMOTENESS

Lloyds Bank Ltd v Budd

[1982] RTR 80, CA
A lorry broke down with clutch trouble on the A1 road and was left all night in a lay-by. Early on the following morning, in daylight but in fog, the driver, Lake, with a mechanic returned to the vehicle to repair it. They found it capable of being driven and decided to take it to a place more convenient for them to do the repair. After a short distance had been done, however, it again broke down and came to a halt on the carriageway blocking it. Because of the fog the mechanic went to the rear of the vehicle to warn traffic. A police car leading a line of vehicles came to a stop when he waved it down. The police officers went to the front of the lorry to attach a tow rope. Three or four minutes later there was a series of collisions at the back of the stationary convoy as vehicles came through the fog and failed to pull up in time. A car in which the plaintiff's husband was a passenger struck a stationary vehicle in front of it and was then struck very violently by a lorry driven by the first defendant, Budd. The plantiff's husband was killed. The judge said it was negligent of Lake to take his lorry

out on to the carriageway and that it created a nuisance, but he considered the nuisance or negligence too remote to be a cause of the accident. He found Budd alone to blame for the death.

HELD, ON APPEAL: Lake's negligence was not too remote. Despite the interval between the convoy coming to a halt and the subsequent collisions the broken down vehicle was a cause of the collisions. Budd was the more blameworthy, however, in driving much too fast in fog. Apportionment of blame: Budd 60%, Lake 40%

Note—See also *Rouse v Squires*, p 198, below and 'Novus actus interveniens,' p 344, below.

Wright v Lodge & Shepherd

[1993] 4 All ER 299, [1993] RTR 123

It was a foggy night and visibility was poor when Mrs Shepherd's mini broke down on the nearside lane of a dual carriageway a short way from Cambridge. It would have been an easy task to push the mini on to the verge. Mr Lodge was driving his Scania lorry at about 60 mph and crashed into the rear of Mrs Shepherd's mini injuring her passenger. The lorry then veered out of control across the central reservation coming to rest on the opposite carriageway whereupon it was struck by other vehicles injuring Messrs Wright and Mr Kerek. Mrs Shepherd's passenger and Mrs Wright and Mr Kerek brought proceedings against Mrs Shepherd and Mr Lodge. Mr Lodge admitted liability but claimed a contribution from Mrs Shepherd. The trial judge held that Mrs Shepherd should contribute 10% in respect of her passenger's claim but not to the claims of Messrs Wright and Kerek. Mr Lodge appealed on the basis that the judge should have had Mrs Shepherd also 10% responsible for the injuries to Messrs Wright and Kerek.

HELD: Appeal dismissed. Mr Lodge's driving was not just negligent but reckless. The presence of Mr Lodge's lorry on the opposite carriageway was wholly attributable to his reckless speed which resulted in the swerve, loss of control and overturn on that carriageway. The presence of Mrs Shepherd's mini did not necessarily become a legally operative cause of the subsequent collision.

Mention was made of the case of *Rouse v Squires* [1973] 2 All ER 903 which established that reckless driving is a different category from negligent driving and that an obstruction which is only a danger to a reckless driver does not constitute a relevant danger (see p 198, below).

3 SPECIAL ROADS

MOTORWAY

Note—The motorways are special roads provided under the Special Roads Act 1949, or the Highways Act 1959, limited to certain classes of vehicles. The special rules applying to traffic on motorways are contained in the Motorways Traffic (England and Wales) Regulations 1982, SI 1982/1163. The use of motorways is restricted to traffic of Classes I and II specified in the Second Schedule to the Special Roads Act 1949, as amended by the Special Roads (Classes of Traffic) Order 1959, SI 1959/1280.

The Special Roads Act 1949, s 12, under which the Motorways Traffic Regulations 1959 were made, was repealed by the Road Traffic Act 1960 and its provisions are now contained in s 17 of the Road Traffic Regulation Act 1984. Vehicles excluded from motorways include pedal cycles, motor cycles not exceeding 50 cc capacity, invalid carriages, certain vehicles carrying oversize loads and agricultural vehicles. Vehicles must be driven in one direction only. Stopping, turning or reversing on a carriageway are forbidden. If a vehicle has to be stopped for certain specified emergencies it must be driven on to the nearside verge and shall not remain there longer than necessary. Learner drivers are forbidden to drive on motorways. No person must go on foot on a motorway except for certain necessary purposes. There are exceptions to and relaxation of the rules in certain specified circumstances, eg to avoid or prevent an accident.

There is a general speed limit of 70 mph (SI 1974/502).

The Highway Code paras 155–186 deal with motorway driving.

Rivers v Cutting

[1982] 3 All ER 69, [1982] 1 WLR 1146, 126 Sol Jo 362, [1983] RTR 105, CA
The plaintiff's car broke down on a motorway: he left it on the verge. A police officer in exercise of powers granted by SI 1968/43, reg 4 arranged for it to be towed away by a local garage employee. The plaintiff alleged that damage was caused thereby in the sum of £716 and sued the police as being vicariously liable for the negligence of the garage. The regulation reads '. . . a constable may remove or arrange for the removal of the vehicle . . .'. The plaintiff claimed that the obligation to ensure the performance of a statutory duty without negligence cannot be discharged by delegating the duty to an independent contractor.
HELD: The constable's duty in exercising the power to arrange for the removal of the car was merely to exercise reasonable care in the choice of the garage. The word 'arrange' authorised the appointment of an independent contractor to do the work. The appointment of a contractor to remove the vehicle was not a delegation of the power but an exercise of the power itself. The police were not vicariously liable for any negligence of the garage in doing the work.

Wallwork v Rowland

[1972] 1 All ER 53, 136 JP 137, 116 Sol Jo 17, [1972] RTR 86, Div Ct
The defendant stopped on the hard shoulder of a motorway to eat sandwiches. He was charged with unlawfully causing his vehicle to remain at rest on a 'carriageway'.
HELD: The hard shoulder of a motorway is part of the 'verge' and not of the 'carriageway'. The 'marginal strip' in the Motorways Traffic Regulations 1959 refers not to the hard shoulder but to the white line which borders the running surface of the nearside lane.

Cornwell v Automobile Association

(2 June 1989, unreported)
The defendant, driving an AA van, was travelling along the hard shoulder of a motorway accompanying a car that was experiencing carburettor problems. When the hard shoulder ran out because of a bridge crossing the motorway, the defendant pulled out from the hard shoulder into the inside lane at a speed of 15 mph. The plaintiff, travelling at 60 mph, collided with the rear of the defendant's van.
HELD: The plaintiff succeeded against the defendant. In the circumstances the defendant's speed was too slow. The plaintiff was not found contributorily negligent.

Concertina collision

Smith v Samuel Williams & Sons

(1972) Times, 3 March (Bristow J)
A recovery vehicle was towing a Scammell lorry in the slow lane of the M1 motorway at about 25 mph at night. Behind was a lorry driven by the plaintiff's husband at 50 mph, followed at two or three lengths by another lorry travelling at the same speed. A concertina collision occurred in which the plaintiff's husband was killed.
HELD: The driver of the rearmost lorry, which had crashed into the back of the deceased's lorry, was undoubtedly negligent in driving much too close, but a careful analysis of the evidence showed that the fatal injuries were those to the deceased's legs, caused by the collision with the Scammell, and that there had been only one blow to the legs. It followed that the first collision was between the deceased's lorry and the Scammell: the subsequent collision had not contributed to the death of the deceased. The action accordingly failed.

NARROW ROAD

Thrower v Thames Valley Bus Co Ltd

[1978] RTR 271, CA
The plaintiff on a dark December evening was driving his car along a narrow lane when he collided with the offside of the defendants' bus travelling in the opposite direction. The lane was 9 feet wide to the centre line on the defendants' side and 8 ft 6 ins on the plaintiff's side. The judge found that the bus may have been an inch or two over the centre line but acquitted the driver of any negligence. There was a restriction order in force prohibiting vehicles more than 6 ft 6 ins wide from using the road but public service vehicles were exempted. He held that the defendants were negligent in failing to give the driver some form of special training or instruction so that he could take special precautions when driving a bus on this narrow road.
HELD: The defendants were not negligent. The road was perfectly adequate to take two vehicles of the width of the two concerned. Other vehicles ahead of the plaintiff had got past safely and it was perfectly possible for him to have done so too.

4 LEARNER DRIVER

PROVISIONAL DRIVING LICENCE

Note—By the Motor Vehicles (Driving Licences) Regulations Act 1981 (SI 1981/952), reg 8, a provisional licence is subject to the condition that the holder shall use it only when under the supervision of a person who holds a licence, not being a provisional licence, authorising him to drive a motor vehicle of the same class as that being driven by the holder of the provisional licence. This person shall, except in the case of a motor cycle or invalid carriage, be present with him in or on the vehicle.

See also paras 36 to 38 of the Highway Code 1993.

DUTY OF CARE

Nettleship v Weston

[1971] 2 QB 691, [1971] 3 All ER 581, [1971] 3 WLR 360, 115 Sol Jo 624, CA
The defendant asked the plaintiff to teach her to drive. He was not a professional instructor. He agreed to do so, having first asked about insurance and been told by the defendant that there was comprehensive insurance which covered him as a passenger. During the defendant's third lesson the plaintiff told her to move off from a halt sign and turn left. She did so but failed to straighten up. Despite the plaintiff's efforts to apply the handbrake and move the steering wheel the car mounted the pavement and struck a lamp-post. The plaintiff was injured. The judge of assize dismissed his claim for damages saying that the only duty the defendant owed him was to do her best and this she had done.
HELD, ON APPEAL: This was not right. The standard of care owed by any driver, whether a learner or not, is that of a driver of skill, experience and care, who is sound in mind and limb, eyesight and hearing, makes no errors of judgment and is free from infirmity. The duty of care is the same to all persons on or near the highway, whether passengers or not and is the same to an instructor, with this exception, that there would be no liability if he had voluntarily agreed to take the risk of injury. The defence of *volenti non fit injuria* is not available unless the plaintiff expressly or impliedly agreed to waive any claim for injury that may befall him. In the present case the plaintiff did not so agree: he asked about insurance to make sure he was covered. But an instructor could be guilty of contributory negligence in for example, not being quick enough to correct errors. Moreover an instructor and learner are jointly concerned in driving the car and together must maintain the same measure of control over the car as an experienced and skilful driver. If an accident happens one or both must have been at fault: in the absence of evidence to distinguish between them they should be held equally to blame. That was the case here and the plaintiff was entitled to half his damages.

Note—Salmon LJ disagreed that the defence of *volenti* was not available against an instructor in the absence of agreement to waive any claim. He held that as an instructor knows the learner has practically no driving experience or skill he is not owed the duty of care to be expected from a skilled driver: the instructor voluntarily agrees to run the risk of injury. But he held that this plaintiff's enquiry about insurance had altered the whole relationship to one in which the defendant accepted responsibility for any injury. Megaw LJ dissented on the question of contributory negligence: he could not see that, on the facts, the plaintiff had done anything wrong.

Volenti is not now a defence available in road accident cases. See *Pitts v Hunt* , p 51, above.

Rubie v Faulkner

[1940] 1 KB 571, [1940] 1 All ER 285, 109 LJKB 241, 163 LT 212, 104 JP 161, 56 TLR 303, 84 Sol Jo 257, Div Ct
The appellant, while in a motor vehicle driven by the holder of a provisional licence (a 'learner driver') who was driving under his supervision in accordance with the Motor Vehicles (Driving Licences) Regulations 1937, reg 16(3)(a) (see now the Motor Vehicles (Driving Licences) Regulations 1976, reg 8), was in a position to see that the driver was about to overtake another vehicle by pulling considerably to the offside at a pronounced bend of the road, but he neither said nor did anything to

prevent it. An accident occurred, and the driver was convicted of driving without due care and attention.

HELD: That the appellant was rightly convicted of aiding and abetting the driver in the commission of the offence.

Per Hilbery J: The Regulation is framed to make some provision for the protection of the public against the dangers to which they are exposed through a car being driven on the road by a driver who is still a learner and therefore assumed to be not fully competent. The supervisor must be intended by the Regulation to have the duty, by supervision, of making up as far as possible the driver's incompetence. In other words, it is the supervisor's duty, when necessary, to do whatever can reasonably be expected to be done by a person supervising the acts of another to prevent that other from acting unskilfully or carelessly or in a manner likely to cause danger to others, and to this extent to participate in the driving.

R v Clark

(1950) Daily Telegraph, 30 May (Sheriff Substitute, Dundee)
A supervisor of an 'L' driver of a motor lorry was held to be the person in charge of the vehicle and convicted of being under the influence of drink to such an extent as to be incapable of having proper control. There was a continuing duty on the part of the supervisor to control the learner's driving which was not interrupted because the learner was driving properly. *Rubie v Faulkner* followed.

Gibbons v Priestley

[1979] RTR 4, QBD (Judge Lymberry QC)
After 18 lessons in a driving school car which had dual controls the plaintiff, a woman of 51, went out with the instructor in her husband's car which did not have dual controls. At a T-junction the plaintiff came to a halt before turning left. On starting forward and turning left she let the clutch in too fast, failed to straighten up and crashed into a tree. The whole incident from start to stop lasted about five seconds. She sustained injury and sued the instructor for damages, claiming that he was negligent in letting her drive on the highway in a car without dual controls and in failing at the time of the accident to take any proper steps to avoid the collision.

HELD: The instructor was not liable because (1) it was not wrong to allow the plaintiff to drive without dual controls in the light of the knowledge he had of the stage her tuition had reached. (2) The passenger supervisor of a learner driver, whether he is a driving instructor or not is not a passenger purely and simply. He has a responsibility of care jointly with the learner driver to other road users in relation to the safe conduct and control of the car on the road. Further, the supervisor and the learner each has a responsibility to the other in the exercise of control over the car in which they are travelling. Circumstances may vary anywhere between nought and 100% as to the comparative blameworthiness of the one as compared with the other. In the short time available the instructor could not reasonably have done more than he did, namely, to shout 'Brake, brake' and pull on the handbrake. (3) The instructor was negligent in failing to recommend the plaintiff to wear her seat belt but this was not a cause of the collision.

Thompson v Lodwick

[1983] RTR 76, QBD
A learner driver who owned a car asked the defendant to sit with him in the car as a

qualified driver. The defendant did not ask about the insurance of the car. He was convicted of 'permitting' the driver to drive without third-party insurance.
HELD, ON APPEAL: The fact that the defendant's presence in the car was necessary to enable the owner to drive lawfully did not mean that he was in a position to permit or refuse the use by the owner of the vehicle. Conviction quashed.

NO SUPERVISION

Verney v Wilkins

(1962) 106 Sol Jo 879, [1962] Crim LR 840 (Winn J)
The infant plaintiff was injured when riding as a passenger in a car driven by the defendant. The car ran out of control and overturned. The defendant held only a provisional licence and there was no one in the car who was a qualified driver.
HELD: There was no actionable claim against the driver merely on the ground that injury had been caused by him and that at the time he was not a fully licenced driver, or was one who had not passed the driving test.

The statutory requirements with regard to learner drivers did not give rise to any cause of action for damages sustained as a result of his driving, whether or not a more skilful driver might have avoided those consequences. The breach of statutory duty per se was not a cause of action. On the facts, however, the defendant had not discharged the onus on him of disproving negligence and was liable.

EXAMINER NOT LIABLE

British School of Motoring Ltd v Simms

[1971] 1 All ER 317, [1971] RTR 190 (Talbot J)
A learner driver was undergoing a driving test by a Ministry of Transport examiner. She approached a road junction governed by a 'Give Way' sign and broken white lines. She failed to see them and drove into the junction. The examiner saw a car approaching and applied the brake. The test car stopped in the path of the other car and was struck, causing another collision with the plaintiff's car. They sued the learner and examiner, alleging negligence against him on the grounds (1) that he failed to ensure that the learner paid regard to the 'Give Way' sign and lines and failed to apply the brake soon enough and (2) that he applied the brakes when it was unsafe and stopped the car in the path of the other car.
HELD: The examiner was not negligent because (1) he is not in the position of a driving instructor but is there to observe if mistakes are made: he should not interfere with the driving except where it is essential in the interests of safety; (2) his application of the brakes was done in the agony of the moment and following the principle in *Jones v Boyce* (p 167, below) and *The Bywell Castle* (1879) 4 PD 219, he was not to be blamed if what he reasonably did in the circumstances turned out to be wrong.

5 LIABILITY FOR CHILDREN

CHILD PEDESTRIANS

Child not negligent

Gough v Thorne

[1966] 3 All ER 398, [1966] 1 WLR 1387, 110 Sol Jo 529, CA
The plaintiff aged 13½ was waiting with her brothers aged 17 and 10 to cross the road. A lorry stopped to allow them to cross. The driver put his right hand out to warn other traffic and beckoned the children to cross. They had got across just beyond the lorry when a car driven by the defendant came past the lorry at speed and hit the plaintiff. The judge held the defendant negligent but said the plaintiff was one-third to blame for having advanced past the lorry into the open road without pausing to see whether there was any traffic coming from her right.
HELD, ON APPEAL: The plaintiff was not to blame at all. Though there was no age below which it could be said that a child could not be guilty of contributory negligence age was a most material fact to be considered. The question whether the plaintiff could be said to be guilty of contributory negligence depended on whether any ordinary child of 13½ could be expected to do any more than she did. If she had been a good deal older she might have wondered whether a proper signal had been given and looked to see whether any traffic was coming, but it was quite wrong to suggest that a child of 13½ should go through such mental processes.

Note—See also *Minter v D & H Contractors,* p 15, above.

Andrews v Freeborough

[1967] 1 QB 1, [1966] 2 All ER 721, [1966] 3 WLR, 110 Sol Jo, 407, CA
An eight year old girl and her brother, aged four, were standing on the pavement edge waiting to cross the road. The defendant was driving her car at 15–20 mph close to the kerb (because of oncoming traffic) and saw the children when she was about 40 yards away. She thought they were waiting to cross though they did not look in her direction. She did not slacken speed or sound her horn. As the car passed the children the girl's head came into violent contact with the windscreen. At the trial of the action the defendant said she saw the girl step off the pavement into the side of the car but the judge did not accept this evidence. He held the defendant to blame (1) for not sounding her horn, (2) for failing to reduce her speed and if necessary stop on seeing the children, (3) for driving too close to the kerb. He found no contributory negligence on the part of the child. On appeal, the defendant did not dispute the finding of negligence in not sounding the horn but disputed the judge's other findings including that of no contributory negligence.

The appeal was dismissed.

Per Willmer LJ: I confess I find it quite difficult to appreciate just how the accident happened if the child remained throughout standing on the kerb. But [the judge's] finding that the child did not step off the kerb was a finding of primary fact, based largely on his view of the quality of the evidence he had heard. In my judgment it is not a finding with which this Court could properly interfere . . . I would only add that if I thought that we could properly find that this child did step off the kerb into the road, I should have needed a good deal of persuasion before imputing contributory negligence to the child having regard to her tender age.

Per Davies LJ: So far as concerns the finding that the defendant was negligent in driving too close to the kerb, it is not easy to see the justification for it save in the light of the judge's conclusion that the little girl while still on the pavement was caught up by the car. Failure to slow or stop is another matter: in the light of the fact that the defendant had seen the children and had failed to call their attention to her presence the judge was entitled to make this finding. On the question whether, as the judge found, the child was caught up by the car or, as the defendant said, she stepped off from the kerb into the side of the car I am bound to say that I incline to the view that it was more probable that the child did step off the kerb into the side of the car. But it is not necessary to express any decided view on this point for the little girl was only eight years of age. Even if she did step off into the car it would not be right to count as negligence on her part such a momentary, though fatal, act of inattention or carelessness.

Prudence v Lewis

(1966) Times, 21 May (Brabin J)
The infant plaintiff aged just under three was struck by the defendant's car on a pedestrian crossing. His mother had been waiting to cross, holding her youngest child in a push chair poised on the edge of the kerb at the crossing: while she looked round for her third child the plaintiff ran on to the crossing and was hit when about 7 feet from the kerb.
HELD: The defendant was wholly to blame. He had seen the mother and children but, though realising that any child was likely to run out, did not blow his horn, thought that they should wait for him and drove on. A child of just under three was incapable of being guilty of contributory negligence.

Jones v Lawrence

[1969] 3 All ER 267
The plaintiff, a boy aged seven, ran across a street 22 feet wide from behind a parked van. The defendant was riding his motor cycle near the crown of the road and was unable to avoid striking the plaintiff, who had failed to see the motor cycle approaching. There was a 30 mph speed limit but the judge found from independent evidence that the defendant's speed was about 50 mph.
HELD: By travelling at such a speed the defendant had deprived himself of the opportunity to avoid the collision by swerving or braking and was negligent. The plaintiff's behaviour was such as one could expect in a normal child of his age momentarily forgetful of the perils of crossing a road and no finding of contributory negligence could be made against him.

Child negligent/contributory negligent

Moore v Poyner

[1975] RTR 127, CA
The defendant was driving his car at 25–30 mph along a street in a poor district in Birmingham on a Sunday afternoon. There was no other traffic. A coach 30 feet long was parked against the nearside pavement and concealed from the defendant an opening between the houses on that side of the road just beyond the front of the coach. As the defendant's car was passing the coach the plaintiff, a child of six, ran from the

opening across the front of the coach into the defendant's path and was struck by the nearside front of the car. The judge held the defendant liable: he should have slowed down or sounded his horn.
HELD, ON APPEAL: The defendant was not liable. The test to be applied to the facts was this: would it have been apparent to a reasonable man, armed with commonsense and experience of the way pedestrians, particularly children, are likely to behave in the circumstances such as were known to the defendant to exist in the present case, that he should slow down or sound his horn, or both? What course of action would he have to take if he was going to make quite certain that no accident would occur? Ought he to have slowed down to such an extent that there could have been no possibility of a child's running out at any moment in front of him and his being unable to stop without striking the child? To do so he would have had to slow down to something like 5 mph. Such a duty of care would be unreasonable; the chance that a child would run out at the precise moment he was passing the coach was so slight as not to require him to slow down to that extent. As for sounding the horn, drivers in traffic are constantly exposed to the danger of pedestrians stepping out in front of parked vehicles. It would be an impossible burden for drivers to sound their horns every time they passed a parked vehicle.

Davies v Journeaux

[1975] 1 Lloyd's Rep 483, [1976] RTR 111, CA
The plaintiff, aged 11½, was struck by the defendant's car when running across the road from the pavement on the defendant's nearside. She had come down a flight of steps to the pavement, which was 3 feet wide. The entrance to the steps was 3 or 4 feet wide. She was struck by the offside front of the car which, after the accident, was parallel with the pavement and 4 ft 9 ins from it. There was a mark on the road behind the nearside rear wheel 22 feet long indicating heavy application of the brakes. The passenger in the nearside front seat of the car saw the plaintiff as she stood momentarily in the entrance to the steps and then dashed across. The defendant did not see her until she was in the act of dashing across; he was then 50 to 60 feet away, travelling at 20 to 25 mph. The judge held him 40% to blame for having failed to see the plaintiff at the moment when his passenger did and failing to sound his horn.
HELD: The fact that the passenger saw the plaintiff a split second before the defendant did not establish a lack of proper care on the defendant's part; he was driving and needed to switch his eyes from one direction to another. Even if he had seen the plaintiff at the same instant it could not be said he should then have sounded his horn; what he did do was to apply his brakes heavily. Having regard to the brake marks he had acted promptly and efficiently. The judge's decision seemed to place a duty on motorists to sound the horn virtually whenever they see a pedestrian, regardless of whether the pedestrian is manifesting an intention of leaving the pavement and dashing across the road. Appeal allowed.

Kite v Nolan

(1982) 126 Sol Jo 821, [1983] RTR 253, CA
The defendant was driving his car on a hot afternoon when he saw an ice-cream van parked on the offside of the road in front of him. He also saw three cars parked on the nearside ahead of the van. He slowed almost to a standstill to allow an approaching car to pass between the van and the parked cars. He then accelerated to about 15 mph. The plaintiff, aged five, ran out in front of him from between the parked cars and was struck by the defendant's car. The judge found that the defendant could not have

avoided striking the plaintiff unless travelling at not more than 5 mph. He held that the defendant was not negligent, referring to *Moore v Poyner* (above). On appeal it was argued that the defendant should have realised the serious risk of a child running out bearing in mind the weather and the attraction of the ice-cream van.
HELD: The judge had decided correctly. He had to determine what was a reasonable standard of care in all the circumstances of the particular case. He would have regard to many factors including the following: (1) the likelihood of a pedestrian crossing the road, considering the allurement of the ice-cream van; (2) the nature of the pedestrian likely to cross, child or adult; (3) the likely degree of injury if struck; (4) the adverse consequences to the public and to the defendant of taking whatever precautions are under consideration. The application of the principles must always depend on the particular circumstances of the case; any decision applying the general standard to particular facts is unlikely to, almost cannot, produce a precedent. The judge had not treated *Moore v Poyner* as a precedent. He had correctly applied the general principle.

Foskett v Mistry

[1984] RTR 1, [1984] LS Gaz R 2683, CA
The plaintiff, a boy of 16 1/2, ran down a parkland slope on to a busy road and collided with the nearside of the defendant's car near the windscreen, sustaining serious injury. The defendant had not seen him before he ran into the car. A driver coming in the opposite direction had seen the plaintiff and thought he was going to run into the road. The judge at first instance dismissed the claim.
HELD, ON APPEAL: The root of liability was negligence, which depended on the facts: reference to authorities in simple running-down cases was unnecessary. Could the defendant be shown to have failed to take reasonable care in all the circumstances? The defendant taking reasonable care ought to have glanced at the open parkland on his left and should have seen the plaintiff when he emerged into his view. A reasonably careful driver would have sounded his horn in the circumstances; if the defendant had seen the plaintiff and sounded his horn probably the accident would have been prevented. The defendant was plainly negligent, though the plaintiff was guilty of contributory negligence to the extent of 75%.
Appeal allowed.

Saleem v Drake

(1993) PIQR 129, CA
The plaintiff was a six year old pedestrian who was severely injured, having been struck by the defendant's mini-bus. The plaintiff had suddenly ran out into the road. The defendant had noticed the plaintiff playing at the side of the road and had slowed down. The defendant had not sounded his horn. The plaintiff's claim failed. The plaintiff appealed.
HELD: The appeal was dismissed. The defendant had satisfied his duty of care towards the plaintiff by slowing down. There was no indication that the plaintiff would rush out and, therefore, the defendant was under no duty to sound his horn.

Armstrong v Cottrell

(1993) PIQR 109, CA
The plaintiff attempted to cross a road, hesitated, and was struck by the defendant's vehicle. The defendant had seen the plaintiff and her friends 'hovering' at the side of the road. The plaintiff's claim had failed. The plaintiff appealed.

HELD: The appeal was allowed. In view of what the defendant had seen, she should have slowed down and sounded her horn. The plaintiff's contributory negligence was assessed at one-third.

ALLUREMENT TO CHILDREN

Rawsthorne v Ottley

[1937] 3 All ER 902 (Hilbery J)
A tip-up lorry in the charge of a single driver had delivered coke in a school playground, and was driving away when a number of boys jumped on to the rear of the lorry causing the tipping part to tip up. Another boy, the plaintiff, had jumped on to the lorry immediately behind the driver's cab, and when the tipping part of the lorry was suddenly released it came down on the plaintiff and crushed his leg. The headmaster of the school had left the boys to play in the playground and had returned into the school premises before the arrival of the lorry. He did not know of the arrival of the lorry. An action for damages was brought against the managers of the school, the headmaster and the owners of the lorry.
HELD: (1) The headmaster was not negligent in leaving the boys in the playground without supervision, nor ought he to have taken steps to stop the lorry from coming during playtime. The headmaster and the managers were accordingly not liable. (2) The owners of the lorry had sent the lorry in the charge of a reasonable adult, and ought not reasonably to have anticipated interference. (3) The driver was not negligent in not looking to see if the boys had jumped on to the lorry, and he could not have anticipated sufficient weight to tip the lorry. The owners of the lorry were, therefore, not liable. (4) A lorry as such is not an allurement to children.

Culkin v McFie & Sons Ltd

[1939] 3 All ER 613 (Croom-Johnson J)
A motor lorry and trailer was carrying sacks of sugar on the highway and sugar was leaking from one sack. A boy aged seven ran off the pavement after the lorry had passed him but not the trailer, and his foot was run over by the trailer. The accident happened in a street in which there were three schools, and on a school holiday. The practice of boys running after the lorries was well known, and the driver of the lorry had frequently had trouble with the boys. There was an alternative route close by. The defendants did nothing to prevent the sugar escaping on to the roadway.
HELD: The lorry was an allurement to the infant and a concealed danger; he was lawfully on the highway and was indulging a natural instinct and not guilty of contributory negligence. Defendants had placed a manifest allurement to children on the highway with an insufficient number of lookout men, and were liable.

Creed v John McGeoch & Sons Ltd

[1955] 3 All ER 123, [1955] 1 WLR 1005, 99 Sol Jo 563 (Ashworth J)
Defendants were contractors for road making on some spare ground or waste land which was freely used by the public and children playing on it. They left a two-wheeled trailer fitted with a towing bar used for removing kerbs, about 6 feet from the roadside kerb. On Saturday afternoon a girl aged five with three other children were playing on the trailer and the girl was injured. The defendants were not occupiers and their duty was higher than that of occupiers on the principle of *Donoghue v Stevenson* ([1932] AC 562). The defendants knew that the trailer was attractive and

dangerous to children who might play on the trailer and be injured, and were negligent in not taking precautions to prevent injury to children, and were liable to damages to the injured girl.

Note—This case in which a motor vehicle is not concerned, bears some resemblance to *Rawsthorne's* case but *Rawsthorne's* case was not cited.

6 DRIVING, MANOEUVRING AND PARKING

OVERTAKING

Sounding horn

Holdack v Bullock Bros (Electrical) Ltd

(1964) 108 Sol Jo 861, affd (1965) 109 Sol Jo 238, CA
In daylight on a straight road a motor scooter was overtaking a motor van when the van swerved to the offside and the scooter collided with the offside front wing of the van. The van driver had not seen the scooter in spite of having two outside mirrors and an interior mirror. The judge held the van driver was negligent in changing course without warning when it was extremely dangerous to do so, but held the scooter rider one-third to blame for having failed to hoot to show his intention to overtake. The scooter rider appealed.
HELD: There was no ground on which the Court of Appeal should interfere. In the ordinary way if a motor scooter was overtaking another vehicle which was going straight along a road there was no need for the scooter to hoot before overtaking if the scooter was giving reasonable clearance. In this case the judge must have come to the conclusion that the movement of the van was such as to put the scooter rider on enquiry as to what the van was going to do.

Distracting driver

Rothwell v Davies Bros (Haulage) Ltd

(1963) 107 Sol Jo 436, [1963] Crim LR 577, CA
The second defendant was in his stationary car when it was struck and damaged by the first defendant's lorry which did not stop. The second defendant, incensed, followed the lorry trying to attract the driver's attention. He drove alongside the lorry flashing his lights, sounding his horn and shouting. The lorry driver's attention was distracted and as a result the lorry collided with the plaintiff's car and injured the plaintiff. The judge found the lorry driver one-quarter to blame and the second defendant three-quarters.
HELD, ON APPEAL by the second defendant: The apportionment could not be disturbed. Motorists must not distract the attention of a driver of a heavy vehicle on a busy road. The second defendant's conduct, though understandable, was foolish and was the substantial cause of the accident.

Jumping the queue

Powell v Moody

(1966) 110 Sol Jo 215, Times, 10 March, CA
Riding his motorcycle along a busy road the plaintiff came up to the tail of a stationary line of traffic consisting of vehicles two abreast which were held up. He proceeded along the offside of the line of traffic, overtaking the stationary vehicles. The defendant, driving a car, came out of a side road on the nearside of the line of traffic to pass through a gap and turn right to go along the main road in the opposite direction. He was given a signal by the driver of a milk tanker to come out and as he was inching his way out the plaintiff, who had not seen the side road, collided with him. The judge held both parties to blame but attributed 80% of the blame to the plaintiff.
HELD, ON APPEAL by the plaintiff: The judge's apportionment was reasonable. Any vehicle which jumped a queue of stationary vehicles was undertaking an operation fraught with great hazard and which had to be carried out with great care. There was always difficulty in such circumstances of seeing what was happening especially emerging from gaps.

Note—Whether any member of the court expressly mentioned the Highway Code (1959), para 29, 'In traffic hold-ups do not "jump the queue"', is not clear from the report. Paragraph 29 is repeated in the Highway Code 1993 at para 91.

Clarke v Winchurch

[1969] 1 All ER 275, [1969] 1 WLR 69, 112 Sol Jo 909, CA
The first defendant's car was parked on its offside of the road, facing the direction in which the first defendant wished to travel. A continuous line of traffic was travelling in the opposite direction and he had to pass through this to proceed on his way. The third defendant, a bus driver driving the second defendants' bus, saw that the first defendant wished to come out and stopped to allow him to do so. The bus driver flashed his headlights at the first defendant who then came out slowly across the front of the bus. When the front of the car was about a yard beyond the offside of the bus the car was struck by a moped ridden by the plaintiff who had overtaken the bus on the offside. The bus driver had looked in his mirror but had not seen the plaintiff. The judge of assize accepted the first defendant's evidence that he was only just crawling out and acquitted him of any blame. He found the plaintiff two-thirds to blame and the bus driver one-third for not giving a hand signal to warn the plaintiff as he said he would have done if he had seen him.
HELD, ON APPEAL: The plaintiff was to blame but the first defendant and the bus driver were not. A cyclist or moped rider is entitled to overtake stationary traffic but to do this warrants a very high degree of care and he must ride in such a way that he can immediately deal with an emergency. When he saw that the bus had stopped the plaintiff ought to have realised that something was going on in front of it and driven accordingly. With regard to the bus driver his flashing his headlights meant merely 'Come on so far as I am concerned'. Having stopped he was under no duty to do anything else and the flashing of the headlights was not a representation that it was clear for the car driver to pull out beyond the offside of the bus. Nor was the bus driver under a duty to give a signal to the moped rider. With regard to the first defendant the judge's finding that he was moving very, very slowly and that he could not have done more justified his being acquitted of negligence.

Note—In a dissenting judgment Russell LJ said the car driver should have stopped with only the tip of his bonnet showing beyond the bus as an indication to overtaking traffic of his presence and should then have paused and listened for any horn sounding before going any further out. He would have held him 20% to blame. The other members of the court also felt there was a good deal of difficulty in finding no blame on the part of the driver but were unwilling to hold that there was anything more the driver could do once the judge's finding was accepted that he came out very, very slowly. In *Worsfold v Howe* (below) the Court of Appeal held that *Clarke v Winchurch* laid down no principle of law.

Leeson v Bevis and Tolchard Ltd

[1972] RTR 373, CA
The defendant's garage was on the north side of Upper Richmond Road with access by an exit 11 feet wide. Their van was being driven out of the exit across the eastbound traffic stream which was at a standstill. A lorry driver had stopped his vehicle so as to leave a substantial gap and had gestured to the defendant's driver to come out. The plaintiff was riding his motor cycle at about 15 mph along the offside of the line of traffic, overtaking the stationary vehicles. As the defendant's van came through the gap, turning right, there was a collision between the motorcycle and the nearside front of the van. The judge held the plaintiff and the van driver equally to blame.
HELD, ON APPEAL: The decision should stand. The plaintiff was doing nothing wrong in overtaking the line of stationary vehicles, but doing that and being aware of this exit and others on to Upper Richmond Road he should have been proceeding with the greatest care and keeping an effective look-out. The van had almost completed its turn when hit and if the plaintiff had been alert he could have swerved to avoid it. The van driver had to perform a difficult and dangerous manoeuvre and very great care was needed: he should have made quite sure that nobody was going across his path in an easterly direction. It was important to realise that the lorry driver's gesture merely meant that he was giving way to the van emerging and not that if the van crossed beyond the shelter of the lorry it would be safe: *Clarke v Winchurch* and *Powell v Moody* (above) were distinguishable on the facts.

HL Motorworks (Willesden) Ltd v Alwahbi

[1977] RTR 276, CA
The plaintiffs' driver stopped at the mouth of a side road, waiting to turn right into the main road. Two cars were stationary side by side in the main road on his right. The driver of one of these waved to him to come out. He drove out across the front of the two cars and when about on the middle line was run into by the defendant's car overtaking the two stationary cars.
HELD: The plaintiffs' driver was not to blame.

Per Cairns LJ: If the driver of one of the cars has given the signal inviting him to come forward, what is he to do? Is he to stay in the mouth of [the side road] disregarding the invitation to come out and wait until there is a complete clearance in both directions in [the main road]? I think that he is entitled to assume that no vehicle will come along on its wrong side of the road making a third line of traffic and overtaking two stationary cars.

Worsfold v Howe

[1980] 1 All ER 1028, [1980] 1 WLR 1175, 124 Sol Jo 646, [1980] RTR 131, CA
At a part of a busy city street where for the northbound traffic the road led to traffic lights at a road junction the nearside lane was for traffic intending to go straight on

and the offside lane for traffic intending to turn right at the junction. The plaintiff was riding his motor cycle in the offside lane; on his left was a line of stationary vehicles held up at the lights. One of the vehicles was a large tanker with a gap ahead of it to allow vehicles to enter the roadway from a railway yard on the left. As the plaintiff overtook the stationary tanker the defendant drove his car across the front of it very slowly so as to cross the northbound lanes and turn right. As his car entered the traffic lane beyond the tanker the plaintiff travelling at a speed more than 10 but less than 30 mph ran into the nearside front of the car which was at an angle. The judge said he would have found the parties equally to blame—the plaintiff for travelling too fast and the defendant for having gone beyond the line of his vision—but for the decision in *Clarke v Winchurch* (p 68, above) which he considered to be on all fours with the present case. He dismissed the plaintiff's claim.
HELD, ON APPEAL, and adopting the dictum of Cairns LJ in *Garston Warehousing v Smart* (p 103, below). The judge was not bound by *Clarke v Winchurch,* which laid down no principle of law. The apportionment of 50-50 suggested by the judge should be accepted.

Overtaking at a road junction

Tocci v Hankard (No 2)

(1966) 110 Sol Jo 835, CA
The plaintiff was riding his moped in a main London street when the defendant's vehicle coming in the opposite direction swerved across the road and struck him. The reason the defendant swerved was that he was in the act of overtaking a scooter travelling in the same direction as himself when the scooter swung to the right to enter a side road. The scooter rider did not stop and could not be identified.
HELD, ON APPEAL: The defendant was not to blame. The rule in the Highway Code not to overtake at road junctions did not apply to side roads such as this of which there were so many in London. One ought not to be critical of what was done on the spur of the moment when a dangerous situation had been created by someone else.

Overtaking horse

Burns v Ellicott

(1969) 113 Sol Jo 490 (Paull J)
The plaintiff was riding her horse on a path at the side of a narrow road. Her right leg was over the edge of the kerb. The defendant driving his car in the same direction as the plaintiff saw another car approaching him from the opposite direction. He slowed down and passed the plaintiff almost brushing her horse. The horse took fright and reared or turned catching its hoofs under the front bumper of the defendant's car. It was badly injured and had to be destroyed.
HELD: The defendant was negligent. If a horse was being ridden in a narrow road a car driver must exercise great caution in passing it. His duty was to slow down and give the horse a wide berth. If he could not do that because a car was coming from the other direction his duty was to wait until the other car had passed.

Haimes v Watson

[1981] RTR 90, CA
The defendant counterclaimed for damages sustained when his car collided with a horse ridden by the plaintiff. He was driving along a road 20 feet wide at about 30 mph. The horse was being ridden in the same direction in the nearside gutter when it shied and moved broadside across the road: the collision was unavoidable. The plaintiff admitted that the shy took the horse temporarily out of his control. There was no plea of scienter in the counterclaim.
HELD: The defendant could not succeed. He had established that the horse had suddenly moved sideways across his bows, and that called for an explanation; but the plaintiff had given one which was adequate to negative any inference of negligence. The county court judge's view that a rider must so control his horse that it will not move sideways if startled and that not so to control the horse was negligence was not the law.

Carryfast Ltd v Hack

[1981] RTR 464 (Ralph Gibson J)
The defendant, an experienced horsewoman, was riding her horse along the narrow grass verge on the nearside of a main road 21 feet wide. The plaintiffs' van was being driven by their employee in the same direction at about 30 mph. When the van had almost reached the horse the driver saw the horse begin to 'dance'; he swerved to the offside, crashing into a lorry approaching from the opposite direction. The plaintiffs claimed against the defendant for the damage to the van. She admitted in evidence that her horse was nervous in traffic but said she could keep the animal under control and that it was on the grass verge all the time before the accident.
HELD: She was not liable. The accident was caused by the plaintiffs' driver's negligence in not being able to slow down sufficiently and stop when he saw the horse 'dancing'. Every case turns on its own facts. It is not negligent of a rider to go on the highway on a horse simply because the rider knows that the horse does not like some traffic noises and may on occasion act as if unsettled, but such a rider may be negligent in taking a horse on to the highway if there is a reasonable risk of the horse getting out of control.

Overtaking signal

Note—The Highway Code formerly contained a hand signal denoting that the driver was ready to be overtaken. The signal was omitted from the 1959 and subsequent editions of the Highway Code, but as some drivers still use it the following case may sometimes be useful.

White v Broadbent and British Road Services

(1957) Times, 29 November, [1958] Crim LR 129, CA
A woman was walking along the pavement at 3.30 pm on a wet and misty afternoon when she was overtaken by a lorry travelling at about 15 mph. She thought it was going to turn into a side street but it drew out to the white line in the centre of the road and stopped as the woman came abreast of it. She crossed the road in front of the stationary lorry and came into the path of a van which was overtaking and passing the lorry. She tried to step back but slipped and fell and was struck by the van and injured. When the lorry driver stopped, he looked to his front and saw the road was clear, and

in his mirror to see if any traffic was coming from behind. The mirror was misty and he wiped it and looked again, saw the van and gave the 'passing' signal to an overtaking driver. He had not seen the woman who had actually started to cross the road when he gave the signal.

The county court judge found the plaintiff one-third to blame; of the remaining two-thirds, the lorry driver 80% and the van driver 20%. The lorry owners appealed. HELD: The overtaking signal did not amount to an authority to the van driver to pass, but it was probable the van driver would proceed, and with greater confidence. The lorry would to some extent obscure the view of pedestrians seeking to cross. The lorry driver's duty was to be on the look-out for pedestrians before he gave the signal. Appeal dismissed; no interference with the apportionment.

Grange Motors Ltd v Spencer

[1969] 1 All ER 340, [1969] 1 WLR 53, 112 Sol Jo, 908, CA
The defendant in his car was approaching a bend in the road. A Post Office van was parked at the bend partly on the roadway. A postman crossed the road towards the van from a house opposite and stood close to it facing the driver's door. The defendant saw him look in the opposite direction and then make a gesture or signal to him which he took to mean that it was safe for him to pass. To do so, giving the postman three feet clearance, the defendant had to go over the centre line of the road. The plaintiff's vehicle came round the bend in the opposite direction and the defendant was unable to avoid colliding with it. The county court judge held the postman wholly to blame for the accident.
HELD, ON APPEAL: He was entitled so to find. The postman owed a duty of care to the defendant, whose car was coming on and he was negligent in giving an invitation to pass at a time and in a position when it was unsafe to give such an invitation. As was said in *White v Broadbent* (above) the driver of a vehicle on a road who makes a signal to another vehicle must have regard to other users of the road before giving that signal and owes a duty to the other driver to that effect, though the extent to which the driver to whom the signal is addressed is entitled to rely on it is a question of fact and degree according to the case. The question must always be, did the driver act with reasonable care?

SPEED

Note—There is a general speed limit of 70 mph on dual carriageway roads (not being motorways), and a general speed limit of 60 mph on single carriageway roads (not being motorways) (SI 1978/1548).

The speed limit of 30 mph on restricted roads is imposed by the Road Traffic Regulation Act 1984, s 81. A restricted road is a road with street lamps 'placed not more than two hundred yards apart' (s 82(1)) but the section provides for various exceptions.

Speed limits on roads other than restricted roads are authorised by s 84, and for vehicles of different classes by s 86. The speed limits at present applicable to various classes of vehicle are contained in the Road Traffic Regulation Act 1984, Sch 5.

Exceeding speed limit not in itself negligence

Tribe v Jones

(1961) 105 Sol Jo 931, 59 LGR 582, Div Ct QB

At 7.20 am when traffic was light the defendant drove his car over half a mile at speeds between 45 and 65 mph. The road was wide, well-surfaced and bounded by common land, but it was subject to a 30 mph speed limit. No accident occurred nor was there evidence of any actual danger to others. The defendant was charged with driving at a speed dangerous to the public contrary to the Road Traffic Act 1960, s 2(1) (now the Road Traffic Act 1972, s 2).

HELD, ON APPEAL (from a dismissal of the charge by the justices): A fast speed was not automatically dangerous although in many cases it might well be so. The justices were entitled to find as they did.

Note—Section 2 of the Road Traffic Act 1972 is repeated as s 2 of the Road Traffic Act 1988.

Barna v Hudes Merchandising Corpn

(1962) 106 Sol Jo 194, [1962] Crim LR 321, CA

The plaintiff, driving his car, wished to turn right from a minor road into a major road. Another car was waiting on the crown of the major road to turn into the minor road. The plaintiff's view to his right was obscured by parked cars. He moved out slowly at a time when the defendant's car was approaching from his right at a speed between 30 and 40 mph, though the road was subject to a 30 mph speed limit. The defendant was unable to pull up in time and ran into the plaintiff's car.

HELD: The defendant was not to blame for the accident. To exceed the speed limit, though an offence, was not in itself negligence imposing civil liability. In the circumstances the defendant's speed was not excessive. He had no reason to suppose that the road would be blocked as it was.

Hurlock v Inglis

(1963) 107 Sol Jo 1023 (Havers J)

The defendant was driving at a speed of 100 mph or more along the M1 motorway when his car got out of control and struck the plaintiff's lorry, causing him injuries. There were skid and tyre marks over 950 feet long. The defendant said he was about to overtake a car travelling in the centre lane when a van swerved in front of it: in trying to avoid the car he was unable to avoid striking the plaintiff's lorry.

The judge found the defendant liable. It was not in itself negligent to drive on the M1 at 100 mph but the defendant had not satisfactorily explained what happened. He had for some reason jammed on his brakes when he was in the outside lane and his car got out of control and for a considerable distance went backwards. Some explanation was called for to account for this extraordinary behaviour. In the absence of a satisfactory explanation he must be held to have been negligent.

Quinn v Scott

[1965] 2 All ER 588, [1965] 1 WLR 1004, 109 Sol Jo 498 (Glyn-Jones J)

On a straight level main road 32 feet wide the defendant was driving his Jaguar car at 70 to 75 mph. He was overtaking another car when he saw, 50 yards ahead, a tree falling across the road from the left. He instinctively swerved to the offside towards the thinner part of the tree, applying his brakes. He crashed into the foliage and lost

control of the car due to the windscreen breaking, the car being filled with leaves and the steering wheel spinning out of his hands. The plaintiff driving a minibus from the opposite direction had seen the tree falling and had pulled up about 40 yards from the centre of the tree. The defendant, coming through the tree out of control, collided with the minibus and the plaintiff was injured.
HELD: The defendant was not negligent. High speed alone is not evidence of negligence unless the particular conditions at the time preclude it. There were no conditions present to make the defendant negligent in overtaking the two cars on his nearside at a speed of 70 to 75 mph. 50 yards was not at that speed sufficient distance in which to pull up when the tree began to fall: the 'thinking distance' shown on the diagrams on the back of the Highway Code could not be applied as a universal rule of thumb where so alarming an event occurs as the unexpected fall of a tree.

Police vehicles

Gaynor v Allen

[1959] 2 QB 403, [1959] 2 All ER 644, [1959] 3 WLR 221, 103 Sol Jo 677 (McNair J)
A pedestrian was injured by a police motor cyclist who was on a road where a 40 mph speed limit was in force. He was travelling at 60 mph or more and was killed as a result of the accident. The case raised the question on which the judge said there appeared to be no authority, of the extent to which the section affected the civil liability of the driver. The defendant contended that there was a difference between a police officer and an ordinary motor cyclist, but the Court negatived this conclusion. The driver was to be judged in exactly the same way as any other driver. He owed a duty to the public to drive with due care and attention and without exposing members of the public to undue danger. The defendant was guilty of negligence and so was the plaintiff, to a lesser extent; apportioned one-third to the plaintiff.

Dyer v Bannell

(1965) 109 Sol Jo 216 (Glyn-Jones J)
The plaintiff was injured when a van she was driving was struck by a police car driven by the defendant, a police constable. It was night time but visibility was good and there was ordinary street lighting. The plaintiff wished to turn right from a main road into a side turning. She switched on her flashing indicators and also made a hand signal. She saw in her driving mirror a taxi cab some distance behind and the reflection of the defendant's car lights behind that. She then began to turn. The defendant was answering a call and was travelling at 45 mph in a built-up area. He overtook the taxi and collided with the plaintiff's van as she turned across his path.
HELD: It was not negligent of a police officer in the execution of his duty to drive at a fast speed; if there was nothing against the defendant except the fact that he was driving at 45 mph or more then it was not negligent. But he must exercise a degree of care and skill proportionate to the speed at which he was driving. He must remember that the ordinary road user in a built-up area would not expect vehicles to drive at that speed and should give audible warning of approach or otherwise make known the presence of a police car. The defendant had not apprehended what the van was doing as quickly as he should have done: he was guilty of want of what was a very high standard of care and skill demanded of a driver at 45 mph in a built-up area. The plaintiff as a reasonable motorist was entitled to suppose it was safe to turn as she had

seen that the next vehicle behind her, the taxi cab, would not be embarrassed by her turn. She need not contemplate that a vehicle still further away would be travelling at such a speed that it would be dangerous to turn. She was not guilty of any contributory negligence. Judgment for the plaintiff.

Note—The Road Traffic Regulation Act 1984, s 87 provides:

'No statutory provision imposing a speed limit on motor vehicles shall apply to any vehicle on an occasion when it is being used for fire brigade, ambulance or police purposes, if the observance of that provision would be likely to hinder the use of the vehicle for the purpose for which it is being used on that occasion.'

Wood v Richards

[1977] RTR 201, 65 Cr App Rep 300, [1977] Crim LR 295, Div Ct
A police patrol driver on a motorway when answering an emergency call decided to overtake a large vehicle by driving on the hard shoulder. In doing so he collided with a lorry standing on the hard shoulder. He was convicted of driving without due care contrary to the Road Traffic Act 1972, s 3. On appeal he claimed that a special standard was applicable to a police officer driving to an emergency.
HELD: Not so. If the Act had meant a different standard to apply it would have said so—as does the Road Traffic Regulation Act 1984 on speed limits by s 87—and it does not.

Note—Section 3 of the Road Traffic Act 1972 is repeated as s 3 of the Road Traffic Act 1988.

Marshall v Osmond

[1983] QB 1034, [1983] 2 All ER 225, [1983] 3 WLR 13, 127 Sol Jo 309, [1983] RTR 475, CA
The plaintiff with other men was a passenger in a car which he knew was stolen. A police car set off in pursuit and stopped alongside the stolen car when the occupants were getting out and running away. The plaintiff was struck by the police car and sustained injury which he claimed was caused by the negligent driving of the defendant, the driver of the police car. The defendant did not intend to injure him.
HELD: He was not entitled to succeed. A police officer driving a car in hot pursuit of a person or persons whom he rightly suspects of having committed an arrestable offence does not owe that person the same duty of care which he owes to a lawful and innocent user of the highway going about his lawful occasions; though he must not deliberately injure such a person unless it is reasonably necessary to do so in order to arrest him.

An appeal was dismissed. Per Sir John Donaldson MR: I do not believe that the defence of *volenti non fit injuria* is really applicable in the case of the police pursuing a suspected criminal. I think that the duty owed by a police driver to the suspect is . . . the same duty as that owed to anyone else, namely to exercise such care and skill as is reasonable in all the circumstances. The vital words in that proposition of law are 'in all the circumstances' and of course one of the circumstances was that the plaintiff bore all the appearance of having been somebody engaged in a criminal activity for which there was a power of arrest.

Note—The Australian case of *Schilling v Lenton* (1988) 47 SASR 88, Supreme Court, is of interest. The plaintiff was being pursued by the defendant, a police officer. Both cars were travelling at a high speed. It was dark and the surface of the road was wet. The plaintiff stopped at a set of traffic lights and the defendant collided with the rear of the plaintiff's vehicle. The plaintiff suffered injuries and sued the defendant.

It was held that the police driver was still under a duty to drive with reasonable care and primary liability rested with him. However, the plaintiff was found a third to blame on the basis that he should have foreseen that the police may well have observed his bad driving and pursued him and that such a pursuit would have involved danger.

Fire engines

Wardell-Yerburgh v Surrey County Council

[1973] RTR 462 (Brabin J)

On a three-lane road in fog which limited visibility to 50 yards the plaintiff's husband was driving a mini-van in the centre lane, slowly overtaking a lorry and trailer 52 feet long. He was following at least one other car. The defendants' emergency tender (fire engine) was being driven in the opposite direction in the centre lane at 50 mph with headlights on and blue light flashing. It was taking tools to rescue trapped persons in crashed vehicles some distance away. A car ahead of the tender moved into its nearside lane to let it through, as did the car ahead of the mini. The tender and the mini collided in the centre of the road, killing the plaintiff's husband. It was argued by the defendants that the tender on such an errand could justifiably be driven in a way which in an ordinary vehicle would be regarded as reckless.

HELD: Following *Gaynor v Allen* (above) the driver of the tender owed to the public the same duty of care as any other driver: he was negligent in driving too fast in fog and not keeping a proper look-out. But the mini driver was the more to blame in the manner of his overtaking. To overtake as the last of three in a fog is liable to result in an accident. He should have delayed overtaking until he could see what was ahead of him. Instead he was moving forward at a slow differential speed in relation to the lorry he was overtaking and could move neither to right nor left when the tender came in sight. All this happening in a second or two he had placed himself in the worst possible position. He was two-thirds to blame, the defendants' driver one-third.

Speed tables

TABLE SHOWING DISTANCE COVERED IN ONE SECOND AT VARIOUS SPEEDS

Miles per hour	*Feet per second*	*Metres per second*
10	14.66	4.39
15	22.00	6.60
20	29.33	8.79
25	36.66	10.99
30	44.00	13.20
35	51.33	15.39
40	58.66	17.59
45	66.00	19.80
50	73.33	21.99
60	88.00	26.40

BRAKING TESTS

Appropriate minimum stopping distances
Four-wheel brakes, pneumatic tyres

Stopping Distances in feet

Road Surface	*Dry Smooth Concrete*	*Macadam Dry*	*Asphalt Dry*	*Asphalt Wet*	*Low Adhesion Surface (Wet)*
Co-efficient of Friction	0.9	0.8	0.7	0.5	0.4
SPEEDS WHEN BRAKES APPLIED IN MPH					
20	15	17	19	27	33
25	23	27	30	42	52
30	33	38	43	60	75
35	45	50	59	82	102
40	60	67	76	107	133
45	75	85	97	135	170
50	93	105	120	167	207
55	112	127	145	202	251
60	134	152	172	240	298

Time lag not allowed for.
Two-wheel brakes approximately double the distance, subject to correction for weight distribution.
Smooth tyres—add about 25%
Solid tyres—add about 33%
For approximate stopping distances in metres multiply by 0.30

Note—The Highway Code gives the following stopping distances in perfect conditions, ie good weather—broad daylight—good dry roads.

Speed	Thinking Distance		Braking Distance		Overall Stopping Distance	
mph	ft	m	ft	m	ft	m
70	70	21	245	75	315	96
60	60	18	180	55	240	73
50	50	15	125	38	175	53
40	40	12	80	24	120	36
30	30	9	45	14	75	23
20	20	6	20	6	40	12

RACE

O'Down v Frazer-Nash

[1951] WN 173, 95 Sol Jo 269 (McNair J)
The course of a road race in Jersey and the regulations were approved by the RAC. The deceased, a doctor, gave his services as a first aid official. He was provided with an RAC handbook for officials giving warning not to set foot on the course, the pavement or road except where their duty required them to do so.

On a practice run the deceased took up a position on the pavement at a road junction opposite a bend where the course took a sharp right-hand bend. The brakes of a car failed and the deceased was killed. There had been no neglect to maintain the car in a fit condition. There was no negligence of the driver. The organisers had performed their duty of protecting their officials against reasonably foreseeable perils. There was no inadequacy in any of their arrangements. The warning in the handbook was adequate. It was a case of familiarity having bred contempt.

The claim against the organisers and the driver failed.

Wilks v Cheltenham Home Guard Motor Cycle and Light Car Club

[1971] 2 All ER 369, [1971] 1 WLR 668, 115 Sol Jo 309, CA
The plaintiff was a spectator at a motor-cycle scramble when he was struck and injured by a machine of a competitor, the second defendant. The machine and rider somehow surmounted a 'wrecking rope', crossed a space of 10 feet and then went under or over another rope barrier before striking the plaintiff. The judge of assize acquitted the organisers (the first defendants) of any blame but held the second defendant negligent on the ground that he lost control of his machine because of excessive speed, inadequate skill or reckless driving. The second defendant appealed.
HELD, ON APPEAL: He was not to blame. A competitor in a race must use reasonable care—but as a competitor he is expected to go all out to win and the degree of care required is that which a reasonable competitor would take in those circumstances. In a race a reasonable man would do everything he could to win but he would not be foolhardy, that is, so conduct himself as to evince a reckless disregard of the spectators' safety. There was no evidence of greatly excessive speed on the part of the second defendant. The fact that he had somehow crossed the two rope barriers did not bring into play the doctrine of *res ipsa loquitur*; the circumstances were vastly different from a case such as *Ellor v Selfridge* (p 35, above) where a motorist mounts the pavement. Appeal allowed.

Harrison v Vincent

[1982] RTR 8, CA
In a motor cycle and combination race the plaintiff was a sidecar passenger. At a point on the course the machines had to be brought down from speeds of 100 mph or more to 30 mph to negotiate a hairpin bend. The rider of the machine applied the brake but due to a defect it failed adequately to slow the machine which went off the course into an escape road. It struck a vehicle projecting into the road injuring the plaintiff severely. The vehicle was placed there to clear away any broken-down equipment. The plaintiff sued the rider and the organisers.
HELD: He was entitled to succeed, (1) against the rider of the machine, since he owed the normal duty of care to the plaintiff, the defect in the brake being one which should

have been rectified beforehand, and (2) against the race organisers for not keeping the escape road clear of obstruction.

Note—See also *White v Blackmore*, p 47, above and *Latchford v Spedeworth International*, p 47, above.

SKIDDING

Note—And see 'Res ipsa loquitur', p 26, above.

A defence of skidding is sometimes raised in answer to a prima facie case of negligence, but the modern tendency is to regard a skid as placing a heavy onus of proof on the defendant. The older cases must be regarded as of doubtful value since *Richley v Faull* (p 82, below).

Defendant held not liable

Hunter v Wright

[1938] 2 All ER 621, CA

The defendant was driving a motor car when it skidded and subsequently mounted the pavement and injured the plaintiff, who was walking thereon. It was found that the skid was not due to any negligence on the part of the defendant, but it was contended that she had been negligent (1) in steering the wrong way to correct the skid, and (2) in accelerating after the skid. Shortly before the accident she had practically stopped at a pedestrian crossing, and was accelerating when the skid occurred. The speed of the car was estimated at 16 to 20 mph, and the car travelled 13 to 20 feet between the skid and the pavement.

HELD, ON APPEAL: The time and space at the disposal of the defendant in which to remedy the skid was so short that it being proved that the skid was not due to any fault of hers, she had discharged the onus of showing how her car came to be on the pavement, and could not be said to have been in any way to blame for the accident. It was decided many years ago that a skidding vehicle is not in law a nuisance, nor is the skidding in itself any evidence of negligence on the part of the driver. There are also cases which have decided that the mounting of a car upon the pavement is prima facie evidence of negligence upon the part of the driver. Here the combination of these matters is considered, and the result is that, when a car mounts the pavement by reason of a skid not due to negligence on the part of the driver, there is no fault for which the driver is responsible, and no action lies in respect of such a skid. Appeal dismissed.

Browne v De Luxe Car Services and Birkenhead Corpn

[1941] 1 KB 549, [1941] 1 All ER 383, 110 LJKB 369, 165 LT 175, 57 TLR 346, 85 Sol Jo 165, CA

A motor car which knocks over a cyclist and carries on into a garage raises a prima facie case of negligence and shifts the onus on to the driver. Where the driver is using skill and care and proceeds to carry out an ordinary simple and perfectly normal manoeuvre, but because of the condition of the road most unexpectedly gets into a skid, the driver is not liable. A skid in itself does not excuse an accident. It may be caused by bad driving, careless driving or over-rapid driving, and the onus is on the driver to prove that the skid was not brought about by one of these causes.

The judge found the treacherous surface was due to long use and wear on granite sets, giving them a highly polished surface which, in wet weather and sometimes in dry weather, became slippery. The highway authority held liable, not the driver.

Custins v Nottingham Corpn

[1970] RTR 365, CA
The plaintiff was waiting for a bus; it was freezing weather and the road was covered with snow. She was standing not on the pavement but about three feet out in the road. The bus driver saw her when he was 70 yards away; he was moving at only 10 mph and slowed down gradually to the place where the plaintiff was standing. He applied slight pressure to the brake and managed to stop the bus, but then it slid sideways and knocked the plaintiff down. The Commissioner of Assize held that as the bus had stopped without difficulty and then slipped sideways the driver had failed to keep the bus under control and was negligent.
HELD: It was impossible to draw an inference of negligence from the evidence accepted by the Commissioner. What more could the driver have done than drive very slowly, keep a proper look-out and apply his brakes gently? There was a camber on the road; when a vehicle starts to skid on an icy road it may take the most unpredictable of courses. It is common knowledge that if you are unlucky when you are driving on an icy road, whatever care you may take, it sometimes by mischance occurs that the vehicle does slide and gets out of control. In these circumstances it does not mean that there is any negligence on the part of the driver. Appeal allowed.

Driver held liable

Liffen v Watson

(1939) 161 LT 351 (Stable J)
The driver of a taxi-cab which was travelling fast suddenly applied his brakes on a wet road causing the cab to skid, and collide with a street refuge. The driver admitted that at this speed a sudden application of the brakes on this wet road was very likely to cause a skid. He gave an explanation of the accident which the court did not accept.
HELD: Where a passenger was injured by a sudden application of the brakes a presumption was raised of negligence or lack of skill. The obiter dictum of Fletcher-Moulton LJ, in *Wing v London General Omibus Co* [1909] 2 KB 652, 78 LJKB 1063, 101 LT 411, 73 JP 429 CA that the mere occurrence of such an accident was not in itself evidence of negligence, and that the fact that an accident had happened either to or through a particular vehicle was by itself no evidence that the fault, if any, which led to it was committed by those in charge of the vehicle went too far. The principle to be applied is stated by Scrutton LJ in *Halliwell v Venables* (p 36, above) that the facts required explanation by the driver of the motor car. The facts in this case required an explanation. The driver's explanation was unacceptable and the passenger was entitled to judgment.

Laurie v Raglan Building Co

[1942] 1 KB 152, [1941] 3 All ER 332, 111 LJKB 292, 166 LT 63, 86 Sol Jo 69, CA
In daylight a heavily laden ten-wheeled lorry was driven at 10 to 12 mph on a broad good road and skidded. The road was in an extremely dangerous condition, as it had snowed and frozen and the surface was like glass. The lorry had no chains on the wheels.

Skidding is not of itself sufficient to displace the prima facie presumption of negligence arising from the vehicle being in a position where it has no right to be. The skid by itself is neutral. It may or may not be due to negligence. If it is shown that the skid happened without the fault of the driver, the prima facie presumption is clearly displaced but merely establishing the skid is not sufficient.
HELD: In the circumstances it was negligent to drive at 10 to 12 mph without chains. It might be unsafe to go at more than foot pace or possibly to proceed at all. If roads are in such a condition that a motor car cannot safely proceed at all, it is the duty of the driver to stop.

Note—Also noted under 'Res ipsa loquitur', p 26, above.

Brayshaw v Pratt

(1947) B No 759 Leeds Assizes, 20 January 1949, Court of Appeal (15 June 1949, unreported), extracted from the shorthand notes of judgments.
The defendant's car was turning a very slight right-hand bend when it suddenly skidded and turned to the right across the road and on to the pavement on the wrong side of the road. The defendant sustained concussion and was unable to give any evidence as to how the accident happened or to what had caused her to go on to the pavement. The car was being driven at average speed and in the proper part of the road. There was no reason to account for the sudden turn to the right.
HELD, ON APPEAL (per Tucker LJ): It is clear from the authorities that the presence of a vehicle on the footpath implies negligence unless and until evidence is given which would entitle the court to infer that notwithstanding the occurrence the driver had in fact been exercising all reasonable care. There was no explanation given as to how or why the vehicle became out of control; or what had caused the driver to apply the brake if the brake was applied before the skid; or that any effort had been made to get out of the skid if the skid started without any application of the brakes, nor any evidence that the defendant had not momentarily taken her eye off the road for some reason or other which caused her to get into a position of difficulty or danger or which might have caused her to apply her brakes. There was a complete absence of any evidence negativing negligence except possibly with regard to the one factor of speed. The defendant had failed to discharge the onus of establishing that the accident happened without any negligence on her part.

London Transport Executive v Foy, Morgan & Co

(1953) L 1572 (7 July 1955, unreported)
Unreported, extracted from the pleadings and shorthand note of judgment. The plaintiff's coach had just pulled up on a particularly bad winter night when there had been ice on the road because of previous snow. It had been snowing and the snow had turned to a certain degree of sleet. It was freezing as well and the road was in such a condition that a police officer had some difficulty in standing. It was a very bad and a very dangerous road. The defendant was driving at 25 mph. He realised that he was on a dangerous road and he was coming to a bend and he had no chance. He was therefore driving in a way that was not showing the care which he ought to have been showing and in such a way as would reasonably avoid a skid.

Per Lord Goddard CJ: People are apt to think that if only they can show that their car skidded, because of certain decisions given a very long time ago, there is an end of the matter. When the cases are examined carefully, it will always be seen that it is only where the skid occurs unavoidably that the driver cannot be held responsible. If he is driving in a way which is asking for a skid, then he is liable.

Richley v Faull

[1965] 3 All ER 109, [1965] 1 WLR 1454, 129 JP 498, 109 Sol Jo 937 (MacKenna J)

On a road which was wet, but not slippery from any other cause, the defendant was driving his Bentley car when it went into a skid. It skidded across the road, turning as it went, into the path of a Hillman car in which the plaintiff was a passenger. The Hillman collided with the Bentley and the plaintiff was injured. The defendant gave no explanation of the reason why his car skidded. He said the same thing had happened two years before when he was driving the same car: he could not explain why.

HELD: The collision was caused by the defendant's negligence. Adopting Lord Greene's reasoning in *Laurie v Raglan Building Co* (above), where a vehicle moves on to the wrong side of the road into the path of another car there is a prima facie case of negligence which is not displaced merely by proof that the defendant's car skidded. But Lord Greene's dictum that a skid by itself is neutral is not acceptable; the unexplained and violent skid is in itself evidence of negligence. It is hardly consistent to hold that the skid which explains the presence of the vehicle on the wrong side of the road is neutral but that the defendant must fail unless he proves that this neutral event happened without his default. On either view, however, the conclusion is the same: the defendant fails if he does not prove that the skid which took him to the wrong place happened without his default.

Butty v Davey

[1972] RTR 75, [1972] Crim LR 48, Div Ct

The defendant was charged with driving without due care and attention. He was the driver of a lorry which skidded to the offside of the road on a shallow left hand bend, colliding with a lorry coming in the opposite direction. The justices, having heard that his speed was not excessive accepted his submission that the accident must have been caused by some unexpected slipperiness of the road due to rain and dismissed the charge.

HELD: On a case stated, the justices had applied their minds to the question whether the lorry was being driven at a reasonable speed in the conditions prevailing and there was no reason to interfere with their decision. *Richley v Faull* (above) had shown that where negligence was concerned proof of a skid was not sufficient to exonerate a driver, but the test in a criminal case was inevitably different. Appeal dismissed.

Plea in defence

The matters complained of by the plaintiff were caused by unavoidable accident.

Particulars

The defendant's car suddenly and without warning skidded upon the wet and greasy road and became uncontrollable, with the result that the defendant although exercising all due care and skill was unable to avoid a collision.

LEADING AND FOLLOWING VEHICLE

Sharp v Avery and Kerwood

[1938] 4 All ER 85, 82 Sol Jo 908, CA
A motor cyclist in company with another motor cyclist carrying a pillion passenger was proceeding from London to Southend. The two motor cyclists agreed that one of them, 'A', should lead the other because he knew the way. The other followed at a distance of about 8 yards. The leading motor cyclist mistook the road and drove on to some waste ground. He then applied his brakes and skidded forward gradually slowing down. The second motor cyclist followed on to the waste ground and collided with the first motor cycle and the pillion passenger on the second motor cycle was injured.
HELD: The first motor cyclist was negligent and in the circumstances there was a duty on him not to mislead the motor cyclist who was following. Verdict against 'A' upheld.

Smith v Harris

[1939] 3 All ER 960, 83 Sol Jo 730, CA
Five motor cyclists were engaged in a treasure hunt. P was apparently clever at finding clues, and it was agreed between them that he should lead the hunt. They were proceeding at about 25 to 30 mph and about 8 yards between each. P overshot a turning and braked hard. He did not swerve either to the left or right to give those behind him a chance of avoiding him. O, who was next, was spreadeagled on the ground to the right of P, and M, who was third, was spreadeagled to the left. H, with the plaintiff as pillion passenger, who was fourth, swerved out to avoid M but ran into O and overturned, and plaintiff was injured. The county court judge held that P was negligent in the way he drew up, and H for not having proper control of his machine, and found each equally to blame.
HELD, ON APPEAL: It was a question of fact. The case *Sharp v Avery* above laid down no fresh principle of law. Appeal dismissed.

Brown and Lynn v Western Scottish Motor Traction Co Ltd

1945 SC 31, 1944 SN 59, Ct of Sess
A motor lorry was travelling along a public street followed at a distance of 25 to 30 feet by a motor omnibus, the speed of both vehicles being approximately 15 mph. The driver of the lorry, in order to avoid a pedestrian, swerved suddenly to the left and pulled up almost instantaneously, and the driver of the omnibus, when he realised that the lorry was stopping, swerved to the right and applied his brakes, but, although he acted with reasonable promptitude, he did not succeed in avoiding a collision. The driver of the lorry had no time to give any signal, and the driver of the omnibus had not seen, and had no reasonable chance of seeing, the pedestrian.
HELD: (Lord Stevenson dissenting): The fact that the driver of the omnibus, although allowing a sufficient space between the vehicles in which to deal with the ordinary exigencies of traffic, had followed the lorry so closely that he could not cope with its exceptionally abrupt stop did not amount to negligence upon his part, and, accordingly, that the owners of the omnibus were not liable to the owners of the lorry for the damage sustained by their vehicle.

Per Lord Cooper: The distance which should separate two vehicles travelling one behind the other must depend upon many variable factors—their speed, the nature of the locality, the other traffic present or to be expected, the opportunity available to the following driver of commanding a view ahead of the leading vehicle, the distance within which the following vehicle can be pulled up, and many other things. The following driver is, in my view, bound, so far as reasonably possible, to take up such a position and to drive in such a fashion, as will enable him to deal successfully with all traffic exigencies reasonably to be anticipated: but whether he has fulfilled this duty must in every case be a question of fact whether, on any emergency disclosing itself, the following driver acted with the alertness, skill and judgment reasonably to be expected in the circumstances.

Jungnikel v Laing

(1966) 111 Sol Jo 19, CA
Lorry A was travelling in the slow lane of the M1 motorway at night when it was run into from behind by lorry B. As a result of the collision lorry B crossed the central island on to the other carriageway and there turned over. The plaintiff's husband driving a mini-truck ran into it and was killed.

As between the two lorry drivers the judge held the driver of lorry B 90% to blame for not keeping a proper look-out but said the driver of lorry A was 10% to blame because he had effected a sudden reduction of speed without warning, as if changing gear.

HELD, ON APPEAL: The driver of lorry A was not at all to blame. Even on the M1 deceleration without warning is not an act of negligence. If a driver was going to make a sudden heavy stop he was under a duty to give warning to traffic behind, but not if he was merely decelerating. Moreover his failure to warn had no causative effect since the driver of lorry B was not keeping a look-out and would not have seen a signal.

Thompson v Spedding

[1973] RTR 312, CA
The plaintiff was riding her moped in a moving line of traffic. There was a Triumph car ahead of her, and in front of that, a Morris driven by the defendant. The Morris pulled up sharply preparatory to turning right. The Triumph was able to pull up safely without colliding with the Morris but the plaintiff could not pull up in time and in trying to avoid the Triumph collided with it and was injured. The judge held the defendant wholly to blame, saying that the plaintiff was not required to ride her moped on the basis that the defendant was suddenly going to stop and put her and the driver in front in jeopardy.

HELD, ON APPEAL: The judge had failed to express correctly the duty of persons driving in a line of traffic; it was to drive at such a distance behind the car in front as to be prepared for foreseeable emergencies. The plaintiff's blame was equal to that of the defendant.

Scott v Warren

[1974] RTR 104, [1974] Crim LR 117, Div Ct
The defendant was driving a car behind a van, both travelling at about 20 to 25 mph. The van driver braked suddenly to avoid a large piece of metal which dropped off a lorry in front. The defendant did not see the metal fall, his vision being obstructed by the van, and he had no warning that the van driver was about to make an emergency stop. He braked but was unable to avoid colliding with the back of the van. The

prosecution, on a charge of driving without due care, presented it as a matter of settled law that if a driver did not leave sufficient space between himself and the vehicle in front to avoid a collision whatever the circumstances, he was guilty of the offence charged; the Highway Code (1968), rr 34 and 35 were relied on.
HELD: The proposition could not be accepted. The words of Lord Cooper in *Brown and Lynn v Western Scottish Motor Traction Co Ltd* (quoted above) indicated a standard to be observed by a following driver appropriate in civil cases. The obligation could not be higher on a criminal charge. In the present case it could not be said the justices were perverse in finding the defendant not guilty of the offence.

Note—The Highway Code 1968, ss 34 and 35 are repeated as paras 57 of the Highway Code 1993.

Parnell v Metropolitan Police Receiver

[1975] 1 Lloyd's Rep 492, CA
The plaintiff was a passenger in a mini-bus being driven about two vehicle lengths behind a large tipper lorry along a road having no crossroads, pedestrian crossing or other interferences. The lorry suddenly stopped for no apparent reason and without warning. The driver of the mini-bus had to brake hard to avoid hitting it and was successful in pulling up 6 feet behind the lorry without his brakes locking. The plaintiff was thrown forward and ricked her neck.
HELD: The test to be applied was that laid down by Lord Cooper in *Brown and Lynn v Western Scottish Motor Traction Co Ltd* (above). The view expressed in *Wooler v London Transport Board* (p 170, below) was relevant to the present case. On the facts the driver was not negligent.

SIGNALLING AND TURNING

Pratt v Bloom

(1958) Times, 21 October, Div Ct
Per Streatfield J: The duty of a driver changing direction is (1) to signal, and (2) to see that no one was incommoded by his change of direction and the duty is greater if he first gives a wrong signal and then changes it.

Overtaking turning vehicle

Sorrie v Robertson

1944 JC 95, 1944 SN 14, 1944 SLT 332, Ct Jus
The Road Traffic Act 1930, s 12, made it an offence to drive 'a motor vehicle on a road without due care and attention or without reasonable consideration for other persons using the road'.

The driver of a motor lorry, who knew that he was being overtaken gradually by a motor cycle, signalled in the appropriate manner that he was about to turn across the road to his right—his intention being to enter a garage 50 yards further on. At that moment he saw the motor cyclist in his driving mirror, but after giving the signal he concentrated his whole attention on turning into the garage. He took no steps to ascertain whether his signal had been observed, and, when he made the turn, the cyclist, who had not observed the signal, was about to pass him, so that a collision resulted. The lorry driver having been convicted of an offence under s 12 of the Act of 1930.

HELD: That the conviction was warranted, in respect that the accused, in view of his knowledge of the overtaking motor cycle, had a duty to observe whether his own signal had been appreciated.

Note—Similar provisions to those in the Road Traffic Act 1930, s 12 are now contained in Road Traffic Act 1988, s 3.

Clark v Wakelin

(1965) 109 Sol Jo 295 (Roskill J)

The plaintiff on a pedal cycle turned right from the nearside of the road and was struck by the defendant who was about to overtake a motor cycle. The plaintiff's statement to the police was 'I looked behind me, let a car go by, put out my hand and turned right.' The defendant said he was about to overtake when the plaintiff put out his hand, turned and never gave him a chance to avoid the accident. No claim was made for a year: a writ was issued after a further year and the action was tried ten months later. The plaintiff said in evidence that the car he let go by was coming towards him from the opposite direction. He relied on the provision in the Highway Code 'Never overtake unless you know you can do so without danger to yourself and others.'

The judge said it was the plaintiff who was in danger from the delay in bringing the action since he had to prove his case. The defendant's version of the accident was to be accepted. A driver was entitled to assume that he could overtake without danger if what he was overtaking gave not the slightest sign that it was going to do something other than what another ordinary careful motorist or motor cyclist might expect. The plaintiff was solely to blame.

Note—See also *Dyer v Bannell*, p 74, below.

Goke v Willett

[1973] RTR 422, CA

On a busy three-lane road in daylight a mini van pulled out into the centre lane to overtake a lorry and trailer travelling in the nearside lane. The mini driver whilst still in the centre lane decided to enter a service station on the offside of the road. He put on his offside indicator and brake, slowing down fairly sharply to enter the further of the two entrances; he had already passed the first entrance before braking. The mini van was then struck from behind by a heavily-laden lorry which had been following the mini van in the centre lane. The lorry driver had been about 100 yards behind the mini van when it braked but the driver had not seen the mini's brake light or trafficator. The mini driver was unaware of the presence behind him of the lorry until after the impact.

HELD: The mini driver was engaged in a most undesirable manoeuvre, turning off the centre lane of a fast road into the second entrance of a service station on the offside. It behoved him to make certain he did it without risk to following or oncoming traffic. In the particular circumstances of this case he ought to have given a hand signal; if he had the lorry driver would probably have seen it and avoided a collision. The Highway Code, insofar as it appears to say that hand signals need never be used when trafficators and brake lights are in good working order, contains unwise advice. There may still be circumstances, as in this case, where the utmost warning to other traffic of one's intentions should be resorted to and a hand signal called for. Proportions of blame: mini driver one-third, lorry driver two-thirds.

Note—But see now the Highway Code 1993, p 57.

Turning out of minor road

Harding v Hinchcliffe

(1964) Times, 8 April, CA
In open flat country early in the morning the plaintiff was riding his motor cycle to school along a class B road and came up behind a bus travelling in the same direction. The bus driver signalled his intention to turn left into a minor road. The plaintiff, wishing to go on along the main road, overtook the bus as it was turning. He was hit by the defendant's car which came out of the minor road as the bus turned into it. The defendant had stopped at the mouth of the lane, intending to turn right into the main road. He had seen the bus approaching for about 150 yards and had waited but when the bus driver showed he was now going to turn into the lane the defendant had driven out. He had not seen the plaintiff, who had been masked by the bus until the moment of collision, nor had the plaintiff seen the defendant. The judge held that the defendant had not been negligent, since he could not have anticipated a motor cyclist being masked by the bus for all that time and distance.
HELD, ON APPEAL: Coming out from a lane into a major road the defendant ought to have waited the few extra seconds necessary to let the bus get completely into the lane because there was always the possibility of a vehicle being masked by the bus. The proper inference was that he was negligent and the boy was not negligent at all.

MacIntyre v Coles

[1966] 1 All ER 723, [1966] 1 WLR 831, 130 JP 189, 110 Sol Jo 315, CA
On a Sunday morning in pouring rain the defendant was driving a heavy lorry along Spon End in the city of Coventry towards a Y junction where The Butts forked off to the right and Spon Street to the left. He intended bearing right into The Butts. There were no road signs indicating the relative importance of these streets but the defendant passed along this route regularly and knew that traffic entering Spon End from Spon Street on his left usually paused at the mouth of Spon Street where there was a 'Keep Left' sign. The plaintiff's husband who did not know the district was riding a motor cycle along Spon Street towards the junction intending to bear right into Spon End along which the defendant was approaching. The plaintiff's husband rode out of Spon Street across the path of the defendant's lorry, which was taking the right fork into The Butts, and was struck by it and killed. The judge of assize held the defendant to be free from blame.
HELD, ON APPEAL: The plaintiff could not succeed. The defendant had given a proper signal that he was turning right, had seen the plaintiff's husband and was proceeding round in the ordinary way. Although it was most unfortunate there were no road signs to indicate how traffic should manoeuvre, the configuration of the road and the 'Keep Left' sign in the mouth of Spon Street did indicate that traffic on Spon End should have priority. Moreover the deceased had the lorry coming from his right: it is a well-recognised and conventional practice that where there is a doubt as to priority, the vehicle which has the other on its right-hand side is the give-way vehicle.

Note—Lang v London Transport Executive was not cited.

The alleged 'well recognised and conventional practice' of giving way to vehicles on the right was said not to exist by Streatfield J but this, like *Lang*'s case, was apparently not brought to the attention of the Court.

Turning into minor road

Simpson v Peat

[1952] 2 QB 24, [1952] 1 All ER 447, [1952] 1 TLR 469, 96 Sol Jo 132, Div Ct
The driver of a motor car on a main road turned to enter a road on his offside and a collision occurred with a motor cyclist coming in the opposite direction. He was prosecuted for driving without due care and attention. The justices found that the defendant had committed an error of judgment in thinking he had left room for the motor cyclist to get through. The defendant contended he could not be guilty for a mere error of judgment, and was acquitted. The prosecutor appealed.
HELD: The expression 'error of judgment' was not a term of art and was of the vaguest possible description. It could mean either a negligent act or one which, though mistaken, is not negligent. A driver might not be using due care and attention although his lack of care may be due to something which could be described as an error of judgment. If he is driving without due care and attention it is immaterial what caused him to do so. The question was whether he was exercising that degree of care and attention which a reasonable and prudent driver would exercise in the circumstances. The question was one of fact and not of law. On the facts, the defendant was cutting across the line of traffic coming from the opposite direction. It was for him to take care that he could execute the manoeuvre in safety.

Case remitted to justices with a direction to convict.

Patel v Edwards

[1970] RTR 425, CA
At a crossroads in town the plaintiff on a pedal cycle wished to turn off the main road into the minor road on his right. He looked behind him and saw a car signalling a left turn and slowing down. He moved towards the centre of the road to make his turn just as the defendant, on a motor cycle, overtook the car, which was then almost stationary. The defendant ran into the plaintiff knocking him on to the pavement on the far corner. The plaintiff had not seen the defendant, nor did the defendant see the plaintiff until he came out in front of him; by that time the defendant was already level with the rear side window of the car. The trial judge said the parties were equally to blame; the plaintiff for his failure to make absolutely certain that it was safe to cross by coming out gently, the defendant overtaking the car when he could not see what was happening ahead of it.
HELD, ON APPEAL: The blame should be apportioned two-thirds to the plaintiff, one-third to the defendant. The judge had not given sufficient weight to the factor that the pedal cyclist was moving in front of a substantially stationary car across a main and important road. Anyone making such a move must naturally take special care to see that he does not get into the path of other traffic. Failure to take such care imports a high degree of culpability.

Challoner v Williams and Croney

[1975] 1 Lloyd's Rep 124, CA
At night on an unlighted road Williams was driving the first of three cars the other two

being driven by friends whom he was leading. He discovered he had taken the wrong route and, seeing a turning on the right, put on his offside flashing indicator preparatory to turning into it so as to go back in the opposite direction. He slowed and moved towards the centre of the road. He looked in his driving mirror when he indicated he was going to turn and looked in the mirror again before he turned. He began to turn into the road on the right without actually stopping; when he was about halfway across the offside half of the road his car was struck by a car driven by Croney which had overtaken both the other cars, Croney not having seen Williams's car ahead until too late. The judge held both drivers equally to blame: he said Williams should have satisfied himself that there was no car overtaking the other two and should have stopped before crossing the offside half of the road.
HELD, ON APPEAL: Williams had done nothing wrong; Croney was wholly to blame.

Brake lights and hand signals

Flack v Withers

(1960) Times, 22 March, CA (reported on another point at [1961] 3 All ER 388, HL)
The infant plaintiff was riding his pedal cycle behind a car driven by the defendant W when the latter pulled up to allow the defendant S to pass him in the opposite direction. The plaintiff ran into the rear bumper of W's car, was thrown to the right and was hit by S's car, sustaining severe injuries. W gave evidence that he looked into his inside mirror but not the wing mirror as he was slowing down, but did not see the plaintiff or any other traffic. His car was fitted with the usual red lights at the back which came on as soon as any pressure was applied to the brake pedal. He had not regarded a hand signal as necessary in the circumstances particularly having regard to his slow speed. At the trial the jury found W 17% to blame for the accident.
HELD, ON APPEAL: There was no evidence to support a finding of negligence against W. A driver would not give more than an occasional glance into his driving mirror. As to the lack of hand signal, W's car was fitted with the usual red lights at the back. It was difficult to accept the view that that might properly be regarded by a jury as evidence of want of care on W's part. The onus of proof on the plaintiff had not been discharged.

Note—The 1993 edition of the Highway Code at p 56 accepts that brake light signals can be used to mean 'I am slowing down or stopping'.

Misleading signals

Another v Probert

[1968] Crim LR 564, Div Ct
The defendant was driving a car along a main road: the 'left turn' indicator was flashing. A police car waiting in a side turning moved out into the main road in reliance on the flashing signal. The defendant drove straight on, colliding with the police car. He defended a charge of careless driving on the ground that the police driver should not have relied on the indicator signal.
HELD: On the prosecutor's appeal, it was careless driving to give misleading signals: the justices must convict.

Note—The Ministry of Transport Driving Manual (1969) warns against reliance on a left turn indicator in such circumstances. It might mean merely that the driver is intending to stop on the left before or *after* the junction as authorised by the 1968 Highway Code.

The Highway Code 1993, para 111 says 'When waiting at a junction, do not assume that a vehicle coming from the right and signalling left will do so. Wait and make sure.'

Wadsworth v Gillespie

[1978] CLY 2534 (Sir Basil Nield)
The defendant, driving a car, came along a minor road to a major road at a junction governed by a 'Give Way' sign. She twice looked to her right along the major road and saw the plaintiff approaching on a motor cycle, his flashing indicator signalling an intended left turn. In reliance on the signal she moved out on to the major road; the plaintiff drove straight on and crashed into her car. He had accidentally turned the indicator on and was unaware it was flashing.
HELD: The defendant was negligent in not looking again to make sure the plaintiff was in fact turning left. The plaintiff was negligent in driving along the main road giving a misleading signal. Liability apportioned two-thirds to the defendant, one-third to the plaintiff.

REVERSING

Liddon v Stringer

(1967) 117 NLJ 464, Div Ct
At the end of its journey a bus had to be reversed into a side road. The conductor stood on the nearside pavement about level with the rear of the bus facing the front and signalled with his arms. The driver watched the conductor and the nearside kerb through his nearside wing mirror and began to reverse at about 3 mph. The conductor walked backwards keeping level with the rear of the bus. When it had moved about 5 yards the conductor signalled to the driver to stop, which he did. The reason for the conductor's signal was that a woman trying to get across to the kerb behind the bus had been knocked down. The driver was convicted by the magistrates of driving without due care and attention.
HELD: Where someone was using someone else as his eyes he was under a duty to see that those eyes were in a position to see what they ought to see. On what was written in the case stated it was difficult to see why the driver had been convicted, but it could not be said that a reasonable bench of justices, who saw the witnesses, could not have reached the conclusion that the driver had not taken steps to see that his 'eyes' were in a position to see. There was no error in law: Per Lord Parker CJ. Appeal dismissed.

NEGLIGENT PARKING

Parking on a bend

Waller v Levoi

(1968) 112 Sol Jo 865, Times, 16 October, CA
The defendant was driving his car on a main road in daylight when he came to a left-handed bend where a side road went off to the left. He had been intending to turn off on to the side road but missed it and went beyond it a little way. He stopped at the kerb on the nearside of the bend to look back at the signpost and his car was run into from

behind by the plaintiff on a motor cycle. The county court judge found the plaintiff 80% to blame and the defendant 20%.
HELD, ON APPEAL: The judge's apportionment of blame should stand. The plaintiff was negligent in failing to see the car in time. The defendant was to blame in stopping on the bend. It was a distinct bend though not sharp; he could have driven on to a straight part of the road and walked back to see the signpost. A car parked on a bend should not cause danger to a person driving carefully but one also owed a duty to careless drivers. A motorist who drove too fast or was temporarily inadvertent could be put in difficulty by a car parked on a bend.

Chop Seng Heng v Thevannasan s/o Sinnapan

[1975] 3 All ER 572, [1976] RTR 193, PC
At 3 am on a winding road in rather misty conditions A was driving his employer's lorry when he required to stop. He chose a spot about 30 feet beyond the exit from a blind left hand bend. He parked the lorry at the nearside with its lights on. There was plenty of room for other vehicles to pass. B drove a lorry round the bend at about 25 mph and crashed into the back of A's lorry, causing severe injuries to the plaintiff, a passenger in B's lorry. The judge at first instance held A 75% to blame and B 25%. On appeal the Federal Court held by a majority that B was wholly to blame. The dissenting member considered A wholly to blame.
HELD, ON APPEAL to the Privy Council: (1) The proposition that a driver who parks a vehicle at night with its lights on where there is room to pass cannot be guilty of negligence is unacceptable. A was to blame for parking too close to the corner. *Waller v Levoi* (above) applied. (2) B was also to blame for taking the bend too fast. Had he been travelling more slowly the impact would have been less heavy and the plaintiff's injuries less severe. (3) As the judge at first instance had not misdirected himself when apportioning blame his 75:25 apportionment should be restored.

Parking at night

Stevens v Kelland

[1970] RTR 445 (Waller J)
In a quiet street V left his van parked on the inside of a bend without lights. C, without noticing the van, parked his car on the outside of the bend near a street lamp a short distance to the north of the van. The gap between the two vehicles, measured along the road, was about 20 feet. S, riding a scooter from the south, saw V's van on his offside and C's car on his nearside and also saw a car driven by Z approaching from the opposite direction on its correct side of the centre line. S saw he could pass C's car safely without himself crossing the centre line and carried on. Z did not see S until he, Z, had pulled over the centre line to pass through the gap. He collided with the scooter as it was passing C's car, jamming it against the car and severely injuring the pillion rider.
HELD: (1) S was not to blame because by the time Z pulled over to pass through the gap he could do nothing to avoid the accident. (2) Z was mainly to blame because he had not seen S in time; he should not have pulled over without ensuring that it was safe to do so. (3) V and C were each partly to blame; V for having parked his van near the elbow of the bend where it blocked the view and was a potential cause of danger, C because by parking his car where he did without noticing the van he had created a hazard. (4) Apportionment of blame was 60% to Z and 20% each to V and C.

Watson v Heslop

(1971) 115 Sol Jo 308, [1971] RTR 308, CA
The defendant parked his car by the nearside kerb of a busy main road 22 feet wide in the hours of darkness. There were no street lights and no speed restrictions. He turned out the lights of the car except for a parking light on the offside. The plaintiff driving his car at 40 mph with dipped headlights failed to see the defendant's car because of the dazzling headlights of approaching traffic and drove straight into it from the rear. The judge of assize held the defendant solely to blame.
HELD, ON APPEAL by the defendant: He was negligent in parking his car there where traffic was passing at speed in both directions: he could foresee that a stationary car might well put traffic in a difficulty. But the plaintiff was also to blame. When he found himself dazzled by approaching headlights he should at once have slowed down to a very slow pace in case there should be someone or something in his path. Moreover, if he had been keeping a proper look-out he should have seen the parking light. He was 30% to blame.

Per Sachs LJ: The defendant should have put his car at least partly on the footway. A parking light was not as good as normal lights.

OPENING DOOR OF VEHICLE

Note—Claims for damages for personal injuries or for damage to passing vehicles caused by the opening of the offside door of a stationary car are extremely common but, perhaps because the negligence is self evident, they rarely result in a reported decision. For examples where a passenger was to blame, see *Brown v Roberts* (p 707, below).

Prosecutions were at one time laid under the Highway Act 1835, s 77 or 78. They are now brought under the Motor Vehicles (Construction and Use) Regulations 1986, reg 105 which provides:
'No person shall open or cause or permit to be opened any door of a motor vehicle or trailer on a road so as to cause injury or danger to any person.'

The regulation does not give a right of action to a person injured by the breach—see *Barkway v South Wales Transport* and *Phillips v Britannia Laundry*, p 204, below. For a case in which justices were held on a prosecutor's appeal to the Divisional Courts to have been entitled to hold that there was a doubt whether opening a car door had caused danger see *Sever v Duffy* [1977] RTR 429.

7 SIGNALS

TRAFFIC LIGHTS

Note—The current regulations providing for traffic light signals are the Traffic Signs Regulations 1981, SI 1981/859, of which reg 31 describes the size colour and type and reg 34 sets out their significance.

Vehicle crossing against red light

Eva Ltd v Reeves

[1938] 2 KB 393, [1938] 2 All ER 115, CA
At a crossing controlled by traffic lights, R approached on his offside at 25 to 30 mph and lights changed to green when he was 20 to 30 yards away. Nearside was occupied

by traffic and R passed these vehicles on offside of road just as they were starting to move. A van was crossing from his left against the red lights. R could not avoid collision.
HELD: R not negligent. He owed no duty to traffic crossing against red light beyond a duty, if in fact he saw such traffic, to take reasonable care to avoid a collision. He was entitled to assume no traffic would be crossing against the lights and could therefore overtake on offside provided no danger to traffic in opposite direction or to traffic turning right. The Traffic Signs Regulations provide that the red signal shall be taken as prohibiting vehicular traffic to proceed until the green signal is shown. Highway Code—'Never overtake at cross roads'—distinguished where traffic is regulated by lights.

Note—Though criticised from time to time this decision has never been overruled.
It has been considered or explained in the following two cases.
See also *Godsmark v Knight Bros,* p 95, below.

Knight v Wiper Supply Services Ltd

(1965) 109 Sol Jo 358 (Havers J)
The plaintiff was riding his moped along Brixton Hill when he came to traffic lights controlling a junction with a road on his left. When he passed the traffic light, the judge found, it was at green but immediately afterwards turned to amber. The defendant's vehicle came out of the side road and struck the plaintiff, injuring him.
HELD: As the light had only just turned amber it must still have been showing red for the defendant's driver when he came out and he was therefore negligent. On the issue of contributory negligence *Eva v Reeves* (above) decided that the driver of a motor vehicle entering a cross-roads with the traffic lights in his favour was not guilty of contributory negligence in colliding with a vehicle entering the cross-roads with the lights against it, since the driver with the lights in his favour was not under any obligation to assume that a driver might be entering the crossroads with the lights against him. The decision had never been criticized in any subsequent decision and accordingly it was unnecessary in this case to consider any question of contributory negligence. The defendants were solely liable.

Davis v Hassan

(1967) 117 NLJ 72, CA
The plaintiff drove across a junction controlled by traffic signals with the green light in her favour. The defendant drove out from the road on her left against a red light and there was a collision. The county court judge held himself bound by *Eva v Reeves* to find wholly in favour of the plaintiff but said that if he had not been so bound he would have held the plaintiff one-third to blame.
HELD, ON APPEAL: (1) It was not necessary in this case to consider whether *Eva v Reeves* was right or wrong. Every case of negligence and certainly every case of traffic accidents had to be decided on its own particular facts. The judge was wrong in thinking himself bound by *Eva v Reeves.* (2) On the facts the judge's finding of the blame against the plaintiff was not justified. The question was whether having the green light in her favour the plaintiff was negligent in not seeing the defendant's car come out of the road on the left. Her attention was focused on the lights and it was a very large junction: it would be wrong to hold her guilty of negligence merely because she did not see the car until the last moment.

Note—Lord Justice Willmer said he wished to make it clear that he was approaching the matter as a jury question and not seeking to lay down a proposition of law. The effect of the decision seems to be that cases which might formerly have been regarded as governed by the principle of *Eva v Reeves* are now simply to be treated as questions of fact.

Sudds v Hanscombe

[1971] RTR 212, CA
The defendant's car entered a crossroads from the east when the traffic lights were in his favour. He passed the primary light but before reaching the centre of the crossroads he had to stop because of an altercation between the drivers of two cars which had stopped there. Those two cars were eventually driven away and the defendant then drove forward to continue over the crossroads. Meanwhile the traffic lights had changed and were red for the road along which he was travelling. The plainitiff's car came to the crossroads from the south: when it was about 10 yards short of the crossing the traffic lights changed to green and he drove straight on. He did not see the defendant's car which had begun to move forward again and there was a collision. The county court judge found against the defendant and held there was no contibutory negligence on the part of the plaintiff.
HELD, ON APPEAL: The plaintiff was entitled to assume when approaching lights which had already changed in his favour that no fresh traffic would enter the junction from the east because the lights there must have been red. On the other hand he was not discharged from his duty of looking to his front to see where he was going and to look out for traffic already in the junction which might obtrude into his path. The crucial question was whether or not the defendant was in a position where a reasonably careful motorist in the plaintiff's position might regard him as a hazard. On the evidence the judge was right in holding the defendant was far enough back from the centre of the crossing that the plaintiff would not suppose he would continue over the junction.

Note—No cases were referred to in the judgments nor were any cited in argument.

Miller v Evans

[1975] RTR 70, CA
Travelling west along the Great West Road, which had dual four-lane carriageways, Miss Pouleuf driving a small Citroen wished to turn right at a cross-roads controlled by traffic lights. Having passed the primary light at green she took up a position in the gap between the two ends of the central reservation, at an angle to cross the eastbound carriageway when it should be safe to do so. When the lights changed to amber and red for eastbound traffic three cars slowed down and stopped. A fourth car driven by Evans travelling in the lane nearest the central reservation drove past the red light at speed and collided with the front of the Citroen. The judge held Miss Pouleuf 15% to blame for the collision on the ground that she must have moved forward, having seen the other cars stop and not having seen Evans's car. She strongly denied having moved at all.
HELD, ON APPEAL: (1) On the evidence, Miss Pouleuf had not moved and was not negligent; (2) even if she had moved forward into the path of Evans's car she was not negligent. Knowing from the fact that the other cars had stopped and the lights had changed to red for eastbound traffic she was under no duty to see if there was traffic in the fourth lane and whether, if there were any, it was travelling at such a speed as to be unlikely to stop at the lights. The clear inference of a reasonably careful motorist

would have been that there was no reason to think that a car in the fast lane would come across against the lights. *Hopwood Homes Ltd v Kennerdine* (below) followed. *Sudds v Hanscombe* (above) supported this view.

Hopwood Homes Ltd v Kennerdine

[1975] RTR 82, CA
The plaintiff, driving a lorry, approached a cross roads where he intended to turn right. The traffic lights were green for him and changed to amber just as he passed the primary light. He came to a stop in the centre of the junction angled to the right ready to continue to make his turn. He looked to his left and saw the defendant's car approaching about 25 yards away. Knowing the traffic lights had turned to red and seeing the car had time to pull up he began to move forward. The car did not stop but continued on past the red light and collided with the lorry. The county court judge held the plaintiff 10% to blame for not having apprehended that the car might not stop at the lights.
HELD, ON APPEAL: The plaintiff was not at all to blame. He had good reason to suppose the car would pull up at the traffic signal. Although as Lord du Parcq said in *Grant v Sun Shipping Co* [1948] AC 549, 'a prudent man will guard against the possible negligence of others when experience shows such negligence to be common', one's experience does not lead one to think that it is a common folly for a driver who has time to pull up at traffic lights to fail to do so. The plaintiff was correct in his assessment when he first saw that car that it had time to stop at the lights which were red and that it was safe for him to move forward.

Duty of drivers when lights changing

Godsmark v Knight Bros (Brighton) Ltd

(1960) Times, 12 May (Barry J)
A, driving a large lorry over 30 feet long, and B, driving a car, were approaching a cross-roads controlled by traffic lights. A from the south, B from the east. When A was well short of the stop line the lights changed from green to amber. He could not safely stop on or short of the line, however, and carried on, though the stop line was about 40 feet from the crossroad and he could have pulled up within the 40 feet. As B approached the cross-roads the lights changed from red to red-and-amber and were showing green when he entered the cross-roads. Thus neither driver disobeyed the rules in the Traffic Signs Regulations as to the significance of light signals. The two vehicles collided at the cross-roads.
HELD: A was two-thirds and B one-third to blame. It must have been obvious to A when the lights changed to amber before he reached the stop line that, if he proceeded, he would for a considerable time be blocking traffic on the east–west road which had received the green light. He should have taken steps to avoid obstruction of traffic lulled into a sense of security by green lights.

B relied entirely on *Eva Ltd v Reeves*. That case did not apply here since it dealt with a vehicle which had entered the cross-roads against the red lights. It might well be that a time arrived when drivers on roads to which green was shown might cease to have any obligation to look left or right to see whether any vehicle was ignoring the regulations. When amber had just been shown to them the position was different. Here the lights had just turned green in favour of B. There was an obligation on B to see that no other vehicles had entered the cross-roads while the lights were amber. B was bound to contemplate that some vehicle which had properly entered the crossroads might still be passing across, although the lights had changed to green.

Radburn v Kemp

[1971] 3 All ER 249, [1971] 1 WLR 1502, 115 Sol Jo 711, CA
The plaintiff, riding a bicycle, came to a large road junction controlled by traffic lights. He wished to enter a street on the opposite side of the junction but the lights were at red. It was a murky wet evening. When the lights changed to green he started forward but by the time he had reached a point about two-thirds of the way over the junction (which was 127 feet across) he noticed the light at the mouth of the street he was aiming for had changed to amber. He was then struck by the defendant's car which had emerged from a street on his left. The defendant had started from this street when the light there changed to green: he had not seen the plaintiff at all. It was admitted that he was negligent but the judge of assize also held the plaintiff to blame to the extent of 50% because he had not seen the defendant's car and if he had, could have stopped.
HELD, ON APPEAL: The plaintiff was not at all to blame. As in *Godsmark v Knight* (above) the defendant, for whom the light had just changed to green, was under a duty to see that there were no vehicles on the crossing which might still be passing across. He had no business, despite the light being in his favour, to enter the junction at all unless he was satisfied that it was safe for him to do so. Once having entered it he had no right to proceed further without taking the utmost care to save harmless people who rightly were already on the junction before he entered it. The defendant had failed to prove that the plaintiff if he had seen the car before the collision could have done anything effective to avoid it.

Smithers v H & M Transport (Oxford) and Hodgkinson

(1983) 133 NLJ 558 (Stocker J)
The defendant's van was stationary in a crossroads junction controlled by traffic lights, waiting to turn right when the lights should change. A motor cyclist was approaching from the opposite direction. The lights had changed for him from green to amber as he crossed the stop line. The van moved into his path and there was a collision.
HELD: The van driver was liable. He had not seen the motor cycle until a split second before impact though he could have seen it if he had looked. It must have been visible before the van was driven off from its angled and stationary position. He should not have driven forward at all so long as the lights were green for traffic coming from the opposite direction over the crossroads.

Duty to pedestrians at traffic lights

Frank v Cox

(1967) 111 Sol Jo 670, CA
At a crossroads controlled by traffic lights Frank began walking across the road on the south side from east to west. The traffic lights had changed and were in his favour. Cox was in his car in the road at the west side of the junction. As soon as the lights changed he drove into the junction and turned right, knocking down Frank who had then almost reached the centre refuge.

HELD: Cox's driving was not only careless: it verged on the monstrous, and Frank was not at all to blame. There is a paramount duty on motorists turning at junctions when the lights showed in their favour to be sure that no pedestrians were crossing the road they were entering. They must observe para 26 of the Highway Code [now the Highway Code (1978), para 60] which requires them when turning at junctions to give precedent to pedestrians who are crossing.

Note—Paragraph 60 of the Highway Code 1978 is replaced by para 68 of Highway Code 1993. See also *Shepherd v West*, p 112, below.

Presumption that lights are working correctly

Wells v Woodward

(1956) 54 LGR 142, Div Ct
Where a court finds that traffic lights are showing green one way, the court is entitled to infer, unless the contrary is proved, that they are showing red the other way.

Tingle Jacobs & Co v Kennedy

[1964] 1 All ER 888, [1964] 1 WLR 638, 108 Sol Jo 196, CA
At a crossroads controlled by traffic lights a car belonging to the plaintiffs collided with a car owned and driven by the defendant. In evidence the plaintiff's driver said that when travelling westwards he saw the traffic light was green in his favour and was crossing the junction when the defendant's car came across his path from the south and ran into it. Two independent witnesses supported the plaintiffs' driver's evidence that the light was green in his favour when he entered the crossing. The defendant and his wife gave evidence that they saw the light in their road change from red to amber and then green and they then went forward into the crossing. There was evidence from a police officer of inspections of the lights on dates before and after the accident when they were working properly. The county court judge accepted that both parties were telling the truth and concluded that the traffic lights could not have been working properly. He apportioned liability equally on the ground that the drivers had failed to keep a proper look-out.
HELD, ON APPEAL: It was plain that one side or the other must have been mistaken. The police evidence was that there had been no trouble with the lights. When you have a device of this kind set up for the public use in active operation the presumption should be that it is in proper working order unless there is evidence to the contrary and there was none here. The case must be decided on the basis that the lights were working properly and there must be a new trial.

Lights not working correctly

Ramoo Son of Erulapan v Gan Soo Swee

[1971] 3 All ER 320, [1971] WLR 1014, 115 Sol Jo 445, PC
At a crossroads controlled by traffic lights a lorry was approaching from the east and a taxi-cab (in which the plaintiff was a passenger) from the north. The lights were not functioning properly: those facing the lorry were showing only a green-amber-green sequence with no red phase; those facing the cab were changing in normal sequence but too rapidly. The lorry driver said he first looked at the lights when he was 40 to

50 feet away and saw them at green only; he was unaware of any malfunction. The plaintiff said he first saw the lights facing the cab when it was 15 feet away and they were green. The cab driver did not give evidence. Both vehicles drove on to the junction at speed and the cab was hit by the lorry, injuring the plaintiff.

HELD: The question was whether either driver should have realised the lights were not working properly and that he must proceed with caution. *Eva v Reeves* (p 92, above) was of no relevance; it merely showed that a driver who enters properly on to a crossing when the lights are in his favour is under no duty to anticipate that another driver may enter the crossing improperly against the lights facing him. The cab driver should have noticed that the lights were changing rapidly and have realised that they were out of order. He should have slowed down but did not. The natural inference in the absence of evidence from him was that he was not keeping a proper look-out. If the lorry driver did not, as he said, see the lights until he was 40 to 50 feet away he too was not keeping a proper look-out. He could not shelter behind the possibility that even if he had looked at them much earlier he may not have been able to deduce that they were out of order. Both drivers were negligent.

Clough v Bussan, ex p West Yorkshire Police Authority

[1990] 1 All ER 431, [1990] RTR 178

A collision occurred at a road junction controlled by traffic lights that were malfunctioning. This malfunction had been reported to the police 34 minutes before the collision. The passenger in one of the vehicles sued the drivers of the two vehicles involved in the collision and one of these obtained leave to join the Police Authority as a third party. This was on the basis that the police had not responded as they should have done. The Police Authority applied to the registrar to strike out the third party notice as disclosing no reasonable cause of action. The registrar dismissed the application. The Police Authority appealed.

HELD: It was established law that the police are under a duty to preserve law and order and to protect life and property because this is their continuing obligation. However, nothing had happened to give rise to a particular duty of care towards this particular individual which he could rely on in respect of the claim made against him by the injured passenger. The fact that the police were informed of the malfunction was not sufficient to impose upon them a duty of care to every motorist who might subsequently use the junction.

See also *Hill v Chief Constable of West Yorkshire* [1989] AC 53, [1988] 2 All ER 238, [1988] 2 WLR 1049, HL for another discussion about the ambit of the police authorities duty of care.

Crossing stop line

Ryan v Smith

[1967] 2 QB 893, [1967] 1 All ER 611, [1967] 2 WLR 390, 131 JP 193, Div Ct

At a crossroads controlled by traffic lights the defendant, driving a bus, passed the primary light and its associated stop line when the light was at green. Before the whole of his bus had passed over the stop line he stopped to allow a vehicle coming in the opposite direction to turn across his front into the road on his left. By the time the road was clear again the traffic light which he had just passed and the secondary light facing him on the far side of the crossroads, had changed to red. He nevertheless

started forward and crossed over the junction. The evidence showed that if he had remained stationary in the position in which he first came to a stop he would not have obstructed traffic wishing to cross the junction from right to left or vice versa. He was convicted of failing to conform to an indication given by the traffic lights, since the Traffic Signals Regulations 1964, reg 34(1)(a) provides that 'the red signal shall convey the prohibition that vehicular traffic shall not proceed beyond the stop line', and the rear end of his bus had crossed the stop line after the light changed to red.
HELD, ON APPEAL: The defendant was rightly convicted. The prohibition relates to any vehicle or any part of any vehicle and is infringed if any part of a vehicle moves forward from one side of the line to the other.

Fire brigade, ambulance and police

Ward v London County Council

[1938] 2 All ER 341 (Charles J)
A fire engine came to a light controlled crossing with the lights against it. The driver had been sounding his gong, seeing no vehicle crossing, proceeded against the red light. A car was entering the crossing from his left with the green light in its favour, turning to its right, and collided with the fire engine.
HELD: The driver of the fire engine was alone to blame. The fact that other traffic gave way to a fire engine was no excuse. The red light was an absolute prohibition.

TRAFFIC SIGNS

Note—The Road Traffic Regulation Act 1984, s 65 authorises a highway authority to place traffic signs and s 36 of the Road Traffic Act 1988 makes it an offence for the driver of any vehicle who fails to conform to the sign.

Lavis v Kent County Council

(1992) 90 LGR 416, CA
The plaintiff motorcyclist suffered severe injuries when he collided with a kerbstone on a sharp bend on Waterloo Road in Vigo, Kent. The plaintiff's Statement of Claim alleged that the defendant council was negligent in that it ought to have erected various signs warning vehicles of the bend.

The defendant authority applied to have the plaintiff's claim struck out as disclosing no cause of action. The Master refused but the council succeeded before the judge on appeal. The plaintiff then appealed.
HELD: The Court of Appeal, considering the Road Traffic Regulation Act 1984, concluded that although the Act did not impose a duty on the authority to erect traffic signals, it did require the authority to take reasonable care in implementing the requirements of the Act. It was a question of fact whether in this instance they were justified in taking no steps to erect signs at this bend and therefore the plaintiff was entitled to pursue the matter further by way of discovery.

Note—The Road Traffic Regulation Act 1984, s 64 deals with traffic signs and defines the expression, which includes any line or mark in the road.

Regulations

Note—The current traffic signs regulations are the Traffic Signs Regulations and General Directions 1981, SI 1981/859, replacing earlier regulations which came into effect as from 1 January 1965. The principle of these regulations is to use symbols to replace words wherever possible in traffic signs. The symbols adopted are, in general, those in use on the continent of Europe.

To understand some of the older cases it is necessary to know that 'Stop' replaces the old 'Halt at Major Road Ahead' sign. It appears on a minor road where traffic emerges into a major road and requires every vehicle (a) to stop at the major road and (b) not to proceed into the major road 'in such a manner or at such a time as is likely to cause danger to the driver of any other vehicle on the major road or as to necessitate the driver of any such other vehicle to change its speed or course in order to avoid an accident with the first mentioned vehicle.'

'Give Way' replaces the old 'Slow Major Road Ahead' sign. Its meaning is the same as that of the 'Stop' sign with the omission of requirement (a).

The Traffic Signs (Speed Limits) Regulations and General Directions 1969, SI 1969/1487, deal with traffic signs relating to speed limits.

Breach not actionable without negligence

Kelly v WRN Contracting Ltd

[1968] 1 All ER 369, [1968] 1 WLR 921, 112 Sol Jo 465 (Ashworth J)
Burke parked his car on a bend opposite double white lines in the road; by so doing he was in breach of the Traffic Signs Regulations 1964, reg 23 [now reg 23 of the 1981 Regulations]. Its nearside wheels were on the pavement and only 3 feet of the width of the car projected into the roadway. It was visible to approaching traffic for at least 100 yards and there was plenty of room for vehicles to pass. O'Connor driving a lorry too fast and possibly failing to see the car until too late got out of control and crashed into a wall injuring the plaintiff, his passenger. O'Connor admitted liability to the plaintiff but claimed a contribution from Burke.
HELD: There was no common law negligence on the part of Burke. There was a breach of reg 23 and as the accident would not have occurred but for parking the car where it was it had a causative effect on the accident. The regulations were designed to avoid accidents and therefore to prevent injury. A breach of the regulations gave rise to civil liability to a person injured by reason of the breach. Liability apportioned 90% to O'Connor, 10% Burke.

Note—But see next case.

Coote v Stone

[1971] 1 All ER 657, [1971] 1 WLR 279, 115 Sol Jo 79, CA
The Various Trunk Roads (Prohibition of Waiting) (Clearways) Order 1963, art 4 provides that 'no person shall . . . cause or permit any vehicle to wait on a clearway'. On a straight stretch of main road which had been designated a clearway the defendant stopped his car close in to the nearside to attend to his small daughter who was feeling sick. After two minutes or so the plaintiff came along in his car from the same direction as the defendant. Being dazzled by the sun he failed to see the defendant's car and crashed into the back of it. The judge held the defendant in breach of the regulation, and said that as the collision would not have occurred if he had not stopped there he was liable.

HELD, ON APPEAL: That was not right. As in *Clarke v Brims* (below) and *Phillips v Britannia Laundry* (p 204, below) the question was whether the regulation was intended to give a civil remedy to a person injured by the breach or whether it imposed only a public duty. The primary object of the Clearways Regulations was to facilitate the passage of traffic, and though this object is not unconnected with the avoidance of danger it was not intended to give rise to any private liability. *Kelly v WRN Contracting Ltd* (above) was wrongly decided and should not be followed.

Effect of traffic sign

Brazier v Alabaster

(1962) Times, 16 January, Div Ct, QBD
A motorist approached a roundabout on a dual-track road. The central intersection of the road ended 62 ft 9 in from the roundabout. Instead of going round the roundabout the motorist made a U-turn between the end of the intersection and the roundabout to get on to the other track of the road. There was a 'Keep Left' sign on the roundabout. He was convicted of failing to conform to an indication given by a traffic signal contrary to s 14 of the Road Traffic Act 1960 (now the Road Traffic Act 1972, s 22).
HELD, ON APPEAL: The conviction could not stand. A traffic sign could only indicate that if a motorist were to pass it he must obey it. As there was not a 'No Entry' sign in the intersection the motorist had the right to use that part of the highway.

Note—Section 22 of the Road Traffic Act 1972 has been replaced by s 36 of the Road Traffic Act 1988.

No warning sign

James v Parsons

[1975] 1 Lloyd's Rep 178 (Kilner Brown J)
Travelling at 40 mph or more in the dark a car driven by the defendant entered an S-bend at the end of which was a hump-backed bridge. There was no warning sign of the bridge, which came as a surprise to the defendant. The car lost contact with the road in passing over the bridge and the plaintiff, a passenger, was injured. It was argued for the defendant that he was not to blame for the result of meeting an unsuspected hazard in the road in these circumstances.
HELD: The defendant should have seen the bridge before he hit it even though not warned about it and should have been driving in such a way that, once he did hit the hump he could have controlled the car and so prevented it from leaving the road.

Slow sign

Buffel v Cardox (Great Britain) Ltd

[1950] 2 All ER 878, 114 JP 564, CA
A cyclist crossing a main road was injured by a lorry on the main road. About 95 yards from the crossing there were in the main road three warning signs consisting of studs in the road with the word 'slow', a cross-road sign and a flashing beacon. The lorry did not slow down before the crossing. Parker J held the cyclist alone to blame.

HELD, ON APPEAL:

Per Bucknill LJ: I do not think that 'slow' means any more than 'proceed with caution'—'proceed at such a speed that you can stop if, when you get to the crossing, you find somebody, or something, in the process of crossing, or about to cross.'

Per Singleton LJ: It is not easy to define the word 'slow'. Its meaning must depend on a variety of circumstances. That which may appear slow to some motorists may strike a pedestrian as fast. I think the fairest way to look on it is that the sign is an indication to the motorist that he is approaching a place of potential danger, and that, therefore, he ought to be driving more slowly than he would drive on a normal open road without any such sign. In other words, his speed ought to be such that he can pull up fairly quickly if someone or something appears from one or other of the crossroads. Appeal allowed.

Traffic entering major road from minor road

Brown v Central Scottish Motor Traction

1949 SC 9, 1949 SLT 66, Ct of Sess

A motor cyclist with pillion passenger was proceeding along a minor road which had a 'Slow, Major Road Ahead' sign and formed the left arm of a Y junction with a major road. He collided with a bus proceeding along the major road at about 25 mph. Each vehicle should have been clearly visible to the other driver. The bus driver did not slow down until the motor cycle emerged from the minor road, when he at once braked and swerved. The pillion passenger was killed, and his father brought proceedings against the bus company. The jury found the bus driver negligent.

HELD, ON APPEAL: There was no evidence of negligence of the bus driver. On the evidence, the bus driver had no opportunity of observing what the motor cyclist was going to do.

Note—Compare *Lang v London Transport Executive* (below).

See also *MacIntyre v Coles*, above.

Lang v London Transport Executive

[1959] 3 All ER 609, [1959] 1 WLR 1168 (Havers J)

A motor cyclist was riding along a minor side road and approaching a major main road. The minor road continued the line of the major road from the junction, where the major road changed direction. About 180 feet from the junction there was a 'Slow, Major Road Ahead' sign. Traffic on the major road was clearly visible from the side road for a distance of 40 yards from the junction. The motor cyclist was proceeding at a speed of 20 mph. There was a 'Slow' sign painted on the major road about 190 feet away from the junction. Just after passing the 'Slow' sign, the bus driver glanced in the direction of the side road and saw some cyclists, but did not look in the direction of the side road again. The bus driver was aware of the 'Slow' sign in the minor road, and he knew that people would suddenly emerge from a side road when it was unwise to do so. The motor cyclist was killed, and his widow sued the bus driver and his employers.

HELD: The deceased was guilty of a high degree of negligence. The bus driver was negligent in not taking the precaution of looking at the traffic in the side road. The judge found the deceased was two-thirds to blame and the bus driver one-third.

Note—See comments of Sachs LJ in *Watkins v Moffat*, p 105, below.

Walsh v Redfern

[1970] RTR 201 (Lyell J)
The defendant was driving an Army lorry and trailer along the main Bath Road late at night. His speed was 35 mph. A car containing six people was being driven along a narrow lane at great speed towards the Bath Road from his left. The defendant saw from the light cast by the car's headlight on the tall hedges on each side of the lane that a car was approaching but owing to the rain and darkness he could form no clear impression of speed and gave no further thought to it. The driver of the car did not stop or slow down but drove straight out on to the main road at speed. The defendant was unable to avoid the car and in the collision four of its occupants were killed.
HELD: The defendant was not at all to blame. There was nothing he could have done to avoid the collision short of slowing right down to such a speed that he could have stopped the lorry and let the car pass across its front when he saw it emerge from behind the hedge. It would be unreasonable to expect him to do so. He was driving on one of the main trunk roads from London to the West of England; it is common knowledge that every minor road which debouches on to a road of this importance has warning signs to approach the major road at slow speed. There was nothing known to the defendant to put him on guard against a lunatic driver who would wholly disregard the warning signs.

Garston Warehousing Co v O F Smart (Liverpool) Ltd

[1973] RTR 377, CA
On a November evening after dark the plaintiffs' car was being driven out of a side street across a main road, which was 26 feet wide and well-lighted, into a street opposite. The main road was a one-way street with traffic travelling only from the car driver's right. As he was about to leave the side street there was on his immediate right against the kerb in the main road a bus which obscured his view to the right. The bus driver gave a flash of his headlights and a hand signal to the car driver to come on. After looking along the nearside of the bus and seeing nothing approaching the car driver switched on his headlights and drove out slowly across and beyond the front of the bus without stopping. When about to enter the street opposite the car was struck violently on its offside by the defendants' van which had overtaken the bus. The van driver had not seen the car until he was 12 to 15 feet away, nor had he noticed a slow-down signal given by the bus driver. The judge held the van driver two-thirds to blame for driving at a speed excessive in the circumstances and failing to see the car earlier; he held the car driver one-third to blame for not stopping when the car was just past the bus and when he would have seen the van approaching.
HELD, ON APPEAL: The apportionment should not be disturbed.

Crossroad collisions

MAJOR ROAD DRIVER NOT TO BLAME

Note—See *Brown v Central Scottish Motor Traction*, p 102, above.

Watson v Everall and Tebbett

(12 July 1960, unreported), CA
In the hours of darkness a motor coach and a van collided at a crossroads where a main road was crossed by a subsidiary road. The van was being driven along the main road

and the coach along the subsidiary road, which had a 'Halt' sign and stop line at the point where the coach emerged on to the main road. Due to his injuries the driver did not remember the actual collision but he remembered turning on his headlights as he left the lights of a town some distance from the crossroads: they would have been visible to the coach driver for at least 70 yards before the crossing. The court found that the coach driver did not halt at the main road but was crossing it at some speed, and without looking out for other traffic, when the van struck the coach on its offside in front of the rear wheel. There was no evidence as to what the van was doing before the impact either as to speed or position on the road, nor did it leave any brake marks on the road. The judge of assize held the drivers equally to blame.

Per Sellers LJ: It depicts the typical case of a vehicle coming out from the side road directly in front of the van which had the right to use that main road expecting that traffic coming out from the side road on the left would conform with the requirements of the law that it should halt and the further requirement that being a side road it should give way to traffic passing on the main road.

Note—The above is taken from a transcript of the full judgment.

Brooks v Graham

(12 March 1964, unreported)
At a crossroads in a built-up area a van was travelling north and a car was travelling west. There was a 'Halt' sign in the van-driver's road, but he did not stop. He drove straight out on to the crossroads at about 20 mph, colliding with the nearside of the car which was travelling at about 15 mph. Neither party saw the other before the collision. The car driver said he looked into the turning on his left as he approached but saw no vehicle at the halt line and carried on. The judge found that car driver 25% to blame for driving at an excessive speed and not keeping a proper look-out.
HELD, ON APPEAL: The driver of the car was not to blame at all. It was impossible to support the judge's conclusion without taking a wholly unrealistic view of traffic conditions as they are. The relative speeds of the vehicles showed that at the moment the car reached the actual crossroads the van could not have reached the halt line. If the car driver had seen it coming towards the crossing he might justifiably have assumed that it would halt when it reached the halt line. The judge had treated the case as though it were one of a collision at an uncontrolled crossroads or a crossroads subject only to a 'Slow' sign. Where there is a 'Halt' sign wholly different considerations apply. If a vehicle on a major road is to approach such a crossroads in such a way that it can stop dead if a vehicle on a minor road fails to observe the 'Halt' sign, it would mean that it would have to slow down to little more than a walking pace and for all practical purposes bring traffic on the major road to a standstill.

Note—Taken from full transcript of judgment.

Gooder v Taylor and Yorkshire Tar Distillers Ltd

(1966) Times, 18 October, CA
At a crossroads where a minor road crossed a major road a van was travelling along the minor road and a tanker along the major road. As the van approached the crossroads the driver slowed down almost to a stop. He looked along the major road but saw nothing coming, pressed the accelerator again and proceeded to cross. The tanker-driver had seen the van approaching the crossroads. He took his foot off the accelerator but, seeing the van slow down as if to stop, put his foot on again to go over

the crossroads. When at the last moment the van moved forward on to the crossroads the tanker driver was unable to avoid hitting it. The judge of assize held the van driver five-sixths to blame for the collision and the tanker-driver one-sixth.
HELD: Allowing the tanker-driver's appeal, he was not to blame at all. He had seen the van slow down and was justified in thinking that the van driver had seen him and was going to let him pass. For the same reason he was not negligent in not sounding his horn. The tanker driver was not negligent in not reducing his speed, for only by slowing down to a very considerable extent could he have avoided the consequences of the van pulling out at the last moment. As he had seen the van slow down as if to allow him to pass he was under no duty to take such drastic action.

Watkins v Moffatt

(1967) 111 Sol Jo 719, [1970] RTR 205n, CA
The plaintiff, a passenger, was injured in a crossroads collision between a Ford van in which he was travelling and an Austin car. The Ford was travelling on the minor road on which there was a 'Slow, Major Road Ahead' sign. The Austin was on the major road. The judge held that the Ford driver was guilty of a high degree of negligence in coming out faster than he should have done but the possibility of danger should have been reasonably apparent to the driver of the Austin if he had been keeping a proper look-out. He held the Austin driver one-third to blame.
HELD, ON APPEAL: It could not be inferred that the driver of the Austin was not keeping a proper look-out. The Ford was on a side road with 'Major Road Ahead' signs and must have been coming so fast that the driver of the Austin, keeping a reasonable look-out on both sides of the road might well not have seen it, and he was not to blame.

Per Sachs LJ: The case is another in which the authority of *Lang v London Transport Executive* (p 102, above) is prayed in aid on behalf of a driver of a vehicle emerging from a side road on to a main road. Whatever may be the correct view of that case on its own facts, a matter on which I would wish to reserve judgment, *Lang*'s case is not a charter in favour of motorists emerging from a side road at speed. That would entail a somewhat unrealistic view of the way reasonably driven traffic uses main roads and would derogate from the great responsibility of those emerging from side roads in relation to main road traffic.

Barclays Bank Ltd v Gaughan and Toole

(8 June 1970, unreported), (James J)
Approaching a crossroads in a rural area in daylight the second defendant was driving his car along the main road at 25 to 30 mph. He knew the minor road on his left had a 'Halt' sign at its mouth. From a point about 35 yards from the junction there was a view through an open fence along the minor road for a similar distance from the junction. The first defendant approaching the crossroads along the minor road at about 50 mph ignored the 'Halt' sign and drove straight on to the junction striking the second defendant's car and killing a passenger. The second defendant, who was paying attention to some horses approaching from the far side of the junction, said he had only a fleeting glimpse of the other car before the collision.
HELD: The second defendant was not at all to blame. He was driving quietly and sensibly on a main road with knowledge of the 'Halt' sign in the minor road. He was faced with the presence of horses. His obligation was to behave reasonably. It was doubtful whether he would have seen anything in the minor road but he had every reason to believe a car in the minor road would stop. The sole responsibility for the accident lay on the first defendant.

Humphrey v Leigh

[1971] RTR 363, CA

The second defendant was driving his car at a steady pace up Gipsy Hill in South London when the first defendant drove out of a side road to cross into a road opposite without stopping or slowing down. There was a collision resulting in injury to the plaintiff. There were no road signs to show that Gipsy Hill was the major road but there was no doubt that it was and that traffic in the side road would as a matter of course slow down and stop. The judge attributed all the blame to the first defendant, who appealed.

HELD: The appeal should be dismissed—the second defendant was in no way negligent.

Per Russell LJ: The question is whether it can be propounded as a matter of law that a person in the position of the second defendant has a duty, if he is to avoid a charge of negligence every time he comes across a side road of this kind leading out of Gipsy Hill, to take his foot off the accelerator and poise his foot over the brake, being prepared to stop short of the crossing. In so far as anything to that effect was said by Lord Justice Ormerod in the case of *Williams v Fullerton* (below) it was an obiter dictum and I personally would not follow it at all; otherwise you would approach in situation in which no traffic moves about the country at any reasonable speed whatsoever.

MAJOR ROAD DRIVER 25% TO BLAME

Williams v Fullerton

(1961) 105 Sol Jo 280, CA

A was driving a car along Richmond Avenue, near King's Cross, London: B was driving a car along Hemingford Road, a minor road which crosses Richmond Avenue at an ordinary cross-roads junction. Hemingford Road had a sign 'Slow—Major Road Ahead'. Despite this B drove on to the cross-roads at a speed estimated between 30 and 60 mph and collided with A's car causing fatal injuries to a passenger. A had approached the junction, which had a conventional cross-roads sign, at a reasonable speed, looked right and left and did not see anything. The trial judge held A 25% to blame and B 75%. A appealed. It was argued on his behalf that a driver on a major road approaching a crossing had no duty to keep a look-out except to see what might reasonably be seen and that there was no obligation to look out for what travelled at an excessive speed.

HELD: The trial judge's finding could not be disturbed. If A's failure had consisted merely in failing to take into account the outrageous driving of B it was at least doubtful if he could be considered negligent. But although he had looked left and right at the crossing he had not, as indicated by the Highway Code, looked right again. Had A looked at the right time or looked properly he must have seen the other car and could have taken avoiding action.

Per Ormerod LJ: If a driver exercised proper care he would approach a crossing with his foot off the accelerator and ready to brake and deal with any traffic from the minor road by slowing down or stopping.

Note—For comment on this decision see *Humphrey v Leigh*, above.

Butters v J H Fenner & Co Ltd

(1967) 117 NLJ 213 (MacKenna J)
At a cross-roads in a built-up area the first defendant's servant was driving a car along a minor road. He failed to see a 'Slow, Major Road Ahead' sign and a large 'Slow', painted on the roadway. He drove straight on to the cross-roads where the car was hit by the second defendant's lorry travelling on the major road. The lorry driver had not looked to his offside as he crossed the junction nor had he slowed down.
HELD: The lorry driver was 25% to blame. He should have looked to his right and slowed down before entering the junction. If he had done so he would have been able to avoid the collision or at least reduce its force.

TRAFFIC FROM RIGHT

There is no rule or custom in this country requiring a driver approaching cross-roads to give way to traffic on his right and allowing him to take precedence over traffic on his left. It would be quite disastrous if some users of the highway observed that practice while others did not. Users of roads of equal importance which crossed one another owed a duty to each other to take care. Even the driver on a major road was not acquitted altogether of the duty of taking care, even though there might be a greater duty on the driver on the minor road. The question of negligence is one of fact. (1954) 98 Sol Jo 380, Times, 29 May (Streatfield J).

White lines

Note—And see 'Traffic signs', p 99, above.

The Road Traffic Regulation Act 1984, s 64 provides that 'In this Act "traffic sign" means . . . any line or mark on a road for' conveying to traffic on roads warnings, information, requirements, restrictions or prohibitions of any kind specified by regulations.

Kirk v Parker

(1938) 60 Ll L Rep 129
If the offside wheels of the defendant's lorry were a little over an imaginary central white line, that is not necessarily negligence if, by driving a car in that position, it is clear you will avoid any collision with vehicles coming in the opposite direction.

Day v Smith

(1983) 133 NLJ 726, QBD
The plaintiff was injured when the car he was driving collided with another on a bend. The deceased's administrator counter-claimed, alleging negligence on the part of the plaintiff. There were no eye witnesses of the accident but there was evidence of some marks on the road. The bend on which the accident occurred was a left hand bend for the plaintiff, the road being 24 feet wide divided by a single central white line.
HELD: On the evidence the plaintiff's car was 3 to 4 feet on the wrong side of the white line at the time of the collision. He was negligent in allowing that to happen and the deceased was not to blame. Judgment for the defendant administrator on the counter-claim.

Dotted line across mouth of road

Note—The Traffic Signs Regulations 1981 provide by regs 21 and 22 that transverse broken white lines across the mouth of a road at a road junction have the effect of a 'Give Way' sign whether or not used in conjunction with a sign.

See *Hardy v Walder*, p 25, above.

Murray v Nicholls

1983 SLT 194 (Outer House)
There was a collision of cars at the junction of a major and a minor road. There had been white lines at the junction but these had not been renewed after roadworks.
HELD: The fact that there had been white lines before was relevant to the issue of foreseeability but not to the existence of a duty. To hold there was such a duty would expose highway authorities to a wide range of liabilities. In any event there was no evidence that either driver was influenced by the existence of the markings at an earlier date. Action dismissed.

Note—But see *Bird v Pearce*, p 264, below.

Double white lines

Note—The Traffic Signs Regulations and General Directions 1981, reg 23 contains the rules of the 'double white line' system of traffic control. Vehicles must not stop on any length of road having a double white line, nor must a vehicle cross a continuous line when it is on the left of a dotted or continuous line as viewed in the direction of travel of the vehicle. There are exceptions to the rule against stopping, including a stop for a person to board or alight, or for the purposes of loading or unloading. It is permissible to cross a continuous line for, inter alia, the purpose of passing a stationary vehicle or entering another road. When the dotted line is on the left a vehicle may cross it provided it is seen by the driver to be safe to do so.

R v Blything Justices, ex p Knight

[1970] RTR 218, Div Ct
The defendant was following two cars and an articulated lorry. He decided to overtake. He did not know he was approaching the beginning of a double white line. He was unable to get back to the nearside until he had driven 40 or 50 yards on the offside of the double white line. He was charged with failing to comply with the Traffic Signs Regulations 1964, reg 23 (now reg 23 of the 1981 Regulations). He said the first of the two cars had accelerated and prevented him from getting back to the nearside in time and that this was an accident giving him a defence under reg 23(4)(a). The magistrate's clerk advised the bench that this defence was not available to a driver who had not first had the double white lines on his offside before crossing them. He was convicted.
HELD, ON APPEAL: The conviction should stand because a driver could not, after putting himself in the wrong by beginning to overtake in such circumstances, claim that he had to continue in the wrong because of some accident. Even so, the magistrate's clerk's advice had been too narrow and was bad. There may be cases (eg when overtaking stationary vehicles) when a man through no fault of his own approaches the double white line on the wrong side of it and never gets back on to his nearside until some distance of the white line has been passed.

West v Buckinghamshire County Council

(1984) Times, 13 November (Caulfield J)
The plaintiff driver, while overtaking, collided with an oncoming vehicle causing the death of the driver of that vehicle, whose personal representatives recovered £160,000 damages. In the present action the plaintiff claimed indemnity from the defendants, the highway authority, for having failed to place double white lines on the road pursuant to their power to do so under the Road Traffic Regulation Act 1967, s 55(1). The Department of Transport had in 1964 recommended that roads less than 20 feet wide should not carry double white lines. At that time the defendants had decided that double white lines were not desirable as the road was less than 20 feet wide. When measured after the accident in 1979 it was found to be more than 20 feet wide. The plaintiff urged that the defendants should have foreseen a gradual widening of the road due to piecemeal repairs and should have measured it after repairs and supplied double white lines, as was done after the accident.
HELD: The defendants were not liable. Although a public body exercising powers given it by statute could owe a duty of care and be liable in damages (per Lord Wilberforce in *Anns v Merton London Borough Council* [1978] AC 728, [1977] 2 All ER 492, [1977] 2 WLR 1024, 121 Sol Jo 377, 75 LGR 555, 243 Estates Gazette 523, 591, HL) a policy decision made pursuant to such statutory powers was a matter of discretion which could not be attacked in the courts. In the present case the defendants had exercised their discretion bona fide and no duty of care arose.

8 PEDESTRIANS

RIGHTS OF PEDESTRIANS

Boss v Litton

(1832) 5 C & P 407
All persons, paralytic as well as others, have a right to walk on the road and are entitled to the exercise of reasonable care on the part of persons driving carriages upon it.

DUTY OF DRIVER

Note—See *Kite v Nolan,* p 64, above.

Kayser v London Passenger Transport Board

[1950] 1 All ER 231, 114 JP 122 (Humphreys J)
A bus driver stopped at a compulsory stop some distance from a pedestrian crossing near where two wide thoroughfares joined the main road. There were two trolley buses ahead, and as the traffic lights turned green he followed the trolley buses. When about one and a half lengths of an omnibus from the traffic lights, he saw plaintiff, a girl of 14, another girl, and a man, hurrying across the road diagonally, holding hands and talking. It was obvious they would have crossed the road before he reached them and he went on. An air raid shelter obstructed his vision and he proceeded very slowly in first gear. The pedestrians scattered but he just caught the plaintiff. According to the evidence, the plaintiff was half-way across, when she suddenly ran

back, probably as the result of traffic in the opposite direction, and ran into the omnibus. She was just off the crossing.

HELD: Where the driver of a vehicle is satisfied that persons who are lawfully entitled to cross the road, whether they are on a pedestrian crossing or not, are out of danger from him if he goes on in the normal course, he is entitled to do so but only at such a pace as will enable him to stop almost immediately should the persons who are crossing do anything dangerous or negligent.

There was no negligence on the part of the driver. Judgment for defendants.

Note—Cf *Foskett v Mistry*, p 65, above.

Baker v Willoughby

[1970] AC 467, [1969] 3 All ER 1528, [1970] 2 WLR 50, 114 Sol Jo 15, HL

The plaintiff wished to cross a main road 33 feet wide in open country. He saw a car approaching from his right about 100 yards away and assumed he had time to cross. He walked out into the centre of the road, paused to look left, and was struck by the defendant's car coming from his right. The defendant had overtaken two other cars at least 200 yards before the point of collision and had the plaintiff in view over that distance. The judge found both parties to blame: the defendant three-quarters because, having the plaintiff in view for 200 yards and taking no evasive action he must have been either driving too fast or not keeping a proper look-out; the plaintiff one-quarter for not waiting for the approaching cars to pass and not looking to his right a second time. The Court of Appeal altered the apportionment to 50-50 on the ground that each party had a view of each other throughout the time the plaintiff was crossing the road to the point of collision and neither did anything about it.

HELD, ON APPEAL to the House of Lords: The judge's apportionment of blame should be restored. There were two elements in an assessment of liability, causation and blameworthiness. A pedestrian had to look to both sides as well as forwards. He was going at perhaps three miles an hour and was rarely a danger to anyone else. A motorist had not got to look sideways and if he was going at a considerable speed must not relax his observation otherwise the consequences might be disastrous. It was quite possible for a motorist to be very much more to blame than the pedestrian.

Mulligan v Holmes

[1971] RTR 179, CA

Two pedestrians began to cross a wide brightly-lit street at night. The distance from the kerb to the central island was 35 feet. There was no satisfactory evidence whether they looked to their right or not. Two cars were approaching. The driver of the first, travelling at 30-40 mph, saw the pedestrians begin to cross when he was about 60 yards away. He slowed slightly but they presented no problem to him and passed across his front. The second car driven by the defendant at a very fast speed, overtook the first car when it was 10 to 15 yards from the pedestrians. The defendant had not seen them before though he could have seen them from 100 yards away if he had looked. They were by that time quite near the central island. They were struck by his car and injured, one fatally. The judge at first instance held that the pedestrians could not have looked to their right and were 50% to blame.

HELD, ON APPEAL: The proportion of contributory negligence should be reduced to 20%. The evidence did not warrant the conclusion that the pedestrians did not look to their right. Nevertheless, they were not blameless: if they had exercised all reasonable care they would have realised that the second car was being driven very quickly and that there was a risk that the driver might not see them and would run them down.

Hurt v Murphy

[1971] RTR 186 (Talbot J)
The plaintiff's wife began to cross the road at a place where her visibility to her left was restricted by a bend to 100 yards. There was no vehicle in sight when she left the pavement. She walked across, looking ahead. The defendant driving his car at a speed very much greater than the 30 mph limit came round the bend and though he applied his brakes he was unable to avoid striking and killing her. She was then just beyond the centre of the road. The defendant admitted his own negligence but alleged contributory negligence.
HELD: The plaintiff's wife was not negligent when she left the pavement because there was then nothing in sight, but there was lack of care on her part in not looking to her left again as she was crossing the road. She was one-fifth to blame.

Williams v Needham

[1972] RTR 387, QBD
The plaintiff at night but in a well-lighted street parked her car with its nearside to the kerb so that she could cross to a shop on the other side. She stood in the roadway on the offside of the car with her back to it and looked to her right. She saw nothing approaching and then looked to her left. She saw three cars approaching and waited until they had passed. Then without looking again to her right she stepped forward to cross the road and was at once hit by the defendant's car coming from her right. The defendant had seen her standing by her car looking away from him and had guessed that she intended crossing the road. He assumed she would look to her right before beginning to cross and he took no precautions against her not doing so. When she stepped forward he was too near to avoid hitting her.
HELD: The plaintiff must bear two-thirds of the blame but one-third must rest on the defendant. He knew that people did sometimes begin to cross without looking and, realising the plaintiff was about to cross, should have drawn her attention to the presence of his car or taken some other precautions against the possibility of her taking a risky step.

Tremayne v Hill

[1987] RTR 131, CA
The defendant drove into a junction past a red traffic light and struck the plaintiff, a pedestrian who had not used the nearby light-controlled pelican crossing, but was crossing the junction diagonally. He alleged that the plaintiff was contributorily negligent for failing to keep a proper lookout and failing to cross at the pelican crossing. The judge held that the accident was entirely caused by the defendant's negligence.
HELD, ON APPEAL: The defendant was wholly to blame. The plaintiff had no reason to anticipate that he would ignore the traffic lights. The defendant was seriously careless and any possible failure to keep a proper lookout was not a contributory factor. Per curiam: There is no legal duty on a pedestrian to cross a junction only at a light-controlled pedestrian crossing. He (or she) is entitled to cross anywhere he wishes provided he takes reasonable care for his own safety.

Note—See also *Fitzgerald v Lane* , p 24, above.

CROSSING AT TRAFFIC LIGHTS

Shepherd v H West & Son Ltd

(1962) 106 Sol Jo 391 (Paull J)
The plaintiff and her 13-year-old daughter wished to cross the road at a junction controlled by traffic lights. They ensured that the traffic lights were showing red and then began to cross in front of a bus which was stationary at the traffic light on the nearside of the road. Whilst they were passing in front of the bus the light changed to red-amber and the bus driver 'revved-up' his engine preparatory to moving off. This alarmed the plaintiff who looked to her right along the offside of the bus and took a step forward to clear the bus in case it moved forward. She was at once struck by the defendant's lorry which was overtaking the bus. The lorry driver's evidence was that the traffic lights were red when he approached, changed to red-amber before he reached the bus and to green as he came alongside it.
HELD: The lorry driver was clearly negligent. A reasonable driver in such circumstances would not have let the front wheels of his lorry get level with the bus until the bus had got half-way across the crossing. To pass a stationary vehicle under such circumstances was a dangerous practice: the danger ought to be realised by all motorists. It was natural for the plaintiff to have tried to get out of the way of the bus when she heard its engine 'revving-up': she could not have taken more than one step forward and was not in any way negligent.

Note—An appeal was dismissed.
See also *Frank v Cox*, p 96, above.

Carter v Sheath

[1990] RTR 12, CA
The defendant who was a good careful driver was approaching a pelican crossing which was showing a green light in his favour. Somewhere close to the pelican crossing the defendant's car struck the plaintiff, a 13 year old boy, who suffered serious injuries. The plaintiff could remember nothing about the accident. Neither the defendant nor his wife, who was sitting in the front passenger seat, saw the plaintiff at all. The judge at first instance commented on the unusual difficulties of the case because of the 'curious paucity of direct evidence as to what exactly happened'. The judge held the defendant 50% to blame for not seeing the plaintiff who was there to be seen and the plaintiff 50% contributorily negligent. Both parties appealed.
HELD: The defendant's appeal was allowed. The plaintiff had not discharged the burden of proving that his injuries were caused by the defendant's negligence. Therefore no question of contributory negligence arose. Lord Brandon of Oakbrooks dictum in *Rhesa Shipping Co SA v Edmonds* [1985] 2 ALR 712, [1985] 1 WLR 948 applied.

NARROW PAVEMENT

Adamson v Roberts

1951 SC 681, 1951 SLT 355, 101 L Jo 511, Ct of Sess
A pedestrian was walking in daylight along a pavement at a point where it was narrowed by a projecting building, and had to put one foot over the edge of the pavement into the gutter in order to pass other pedestrians. As she did so, she was

struck from behind by a motor van. The van did not encroach upon or over the kerb. In the Outer House of the Court of Session the action was dismissed ((1951) 101 LJ 330).
HELD, ON APPEAL: In the circumstances a special duty was imposed upon the driver in relation to the speed at which he travelled, the warning which he gave and the part of the road on which he directed his vehicle. Appeal allowed.

Note—See also 'Vehicle overlapping pavement', p 35, above.

STANDING ON KERB

Chapman v Post Office

[1982] RTR 165, CA
The plaintiff was struck by the projecting driver-mirror of a passing vehicle when standing on the kerb at a bus stop. She sustained a severe blow to her arm. At the trial of her claim for damages the judge said she must have been leaning over the carriage way and found her equally to blame with the driver of the vehicle.
HELD, ON APPEAL: She was not at all to blame. A person standing on a kerb is not guilty of negligence if struck even if leaning out or having her back to the traffic, nor even if she went an inch or two into the roadway.

NOT USING PEDESTRIAN CROSSING

Snow v Giddins

(1969) 113 Sol Jo 229, CA
The plaintiff began to cross the road near a road junction and not far from a pedestrian crossing which had a central refuge. He threaded his way through the northbound traffic, which was stationary and then stood in the middle of the road just over the centre line looking to his left for any approaching south-bound traffic. Whilst standing there he was struck from his right by a motor cycle ridden by the defendant, who was travelling north overtaking the stationary vehicles. The county court judge held the defendant wholly to blame, rejecting, inter alia, a suggestion that the plaintiff was negligent in not using the pedestrian crossing.
HELD, ON APPEAL: The plaintiff was not negligent in failing to use the pedestrian crossing but he was negligent in taking on himself the hazard of being marooned in the centre of the road at the mercy of on-coming traffic instead of crossing where there was a central refuge: He was 25% to blame. A pedestrian who elected not to use a crossing took upon himself a higher standard of care.

PEDESTRIANS RUNNING

Brophy v Shaw

(1965) Times, 25 June, CA
Shortly before midnight the plaintiff and a friend had taken part in a street brawl and the plaintiff had struck and injured an elderly man. The police being about to apprehend them the plaintiff and friend ran away. They ran along the pavement past a bus which was just pulling away from a stop and shortly afterwards darted out into

the carriageway, running across at an angle of 45 degrees. The road had dual carriageways and the defendant was driving his car at about 30 mph keeping close to the offside. He failed to see the men crossing from his left, even though his headlights were on, until they had got a substantial way across the road. They ran right across in front of his car and were hit by it. The plaintiff was seriously injured and his friend killed.

HELD: The defendant was not liable. It had been alleged that he should have seen the men running along the pavement, but his duty, like that of any other road user, was to exercise reasonable care. He was not under a duty to be a perfectionist. It was going too far to say he should have observed the negligence and irresponsible action of the two men earlier than he did.

WALKING ON ROAD AT NIGHT

Powell v Phillips

[1972] 3 All ER 864, 116 Sol Jo 713, CA

The plaintiff and a friend were walking along a poorly-lit street at night on the left-hand pavement. From time to time because of snow and slush on the pavement they walked in the roadway near the kerb. Whilst so doing the plaintiff was hit from behind by the defendant's car, which was travelling at speed and did not stop. It was argued for the defendant that the plaintiff was guilty of 25% contributory negligence because she was not complying with the rules for pedestrians in the Highway Code: she was walking next to the kerb with her back to traffic, not wearing or carrying anything white.

HELD: She was not, on the facts, guilty of contributory negligence. Though the Road Traffic Act 1960, s 74(5) (now replaced by s 37(5) of the 1972 Act) enables a party to rely upon a breach of the Highway Code as tending to establish or negative liability, a breach creates no presumption of negligence calling for an explanation, still less a presumption of negligence contributing to causing an accident or injury. A breach is just one of the circumstances on which a party can rely in establishing the negligence of the other and its contribution to causing the accident or injury. It must not be elevated into a breach of statutory duty. In the present case, the plaintiff had not failed to take reasonable care for her own safety in walking a few feet out in the road for about 20 yards when it got too slushy; even if it did amount to negligence it made no real contribution to the accident.

Note—Section 37(5) of the 1972 Act has been replaced by s 38(7) of the Road Traffic Act 1983.

Kerley v Downes

[1973] RTR 188, CA

The plaintiffs were father and son, the latter aged 13. At night they left the lighted entrance to a fairground adjoining a straight country road and walked along a grass verge alongside the road for a distance and then along the left hand edge of the road for 20 yards or so preparatory to crossing to the other side at a place where there was an isolated street lamp. Before they reached it they were struck from behind by the defendant's car. The judge declined to find the plaintiff father negligent either for his own safety or in respect of his son's.

HELD: The judge was right. Following *Parkinson v Parkinson* (below) and *Powell v Phillips* (above) mere contravention of the recommendation in the Highway Code to walk on the right of the road and not to walk with your back to the traffic did not create a presumption of negligence.

PEDESTRIAN LIABLE TO MOTORIST

Eames v Cunningham and Capps

(1948) Eastern Daily Press, 1 June, 82 Sol Jo 314 (Croom-Johnson J)
At 5.10 pm on 20 November 1946, a motor cyclist with pillion passenger collided with a pedestrian and the pillion passenger, a plasterer, was killed. His widow sued the motor cyclist and the pedestrian. A witness who was walking with the pedestrian gave evidence that when he saw the lights of the motor cycle approaching, he shouted 'Look out!' and stepped back. He had taken about one step into the road and the pedestrian was about to step in front of him. The pedestrian, who had a dog on a lead, seemed to hesitate for about a second and was struck by the motor cycle. Another witness said the pedestrian seemed to hesitate when the motor cyclist sounded his hooter, turned as if to speak to the first witness and then took another step forward. There was a good headlight on the motor cycle.

The motor cyclist said the pedestrian walked into the road, hesitated and then stepped forward. He was travelling slowly and had sounded his hooter. He could have avoided the pedestrian if he had stood still or stepped back like the other man. The pedestrian said he saw a light but thought it was a bicycle, not a motor cycle. He tried to make for the opposite pavement. If he had known it was a motor cycle he would have stopped till it had gone by.

HELD: The motor cyclist was not guilty of negligence; the pedestrian and the first witness stepped off the pavement with their minds on something else and got into the way of the motor cyclist. Judgment against pedestrian with costs; judgment for motor cyclist without costs.

Barry v MacDonald

(1966) 110 Sol Jo 56, Times, 15 January (MacKenna J)
The plaintiff's husband, riding a motor scooter, was killed when he collided with the defendant and his infant son when they were walking across the road. The defendant's statement to the police was 'I stepped off the kerb without looking and the next thing I was flying. It was entirely my fault.' In evidence he said he looked to his right but could not explain why he did not see the scooter.

HELD: The defendant was to blame in stepping from the footpath without ensuring it was safe to do so. It had been suggested that the plaintiff's husband was riding too close to the nearside and should have been nearer the middle of the road in case a pedestrian should step off the grass verge. It was not certain how close he was to the verge but if he were within a few feet it could not be said he was negligent. The defendant's negligence was the sole cause of the accident.

Note—See also *Green v Hills*, p 45, above.

Parkinson v Parkinson

[1973] RTR 193, CA

The defendant was driving his car along a straight unlighted road at night. He saw ahead of him on the nearside of the road two women pedestrians walking in the same direction as he was travelling but failed to see until too late two men walking about 20 yards behind them, the outer about 4 ft 6 ins from the edge of the road. The road was 25 feet wide. There was a grass verge on the left of the road but only a hedge on the right. The judge found the defendant wholly to blame. On appeal it was argued that the pedestrians were negligent in not following the advice in the Highway Code to walk on the right of the road so as to face the oncoming traffic.

HELD: There were no grounds for finding contributory negligence. Even if the outside pedestrian was 4 ft 6 ins out it did not amount to negligence when the road was 25 feet wide. It is depriving pedestrians of their natural rights as highway users to say they must walk on the right and are not entitled to walk on the nearside. The mere fact that a pedestrian walks on the left side of a country road is not necessarily negligent; it depends on the circumstances. In the present case there was a grass verge on the left on to which one could move in an emergency but only a hedge on the right.

PEDESTRIAN CROSSINGS

Precedence of foot passengers

Note—The Road Traffic Regulation Act 1984, s 25 provides for power to make regulations with respect to the precedence of vehicles and foot passengers respectively.

See the 'Zebra' Pedestrian Crossings Regulations 1971 (SI 1971/1524) printed in the ninth edition at p 93.

Regulation 8 gives precedence to foot passengers only on an 'uncontrolled zebra crossing', ie a zebra crossing not controlled for the time being by a policeman or traffic warden. 'Pelican' crossings are provided for by different regulations. The following cases deal with uncontrolled crossings.

Regulation 4, both of the 1954 Regulations and of the 1951 Regulations, was in similar terms to reg 8 of the 1971 Regulations.

It is always worth checking that these regulations have been complied with.

Leicester v Pearson

[1952[2 QB 668, [1952] 2 All ER 71, 116 JP 407, [1952] 1 TLR 1537, 96 Sol Jo 397, Div Ct

A pedestrian on a crossing was struck by a car. The lighting was poor, it was raining, the road surface wet and in poor condition, one side of the road flanked by trees causing shadows and the other side lighted from shop windows, and the pedestrian was crossing from the darker to the lighter side. The magistrate found the driver was exercising all due care, keeping a proper look-out, and driving without negligence and the accident happened because the car skidded and it was not his fault that he did not accord precedence. The prosecutor appealed.

HELD: The Pedestrian Crossings (General) Regulations 1951, reg 4 (see now reg 8 of the 1971 Regulations), although it appears in terms to be absolute, does not impose an absolute duty, but a duty to take reasonable steps to let the foot passenger have precedence. A driver might do everything required of him but might skid or be pushed forward by a car. It is not a regulation prohibiting the doing of some specific act but one for controlling the order of traffic and indicating precedence. Although it would only be in an exceptional case that a magistrate would be able to find the failure to see a foot passenger was not due to failure to keep a proper look-out, it might be inevitable or due to some circumstance over which the driver had no reasonable or possible control. The finding of the magistrate of no negligence was by itself an answer. Appeal dismissed.

Note—This decision can be misleading unless the following seven cases are also read.

Gibbons v Kahl

[1956] 1 QB 59, [1955] 3 All ER 345, [1955] 3 WLR 596, 120 JP 1, 99 Sol Jo 782, Div Ct

A trolley bus driver pulled up at a pedestrian crossing because three children stepped on to the crossing when he was 20 or 25 yards away. He signalled following traffic to slow down, stopped and waved the children to cross. A motorist proceeding in the same direction as the bus saw the driver's signal but did not see the children and struck one of the children who was 22 feet across on a 33 feet road. He was prosecuted for driving without due care and attention and failing to accord precedence to a pedestrian. The justices dismissed both summonses as they were not satisfied he was negligent.

HELD, ON APPEAL: The appeal court would not interfere on the first decision as they could not say the finding was perverse. There must be a conviction on the second charge. A breach of the regulations does not necessarily mean careless driving: *Leicester v Pearson* (above) was a very special case on very peculiar facts.

It is the duty of any motorist approaching a pedestrian crossing to approach it in such a way that he can deal with the situation on the crossing when he gets there. He must be in such a position and driving at such a speed that if anybody is on the crossing he is in a position to stop.

Note—Overtaking at zebra crossings was not then an offence, as it is now under reg 10 of the 1971 Regulations.

Lockie v Lawton

(1959) 124 JP 24, 103 Sol Jo 874, 57 LGR 329, Div Ct QBD

The defendant, driving a trolley-bus, approached an uncontrolled crossing. A lorry reversing out of a side street on his offside of the road obscured at least half his view of the crossing. An old man, partially blind and deaf, was making his way over the crossing from the offside of the road. The defendant did not see the man until he had reached the crown of the road. Though the defendant then applied his brakes violently he was unable to avoid striking the man. The magistrates dismissed a charge of failing to give precedence to the foot-passenger contrary to reg 4 (of the 1954 Regulations: now reg 8 of the 1971 Regulations).

HELD, ON APPEAL: The magistrates should convict. *Leicester v Pearson* (above) was a decision that the duty under reg 4 is a duty only to take reasonable steps to let the pedestrian have precedence, but it was a case on very special facts. What are and what are not reasonable steps must be viewed in the light of the clear duty which arises from reg 4, namely the duty laid down in *Gibbons v Kahl* (above) to drive at such a speed that one can stop if there is in fact a pedestrian there, albeit he is hidden from one's view. On the facts of the present case it was the driver's duty to drive at such a speed as to be able to stop when the old man emerged from behind the lorry.

Scott v Clint

(1960) Times, 28 October, Div Ct
A lorry was approaching a pedestrian crossing at 15-20 mph. When it was only 10 yards from the crossing two children stepped on to the crossing without looking to their right and started to cross. The driver did his best to avoid them but was unable to avoid hitting one of them.
HELD: Regulation 4 of the Pedestrian Crossing Regulations 1954 laid down an absolute duty. Once a pedestrian is on a crossing the driver of any vehicle approaching that crossing must accord him precedence, however unexpectedly or suddenly he crosses. The driver was guilty of an offence.

Hughes v Hall

[1960] 2 All ER 504, [1960] 1 WLR 733, 124 JP 411, 104 Sol Jo 566, Div Ct
The respondent was driving a car, at a reasonable and proper speed towards a pedestrian crossing. He had passed over the studs indicating the approach to the crossing when a woman stepped off the nearside pavement on to the crossing without looking to right or left and began to walk over the crossing. The respondent applied his brakes at once but was unable to pull up in time to avoid hitting her. On a charge under the Pedestrian Crossings Regulations 1954, reg 4 the respondent pleaded that (1) in passing over the approach studs he had come within the limits of the crossing before the woman stepped on to it and there was no case to answer; (2) on the authority of *Leicester v Pearson* (p 116, above) the duty imposed by reg 4 was not absolute.
HELD: (1) The limits are not the approach studs but the studs which border the striped crossing; (2) on the latest decisions of the Divisional Court reg 4 imposes an absolute duty and it is quite immaterial whether there is any evidence of negligence or failure to take reasonable care. Offence proved.

Levy v Hockey

(1961) 105 Sol Jo 157 (Nield J)
The plaintiff was knocked down and injured on an uncontrolled pedestrian crossing by a car driven by the defendant who overtook three other cars that were slowing down. The defendant pleaded that his failure to pull up in time was due to a latent defect in the braking system of his car, not discoverable by the exercise of reasonable care, so that the brakes failed to operate properly when he applied them.
HELD: In so far as the claim was based on a breach of the Pedestrian Crossings Regulations 1954, reg 4, the question arose of impossibility. If the Court were satisfied that, owing to a latent defect, a situation arose in which it was impossible for a driver to accord precedence to a foot passenger there would be no breach of the statutory duty so as to give rise to a right to damages. On the particular facts of this case, however, there was no latent defect.

Note—See note after *Gibbons v Kahl* (p 117, above). Regulation 4 of the 1954 Regulations has been replaced by reg 8 of the 1971 Regulations (p 116, above).

Neal v Bedford

[1966] 1 QB 505, [1965] 3 All ER 250, [1965] 3 WLR 1008, 129 JP 534, Div Ct
Two pedestrians began to walk across a pedestrian crossing. When they were about a third of the way across they stopped to allow a car coming from their right to pass over the crossing in front of them. The defendant was driving a car behind the one

which the pedestrians had allowed to pass and he began to follow it over the crossing. As he did so the pedestrians started to walk forward again and one was struck by his car on the crossing. A charge against him of failing to accord precedence to the pedestrians on the crossing was dismissed, the magistrates being of the opinion that the pedestrians had waived their precedence. The prosecutor appealed.
HELD: Regulation 4 imposed an absolute duty on motorists to accord precedence to pedestrians on an uncontrolled crossing. The justices had taken the view that the defendant was misled into thinking that the pedestrians had stopped to let him pass. Whether he genuinely thought they would let him pass was irrelevant. His absolute duty was to allow the pedestrians to cross. They had not waived their precedence by signalling him to pass; they had started walking. There must be a conviction.

Note—Regulation 4: see now reg 8 of the 1971 Regulations.

Burns v Bidder

[1967] 2 QB 227, [1966] 3 All ER 29, [1966] 3 WLR 99, 130 JP 342, 110 Sol Jo 430, Div Ct
The defendant was charged with failing to accord precedence to a pedestrian on a pedestrian crossing contrary to reg 4. When driving his car he had overtaken a bus which was waiting at a pedestrian crossing for people to cross, and had gone straight over the crossing without stopping, striking a pedestrian. He alleged that his brakes had failed, though a police officer testing them afterwards found nothing wrong. The magistrate said he was not satisfied the brakes had not failed but that the duty under the regulation was absolute and the defendant was guilty of the offence charged.
HELD, ON APPEAL: Regulation 4 does not impose an absolute duty come what may; there is no breach of the obligation under the regulation in circumstances where the driver fails to accord precedence to a pedestrian on the crossing solely because his control of the vehicle is taken from him by the occurrence of an event which is outside his possible or reasonable control and in respect of which he is in no way at fault. As Nield J said in *Levy v Hockey* (above) reg 4 must be read subject to the principle as to impossibility. Examples include a driver stung by a swarm of bees or suffering a sudden epileptic form of disabling attack, or a vehicle being knocked forward on to the crossing by another vehicle hitting it from behind, or a sudden removal of control occasioned by a latent defect of which the driver did not and could not reasonably know. But beyond that limited sphere the obligation of the driver can properly be described as absolute. *Gibbons v Kahl* (p 117, above), *Scott v Clint* (p 118, above), and *Hughes v Hall* (p 118, above) were all cases where the driver was in control of the vehicle as a driver and no special feature had occurred to take control of the vehicle out of his hands. *Leicester v Pearson* (p 116, above) had not been overruled but it remained a very special case. In the present case the magistrate was not satisfied the brakes had not failed and the conviction must be quashed.

Note—See note following previous case.

Moulder v Neville

[1974] RTR 53, Div Ct
The defendant was driving his car towards an uncontrolled (ie 'zebra') crossing and was within the area marked by the zig-zag lines when a pedestrian stepped on to the crossing. The defendant continued over the crossing, missing the pedestrian by a foot. On a charge of failing to give precedence he claimed that the area between the

zig-zag lines was part of the crossing and that when a vehicle was within the controlled area (ie between the zig-zag lines) no pedestrian should move on to the crossing.
HELD: This was a similar contention to that made under the 1954 Regulations in *Hughes v Hall* (above) and was wrong. The roadway between the zig-zag lines was not part of the crossing. If a pedestrian gets on to the striped area before the car gets on to the striped area the driver must give the pedestrian priority.

Crank v Brooks

[1980] RTR 441, QBD
A person who is walking across a pedestrian crossing pushing a bicycle having started on the pavement on one side on foot and pushing the bicycle with both feet on the ground is a 'foot passenger' within the meaning of the 'Zebra' Pedestrian Crossings Regulations 1971.

Negligence of pedestrians

Note—In view of the considerable changes in the Pedestrian Crossings Regulations since 1951 cases decided before that date are of little value. The following cases are a guide to present law and practice where the pedestrian plaintiff is guilty of negligence.

Regulation 4 of the 1954 Regulations referred to in the following cases has been replaced by reg 8 of the 1971 Regulations which is in similar terms (p 116, above).

Bassett v Victoria Wine Co

(1958) Times, 6 February, CA
A woman pedestrian aged 60 was crossing the road on a zebra pedestrian crossing. On her right was a parked car between the crossing and the line of studs, contrary to reg 6 [which was similar in effect to reg 9 of the 1971 Regulations, above. Whilst on the crossing she was struck by a van, the driver of which could not see the plaintiff because of the stationary car. She looked to the right before crossing and saw nothing. She was struck in the middle of the crossing. She claimed against the owners of the van, but no reliance was placed on reg 4. The claim was based on common law negligence and nothing more. The county court judge held the van driver was not negligent. The plaintiff appealed.
HELD: This was a matter of common law and the plaintiff must prove the defendants at fault. Drivers could not be expected to stop when they got to crossings if their view was obscured, but they must drive at a speed which took into consideration that a person might emerge from behind the stationary vehicle and that such person had precedence under the regulations. The county court judge found there was no evidence of excessive speed. It was a question of degree what was a proper speed in the circumstances and this was eminently a matter for the judge. Appeal dismissed.

Kozimor v Adey

(1962) 106 Sol Jo 431 (Megaw J)
The plaintiff, a woman of 40, ran on to an uncontrolled pedestrian crossing in front of the defendant's car. The car was travelling at about 25 mph and was about 15 yards away when the plaintiff began to cross. The defendant applied his brakes and swerved to the right but was unable to avoid hitting the plaintiff.

HELD: (1) The defendant was not guilty of any negligence from the point when the plaintiff ran on to the crossing. (2) Having collided with the plaintiff when she was crossing he was guilty of a breach of the Pedestrian Crossing Regulations 1954, reg 4. Under those regulations there was an absolute duty on a driver to drive at such a speed and keep such a look-out that he might be able to allow uninterrupted crossing to any pedestrian who set foot on the crossing intending to cross. He could only be certain of avoiding a breach by approaching the crossing at such a slow speed that he could stop in time to avoid any pedestrian however unexpected and however foolish. (3) His breach of the regulations was a cause of the plaintiff's injuries but another cause was the plaintiff's failure to take care for her own safety, and the Court had to consider how far, if at all, the breach was the cause of the injury. Because of the policy behind the regulations there was a measure of moral responsibility on the defendant because his duty was to anticipate and provide against even so unexpected an occurrence. The proportion of responsibility was 75% to the plaintiff and 25% to the defendant.

Lawrence v W M Palmer (Excavations) Ltd

(1965) 109 Sol Jo 358 (Phillimore J)
The plaintiff, aged 77 and deaf, was crossing the road on a pedestrian crossing when she was struck by the rear nearside of the defendant's lorry, which came from her right. She was found after the accident lying on the road 11 feet from the pavement she had left and eight or nine feet from the crossing.
HELD: Her injuries indicated a considerable impact from which one might have expected her to be thrown to some extent backwards in the direction she had come. The accident could not have happened in the way it had if the driver had been keeping a proper look-out since she must have been on the crossing before the lorry came on to it. Under the regulations she was entitled to precedence and accordingly there was an element of negligence and breach of statutory duty for which the defendants were liable. The plaintiff was guilty of some contributory negligence in failing to see the lorry and proceeding without regard to whether there was other traffic on the road. Defendants two-thirds to blame, plaintiff one-third.

Maynard v Rogers

[1970] RTR 392 (Mocatta J)
Shortly after midnight in a not-very-well-lit street the plaintiff, aged 19, stepped on to a pedestrian crossing without first looking to her right. She was hit by the defendant's car coming from her right. She was not far from the pavement she had left and the defendant had very little opportunity of avoiding the accident. The plaintiff must have been able to see his car if she had looked.
HELD: Although the major proportion of the blame must rest on the plaintiff it was possible that if the defendant had sounded his horn she might have been able to jump back. Moreover (following *Kozimor v Adey* (above)) there was a breach of statutory duty, namely, reg 4 of the 1954 Regulations, inasmuch as the plaintiff when struck was on an uncontrolled pedestrian crossing. Plaintiff two-thirds to blame, defendant one-third.

Jankovic v Howell

[1970] CLY 1863 (Ormerod J)
The plaintiff, crossing a road by a pedestrian crossing, walked over the central island without pausing and on to the other half of the crossing, where he was struck by the defendant's scooter.
HELD: It was superfluous to hoot or take evasive action every time a pedestrian approaches a refuge. Judgment for the defendant.

Clifford v Drymond

[1976] RTR 134, CA
Whilst walking across the road on a zebra crossing the plaintiff was struck by a car coming from her right. She was thrown or carried 45 feet and sustained serious injuries. She was 10 feet on to the crossing when hit. The judge found on the available evidence that the car, travelling not more than 30 mph had been about 75 feet away when the plaintiff began to cross. He considered whether the plaintiff was guilty of contributory negligence in stepping on to the crossing when the approaching car was within 75 feet to 80 feet and decided she was not.
HELD, ON APPEAL: The plaintiff should bear 20% of the blame. Rules 13 and 14 of the 1968 Highway Code require a pedestrian not only to allow vehicles plenty of time to slow down or stop before starting to cross but also to look right and left while crossing. If the plaintiff did not look at the approaching car she was negligent; if she did look she should have seen the car was near enough to make it doubtful whether it would pull up. She must also have been guilty of a measure of negligence in having failed to keep the car under observation as she proceeded to cross the road. If she had she would have seen it was not going to stop and could have allowed it to pass.

Note—For the Highway Code 1968, rr 13 and 14 see now the 1993 Code paras 11 and 12.

Push button controlled crossing

Note—The 'Pelican' Pedestrian Crossing Regulations and General Directions 1969, SI 1969/ 888, contain rules governing precedence at pedestrian crossings where a pedestrian may operate traffic lights by a push button control so as to require vehicular traffic to come to a stop. By reg 6(1)(c) a driver of a vehicle is prohibited from driving on to the crossing when a vehicular traffic light signal is showing a red light. By reg 6(1)(d) every foot passenger on the carriageway within the limits of the crossing has precedence over any vehicle whilst the vehicular traffic light is showing a flashing amber light. The effect is that a pedestrian has precedence during both the red and flashing amber periods of the vehicular traffic light signal.

The 'Pelican' Pedestrian Crossing Regulations and General Directions 1969 (and 1979) have been revoked and replaced by the 'Pelican' and Pedestrian Crossing Regulations and General Directions 1987, SI 1987/ 16.

Oakley-Moore v Robinson

[1982] RTR 74, Div Ct
The defendant's car ran out of petrol. He stopped it within the limits of a Pelican crossing and went away. He was convicted of leaving it within the approach limits of the crossing. On appeal he contended he had been 'prevented from proceeding by circumstances beyond his control' (the 'Pelican' Pedestrian Crossing Regulations, reg 9(2)).

HELD: Though a latent defect unknown to the driver could be a defence, as indicated in *R v Spurge* (p 214, below) and *Burns v Bidder* (p 119, above), the present case was not one of latent defect. The amount of petrol in a motor car is something which is at all times plainly within the control of the driver.

School crossings

Note—(Road Traffic Regulation Act 1984, ss 26, 27 and 28, replacing earlier enactments).

Operate between 8 am and 5.30 pm.

Patrol appointed by the authority (s 28) may require a vehicle to stop by exhibiting prescribed sign.

The School Crossing Patrol must be in uniform.

Signs prescribed by SI 1982/859.

Hoy v Smith

[1964] 3 All ER 670, [1964] 1 WLR 1377, 129 JP 33, 108 Sol Jo 841, 62 LGR 661, Div Ct
'Exhibiting' does not necessarily mean that the sign should be held full face to the oncoming traffic; it is sufficient if the sign is held in such a way that the driver can see the words 'Stop: children crossing' on the sign.

Toole v Sherbourne Pouffes Ltd

[1971] RTR 479, CA
The plaintiff, aged six, came out of school, which was beside a busy main road, and was taken by a teacher with other children to a pedestrian crossing. At the crossing was a school crossing patrol, an elderly man. He stood at the side of the road with the children, waiting until he could step forward with his sign board to stop the traffic. The first defendant's van was approaching. The driver saw the patrol waiting at the side of the crossing so he carried on to pass over the crossing at about 30 mph. Suddenly the plaintiff darted across the road on the crossing and was hit by the van. The judge held the first defendant's driver free from blame and held the second defendants, the school authority who employed the patrol, liable by reason of his negligence.
HELD: Dismissing the appeal, the patrol man had not done enough to keep the children under control. If he had been really exercising proper charge and keeping them back the plaintiff would not have made the sudden dart into the road. Moreover, the second defendants, on this most critical part of the case, had not called the patrol man to give evidence.

Franklin v Langdown

[1971] 3 All ER 662, 135 JP 615, 115 Sol Jo 688
When the crossing patrol is correctly displaying the 'Stop: children crossing' sign a motorist must stop and not move on again until the sign has been removed.

Wall v Walwyn

[1974] RTR 24, [1973] Crim LR 376.
An offence is committed if the driver fails to stop whether the children are impeded or not.

CHAPTER 3

Vicarious Liability

1 MASTER AND SERVANT

The doctrine of vicarious liability provides that an employer is liable for damage caused by the torts of any employee, whilst acting in the course of his employment.

WHO IS AN EMPLOYEE

Note—The more traditional nomenclature for the employer/employee relationship is that of master and servant. A servant is defined in *Salmond on Torts* as:

'Any person employed by another to do work for him on terms that he, the servant, is to be subject to the control and direction of his employer in respect of the manner in which his work is to be done.' (15th edn, p 647 and repeated in the 19th edn at p 511).

A person paid to do something may be a servant or an independent contractor. It is often stated that a servant is employed under a contract of services whereas an independent contractor is employed under a contract for services. There is no single test which can be applied. The degree of control is important but is only one of the factors to consider.

'The most that can be said is that control will no doubt always have to be considered, although it can no longer be regarded as a sole determining factor; and that factors which may be of importance are such matters as whether the man performing the services provides his own equipment, whether he hires his own helpers, what degree of financial risk he takes, what degree of responsibility for investment and management he has, and whether and how far he has an opportunity of profiting from sound management in the performance of his task': *Winfield on Tort* (19th edn) p 546 quoting *Marketing Investigations Ltd v Minister of Social Security* [1969] 2 QB 173, [1968] 3 All ER 732, [1969] 2 WLR 1, 112 Sol Jo 905.

Egginton v Reader

[1936] 1 All ER 7 (Lewis J)
A commercial traveller who owned a car worked for a company under an oral agreement subject to one week's notice. He received no salary but was paid £1 a week towards running expenses of the car and 6% commission on sales. He worked for no one except the company. He called on his own customers but he also sometimes called on firms whose names were given him by the manager of the company, although under no obligation to do so. When an accident occurred, he was on his way to see a customer and had in his car goods of the company to show those customers. He was at liberty to refuse to call on anyone if he did not wish and could travel when and where he liked, and need not work at all unless he chose.
HELD: The company were not liable for his negligence.

Ready Mixed Concrete Ltd v Minister of Pensions

[1968] 2 QB 497, [1968] 1 All ER 433, [1968] 2 WLR 775, 112 Sol Jo 14 (MacKenna J)
The owner of a lorry worked for the appellant company under a written contract which described him as an independent contractor. It required him to make his lorry available for the purpose of carrying concrete for the company, to maintain it in good order at his own expense and to hire a driver to drive it when he himself was not available to do so: he was to be paid per mile for the concrete he delivered.
HELD: A contract of service existed if three conditions were fulfilled (1) an agreement by the servant to provide his own work and skill to perform some service in consideration of remuneration; (2) agreement that in performance of the service he would be subject to control sufficiently to make the other the master, (3) the other provisions of the contract are consistent with a contract of service. In classifying the contract a judge might take into account other matters besides control. In the present case the driver had ownership of the assets, the chance of profit and the risk of loss. He had sufficient freedom in the performance of the obligations under the contract to qualify as independent contractor. He was a 'small businessman' not a servant.

Challinor v Taylor

[1972] ICR 129, 116 Sol Jo 141, 7 ITR 104
A taxi driver had an agreement with the owner of a taxi whereby he paid to the owner 65% of the fares registered on the clock plus the cost of an employee's national insurance stamp. The owner paid for fuel and maintenance. The driver kept the balance of the takings plus all the tips. He was assessed income tax under Sch D as a self-employed person. No memorandum of the terms of employment was supplied to him under the Contracts of Employment Act 1963. The owner never exercised any control over where or for how long the driver plied for hire. When the owner sold the cab the driver claimed a redundancy payment under the Redundancy Payments Act 1965 as an 'employee'.

HELD: He was not an employee. In deciding whether someone was an employee or an independent contractor many factors had to be taken into account of which actual control or the right to control the way in which the work was performed was only one. Whether the contract was one of service depended in the last resort on whether an ordinary person would so consider it in the light of his experience and knowledge.

Global Plant Ltd v Secretary of State for Health and Social Security

[1972] 1 QB 139, [1971] 3 All ER 385, [1971] 3 WLR 269, 115 Sol Jo 506 (Lord Widgery CJ)
For a period up to 1968 the appellants, a company which hired out earth-moving machines with drivers, employed Summers as a driver at a weekly wage and on terms which amounted to a contract of service. In that year he asked to be self-employed as a sub-contractor. Thereafter he stamped his own insurance card at the self-employed person's rate, paid his own income tax under Sch D and was paid at a much enhanced hourly rate, but without travelling expenses, sick pay or provision for holidays. He drove the company's machines as before on sites selected by them under the control of the site foreman or agent. He was not expressly under any duty to work at all but the intention was that he should work exactly as he had before. A determination was made by the Secretary of State for Social Services under the National Insurance Act 1965 that Summers was still a person employed under a contract of service.
HELD: There was no error in law in the Minister's decision.

Note—After commenting that 'the idea of the degree of control exercised by the employer over the servant being a decisive factor in this question has been very largely modified'. Lord Widgery quoted with approval a passage from Cooke J's judgment in *Market Investigations Ltd v Minister of Social Security* [1969] 2 QB 173, [1968] 3 All ER 732, [1969] 2 WLR 1, 112 Sol Jo 905: 'factors which may be of importance are such matters as whether the man performing the services provides his own equipment, whether he hires his own helpers, what degree of financial risk he takes, what degree of responsibility for investment or management he had and whether and how far he has an opportunity of profiting from sound management in the performance of his task'.

Roberts v Warne

[1973] RTR 217, Div Ct
Roberts, a hire-car driver, made an agreement with Davies, who ran a hire-car booking office, having the following elements: Roberts would drive Davies's car for the purpose of carrying passengers who booked in at Davies's Need-a-cab office. Roberts would be on call or attend at the office regularly at agreed times on every weekday except Fridays and Saturdays and would then drive a car as directed by Davies's office: Davies would ensure that Roberts was covered by Davies's own insurance: Roberts would be entitled to 50% of the takings from passengers whom he drove and would pay his own national insurance contributions and income tax.
HELD: The question whether Roberts was employed by Davies under a contract of service or not could be decided by asking: Whose business was it that was being carried on? What they had agreed was that Davies was to supply the car and booking facilities and Roberts was to do the work and they were to split the proceeds 50-50; the answer to the question was that it was the business of both of them. It was not a contract of service, it was a co-adventure.

Ferguson v Dawson

[1976] 1 Lloyd's Rep 143 (Boreham J)
The plaintiff was a building worker 'on the lump'. He was injured when working for the defendants who were building contractors. Both the plaintiff and the defendants regarded and named him as a 'self-employed labour only contractor'. The plaintiff paid his own national insurance stamp as a self-employed person and his wages were paid free of tax.
HELD: Where all the other indicia mentioned by MacKenna J in *Ready Mixed Concrete v Ministry of Pensions* (p 126, above) point to the relationship being that of master and servant then it was in reality a contract of service.

Massey v Crown Life Insurance Co Ltd

[1978] 2 All ER 576, [1978] 1 WLR 676, 121 Sol Jo 791, CA
From 1971 to 1973 the appellant worked as branch manager for the respondent insurance company which treated him as a servant, paying his wages and deducting tax. From 1973 onwards he carried on doing the same job but as an independent contractor under a new agreement at his own instance to enable him to be taxed under Sch D. Later he was dismissed and sought compensation for unfair dismissal.
HELD: He was not an employee and could not claim compensation. Where a perfectly genuine agreement had been entered into at his instance and for his benefit he could not afterwards claim the relationship was something other than what the agreement stated. *Ferguson*'s case (above) was different; there the contract was so unspecific that the way the parties had acted was the only thing to go by.

Young & Woods v West

[1980] IRLR 201, CA
West, a sheet metal worker, asked for his employers to treat him as self-employed. His salary was paid with no deductions and he received no holiday entitlement or sick pay, nor did the company disciplinary procedures apply to him. West's employment was terminated by the company and he applied for unfair dismissal compensation before an industrial tribunal. West succeeded in establishing that the tribunal had jurisdiction to hear his case as an employee. The company appealed this finding.
HELD: West was an employee as defined by statute and was not self-employed. His working conditions were exactly the same as those of his co-workers and who were subject to PAYE and the court stated that he could not be regarded as being in a business on his own account.

SCOPE OF EMPLOYMENT

Note—For the doctrine of vicarious liability to operate, any tort for which the employer will be responsible must be committed by the employee in the course of his employment. The court considers the facts of each case in determining this but one test is cited with approval in *Salmond on Torts* (15 edn) p 621:

'If the unauthorised and wrongful act . . . is not so connected with the authorised act as to be a mode of doing it, but is an independent act, the master is not responsible; for in such a case the servant is not acting in the course of his employment, but has gone outside of it'.

Employee driving on employer's business

Joel v Morison

(1834) 6 C & P 501
The plaintiff was knocked down and injured by the defendant's horse and cart driven by his servant when a considerable distance from its usual route.

Per Parke B: The master is only liable where the servant is acting in the course of his employment. If he was going out of his way against his master's implied commands when driving on his master's business he will make his master liable, but if he was going on a frolic on his own, without being at all on his master's business, the master will not be liable.

Verdict for the plaintiff.

Note—See also *Aitchison v Page Motors Ltd*, p 145, below.

Limpus v London General Omnibus Co Ltd

(1862) 1 H & C 526, 32 LJ Ex 34, 7 LT 641
Defendants' driver, in breach of his instructions not to hinder or obstruct other omnibuses, purposely pulled across the road to stop another omnibus passing.
HELD: A case of improper driving in the course of the employment and the master was liable.

Note—See also *Ilkiw v Samuels*, p 141, below.
And see *McKean*'s case, below.

Storey v Ashton

(1869) LR 4 QB 476, 10 B & S 337, LLQB 223 (Lush J)
Defendant, a wine merchant, sent his carman and clerk with a horse and cart to deliver some wine, and bring back some empty bottles; on their return, when about a quarter of a mile from defendant's offices, the carman, instead of performing his duty and driving to defendant's offices, depositing the bottles, and taking the horse and cart to the stable in the neighbourhood, was induced by the clerk, it being after business hours, to drive in quite another direction on business of the clerk's; and whilst they were thus driving, plaintiff was run over, owing to the negligence of the carman.
HELD: Defendant was not liable, for the carman was not doing the act, in doing which he had been guilty of negligence, in the course of his employment as servant. The question in all such cases as the present is whether the servant was doing that which the master employed him to do.

McKean v Raynor Bros Ltd (Nottingham)

[1942] 2 All ER 650, 167 LT 369, 86 Sol Jo 376
A servant who was a general utility hand was instructed by his employer to take and drive one of the employer's lorries and meet a convoy and deliver a message to them. Without permission from his employer, he used his father's private car and was involved in an accident. He had used a private car on other occasions on the employer's business, and had never been told not to use a private car for those purposes.

HELD: The workman was doing an authorised act in an unauthorised but not a prohibited way, and the employer was liable. Hilbery J cited *Bayley v Manchester Rly Co*:

'Where a servant is acting within the scope of his employment, and in so acting does something negligent or wrongful, the employer is liable even though the acts done may be the very reverse of that which the servant was actually directed to do.'

He also cited *Limpus v London General Omnibus Co* above:

'The law casts upon the master a liability for the act of the servant in the course of his employment; and the law is not so futile as to allow a master, by giving secret instructions to his servant, to discharge himself from liability.'

Note—Followed in *Harvey v O'Dell*, p 156, below.

A & W Hemphill v Williams

[1966] 2 Lloyd's Rep 101, HL
The defendants sent their lorry and driver to fetch a party of boys, of whom the plaintiff was one, from Benderlock in Argyll, where the boys had been camping, back home to Glasgow. Impliedly, the driver's orders were to return by the most direct route. Some of the boys asked him to return through Stirling which required a detour: the driver asked the adult in charge of the boys (who was not returning in the lorry) but was refused permission. On the journey some of the boys (but not the plaintiff) persuaded the driver to go to Stirling and then to Dollar before returning to Glasgow. An accident occurred on the way to Dollar in which the plaintiff was seriously injured. The boys' object in going via Stirling and Dollar was to see some Girl Guides who had been camping near to the boys and who were returning home to Dollar by train on the same day. The defendants denied they were vicariously liable for the driver's negligent driving on the ground that he was acting outside the scope of his employment.
HELD: It is a question of fact and degree in each case whether the deviation is sufficiently detached from the master's business to constitute a frolic of the servant unconnected with the enterprise for which he was employed. In *Storey v Ashton* (above) the continued presence in the cart of the master's empty wine bottles was not considered a compelling factor in deciding the question of degree as to how far the deviation could be held to absolve the master from vicarious responsibility: had the property in the cart been some more important or valuable or dominant cargo the result might well have been different. In the present case the presence of passengers whom the servant as such was charged to drive to their ultimate destination made it impossible (at all events, provided they were not all parties to the plans for deviation) to say that the deviation was entirely for the servant's own purposes. Their presence and transport was a dominant purpose of the authorised and, although they were transported deviously, continued to play an essential part. The defendants remained liable for the driver's negligence.

Note—The form of a plea in defence can be as follows:

'The driver was in the general employment of the defendants as a . . . but at the time of the occurrence complained of he was not driving for or on behalf of or with the authority of the defendants nor within the scope of his employment by them but was using the vehicle for his own purposes.'

General Engineering Services Ltd v Kingston and St Andrew Corpn

[1988] 3 All ER 867, [1989] 1 WLR 69, [1989] IRLR 35, 133 Sol Jo 20, PC
The plaintiff's premises were burning gently. The Fire Brigade were called; they were some three and a half minutes' drive away from the fire. Because of an industrial dispute the firemen were operating a 'go-slow' policy which entailed their stopping and starting so that the journey took them 17 minutes. As a result, the appellants' property was completely destroyed by fire instead of suffering slight damage. They brought an action against the local authority alleging liability for the behaviour of their employees.
HELD: The firemen were not acting in the course of their employment. The way in which they drove to the fire was not merely a wrongful mode of doing an authorised act but was so unconnected with their authorised task of driving to the emergency as quickly as possible that it did not amount to performing this task at all.

Smith v Stages

[1989] AC 928, [1989] 1 All ER 833
The first defendant and M, who were based in Staffordshire, were instructed by their employer to drive to Wales for a week's work. They were told to commence work on Tuesday, 23 August 1977 at 8 am. The men travelled down the preceding Monday and were given expenses equivalent to the return rail fare, together with a day's pay. No stipulations were made as to how they should travel and they went in the first defendant's car. The men then worked through the week until 8.30 am on the following Monday morning. The men were paid for sleeping and travel time on their return journey.

They had to report back for work to Staffordshire on the Wednesday morning and they set off on the Monday in the first defendant's car. An accident occurred and M suffered serious injuries. M subsequently died from connected causes. His widow claimed damages against the employers of the driver. At first instance the judge found that the defendant was not acting in the course of his employment when driving and dismissed the widow's claim. She appealed.
HELD: An employee paid by his employer to travel to a workplace different from his usual one to carry out a job, who was also paid wages for the return journey was acting in the course of his employment. It did not matter that the defendant in this case could decide the mode and time of travel. The defendant was acting in the course of his employment when driving the deceased to Pembroke and back. The driver's employers were vicariously liable for his negligence.

Employee acting within course of employment

Aldred v Nacanco

[1987] IRLR 292, CA
The plaintiff was standing in the wash room at work with her back very close to a slightly unstable wash–basin. A fellow employee entered the room and, to startle the plaintiff, pushed the wash–basin. The rim struck the upper part of one of the plaintiff's thighs, without causing any bruising, but the plaintiff turned round quickly to see what had happened and in some way twisted her back causing injury. The plaintiff alleged that the defendants were vicariously liable for the action of the fellow employee. Her claim was dismissed and she appealed.

HELD: The plaintiff's claim failed: the act of the fellow employee was a deliberate act which had nothing whatsoever to do with anything she was employed to do. Her employers were not vicariously liable for her behaviour.

Irving & Irving v Post Office

[1987] IRLR 289, CA
E was employed by the Post Office as a mail sorter. Whilst sorting mail he came across an envelope addressed to the plaintiffs who were his neighbours and were of Jamaican origin. E did not like them and wrote an offensive racist remark on the envelope. The plaintiffs brought an action against the Post Office under the Race Relations Act seeking a declaration, injunction and damages. The case was dismissed in the county court on the basis that E was not acting in the course of his employment when he wrote the abusive remark. The plaintiffs appealed.
HELD: An employer's vicarious liability for the unauthorised acts of employees depends on whether the act was merely unauthorised or whether it was entirely outside the scope of the employment. On the facts E's actions could not be seen as a prohibited mode of carrying out his obligations. The writing of the racist comments formed no part of the performance of E's duties even though his employment provided the opportunity to do them. The appeal was dismissed.

Fellow employee driving

Beard v London General Omnibus Co

[1900] 2 QB 530, 69 LJQB 895, 83 LT 362, 16 LTR 499, CA
At the end of a journey, the conductor of an omnibus belonging to defendants, in the absence of the driver, and apparently for the purpose of turning the omnibus in the right direction of the next journey, drove it through some by-streets at a considerable pace, and while so doing negligently ran into and injured plaintiff. Plaintiff gave no evidence that the conductor was authorised by the defendants to drive the omnibus in the absence of the driver.
HELD: Plaintiff had not discharged himself from the burden cast upon him of showing that the injury was due to the negligence of a servant of defendants acting within the scope of his employment, and defendants were entitled to judgment.

Note—If the conductor had merely been turning the vehicle round at the terminus in preparation for the next journey in the circumstances of the driver's absence it is doubtful whether the decision, at least in these days, would have gone the same way: Per Sellers LJ in *Kay v ITW Ltd*, p 137, below.

See also *Ricketts v Tilling*, p 141, below.

Driver going for food

Higbid v R C Hammett Ltd

(1932) 49 TLR 104, CA
Delivery boy employed by firm of butchers used employers' cycle with their permission to ride home to his dinner and negligently rode into plaintiff.
HELD: Under Shop Acts employers had no power to say how servant should use his dinner hour. Servant was using cycle for his own purposes and not doing something

in the course of employers' business and (reversing judgment of Roche J and a common jury) employers were not liable.

Crook v Derbyshire Stone Ltd

[1956] 2 All ER 447, [1956] 1 WLR 432, 100 Sol Jo 302 (Pilcher J)
The driver of a motor lorry on a journey stopped shortly before 8 am and crossed the road to a cafe on the other side. A motor cyclist collided with him and both were injured. The practice of drivers stopping at wayside cafes to obtain refreshment was well known to the driver's employers and impliedly sanctioned by them.
HELD: The driver was not employed on the employer's business. When he left the lorry he had no further duty to perform on his employer's account until he returned to the lorry and resumed his journey. The employers were not liable for his negligence.
Century Insurance Co case distinguished.

Note—This case was distinguished in the case of *Staton v National Coal Board* (below). See also *British Transport Commission v Maxine & Co Ltd*, p 143, below.

Hilton v Thomas Burton Ltd

[1961] 1 All ER 74, [1961] 1 WLR 705, 105 Sol Jo 322 (Diplock J)
The plaintiff's husband was killed when riding in a lorry driven by the second defendant who was an employee of the first defendants, the owners of the lorry. The accident was caused by the negligent driving of the second defendant. The plaintiff's husband was a foreman in charge of a gang of men engaged on demolition some miles from the employer's premises. After working for some time, four of the men including the plaintiff's husband and the second defendant decided to go in the lorry to a cafe seven miles away to have some tea. Before arriving there they decided there was not enough time as they had to pick up some other men who were still working at the site. They turned round and were on the return journey when the accident happened. A director of the first defendants gave evidence that he permitted the employees to use the lorry for any reasonable purpose including going to get refreshment: the second defendant was an authorised driver.
HELD: Following *Higbid v R C Hammett Ltd* (above), the second defendant was not at the time of the accident doing something he was employed to do. He, the plaintiff's husband and the other men in the lorry were out on a frolic of their own and the first defendants were not vicariously liable for his negligent driving.

Elleanor v Cavendish Woodhouse Ltd and Comerford

[1973] 1 Lloyd's Rep 313, CA
The second defendant was a salesman employed by the first defendants. He worked ordinary business hours in his employers' shop in Darlington but was also required to do some canvassing during evenings within the radius of thirty miles, using his own car. Sometimes he went with another salesman, a practice known to their employers which led to better results. One evening he took another salesman Smith on canvassing some distance from Darlington. The canvassing finished by 8 pm and they then called at one or more public houses for food and drink. On the way home there was an accident at about 9.30 pm caused by the second defendant's negligence.
HELD: The employers were vicariously liable. On the evidence the second defendant was under a duty as an employee to bring his fellow-salesman back to Darlington and was therefore doing something which he was employed to do.

Employees injured on employers' premises outside working hours

British Transport Commission v Ministry of Supply

(1951) R 1007, Nottingham Summer Assizes, 25 June 1956
The driver of a railway locomotive at the defendant's depot drove his engine to the canteen in his lunch hour. On the way he negligently ran into and damaged the plaintiff's lorry.
HELD: He was acting within the scope of his employment. He had a meal break and had to have a meal at the canteen built for that purpose. He was doing what he was employed to do - driving a locomotive. *Higbid*'s case (p 132, above) distinguished. In that case the servant had left work and gone home: Per Finnemore J.

Note—The case is not reported but is mentioned in *The Times* and other papers of 26 June 1956.

Staton v National Coal Board

[1957] 2 All ER 667, [1957] 1 WLR 893, 101 Sol Jo 592 (Finnemore J)
A workman was in regular employ of a colliery as a first-aid man. He was on night shift from 10.30 pm to 8 am. Friday afternoon between 1 pm and 5 pm was the proper time for the men employed at the colliery to collect their week's wages. On Friday he finished his shift at 8.30 am. In the afternoon he proceeded to the colliery for his wages. He called at the Time Office in the colliery premises and then proceeded on his cycle to the General Office where the pay office was situated. On the left-hand side of the road was a bus park where some buses were parked waiting to take home the miners who had finished the day shift. The workman left the road to proceed across the bus park and decided to ride through the space between the second and third buses.

A miner employed by the colliery who had finished his work on the day shift, was seated in one of the buses, when he suddenly remembered something which required him to go back across the road to one of the offices. He came round the front of the bus and was knocked down in collision with the cycle, and sustained injuries from which he died.
HELD: The accident arose in the course of the employment of the first-aid man rendering his employers liable to the defendants of the injured man. He had finished his manual work and was riding his cycle across the employers' premises to collect the wages the employers had contracted to pay him and was still in the course of his employment. There had been nothing to break the course of his employment. It was in the interests of the employer as well as the employee that a workman should receive his wages and receive them at a convenient place and at a convenient time. He was not on the Queen's highway on his way to his place of employment to get his wages but was actually on his employers' premises going to the place which the employers had said was the place to which he was required to come in order to draw his wages. The case of *Crook v Derbyshire Stone Ltd* (p 133, above) was quite different on the facts.
SEMBLE: If a workman was off the employers' premises, eg on the Queen's highway on his way to his place of employment, he would not be in the course of his employment.

Note—See also *British Transport Commission v Maxine & Co Ltd*, p 143, below.

PROHIBITED ACTS

Note—There may be situations where the employer has given instructions which prohibit certain acts. Whether such an instruction prevents an action from being within the scope of employment depends on whether the employer's instructions prohibit a particular way of carrying out the task or restricts the class of acts which the employee has to perform.

Prohibited acts within scope of employment

Canadian Pacific Rly Co v Lockhart

[1942] AC 591, [1942] 2 All ER 464, PC
The plaintiff was a child who was knocked down by a car driven by one of the defendants' employees. The defendants were a railway company and the employee was a handyman who used to do various repair jobs at different railway stations. On the day of the accident he was required by his employers to take a newly-made key to a station a few miles away and see if it would fit the lock it was made for. He could have travelled by rail, and was expected to do so, but instead he chose to go in his own car. The employers did not object to employees using their own cars, but had twice issued a firm instruction that they must not use a car if it was not covered by third-party insurance. On this occasion the employee's car was not covered by third-party insurance.

HELD: The employers were liable. The principles were set out in *Salmond on Torts*: A master, as opposed to the employer of an independent contractor, is liable even for acts which he has not authorised provided they are so connected with acts which he has authorised that they may rightly be regarded as modes—although improper modes—of doing them. In other words, a master is responsible not merely for what he authorises his servant to do, but also for the way in which he does it. On the other hand, if the unauthorised and wrongful act of the servant is not so connected with the authorised act as to be a mode of doing it, but is an independent act, the master is not responsible; for in such a case the servant is not acting in the course of his employment but has gone outside it.

The first consideration is the ascertainment of what the servant was employed to do. The existence of prohibitions may, or may not, be evidence of the limits of the employment. If the prohibition had absolutely forbidden the servant to drive his motor car in the course of his employment it might well have been maintained that he was employed to do carpentry work and not to drive a motor car, and that, therefore, the driving of a motor car was outside the scope of his employment, but it was not the acting as driver that was prohibited but the non-insurance of the motor car, if used as a means incidental to the execution of the work which he was employed to do. It follows that the prohibition merely limited the way in which, or by means of which, the servant was to execute the work which he was employed to do, and that breach of the prohibition did not exclude the liability of the master to third parties.

Note—The above quotation from *Salmond on Torts* was adopted by the Court of Appeal in the following case:

London County Council v Cattermoles (Garages) Ltd

[1953] 2 All ER 582, [1953] 1 WLR 997, 97 Sol Jo 505, CA
At a garage a workman was employed as a general garage hand, including moving

cars by pushing them or giving guidance to the drivers, eg when reversing. He was not competent to drive, had no licence, and had been forbidden to do so. A van was stationary at the petrol pumps and he moved the van to enable two lorries to obtain petrol. He got into the van, started the engine, drove the van and went on to the highway. He had not intended to go on the highway, but to keep inside the garage, but did so intending to return behind the lorries. On the highway he collided with the plaintiff's van.
HELD: The terms of the employment were not precise. The prohibition about driving was not a limitation of the scope of the employment but a subsequent prohibition when the employers discovered he had no qualification for driving and his employment could not be limited to pushing cars by hand and not by other means including driving them. The use of the van's own engine to do shunting was not something independent of the job of shunting but was an unauthorised or prohibited means of doing an authorised job. The fact that the workman did not intend to go on to the highway but this was accidental did not alter the result even though the servant was doing something unlawful, having no licence. The job was not something quite different in its nature and character from the driving of motor cars. The employers were liable.

Mulholland v William Reid and Leys

1958 SC 290, 1958 SLT 285 (Ct of Sess, Inner House)
An apprentice working with a journeyman, both in the employ of the defenders, offered to move a van which was in the way. He had never driven a vehicle before and had no authority to do so, but the journeyman made no objection. He started up the van and fatally injured the husband of the pursuer.
HELD: He was acting within the scope of his employment and his employers were liable. *London County Council v Cattermoles (Garages) Ltd* followed.

Spencer v Curtis Bros

(1962) 106 Sol Jo 390, CA
The plaintiff, a farmer, was helping the defendant, who was a neighbour of his, to harvest grain on the defendant's farm. The plaintiff was driving his own combine harvester on which the defendant's employee H was riding for the purpose of filling bags with grain: this was part of the operation of using the harvester. H had been shooting earlier in the day and had his gun with him. The defendant realising the danger of carrying the gun on the machine, told H not to do so: in disobedience of this order H had nevertheless put his gun on the floor of the machine. As the plaintiff was driving the machine the gun went off and he was seriously injured. Negligence on the part of H was admitted. It was contended for the defendant that the taking of the gun on the machine was not an act in the scope of H's employment but was something entirely independent.
HELD: In taking the gun on the machine H had added an additional danger to the risks of the work and the defendant was liable. It had been said that *Jefferson v Derbyshire Farmers Ltd* (below) and *Century Insurance Co Ltd v Northern Ireland Road Transport Board* (p 129, below) were distinguishable because the act which caused the damage in those cases was one which could be done while the proper work was being carried on, but there was no real distinction. The true test was defined by Lord McNaghten in *Lloyd v Grace Smith & Co* [1912] AC 716, when he said that the words 'scope of employment . . . must be used liberally'.

Note—And see *Harvey v O'Dell*, p 156, below.

Kay v ITW Ltd

[1968] 1 QB 140, [1967] 3 All ER 22, [1967] 3 WLR 695, 111 Sol Jo 351, CA
The defendants employed a man named Ord to drive small trucks inside their works. A large diesel lorry belonging to another company came to the works for loading and was parked on a ramp with its back facing the closed doors of a warehouse. The plaintiff (a storeman in the defendants' employment) and the lorry driver were loading the lorry. Ord came to the ramp with a fork lift truck to take it into the warehouse where it was normally kept. Without asking or even looking for the driver he got into the cab of the lorry and turned the key to start the engine: his intention was to move the lorry so that he could drive the fork lift into the warehouse. The lorry had been left in reverse gear and at once started backwards pinning the plaintiff against the warehouse doors. The defendants' case was that Ord was acting outside the scope of his employment in trying to move the lorry: they conceded that he was entitled to move light or small obstructions.
HELD: Ord was acting in the scope of his employment and the defendants were liable. Though his entering the cab and starting the engine was foolhardy and unnecessary the question was whether, as in *Lockhart v CPR* it was a mode, though an improper one, of doing the work he was employed to do. It was not conclusive that what he was doing was in the employers' interest or was done during working hours. It was a border-line case but he was trying to move the lorry so as to take the fork lift truck into the warehouse and his conduct was not so gross or extreme as to take the act outside what he was employed to do.

Note—See also *East v Beavis Transport*, p 142, below and *Harrison v Michelin Tyre Co Ltd* [1985] 1 All ER 918.

Iqbal v London Transport Executive

(1973) 16 KIR 329, CA
The plaintiff, a bus driver employed by the defendants, found he could not get his bus out of the garage to begin work until the bus behind it had been moved. He asked the conductor, Carberry, to get someone from the engineering department to move the other bus. Instead, Carberry, who had never driven a bus before, tried to move it himself. He started it and it crushed the plaintiff, who was standing between it and his own bus. There was a clear instruction, adequately published, 'In no circumstances is a conductor allowed to drive a bus'.
HELD: The defendants were not vicariously liable for Carberry's negligence. It was not a case within the principle set out in *Salmond on Torts* (quoted in *Canadian Pacific Rly v Lockhart* (above)) of his having improperly done what he was authorised to do. The defendants' prohibition did not merely deal with conduct within the sphere of employment; it was a prohibition which limited the sphere of his employment.

Compton v McClure

[1975] ICR 378 (May J)
The first defendant was employed at the second defendants' factory. On arriving at work and in attempting to clock on in time he drove too fast and on the wrong side of the factory road to the car park and knocked the plaintiff down. The second defendants had imposed a speed limit and the first defendant had been warned several times for speeding.
HELD: (1) The accident was caused by the first defendant's negligent driving; (2) the second defendants had not been negligent as they had taken reasonable precautions

to protect persons using the roadway; (3) the second defendants were vicariously liable for the first defendant's negligent driving because he was acting in the course of his employment in entering the factory gates to clock on for the purposes of his employers' business.

Coult v Szuba

[1982] ICR 380, [1982] RTR 376, QBD, Div Ct
While driving his car from the clocking on point to his place of work two miles away the defendant had an accident on a private road. It was alleged for the purpose of a prosecution under the Health and Safety at Work etc Act 1974 that he was 'in the course of his employment'.
HELD: The phrase was not easily defined. The precise meaning of the words had to be extracted by looking at the facts in each case in the context of the legislation. It was not a matter of law that once the defendant had clocked on his course of employment must have started. The finding of the justices that he was not in the course of his employment could not be said to be wrong in principle.

Harrison v Michelin Tyre Co Ltd

[1985] 1 All ER 918, [1985] ICR 696, QBD
The defendants' employee Smith, pushing a hand truck along a passageway at their premises, turned the truck a couple of inches and pushed the edge under a duckboard on which the plaintiff was standing, tipping it up and causing the plaintiff injury. Smith was pushing the truck along the passageway as part of his job but admitted in evidence that pushing the edge under the duckboard was done purely as a joke.
HELD: The defendants were vicariously liable for his act. The movement by Smith from the passageway, a quick turn right of about 2 inches at most, was done in the course of his employment.

Prohibited acts outside scope of employment—giving lifts

Wright v International Tea Co

(27 October 1943, unreported) (Croom-Johnson J)
The driver of a trade vehicle which had no provision for passengers in the ordinary sense gave a lift to a pedestrian, who sat on a sort of continuation of the driver's seat. The driver had been warned on two occasions by his employers that he must not take up passengers, and on one occasion that it would cause some difficulty about the insurance policy.
HELD: The driver's act was in defiance and disobedience of a precise prohibition. The scope of the authority must be measured by reference to the ordinary duties of such a man. He had no authority from his employers nor had he been held out by anybody as having authority to pick up passengers, and no such authority was to be implied. The plaintiff ought to have known she had no authority to get into the van and must take the consequences of her own neglect. The case was one of a prohibition which limited the sphere of employment and not a prohibition of conduct within the sphere of employment. In his judgment the judge referred to the two following cases.

Houghton v Pilkington

[1912] 3 KB 308, 82 LJKB 79, 107 LT 235, 28 TLR 492, 56 Sol Jo 633
Plaintiff at the request of a servant of defendant, got into defendant's cart, which was then in charge of the servant, in order to render assistance to another servant of defendant who had been rendered unconscious by an accident. Plaintiff fell out of the cart and was injured through the negligence of the servant in charge of the cart causing the horse to start.
HELD: The existence of the emergency gave no implied authority to the servant to invite the plaintiff into the cart and defendant was not liable.

Lygo v Newbold

(1854) 9 Exch 302, 23 LJ Ex 108
Plaintiff, a person of full age, contracted with defendant to carry certain goods for her in his cart. Defendant sent his servant with the cart, and plaintiff, by the permission of the servant, without defendant's authority, rode in the cart with her goods. The cart broke down and plaintiff was injured.
HELD: The defendant had not contracted to carry the plaintiff, and as she had ridden in the cart without his authority, he was not liable. The plaintiff had no business to get up into the cart without defendant's permission.

Twine v Beans's Express Ltd

(1946) 175 LT 131, 62 TLR 458, CA
Defendants provided a motor van and driver for a bank on terms that they accepted no liability for passengers other than employees of the defendants. The driver was forbidden to take any such passengers and a notice was on the dashboard of the van. The driver took a passenger, an employee of the bank, first informing him it was at his own risk.
HELD: Defendants were not liable; they owed no duty to the passenger: it was outside the scope of the driver's employment to extend the liability of the defendants to the passenger who was a trespasser: Per Uthwatt J ([1946] 1 All ER 202, 174 LT 239).
ON APPEAL: Only limited classes of persons were entitled to be carried on this van and it was clear that the deceased was not one of those persons. The driver, in giving the lift to T, was clearly not acting within the scope of his employment and his employers were consequently not liable.

Note—See also *Baker v Provident Accident* [1939] 2 All ER 690, 64 Ll L Rep 14, 83 Sol Jo 565.

Conway v George Wimpey & Co

[1951] 2 KB 266, [1951] 1 All ER 363, 95 Sol Jo 156, [1951] 1 TLR 587, CA
Defendants were the main contractors for the building of an aerodrome and provided motor lorries to convey their workmen to their place of work. In the cab was a notice as follows: 'The driver of this vehicle has strict orders to carry no passengers other than employees of G. Wimpey & Co Ltd during the course of and in connection with their employment. Any other person travelling on this vehicle does so at his own risk.' The driver had also received express instructions to carry defendants' men only.

A workman of another contractor on the same site hailed the lorry and was permitted by the driver to ride on it, and was injured by the driver's negligence. It was not unusual for men not employed by defendants to get lifts on defendants' lorries but it was not established that the drivers in general knowingly carried men other than defendants' servants, or that the driver in this case knew that the plaintiff was not in the defendants' employ. The defendants themselves were not aware of such use by other men.

HELD: The fact that in *Twine*'s case (above) the plaintiff was informed by the driver that he had no right to travel on the van was immaterial. The argument that the plaintiff could not be a trespasser unless he knew he was one was unfounded in law. It is elementary that if A, professedly acting on behalf of B, purports to give leave to enter on B's land, and A has no actual authority to do so, the person receiving permission who acts on the permission is a trespasser, and none the less so because he does not know of A's want of authority. To establish an apparent authority binding on the driver's employers the plaintiff must show, (1) knowledge of the defendants of a practice by their drivers of disregarding the prohibition; (2) acquiescence by the defendants in the practice, (3) acquiescence in such a manner as to represent to the plaintiff that the driver's authority was not limited to carrying the defendants' men. There was no evidence to establish the first proposition, apart from the others. The fact that four of the defendants' workmen gave evidence that they knew of the practice did not impute knowledge to the defendants; nor that a practice of this kind must inevitably grow up. There was clear evidence that they did not know. The plaintiff never ceased to be a trespasser.

On the contention that the driver's act was within the scope of his employment, it was pointed out by Uthwatt J in *Twine*'s case that the driver's act was outside the scope of his employment. Taking men other than the defendants' employees on the vehicle was not merely a wrongful mode of performing an act of the class which the driver was employed to perform, but was the performance of an act of a class which he was not employed to perform at all. The act was outside the scope of the employment for the same reason as in *Twine*'s case. The case of *Limpus v London General Omnibus Co* did not apply. The case of *Hay (or Bowhill) v Young* (p 6, above) mentioned by the trial judge had nothing to do with the responsibility of employers for the acts of their servants. Appeal dismissed.

Rose v Plenty

[1976] 1 All ER 97, [1975] 1 WLR 141, 119 Sol Jo 592, CA

The second defendant employed the first defendant as a milkman. Notices at the depot made it clear that roundsmen were not allowed to take children on vehicles. Despite this the first defendant took the plaintiff, a boy of 13, on his milk float, paying him a few shillings for help in delivering milk. Whilst being carried on the vehicle the plaintiff was injured by the first defendant's negligence.

HELD, ON APPEAL (Lawton LJ diss): There was vicarious liability on the second defendant. The prohibited act, namely taking the boy on the float to help him deliver milk was done by the milkman in the course of his service and for the employer's purposes. *Twine v Beans's Express* and *Conway v Wimpey* (above) were cases where a driver had given a lift to someone else contrary to a prohibition and not for the purposes of the employers. The prohibition on the milkman against employing boys to help him was not one which defined or limited his sphere of employment, which was to go round the rounds delivering milk. This distinguished it from such cases as *Iqbal v London Transport* (p 137, above).

Unauthorised person driving

Ricketts v Tilling

[1915] 1 KB 644, 84 LJKB 342, 112 LT 137, 31 TLR 17, CA
At the end of a journey the conductor of an omnibus belonging to the defendant, in the presence of the driver, who was seated beside him, for the purpose of turning the omnibus in the right direction for the next journey, drove it through some by-streets so negligently that it mounted the foot-pavement and knocked down and seriously injured plaintiff, who was standing there. At the trial the judge upon the authority of *Beard v London General Omnibus Co* (p 132, above) held there was no evidence that the conductor had any authority from defendants to drive the omnibus and entered judgment for defendants.
HELD: There was evidence of negligence on the part of the driver in allowing the omnibus to be negligently driven by the conductor and there must therefore be a new trial.

Ilkiw v Samuels

[1963] 2 All ER 879, [1963] 1 WLR 991, 107 Sol Jo 680, CA
The defendants' lorry was driven to the premises of the plaintiff's employers to load bags of sugar. The defendants' driver Waines put the lorry under a conveyor and then stood in the back of the lorry to load bags from the conveyor. When sufficiently loaded the lorry had to be moved. Samuels, a fellow employee of the plaintiff's and not employed by the defendants, offered to move it. Waines allowed him to do so without asking whether he could drive. In fact Samuels could not drive and after starting the lorry could not stop it. It crushed the plaintiff, who was working nearby, against another conveyor causing him serious injury. Waines remained in the back of the lorry throughout. He had been expressly forbidden by his employers to let anyone other than himself drive the lorry.
HELD: (1) Waines was negligent in allowing Samuels to drive without inquiring whether he was competent: the defendants were vicariously liable for his negligence because it was a mode, though an improper mode, of performing the duties on which he was employed namely, to have charge and control of the lorry. It was therefore a negligent act within the scope of his employment.

Per Willmer LJ: Waines was employed not only to drive but also to be in charge of his vehicle in all circumstances during any such times as he was on duty. That means to say that, even when he was not himself sitting at the controls, he remained in charge of the lorry and in charge as his employers' representative. His employers must remain liable for his negligence so long as the vehicle was being used in the course of their business. As I understand the authorities, the employers escape liability if, but only if, at the time of the negligent act, the vehicle was being used by the driver for the purpose of what had been called a 'frolic' of his own. That is not this case. Here, at the material time, this vehicle was in fact being used in the course of the defendants' business. In those circumstances it appears to me that there is no ground on which the defendants can escape liability for Waines' negligence.

(2) Even if Samuels had been a competent driver but negligent on that occasion, Waines would still have been negligent for the reason given in *Ricketts v Tilling* (above) that it was his duty to prevent another person from driving, or, if he allowed another person to drive, to see that he drove properly. This also was negligence within the scope of his employment.

(3) Per Diplock LJ: It was not necessarily negligent of Waines to allow Samuels to drive; even if it were, the employers would not be vicariously liable since the selection of a person to drive was not part of Waines's duties—indeed he was forbidden to let anyone else drive. But the employers were liable to the plaintiff on the broader ground that the lorry was being driven negligently while being used for the purposes of the defendants' business under the control of their servant Waines, he being employed to take charge and control of the vehicle while engaged on the task being performed when the accident took place. Liability would be the same even if Samuels had been a highly experienced driver, provided his negligent driving on this occasion was the cause of the plaintiff's injuries.

(4) The fact that the defendants had expressly forbidden Waines to let anyone else drive was immaterial since it was no more than a direction as to the mode in which the servant was to perform the duty. *Limpus v LGOC* (p 129, above) followed.

East v Beavis Transport Ltd

[1969] 1 Lloyd's Rep 302, CA

Two lorries stood back to back at Boston docks being loaded with produce by dockers and others. It was required to move one of them, owned by Beavis, to let the tailboard down. Beavis's driver Rose gave permission to Sellars, a docker employed by Andersons, to move it. Sellars reversed into the other lorry, squashing the plaintiff against it and injuring him.

HELD: Rose was negligent because he was in charge of the lorry and even if it was in order for a docker to move the lorry he should have directed him. He was responsible for the movements of the lorry and Beavis were vicariously liable. Sellars was equally negligent because he could not see properly when reversing and made no arrangement with Rose to direct him. His employers Andersons were vicariously liable for his negligence because although they did not employ him to drive lorries his act had a close connection with what he was employed to do, namely, the loading of lorries (following *Kay v ITW Ltd*, p 137, above).

Lifts given to licensee

Young v Edward Box & Co

[1951] 1 TLR 789, CA

The plaintiff was employed by the defendants in unloading at a quarry. It was the plaintiff's business to make his own way to the place of work. It was necessary to work on Sundays and it was difficult for the plaintiff and other workmen to get to and from the place on a Sunday. The defendants' foreman arranged for a lorry of the defendants, driven by the defendants' driver, to pick up workmen to take to work and take them home from work, and this took place for some seven or eight Sundays before the accident. The place where the plaintiff was picked up was on the lorry's normal route. On a Sunday the plaintiff whilst a passenger on the lorry was injured by the negligence of the lorry driver. Defendants' traffic manager denied that he had given any instructions for men to be carried, and the foreman had no authority to do so.

HELD (per Somervell and Singleton LJJ): The plaintiff was a licensee on the lorry and not a trespasser; he was there by permission of the foreman and this was plainly within the ostensible authority of the foreman.

Per Denning LJ: The foreman had no authority to let the men travel on the lorry and the men were therefore trespassers so far as the employers were concerned; but the defendants were liable because the driver was acting in the course of his employment in giving the plaintiff a lift. It would not have been in the course of his employment to give a lift to a hitch-hiker, but it was to give a lift to the men on the job.

Defendants held liable to the plaintiff caused by negligence of the driver.

Miller v Liverpool Co-operative Society Ltd

[1940] 4 All ER 367 (Stable J); affd [1941] 1 All ER 379n
Plaintiff had been in the habit of waking up a driver who in return gave him a lift to his place of work. The owner knew this, had seen him on a number of occasions, had not taken the slightest exception and had acquiesced in what had become an established practice. The owner had not given express permission. The passenger was not a trespasser but a licensee; the driver was on the owner's business and the owner was liable.

Smoking at work

British Transport Commission v Maxine & Co Ltd

(1963) 107 Sol Jo 1024 (McNair J)
Premises held by the defendants on licence from the plaintiffs were damaged by fire caused by the defendants' workman who had carelessly thrown down a lighted match. The incident occurred on a Friday, the day on which the workman received his pay. He had been given notice in the previous week and his employment was to end on that Friday. He finished his day's work by 4.30 pm and his pay would not be ready for collection until 4.45. While waiting he went to another part of the premises to say goodbye to friends. It was during this call that he threw away the lighted match. The plaintiffs claimed that the defendants' were vicariously liable for his negligence.
HELD: He was not acting in the scope of his employment when he threw away the match. The test was whether the negligence arose in the course of work being done for the employer or was incidental to it. Although the workman here was entitled to go to the warehouse to see his friends and although he had to wait for his pay packet it was unrealistic to say that he was then performing any work for his employers or doing any act incidental to it. *Staton*'s case (p 134, above) was distinguishable on the basis that there the workman and the employers had an interest in the workman receiving his wages.

Note—See also *Century Insurance Co v Northern Ireland Road Transport Board*, p 229, below.

Jefferson v Derbyshire Farmers Ltd

[1921] 2 KB 281, 90 LJKB 1361, 125 LT 775, CA
The owner of a motor garage leased it to a firm of motor engineers, who agreed with defendants to give them the use of it as a garage for motor lorries. A youth employed by defendants in the garage, while drawing motor spirit from a drum into a tin, struck a match, lit a cigarette and then threw the match on the floor. This set light to some oil and petrol lying about the floor; the fire spread to the motor spirit flowing from the drum and the garage and its contents were consumed. An action was brought by

the owner and the lessees of the garage against the defendants for the negligence of their servant.

HELD: The servant being engaged in an act which was within the scope of his employment and required special caution, and having failed to exercise caution, was guilty of negligence in the course of his employment and defendants were liable for the resulting damage.

Note—In *Williams v Jones* (1865) 3 H & C 602 the defendant's carpenter while working in plaintiff's shed lighted a pipe from a match with a shaving which he accidentally dropped and the shed was burned down. It was there held that the negligent act was not within the scope of his employment. This case is now overruled by *Jefferson*'s case.

UNLAWFUL ACTS OF EMPLOYEES

Note—It was thought an employer could not be vicariously liable for the theft by an employee. However, there are circumstances in which a theft may be deemed to be committed by an employee in the course of his employment, for example where that employee has been entrusted with another's property for his safe keeping.

Breach of duty of safe custody

Central Motors Glasgow Ltd v Cessnock Garage Co

1925 SC 796, 1925 SN 103, 1925 SLT 563

The plaintiffs entrusted their car to the defendants, who were garage proprietors, for a single night for custody for reward. The defendants' night watchman, in defiance of express orders, took the car out on a frolic of his own, became intoxicated, and smashed up the car. The defendants pleaded the servant was acting outside the scope of his authority.

Per Lord Cullen: A person who is a servant has always a purely personal and independent sphere of life and action and at any particular time may be acting in that sphere and not in his sphere of service and if he is so acting his master cannot be responsible for what he does. This is simple enough; but what is often so difficult is to determine in a question with a third party within which sphere a particular act falls. The question is not to be answered merely by applying the test whether the act in itself is one which the servant was employed or ordered or forbidden to do. The employer has to shoulder responsibility on a wider basis; and he may and often does become responsible to third parties for acts which he has expressly or implicitly forbidden the servant to do. A servant is not a mere machine continually directed by his master's hand but is a person of independent volition and action; and the employer when he delegates to him some duty which he is himself under an obligation to discharge must take the risk of the servant's actions being misdirected when he is, for the time, allowed to be beyond his master's control. It remains necessary that the servant's act be one done within the sphere of his service but it may have that character although it consists in doing something the very opposite of what the servant has been intended or ordered to do, and which he does for his own private ends. The servant is a bad servant who has not faithfully served, but has betrayed, his master. Still, *quoad* the third party injured, his dishonest act may fall to be regarded as an ill way of executing the work assigned to him and which he has been left with power to do well or ill.

Note—This decision can be misleading if regarded merely as a case of the liability of an employer for a prohibited act. The judgment in *Adams (Durham) Ltd and Day v Trust Houses Ltd* shows that the essence of this case was that the contract was one of custody. The defendants had delegated the safekeeping of the car to their servant and were liable for his betrayal of that duty. The position of a third party injured by the servant's negligent driving might have been different.

The correctness of this view is supported by the following case:

Aitchison v Page Motors Ltd

(1935) 154 LT 128, 52 TLR 137 (Macnaghten J)

The defendants were a garage company who sent the plaintiff's car to the makers' works at Fulham for repair. The defendants' service manager collected the car at 7 pm on Friday evening to deliver it to the plaintiff at Epsom. At 11 pm on Friday, driving the car with two friends as passengers, he collided with a bus at Balham; all three were killed, and the plaintiff's car was destroyed.

HELD: The manager was acting in the course of his employment and within the scope of his authority when he took delivery of the car. In breach of his duty he used it for some private purpose of his own, and whilst he was so using it the accident happened. The defendants as his employers were liable to the plaintiff for the manner in which he conducted himself in performing the service of delivering the car.

Morris v C W Martin & Sons Ltd

[1966] 1 QB 716, [1965] 2 All ER 725, [1965] 3 WLR 276, 109 Sol Jo 451, [1965] 2 Lloyd's Rep 63, CA

The plaintiff's mink fur was sent to the defendants for cleaning. They delegated the task of cleaning it to an employee, who stole it. It was not recovered and the plaintiff sued for its value. The county court judge held that the employee was not acting in the scope of his employment in stealing the fur and that the defendants were not liable for his wrongful act.

HELD, ON APPEAL: The defendants had accepted the fur as bailees for reward in order to clean it. They put the employee as their agent to clean the fur and take charge of it whilst doing so. The manner he conducted himself in doing that work was to convert it: it was done in the scope or course of his employment and the defendants were liable for his wrongful act.

Lord Denning MR drew attention to the fact that if the owner of a car takes it to a garage to be repaired and it is repaired by a garage hand who then takes it out on a 'frolic of his own' and collides with a motor cycle the owner of the car can sue the garage proprietor for any damage to the car (as in *Central Motors v Cessnock*, above) but the motor cyclist cannot sue the garage proprietor for damage to the motor cycle (citing *Storey v Ashton*, p 129, above). He continued: I ask myself, How can this be? How can the servant, on one and the same journey, be acting both within and without the course of his employment? Within *qua* the car owner. Without *qua* the motor cyclist. It is time we got rid of this confusion. And the only way to do it, so far as I can see, is by reference to the duty laid by the law on the master. The duty of the garage proprietor to the owner of the car is very different from his duty to the motor cyclist. He owes to the owner of the car the duty of a bailee for reward, whereas he owes no such duty to the motor cyclist on the road. He does not even owe him a duty to use care not to injure him. If you go through the cases on this difficult subject, you will find that, in the ultimate analysis, they depend on the nature of the duty owed by the master towards the person whose goods have been lost or damaged.

Theft by employee

United African Co v Saka Owoade

[1955] AC 130, [1957] 3 All ER 216, [1955] 2 WLR 13, 99 Sol Jo 26, [1954] 2 Lloyd's Rep 607, PC
A transport contractor authorised a customer to hand goods to his driver and clerk, who received goods for carriage. The goods were never delivered and the clerk and driver were convicted of stealing the goods.
HELD: The goods were converted in the course of the employment and the contractor was liable to the customer.

Grundy (Teddington) v Fulton

[1981] 2 Lloyd's Rep 666 (Stuart-Smith J); affd [1983] 1 Lloyd's Rep 16, CA
The plaintiff company claimed under an insurance policy which covered theft of goods from its premises. The goods had been stolen by drivers deviating from their routes and failing to make deliveries.
HELD: The plaintiffs could not succeed. 'Theft' in the policy of insurance must be given the same meaning as in criminal law and in that law the theft took place when the driver deviated from his route.

Note—See also *Morris v C W Martin & Sons Ltd,* p 145, above.

Heasmans v Clarity Cleaning Co Ltd

[1987] IRLR 286, CA
The defendants were contract cleaners who had contracted to clean the plaintiff's offices and equipment. One of the defendants' employees made telephone calls from the plaintiff's offices costing a total of £1,400 for which the plaintiff was liable. The terms of the contract between the parties stipulated that the defendants were strictly liable for acts of their employees while on the premises of the plaintiff although there were no specific clauses which related to these circumstances. It was held in the county court that the defendants were vicariously liable under the terms of the contract or alternatively there was an implied term to this effect. The defendants appealed.
HELD: The defendants could not be vicariously liable for tortious or criminal acts committed by an employee which were wholly outside the scope of his employment, merely because the employment provided the employee with the opportunity to commit the act. It was necessary to show a link between the circumstances of the employment and the tortious act which went beyond mere opportunity. Furthermore, the judge in the county court was mistaken in his alternative findings since the term he implied was collateral and did not go to the specific root of the contract. The appeal was allowed.

Assault by servant

Bayley v Manchester, Sheffield and Lincolnshire Rly Co

(1873) LR 8 CP 148, 42 LJCP 78, 28 LT 366
A railway passenger was pulled violently out of a railway carriage by a porter under the erroneous impression that the passenger was in the wrong carriage. The byelaws did not authorise any such action. Employers held liable.

Per Willes J: A person who puts another in his place to do a class of acts in his absence, necessarily leaves him to determine, according to the circumstances that arise, when an act of that class is to be done, and trusts him for the manner in which it is done; and consequently he is held answerable for the wrong of the person so entrusted either in the manner of doing such an act, or in doing such an act under circumstances in which it ought not to have been done; provided that what was done was done, not from any caprice of the servant, but in the course of his employment.

Note—Hilbery J in *Warren*'s case, below, pointed out that the words 'in the course of the employment' should be read in the light of the judgment of Scrutton LJ, in *Poland*'s case.

Poland v John Parr & Sons

[1927] 1 KB 236, 96 LJKB 152, 136 LT 271, CA
A carter employed by defendants was walking behind a wagon driven by one of the defendants carrying bags of sugar. The carter honestly thought a boy of twelve, walking beside the waggon, was pilfering the sugar, struck the boy on the neck and knocked him under the wagon.
HELD: Master liable: the servant had implied authority to protect his master's property; the method was mistaken and excessive, and even amounted to a crime; it was not so excessive as to take it outside the authority; it was an unauthorised mode of doing an authorised act.

Per Bankes LJ: A master is not responsible for a wrongful act done by his servant unless it is done in the course of his employment. It is deemed to be so done if it is either (a) a wrongful act authorised by the master, or (b) a wrongful and unauthorised mode of doing some act authorised by the master.

Per Scrutton LJ: To make an employer liable for the act of a person alleged to be his servant the act must be one of a class of acts which the person was authorised or employed to do. If the act is one of that class the employer is liable, though the act is done negligently or, in some cases even if it is done with excessive violence. But the excess may be so great as to take the act out of the class of acts which the person is authorised or employed to do.

Warren v Henlys Ltd

[1948] 2 All ER 935, [1948] WN 449, 92 Sol Jo 706 (Hilbery J)
The plaintiff driving one vehicle and his servant driving a second vehicle called at a garage for petrol. After the first vehicle was supplied, the plaintiff drove a short distance to allow the second vehicle across to the pump. The attendant ran after the plaintiff, swore at him and accused him of trying to get away without paying or surrendering coupons. The attendant refused to supply petrol to the second vehicle and they repaired to the cash desk where the plaintiff paid and gave up coupons. The plaintiff then noticed a police car was passing, drove after it, and brought a police constable back, apparently thinking the police could take action. Finding this was not so, the plaintiff told the attendant he would report him to his employers. The attendant then assaulted the plaintiff.
HELD: The plaintiff's business with the defendants had ended, and going for the police was a matter personal to the plaintiff and the attendant. The employers were not liable.

EMPLOYER'S LIABILITY FOR LOANED SERVANT

Note—Where an employer lends an employee to another employer on a temporary basis, the question arises as to which employer will be vicariously liable for the employee's negligence. This is a question of fact and the court will consider who has the power of control, look at by whom he is engaged and paid and who has the right to discharge the employee. In general terms it will be difficult for the main employer to pass responsibility to the temporary employer.

Parker v Miller

(1926) 42 TLR 408, CA (Scrutton LJ)
Ever since *Quarman v Burnett* (1840) 6 M & W 499, the law had been that right to control, not actual physical control, was the test of agency in cases of negligence.

Main employer liable

Century Insurance Co v Northern Ireland Road Transport Board

[1942] AC 509, [1942] 1 All ER 491, 111 LJPC 138, 167 LT 404, 72 Ll L Rep 119, HL
A Board entered into a written contract with distributors to supply tankers, with drivers, who should accept and obey the orders of the distributors regarding delivery to their customers: the Board should dismiss any employee disregarding or failing to obey such orders; the distributors provided garage accommodation; the tankers were painted and the drivers wore uniform to identify them with the distributors.

Per Lord Simon: Applying *Donovan v Laing* [1893] 1 QB 629, the test is in whose employment the man was at the time when the acts complained of were done, in the sense that by the employer is meant the person who has a right at the moment to control the doing of the act. And applying *Moore v Palmer* (1886) 2 TLR 781 the great test was this—whether the servant was transferred or only the use and benefit of his work.

Per Lord Wright: This was a contract for carriage and delivery with their own servants and not for the hiring out of lorries and men or lending them to the distributors to enable them to effect delivery. The question is, who is the 'superior' in the particular instance? The facts of one case can never rule another case. The contractor may contract to do the work, the means being left to him, or he may place his servants and plant under the control of another, that is, he may lend them and in that case he does not retain control of the work. Citing *Quarman v Burnett* (1840) 6 M & W 499: A job-master contracted with two ladies to send horses and a driver for their coach. The ladies were intended to direct the times when and the places to and from which they took their drives. That was certainly a measure of control, but what was there transferred was the use and benefit of the coachman's work. The coachman did not become the servant of the ladies. The authority of that case had never been questioned. Following Lord Herschell in *Cameron v Nystrom* [1893] AC 308: Has there been a transfer of the man's services from his general employer to the other who is said to be his temporary employer? It is, I think, clear that the presumption is all against there being such a transfer.

HELD: The Board were independent contractors undertaking by the use of their own vehicles and by the activities of their own servants to make the deliveries, and not that of people lending vehicles and drivers for the hirers to direct.

Note—For facts see p 229, below. See also *Harris v Continental Express Ltd* [1961] 1 Lloyd's Rep 251.

Stitt v Woolley

(1971) 115 Sol Jo 708, CA
Stitt, Woolley and another man G, were members of a local authority fire brigade and were required by their terms of service 'to attend promptly at the station in response to a call at any time'. On the night in question the fire bells rang in their homes. Woolley went, as usual, in his car, with G in the front passenger seat and Stitt in the back. On the way to the fire station G suddenly grasped the steering wheel. There was a struggle: the car crashed into a bridge and Stitt was injured. He claimed not only against Woolley but against the local authority as being vicariously liable for Woolley's or G's negligence.
HELD: Woolley was not negligent. In respect of the local authority's liability for G's acts the men were, in the special circumstances of the case, on duty once they left their homes in answer to an emergency call since it was part of their duty to get to the station as quickly as possible. It was different from the case of a man going to work and was an exception to the rule that a workman was not usually employed until he reached his place of business. It was a case like *Blee v LNER* (below). But it could not be said that G's extraordinary action was within the course of his employment and the employers were not liable for it.

Keppel Bus Co Ltd v Sa'ad bin Ahmad

[1974] 2 All ER 700, [1974] 1 WLR 1082, [1974] RTR 504, PC
In the course of a bus journey the conductor, a servant of the appellant bus company, spoke sharply to a lady passenger and was reproved for doing so by another passenger, the respondent. An altercation then broke out between the conductor and respondent in which they aimed blows at each other, but they were separated by other passengers. Later, whilst collecting fares, the conductor abused the respondent, using a very rude Chinese expression. The respondent stood up, told the conductor not to use the expression and sat down again. The conductor then hit him with the ticket-punch causing serious injury to his eye. The respondent was awarded damages against the appellants as vicariously liable for the conductor's act on the ground that he was acting, even though in a high-handed manner, in the course of his duty to keep order among the passengers.
HELD, ON APPEAL to the Privy Council: The appellants were not vicariously liable. To describe the conductor's act as quelling disorder was impossible on the evidence; if anyone was keeping order in the bus it was the passengers. The evidence fell far short of establishing an implied authority in the conductor to take violent action where none was called for, nor was there present in the bus an emergency situation calling for forcible action justifiable upon any express or implied authority with which the appellants could be said on the evidence to have clothed him.

Note—See also *Racz v Home Office* [1994] 1 All ER 97, HL.

Marney v Campbell Symonds & Co Ltd

(1946) 175 LT 283, 62 TLR 324, 90 Sol Jo 467 (Hilbery J)
The Minister of War Transport under the Defence Regulations requisitioned a motor car belonging to garage proprietors and directed them to deliver the car to a specified

address and provide a driver and fuel for that purpose. Directions were given in case of breakdown and forms of request to traders to supply requisites and to the police to assist, the cost being chargeable to the officer commanding the unit to which the vehicle was consigned. As the car had no road licence, a disc was provided in lieu. 'On His Majesty's Service only'.
HELD: Following *Century Insurance Co v Northern Ireland Transport Board* and *Hewitt v Bonum* there was no transfer of service. The driver remained the servant of the garage proprietor.

Nicholas v F J Sparkes & Son

[1945] KB 309n, CA (reported with *Dowd* and *McFarlane*'s cases, below)
Plaintiff's employers. Currans Industries Ltd, hired from defendants from two to nine lorries per week, by telephoning and saying how many lorries they required a week. The drivers were told to work for a week at Currans. A driver was told to work there and accept orders as other lorry drivers and had been working only for Currans for three months or more with the same lorry. Defendants could take him away or give him a holiday. Plaintiff was injured on a private roadway of Currans premises by defendants' lorry. The county court judge held the driver was under the control of Currans and the defence of common employment succeeded.
HELD, ON APPEAL reversing the county court decision: Where the particular employer directs the driver as to time and place but has no control over the driver's art of driving, the general employer is liable. If, however, the particular employer has detailed control over the manner in which the servant does the work, complying with his orders and not acting except on his orders, the particular employer is liable.

The driver was exercising his own discretion as driver, and Currans had nothing to do with the mistake he made as driver.

The onus is on the general employer. This is particularly so in the case of a vehicle where the driver is in sole charge and he alone is allowed to drive. It is placed under his control by the general employer who relies on him to use his own skill and exercise his own discretion in driving.

Mersey Docks and Harbour Board v Coggins and Griffiths (Liverpool) Ltd

[1947] AC 1, [1946] 2 All ER 345, HL
Coggins and Griffiths hired from the Dock Board a crane and driver who was engaged and paid by the Board. A third party employed by a firm of forwarding agents was injured by the negligence of the crane driver and obtained judgment against the Board. The Board appealed.

Per Viscount Simon: In applying the doctrine of *respondeat superior*, prima facie the responsibility for the negligence of servants engaged and paid by a general employer or permanent employer is on that employer, and the burden of proving that the responsibility has shifted to the hirer rests on the general employer. That burden is a heavy one and can only be discharged in quite exceptional circumstances. I prefer, instead of the test applied by the Court of Appeal following *Nicholas'* case, the test where the authority lies to direct, or to delegate to, the workman, the manner in which the vehicle is driven. It is this authority which determines who is the workman's 'superior'.

In this case, the servant was exercising his own discretion as driver, a discretion vested in him by his general employers, and the mistake he made had nothing to do with the hirers. If, however, the hirers had intervened to give directions how to drive and the driver *pro hac vice* had complied with them the hirers might have been liable, as joint tortfeasors.

The contract between the parties provided that the hirers of the crane and workman must take all risks and the workman shall be the servant of the hirers. This contract does not affect the rights of third parties. Appeal dismissed.

Chowdhary v Gillot

[1947] 2 All ER 541, 63 TLR 569 (Streatfield J)
The plaintiff for 10 or 12 years had been a valued customer of the Daimler Co. He was in the habit of taking his Daimler car to their works and leaving it with them for servicing and repairs. Before the war the Daimler Co drove the plaintiff to the nearest railway station as a courtesy service in their own car with their own driver. During the war, their servant drove the plaintiff in his own car to the station and would then drive the car back to the works. On the way to the station an accident occurred by the negligence of the servant, and the plaintiff and a third party were injured.
HELD: Although the burden of proof of transfer of a servant is not so heavy when the servant alone is hired, as opposed to the man plus the machine, it remains a heavy burden. The burden of proof was on the plaintiff to show that he had abandoned his right to control or had contracted himself out of that right.

(1) The Daimler Co were in possession of the car as bailees; (2) plaintiff had no right to control the bailees' servant; (3) plaintiff was doing no more than receive courtesy service; (4) plaintiff was not in a position to exercise control.

The fact that he could have ordered him to drive more carefully if he was driving dangerously, or more slowly if at an uncomfortable or dangerous speed would be no more than the common prudence that a hirer would exercise towards a taxi driver, who is not the servant of the fare. He could not have ordered the driver to stop and wait half an hour, or deviate and wait while he visited a patient, or drive to a more distant place for his own purposes. If the Daimler Co had a regulation limiting the driving of customer's cars to a speed of, say, 20 mph and plaintiff had ordered the driver to drive faster to catch a train, the driver could have refused.

Distinguishing *Pratt v Patrick* (p 158, below) and *Samson v Aitchison* (p 158, below), the driver remained the servant of the Daimler Co.

O'Reilly v ICI

[1955] 3 All ER 382, [1955] 1 WLR 1155, 99 Sol Jo 778, CA
A driver's employers had a contract with customers whereby they set aside lorries and drivers for almost exclusive use of the customers. The lorries were painted a special colour and bore the name and trade mark of the customers.
HELD: Adopting the judgment of Lord Porter in *Mersey Docks & Harbour Board v Coggins and Griffiths* (p 150), the driver remained in the employ of the general employers. The temporary employer had got the right to dictate not only what the servant was to do but also how he was to do it.

Denham v Midland Employers Mutual Assurance Ltd

[1955] 2 QB 437, [1955] 2 All ER 561, [1955] 3 WLR 84, 99 Sol Jo 417, [1955] 1 Lloyd's Rep 467, CA
Eastwoods Ltd, brickmakers, contracted with Le Grand Co, arterial well engineers, to perform work on their property, and agreed to provide one unskilled labourer to assist two skilled drillers of Le Grand Co free of charge. The labourer was selected

by and paid by Eastwoods; they alone could suspend or dismiss him; they kept his insurance cards and paid for his insurance stamps. He was not asked nor did he consent to a transfer of his contract of service; if he was not paid his wages, or was wrongfully dismissed, he could sue Eastwoods and no one else; if he failed to turn up, Eastwoods alone could sue him. The labourer was killed in circumstances whereby Le Grand Co were liable to his widow by reason of negligence of Le Grand Co or their servants.

Le Grand Co had a policy of insurance against employers' liability with the first defendants indemnifying them in respect of injury to any person under a contract of service with them by accident arising out of and in the course of his employment by them. They also had a public liability policy with the second defendants, which excluded liability in respect of any person under a contract of service with them by accident arising out of and in the course of employment by them. Each insurer contended the other was liable to indemnify.

HELD, ON APPEAL: There was no contract of service with Le Grand and they were not entitled to recover from the first insurers. The contract of service was with Eastwoods. The second defendants were liable under the public liability policy.

Treadaway v Dike and Ramsgate Corpn

[1967] 1 Lloyd's Rep 564

Per Paull J: In my judgment, the law is reasonably simple. It is this: if I hire a machine together with its driver, who from the essence of the case is an expert, and must be an expert in the driving of the machine, and there are no special terms with regard to what shall be the position between the driver and the firm to whom he is hired, then so long as he is driving that crane or that machine the person from whom it is hired is liable for the driver's negligence.

Savory v Holland, Hannen and Cubitts (Southern) Ltd

[1964] 3 All ER 18, [1964] 1 WLR 1158, 108 Sol Jo 479, CA

The defendants, building contractors, were clearing a large site to build a factory. They encountered rock, and engaged sub-contractors to blast it out. The sub-contractors sent the plaintiff, a skilled blaster, to do the job. He brought his own equipment but the defendants provided flagmen. The sub-contractors employed him, paid him and had power to dismiss him. The defendants could decide what rock they wanted him to blast but had no right to dictate to him how the actual blasting should be done. He was injured when he slipped whilst walking down a bank after acting as a flagman. He claimed damages on the grounds that the defendants had not provided enough flagmen nor a ladder to climb the bank in spite of his having asked for both. The judge held that he was a servant for the time being of the defendants and that they were liable.

HELD, ON APPEAL: The plaintiff was not a servant of the defendants either for the time being or at any time. He remained throughout the servant of the sub-contractors, his general employers, and the defendants were not liable.

Per Diplock LJ: The doctrine of master and servant *pro hac vice* today seems to me to be relevant only to a question of vicarious liability: it is a mere adjunct of the doctrine or *respondeat superior* for determining whether A is the superior of B.

Note—See also *Garrard v A E Southey & Co and Standard Telephones and Cables Ltd* [1952] 2 QB 174, [1952] 1 All ER 597, [1952] 1 TLR 630, 96 Sol Jo 166, and *Johnson v A H Beaumont*

[1953] 2 QB 184, [1953] 2 All ER 106, [1953] 2 WLR 1153, 97 Sol Jo 389, [1953] 1 Lloyd's Rep 546.

County Plant Hire Ltd v Jackson

(1970) 114 Sol Jo 263, CA
The defendant, a quarry owner, hired an excavator and driver from the plaintiffs who substituted an excavator and driver hired by them from the third parties. The driver was given orders for his work by the defendant but in negligently carrying them out damaged some equipment of the defendant. The plaintiffs sued for unpaid hire charges whereupon the defendant counterclaimed for the damage to his equipment and made the same claim against the third parties. The judge held that the defendant could not succeed in either claim because he was the person giving orders to the driver.
HELD: When the driver was driving the excavator he was acting in the course of that employment by the third parties; the mere fact that directions were given by the defendant as to what to do did not take the matter out of the course of that employment. If he had given wrong directions it might amount to contributory negligence. Judgment for the defendant against the third parties.

Ready Mixed Concrete v Yorkshire Traffic Licensing Authority

[1970] 2 QB 397, [1970] 1 All ER 890, [1970] 2 WLR 627, 134 JP 293, 114 Sol Jo 111, Div Ct
The appellants had a contract with a haulage contractor for collection, carriage and delivery of their goods to customers. He was bound by terms of the contract to abide by all reasonable directions from the appellants for deliveries and to keep his vehicle clean and in good condition. He could, with the appellants' consent employ another suitable person to drive the vehicle, for whose acts the contractor would be responsible.

The contractor was ill for a month during the period of contract and unable to drive. The appellant sent Stacey, one of their own employees, to drive the truck during his illness. Stacey was given the keys by the contractor who told him to look after the vehicle. He could have refused to have Stacey drive it if he wished. The appellants continued to pay Stacey's wages, stamp and SET. They deducted 15s a load from the payments to the contractor being an agreed amount to cover all expenses.
HELD: Stacey was throughout the servant of the appellants. Although prima facie the owner of a vehicle is the person who has the authority to give directions as to how it is to be driven it is not the sole or decisive test. There is a presumption against transfer of a servant to a temporary employer. In the present case the appellants whilst continuing to pay Stacey lent him to the contractor to perform particular deliveries. It was not a case of a transfer of the servant but merely of the use and benefit of his work.

McConkey v Amec plc

(1990) Times, 28 February, CA
The plaintiff was injured by equipment falling from a crane. His employers ('the hirers') had hired the crane and driver. The plaintiff sued both the hirers and the owners of the crane and driver.

The terms of the contract between the parties incorporated the model conditions agreed between the Contractors Plant Association and the Federation of the Civil Engineering Contractors. The relevant clauses were:

'5(a) Unless notification . . . to the contrary is received . . . the plant shall be deemed to be in good order . . .'

'8 When a driver or operator is supplied by the owner with the plant, the owner shall supply a person competent in operating the plant and such person shall be under the direction and control of the hirer . . .'

'13(a) . . . Nothing in this clause affects the operation of clauses 5, 8 . . . of this agreement . . .'

The judge accepting that the driver of the crane was not at the relevant time a competent operator within the terms of clause 8, nevertheless found that the owners had a complete indemnity from the hirers. The hirers appealed.
HELD: The driver of the crane was an employee of the owners who were vicariously liable for the damage caused by his negligence. The agreement was to be read to the affect that if the owners supplied an incompetent operator or defective equipment then such operator was not to be regarded as a servant or agent of the hirer and the owner remained vicariously liable for his negligence.

Note—But see the two earlier decisions of *Philips Products Ltd v Hyland* and *Thompson v T Lohan,* below, where the indemnity was effective.

Effects of express contractual terms

Thompson v T Lohan (Plant Hire) Ltd

[1987] 2 All ER 631, [1987] 1 WLR 649 [1987] IRLR 148, 131 Sol Jo 358, CA
The plaintiff's husband, an excavator driver, was killed in a quarry accident. The accident was due to the negligence of another excavator driver. Both drivers were hired by the second defendants from the first defendants. The hire contract in *Philips Products v Hyland* (above) had similar conditions; the drivers were to be regarded as the hirer's servants and the hirer would be responsible for all claims arising in connection with the operation of the plant by the drivers. The second defendants submitted that this was contrary to s 2(1) of the Unfair Contract Terms Act 1977 in that it purported to exclude the first defendants' liability for death or personal injury.
HELD, ON APPEAL: This argument failed. Whilst an employer cannot exclude liability for the acts of his employee as between himself and the general public this does not prevent the parties to a contract of hire from determining between themselves who is to be liable for the negligent acts of a hired employee. *Arthur White (Contractors) Ltd v Tarmac Civil Engineering Ltd* [1967] 1 WLR 1508 applied. The clause was not contrary to s 2(1) of the Unfair Contract Terms Act 1977. The plant owner was not excluding liability for negligence, merely transferring the burden of compensation to the hirer by a commercial arrangement. The plaintiff was not prejudiced because she could enforce judgment against the second defendant.

EMPLOYEES' LIABILITY TO EMPLOYER FOR THEIR NEGLIGENT ACTS

Note—Employees are subject to an implied term that they will exercise reasonable care when performing the duties required under their contract of employment. Where the negligence of an employee leads to the employer being found vicariously liable to a third party, then at common law the employer is entitled to be indemnified for the loss attributable to the employee's breach of contract.

Ryan v Fildes

[1938] 3 All ER 517 (Tucker J)
A schoolmistress, the servant of the school managers, boxed the ears of a schoolboy and caused injury. The boy sued the schoolmistress and the school managers and recovered against both defendants. The managers recovered 100% contribution from the schoolmistress.

Jones v Manchester Corpn

[1952] 2 QB 852, [1952] 2 All ER 125, [1952] 1 TLR 1589, CA
Per Singleton LJ: It may well be that in the ordinary simple case a servant must indemnify his master against his wrongful acts for which the master is made liable. A chauffeur who, through negligence, causes damage for which his employer is held responsible may well be liable to his master. On the other hand, if the chauffeur is young and inexperienced, and is suddenly told to drive another and bigger car, or lorry, which he does not understand, and an accident follows, it is by no means certain that the employer would be entitled to an indemnity. The statement in Salmond on the *Law of Torts* (15th edn) p 620, that a master should generally be able to sue his servant for indemnity cannot apply if the master has himself contributed to the damage or if some other employee has contributed to the damage.

Semtex Ltd v Gladstone

[1954] 2 All ER 206, [1954] 1 WLR 945, 98 Sol Jo 438 (Finnemore J)
The defendant was a driver employed by the plaintiffs. By the negligent driving of the defendant, personal injuries were caused to other workmen of the plaintiffs. The plaintiffs, by the insurers of their employers' liability policy, settled claims amounting to £9,360, and sued the defendant for that sum. The defendant was indemnified by the plaintiffs' motor policy, and these insurers were the real defendants. The employers claimed from the servant driver indemnity at common law or contribution of 100% under the Law Reform (Married Women and Tortfeasors) Act 1935, s 6(2).
HELD: It was clear law that a master could sue his servant for negligence. This right applies to moneys paid by the master for such negligence to other parties as well as to the master himself as in *Digby v General Accident* (p 854, below), whether treated as a breach of contract by the servant, or a case of contribution of 100%. It was immaterial whether the plaintiff's claim was based on a breach of the contract of service which placed the driver under a duty to drive carefully, or whether as between tortfeasors, for in either event they were entitled to recover the whole of the damages which they had been forced to pay owing to his negligence.

Lister v Romford Ice and Cold Storage Co Ltd

[1957] AC 555, [1957] 1 All ER 125, [1957] 2 WLR 158, 101 Sol Jo 106, [1956] 2 Lloyd's Rep 505, HL
The driver of a motor lorry went to a yard off the highway to collect goods. His father, in the same employ, went with him. In the yard the father was injured whilst the driver was backing the lorry. The father sued the employers and recovered damages. The employers sued the driver claiming indemnity in contract and in negligence.
HELD: The employers were entitled to an indemnity from the driver.

Per Viscount Simmonds: In my opinion the case of *Semtex Ltd v Gladstone* (above) was rightly decided. It is clear that it was an implied term of the contract that the appellant would perform his duties with proper care (*Harmer v Cornelius* (1858)

5 CBNS 236). This includes a servant employed to drive a lorry. There is no distinction between possessing skill and exercising it. Skill embraces care. In this case it is immaterial whether the cause of action lies in contract or in tort. The servant owes a contractual duty of care to his master, and breach founds an action for damages for breach of contract. A single act of negligence may give rise to a claim either in tort or for breach of a term express or implied in a contract. The respondents are entitled to recover the damage for breach of contract, unless the damage is too remote or there is some other intervening factor which precludes recovery. The damages are not too remote. With regard to the implication of some implied term, I cannot accept the implication that the respondents would indemnify the appellant for any act in the course of his employment, nor that the appellant would receive the benefit of any contract of insurance effected by them, nor that the employer was bound as a reasonable man to effect such an insurance. The fact that one party to a contract is insured is to be disregarded.

Note—This case led to considerable concern at the prospect of insurers enforcing employers' rights against employees with detrimental consequences for industrial relations. Employers' liability insurers subsequently entered into a 'gentleman's agreement' not to pursue such claims unless there was evidence of 'collusion or wilful misconduct': Michael A Jones *Torts*.

Harvey v R G O'Dell Ltd

[1958] 2 QB 78, [1958] 1 All ER 657, [1958] 2 WLR 473, 102 Sol Jo 196, [1958] 1 Lloyd's Rep 273 (McNair J)
The plaintiff was in the employ of the defendant company. Galway was also in the company's employ as a storekeeper at their works. The defendant company were builders and repairers of barges with works at Battersea, but also did general work away from the works. If the outside work necessitated the use of substantial materials, or heavy tools, the men were conveyed by the company's lorry or van, but in other cases the men made their own arrangements for travel and were reimbursed the cost of travel by public transport, whether they used it or not. Galway owned a motor cycle combination which he used to travel to and from work, from time to time on the employers' business to collect materials, and sometimes for travelling to and from an outside repairing job. He paid his own money for petrol and maintenance but when on business was allowed a travelling allowance based on the cost of public transport. The plaintiff was Galway's assistant. The defendants' manager told Galway he would like him to go the following day to repair a fence round a caravan at Hurley, some five to six miles from Maidenhead, and to take the plaintiff with him. Galway was free to refuse, but agreed. The same evening he told the plaintiff to make arrangements with Galway to accompany him. On 29 February 1952, Galway collected a brace and bit and some tools from the store, put them in the sidecar and proceeded with the plaintiff to Hurley, where they worked for four or five hours, and Galway then told the plaintiff they would have to go to Maidenhead for more tools and materials. At Maidenhead the plaintiff got out at a cafe and Galway rejoined him about half-an-hour later, when they both had a meal of coffee and sandwiches. On the way back to Hurley the combination collided with a car, and Galway was killed. The accident was due in part to the negligence of Galway.

The judge held (1) Galway was using the combination on behalf of his employers; (2) Galway was acting within the scope of his employment in the journey from London to Hurley; (3) the journey from Maidenhead to Hurley was fairly incidental to the work.

The defendants sued Galway's administratrix in third party proceedings for an indemnity.

HELD: The authorities, including *Lister v Romford Ice and Cold Storage Co Ltd* were cases where the servant was employed as a driver. Galway was engaged as a storekeeper. Making his motor cycle available to his employers from time to time as a concession, did not imply into his contract of employment a term that he would use reasonable care and skill in driving or that he had impliedly agreed to indemnify his employers against liability arising from his negligent driving. There is no right to indemnity on the facts in this case.

But there was a right to contribution as a joint tortfeasor under the Law Reform (Married Women and Tortfeasors) Act 1935, s 6(1)(c). The right of contribution between tortfeasors is a right *sui generis* conferred by statute. They are not proceedings in respect of a cause of action in tort. The claim of the plaintiff against the company and Galway's administratrix was as against joint tortfeasors. The company's liability is purely vicarious, and the company was entitled to judgment for 100% contribution, ie an indemnity against their liability under the judgment in action, with costs of action and third party proceedings.

2 OWNER'S LIABILITY FOR DRIVER

PRIMA FACIE LIABILITY

Note—An owner of a vehicle does not incur a liability for damage caused by it, merely by being the owner. It must be established that the driver of the vehicle was driving it as the servant or agent of the owner: see Du Pareq in *Hewitt v Bonvin* p 160, below.

Barnard v Sully

(1931) 47 TLR 557

Where a plaintiff in an action for negligence proved that damage has been caused by the defendant's motor car, the fact of ownership of the motor car is prima facie evidence that the motor car, at the material time, was being driven by the owner, or by his servant or agent.

Per Scrutton LJ: The more usual fact is that a motor car is driven by the owner or the servant or agent of the owner and therefore the fact of ownership is some evidence fit to go to the jury that at the material time the motor car was being driven by the owner of it or by his servant or agent. But it is evidence which is liable to be rebutted by proof of the actual facts.

Note—Applied in *Elliott v Loake* [1983] Crim LR 36, a criminal case, and more recently applied in *Pask v Keefe & Stewarts Garages* (23 April 1985, unreported) (Webster J).

Rambarran v Gurrucharran

[1970] 1 All ER 749, [1970] 1 WLR 556, 114 Sol Jo 244, [1970] RTR 195, PC

The defendant owned a car which he allowed his sons to use at any time. He himself did not drive. An accident occurred when his son Leslie was driving. The defendant gave evidence at the trial, accepted by the trial judge, that he did not know Leslie was out in the car on the day in question; it had not been used for his own purposes on that day and he was not at his home where the car was kept. The Guyana Court of Appeal by a majority held that the defendant had not rebutted the prima facie case of agency arising from the fact of ownership of the car, as in *Barnard v Sully* (above), since he had left the court without evidence as to the journey during which the accident occurred.

HELD ON APPEAL to the Privy Council: The defendant was not liable. A plaintiff must establish, if he is to make the owner liable, that the driver was driving the car as the servant or agent of the owner and not merely on his own concerns. Although in the absence of other evidence an inference can be drawn from ownership that the driver was the servant or agent of the owner there was evidence from the defendant that the car was not being used for his purposes on the day of the accident and this was sufficient to rebut the inference. It was not necessary additionally that he should prove what Leslie's object was in using the car; once he had proved that Leslie was not driving as his servant or agent then Leslie's actual purpose on that day was irrelevant. Appeal allowed.

OWNER IN CAR

Samson v Aitchison

[1912] AC 844, 82 LJPC 1, 107 LT 106

Where the owner of a vehicle, being himself in possession and occupation of it, requests or allows another person to drive, this will not of itself exclude his right and duty of control, and therefore, in the absence of further proof that he has abandoned that right by contract or otherwise, the owner is liable as principal for damage caused by the negligence of the person actually driving.

In his judgment which was approved by the Privy Council, the trial judge said: 'I think that where the owner of an equipage, whether a carriage and horses or a motor, is riding in it while it is being driven, and has thus not only the right to possession but the actual possession of it, he necessarily retains the power and the right of controlling the manner in which it is to be driven, unless he has in some way contracted himself out of his right, or is shown by conclusive evidence to have in some way abandoned his right. If any injury happens to the equipage while it is being driven, the owner is the sufferer. In order to protect his own property if, in his opinion, the necessity arises, he must be able to say to the driver, "Do this," or "Don't do that." The driver would have to obey, and if he did not the owner in possession would compel him to give up the reins or the steering wheel. The owner, indeed, has a duty to control the driver. . . . The duty to control postulates the existence of the right to control. If there was no right to control there could be no duty to control. No doubt if the actual possession of the equipage has been given by the owner to a third person - that is to say, if there has been a bailment by the owner to a third person - the owner has given up his right of control': (quoted in *Chowdhary*'s case.)

Pratt v Patrick

[1924] 1 KB 488, 93 LJKB 174, 130 LT 735 (Acton J)

Defendant was in his motor car, with him, on his invitation, being two friends, E and P. E drove the car and, owing to his negligence, it collided with another vehicle and P sustained injuries from which he died. P's widow sued defendant under the Fatal Accidents Act for damages.

HELD: As defendant was in the car, and there was no evidence that he had abandoned his right of control, he was liable notwithstanding that by a casual delegation he had entrusted its actual management and mechanical control to E.

Note—In that case [*Pratt v Patrick*] there was a delegation of the control of the car by the owner to a casual driver while the owner himself remained in the car ready to control, if he was so minded, or to direct the driver. There was no question of the car having been handed over to anybody. There was no evidence there of any abandonment by the owner of his right to control it. Per Streatfield J in *Chowdhary's* case (p 151, above).

Trust Co Ltd v de Silva

[1956] 1 WLR 376, 100 Sol Jo 262, [1956] 1 Lloyd's Rep 309, PC
Insurers employed canvassers on commission but no salary, and field officers with a small salary and overriding commission who supervised their canvassers. Either selected a doctor to examine proposers for life insurance. A doctor was a passenger with a field officer in a car of the field officer driven by a canvasser, and was injured.
HELD: The field officer was a servant of insurers and was acting in the course of and for the purposes of his employment; he had the right to exercise control over the driver and was in control of the car. Insurers were liable to the doctor for injuries caused by the negligent driving of the canvasser.

Haydock v Brown

(1939) Times, 24 May, Manchester Guardian, 24 May (Croom-Johnson J)
The owner of a car gave permission to A (her son) to drive the car. A was in the car which was being driven by B. A was bailee of the car and had the right to possession of it. There is no difference whether the right to possession is as owner, hirer, or gratuitous bailee. If he is in the car, he must be taken to have retained his right of control, and if he has the right of control, he is liable for a person who must be deemed to be driving on his behalf and under his control.

OWNER NOT IN CAR

Loan of car

Britt v Galmoye and Nevill

(1928) 44 TLR 294, 72 Sol Jo 122
A had been in the employment of B as a van driver. B lent A his private car after the day's work was finished to take A's friends to a theatre. A, by his negligent driving, injured the plaintiff.
HELD: As the journey was not on the master's business, and the master was not in control, he was not liable for his servant's act.

Hillman v Walls

(1938) 5 LJCCR 167
Defendant owned a car and lent it to a fellow servant H to go home to lunch. H returned by other means. At the owner's request H brought the car back to work next morning, and on the way injured the plaintiff. H disappeared and the plaintiff sued the defendant alleging defendant had the right to control.

HELD: Following *Higbid v Hammett* (p 132, above), defendant was not in control and H was not his servant or agent.

Driving with consent, owner not liable

Hewitt v Bonvin

[1940] 1 KB 188, 109 LJKB 223, 161 LT 360, 56 TLR 43, 83 Sol Jo 869, CA
A son was driving his father's car with the consent of the father. Lewis J, held that as he was driving with the consent of the father, he was the father's agent on that journey. The Court of Appeal reversed the decision.

Per MacKinnon LJ: A man may, of course, be temporarily employed as a servant without remuneration. If I say to a friend, or to my son, 'The chauffeur is ill and cannot come. Will you drive me in my car to the station?' he is no doubt *pro tempore* my servant, and he is doing my work for me. But a servant must at the moment of his act be doing work for his employer. The plaintiff must establish (1) that the son was employed to drive the car as his father's servant, and (2) that he was, when the accident happened, driving the car for the father, and not merely for his own benefit and for his own concerns.

Per du Parcq LJ: It is plain that the ownership of the car cannot of itself impose any liability on the owner. The owner, without further information, is prima facie liable, because the court is entitled to draw the inference that the car was being driven by the owner, his servant or agent, but when the facts are given in evidence the court is not left to draw an inference. The owner is liable if the driver had authority, express or implied, to drive on the owner's behalf. This depends not on ownership, but on the delegation of a task or duty. Permission to drive the car is consistent with a mere loan or bailment. The relationship of father and son is not of itself evidence of agency.
HELD: The father was not liable.

Note—See also *Rambarran v Gurrucharran*, p 157, above. The following is a form of a Plea in a Defence denying agency:

'The driver of the defendant's car was not the servant or agent of the defendant. The defendant lent the car to the said driver, who was driving the car merely for his own benefit and for his own concerns and was not driving the car for the defendant. The defendant disclaims all legal liability for the acts of the said driver.'

Klein v Caluori

[1971] 2 All ER 701, [1971] 1 WLR 619, 115 Sol Jo 228, [1971] 1 Lloyd's Rep 421, [1971] RTR 354 (Lyell J)
The defendant's car was borrowed and driven away without his knowledge or consent by a friend. An hour or two later the friend telephoned the defendant and told him he had taken the car. The defendant told him curtly to bring it back. On the way back the car collided with the plaintiff's stationary car and damaged it. The plaintiff claimed that the defendant was vicariously liable on the ground that his friend was his agent in driving the car because in bringing it back he was driving for the purposes of the owner, the defendant.
HELD: The return journey was part and parcel of the whole enterprise, namely, the borrowing of the car. A mere permission to drive a car does not make the driver the agent of the person giving permission. Whether or not the borrowing had been with

consent the return journey was for the purposes of the borrower only. It could make no difference that the defendant told the friend to bring the car back; it was merely a reminder of his duty to do so.

Driving on owner's business

Smith v Moss

[1940] 1 KB 424, [1940] 1 All ER 469, 109 LJKB 271, 162 LT 267, 56 TLR 305, 84 Sol Jo 115 (Charles J)
B bought a car which was garaged at her son's house and the son was the only driver. The car was used to convey the mother, son and son's wife home from a party. The mother was taken to her house and the son drove the wife in the car to the son's house. The wife was injured and sued the mother.
HELD: The driver was the agent of the owner. It was by her direction that he took her to the party, and it was by her direction that he took her back from the party. He had not ceased to be acting for her. The wife was entitled to recover.

Ormrod v Crosville Motor Services Ltd

[1953] 2 All ER 753, [1953] 1 WLR 1120, 97 Sol Jo 570, CA
The owner of a car who was taking part in the Monte Carlo rally arranged with a friend for the friend to drive the car, with the friend's wife as passenger, in the friend's own time and manner, and meet him at Monte Carlo before the end of the rally, after which the car would be used for a holiday in Switzerland of these three persons. A suitcase belonging to the owner was carried in the car. On the journey in England the car was involved in a collision and the owner of the other vehicle sued the car owner for damages caused by the negligent driving of the friend.
HELD: The friend driving was not the servant of the owner. To render the owner liable there must be something more than the granting of the mere permission but it is not necessary to show a legal contract of agency. It is, however, sufficient where there is a social or moral obligation (per du Parcq LJ in *Hewitt v Bonvin* (above)), to drive the owner's car. A request to the friend to drive the car, and compliance with the request, makes the friend the agent of the owner, since the owner has an interest in the request being complied with. The driving was for the owner's benefit, and the owner is liable for the driver's negligence.

Per Singleton LJ: Mere consent is not proof of agency. Here the purpose was that the car should be used by the owner or for the joint purposes of the plaintiff and the owner when it reached Monte Carlo. The male plaintiff was driving for the purposes of the owner or the joint purposes of the owner and himself.

Per Denning LJ: An owner may be liable although the driver is not his servant. The owner is also liable if the driver is, with the owner's consent, driving the car on the owner's business or for the owner's purposes. Here it was partly for the driver's own purposes and partly for the owner's purposes. The contention that because the driver started two or three days earlier for his own purposes the owner is not liable fails. The law puts an especial responsibility on the owner who allows it to go on the road in charge of someone else. If it is being used wholly or partly on the owner's business or for the owner's purposes, the owner is liable. He only escapes when it is to be used for purposes in which he has no interest or concern (*Hewitt v Bonvin*). The trip to Monte Carlo must be considered as a whole.

Carberry v Davies

[1968] 2 All ER 817, [1968] 1 WLR 1103, 112 Sol Jo 445, CA
The owner of a car was a coal-merchant who had three lorries for delivery of coal one of which was driven by his employee H, who was a servant at a wage. The owner also had a Ford car which he regarded as the family car and which he wanted all his family to use as far as practicable. But he would not allow anyone to drive it except himself and H. When his son aged 16 wanted to go out in the car he could do so provided H drove it. On one such occasion it collided with the plaintiff and H was held to blame. Was the car-owner vicariously liable for H's negligence?
HELD: The principle was stated by Singleton LJ in *Ormerod v Crosville Motor Services* (above): 'the driver of a motor car must be doing something for the owner of the car to become an agent of the owner'. The present case turned on how the arrangement was made. Did the car-owner make the arrangement with H, so that his son could have the use of the car or was it the son who made the arrangement and simply asked his father's permission? On the facts it was the father who made the arrangement and he was liable for H's negligent driving.

Vandyke v Fender

[1970] 2 QB 292, [1970] 2 All ER 335, [1970] 2 WLR 929, 134 JP 487, 114 Sol Jo 205, CA
On the facts set out on p 738, below, the Court of Appeal held, following *Ormerod v Crosvill Motor Services* (above) that Fender was the agent of the second defendants when driving the car owned by them for a purpose in which they had an interest and they were vicariously liable for his negligent driving whether or not he was driving in the course of his employment.

Responsibility of spouse

Morgans v Launchbury

[1973] AC 127, [1972] 2 All ER 606, [1972] 2 WLR 1217, 116 Sol Jo 396, HL
Mrs Morgans, the defendant, owned a car which was registered and insured in her name. Both she and her husband regularly used it, he more than she. She regarded it as being their car jointly, rather than hers. He used it for going to work. One evening he telephoned her from his place of work, saying he was going out for the evening. He visited various public houses and at one of them, conscious that he ought not to drive, asked a friend named Cawfield to act as his chauffeur for the rest of the evening. Later he and Cawfield left a public house in the car with the plaintiffs as passengers and were travelling to a town some miles away, not in a homeward direction, when an accident occurred due to Cawfield's negligent driving. The defendant's husband and Cawfield were killed, the plaintiffs injured. The defendant had been promised by her husband that if ever he had had too much to drink when out with the car he would get someone who was sober to drive. The Court of Appeal held the defendant vicariously liable for Cawfield's negligent driving on the grounds inter alia that it was a 'family car' and that she had an 'interest and concern' in the purpose for which it was being driven.
HELD: Allowing the appeal, there was no authority for accepting the 'interest and concern' or 'family car' arguments, which have no validity in English law. An owner's vicarious liability for the negligence of the driver was correctly and

accurately stated by MacKinnon LJ and du Parcq in *Hewitt v Bonvin* (p 160, above). The understanding between Mr and Mrs Morgans that when unfit he would get someone else to drive was no basis for holding that Cawfield had been delegated to drive as agent for her, and she was not vicariously liable for his negligence.

Norwood v Navan

[1981] RTR 457, CA
Mrs Navan had her husband's consent to use his car. She went out in it for the afternoon with two friends to a neighbouring town, first to visit a fortune-teller and then on a shopping expedition. On the return journey by her negligent driving she caused injury and loss to the plaintiff. He claimed damages against both Mr and Mrs Navan. She allowed judgment against her to go by default but her husband denied any vicarious liability for her negligence. The county court judge held he was liable in that the shopping she had done was in the interests and for the purpose of both of them. There was a sufficient use of the car for his purposes to make her his agent: he was vicariously liable for her negligent driving.
HELD, ON APPEAL: This was not right. The idea of a 'matrimonial car' formulated by Lord Denning in *Launchbury v Morgans* (above, sub nom *Morgans v Launchbury*) had been rejected by the House of Lords. The law there laid down by the Lords is based on proper proof of agency. The facts in the present case did not amount to such proof. Mrs Navan was at very most doing only general shopping. It would be absurd in such a case for the court to examine the contents of her shopping basket to see what she had bought. There was no vicarious liability on Mr Navan.

Delegation of liability

Norton v Canadian Pacific Steamships Ltd

[1961] 2 All ER 785, [1961] 1 WLR 1057, 105 Sol Jo 442, CA
The plaintiff claimed damages for injuries he received by the negligent driving of an electric bogie by a porter named Morris on the Prince's landing stage at Liverpool. Morris was one of 180 porters plying for hire on the landing stage. Though requiring a licence from the Liverpool City Council to act as such the porters were an independent body of men not in the general employment of anyone. The defendants were ship owners whose vessels used the landing stage for the disembarkation of passengers. They paid for the porters' services in handling passengers' luggage by a single payment per ship to the senior head porter who was responsible for distributing the money among the porters in whatever manner they had agreed. The electric bogie was one of the seven in use by the porters. Four had been provided by the defendants and the Cunard Line jointly and three by the manufacturers of the bogies. They were all used indiscriminately by the porters. The bogie Morris was driving at the time of the accident happened to be one of the four belonging to the defendants and the Cunard Line. The accident occurred when Morris was using it to transfer luggage from the defendant's ship to a conveyor on the landing stage. In the Court of first instance the plaintiff alleged that Morris was a servant of the defendants, but the judge held that he was not. This finding was not appealed against. The judge found in favour of the plaintiff on the ground that the bogie belonged to the defendants (as joint owners with the Cunard Line) and that in the circumstances Morris was driving as their agent at the time of the accident, following *Ormrod v Crosville Motor Services Ltd* (above).

HELD, ON APPEAL: The defendants were not liable. Morris never lost his independence as a licensed porter and was in complete control of the services he was rendering; he was using the bogie purely for the better or easier performance of the duties for which he was engaged and paid. The defendants had not assumed any obligation or undertaken any task of driving and using the bogies and had not delegated such task to the porters. There was clear and emphatic evidence that the defendants did not exercise any control or have any right to control the licensed porters in respect of the manner in which they were to move the luggage or use the bogies. Ownership of the bogie was insufficient in itself to create liability for its negligent use. The principle in *Ormrod*'s case is that of the delegation of a task or duty as in *Hewitt v Bonvin* (p 160, above). The owner of a car who takes or sends it on a journey for his own purposes owes a duty of care to other road users and is liable for the negligent driving of the car whether by himself or by an agent to whom he had delegated the driving. In the present case there was no such delegation.

Liability of repairer

McManus v Weinbert

(1940) Post Magazine, 621, 11 May
W's policy was O O D. Repairers sent driver who was driving car from W's house to repairers when plaintiff was injured. Lewis J held W had no right to control the driver. The right of control remained with the repairers who were the employers of the driver on the journey and repairers were liable.

Principal not the owner of vehicle

Nottingham v Aldridge

[1971] 2 QB 739, [1971] 2 All ER 751, [1971] 3 WLR 1, 115 Sol Jo 328, [1971] 1 Lloyd's Rep 424 (Eveleigh J)
The plaintiff and the first defendant were apprentices employed by the Post Office (the second defendants). They were required by the terms of their service to attend a residential course of training some distance from home. They were allowed home for the weekend but had to be back at the training centre by Sunday night. They were returning on Sunday evening in a car driven by the first defendant when an accident occurred in which the plaintiff was injured. The car belonged to the first defendant's father. In accordance with Post Office regulations the first defendant was entitled to be, and was, paid 3d per mile for the cost of travel by car and an additional 1d per mile for conveying the plaintiff. The plaintiff claimed that the Post Office were vicariously liable for the first defendant's negligence either (1) as their servant or (2) as their agent, driving the car for their benefit.
HELD: (1) Although the first defendant was the servant of the Post Office in that he had with them a contract of service he was not at the relevant time acting as such and the relationship of master and servant did not exist. (2) The Post Office were not so involved in the carriage of the plaintiff as to make the first defendant their agent. While ownership of motor vehicle is not essential in all cases to make a principal liable for the acts of his agent in driving it for his benefit the fact of ownership is of value in determining whether or not the driver was driving independently or on behalf of the principal. Where (as here) the principal is not the owner of the vehicle it must

be established that the driver was driving in a genuinely representative capacity, that is, as an agent for and on behalf of the principal and as one to whom there has been a delegation of a task or duty. That was not the case here and the Post Office were not liable.

TAXIS

Liability of proprietor for negligence of drivers in London

Gates v Bill

[1902] 2 KB 38, 71 LJKB 702, 87 LT 288, 50 WR 546, 18 TLR 592, 46 Sol Jo 498, CA and other cases
Under the London Hackney Carriages Act 1843, so far as the public is concerned, the registered proprietor, and also the actual proprietor, of a hackney carriage is responsible for the acts of the driver whilst he is plying for hire, as if the relationship of master and servant exists between them, even though it does not in fact exist.

Liability of proprietor for negligence of driver outside London

Bygraves v Dicker

[1923] 2 KB 585, 92 LJKB 1021, 129 LT 688, Div Ct
Outside London the Town Police Clauses Act 1847, provides that the registered proprietor must be treated as the employer of the driver for the purpose of claims by members of the public in respect of damage by the negligence of the driver.

Note—By the London Cab Order 1934, dated 11 December 1934, S R & O 1934/1346, made pursuant to the Metropolitan Public Carriage Act 1869 (32 & 33 Vict, c 115) and the London Cab and Stage Carriage Act 1907 (7 Edw 7, c 55), which applies by para 2 to a motor cab in the City of London and Metropolitan Police District, it is provided by r 8 as follows:

'**8** (1) The liability to third parties to which this paragraph relates is any liability (other than a contractual liability) incurred by the owner or driver of a cab, as a consequence of the user of the cab, in respect of

(a) the death or bodily injury to any person, other than a person employed by the owner of the cab whose death or injury arises out of and in the course of his employment, and
(b) damage to animals or to property not belonging to the cab-owner or cab-driver nor held in trust by him nor under his charge or control not being conveyed in the cab, and not being damage to any bridge, weighbridge, viaduct, or road, or any property thereunder.

(2) Subject as hereinafter provided there shall be in force in relation to every cab a policy of insurance issued by an insurer approved by the [Assistant Commissioner] which insures the owner of the cab and any other person who drives the cab with his permission in respect of any liability to third parties to which this paragraph relates: provided that

(a) a policy of insurance or a security complying with Part II of the Road Traffic Act 1930, as amended by any subsequent Act, shall be a sufficient fulfilment of the requirements of this paragraph in respect of so much of the liability as it covers, and
(b) any other liability to which this paragraph relates shall not be required to be covered for an amount in excess of £10,000 in respect of any claim or series of claims arising out of any one accident or occurrence.

(3) The [Assistant Commissioner] may, in any case where he is satisfied that the financial position of the owner of a cab is such as to enable him and the cab-driver to meet without insurance any liability to third parties to which this paragraph relates, or any part of that liability, direct that the requirements of this paragraph (not being requirements of Part II of

the Road Traffic Act, 1930, as amended by any subsequent Act) either shall not apply in relation to that cab or shall apply with such modifications as he may direct, and in any case such case those requirements shall either have no effect or have effect as so modified as the case may be.'

Mini-cabs

Rogers v Night Riders

[1983] RTR 324, CA
The defendants were a firm operating a minibus service, holding themselves out to the general public as a car hire firm. The plaintiff telephoned them for a car to take her to Euston station. A car was sent and the plaintiff travelled in it. En route a door flew open, struck a parked vehicle and bounced back, injuring the plaintiff's hand. The car belonged to the driver; he was not the defendants' employee and the defendants had no control over the management of the car. The county court judge found that there had been a failure to maintain the car properly but also that the driver was an independent contractor for whose negligence the defendants were not liable. HELD, ON APPEAL: This was not right. It was not a case of vicarious liability; it was a case of a primary duty on the part of the defendants. They had undertaken to provide a car and driver to take the plaintiff to her destination and they owed her a duty to take care to see that the vehicle was safe and reasonably fit for that purpose. It was immaterial whether the duty was put in contract or in tort: it was a duty the defendants could not delegate. The situation would have been different if the true nature of the defendants' business had been known to the plaintiff, but it was not.

3 LIABILITY OF PARENT

Note—A parent as such is not liable for the negligence of their child, unless the child is their servant or agent. A parent is liable for his own negligence and further is under a duty to exercise such control over the children as a prudent parent would exercise. The age of the child is a material factor to be taken into account.

Donaldson v McNiven

[1952] 2 All ER 691
Parents are not responsible for the torts of their children.

Bebee v Sales

(1916) 32 TLR 413
They are only responsible when they have themselves done something wrong, eg if they have been guilty of lack of that supervision to be expected of reasonable and prudent parents.

Note—See *Carmarthenshire County Council v Lewis*, above.

CHAPTER 4

Passengers

DUTY TO PASSENGERS

Note—A person who undertakes to carry another person in a vehicle either gratuitously or for reward will be liable to that other party if he causes him damage by negligence. The duty is to use reasonable care and skill for the safety of the passengers during the period of carriage. There is no absolute duty.

Jones v Boyce

(1816) 1 Stark 493, 18 RR 812
A passenger in a coach was, by negligence of the coach proprietor in failing to provide proper means of conveyance placed in a perilous position, and he leaped from the coach and was injured. This is the result of the negligence of the coach proprietor in providing a coupling rein that was defective.

Per Lord Ellenborough: to enable the plaintiff to sustain the action it is not necessary that he should have been thrown off the coach; it is sufficient if he was placed by the misconduct of the defendant in such a situation as obliged him to adopt the alternative of a dangerous leap or to remain at certain peril; if that position was occasioned by the default of the defendant the action may be supported. The question is, whether he was placed in such a situation as to render what he did a prudent precaution for the purpose of self-preservation.

Ludditt v Ginger Coote Airways Ltd

[1947] AC 233, [1947] 1 All ER 328, [1947] LJR 1067, 177 LT 334, 63 TLR 157, PC
The liability of a common carrier of passengers was settled by the decision of *Readhead v Midland Rly Co* (below). It is more limited than that of a common carrier of goods. His obligation is to carry 'with due care'. One reason, no doubt, is that the carrier of goods is a bailee of the goods but not of passengers (citing *Grand Trunk Rly*

Co of Canada v Robinson [1915] AC 740, 84 LJPC 194, 113 LT 350, 31 TLR 395). In the case of a railway company a breach can be regarded as a breach of an implied contract, or of a duty imposed by the general law and in the latter case as in form a tort. This general duty, subject to any statutory restrictions, can be superseded by a specific contract. The carrier is not precluded from making a special contract with his passengers.

Joint enterprise for crime

Ashton v Turner

[1981] QB 137, [1980] 3 All ER 870, [1980] 3 WLR 736, 124 Sol Jo 792, [1981] RTR 54 (Ewbank J)
After an evening of heavy drinking in public houses and clubs, Ashton, Turner and McLune returned to McLune's home in his car, driven by Turner. There Ashton suggested going out to burglarise a shop. Turner agreed but McLune said he would have nothing to do with it and went to bed. The other two then drove off in McLune's car. They chose a suitable shop, smashed the window and stole goods from it. They went back to the car and Turner drove it, Ashton in the passenger seat. They were pursued by a taxi and in travelling at a high speed to get away from the taxi, skidded and crashed. Ashton was badly injured. He sued Turner for damages for negligent driving.
HELD: (1) The law of England may in certain circumstances not recognise the existence of a duty of care by one participant in a crime to another participant in the same crime in relation to an act done in connection with the commission of that crime; the law is based on public policy. In the present case no duty of care existed between Turner and Ashton during the course of the burglary and the subsequent flight in the get-away car. (2) The maxim *volenti non fit injuria* could on the facts of this case, where two burglars had been drinking and were fleeing in a get-away car, apply to give a complete defence; and this was so despite the Road Traffic Act 1972, s 148(3). (3) If (1) and (2) were wrong the plaintiff would still on the facts be guilty of contributory negligence to the extent of 50%.

See also *Pitts v Hunt* and *Morris v Murray*, p 49, below.

Note—Section 148(3) of the Road Traffic Act 1972 has been replaced by s 149 of the Road Traffic Act 1988 which became effective on 15 May 1989.

LIABILITY OF PASSENGER FOR NEGLIGENCE OF DRIVER

Scarsbrook v Mason

[1961] 3 All ER 767, 105 Sol Jo 889 (Glyn-Jones J)
The defendant was a passenger in a car which, due to the negligence of the driver, ran off the road and injured the plaintiffs who were standing on the footway. The judge found that the defendant had joined the other occupants of the car for a trip to Southend: he had paid 4s towards the cost of petrol and he was accepted by the others as an equal member of the party, all equally concerned in the trip, one of whom was to drive on behalf of all the others. The owner was not present, the car having been driven away by someone without his consent about three days previously.

HELD: The members of the party were jointly and severally liable for the manner in which the car was driven and the plaintiffs were entitled to succeed against the defendant as a member of the party, on the ground that the driver was acting as agent for each and all the members of that party.

Bown v Chatfield

[1963] CLY 2348, CC
The defendant and another man took the plaintiff's car from a car park without his consent. The car was damaged whilst being driven by the other man with the defendant as a passenger. The plaintiff relied on *Scarsbrook v Mason* (above). The defendant gave evidence that he was drunk when the car was taken from the car park and remembered nothing of the journey. The judge held that the driver is agent for the passengers only when they are equal members of the venture. On the facts the defendant was not an equal member and was not liable.

PASSENGERS ON PUBLIC TRANSPORT

Duty of driver

Parkinson v Liverpool Corpn

[1950] 1 All ER 367, [1950] WN 43, 66 TLR 262, 94 Sol Jo 161, CA
The driver of an omnibus applied his brakes with some suddenness to avoid running over a dog. The dog came from the nearside and the driver saw it about 20 yards away. It appeared to be crossing in front of the bus and the driver took his foot off the accelerator and passed behind the dog. Having cleared the bus, the dog suddenly came back across the front of the bus when the driver was some 5 or 6 yards away, whereupon the driver applied his brakes with some suddenness and stopped the bus. A male passenger aged 65 had risen from his seat to be ready to alight and was walking along the gangway. He was thrown to the floor and broke two ribs. The conductor was also thrown to the floor but the seated passengers were not inconvenienced.

Pritchard J held the test was not whether the driver owed a duty to the dog and a greater duty to the passengers. The test was: Did the driver act reasonably or unreasonably by doing something which a reasonable person would do? The judge held that the driver acted as a reasonable person in an emergency and there was no negligence.
HELD, ON APPEAL: If there had been no explanation there was a prima facie inference of negligence but the driver had given an explanation. The proper test had been applied of an ordinary, reasonable, careful driver. The argument based upon *Sutherland*'s case (below) that there was a paramount duty to the passengers and that it is not an answer to say it was to avoid a dog, was not accepted. There were two differences on the facts: (1) the passengers had not had time to get to their seats; (2) it was a case of a magnetic brake on a tramway car which had extremely sudden consequences. Although drivers act instinctively they are required to go through some process of reasoning. The driver's evidence was that he would try to save the animal's life without endangering anybody else. He had applied his mind to the question of endangering anyone else when faced with an emergency of this kind. Appeal dismissed.

Glasgow Corpn v Sutherland

[1951] WN 111, 95 Sol Jo 204, HL
A passenger boarded a tramcar at a stopping place and soon after it moved off a dog which had been running alongside darted in front. The driver applied his magnetic brake and brought the car to a sudden stop. The passenger had not had time to take her seat and was thrown to the ground and injured.

Per Lord Simmonds: It was a question of fact whether the driver had acted with the skill and care of a reasonable driver and the findings showed that he had not. This opinion did not either doubt or affirm *Parkinson*'s case, above.

Challen v Bell and London Transport Executive

(1954) Times, 6 February (Pilcher J)
A pedestrian stepped in front of an omnibus causing it to stop suddenly. The plaintiff was a passenger and was thereby injured. The plaintiff sued London Transport Executive and the pedestrian. Pedestrian found alone to blame; judgment against pedestrian and for LTE.

Wooller v London Transport Board

[1976] RTR 206, CA
The defendant's bus was being driven along Lewisham Way in the rush hour at about 25 mph. It was about half a bus-length behind a lorry. Some passengers in the bus, of whom the plaintiff was one, were standing ready to get off at a stop 150 yards ahead. Suddenly a pedestrian stepped off the pavement on to a pedestrian crossing in front of the lorry. The lorry pulled up suddenly and the bus driver applied his brakes hard and stopped without hitting the lorry. The plaintiff, who was not holding on, was thrown over by the sudden stop and injured. The judge held the bus driver two-thirds to blame for driving too close to the lorry.
HELD, ON APPEAL: The bus driver was not to blame at all. It was a case like *Parkinson v Liverpool Corpn* (above). The bus was a reasonable distance behind the lorry and the driver was able to pull up in this emergency without hitting it. The suggestion that the bus should keep such a distance from the lorry that it could pull up without having to brake suddenly was a counsel of perfection which ignored modern traffic conditions.

Barry v Greater Manchester Passenger Transport Executive

(19 January 1984, unreported: taken from full transcript), CA
As the driver of a bus approached a bus stop where he intended to stop he saw ahead on the pavement three girls with two dogs, one on a lead, the other not. He was driving slowly, at about 15 mph, because he was approaching the stop. Just as he was about to pass the girls and dogs one of the dogs dashed out into the road in front of him. Instinctively he stepped on the brake; the plaintiff passengers who had risen from their seats intending to alight were thrown to the floor and injured. The judge held the driver not to blame; he had acted on instinct—the instinct to preserve life whether of a dog or of a child or whatever it may be. 'Anybody who has driven for any length of time knows perfectly well that when such an emergency arises you go for the brakes.' It was argued on appeal that the judge should not have equated the attitude of a driver to a dog as it should be to a child; the driver should have taken a conscious decision as he approached the group that if a dog ran out he would drive on rather than risk injuring his passengers.

HELD: This would be a totally unrealistic expectation utterly divorced from the way in which reasonable people conduct their affairs. Three young people and two dogs standing on a pavement do not call for any special adjustment of the driving of a bus. A dog suddenly dashing out is an uncovenanted happening. The judge approached the case on the right lines: the driver was taken by surprise and reacted instinctively. Passengers on public transport take the risk that the driver may effect emergency braking causing inconvenience. Although the facts in *Parkinson*'s case (above) were different the judge was right to have regard to that decision as a guide. Appeal dismissed.

Entering the vehicle

Geeves v London General Omnibus Co

(1901) 17 TLR 249, 190 LT Jo 15, CA
A passenger was starting to go upstairs on an omnibus when the conductor asked him whether all was well. The passenger replied, 'Yes, go on.' The vehicle started with a jerk and the passenger fell. The passenger was held entitled to recover.

Degan v Borough of Dundee

(1940) 190 LT Jo 15
A passenger was thrown off his balance by a number of workmen who boarded an omnibus as he was making his way towards a seat. The court held the bus company not liable. The plea that the presence in an omnibus of 20 or 30 workmen placed on the bus company a duty for special measures of caution by police or a special staff was fantastic.

Note—See also *Glasgow Corpn v Sutherland*, p 170, above.

Davies v Liverpool Corpn

[1949] 2 All ER 175, 93 Sol Jo 373, CA
Five women were waiting to board a tramcar at a request stop. Three of them had boarded it and the plaintiff had one foot on the step, when an unidentified and unauthorised passenger rang the bell to restart the car and the plaintiff was injured. The conductor was collecting fares on the upper deck. The judge found that the conductor made no endeavour to come from the top deck for the purpose of restarting the car and, notwithstanding the number of persons waiting to board it, showed gross indifference to the safety of the passengers. The car was stopped for an appreciable time and the conductor could have come down to see that it was safe, and in breach of his admitted duty and without sufficient excuse was absent from the place where he should have been.
HELD, ON APPEAL: It is desirable, unless there are some special circumstances which make it impracticable or impossible, for the conductor to be on the platform at a stopping place, because he is the only person authorised to give the starting signal. The conductor might reasonably have foreseen such a happening if he did not come down quickly. Appeal dismissed.

McLaughlin v Glasgow Corpn

1963 SLT (Sh Ct) 53
The defendants' bus started as the pursuer was boarding it and before she had reached a position of safety on the platform. A witness said in evidence that the conductress had rung the bell for the driver to proceed, and it was argued for the defenders that it could not be negligent for him to do so.
HELD: A bell from the conductress only authorised the driver to proceed and did not absolve him from a duty to exercise reasonable care. So far as he was able to do so from his position and with the assistance of his mirrors, he must still take care. In any event it had not been established that the bell had been rung and for the bus to start while the pursuer was in the act of boarding was negligent.

Guinnear v London Passenger Transport Board

(1948) 92 Sol Jo 350, Times, 10 April (Lynksey J)
The plaintiff signalled a Green Line bus to stop at a request stop in Limpsfield. The bus driver slowed down and drew in towards the plaintiff, but signalled to him that he was going to stop farther on. The plaintiff failed to see the signal and attempted to board the bus while it was still moving at 3 or 4 miles an hour. The bus then accelerated and the plaintiff fell from it into a trench, which had been dug in the road just in front of the request stop, and suffered personal injuries.
HELD: The driver of the bus was negligent in accelerating before he had made sure of the plaintiff's safety, and the plaintiff was negligent in boarding a moving bus; each party was equally to blame. Award one-half of assessed damage.

Passengers injured en route

Baird v South London Tramways Co

(1886) 2 TLR 756, 190 LT Jo 15
A conductor who calls out the name of a stopping place which a tramcar is approaching does not thereby invite a passenger to alight.

Folkes v North London Rly Co

(1892) 8 TLR 269
A passenger who stood by an open door of a tram as it slowed down and was thrown out because it stopped with a jerk was held not entitled to recover.

Note—This case was afterwards doubted but not reversed, 190 LTJ 15.

Hall v London Tramways Co Ltd

(1896) 12 TLR 611, 190 LT Jo 15, CA
If, after a bell is rung, the driver slows down 'almost to a standstill' he is bound to look round and see whether the passenger is safe.

Note—208 LTJ 15 adds that the plaintiff asked the conductor to stop; he rang his bell and went upstairs, but the tram never came to a standstill and the driver accelerated suddenly, jerking the passenger off. This was a case of a horse tram. The Court of Appeal said there was no rule that a passenger must sit still until the vehicle actually stops.

Western Scottish Motor Traction v Allam

[1943] 2 All ER 742, 60 TLR 34, 87 Sol Jo 399, HL
A passenger was standing in a motor omnibus near the doorway which was in the forward part just behind the driver's cabin. The door had not been closed. There were no vacant seats, but he was not holding on to any part of the vehicle. The vehicle was not provided with rails or straps. He was thrown through the doorway into the road while it was being driven round a curve.
HELD: The driver was negligent in driving round the bend at high speed and there was no contributory negligence. The decision was upheld in the House of Lords.

Per Viscount Simon LC: The driver was not entitled to sway round the corner at what speed he liked so long as that speed was safe for passengers who were seated or holding on to some portion of the vehicle. The duty of reasonable care owed by the driver to those on board extends to all passengers whether they are 'holding on' or not. There may well be a case, eg of a person with a baby in his arms, where a standing passenger had no free hand with which to hold on.

Johnstone v Western Scottish Motor Traction Co Ltd

(1955) 105 L Jo 762, Outer House, Ct of Sess
A man was killed when he was flung through the open door of the defendants' omnibus in which he was travelling as a passenger. The omnibus was a single decker to which access was obtained through a doorway at the front end of the nearside, the open doorway being fitted with a folding door which opened inwards and forwards. When the deceased and his wife (who was the pursuer in this action) entered the bus there was standing room only and the deceased took his position inside the bus but near the doorway. He stood with his back against the forward partition without apparently holding on. About 170 yards from the bus stop the road turned to the left, passed under a railway bridge and then turned to the right. The accident occurred as the bus was emerging from the railway bridge and was steering on a right lock. The pursuer contended inter alia that the fact of the deceased's accidental exit from the omnibus while in motion, being something that did not happen in the ordinary course of things, amounted prima facie to evidence of fault on the part of the defendants and she prayed in aid the maxim *res ipsa loquitur*. Reference was also made to *Western Scottish Motor Traction Co Ltd v Allam*.

In rejecting the contention Lord Walker observed that in the case referred to it was proved independently that the omnibus had been driven at too great a speed. The only useful proposition extractable from the decision related to the standard of care required of a driver. The driver, it was held, must exercise care to avoid ejecting a passenger even although the passenger was standing without holding on. The decision was not, however, in his Lordship's opinion, an authority for the view that the fact of a passenger's accidental exit from an omnibus in motion was prima facie evidence of negligence on the part of the driver or conductor.

Wragg v Grout and London Passenger Transport Board

(1966) 116 L Jo 752, CA
The plaintiff boarded a bus at a request stop and decided to go upstairs. As she was mounting the stairs the conductor rang the bell and the bus started. It had covered about 40 yards and had reached a speed of about 20 mph when on rounding a slight right-hand bend it swayed to the left. The plaintiff had not quite reached the top of the

stairs; she was not holding on and fell back down the stairs breaking her leg. The road had a camber so that as the bus started from the bus stop it would tend to be leaning to the left. On passing the mouth of a side road it would straighten up and would sway to the left again after passing the side road and on entering upon the right-hand bend. HELD: It must be common knowledge that when a bus was being driven in a normal fashion movements of the body of the bus could be felt and that as it went round the bend even at a moderate speed it would not be unusual for it to sway to the left. Anyone standing or just about to sit down would be inconvenienced by the sway and might momentarily lose his balance; that was even more true of anyone mounting the stairs whilst holding two bags in one hand as the plaintiff did and momentarily not holding on to the rail. It was impossible to say that if a person did fall down that that was evidence of negligence against the bus driver. If there was evidence of an extra-ordinary swerve or sway, that might be evidence of negligence on the basis of *res ipsa loquitur. Western Scottish Motor Traction v Allam* (above) was no authority for saying that if there was any movement of the bus while people were standing or walking to their seats it was evidence that the driver was not driving the bus carefully. In the absence of a finding that the driver was driving too fast or that the movement or sway was wholly exceptional there was no ground for holding the driver negligent. *Allam's* case was quite different. In that case the bus was going too fast.

Alighting from vehicle

Holland v North Metropolitan Tramway Co

(1886) 3 TLR 245, 190 LT Jo 15
It is negligence for a tram conductor to start his vehicle whilst a passenger is getting off.

Hett v McKenzie

1939 SC 350
A passenger, while getting out of the rear of a car, put his hand on the pillar between the rear and front door. The driver slammed the front door and injured the passenger's fingers, not knowing they were there. The driver was held liable.

Mottram v South Lancashire Transport Co

[1942] 2 All ER 452, 86 Sol Jo 321, CA
About 10.30 pm on 7 September 1941, the plaintiff followed a male passenger down the stairs from the upper deck of a bus to dismount at a request stop. The male passenger rang the bell once, and the bus slowed down, but just as he was getting off, he rang the bell twice (the signal to proceed). The plaintiff proceeded to alight after him but the bus did not stop and gathered speed, and plaintiff was thrown and injured. The conductress was collecting fares on the upper deck.
HELD: No negligence of conductress; it was putting the duty too high to say that she should go down to the platform to see people off in safety.

Jude v Edinburgh Corpn

1943 SC 399, Ct of Sess
In an action against the owners and operators of an omnibus service for damages in respect of injuries sustained through falling from one of their omnibuses, the pursuer

averred that, as the omnibus approached the stopping place at which she wished to alight, she was standing on the upper of two steps below the platform, holding the handrail, preparatory to alighting. Instead of stopping, the omnibus suddenly and without warning swerved violently, first to the right and then to the left, in order to pass another omnibus already at the stopping place. As a result of this swerve, the pursuer was thrown on to the roadway and injured. The conductress, who saw where the pursuer was standing, did not suggest that she should leave the step, the stance usually taken by passengers intending to alight, and the only one from which a notice warning passengers against alighting before the omnibus stopped was legible.
HELD: That the pursuer's averments disclosed that she had been guilty of contributory negligence in placing herself in a position of danger on the step of a vehicle in motion; and action dismissed.

Massie v Edinburgh Corpn

(1950) 100 L Jo 665, Ct of Sess
A man boarded a bus which had a door at the front, and sat beside a friend on the front nearside seat next the gangway. In front of him was a metal shield and an upright stretching to the roof for passengers to hold on to. He got up to leave, holding the upright with his left hand, and, as the bus turned a corner, he fell out of the open door and was killed.
HELD: The conductor was not under an absolute obligation to keep the door shut; he had no reason to anticipate that the deceased might fall through the open door, there being no standing passengers. Nor was there evidence that it should have been apparent to the conductor that the deceased was unwell and might fall. The owners of the bus were under no liability.

Prescott v Lancashire United Transport Co

[1953] 1 All ER 288, [1953] 1 WLR 232, 97 Sol Jo 64, CA
The plaintiff and her husband were passengers on the defendants' single-decker bus, which was full. All the seats were occupied and some five or eight people were standing. The door was at the front. The husband told the conductor that they wished to alight at the next request stop. The conductor rang the bell and told them to wait until the bus stopped. Owing to road works, marked with red lights, and driving conditions, the bus stopped 20 or 25 yards short of the request stop right into the kerb. Unknown to the driver and conductor, but known to the plaintiff and her husband, it had for some time been customary for other buses to stop for passengers to alight at that point short of the request stop on account of the road works. The plaintiff and her husband assumed the bus had stopped for them to alight. The husband alighted and as the plaintiff was alighting, the bus re-started and the plaintiff was injured. The driver was unaware of the accident. The conductor had closed the door at the previous stop and had not noticed anyone opening the door.
HELD: There was no evidence of negligence of the driver. The conductor was negligent. His statement to the husband to 'wait until the bus stops' was a clear invitation to the plaintiff and her husband to alight when the bus did stop. When the bus stopped short of the request stop, the conductor ought either to have warned the passengers or communicated with the driver. The conductor could see the husband had got off and that there were others waiting to get off.

Adopting the statement of Goddard LJ in *Mottram*'s case:

'After the man had given the signal for the bus to stop, and if the bus had stopped, it would have been the duty of the conductress to see that no one else was getting off before giving the signal for the bus to start again. In this case the bus never did stop.'

Before it could stop, the officious passenger gave the signal for the bus to start again.

The conductor was negligent and the defendants were liable.

Wyngrove v Scottish Omnibuses Ltd

1966 SC (HL) 47

The appellants' bus was of a type having a rear door which gave access from and to a rear platform. The doorway was 3 ft 3 in wide. The door was kept open along parts of the route where stops were frequent. There was no central pillar in the doorway but there were nine handholds available to passengers on the platform. The respondent's husband came on to the platform ready to alight at the next stop. The door was open. There were two handholds on the right but he failed to grasp either and fell out. The bus was being driven smoothly at the time. In the courts below the judges took the view that if there had been a central pillar the accident would have been prevented and the appellants were negligent.

HELD, ON APPEAL: The well established principles of law on the duty of a person towards passengers showed that he must take all precautions for their safety and anticipate such degree of inadvertence on their part as experience showed to be not uncommon. But he was entitled to have regard to his own experience and that of others in a similar situation with regard to what precautions had been found hitherto to be adequate. It was clearly foreseeable that a person leaving his seat in a moving bus may lose his balance and, if near the door, may fall out. The recognised means of enabling him to save himself was to provide handholds, of which there were nine on the platform of this bus. Over a period of years no accident had been attributed to the absence of a central pillar and it would have been unreasonable to fit one. Appeal allowed.

CONTRIBUTORY NEGLIGENCE

Generally

Davies v Swan Motor Co (Swansea) Ltd

[1949] 2 KB 291, [1949] 1 All ER 620, 65 TLR 278, CA

A workman was riding on steps on the offside of his employers' dust lorry, contrary to regulations. An overtaking omnibus collided with the lorry and the workman sustained fatal injuries. His widow sued the bus company, who joined the employers and their driver as third parties. The judge held the bus company negligent; that the deceased was not negligent; that the lorry owners were not liable by reason of the doctrine of common employment; and that the lorry driver was not liable because deceased was in the position of a trespasser.

HELD ON APPEAL: The deceased, the bus driver and the lorry driver, were all negligent; the bus driver for overtaking on a bend in a narrow lane without warning and before receiving a signal; the lorry driver for turning suddenly across the road without making proper use of his mirror and without giving sufficient warning; the deceased for taking up a dangerous position by riding on the offside step. The plaintiff contended that the deceased owed no duty to the bus driver not to stand on the step,

and that the bus driver had the last opportunity of avoiding the accident, and that the plaintiff's damages should not be apportioned as against the bus company.
HELD Per Bucknill LJ citing Charlesworthy on the *Law of Negligence* (2nd edn) p 464, and Atkin LJ in *Ellerman Lines Ltd v Grayson* [1919] 2 KB 514; affd sub nom *H & C Grayson v Ellerman Line Ltd* [1920] AC 466, 123 LT 65, HL:

'The doctrine of contributory negligence cannot, I think, be based upon a breach of duty to the negligent defendant. It is difficult to suppose that a person owes a duty to anyone to preserve his own property. He may not recover if he could reasonably have avoided the consequences of the defendant's negligence.'

Apportionment between plaintiff and the defendants; lorry driver four-fifths to blame; deceased one-fifth; of the four-fifths between defendants (adopting that of trial judge) lorry driver two-thirds to blame bus driver one-third.

Jones v Livox Quarries Ltd

[1952] 2 QB 608, [1952] 1 TLR 1377, 96 Sol Jo 344, CA
A workman in a quarry proceeding to the canteen jumped on the back of a traxcavator (which did work similar to an excavator) and stood on the towbar at the back holding on to two uprights. In so doing, he was acting in defiance of orders. A dumper ran into the back of the traxcavator and the plaintiff was injured. Hallett J held the driver of the dumper was negligent and plaintiff contributed to extent of 15%. Both parties appealed and both appeals were dismissed.

Per Denning LJ: Contributory negligence depends on foreseeability and the plaintiff must take into account the possibility of others being careless. The consequences did not depend on foreseeability but on causation. The question in every case was: what faults were those which caused the damage? Was the plaintiff's fault one of them? That necessity was shown by the word 'result' in s 1(1) of the 1945 Act. There was no clear guide to causation. It was a matter of common sense depending on the facts. Foreseeability was not the decisive test of causation though it was often a relevant factor. The plaintiff's injury was due in part to the fact that he chose to ride on the towbar instead of walking. His position was similar to that of the plaintiff in *Davies'* case. One of the causes was the plaintiff's negligence in riding on the towbar.

Dawrant v Nutt

[1960] 3 All ER 681, [1961] 1 WLR 253, 105 Sol Jo 129 (Stable J)
The plaintiff was a passenger in the side-car of a motor cycle combination driven by her husband when it collided with a car driven by the defendant. The accident happened at a dark part of the road after 9 pm on 30 August. Due to some defect neither the headlight nor the side light on the motor-cycle combination was alight: both the plaintiff and her husband had been aware of this for some time before the collision. The plaintiff was injured and her husband was killed. In actions, heard together, for damages for the plaintiff's personal injuries and as administratrix of her husband's estate for damages under the Fatal Accidents and Law Reform Acts the judge held the defendant and the plaintiff's husband equally to blame for the collision. On the question of the plaintiff's own contributory negligence in knowingly riding in an unlighted vehicle:
HELD: It was sufficient to say that it was unwise of the plaintiff to travel in a motor vehicle which she knew to be improperly lighted. That would not amount to a defence

unless there was a legal duty imposed on the plaintiff, vis-a-vis other possible users of the highway, not to do so; in other words, a legal duty to take reasonable care for her own safety. Having regard to *Dann v Hamilton* (above) and the reason behind it, the plaintiff did owe a duty and was in breach of it in knowingly travelling in an unlighted combination. But the proportion of negligence to be attributed to the driver and passenger of an unlighted vehicle was not necessarily the same. On the facts of the present case, the plaintiff's share of the blame vis-a-vis the defendant was one-quarter.

Note—G H L Fridman points out (117 NLJ at 1079) that the plaintiff's contributory negligence could not consist in a breach of a duty to other road users not to travel in an unlighted vehicle, for she owed none. It consisted in her disregard for her own safety.

Madden v Quirk

[1989] 1 WLR 702, 133 Sol Jo 752, [1989] RTR 304
The plaintiff was one of several passengers in the open back of a pick-up truck being driven along a main road by the first defendant. As the pick-up truck went to overtake a vehicle a car emerged from its offside. The emerging car swerved and avoided a collision with the truck. However, a second vehicle driven by the second defendant following behind this car took no evasive action and collided with the truck. As a result of this collision the plaintiff was thrown from the back of the truck and severely injured.

The first defendant pleaded guilty to carrying passengers in a dangerous manner contrary to s 40(5) of the Road Traffic Act 1972 and reg 100(1) of the Road Vehicles (Construction and Use) Regulations 1986. The first defendant was also convicted of driving without due care and attention.

The plaintiff accepted that he was 5% contributorily negligent and the trial judge found that both defendants were negligent. The judge then considered the question of contribution as between the defendants.
HELD: The negligence of the first defendant was to be assessed at 80% and that of the second defendant at 20%. However, in considering the Civil Liability (Contribution) Act 1978 the judge felt that the primary duty of care was on the driver rather than the passenger pursuant to reg 100(1) of the 1986 Regulations. Therefore he found that the first defendant was to be regarded as additionally negligent and in the circumstances the first defendant's contribution was increased to 85% and that of the second defendant reduced to 15%.

Note—Section 40(5) of the Road Traffic Act 1972 is now found at s 42(1) of the 1988 Act.

When drivers affected by drink

Owens v Brimmell

[1977] QB 859, [1976] 3 All ER 765, [1977] 2 WLR 943, 121 Sol Jo 338, [1977] RTR 82 (Tasker Watkins J)
The plaintiff and defendant were friends, both about 20 years of age, who at times drank together in public houses and clubs. One evening they went together visiting various public houses and a club, which they left in the defendant's car at about 2 am. By that time each had drunk about eight pints of beer. A short distance from the club the defendant overtook another car and in bringing his car to the nearside lost control and ran into a lamp post. The plaintiff was very seriously injured.

HELD: (1) It must be inferred that the effect of alcohol on the defendant's ability to drive was the cause of his losing control; (2) it was a clear case of contributory negligence on the part of the plaintiff either on the ground that the minds of both parties behaving recklessly were so befuddled by drink as to rid them of clear thought and perception or that the plaintiff should have foreseen the risk of being hurt by riding as a passenger with the defendant. But in such a case the driver, who alone controls the car and therefore has it in him whilst in drink to do great damage must bear by far the greater responsibility. The plaintiff's damages would be reduced by 20%.

Thomas v Fuller

(7 February 1977, unreported (Cantley J) (taken from full transcript of judgment))
The plaintiff, defendant and a friend spent an evening at a public house drinking. They were all habitual drinkers there, and on this evening, just before Christmas, they drank even more than usual, mainly spirits, amounting to about £45 worth. The plaintiff and defendant in the course of the evening began to think it a good idea to drive to Scotland on the M1. They borrowed the friend's car. They called at the plaintiff's house where they had more to drink and then set off. A few miles along the M1 the car ran into the back of a lorry. Each man said the other was driving; the driver was in fact the defendant. The plaintiff was seriously injured.
HELD: The cause of the accident was drink and the parties were on a drunken frolic. In putting himself as a passenger in a car driven by his drinking companion at the end of such an evening the plaintiff showed recklessness for his own safety. But although it was a joint venture it would be wrong to apportion the damages equally between them. The driver of a car is in control and it is he who is primarily responsible for its being properly driven. A fair adjustment even though this was a bad case of its type would be to hold the plaintiff 25% to blame for his injuries.

Buckingham v D'Souza

(18 July 1978, unreported) (taken from full transcript)
The plaintiff aged 16 1/2 and the defendant aged 19 went out together for the evening in the defendant's car. Despite his being the younger the plaintiff was the dominant partner in the expedition; they were out to find girls. After pints of lager in two public houses they went to a dance hall at about 10 pm. Between bouts of dancing they bought drinks and sat at a table drinking. They had further pints of lager as well as vodka and lime. They left the hall at 2 am, two girls in the back of the car. On a clear road with no other traffic present the car, driven by the defendant, ran off the road and overturned: the plaintiff suffered injury causing permanent paralysis below neck level. At about 5.30 am a blood test showed the defendant's alcohol level to be 150 mg. At trial expert evidence was given that it must have been at least 190 at the time of leaving the dance hall.
HELD: The amount the boys had had to drink by the time they left the dance hall was enough to have considerably affected the defendant's ability to drive and for it to be visible to anyone who was watching out for it. A passenger knows, or should know, that any drinking substantially beyond the permitted limit is likely to result in an accident. The plaintiff must bear some responsibility; his damages should be reduced by 20%. If it had been a case of two boys setting out on a pub-crawl a higher degree of contributory negligence would have been appropriate: per Jupp J.

Traynor v Donovan

[1978] CLY 2612 (Sheldon J)
The plaintiff suffered severe injuries when travelling as a front seat passenger in a car driven by the defendant. She had first met him in a public house only half an hour previously. The defendant was found to have a blood/alcohol level of 168 milligrammes but she had not noticed before accepting a lift any sign that his driving ability might be impaired. She called police evidence to confirm that symptoms of such excessive consumption of alcohol were not necessarily apparent to a lay person. There was medical evidence that her injuries had she been wearing a seat belt would have been different but no less serious.
HELD: There should be no deduction for contributory negligence from the plaintiff's damages.

Malone v Rowan

[1984] 3 All ER 402 (Russell J)
At about 8.15 pm the defendant was driving his small van with five friends as passengers when he lost control of the vehicle. One of his passengers, the plaintiff's husband, was thrown out and killed. The party had been out since morning. Between 12.30 and 3.30 pm they had been in public houses where the defendant drank four pints of lager; in the evening he had a further three half-pints. A blood-alcohol test showed that at the time of the accident he would have had at least 148 mg per 100 ml of blood. The surviving passengers said in evidence they knew the defendant had been drinking but not how much; they did not consider him unfit to drive and said there was nothing unusual in his manner of driving.
HELD: The facts were far removed from those of *Owens v Brimmell* (above). There was no direct evidence of the deceased's knowledge of what the defendant had consumed or whether he appreciated the risk he was running. The burden of proof was on the defendant. There should be no reduction of damages for contributory negligence.

Meah v McCreamer

[1985] 1 All ER 367, [1985] NLJ Rep 80
The plaintiff was seriously injured when a car in which he was a passenger, driven by the defendant, crashed into a tree. The two men had been out drinking before the accident: the plaintiff ought to have realised that the defendant was unfit to drive. The defendant was tested and found to have excess alcohol in his blood. Subsequently he disappeared and could not be found; his insurers through their solicitor contested the action. They pleaded that the plaintiff was negligent in accepting a lift when he knew the defendant was drunk. It was argued on behalf of the plaintiff that the plea was an admission of a criminal offence on the part of the defendant and that as the solicitor had perforce received no express instructions from him he was not able to make such a plea.
HELD: The insurance policy gave the insurers 'full discretion' in the conduct of proceedings. Although *Groom v Crocker* (p 883, below) showed that a solicitor was nevertheless bound in such case by a general duty to his client it was not inconsistent with that duty to plead contributory negligence. It was merely a plea that if the defendant were found to have been negligent the plaintiff was negligent in accepting a lift; indeed not so to plead would be inconsistent with the duty to the defendant not to incur more damages than justice required. The plaintiff's damages should be reduced by 25%.

Note—See also *Morris v Murray* (p 49, above) and *Pitts v Hunt* (p 51, above).

Stinton v Stinton

(1992) Times, 5 August
The plaintiff was injured when a passenger in a car belonging to and driven by his brother. The plaintiff's brother had just acquired the car but had not acquired any insurance. The plaintiff was aware that his brother did not have any insurance and that he and his brother would be using the car as a joint means of transport during an evening over the course of which much drink was consumed. The plaintiff's brother lost control of the car due to his inebriated condition and the plaintiff sued his brother and the MIB.
HELD: The plaintiff obtained a judgment against his brother with a one-third deduction for contributory negligence but his claim against the MIB failed. See Chapter 19.

SEAT BELT

Froom v Butcher

Note—The question whether the omission to wear a seat belt was reason for reducing the plaintiff's damages was argued in a number of cases heard in courts of first instance and gave rise to several conflicting decisions. The question eventually came before the court in *Froom v Butcher* on the 21 July 1975.

Froom v Butcher

[1976] QB 286, [1975] 3 All ER 520, [1975] 3 WLR 379, 119 Sol Jo 613, CA
A head-on collision occurred, wholly by the negligence of the defendant, between his car and a car driven by the plaintiff. The injuries sustained by the plaintiff included an abrasion of the scalp, fracture of the fourth right rib and fracture of a bone in the right hand. He was not wearing the seat belt fitted in the car for his use. He said he did not like wearing one and had heard of cases where belts had caused danger. The judge held on the medical evidence that the injuries might have been slighter if the belt had been worn; the issue was whether the driver's omission to wear the belt constituted negligence or lack of care. There were two bodies of opinion of which the dominant opinion was that belts should be worn. Nevertheless proper respect should be paid to the minority view; the courts were not justified in invading the freedom of choice of a motorist by holding it to be negligence or lack of care or fault to act on an opinion firmly and honestly held and shared by many other sensible people. The plaintiff's damages should not be reduced ([1974] RTR 528).
HELD, ON APPEAL: The judge's view was not right. In determining responsibility the law took no notice of the views of the particular individual. It required everyone to exercise all such precautions as a man of ordinary prudence would observe. As it is compulsory for every motor car to be fitted with seat belts Parliament must have thought it sensible to wear them. The material before the court about the value of wearing a seat belt showed plainly that everyone in the front seats of a car should wear one. The Highway Code advised wearing them. Wearing them only when there was a high risk as on a motorway in a fog was not enough; every time a car went out on the road there was a risk of accident. Forgetfulness was no excuse but there might be exceptional cases where a person might be excused from wearing a belt—for example, an unduly fat man or pregnant women. Apart from such cases a person failing to wear a seat belt should accept some share of responsibility for the damage

if it could have been prevented or lessened by wearing one. The question how much the share should be should not be prolonged by an expensive inquiry into the degree of blameworthiness. If the injuries would have been prevented altogether by wearing a seat belt the reduction should be 25%. If the evidence merely showed that the injuries would have been a good deal less by wearing a belt damages should be reduced by 15%. In the present case 20% would be right. In the case of passengers a driver might have a duty to invite his passenger to fasten the seat belt but adult passengers should know they ought to wear a seat belt without being told.

Condon v Condon

[1978] RTR 483 (Bristow J)
The plaintiff, a front seat passenger in the defendant's car, sustained injury to her right eye when the car struck a telephone pole. She was not wearing a seat belt. In a medical report a doctor said she would probably not have sustained such a severe injury had she been wearing a seat belt. The defendant called no evidence on the point. The plaintiff said she could not bear to wear a seat belt because of her fear of being trapped in the event of an accident.
HELD: If the defence wished to rely on a seat belt contributory negligence plea then in the absence of a clear admission it must elicit some evidence at the trial to enable the court to form a conclusion about it. The doctor had not said on what basis he expressed his opinion. On the available evidence it was unlikely that not wearing a seat belt had anything to do with the eye injury at all. Even if it had the damages should not be reduced because the plaintiff's phobia made her an 'extraordinary case' such as Lord Denning had visualised in *Froom v Butcher* (above). Her not wearing a seat belt was not a failure on her part to take reasonable care for her own safety.

Patience v Andrews

[1983] RTR 447, CA (Croom-Johnson J)
Where a plaintiff who was not wearing a seat belt suffered injuries the court had to examine the injuries actually suffered, assess compensation and then make a deduction depending on the extent to which those injuries had been caused or contributed to by the failure to wear the seat belt. It was not open to the court to reduce that percentage by speculating upon what other injuries the plaintiff might have suffered had he been wearing a seat belt, otherwise there would be 'an imponderable diminution' of the effect of the rule set out in *Froom v Butcher* (above).

Salmon v Newland

(1983) Times, 16 May (Michael Davies J)
The plaintiff suffered a perforating injury to his right eye resulting in total loss of useful vision in that eye, multiple facial injuries resulting in scarring and a continuing anxiety state. The injuries were sustained in a head-on collision of cars in one of which she was a passenger. She was not wearing a seat belt.
HELD: She was guilty of contributory negligence. Even though there was no medical evidence on the point, her injuries would have been a good deal less severe if she had been wearing one. Although Lord Denning had said in *Froom v Butcher* (above) that 15% was an appropriate reduction in such cases it was not high enough in this case; the reduction should be 20%. Additionally the cost of a convalescent holiday was recoverable in damages when, without it, her general condition might now be a good

deal worse. Award for pain suffering and loss of amenity £18,500; loss of future earnings £54,000, special damages £11,414 all subject to 20% reduction for contributory negligence.

Eastman v Southwest Thames Area Authority

(1990) 135 Sol Jo LB 99, [1991] RTR 389, CA
A passenger travelling in the front seat of an ambulance who sustained injuries for which the driver was in no way to blame, and which would have been avoided had she worn a seat belt was not entitled to recover damages from the Health Authority for the ambulance driver's failure to advise her to wear a belt. Seats in the rear part of the ambulance are equipped with seat belts: the plaintiff chose to occupy a seat in the front which did not have a belt. Above the seats was a notice which read 'For your own safety use the seat belts provided'. The question was whether in the circumstances it could fairly be said that the defendants had not exercised reasonable care in failing to draw attention to the seat belts, which were there to be seen. Lord Justice Russell could not accept the judge's decision at first instance that the ambulance attendant was under any obligation to point out the seat belts and the notice. In his Lordship's view no negligence had been demonstrated.

Decisions before Froom v Butcher

Toperoff v Mor

[1973] RTR 419 (Judge Dean QC)
The plaintiff wore a seat belt for most of the journey at the instance of the defendant, but omitted to refasten the belt after a short stop. Damages reduced by 25%.

Pasternack v Poulton

[1973] 2 All ER 74, [1973] 1 WLR 476, [1973] 1 Lloyd's Rep 439, QBD
The plaintiff usually wore seat belts but was unaware of their existence in the defendant's car. The duty of care lay with the defendant to point them out but damages were reduced by 5% since the plaintiff had failed to look.

Parnell v Shields

[1973] RTR 414 (Wein J)
The plaintiff's husband was killed when he was thrown from a van in a collision caused by the defendant's negligence. Damages were reduced by one-fifth since the deceased ought to have guarded against the folly of other drivers by wearing a seat belt.

McGee v Francis Shaw & Co Ltd

[1973] RTR 409 (Kilner-Brown J)
Had the plaintiff been wearing a seat belt he would have sustained no injury and he had, in fact, worn one previously in this vehicle. Damages were reduced by one-third.

Challoner v Williams and Croney

[1974] RTR 221 (Shaw J)
It was found that the defendants had not proved whether the plaintiff was wearing a

seat belt and whether, if she had been wearing one, it would have affected the injuries sustained. Therefore there was no reduction for contributory negligence.

Smith v Blackburn

[1974] 2 Lloyd's Rep 229 (O'Connor J)
It was for the defendant to show the plaintiffs had not been wearing seat belts and if the defendant failed to do this then there was no reduction.

Drage v Smith & Drage

[1975] 1 Lloyd's Rep 438 (Stabb J)
The plaintiff did not wear a seat belt because it was only a short journey. The plaintiff ought reasonably to have anticipated the risk. Damages were reduced by 15%.

Statutory regulations

ROAD TRAFFIC ACT 1988, SS 14 AND 15

14 Seat belts: adults (1) The Secretary of State may make regulations requiring, subject to such exceptions as may be prescribed, persons who are driving or riding in motor vehicles on a road to wear seat belts of such description as may be prescribed.
(2) Regulations under this section—
(*a*) may make different provisions in relation to different classes of vehicles, different descriptions of persons and different circumstances,
(*b*) shall include exceptions for—
(i) the users of vehicles constructed or adapted for the delivery of goods or mail to consumers or addresses, as the case may be, while engaged in making local rounds of deliveries,
(ii) the drivers of vehicles while performing a manoeuvre which includes reversing,
(iii) any person holding a valid certificate signed by a medical practitioner to the effect that it is inadvisable on medical grounds for him to wear a seat belt,
(*c*) may make any prescribed exceptions subject to such conditions as may be prescribed, and
(*d*) may prescribe cases in which a fee of a prescribed amount may be charged on an application for any certificate required as a condition of any prescribed exception.
(3) A person who drives or rides in a motor vehicle in contravention of regulations under this section is guilty of an offence; but, notwithstanding any enactment or rule of law, no person other than the person actually committing the contravention is guilty of an offence by reason of the contravention.
(4) If the holder of any such certificate as is referred to in subsection (2)(*b*) above is informed by a constable that he may be prosecuted for an offence under subsection (3) above, he is not in proceedings for that offence entitled to rely on the exception afforded to him by the certificate unless—
(*a*) it is produced to the constable at the time he is so informed, or
(*b*) it is produced—
(i) within seven days after the date on which he is so informed, or
(ii) as soon as is reasonably practicable,
at such police station as he may have specified to the constable, or
(*c*) where it is not produced at such police station, it is not reasonably practicable for it to be produced there before the day on which the proceedings are commenced.
(5) For the purposes of subsection (4) above, the laying of the information or, in Scotland, the service of the complaint on the accused shall be treated as the commencement of the proceedings.
(6) Regulations under this section requiring the wearing of seat belts by persons riding in motor vehicles shall not apply to children under the age of fourteen years.

15 Restrictions on carrying children not wearing seat belts in motor vehicles (1) Except as provided by regulations, where a child under the age of fourteen years is in the front of a motor vehicle, a person must not without reasonable excuse drive the vehicle on a road unless the child is wearing a seat belt in conformity with regulations.
(2) It is an offence for a person to drive a motor vehicle in contravention of subsection (1) above.
(3) Except as provided by regulations, where a child under the age of fourteen years is in the rear of a motor vehicle and any seat belt is fitted in the rear of that vehicle, a person must not without reasonable excuse drive the vehicle on a road unless the child is wearing a seat belt in conformity with regulations.
(4) It is an offence for a person to drive a motor vehicle in contravention of subsection (3) above.
(5) Provision may be made by regulations—
(*a*) excepting from the prohibition in subsection (1) or (3) above children of any prescribed description, vehicles of a prescribed class or the driving of vehicles in such circumstances as may be prescribed,
(*b*) defining in relation to any class of vehicle what part of the vehicle is to be regarded as the front of the vehicle for the purposes of subsection (1) above or as the rear of the vehicle for the purposes of subsection (3) above,
(*c*) prescribing for the purposes of subsection (1) or (3) above the descriptions of seat belt to be worn by children of any prescribed description and the manner in which such seat belt is to be fixed and used.
(6) Regulations made for the purposes of subsection (3) above shall include an exemption for any child holding a valid certificate signed by a medical practitioner to the effect that it is inadvisable on medical grounds for him to wear a seat belt.
(7) If the driver of a motor vehicle is informed by a constable that he may be prosecuted for an offence under subsection (4) above, he is not in proceedings for that offence entitled to rely on an exception afforded to a child by a certificate referred to in subsection (6) above unless—
(*a*) it is produced to the constable at the time he is so informed, or
(*b*) it is produced—
(i) within seven days after the date on which he is so informed, or
(ii) as soon as is reasonably practicable,
at such police station as he may have specified to the constable, or
(*c*) where it is not produced at such police station, it is not reasonably practicable for it to be produced there before the day on which the proceedings are commenced.
(8) For the purposes of subsection (7) above, the laying of the information or, in Scotland, the service of the complaint on the accused shall be treated as the commencement of the proceedings.
(9) In this section—
'regulations' means regulations made by the Secretary of State under this section, and
'seat belt' includes any description of restraining device for a child and any reference to wearing a seat belt is to be construed accordingly.
(10) This section is affected by Schedule 5 to the Road Traffic (Consequential Provisions) Act 1988 (transitory modifications).

Note—The Motor Vehicles (Wearing of Seat Belts in Rear Seats by Adults) Regulations 1991, made under s 14(1)(2) of the Road Traffic Act 1988 require adults to wear seat belts in the rear seats of specified vehicles where they are fitted, as from 1 July 1991.

Webb v Crane

[1988] RTR 204, QBD
A newsagent driving to collect bundles of newspapers and returning to his premises must wear a seat belt as he is not 'making local rounds of deliveries' for the purposes of the exception under s 33A of the Road Traffic Act 1972 (now s 14 of the Road Traffic Act 1988). The word 'rounds' means a series of visits or calls such as those

made by milkmen, bakers or postmen. It does not include a newsagent driving to collect bundles of newspapers for distribution and returning to his premises.

Capps v Miller

[1989] 2 All ER 333, [1989] 1 WLR 839, [1989] RTR 312, CA
The plaintiff was waiting on a moped in the centre of the road to turn right when he was struck from behind by the defendant's car. Because the plaintiff had not fastened his crash helmet properly it came off in the accident and he suffered severe brain damage. The judge found that if the helmet had been properly secured the plaintiff's injuries would have been much less severe but that the plaintiff's contributory negligence should be disregarded. The defendants appealed.
HELD: The judge failed to take into account the plaintiffs breach of statutory duty in failing to fasten the helmet. The plaintiff's chin strap was unfastened contrary to reg 4(a) of the Motorcycles (Protective Helmets) Regulations 1980, SI 1980/1279. The appropriate reduction for contributory negligence in this case was 10% although it could not be precisely determined how much the plaintiff's injuries could have been lessened if the helmet had remained on. It was appropriate to apply the dicta in *Froom v Butcher* on the reduction of damages for not wearing a seat belt in a case where a crash helmet was not worn or not properly worn.

No belts fitted

Hoadley v Dartford District Council

(1979) 123 Sol Jo 129, [1979] RTR 359, CA
The plaintiff, driving his 1963 Ford van, was injured when it was forced into a lamp post following a collision with the defendant's vehicle. He was awarded damages. The van was not fitted with seat belts as there was no statutory obligation to do so: the relevant Road Vehicles (Construction and Use) Regulations did not call for seat belts in vehicles registered before 1966. The defendants appealed, contending that the plaintiff ought to have fitted his van with seat belts.
HELD: It would not be right to extend the principle in *Froom v Butcher* (above) to hold that a person was failing to take proper care for his own safety by not having had seat belts fitted to a vehicle in respect of which there was no statutory obligation to do so. *Froom*'s case merely applied the principle that the law required everyone to exercise all such precautions as a man of ordinary prudence would observe. Such a man would not necessarily fit a belt to his vehicle when the law did not require that to be done, or not drive his car until seat belts were fitted. Appeal dismissed.

Tripping on seat belt

Donn v Schacter

[1975] RTR 238 (Phillips J)
The defendant's car had seat belts for the front seats, fitted in the usual position on the central door pillar on each side. They were rarely used and were normally left hooked up on each pillar. The plaintiff when being given a lift home by the defendant was travelling in the rear offside seat; at the end of the journey when alighting she caught her foot in the nearside seat belt and fell, sustaining injury.

HELD: The defendant was not liable. On the evidence that the seat belt was probably hooked up the driver was not in breach of duty to the passenger either in allowing it to remain in that condition or failing to warn the plaintiff about it. Even if the belt was not hooked up but was on this isolated occasion lying loose on the floor there was no obligation on the driver to make a visual check or to warn the passenger to make sure the seat belt was satisfactory.

McCready v Miller

[1979] RTR 186, CA
The plaintiff, a woman of 53, travelled home at night in the defendant's minicab. She occupied the rear nearside seat. The car was an ordinary saloon car with a seat belt on the nearside central pillar properly hooked up out of use. When alighting at the end of the journey the plaintiff's left foot caught in the belt and she fell out on to the pavement, breaking her ankle. The street lighting was poor and the interior light of the car was not on. The judge held that the defendant was under no duty to see that the seat belt was not loose or warn the plaintiff or switch the interior light on, but was entitled to assume that a passenger would do what was necessary to avoid the hazard.
HELD, ON APPEAL: This was not right. The driver of a car carrying passengers has a duty to take reasonable care to provide a vehicle which is safe for them when getting into it, riding in it and getting out of it. The duty depends on the circumstances but it cannot be lower than the common duty of care defined in the Occupiers' Liability Act 1957, s 2(2) and may be higher on a driver who carries passengers for hire. The decision in *Donn v Schacter* (above) may have been right on the facts but is no authority for saying that the driver's duty does not include a duty to see that the hazard or obstruction caused by a seat belt is avoided or reduced. The defendant was under a duty to reduce the reasonably foreseeable risk by switching on the interior light or by warning the plaintiff or both.

CONTRACTING OUT OF LIABILITY

PUBLIC PASSENGER VEHICLES ACT 1981

29 Avoidance of contracts so far as restrictive of liability in respect of death of or injury to passengers in public service vehicles A contract for the conveyance of a passenger in a public service vehicle shall, so far as it purports to negative or to restrict the liability of a person in respect of a claim which may be made against him in respect of the death of, or bodily injury to, the passenger while being carried in, entering or alighting from the vehicle, or purports to impose any conditions with respect to the enforcement of any such liability, be void.
1 Definition of 'public service vehicle' (1) Subject to the provisions of this section, in this Act 'public service vehicle' means a motor vehicle (other than a tramcar) which -
(a) being a vehicle adapted to carry more than eight passengers, is used for carrying passengers for hire or reward, or
(b) being a vehicle not so adapted, is used for carrying passengers for hire or reward at separate fares in the course of a business of carrying passengers.

Note—Similar provisions (repealed) were contained in the Road Traffic Acts 1930 and 1960. Compare this with s 149 of the Road Traffic Act 1988 which replaces s 148 (3) of the Road Traffic Act (1972). Note also the provisions of s 2(1) of the Unfair Contract Terms Act 1977.

Wilkie v London Passenger Transport Board

[1946] 1 All ER 650, 175 LT 331, 110 JP 215, 62 TLR 327, 90 Sol Jo 249 (Lord Goddard CJ); affd [1947] 1 All ER 258, [1947] LJR 846, 177 LT 71, 111 JP 89, 63 TLR 115, 45 LGR 170, CA

Plaintiff was a clerk in the employ of the LPTB and was given a free pass for use on their omnibuses. The pass contained the following condition. 'No 6. It is issued and accepted on condition that neither the London Passenger Transport Board nor their servant are to be liable to the holder or his or her representative for loss of life, injury or delay or other loss of or damage to property howsoever caused.' The pass was subject to the right of the Board at any moment to cancel it if they thought fit. The condition did not apply in the case of an employee while using the pass in the course of his or her employment or on the business of the Board.

Plaintiff was injured as a passenger whilst on vacation.

HELD: There was no contract and the Road Traffic Act 1930, s 97 (which was in the same terms as the Public Passenger Vehicles Act 1981, s 29 p 187, above) did not apply. The pass was a mere privilege or licence and no part of the plaintiff's contract of employment.

HELD, ON APPEAL: The condition came into operation as soon as the plaintiff began to enjoy any of the benefits and included taking such steps as would enable him to obtain those benefits and included boarding the bus. There was no contractual animus in the pass. It was nothing but a licence subject to a condition and s 97 had no application.

Per Bucknill LJ: There must be some limitation on the wide terms of the condition. It would be reasonable that it should only apply when the pass-holder is using the pass.

Cosgrove v Horsfall

(1945) 175 LT 334, 62 TLR 140, CA

An omnibus driver in the employ of the Board was travelling for his own purposes as passenger on one of the Board's buses with a similar pass. He sued and recovered against the driver. The condition did not avail the driver who was not a party to the contract nor were the Board his agents in making the contract.

Per du Parcq LJ: It is, to say the least, doubtful whether the deposit under s 35(4) of the 1930 Act (now the Road Traffic Act 1972, s 144(1), below) can be made available to meet the judgment.

Note—Section 144(1) of the Road Traffic Act 1972 has now been replaced by s 144(1) of the Road Traffic Act 1988.

Mayor v Ribble Motor Services Ltd

(1958) Times, 16 October, CA

A bus conductress was injured whilst a passenger in an omnibus belonging to her employers by the negligence of the bus driver. She was a member of a darts team and was being carried gratuitously subject to the express condition that the employers should be under no duty to carry her with care or safety and were to be free from all liability to her arising from personal injuries or loss or damage to her property, however caused. They had agreed to provide transport for sporting events.

HELD: Section 97 (of the 1930 Act) did not apply, since there was no contract. The document containing the condition used the word 'agreed' but this did not of itself have a contractual import and did not make the document a term of the plaintiff's contract of employment. It merely expressed willingness to provide transport, and was not taking any obligation on itself. The same defence applied to the claim based on the Law Reform (Personal Injuries) Act 1948, s 1(3).

Note—The provisions of the Road Traffic Act 1930, s 97 are now contained in the Public Passenger Vehicles Act 1981, s 29.

Genys v Matthews

[1965] 3 All ER 24, [1966] 1 WLR 758, 110 Sol Jo 332 (Liverpool Court of Passage)
The Liverpool Corporation granted the plaintiff a free pass on Corporation buses on the following conditions: 'The pass is issued and accepted on the understanding that it merely constitutes and grants a licence to the holder to travel on the Liverpool Corporation's buses with and subject to the conditions that neither the Liverpool Corporation nor any of their servants or agents . . . are to be liable to the holder . . . for . . . injury . . .' The plaintiff was injured when travelling on a Corporation bus due to the negligence of the defendant, the driver of the bus, who was a servant of the Corporation.
HELD: Following *Cosgrove v Horsfall* (above) the defendant was not protected by the terms on which the pass was issued. Even though the pass may be only a licence and not a contract the condition could only be enforced by a party to it. This was the effect of, inter alia, *Scruttons v Midland Silicones* (p 318, below) and *Adler v Dickson* [1955] 1 QB 158, [1954] 3 All ER 397, [1954] 3 WLR 696, 98 Sol Jo 787, [1954] 2 Lloyd's Rep 267, CA.

Gore v Van der Lann

[1967] 2 QB 31, [1967] 1 All ER 360, [1967] 2 WLR 358, 110 Sol Jo 928, CA
The plaintiff was an old-age pensioner who had been given a free pass by the Liverpool Corporation to travel on its buses. The defendant was a bus conductor employed by the Corporation. Due to his negligence the plaintiff was injured when boarding a bus. The Corporation intervened in the action claiming an order to stay on the ground that the free pass was issued on the express condition that the Corporation and its servants should be under no liability for injury to the plaintiff.
HELD: (1) The free pass in this case, unlike that in *Wilkie v LPTB* (above) was a contract. It was issued in response to a written application, was couched in the language of contract, calculated to impress upon the plaintiff that she was entering into a legally binding agreement. Consequently the exclusion of liability was void under the Road Traffic Act 1960, s 151; (2) a stay could be granted (under the Supreme Court of Judicature (Consolidation) Act 1925, s 41) only if the prosecution of the action amounted to a fraud on the Corporation either (a) because the plaintiff had agreed with the Corporation for good consideration not to bring the action or (b) because the Corporation would in law be obliged to indemnify the defendant against liability to the plaintiff. As to (a) no express or implied agreement had been made out. As to (b) there was no such legal obligation on the Corporation. They were not entitled to a stay.

Note—The Road Traffic Act 1960, s 151 is repealed and is repeated in the Public Passenger Vehicles Act 1981, s 29. The provisions of the Supreme Court of Judicature (Consolidation)

Act 1925, s 41 relating to a stay of proceedings are now contained in the Supreme Court Act 1981, s 49(3).

EXCLUSION OF PASSENGER LIABILITY INEFFECTIVE

ROAD TRAFFIC ACT 1988, S 149

149(1) This section applies where a person uses a motor vehicle in circumstances such that under section 143 of this Act there is required to be in force in relation to his use of it such a policy of insurance or such a security in respect of third-party risks as complies with the requirements of this part of this Act.
(2) If any other person is carried in or upon the vehicle while the user is so using it, any antecedent agreement or understanding between them (whether intended to be legally binding or not) shall be of no effect so far as it purports or might be held—
(a) to negative or restrict any such liability of the user in respect of persons carried in or upon the vehicle as is required by section 145 of this Act to be covered by a policy of insurance, or
(b) to impose any conditions with respect to the enforcement of any such liability of the user.
(3) The fact that a person so carried has willingly accepted as his the risk of negligence on the part of the user shall not be treated as negativing any such liability of the user.
(4) For the purposes of this section—
(a) references to a person being carried in or upon a vehicle include references to a person entering or getting on to, or alighting from, the vehicle, and
(b) the reference to an antecedent agreement is to one made at any time before the liability arose.

Note—In *Gregory v Kelly* (p 22, above) a defence of *volenti* was raised. Kenneth Jones J said 'I can deal with that very shortly because it is now agreed between counsel, as I understand it, and I certainly so judge, that s 148(3) of the Road Traffic Act 1972 has the effect of depriving the defendant of that defence'. In *Ashton v Turner* (p 168, above) Ewbank J declined to accept that the subsection deprived the owner of the car of the defence of *volenti* having regard to the special facts of that case, namely 'two burglars who had been drinking and were fleeing in a getaway car'.

See also *Winnick v Dick*, p 48, above.

Section 148(3) has been replaced by s 149 of the Road Traffic Act 1988.

CHAPTER 5

Lighting of Vehicles

LIGHTS ON VEHICLES

Note—Paragraph 131 of the Highway Code 1993 states that you must:

(a) make sure all your lights are clean, that they work and that your headlights are properly adjusted—badly adjusted headlights can dazzle other road users and may cause accidents;

(b) use sidelights between sunset and sunrise;

(c) use headlights at night (between half an hour after sunset and half an hour before sunrise) on all roads without street lighting and on roads where the street lights are more than 185 metres (600 ft) apart or are not lit;

(d) use headlights or front fog lights when visibility is seriously reduced, generally when you cannot see for more than 100 metres (328 ft).

Paragraph 132 of the Highway Code 1993 states that you should also:

(a) use headlights at night on lit motorways and roads with a speed limit in excess of 50 mph;

(b) use dipped headlights at night in built-up areas unless the road is well lit;

(c) cut down glare. If your vehicle has dim-dip, use it instead of dipped headlights in dull daytime weather and at night in built-up areas with good street lighting;

(d) dip your headlights when meeting vehicles or other road users and before you dazzle the driver of a vehicle you are following;

(e) slow down or stop if you are dazzled by oncoming headlights.

Checking lights

Sieghart v British Transport Commission

(1956) 106 L Jo 185 (Finnemore J)

On a dark and rainy night the defendants' driver stopped his lorry for the purpose of adjusting his windscreen wiper. He stopped on a straight length of road with a visibility of not less than 20 to 30 yards and parked correctly on his nearside. The driver did not know and had no reason to suspect that at the time his rear lamp was unlit. The lorry had been checked at the depot a few miles back. Having glanced in both directions and seen that no traffic was approaching the driver descended from his cab. As he reached up to move the windscreen wiper, the car driven by the plaintiff struck the back of the lorry and he and his wife, the second plaintiff, received injuries.

HELD: The statement regarding stopping at night in the Highway Code (p 65 in 1978 edn) 'see that your side and tail lamps are alight' did not require that a driver who was stopping only for a minute or two and had no reason to suspect that his lamps were not alight should, immediately he stopped, examine the vehicle's rear lights, and that in the circumstances the lorry driver was not guilty of negligence and had not created a nuisance on the highway. Judgment for defendants.

Note—See now paras 138 to 141 inclusive of the Highway Code 1993.

Parked with headlights on

Chisman v Electromotion (Export) Ltd

(1969) 113 Sol Jo 246, CA
In the hours of darkness on a straight main road the defendant's lorry was parked on the wrong side of the road with its headlights on. It was visible 700 yards away. The plaintiff driving a mini struck the lorry full tilt. The judge said it was a case of almost maximum negligence on the part of both parties and apportioned liability equally.
HELD, ON APPEAL: The court declined to alter the judge's decision. The attempt to plead that the plaintiff should be found wholly to blame was just one more attempt to bring into the law the doctrine of last opportunity. The court would decline to administer the kiss of life to that doctrine. To put a lorry with its lights on on the wrong side of the road was plain and obvious negligence. There was also negligence on the part of the plaintiff. The court had the power to apportion the damages if it was satisfied that the apportionment was wrong but started with the presumption that the judge was right. In this case he was.

Headlights not dipped

Saville v Bache

(1969) 113 Sol Jo 228, Times, 28 February, CA
The first defendant was driving along an unlighted B road at night, using dipped headlights. The second defendant was approaching in the opposite direction, also on dipped headlights. When he was about 100 yards from the first defendant he (as the judge found) turned his headlights on to main beam. The first defendant was dazzled and collided with the plaintiff whom he had not seen and who was standing with his bicycle at the side of the road. The second defendant denied that he had put his headlights on full beam; he said they were dipped all the time. The judge, rejecting his evidence, held him one-third to blame.
HELD: Dismissing his appeal, it was good manners and good driving to approach another vehicle with headlights dipped. There could be circumstances when a driver had to put his lights on full beam but the second defendant was negligent unless he had a good reason for doing so. He had not given a reason; he had merely denied it.

Headlights in fog

Burgess v Hearn

(1965) Guardian, 25 March, CA
The plaintiff, riding a motor cycle combination, was injured when he collided with

the offside wing of the defendant's car, which was travelling in the opposite direction. The accident happened in thick fog with visibility of 10 to 15 yards. The plaintiff was travelling at 25 mph and the defendant at 15 mph. The plaintiff had a dipped headlight on but the defendant was showing sidelights only. There had been a collision shortly before on the plaintiff's side of the road between a van and a car. The plaintiff ignored the wave of a man who had come to wave people down and had to swerve round the car and then pass the van. It was at this point when the bulk of his motor cycle was on the wrong side of the road that he saw the defendant's car at very short range. The judge found the parties equally to blame, holding the defendant negligent for not having his headlights on and the plaintiff for his speed and for blindly pulling out on to the wrong side of the road.
HELD, ON APPEAL by the defendant: (1) The judge was justified in finding the defendant negligent in not having dipped headlights on. Paragraph 111 of the Highway Code (1978) recommended headlights in mist or fog and though not of statutory force it was of assistance in assessing proper road usage. Moreover there was evidence that it was police policy to use headlights in fog and other road users at the trial had said they were using dipped headlights. But (2) even if the defendant had had his headlights on it would not have prevented the accident since the vehicles were so far apart when the plaintiff pulled out on to the wrong side of the road that he would not have been able to see the headlights. Appeal allowed.

Note—The use of headlights when visibility is seriously reduced is now compulsory. See the Road Vehicles Lighting Regulations 1989 and paras 131–136 of the Highway Code 1993.

The use of sidelights only is not a compliance with the regulations: see *Swift v Spence* [1982] RTR 116.

The Highway Code 1968, para 34 provides 'Never drive so fast that you cannot stop well within the distance you can see to be clear.' It is repeated in the Highway Code 1993, para 57.

Section 37(5) of the Road Traffic Act 1972 has been replaced by s 38(7) of the Road Traffic Act 1988.

Stationary lorry on clearway

Butland v Coxhead

(1968) 112 Sol Jo 465, Times, 8 May (Browne J)
The plaintiff, a learner, was riding a scooter on a clearway on the main London–Portsmouth road in the hours of darkness when he ran into the back of the defendants' stationary lorry. The lorry had broken down and could not be moved. Before the plaintiff's accident another vehicle had collided with the lorry's offside rear and damaged the rear lamp, but the lamp had been repaired and when the plaintiff ran into the lorry both rear lamps were on and visible from a reasonable distance.
HELD: The defendants were not liable. Though a stationary lorry, even with normal tail lights, was a danger to traffic on a fast road and on a bad night, the lorry could not move after it had broken down and the defendants were not negligent in not parking in a side road or on the verge. There was no evidence of a practice among lorry owners to provide torches or flashing lamps. The case of *Moore v Maxwells* (p 195, below) was stronger than the present case. It would be a very good thing if heavy lorries were required to carry some form of warning lamp but no regulations existed to that effect; there was no negligence on the part of the defendants.

Parking without lights

Note—As from 30 April 1972 all rules and regulations relating to parking without lights were standardised. Cars and goods vehicles not exceeding 1525 kg unladen, invalid carriages and motorcycles may be parked without lights on a road provided that:
(a) the road is subject to a speed limit of 30 mph or less;
(b) the vehicle is parked at least 10 m (32ft) away from any junction, close to the kerb and facing in the direction of the flow of traffic, or
(c) in a recognised parking place.
Other vehicles and trailers, and all vehicles with projecting loads, must not be left on a road at night without lights.

The current regulations are contained in the Road Vehicles Lighting Regulations 1989 and at paras 142 and 143 of the Highway Code 1993.

For the lighting-up time at any particular place and date, apply to Royal Greenwich Observatory, Madingley Road, Cambridge CB3 OEZ (Fax No: 0223 374700) marked 'Public Information'.

UNLIGHTED VEHICLES

Failure of lights

Henley v Cameron

[1948] WN 468, [1949] LJR 989, 65 TLR 17, CA
Defendant's car ran out of petrol on the road from Market Drayton to Newcastle about midnight. By 1 am the batteries had run down and there were no lights on the car. The road was 19 ft wide with 3 in kerb and a 5 ft grass verge in a cutting with hedges and trees 15 feet high. The car was left with its rear near wheel close to the kerb and front near wheel about 1 foot out, the front wheels being turned in slightly to the off. There was a turning into a lane 20 or 30 yards away. Lighting up time was 4.20 pm to 7.50 am. At about 6 am deceased riding a motor cycle combination collided with the car. A police officer said the car could have been placed in the mouth of the lane or on the verge. Henn Collins J found the deceased alone to blame.
HELD, ON APPEAL:

Per Tucker LJ: Defendant was negligent in leaving the car unlighted in that position in the hours of darkness when it could have been moved, and the car constituted a nuisance. The absence of a light was prima facie a cause contributing to the accident. The fact that a car driver runs into a stationary unlighted vehicle does not establish that he is solely to blame. It is a question of fact depending on the particular circumstances.

Per Singleton LJ: There was evidence of two witnesses of the difficulty of seeing a car in that position. The negligence of both continued up to the time of the accident.
HELD by a majority: defendant two-thirds; deceased one-third to blame.

Hill-Venning v Beszant

[1950] 2 All ER 1151, [1950] WN 538, 66 (pt 2) TLR 921, 94 Sol Jo 760, CA
A motor cyclist was riding along the road from Guildford to Farnham when his lights failed. He thought it would only mean changing the bulb in the headlight, but discovered that the tail light was also out, and that there was a fault in the electric wiring. Still thinking the fault could be quickly repaired, he did not move his motor cycle, which was standing with its offside some three feet from a wide grass verge. The road was wide and straight and he would have had no difficulty in removing it

on to the verge which was level with the highway. While repairing the wiring, he observed some five minutes after stopping, the light of a vehicle coming from behind, which was a dipped headlight of the plaintiff's motor cycle. The plaintiff failed to see the defendant's motor cycle in time to avoid it. It was not disputed that the plaintiff was negligent, but the plaintiff contended the defendant was negligent in not removing the motor cycle on to the grass verge and leaving an obstacle on the road. Parker J held the defendant had not been guilty of negligence.

HELD, ON APPEAL:

Per Cohen LJ: It might not have been negligent not to have moved the motor cycle merely to change the bulb, but when he found the breakdown in the electric wiring, it was his duty to move it on to the grass verge, and when he saw a light and knew a vehicle was coming, he should have taken the precaution of moving it off the road. A court has to be very careful before taking the view that there is no negligence in leaving an obstacle on the road after lighting up time when it is not plainly visible to approaching vehicles without the aid of full headlights and when it could easily be moved off the road. I think the defendant was responsible to the extent of one-third.

Per Denning LJ: It is clear beyond controversy that his unlighted motor cycle was a danger on the road. Any unlighted bicycle on a fast motor road is a danger to traffic. This is a proposition not of law, but of common sense. It is prima facie evidence of negligence and the onus is on him to show how it came to be unlighted and why he could not move it out of the way or give warning to on-coming traffic. I should have been inclined to apportion the responsibility two-thirds to the unlighted vehicle as in *Henley v Cameron*, but in deference to my brothers I do not dissent from the proportions suggested by Cohen LJ.

Appeal allowed.

Moore v Maxwells of Emsworth Ltd

[1968] 2 All ER 779, [1968] 1 WLR 1077, 112 Sol Jo 424, CA

On a clear evening in the hours of darkness the defendants' lorry was being driven along an unlit dual-track road by their driver when a passing motorist signalled that there was something wrong. The driver stopped at the nearside of the road and found his rear light was out. In checking whether a plug was connected he fused all the obligatory lights. He began to repair the plug whilst his mate stood at the back of the lorry to warn approaching vehicles. The plaintiff driving a chassis failed to see the lorry until too late and crashed into the back of it. The defendants' driver had checked his lights before starting the journey and again at lighting-up time and found them working properly.

HELD: The defendants were not liable. The presence of an unlighted vehicle on the highway called for an explanation from the defendants and to that extent the onus of proof was on them, but the driver had given an explanation, namely, the failure of the lighting system. There was no further onus of proving regular servicing of the vehicle. Nor were the defendants negligent in not supplying torches or flashing warning lights, there being no evidence that it was customary to do so. The driver was not negligent in not driving on to the verge as it was soft and the lorry heavy. He acted reasonably in assuming it would not take long to mend the fuse rather than drive on with no lights to a place where there was street lighting.

Note—See also *Brown v Thompson,* p 25, above and *Parish v Judd,* p 199, below. And see *Jordan v North Hampshire Plant Hire,* p 197, below.

Lee v Lever

[1974] RTR 35, CA
The plaintiff's car developed an electrical fault and as a result came to a stop at night by the nearside verge (to which the plaintiff had steered it) of a well-lighted road which was a clearway. There were no lights on the car; he took the battery to a garage on the other side of the road for recharging. Twenty minutes later the defendant driving his car at about 30 miles an hour did not see the plaintiff's car in time and crashed into the back of it. The county court judge held the plaintiff wholly to blame; he said the plaintiff had not discharged the onus of proof placed on him by Denning LJ's ruling in *Hill-Venning v Beszant* (quoted above).
HELD, ON APPEAL: The plaintiff was negligent in failing to borrow a red lamp from the garage to put by his car and perhaps (as the county court judge held) for failing earlier to see the warning red light on the dashboard and failing to push the car to the verge; but the defendant was also to blame for not seeing the plaintiff's car in time to pull up. The proper proportions of blame were 50-50.

Per Buckley LJ: I do not think normal experience leads one to the conclusion that it is safe to assume that no one will ever park in a part of the roadway which is classified as a 'Clearway', and it is incumbent upon every user of such a roadway to drive in a way which enables him to meet an emergency or hazard presented by the fact that someone has parked—it may be for unavoidable reasons, such as a breakdown—in the 'Clearway'.

Ill-lit lorry across highway

Harvey v Road Haulage Executive

[1952] 1 KB 120, 95 Sol Jo 759, CA
On a foggy morning in November 1949, shortly after sunrise, the defendants' lorry, 22 feet long and 7 feet wide was towed from a car park on to the highway in order to start the engine. The towing vehicle left, and the lorry remained standing with the engine running for about five minutes to warm up. The road was 30 feet wide, divided into three 10 foot strips by two white lines. The lorry was on the slant athwart the road, the near rear wheel being 5 ft from the nearside kerb, the near front wheel 7 ft from this kerb and the off front wheel 14 ft out into the road nearly half-way across, straddling across the nearside white line. Visibility only extended to 11 or 12 yards. The plaintiff was riding a motor cycle at 18 or 20 mph along the nearside white line, came from behind, saw the lorry when within 11 or 12 yards and thought it was moving. It was impossible to overtake it on the offside, since he could not see a clear way through on-coming traffic. There was a dispute whether the red rear light was on, and without coming to a firm conclusion, the judge assumed the light was on. Slade J found the plaintiff was driving too fast in the fog and that he was also negligent in failing to avoid the impact when he had seen the lorry. He made no finding whether the lorry driver was also at fault in leaving the lorry in a dangerous position athwart the road. Assuming he was, this had created a static position which the plaintiff could have avoided. He dismissed the action.
HELD, ON APPEAL: The lorry driver was at fault. He ought to have brought the lorry wholly within the nearside lane. The finding below seemed a reversion to the doctrine of 'last opportunity' which was obsolete. If a motorist saw an obstruction on the road and purposely and recklessly ran into it, he could not recover, but if he were merely

negligent in not taking steps to avoid it, the damage was the result partly on his own fault and also partly the fault of the person leaving the obstruction on the road. Both parties were equally to blame.

Barber v British Road Services

(1964) Times, 18 November, CA
The defendants' driver, stopping at a lorry drivers' cafe on the Oxford-Banbury road at 3 am on a dark and rainy morning, decided to turn his lorry round and back it into the car park. The lorry was 30 feet long and the road 32 feet wide. The manoeuvre took one and a half minutes and involved having the lorry at right angles covering the whole road in both directions. Whilst the lorry was across the road the plaintiff driving a lorry from Banbury failed to see it in time and crashed into it, sustaining serious injuries. The judge of assize held that the defendants' driver was not negligent.
HELD, ON APPEAL: If at night there was an obstruction across a fast main road, that was prima facie evidence of negligence and it was up to the person who put it there to explain how it came there without negligence. The defendants' driver had not given any sufficient explanation. The length of time required to reverse a lorry of this size made the manoeuvre inevitably dangerous. The defendants were not entitled to assume that any person driving along that road at that time of night would be driving at a moderate speed and keeping a good look-out. Permanent lights showing sideways were contrary to the law but some temporary lateral light could have been shown either by torches carried by someone from the cafe or at the side of the vehicle. Blame should be apportioned as to two-thirds to the plaintiff and one-third to the defendants.

Jordan v North Hampshire Plant Hire Ltd

[1970] RTR 212, CA
After a stop at a cafe on the west side of a fast and busy main road in the hours of darkness the defendants' driver wished to resume his journey south. The lorry was an articulated vehicle 35 feet long. It had a flashing light on the cab roof but no other lights showing to the side. There were three reflectors on the side of the trailer. The driver had to drive slowly across the road which had double white lines in the middle and then turn right using the grass verge on the other side to get enough room to make the turn. The manoeuvre would take 10 to 15 seconds during which the lorry would block the carriageway. The plaintiff, driving his car from the south at about 60 mph approached the scene round a slight left hand bend which limited visibility to about 300 yards. He failed to see the lorry in time and struck the back end of the trailer. The county court judge found the two drivers equally to blame. The defendants appealed.
HELD, by the Court of Appeal: (1) It was quite wrong for the defendants' driver to have pulled into a cafe on his offside of the road when the curve was such that only rarely, if at all, could he pull out again without creating grave risks; (2) the lorry was quite insufficiently lit to give proper warning to a driver coming from the south. The flashing light might confuse, and at the time of the accident was in the other traffic lane; the three reflectors had swung round by the time the plaintiff arrived and would not show, and there was no other light which showed; (3) the lorry driver's mate could have flashed a torch as a warning. There have been changes in outlook since *Moore v Maxwells* (above) and the defendants were negligent in not using warning lights in such circumstances as the present. The appeal was hopeless. The plaintiff (who had not cross-appealed) was unlucky to have had his damages docked by as much as one-half.

Rouse v Squires

[1973] QB 889, [1973] 2 All ER 903, [1973] 2 WLR 925, 117 Sol Jo 431, CA
On the M1 motorway at night an articulated lorry driven by Allen got out of control and came to a stop in a position blocking the middle and fast lanes. A car collided with it in the centre lane and remained there with rear lights on. Another lorry stopped in the nearside lane short of Allen's lorry with its headlights on to illuminate the stationary vehicles. Squires then came along driving his employer's lorry, he saw the vehicles ahead when 400 yards away but did not realise two lanes were obstructed. At 150 yards away he saw the vehicle in the nearside lane, braked and moved into the centre lane. He then realised that lane was also blocked; he applied the brake harder, went into a skid and hit the lorry on the nearside, killing the plaintiff's husband who was standing in front of it. The judge held Squires wholly to blame; the fact that Allen caused an obstruction was not, bearing in mind the circumstances, a factor which contributed to the fatal accident.
HELD, ON APPEAL: There was no break in the chain of causation between the negligent driving of Allen and the death of the plaintiff's husband. If a driver so negligently manages his vehicle as to obstruct the highway and constitute a danger to other road users including those who are driving too fast or not keeping a proper look-out (but not those who deliberately or recklessly drive into an obstruction as in *Dymond v Pearce* (p 281, below)) then the first driver's negligence may be held to have contributed to the causation of the accident of which the immediate cause was the negligent driving of a vehicle which collided with it. Where a party guilty of prior negligence has created a dangerous situation which is still continuing to a substantial degree at the time of the accident which would not have happened but for the continuing danger he is responsible as well as the party subsequently negligent. *Harvey v Road Haulage Executive* (p 196, above) and *Barber v British Road Services* (p 197, above) followed. Allen held 25% to blame.

Lancaster v HB and H Transport Ltd

[1979] RTR 380, CA
The defendants' driver had to deliver a lorry load of potatoes to a farm on the east side of the A1 road. To do so he came to the A1 from the west on a side road and wished to cross to a road on the opposite side of the double carriageway. It was early on a February morning, still getting light. Mist reduced visibility to between 50 and 100 yards; the roadway was wet. The articulated lorry had its headlights on but only a small marker light and orange reflector on the side. It crossed the north-bound carriageway and stopped in the intersection to allow cars to pass before starting to cross the southbound carriageway. When he started forward the driver could see no headlights to his left but when part-way over he saw the headlights of a car approaching at quite a fast speed. He thought it best to continue; the car did not stop but crashed into and underneath the trailer. It left no brake marks. The car driver was killed. The lorry would take 12 seconds to cross the carriageway. The judge at first instance considered the lorry driver not to blame.
HELD, ON APPEAL: The lorry driver was negligent in taking the lorry across the A1 in such poor conditions of visibility. He knew that vehicles coming towards him and which he could not see—even 150 yards away at 30 mph—would be on him before he could get clear of the carriageway. He could have found out, had he asked, that he could cross the A1 by slip roads and a bridge a couple of miles to the north. Allegations of contributory negligence on the grounds of excessive speed and the car

driver's failure to brake were not adequately established by the defendants' evidence. It was too much to expect of the car driver that he should realise that disembodied headlights passing from the right to left across his front indicated no less than 50 feet of a slow moving vehicle blocking the carriageway.

Unlighted vehicle on road: duty of care

Drew v Western Scottish Motor Traction Co

1947 SC 222, 1947 SLT 92
On a dark morning in December, just before daybreak and the end of lighting-up time, a bread van was delivering bread at a shop situated on a main road in a built-up area. The van was drawn up facing west close to the south kerb. Although its rear lamp was lit, it was completely obscured by the lower half of the open back door which folded downwards. An omnibus coming from the east ran into the back of the van and inflicted fatal injuries on a boy who was unloading bread. The court found the owners of the omnibus to blame in respect that their driver had failed to maintain a proper look-out, and the van owners in respect that they had allowed their vehicle to be on the road during lighting-up time with a rear light which was invisible; proportions 50-50.

Parish v Judd

[1960] 3 All ER 33, [1960] 1 WLR 867, 124 JP 444, 104 Sol Jo 664, CA
On a dark night at about 10 pm the defendant was driving along a main road when without negligence on his part the lighting system of his car failed completely. A passing lorry stopped and the driver offered him a tow to a service station. The defendant accepted and the lorry began to tow the defendant's car. Before reaching the service station the lorry driver stopped to see if the defendant was all right. He chose a place just beyond a street lamp, which illuminated the rear of the defendant's car. When the two vehicles had been stationary about a minute a car driven by the plaintiff's husband ran into the back of the defendant's car and the plaintiff, who was a passenger, was injured.
HELD: (1) The mere fact that an unlighted vehicle is found at night on a road is not sufficient to constitute a nuisance; there must also be some fault on the part of the person responsible for the vehicle; (2) the presence on a dark road at night of a wholly unlit vehicle is prima facie evidence of negligence on the part of the person responsible for the vehicle; (3) the whole basis of the claim, both in negligence and in nuisance, must be the existence of danger. On the facts, no danger was presented by the presence of the defendant's motor car on that road at that place at that time.

Fotheringham v Prudence

[1962] CLY 2036, CA
The defendant was driving a lorry after dark when a wheel came off. He had to draw in on the nearside of the road just past a bridge. There were no rear lights on the lorry and no reflectors. The nearest street lamp was 12 yards away on the other side of the road. The plaintiff riding a motor cycle at 10 to 12 mph ran into the back of the stationary lorry and was injured. Elwes J found the defendant wholly to blame. The Court of Appeal refused to disturb the finding: there was ample evidence of negligence and causation and the plaintiff was not guilty of contributory negligence.

Hill v Phillips

(1963) 107 Sol Jo 890, CA
The plaintiff was injured when a car in which she was a passenger collided with a stationary trailer during the hours of darkness. The trailer had broken down and had been pushed by the driver of the towing lorry on to a 4 ft 6 in grass verge. As the trailer was 8 feet wide it protruded 3 ft 6 in into the roadway. The lorry driver had gone in the lorry to find a garage and left the trailer unlighted. The driver of the car, driving with dipped headlights at 30 mph, did not see the trailer until he was a car's length away. The judge held the lorry driver wholly to blame, saying that a motorist was not negligent if he did not see what was not visible.

On appeal, the drivers were held equally to blame. The car driver was plainly negligent in failing to keep a proper look-out. When driving with dipped headlights in country roads motorists should drive so that they can see unlighted obstructions. Although unlighted obstructions should not be on country roads their presence was to be anticipated, eg cyclists without lights or men in dark clothes.

The lorry driver was negligent in leaving an unlighted obstruction which was a danger to oncoming traffic. He should have done something to illuminate the trailer; he could have left the lorry behind it with the lights on. It might be that drivers of heavy lorries should have lamps with them as a precaution in case their lights failed.

Young v Chester

[1974] RTR 70, CA
The defendant was driving his car on a fast, wide road at night when the engine stopped and he came to a standstill by the nearside verge but not on it. He then attempted to re-start the engine by operating the self-starter. The plaintiff driving his van in the nearside lane from the same direction at 45 to 50 mph saw the two rear lights of the defendant's car when he was about 400 yards away and they seemed to him to disappear. He thought the car must have turned off on to a slip road. He did not see it again until he was quite close. He applied his brakes heavily but struck the car, pushing it 57 feet. The judge concluded that the apparent disappearance of the car's rear lights was due to the defendant's use of the self-starter, causing the lights to dim or go out and that the defendant was 60% to blame.
HELD, ON APPEAL by the defendant: The judge was entitled to find as he did.

Hannam v Mann

[1984] RTR 252, CA
The plaintiff, riding a motor cycle in the hours of darkness, followed a car out of a side road turning left into a well-lit major road. When in the major road the car's offside traffic indicator light came on. The plaintiff, watching the car and thinking it about to turn right, took his eyes momentarily off the road ahead and crashed into the defendant's car parked without lights against the nearside kerb. The car driver was not turning right; he was merely indicating to show that he was moving out to pass the defendant's car. Although the defendant's car was illuminated by a street lamp opposite it was illegally parked since it was only 5 yards from a road junction, contrary to the Road Vehicles Lighting (Standing Vehicles) (Exemption) General Regulations 1975, reg 4. The judge found the defendant 25% to blame on the ground that if the rear lights of his car had been on they might just have drawn the plaintiff's attention to the car and enabled him to avoid it. The defendant appealed.

HELD: The appeal should be dismissed. The car, unlit and in the position where it was, constituted a nuisance. The judge had asked himself the right question, would the accident have been avoided if the car had been lit? He was entitled to draw the inference that it might and it would be wrong to interfere with that decision or, in the Court of Appeal, to alter the assessment of the degree of blame.

Note—The Road Vehicles Lighting (Standing Vehicles) (Exemption) General Regulations 1975 have been superseded by the Road Vehicles Lighting Regulations 1989. See also paras 142 and 143 of the Highway Code 1993.

CHAPTER 6

Defective Vehicles

STATUTORY DUTIES

ROAD TRAFFIC ACT 1988, S 41

41 (1) The Secretary of State may make regulations generally as to the use of motor vehicles and trailers on roads, their construction and equipment and the conditions under which they may be so used.

Subsections (2) to (4) below do not affect the generality of this subsection.

(2) In particular, the regulations may make provision with respect to any of the following matters—

(a) the width, height and length of motor vehicles and trailers and the load carried by them, the diameter of wheels, and the width, nature and condition of tyres, of motor vehicles and trailers,

(b) the emission or consumption of smoke, fumes or vapour and the emission of sparks, ashes and grit,

(c) noise,

(d) the maximum weight unladen of heavy locomotives and heavy motor cars, and the maximum weight laden of motor vehicles and trailers, and the maximum weight to be transmitted to the road or any specified area of the road by a motor vehicle or trailer of any class or by any part or parts of such a vehicle or trailer in contact with the road, and the conditions under which the weights may be required to be tested,

(e) the particulars to be marked on motor vehicles and trailers,

(f) the towing of or drawing of vehicles by motor vehicles,

(g) the number and nature of brakes, and for securing that brakes, silencers and steering gear are efficient and kept in proper working order,

(h) lighting equipment and reflectors,

(j) the testing and inspection, by persons authorised by or under the regulations, of the brakes, silencers, steering gear, tyres, lighting equipment and reflectors of motor vehicles and trailers on any premises where they are (if the owner of the premises consents),

(k) the appliances to be fitted for—

  (i) signalling the approach of a motor vehicle, or

  (ii) enabling the driver of a motor vehicle to become aware of the approach of another vehicle from the rear, or

  (iii) intimating any intended change of speed or direction of a motor vehicle, and the use of any such appliance, and for securing that any such appliance is efficient and kept in proper working order,

(l) for prohibiting the use of appliances fitted to motor vehicles for signalling their approach, being appliances for signalling by sound, at any times, or on or in any roads or localities, specified in the regulations.

(3) The Secretary of State may, as respects goods vehicles, make regulations under this section—

(a) prescribing other descriptions of weight which are not to be exceeded in the case of such vehicles, . . .

(4) Regulations under this section with respect to lighting equipment and reflectors—

(a) may require that lamps be kept lit at such times and in such circumstances as may be specified in the regulations, and

(b) may extend, in like manner as to motor vehicles and trailers, to vehicles of any description used on roads, whether or not they are mechanically propelled.

ROAD VEHICLES (CONSTRUCTION AND USE) REGULATIONS 1986

Note—These Regulations are intended to conform with European Community law. They came into force on the 11 August 1986. As appears from cases set out below, breach of the Regulations does not give rise of a cause of action for damages.

Part I of the new Regulations deals with preliminaries and interpretation. Part IIA deals with dimensions of vehicles, Part IIB with brakes, Part IIC with wheels and tyres, Part IID with steering, Part IIE with vision, Part IIF with instruments and equipment, Part IIG with fuel, Part IIH with minibuses, Part II.I with power to weight ratio, Part IIJ with protective systems, and Part IIK with control of exhausts. Part III deals with plates and markings, Part IVA deals with laden weight, Part IVB with dimensions of laden vehicles, Part IVC with trailers and sidecars, Part IVD with gas propulsion systems, Part IVE with control of noise, and Part IVF with avoidance of danger. The Parts are supplemented by 12 Schedules.

Included are regulations which require that a vehicle must not be driven backwards further than may be requisite for the safety or reasonable convenience of the occupants or of other vehicles on the road (reg 106); that during the hours of darkness vehicles must not stand on a road otherwise than with the nearside of the vehicle as close as may be to the edge of the carriageway (reg 101); that a motor vehicle not attended by a person licensed to drive it must (subject to some necessary exceptions) have the engine stopped and the brake set (reg 107); and that no person shall open any door of a motor vehicle so as to cause injury or danger to any person (reg 105). Part III gives power to a police officer or vehicle examiner to test and inspect the brakes, silencers, steering gear, tyres, lighting equipment and reflectors either on 48 hours' notice or in any event within 48 hours of an accident in which the vehicle had been involved.

Phillips v Britannia Hygienic Laundry

[1923] 2 KB 832, 93 LJKB 5, 129 LT 777, 39 TLR 530, 68 Sol Jo 102, CA

The axle of the defendants' motor lorry broke, causing a wheel to come off and damage the plaintiff's van. He claimed damages for breach of a clause of the Motor Cars (Use and Construction) Order 1904 made under the Locomotives on Highways Act 1896: 'The motor car and all the fittings thereof shall be in such a condition as not to cause . . . danger to any person on the motor car or on any highway.'

HELD: Breach of the regulation did not give rise to a civil cause of action because (per Bankes LJ) it was a rule for the protection of the public at large and not a particular class: the public using the highway is not a class; it is itself the public: per Atkin LJ. Whether a person aggrieved by a breach of the duty has a right of action depends on the intention of the Act. The duty the Regulations were intended to impose was not a duty enforceable by individuals injured, but a public duty only, the sole remedy for which was the remedy provided by way of fine.

Barkway v South Wales Transport Co Ltd

Per Lord Normand: The Regulations give no right of action to persons injured by breach of a regulation.

Note—Noted fully at p 37, above.

Winter v Cardiff RDC

[1950] 1 All ER 819, 114 JP 234, 49 LGR 1, HL
Per Lord Porter: The statement of claim also contained an allegation that the respondents had been guilty of a breach of statutory duty in that the requirements of the Motor Vehicles (Construction and Use) Regulations 1941, reg 67 had not been complied with. This last contention, however, was not persisted in save as providing a standard with reference to which the requisite care to be observed could be estimated. So regarded, it merges in the question whether the respondents were guilty of negligence for which the responsibility was theirs, though the actual immediate cause of the injury was the negligence of a fellow servant.

Tan Chye Choo v Chong Kew Moi

[1970] 1 All ER 266, [1970] 1 WLR 147, 113 Sol Jo 1000, PC
The respondent bought a taxi as an investment in November 1960. It was driven and maintained by an employee. In October 1961 it was examined by the registrar of motor vehicles who reported that it was satisfactory in all respects. On 28 January 1962 it suddenly swerved out of control when being driven by the respondent's servant, colliding with a car travelling in the opposite direction and killing two of the occupants. The cause of the swerve was the collapse of the nearside ball joint of the steering gear due to excessive strain placed upon it by the modification to the spring seating done when the original petrol engine was replaced by a heavier diesel engine. This modification had been done before the respondent bought the car and was not of a kind which any ordinary inspection would have revealed.
HELD: The respondent had not been negligent and was not liable. On an alternative claim that she was liable in damages for breach of a statutory rule requiring the condition of the car to be at all times 'such that no danger is caused or likely to be caused to any person' the case was impossible to differentiate from *Phillips v Britannia Laundry* (above). The statutory rule was not one which gave a civil cause for action.

Sale of secondhand car

Badham v Lambs

[1946] KB 45, [1945] 2 All ER 295, 115 LJKB 180, 173 LT 319, 61 TLR 569, 89 Sol Jo 381 (du Parcq LJ in KBD)
In July 1944 plaintiff bought a secondhand car from defendants, and the contract of sale contained a term eliminating any warranty of quality or fitness. After driving 27 miles plaintiff was involved in a collision owing to a defect in the braking system which caused him loss, and claimed to recover his loss from defendants.

HELD: (1) The contract was a defence apart from breach of statutory duty. (2) There was a breach of statutory duty but the Act had provided a specific remedy, and this deprived the subject of any other form of remedy. Applying *Phillips v Britannia Hygienic Laundry* judgment was given for defendants.

Note—The Road Traffic Act 1930, s 3(1) (now replaced by s 42(1) of the Road Traffic Act 1988) made it unlawful to use a motor vehicle which does not comply with the Regulations as to construction, weight and equipment.

The Road Traffic Act 1934, s 8(1) (now replaced by s 75 of the 1988 Act) made it unlawful to sell or supply a motor vehicle in such a condition that its use would be unlawful under s 3 of the 1930 Act.

Section 30 of the 1930 Act (now replaced by s 41(1) of the 1988 Act) empowered the Minister to make regulations as to the number and use of brakes, and for securing their efficiency and maintenance.

Section 113 of the 1930 Act provided penalties for offences under that Act.

Regulations 39 and 68 of the 1947 Regulations (now regs 64 and 101 of the 1978 Regulations) require (1) an efficient braking system, and (2) maintenance in efficient working order, respectively.

Vinall v Howard

[1954] 1 QB 375, [1954] 1 All ER 458, [1954] 2 WLR 314, 98 Sol Jo 143, CA
Plaintiff sold to defendant a secondhand motor car which had defects in the speedometer, brake and silencer. Both parties were aware of the defects at the date of sale. Defendant gave a cheque in payment but stopped payment of the cheque and plaintiff sued for the amount of the cheque. Streatfield J held the sale was unlawful under s 8(1) of the 1934 Act (now s 75(1) of the 1988 Act).
HELD, ON APPEAL by the defendant: The defects were not in the original construction and equipment of the car but neglect of proper maintenance, a failure to keep in working order. They did not come under Part II of the Regulations made under s 3 of the 1930 Act but arose under Part III made under s 30 of the 1930 Act. The defects did not fall within s 3 and the contract was not unlawful under s 8(1) of the 1934 Act.

Note—The Road Traffic Act 1988, s 75(7) provides: 'Nothing in the preceding provisions of this section shall affect the validity of a contract or any rights arising under a contract.' There was no such provision in the 1930 Act.

Business Applications Specialists Ltd v Nationwide Credit Corpn Ltd

[1988] RTR 332, CA
The defendants sold the plaintiffs a Mercedes car on hire purchase for £14,850. The car was two and half years old and had apparently covered 37,000 miles. After being driven for 800 miles by the plaintiffs, the car broke down and was found to have burnt out valves and worn oil seals. The cost of repair was £635. The plaintiffs sued for damages for breach of the implied condition of merchantable quality under s 14(2) of the Sale of Goods Act 1979.
HELD: The correct test of merchantable quality for a secondhand car is not simply that it should be reasonably fit for the purpose of being driven along a road. Section 14(6) of the Sale of Goods Act 1979 had materially changed the law, and it was now necessary to consider also the comfort, ease of handling and appearance of the car. However, the buyer of a second-hand car must expect defects to arise sooner or later, and in this case there was no evidence that the car was not of merchantable quality when it was sold. The plaintiffs' case was dismissed.

M O T inspection

Note—Section 43 of the Road Traffic Act 1972 has been replaced by s 45 of the 1988 Act: s 44 of the 1972 Act has been replaced by ss 47–48 of the 1988 Act.

The Road Traffic Act 1972, s 43, replacing the Road Traffic Act 1960, s 65, contains provisions for the purpose of ascertaining whether the prescribed statutory requirements relating to the construction and condition of motor vehicles are complied with. Subsection 2 of the section enables the Secretary of State to make provision by regulations for the examination of vehicles and the issue of test certificates. Section 44 makes it an offence to use on a road a vehicle to which the section applies and in respect of which no test certificate has been issued within the previous 12 months. The section applies to vehicles registered more than ten years but enables the Minister by regulation to substitute a shorter period. The period is at present three years.

The Motor Vehicles (Tests) Regulations, SI 1981/1694, have been made under s 43. They provide, inter alia, for examiners to be authorised to carry out tests at vehicle testing stations, requirements as to vehicles submitted for examinations and the manner of carrying out the examinations. Regulation 14 provides that when a vehicle has been submitted for examination the authorised examiner shall have the same responsibility for loss of or damage to the vehicle or to any other property, or personal injury, arising out of the use of the vehicle in connection with the carrying out of the examination as would rest on a person who had undertaken for payment to accept the custody of the vehicle and to carry out the same examination under a contract making no express provision with respect to the incidence of liability as between the parties thereto for any such loss, damage or injury.

This provision would appear to exclude the operation of any 'owners risk' notices or other exemptions from liability which may be displayed at garages and service stations which are also authorised vehicle testing stations whilst a vehicle is being tested or is in the custody of the examiner for the purpose of carrying out the test.

Rowley v Chatham

[1970] RTR 462 (Shaw J)
On 6 March the defendant, an authorised examiner under the Motor Vehicles (Test) Regulations 1960, issued a test certificate relating to the plaintiff's husband's motor van. On 31 March the plaintiff's husband was driving the van when it steered into the path of an approaching lorry and he was killed. It was found that the upper and lower ball race cages of the steering column had broken down. There was evidence that this state of affairs had existed at the time of the test on 6 March.
HELD: (1) On the evidence adduced by the defendant, the tests required by the 1960 Regulations were properly and duly applied and would not have revealed that there was a fault or defect in the steering. (2) The relationship between the examiner and the owner of the vehicle is a contractual one but the duty owed by the examiner is prescribed by the Regulations and is limited to certifying the condition of the vehicle at the date of the examination. Any representation expressed or implicit in the certificate cannot be relied upon (as in the present case) some weeks later. The purpose of the Road Traffic Act 1960, s 66 is to protect the public from unroadworthy vehicles, not to provide motorists with a cheap means of being advised on the condition of their own vehicles. Judgment for the defendant.

Note—See also *Rees v Saville*, p 216, below.

Artingstoll v Hewen's Garages Ltd

[1973] RTR 197 (Kerr J)
On 13 December 1967, the plaintiff delivered his car to the defendants, who were authorised examiners for the annual MOT test. After the test they issued a notification

of refusal of a certificate saying that the nearside front hub bearing needed renewal. The plaintiff obtained a new bearing and the defendants fitted it. Without further test they then issued a test certificate on 14 December. Five weeks later during which the plaintiff had driven the car 700 miles it suddenly veered across a busy main road and collided with an approaching vehicle, injuring the plaintiff. It was found that steering joints were loose. The plaintiff sued the defendants for damages for personal injury. HELD: Following *Rowley*'s case (above) (1) there is a duty on an examiner in contract to carry out the test properly and with reasonable skill and care and the issue of a test certificate bearing the prescribed wording also imports a warranty that the statutory requirements prescribed by the regulations were complied with at the date of the examination; (2) though a claim for damages either in contract or tort may be difficult to establish because of the lapse of time there is no reason in principle (contrary to the view expressed in *Rowley*'s case) why substantial (as distinct from nominal) damages should not be recovered by a plaintiff who can prove a failure to carry out the examination with proper skill and care and the issue of a test certificate which should not have been issued and that loss and damage were thereby caused; (3) if a plaintiff himself was guilty of some degree of carelessness in driving at the time of the accident the court can make an apportionment as between the causative faults under the Law Reform (Contributory Negligence) Act 1945 even if the claim is regarded as lying solely in contract; (4) on the facts of the present case the plaintiff had failed to prove any breach of contract or duty in relation to the brakes or steering. Action dismissed.

Note—But see *Basildon District Council v Lesser*, p 12, and *Maritrans A B v Comet Shipping*, p 14, above.

Section 66 of the Road Traffic Act 1960 is now s 188 of the Road Traffic Act 1988.

OCCUPIERS' LIABILITY ACT 1957

Note—Section 1(3)(a) applies the duty of an occupier to visitors to the person having control over any vehicle. Section 5(2) applies that section to vehicles. The motorist is therefore concerned in respect of passengers, and also in respect of damage caused to his vehicle where he visits premises. The relevant sections of the Act are set out below.

The Act abolished the distinction between invitees and licensees, and enacted the same duty to every visitor, a 'common duty of care', which is a duty to take such care as in all the circumstances of the case is reasonable to see that the visitor will be reasonably safe in using the premises for the purpose for which he is invited or permitted to be there. Note that, in respect particularly of s 2, the Unfair Contract Terms Act 1977 prohibits the exclusion or restriction by a term of a contract or by notice of liability for death or personal injury resulting from negligence, where such liability arises in the course of business.

Relevant sections of the Act

2 Extent of occupier's ordinary duty (1) An occupier of premises owes the same duty, the 'common duty of care', to all his visitors, except in so far as he is free to and does extend, restrict, modify or exclude his duty to any visitor or visitors by agreement or otherwise.
(2) The common duty of care is a duty to take such care as in all the circumstances of the case is reasonable to see that the visitor will be reasonably safe in using the premises for the purpose for which he is invited or permitted by the occupier to be there.
(3) The circumstances relevant for the present purpose include the degree of care and of want of care, which would ordinarily be looked for in such a visitor, so that (for example) in proper cases—

(a) an occupier must be prepared for children to be less careful than adults; and
(b) an occupier may expect that a person, in the exercise of his calling, will appreciate and guard against any special risks ordinarily incident to it, so far as the occupier leaves him free to do so.

(4) In determining whether the occupier of premises had discharged the common duty of care to a visitor, regard is to be had to all the circumstances, so that (for example)—

(a) where damage is caused to a visitor by a danger of which he had been warned by the occupier, the warning is not to be treated without more as absolving the occupier for liability, unless in all the circumstances it was enough to enable the visitor to be reasonably safe; and
(b) where damage is caused to a visitor by a danger due to the faulty execution of any work of construction, maintenance or repair by an independent contractor employed by the occupier, the occupier is not to be treated without more as answerable for the danger if in all the circumstances he had acted reasonably in entrusting the work to an independent contractor and had taken such steps (if any) as he reasonably ought in order to satisfy himself that the contractor was competent and that the work had been properly done.

(5) The common duty of care does not impose on an occupier any obligation to a visitor in respect of risks willingly accepted as his by the visitor (the question whether a risk was so accepted to be decided on the same principles as in other cases in which one person owes a duty of care to another).

(6) For the purpose of this section, persons who enter premises for any purpose in the exercise of a right conferred by law are to be treated as permitted by the occupier to be there for that purpose whether they have in fact his permission or not.

3 Effect of contract on occupier's liability to third party (1) Where an occupier of premises is bound by contract to permit persons who are strangers to the contract to enter or use the premises, the duty of care which he owes to them as his visitors cannot be restricted or excluded by that contract, but (subject to any provision of the contract to the contrary) shall include the duty to perform his obligations under the contract, whether undertaken for their protection or not, in so far as those obligations go beyond the obligations otherwise involved in that duty.

(2) A contract shall not by virtue of this section have the effect, unless it expressly so provides, of making an occupier who has taken all reasonable care answerable to strangers to the contract for dangers due to faulty execution of any work of construction, maintenance or repair or other like operation by persons other than himself, his servants and persons acting under his direction and control.

(3) In this section 'stranger to the contract' means a person not for the time being entitled to the benefit of the contract as a party to it or as the successor by assignment or otherwise of a party to it, and accordingly includes a party to the contract who has ceased to be so entitled.

5 Implied term in contracts (1) Where persons enter or use, or bring or send goods to, any premises in exercise of a right conferred by contract with a person occupying or having control of the premises, the duty he owes them in respect of dangers due to the state of the premises or to things done or omitted to be done on them, in so far as the duty depends on a term to be implied in the contract by reason of its conferring that right, shall be the common duty of care.

(2) The foregoing subsection shall apply to fixed and movable structures as it applies to premises.

(3) This section does not affect the obligations imposed on a person by or by virtue of any contract for the hire of, or for the carriage for reward of persons or goods in, any vehicle, vessel, aircraft or other means of transport, or by virtue of any contract of bailment.

Note—The Occupiers' Liability Act 1984 requires an occupier of premises 'to take such care as is reasonable in all the circumstances' to see that a person (not being his visitor within the meaning of the 1957 Act) does not suffer injury on the premises by reason of a danger of which the occupier knows or has reasonable grounds to believe exists when he knows or has reasonable grounds to believe the other may be in its vicinity. The duty can be discharged in an appropriate case by a warning. 'Premises' includes any fixed or movable structure and 'movable structure' includes 'any vessel, vehicle or aircraft'. No duty is owed under the Act to persons using the highway.

CONSUMER PROTECTION ACT 1987

The Consumer Protection Act 1987, Part I, ss 1–9 implements provisions contained in the European Communities Directive on product liability dated 25 July 1985, No 85/374/EEC. Section 1 defines the meaning of products and producers. Section 2 imposes civil liability on producers and importers into the EEC for damage caused by defective products. Section 3 provides that there is a defect in a product if its safety is not such as persons are generally entitled to expect. Section 4 provides certain defences to liability under the Act. Section 5 limits liability under the Act to damage in respect of death, personal injury, or damage to property intended for private use exceeding £275. Section 6 causes the Act to apply to certain enactments including the Law Reform (Miscellaneous Provisions) Act 1934, and the Fatal Accidents Act 1976. The Act also applies to the Congenital Disabilities (Civil Liability) Act 1976 and the Limitation Act 1980, among others. Section 7 prohibits a person who is liable for damage caused by a defective product from limiting or excluding his liability by any contract term or similar provision. Section 8 contains the power for Part I of the Act to be modified if modifications are made to the Directive. The Crown is bound by Part I of the Act under s 9.

CONTRACTUAL LIABILITY

Repairer

GH Myers & Co v Brent Cross Service Co

[1934] 1 KB 46, [1933] All ER Rep 9, 103 LJKB 123, 150 LT 96, Div Ct (Swift and du Parcq JJ)

The owner of a motor car in October 1932, handed his car to repairers to cure a 'knock' in the engine and renew any part which in their opinion required replacement. The repairers obtained from the manufacturers six connecting rods which they fitted to the engine. On 9 November 1932, one of the rods broke causing extensive damage to the engine. The owner claimed £62 18s 0d for the cost of repairing the car and consequential damage. The county court judge found that one connecting rod was defective but was due to an undiscoverable latent defect.

HELD: This was not a contract for the sale of goods but a contract for work and labour in the course of which goods were supplied. The liability of a person supplying goods in the course of doing work and labour is certainly not less than the liability of the person selling goods. He warrants that the material which he uses will be of good material and reasonably fit for the purpose for which he is using them, unless the contract excluded any such warranty, and the person is liable if there is any defect in the materials supplied, even if it was one which reasonable care could not have discovered.

The case was remitted to the county court judge to decide whether the defendants were contracting in such a way as to bind themselves to exercise their own skill and judgment with reference to the selection of the material, or whether they were bound to get the materials from the original manufacturers of the car.

Stewart v Reavell's Garage

[1952] 2 QB 545, [1952] 1 All ER 1191, [1952] 1 TLR 1266, 96 Sol Jo 314 (Sellers J)
The plaintiff was the owner of a Bentley speed model and took the car to defendants, who were experienced car repairers to whom the car was well known, to have the brake-drums and brake-shoes relined. This was specialist's work which to the knowledge of the plaintiff the defendants did not undertake. Plaintiff suggested that the work should be done by a firm who advertised cast-iron linings for Bentley brake-drums and informed the defendants that a cast-iron sleeve, which would be cut from a tube with no weld, would be preferable. The price quoted by this firm was too high and the defendants with the plaintiff's consent obtained a quotation from a firm who normally did this work for them. Defendants recommended this firm to plaintiff and plaintiff accepted their advice without knowing that this method involved welding, which was not suitable for this make of car. The sub-contractors did not fit the offside front brake lining properly. The day after the car was delivered to the plaintiff, the faulty lining caused an accident and the car was damaged. The defendants contended that their only duty was to take reasonable care to employ a suitable sub-contractor and that they were entitled to assume without further detailed examination that their work would be satisfactory.
HELD: The contract was for work done and materials supplied. The standard of care in the case of a sale of goods was stated by Lord Wright in *Cammell Laird & Co Ltd v Manganese Bronze and Brass Co Ltd* [1934] AC 402, [1934] All ER Rep 1, 103 LJKB 289, 151 LT 142. The standard of proof was equally applicable in this case. The law was also stated by du Parcq J in *GH Myers & Co v Brent Cross Service Co* (above). There might be an implied warranty of absolute fitness for the intended purpose if the circumstances showed that the particular purpose was made known to the repairer, and that the work of repair was of the type which the repairer held himself out to perform, either by himself or sub-contractor, and if the circumstances showed that the purpose was made known so as to show that the customer relied on the repairer's skill and judgment. Such a reliance must be brought home to the mind of the repairer that he was relying on him in such a way that the repairer must be taken to have contracted on the footing that the reliance was to be the basis of the contract. It was their duty in the circumstances to provide good workmanship, materials of good quality, and a braking system reasonably fit for its purpose, and they failed to do so by reason of the faulty offside front brake-drum lining. In fact, though unwittingly, they handed over to the plaintiff a highly dangerous vehicle. Judgment for the plaintiff for £283 3s 4d.

Note—68 LQR 297 points out that a repairer will be protected if he used replacement material supplied by the makers of the car because he is entitled to assume it will be suitable, but if obtained from an independent contractor, it is his duty to see that it is adequate for its purpose. He is being paid for expert supervision, which is not properly performed if all he does is to rely on the skill of a third person.

Taylor v Kiddey

(1968) 118 NLJ 134, CA
In November 1965 the plaintiff bought a secondhand car from the defendant who warranted that it was 'in tiptop condition and really roadworthy'. On 3 February 1966 the defendant gave the car a routine 3,000-mile service, one item of which was checking the steering. On 4 April 1966 while the plaintiff was driving, the nearside front wheel came off because the securing bolts had been insufficiently tightened; she

was injured and the car wrecked. She claimed damages. There was no evidence that anything had happened, such as the changing of a wheel, between November 1965 and the accident which might have caused the wheel bolts to be left insufficiently tightened.
HELD: The plaintiff was entitled to damages because (1) on the evidence it was clear that the bolts had been loose when the car was sold by the defendant and he was thus in breach of warranty; (2) it was part of the duty of a garage when carrying out a service which included checking the steering to test the front wheels to ensure that the securing bolts were tight.

Hirer

Spear v Self Motoring Ltd

(1947) S No 27, 15 March 1948 (Mr Commissioner Sachs KC)
Plaintiff hired from defendants, whose business was to let out private cars on hire a 1938 hp car to drive from Norwich to Cambridge, a distance of 61 miles. After driving 54 miles, the steering gear failed and the car swerved across the road into an oncoming vehicle. The plaintiff was very seriously injured. The car was eight years old and had been in heavy use. The accident was due to the steering mechanism being defective, whereby a ball joint by which the drag link is joined to the steering side arm (the rear drag link joint) came apart, due to severe wear and strain.
HELD: The car was unsuitable for the purpose for which it was hired, due to the negligence of the defendants in failing properly to examine it and service it. The defendants were liable for breach of implied warranty that the car was reasonably fit for the purpose (even if the defect is latent), and for negligence in failing to take any adequate steps to keep the car in safe and efficient condition. There was not any servicing system. The ball joints had not been properly attended to. Verdict for plaintiff. *Myer*'s case p 210, above, followed.

Reed v Dean

[1949] 1 KB 188 (Lewis J)
There is an implied warranty of fitness on the hire of a chattel, that it shall be as fit for the purpose for which it was hired as reasonable care and skill can make it.

Moons Motors Ltd v Kiuan Wou

[1952] 2 Lloyd's Rep 80, CA
Defendant hired a car from plaintiffs and received a card showing prices, etc and the car showed that prices included petrol and insurance. Defendant signed an agreement which contained at the bottom the words: 'The terms and conditions of hire can be seen overleaf' in quite clear print. The defendant was never given a copy of the agreement.

The agreement started by saying: 'It is agreed that the owner will let subject to the following questions which constitute a proposal for insurance being answered by the hirer to the satisfaction of the owner and the insurance company concerned and the hirer will take on hire . . .'. Clause 8 said: 'The hirer has completed the proposal for insurance incorporated in this agreement and a policy of insurance is in force in relation to the use of the car by the hirer but nothing herein contained shall confer or give rise to any rights against the owner by way of indemnity . . .'.

The insurance was for third party only. The car was damaged in an accident and the plaintiffs sued the defendant for the damage. The county court judge found that the defendant never had an opportunity to read the condition and never read it and it was never brought to his notice.

HELD: The statement that the price included insurance amounted to a warranty that the defendant would be covered against all normal risks. Read together, clauses 7 and 8 had the effect that the hirer is responsible for the cost of repairs but entitled to look to an insurance company in respect of the usual risks on the usual terms. 'A policy of insurance in relation to the use of the car' means a policy covering normal risks. Defendant was not liable.

Vehicles on hire purchase

Brown v Sheen & Richmond Car Sales Ltd

[1950] 1 All ER 1102 (Jones J)

The plaintiff arranged to obtain a car from motor car dealers who represented that the car was in perfect condition. The transaction was completed by a hire purchase agreement. The plaintiff paid all instalments and the car became his property. The car was not in perfect condition and the plaintiff was compelled to have considerable repairs done to it. He sued the dealers for damages for breach of warranty.

HELD: The warranty had induced the plaintiff to enter into the agreement and the dealers were liable for the difference between the amount paid and the amount the plaintiff would have paid if the warranty had not been given.

Andrews v Hopkinson

[1957] 1 QB 229, [1956] 3 All ER 422, [1956] 3 WLR 732, 100 Sol Jo 768 (McNair J)

On 11 September 1952, plaintiff arranged to obtain from defendant, a dealer in secondhand cars, a 1934 car. Plaintiff told defendant that he did not know a great deal about cars. Defendant took plaintiff and a friend for a drive for about 5 miles in the car and said 'It's a good little bus. I would stake my life on it. You will have no trouble with it'. Plaintiff agreed to a price of £150 for the car, payable as to £50 the next day, the balance to be by hire purchase. On 12 September 1952, the £50 was paid and a hire-purchase agreement completed. This agreement provided that acceptance of delivery should be conclusive evidence that the car was complete and in good order and condition and in every way satisfactory, and the plaintiff signed the agreement.

On 19 September 1952, the plaintiff was driving the car when it suddenly swerved and collided with a lorry. The car was wrecked and the plaintiff seriously injured. Plaintiff sued defendant for damage to car and personal injuries. The judge found the defective condition of the drag-link joint was the cause of the accident.

HELD: The words used amounted to a warranty that the car was in good condition and reasonably safe for use on the highway. There was an implied warranty similar to that implied on a sale of goods and the plaintiff had acted on this warranty in entering into the agreement and could enforce the warranty. *Brown*'s case (above) followed. The plaintiff's personal injuries were a direct and natural result of the breach and the plaintiff was entitled to recover on this ground. The defendant was also liable for negligence in delivering the car in a dangerous condition when he could have discovered the condition by reasonable care and he had failed to have the car examined or warn the plaintiff that it had not been examined. *Herschtal*'s case followed. Judgment for plaintiff.

Latent defect

Note—The Occupiers Liability Act 1957, s 1(3)(a) applies the duty of an occupier to his visitors to any person having control of any vehicle.

The Latent Damage Act 1986 has no application to personal injury cases, but on limitation generally see pp 509-511, below.

If an accident is due to a latent defect which was not discoverable by reasonable care, there is no negligence. For example, it is sufficient that a carrier should adopt the best known apparatus, kept in perfect order and worked without negligence by the servants he employs. If the carrier does this then he is not responsible for the consequences of an extremely rare and obscure accident which could not have been prevented by any reasonable means. Having said that, there is a higher degree of duty on the carrier. (See *Readhead v Midland Rly Co* (1869) LR 4 QB 379, 38 LJQB 169, *Hyman v Nye* (1881) 6 QBD 685, 44 LT 919, 45 JP 554 and *Newberry v Bristol Tramways and Carriage Co Ltd* (1912) 107 LT 801, 29 TLR 177, 57 Sol Jo 172 (9th edn) pp 240-41.)

R v Spurge

[1961] 2 QB 205, [1961] 2 All ER 688, [1961] 3 WLR 23, 125 JP 502, 105 Sol Jo 469, CCA

The appellant was driving his sports car round a very sharp and dangerous left hand bend. The car went over the double white lines in the centre of the road and collided with an oncoming motor scooter. His defence was that he decided to take the bend at a snail's pace and applied the brakes somewhat vigorously; the application of the brakes pulled the car on to its wrong side of the road in such a fashion that it was impossible for him to control it. Expert witnesses gave evidence that the brakes were in very bad condition and that vigorous application at 30 mph pulled the car fairly violently to its offside. The appellant had taken delivery of the car only a few days before.

HELD: (1) There is no real distinction between a man being suddenly deprived of all control of a motor car by some sudden affliction to his person and being so deprived by some defect suddenly manifesting itself in the motor car, but (2) cases in which a mechanical defect can be relied on as a defence to a charge of dangerous driving must be rare. The defence has no application where the defect is known to the driver or should have been discovered by him had he exercised reasonable prudence; (3) the appellant could not succeed because he admitted he was aware of the tendency of the car to pull to the right when its brakes were applied.

Hougham v Martin

(1964) 108 Sol Jo 138, Div Ct

The defendant was driving a Ford Anglia car along a main road when it gradually moved over to its offside of the road and collided with a vehicle travelling in the opposite direction. The defendant said she had no recollection of the accident. In answer to a charge of driving without due care and attention it was argued in her favour that the accident might have been caused by a mechanical defect to which modern mass-produced vehicles were prone but which it was not possible to specify. The justices dismissed the information.

On a case stated the Divisional Court directed the justices to convict. The mere suggestion that modern mass-produced vehicles were prone to mechanical defects did not give rise to a reasonable doubt and was merely fanciful.

Pearce v Round Oak Steel Works Ltd

[1969] 3 All ER 680, [1969] 1 WLR 595, 113 Sol Jo 163, CA
The plaintiff, a factory worker, was injured when a piece of a machine fell on his foot. The fall was caused by the breakage of a bolt due to a latent defect not discoverable by reasonable inspection. The plaintiff pleaded *res ipsa loquitur* and called as a witness a metallurgist who said the machine had been made in 1930 and bought by the defendants in 1959. He said there may have been drawings which would have given information about the material from which the bolt was made. The defendants called no evidence. The county court judge said the plaintiff had given sufficient evidence to put the burden on the defendants to show they had taken reasonable precautions. They had called no evidence and the plaintiff was entitled to succeed.
HELD, ON APPEAL: The judge's approach to the problem was right. Even though there is a latent defect the defendants must prove that the accident happened despite all reasonable care on their part: this means reasonable care not only in inspection and maintenance but also when they bought the machine. They must prove that in acquiring the machine and in their dealings with it they had taken reasonable care to see that it was in good order and condition. They ought to have called evidence about the circumstances in which they acquired the machine. Appeal dismissed.

Henderson v Henry E Jenkins & Sons and Evans

[1970] AC 282, [1969] 3 All ER 756, [1969] 3 WLR 732, 113 Sol Jo 856, HL
A lorry driver applied the brakes of the lorry on a steep hill but they failed to operate. As a result the lorry struck and killed a man who was emerging from a parked vehicle. His widow sued the lorry owners who denied liability on the ground that the brake failure was due to latent defect not discoverable by reasonable care on their part. The lorry was five years old and had done at least 150,000 miles. The brakes were hydraulically operated. It was found after the accident that the brake failure was due to a steel pipe bursting at a point where corrosion had reduced the thickness of the wall of the pipe from .7mm to .1mm. The corrosion had occurred where it could not be seen except by removing the pipe completely from the vehicle and this had never been done. Expert evidence showed that it was not a normal precaution to do this if, as was the case, the visible parts of the pipe were not corroded. The corrosion was unusual and unexplained. An expert witness said it must have been due to chemical action of some kind such as exposure to salt from the roads in winter or on journeys near the sea or from leakage of corrosive liquids from particular kinds of loads. The judge of assize held there was no negligence on the part of the lorry owners. The Court of Appeal, by majority, agreed.
HELD, ON APPEAL to the House of Lords: The defendants had not discharged the burden of proof which lay on them of showing they had taken all reasonable care and that despite this the defect remained hidden. The evidence showed that something unusual must have happened to cause this corrosion: it was caused by some chemical agent. So it was necessary for the defendants to show that they neither knew nor ought to have known of any unusual occurrence to cause the breakdown. They had given no evidence at all of the history of the vehicle or the loads it had carried. It might have been sufficient for them to prove that they had a proper system for drivers reporting all occurrences but they had not done this. They chose to leave the case in a state

where, for all they knew, the lorry might have been carrying carboys of acid regularly or had been coming into contact with sea water or salt frequently or had been engaged in carrying cattle. They had to prove that in all the circumstances of which they knew or ought to have known they had taken all proper steps to avoid danger. They had failed to do that and the plaintiff must succeed.

Note—See also *Barkway v South Wales Transport Co*, p 37, above.

Rees v Saville

[1983] RTR 332, CA
The defendant was driving his car when it suddenly swerved to the right and struck the plaintiff's parked car causing substantial damage for which the plaintiff claimed. The accident was caused by the failure of a ball joint on the steering mechanism of the front offside wheel of the defendant's car. The car was eight years old but he had owned it only a month or less; he had bought it privately. He was not an engineer but he had inspected it before purchase and found no defects. It had an MOT certificate three or four months old. Expert evidence was that the worn condition of the ball joint was not easily discoverable on inspection, but should have been detected on the MOT test. The defendant said in evidence that he had noticed no symptoms of wear on the ball joint which might be shown by uneven tyre wear or otherwise and that 'it was a natural assumption from the MOT certificate that the vehicle was okay'. The judge said the test of negligence was what a reasonable motorist could be expected to do. He held there was no negligence on the part of the defendant.
HELD, ON APPEAL: The judge was entitled so to hold. (1) The question of onus matters only when there is a question of fact on which no evidence is called on one side or the other. In this case credibility of the evidence was established at the trial and it merely remained for the court to decide whether, on the facts proved or admitted, the defendant was negligent. *Henderson v Jenkins* (p 215, above), and *Barkway v South Wales Transport* (p 37, above) were distinguishable. In *Henderson*'s case the plaintiff established the cause of the corrosion but the defendants called no evidence. In *Barkway's* case negligence was proved against the defendant's servants or agents. (2) It had been said against the present defendant that he should have placed no reliance on the MOT certificate. A valid MOT certificate was a factor which must be taken into account in deciding whether or not it was necessary for the defendant himself to submit the car to an expert for inspection. On the facts of the present case the defendant was not negligent in failing to have a further inspection of the vehicle.

TORTIOUS LIABILITY

Manufacturers and repairers

Malfroot v Nozal

(1935) 51 TLR 551, 74 Sol Jo 610 (Lewis J)
While the male plaintiff, the owner of a motor cycle to which a few days previously the defendants had fitted a side-car, was driving the combination along a public road, the side-car became detached from the motor cycle. Both the male plaintiff and the female plaintiff who was a passenger in the side-car, sustained personal injuries. An action was brought for damages.

HELD: That the defendants were guilty of negligence in fitting the side-car to the motor cycle, that they were liable to the male plaintiff in contract and in tort, and to the female passenger in tort. The principles enunciated in *Donoghue v Stevenson* were applied: per Lewis J.

Herschtal v Stewart and Ardern Ltd

[1940] 1 KB 155, [1939] 4 All ER 123, 161 LT 331, 56 TLR 48, 84 Sol Jo 79 (Tucker J)

The plaintiff who was a director of, and had a controlling interest in, a company known as UP Ltd acquired on its behalf a reconditioned motor car from a company known as S & A Services Ltd. The latter company acquired the car from the defendants for the purpose of hiring it out on hire purchase terms to UP Ltd. The defendants knew that the car was going to be used chiefly by the plaintiff, and they knew that it was going to be so used immediately. On the morning after the deliver of the car, before it had been driven more than a few miles, and while it was being driven by the plaintiff, the nearside rear wheel came off, whereby the plaintiff suffered damage. There was no evidence that anything had happened between the time when the car was delivered by the defendants and the time of the accident. At the time of delivery the plaintiff had signed, for and on behalf of UP Ltd, a form of receipt stating that the car was accepted as being in good condition and as seen, tried and approved.

HELD: (1) The form of receipt did not protect the defendants in a claim of negligence by the plaintiff, however it might affect their contractual liability with UP Ltd. (2) The defendants were liable in negligence under the rule in *Donoghue v Stevenson*, because, although the plaintiff was given an opportunity to examine the car for the purpose of discovering any defects, yet the defendants never anticipated that there would be any such examination.

Note—In the above case the Motor Vehicles (Construction and Use) Regulations 1937, reg 67 (now the Road Vehicles (Construction and Use) Regulation 1986), and the Road Traffic Act 1934, s 8 were referred to, but counsel for the plaintiff conceded that the plaintiff could not succeed without proof of negligence in view of *Phillips v Britannia Hygienic Laundry* (below). See also *Andrews v Hopkinson*, p 213, above.

Lexmead (Basingstoke) Ltd v Lewis

[1982] AC 225, [1981] 1 All ER 1185, [1981] 2 WLR 713, 125 Sol Jo 310, [1981] 2 Lloyd's Rep 17, [1981] RTR 346, HL

The first defendant was the owner of a Landrover and trailer being driven by his employee the second defendant when the trailer became detached and ran out of control into collision with a car in which the plaintiffs were travelling. The coupling which failed had been designed and manufactured by the third defendants and sold to the first defendant by retailers, the fourth defendants. The judge found, on the evidence, that the coupling was defective in design and dangerous in use and that the defects were readily foreseeable by an appropriately skilled engineer; the manufacturers were negligent and liable to the plaintiffs in tort for the personal injuries sustained. He also found the owner liable in that he had allowed the coupling to be used for some months in a damaged condition without having it repaired or even finding out if it was safe to use in such condition. Apportionment: 75% blame on the manufacturers, 25% on the owner. The retailers were not liable to the plaintiffs because (1) the coupling in question was a standard fitting for a Landrover and the defects would call for a knowledge of design they did not possess, and (2) when servicing the vehicle they were not required without specific mention to inspect the coupling.

In third party proceedings the owner claimed indemnity from the retailers for breach of the Sale of Goods Act 1893, s 14, the retailers having supplied the coupling as fit and suitable for the owner's requirements. The judge held that there was a breach of s 14(1) of the 1893 Act in that the coupling was unsuitable and unfit for the purpose but the owner's act in continuing to use the coupling when he realised, or ought to have realised, that it was broken was not within the contemplation of the parties when the contract was made. *Mowbray v Merryweather* [1895] 2 QB 640 was authority for saying that the owner's liability to pay damages to the plaintiffs was a natural consequence of the breach of s 14 and entitled the owner to indemnity, but not where the damage was also due to an act not within the contemplation of the parties, namely, the use of the coupling in a damaged condition. The owner's claim against the retailers failed. The Court of Appeal disagreed, holding that as the owner's conduct was not so unreasonable as to be beyond the contemplation of the retailers there was no break in the chain of causation and the dealers were liable to indemnify him.

HELD, in the House of Lords: This was not right. The first inquiry to be made was what were the terms of the warranty which was said to have been broken? It was that the coupling as fixed to the Landrover should be reasonably fit for towing trailers fitted with the appropriate type of attachment. This warranty was continuing up to the time when the owner learnt of its damaged condition. After this damage became apparent to him the only warranty he could have relied on was one which warranted that the coupling could continue to be safely used even in a damaged state—an obvious impossibility. The issue of causation on which the owner's claim against the dealers depended was whether it resulted from the dealer's breach of warranty, and manifestly it did not; it resulted from his own negligence in using the coupling in a damaged state.

Bernstein v Pamson Motors (Golders Green) Ltd

[1987] 2 All ER 220, [1987] RTR 384, [1987] BTLC 37, QBD

The plaintiff purchased a new Nissan motor car from the defendants which he collected from them on 7 November 1984. On 3 January 1985, the plaintiff made his first long journey in the car, which had covered a little over 100 miles. On the motorway, the camshaft seized up and the car had to be towed home. It was found that a drop of mastic sealant had blocked the lubrication system in the manufacturing process. On 4 January 1985, the plaintiff sought to reject the car as not being of merchantable quality under s 14 of the Sale of Goods Act 1979. During January, the car was repaired under warranty at not cost to the plaintiff. The plaintiff refused to accept the car, on the ground that the defect could have caused unknown damage to the engine, and that certain minor problems consequent on the defect had not been rectified.

HELD : The car was not of merchantable quality at the time of sale, but the defect was not one of a progressive nature. After repair, the car was effectively as good as new. The proper test of merchantability is the condition of the car at the time of delivery. This depends on whether the car was safe to drive, whether the defect or defects could be repaired satisfactorily, whether other potential damage might arise, and the time and expense of the repairs. Whether the defect was immediately apparent or not is immaterial. The plaintiff had accepted the car under s 35 of the Sale of Goods Act 1979 and his claim was limited to damages only, not rescission of the contract. Section 35 allowed a reasonable practical interval in commercial terms to inspect and return the goods, and on the facts the plaintiff had had this opportunity. *Bartlett v Sidney Marcus Ltd* [1965] 2 All ER 753 considered.

Rogers v Parish (Scarborough) Ltd

[1987] QB 933, [1987] 2 All ER 232, [1987] 2 WLR 353, 131 Sol Jo 223, CA
In November 1981 the plaintiffs bought a new Range Rover with the benefit of a manufacturers' warranty which promised free replacement or repair of parts if necessitated by manufacturing or material defect. The warranty was specifically stated not to affect the purchaser's statutory rights. After a few weeks the first Range Rover was replaced by another, which proved no more satisfactory. The original contract and warranty still applied. In May 1982, by which time several repair attempts had failed to correct problems with the engine and gearbox, the plaintiffs rejected the car as not being of merchantable quality within s 14(6) of the Sale of Goods Act 1979. The judge held that the car was of merchantable quality because the Range Rover was capable of being repaired (so it was not unfit for its normal purposes), that the plaintiffs should have taken it to another dealer to repair it (if they were unhappy with the defendants) and that as they had driven over 5,000 miles in the first six months, the plaintiffs had had plenty of use from the vehicle. The plaintiffs appealed.
HELD, ON APPEAL: Appeal allowed, for two reasons: (1) In considering whether this vehicle was of merchantable quality, the judge should not merely have considered it as a means of transport, but taken account of the expectations flowing from the purchase of a new Range Rover for comfort, ease and appearance. On this test, the vehicle failed. (2) The existence of the warranty was irrelevant—it was only an addition to the purchaser's rights.

R & B Customs Brokers Co Ltd v United Dominions Trust Ltd (Saunders Abbott (1980) Ltd, third party)

[1988] 1 All ER 847, [1988] 1 WLR 321, 132 Sol Jo 300, [1988] RTR 134, CA
The plaintiff was a private company owned by Mr and Mrs B, the defendant a finance company and the third party motor dealers. On 21 September 1984 Mr B arranged on behalf of the plaintiff to buy a Colt Shogun car on hire purchase, and drove the car away on the same day. Contracts between the plaintiff and the defendant, and between the defendant and the third party only came into existence on 3 November 1984 when the necessary documents were signed by all parties. By late October it became evident that the car roof leaked badly. The dealers tried unsuccessfully to repair this but it was incurable. In February 1985, Mr B rejected the car and asked for his money back. The judge found that the car was unfit for its purpose, which was ordinary use on English roads. The defendant appealed.
HELD: Appeal dismissed. The car was not of merchantable quality, in breach of the implied condition in s 14(2) of the Sale of Goods Act 1979. The relevant date was 3 November, and although the plaintiff, through Mr B, was aware that the roof leaked before then, this did not prevent it from relying on this condition, since Mr B did not know that the leak was incurable. There was also breach of the condition in s 14(3) of the Act, that the car was fit for its purpose. The exception to that condition which applied where it was unreasonable for the buyer to rely on the seller's skill and judgment was not fulfilled, because there was no indication that Mr B had ceased to rely on the motor-dealer's skill and judgment by 3 November. The implied conditions in s 14(2) and (3) could not be excluded by arguing that the plaintiff was not 'dealing as consumer' within s 12 of the Unfair Contracts Terms Act 1977 because the plaintiff

did not make the contract 'in the course of a business' under s 12(1)(a) of that Act. The latter phrase should be construed in a restricted sense as being an activity integral to the purchaser's business or a regular course of dealing in an activity incidental to it. Neither of these criteria was fulfilled here.

Intermediate examination

Vaile Bros v Hobson Ltd

[1933] All ER Rep 447, [1933] 149 LT 283, Div Ct
The plaintiffs had sent a carburettor to the defendants for repair. In use one of the connecting rods broke, the engine raced out of control, the flywheel broke and extensive damage was done. The county court judge found that the engine switch was not connected to the dashboard, with the result that the damage could not be prevented by switching off the engine. He held this to be contributory negligence and absolved the defendants from liability. On appeal, this was reversed and it was held that the repairer could not escape liability for a defective repair by pointing to another defect for which he was not liable.

Stennett v Hancock and Peters

[1939] 2 All ER 578, 83 Sol Jo 379 (Branson J)
The owner of a motor lorry took a wheel of the lorry, the flange of which had come off, to a motor repairer with instructions to reassemble it. The repairer's assistants reassembled and replaced it on the lorry, and the lorry owner's servant drove the lorry away. An hour or two later, the flange came off while the lorry was being driven on the highway by the lorry owner's servant, and, bowling along the road, it mounted the pavement and hit the female plaintiff, injuring her. There was no evidence that anything had happened between the time when the lorry was taken out of the garage and the time of the accident which might have caused the wheel to become dislodged. HELD : (1) Following *Phillips v Britannia Hygienic Laundry* (p 204, above) the lorry owner having entrusted the repair of the lorry to a competent repairer, he was not liable for either negligence or nuisance to a person who suffered injury upon the road by reason of the competent repairer having been negligent. (2) The lorry owner, or the person who was going to take the vehicle on the road, was not under a duty to ascertain for himself, in so far as his capabilities allowed him to do so, whether the competent repairer had competently repaired the lorry. (3) Following *Donoghue v Stevenson* and distinguishing *Earl v Lubbock* ([1905] 1 KB 253) the repairer was liable to the persons who suffered injury on the road as a result of his negligence, as he was in the same position as that of the manufacturer of an article sold by a distributor in circumstances which prevented the distributor or ultimate purchaser or consumer from discovering by inspection any defect in the article.

Aspin v J Bretherton & Sons

(1947) Policy Holder Law Supplement, 24 December (Streatfield J)
On 24 June 1946, the owners sent their lorry to the repairers to have the brakes relined, which involved dismantling, reassembling and replacement as necessary. The following day the repairers fitted a new drum and replaced roller bearings. On 22 July 1946, the owners sent the lorry to the repairers for special greasing. The owners did the maintenance work and greased once a week and tested for end play. On 24 July

1946, the lorry had travelled 2,059 miles, when the front offside wheel came off causing the lorry to collide with a bus. A passenger in the bus was injured and sued the lorry owners and the repairers.
HELD: The owners' explanation excluded them from liability. The lorry driver was not negligent. The condition of the thrust washer put the repairers on inquiry. There was not anticipation of examination by the owners and they were not bound to inspect after 2,059 miles and within a month. Time and distance were questions of fact. The repairers were negligent and were liable to the passenger.

Donnelly v Glasgow Corpn

1953 SC 107, 1953 SLT 161
An omnibus belonging to a local authority overturned owing to a broken front spring. In an action for damages arising out of the accident, the local authority sought to blame the manufacturers of the spring, on the ground that two usual and normal safety devices connected with the spring had been omitted in the construction of the chassis.
HELD: The defect was clearly one which could have been detected by an examination of the bus after it came into the hands of the local authority, they having competent mechanics expert in the maintenance of public service vehicles. As a result the chain of causation between the manufacturers and the persons injured was broken, since there had been an opportunity for intermediate examination. No fault, therefore, could be placed at the door of the manufacturers. The contention of the local authority rejected.

Davie v New Merton Board Mills

[1959] AC 604, [1959] 1 All ER 346, [1959] 2 WLR 331, 103 Sol Jo 177, [1959] 2 Lloyd's Rep 587, HL
The plaintiff, a maintenance fitter in the employ of the first defendant, was injured when using a drift, a tool for separating pieces of metal. At the second blow by a hammer, a particle of metal flew off the head of the drift and entered his left eye resulting in the loss of all useful vision in that eye. The accident occurred on 8 March 1953. The drift had been purchased by the employers from a reputable firm of suppliers in 1946, who had purchased it in 1946 from a firm of reputable and old established toolmakers. The drift appeared to be in good condition but was excessively hard for its purpose owing to negligence in its manufacture. The employers were unaware of the defect and could not reasonably have discovered it.
HELD: The employers were not liable. No intermediate examination of the tool between the time of its manufacture and the time of its actual use was reasonably to be expected. It was unreasonable to expect an employer to test a drift for hardness before issuing it to his employee. No examination short of a test would have revealed the danger existing in this particular drift.

Note—The duty of an employer to a workman is admittedly higher than the owner of a car to a passenger, but the decision may be a guide to the defence of a car owner.

The Employer's Liability (Defective Equipment) Act 1969 (which came into force on 25 October 1969), s 1(1)–(3) provides as follows:
'**1 Extension of employer's liability for defective equipment** (1) Where after the commencement of this Act—
(a) an employee suffers personal injury in the course of his employment in consequence of a defect in equipment provided by his employer for the purposes of the employer's business; and

(b) the defect is attributable wholly or partly to the fault of a third party (whether identified or not),

the injury shall be deemed to be also attributable to negligence on the part of the employer (whether or not he is liable in respect of the injury apart from this sub-section), but without prejudice to the law relating to contributory negligence and to any remedy by way of contribution or in contract or otherwise which is available to the employer in respect of the injury.

(2) In so far as any agreement purports to exclude or limit any liability of an employer arising under subsection (1) of this section, the agreement shall be void.

(3) In this section—

"business" includes the activities carried on by any public body;

"employee" means a person who is employed by another person under a contract of service or apprenticeship and is so employed for the purposes of a business carried on by that other person, and "employer" shall be construed accordingly;

"equipment" includes any plant and machinery, vehicle, aircraft and clothing;

"fault" means negligence, breach of statutory duty or other act or omission which gives rise to liability in tort in England and Wales or which is wrongful and gives rise to liability in damages in Scotland; and

"personal injury" includes loss of life, any impairment of a person's physical or mental condition and any disease.'

Clarkson v William Jackson & Sons Ltd

(1984) Times, 21 November, CA

The Employer's Liability (Defective Equipment) Act 1969 does not give employees a new cause of action. The scheme of the Act is to prevent an employer escaping liability when the fault in the equipment was the fault of the supplier or manufacturer and not of the employee.

Knowledge of dangerous condition

Hurley v Dyke

[1979] RTR 265, HL

The defendant was a garage owner near Malvern. On 28 September a man named Halford driving an old Reliant three-wheeled car called at the garage because the carburettor was leaking. Both looked at the car and noticed it was down on one side. The defendant said Halford could not drive it like that. Halford said he would scrap the car and the defendant then paid him £10 for it. On 8 October, the carburettor having been repaired, the defendant took the car to a car auction at Tewkesbury, putting a reserve of £40 on it. It was offered for sale at auction on the terms 'To be sold as seen and with all its faults and without warranty'. Jones, a motor dealer, bought it for £40 intending to use it for spares, but after the sale Nigel Clay, a young man who had tried unsuccessfully to bid for the car, offered Jones a further £10 and Jones sold it to him. Clay drove it to Coventry where he lived and a week later to Surrey to see a friend. On 16 October he was driving the car with the plaintiff as passenger when the nearside of the chassis collapsed causing the car to go out of control. Clay was killed and the plaintiff very seriously injured. The judge at first instance held the defendant liable on the ground that, knowing the car was dangerous to drive, he had not ensured that the auctioneer made it clear that what was being sold was an unroadworthy vehicle. The Court of Appeal held there was no liability on the

defendant. The warning given by the auctioneer was sufficient to bring home to the mind of any reasonable immediate buyer from the defendant that the car should not be put upon the road without intermediate examination. The defendant's duty did not extend beyond any first buyer from him.
HELD, ON APPEAL to the House of Lords: The defendant was not liable. The case turned on the question of fact as to the extent of the defendant's knowledge of the nature of the defect in the car when he put it up for auction. The highest that the defendant's knowledge could be put was an awareness of the public danger of driving the car without further examination. The warning given at auction that it was to be sold 'as seen and with all its faults' was adequate to satisfy any duty of care owed by the defendant to the plaintiff.

Safety glass

Grenfell v Meyrowitz

[1936] 2 All ER 1313, CA
'Safety glass' means made from laminated glass, and there is no warranty of absolute safety in these words.

Evans v Triplex Safety Glass Co Ltd

[1936] 1 All ER 283 (Porter J)
The plaintiff bought a motor car in June 1934, with a windscreen made of 'Triplex Toughened Safety Glass'. The windscreen was fitted by the Vauxhall Motor Co. On 27 July 1935, whilst he was driving the car, the windscreen, suddenly and for no apparent reason, broke into many fragments and injured the second plaintiff, wife of the first plaintiff. The plaintiffs brought an action in negligence against the defendants. There was no claim in contract against the vendors of the car.
HELD: A number of causes might have brought about the disintegration. The suppliers of the car had every opportunity to examine the windscreen. I do not find any negligence proved against the defendants. Verdict for defendants with costs.

Remedies

Shine v General Guarantee Corpn Ltd (Reeds Motor Co (a firm), third party)

[1988] 1 All ER 911, [1988] BTLC 1, CA
The defendant finance company purchased a Fiat X19 car from the third party and let it to the plaintiff under a hire purchase agreement dated 15 September 1982. The car was first registered in January 1981, but in January 1982 it was submerged in water for 24 hours and was treated as an insurance write-off. The third party were not aware of this when they sold the car to the defendants. The plaintiff subsequently sued the defendants for breach of the implied term of merchantable quality under s 14(2) of the Sale of Goods Act 1979.
HELD: A car is not merely a means of transport but is also an investment, and in this case, a specialist car for the enthusiast. The car was not of merchantable quality and the plaintiff was entitled to damages (to be reassessed by the judge at first instance) but not for rescission of the contract, since he had accepted the car by using it for a substantial period of time after discovering the breach.

CHAPTER 7

Fire Damage

FIRES PREVENTION (METROPOLIS) ACT 1774

Note—Liability for damage to property by fire may be founded in negligence; or, where there is an escape of fire due to a non-natural use of land, there may be liability without negligence. If negligence is relied on, the burden of proof is on the plaintiff (Fires Prevention (Metropolis) Act 1774). Both grounds of liability were considered in *Musgrove v Pandelis*, where the fire began in a motor car.

The Fires Prevention (Metropolis) Act 1774 (which applies to the whole country) provides that no action shall lie against a person on whose land any fire 'shall accidentally begin'. The Act has been interpreted to mean that such a person shall not be liable merely because the fire began on his premises; if the plaintiff cannot prove negligence he will not succeed unless he can bring his case within the principle of strict liability for the escape of the fire, against which the Act gives no protection.

Musgrove v Pandelis

[1919] 2 KB 43, 88 LJKB 915, 120 LT 601, 35 TLR 299, 63 Sol Jo 353, CA
Plaintiff occupied rooms over a garage. Part of the garage was let to defendant, who kept a motor car there. Defendant's servant, who had little skill as a chauffeur, having occasion in the course of his employment to move the motor car, started the engine, and from some unexplained cause, and without negligence on the part of the servant, the petrol in the carburettor caught fire. If the servant had promptly turned off the tap leading from the petrol tank to the carburettor, the fire would have harmlessly burnt itself out. But he failed to do this; and the fire spread and burnt the car, the garage and plaintiff's rooms and furniture. Plaintiff brought an action for damages. Defendant pleaded that the fire accidentally began within the meaning of the above enactment. The judge at the trial found that defendant's servant was negligent in not promptly turning off the petrol tap.
HELD: (1) The Fires Prevention (Metropolis) Act 1774 did not protect a person who brought upon his premises an object likely to do damage if not kept in control, and a motor car ready to start, or such a car in charge of an unskilled chauffeur, was an

object of that kind; (2) the fire which caused the damage was not that which took place in the carburettor, but was the fire which spread to the car; and this fire did not begin accidentally but was caused by the negligence of the defendant's servant.

Mulholland and Tedd Ltd v Baker

[1939] 3 All ER 253, 161 LT 20 (Asquith J)
Asquith J in a case of a 20-gallon drum of paraffin catching fire in the yard of a shop, adopted the decision in *Musgrove v Pandelis* (above) that it is not necessary to prove negligence where the defendant has brought on his premises an object likely to do damage if it is not kept under control and that object catches fire, but as he had already found negligence of the defendant, his decision was really obiter.

Sinclair v Juner

(1952) 101 L Jo 706, Ct of Sess First Div
The principles of the Act of 1774 do not apply to Scotland in as much as it is deemed that a fire is accidentally begun.

Williams v Owen

[1956] 1 All ER 104, [1955] 1 WLR 1293, 99 Sol Jo 890 (Finnemore J)
Plaintiff was a guest at a hotel and his car was in the hotel garage. The car was destroyed by fire. He sued the hotelkeeper for damages for its loss. His claim was based on the responsibility of an innkeeper at common law for the goods of his guests. The defendant claimed to be protected by the Fires Prevention (Metropolis) Act 1774, s 86, which prohibits the bringing of proceedings against a person on whose premises a fire accidentally begins 'any law, usage or custom to the contrary notwithstanding'. In a corner of the garage was a small boiler for heating water for rooms above the garage occupied by the staff. The boiler had a closing door and was surrounded by a concrete wall 7 ft 6 in high, and it was stoked from the far side where there was a ramp. The boiler was lit about noon and stoked until 2.30 pm when it was shut down and the fire allowed to die out, and was usually out by 8 pm. The fire broke out about 11.30 pm.
HELD: That the innkeeper's liability at common law was a custom within the meaning of s 86, and that accordingly the defendant's liability was limited, in the case of damage by fire, to non-accidental fires. The Act of 1774 applied and plaintiff had not proved negligence. Verdict for defendant.

Perry v Kendricks Transport Ltd

[1956] 1 All ER 154, [1956] 1 WLR 85, 100 Sol Jo 52, CA
Garage and coach proprietors had left a coach for three months on their parking ground adjoining waste land. People crossing the waste land might go through the vehicle park, though they had no right to do so. When left, the tank was emptied of petrol and the cap of the tank replaced. There was regular inspection of the park and vehicles. A boy aged ten saw two other boys near the coach and went towards them. As he neared them, they jumped away and there was an explosion and he was dreadfully burned. The court concluded that the cap had been removed by someone before the accident and found there was no negligence of the proprietors. It was also contended that the case came within the rule in *Rylands v Fletcher* which contention failed.

HELD, ON APPEAL: Assuming the removal of the cap and the throwing of a lighted match was done by the two boys mischievously and deliberately, it was not something the defendants ought to have anticipated and the rule did not apply to the wrongful acts of third parties over whom the defendants had no control.

Per Parker LJ: Although the decision in *Musgrove v Pandelis* (p 225, above) has been the subject of some criticism, it is still binding on the Court of Appeal, nor do I think it is open to this court to hold that it does not apply to personal injury.

Note—Followed by Pearce J in *Adcock v Loveridge* (1956) Times, 21 June.

Sturge v Hackett

[1962] 3 All ER 166, [1962] 1 WLR 1257, 106 Sol Jo 568, 183 Estates Gazette 161, CA

The tenant of a flat forming part of a house wished to destroy a bird's nest in a cornice on the exterior of his flat. He stood on the roof of a porch (not forming part of his flat) below the cornice, lit some paraffin-soaked rags and then applied them at the end of a stick to the nest. The nest caught fire and a piece of burning straw entered the roof-space, setting fire to the house, which was burnt down. In an action arising from the destruction of the house a question arose whether the fire started on the premises (ie the flat) of which he was occupier.

HELD: Following *Musgrove v Pandelis* the relevant fire for the purposes of the old common law liability of allowing fire to escape from one's premises is the fire which gets out of control—not the match or other means used for lighting the fire which gets out of control. The paraffin rag was merely the means by which he ignited the nest. What got out of control and spread was the new fire which he started when he applied the paraffin rag to the base of the nest.

Mason v Levy Auto Parts of England

[1967] 2 QB 530, [1967] 2 All ER 62, [1967] 2 WLR 1384, 111 Sol Jo 234, [1967] 1 Lloyd's Rep 372

The plaintiff's house and garden adjoined the defendant's premises on which they stored large quantities of machinery and spare parts. The machinery was coated in grease and packed in paper and was contained in wooden packing cases. There were quantities of other combustible materials including tarpaulins and inflammable liquids. Fire broke out among this material through no ascertainable cause and spread to the plaintiff's property causing damage.

HELD: The defendants had the protection of the Fires Prevention (Metropolis) Act 1774, against a claim based on their negligence in causing the fire or allowing it to spread: the onus of proof of negligence was on the plaintiff and he had failed to discharge it. But the Act did not give protection to a defendant who in the course of some non-natural use of the land had brought on to it things likely to catch fire and had kept them there in such conditions that if they did catch fire the fire would be likely to spread to the plaintiff's land (*Musgrove v Pandelis*). In the present case having regard to the amount of combustible material, the way in which it was stored and the character of the neighbourhood the defendants' use of their land was non-natural and they were liable for the damage done to the plaintiff's premises by the escape of the fire.

H and N Emanuel Ltd v Greater London Council

[1971] 2 All ER 835, 115 Sol Jo 226, 218 Estates Gazette 1413, [1971] 2 Lloyd's Rep 36, CA

A demolition contractor was removing prefabricated bungalows under contract with the Ministry of Works from land belonging to the defendant council. In breach of a term of his contract with the Ministry he lit a rubbish fire and negligently allowed sparks to fly on to the plaintiffs' adjoining property causing fire damage to buildings and vehicles. He had no contract with the defendants but he was on the site with their permission. Their foreman had the keys of the prefabs and anyone wishing to do anything with them had to get his permission. There was evidence that it was a standard practice of demolition contractors to light fires when clearing sites.

HELD: It has been the law for centuries that an occupier of premises is liable for an escape of fire caused by anyone other than a 'stranger', though since the Fires Prevention (Metropolis) Act 1774 the escape must be negligent. The contractor was negligent: was he a 'stranger' ie a person who acts in a way contrary to anything which the occupier could anticipate? As there was a standard practice among demolition men to burn rubbish and as they were on the site with the leave and knowledge of the defendants they were not 'strangers'. The defendants were occupiers and had control over the activities of the contractor. They were liable to the plaintiffs.

RYLANDS V FLETCHER

Collingwood v Home and Colonial Stores

[1936] 3 All ER 200, 155 LT 550, 53 TLR 53, 56 Ll L Rep 105, CA

The dicta in the judgments in *Musgrove*'s case which suggested that the principle of *Rylands v Fletcher* applied, have been criticised as follows:

Per Lord Wright MR: I confess, however, I find some difficulty about the other ground (than negligence) on which the decision was based though, if it were necessary, I should follow the ruling of the Court of Appeal.

Per Romer LJ: I think at some time it will be desirable if the House of Lords would consider the case of *Musgrove v Pandelis*, so far as the decision in that case was based upon *Rylands v Fletcher* (1) that a motor car is a dangerous thing to bring into a garage, and (2) that the use of one's land for the purpose of erecting a garage and keeping a motor car there is not an ordinary and proper use of the land, are two propositions which, but for that authority, I should myself respectfully have doubted.

Read v J Lyons & Co Ltd

[1947] AC 156, [1946] 2 All ER 471, [1947] LJR 39, 175 LT 413, 62 TLR 646, 91 Sol Jo 54, HL

A worker was injured in a munition factory by the explosion of a shell. She claimed that the employers were liable without proof of negligence under the principle of *Rylands v Fletcher*.

HELD: Two conditions were necessary (1) escape from the place of occupation, and (2) non-natural use of the land, and there was no 'escape'.

Per Lord Porter: Furthermore, in *Musgrove v Pandelis* it was held that a motor car brought into a garage with full tanks was a dangerous object, a conclusion which, as Romer LJ pointed out in *Collingwood v Home and Colonial Stores*, involves the propositions that a motor car is a dangerous thing to bring into a garage and that the use of one's land for the purpose of erecting a garage and keeping a motor car there is not an ordinary or proper use of the land.

My Lord, if these questions ever come directly before this House it may be necessary to lay down principles for their determination. For the present I need only say that each seems to be a question of fact . . . and . . . all the circumstances of the time and place and practice of mankind must be taken into consideration so that what might be regarded as dangerous or non-natural may vary according to those circumstances.

The question whether the principle applied to personal injuries was left open. Lord Macmillan did not think it had ever been laid down that it did; and if the foundation was to be found in the injunction *sic utere tuo ut alienum non laedas*, it was manifest it did not apply to personal injuries.

Lord Porter said this point was not in issue and the cases where it had been thought to apply, *Shiffman v Order of St John* [1936] 1 All ER 557, 80 Sol Jo 346 and *Miles v Forest Rock Granite Co (Leicestershire) Ltd* (1918) 34 TLR 500, 62 Sol Jo 634 may some day require examination.

Note—See also *Dunne v North Western Gas Board*, below.

LIABILITY FOR NEGLIGENCE

Note—Charlesworth on Negligence (7th edn) para 12-120 says 'the burden of proving that the origin of a fire was caused by the negligence of the occupier, or his servants, agents or independent contractors, for whose acts or omissions he would be vicariously liable, rests firmly on the plaintiff'. The cases cited in support are *Becquet v MacCarthy* (1831) 2 B & Ad 951 and *Musgrove v Pandelis* (p 225), *Collingwood v Home and Colonial Stores* (p 228) and *Williams v Owen* (p 226, below).

But in the case of bailment the onus is on the bailee. See below, *Hyman v Benedyk* (p 232) and *Smith v Taylor* (p 233).

Roskill v Cook

(1932) 43 Ll L Rep 511 (de Parcq J)
A fire occurred in the plaintiff's house. The plaintiff suggested that the fire originated in a wood block in the party wall. The defendant suggested it arose from an electric installation in the plaintiff's house.
HELD: The plaintiff had failed to discharge the onus of proof of the cause of the fire.

Note—See also *Jefferson v Derbyshire Farmers Ltd*, p 143 above and *British Transport Commission v Maxine*, p 143, above.

Century Insurance Co v Northern Ireland Road Transport Board

[1942] AC 509, [1942] 1 All ER 491, 111 LJPC 138, 167 LT 404, 72 Ll L Rep 119, HL
Policy covered use of motor tanker including loading and unloading not beyond the limit of the carriageway or thoroughfare. The driver backed a petrol lorry into the garage of a customer, inserted the nozzle of the delivery hose into the manhole of the customer's storage tank and turned on the stopcock at the side of the tanker. While petrol was flowing from the tanker to the tank, he lit a cigarette, and threw the lighted match on the floor of the garage, which ignited material on the floor of the garage and set fire to the petrol at the nozzle. He drove the tanker out of the garage and stopped

with the fore-wheels in the water channel and jumped off. An explosion occurred causing damage to the tanker and to property of third parties.
HELD: (1) This was negligence in the discharge of his duties and the master was responsible. It need not be an act for the employer's benefit. (2) The damage was caused by the use of the tanker including loading and unloading.

Sochaki v Sas

[1947] 1 All ER 344 (Lord Goddard CJ)
A lodger went out leaving a fire burning in his room, and was away two or three hours. There was no evidence that he made up the fire in an unusual way or built up any enormous fire. While he was out a fire took place, probably caused by a spark jumping from the fire and setting fire to the floorboards. There was no fire guard or iron fender. There was an ordinary, natural, proper, everyday use of the fireplace.
HELD: No evidence of negligence. The lodger was not liable under *Rylands v Fletcher*, and the doctrine of *res ipsa loquitur* did not apply. The lodger was not liable.

Anglo-Saxon Petroleum Co v Admiralty Comrs

[1947] KB 794, [1947] 2 All ER 465, [1948] LJR 153, 80 Ll L Rep 459, CA
An oil tanker during the war stranded in Alexandria Harbour. The naval authorities took complete control of the salvage operations and lightened the ship by forcing petrol by air pressure out of the tanks with the result that there was one-sixteenth of an inch of petrol over two square miles of sea. Two tugs were sent to the stranded vessel. The petrol caught fire. The cause of the fire could not be determined. Probable causes were (1) smoking, both lighting and from burning cigarette ends thrown away; (2) galley fires; (3) sparks from the funnel of the tugs; (4) sparks from any blow of steel against steel; (5) electric sparks from the tug's degaussing coils. The plaintiffs were unable to say which one was the actual cause.
HELD: The plaintiffs were entitled to succeed if they established a balance of probability that the source of the ignition emanated from the tugs rather than from the ship. In one sense it was a new point but it depended on well-established principles. Verdict for plaintiffs upheld.

Yachuk v Oliver Blais Co Ltd

[1949] AC 386, [1949] 2 All ER 150, 65 TLR 300
Petrol suppliers were held liable for injuries sustained by a 9 year old boy when he used petrol supplied by them to make a torch and subsequently burned himself. The boy had obtained the petrol by falsely stating that his mother needed it as her car had broken down. The court decided that the suppliers had been negligent in entrusting a substance so highly inflammable to a young child, putting temptation in his way, and subjecting him to the risk of injury.

Balfour v Barty-King

[1957] 1 QB 496, [1957] 1 All ER 156, [1957] 2 WLR 84, 101 Sol Jo 62, [1956] 2 Lloyd's Rep 646, CA
A large country house had been divided into separate dwelling houses. The defendant occupied one part and the plaintiff occupied another part which adjoined and was contiguous to the defendant's part. The water system of the defendant's house became frozen and he employed an independent contractor to do the necessary work. The cisterns were in a loft which contained combustible material. The contractor's

men used a blowlamp, which set fire to the material. The fire spread to the roof and so to the plaintiff's house and caused considerable damage to it. The trial judge found that the contractor's men were negligent in using a blowlamp near to combustible material. He held the defendant was liable to the plaintiff for the damage. The defendant appealed.

HELD: There was no direct authority. From very early times the law recognised a special duty to guard against escape of fire. The curfew was imposed as a precautionary measure. *Musgrove v Pandelis* (p 225, above) held that the statutory exception of accidental fire leaves the other heads of liability at common law untouched. It is clear that at the present day a person in whose house a fire is caused by negligence is liable if it spreads to that of his neighbour, whether the negligence is his own or that of his servant or guest but not a stranger. A trespasser would be a stranger, but an employed contractor cannot be in any better position than a guest. Here the defendant had control of the contractor in that he chose him, invited him to his premises to do the work, and could have ordered him to leave at any moment. The defendant is liable to the plaintiff for the plaintiff's damage.

Goldman v Hargrave

[1967] 1 AC 645, [1966] 2 All ER 989, [1966] 3 WLR 513, 110 Sol Jo 527, [1966] 2 Lloyd's Rep 65, PC

On 25 February a tree on the appellant's land was struck by lightning and caught fire 84 feet above the ground. The appellant had the tree felled on the following day to deal with the blaze but instead of putting the fire out with water, which he could have done on the morning of the 25th at the latest, he preferred to burn it out. On 1 March the wind rose, reviving the fire, which then spread to the respondent's adjoining properties causing damage.

HELD: (1) There is a general duty of care on occupiers in relation to hazards occurring on their land, including that of fire, and whether natural or man-made, to remove or reduce such hazards. The duty is based on knowledge of the hazard, ability to foresee the consequences of not checking or removing it, and the ability to abate it. What is reasonable for the occupier to do depends on his circumstances: he should not be held liable unless it is clearly proved that he could, and reasonably in his individual circumstances should, have done more. In the present case it was well within the capacity and resources of the appellant to put the fire out on 26 or 27 February and he was liable to the respondents for not having done so; (2) The Fires Prevention (Metropolis) Act 1774 relieved an owner from liability for a mere escape of fire but not from a claim for damages for negligence—*Musgrove v Pandelis* (p 225, above). In the present case the fire which damaged the respondents' property was that which arose on 1 March as a result of the negligence of the appellant, and the statutory defence failed.

Note—See also *Sturge v Hackett*, p 227, above.

Leong Bee & Co v Ling Nam Rubber Works

(1970) 114 Sol Jo 806, [1970] 2 Lloyd's Rep 247, PC

A fire started on the respondents' premises at night and spread to the appellants' building 14 feet away. There was no evidence to show how the fire began.

HELD: The burden of proof lay on the appellants (as original plaintiffs) as to both negligence and nuisance. Their task at the trial was to establish (1) that the respondents themselves or some person for whose conduct they were answerable had been guilty of some negligent act or omission which was a cause either of the commencement of the fire or of its spreading to the appellants' premises, or (2) that the respondents had caused or permitted to exist on their premises a source of fire danger giving rise to a reasonably foreseeable risk of material injury. On the evidence given at the trial the fire was not caused by the respondents' negligence or nuisance. Their only remaining duty was under the principle explained in *Goldman v Hargrave* (p 231, above) and based on knowledge of the fire, foreseeability of the consequences of not checking it and ability to abate it. Although the respondents' nightwatchman became aware of the fire and could foresee the consequences there was nothing he could then do which would have saved the appellants' building. The respondents were not liable.

Ogwo v Taylor

[1988] AC 431, (1987) 3 All ER 961 HL
The defendant negligently set fire to his house. The trial judge found that it was an ordinary house and an ordinary fire. The plaintiff, a fireman, suffered injuries while tackling the blaze and brought an action in negligence against the defendant.

The trial judge found for the defendant on the basis that although he had been negligent the injury to the plaintiff was not a foreseeable consequence of this negligence. The plaintiff won on appeal and the defendant appealed to the House of Lords.

HELD: Where an occupier negligently causes a fire and a fireman is injured when attempting to put out this fire, the occupier is liable if it was foreseeable that the fireman would attend to extinguish the fire. The same is true whether the fireman is exposed to exceptional or merely ordinary risks undertaken by firemen. There may, however, be an element of contributory negligence where the fireman recklessly exposes himself to unnecessary danger.

LIABILITY OF BAILEE

I and J Hyman (Sales) Ltd v A Benedyk & Co Ltd

[1957] 2 Lloyd's Rep 601 (Judge Malcolm Wright), Lambeth CC
Rags belonging to the plaintiffs, rag and general merchants, were being processed in defendants' premises by the defendants. Fire broke out on the defendants' premises and the plaintiffs' goods were damaged. It was common ground that the defendants were bailees for reward. The likely cause of the fire was by a cigarette or match carelessly disposed of by defendants' labourer, but the judge did not think this was proved. Defendants contended that, under the 1774 Act, the onus was on the plaintiffs to prove negligence.

HELD: At common law the onus was on defendants as bailees to prove absence of negligence.

The onus was on the defendants to show that the fire was accidental. In *Charlesworth on Negligence* (3rd edn) p 298, it is stated the burden of proving negligence is on the plaintiff (*Williams v Owen*, above). Apart from inn-keeper's liability, that was not a case of bailor and bailee.

When defendants seek to rely on the statute, in a case where the law requires them to prove the absence of negligence, the duty lies on them to prove the defence they have set up. Judgment for plaintiffs.

Note—See now paras 12-120 of *Charlesworth on Negligence* (8th edn).

Smith v Taylor

[1966] 2 Lloyd's Rep 231 (Blain J)
The plaintiff left his car for repair at the defendant's garage. Whilst the mechanic was draining the petrol tank a quantity of petrol spilled on to the floor. A short time later the car burst into flames and was destroyed. The cause of the fire was not ascertained. HELD: The defendant being a bailee was at common law under a liability to establish that when a vehicle entrusted to his care was damaged that did not happen through negligence on his part or that of his servant or agent. It was therefore, necessary, even when the plaintiff's expert witness could not establish the probable cause of the fire, for the defendant, if he sought to escape liability, to call evidence. The mechanic knew that petrol vapour was dangerous in the presence of an electric lamp such as he was using and his failure to take the necessary steps to prevent a quantity of petrol spilling on the floor was negligence. The defendant was liable.

CHAPTER 8

Animals on the Highway

INTRODUCTION

The common law rules which formerly determined the liability of owners for damage caused by animals were amended and partially codified by the Animals Act 1971, which came into force on 1 October 1971. The owner of an animal has a duty to take reasonable care to control or restrain the animal so that it does not cause damage or injury to persons using the highway. The old common law rule that an owner is under no duty to prevent his animals from straying on to the highway is abolished.

The Dangerous Dogs Act 1991, which came into force on 12 August 1991, further determined the liability of owners or keepers for damage caused by dogs.

Those sections of the Acts which are or may be relevant to motor claims are as follows.

THE ANIMALS ACT 1971

1 New provisions as to strict liability for damage done by animals (1) The provisions of ss 2 to 5 of this Act replace—

(a) the rules of the common law imposing a strict liability in tort for damage done by an animal on the ground that the animal is regarded as ferae naturae or that its vicious or mischievous propensities are known or presumed to be known;

(b) . . .

(c) . . .

(2) Expressions used in those sections shall be interpreted in accordance with the provisions of s 6 (as well as those of s 11) of this Act.

2 Liability for damage done by dangerous animals (1) Where any damage is caused by an animal which belongs to a dangerous species, any person who is a keeper of the animal is liable for the damage, except as otherwise provided by this Act.

(2) Where damage is caused by an animal which does not belong to a dangerous species, a keeper of the animal is liable for the damage, except as otherwise provided by this Act, if

(a) the damage is of a kind which the animal, unless restrained, was likely to cause or which, if caused by the animal, was likely to be severe; and
(b) the likelihood of the damage or of its being severe was due to characteristics of the animal which are not normally found in animals of the same species or are not normally so found except at particular times or in particular circumstances; and
(c) those characteristics were known to that keeper or were at any time known to a person who at that time had charge of the animal as that keeper's servant or, where that keeper is the head of a household, were known to another keeper of the animal who is a member of that household and under the age of sixteen.

5 Exceptions from liability under sections 2 to 4 (1) A person is not liable under ss 2 to 4 of this Act for any damage which is due wholly to the fault of the person suffering it.
(2) A person is not liable under s 2 of this Act for any damage suffered by a person who has voluntarily accepted the risk thereof.

6 Interpretation of certain expressions used in sections 2 to 5 (1) The following provisions apply to the interpretation of ss 2 to 5 of this Act.
(2) A dangerous species is a species—
(a) which is not commonly domesticated in the British Islands; and
(b) whose fully grown animals normally have such characteristics that they are likely, unless restrained, to cause severe damage or that any damage they may cause is likely to be severe.
(3) Subject to sub-s (4) of this section, a person is a keeper of an animal if—
(a) he owns the animal or has it in his possession; or
(b) he is the head of a household of which a member under the age of sixteen owns the animal or has it in his possession;
and if at any time an animal ceases to be owned by or to be in the possession of a person, any person who immediately before that time was a keeper thereof by virtue of the preceding provisions of this subsection continues to be a keeper of the animal until another person becomes a keeper thereof by virtue of those provisions.
(4) Where an animal is taken into and kept in possession for the purpose of preventing it from causing damage or of restoring it to its owner, a person is not a keeper of it by virtue only of that possession.
(5) Where a person employed as a servant by a keeper of an animal incurs a risk incidental to his employment he shall not be treated as accepting it voluntarily.

8 Duty to take care to prevent damage from animals straying on to the highway (1) So much of the rules of the common law relating to liability for negligence as excludes or restricts the duty which a person might owe to others to take such care as is reasonable to see that damage is not caused by animals straying on to a highway is hereby abolished.
(2) Where damage is caused by animals straying from unfenced land to a highway a person who placed them on the land shall not be regarded as having committed a breach of the duty to take care by reason only of placing them there if—
(a) the land is common land, or is land situated in an area where fencing is not customary, or is a town or village green; and
(b) he had a right to place the animals on that land.

10 Application of certain enactments to liability under sections 2 to 4 For the purposes of the [Fatal Accidents Act 1976] the Law Reform (Contributory Negligence) Act 1945 and the [Limitation Act 1980] any damage for which a person is liable under ss 2 to 4 of this Act shall be treated as due to his fault.

11 General interpretation In this Act—

'common land' and 'town or village green' have the same meanings as in the Commons Registration Act 1965;

'damage' includes the death of, or injury to, any person (including any disease and any impairment of physical or mental condition);

'fault' has the same meaning as in the Law Reform (Contributory Negligence) Act 1945;

'fencing' includes the construction of any obstacle designed to prevent animals from straying;

'species' includes sub-species and variety.

12 Application to Crown (1) This Act binds the Crown, but nothing in this section shall authorise proceedings to be brought against Her Majesty in her private capacity.
(2) Section 38(3) of the Crown Proceedings Act 1947 (interpretation of references to Her Majesty in her private capacity) shall apply as if this section were contained in that Act.
[*The Act does not apply to Scotland.*]

Wallace v Newton

[1982] 2 All ER 106, [1982] 1 WLR 375, 126 Sol Jo 101 (Park J)
The plaintiff was employed as a groom, handling horses belonging to her employer which were used for show jumping. On an occasion when she was leading a horse into a horsebox it suddenly leaped or lunged forward, crushing her arm against a bar in the trailer. The injury was serious. She claimed damages under the Animals Act 1971, s 2(2)
HELD: By s 2(2)(b) the plaintiff had to establish that the likelihood of the damage was due to characteristics of the animal which were not normally found in horses. This did not mean the horse had to be shown to have a vicious tendency to injure people by attacking them; it was sufficient to show that it had characteristics of a kind not usually found in horses. There was evidence that during the period the plaintiff had the horse in her charge its behaviour was unpredictable and unreliable and that the owner, the defendant, knew of it. The plaintiff was entitled to succeed.

Davies v Davies

[1975] QB 172, [1974] 3 All ER 817, [1974] 3 WLR 607, 118 Sol Jo 717, CA
Alongside a main road was a large area of common land. Owners of a nearby farm were entitled to put animals on the common for grazing and were registered for that purpose under the Commons Registration Act 1965. Sheep got on the road from the common; the plaintiff in his car collided with them without negligence on his part and his car was damaged. The defendant, who was a son of the owner of the farm by whom he was licensed to have sheep on the farm, was charged under the Highways Act 1959, s 135 and pleaded guilty. The plaintiff sued for the damage to his car.
HELD: The defendant was not liable. He had the right to place sheep on the common and so was protected by the Animals Act 1971, s 8(2). A conviction under the Highways Act did not make him liable for a civil offence. Being licensed to put sheep on the common was sufficient to apply s 8(2); the protection was not limited to persons actually having title to the land.

Curtis v Betts

[1990] 1 All ER 769, [1990] 1 WLR 459, CA
The ten year old plaintiff was injured in an attack by his neighbours' bull mastiff as the dog was being loaded in a Land Rover for its usual walk in the park. The judge found the defendants liable under s 2(2) of the Animals Act 1971 though he accepted that there had been no failure on their part to control the dog.

The second part of s 2(2)(a) was satisfied by showing that damage from a bite was likely to be severe in view of the type of breed and on the evidence the dog was territorially possessive, in particular of the area near to the Land Rover. This was a characteristic not normally found in bull mastiffs except at particular times or in particular circumstances. This was sufficient to bring the claim within the second limb of s 2(2)(b) and judgment was given for the plaintiff once the judge had decided that the dog's nature was known to the defendant owner.

Hunt v Wallis

(1991) Times, 10 May, QBD
The plaintiff was injured when the defendant's border collie collided with him. The judge rejected his argument that s 2(2)(b) of the Animals Act 1971 required the court to compare the characteristics of a border collie with dogs in general. Mr Justice Pill took the view that the proper test was to look at the nature of other dogs of that breed, where a particular breed could be identified, to see whether he had unusual characteristics. Judgment for the defendant.

DANGEROUS DOGS ACT 1991

The relevant sections of this Act were brought into force on 12 August 1991 by the Dangerous Dogs Act 1991, SI 1991/1742:

'**3 Keeping dogs under proper control** (1) If a dog is dangerously out of control in a public place—
(a) the owner; and
(b) if different, the person for the time being in charge of the dog,
is guilty of an offence, or, if the dog while so out of control injures any person, an aggravated offence, under this subsection.
(2) In proceedings for an offence under subsection (1) above against a person who is the owner of a dog but was not at the material time in charge of it, it shall be a defence for the accused to prove that the dog was at the material time in the charge of a person whom he reasonably believed to be a fit and proper person to be in charge of it.
(3) If the owner or, if different, the person for the time being in charge of a dog allows it to enter a place which is not a public place but where it is not permitted to be and while it is there—
(a) it injures any person; or
(b) there are grounds for reasonable apprehension that it will do so,
he is guilty of an offence, or, if the dog injures any person, an aggravated offence, under this subsection.
(4) A person guilty of an offence under subsection (1) or (3) above other than an aggravated offence is liable on summary conviction to imprisonment for a term not exceeding six months or a fine not exceeding level 5 on the standard scale or both; and a person guilty of an aggravated offence under either of those subsections is liable—
(a) on summary conviction, to imprisonment for a term not exceeding six months or a fine not exceeding the statutory maximum or both;
(b) on conviction on indictment, to imprisonment for a term not exceeding two years or a fine or both.
(5) It is hereby declared for the avoidance of doubt that an order under section 2 of the Dogs Act 1871 (order on complaint that a dog is dangerous and not kept under proper control)—
(a) may be made whether or not the dog is shown to have injured any person; and
(b) may specify the measures to be taken for keeping the dog under proper control, whether by muzzling, keeping on a lead, excluding it from specified places or otherwise.
(6) If it appears to a court on a complaint under section 2 of the said Act of 1871 that the dog to which the complaint relates is a male and would be less dangerous if neutered the court may under that section make an order requiring it to be neutered.
(7) The reference in section 1(3) of the Dangerous Dogs Act 1989 (penalties) to failing to comply with an order under section 2 of the said Act 1871 to keep a dog under proper control shall include a reference to failing to comply with any other order made under that section; but no order shall be made under that section by virtue of subsection (6) above where the matters complained of arose before the coming into force of that subsection.

6 Dogs owned by young persons Where a dog is owned by a person who is less than sixteen years old any reference to its owner in section 1(2)(d) or (e) or 3 above shall include a reference to the head of the household, if any, of which that person is a member or, in Scotland, to the person who has his actual care and control.

10 Short title, interpretation, commencement and extent (2) In this Act—

"advertisement" includes any means of bringing a matter to the attention of the public and "advertise" shall be construed accordingly;

"public place" means any street, road or other place (whether or not enclosed) to which the public have or are permitted to have access whether for payment or otherwise and includes the common parts of a building containing two or more separate dwellings.

(3) For the purposes of this Act a dog shall be regarded as dangerously out of control on any occasion on which there are grounds for reasonable apprehension that it will injure any person, whether or not it actually does so, but references to a dog injuring a person or there being grounds for reasonable apprehension that it will do so do not include references to any case in which the dog is being used for a lawful purpose by a constable or a person in the service of the Crown.'

In addition to the Dangerous Dogs Act 1991, s 27 of the Road Traffic Act 1988 remains in force:

'**27 Control of dogs on roads** (1) A person who causes or permits a dog to be on a designated road without the dog being held on a lead is guilty of an offence.

(2) In this section "designated road" means a length of road specified by an order in that behalf of the local authority in whose area the length of road is situated.

(3) The powers which under subsection (2) above are exercisable by a local authority in England and Wales are, in the case of a road part of the width of which is in the area of one local authority and part in the area of another, exercisable by either authority with the consent of the other.

(4) An order under this section may provide that subsection (1) above shall apply subject to such limitations or exceptions as may be specified in the order, and (without prejudice to the generality of this subsection) subsection (1) above does not apply to dogs proved—

(a) to be kept for driving or tending sheep or cattle in the course of a trade or business, or

(b) to have been at the material time in use under proper control for sporting purposes.

(5) An order under this section shall not be made except after consultation with the chief officer of police.

(6) The Secretary of State may make regulations—

(a) prescribing the procedure to be followed in connection with the making of orders under this section, and

(b) requiring the authority making such an order to publish in such manner as may be prescribed by the regulations notice of the making and effect of the order.

(7) In this section "local authority" means—

(a) in relation to England and Wales, the council of a county, metropolitan district or London borough or the Common Council of the City of London, and

(b) (*applies to Scotland only*).

(8) The power conferred by this section to make an order includes power, exercisable in like manner and subject to the like conditions, to vary or revoke it.'

R v Knightsbridge Crown Court, ex p Dunne
Brock v DPP

[1993] 4 All ER 491, [1994] 1 WLR 296

The court was entitled to consider the American Dog Breeders Association guide to breeds when deciding whether a dog fell within the definition of 'type' contained within s 1(1) of the Dangerous Dogs Act 1991. It was wrong to approach these cases on the basis that type was restricted to breed for it had much wider connotations; the court should look at the evidence adduced by the parties to see if the dog had characteristics which were substantially similar to those of the breed in general.

OWNER'S DUTY OF CARE

Common law

Deen v Davies

[1935] 2 KB 282 at 295
Per Romer LJ: The general principle is established that the owner of an animal which he brings on to the highway must use all reasonable care to prevent the animal doing damage.

Note—For facts see p 246, below.

Davies v Davies

[1975] QB 172, [1974] 3 All ER 817, [1974] 3 WLR 607, 118 Sol Jo 717, CA
Alongside a main road was a large area of common land. Owners of a nearby farm were entitled to put animals on the common for grazing and were registered for that purpose under the Commons Registration Act 1965. Sheep got on the road from the common; the plaintiff in his car collided with them without negligence on his part and his car was damaged. The defendant, who was a son of the owner of the farm by whom he was licensed to have sheep on the farm, was charged under the Highways Act 1959, s 135 and pleaded guilty. The plaintiff sued for the damage to his car.
HELD: The defendant was not liable. He had the right to place sheep on the common and so was protected by the Animals Act 1971, s 8(2). A conviction under the Highways Act did not make him liable for a civil offence. Being licensed to put sheep on the common was sufficient to apply s 8(2); the protection was not limited to persons actually having title to the land.

DOGS

Fardon v Harcourt-Rivington

(1932) 146 LT 391, [1932] All ER Rep 81, 48 TLR 215, 76 Sol Jo 81, HL
Defendant parked his saloon car in a street with its back against the pavement. The car was left shut with a dog inside it. There was no evidence that the dog had a vicious propensity. When plaintiff, who had parked his car near defendant's car, was walking past defendant's car the dog, which had been barking and jumping about the car, jumped up against a window in the rear of defendant's car, smashing a panel, whereby a glass spinter flew out and entered plaintiff's eye, with the result that plaintiff lost his eye. An action for damages for personal injuries was brought.
HELD: The danger of a piece of glass being knocked by a dog out of a small window at the back of the car and of a splinter of glass hitting a passer-by on the pavement was such an unlooked-for event that no reasonable man could say that a person ought to be convicted of negligence for not taking any precautions against it. A person must guard against reasonable probability of danger; he was not bound to guard against a fantastic possibility.

Howarth v Straver

(16 November 1953, unreported) (Croom-Johnson J)
The plaintiff was riding a motor cycle with a pillion passenger at 10.40 pm on 14 October 1951, along Bagshot Road, Cobham at not more than 40 mph. The defendant's golden retriever dog was loose and uncontrolled and roaming about the road. It ran across the road from the right, swerved to go behind the motor cycle and then came back and hit the motor cycle. The plaintiff in trying to avoid it ran into the hedge on the left-hand side of the road and was injured. He sued the defendant for damages alleging that the dog was of a mischievous nature. The judge found the dog was not vicious in the ordinary sense of the term. Citing *Deen v Davies* (p 246, below) if an animal owner knows that it has a tendency to run into cyclists or other passengers on the highway, it cannot avail him to say that it was not vice, but a frolicsome disposition, or perhaps mere blundering, which caused the harm. A cyclist gave evidence that the dog had previously got in his way, and a woman that the dog ran round bicycles and people and that she had complained to the defendant. The judge found it was a nuisance to people and a potential source of danger and gave a verdict for plaintiff.

In the case of *Adam v Chiddingfold Farmers Foxhounds*, a motorist driving at 35 to 40 mph along the Portsmouth Road near Wisley, saw a fox run across the road 20 or 30 yards ahead of him. He did not realise it was a fox until a pack of hounds dashed into the road after it, when he was about 10 to 15 yards away. He could not avoid them and sustained damage to his car and sued for £22 10s 6d. Judge Gordon Clark found that all reasonable precautions had been taken. The huntsmen and hounds were legitmate users of the highway and there was nothing improper in allowing hounds on a road of this sort. Judgment for defendants: (1955) Times, 5 November.

Gomberg v Smith

[1963] 1 QB 25, [1962] 1 All ER 725, [1962] 2 WLR 749, 106 Sol Jo 95, CA
At about 6.30 pm at Roman Road, Bow, London, the defendant opened the door of his shop. His dog, a large St Bernard, shot out and ran across the road. The defendant followed, shouting at the dog, which eluded him and ran back across the road, colliding with the plaintiff's van and causing damage. In a solicitor's letter and in his defence in the action the defendant alleged, untruthfully, that he had the dog on a lead. In the county court the judge held, following *Searle v Wallbank* (p 249, below), that there was no liability on the defendant if the dog escaped on to the highway and that there was no evidence either how the dog got out or that the defendant was taking it on to the highway.
HELD, ON APPEAL: The evidence of a witness that the defendant and dog came out together, and the fact that the defendant had not alleged in his defence that the dog escaped, amounted to evidence that he had brought the dog on to the highway. He had failed to keep it under control and was liable, following *Deen v Davies* (p 246, below).

Lister v Vergette

(1964) Times, 12 June (Thompson J)
The plaintiff was injured when he was knocked off his moped by the defendant's dog, which emerged suddenly from the gateway of the defendant's house. It was the dog's habit to accompany the tractor drivers on their rounds to the farm fields. On the day of the accident she had returned to the yard. A tractor was being taken out and she probably thought she was being left out and ran out to join the tractor driver. The plaintiff's case was based on *Brock v Richards* [1951] 1 KB 529 and dicta of Pearson LJ in *Ellis v Johnstone* (above).
HELD: The judge found that the defendant was not aware of the dog's 'unwelcome attitude to users of the highway' nor of any previous incidents she may have caused. The plaintiff's claim failed.

Smith v Ainger

(1990) Times, 5 June, CA
The plaintiff sustained a fractured left leg after being knocked over by Sam, an aggresive dog, owned by the defendant. The plaintiff sought to rely on s 2(2)(a), of the Animals Act 1971 on the basis that the damage caused was likely if the dog was not restrained, or was likely to be severe. Neill LJ said that the two issues to consider were:
(1) Was personal injury to a human a kind of damage which the defendant's dog unless restrained, was likely to cause?
(2) Was personal injury to a human, if caused by that dog likely to be severe?

The judge at first instance had been satisfied on the evidence that Sam was likely to attack another dog even without provocation. If Sam did attack the other dog there was a 'material risk' that the owner of the other dog would seek to defend his animal and would be injured as a result of that intervention. The fact that previous injuries inflicted by Sam were quite minor was considered irrelevant as damage caused by a large dog such as an alsatian was likely to be severe within the meaning of s 2(2). Judgment for the plaintiff.

COWS

Note—The nature of the liability for cattle trespass was defined in *Street on Torts* as follows: 'Where cattle trespass upon the land of the plaintiff or, even without trespassing on his land, consume produce which by being severed from land has become his chattel, the person in possession of the cattle is liable for the consequences of those acts irrespective of whether his conduct be intentional, negligent or accidental.'

The definition of cattle was held to extend to cows, bulls, goats, swine, sheep, horses, asses, domestic fouls, geese, turkey, ducks and peacocks, but not to dogs (*Brown v Giles* (1823) 1 C & P 118) or to cats (*Buckle v Homes* [1926] 2 KB 125, CA).

Ludlam v Peel

(1939) Times, 10 October
Cattle belonging to a farmer were customarily driven from the farm for about a mile along the Great North Road to a field. Six cows were being driven along the grass verge at the side of the road. A motor car was being driven along the road in the opposite direction. When the car was a few yards away, one cow suddenly ran out across the road in front of the car and a collision occurred. The county court judge

based on the judgment of Lord Moncrieff in *Harpers v GNR of Scotland* (1886) 13 R (Ct of Sess) 1139, held it was not necessary to prove actual negligence, and there was a duty to control the cows on the highway, and the farmer had failed to keep them under proper control.
HELD, ON APPEAL: It was necessary to prove negligence. The owner had employed a competent drover and there was no evidence of failure to take reasonable care. The county court judge had sought to impose an absolute duty which did not exist in law.

Imrie v Clark

(24 October 1939, unreported) (Lord Patrick)
A motor cyclist at 5.45 am whilst it was dark, collided with cattle on the road. The owner of the cattle had opened a gate between the field and the road to allow the cattle to emerge and proceed along the road to the farm. The owner remained in the field and took no steps to warn drivers of vehicles in the road.
HELD: The cattle were entitled to use the road for passage as much as motor cars or pedestrians. The law does not require or custom prescribe that warnings should be given of cattle on the road or that in the dark the cattle owner must place lights on the road or give signals to warn traffic.

Note—But see next case.

Harrison v Jackson

(1947) 14 LJNCCR 242 (Judge Peel KC)
About 5.45 am on 12 October 1946, the plaintiff was driving his motor car along the highway from Kirkby Lonsdale to Carnforth. On the nearside ahead was an open gate to a field, and about 30 or 40 yards inside the gate 'a bunch' of about 30 cows. On the offside nearly opposite the field gate was the gate from the farm yard to the road. This gate was open. The plaintiff inferred that the cows had just come from the farm to the field. There was no one on the road. A high wall prevented the plaintiff seeing into the farm yard. The plaintiff reduced his speed to 10 or 15 mph in case any other cows emerged. Just short of the farm gate two other cows came out at a fast speed close together and side by side. One cow was probably playing with or molesting the other. The plaintiff applied his brakes. One cow went straight into the car at the offside end of the windscreen and the other landed right across the bonnet. Immediately after the acccident a German prisoner who did not understand English was in the farm yard walking towards the gate. What was taking place was a routine operation of the farm. Whether the car had actually come to rest at the moment of impact was immaterial.
HELD: This was not a case of cattle straying on to the highway but of their being put on to and across the highway and of being sent by defendant's men across it. The defendant was not any the less liable by letting his cattle wander back unattended than if they had been driven.

Following Romer LJ's dictum in *Deen v Davies* (quoted on p 246, below) which was approved by Lord Porter in *Searle v Wallbank*, the defendant had failed in his duty to users of the highway to ensure that reasonable care was taken in the control of his cows crossing the highway. It would have been reasonable to have a man on the road to warn approaching traffic, especially as the corner at the gateway was blind. A man placed in the roadway would have been able to prevent the cows dashing out, or halt the plaintiff's car. Judgment for plaintiff.

Note—See also *Andrews v Watts*, p 245, below.

Wright v Callwood

[1950] 2 KB 515, 66 TLR (pt 2) 72, 94 Sol Jo 420, CA
The defendant, a farmer, drove two calves out of a field on to the highway, then to the right for a few yards along the highway, and then to the left through a gateway into a drive some 14 feet wide and 50 feet long to the farm. A lorry was stationary in the farm yard and the engine was started and frightened the calves which ran back down the drive, the defendant following close behind with a stick attempting to get in front of them. The plaintiff was cycling along the highway passing the gateway. One of the calves ran out about a yard in front of her cycle and the second knocked her off her machine. A veterinary surgeon gave evidence that a calf ran away just like a young horse, and more men were needed to drive them.

The county court judge considered there were special circumstances which imposed a special duty and referred to the judgment of Greer LJ in *Sycamore v Ley* (1932) 147 LT 342; the defendant ought to have closed the gates or had a man to assist, and gave judgment for the plaintiff.

HELD, ON APPEAL: There was no evidence the defendant knew that the motor lorry was in the yard and that its engine might be started; there were no special circumstances. Appeal allowed.

Thorp v King Bros

(1957) Times, 23 February (Stable J)
A cow unloaded from a transport vehicle at Guildford Market ran away without any negligence in the unloading. It turned into a cul-de-sac where it was frightened by a number of people shouting and waving their arms and it turned into the main street and trotted quietly along and turned into a car park. The sound of a motor horn sent it into another road and over a pedestrian crossing. A pedestrian on the crossing was knocked down by the cow and injured. He claimed damages from the owner of the cow and the transporters.

HELD: The cow had never shown any sign of vice. It had been driven frantic by the behaviour of the people.

Verdict for both defendants.

Martin v Zinn

(1960) Times, 9 March, CA
The plaintiff, riding a 1935 motor cycle with a light which shone for 50 yards, collided in the dark with one of the defendant's cows which was crossing a narrow public road which divided two of the defendant's fields. The defendant's practice was to allow his cows to cross in threes. He stood by the gate holding a lamp until the third cow was in the road, when he would follow behind.

HELD: The plaintiff was to blame for the accident. He was riding an old fashioned motor cycle with a headlamp which for country lanes was inadequate. The defendant had stationed himself by the gateway of his farm and was holding a lamp which could be seen by traffic on the road. The plaintiff knew the locality and should have anticipated that cows might be on the road.

Friend v Facey

(1963) Times, 19 March, CA
The plaintiff was driving his car along the main Ilfracombe-Barnstaple road at about 40 mph when a cow suddenly galloped out of a gateway on his nearside whilst being taken to the farm for milking. He jammed on his brakes at once but struck the cow, injuring it and damaging the car. The county court judge found the farmer to blame for not having two men to take the cows home to milk: it was not sufficient to leave the job to his 17 year old son as he had done. He found the plaintiff equally to blame for not avoiding the cow by swerving to the offside. The Court of Appeal agreed that the farmer was negligent for the reasons given but held the plaintiff free from blame. His speed was not too fast on that road, the warning he received was nil and it would be asking too much to say he was negligent because he did not swerve.

Andrews v Watts

[1971] RTR 484 (Karminski LJ)
The owner of some cattle wanted to fetch them from a field some distance from her farm. She took two men to help her. It was a dark evening in November. They got the cattle out from the field on to the road, one man walking at the front and the other at the rear of the herd. Neither man was carrying a light of any kind. The owner had parked her car in the road at the gateway with dipped headlights on facing away from the herd. She stood there herself to warn approaching traffic. A car came along at about 40 mph and the cattle owner waved it down. The driver, a 19 year old girl took fright; she was dazzled by the headlights and seeing nothing beyond thought it must be some kind of hold-up. Her own headlights were dipped. She went on faster and ran into the man at the rear of the herd who by that time was about 50 yards from the gateway. He was killed.
HELD: On a claim by the widow, both the driver and the cattle-owner were to blame. The driver should have realised that the waving-down and the headlights might be a warning of an obstruction; she should have reduced her speed and put her headlights on full beam. The cattle-owner had brought the cows on to the road, had failed to provide the men with any lights (contrary to the advice in the Highway Code) and had pointed the headlights away from the cattle instead of illuminating them. She was two-thirds to blame and the driver one-third. The deceased was not to blame at all.

HENS

Hadwell v Righton

[1907] 2 KB 345, 76 LJKB 891, 97 LT 133, 71 JP 499, 23 TLR 548, 51 Sol Jo 500, 5 LGR 881 (Bray J)
Plaintiff was riding carefully a bicycle on a highway, upon the footpath of which were some fowls belonging to defendant, who occupied premises on the side of the road opposite to the footpath. As plaintiff got abreast of the fowls a dog belonging to a third party frightened the fowls, one of which flew into the spokes of the machine, causing it to upset, whereby plaintiff suffered personal injury and the bicycle was damaged. Defendant knew the fowls were in the habit of straying on the road.
HELD: (1) Even if the fowls were not lawfully on the highway, the damage which happened was not of such a nature as was likely to result from their unlawful presence there, and such damage was too remote. (2) Plaintiff could not recover.

Quaere whether it is unlawful for the occupiers of land adjoining a highway to allow their poultry to stray upon the highway.

Cases in which plaintiff was the owner of the soil on which the trespass was committed are not in point; for here the cyclist had no interest in the soil of the highway.

HORSES

Holmes v Mather

(1875) LR 10 Exch 261, 44 LJ Ex 176, 33 LT 361
Plaintiff was walking along a public street when defendant, seated on the box of his carriage which was drawn by two horses and driven by a man then under his control, came down a cross street. The horses, frightened by the barking of a dog, ran away. The driver was unable to hold them in, but told defendant to leave them to him. Defendant accordingly sat passive, while the driver, trying to turn the horses so as to prevent them from running into a shop window opposite, pulled them aside toward the spot where plaintiff then happened to be, but on nearing her, endeavoured vainly to draw them away from her. They ran against her, and she being hurt, sued defendant for negligence and trespass. The jury found defendant free from negligence, and that the occurrence was a mere accident.
HELD: He was not liable in trespass.

Deen v Davies

[1935] 2 KB 282, [1935] All ER Rep 9, 104 LJKB 540, 153 LT 90, 51 TLR 398, 79 Sol Jo 381, CA
The defendant, a farmer, rode his pony into a neighbouring large town and stabled it there whilst he did business in the town. Instead of tethering it to a staple provided for the purpose he tied it to a piece of wood which he believed to be firmly nailed to the wall of the stable. Whilst he was away the pony broke the piece of wood away from the wall and went out into the street to return home. Though of docile disposition it caused the plaintiff to fall when stepping from the pavement and she sustained injury. The county court found that the pony, whilst not exhibiting any savage tendencies, had acted in a way in which a pony might be expected to when unattended on a roadway in a town. The defendant had been negligent in not tying up the pony properly in the stall and his negligence had led to the pony getting on to the roadway unattended and injuring the plaintiff. He awarded the plaintiff damages.
HELD, ON APPEAL: This was not a case of an animal being depastured on land adjoining the highway and escaping or straying on to it: it was one of a different class of case in which the owner himself has brought the animal upon the highway. In this type of case the owner has a duty to take reasonable care that the animal does not damage other parties. Reasonable care in the country may not be reasonable care in the town. The defendant had brought his horse upon the highway and rode it into a town. When he tethered it in the stable he had not secured it properly and thereby failed to discharge the duty he owed to the public. The duty began when he took the horse on to the highway and did not come to an end when he tethered it in the stable. Appeal dismissed.

Annells v Warneford

(1958) Times, 7 May, [1958] CLY 104, CA
Two children were trying to catch a pony which was in a field; but the pony slipped past one of them, ran down a lane and into a main road where it collided with a motor car. The driver of the car sued in negligence.
HELD: Although the children had been under a duty to take reasonable care to prevent the pony going down the lane and into the road they had fulfilled that duty. Appeal dismissed.

Landau v Railway Executive

(1949) 99 L Jo 233, Clerkenwell CC (Judge Earengey)
A railway carman took his horse and cart on his usual collection and delivery round into a manufacturer's yard. The yard was paved with stone sets, and sloped down to an archway, where there was a gatekeeper. The cart was backed up to a loading bank at right angles to the slope, and a nosebag was put on the horse, and a chain on the rear wheel, but without the brake applied. The horse had been bought about two years previously with a warranty that it was quiet. It had been driven frequently by the carman who had never known it to bolt before. After the horse had been left unattended for about five minutes, it ran through the archway into the highway and caused damage.
HELD: The brake was fitted for the obvious purpose of reinforcing the chain on difficult ground, or in cases of emergency, and the yard was clearly dangerous ground. *Deen v Davies* was not doubted by the Court of Appeal in *Brackenborough v Spalding UDC* and was approved by Lord Porter in *Searle v Wallbank.* Railway Co held liable.

Bativala v West

[1970] 1 QB 716, [1970] 1 All ER 332, [1970] 2 WLR 8, 113 Sol Jo 856 (Bridge J)
The defendant, the proprietor of a riding school, organised a gymkhana in a field. The part of the field used was some distance from a road and separated from it first by a rope to control spectators and then by a hedge with an open gateway in it. In a race in which competitors had to saddle their ponies a saddle slipped and caused the pony to bolt, clearing the rope and running out into the road where it collided with the plaintiff's car.
HELD: The defendant was liable. She was aware of the risk; a slipping saddle was a well-known hazard and if this happened the horse would probably run away in fear. Each link in the chain of causation was reasonably foreseeable and she was negligent by ordinary standards. She had relied on the rule as laid down in *Searle v Wallbank* (p 249, below) that there was no duty to prevent the escape of animals on to the highway, but an owner could still be liable if he could be shown to have failed in his duty to take care. Most cases in which the rule in *Searle v Wallbank* had been held to apply were cases in which the animal had strayed from a situation in which it had been properly left to its own devices. Different considerations arose when the animal escaped from a situation in which it was under direct human control. The present case could be decided in accordance with the ordinary principles of negligence and the plaintiffs were entitled to damages.

SHEEP

Heath's Garage Ltd v Hodges

[1916] 2 KB 370, 85 LJKB 1289, 115 LT 129, 32 TLR 570, 60 Sol Jo 554, CA
An owner or occupier of land adjoining highway (ie putting aside cases where, either by a local Enclosure Act, or by prescription, or otherwise, a duty to fence is imposed) is not bound to fence so as to prevent animals like sheep straying upon the highway.

While the plaintiff's motor car was being driven along a highway in the daylight at the rate of 16 to 20 mph, the driver saw in front of him on the road a number of sheep untended. He put on his brakes and almost immediately thereafter two sheep, which had apparently been left behind by the others, jumped from the bank on the near side and one of them ran in front of the car and broke part of the steering gear, in consequence of which the driver lost control, and the car ran into the bank and was damaged. The sheep were the property of the defendant, who was subsequently prosecuted and fined under the Highway Act 1864, s 25, for having allowed them to stray on the highway. In an action against the defendant by the plaintiffs in respect of the damage to the car, the county court judge found (1) the sheep escaped on to the highway from defendant's field owing to a defective hedge; (2) it was the natural tendency of sheep which were untended to run across or otherwise endanger vehicles in a road, and it was common knowledge that when sheep find themselves separated from the flock they have almost a mania for rejoining it, regardless of intervening traffic; (3) defendant had been guilty of negligence, or had committed a nuisance, in allowing sheep to stray on to the highway, and the accident was the natural consequence thereof, and he held the defendant was liable.
HELD, ON APPEAL: (1) Whether the action was sought to be based on negligence or on a nuisance to the highway, it was not breach of duty by defendant, not to keep his sheep from straying on to the highway; (2) an animal like a sheep, by nature harmless, could not fairly be regarded as likely to collide with a motor car, and defendant could not be held liable on that footing; (3) (per Avory J) the tendencies of sheep as found by the county court judge were not a vicious or mischievous propensity within the decided cases.

But see note following *Hoskin v Rogers* on p 250.

Frazer v Pate

1932 SC 748, 60 SLR 470
A motor cyclist was injured by a collision in daylight with a sheep upon a public road. Pursuer averred that defender was negligent in knowingly failing to keep his fences in such repair as would prevent his sheep from straying on to the road, in any event in allowing his sheep to graze upon the road.
HELD: The accident was not the natural and probable result of the negligence alleged.

McGowan v Gilmore

[1953] CLY 117, Cty Ct
A farmer's ram escaped on to the highway in the hours of darkness. The defendant went in his car in pursuit and, whilst chasing it, the ram collided with and damaged the plaintiff's car.
HELD: Defendant had not brought the ram on to the highway. He was reasonably and properly attempting to take possession and control of it but had not succeeded in doing so at the time of the accident. The defendant was not negligent.

STRAYING ANIMALS

Searle v Wallbank

[1947] AC 341, [1947] 1 All ER 12, HL
A cyclist was injured by a horse which strayed from a field adjoining the highway through a defective fence.
HELD: (1) The owner of a field abutting on the highway is under no prima facie legal obligation to users of the highway so to keep and maintain his hedges and gates along the highway as to prevent his animals from straying on to it; (2) nor to take reasonable care to prevent his animals (not known to be dangerous) from straying on to the highway.

Note—The cases of *Hughes v Williams* and *Brock v Richards* ((6th edn) pp 210 and 213 respectively) may now be regarded as obsolete. The following case may still be of value:

Fitzgerald v E D and A D Cooke Bourne (Farms) Ltd

[1964] 1 QB 249, [1963] 3 All ER 36, [1963] 3 WLR 522, 107 Sol Jo 459, 188 Estates Gazette 209, CA
The plaintiff was crossing a field by a public footpath when she was knocked down by a filly belonging to the defendants. She did not receive serious physical injury but was frightened and subsequently suffered a nervous breakdown. The filly was one of two normally pastured in the field. It had not attacked the plaintiff but galloped up to her, swerving and prancing in a playful way, striking her with its shoulders and knocking her down. There was some evidence of similar behaviour to a person on the footpath on a previous occasion. The judge held that the horses were not vicious but had a natural propensity to gallop up to people who walked across the field: their behaviour was what could be expected of young animals of that sort of breeding. He held that the defendants were liable on the basis that they knew of the potential danger of the horse doing to the plaintiff what it did.

On appeal the decision was reversed. The plaintiff's case was put in two ways (1) that the filly was a dangerous animal to the knowledge of the defendants and that accordingly they were under strict liability as for an animal *ferae naturae*; (2) that they were liable in negligence on the ground that they ought reasonably to have foreseen and guarded against an accident of the kind that occurred.
HELD: On the first point, the filly was not vicious but was merely indulging its natural propensity to be playful. It was not attacking or showing hostility. The fact that it conduct was frightening to the plaintiff or others did not make it a dangerous animal so as to place the defendants under strict liability. On the second point the footpath was similar to a highway in the unfenced condition in which highways existed when the common law developed. *Searle v Wallbank* (above) made it clear beyond doubt that the owner of animals pastured in the vicinity had no duty to prevent them from straying on to the highway, but it was envisaged in that case that an action for negligence might lie if, in the particular circumstances of the particular case, the owner of a particular animal ought reasonably to foresee that, having regard to its peculiar propensities, it may cause injury otherwise than by merely straying if it escaped on to a highway. To establish such a case in negligence it was not sufficient to show a 'reasonable possibility' of injury: it must be shown that there was a real likelihood of injury which ought to have been foreseen. In the present case the evidence proved nothing against the defendants to show that they ought reasonably to have foreseen the likelihood of injury except in so far as they must be taken to have

had a general knowledge of the behaviour of fillies of this class; this was not sufficient to make them liable.

Hoskin v Rogers

[1985] LS Gaz R 848, Times, 25 January, CA
The plaintiff motorcyclist was injured when he collided with the body of a heifer killed by another vehicle. It had strayed on to the highway through inadequate fencing from adjoining land owned by the second defendant. The accident occurred in October; the land had been let to the first defendant on a 'grass purchase' agreement since May, when the fence was reasonably stockproof. The judge held the first defendant alone liable.
HELD, ON APPEAL: The duty of care on the second defendants as owners of the land was to take reasonable care to see that the land was fenced adequately so as to prevent stock they knew was going to be on the land from straying on to the highway. There was no breach of that duty by the second defendants in May when the agreement was negotiated. Thus the question was whether it had been shown that by the date of the accident they had been put on notice that the fencing was by then inadequate. The evidence did not establish that this was so; the second defendants were not in breach of their duty of care. Appeal dismissed.

Note—The rule at common law that the owner of animals on land adjoining a highway had no duty to prevent them from straying on to it received its most authoritative statement in *Searle v Wallbank* (below). The rule was abolished as from 1 October 1971 by the Animals Act 1971, s 8(1) (p 236, above) but there are exemptions in sub-s (2).

CHAPTER 9

Highways: Dangers and Obstructions

1 LIABILITY OF HIGHWAY AUTHORITY

NON-REPAIR

Note—The responsibilities of the highway authority are now largely governed by the Highways Act 1980. Consolidating the 1959–1971 Acts and other related enactments it gives effect to certain recommendations made by the Law Commission. However, at common law a highway authority was not liable for damage or injury caused by disrepair of the highway if the disrepair was the result of non-feasance and not misfeasance. It was not liable, that is, for failing to repair the highway but only for doing work negligently and thus causing the danger. This freedom from liability for non-repair came to an end on 3 August 1964 (except in cases where the damage arose from an event occurring before that date), as a result of the Highways (Miscellaneous Provisions) Act 1961, s 1. That section was repealed and replaced in part by s 58 of the Highways Act 1980 (p 256, below).

The rule at common law

Note—Only sufficient cases are quoted here as may explain the old rule. A full digest of the old cases will be found in the 5th edition of this work.

Russell v Men of Devon

(1788) 2 Term Rep 667
No action will lie by an individual against the inhabitants of a county for an injury sustained in consequence of a county bridge being out of repair.

Note—The rule was based solely on the historical reason that in the past it was difficult to levy on the unincorporated inhabitants of the county.

Simon v Islington Borough Council

[1943] 1 KB 188, [1943] 1 All ER 41, CA (Scott LJ)
The principle that a highway authority is not liable for non-feasance is that the immunity descended to it as the lineal successor, first, of the surveyor of highways, and before him, of the inhabitants at large. It is limited to duties as highway authority. It extends only to damage due solely to the non-repair of the road *qua* road. It does not extend to acts or defaults of the highway authority in connection with any duties except characteristic highway duties such as that of repairing the road. It does not apply in connection with the public health duties, eg in connection with sewers: nor with the duty of protecting the public from falling into an unfenced pit alongside the high road; nor with duties imposed by the Road Traffic Acts.

Note—For facts see p 267, below.

Burton v West Suffolk County Council

[1960] 2 QB 72, [1960] 2 All ER 26, [1960] 2 WLR 745, 124 JP 273, 104 Sol Jo 349, 58 LGR 175, CA
The plaintiff was injured when his car skidded, without negligence on his part, on a road covered, at the place of the accident, by a thin film of ice. The defendants, who were the highway authority, had carried out some road drainage work some months previously by which the drainage had been improved but there was still a tendency to flooding and the road surface tended to keep damp from water which ran off the adjoining land. If more drainage work had been done this tendency would have been reduced and the accident would probably not have occurred. The plaintiff claimed damages on the grounds (1) that the failure to complete the drainage work amounted to misfeasance; (2) that the defendants failed to give warning of the dangerous state of the road.
HELD: (1) If a highway authority does work on a road by way of repair or reconstruction, it must be done properly and in such a way as not to cause danger on the road, but this does not mean that where some work has been done and done properly to improve the

drainage of the road the defendants should be held liable for failing to do further work which would result in further improvement of the drainage. It was not misfeasance but non-feasance. (2) The defendants were under no duty to warn the plaintiff of the icy conditions of the road.

Statutory duty: Highways Act 1980

Section 41(1) of the Highways Act 1980 provides that:

'**41** (1) The authority who are for the time being the highway authority for a highway maintainable at the public expense are under a duty . . . to maintain the highway.'

By s 329(1) 'maintain' includes 'repair'.

Highways which are maintainable at the public expense are further defined by s 6 of the 1980 Act. These in essence, comprise all highways which were maintainable at the public expense before the 1980 Act and in addition:

(a) any highway constructed by or on behalf of the highway authority;
(b) any highway constructed by the Council pursuant to Part II of the Housing Act 1985;
(c) any highway which is not designated a trunk road or special road; and
(d) a footpath or bridle-way created by specific order or dedicated as a highway for the purposes of the Act.

Griffiths v Liverpool Corpn

[1967] 1 QB 374, [1966] 2 All ER 1015, [1966] 3 WLR 467, 110 Sol Jo 548, CA

The plaintiff was walking along the pavement of a street when she slipped or tripped on a flag-stone and fell, sustaining injury. The flag-stone rocked when walked on and when at rest one of its edges protruded half an inch above the adjacent flag-stone. She sued the highway authority. The county court judge on the evidence of a surveyor and of a highway superintendent found as a fact that the flag-stone was dangerous. The highway superintendent said there was no system of inspection and that inspection should be done every three months. The reason it was not was that it was not possible to get tradesmen to do the repair work, though there was no difficulty in getting sufficient labourers to do the inspection. If the flag-stone in question had been discovered it could have been made safe even by a labourer.

HELD: The Highways Act 1959, s 44 imposed a duty on the defendants, the highway authority, to keep the pavement in repair. This action was based on a breach of that duty. The Highways (Miscellaneous Provisions) Act 1961, abrogated the old rule exempting highway authorities from liability for non-repair of highways and therefore, since the flag-stone was dangerous, the defendants were liable to the plaintiff absolutely and without proof of negligence unless they could establish a defence under s 1(2) and (3) of the Act. To establish the defence it was not necessary that the highway authority should prove they had taken such care as was reasonably necessary to make the highway safe: it would be sufficient for them to prove that they had taken such care as, in all the circumstances, they reasonably could. If through no fault of theirs they had been unable to take steps to make the highway safe, they would escape liability. In the present case the defendants, though unable to get tradesmen, could have employed labourers to deal with dangers such as the one in question and had not established a defence under sub-ss (2) and (3). Judgment for the plaintiff upheld.

Note—The finding of fact that the flag-stone was dangerous was not appealed. All the Appeal Judges expressed doubts whether they themselves would have made such a finding. See *Meggs v Liverpool Corpn* and *Littler v Liverpool Corpn*, p 259, below. The Highways Act 1959 was repealed as from 1 January 1981 by the Highways Act 1980. Section 44(1) of the 1959 Act is re-enacted in s 41(1) of the 1980 Act.

Pitman v Southern Electricity Board

[1978] 3 All ER 901, 143 JP 156, 122 Sol Jo 300, 76 LGR 578, CA
The plaintiff, aged 78, was walking at dusk along the pavement in the village where she lived when she tripped on a metal sheet which the defendants' employees had placed over a hole. It was only 1/8 inch proud of the surrounding surface. The place was unlighted.
HELD: She was entitled to damages. The difference between this case and those of *Meggs* and *Littler* (below) was that she tripped on an unexpected condition and level of the pavement—unexpected because as an inhabitant of the village she had become accustomed to the state of affairs there and on the evening in question was faced with a new and unexpected hazard.

Note—However, a breach of this duty only gives rise to an action for damages for personal injury or as a result of damage to property and does not include economic loss (see *Wentworth v Witts County Council*, above).

FLOODING

Burnside v Emerson

[1968] 3 All ER 741, [1968] 1 WLR 1490, 133 JP 66, 112 Sol Jo 565, CA
The plaintiff and first defendant were driving their cars in opposite directions on a main road and were about to pass each other. It had been raining hard for some hours and a pool of water had formed extending half-way across the road on the first defendant's side. He was travelling at about 50 mph. As his car struck the water it swerved across the road into collision with the plaintiff's car. The second defendants were the highway authority. Their attention had been drawn before the accident to the tendency of the road to become flooded at that point in wet weather, due to bad positioning of a drain and a failure by the second defendants' employees to keep the grips or gulleys in good condition and to keep the ditch cleaned out.
HELD: The second defendants were liable for their failure to fulfil the duty to maintain the highway placed upon them by the Highways Act 1959, s 44(1). An action under the section requires three things: (1) The plaintiff must show the road was dangerous for traffic, that is to say, in a state in which injury may reasonably be anticipated to persons using the highway: foreseeability is an essential element. (2) The plaintiff must prove that the dangerous condition was due to a failure to maintain which includes a failure to repair. (3) If there is a failure to maintain the highway authority is prima facie liable but can escape liability if it proves that it took such care as in all the circumstances was reasonable, having regard to the Highways (Miscellaneous Provisions) Act 1961, s 1(3). The pool of water was admitted by the second defendants' surveyor at the trial to be a danger to traffic and the existence of the pool was due to their failure to maintain the drainage system in a satisfactory condition. They were liable, but the first defendant was also negligent in driving too fast. Blame apportioned two-thirds to the first defendant and one-third to the second defendants.

Tarrant v Rowlands

[1979] RTR 144 (Cantley J)
The first defendant was driving his car at dusk at 40 mph along the A6 road when he ran into a pool of water on the road which he had not seen. He lost control of the steering and crashed head-on into a van driven by the plaintiff. Both were injured. It had been a wet day but the rainfall had not been of exceptional severity. The pool extended about 30 feet along the road and covered it to about the middle on the first defendant's side. It was about 5 inches deep at the deepest. There was evidence that water was usually found lying in that place on the road after a good deal of rain. The supervising foreman of the highway authority, the second defendants, said that there was regular inspection of the road once a month and before the accident he was unaware of any drainage problems in this area of the road.
HELD: The principles to be followed were those laid down in *Burnside v Emerson* (above) applying the Highways Act 1959, s 44 (now Highways Act 1980, s 41) and the Highways (Miscellaneous Provisions) Act 1961, s 1 (now Highways Act 1980, s 58). The evidence that water was frequently found on the road at that place showed that the second defendants 'could reasonably have been expected to know' that the condition of the highway 'was likely to cause danger to users of the highway' (s 1(3)(d) of the 1961 Act). If they did not know then the system of inspection had broken down and they had some responsibility for the accident. The first defendant was also to blame for failing to see the pool. He was driving too fast in the conditions prevailing. Division of responsibility 50-50.

Morris v Thyssen (GB) Ltd

[1983] Abr 2418 (Booth J)
A van driver lost control of his vehicle when it hit a large pool of water on the road caused by flooding. He blamed the highway authority.
HELD: The flooding was a serious hazard which was reasonably predictable from the low-lying nature of the road and the weather conditions. The authority had direct knowledge of the serious extent of the flood from the police and their own employees. The one flood sign displayed in a nearby lay-by was not an adequate warning. Authority two-thirds liable, van driver one-third.

DEFECTIVE ROAD EDGES

Stovin v Wise

[1994] RTR 209
Prior to the plaintiff suffering serious injuries in a road traffic accident, the local authority had identified the need to improve visibility at the junction where the accident occurred. Unfortunately the consent of the owners of the bank of land in need of removal, British Rail, had not been given by the time of the accident and the judge at first instance held that the local authority had breached their common law duty to protect the safety of road users by failing to carry out the necessary steps.
HELD, ON APPEAL: The Court of Appeal agreed with the judge, though rejected the contention that the local authority were also in breach of s 41(1) of the Highways Act 1980 in that they had failed to maintain the highway as the land in question did not fall within s 41. Having accepted the need for improving visibility they should have completed the works within a reasonable time.

Rider v Rider

[1973] QB 505, [1973] 1 All ER 294, [1973] 2 WLR 190, 117 Sol Jo 71, CA
The plaintiff was badly injured when a car in which she was a passenger on a narrow lane at night swung across the road and collided with an approaching vehicle. The lane was commonly used as a secondary traffic route but the highway authority had done no repair work for at least six months. The edges of the tarmac had broken away in places causing gaps where the nearside wheels of vehicles would pass; the judge accepted that the driver's loss of control was due to this state of disrepair. He held the highway authority two-thirds to blame.
HELD: Dismissing the highway authority's appeal, the judge was right. They had failed to perform their statutory duty under the Highways Act 1959, s 44 to keep the highway in repair. They had further failed to discharge the duty implied in the Highways (Miscellaneous Provisions) Act 1961, s 1(2) to maintain the road in such a way as to secure that there was no danger for traffic. Whether part of the highway is a danger for traffic is a question of fact to be decided in a commonsense way; but it was not correct that the test of danger is the risk to a careful driver. The duty of maintaining the highway free of danger is owed to all users who use the highway in the way normally to be expected of them—including some who may be rated as negligent. In the present case a finding of one-third negligence on the part of the car driver was justified on the ground that, with knowledge of the state of the lane he should have been going more slowly.

STATUTORY DEFENCE: 'REASONABLE CARE'

Section 58 of the 1980 Act provides a defence where the highway authority can show that it took reasonable care to ensure that the highway was not hazardous to users.

HIGHWAYS ACT 1980, S 58

58 Special defence in action against a highway authority for damages for non-repair of highway (1) In an action against a highway authority in respect of damage resulting from their failure to maintain a highway maintainable at the public expense, it shall be a defence (without prejudice to any other defence or the application of the law relating to contributory negligence) to prove that the authority had taken such care as in all the circumstances was reasonably required to secure that the part of the highway to which the action relates was not dangerous for traffic.
(2) For the purposes of a defence under subsection (1) above, the court shall in particular have regard to the following matters:
(a) the character of the highway, and the traffic which was reasonably to be expected to use it;
(b) the standard of maintenance appropriate for a highway of that character and used by such traffic;
(c) the state of repair in which a reasonable person would have expected to find the highway;
(d) whether the highway authority knew, or could reasonably have been expected to know, that the condition of the part of the highway to which the action relates was likely to cause danger to users of the highway;
(e) where the highway authority could not reasonably have been expected to repair that part of the highway before the cause of action arose, what warning notices of its condition had been displayed;
but for the purposes of such a defence it is not relevant to prove that the highway authority had arranged for a competent person to carry out or supervise the maintenance of the part of

the highway to which the action relates unless it is also proved that the authority had given him proper instructions with regard to the maintenance of the highway and that he had carried out the instructions.
(3) This section binds the Crown.

Subsection (4) excludes the operation of the section from damage following the breakage or opening of a street and resulting from an event before the completion of reinstatement required by the Public Utilities Street Works Act 1950, s 7(2).

Note—Section 7(2) of the Public Utilities Street Works Act 1950 has now been replaced by s 70 of the New Roads and Street Works Act 1991.

Statutory defence: inspection

Pridham v Hemel Hempstead Corpn

(1970) 114 Sol Jo 884, 69 LGR 523, CA
The plaintiff was pushing a pram along the pavement of a residential road when she caught her foot in a hole and was injured. In answer to her claim for damages for breach of the Highways Act 1959, s 44 the defendants, the highway authority, pleaded the statutory defence in s 1(2) of the 1961 Act. They gave evidence that two men were employed full time on inspection of roads and that residential roads were inspected every three months. The judge concluded on examination of the figures of mileage of roads and hours of work that residential roads could have been inspected monthly and held that the defendants had not established the statutory defence.
HELD, ON APPEAL: It was wrong to depart from the words of the section, in which the test is reasonableness. The system was reasonable and the fact that it was practicable to inspect more frequently did not make the system unreasonable. Appeal allowed.

Note—The duties imposed on the highway authority to inspect the highway have been tightened by the Code of Practice for Inspections (1992) which came into force on the 1 January 1993. See also ss 70–72 of the New Roads and Street Works Act 1991.

Bramwell v Shaw

[1971] RTR 167 (Ackner J)
On a busy road carrying heavy commercial traffic at Millwall, London, one-half of the roadway was obstructed by fenced-off roadworks in which the plaintiff was working. An articulated lorry driven by the first defendant had to pull over to the offside lane, which was about 10 feet wide, to pass the obstruction. The road surface was nearing the end of its life and was a patchwork of old cobbles, tarmac, concrete and asphalt. As the first defendant drove through the gap at 15 to 20 mph the offside wheels of the lorry ran into a depression in the road surface struck a tree growing near the edge of the road and fell off on to the plaintiff.
HELD: (1) The first defendant was negligent in that he drove too fast. If he had driven more slowly he would have seen the hole and could have avoided it. (2) The highway authority (the third defendants) were in breach of their statutory duty under the Highways Act 1959, s 44 to maintain the highway. They were unable to rely on the defence afforded by the Highways (Miscellaneous Provisions) Act 1961, s 1(2) because they had failed to take 'such care as in all the circumstances was reasonably required' to make the road safe. The traffic which could be expected to use the road was heavy; at the particular point where the accident occurred there was especially

heavy wear and tear and it should have been inspected pretty well daily: if it had been the depression would have been seen in time and could have been repaired. (3) The first defendant was the more to blame: proportions 60% first defendant, 40% third defendants.

Note—For references to the Highways Act 1959, s 44 and Highways (Miscellaneous Provisions) Act 1961, s 1, see notes to pp 253 and 259 above.

Jacobs v Hampshire County Council

(1984) Times, 28 May (Skinner J)
A cyclist was injured when the front wheel of his cycle went into a hole at the edge of the road caused by water penetration. The highway authority had inspected the road at six-monthly intervals, having regard to the type of area in which the road lay and the likely extent and type of use of the road.
HELD: To establish a defence under the Highways Act 1980, s 58 the authority should have also taken into account in deciding the frequency of inspections, the design of the road. Tarmac adjoining cobbles at the edge made it especially vulnerable to water penetration, capable of causing damage within two months. The defence was not established.

Failure to establish breach

A plaintiff must establish that the highway authority failed to ensure that the highway was free of danger to all users. There will not usually be a cause of action where a person trips as a result of fractional differences in the levels of flagstones in a pavement.

Meggs v Liverpool Corpn

[1968] 1 All ER 1137, [1968] 1 WLR 689, 132 JP 207, 111 Sol Jo 742, 65 LGR 479, CA
The plaintiff tripped on uneven flag-stones of a pavement in the highway. One of them had sunk three-quarters of an inch. She sued the highway authority. The judge found as a fact that the state of the pavement was not such as to indicate a failure by the highway authority to discharge its duty.

Her appeal was dismissed. The Highways Act 1959, put the duty to maintain on the highway authority and the Act of 1961 had abrogated the non-feasance rule. If a highway was in a dangerous condition so that it was not reasonably safe for traffic or people going along it there was prima facie a breach of the obligation to maintain or repair. But in order to get a claim going the plaintiff must at least show that the highway or pavement was not reasonably safe and that it was dangerous to traffic. The judge had examined the evidence and, having regard to the fact that thousands had used the pavement and no one had reported it, had said he was not satisfied the highway authority was in breach of its duty. That was a finding of fact: everyone had to take account of unevenness in a pavement here and there, and there was no reason for discharging the judge's finding.

Note—Section 44 of the 1959 Act is now replaced by the Highways Act 1980, s 41(1) in similar terms.

Littler v Liverpool Corpn

[1968] 2 All ER 343, 66 LGR 660 (Cumming-Bruce J)
The plaintiff, aged 19, was running along the pavement of a street when he tripped and fell. The pavement was of York stone about 80 years old. The only defect was a triangular depression half-an-inch deep measuring about 3 inches along its longest side. He alleged against the defendants, the highway authority, a failure to maintain contrary to the Highways Act 1959, s 44, and negligence.
HELD: To establish a cause of action for failing to maintain the highway the plaintiff must prove that it was dangerous to relevant traffic (*Meggs*'s case (above)). The test is reasonable foreseeability of danger. It is a mistake to isolate and emphasise differences in level between the flagstones of a pavement unless the difference is such that a reasonable person who considered it would regard it as a real source of danger. Differences of about an inch may cause a stumble but they have to be accepted. A pavement is not to be judged by the standards of a bowling green. The evidence in the present case did not establish that the pavement was dangerous.

Note—See also *Ford v Liverpool Corpn* (1972) 117 Sol Jo 167 where the highway authority was held not liable when a pedestrian slipped over on a one inch ridge where tarmac of the roadway abutted on a metal grid. See also *Griffiths v Liverpool Corpn*, p 253, above.

Whiting v Hillingdon London Borough Council

(1970) 114 Sol Jo 247, 68 LGR 437 (James J)
In April 1966 the plaintiff was walking along a footpath when, to pass another person, she stepped to the side of the path and sustained injury to her leg on a tree stump hidden by foliage. She sued the defendants, the highway authority, both under the Occupiers' Liability Act 1957 and for breach of the Highways Act 1959, s 44. The defendants had inspected the path in the summer of 1964 and 1965 and repaired it in February 1966 without noticing the tree stump.
HELD: (1) The only basis for the defendants' occupation of the path (of which they were not owners) was their duty of maintenance under the Highways Act 1959, s 44(1) and that did not render them occupiers for the purpose of the 1957 Act. (2) As the defendants' officer could not remember seeing the tree stump in February 1966 the tree must have been cut down after that date. It was not reasonable to expect another inspection between February and April 1966 when the accident happened. Action dismissed.

Haydon v Kent County Council

[1978] QB 343, [1978] 2 All ER 97, [1978] 2 WLR 485, 121 Sol Jo 849, CA
The plaintiff was descending a steep footpath coated with snow and ice when she slipped and broke her ankle. She claimed damages from the highway authority, relying on the duty in the Highways Act 1959, s 44 'to maintain the highway'. Section 295 says '"Maintain" includes repair'. [The Highways Act 1980, s 329 says '"maintenance" includes repair and "maintain" and "maintainable" are to be construed accordingly'.]
HELD: The duty under s 44 was to repair and also maintain. The statutory obligation included clearing snow and ice or providing temporary protection by gritting, but whether there had been a breach of that duty was a question of fact and degree on the

facts of each case. The plaintiff must prove either that the authority was at fault apart from merely failing to take steps to deal with the ice, or that having regard to the nature and importance of works sufficient time had elapsed to make it prima facie unreasonable for the authority to have failed to take remedial measures. In the present case not sufficient time had elapsed after the onset of the icy conditions having regard to the authority's heavy commitments to keep major roads in its area safe and clear.

Bartlett v Department of Transport

(1985) 83 LGR 579, 82 LS Gaz R 849 (Boreham J)
The plaintiff's husband was killed in a road accident on the A34 road due, at least in part, to the icy, slippery condition of the road surface. The roadway had not been gritted because the defendants were in dispute with the employees, members of the National Union of Public Employees, who had forbidden all work on the A34. The plaintiff alleged a breach of the Highways Act 1959, s 44 (now the Highways Act 1980, s 41(1)).
HELD: The defendants were not liable. An action for breach of s 44 could succeed only if the failure to maintain was related to want of repair or if an obstruction caused or contributed to want of repair. The plaintiff could not complain of any breach of the employees' duty to the defendant unless it was induced or condoned by the employers and, on the facts, this was not the case.

Mills v Barnsley Metropolitan

(1992) PIQR P291, CA
The plaintiff tripped and fell when the heel of her shoe caught in a hole in the pavement, caused by a missing corner of a paving brick. The local authority admitted a duty to maintain the highway (Highways Act 1980, s 41) and accepted the definition of maintenance as set out in s 329(1). Per Lord Justice Steyn: 'In order for a plaintiff to succeed against a highway authority in a claim for personal injury for failure to maintain or repair the highway, the plaintiff must prove (a) the highway was in such a condition that it was dangerous to traffic or pedestrians in the sense that, in the ordinary course of human affairs, danger may reasonably have been anticipated from its continued use by the public; (b) the dangerous condition was created by the failure to maintain or repair the highway; and (c) the injury or damage resulted from such a failure. Only if the plaintiff proves these *facta probanda* does it become necessary to turn to the highway authority's special defence under s 58(1) of the 1980 Act, namely that the authority had taken such care as in all the circumstances was reasonably required to secure that that particular part of the highway was not dangerous to traffic. On this aspect, the burden rests on the highway authority.'

James v Preseli Pembrokeshire

(1992) Independent, 16 November, CA
The court yet again reminded the parties involved in 'tripping' cases that each turns on its own individual facts. If a pedestrian were to succeed in an action for damages he must first of all identify the hazard which caused him to fall and then establish that the local authority had failed in their duty to maintain the highway by removing a danger to users of the highway.

Per Lord Justice Ralph Gibson: 'Thus the test of dangerousness is one of reasonableness of harm to the users of the highway but in drawing the inference on dangerousness the court must not set too high a standard.'

MISFEASANCE

Note—A highway authority constructing a road for public use under statutory powers owes a duty to the public to take reasonable care to construct the road properly. The Highways Act does not make an authority liable for acts of misfeasance committed by its predecessors.

McClelland v Manchester Corpn

[1912] 1 KB 118, 81 LJKB 98, 105 LT 707, 28 TLR 21 (Lush J)
A street within the district of the defendants, a municipal corporation, was dedicated to the public by its owner. Across the end of the street was an unfenced natural ravine. In 1904 the defendants took over the street under the provisions of a private Act of Parliament similar to those contained in the Public Health Act 1875, and paved and made it up and subsequently maintained it. They also lighted it under their statutory powers, which authorised them to do such acts as they should think necessary for lighting their district. In 1910 a motor car containing the plaintiff while being driven along the street at night fell over the ravine in consequence, it was alleged, of the ravine being unfenced and the street being insufficiently lighted. In an action by the plaintiff to recover damages for injuries sustained the jury found that the street as made up and constructed was a danger to persons using it, that the unfenced ravine was a hidden trap, and that the defendants had not taken proper care to warn the public of danger.
HELD: That the effect of the findings of the jury was that the defendants in taking over and making up the street and leaving it in a dangerous condition had been guilty of misfeasance, and also that they had acted negligently in the performance of their statutory duties with regard to maintaining and lighting the street, and that the plaintiff was, therefore, entitled to judgment.

Note—See also *Burton v West Suffolk CC*, p 252, above.

Baxter v Stockton-on-Tees Corpn

[1959] 1 QB 441, [1958] 2 All ER 675, [1958] 3 WLR 275, 102 Sol Jo 562, CA
A motor cyclist at about midnight collided with the kerb of an approach island adjacent to a roundabout on the highway and sustained fatal injuries. His widow sued the defendants as the highway authority alleging negligence in failing to light or give warning of a concealed danger or trap. The highway was constructed between 1938 and 1940 by the Durham County Council under the Development and Road Improvement Funds Act 1909, ss 8 and 10, as amended by the Roads Act 1920, s 4 and Sch 1, as a main road repairable by the inhabitants at large. The Local Government Act 1929, s 29(1), substituted 'county road' for 'main road'. In 1941 the defendants took over the highway from the county council under the Local Government Act 1929, s 32 and thereby became the highway authority and responsible for its maintenance and repair.
HELD: If there had been negligence of the county council in the construction of the road and they were still in charge of it, and a person sustained injury in consequence, there might be liability on the principle of negligence in the performance of statutory powers. The Court of Appeal was not satisfied that such a case could have been made out, but if it could, the defendants could not be liable on that principle, as they were not the constructors of the road. The plaintiff's claim on the basis that if a highway authority place an obstruction on the highway, they have a duty to light or otherwise protect the public, had no application because the defendants had done no positive act,

but merely kept the island as they found it. The theory that the defendants inherited any such duty from the county council is untenable in view of *Nash v Rochford Rural Council*. The defendants could only be liable by virtue of some express words in the Act under which the road became vested in them. There was nothing in s 32 of the Act of 1929 to impose on an urban district council taking over a county road any special obligation as to maintenance so as to exclude the ordinary immunity for mere non-feasance. Appeal of defendants from judgment of Barry J awarding £4,500 to the widow, allowed.

Note—In so far as this decision was based on the immunity of a highway authority from liability for non-feasance it is no longer good law. It is still effective on the point that a highway authority constructing a road for public use under statutory powers owes a duty to the public to take reasonable care to construct the road properly, but the Acts do not make such an authority liable for acts of misfeasance committed by its predecessors.

Gradient across road

Scottish Omnibuses Ltd v Midlothian County Council

(1955) 105 L Jo 90, Ct of Sess, Outer House
A motor omnibus was proceeding along a road which turned to the right and 90 yards further on, going downhill, crossed a bridge over a river. The outer side of the turn was 2 feet higher than the inner side making a gradient of about one in ten across the road. The road was icebound and at the turn the bus skidded and slipped down the road, collided with the parapet of the bridge and fell into the river.
HELD: The highway authority were under no duty to construct a roadway to prevent such an occurrence.

Negligent repair causing subsidence

Leech v Bristol Corpn

(1932) Post Magazine, 6 February
At the Bristol County Court a motor cyclist was awarded damages in his action against the Bristol Corporation in respect of personal injuries and material damages sustained owing to the alleged misfeasance of the Corporation as surveyors of highways in Bristol. The motor cyclist alleged that the Corporation, by servants or agents, repaired a part of a lane by placing loose gravel on the tarred surface in such a manner as to render it dangerous, so that it could not be properly and safely traversed by the public. While driving over the repaired patch of road, the motor cycle skidded, as a result of which he was injured and his machine and clothing were damaged.

The Corporation denied negligence, pleading that if plaintiff had kept a proper lookout he would have seen that part of the road had been recently tarred and covered, and would have escaped the risk of accident, if any. Evidence was given by an omnibus driver to the effect that the chippings were very loose, and where vehicles had gone through them the wheels had caused ridges. Another motor cyclist said in evidence that on the day following the accident he drove over the re-surfaced part of the road, and in turning the bend where the accident happened he had difficulty in controlling his machine. The chippings were loose, and he estimated that there was a depth of about 3 inches of chippings on the road.

Newsome v Darton UDC

[1938] 3 All ER 93, 159 LT 153, 54 TLR 945, 82 Sol Jo 520, CA
In July 1933, the defendants had made a trench in a highway for the purpose of executing certain drainage work. The excavation was filled in, and in 1935, when the surface was tar-sprayed and chippings were rolled in with a steam roller, the surface was said to be level. In 1936, a depression or hole had formed at the place where the work had been done, and the jury found that the highway at this place was dangerous to those using it with due care. The jury also found that, although the original work was executed without negligence, the dangerous condition was due to the work of the defendants, and that the defendants were negligent in not discovering and taking steps to remedy the danger. The plaintiff having been thrown from his bicycle and injured by reason of the subsidence of the road at the place in question, brought an action against the defendants as the highway authority responsible for the repair of the road.
HELD: There was a duty on the defendants to make good the inevitable subsidence from their work in 1933, and they were negligent in not discovering, and in not taking steps to remedy, the danger. The jury had found that the subsidence was due to the excavations made by the highway authority. If the authority interferes with the structure of the road, then the operation of restoring it to the condition in which it was before such interference includes the remedying of a subsequent subsidence, although the subsidence was two years after the excavation and the accident three years after the excavation.

Birmingham v East Ham Corpn

(1961) 60 LGR 111, CA
The plaintiff was injured when walking across a public highway for which the defendants were the appropriate authority. His foot went into a hole 9 inches wide by 6 inches deep. Four days previously the highways superintendent of defendants had noticed a depression at the same spot. He had at once arranged for repairs which had been carried out. The loose earth beneath the surface was taken out until a solid base was reached. The sides of the excavation were made firm and the hole filled and 'punnelled' firm. An asphalt topping was put on and levelled with the wheel of a vehicle. There was evidence that rats were active in the vicinity and that there was a rat run nearby.
HELD: The defendants were not liable. The mere fact that the surface had sunk so soon after the work was done was not conclusive that the work had not been satisfactorily carried out. There was direct evidence that the work had been properly done and there was evidence about the rat run which could provide an explanation how the cavity could arise. The defendants were not under a further duty in the circumstances to take special precautions against the rats, eg by mixing broken glass with the filling.

Bright v A-G

(1971) 115 Sol Jo 226, [1971] RTR 253, 69 LGR 338, [1971] 2 Lloyd's Rep 68, CA
The plaintiff was riding his motor cycle down a road which had formerly been part of the A1 road when he lost control due to longitudinal ridges on the road surface and was injured. The road had ceased to be a trunk road about two years earlier and the Ministry of Transport had instructed the local authority as its agent to remove double white lines which had divided two lanes of traffic. The local authority had done so about four months before the accident by covering the lines with asphalt. Summer traffic had compacted the asphalt between the lines, creating the ridges. An expert

gave evidence that the groove between the ridges presented a serious and foreseeable danger to motor cycles. The judge at first instance held the Ministry to blame for not having given instructions to the local authority on how the work should be done.
HELD, ON APPEAL: The case turned on its own special facts. The Ministry was not negligent since the local authority was quite capable of doing the work properly. The negligence was that of the workmen who had failed to chip off the lines but had merely covered them up. The local authority was liable for the negligence of its workmen and the Ministry, as principals, must accept responsibility.

Per Lord Denning: If it were not for the special circumstances of this case I would have held the defendant not liable. The law still is that a highway is not to be considered to be dangerous simply because it is uneven, or not level, or has patches or undulations, or has been dug up for pipes and been filled in, or because the surface is bad. Road users cannot expect it to be as level as a bowling green. They must take the rough with the smooth. A highway is only to be considered dangerous when there is something which may be regarded as a trap into which an ordinary careful person may fall.

Note—In *Rider v Rider* (p 256, above) members of the Court of Appeal disagreed with the final sentence of the passage from Lord Denning's judgment in *Bright's* case; they did not accept as a matter of law that a danger for traffic cannot exist unless the road conditions constituting it would be a trap for the careful driver. Highway authorities must not provide only for those who use reasonable care.

McLaughlin v Strathclyde Regional Council

[1992] Lexis, SLT 959
Mrs McLaughlin brought an action for damages against Strathclyde Regional Council when she fell and injured herself as she crossed the road. At some point after the construction of the road, a metal framed drainage gully had been placed in the road surface, and the area around it had been infilled and re-tarmacked. Over the years the infill had subsided and at the time of the accident there was a difference in height between the existing roadway and the replaced tarmac of between 1–2 inches. In the court's view that was insufficient to create a liability for the local authority.

Per Lord Coulsfield: 'I think it is clear that a road authority is not required to keep all pavements, far less all parts of the road surface, absolutely flat and even.'

Relevance of previous accidents

Alexander & Sons v Dundee Corpn

1950 SC 123, 1950 SLT 76, Ct of Sess
In an action for negligence against a highway authority, averments that various other road accidents had taken place in the recent past on the stretch of road in question were held relevant and could properly be admitted to proof.

Traffic systems

Bird v Pearce

[1979] RTR 369, 77 LGR 753, CA
At a crossroads where Downs Lane crossed the Bruton Road the first defendant's car entering the crossroads from Down Lane was struck by the second defendant's car

travelling along the Bruton Road. Both roads were unclassified. The traffic system laid out by the highway authority gave priority to the Bruton Road by double dotted white lines at the mouth of side roads, but at this crossroads the white lines had been obliterated by resurfacing about a month before the accident and not yet repainted. As between the defendants the first defendant was found 90% to blame. In third-party proceedings he sought contributions from the highway authority.

HELD: It was foreseeable that there was a risk of drivers misunderstanding their priorities at a crossroads junction—a greater risk than in the days before there had been any signs at all at the mouths of the side roads along a major road. The highway authority had created a pattern of traffic flow which did not exist before they placed white lines on the roads, a pattern which drivers could be expected to rely on. The highway authority was under a duty of care to the plaintiff to prevent injury from the potentially dangerous situation resulting from the removal of the white lines. They failed to erect any warning sign. The authority should contribute one-third to the damages paid by the first defendant.

Note—See also *Murray v Nicholls*, p 108, above.

Lavis v Kent County Council

(1992) Lexis, 90 LGR 416, CA

The plaintiff motorcyclist suffered severe injuries when he collided with a kerbstone on Waterloo Road near Vigo, Kent. The road markings were minimal and, in the plaintiff's submission, inadequate in warning of the potential danger to road users.

On appeal from the Master, the statement of claim was struck out for failing to disclose a reasonable cause of action. The Court of Appeal, considering the Road Traffic Regulation Act 1984, concluded that although the Act did not impose upon a local authority a duty to erect traffic signs, it did require them to implement the regulations with reasonable care. It was a question of fact whether in this instance they were justified in taking no further steps and it was only right that the plaintiff be allowed to investigate the matter by way of discovery.

Road not taken over

Coleshill v Manchester Corpn

[1928] 1 KB 776, 97 LJKB 229, 138 LT 537, 44 TLR 258, CA

The defendants in execution of a housing scheme were laying out a new road running eastwards from a certain highway and closed at its eastern end by a quickset hedge. Footpaths had already been laid out and edged with kerbstones; houses were being built on the northern side and heaps of earth and building materials made the footpath on this side impassable; the footpath on the south side was still unfinished, but was traversable; it was bounded by a fence of wooden posts and bars; the middle of the road was levelled but not metalled; across it, for laying an electric cable, the defendants had cut a trench which they left unfenced and by night unlighted. They did not prevent persons, whether intending occupiers of houses or others, from walking down the new road. The plaintiff on a September evening while there was still daylight, walked with a companion down the highway and into the new road along the southern footpath. Through a gap in the fence they went across other land occupied by the defendants to a golf course. They returned somewhat hurriedly when it was growing dark, and the plaintiff fell into the trench and was injured.

HELD: That the trench being apparent to all, there was nothing in the nature of a concealed danger or 'trap', and that therefore the defendants were not liable to the plaintiff, who was a mere licensee.

Adjacent occupier

Macfarlane v Gwalter

[1959] 2 QB 332, [1958] 1 All ER 181, [1958] 2 WLR 268, 122 JP 144, 102 Sol Jo 123, 56 LGR 160, CA
A pedestrian walking along the footpath slipped through an iron grating which formed part of the pavement. The grating was old and in bad condition. The defendant was the occupier of the adjacent building.

The Public Health Acts Amendment Act 1890, s 35(1) (now replaced by the Highways Act 1980, s 180(5), which is in similar terms), provided as follows—

'All vaults, arches, and cellars under any street, and all openings into such vaults, arches, or cellars in the surface of any street, and all cellarheads, gratings, lights and coal holes in the surface of any street, and all landings, flags, or stones of the path or street supporting the same respectively shall be kept in good condition and repair by the owners or occupiers of the same, or of the houses or buildings to which the same respectively belong.'

The grating covered a small open area and its purpose was to provide light for the cellar window of the defendant's premises.
HELD: The defendant was liable under the Act whether the street had been dedicated or not.

Scott v Green & Sons

[1969] 1 All ER 849, [1969] 1 WLR 301, 113 Sol Jo 73, CA
A lorry backed on to the pavement outside the defendant's premises cracking a paving stone over the defendants' cellar. A few minutes later the plaintiff, walking along the pavement, stepped on it and it gave way. She was injured and sued for damages for breach of the Highways Act 1959, s 154(5) (now replaced in similar terms by the Highways Act 1980, s 180(5)) which provides 'every vault, arch and cellar under a street . . . and all landings flags or stones . . . by which they are supported . . . shall be kept in good condition and repair by the owner or occupier . . . of the premises to which it belongs'.
HELD: The subsection placed no absolute liability on the occupier in case of a breach. It merely gives control of the flagstone over the cellar to the owner or occupier so as to enable him to repair it whether the pavement had been dedicated to the public or not. Being in control of it he can be liable in negligence or nuisance but where, as here, there was no negligence or nuisance on the part of the defendants at all they were not liable.

Works by contractors

Penny v Wimbledon UDC and Iles

[1899] 2 QB 72, 68 LJQB 704, 80 LT 615, CA
A district council, acting under the Public Health Act 1875, s 150, employed a

contractor to make up a highway which was used by the public but had not become repairable by the inhabitants at large. In carrying out the work the contractor negligently left on the road a heap of soil, unlighted and unprotected. A person walking along the road after dark fell over the heap and was injured. An action was brought against the district council and the contractors to recover damages for the injuries sustained.
HELD: As, from the nature of the work danger was likely to arise to the public using the road, unless precautions were taken, the negligence of the contractor was not casual, or collateral to his employment, and the district council were liable.

Note—See also *Salisbury v Woodland*, p 275, below.

Tramways

Browne v De Luxe Car Services and Birkenhead Corpn

[1941] 1 KB 549, [1941] 1 All ER 383, 110 LJKB 369, 165 LT 175, 57 TLR 346, 85 Sol Jo 165, CA
The Tramways Act 1870, s 28 provides that if the undertaking or any part is abandoned and taken up, the undertakers shall within six weeks fill in and make good to the satisfaction of the road authority and restore to its former condition.

Undertakers abandoned in 1932. They did not pull up the rails, but everything else connected with the tramway disappeared, and only the steel rails in the ground were left, and these were covered up with tar.
HELD: The tramway still belonged to the Corporation and the track still remained in the road, and there was nothing in the section or the Act to divert them from maintaining the roadway. The Corporation were under a liability for what, apart from the statute, would be a nuisance. They could take up the tram rails and make good the surface and then their obligation as a tramway company would end and be that of a local authority.

Simon v Islington Borough Council

[1943] 1 KB 188, [1943] 1 All ER 41, 112 LJKB 337, 168 LT 65, 59 TLR 87, 87 Sol Jo 92, CA
Undertakers abandoned a tramway and pursuant to the provisions of the London Passenger Transport Act 1933, the defendants took over. By the provisions of the Act they indemnified the undertakers. A cyclist was fatally injured owing to the defective condition of the tramway track.
HELD, ON APPEAL: The tramway equipment was foreign to the highway. The defendants took over something which was an artificial work. It had become incongruous foreign matter in a modern road, and a mere obstruction to traffic. The principle of non-feasance did not apply and the defendants were liable.

CONTRIBUTORY NEGLIGENCE BY THE PLAINTIFF

There is a natural reluctance on the part of the courts to find contributory negligence. In *Almeroth v Chivers & Sons Limited* [1948] 1 All ER 53, CA it was held on appeal that a man crossing the road had not failed to take reasonable care simply by looking down at his feet. Unless, therefore, specific allegations can be made against the plaintiff general allegations of contributory negligence are unlikely to succeed.

Campbell v Inverness District Council

[1993] Court of Session, Outer House 10 February (reported on Lexis)
The District Council agreed to carry out certain repairs to one of their properties which was subject to a tenancy agreement. Mr Campbell, an employee of the local authority, attended the premises to assess what works were necessary. On a subsequent visit to check the progress of the works he fell and injured himself when he stepped on to a stair which had had the tread removed, thus making it unsafe.

The Court of Session, Outer House, concluded that on the evidence the local authority, through their employees, had been negligent in leaving the staircase in such a condition without giving any warning to potential users, but that the plaintiff was himself negligent to the extent of 25%, for he knew that works may well have been carried out to the staircase and he should therefore have paid particular attention to where he was walking.

DEDICATION OF HIGHWAY

Note—The textbook writers accept that there is no liability on the owner of the soil when the public are permitted to use a way over the land. *Salmond on Torts* says:

'Passengers on a highway across land in private ownership stand in a class apart. Apart from statutory modifications of the common law, a highway is merely a public right of way over land which remains in the occupation of the owner of the land. It is well established that such an occupier is under no responsibility as such towards users of the highway for its safety and is not liable for dangers thereon whether they exist at the time of dedication or come into existence later.'

Citing *Gautret v Egerton* (1867) LR 2 CP 371, 36 LJCP 191, Willes J: If I dedicate a way to the public which is full of ruts and holes, the public must take it as it is.

Holden v White

[1982] QB 679, [1982] 2 All ER 328, [1982] 2 WLR 1030, 126 Sol Jo 230 CA
The only means of access to cottages in a row extending at right angles to the highway was over a strip of land belonging to the owner of the cottage nearest the highway. A milkman visiting one of the further cottages was injured on the right of way when his foot went through a defective manhole cover.
HELD: He was not entitled to damages against the owner of the strip of land, whether or not she was the occupier, because he was not her 'visitor' for the purposes of the Occupiers' Liability Act 1957. She did not owe the common duty of care to him; it was entirely unreal to regard her, as servient owner, as having in any sense issued any invitation or permission to a person who entered the land in exercise of the dominant owner's right of way.

Note—See also *Greenhalgh v British Railways Board* (p 269, below).

RAILWAY BRIDGES

North Staffordshire Rly Co v Dale

(1858) 8 E & B 836
The roadway over a bridge is part of the bridge so that the railway company is obliged not only to maintain the structure of the bridge, but also the road surface going across it.

Note—Followed by CA in *Bury Corpn v London and Yorkshire Rly Co* (1888) 20 QBD 485.

London and North Western Rly Co v Skerton

(1864) 5 B & S 559
A railway company which, in carrying a railway over a highway by a bridge, lowered the level of the highway, were not bound to keep the slope of the road in repair as being a part of the approaches on each side of the bridge.

Swain v Southern Rly Co

[1939] 2 KB 560, [1939] 2 All ER 794, 108 LJKB 827, 160 LT 606, 55 TLR 805, 83 Sol Jo 476, CA
Plaintiff was riding his bicycle on a road, a bridge carrying the road over a railway which was repairable by the railway company pursuant to their private Act. Plaintiff was thrown from his bicycle because the wheels got into a rut about 3 inches deep and from 6 to 9 inches wide, which was a dangerous rut. The accident was caused by the want of repair of the road.
HELD: By the Railways Clauses Consolidation Act 1845, s 46, the railway company were liable for non-feasance as well as misfeasance. The road was in a condition which would have been dangerous to traffic as it was when the bridge was constructed. The duty is to maintain in the state when originally constructed and that necessarily implies an absence of dangerous ruts. The railway company were liable.

Lewys v Burnett and Dunbar

[1945] 2 All ER 555, 173 LT 307, 61 TLR 527, 89 Sol Jo 415 (Croom Johnson J)
A road ran under a railway bridge, the headroom of which, by the Act authorising the construction of the railway, was required to be not less than 9 feet, and had been 9 ft 3 in. The road authority had repaired the road and reduced the headroom to 8 ft 9 in and fixed a notice to the bridge '8 ft 9 in headroom'. A passenger on a lorry was killed by his head coming into contact with the bridge.
HELD: The lorry owner was liable for failing to warn, and the highway authority for negligently performing the statutory duty to repair; proportions 50-50.

James v Durkin (Civil Engineering Contractors) Ltd

(1983) Times, 25 May (Michael Davies J)
The driver of a skip lorry owned by the defendants was killed when part of the lorry slightly over 12 feet high struck a bridge of 11 ft 6 ins in clearance, causing the vehicle to overturn. There was no notice in the cab of the lorry to indicate the height of the lorry.
HELD: A vehicle of such a height should have a clear warning notice, and the defendants were liable. Damages should be reduced by 50% because the driver approached the bridge at too high a speed having regard to the height of the lorry.

Greenhalgh v British Railways Board

[1969] 2 QB 286, [1969] 2 All ER 114, [1969] 2 WLR 892, 113 Sol Jo 108, CA
The plaintiff was walking across the defendants' bridge over their railway when she fell and was injured owing to the bad condition of the road surface. The bridge had been built in 1873 as an accommodation bridge for adjoining landowners under the Railways Clauses Consolidation Act 1845, s 68. In the course of time the public had acquired a right of way across the bridge. The local authority built large housing

estates on each side of the railway with good approach roads to the bridge. The plaintiff lived on one of the estates some distance from the bridge.
HELD: (1) The defendants' duty under s 68 was only to 'owners and occupiers of lands adjoining the railway' and the plaintiff was not in that category; (2) the plaintiff was not a 'visitor' on the bridge for the purposes of the Occupiers' Liability Act 1957. A person is a 'visitor' only if at common law he would be regarded as an invitee or licensee. This does not include a person who, like the plaintiff, crosses land in pursuance of a public right of way (citing dictum of Willes J in *Gautret v Egerton*, quoted on p 268, above). Judgment for the defendants.

Note—The duty to maintain bridges can rest either with the highway authority or with a particular bridge authority for example British Railways Board.

Section 46 of the Railways Clauses Consolidation Act 1845 imposed a duty on railway companies to maintain bridges for which they were responsible in the state in which they were originally constructed.

2 STREETWORKS: REINSTATEMENT

INDEPENDENT CONTRACTORS

The duty to maintain the highway under s 41(1) of the 1980 Act is absolute and cannot be delegated. Nevertheless where prima facie liability is established against the highway authority they may be entitled to an indemnity if contractors were working on site at the time of the accident. The highway authority will need to demonstrate that:
(a) they used independent contractors to carry out the works;
(b) they exercised reasonable care when choosing the contractors;
(c) those contractors were de facto responsible for any alleged negligent act or omission; and
(d) the contractors were competent.

McNair v Dunfermline Corpn

(1954) 104 L Jo 66
The fact that a Gas Board failed to discharge its obligation under s 7(2)(c) to reinstate the pavement does not diminish the responsibility of the highway authority who have the paramount interest.

STREETWORKS CODE

Until 12 December 1992 streetworks and reinstatements were governed by the Public Utilities Street Works Act 1950. Section 7(2) of the Act provided that where a highway authority instructed an undertaker to carry out works on the highway the undertaker was obliged on completion of the works to 'reinstate and make good' the relevant part of the highway.

The undertakers were further specifically obliged to:
(a) begin reinstatement as soon as reasonably practicable following the completion of the works;

(b) afford facilities to the highway authority to supervise the reinstatement and to reinstate the highway to the satisfaction of the authority;
(c) make good any tunnelling works to the original surface level (subject to the Third Schedule of the 1950 Act).

The obligation was to reinstate to the same condition as before works commenced (s 30(4)). Section 39(1) of the 1950 Act further defined 'reinstatement and making good' to include temporary or interim restoration.

The Third Schedule of the 1950 Act

Reinstatement and making good by highway authority after execution of works

The obligation on the undertakers was to reinstate permanently the highway unless the highway authority notified the undertaker that they wished to carry out the permanent reinstatement themselves.

Such notification was deemed to have been given where the contract between the undertaker and authority provided that the Third Schedule would apply.

Section 2(2) of the Third Schedule defined interim restoration as 'works which were necessary to ensure that the highway was safe until such time as it was permanently reinstated'.

'Permanent reinstatement' was conversely defined as any works of reinstatement and making good executed on any occasion otherwise than with a view to the works being superseded by further work to be executed shortly thereafter.

If the plaintiff could show that the cause of an accident was the negligent reinstatement of the highway then the highway authority could look to the undertaker for an indemnity. The extent of the indemnity would, however, depend on the degree of supervision exercised by the highway authority during and after the reinstatement.

STANDARD OF REPAIR

(i) *No cause of action for breach*

Keating v Elvan Reinforced Concrete Co Ltd

[1968] 2 All ER 139, [1968] 1 WLR 722, 112 Sol Jo 193, CA

The plaintiff fell into a trench dug by the defendants and was injured. Part of the barricade and lamps erected by the defendants had been knocked down by someone else and they were in no way to blame. The Public Utilities Street Works Act 1950, s 8(1)(a) required the defendants to ensure that the trench was adequately fenced and guarded and lighted. The plaintiff claimed that this duty was absolute, that the defendants were in breach of it and that he was entitled to damages.

HELD: The plaintiff's contention failed. The section was part of the group of sections which comprised the Street Works Code and it was only in s 8 that provisions for safety were made, provisions little different from those of common law except for the possibility that they might be absolute. Having regard to the statute as a whole there was no intent to create a cause of action for breach of statutory duty.

An appeal was dismissed. The proper approach to the case, said the Court of Appeal, was to ask whether on a true construction of the statute as a whole the duties were public duties only or whether a right of action by an individual ought to be implied. Examination of ss 3–14 of the Act, which comprised the 'Street Works Code' showed that they were enacted for the purpose of providing protection for certain public authorities concerned with streets. There was no suggestion that any part of it was enacted for the protection of individuals who may suffer injury owing to defective precautions taken with regard to excavations in the streets. Moreover, s 8(3) provided for a penalty on conviction of undertakers who failed to comply with s 8(1) and sub-s (4) gave a civil remedy to an authority against undertakers who failed to satisfy an obligation under s 8(1). Neither in sub-s (3) or (4) was there any mention or suggestion that any private individual would have any remedy or right of action under the section.

Cohen v British Gas Corpn

[1978] CLY 2053 (Judge Lymbery QC)
The defendants temporarily reinstated an excavation which they had made on a public road and gave notice to the local authority under the provisions of the Public Utilities Street Works Act 1950. The excavation was about 5 ft by 3 ft and the filling had sunk causing a depression of about 1 in. The plaintiff alleged he tripped over the temporary reinstatement.
HELD: Inevitably in a roadway one finds undulations: the surface is not to be judged by the standards of a bowling green. A depression of 1 in was not dangerous.

Cressy v South Metropolitan Gas Co

(1906) 94 LT 790, Div Ct
Under the Gasworks Clauses Act 1847, undertakers had power to break up roads and reinstate. Under the Metropolis Management Act 1855, s 114 (now repealed), the borough council had power to step in and do repairs.

A gas company had excavated in a street, and the local authority had stepped in and reinstated. Owing to the negligent filling in of the excavation, a hole was caused and the plaintiff was injured by stepping into the hole. She sued the gas company.
HELD: The legislature before the 1855 Act contemplated a trading company for its own profit interfering with a street and made provision for the protection of the public if the authorised work was not properly done. The effect of the 1855 Act was that this obligation was subject to the provision 'unless the local authority step in and do the work' at the expense of the gas company, which the local authority are entitled to do if they please. This included maintenance, because the Act uses the words 'making good', and it is not made good until it is in a permanent condition so far as practicable. The gas company could not do the work and were not liable.

Note—Similar provisions to those of s 114 of the Metropolis Management Act 1855 were contained in Sch 3 to the Public Utilities Street Works Act 1950. See now ss 70–72 of the New Roads and Street Works Act 1991.

Brame v Commercial Gas Co

[1914] 3 KB 1181, 84 LJKB 570, 111 LT 1099, Div Ct
A metropolitan borough council, acting under s 114 of the 1855 Act, passed a resolution to the effect that where the surface of any street in the borough was opened by a gas company, they would themselves undertake the work of reinstatement. Subsequently to the date of this resolution, a gas company having finished laying their pipes under the pavement of a street in the borough, notified the council that reinstatement was necessary. The plaintiff was injured owing to the pavement being out of repair after such notice had been given. She sued the gas company
HELD: The resolution of the borough council did not release the gas company from its obligation under the Gasworks Clauses Act on the expiration of a reasonable time after they had received notice from the gas company that reinstatement was necessary.

Before such a release could be effected, it was necessary that the company should be dismissed from the control of the reinstatement by the council, and the work undertaken by the council.

(ii) *Sanitary authority*

Shoreditch Corpn v Bull

(1904) 90 LT 210, 20 TLR 254
Appellants, who were both the sanitary and the highway authority, dug a trench along a road under their control for the purpose of laying a sewer. When the work was completed they filled in the trench and opened the road for traffic. About a week afterwards the respondent was driving along the road in a cab at night. The driver found that part of the road where the trench had been opened was soft, and crossed on to the other side, and ran into a heap of rubbish, with the result that the cab was overturned and the respondent was injured. The rubbish had been wrongfully deposited in the road without the permission of appellants, but they knew it was there, and had not lighted or fenced it. The jury found that the part of the road where the trench had been opened had been properly filled in, but had been rendered soft by subsequent rain, and was dangerous to traffic at the time of the injury.
HELD: Appellants were liable for the injury.

(iii) *Water Board*

Rider v Metropolitan Water Board

[1949] 2 KB 378, [1949] 2 All ER 97 (Devlin J)
On 8 July 1944, undertakers broke the tarred surface of the pavement to repair a stop-cock box and excavated a hole 2 ft square by 18 ins deep. They refilled and consolidated, and also made the surface good temporarily by laying gravel to a depth of 4 ins. On 10 July 1944, they gave notice to the Wandsworth Borough Council under the Waterworks Clauses Act 1847, s 30 that the surface had been broken open and required immediate reinstating. This notice should be three days before starting the work, except in emergency, when it may be given as soon as possible after starting. This occasion was treated as an emergency. On 15 August 1944, the Council did the work of renewing the surface; they removed the temporary surface of gravel and put tar with a topping of finer material. About 5.30 pm on 29 December 1946, a very foggy night, the plaintiff tripped over the lid of the box, which projected and formed a danger due to the negligence of the Council in laying the topping. The Council was acting under the Metropolis Management Act 1855, s 114.
HELD: Following *Cressy*'s case and *Brame v Commercial Gas Co*, the undertakers are absolved from all liability under s 32 of the 1847 Act, which is qualified by s 114 of the 1855 Act, and should be read as if subject to the proviso 'unless the local authority step in and do the work', but not until the work is actually taken over by the Council (*Brame*'s case). Section 114 applies although the Council only did part of the work, ie reinstatement of the surface, as distinct from filling in a firm base done by undertakers. It applies to both these two operations separately, and so does s 32 of the 1847 Act. (Judgment for defendants.)

Note—See note after *Cressy*'s case, above.

WATER ACT 1945

Third Schedule, Part VI

22 Power to break open streets Subject to the provisions of this Part of this Schedule, the undertakers may within their limits of supply for the purpose of laying, constructing, inspecting, repairing, renewing or removing mains, service pipes, plant or other works, and outside those limits for the purpose of laying any mains which they are authorised to lay and of inspecting, repairing, renewing or removing mains, break open the roadway and footpaths of any street, and of any bridge carrying a street, and any sewer, drain or tunnel in or under any such roadway or footpath, and may remove and use the soil or other materials in or under any such roadway or footpath:

Provided that they shall in the exercise of the powers conferred by this section cause as little inconvenience and do as little damage as may be, and for any damage done shall pay compensation to be determined, in case of dispute, by arbitration.

27 Remedies where undertakers fail to comply with foregoing requirements (1) If the undertakers fail to comply with, or contravene, any of the foregoing provisions of this Part of this Schedule, they shall, without prejudice to their civil liability if any, to a person aggrieved, be liable to a fine not exceeding five pounds, and to a further fine not exceeding five pounds for each day on which the offence continues after notice thereof has been given to them by, or by an officer or agent of, the persons aggrieved.

The fine is increased to 'level 1 on the standard scale' by Criminal Justice Act 1982, s 46.

Wells v Metropolitan Water Board

[1937] 4 All ER 639 (Humphreys J)

The plaintiff was injured through tripping over the cover-plate of a valve-box, belonging to the defendant water board. When the cover of this valve-box was closed it was in no way objectionable or dangerous, but on this occasion someone, presumably a child, had opened the cover and, when open, it projected some 3 or 4 ins above the surface of the road. The cover could be opened quite easily, and was not fitted with any locking device, and there was evidence that the fitting of a locking device was both possible and reasonable.

HELD: (Distinguishing *Simpson v Metropolitan Water Board* (1917) 15 LGR 629) the plaintiff's injuries were caused by the negligence of the defendant.

Longhurst v Metropolitan Water Board

[1948] 2 All ER 834, [1948] WN 418, 112 JP 470, 64 TLR 579, 92 Sol Jo 633, HL

A stopcock below a public footway, belonging to and controlled by water undertakers, developed a leak. The escaping water dislodged the paving stones of the footway from their seatings. The practice of the undertakers was to take up only so much of the highway as was necessary to repair the leak, making good the surface temporarily, and notify the highway authority to effect permanent repairs, and until they did so, maintain a warning to the public of any danger. The work of repairing the leak was completed in a day, but the undertakers did not think it their duty to render safe the loosened stones in the pavement which it was not necessary to remove to repair the leak. They did not give warning to the public of the dangerous condition of those stones. The local authority received notice about 10 am the day after the repairs had been completed, but before they had time to begin the permanent repairs, the plaintiff tripped over a loose paving stone and was injured.

The Waterworks Clauses Act 1847, s 28 gave the Board power to break up the pavement and to repair. Section 32 (see now Public Utilities Street Works Act 1950,

s 8) required them to reinstate and to fence or guard and to light at night to warn passengers and keep in repair for three months.
HELD: The defendants were not liable: there was no evidence or inference that the undertakers knew or ought to have known of the danger. No negligence being proved, the only remaining basis of claim lay in nuisance. Even in the case of a private individual liability for nuisance without negligence is not readily established, but statutory authorities acting under statutory powers are under a more limited liability (*Geddis v Bann Reservoir Proprietors* (1878) 3 App Cas 430). No action lay for damage caused by doing an act authorised by the legislature unless done negligently. In *Green v Chelsea Waterworks Co* (1894) 70 LT 547, 10 TLR 259, undertakers were not liable for a burst main. The obligation under s 32 only requires the undertakers to reinstate and repair such portion of the road as they had taken up.

Per Lord du Parcq: There might be a duty to warn in an emergency where undertakers knew or had means of knowledge not available to the highway authority.

Note—The 1847 Act was repealed by the Water Act 1945, but the repeal does not apply to individual undertakers except by order of the Minister. Sections 30–34 are now repealed by the Public Utilities Street Works Act 1950, itself now repealed by the New Roads and Street Works Act 1991.

Dunne v North Western Gas Board

[1964] 2 QB 806, [1963] 3 All ER 916, [1964] 2 WLR 164, 107 Sol Jo 890, 62 LGR 197, CA
The plaintiffs were injured by a gas explosion in a street in Liverpool. It was caused by a leakage of gas from a gas main into a sewer due to a leak from a water main. Both the judge of first instance and the Court of Appeal held there was no negligence on the part of either the gas board or the water undertakers, but the judge held the gas board liable in nuisance and the water undertaker liable under the doctrine in *Rylands v Fletcher*.
HELD, ON APPEAL: The defendants supplied gas and water under statutory authority. If in such cases there was an accident occurring as the result of statutory operations without negligence on the part of the statutory undertakers there could be no liability. Quoting Lord Blackburn in *Geddis v Bann Reservoir Proprietors*, 'No action will lie for doing that which the legislature has authorised, if it be done without negligence although it does occasion damage.' *Rylands v Fletcher* did not apply; that case imposed liability for the negligence of an independent contractor on a landowner who for his own purposes collected things on his land which escaped. Those were not the facts in the present case.

Note—But see comments of Robert Goff J on *Geddis*'s case in *Fellowes v Rother District Council* [1983] 1 All ER 513 at 518–20.

(iv) *Liability after 12 months*

Hartley v Rochdale Corpn

[1908] 2 KB 594, 77 LJKB 884, 99 LT 275, 72 JP 343, 24 TLR 625, 6 LGR 858
A corporation had power to supply and supplied water outside their area. They filled up an excavation, and under the Waterworks Clauses Act their liability to remedy post-work subsidence ceased after 12 months. During the 12 months subsidence

occurred and the Corporation employed the local council of the area to repair. Twenty months after the expiry of the 12 months the plaintiff was injured.
HELD: The local council had repaired as agents for the Corporation; the road had been out of repair since the 12 months expired, and the defendant Corporation were liable.

THE NEW ROADS AND STREET WORKS ACT 1991

The Public Utilities Street Works Act 1950 has now been repealed and replaced by the New Roads and Street Works Act 1991. The 1991 Act effects changes for both local authorities and public utilities and their sub-contractors. The Act came into force on 1 January 1993 together with three codes of practice:
(i) Specification for the Reinstatement of Openings in Highways.
(ii) Measures necessary where apparatus is effected by Major Works (Diversionary Works).
(iii) Code of Practice of inspection.

Reinstatement

Section 70(1) and (2)

70(1) It is the duty of the undertaker by whom streetworks are executed to reinstate the street.

70(2) The undertaker shall begin the reinstatement as soon after the completion of any part of the street works as is reasonably practicable and shall carry on and complete the reinstatement with all such dispatch as is reasonably practicable.

(iii) He shall before the end of the next working day after the day on which the reinstatement is completed inform the street authority that he has completed the reinstatement of the street stating whether the reinstatement is permanent or interim.
(iv) If it is interim he shall complete the permanent reinstatement of the street as soon as reasonably practicable and in any event within six months (or such other period as may be prescribed) from the date on which the interim reinstatement was completed; and he shall notify the street authority when he has done so.
(v) The permanent reinstatement of the street shall include in particular the reinstatement of features designed to assist people with a disability.

Interim reinstatement is defined in the Codes of Practice as 'the orderly placement and proper compaction of reinstatement layers to finished surface level including some temporary materials'.

Permanent reinstatement is defined as 'the orderly placement and proper compaction of reinstatement layers up to and including the finished level'.

Under s 71 of the Act the standard of reinstatement must conform with the Approved Code of Practice (the Specification for the Reinstatement of Openings in Highways) which sets out general performance requirements and detailed reinstatement, inspections, methods and materials for various types of roads.

Guarantee period

Section 1.2.1 of the Specification for the Reinstatement of Openings in Highways requires the undertaker to ensure that:
(a) the interim reinstatement conforms to prescribed standards until the permanent reinstatement is completed and that,

(b) the permanent guarantee period shall run for two years following completion of the reinstatement or for three years in the case of deep openings.

The effect of the new legislation therefore is to shift the burden of responsibility for reinstatement from the highway authority to the undertaker.

Notwithstanding that, the street authority may still be at risk for any residual responsibility they have retained for supervising or signing off the temporary or permanent reinstatement works or for carrying out periodical inspections.

3 OBSTRUCTIONS AND DANGERS ON HIGHWAY

WHAT CONSTITUTES AN OBSTRUCTION

Unlighted obstruction in highway

Polkinghorn v Lambeth Borough Council

[1938] 1 All ER 339, 158 LT 127, 54 TLR 345, 82 Sol Jo 94, CA

An illuminated bollard at one end of a tram refuge had been damaged in an accident. The defendant council had placed a light upon it, but the light had, for some unexplained reason, gone out. As a result of this, the plaintiff's motor car collided with the bollard, and the plaintiff was injured.

HELD: The defendant council having erected the refuge and bollards, were under a continuing duty to keep them adequately lighted. They were, therefore, liable to the plaintiff in respect of the injury he had sustained. Farwell J said he would prefer to deal with the case as one of negligence rather than as a case of breach of any statutory duty, and held that it was common law negligence.

Fisher v Ruislip-Northwood UDC and Middlesex County Council

[1945] KB 584, [1945] 2 All ER 458, 173 LT 161, 62 TLR 1, 89 Sol Jo 434, CA

The defendant local authority had lawfully erected a surface shelter in the highway under the Civil Defence Act 1939, s 9. There was a warning light at each corner which could be turned on and off by a switch inside the shelter, which it was the duty of the air-raid wardens to switch on at the appointed time. The shelter was sometimes lighted and sometimes not lighted. The plaintiff driving a car in the hours of darkness with due care and on the proper side of the road collided with the shelter which was unlighted. He was a complete stranger to the district and had never been in the road before.

HELD, by the Court of Appeal: On undertakers who were given statutory power to construct works a legal duty was imposed that reasonable care should be taken so to construct and maintain the works as to render them safe and not dangerous to the public though no such duty was imposed by the statute itself or by the common law; except in cases where the statute excluded the duty of taking care. The duty to take reasonable care to prevent danger to the public was present throughout; the date of the erection of an obstruction and the purpose for which it was intended to be used (apart from special circumstances or special language in the statute), were immaterial. So long as the streets were properly lit, the duty was ipso facto performed, but when the street lighting was suspended for any reason, whether by lighting restrictions, the exercise of an option on the part of the local authority not to light, or accidental breakdown, it became the duty of the local authority to take such steps to safeguard the public by special danger lights or otherwise, as in the circumstances of the case were reasonably possible.

The respondents were responsible for the shelter and were under a duty to take reasonable steps to warn the public of its existence and that duty was not performed, and they were liable to the appellant. Appeal allowed.

Whiting v Middlesex County Council and Harrow UDC

[1948] 1 KB 162, [1947] 2 All ER 758, [1948] LJR 242, 112 JP 74, 63 TLR 614, 92 Sol Jo 41, 46 LGR 136 (Croom-Johnson J)
A motor cyclist during the hours of darkness when public lighting was unrestricted, collided with an air-raid shelter which was built partially on the footway to the extent of about 1 foot and jutted out into the roadway for about another 6 feet. It was near a street lamp which threw a shadow into the roadway causing a pool of darkness. An electric bulb showing a red light was built in, protected from outside by a wire mesh grill, and inside two screws would have to be removed to remove the red glass covering the lamp. The lamp was for some reason extinguished. The light had been destroyed over and over again by mischievous persons, and other accidents had occurred. The defendants ordered workpeople to put the light back, but it was repeatedly destroyed to the knowledge of the defendants.
HELD: Defendants had not taken reasonable steps. What they did was equivalent to taking no steps at all. The duty is not a duty to light but a duty to take reasonable steps to prevent the obstruction becoming a danger to the public; to ensure that a warning is given. Lighting is no doubt the obvious and simplest measure of precautions during the hours of darkness. It may be the only possible effective precaution. There may be other steps which would be as effective.

'Properly lit' (see *Fisher*'s case) applies when the street lighting is effective to fulfil the duty. Here the public lighting resulted in something like a trap and the structure remained a danger. The defendants could not say—we will put the lighting back and, until somebody destroys it again, we have performed our duty. Defendants were liable.

Roadworks as an obstruction

Note—See *Fisher v Ruislip-Northwood UDC and Middlesex County Council* [1945] KB 584, [1945] 2 All ER 458, 173 LT 161, 62 TLR 1, 89 Sol Jo 434, CA, above.

Murray v Southwark Borough Council

(1966) 65 LGR 145 (MacKenna J)
In a street in Rotherhithe, London, reasonably well lit by sodium lighting of orange colour the plaintiff saw lines of red lamps dividing the road into two lanes. He was using only the sidelights of his car. He drove into the nearside lane, which was out of use for repairs, and though finding the surface rough drove on for ten yards or so until the front wheels fell into an excavation a foot deep. Some hooligans had removed a trestle and lamps which had been placed across the entrance to the nearside lane by the defendant highway authority to divert traffic into the offside lane.
HELD: The plaintiff was not negligent either in not using headlights or in failing to see the excavation. The defendants were negligent in not providing enough watchmen in an area where hooliganism was common.

Lilley v British Insulated Callenders Construction Co Ltd

(1968) 67 LGR 224, CA
The plaintiff was injured when at about 10.50 pm his car collided with an obstruction left in the road by the defendants. The plaintiff said there were no lights or guard rail round the obstruction. The defendants brought evidence that at 8.30 pm barriers were in position and lights were burning.
HELD, ON APPEAL: The real issue was whether the defendants ought to have had a man to inspect the lights periodically during the night. There was evidence that the defendants did so at their main sites, but this accident had taken place in a quiet residential road. The defendants had taken reasonable precautions and were under no obligation to send a man to inspect the site.

Street lighting

Note—Outside the Metropolis, the lighting of streets comes under the provisions of the Public Health Act 1875, s 161:

'Any urban authority may contract with any person for the supply of gas, and other means of lighting the streets, market and public buildings in their district, and may provide such lamps, lamp posts and other materials and apparatus as they may think necessary for lighting the same.

Where there is not any company or person (other than the urban authority) authorised by or in pursuance of any Act of Parliament, or any order confirmed by Parliament, to supply gas for public and private purposes, supplying gas within any part of the district of such authority, such authority may themselves undertake to supply gas for such purposes or any of them throughout the whole or any part of their district; and if there is any such company or person so supplying gas, but the limits of supply of such company or person include part only of the district, then the urban authority may themselves undertake to supply gas throughout any part of the district not included within such limits of supply. . . .'

Sheppard v Glossop Corpn

[1921] 3 KB 132, CA
The defendants had placed a lamp on a place which was dangerous when not lighted, but extinguished it every night soon after 9 pm in accordance with a resolution passed by the authority.
HELD: The section confers upon urban authorities a discretion but imposes on them no obligation to light the streets in their districts; consequently the defendants who had begun were not bound to continue to light the street; and having done nothing to make the street dangerous they were under no obligation whether by lighting or otherwise, to give warning of danger.

Note—See also *Burton v West Suffolk CC* (p 252, above).

Dangerous position of road sign

Hughes v Sheppard, Morley v Sheppard

(1940) 163 LT 177, 104 JP 357, 56 TLR 810, 84 Sol Jo 490, 38 LGR 336
The employees of a county council acting as agents for the Minister of Transport were engaged in painting a white line down the centre of a trunk road for which by virtue of the Trunk Roads Act 1936, the Minister was the highway authority. The men

having left their work for the midday rest, the newly-painted line was marked by a series of cans filled with sand in which red flags were fixed. A motor driver, having failed to see the cans, collided with the first as he approached, and then with another car coming towards him.

In actions brought against him, and against the county council and Minister of Transport for negligence, it was contended that the council and the Minister were guilty of negligence in not giving clear indication of the presence of the cans and flags and of nuisance.

HELD: (1) The painting of the white lines was, whether or not an 'improvement' within the Trunk Roads Act 1936, within the powers of the Minister as highway authority; it was no more than what was reasonably necessary to the process of painting the line to indicate that such work was in progress by means of the cans and flags; and the placing of the cans and flags did not constitute negligence or nuisance; (2) in any event, even if the placing of the cans and flags along the line constituted a nuisance, the only person liable to plaintiffs was defendant driver by reason of his negligence in failing to see the cans and flags in time to avoid the accident.

Levine v Morris

[1970] 1 All ER 144, [1970] 1 WLR 71, 113 Sol Jo 798, [1970] RTR 93, CA
The first defendant driving a car on a main road towards a roundabout in heavy rain got into a skid and crashed into massive concrete columns supporting a road sign erected by the Ministry of Transport, killing a passenger. He was held 75% to blame and the Ministry 25%.

The Ministry's appeal was dismissed. They owed a duty to take reasonable care, when there were sites for signs equally good as regards visibility, not to select the one which involved greater hazards to the motorist. It was well known that at high speeds there was a risk of motorists going off the road in bad weather. The chances of such accidents should always be borne in mind by the Ministry and the extent of such chances assessed. In the present case anyone skilled in road design would foresee that drivers who had not the fullest degree of skill might leave the road. The danger could have been averted by siting the sign where the risk was diminished.

DEFENCE OF STATUTORY OBSTRUCTION

Note—A defence may be available where the obstruction complained of by the plaintiff has been legalised by an Act of Parliament (*Great Central Railway Company v Hewlett*, below).

Great Central Rly Co v Hewlett

[1916] 2 AC 511, 85 LJKB 1705, 115 LT 349, 32 TLR 707, 60 Sol Jo 678, HL
A railway company erected in the public highway certain gate posts from which collapsible steel gates could be run across the road so as to close the entrance to the station yard. These posts were erected by the company in contravention of their special Act and in 1901 were judicially held to be an obstruction to the highway. In 1902 the company obtained an Act which empowered them to 'maintain' the posts and gates and to replace them when necessary on the same site. A licensed taxicab driver, while lawfully driving his cab on a dark rainy night along the public highway into the station yard, collided with one of these posts, which was practically invisible owing to the darkening of the street in compliance with the Reduction of Lighting Regulations and thereby damaged his cab. The post was in the condition in which it

was at the time of the passing of the Act in 1902. An action was brought by the cab driver against the railway company for damages for negligence.
HELD: The accident arose, not from any overt act of the company, but from the existence of the gate post which had been legalised by the Act of 1902, coupled with the diminution of light necessitated by the exigencies of the War; the mere power to maintain the post imposed no obligation on the company to take reasonable precautions to warn the public of its existence; and the company was not guilty of negligence.

OTHER DANGERS

Excavations adjacent to highway

Caseley v Bristol Corpn

[1944] 1 All ER 14, CA
The duty of an occupier of land is to fence any dangerous excavation adjoining the highway, and this may extend to a danger close to though not actually adjoining.

A man wandered in a fog from the highway and fell into a dock basin 47 feet from the highway.
HELD: There was no duty to fence unless the danger was so near the highway that a man making a false step, or overcome by temporary giddiness, would fall into the excavation.

Ball from playing field on highway

Hilder v Associated Portland Cement Manufacturers Ltd

[1961] 3 All ER 709, [1961] 1 WLR 1434, 105 Sol Jo 725; 179 Estates Gazette 445 (Ashworth J)
The defendants allowed their field adjoining a busy road to be used as a playing field by children. The field was separated from the road by a three-foot wall and a line of poplar trees. Two boys aged nine and ten were playing with a football using a poplar tree as one goal post and a stick as the other. In the course of the game one of the boys kicked the ball on to the road. The plaintiff's husband was riding by on a motor cycle: he was thrown off by the ball and killed.
HELD: The defendants were liable in negligence. The test was whether the defendants were shown to have failed to take reasonable care in all the circumstances. The relevant circumstances included the situation of the field and the road, the amount of traffic using the road, the ages of the children using the field, the nature of their amusements and the frequency with which the field was used. A reasonable man would come to the conclusion, on the facts given in evidence, that there was a risk of damage to persons using the road which was not so small that he could disregard it.

Danger created by independent contractor

Salsbury v Woodland

[1970] 1 QB 324, [1969] 3 All ER 863, [1969] 3 WLR 29, 113 Sol Jo 327, CA
The first defendant was the owner of a house adjoining a public highway. He wished to have a hawthorn tree removed which stood in the front garden 28 feet from the

roadway. His wife found some tree-fellers and engaged one of them (the second defendant) to do the job. He failed to lop the branches sufficiently before bringing the tree down and as a result it fouled and broke two telephone wires running to the house from a post on the other side of the road. The wires hung across the roadway and the plaintiff, a bystander, went to remove them. Before he reached them he saw the third defendant coming in his car at fast speed towards the wires. He flung himself down on the grass verge to avoid being struck by the wires and injured his back. The second defendant did not contest the action. The judge held the first defendant was liable for the second defendant's negligence even though he was an independent contractor. He said that when the very act which is required to be done by the independent contractor contains a risk of injury to others the principal is liable if injury results from negligence in performing it.
HELD, ON APPEAL: The judge's statement of principle was too wide. The first defendant was not himself negligent and could not be liable unless the case was within the special categories of case in which the principal was liable for the contractor's lack of care in doing the work. Only two such categories were relevant to the present case: (1) 'extra hazardous acts'—those acts so hazardous that the law has seen fit to impose direct liability on the principal. The present case did not come into that category. The job if done with elementary caution by skilled men presented no hazard to anyone at all. (2) Dangers created in a highway. Such cases are all found on analysis to be cases where the work being done was in a highway and of a character which would have been a nuisance unless authorised by statute. This case was not one of work done in a highway. There was no sound authority for saying that there is an additional class of case of liability where the principal commissions work to be done *near* a highway.

Fire engine parked

Amos v Glamorgan County Council

(1967) 66 LGR 166, CA
The plaintiff, a youth of 19, was riding his motor cycle when he collided with the defendants' stationary fire engine. The accident happened in broad daylight. The fire engine was properly parked at the kerb, having been called to a fire at a nearby house. It had been there only two minutes or so and had two blue flashing lights on top. The plaintiff had a view of it for at least 80 yards. There was heavy rain and the plaintiff was not wearing his spectacles. The Commissioner of Assize found the defendants one-half to blame for omitting to put a red warning light on the road to give oncoming traffic early warning of the presence of the fire engine.
HELD, ON APPEAL: The defendants were not to blame at all. The fire brigade had to give priority to those in peril from fire and in the circumstances the flashing signal from the fire engine was a sufficient warning of its presence. Bad weather conditions did not justify a motor cyclist for failing to keep a proper look-out: they required him to proceed more carefully.

Ice on road

Manchester Corpn v Markland

[1936] AC 360, [1935] All ER Rep 667, 104 LJKB 480, HL
The Manchester Corporation were the statutory authority for the supply of water. A service pipe in a road burst and caused a pool of water to form in the road. The water

lay unheeded for three days. On the third day a frost occurred, the water froze, and on the ice so formed a motor car skidded and knocked down and killed a man. The Corporation were not informed until after this accident that the service pipe had burst.
HELD: The driver of the car was not guilty of negligence, but the Corporation were liable for not having taken prompt steps to attend to the leak and so to prevent the road from becoming dangerous to traffic.

Lambie v Western Scottish Motor Traction Co

(1944) SC 415
Ice formed on the pavement from washing of buses in a neighbouring garage. A pedestrian slipped on the ice and was injured.
HELD: The bus company were liable.

Lamp-posts

Davies v Carmarthenshire County Council

[1971] RTR 112, CA
The plaintiff was driving her car up a hill at about 17 mph into the setting sun. The road had recently been widened by the defendants who had left a lamp-post in its original position about 5 feet out from the new edge of the road. The plaintiff completely failed to see it and drove straight into it. The county court judge held the defendants wholly to blame. They appealed on the issue of contributory negligence.
HELD: The plaintiff was not so dazzled by the sun that she had no visibility at all: if she were then it was negligent to go ahead except at a minimal pace. She was not driving completely blind and should have seen the lamp-post at the speed she was travelling and avoided it. But the blameworthiness of the defendants in leaving the obstacle in the road without any sufficient warning to motorists was very much greater. Proportion 80% defendants, 20% plaintiff.

Slates on highway

Almeroth v W E Chivers & Sons Ltd

[1948] 1 All ER 53, 92 Sol Jo 71, CA
Contractors left a small pile of slates by the kerb which was between 4 and 6 inches high. The pile did not overtop the kerb. The plaintiff crossing the road in daylight tripped over the pile which he had not previously seen and did not notice as he was stepping up on to the kerb, and was injured. There was no evidence that the defendants' work could not be carried on in any other way.

Lewis J held the heap constituted a nuisance but that the accident was due solely to the negligence of the plaintiff because he did not see the pile.
HELD, ON APPEAL: A pedestrian is not bound to keep his eyes on the ground or look constantly down to his feet to see whether or not there was any obstacle in his path. The small heap did not cause an obstruction in that it prevented or impeded the flow of traffic or the passage of pedestrians, but it constituted a nuisance which might easily not be noticed by a reasonably careful person. There was no evidence of negligence of the plaintiff. The defendants were guilty of negligence and nuisance. Appeal allowed.

Prince v Gregory

[1959] 1 All ER 133, [1959] 1 WLR 177, 103 Sol Jo 130, CA
Defendant left a pile of lime mortar in the gutter outside his house pending his use of it presumably for repairs. The plaintiff was a boy aged ten. Another boy aged 14 picked up some of the mortar and threw it at the plaintiff and injured him.
HELD: The defendant could not reasonably be expected to apprehend danger to children from the lime mortar being left where it was, pending its use for a useful purpose. Defendant not liable.

Smoke on highway

Holling v Yorkshire Traction Co Ltd

[1948] 2 All ER 662 (Oliver J)
The second defendants were owners of coke ovens on the north side of and about 50 yards from the main road from Sheffield to Manchester. The operations produced masses of steam and smoke about every three-quarters of an hour. In normal weather the clouds of vapour rose and blew over the road at a height which did not inconvenience traffic, but on comparatively rare occasions they passed low and involved vehicles on the road.

On 22 February 1947, about 3 pm, an omnibus of the first defendants and a private car travelling in opposite directions collided in the middle of a particularly dense cloud of grey smoke and steam, which amounted to complete obscurity. The omnibus driver could not see the car even after he had run into it. Two passengers in the car were killed and their widows brought proceedings against both defendants.
HELD: There was no negligence of the driver of the private car.

With regard to the second defendants, the discharge of vapour was a nuisance. It was not an incident of the ordinary and lawful use of land, nor a case of lawful user of the highway. The smoke clouds had persisted all day and were obvious. The second defendants were also negligent. They could have posted a man at each of the affected area to warn traffic.

As to the first defendants, the accident occurred during one of the most severe winters in human memory. The road surface was extremely treacherous and dangerous demanding the utmost care from drivers. Any sudden application of the brakes unless the speed was very moderate would certainly precipitate a skid. Visibility apart from the smoke was quite good. The omnibus driver was negligent (1) in driving on the wrong side of the road; (2) in going too fast; (3) in failing to observe and guard against the vapour cloud in time to take effective action.

Rollingson v Kerr

[1958] CLY 2427
A collision occurred between two vehicles going in opposite directions on a straight stretch of road. Defendant's servant had lit a bonfire of hedge clippings, causing dense smoke to blow across the road, and it was in the midst of this that the collision took place. The judge found the defendant guilty of negligence and the defence of *volenti non fit injuria* failed, and that neither driver was guilty of contributory negligence.

Holling's case followed; *Heywood v London North Eastern Rly Co* (1926) Times, 1 December not followed.

Hall & Co Ltd v Ham Manor Farm Ltd

(1966) 116 L Jo 838, Chichester CC (Judge Talbot)
The plaintiffs' lorry collided with another lorry in thick smoke on the main Worthing-Chichester road. The smoke came from the defendants' adjacent field where stubble was being burnt; it was patchy but in one area visibility on the road was reduced practically to nil.
HELD: (1) In so far as the claim lay in negligence it failed because the defendants' servants had taken all reasonable precautions to avoid any dangers and the enveloping of the road with thick smoke was not only foreseen but was of short duration and was a temporary hazard which could be seen by those travelling along the road; (2) if an action lay in nuisance it could do so only as a public nuisance from which the plaintiffs had suffered damage. It was impossible to hold that the thick smoke which covered the road for such a short space of time could be classed as such an interference with the public right as to warrant it being classed as a public nuisance: the facts were wholly different from *Holling v Yorkshire Traction Co Ltd* (above); (3) the rule in *Rylands v Fletcher* was not applicable where the defendants were making an ordinary and proper use of their land. Judgment for the defendants.

Perkins v Glyn

[1976] RTR ixn, [1976] CLY 1883
The plaintiff, riding a motor cycle, collided with a stationary car when his vision was obscured by smoke from stubble burning in a field owned by the defendant. The smoke was blowing in gusts across the road for a distance of 150 yards or so.
HELD: (1) Burning stubble was not a non-natural user of land. (2) The defendant was not negligent. He could not always wait until the wind was blowing away from the road; warning was not necessary as the smoke was visible a mile away and the plaintiff had already ridden through 100 yards of it. (3) On the question of nuisance, a motorist must expect to be obstructed occasionally and the defendant could not be said to have set a trap. The claim failed. Per Judge Pennant.

Road repairs

Maher v Hurst

(1969) 113 Sol Jo 167, 67 LGR 367, CA
On the Watford by-pass, a road wide enough to take three lines of traffic, asphalting contractors were spreading asphalt by means of a large machine which spread a strip 10 feet wide. It operated on one lane at a time leaving the other two lanes open for traffic. The contractors had put the usual warning signs out to warn oncoming traffic and so placed as to funnel the traffic into the two open lanes. The plaintiff, an employee of the contractors was standing at the side of the strip being spread, on the road surface of the middle lane which was being used by traffic. A lorry began to pass the roadworks using the middle lane with the spreader on its nearside. The driver saw a coach approaching at a time when a cloud of steam came up from the hot asphalt causing serious injury. The judge said the driver was going too fast but accepted the suggestion that the contractors should have put up a barrier of tripods on the middle lane to protect the plaintiff. He held the contractors three-quarters to blame.
HELD: The contractors were not to blame at all. They were carrying out the usual system for such work by which two lanes were left clear for traffic. There was no

evidence of similar accidents. If tripods were put in the middle lane traffic on this very important road would be reduced to one line: it would cause such inconvenience to the public that it should not be done unless the risk to the men was so great as to warrant it. There was no evidence of such risk. The accident was caused solely by the driver's negligence in driving too fast.

Traffic studs

Skilton v Epsom and Ewell UDC

[1937] 1 KB 112, [1936] 2 All ER 50, 106 LJKB 41, 154 LT 700, 52 TLR 494, 80 Sol Jo 345, CA
A traffic stud, placed in a road by authority of the Road Traffic Act 1930, s 48 (now the Road Traffic Regulation Act 1984, s 65), caused an accident through being defective.
HELD: The defective stud was a nuisance and Council was liable.

Supermarket shopping trolley

Devon County Council v Gateway Foodmarkets

(1990) 154 JP 557, DC
HELD: that a supermarket's shopping trolley rank can be an obstruction under s 137 (1) of the Highways Act 1980.

NUISANCE ON HIGHWAY

Definition of nuisance

Harper v GN Haden & Sons Ltd

[1933] Ch 298, 102 LJCh 6, 148 LT 303, 96 LP 525, 76 Sol Jo 849, 31 LGR 18, CA
The law relating to the user of highways is in truth the law of give and take. Those who use them must, in doing so, have reasonable regard to the convenience and comfort of others, and must not themselves expect a degree of convenience and comfort only obtainable by disregarding that of other people. They might expect to be obstructed occasionally. It is the price they pay for the privilege of obstructing others.

Searle v Wallbank

[1947] AC 341, [1947] 1 All ER 12, [1947] LJR 258, 176 LT 104, 63 TLR 24, 91 Sol Jo 83, HL (Lord du Parcq)
An underlying principle of the law of the highways is that all those lawfully using the highway, or land adjacent to it, must show mutual respect and forbearance. The motorist must put up with the farmer's cattle; the farmer must endure the motorist. It is commonly part of a man's legal duty to his neighbour to tolerate the untoward results of his neighbour's lawful acts. These observations are, I think, relevant not only to the issue of negligence, but also to the allegation of nuisance. The stray horse on the road does not seriously interfere with the exercise of a common right, and is no more a nuisance in law, merely by reason of its presence there, than the fallen

carthorse or its modern analogue, the lorry which has temporarily broken down. The same considerations which guided the Court of Appeal in *Maitland v Raisbeck* [1944] KB 689 are, I think, applicable here.

Howard v Walker

[1947] KB 860, [1947] 2 All ER 197, [1947] LJR 1366, 177 LT 326, 63 TLR 518, 92 Sol Jo 494 (Lord Goddard CJ)
I can think of no better definition of nuisance than this, given in Winfield's textbook on the *Law of Tort* (3rd edn) p 426: 'Nuisance is the unlawful interference with a person's use or enjoyment of land, or of some right over, or in connection with it.' If a person's right of free passage over a highway is subject to interference he has an action, just as he would have if a private right of way of which he was the grantee was obstructed.

Jacobs v London County Council

[1950] 2 KB 353, [1959] 1 All ER 737, [1950] WN 170, 66 TLR 659, HL
It will help to keep sight of the differences between cases of nuisance and cases of negligence if two propositions are maintained—(1) that negligence is not necessarily an element in nuisance, and (2) that, where the nuisance in respect of which a private person sues is a 'public nuisance', he has no personal right of action unless he can prove special damage beyond that suffered by other members of the public.

Note—'A nuisance to a highway consists either in obstructing it or in rendering it dangerous:' *Salmond, Torts* (14th edn) p 124, quoted by Sir Raymond Evershed MR in the following case.

Trevett v Lee

[1955] 1 All ER 406, [1955] 1 WLR 113, 99 Sol Jo 110, CA
Per Sir Raymond Evershed MR: It is well established that a private individual can only sue in respect of a public nuisance if he suffers some special damage as a result of it.

If I make a small hole in the highway difficult to see, or put some greasy substance on it, so that treading in the hole or on the substance is liable to cause a man as a natural consequence to fall, then it may be that I have caused a nuisance to the highway, not by obstructing it, but by rendering it dangerous.

It is not open to doubt that in a claim for damages based on nuisance the defendant may set up and rely on a fault consisting of what is commonly called contributory negligence so as to reduce or extinguish his own liability.

Overseas Tankship (UK) Ltd v Miller Steamship Co Pty (The Wagon Mound (No 2))

[1967] 1 AC 617, [1966] 2 All ER 709, [1966] 3 WLR 498, 110 Sol Jo 447, [1966] 1 Lloyd's Rep 657, PC
Per Lord Reid: Although negligence may not be necessary [to establish nuisance], fault of some kind is almost always necessary and fault generally involves foreseeability, eg in cases like *Sedleigh-Denfield v O'Callaghan* ([1940] AC 880) the fault is in failing to abate the nuisance of which the defendant is or ought to be aware as likely to cause damage to his neighbour. The present case is one of creating a danger to persons or property in navigable waters (equivalent to a highway) and there it is admitted that fault is essential—in this case the negligent discharge of the

oil. . . . So in the class of nuisance which includes this case foreseeability is an essential element in determining liability.

Note—The events giving rise to the action were the same as in *Overseas Tankships (UK) v Morts Dock* (p 332, below). In *The Wagon Mound (No 2)* the respondent plaintiffs were owners of two ships damaged by the fire.

What constitutes a nuisance

VEHICLE PARKED ON ROADWAY

Dymond v Pearce

[1972] 1 QB 496, [1972] 1 All ER 1142, [1972] 2 WLR 633, 116 Sol Jo 62, [1972] RTR 169, CA

The defendants' driver fetched a large loaded lorry from their depot at 6 pm and parked it near his home ready for an early start next morning. It was parked on the outside of a shallow bend on an urban road having two carriageways each 24 feet wide. Before lighting-up time the driver turned on the lights. The lorry was under a street light and was visible for at least 200 yards to approaching traffic: it was 7½ feet wide leaving at least 16 feet of the carriageway unobstructed. After lighting-up time a motor cyclist, looking round at someone on the pavement, failed to see the lorry and crashed into it. The plaintiff, his passenger, was injured. He based his claim on two grounds: (1) that the lorry was negligently parked and (2) that the lorry was an obstruction and amounted to a common law nuisance, actionable without proof of negligence. The trial judge held that (1) in the manner in which the lorry was parked there was no foreseeable danger and no negligence; (2) the mere parking of the lorry on the nearside of the road where it was not foreseeably dangerous did not amount to nuisance at common law; (3) the sole cause of the accident was the motor cyclist's failure to look where he was going.

HELD, ON APPEAL: (1) The judge was right in finding that the defendants and their driver had not been negligent in parking the lorry at that place in the way they did; (2) there were two categories of nuisance on a highway, an obstruction which constituted a danger and an obstruction without danger. It was important to remember the two categories when looking at the authorities. In neither category was it necessary to prove negligence as an ingredient, and in both proof of what was prima facie a nuisance laid the onus on the defendant to prove justification. Neither category was actionable unless the plaintiff could prove damage had been caused to him. Leaving aside the special position of frontagers (and the driver in this case was not a frontager) the common law rights of users of the highway were normally confined to use for passage and repassage and incidents reasonably associated with such use. Leaving a large vehicle on the highway prima facie resulted in a nuisance, for it narrowed the highway: in the present case the lorry constituted a nuisance at the time the motor cyclist ran into it but that did not render the defendants liable to the plaintiff because, as the judge had found, the nuisance was not the cause of the accident—the sole cause was the motor cyclist's negligence. In most cases that was an inevitable conclusion once negligence on the part of a stationary vehicle was negatived. Nevertheless (per Edmund Davies LJ) a person creating a highway obstruction must be alert to the possibility that weather changes or the actions of third parties might convert what was originally a danger-free obstruction into a grave traffic hazard. In the present case the lorry parked as it was did not present a danger to those using the highway in the manner in which they could be reasonably expected to use it. Appeal dismissed.

Note—In *Dymond v Pearce* Sachs LJ considered that there were two categories of nuisance: either an obstruction which was not dangerous, or one which was. Edmund Davies LJ in the same case thought an obstruction in a highway did not become a nuisance unless it was shown to be dangerous. This difference of view was alluded to in the cases of *Wills v T F Martin (Roof Contractors) Ltd* (1972) 116 Sol Jo 145 (Forbes J) and *Drury v Camden Borough Council* [1972] RTR 391 (May J).

BUILDER'S SKIP ON ROADWAY

Saper v Hungate Builders Ltd

[1972] RTR 380 (Cantley J)
King was driving his car in the hours of darkness along a residential road with the plaintiff as passenger when he collided with a builder's skip which he did not see in time to avoid. The skip had been placed partly on the grass verge and partly on the roadway by the owners who had delivered it on the instructions of the hirers. The hirers were builders doing work on a nearby house. They arranged for the house-owner, their customer, to put a lamp at each offside corner of the skip. Two motorists passing the skip two to three hours before the accident had seen the skip only just in time to swerve and avoid it.
HELD: The provision of two lamps which so many persons failed to see was not adequate lighting. An object like a skip was very dangerous unless proper warning was given by lighting which would be readily and instantly apparent: this skip in its position and condition was a nuisance in the highway. The fact that King failed to see it was not fatal to his claim, but driving at a reasonable speed and being alert as a driver should be at night he should have seen it. He was 40% to blame. The builders were liable as having taken detailed charge of the safety precautions. The owners of the skip were equally to blame with the builders having put the obstruction in the carriageway and left it there; they were under a duty to light it and could not escape liability by delegating the duty to someone else. The house-owner was not liable; he had merely done what he was asked to do.

Note—In *Dymond v Pearce* (above) Sachs LJ considered there were two categories of nuisance: either an obstruction which was not dangerous, or one which was. Edmund Davies LJ in the same case thought an obstruction in a highway did not become a nuisance unless it was shown to be dangerous. This difference of view was alluded to in the following two cases.

Wills v TF Martin (Roof Contractors) Ltd

(1972) 116 Sol Jo 145, [1972] RTR 368 (Forbes J)
Riding a moped in the hours of darkness along a residential road which was poorly lit the plaintiff collided with a skip which he had not seen. It was on the nearside of the roadway and the plaintiff said it was unlighted. He was injured and claimed damages in nuisance and negligence against the roofing contractors who had put it there.
HELD: Applying *Dymond v Pearce* (above), you have first to consider whether the presence of the skip on the highway is a nuisance. If the plaintiff satisfies that burden he has still to show, according to Edmund Davies LJ (in *Dymond*'s case), that the

obstruction was also a dangerous obstruction. The last link in the chain is that the plaintiff must satisfy the court that the obstruction was at least a cause of the accident. A skip placed on a highway is in a different category from a parked vehicle. It has no business to be on a highway at all; to deposit a container of that character on the highway creates a nuisance. The skip was a nuisance because it was occupying a section of the highway which ought not to be obstructed in that way. If unlit in this position on the road it would be potentially dangerous, but on the evidence it was not established that it was unlighted. The sole cause of the accident was the plaintiff's failure to look where he was going and the claim failed.

Drury v Camden Borough Council

[1972] RTR 391 (May J)
The defendant Council had placed a skip against the nearside kerb of a one-way street 35 feet wide. It was 6 feet wide and of much the same colour as the road surface and unlighted: the street lighting was adequate but not good. The plaintiff riding a scooter in the early morning before it was light failed to see the skip in time and collided with it.
HELD: As a matter of law, adopting Sachs LJ's view in *Dymond*'s case, the skip was an obstruction and as such constituted a nuisance; it did not matter either that it occupied only 6 feet of a 35 foot-wide road, nor that the street lighting was or was not good. If the view of Edmund Davies LJ in *Dymond*'s case was correct, and in any event on the alternative claim in negligence, it was necessary to decide further whether the obstruction was dangerous. On the facts and the evidence it was. The final question was one of causation: did the presence of the skip play any causative part in the occurrence of the accident or was the plaintiff's failure to keep a proper lookout the sole cause? Bearing in mind all the circumstances, the nature of the road, the lighting and the amount of traffic which had avoided the skip, the existence of the nuisance did play a part but the plaintiff was 50% to blame in failing to keep as good a lookout as he should.

LORRY DROPPING ACID

Pope v Fraser and Southern Rolling and Wire Mills Ltd

(1938) 55 TLR 324, 83 Sol Jo 135
Lorry on highway loaded with carboys of sulphuric acid. Without driver's knowledge and without negligence, one carboy became cracked and the acid ran into the road. After going some distance, the driver was told of the leakage, but did not return for nearly half an hour and took no steps to warn persons on the highway of the danger. In the interval, plaintiff on a motor cycle saw the patch of acid extending across the road, but thought it was water. His machine skidded in the acid and he fell and was burned.
HELD: The driver could have discovered the leakage when he stopped and it was his duty to go back and warn traffic, and defendants were liable.

SMOKING EXHAUST

Tysoe v Davies

[1984] RTR 88, [1983] Crim LR 684 (Skinner J)
The defendant was driving a horsebox which was emitting dense clouds of smoke. A Landrover was travelling behind the horsebox. The plaintiff riding a moped came up behind the Landrover and, thinking it was that vehicle that was causing the smoke, overtook it. Because of the smoke he failed to see the horsebox and crashed into it, sustaining injury. He claimed in negligence and public nuisance.
HELD: The defendant was negligent in driving the horsebox when it was dangerous to do so: it would have been neither difficult nor expensive to have it towed. As to public nuisance the plaintiff was entitled to sue because (1) the clouds of smoke made the highway less commodious to other road users; (2) they were a dangerous obstruction; and (3) the defendant had acted unreasonably. The plaintiff was 20% to blame for failing to keep a proper look out.

4 LEVEL CROSSINGS

Note—Reference should be made to the Highway Code. It contains detailed instructions for the guidance of drivers at all types of railway level crossing.

PUBLIC CROSSINGS

The Railways Clauses Consolidation Act 1845

Note—The Railways Clauses Consolidation Act 1845, s 47, provides as follows:

'47 Provisions in cases where roads are crossed on a level If a railway cross any turnpike road or public carriage road on a level, the company shall erect and at all times maintain good and sufficient gates across such road, on each side of the railway, where the same shall communicate therewith, and shall employ proper persons to open and shut such gates; and such gates shall be kept constantly closed across such road on both sides of the railway, except during the time when horses, cattle, carts, or carriages passing along the same shall have to cross such railway, and such gates shall be of such dimensions and so constructed as when closed to fence in the railway, and prevent cattle or horses passing along the road from entering upon the railway; and the person intrusted with the care of such gates shall cause the same to be closed as soon as such horses, cattle, carts, or carriages shall have passed through the same. . . .'

Ellis v Great Western Rly Co

(1874) LR 9 CP 551, 43 LJCP 304, 30 LT 874 Ex Ch
Railway companies operate under statutory powers and are not analogous to ordinary road traffic cases.

Liability to railway passengers

Stubley v London and North Western Rly Co

(1865) LR 1 Exch 13, 4 H & C 83, 35 LJ Ex 3, 13 LT 376, 29 JP 808, 14 WR 133, 11 Jur NS 956
The railway company are bound, as to rate of speed, and signalling or whistling, or other ordinary precautions, to do everything reasonably necessary to secure the safety of persons using the crossing. The persons who cross the line take the risk, but the railway company must not do anything to prevent such persons from taking care of themselves or expose them to greater peril than that of a level crossing, or they then impose upon themselves an obligation to take other than the usual precautions (*Cliff v Midland Rly Co* (1870) LR 5 QB 258, 22 LT 382, 34 JP 357, 18 WR 456). There is no general duty on railway companies to place watchmen at public footways crossing the railway on the level.

Knapp v Railway Executive

[1949] 2 All ER 508, CA
By the Brighton and Chichester Railway Act 1844 (7 & 8 Vict, c 67) and an Order made under the Act, it was provided that at a level crossing on a public highway the railway company should maintain gates closed across each end of the highway except when trains passed across the road, and employ persons to open and shut the gates so that carriages passing along the highway should not be exposed to danger or damage by trains. The Order was made under a proviso in the Act giving power when 'it will be more conducive to the public safety'. The plaintiff driving a motor car approached when the gates were closed and stopped about a car length away, but the car moved slowly down the slope and struck the gate. The gate was not securely fixed as it should have been and swung across the line, and was struck by a train and the train driver was injured. The driver sued the plaintiff who settled the action and claimed contribution from the railway company.
HELD: The purport of the Act was to protect road users and not persons travelling on the railway. There was an important difference between the 1844 Act and s 47 of the 1845 Act (above), which is in general terms, and s 274 of the 1844 Act which was quite clearly for the protection of users of the highway. Section 68 of the 1845 Act (see *Copps v Payne*, below), which requires the railway company to maintain works for the accommodation of owners and occupiers of adjoining lands, does not impose a duty to fence as to passengers. Citing *Buxton v North Eastern Rly Co* (1868) LR 3 QB 549, 9 B & S 824, 37 LJQB 258, 18 LT 795, a passenger injured through a truck striking a bullock which had got on to the line through a defective fence held not entitled to recover from the railway company. The train driver had no right of action under the Act, and the plaintiff was not entitled to contribution.

Level crossing replaced by subway

Law v Railway Executive and Chigwell UDC

[1949] WN 172, 65 TLR 288, 93 Sol Jo 251 (Hallett J)
A cyclist at 10 pm on 5 October 1949, collided with a pavement and wall which formed part of a sub-way substituted under statutory authority for a public level

crossing. By agreement the county council built the wall and pavement; the railway company were responsible for maintenance of the sub-way and the UDC for lighting. HELD: The railway company would not have been under any legal liability to light the gates, but that did not apply to the wall and pavement; there was no obligation on the UDC to light the road, the UDC and railway company were partners in the works and therefore shared in any liability. They had not taken all reasonable precautions to render it safe, and were liable. The plaintiff knew the obstruction was there and was also negligent. Apportionment 50-50.

Private accommodation crossing becoming public crossing

Note—The Railways Clauses Consolidation Act 1845, s 68, which deals with accommodation crossing provides:

'The company shall make and at all times thereafter maintain the following works for the accommodation of the owners and occupiers of lands adjoining the railway. . . .'

The works include gates. Section 75 provides a penalty if a person using the gates omits to shut and fasten them.

Copps v Payne

[1950] 1 KB 611, [1950] 1 All ER 246, 66 TLR 217, 94 Sol Jo 147, Div Ct
At the time the railway was built, it crossed an occupation road, and gates were erected as an accommodation crossing. Subsequently the road became a public highway. The defendant opened the gates on both sides of the crossing and he and the carriage under his care passed over the crossing. He failed to close the gates. He was prosecuted under s 75. The justices held the obligation was on the railway company and dismissed the summons.
HELD, ON APPEAL: This did not create a liability on the railway company under s 47 in respect of a public carriage road. Their liability remained limited to that under s 75. The test was the liability at the time of the construction of the railway. Case remitted to justices to convict.

Lloyds Bank Ltd v Railway Executive

[1952] 1 All ER 1248, [1952] 1 TLR 1207, 96 Sol Jo 313, CA
Deceased was killed by a railway train whilst driving his motor car across a railway at C. There were gates at the crossing which had to be operated by those using them and a friend travelling with deceased got out of the car to open the gates. The visibility was bad but the deceased without waiting for his friend to signal him, started to cross the level crossing when a train came into collision with the car. Lloyd-Jacob J held the Railway Executive were in breach of their statutory duty and were negligent at common law, but deceased was guilty of contributory negligence and held the Railway Executive 75% to blame.
HELD, ON APPEAL: Apart from statute the defendants were under a duty at common law to prevent danger at these crossings. As the danger increases, so must their precautions increase. They were not bound to turn the crossing into a public level crossing but they must take all reasonable requirements in the shape of warnings, whistles and so forth. Appeal dismissed.

PRIVATE ACCOMMODATION CROSSINGS

Knight v Great Western Rly Co

[1943] 1 KB 105, [1942] 2 All ER 286 (Tucker J)
There is a duty to take reasonable precautions, but the nature of the precaution and the degree of care required are not the same as for a public crossing and may vary very considerably. The difference is merely in the degree of care which is required in the circumstances. There may be cases where, owing to a sharp turn in the railway or the presence of a large number of trees in a cutting obstructing the view, precautions should be taken, but there is no rule that at any private crossing the railway company is bound to use special precautions of some kind. The distance of vision owing to fog was limited to a space of from 30 to 50 yards, and the engine was proceeding at 30 mph. The driver knew of the crossing and that cows were driven across it daily. He had blown his whistle at the whistle board 440 yards from the crossing. He had received the appropriate fog signal, that the line was clear from the railway point of view.

HELD: It was not negligent that he could not pull up within the distance of his vision.

Citing *Cliff v Midland Rly Co* (1870) LR 5 QB 258, 22 LT 382:

'The railway company are to work the railway in a reasonably proper manner; and in crossing a footway on a level the company are bound, as to the mode of working their railway, as to the rate of speed, the provision of men to give warning of approach, the position of warning signals such as a whistle board, and signalling or whistling, or other ordinary precautions to do everything reasonably necessary for the safety of persons crossing.'

Liddiatt v Great Western Rly Co

[1946] KB 545, [1946] 1 All ER 731, CA
The plaintiff's servant was driving eight cattle across a private accommodation crossing over a single track railway line. This crossing was 160 yards east of a public level crossing. There was a signal box, 1,030 yards and a signal 700 yards west of the public crossing. The public crossing gate and the signal were operated by a crossing keeper. The gate of the accommodation crossing on the south side, but not on the north side, was visible to the crossing keeper. The crossing keeper did not have any regard to the accommodation crossing.

HELD: The railway company were under no duty to place a watchman or keeper at the accommodation crossing; nor was there any evidence that the crossing was so placed as to impose on the railway company the duty to take some greater precaution at this spot than is usual in the normal working of a railway. The fact that it was only 160 yards from a public crossing did not enlarge or extend the obligations or duties of the company or the crossing keeper.

Smith v Smith and Railway Executive

[1948] WN 276, 92 Sol Jo 499 (Hilbery J)
The plaintiff was a passenger in a car driven by the first defendant in a private lane over a railway line of the second defendants at an accommodation crossing. The gates were open to the lane. A train ran into the motor car and the plaintiff was injured. The lane had been regularly used by occupiers of the adjacent land and their servants and visitors. The railway company had constructed the gates to close the lane when a train

was approaching and provided a hut for a servant whose duty was to open and shut the gates. The servant left duty at 6 pm and the accident occurred in daylight about 9.40 pm on 10 July 1941. About two years before the accident a swimming pool had been constructed about 100 yards from the crossing and the lane was largely used by private motorists visiting the pool and this must have been known to the railway company's servants, but they took no action to prevent it except to put up a notice near the crossing marked 'Beware of the trains.'
HELD: Citing Pickford J, in *Jenner v South East Rly Co* (1911) 105 LT 131, there was a duty cast on a railway company to take reasonable precautions at an accommodation crossing. The judge rejected the contention of the railway company that their only duty was to refrain from obstructing a right of way. *Johnson v London Midland and Scottish Rly Co* (7 May 1926, unreported) distinguished. In that case the plaintiff was the occupier of land adjacent to the road, knew all about the crossing and was guilty of contributory negligence. The judge found both defendants to blame, and apportioned the blame as to three-fifths to the railway company and two-fifths to the motor driver.

Smith v London Midland and Scottish Rly

[1948] SC 125, 1948 SLT 235, Ct of Sess
A railway company has a duty at every level crossing where members of the public have a right to be to take all reasonable precautions in train operations (and perhaps in other respects) to reduce the danger to a minimum, the nature of the precautions required and the question whether the duty has been fulfilled depending on the circumstances of each case. *Cliff v Midland Rly Co* applied.

Lloyds Bank Ltd v British Transport Commission

[1956] 3 All ER 291, [1956] 1 WLR 1279, 100 Sol Jo 748, CA
A railway built about one hundred years ago crossed a lane to a farm and four cottages and an accommodation crossing was provided for the occupants. Gates were installed, which were regularly closed but were occasionally left open. A ganger who patrolled the line daily inspected the gates and closed them if open. There was a distance of vision to the left for about 350 yards. Owing to the acute angle the car driver would have the difficult task of looking behind across his left shoulder to see if anything was coming along the line.

A car driver when it was quite dark drove his car with his headlights on. The gate had been left open by some unknown person and the driver drove straight through. When crossing the second line of rails the car was hit broadside by a train coming from his left, and the driver killed. His widow sued the railway authorities and contended the crossing had special peculiarities which called for safeguards; that there was negligence in the management of the railway and also negligence of the engine driver; that there ought to have been a whistle board; that the driver ought to have seen the headlights of the car, and that the bend in the railway line and the crossing called for special precautions.
HELD: The railway authority had fulfilled their duty; the engine driver's look-out was properly directing his attention to the signals; he did whistle 175 yards from the crossing; the bend was immaterial as the car driver could see for 350 yards; the driving of a train and of a motor car were two different things. The learned judge was correct in finding that the engine driver was not negligent and that the accident was due solely to the negligence of the car driver in failing to stop in the 30 feet between the gate and the actual line. The facts in the cases of *Smith v London Midland and Scottish Rly Co*

(above) and *Lloyds Bank Ltd v Railway Executive* (p 286, above) were different. Appeal dismissed.

Hazell v British Transport Commission

[1958] 1 All ER 116, [1958] 1 WLR 169, 102 Sol Jo 124 (Pearson J)
A farm tractor was being driven across an accommodation crossing, on a single branch line. On a stretch of 16 miles there were 33 level crossings most of which were accommodation crossings. Possibly two or three farm vehicles used the crossing each day. The gates were padlocked except when opened by a user. The crossing was so wide that the tractor could stand between the gates and the railway line. Shortly before the crossing the line ran round a left-hand bend with a slow down gradient of about 1 in 500. In ordinary weather the train could be seen several hundred yards away. There was a bad fog, visibility varying from place to place. As the tractor was being driven over the line a train ran into it. The train driver had shut off steam and was coasting, there being a station about a mile or one and a half miles ahead, so that the sound of the exhaust blast had ceased; the line was wet so that the train made less noise than usual, and the effect of the fog was to smother the sound to some extent, but the train could have been heard by anyone at the crossing if there was no other noise, and the judge drew the inference that the tractor driver failed to switch off his engine.
HELD: The principle to be applied is that in the absence of special circumstances, the engine driver is not expected to reduce speed or whistle, and the Commission are not expected to erect a whistle-board. An engine driver is not expected to reduce speed to five miles an hour because of fog. If the engine driver is aware of something on, or likely to come on, the line, he must take proper steps to avoid an accident. There are no special circumstances in this case, and no liability on the Commission or the engine driver, and the action fails.

Kemshead v British Transport Commission

[1958] 1 All ER 119, [1958] 1 WLR 173, 102 Sol Jo 122, CA
An accommodation level crossing for a road leading to a farm and some farm cottages had a notice on the gates requiring users to shut and fasten the gates. The plaintiff was a passenger in a car going to the farm. He had used the crossing on at least twenty occasions and knew of the notice. The gates had been left open by some person unknown and apparently the car driver crossed without stopping. It was a foggy morning and as the car crossed the railway lines, a train ran into it. The plaintiff and driver were severely injured and another passenger was killed. The plaintiff alleged that no whistle was sounded and no indication was given of the approach of the train.
HELD: At an accommodation crossing there is no obligation on a railway company to supply watchmen or have signals or bells, nor to whistle unless there are special circumstances where people may reasonably be expected. Citing Scrutton LJ in *Burrows v Southern Rly Co* ((1933), unreported, read by Tucker J in *Knight v Great Western Rly Co* (p 287, above)) a sharp turn in the railway, or the presence of a large number of trees in a cutting obstructing the view might call for some reasonable precautions even at a private crossing. There was nothing calling for special precautions. The presence of fog calls for special precautions by the person crossing. There were no special conditions applying to this crossing. There must be judgment for the Commission.

Skeen v British Railways Board

[1976] RTR 281 (Latey J)
Three cottages were reached by crossing a railway at an accommodation crossing approached down a lane from which the railway could not be seen. At the crossing the visibility to the right along the railway was limited to 100 yards by a sharp curve. On 14 June a van was being driven over the crossing when it was hit by a train from the right travelling at about 50 mph. The van driver and passenger were both killed. Though there had been no previous accidents the occupier of one of the cottages had complained to British Railways about seven weeks earlier about the danger at the crossing. A meeting had been held with British Railways representatives when it was agreed that the crossing was dangerous. Various safety precautions were canvassed such as the erection of whistle boards or the provision of a telephone to the signal box, but nothing had been done. The defendants pleaded that both the van driver and passenger were negligent in not having the passenger cross the line on foot and direct the driver from the other side, from which visibility of trains was 200 yards.
HELD: There was a duty on the defendants to take reasonable care not to imperil those using the crossing. What is reasonable depends on the particular circumstances of the crossing, its layout and any special dangers. The fact of there having been no previous accident was immaterial since the danger was admitted seven weeks earlier. Precautionary measures should have been taken as a matter of urgency. The direct telephone to the signal box was the best method as was in fact done after the accident. The defendants were liable in negligence. The passenger was not negligent since decisions are in the hands of the driver of a motor vehicle. The driver was not negligent in not sending the passenger across the line to direct him because the increase in visibility would have reduced the danger so minimally as to be insignificant.

5 TREES

FALLING BRANCH

Noble v Harrison

[1926] 2 KB 332, 95 LJKB 813, Div Ct
A branch of a beech tree growing on the defendant's land overhung a highway at a height of 30 feet above the ground. In fine weather the branch suddenly broke, fell upon the plaintiff's vehicle, which was passing along the highway, and damaged it. In an action by the plaintiff claiming in respect of the damage to his vehicle, the county court judge found that neither the defendant nor his servants knew that the branch was dangerous, and that the fracture was due to a latent defect not discoverable by any reasonably careful inspection, but he held that the defendant was liable (1) upon the principle of *Rylands v Fletcher* and (2) for a nuisance.
HELD: (reversing the decision of the county court judge): (1) That the *Rylands v Fletcher* principle had no application, inasmuch as a tree was not in itself a dangerous thing, and to grow trees was one of the natural uses of the soil; (2) that the mere fact that the branch overhung the highway did not make it a nuisance seeing that it did not obstruct the free passage of the highway, and although the branch proved to be a danger the defendant was not liable, inasmuch as he had not created the danger and

had no knowledge, actual or imputed, of its existence. (*Barker v Herbert* [1911] 2 KB 633 applied.) (Observations of Best J in *Earl of Lonsdale v Nelson* (1823) 2 B & C 302 and *Tarry v Ashton* (1876) 1 QBD 314, distinguished.)

FALLING TREE

Cunliffe v Bankes

[1945] 1 All ER 459 (Singleton J)
A motor cyclist riding along a road in the dark collided with a tree which had fallen across the road. It was an elm, 50 years old, about 40 feet high, growing about 20 feet inside a park wall 6 feet high. It had been attacked by honey fungus. The estate agent had inspected each year when the trees were in foliage, which was performing his duty, but the tree showed no sign of danger.
HELD: No evidence of negligence. As to nuisance, the defendant was not liable unless (1) he caused the nuisance, or (2) by the neglect of some duty he allowed it to arise, or (3) when it has arisen without his own act or default, he omits to remedy it within a reasonable time after he became or ought to have become aware of it.

Brown v Harrison

[1947] WN 191, 177 LT 281, 63 TLR 484, CA
The plaintiff was walking along the highway when he was injured by the fall of a tree growing in a spinney on the side of the road. At about the time of the accident there was a gust of wind at 58 mph registered at an observatory 10 or 15 miles away, and two other perfectly sound trees in the neighbourhood were blown down.

The defendant owner of the tree was in the habit of passing the spinney daily and often in and about it, and it never occurred to him that the tree was a source of danger or he would have removed the danger. It did not occur to anyone that there was any real likelihood of danger.
HELD: The tree was in a defective and therefore dangerous condition. There is no duty on the landowner to have a periodical examination by an expert. It is impossible to define the duty to call in expert advice and have expert examination, but in the ordinary case a landlord discharges his duty if he takes reasonable steps to remove any dangers of which he becomes aware, but if there is a danger which is apparent, not only to the expert but to the ordinary layman, which the ordinary layman can see with his own eyes if he chooses to use them, and he fails to do so, and injury is occasioned to someone on the highway, the owner is responsible.

The tree had the appearance of being dead at the top for many years. It was not quite dead all the way down, but the leaf in spring was very restricted and less than a normal healthy tree and did not blossom. The ordinary layman with ordinary powers of observation would have noted this, and that it could fall across the highway. In *Noble v Harrison* it was said a tree in decay may become a dangerous object. If the owner knew of the danger and did not remedy it, his liability would be established beyond controversy. This tree by reason of its decay had become a dangerous object, sufficiently apparent to impose on the landowner the duty of taking precautionary measures. The defendant was liable (1946) Birmingham Assizes, 11 December (Stable J).
HELD, ON APPEAL: The landowner's duty was correctly stated that if there was a danger apparent, not only to the expert, but to the ordinary layman, if he chose to notice it, the owner should take precautionary measures. A dying tree at a certain stage became a danger which should be apparent to the ordinary landowner.

Lambourn v London Brick Co

(1950) 156 Estates Gazette 146
The plaintiff's husband was killed in a collision with elm trees that had been blown across a road from the defendants' land.
HELD: There was nothing to indicate to the defendants that the trees were dangerous; defendants not liable.

Caminer v Northern and London Investment Trust Ltd

[1951] AC 88, [1950] 2 All ER 486, 66 TLR (pt 2) 184, [1950] WN 361, 94 Sol Jo 518, HL
A large elm tree in the forecourt of a block of flats fell on a car passing along the highway. The wind was blowing in strong squally gusts from time to time but was not exceptional. Defendants became owners in 1940. The tree was a large, well-grown elm between 120 and 130 years old. After it fell it was evident that the base of the tree had been affected by a disease not uncommon in an elm tree of elm butt rot. The disease was of long standing and must have been in the roots long before the defendants became owners. There was nothing in the appearance of the tree to indicate that it was in any way diseased. The tree carried a crown of about 35 feet. It had not been trimmed or lopped for a great many years. Elms are shallow-rooted trees and notoriously treacherous and apt to fall. The owners shortly before the accident had given orders to lop and top the trees in the forecourt and but for the Easter holidays this tree would probably have been pollarded or topped before the accident. There was evidence that elm trees should be inspected every five to seven years.
HELD, ON APPEAL to the House of Lords: The defendants were not liable.

Per Lord Porter: I cannot accept the view that the defendants were negligent merely because they failed to call in an expert to advise as to the possible existence of an unsuspected and undiscoverable disease, even though an expert, if called in, might have recommended topping and lopping.

I do not regard the evidence as establishing that elm trees are so plainly a danger as to require their being lopped and topped lest they should fall, though to all external appearance they are sound and no inspection would raise a doubt as to their general condition.

Per Lord Oaksey: The defendants had performed their duty by employing a well-known firm of estate agents to manage this property and they in turn employed a timber contractor.

Quinn v Scott

[1965] 2 All ER 588, [1965] 1 WLR 1004, 109 Sol Jo 498 (Glyn-Jones J)
At a place where the Doncaster-Nottingham road runs alongside Clumber Park a belt of trees inside the park bordered the road. They included a beech tree about 200 years old having four or five limbs growing 70 feet or so almost vertically from the top of a bole about 20 feet high. On a windy day part of the tree split away from the rest and fell across the road causing a collision of vehicles in which the plaintiff was injured. The tree had reached an age at which decay could be apprehended. There was, before the accident, some appearance of unhealthiness in the thinness of the foliage and indications of die-back, but these had not been reported to the owners, the National Trust.
HELD: (1) A landowner on whose land this belt of trees stood, adjoining a busy highway, was under a duty to provide himself with skilled advice about the safety of the trees; (2) the National Trust had fulfilled this duty by employing a forestry

adviser, a land agent, a forester and seven woodmen who inspected the tree several times a year; but (3) there had been a failure to report the signs of decay to the land agent and the Trust should have known of them; (4) a reasonable landowner with knowledge of these signs would have had the tree felled. The National Trust must be held liable.

Lynch v Hetherton

(1991) 2 IR 405
The plaintiff was driving along the defendant's land when a tree fell and damaged his car. Externally this tree showed no signs of decay but was rotten on the inside. The trial judge found the defendant liable to the plaintiff but reduced the plaintiff's award for contributory negligence. The defendant appealed.
HELD: The plaintiff's claim should fail. The defendant regularly inspected his trees and exercised the degree of care which a reasonable and prudent landowner would have exercised in ensuring his trees were not a danger to the users of the highway.

DAMAGE FROM POLLEN

Coachcraft v Lancegays Safety Glass Co

(1938) City Press, 15 July, City of London Ct
Repairers placed car under lime tree. Lime pollen fell or was driven on to the car by rain. The acid concentration from the lime pollen pitted and damaged the cellulose and lacquer treatment of the car body.
HELD: Repairers were negligent as bailees and liable for damage.

COLLIDING WITH TREE

Radley v London Passenger Transport Board

[1942] 1 All ER 433, 166 LT 285, 106 JP 164, 58 TLR 364, 86 Sol Jo 147 (Humphreys J)
On a country road an overhanging branch of a tree on the side of the road broke a window in a bus and injured a passenger. The accident occurred at midday, and the tree was clearly visible along the road. A witness said he had seen the defendants' buses brush against the trees on the road on several occasions. The defendants submitted no case and called no evidence.
HELD: Prima facie case of negligence and defendants were liable. It was immaterial that the obstruction was not on the ground. It was visible to the driver. It might be different if a branch broke off suddenly in a gale.

Hale v Hants and Dorset Motor Services Ltd

[1947] 2 All ER 628, CA
Plaintiff was a passenger on top of a bus. Just after the bus moved off from a stop, the near side upper deck came in contact with the branches of a tree standing on the edge of the pavement and glass on the upper deck was broken. A splinter entered plaintiff's eye, which had to be removed. He sued the bus company and the corporation.

The judge of assize held that the corporation ought to have contemplated that a bus would pull close to the tree near a bus stop, and should have pruned a badly shaped tree leaning towards the highway. The road camber caused the bus to tilt slightly, but the bus would hit the overhanging branch apart from the camber.

He held the corporation two-thirds, and the bus company one-third, to blame.

Both defendants appealed. On appeal it appeared from the evidence that the projection of the branches was 7½ and 6½ ins respectively. It was at night. There was a brilliant street lamp between the driver and the tree as he came round a roundabout.

HELD, ON APPEAL: The corporation had planted the tree on the side of the highway under the provisions of the Road Improvement Act 1925, s 1(1) (now replaced by the Highways Act 1980, s 96) which empowers a highway authority to cause trees to be planted in any highway maintainable by them. Section 1(2) (now replaced by the Highways Act 1980, s 96(6)) is as follows: 'No such tree . . . shall be placed, laid out or allowed to remain in such a situation as to hinder the reasonable use of the highway by any person entitled to the use thereof.'

HELD: The passengers on the omnibus were persons entitled to the use of the highway, the omnibus was making reasonable use of it, the tree hindered reasonable use and the corporation had allowed the tree to remain in that position. It was not unreasonable for the driver to drive very close to the kerb. It was only the tree which made the danger. The driver was not to be blamed for not observing and estimating the overhang, but he knew the trees were potential sources of danger and should have acted on the footing that it might overhang and give it a wide berth. Both appeals dismissed.

J H Dewhurst Ltd v Ratcliffe

(1951) 101 L Jo 361 (Judge Reid)

Plaintiffs' motor car in daylight and clear weather was being driven along a road 16 to 18 feet wide at 20 to 25 mph, when a single-deck omnibus approached from the opposite direction. The car driver in passing brushed the hedge on the near side with the car and collided with a tree stump nearly 4 feet high which was 1 or 2 inches inside the hedge and hidden by the leaves and foliage. Plaintiffs sued the defendant who was the owner and occupier of the farm adjoining the road. The tree stump was wholly on the defendant's land but did not overhang the road although it was less than 6 inches clear of it. The defendant trimmed the top and inside of the hedge and the local council cut back the hedge from the road.

HELD:The claim in negligence failed because defendant owed no legal duty to the plaintiffs. As regards nuisance, the car driver was not entitled to brush innocent looking leaves and twigs at the roadside and complain if he sustained damage because of something lying behind them. Verdict for defendant.

British Road Services Ltd v Slater

[1964] 1 All ER 816, [1964] 1 WLR 498, 108 Sol Jo 357 (Lord Parker CJ)

A lorry belonging to the plaintiffs was being driven at night along the A41 road at a place where it adjoined farm land belonging to the defendants. The roadway was 20 feet wide: along the side of it was a strip of gravel a foot wide beyond which was a grass verge or bank. Standing in the verge about 2 ft 6 in from the gravel edge was an oak tree of considerable age which had a stout branch growing towards the road for about 2 feet and then turned upwards. The driver of the lorry on approaching this place had to keep well to the nearside to avoid another of the plaintiff's lorries which was approaching from the opposite direction. As the first lorry passed the tree a packing case stacked on the back of the lorry struck the branch causing another packing case to fall off into the path of the lorry. Damage was caused both to this lorry and the packing case, for which the plaintiffs claimed against the defendants on the ground that they had created or continued a nuisance in the form of the branch of the tree. The defendants had owned the land on both sides of the road since 1936 but the tree had been sown long before that, but not before the highway, which was ancient, had been dedicated. Neither the defendants nor the highway authority nor the driver of the lorry (who had very frequently passed along the road) had ever considered the branch to be a hazard.

HELD: (1) Looked at objectively, the branch prevented the convenient use of the highway and was a nuisance; (2) even though the highway authority might have a right or duty to remove obstructions the defendants were not sufficiently dispossessed of the verge or of the tree to exonerate them from liability for an obstruction created by the branch; (3) although the branch was a nuisance the defendants could not be presumed to know of it because no one had ever thought it was a hazard. Only the fortuitous circumstance that two heavy lorries happened to meet at that point in the dark had shown this. The defendant had not created the nuisance since the tree was already there when they acquired the land. They could be liable for continuing it only if they had knowledge or means of knowledge so that they knew or should have known of the nuisance in time to correct it and obviate its mischievous effects (quoting Lord Wright in *Sedleigh-Denfield v O'Callaghan* [1940] AC 880). This rule was not limited to cases where the nuisance was due to a hidden defect but applied also where, as here, the defendants had no reason to suppose it was a nuisance. The defendants were not liable.

CHAPTER 10
Bailments

1 INTRODUCTION

Note—Bailment is a delivery of goods from one person, called the bailor, to another person called the bailee, for some purpose, upon a condition, express or implied, that, after the purpose has been fulfilled, they shall be redelivered to the bailor, or otherwise dealt with according to his directions, or kept till he reclaims them.

Bailments are of three kinds:

(1) Those for the exclusive benefit of the bailor; as, if A leaves plate with B to keep safely and securely without reward. He, the bailee, is only responsible in respect of gross negligence.

(2) Those for the mutual benefit of bailor and bailee; as, if C lets a horse to D for so much per hour; or if E gives F (a tailor) clothes to repair, in the course of his trade, etc. The bailee must exercise ordinary care.

(3) Those for the exclusive benefit of the bailee; as, if G lends H a book to read, without reward. The bailee is responsible for even slight negligence.

Questions of bailment may arise in the case of a car park, of a carrier, of owner's risk and contracting out of negligence, or garage of cars, and of repairs to car, as well as in keeper cases.

The onus is on the bailee to prove that loss or damage to the goods has occurred without negligence on his part.

Metaalhandel v Ardfields Transport Ltd

[1988] 1 Lloyd's Rep 197, [1987] 2 FTLR 319
The defendants were asked to collect goods on behalf of the plaintiffs and store them at their warehouse. In fact they took them to the second defendant's premises from where they were subsequently stolen.

Gatehouse J concluded on the evidence that the defendants were not bailees of the goods, as they were never actually in their possession. The defendants had entered into an authorised subcontract and thus became 'quasi-bailees'. Whilst that entitled the defendants to subcontract performance of a contract, they remained responsible for the faults of the subcontractor, and in this case the defendants were liable to the plaintiffs.

Transcontainer Express v Custodian Security

[1988] 1 Lloyd's Rep 128, [1988] 1 FTLR 54, CA
The plaintiffs subcontracted part of a carriage of goods contract to Crossland Haulage Limited. Those subcontractors deposited the sealed load at premises protected by the defendant security company. The container was subsequently stolen whilst there and the plaintiffs brought an action for breach of the duty of care they were owed by the defendants or in the alternative for breach of duty as sub-bailees to take all reasonable care of the container and its contents.

Boreham J dismissed the plaintiff's claim. They were not bailees and their duty to the owners of the goods was in contract only. It therefore followed that the defendants were not sub-bailees and their limited duty only extended to the owners. The Court of Appeal dismissed the appeal for there was no evidence that Crossland were anything other than subcontractors, and the plaintiffs had failed to establish 'possessory title' in the goods, as defined by Lord Brandon in *Leigh & Sullivan Ltd v Aliakmon Shipping Ltd, The Aliakmon* [1986] 2 Lloyd's Rep 1.

2 BAILEE'S LIABILITY FOR LOSS OR DAMAGE

ONUS OF PROOF ON BAILEE

Coldman v Hill

[1919] 1 KB 443, 88 LJKB 491, 120 LT 412, CA
The plaintiff sent cattle to the defendant for agistment. Two cows were stolen without default of the defendant but he did not report the loss to the plaintiff or the police nor make any effort himself to find them.

HELD: The defendant was liable. He was to blame for not reporting the loss or trying to trace the cows, and it was no defence that the plaintiff could not prove that the cows would have been traced if this had been done. The onus was on the defendant to prove, if he could, that the cows would not have been recovered if he had made enquiries.

Global Dress Co Ltd v Boase & Co Ltd

[1966] 2 Lloyd's Rep 72, CA
The defendants, master porters, received 30 cases of dresses for the plaintiffs at their dockside shed. A few days later one case was found to be missing. The county court

judge found that the defendants' security system was good but said he could not understand how the case could have been removed without being seen if the watchman, checkers or others of the defendants' servants were doing their duty properly. He held the defendants had not discharged the onus on them as bailees.
HELD, ON APPEAL: The judge's decision should not be upset. The onus was on the defendants as bailees to show that they had taken reasonable care of the plaintiffs' goods. It was not sufficient for them to prove that their system was to have a watchman on duty. There was evidence on which the judge could find that the watchman had not been sufficiently vigilant but even if he had been left in doubt on this point the defendants still could not have succeeded because the onus was upon them.

British Road Services Ltd v AV Crutchley & Co Ltd

[1968] 1 All ER 811, [1968] 1 Lloyd's Rep 271, CA
The plaintiffs arranged for the defendants to receive a lorry load of whisky worth £9,000 at their warehouse preparatory to being loaded on board ship for export. The whisky was unloaded from the lorry on to a trailer which was left overnight, with tractor attached, facing the doors of the warehouse ready to be driven to the ship on the following morning. During the night thieves entered the warehouse through a skylight, opened the doors and drove away the whole load. The defendants had a contract with third parties to send a patrolman to the premises from time to time during the night but he had failed to make all the visits required of him.
HELD: The onus was on the defendants to prove that the loss did not result from negligence on their part (*Coldman v Hill*, above). On the facts, the defendants' system of protection was not adequate in relation to the special risks involved and they had failed to discharge the burden on them of proving that the loss was not caused by negligence on their part. The defendants must accept responsibility for the negligence of the third party's patrolman even though they were independent contractors. A bailee cannot escape from the responsibility for taking proper care of the goods bailed merely by employing sub-contractors for that purpose.

Transmotors Ltd v Robertson Buckley & Co Ltd

[1970] 1 Lloyd's Rep 224 (Mocatta J)
The defendants, road hauliers, contracted with the plaintiffs to deliver consignments of food by lorry from Liverpool to places in the London area. The defendants' driver, Davenport, left Liverpool at 5 am; late in the afternoon he reported to Plumstead Police Station that his lorry and load had been hijacked when he stopped on a lay-by on the A4 near Maidenhead at about 1 pm. He said he had been forced into a van and dumped four hours later at Woolwich. His lorry was found empty at Bow the following day. There was no evidence to corroborate his story but it was not positively disproved. He had been convicted of theft when working as a docker some months earlier and his employees knew of this when they engaged him. His account of his movements up to the time of the hijacking was unsupported by any other evidence. Nine months after the hijacking he was sacked by the defendants after another conviction for theft. The plaintiffs claimed for the loss of the goods.
HELD: If the servant of a bailee in the course of his employment stole goods bailed then the bailee was liable to the bailor for the loss of the goods—*Morris v Martin* (p 145, above). In order for a bailee to escape liability he had to prove he had taken all reasonable care in relation to the goods including proof that the goods had not been stolen by his employees (though it was highly desirable that the bailors should give

specific notice of their intention to allege theft, if that was their case, either in the pleadings or otherwise). It was not necessary for the court to decide positively whether Davenport was a party to the theft but merely whether on the balance of probabilities the defendants had exercised reasonable care in regard to the goods and their safety and had negatived Davenport having acted as an accomplice. On the evidence the defendants had not discharged the burden of proof upon them. Judgment for the plaintiffs.

REPAIRER

Cooper v Dempsey

(1961) 105 Sol Jo 320, CA

The defendant had a garage, petrol station and café on a main road 12 miles from Plymouth. Behind the premises was a yard used as a car park with access from it to a minor road through a gate. The yard was used for storing the defendant's own vehicles and for parking cars of café patrons and cars brought in for repairs. The plaintiff took his car for repair on 18 October 1959, and left it on the defendant's premises. The defendant left it in the car park with the ignition key in the switch, the doors unlocked and without supervision. Between 5.30 pm and 10 pm on 21 October it was stolen and was later found elsewhere in a damaged condition. The county court judge held that the defendant had done his duty as a custodian of the car.

HELD, ON APPEAL: The test was what a reasonable and prudent man looking after his own property would do. Leaving the car in the yard unsupervised and with the ignition key in the switch was not exercising proper care. The defendant had not discharged the onus of proving that without the absence of reasonable care this car had disappeared. The plaintiff was entitled to damages for the damage to the car which was not too remote. The damage was foreseeable.

Cowan v Blackwill Motor Caravan Conversions Ltd

[1978] RTR 421, CA

The plaintiff took his motor caravan to the defendants for repair. It was difficult to engage any of the forward gears and the reverse gear could not be engaged at all. The defendants told him to leave it in a sidestreet alongside their wired-in compound. He was told they would put it in the compound as soon as possible. The sidestreet was a cul-de-sac; the vehicle was left facing downhill towards the dead end. It was not put in the compound on the following day because other vehicles were put in in preference to the plaintiff's, since it could not be taken away except by pushing it backwards uphill. On the second night there it was stolen.

HELD: The issue was whether the defendants, as bailees of the vehicle, had discharged the onus of showing that the vehicle was lost without negligence on their part. The standard of care required of the defendants was that which was to be expected in the relevant circumstances from a prudent owner, and was no greater than the standard exhibited by thousands of vehicle owners who immobilise their vehicles appropriately by steering locks, locking doors, removing the distributor arm or by other means. On the facts the defendants had not been negligent.

Idnani v Elisha (t/a Grafton Service Station)

[1979] RTR 488, CA

The defendant was proprietor of a service station on a main route out of London, comprising a forecourt, two petrol pumps, a kiosk and two repair bays. The enclosed premises where vehicles would be under lock and key could accommodate only three vehicles: the defendant handled many more than this and there were often seven or eight vehicles left out on the forecourt overnight. The plaintiff, a motor dealer for whom the defendant had previously repaired vehicles, took a Jaguar E-type car to him for repair. The defendant removed the cylinder head in the course of the repairs; consequently the car could not be moved under its own power. It was left locked on the forecourt. Overnight someone towed it away; when subsequently recovered it had been severely damaged by the removal of components. The plaintiff sued for the damage done. In the pleadings both parties pleaded contractual terms; the plaintiff that it was an express term of their dealings with each other that no car of his would be left out on the forecourt overnight; the defendant that there was a term to be implied from their dealings that he was at liberty to keep a car entrusted to him by the plaintiff on the forecourt overnight. In the course of the hearing both these pleas were expressly abandoned. The county court judge nevertheless held as a fact that the plaintiff did tell the defendant that he wanted his cars kept in at night. The judge said it was in every way foreseeable that someone would come on the forecourt and help themselves to components from the car. He held that the defendant had not discharged the burden of proof on him to show that he had discharged the duty of care he owed as bailee.

HELD, ON APPEAL: This was not right. The finding of the judge that the plaintiff had asked for his cars to be kept in at night, taken with his express abandonment of the alleged contractual term, must imply that the defendant had not given the plaintiff reason to believe that he would do so. Whether there was negligence or not depended on the circumstances of any particular case; the degree of risk on the one hand had to be balanced against the degree of practicability of taking effective steps to prevent that loss on the other. Was it in all the circumstances reasonably practicable for lock-up accommodation? The decisive consideration was that the car was not placed inside because it was immobile and difficult to manoeuvre in the morning to get out. The judge had given too little consideration to the practical difficulties confronting the defendant of which the plaintiff was well aware. Appeal allowed. *Cowan v Blackwill Motor Caravan Conversions Ltd* (above) applied.

Note—See also *Smith v Taylor*, p 233, above.

HOTEL KEEPER

Adams (Durham) Ltd and Day v Trust Houses Ltd

[1960] 1 Lloyd's Rep 380

The second plaintiff, driving a car owned by the first plaintiff, arrived at the defendant's hotel some time after 10 pm to stay the night. The night porter unlocked the hotel garage for him and he put the car in. The night porter locked the garage and remained in possession of the keys. There was a charge of 2s for using the garage. During the night the night porter took the car out for some purpose of his own, ran into a traffic island and wrecked it.

HELD: (1) There was a bailment of the car to the defendants, not a mere licence to park the car on the defendant's premises. *Ashby v Tolhurst* (p 305, below) distinguished. (2) As bailees for safe custody for reward the defendants were under a legal obligation to take all reasonable care of the plaintiff's car. They had delegated the safe custody of the car to their night porter and were liable not so much as being vicariously responsible for his torts when driving about the streets, but on the basis that they had entrusted to him the fulfilment of their own contractual duty and that duty was not performed. *Central Motors, Glasgow Ltd v Cessnock Garage Co* (above), followed. (3) On the facts, clauses excluding liability for the defendants had not been brought to the notice of the second plaintiff and did not form part of the contract, but even if they had, there was a fundamental breach of the contract of bailment bringing it to an end along with any conditions forming part of it.

Note—There is statutory liability on a hotel proprietor under the Hotel Proprietors Act 1956 to make good loss or damage to a guest's property even when not due to fault of the proprietor or his staff, but by s 2(2) of the Act this liability does not extend to any vehicle or any property left therein.

COACH PROPRIETOR

Houghland v RR Low (Luxury Coaches) Ltd

[1962] 1 QB 694, [1962] 2 All ER 159, [1962] 2 WLR 1015, 106 Sol Jo 243, CA
The plaintiff was a passenger in the defendant's motor coach on a journey from Southampton to Hoylake. Her suitcase was put with other passengers' luggage in the boot of the coach at Southampton and the boot was locked. When the coach stopped during the journey for the passengers to take tea it could not be restarted. The defendants' driver telephoned the defendants who sent a relief coach. Whilst the driver of the relief coach was having his tea the driver of the first coach with the help of the passengers transferred the luggage from the boot of his coach to the boot of the other which was then locked. When the relief coach arrived at Hoylake the plaintiff's suitcase was not in the boot and could not be found. She claimed the value of the case and contents from the defendants.
HELD: The defendants were liable. They were bailees of the suitcase and had failed to discharge the onus which was on them of proving that the suitcase had been lost without default on their part. It made no difference whether the case was put in detinue or whether it was treated as an action for negligence. It had been admitted in argument that the plaintiff, by proving the delivery of the suitcase at Southampton and its non-return on the arrival of the coach at Hoylake, made out a prima facie case. That prima facie case stood unless and until it was rebutted. The burden was on the defendants to adduce evidence in rebuttal. They could discharge that burden by proving that what in fact did happen happened without any default on their part or by showing that, although they could not put their fingers on what actually did happen to the suitcase, nevertheless, whatever did occur occurred notwithstanding all reasonable care having been exercised by them throughout the journey. The first coach had stood for three hours in the dark waiting for the relief coach and the luggage had then been transferred by passengers and stowed in the relief coach by one driver only, with no supervision at all over the unloading of the first coach. The defendants had failed to discharge the onus of proof on them.

BAILEE'S OWN LOSS

O'Sullivan v Williams

[1992] 3 All ER 385, [1992] RTR 402
The defendant's excavator badly damaged the first plaintiff's car (which at the time

was parked outside the second plaintiff's home) when it fell off his trailer. The first plaintiff sought to recover the value of the car and damages for loss of use. The second plaintiff (his girlfriend) who had borrowed the vehicle whilst he was on holiday claimed for loss of use and for nervous shock.

The trial judge dismissed the nervous shock claim but awarded £400 in respect of the loss of use, despite the fact that the first plaintiff's claim had already been settled. The Court of Appeal allowed the defendant's appeal, for a bailee could not recover damages in circumstances where that loss had already been recovered by the bailor. It was for the bailor to account to the bailee if there were an enforceable agreement between them.

Note—The Court of Appeal accepted that the second plaintiff had 'possessory title' in the vehicle as bailee at the time of the damage.

3 CAR PARK

LIABILITY FOR LOSS BY THEFT

Ashby v Tolhurst

[1937] 2 KB 242, [1937] 2 All ER 837, 106 LJKB 783, 156 LT 518, 53 TLR 770, 81 Sol Jo 419, CA
The owner of a car left it on a private parking ground, paid 1s and received a ticket from the attendant headed 'Seaway Car Park, Car Park Ticket' containing receipt for 1s and the provision: 'The proprietors do not take any responsibility for the safe custody of any cars or articles therein nor for any damage to the cars or articles however caused . . . all cars being left in all respects entirely at their owners' risk.'

The car park attendant handed the car to a man who described himself as the owner's friend. The car was locked and this man had not the ticket nor the key, but was able to put his hand through the windscreen and free the car. The negligence of the attendant was admitted.
HELD, by Court of Appeal: (1) Relation of parties was licensor and licensee and car park proprietor was under no liability whatever for the car; (2) there was not a misdelivery of the car; (3) assuming there was a contract of bailment and of misdelivery of car, the conditions on the ticket relieved proprietors of all liability; (4) no term could be implied that the car should not be parted with without production of the ticket.

Note—See also *Adams (Durham) Ltd and Day v Trust Houses Ltd*, p 303, above.

Preston v Ascot Central Car Park Ltd

(1954) Times, 28 January (Pilcher J)
The plaintiff on 18 June 1952, went to Ascot races and left his car in the car park of the Ascot Central Park Ltd, to whom he had paid 15s and received a ticket with the words on it 'The proprietor does not hold himself responsible for any damage to the motor car, or loss by fire or theft of any property stored here, but all due care will be taken.' The car was stolen.

HELD: There was no sufficient delivery to constitute a contract of bailment; the plaintiff had locked the doors and closed the windows to prevent the car being tampered with. There was only a licence to park and no duty was owed to the car owner. The words 'all due care will be taken' merely meant that the attendant would be careful in parking and unparking cars, and no more; *Ashby v Tolhurst* followed.

BRS (Contracts) Ltd v Colney Motor Engineering Co Ltd

(1958) Times, 27 November, CA
A lorry which was carrying cigarettes worth £32,000 from Ashton-under-Lyme to London, stopped for the night at the defendants' car park. The place where the lorry had been parked consisted of a large floodlit yard surrounded by a fence 6 feet high, topped with barbed wire. There was an adjacent petrol station, and an attendant was on duty night and day. Whilst the lorry was parked, part of the load, of the value of £312, was stolen. A standard charge of 1s 6d a night was made for parking irrespective of the value of the contents of the lorry, which was locked up by the driver, who kept the keys and who drove away when he liked. At the trial of an action by the lorry owners the judge held the lorry had been bailed and awarded them £312.
HELD, ON APPEAL: The defendants exercised no control over the lorry. There was no bailment. The facts pointed to the place being a car park rather than a place in the nature of a closed garage. Appeal allowed.

Note—See also *Cooper v Dempsey*, p 302, above.

BG Transport Service v Marston Motor Co

[1970] 1 Lloyd's Rep 371 (Bean J)
The defendants were owners of a large garage with a car park at the rear enclosed by fencing. Drivers could leave vehicles in the car park on payment or by pre-arrangement. A driver on parking a vehicle paid a charge and received a ticket which bore a printed notice relieving the defendants of liability for all risks and losses and containing the words 'On production of this ticket by any person, the vehicle be released to the bearer. No responsibility can be accepted by us for any delay in releasing the vehicle resulting from the loss of this ticket.' The plaintiffs' driver left a loaded van in the car park overnight having paid the charge and received a ticket. On returning the following morning he found the van had gone. The defendant's night watchman, who had come on duty at midnight, said that at about 2 am he was in the petrol pump attendant's office where the keys of parked vehicles were kept when a man knocked and asked for the keys of the vehicle, mentioning the number of the ticket. The man had then taken the keys and driven the vehicle away. He had not surrendered, nor been asked for, the driver's part of the ticket. There was evidence that not all drivers left their keys in the office nor, if they were regular parkers, did they always have tickets. The plaintiffs claimed the value of the load, which was stolen, on the basis that there was a bailment and that the defendants were at fault in parting with the vehicle without receiving or seeing the ticket. They cited an Australian case of *City of Sydney v West* (1965) 144 CLR 481 in which there was held to have been a bailment where the attendant at the exit from a parking station was under a duty not to permit vehicles to proceed out of the parking station except on production of a ticket.
HELD: The present case was one of a licence only and not a bailment. The case of *Ashby v Tolhurst* (above) was on one side of the line between licences and bailments and the Australian case was on the other. The *Ashby v Tolhurst* style of parking, with a

nominal payment and no formalities to collect the car, would result in a licence; equally, parking within a bounded area in circumstances under which there is no access to the vehicle except through a special entrance, and where the vehicle can be withdrawn by presentation of a ticket and not otherwise, is a bailment. The present case was similar to *BRS (Contracts) Ltd v Colney Motor Engineering Co Ltd* (p 306, above). The words on the ticket did not mean that a vehicle would only be handed over in exchange for a ticket; nor, on the evidence, did the ticket play but a small part in the running of the car park.

Note—See also *James Buchanan Co Ltd v Hay's Transport Services Ltd* [1972] 2 Lloyd's Rep 535.

Fred Chappel Ltd v National Car Parks Ltd

(1987) Times, 22 May, QBD
The plaintiffs' employee parked a vehicle in a car park run by the defendants. The car park had two attendants but no barrier; ready access to the cars could be gained through the perimeter of the car park. The plaintiffs' employee paid a charge of £2, and parked the vehicle subject to the defendants' standard terms and conditions which purported to transfer custody of the vehicle to them. The vehicle was stolen and the plaintiffs sued the defendants for negligence and breach of contract.
HELD: The claim failed. Despite the wording of the standard terms and conditions, the contract was merely a licence to park, not a bailment of the vehicle. Custody of the vehicle had not been transferred to the defendants. The defendants had reserved the right not to release the vehicle without production of the ticket, but this did not imply a positive obligation to the plaintiff not to allow the vehicle to leave the car park without production of the ticket. It appeared that the vehicle had been stolen by an expert thief. In the circumstances the defendants were not negligent or in breach of contract.

4 CARRIERS

VEHICLES LEFT UNATTENDED

WLR Traders Ltd v B & N Shipping Agency Ltd

[1955] 1 Lloyd's Rep 554 (Pilcher J)
Plaintiffs contracted with forwarding agents, who sub-contracted with private carriers, to collect three cartons of nylon stockings from plaintiffs' London warehouse and deliver at Millwall Docks. The goods, with other goods, were taken on an open lorry, which was left by the driver in Euston Road while he went to a nearby shop on a private errand to buy a hammer. He removed the ignition key pursuant to his employees' instructions and was absent for three or four minutes during which time the lorry with its load was stolen.
HELD: The carriers as bailees of the goods had failed to prove that the loss occurred without their negligence. Lorries containing goods are often stolen when left unattended. The driver ought to have anticipated that the load was probably valuable. He had no reason to stop. He must be taken to have known that lorry thieves are active

in London; that ignition keys are easily procurable; that removing the ignition key would not foil a thief for more than half a minute; he might have removed a vital part of the electrical mechanism. His employers should have taken further precautions by instructions to drivers if obliged to leave their lorries unattended. The carriers were liable to the plaintiffs for the loss of their goods.

Lee Cooper Ltd v CH Jeakins & Sons Ltd

[1967] 2 QB 1, [1965] 1 All ER 280, [1965] 3 WLR 753, 109 Sol Jo 794, [1964] 1 Lloyd's Rep 300 (Marshall J)
The plaintiffs instructed a firm of shipping agents with whom they normally did business to forward some goods from London to Eire. For a part of the journey the shipping agents engaged the defendants, who were hauliers, to carry the goods in their lorry. The driver stopped on the journey and left the lorry unattended. As a result the goods were stolen. The contracts between the plaintiffs and the shippers, and between the shippers and the defendants, both contained exclusion clauses. The judge found that the theft was due to the driver's negligence and that, there being no contractual relationship between the plaintiffs and defendants, the defendants had no protection from the exclusion clauses, nor were plaintiffs owed any duties by the defendants in contract. Could the plaintiffs succeed in tort?
HELD: Lord Atkin's famous dictum in *Donoghue v Stevenson* was wide and flexible and the plaintiff's case was within it: 'The law of torts exists to prevent men from hurting one another, whether in respect of their property, their persons, their reputation or anything else that is theirs.' The defendants were bailees for reward of the plaintiff's goods though their contractual duty was owed to the shippers. They knew from previous trading that the shippers were continuously handling their customers' goods and not their own. They knew from the delivery notes that the plaintiffs were the owners of the goods. They owed the plaintiffs a duty of care which was breached by their driver's negligence. Judgment for the plaintiffs.

Learoyd Bros & Co Ltd v Pope & Sons Ltd

[1966] 2 Lloyd's Rep 142 (Sachs J)
The plaintiffs wished to send 12 bales of worsted from Huddersfield to London Docks. They contracted for the carriage with Hanson Haulage Ltd who, for the last stage of the journey hired a lorry and driver from the defendants. The lorry was loaded with the bales and other goods some of which were for Mark Brown's Wharf, off Tooley Street. The driver parked his vehicle in Tooley Street and left it unattended whilst he went to the wharf office 75 yards away, which he knew would not be open for another 10 minutes or so. When it did open he took 15 minutes to transact his business. When he returned to the place where he had left the lorry it had gone. When it was found later the bales had been stolen.
HELD: (1) The defendants were bailees of the goods in relation to the plaintiffs; (2) whatever were the terms of the contract between Hanson Haulage and the defendants, the driver, so far as the plaintiffs were concerned, remained a servant of the defendants who were liable for his negligence; (3) the driver was negligent in leaving the vehicle when he knew the office was not yet open, not keeping it under observation and locking it properly; (4) the defendants were negligent in not fitting the vehicle with brake lock devices. The defendants were liable to the plaintiffs for the value of the goods lost.

Note—See also *Bontex Knitting Works v St John's Garage* (p 328, below) and *Colverd v Anglo-Overseas Transport Ltd* (p, 321, below).

In *Pye Ltd v BG Transport Service Ltd* [1966] 2 Lloyd's Rep 300 Browne J held that a driver who left his lorry unattended in Berner Street, Stepney for 20 minutes was negligent in not operating the 'petro-mag' (an anti-theft device cutting off petrol and ignition) before leaving it, though he locked the cab. By contrast Roskill J in *Presvale Trading Co Ltd v Sutch and Searle Ltd* [1967] 1 Lloyd's Rep 131 held the driver of a lorry who locked the cab when leaving it in a locked garage in Peckham overnight was not negligent merely by leaving the 'Waso' steering lock on the lorry unsecured.

COMMON CARRIERS

Great Northern Rly Co v LEP Transport

[1922] 2 KB 742, 91 LJKB 807, 127 LT 664, 38 TLR 711, CA
The liability of a common carrier for loss, injury, or delay in respect to the goods carried may be varied by contract. If the contract be such as to obliterate or destroy the character of a common carrier, he must be regarded for the purposes of that particular contract as a private carrier but if the contract does not so obliterate or destroy that character, and merely limits his liabilities in some respects, in all other respects remains under a common carrier's liability.

Ludditt v Ginger Coote Airways Ltd

[1947] AC 233, [1947] 1 All ER 328, [1947] LJR 1067, 177 LT 334, 63 TLR 157, PC
A common carrier is one who undertakes to carry goods of all persons indifferently for hire. The question whether the liability of a common carrier has been undertaken in any particular case is one of fact and not of law. A common carrier is an insurer of the goods he carries, but not of passengers. If he is not a common carrier, a carrier is not liable for accidental damage by fire.

By the custom of the realm a common carrier of goods was at common law 'bound to answer for the goods at all events . . . The law charges this person thus entrusted to carry goods against all events but acts of God and of the enemies of the King': *Readhead v Midland Rly Co* (1869) LR 4 QB 379, 38 LJQB 169.

The common carrier of goods was at common law free to limit his stringent obligations by special contract. He could insist on making his own terms and refuse to carry except on those terms, subject to any statutory provisions.

5 LIEN OF REPAIRER

Hatton v Car Maintenance Co Ltd

[1915] 1 Ch 621, 84 LJCh 847, 110 LT 765, 30 TLR 275, 58 Sol Jo 361
The owner of a motor car had an agreement with a company under which the latter were for three years to maintain the car and its accessories, provide a driver who was to be the company's servant, and do the necessary repairs. The owner was to pay the

company a fixed annual sum up to a limited mileage and at a rate for every mile beyond the limit. The car when in London was kept at the company's garage, and whether the owner was in London or elsewhere she took the car out when and as she liked. An amount having become due by the owner under the agreement, the company took possession of the car and claimed a lien on it for the amount due.
HELD: (1) Inasmuch as what the company did to the car was not to improve it, but only to maintain it in its former condition, the company had no lien on the car; (2) even if the company had a lien, their lien would have been lost by the arrangement acted on, under which the owner was entitled to take away the car as and when she pleased.

Re Southern Livestock Producers Ltd

[1963] 3 All ER 801, [1964] 1 WLR 24, 108 Sol Jo 15
Per Pennycuick J: It is perfectly clear that unless a bailee can establish improvement he has no lien. If this matter were free from authority it would, I think, be tempting to draw the line in rather a different place so as to cover the case where a person by the exercise of labour and skill prevents a chattel from deteriorating. . . . However, it is quite impossible for me at this time of day to introduce that sort of modification into a well-established principle.

BAILEE ORDERING REPAIRS: LIEN AGAINST OWNERS

Tappenden v Artus

[1964] 2 QB 185, [1963] 3 All ER 213, [1963] 3 WLR 685, 107 Sol Jo 572, CA
The plaintiff, a motor dealer, owned a motor vehicle which A wished to take on hire purchase. Requiring to use it at once on his business and having insufficient cash to pay the necessary deposit, A was allowed by the plaintiff to take it away and use it pending completion of a hire-purchase agreement. It was also stipulated by the plaintiff that A should tax and insure the vehicle and he did so. Two days later A was using the vehicle when it broke down. He arranged for repairers to take it to their garage and repair it. After doing so they rendered an account for £40 to A which was unpaid. After some weeks (the bailment to A having been terminated) the plaintiff traced the vehicle to the repairers who refused to give it up whilst the bill for repairs remained unpaid, claiming to exercise their repairer's lien. The plaintiff sued the repairers for a return of the van and damages for its detention.
HELD: The repairer was entitled to assert his lien against the plaintiff. Where possession of goods is given to a repairer not by the owner but by a bailer the test whether the repairer can assert his lien against the owner is whether the owner authorised the bailee either expressly or as a necessary incident of the bailment to give possession of the goods to the repairer. A had received the vehicle from the plaintiff as a bailee with the right to use it for all reasonable purposes and in all reasonable ways, and among those ways was the right to get the vehicle repaired when necessary (*Bowmaker Ltd v Wycombe Motors* (below) per Goddard CJ). There was consideration for the bailment in that A had taxed and insured the vehicle. On the day in question A lawfully had possession of the vehicle and could not use it for the purposes of the bailment unless he were to have it repaired: the giving of actual and lawful possession of the vehicle to the repairer for the purpose of effecting repairs necessary to render if roadworthy was an act reasonably incidental to his use of the vehicle.

HIRE PURCHASE

Green v All Motors Ltd

[1917] 1 KB 625, 86 LJKB 590, 116 LT 189, CA
P was the hirer of a car under a hire-purchase agreement with the plaintiff, one of the terms of which was that he should keep the car in good repair and working condition. The car having been damaged in an accident P sent it to the defendant for repair at a time when no default had been made in the payment of instalments. Before the repairs had been completed the plaintiff as owner demanded the return of the car. The defendant completed the repairs and refused to deliver up the car until they were paid for, claiming a lien.
HELD: The defendant had a valid lien on the car for the cost of the repairs. The hirer of a chattel is entitled to have it repaired so as to enable him to use it in the way in which such a chattel is ordinarily used. In this case there was an additional contractual duty to keep the car in repair. Thus the hirer had by contract a duty as well as a right until the hire was terminated to have the car repaired, with the ordinary consequence of giving the repairer a lien on the car for the proper cost of repairs not only against himself but also against the owner.

Bowmaker Ltd v Wycombe Motors Ltd

[1946] KB 505, [1946] 2 All ER 113, 115 LJKB 411, 175 LT 133, 62 TLR 437, 90 Sol Jo 407, Div Ct
A hire-purchase company determined the hire of a car for default in payment of instalment, but the hirer retained possession of the car. After the determination the hirer instructed repairers to repair the car. Repairers claimed a lien against the hire-purchase company. The hire-purchase agreement contained a condition that the hirer had no authority from the company to create a lien for repairs.
HELD: Whilst the hiring was in existence and the hirer entitled to possession, the lien would have been good, and the condition would not affect the repairer, but when the hire had been determined, the hirer has no right to the car and there is no lien.

CHAPTER 11

Exclusion Clauses

1 INTRODUCTION

Note—Clauses which exclude liability for loss or damage are a common feature in many types of contract, including those for repair, hire or storage of vehicles or for the carriage of goods. In considering the effect of such clauses the points most commonly met with are:
(1) whether the words of the clause are effective to exclude liability for negligence;
(2) whether there has been a fundamental breach of contract rendering the clause inoperative;
(3) whether the clause has been effectively brought to the notice of the other contracting party;
(4) applicability of the Unfair Contract Terms Act 1977.
The cases relevant to (1) are at pp 314–318, below, (2) at pp 319–323, below, and (3) at pp 323–327, below.

UNFAIR CONTRACT TERMS ACT 1977

Where in respect of contracts made on or after 1 February 1978 (or where non-contractual notices are concerned) liability arises for any loss or damage suffered on or after that date, clauses or notices purport to exclude liability for loss or damage, the provisions of the Unfair Contract Terms Act 1977 will call for consideration. The essence of the Act is contained in sub-ss (1) and (2) of s 2:

'(1) A person cannot by reference to any contract term or to a notice given to persons generally or to particular persons exclude or restrict his liability for death or personal injury resulting from negligence.
(2) In the case of other loss or damage a person cannot so exclude or restrict his liability for negligence except in so far as the term or notice satisfies the requirement of reasonableness.'

The test of 'reasonableness' is explained in s 11. A term of a contract must be 'fair and reasonable . . . having regard to the circumstances which were or ought reasonably have been known to or in the contemplation of the parties when the contract was made'. A non-contractual notice must be 'fair and reasonable . . . having regard to all the circumstances obtaining when the liability arose or (but for the notice) would have risen'. In relation to contracts (other than sale or hire purchase) s 2 applies only to 'business liability', defined in s 1(3): 'liability for breach of obligations or duties arising—

(a) from things done or to be done by a person in the course of a business (whether his own business or another's); or
(b) from the occupation of premises used for business purposes of the occupier.'

Contracts of insurance are excluded altogether from the controls in the Act.

2 CONSTRUCTION OF CLAUSE

Ailsa Craig Fishing Co Ltd v Malvern Fishing Co Ltd

[1983] 1 All ER 101, [1983] 1 WLR 964, 127 Sol Jo 508, [1983] 1 Lloyd's Rep 183n, 1982 SLT 377, HL
Per Lord Wilberforce: Whether a condition limiting liability is effective or not is a question of construction of that condition in the context of the contract as a whole. If it is to exclude liability for negligence, it must be most clearly and unambiguously expressed, and, in such a contract as this (a contract between a security company and owners of a fishing vessel to provide a security service for the vessel when in harbour), must be construed *contra proferentem*. . . . But I venture to add one further qualification, or at least clarification: one must not strive to create ambiguities by strained construction. . . . The relevant words must be given, if possible, their natural, plain meaning. Clauses of limitation are not regarded by the courts with the same hostility as clauses of exclusion; this is because they must be related to other contractual terms, in particular to the risks to which the defending party may be exposed, the remuneration which he received and possibly also the opportunity of the other party to insure.

NEGLIGENCE NOT EXPRESSLY MENTIONED

Rutter v Palmer

[1922] 2 KB 87, CA
The defendant was a garage owner with whom the plaintiff deposited his car for sale on commission. The contract of bailment included a clause 'Customers' cars are driven by [the defendant's] staff at customers' sole risk'. Whilst being demonstrated to a possible purchaser the car was badly damaged by the negligent driving of the defendant's driver.

HELD: The clause protected the defendant from liability for the damage. Since an ordinary bailee is not liable for the acts of his servants unless they are negligent the clause covered negligent acts because otherwise the words would have no effect.

Per Scrutton LJ: In construing an exemption clause certain general rules may be applied: First the defendant is not exempted from liability for the negligence of his servants unless adequate words are used; second, the liability of the defendant apart from the exempting words must be ascertained; then the particular clause in question must be considered; and if the only liability of the party pleading the exemption is a liability for negligence, the clause will more readily operate to exempt him.

Canada SS Lines v R

[1952] AC 192, [1952] 1 All ER 305, 96 Sol Jo 72, [1952] 1 Lloyd's Rep 1, [1952] 1 TLR 261, PC

(1) If the clause contains language which expressly exempts the person in whose favour it is made from the consequences of the negligence of his own servants, effect must be given to that provision.

(2) If there is not express reference to negligence, the court must consider whether the words used are wide enough in their ordinary meaning, to cover negligence on the part of the servants of such person. If a doubt arises at this point, it must be resolved against such person.

(3) If the words used are wide enough for the above purpose, the court must then consider whether 'the head of damage' may be based on some ground other than that of negligence, as stated by Lord Greene in *Alderslade v Hendon Laundry* [1945] KB 189. The 'other ground' must not be so fanciful or remote that such person cannot be supposed to have desired protection against it, but subject to this qualification, which is, no doubt, to be implied from Lord Greene's words, the existence of a possible head of damage other than that of negligence is fatal to such person even if the words are, prima facie, wide enough to cover negligence on the part of his servants.

Note—See also *Clement Shaw & Co v Joseph C Mount & Co* (below). For consideration of the three tests see *Smith v South Wales Switchgear Ltd* [1978] 1 All ER 18, [1978] 1 WLR 165, 122 Sol Jo 61, HL. See also (applying the tests) *Lamport & Holt Lines Ltd v Coubro & Scrutton (M & I) Ltd, The Raphael* [1981] 2 Lloyd's Rep 659; affd [1982] 2 Lloyd's Rep 42, [1982] Com LR 123, CA and *George Mitchell (Chesterhall) Ltd v Finney Lock Seeds Ltd* [1983] QB 284, [1983] 1 All ER 108, especially Kerr LJ at 125, and [1983] 2 AC 803, [1983] 2 All ER 737, [1983] 3 WLR 163, [1983] 2 Lloyd's Rep 272, HL.

In *Mark Rowlands Ltd v Berni Inns Ltd* [1985] 3 All ER 473, the operation of a fire insurance policy (which clearly covered fires caused both accidentally and negligently), in conjunction with the lease which required cover to be obtained, resulted in the loss of the right to recover damages in negligence. There was no relevant exemption clause.

Hollier v Rambler Motors (AMC) Ltd

[1972] 2 QB 71, [1972] 1 All ER 399, [1972] 2 WLR 401, 116 Sol Jo 158, [1972] RTR 190, CA

The plaintiff arranged with the defendants by telephone for them to do some repair work to his car. The defendants told him to send it to their works; no other terms were discussed or agreed. The plaintiff sent his car. Whilst it was in the defendants' works it was damaged by fire caused by their negligence. On three previous occasions over a period of five years the defendants had done work to the plaintiff's car and each time had obtained his signature on an invoice containing the words (which the plaintiff had

never read) 'The company is not responsible for damage caused by fire to customers' cars on the premises'. They claimed that this was a course of dealing which imported the exclusion of liability into the oral agreement.
HELD: (1) Following *McCutcheon v David MacBrayne Ltd* (p 325, below) there was not such a frequent and consistent course of dealing as could import the term into the oral contract. (2) Even if the words used had formed part of the contract they were not effective to exclude liability. For a clause to exclude liability for negligence the language should be so plain that it clearly bears that meaning. If negligence is not mentioned the question is whether the exemption clause would convey to any ordinary literate and sensible person that the garage was excluding liability for their negligence. It is not correct that if the only liability which coud arise would lie in negligence and nothing else the clause *must* be construed as extending to that head of damage (as Lord Greene appeared to say in *Alderslade's* case [1945] KB 189); in such a case the clause would merely, as Scrutton LJ said in *Rutter v Palmer* (p 314, above), *more readily* operate to exempt him'. In the present case an ordinary man would consider the clause meant that the mere fact that there was a fire would not make the garage liable, not that the defendants were excluding liability for a fire caused by their own negligence. Alternatively the words could be given ample content by construing them as a warning or a statement of fact that the garage was not liable for fire in the absence of negligence. Judgment for plaintiff.

'ANY CAUSE WHATSOEVER'

Clement Shaw & Co v Joseph C Mount & Co

(1949) 82 Ll L Rep 995 (Lord Goddard CJ)
Defendants were warehousemen and agreed to store motor lorries of the plaintiffs and that they would 'drain the radiators on arrival' and accept the lorries at 'owner's risk'. The printed conditions exempted from liability for negligence, which probably did not add anything to the words 'owner's risk' (see *McCawley v Furness Rly Co* (1872) LR 8 QB 57, considered and applied in *Rutter v Palmer*). The defendants would have been liable for nothing but negligence and the term 'at his own risk' excluded all liability for negligence. The lorries had separate drainage for radiator and cylinder blocks and the latter were not drained. Frost damage ensued.
HELD: Defendants had carried out their contract by draining the radiators. They were unaware of the drainage system of the cylinder blocks. They were not told to drain the cylinder blocks and knowledge could not be imputed to them. There was no negligence and no breach of contract, and if there had been, the exemption clause and the 'owner's risk' term protected them. Breach of contract might arise in the case of a garage proprietor.

Note—Denning LJ in *White v John Warrwick & Co* ([1953] 2 All ER 1021, [1953] 1 WLR 1285, 97 Sol Jo 740, CA) pointed out that 'if a transport company expressly stipulates with the plaintiff for exemption from liability for damage, *however caused*, the plaintiff cannot overcome that exemption by suing in negligence instead of contract'.

AE Farr Ltd v Admiralty

[1953] 2 All ER 512, [1953] 1 WLR 965, 97 Sol Jo 491 (Parker J)
Plaintiffs contracted with the Admiralty for the construction of a jetty. The contract included a clause that the plaintiffs should be responsible for any loss or damage to

the works arising from any cause whatsoever. The works were damaged by the negligent navigation of an Admiralty vessel.
HELD: The words 'any cause whatsoever' were as wide as they could be and included negligent navigation of a ship by an Admiralty servant.

Wright v Tyne Improvement Comrs and Osbeck & Co Ltd

[1968] 1 All ER 807, [1968] 1 WLR 336, [1968] 1 Lloyd's Rep 113, CA
The plaintiff was in a railway wagon into which a sling of timber was being lowered by means of a crane when the wagon moved and he was pushed off by the suspended timber, sustaining injury. The wagon was under the control of the first defendants and was moved by their employee, a capstan operator. He should not have moved the wagon at the time of the accident; his negligence was the sole cause of the accident and the plaintiff was awarded damages against the first defendants. The crane from which the timber was suspended had been hired by the first defendants to the second defendants, the plaintiff's employers, by a contract containing the words 'We [the second defendants] hereby agree to bear the risk of and be responsible for all damages injury or loss whatsoever howsoever and whensoever caused arising directly or indirectly out of or in connection with the hiring or use of the said crane.'
HELD: The words 'whatsoever and whensoever caused' were wide enough to give an indemnity against damage, injury or loss due to negligence of the first defendants' servant and they were entitled to be indemnified by the second defendants.

Indemnity clause

Gillespie Bros Ltd v Roy Bowles Transport Ltd

[1973] QB 400, [1973] 1 All ER 193, [1972] 3 WLR 1003, 116 Sol Jo 861, CA
A condition of a contract of carriage provided: 'The trader . . . shall keep the carrier indemnified against all claims or demands whatsoever by whomsoever made . . . ' Goods were lost by negligence of the carriers' servant and the owners successfully sued for the amount of their loss. The carriers sought indemnity from the traders.
HELD: If the words of the clause were sufficient to show an express agreement to indemnify the carriers even against claims arising from the negligence of their own servant, effect must be given to them. The use of the word 'whatsoever' in the phrase 'all claims or demands whatsoever' signified an intention that the indemnity was to extend to all claims of whatsoever kind without exception. The first of the requirements propounded in *Canada SS Lines v R* (p 315, above) was satisfied and it was unnecessary in this case to apply the second and third.

Words not effective

Chowdhary v Gillot

[1947] 2 All ER 541, 63 TLR 569
The plaintiff for 10 or 12 years had been a valued customer of the Daimler Co. He was in the habit of taking his Daimler car to their works and leaving it with them for servicing and repairs some three or four times every year. He stated his requirements verbally or brought a rough list, and these were transferred to a 'Repair form', which he signed or which was posted to him for signature. He never read the conditions but supposed they contained ordinary garage contract conditions.

Condition 4 was: If a customer's car and/or chassis shall be driven at any time by one of the company's employees, the employee shall be deemed for all purposes to be the servant of the customer who shall be entitled to all rights and shall discharge all liabilities incident to that relationship.

On 23 November 1944, the plaintiff did not sign any order form. The company's servant drove him in his car to the station, and on the way an accident occurred by the negligence of the servant, and the plaintiff and a third party were injured.

HELD: Plaintiff had not signed the form. Even if he is to be taken to have contracted on the usual terms, condition 4 did not refer to the circumstances. On a repair order, it refers to driving incidental to the repairs, eg, on test or from one garage to another.

Extent of 'owner's risk'

Michaelides v Henleaze Park Garage Ltd

(1954) 104 L Jo 412 (Paton J), Bristol County Court

The plaintiff claimed damages for the damage done to his car by negligence on the part of the defendant's employee when driving a car belonging to the third party, Anstey, on a test run after repairs. The defendants settled the plaintiff's claim and then claimed indemnity from Anstey in third-party proceedings on the basis of a term in the contract for repair to be implied from a notice 'customers' cars garaged and driven at owner's risk'.

HELD: Anstey was not liable. The words 'owner's risk' were appropriate to absolve the defendants for damage *to* Anstey's car but wholly insufficient to fix him with liability for damage done *with* the car.

EXEMPTION NOT EFFECTIVE AGAINST THIRD PARTY

Cosgrove v Horsfall

(1945) 175 LT 334, 62 TLR 140, CA

An omnibus driver in the employ of the Board was travelling for his own purposes as passenger on one of the Board's buses with a similar pass. He sued and recovered against the driver. The condition did not avail the driver who was not a party to the contract nor were the Board his agents in making the contract.

Per du Parcq LJ: It is, to say the least, doubtful whether the deposit under s 35(4) of the 1930 Act can be made available to meet the judgment.

Note—See *Cosgrove v Horsfall*, p 318, above.

Liability for death or personal injury: see now Unfair Contract Terms Act 1977, s 2(1).

Third party cannot claim benefit of clause

Scruttons Ltd v Midland Silicones Ltd

[1962] AC 446, [1962] 1 All ER 1, [1962] 2 WLR 186, 106 Sol Jo 34, [1961] 2 Lloyd's Rep 365, HL

The appellants, who were stevedores, damaged a drum of chemicals belonging to the respondents whilst in transit under a bill of lading with carriers by the terms of which the liability of the carriers for damage was limited to 500 dollars. The word 'carriers'

was expressed to include any person acting as carrier or bailee. The agreement between the carriers and the appellants provided that the appellants should have the protection of the 'terms conditions and exceptions of the bill of lading'. The appellants claimed the benefit of the limitation against the respondents.
HELD: As the appellants were not parties to the bill of lading they could not claim the benefit of a term contained in it.

Note—However, it may be that the stevedores could be protected by an exclusion clause contained in a contract of carriage to which they were not a party if the carrier contracted as an agent on their behalf.

See *New Zealand Shipping Co v AM Satterthwaite & Co Ltd* [1975] AC 154.

EFFECT OF ORAL VARIATION

Mendelssohn v Normand Ltd

[1970] 1 QB 177, [1969] 2 All ER 1215, [1969] 3 WLR 139, 113 Sol Jo 263, CA
The plaintiff left his car in the defendants' garage whilst he went away to have lunch. He wanted to lock the car but the garage attendant, employed by the defendants, said it was contrary to the rules and would not let him. He told the attendant there were valuables in the car and gave him the keys on the understanding that he would lock the car after moving it. The plaintiff was given a ticket, as on previous occasions when he used the garage, bearing the printed conditions: '1. The [defendants] will not accept responsibility for any loss or damage sustained by the vehicle its accessories or contents however caused. 6. No variation of these conditions will bind the [defendants] unless made in writing signed by their duly authorised manager.' When the plaintiff reclaimed the car he found it unlocked and some valuables were missing.
HELD: The plaintiff was entitled to damages for the loss. Although the printed terms were part of the contract the promise of the attendant to see that the contents were safe took priority over any printed condition. The oral promise had a decisive influence on the transaction since it induced the plaintiff to contract and it would be unjust to allow the maker to go back on it. The defendants were additionally liable in having deviated from the contract—they had agreed to keep the car locked and had failed to do so.

3 FUNDAMENTAL BREACH

Note—Note the Unfair Contract Terms Act 1977, s 9(1):

'Where for reliance upon it a contract term has to satisfy the requirement of reasonableness, it may be found to do so and be given effect accordingly notwithstanding that the contract has been terminated either by breach or by a party electing to treat it as repudiated.'

Suisse Atlantique Societe d'Armement Maritime SA v Rotterdamsche Kolen Centrale NV

[1967] 1 AC 361, [1966] 2 All ER 61, [1966] 2 WLR 944, 110 Sol Jo 367, [1966] 1 Lloyd's Rep 529, HL
A demurrage clause in a contract of charter provided for the calculation of payments for delays in loading and unloading the ship. The shipowners, alleging a fundamental breach of the contract but electing to continue the charter, claimed that damages for

the breach were not limited to the payments in the demurrage clause since it was an exemption clause and could not apply where there had been a fundamental breach. The House of Lords rejected the argument and disapproved of observations of members of the Court of Appeal in *Charterhouse Credit Co Ltd v Tolley* [1963] 2 QB 683, [1963] 2 All ER 432, [1963] 2 WLR 1168, 107 Sol Jo 234, *Karsales (Harrow) Ltd v Wallis* [1956] 2 All ER 866, [1956] 1 WLR 936, 100 Sol Jo 548, CA, *Yeoman Credit Ltd v Apps* [1962] 2 QB 508, [1961] 2 All ER 281, [1961] 3 WLR 94, 105 Sol Jo 567, CA and other cases appearing to assert a rule of law that where there is a fundamental breach of a contract the party in breach can never rely on the terms of an exemption clause contained in the contract. If the other party elects to treat the contract as still in being then the question whether the party in breach can claim the benefit of the terms of the exemption clause depends on the true construction of the clause in its context. Such clauses must be construed strictly and will not normally be found applicable to cases of fundamental breach, but where suitable words are used it is not impossible as a matter of law that such a clause may have effect even where a fundamental breach has occurred.

Photo Production Ltd v Securicor Transport Ltd

[1980] AC 827, [1980] 1 All ER 556, [1980] 2 WLR 283, 124 Sol Jo 147, [1980] 1 Lloyd's Rep 545, HL

Securicor contracted with Photo Production to provide a night patrol at their premises, a factory containing much paper and cardboard. The patrolman employed by Securicor when on his rounds deliberately set fire to some paper in a cardboard box; the fire spread and the factory was burned down. It was conceded by Securicor that in the absence of contractual terms to the contrary they would be liable for the act of the patrolman. They claimed the benefit of two exemption clauses which excluded or reduced their liability.

It was held in the Court of Appeal that the words of the clauses if applicable were effective to protect Securicor but by the patrolman's act they were guilty of a breach which went to the root of the contract; instead of safeguarding the premises they had burned them down. They could not rely on the exemption clauses.

HELD, ON APPEAL to the House of Lords: This was wrong. The question whether, and to what extent, an exclusion clause is to be applied to a fundamental breach, or breach of a fundamental term, or indeed to any breach of contract, is a matter of construction of the contract. This is the correct rule, established in *Suisse Atlantique v Rotterdamsche Kolen* (above). Parties should be left free, when risks are normally borne by insurance, to apportion the risks as they think fit and according to the contractual provisions they have themselves made. In the present case the words of the clause were perfectly clear and relieved Securicor from liability for the patrolman's act.

Note—The effect of the decision was discussed at length in *George Mitchell (Chesterhall) Ltd v Finney Lock Seeds Ltd* [1983] QB 284, [1983] 1 All ER 108, [1982] 3 WLR 1036, 126 Sol Jo 689, [1983] 1 Lloyd's Rep 168, CA.

Per Kerr LJ: Beginning with the *Securicor* case [1980] AC 827, it is in my view perfectly clear that this has wholly laid to rest the doctrine of 'fundamental breach' in one respect at least. It has abrogated the supposed rule, exemplified most signally by the decisions of this court in *Harbutt's Plasticine Ltd v Wayne Tank and Pump Co Ltd* [1970] 1 QB 447, [1970] 1 All ER 225, and *Wathes (Western) Ltd v Austins (Menswear) Ltd* [1976] 1 Lloyd's Rep 14, that a breach which can be described as fundamental, or a breach of one of the terms of the contract which can be so described, caused any exemption clause to cease to be applicable and capable of being relied upon; and—further—that this is so whether the innocent party treats the breach as a repudiation of the entire contract or whether it affirms the contract. It is now clear law that, whatever the nature of the breach, an exemption clause can never 'terminate' or 'cease to have effect', but remains to be construed to order to decide whether or not the parties intended that its terms should apply to the breach in question. Thus, such commonly used expressions as 'the defendants cannot rely on the clause' must now be treated as suspect, unless they mean no more than that the clause, on its true construction, does not apply to the breach in question. Further, as pointed out by Lord Diplock in the *Securicor* case [1980] AC 827, if the expression 'fundamental' is to be retained in any context whatever, it should be confined to cases of anticipatory breach, ie to breaches which entitle the innocent party to treat the contract as at an end and to absolve him from any further performance of its terms; but not in any context which bears on the continuing effect of an exemption clause.

The decision of the Court of Appeal was affirmed in the House of Lords [1983] 2 AC 803, [1983] 2 All ER 737, [1983] 3 WLR 163, [1983] 2 Lloyd's Rep 272, where Lord Bridge said 'The *Photo Production* case gave the final quietus to the doctrine that a "fundamental breach" of contract deprived the party in breach of the benefit of clauses in the contract excluding or limiting his liability.'

NO FUNDAMENTAL BREACH

Colverd & Co Ltd v Anglo-Overseas Transport Co Ltd

(1961) 105 Sol Jo 1010, [1961] 2 Lloyd's Rep 352 (Barry J)

The defendants were forwarding agents for the importation of watches from Switzerland by the plaintiffs under arrangements first made in 1955. A consignment of watches arrived at London Airport on 17 February 1958 and was collected by the defendants in their vehicle on 21st and taken to a depot at Finsbury. On 24th it was loaded with other cases of goods on another of their vehicles for delivery to the plaintiffs. The driver made various other calls first and still had the plaintiffs' watches in his van when he stopped for lunch near Oxford Street. He parked the van without locking it and was absent 40 minutes. When he returned the van was gone and the plaintiffs' watches were never recovered. There were exclusion clauses in the contract of carriage which it was admitted excluded the defendants' liability unless there could be said to be a fundamental breach of the contract.

HELD: There was no fundamental breach and the defendants were not liable. The driver of the van was negligent but any negligence for which the defendants would, but for the exclusion clauses, have been liable was in the course of carrying out their contract. This was a contract spread over a number of days and included duties other than the delivery of the goods. The isolated lapse on the part of the driver could not be said to go to the root of the contract.

Hollins v J Davy Ltd

[1963] 1 QB 844, [1963] 1 All ER 370, [1963] 2 WLR 201, 106 Sol Jo 1033 (Sachs J)

The plaintiff garaged his car at the defendants' premises on the terms of a written contract which provided for payment every four weeks and contained conditions excluding the defendants' liability 'for loss of or damage to customer's goods, however caused' and from 'responsibility for loss or misdelivery of . . . any vehicle . . . whilst in our hands . . . arising from any cause including negligence'. A man came to the garage and was allowed by the garage attendant, a servant of the defendants, to drive away the car on his representing that he had been sent by the plaintiff to collect it. He was in fact a thief and the car was lost. It was admitted that the attendant, though

acting honestly had been negligent in allowing the man to take it. In this action the plaintiff alleged that the circumstances amounted to a fundamental breach of the contract which disentitled the defendant to rely on the exclusions in the contract.
HELD: The honest error of the attendant leading him to give the permission to take the car away was not a fundamental breach of the contract. A person doing an act honestly intending to do his best to carry out the intent of the contract cannot, merely because he is deceived, be said to be deliberately breaking the contract. In cases of fundamental breach there is a deliberate disregard of bounden obligations. The attendant honestly believed the man represented the plaintiff: if he had known the man had no authority or not actively believed him to have authority the case would have been different. There was both a loss and misdelivery of the car and each was covered by the exemption clause.

John Carter (Fine Worsteds) Ltd v Hanson Haulage (Leeds) Ltd

[1965] 2 QB 495, [1965] 1 All ER 113, [1966] 2 WLR 553, 109 Sol Jo 47, [1965] 1 Lloyd's Rep 49, CA
The defendants were private carriers who accepted goods from the plaintiffs for carriage from Bradford to London Docks subject to the terms of a contract which provided that 'the liability of the contractor in respect of loss of or damage of the goods . . . shall in any case be limited as follows . . . to the sum of £50 per gross cwt and pro rata for any part of a cwt of the goods so lost or damaged'. The goods were taken by the defendants to their London depot and transferred to a lorry driven by a man whom they had taken into employment only two days before. He had given some details of former employment but the defendants had not checked them or asked for a reference. He had a conviction, unknown to the defendants, for breaking and entering and his object in entering the defendants' employment was to steal the first load he was entrusted with. He drove the load including the plaintiffs' goods to an arranged meeting place with friends who stole them. The defendants paid the plaintiffs a sum calculated on the terms of the limitation of liability in the contract but the plaintiffs sued for the balance. The county court judge held that the defendants' failure to make proper inquiries about the driver before employing him was negligence amounting to a fundamental breach of the contract and the limitation of liability did not apply.
HELD, ON APPEAL: (1) The defendants were negligent as found by the county court judge, but (2) this negligence could not amount to a fundamental breach. The defendants, in employing the driver, were not abandoning the contract or deviating from the performance of it; they were attempting, albeit negligently, to carry it out. (3) The theft itself did not constitute a fundamental breach of the contract by the defendants since it was not their act but the act of their driver: to amount to a fundamental breach there must be a deliberate breach of the contract which can be imputed to the contracting party personally. (4) The words of the contract limiting liability were effective to cover loss by theft.

Gillette Industries Ltd v WH Martin Ltd

[1966] 1 Lloyd's Rep 57, CA
The defendants, who were forwarding agents, contracted with the plaintiffs to collect 19 containers of goods from a ship arriving at Liverpool and to deliver them to Reading. Their normal practice was to arrange transport by employing sub-contractors known to them. Transport of 16 of the containers was arranged in this way but for the last three, being unable to find anyone else, they employed two men who were

available for work with a lorry in the Liverpool 'lorry pool', a parking space where lorries and drivers waited for any work that may be available. The defendants saw that the lorry had an 'A' licence bearing the name of a transport company and interviewed the two men though without seeing their driving licences or taking their names and addresses. The two men took the containers but did not deliver them to Reading. The containers were found at Leytonstone a few days later with some of their contents missing. The contract between the plaintiffs and defendants contained a clause exempting the defendants from liability for loss or damage to goods 'unless such loss or damage occurs whilst the goods are in the actual custody of the company [ie the defendants] and under their actual control and unless such loss or damage is due to wilful negligence or default of the company or their own servant'. The plaintiffs sued for damages for the loss of goods, claiming that by handing them over to two unknown men without taking any adequate steps to satisfy themselves as to the bona fides or honesty of the men the defendants were in fundamental breach of the contract and could not rely on the exemption clause.
HELD: Following *John Carter v Hanson Haulage* (p 322, above) any negligence on the part of the defendants in failing to make proper inquiries about the two men amounted to no more than negligence in the performance of the contract and was not a fundamental breach. The defendants were accordingly protected by the exemption clause.

4 REASONABLENESS

Phillips Products Ltd v Hyland

[1987] 2 All ER 620, [1987] 1 WLR 659n, (1984) 129 Sol Jo 47, [1985] LS Gaz R 681, CA
The plaintiffs hired an excavator and driver from the second defendants. The driver negligently drove the excavator, damaging the plaintiffs' buildings. It was a condition of the contract of hire that the driver (who was the first defendant) would be under the direction and control of the plaintiffs, the hirers, and that they would be responsible for all the claims arising in connection with the operation of the plant by the driver.
HELD, ON APPEAL: Having regard to the Unfair Contract Terms Act 1977, s 11(1) the second defendants had to show that the condition was a fair and reasonable one in the light of the circumstances which were or ought to have been known to both parties when the contract was made. The judge had examined all the relevant circumstances and was not satisfied that it was. The question was not whether the condition was valid or invalid in any and every contract of hire between hirer and plant owner. The question was whether the second defendants' exclusion of liability satisfied the requirement of reasonableness imposed by the Act. The judge was not plainly or obviously wrong in his conclusion. Appeal dismissed.

Note—See also *Stevenson v Nationwide Building Society* (1984) 128 Sol Jo 875, 272 Estates Gazette 663—reasonableness of a disclaimer in an application form for a building society loan.

Thompson v T Lohan (Plant Hire) Ltd

[1987] 2 All ER 631, [1987] 1 WLR 649, [1987] IRLR 148, 131 Sol Jo 358, CA
The plaintiff's husband, an excavator driver, was killed in a quarry accident. The accident was due to the negligence of another excavator driver. Both drivers were hired by the second defendants from the first defendants. The hire contract in *Phillips*

Products v Hyland (above) had similar conditions; the drivers were to be regarded as the hirers' servants and the hirer would be responsible for all claims arising in connection with the operation of the plant by the drivers. The second defendants submitted that this was contrary to s 2(1) of the Unfair Contract Terms Act 1977 in that it purported to exclude the first defendants' liability for death or personal injury. HELD, ON APPEAL: This argument failed. Whilst an employer cannot exclude liability for the acts of his employee as between himself and the general public this does not prevent the parties to a contract of hire from determining between themselves who is to be liable for the negligent acts of a hired employee. *Arthur White (Contractors) Ltd v Tarmac Civil Engineering Ltd* [1967] 1 WLR 1508 applied. The clause was not contrary to s 2(1) of the Unfair Contract Terms Act 1977. The plant owner was not excluding liability for negligence, merely transferring the burden of compensation to the hirer by a commercial arrangement. The plaintiff was not prejudiced because she could enforce judgment against the second defendant.

5 NOTICE OF EXEMPTION CLAUSE

Note—As part of the test of 'reasonableness' the Unfair Contract Terms Act 1977, s 2 includes among relevant matters 'whether the customer knew or ought reasonably to have known of the existence and extent of the terms . . .' In reference to this s 11(2) expressly 'does not prevent the court or arbitrator from holding, in accordance with any rule of law, that a term which purports to exclude or restrict any relevant liability is not a term of the contract', eg because adequate steps had not been taken by the other party to draw his attention to it.

TICKET CASES

Thompson v London, Midland and Scottish Rly Co

[1930] 1 KB 41, 98 LJKB 615, 141 LT 382, CA
The plaintiff's niece, who accompanied plaintiff, took an excursion ticket for plaintiff, who could not read.

On the ticket was printed (inter alia) 'Excursion. For conditions see back.' On the back were printed (inter alia) the words 'Issued subject to the conditions and regulations in the company's time tables and notices and excursion and other bills'. On the excursion bill were printed (inter alia) the words, 'Excursion tickets are issued subject to the notices and conditions shown in the company's current time tables'. In the company's timetable (which could be obtained for 6d each) were printed the words 'Excursion tickets . . . are subject to the condition that neither the holders nor any other person shall have any right of action against the company . . . in respect of . . . injury (fatal or otherwise), loss, damage or delay however caused'.
HELD: The fact that the plaintiff could not read did not avail her in any degree. Sufficient notice of the condition had been given to the plaintiff and she was bound by it. Appeal against judgment for defendants dismissed.

Note—See now Unfair Contract Terms Act 1977, p 313, above.

Sugar v London, Midland & Scottish Rly Co

[1941] 1 All ER 172, 164 LT 311, 57 TLR 197, 85 Sol Jo 32 (Viscount Caldecote LCJ)
The words on the face of a railway ticket reading 'For conditions see back, Day Excursion', were obscured and blotted out by the date stamp.

HELD: Reasonable notice had not been given and the passenger was not bound.

McCutcheon v David MacBrayne Ltd

[1964] 1 All ER 430, [1964] 1 WLR 125, 108 Sol Jo 93, [1964] 1 Lloyd's Rep 16
The appellant, McCutcheon, wished to have his car sent from Islay to the Scottish mainland by the respondent's steamship service. The carriage was arranged by his brother-in-law, McSporran, who went to the representatives' office on Islay and there saw the purser of their vessel, who quoted a freight charge for the journey. McSporran paid the amount of the freight, was given a receipt and delivered the car to the respondents. By an oversight he was not shown or asked to sign the respondents' 'risk note' a document containing an effective exclusion of liability for negligence. McCutcheon and McSporran had each consigned goods on previous occasions. McCutcheon had always signed the risk note though he had not read it; McSporran had sometimes been presented with the risk note to sign (and had signed it) and sometimes not; he had never read it. Both knew the note contained conditions.

The respondent's vessel sank by reason of their servants' negligence and the car was lost. In this action by McCutcheon for its value the respondents contended that by reason of the knowledge of the risk note gained by McCutcheon and McSporran in the previous transactions the appellant was bound by the conditions in it.
HELD: McCutcheon was not bound by the conditions in the risk note which formed no part of the contract. The course of dealing on earlier occasions is often relevant in determining contractual relations but not where, as here, the respondents had omitted to ask the appellant's agent to sign the document which would have been protection. If McSporran had known that the respondents always required a risk note to be signed and knew the purser was simply forgetting to submit it to him the result might be different; but there had been no constant course of dealing. He was offered an oral contract without any reference to conditions and accepted the offer in good faith.

Per Lord Devlin: There can be no conditions in any contract unless they are brought into it by expression, incorporation or implication. They are not brought into it simply because one party has inserted them into similar transactions in the past and has not given the other party any reason to think he will not want to insert them again. . . . If a man is given a blank ticket without conditions or any reference to them, even if he knows in detail what the conditions usually exacted are, he is not, in the absence of any allegation of fraud or of that sort of mistake for which the law gives relief, bound by such conditions.

Note—See also *Hollier v Rambler Motors* , p 315, above.

The Eagle

[1977] 2 Lloyd's Rep 70, QBD (Deputy Judge Mr Michael Ogden, QC)
The plaintiff was injured by the negligence of the defendants when on a cruise on their ship. The booking for the cruise had been made for the plaintiff by a friend. When making the booking he had seen a brochure issued by the defendants drawing attention to the conditions of carriage to be seen in the defendants' offices. When he eventually received the ticket he saw for the first time that there was a condition exempting the defendants from liability for negligence.
HELD: (1) He was agent for the plaintiff and his knowledge was binding on her; but (2) the contract was completed at the time of the booking, not delivery of the tickets,

and the ticket was not a contractual document; (3) mere knowledge that there were conditions was not sufficient in the circumstances to make them terms of the contract, and (4) even if that were wrong the brochure did not fairly bring home to passengers the existence of the exemption clause and the plaintiff was not bound by it.

The Dragon

[1979] 1 Lloyd's Rep 257 (Brandon J)
On 19 January 1971 the plaintiff's husband booked passages for himself, the plaintiff and their children on the defendant's vessel for the 7 July through their agents. He was not notified of any conditions of carriage. In June he received the tickets by post together with conditions of carriage exempting the defendants from liability for injury to a passenger. He did not notice or read the conditions.
HELD (following on this point *The 'Eagle'*, above): It would be wrong to hold that there was no concluded contract until the plaintiff's husband received and accepted the tickets sent him in June. The contract was concluded in January when no notice of the conditions was given. The defendant could not subsequently, by issuing a ticket containing the conditions, introduce them into the contract when it was not subject to them originally.

NOTICE-BOARDS

The Humorist

[1944] P 28, 113 LPJ 41, 171 LT 85, 60 TLR 190, 77 Ll L Rep 189 (Pilcher J)
'Notice to barge owners' on a notice-board 6 ft by 4 ft 10 ins was exhibited on the wall of a mill adjacent to a wharf. A barge lay alongside the wharf after loading, and was damaged by the defective berth. The writing on the notice-board was faded and it was difficult to read. The plaintiff's lightermen had not observed the notice board at all.
HELD: Defendants had not taken reasonable steps to bring the conditions on the board to the notice of casual invitees and plaintiffs were not affected with knowledge of its terms either as constituting a modification of the conditions of the invitation or as a warning to frequenters of the premises.

Furley v Victoria Garage Co

(1948) 98 L Jo 94, Bristol CC
The exhibition of notices at a garage to the effect that cars are accepted for storage at the owner's risk is not sufficient to limit the common law liability of the garage proprietors as bailees for reward, in the absence of positive evidence that the plaintiff saw and assented to the condition contained in the notices. The notices exhibited by the defendants constituted no defence unless it could be shown that the plaintiff had read one or more of them, and had assented to these terms being incorporated in the contract when he left his car in the defendants' custody. The judge found as a fact that the plaintiff had not at that time seen any one of the notices, and therefore that the restriction on the defendants' liability was not a term of the contract.

Cawood, Wharton & Co Ltd v Samuel Williams & Sons, The Cawood III

[1951] P 270, [1951] 1 TLR 924, [1951] 1 Lloyd's Rep 350, 95 Sol Jo 337 (Willmer J)
The plaintiffs, lightermen, contracted with the defendants, wharf owners, to provide

a lighter to be loaded by defendants at the defendants' jetty. The lighter was sunk by a projecting bolt of a timber fender at the jetty. A printed clause in the defendants' letter forming part of the contract provided that the defendants should not be liable for damage howsoever caused, even by their negligence, in relation to any goods handled by them. They also relied on a notice exhibited at the jetty that all lighters used the premises solely at their own risk and defendants would not be liable for any damage howsoever caused even by their negligence, and that the owners of lighters would indemnify them against all claims.
HELD: The notice was not a defence. (1) The onus of providing a previous course of business was on the defendants and had not been discharged; (2) it was not proved that any person representing the plaintiffs (other than the lightermen) ever had the terms of the notice brought to their attention, or ever had a fair opportunity of seeing or reading it; a lighterman was not an agent of the plaintiffs to receive such a notice; (3) the defendants had not included a clause in the terms of the notice in the contract; (4) the exceptions in the contract implied that they were the only exceptions. Judgment for plaintiffs.

Note—In some reports *Catwood for Cawood.*

Smith v Taylor

[1966] 2 Lloyd's Rep 231 (Blain J)
The plaintiff's car broke down. He walked to a nearby garage for help. A mechanic came with a breakdown vehicle and towed the car to the garage, the plaintiff steering it. It was towed into a yard at the side of the garage where the plaintiff said 'Do whatever is necessary' and then went away. He was known at the garage, where he had a monthly account, though he had used it in the past solely for the purchase of petrol. He had occasionally entered a small office when paying his petrol account but had not seen a notice displayed in the office window which relieved the garage owner of liability for damage by negligence to cars being repaired. Whilst the plaintiff's car was being repaired it caught fire due to the mechanic's negligence and was destroyed.
HELD: The notice did not apply. There was an onus on the garage owner if he wished to cover himself contractually to display the notice of conditions so as to bring it to the attention of persons who were likely to be making use of the garage in a way to which the conditions were relevant. When the plaintiff had been in the office it was simply for the purpose of paying for petrol and he had not had occasion then to concern himself with his position if he were going to be a regular user of the garage or workshops. When he was towed in to use the garage for the first time as a repair shop he went only in the yard, where there was no such notice. No previous use he had made of the premises was such as to impose on him any duty to make himself aware of what had been shown on the notice on the office window.

Thornton v Shoe Lane Parking Ltd

[1971] 2 QB 163, [1971] 1 All ER 686, [1971] 2 WLR 585, 115 Sol Jo 75, CA
The plaintiff, wishing to park his car, drove it to the defendants' automatic car park. There was a notice outside giving the charges and saying that all cars were parked at owners' risk. He drove up to the entrance where a machine automatically extruded a ticket which he took. He then drove on further and the car was taken up in a lift. In addition to instructions how to reclaim the car the ticket bore the words in small print 'This ticket is issued subject to the conditions of issue as displayed on the premises'. These (which he could have found if he had looked for them) included a condition

excluding liability for any injury. When he returned to the premises to reclaim the car he sustained personal injuries due to the defendants' negligence.

HELD: The defendants could not claim the protection of the condition because they had not taken adequate steps to bring it to the plaintiff's notice. They should have posted a prominent notice at the entrance, or used something like red ink on the ticket. The first attempt to bring the conditions to his notice was when it was almost impossible for him to leave. Moreover (per Lord Denning) the plaintiff had accepted the offer when he drove into the appropriate line or place; the ticket then issued was merely a receipt which could not alter the terms.

Note—In *Interfoto Picture Library Ltd v Stiletto Visual Programmes Ltd* [1988] 1 All ER 348, CA it was held, applying *Thornton*, that if one of a number of printed conditions was particularly onerous, adequate steps must be taken to bring it to the attention of a contracting party. People hardly ever troubled to read printed conditions on a ticket or delivery note or similar document. In *Interfoto*, nothing was done to draw attention to a particularly onerous condition so it did not become part of the contract.

HIRE-PURCHASE AGREEMENTS

Bontex Knitting Works v St Johns Garage

[1944] 1 All ER 381n, 60 TLR 253, CA

Plaintiffs, a firm of manufacturers, contracted with defendants, motor contractors, for the hire of a motor van and driver by time or by mileage. The defendants' document contained a clause, 'We do not hold ourselves responsible for the loss or damage to goods while on our lorry.' The plaintiffs instructed the driver as to the parcels to be delivered with addresses and documents. The contract was to deliver forthwith and immediately, and was estimated to take 2 ½ hours. On the journey the driver parked the van, removed the ignition key, but took no further precautions against theft. From 11 am or 11.15 am to 12 noon or 12.20 pm, he was absent from the van, which disappeared.

HELD, ON APPEAL: As the job was estimated not to occupy more than 2½ hours, and paid for on a time basis, there must be implied a term that the delivery should be forthwith and immediate and should go on continuously. Judgment of Lewis J [1943] 2 All ER 690, 60 TLR 44, in the court below was upheld.

Note—But see *Colverd v Anglo-Overseas Transport,* below.

Lowe v Lombank Ltd

[1960] 1 All ER 611, [1960] 1 WLR 196, 104 Sol Jo 210, CA

The plaintiff, a widow aged 65, went to a motor car dealer to buy a second-hand car. She was offered a car at £200 which the dealer said was in perfect condition. She wanted hire-purchase facilities and was required by the dealer to sign a form of hire-purchase agreement issued by the defendants. She signed without reading it. The car was later delivered to her and she signed a delivery receipt. The car turned out to be utterly unroadworthy, though to the plaintiff the defects would not have been apparent on reasonable inspection. The plaintiff sued for damages for breach of the implied condition of fitness in the Hire-Purchase Act 1938, s 8(2).

HELD: (1) Clauses in the hire-purchase agreement which purported to exclude conditions and warranties, express or implied, were not brought to the plaintiff's notice as required by s 8(3) of the Act and the defendants could not rely on them; (2) the plaintiff had made known to the owners the particular purpose for which the goods were required since the agreement itself contained terms appropriate to the use of the car as a means of transport; and (3) there was a breach of the implied warranty of fitness in s 8(2); (4) the plaintiff was not estopped from relying on the defects as proof of the breach of warranty by having signed a delivery receipt acknowledging that the car was in good order and condition, because it was not the case that the defendants had entered into the hire-purchase agreement in reliance on the terms of the receipt.

Note—For implied term as to fitness in hire-purchase agreements see now Supply of Goods (Implied Terms) Act 1973, s 10 as amended by the Supply of Goods and Services Act 1982, s 17.

Astley Industrial Trust Ltd v Grimley

[1963] 2 All ER 33, [1963] 1 WLR 584, 107 Sol Jo 474, CA
The defendant, a haulage contractor in a fair way of business, went to a dealer to obtain a tipping lorry on hire purchase. He said he had not done tipping before and that he could afford to take a lorry in the £500-£700 range. The dealer recommended him to take a Bedford lorry, six years old, and the defendant agreed to do so. The dealer sold the vehicle to the plaintiffs, a hire-purchase company, from whom the defendant agreed to hire it under a hire-purchase agreement which expressly excluded any warranty as to description, repair, quality or fitness for any purpose. The defendant noticed defects in the clutch, starter and tipping mechanism which the dealer said he would put right. After the lorry had been left with him on two occasions the defects were still not put right and the defendant took the lorry away, under protest, and began to use it for carrying hardcore. He drove it 150 miles to a place where for some weeks he used it to carry hardcore from a quarry. This was very heavy work which could quickly wear out even a new vehicle. A number of defects showed themselves and breakdowns occurred requiring repairs which cost the defendant a total of £55 in three months.
HELD: The plaintiffs were entitled to succeed: there was an implied condition or fundamental term that they were letting on hire a Bedford tipper, but the vehicle, though not free from defects, complied with that description and was capable of use as such. There was no fundamental breach and the plaintiffs were entitled to rely on the express exclusion of warranties in the hire-purchase agreement.

G Montague (Southern) Ltd v Warren

(1965) Times, 5 February, CA
The defendant, a chauffeur, took on hire purchase a Ford car. He paid three monthly instalments and drove the car 1,200 miles before beginning to complain about the condition of the car. His complaint was that he had to keep having the car repaired. He took the car back to the dealers from whom he had obtained it and paid no further instalments. To an action for recovery of arrears he pleaded a fundamental breach in that the condition of the car made it unroadworthy.
HELD: He had driven it 1,200 miles: there was no fundamental breach.

Porter v General Guarantee Corpn Ltd

[1982] RTR 384 (Kilner Brown J)
The plaintiff took a secondhand car on hire purchase from motor dealers. The dealers

represented that the car was in excellent condition, knowing that he wished to use it as a minicab. The car was not in fact in excellent condition.
HELD: The representation in the context of intended use as a mini-cab was sufficiently important in the minds of both parties to make it a fundamental term, breach of which entitled the plaintiff to repudiate the contract. He was entitled to judgment against the hire-purchase company as the contract was between him and them, they having utilised the services of the dealers and being bound by any representations made by them. As the agreement was a consumer credit agreement under the Consumer Credit Act 1974 the hire-purchase company were entitled as creditors to be indemnified by the dealers who were suppliers to the debtor.

SUB-CONTRACT

Davies v Collins

[1945] 1 All ER 247, 114 LJKB 199, 172 LT 155, 61 TLR 218, 89 Sol Jo 152, CA
Where a cleaner of clothes entered into a contract containing an owner's risk clause and limiting liability to ten times the cost of cleaning, the defendant had sent the work to sub-contractors. A contract might be for work to be done by the defendant himself, or by sub-contractors. The wording here that 'every care is exercised in cleaning' referred to the defendant himself. The contract excluded any right to get the work done by sub-contractors, though not for ancillary matters such as a carrier to take the goods back.
HELD: The clause did not relieve from negligence of sub-contractors and the defendant was liable.

Edwards v Newland & Co

[1950] 2 KB 534, [1950] 1 All ER 1072, 66 TLR (pt 2) 321, 94 Sol Jo 351, CA
B agreed with A for reward to store A's furniture. B stored the furniture with C. C's premises were bombed and C wrote to B advising the removal of the furniture. B wrote to A with the same advice but without informing A that the storage was not with B, and enclosing the account to date. A was on military service and his wife sought to remove the goods but was denied access until the account was paid. When the goods were delivered up, a number of articles were missing.
HELD: (1) B was in breach of his contract ab initio by undertaking to be a bailee and not acting as such; (2) the personal care and skill of B was of the essence of the contract and B was in breach of his contract in employing a sub-contractor.

Denning LJ pointed out that a repairer of a motor car can often reasonably sub-contract and send away a part of it to another firm for repairs; a carrier of goods would be entitled to make a sub-bailment and might need to entrust them to another carrier for part of the journey; a hirer of goods might often lawfully sub-hire. It depends on the circumstances of the particular case.

B held liable to A.

CHAPTER 12

Damages: General Principles and Damage to Property

1 FORESEEABILITY

INTRODUCTION

The present law of foreseeability derives from the decision in *Wagon Mound (No 1)* (or *Overseas Tank Ship (UK) Ltd v Morts Dock & Engineering Co Ltd*) (see below). This modified the judgment in *Re Polemis* [1921] 3 KB 560 by establishing that if a defendant could have anticipated damage by fire resulting from their action then they would be liable for that damage. This view was confirmed by a series of later cases including *Hughes v Lord Advocate* [1963] 1 All ER 705 HL, the *Wagon Mound (No 2)* (see below) and *Wieland v Cyril Lord Carpets Ltd* (see below). Therefore a defendant will only be liable for harm if it is of a kind, type or class foreseeable by the reasonable man.

As well as the cases mentioned below reference should also be made to the introduction to Chapter 1.

See also Lord Goff's Judgment in *Cambridge Water Company v Eastern Counties Leather* [1994] 1 All ER 53 where he imported the test of foreseeability into actions under nuisance and *Rylands v Fletcher*.

CASES ON FORESEEABILITY

Overseas Tankship (UK) Ltd v Morts Dock and Engineering Co Ltd (The Wagon Mound)

[1961] AC 388, [1961] 1 All ER 404, [1961] 2 WLR 126, 105 Sol Jo 85, [1961] 1 Lloyd's Rep 1

The respondents were owners of a wharf which they used for their business of ship repairing. The appellants were charterers of a vessel which was discharging petroleum products and taking in furnace oil at another wharf about 600 feet away. By carelessness of the appellants' servants a large quantity of furnace oil was allowed to spill into the water and spread over the surface, particularly along the foreshore near and under the respondents' wharf. Molten metal from welding operations on the respondents' wharf fell on some cotton waste or rag floating on debris beneath the wharf and set it alight. Flames from the cotton waste ignited the furnace oil on the water, as a result of which a conflagration developed which damaged the respondents' wharf. The appellants did not know and could not reasonably be expected to have known that the furnace oil was capable of being set on fire when spread on water. There was other damage directly caused by the oil but not caused by the fire, though the respondents had not claimed for it. The Supreme Court of New South Wales, following the decision in *Re Polemis*, held that the appellants were liable for the fire damage.

HELD, ON APPEAL to the Privy Council: the respondents were not liable for the fire damage. The *Polemis* decision should no longer be regarded as good law. If a defendant is guilty of negligence he is liable only for those consequences of his act which were reasonably foreseeable. It is, no doubt, proper when considering tortious liability for negligence to analyse its elements and to say that the plaintiff must prove a duty owed him by the defendant, a breach of that duty by the defendant, and consequent damage. But there can be no liability without damage. It is not the act but the consequences on which tortious liability is founded. The test of liability for the consequences of a negligent act is the foreseeability of the damage which in fact happened.

Doughty v Turner Manufacturing Co Ltd

[1964] 1 QB 518, [1964] 1 All ER 98, [1964] 2 WLR 240, 108 Sol Jo 53, CA

In the heat treatment department of the defendants' works was a sodium cyanide bath containing molten liquid at 800°C. Whilst changing electrodes in the bath a workman allowed a cover of asbestos cement to fall into the bath. After a minute or two there was an eruption in the bath and hot liquid was blown off, injuring the plaintiff. No one

knew before this accident that asbestos cement caused an explosion of this kind in sodium cyanide. The judge said the defendants were not to blame for not appreciating that the immersion of the cover would produce an explosion but held that the workman was negligent in letting the cover fall into the bath and that the defendants were liable for his negligence.
HELD, ON APPEAL: Even if the act of the workman in allowing the cover to fall in was negligent there was no liability on the defendant because the evidence showed that nobody supposed that the cover could not be safely immersed in the bath. The *Wagon Mound* (above) showed that *Re Polemis* was no longer good law: the essential factor in determining liability was whether the damage was of such a kind as the reasonable man should have foreseen.

Stewart v West African Terminals Ltd

[1964] 108 Sol Jo 838, [1964] 2 Lloyd's Rep 371, CA
The plaintiff, a boiler maker, was going aboard a vessel to fetch his tools when he involuntarily put his hand on a derrick wire to support himself whilst pushing aside another wire which was blocking his path. As he did so the derrick wire moved and injured his hand in a block. The stevedores argued that the risk of injury was not reasonably foreseeable.
HELD: There was evidence that the plaintiff's way to his tools was obstructed by the stevedores' negligence. Since *The Wagon Mound* a person was not responsible for the consequences of negligence unless they were reasonably foreseeable—subject to this, that it was not necessary for the precise concatenation of circumstances to be envisaged if the consequence was one which was within the general sphere of contemplation and not of an entirely different kind which no one could anticipate. The plaintiff's accident was within the sphere of contemplation for which the stevedores were liable.

Slatter v British Railways Board

[1966] 2 Lloyd's Rep 395 (Sachs J)
The plaintiff was a wagon examiner at the defendants' goods yard. He was inspecting a broken wagon on a railway line in the yard when he was startled by the noise of a violent crash as three loaded wagons were shunted into the other wagons on the line. He stumbled forward and his hand went on to the line where it was run over by the wheel of the wagon. It was known by the shunter that the plaintiff was in the vicinity.
HELD: The injury was a foreseeable result of allowing the wagons to crash into each other. It was foreseeable that someone would be startled by the crash and it was 'on the cards' that they would jump or stumble and by so doing might well be injured.

Overseas Tankship (UK) Ltd v The Miller Steamship Co Pty, The Wagon Mound (No 2)

[1967] 1 AC 617, [1966] 2 All ER 709, [1966] 3 WLR 498, 110 Sol Jo 447, PC.
As the result of the same fire as gave rise to the action and appeals in *Overseas Tankship (UK) Ltd v Morts Dock* (p 332, above) a ship belonging to the Miller Steamship Co Pty was damaged. On trial of their action the judge found that: (1) the officers of the *Wagon Mound* who allowed the oil to escape would regard furnace oil as very difficult to ignite on water; (2) in their experience this had very rarely happened; (3) they would have regarded it as a possibility which could become an actuality only in very exceptional circumstances. He held that the damage was not reasonably foreseeable by them.

HELD, ON APPEAL to the Privy Council: A risk cannot be regarded as not reasonably foreseeable merely because it is remote. If a real risk exists but is one that could only happen in very exceptional circumstances the defendant is not justified in dismissing the risk from his mind and doing nothing about it in circumstances where action to eliminate it presents no difficulty, involves no disadvantage and requires no expense. A reasonable man would weigh the risk against the difficulty and expense of eliminating it. In the present case no question of balancing advantages and disadvantages arose: it was both the interest and duty of the appellant defendants' servants to stop the discharge of oil immediately. In *The Wagon Mound (No 1)* the Board were not concerned with degrees of foreseeability because the finding there was that the fire was not foreseeable at all. In the present case the findings of fact showed some risk of fire would have been present in the mind of a reasonable man in the shoes of the defendants' servants. The defendants were liable.

Vacwell Engineering Co Ltd v BDH Chemicals Ltd

[1971] 1 QB 88, [1969] 3 All ER 1681, [1969] 3 WLR 927, 113 Sol Jo 639 (Rees J)
The defendants supplied a quantity of boron tribromide, a substance which explodes in contact with water, to the plaintiffs for industrial use in glass ampoules. They gave no warning of its explosive character. The plaintiffs put a large number of the ampoules in water to remove the labels. Somehow an ampoule broke causing others to break and bringing about a vast explosion. The defendants could have foreseen that, in the ordinary course of handling, an ampoule might come into contact with water and cause a minor explosion, but a violent and damaging explosion of the size which actually occurred was not reasonably foreseeable.
HELD: Following *Smith v Leech Brain & Co* (below) an explosion and some damage to property being foreseeable it was immaterial that the magnitude of the former and the extent of the latter were not. The defendants were liable for the whole of the damage done.

Note—An appeal was settled before the end of the hearing on the basis that that part of Rees J's judgment dealing with remoteness of damages in negligence should not be challenged. See [1970] 3 All ER 533.

THE RULE APPLIED TO PERSONAL INJURY CASES

Burden v Watson

1961 SLT (Notes) 67
The driver of a bus which collided with a motor cycle suffered a coronary thrombosis due to shock. It was contended on behalf of the motor cyclist that such an injury was not reasonably foreseeable.
HELD: Though the loss alleged to have been suffered must always be subject to the test of foreseeability it need not be shown that the wrongdoer ought to have foreseen the precise type of physical injury suffered. The position might well be different if the loss sustained as a result of the accident was of a type which a reasonable man would not be expected to foresee, eg through being unable to keep an appointment or attend a meeting.

Smith v Leech Brain & Co Ltd

[1962] 2 QB 405, [1961] 3 All ER 1159, [1962] 2 WLR 148, 106 Sol Jo 77 (Lord Parker CJ)
The plaintiff's husband received a burn on the lip in the course of his work due to the negligence of the defendants. The burn healed but later became ulcerated and cancerous. An operation was done to remove the cancer but secondary cancers developed and after further operations the plaintiff died about three years after sustaining the burn. In an action under the Fatal Accidents and Law Reform Acts the judge found that the burn was the promoting agency of the cancer in tissues which already had a pre-malignant condition as a result of the deceased's having worked in a gasworks. It was contended by the defendants that *The Wagon Mound* (p 332, above) disentitled the plaintiff to recovery damages since the defendants could not reasonably have foreseen that the burn would cause cancer and that the deceased would die.
HELD: In *The Wagon Mound* the Privy Council did not have the 'thin skull' cases in mind. It has always been the law of this country that a tortfeasor takes his victim as he finds him: there is not a day goes by where some trial judge does not adopt that principle. If the Privy Council had any intention of making an inroad on that principle they would have said so. On the contrary a distinction was drawn in their advice between type of injury and extent of damage. The test was not whether the defendants could reasonably have foreseen that a burn would cause cancer and that the deceased would die: the question was whether the defendants could reasonably foresee the type of injury which he suffered, namely, the burn. The plaintiff was entitled to damages for her husband's death.

Warren v Scruttons Ltd

[1962] 1 Lloyd's Rep 497 (Paull J)
The plaintiff, a dockworker, was handling a wire rope when his finger was pricked by a projecting strand of wire. The wound became poisoned, causing a generalised poisoning of the system with a high temperature. Part of the injured finger had to be cut off and there was continuing tenderness. In his teens the plaintiff had suffered from ulceration of the right eye leaving some weakness of vision. The high temperature and poisoning of the system following the injury to the finger caused a further ulcer with some resulting deterioration of the vision. The medical evidence was that an eye which had once suffered ulceration may always get further ulcers if some condition of the body causes a high temperature. The defendants having been found liable for the injury to the finger it was argued on their behalf that (on the principle of *The Wagon Mound*, p 332, above) the eye condition was not a foreseeable result of the pricking of the finger and damages for the eye condition should not be awarded against them.
HELD (following *Smith v Leech Brain*, above): The defendant's argument was not right. You must look to the type of damage to see whether it was one which could reasonably be anticipated. The type of damage here was a pricked finger. Once it was found that that damage could have been reasonably anticipated then any consequence which resulted because the individual had some peculiarity was a consequence for which the tortfeasor was liable. Nevertheless the fact that any febrile condition which the plaintiff suffered, eg a high temperature brought on by a very serious cold, would

produce the same condition as the accident did must be taken into account in assessing damages. Award £850 plus special damages of £41.

Bradford v Robinson Rentals Ltd

[1967] 1 All ER 267, [1967] 1 WLR 337, 111 Sol Jo 33, (Rees J)
In very cold weather on roads made difficult by ice and snow the plaintiff was required by his employers, the defendants, to take an old Austin van from Exeter to Bedford, a distance of 240 miles, and bring back a new one. This was not his normal work. Neither vehicle had a heater. The plaintiff protested against having to do the journey in such weather but the defendants insisted. The journey took two days. Owing to the prolonged exposure to very low temperatures the plaintiff sustained injury to his health by 'frost bite' or cold injury. There was no evidence that before the plaintiff started the journey either the plaintiff himself or the defendants actually contemplated that the plaintiff might suffer from 'frost bite' if he were required to carry out the journey.
HELD: Any reasonable employer would know that if the plaintiff were required to carry out the journey he would be subjected to a real risk to his health from prolonged exposure to the exceptional cold—for example a common cold, or pneumonia or chilblains. The law does not require that liability for its consequences is attributed. *Salmond on Torts* (14th edn) p 719 conveniently states the principle to be followed since *The Wagon Mound* (p 332, above): 'It is sufficient if the type, kind, degree or order of harm could have been foreseen in a general way. The question is, was the accident a variant of the perils originally brought about by the defendant's negligence?' In the present case the defendants knew that the plaintiff was being called upon to carry out an unusual task which would be likely to expose him for prolonged periods to extreme cold and considerable fatigue. By sending him on this journey they exposed him to a reasonably foreseeable risk of injury arising from such exposure. He sustained injury from it and was entitled to damages.

Note—See also *Malcolm v Broadhurst*, p 383, below.

Tremain v Pike

[1969] 3 All ER 1303, [1969] 1 WLR 1556, 113 Sol Jo 182 (Payne J)
The plaintiff, a farm worker, contracted Weil's disease by handling materials contaminated by rat's urine. The disease was not a reasonably foreseeable result of rat infestation.
HELD: This was not a case like *Smith v Leech Brain* (p 335, above) or *Bradford v Robinson Rentals* (above) in which the risk of injury from a burn or from extreme cold was foreseeable and in which it was only the degree of injury or the development of the sequelae which was not foreseeable. In the present case the risk of the initial infection was not foreseeable and was entirely different in kind from other possible injuries from rat infestation. The plaintiff was not entitled to succeed.

SECOND INCIDENT

Wieland v Cyril Lord Carpets Ltd

[1969] 3 All ER 1006 (Eveleigh J)
The plaintiff, a lady of 57 years of age was a passenger in a bus when she was thrown forward and sustained injury to her neck. She was treated at hospital where, two days

later, she was fitted with a collar. On the same day whilst descending some stairs she fell and injured her ankles. The cause of her fall, the judge found, was that whilst wearing the collar she was unable properly to judge the position of the steps when wearing her bifocal lens spectacles. The defendants contended that the injury to the ankles was not due to their negligence; alternatively it was not foreseeable, relying on *The Wagon Mound.*

HELD: (1) The fall and resultant injury was caused by the defendants' negligence. The plaintiff's ability to negotiate stairs had been impaired and this caused the fall. It had long been recognised that injury sustained in one accident may be the cause of a subsequent injury, eg the injury sustained by accident victims on the operating table. It is always a question for the court to decide on the facts whether the accident did cause the second injury; *Hogan v Bentinck Collieries* (p 384, below). (2) *The Wagon Mound* decided that damages can only be recovered if the injury complained of was an injury of a class or character foreseeable as a possible result of the negligence. 'The injury complained of' means that personal injury, loss or damage which the law requires to constitute the tort of negligence. *The Wagon Mound* is not to be read as dealing with the extent of the injury or the degree to which it has affected the plaintiff, still less as requiring foreseeability of the manner in which that original injury has caused harm to the plaintiff. In determining liability for the possible consequences of the injury it is not necessary to show that each consequence was within the foreseeable extent or foreseeable scope of the original injury in the same way as the possibility of injury must be foreseen when determining whether or not the defendant's conduct gives a claim in negligence. The present case was concerned with the extent of the harm suffered by the plaintiff: the injury and damage suffered because of the second fall were attributable to the original negligence. (3) Another way of putting it is to say that it is foreseeable that one injury may affect a person's ability to cope with the vicissitudes of life and thereby be a cause of another injury. Foreseeability of this general nature will suffice.

McKew v Holland and Hannen and Cubitts (Scotland) Ltd

[1969] 3 All ER 1621, 1970 SC (HL) 20, 1970 SLT 68

On 14 February owing to the defender's negligence the pursuer sustained minor injuries to his left leg. On several occasions following the injury his left leg for a short time went numb and he lost control of it. On 5 March as he was about to descend a staircase he felt his leg give way again. To avoid a fall he jumped down the flight of stairs and sustained severe injury.

HELD: The defendant was not liable in damages for the second injury. The pursuer was acting unreasonably in choosing to descend the staircase without taking precautions against the possibility that his leg might give way. His unreasonable conduct was a *novus actus interveniens*.

Per Lord Reid: I do not think that foreseeability (of the defender) comes into this. A defender is not liable for a consequence of a kind which is not foreseeable. But it does not follow that he is liable for every consequence which a reasonable man could foresee. . . . It only leads to trouble if one tries to graft on to the concept of foreseeability some rule of law to the effect that a wrongdoer is not bound to foresee something which in fact he could readily foresee as quite likely to happen. For it is not at all unlikely or unforeseeable that an active man who has suffered such a disability will take some quite unreasonable risk. But if he does, he cannot hold the defender liable for the consequences.

Note—See also 'novus actus interveniens', p 344, below.

CONTRACT AND TORT CONTRASTED

Koufos v C Czarnikow Ltd, The Heron II

[1969] 1 AC 350, [1967] 3 All ER 686, [1967] 3 WLR 1491, 111 Sol Jo 848, HL

The respondents chartered the appellant's ship to carry a cargo of sugar to Basrah. Owing to a deviation amounting to a breach of contract the ship arrived nine days later than anticipated. The price of sugar at Basrah fell during that period and the respondents obtained less for the cargo than if the ship had arrived on time. At the time the contract was made the appellant did not know what the respondents were going to do with the sugar but he knew there was a market in sugar at Basrah and could have assumed if he thought about it that the sugar would be sold there. The price might have gone up or down—there was an even chance of either happening.

HELD: The loss was not too remote and the appellant was liable for it.

Per Lord Reid: In cases [of contract] like *Hadley v Baxendale* (1854) 9 Exch 341 or the present case it is not enough that in fact the plaintiff's loss was directly caused by the defendant's breach of contract. It clearly was so caused in both. The crucial question is whether, on the information available to the defendant when the contract was made, he should, or a reasonable man in his position would, have realised that such a loss was sufficiently likely to result from the breach of contract to make it proper to hold, that the loss flowed naturally from the breach or that loss of that kind should have been within his contemplation. The modern rule in tort is quite different and it imposes a much wider liability. The defendant will be liable for any type of damage which is reasonably foreseeable as liable to happen even in the most unusual case, unless the risk is so small that a reasonable man would in the whole circumstances feel justified in neglecting it; and there is a good reason for the difference. In contrast, if one party wishes to protect himself against a risk which to the other party would appear unusual, he can direct the other party's attention to it before the contract is made. . . . In tort, however, there is no opportunity for the injured party to protect himself in that way, and the tortfeasor cannot reasonably complain if he has to pay for some very unusual but nevertheless foreseeable damage which results from his wrongdoing.

Hargreaves Vehicle Distributors Ltd v Holbrook

[1970] RTR 380, CA

The defendant was acquiring a lorry by hire purchase and was using it as his only means of livelihood. It was badly damaged in an accident and was taken to the plaintiffs' garage for repair on 4 April. An estimate was agreed with the defendant's insurers on 24 April but the plaintiffs did not order essential parts until 17 May. They completed the work on 10 September but did not tell the defendant until 14 October. When he collected it he found the work had not been satisfactorily done. Meanwhile because of the delay he had been unable to keep up his payments to the hire-purchase company who in January repossessed themselves of the vehicle and obtained judgment against the defendant for £418. The plaintiffs sued for £10 excess under his insurance policy: the defendant counterclaimed in the amount of his loss.

HELD: The plaintiffs knew it was a commercial vehicle and that when it was not available there would be loss of profit or other monetary loss to the defendant. They were under a contractual obligation to return the vehicle properly repaired within a reasonable time and the delay of at least two months was a breach of that duty.

Whether or not they were aware of the precise circumstances of the hire purchase they were liable to the defendant for the amount of his loss.

Note—See also *Charnock v Liverpool Corpn,* p 871, below.

Batty v Metropolitan Realisation Ltd

[1978] QB 554, [1978] 2 All ER 445, [1978] 2 WLR 500, 112 Sol Jo 63, CA
The *ratio decidendi* of *Esso Petroleum Co Ltd v Mardon* ([1976] QB 801, [1976] 2 All ER 5, [1976] 2 WLR 583, 120 Sol Jo 131) necessarily requires that the mere fact the plaintiffs have obtained judgment for breach of contract does not preclude them from the entitlement which would have existed, apart from contract, to have judgment entered in their favour also in tort, assuming, eg that the plaintiffs had established a breach by the defendant of a common law duty of care owed to the plaintiffs.

2 CAUSATION OF DAMAGE

Note—The test of foreseeability determines liability in damages for the result of a wrongful act. An entirely separate question is whether a particular form of loss is a sufficiently direct result of the wrongful act as to give the plaintiff a right to be compensated for that loss.

DAMAGE MUST RESULT FROM THE WRONGFUL ACT

Carslogie SS Co v Royal Norwegian Government

[1952] AC 292, [1952] 1 All ER 20, [1951] WN 609, [1951] 2 TLR 1099, 95 Sol Jo 801, HL
The elementary principle is that it is for the plaintiff in an action for damages to prove his case; to show affirmatively that damage under any particular head has resulted from the wrongful act of the defendant.

Note—See *Meah v McCreamer (No 2)* [1986] 1 All ER 943, p 398, below.

Organic Research Chemicals Ltd v Ricketts

[1961] Times, 16 November, CA
The plaintiffs had handed their car to the defendant to repair when it broke down. The car was towed to the defendant's garage. Attempts were made to restart it which caused further extensive damage to the engine. The first breakdown was due to a broken camshaft which would have cost £30 to replace. The extensive damage caused by the defendant's attempt to restart it made necessary the fitting of a re-conditioned engine at a cost of £61. The county court judge awarded the plaintiffs the whole cost of the engine. On appeal the Court of Appeal reduced the award to £31 being the difference between the cost of the re-conditioned engine and the cost of replacing the camshaft. It was impossible to say that the plaintiffs had suffered £61 damages, since the engine needed £30 spent on it before the damage was done. What they had suffered was the difference between the £61 for the re-conditioned engine and the £30 they would have had to pay anyhow. *The Bernina* (1886) 6 Asp MLC 65 and *The*

Munster (1896) 12 TLR 264 were distinguishable on the grounds that the pre-existing damage to this car had rendered it completely immobile.

Performance Cars Ltd v Abraham

[1962] 1 QB 33, [1961] 3 All ER 413, [1961] 3 WLR 749, 105 Sol Jo 748, CA
The plaintiffs' car was damaged in a collision with the defendant's car for which the defendant admitted he was to blame. The damage was such that the whole of the lower part of the plaintiffs' car would need to be resprayed to put it right, at a cost of £75. A short time before this accident the plaintiffs' car had been damaged in another collision and needed a re-spray of the whole of the lower part to put that damage right. The respray had not been done at the time of the second accident. A judgment had been obtained for £75 against the person responsible for the first accident but was unsatisfied. The plaintiffs claimed they were entitled to £75 damages from the present defendant as one of two separate tortfeasors who must each be liable for the consequences of his own tortious act.
HELD: The defendant was not liable for the cost of the re-spray. The necessity for re-spraying was not the result of the defendant's wrongful act because the necessity already existed. The second collision had put no extra burden on the plaintiffs in the matter of re-spraying, for the earlier collision had already imposed the burden of re-spraying on them. The rights of the plaintiffs against the person who caused the first collision were not completely collateral and the quotation from *Mayne on Damages* referred to by Asquith LJ in *Shearman v Folland* (p 437, below) did not apply here. The principle to be applied was that adopted by the House of Lords in *Carslogie SS Co v Royal Norwegian Government* (above).

Note—See also *Hodgson v General Electricity Co Ltd* and *Jobling v Associated Dairies Ltd*, p 387, below.

Cutler v Vauxhall Motors Ltd

[1971] 1 QB 418, [1970] 2 All ER 56, [1970] 2 WLR 961, 114 Sol Jo 247, CA
In November 1965 the plaintiff sustained a graze on the right ankle in an accident at work. It healed in a fortnight and he was not off work. In May 1966 he had pain in the right leg. He was found to have a varicose condition of both legs. An ulcer formed on the site of the original graze and because of this he was advised to have an immediate operation on both legs to cure the varicose condition. This was done in September 1966. The varicose condition was not the result of the accident but the ulcer was, and it was also the reason for having the operation done at once, though even if the accident had never occurred the operation would have been necessary by 1970 or 1971. The plaintiff lost wages amounting to £173 when the operation was done. The judge awarded him £10 for the graze but nothing for the discomfort of the operation or the resultant loss of wages.
HELD, ON APPEAL: The judge was right. The task of the court is to assess the totality of the damages to be awarded and to do so the court must have regard to future probabilities. There was no reasonable ground for supposing that if the accident had not happened the plaintiff would not have survived to 1970 or 1971 and then lose a sum at least equivalent to the £173. If the plaintiff were awarded £173 in this action the defendants would be recouping him for a loss which in all probability he would have had to bear even if the accident had not occurred.

Kay's Tutor v Ayrshire and Arran Health Board

[1987] 2 All ER 417, 1987 SLT 577, HL
In November 1987, the appellant's son, Andrew, aged two years five months, contracted meningitis and was admitted to the defendants' hospital. While seriously ill, he was injected with a massive overdose of penicillin, causing temporary paralysis and convulsions. The mistake was immediately rectified and he recovered from the meningitis, but became severely deaf. The appellant sued the respondents in negligence on the grounds that the overdose of penicillin had caused the deafness.
HELD, ON APPEAL: There was no satisfactory evidence that an overdose of penicillin would have caused Andrew's deafness, or indeed that an overdose of penicillin had ever caused deafness. On the other hand, even when meningitis was treated correctly, deafness frequently occurred as an inevitable result. Accordingly, the appeal must be dismissed. In this case, there were two competing causes of injury: the overdose, which was a tortious cause, and the result of the illness, which was not. The court could not presume that the tortious cause was responsible for the injury if this was not substantiated by the evidence.

IIMPECUNIOSITY

Liesbosch, Dredger v Edison SS

[1933] AC 449, 102 LJP 73, 149 LT 49, HL
While the dredger 'L' was lying moored alongside the breakwater at Patras Harbour the steamship 'E' fouled the dredger's moorings and carried her out to sea, where she sank and was lost. The owners of the 'E' admitted sole liability for the loss. The 'L' had been bought in 1927 for £4,000 by her owners, who had spent a further £2,000 in bringing her to Patras. They were a syndicate of civil engineers. Under a contract with the Patras Harbour Commissioners they were engaged in construction work in the harbour, for which a dredger was necessary and for which they were using the 'L'. The contract provided for completion of the work within a specified time. The loss of 'L' stopped the work and, being unable from want of funds to purchase any suitable dredger which was for sale, on 4 May 1929, they hired a dredger, the 'A' which was lying in harbour at Carlo Forte, Sardinia, to take the place of the 'L'. The 'A' was more expensive in working than the 'L' and required the attendance of a tug and two hopper barges. The 'L' was sunk on 26 November 1928. The 'A' got to work on the harbour on 17 June 1929.
HELD: The measure of damages was the value of the 'L' to her owners as a profit-earning dredger at the time and place of her loss; and that it should include: (1) A capital sum made up of (a) the market price on 26 November 1928 of a dredger comparable to the 'L'; (b) the cost of adapting the new dredger and of transporting and insuring her from her moorings to Patras; and (c) compensation for disturbance and loss suffered by the owners of the 'L' in carrying out their contract during the period between 26 November 1928 and the date on which the substituted dredger could reasonably have been available for use at Patras, including in that loss such items as overhead charges and expenses of staff and equipment and the like thrown away, but neglecting any special loss or extra expenses due to the financial position of one or other of the parties. (2) Interest upon the capital sum from 26 November 1928.

If the appellants' financial embarrassment is to be regarded as a consequence of the respondents' tort, I think it is too remote; but I prefer to regard it as an independent cause, though its operative effect was conditioned by the loss of the dredger (Lord Wright).

Note—The point was neatly put in arrangement that the defendants were liable for restitution but not to pay for destitution.

It is common to find a plaintiff claiming for continuing loss of use because he had not the means to pay for repairs. It is submitted this cannot be recovered. But see the following cases.

Clements v Bawns Shipping Co

(1948) 81 Ll L Rep 232 (Denning J)
A ship was sold by fraudulent misrepresentation. The purchaser sued for damages, including loss of profit-earning capacity. The plaintiff was too poor to be able to expend the money on repairs for two years, nor up to the date of trial.
HELD: The consequences of his own poverty were not damages resulting from the tort of the defendant. The *Liesbosch* case (above) followed.

The judge allowed for loss whilst the boat was being repaired, whilst arrangements were being made for it, and whilst obtaining the necessary parts for the engine.

Robbins of Putney v Meek

[1971] RTR 345 (John Stephenson J)
The defendants ordered from the plaintiffs, motor dealers, a Bentley car at a price of £7,510. In breach of the contract they refused to accept it and the plaintiffs had to find another buyer. They were short of liquid capital and purchase of the car had caused them to exceed the limit of their overdraft. After two months of advertising it at figures well over £6,000 they sold it to a dealer at £5,750. In reply to the plaintiffs' claim for loss of profit the defendants said that because of impecuniosity they had sold too quickly and should not have sold it until they could get its full value.
HELD: In relation to mitigation of damages (as distinct from measure of damages) the wrongdoer must take his victim as he is. The plaintiffs, with the maximum limit fixed for their overdraft and their lack of liquid capital, had acted reasonably in selling the car as they did and were entitled to recover from the defendants the amount of the loss.

Dodd Properties (Kent) Ltd v Canterbury City Council

[1980] 1 All ER 928, [1980] 1 WLR 433, 124 Sol Jo 84, 253 Estates Gazette 1335, CA
A building owned by the plaintiffs was damaged by building work next door carried out by the defendants, who eventually admitted liability to pay damages. The damage was done in 1968 and repairs could have been done in 1970 when they would have cost £11,375. For various reasons, including financial stringency (short of impecuniosity or financial embarrassment) the plaintiffs had not done repairs at the time of the hearing in 1978. By then the cost of repairs had gone up to £30,000.
HELD: Though the general principle is that damages are to be assessed as at the date the damage occurs it is not a universal rule and is subject to many exceptions and qualifications. Where there is a material difference between the cost of repairs at the date of the wrongful act and the cost when the repairs can, having regard to all relevant circumstances, first reasonably be undertaken it is the latter time at which the cost of repairs should be taken in assessing damages. On the facts the plaintiffs had good commercial reasons for not doing the repairs before the case was heard and were entitled to damages based on cost of repairs at £30,000. The decision in the *Liesbosch* case (above) was not applicable: in that case the excess loss flowed directly from the lack of means and not from the tortious act.

Note—See also *London Congregational Union v Harriss and Harriss (a firm)* [1985] 1 All ER 335.

Perry v Sidney Phillips & Son (a firm)

[1982] 3 All ER 705, [1982] 1 WLR 1297, 126 Sol Jo 626, 263 Estates Gazette 888, CA
The plaintiff bought a house on the strength of a report from the defendants that it was sound. In fact it suffered from a number of defects causing him anxiety and distress for which he claimed damages. It was pleaded for the defendants that he could have cut his losses by selling or having repairs done and that if lack of means prevented him from doing this the *Liesbosch* case was a bar to his recovering.
HELD, per Kerr LJ: It was reasonable for the plaintiff not to do any repairs by the time of the trial, and those reasons went beyond his lack of means. In any event it seems to me that the authority of what Lord Wright said in the *Liesbosch* case is consistently being attenuated in more recent decisions of this court, in particular in *Dodd Properties v Canterbury CC* (above). . . . If it is reasonably foreseeable that the plaintiff may bc unablc to mitigatc or remedy the consequences of the other party's breach as soon as he would have done if he had been provided with the necessary means to do so from the other party, then it seems to me that the principle of the *Liesbosch* case no longer applies in its full vigour.

Ramwade Ltd v WJ Emson & Co Ltd

[1987] RTR 72 [1986] LS Gaz R 2996, CA
The plaintiff's skip lorry was written off in an accident. The defendants, their insurance brokers, had failed to arrange comprehensive insurance cover and insurers correctly rejected the claim for the value of the lorry. The plaintiffs obtained judgment against their brokers for their losses flowing from the failure to obtain comprehensive cover. Damages were assessed to include amounts paid by the plaintiffs to hire replacement vehicles. The defendants appealed against this award; the plaintiffs conceded that a comprehensive policy would not have covered the cost of hiring replacement vehicles.
HELD: The appeal succeeded. It might seem superficially attractive to argue that the payment of hire charges was a foreseeable result of the broker's failure to arrange insurance, because of the resultant delay in payment, but correctly the foreseeable loss was the amount that the insurers would have paid. The hire charges were incurred either because the plaintiffs could not afford to buy a substitute vehicle or because the damages were not paid at the proper time, so the plaintiffs would be seeking to recover damages for non-payment of damages.

Note—In *London Congregational Union v Harriss and Harriss* (*a firm*) [1985] 1 All ER 335, Judge Newey OR assessed damages to reflect the cost of repairs when they could first reasonably have been undertaken.

This approach taken to the measure of damages was not questioned, although much of the judgment was the subject of a partially successful appeal.

Mattocks v Mann

[1993] RTR 13, CA
The plaintiff's two door Peugeot GTI was badly damaged in a road traffic accident for which the defendant admitted responsibility. The plaintiff needed a replacement vehicle and first hired a four-door saloon model for some 20 weeks exchanging it thereafter for a smaller two-door vehicle. The plaintiff claimed the full hire costs to the date when the defendant's insurance company provided money to pay for the

repairs to her vehicle. The plaintiff argued that she was unable to meet these repair costs herself.

Assessing the damages the Master (i) disallowed the extra cost of hiring the four-door saloon but (ii) allowed the claim for hire charges incurred for the period after the completion of the repairs to the plaintiff's vehicle to the time when the defendant released money to pay for the work. Both parties appealed.

HELD: (i) The Master applied the wrong test. It was not relevant that the plaintiff could have managed with the smaller vehicle hired after the saloon. The proper test was to look at whether or not the plaintiff had acted reasonably in hiring the saloon in the first place. There was nothing to indicate that the hiring of the saloon was unreasonable in the circumstances, particularly as it was still over £200 a week cheaper than if the plaintiff had hired a replacement Peugeot GTI.

(ii) The law of damages had moved on since the decision in the *Liesbosch* case. The plaintiff's impecuniosity in this case could not be said to be the sole cause of the need to hire an alternative vehicle but:

'In these days when everybody looks to one or other of the insurers of vehicles involved in an accident, it is clearly contemplated that where the cost of repairs are of the substantial kind involved in this case, the source of payment of that cost will be the insurers. Looking here at the whole history of events, one cannot isolate the plaintiff's inability to meet the cost of those repairs and say that that brought an end to the period for which it was reasonable that the second defendant's insurers should be liable': per Beldam LJ.

The plaintiff was awarded her hire charge claim in full.

NOVUS ACTUS INTERVENIENS

Intervening act of third party

Note—The chain of causation between the defendant's wrongdoing and the plaintiff's damage may be broken if the immediate cause of the damage was the act of a third party.

Home Office v Dorset Yacht Co Ltd

[1970] AC 1004, [1970] 2 All ER 294, [1970] 2 WLR 1140, 114 Sol Jo 375, [1970] 1 Lloyd's Rep 453, HL

A party of borstal trainees were working on Brownsea Island under the supervision and control of three borstal officers employed by the appellants. During the night seven of the trainees escaped and went on board a yacht they found nearby. They set it in motion and collided with the respondent's yacht which was moored in the vicinity, causing damage.

HELD: The appellants were liable for the damage.

Per Lord Reid: The ground of liability is not responsibility for acts of the escaping trainees; it is liability for damage caused by the carelessness of these officers in the knowledge that their carelessness would probably result in the trainees causing damage of this kind. So the question is really one of remoteness of damage . . . [and] to what extent the law regards the acts of another person as breaking the chain of causation between the defendants' carelessness and the damage of the plaintiff. . . . It has never been the law that the intervention of human action always prevents the ultimate damage from being regarded as having been caused by the original carelessness. The convenient phrase *novus actus interveniens* denotes those cases where such action is regarded as breaking the chain and preventing the damage from being held to be caused by the careless conduct. But every day there are cases where, although one of the connecting links is deliberate human action, the law has no difficulty in holding that the defendant's conduct caused the plaintiff loss. . . . What then is the dividing line? . . . The cases show that, where human action forms one of the links between the original wrongdoing of the defendant and the loss suffered by the plaintiff, that action must at least have been something very likely to happen if it is not to be regarded as *novus actus interveniens* breaking the chain of causation. I do not think that a mere foreseeable possibility is or should be sufficient, for then the intervening human action can be more properly regarded as a new cause than as a consequence of the original wrongdoing. But if the intervening action was likely to happen I do not think it can matter whether that action was innocent or tortious or criminal.

Note—See also *Robinson v Post Office*, p 384, below, and *Lloyds Bank v Budd*, p 55, above.

West v Hughes of Beaconsfield Ltd

[1971] RTR 298 (Mocatta J)
In the hours of darkness the plaintiff, on a bicycle, wished to turn right from a busy road into a side road. When in the centre of the main road before turning he was struck from behind by a van and knocked over. He got up, picked up his bicycle, and was then hit and very severely injured by a car which was following the van. Neither driver saw him before the collisions though they were using headlights and there was nothing to prevent them from seeing him. The judge held both drivers to have been negligent. It was argued for the van driver that (1) the car driver's negligence was a *novus actus*, alternatively (2) as the most serious injuries were caused by the car the car owner should bear the major part of the responsibility.
HELD: (1) Although all the grave injuries were directly caused by the car there was not such a break in the chain of causation that the van driver could be held liable only for nominal damages. If a driver in a line of traffic on a busy road at night negligently knocks down a cyclist it is plainly foreseeable that the next following vehicle may injure the rider. The fact that the following driver could have avoided the cyclist if he had been keeping a proper look-out does not make his negligence a *novus actus*. (2) The negligence of each driver was causative of the plaintiff's injuries: as the van driver had a better opportunity of seeing the plaintiff than the car driver he should bear 55% of the responsibility and the car driver 45%.

Lamb v Camden London Borough Council

[1981] QB 625, [1981] 2 All ER 408, [1981] 2 WLR, 1038, 125 Sol Jo 356, CA
The plaintiff owned a house in a good neighbourhood. She let it to a tenant and went to America. Some months later the defendant council in doing work for renewal of a sewer damaged a water main. Water caused a subsidence of the house: it was not safe to live in and the tenant left. Repair work was not done until some years later. During the intervening period the house was locked up but squatters broke in and caused considerable damage to the interior. The council admitted liability for nuisance. The plaintiff claimed damages for the cost of repairs made necessary by the subsidence and in addition damages for the cost of making good the damage done by the squatters.
HELD: The defendants were not liable for the damage done by the squatters: it was too remote. Applying Lord Reid's test in *Home Office v Dorset Yacht Co* (above) the

squatters' actions, though 'foreseeable', were not 'likely', the house being in a neighbourhood where squatting had not formerly occurred. But even Lord Reid's test may not be adequate where the fresh damage had been caused by the intervening act of a third party. A court may require a degree of likelihood amounting almost to inevitability before it fixes a defendant with responsibility for the act of a third party over whom he has and can have no control.

Note—Applied in *P Perl (Exporters) Ltd v Camden London Borough Council* [1984] QB 342, [1983] 3 All ER 161, [1983] 3 WLR 769, 127 Sol Jo 581, CA. See also *Ward v Cannock Chase District Council* [1985] 3 All ER 537.

Knightley v Johns

[1982] 1 All ER 851, [1982] 1 WLR 349, 126 Sol Jo 101, [1982] RTR 182, CA
Johns was driving his car through a tunnel having two carriageways when it overturned, blocking most of the northbound carriageway. The accident was admittedly due to his negligent driving. The driver of a following car reported the accident by telephone to the police control centre whence a message was transmitted by radio to the plaintiff, PC Knightley, a police officer on a motor cycle. He entered the tunnel, saw the situation, and then left it to radio further information to the control centre. On returning to the scene he found that Inspector Sommerville, the third defendant, had already arrived with other police officers. The inspector said to him and another officer 'I have forgotten to close the tunnel; you go back and do it.' The two officers then rode south, in the opposite direction to the traffic stream. The plaintiff collided with an oncoming car near the entrance and was injured. There were in existence standing orders presumably known to the inspector (who, though present at the trial, did not give evidence) specifying a procedure and precautions for dealing with accidents in the tunnel. They required, inter alia, the tunnel to be closed at the outset, for officers to go on foot only and for 'emergency vehicles' to be accompanied by an officer only when all traffic had been stopped. The trial judge held that the police officers were not negligent, that the whole sequence of events flowed from Johns's negligence, and that he was liable in damages to the plaintiff.
HELD, ON APPEAL: The decision was not right. The inspector was negligent in not closing the tunnel and in ordering or allowing his subordinates to do a very dangerous thing contrary to standing orders. The question to be answered was whether his negligence was concurrent with the negligence of Johns or whether the acts and omissions of the plaintiff and the inspector were new causes which broke the chain of causation. In considering the effects of carelessness the test is reasonable foreseeability; in this case, whether the whole sequence of events was a natural and probable consequence of Johns's negligence and a reasonably foreseeable result of it. Negligent conduct is more likely to break the chain of causation than conduct which is not; positive acts will more easily constitute new causes than inaction. The inspector's negligence was not a concurrent cause running with Johns's negligence, but a new cause interrupting the effect of it. The judge's decision carried Johns's responsibility too far. The inspector, not Johns, was liable in damages to the plaintiff.

Smith v Littlewoods Organisation Ltd

[1987] 1 All ER 710, [1987] NLJ Rep 149, HL
Littlewoods purchased the Regal Cinema, Dunfermline to demolish it and build a supermarket. It was left empty and unattended from the end of the third week of June

1986; by the beginning of July there was obvious evidence that it was being regularly broken into and vandalised, but no-one told Littlewoods or the police, nor were they told that a small fire had been stamped out. On 5 July 1986, after further acts of vandalism, a fire was deliberately started which razed the cinema and damaged adjoining buildings. The owners of these buildings claimed damages on the grounds of Littlewoods' negligence, contending that it was reasonably foreseeable that the cinema would be entered by vandals (or even just children) who would start fires which would spread to adjoining property.
HELD: The appellants could not recover damages from Littlewoods. (i) On the information available to Littlewoods, these events were not reasonably foreseeable to them; they were under a general duty to take reasonable care to ensure that their premises were not a source of danger to neighbours but the existence of any more specific duty to prevent this type of damage must depend on the circumstances—here no such specific duty was owed. (ii) (Per Lord Mackay) Where damage is the result of unpredictable human conduct ('every society will have a sprinkling of people who behave most abnormally'), what the reasonable man is bound to foresee is the highly likely result of any error of his own, not the merely possible. The more predictable the behaviour the more foreseeable the result. (iii) (Per Lord Goff) Liability in negligence for damage deliberately caused by others could only exist in special circumstances, for example, where there is a special relationship (as between borstal officers and trainees in *Home Office v Dorset Yacht Co Ltd*, p 344, above), where a defendant negligently creates a source of damage (leaving a horse in a crowded street, as in *Haynes v Harwood*, p 46, above) or where (as in *Goldman v Hargrave*, p 231, above) a defendant knows of a fire started by others on his premises, but fails to take reasonable steps to prevent it damaging adjoining property.

Note—For a detailed analysis of the judgments, see (1989) LQR 104 at 105, where it is suggested that Lord Mackay raises, for the first time, the possibility of a duty being owed by the owner of premises to prevent third parties damaging adjoining property.

Intervening act of plaintiff

Note—See cases at p 386, below, under heading 'Refusal to undergo operation'.

Malcolm v Dickson

(1951) 112 Post Magazine 249, Ct of Sess
The painter employed in painting premises set fire to the woodwork with a blowlamp. The deceased, who was living in the house, went upstairs to save some personal belongings. He was overcome by fumes and collapsed and was burned to death.
HELD: The death was too remote from the alleged negligence. Logically, the loss of a battle, or even a kingdom, might be traced to the absence of a nail in a horse's shoe, but strict logic is not a safe guide. There is a danger of the courts being driven stage by stage to undue lengths in the direction of allowing the inclusion of more and more remote consequential items of loss.

3 ECONOMIC LOSS

Note—Mere economic loss unaccompanied by damage to the plaintiff's person or property is irrecoverable in an action for negligence.

Negligent conduct

Brandon Electrical Engineering Co v Wm Press & Son

(1956) 106 L Jo 332 (McKee)
Public works contractors broke water main under highway which put electric cable out of action and plaintiff's factory stopped for some hours. Plaintiffs could not recover damages for wasted wages and loss of production.

Weller & Co v Foot and Mouth Disease Research Institute

[1966] 1 QB 569, [1965] 3 All ER 560, [1965] 3 WLR 1082, 109 Sol Jo 702, [1965] 2 Lloyd's Rep 414
The defendants allowed foot and mouth virus to escape into the atmosphere. As a result the Minister of Agriculture ordered the Guildford and Farnham cattle markets to be closed: the plaintiffs were auctioneers there and lost business by reason of the closure.
HELD: The plaintiffs could not recover damages from the defendants. A great volume of authority both before and after *Donoghue v Stevenson* [1932] AC 562 was to the effect that a plaintiff suing in negligence for damages suffered as a result of an act or omission of the defendant could not recover if the act or omission did not directly injure, or at least threaten directly to injure, the plaintiff's person or property but merely caused consequential loss, as, for example, by upsetting his business relations with a third party who was the direct victim of the act or omission. A duty of care which arose from a direct injury to person or property was owed only to those whose person or property might foreseeably be injured by a failure to take care. If the plaintiff could show that the duty was owed to him, he could recover both direct and consequential loss which was reasonably foreseeable and there was no reason for saying that proof of direct loss was an essential part of the claim. The plaintiff had, however, to show he was within the scope of the defendant's duty to take care. In the present case the duty to take care to avoid an escape of virus was owed to the owners of cattle which might be infected by the virus. The plaintiffs were not owners of cattle and had no proprietary interest in anything that might conceivably be damaged by the virus if it escaped.

Note—See also *Lee Cooper v CH Jenkins & Sons Ltd*, p 308, above.

British Celanese Ltd v Hunt

[1969] 2 All ER 1252, [1969] 1 WLR 959, 113 Sol Jo 368 (Lawton J)
The plaintiffs and the defendants both occupied premises on an industrial estate about 150 yards apart, supplied with electricity from a sub-station about 100 yards from the plaintiffs' premises. Metal foil strips were blown by the wind from the defendants' premises on to busbars at the sub-station and caused a breakdown in the electricity supply to the plaintiffs' factory. Material solidified in their machines which had to be

cleaned. They claimed damages for loss of production and profit. Metal foil strips had been blown into the sub-station on a previous occasion and the electricity board had warned the defendants that it could cause a failure of electricity supply to premises on the estate.
HELD: The damages claimed were not too remote. The solidifying of material in the machines was damage to property and the loss claimed for was not merely economic. Unlike the plaintiff in *Weller*'s case (above) the present plaintiffs were direct victims of the negligence alleged. In the present case, too, the defendants owed the plaintiffs a duty of care because they foresaw or ought to have foreseen that the interruption of power supplies would injure the plaintiffs' property.

SCM (UK) Ltd v WJ Whittall & Son Ltd

[1971] 1 QB 337, [1970] 3 All ER 245, [1970] 3 WLR 694, 114 Sol Jo 706, CA
The defendants were digging a trench in a road adjoining a number of factories of which the plaintiffs' was one. In the course of the work the defendants damaged an electric cable, causing a power failure in the plaintiffs' factory. Molten material solidified in the machines causing physical damage to the plaintiffs' materials and tools. They claimed damages, confining the claim to the physical damage and to economic loss directly consequential on that physical damage.
HELD: The plaintiffs were entitled to recover. The defendants owed them a duty of care not to damage the cable because they knew that if they damaged it the current would be cut off and damage would be suffered by the factory owners. It was immaterial that the factory was not liable to be directly injured. A man may owe a duty of care to those whom he foresees may be indirectly injured as well as to those whom he foresees may be directly affected. But (per Lord Denning) when the plaintiff has suffered no damage to his person or property, but has only sustained economic loss, the law does not usually permit him to recover that loss; this is not because no duty of care is owed to him but because it is too remote to be a head of damage. *Weller's* case (above) depends on remoteness, not duty of care; similarly *Electrochrome v Welsh Plastics* (above).

Per Winn LJ: There is no liability (except in the special case of negligently uttered false statements) for unintentional negligent infliction of any form of economic loss which is not consequential on foreseeable physical injury or damage to property. *British Celanese Ltd v Hunt* (above) approved.

Spartan Steel and Alloys Ltd v Martin & Co (Contractors) Ltd

[1973] QB 27, [1972] 3 All ER 557, [1972] 3 WLR 502, 116 Sol Jo 648, CA
The plaintiffs' factory was supplied with electricity by a direct cable from the power station. The defendants were doing work in a road about a quarter-mile from the factory and negligently damaged the cable causing the power supply to the factory to be cut off for 14 hours. As a result the plaintiffs suffered loss from (1) damage to metal in an electric furnace; (2) loss of profit on that melt of metal; (3) loss of profit on metal which they would have subsequently melted during the period the power was off.
HELD: The plaintiffs were entitled to damages under heads (1) and (2) but not head (3). The loss under head (3) was economic loss independent of the physical damage to the metal in the furnace when the power failed.

Note—See also *Muirhead v Industrial Tank Specialities*, p 4, above.

Simaan General Contracting Co v Pilkington Glass Ltd (No 2)

[1988] QB 758, [1988] 1 All ER 791, [1988] 2 WLR 761, 132 Sol Jo 463, CA
The plaintiffs were main contractors for the construction of the Al-Oteiba Building in Abu Dhabi, which was to be walled in green glass. They subcontracted the installation of the glass to another company who bought it from Pilkingtons. Simaan sued the defendants in negligence, alleging that Pilkingtons, as the specified suppliers of the glass units, owed them a duty to take reasonable care to avoid defects in the units which (it was assumed for the purposes of a preliminary issue) had caused the plaintiffs economic loss. Did they? The defendants appealed against the judge's finding that they did.
HELD, ON APPEAL: They did not. There was no special relationship between plaintiff and defendant—the plaintiffs had merely instructed their subcontractor to buy the units from Pilkingtons because they were contractually obliged to do so and Pilkingtons had assumed no direct responsibility to the plaintiffs for the units.

Physical damage to property

D & F Estates Ltd v Church Comrs for England and Wales

[1989] AC 177, [1988] 2 All ER 992, [1988] 3 WLR 368, HL
The plaintiffs owned a flat in Gloucester Square, London. It was built between 1963 and 1965. Wates Ltd were the main contractors. The plaster work was incorrectly applied by their subcontractors: in 1980 the plaster was found to be loose and some fell. The plaintiffs sued Wates for damages for negligence to cover the cost of replacing the plaster and some consequential losses.
HELD: The cost of repairing the plaster incurred by the plaintiffs was pure economic loss, not recoverable in tort. There is no right of action in tort for the cost of rectifying a negligently-caused defect where that defect has not caused personal injury or physical damage to other property. Damages for personal injury and for damage to extraneous property remain recoverable under the conventional *Donoghue v Stevenson* principles.

Greater Nottingham Co-operative Society v Cementation Piling and Foundations Ltd

[1989] QB 71, [1988] 2 All ER 971, [1988] 3 WLR 396, 132 Sol Jo 754, CA
The plaintiffs employed contractors to execute extension works at their premises in Lumley Road, Skegness. Cementation were the piling contractors but entered into a direct collateral agreement with the plaintiffs, covering standards of design, workmanship and materials. A Cementation employee negligently operated the piling equipment and caused damage to the Windsor Restaurant next door. This had two effects: (1) the plaintiffs had to compensate the restaurant owners for damage to their property; and (2) the building contract was delayed, causing the plaintiffs economic loss. The plaintiffs claimed against Cementation, in negligence, under both heads and were successful before an official referee.
HELD, ON APPEAL: That the plaintiffs' economic loss, although a reasonably foreseeable consequence of Cementation's pecuniary loss unconnected with any damage to the plaintiffs' own property. Moreover, the collateral agreement between the plaintiffs and Cementation illustrated the lack of any assumption (voluntary or otherwise) by Cementation of any responsibility for economic loss and thus that no duty in tort

should be imposed. (*Spartan Steel and Alloys Ltd v Martin, Junior Books Ltd v Veitchi Co Ltd* (above) and *Muirhead v Industrial Tanks Specialities Ltd* (p 4, above) distinguished).

Murphy v Brentwood District Council

[1990] 2 All ER 908, HL
The plaintiff purchased a house built on an infilled site. The house had been built on a concrete raft foundation. The plans for this foundation had been approved by the defendant Council following discussions with consulting engineers. Some 11 years after the purchase the plaintiff noticed cracks in his house caused by the failure of the foundations. The plaintiff sold his house subject to the defect for £35,000 less than its market value in sound condition and sued the Council. The plaintiff claimed that he and his family had suffered an imminent risk to health and safety due to the fact that the soil pipes had broken and there was a risk of further breakages. The judge found for the plaintiffs and this was upheld on appeal. The Council appealed to the House of Lords.
HELD: The plaintiff's claim failed. The defects were defects within the structure of the property and had not caused either damage to other property or physical injury. Thus the plaintiff's loss was purely economic and not recoverable. The Council owed no duty of care to the plaintiff when it approved the plans for the foundations for his house.

'I see no reason to doubt that the principle of *Donoghue v Stevenson* does indeed apply so as to place the builder of premises under a duty to take reasonable care to avoid injury through defects in the premises to the person or property of those whom he should have in contemplation as likely to suffer such injury if care is not taken': per Lord Keith.

Special relationship

Caparo Industries plc v Dickman

[1990] 1 All ER 568, HL
The plaintiffs both held shares in Fidelity plc. The defendants were the company's auditors. The plaintiff relied on the defendant's accounts to purchase further shares in Fidelity plc and eventually mount a successful take over bid for the company. The plaintiff alleged that the accounts were misleading and inaccurate in that they showed a pre-tax profit whereas they should have recorded a loss. The plaintiff claimed that had they been aware of the proper figures they would not have purchased the further shares and made the take over bid. The court was asked to decide whether the auditors owed a duty of care to the plaintiff.
HELD: The defendant auditors owed no duty of care to shareholders in the company or to members of the public in respect of the accuracy of the accounts. The accounts were prepared for the shareholders of the company to assist them in controlling and managing that company, not to promote the interests of potential investors.

'. . . the necessary relationship between the maker of a statement or giver of advice (the adviser) and the recipient who acts in reliance on it (the advisee) may typically be held to exist where (1) the advice is required for a purpose, whether particularly specified or generally described, which is made known, either actually or inferentially to the adviser at the time when the advice is given, (2) the adviser knows, either actually or inferentially, that his advice will be communicated to the advisee, either specifically or as a member of an ascertainable class, in order that it should be used by the advisee for that purpose, (3) it is known, either actually or inferentially, that the advice so communicated is likely to be acted on by the advisee for that purpose without independent inquiry and (4) it is so acted on by the advisee to his detriment': per Lord Oliver.

Note—See also *Candler v Cran Christmas & Co* [1951] 2 KB 164, [1951] 1 All ER 426, CA and *Hedley Burn & Co Ltd v Heller & Partners Ltd* [1964] AC 465, [1963] 2 All ER 575, [1963] 3 WLR 101, HL.

Smith v Eric S Bush (a firm)

[1990] 1 AC 831, [1989] 2 All ER 514, HL
Mrs Smith purchased a house with the assistance of a building society mortgage. The building society instructed a building surveyor from the defendant firm to value the property for which Mrs Smith paid a fee of £36.89. The report stated that the house did not require any essential repairs. Mrs Smith did not obtain her own independent surveyors report but purchased the house in reliance upon the defendant's findings. Unfortunately two chimney breasts had been removed but the chimney breast in the loft and the chimneys had not been supported. Eighteen months after purchase the bricks from the chimneys collapsed and caused damage.

The question to be asked was did the defendant owe a duty of care to the plaintiff? The defendant sought to rely upon a clause excluding liability.

HELD: The defendant valuer did owe a duty of care to the plaintiff. The valuer assumed a responsibility to both the building society and the plaintiff by agreeing to carry out the valuation for mortgage purposes. He knew that the valuation fee had been paid by the plaintiff and he knew that the valuation would probably be relied upon by the plaintiff in order to decide whether or not she would purchase the property. The plaintiff, who had paid the fee, was entitled to rely upon the professional skill and advice given by the defendant valuer.

The disclaimer of liability was subject to the test of reasonableness as defined by s 11(3) of the Unfair Contract Terms Act 1977. The defendant valuer had been paid for his services. It was common knowledge that 90% of purchasers relied on the mortgage valuation to purchase their property and did not commission their own survey. Many purchasers could not afford a second valuation. It was therefore inevitable that a great many purchasers would rely upon the mortgage valuation commissioned by the building society. Furthermore the defendant valuer knew that failure on his part to exercise reasonable care and skill would be disastrous to the purchaser. Therefore the disclaimer was not effective to exclude liability for the negligence of the valuer.

Note—This decision only relates to the cheaper end of the housing market.

4 MITIGATION

THE RULE

British Westinghouse Co v Underground Electric Rlys Co

[1912] AC 673, 81 LJKB 1132, 107 LT 325, HL
In assessing damages in contract, the fundamental basis is compensation for pecuniary loss naturally flowing from the breach, but this is qualified by plaintiff's duty to take all reasonable steps to mitigate the loss consequent on the breach and he cannot claim any part of the damage which is due to his neglect to take such steps. If the action which he has taken has actually diminished his loss, such diminution may be taken into account even though there was no duty on him to act.

Pomphrey v James A Cuthbertson

1951 SC 147, 1951 SLT 191, Ct of Sess
Pursuer claimed (1) the cost of a vehicle which he had bought to replace his damaged car; (2) the cost of adapting it to his purposes; and (3) hire charges until replacement; less the scrap value of his damaged car.
HELD: This was the wrong basis; the correct basis being either the cost of repair plus hire charges, or the market value of the damaged car immediately before the accident, plus hire charges until replaced, less its scrap value.

The Pacific Concord

[1961] 1 All ER 106, [1961] 1 WLR 873, 105 Sol Jo 492, [1960] 2 Lloyd's Rep 270
The plaintiffs' vessel was damaged in a collision with the defendants' vessel for which the defendants admitted liability. The repairs (for which there was no urgency) were carried out at London where repair charges were about 50% more than at Newcastle where the plaintiffs could have had them done if they had taken reasonable precautions to give adequate notice to stem a dry dock. Moreover by having the repairs done before the cancellation of a charter party instead of after it they lost £2,319 profit on the charter.
HELD: The plaintiffs' duty was to make such arrangements for the repair of the damage as a prudent uninsured owner would make for himself. It was an unreasonable decision to have the repairs done when and where the plaintiffs had them done: they were not entitled to recover from the defendants the additional expense by having them done at London, nor the loss of profit on the charter party. *Dunkirk Colliery Co v Lever* (above) applied.

Bellingham v Dhillon

[1973] QB 304, [1973] 1 All ER 20, [1972] 3 WLR 730, 116 Sol Jo 566 (Forbes J)
The plaintiff was a driving school proprietor. In 1967 he was negotiating to install an electronic simulator to teach driving but because of injuries he had sustained in an accident for which the defendant was responsible the negotiations broke down. A simulator would have cost him £1,824 a year for five years and then £71 per year. In 1971 he was able to, and did, buy one outright secondhand from a company in liquidation. But for this purchase his net loss of profit on simulator teaching would be £2,774; if the defendant was entitled to take the purchase of the secondhand simulator into account the loss was nil. It was argued for the plaintiff that sums which

came to him as a result of the tortious act and would not have come to him but for the tort were not to be taken into account.
HELD: The plaintiff had a duty to mitigate his damage by buying equipment just as much when that damage arose in tort as if it had arisen in contract. Applying the principles set out by Lord Haldane in *British Westinghouse v Underground Electric Railways Co* (above) the damages were to be arrived at by subtracting the profits the business earned after the wrong had been suffered from the profits the business would have earned on the hypothesis that the defendant's wrong had not reduced them, looking at the whole of the facts and ascertaining the result. On this basis no loss arose on the simulator venture.

HIRE OF REPLACEMENT VEHICLE

Macrae v HG Swindells

[1954] 2 All ER 260, [1954] 1 WLR 597, 98 Sol Jo 233 (Barry J)
A garage negligently or by breach of contract damaged a customer's car which was with the garage for repairs. The garage lent the customer another car until it was properly repaired. The customer's servant negligently drove the lent car and it was destroyed in an accident. The garage obtained judgment against the customer for the value of the lent car. No other car was offered by the garage and the customer hired another car till he received his car back and sued the garage for the amount of the hire charges incurred.
HELD: The hire was the result of the negligence or breach of contract of the garage and not the result of the negligence of the customer's servant; the reason the lent car ceased to be available was irrelevant.

Watson Norie Ltd v Shaw

(1967) 111 Sol Jo 117, CA
The plaintiff company's Jensen car, used by the managing director was damaged by the defendant's negligence. The company hired a Rover and later a Jaguar car for seven weeks at £40 per week whilst it was being repaired, these cars being of equivalent value and prestige to a Jensen. The defendants objected that the amount was unreasonable and the plaintiffs had failed to mitigate their damage. There was evidence that a Triumph Herald could be hired at £17 10s per week or a Ford Zephyr at £25 per week. The county court judge thought it was not reasonable to expect the plaintiff to use the Triumph but that the Ford would have been suitable. He considered the plaintiffs had been casual in hiring a replacement, not having made inquiries to find out if a suitable car could be obtained more cheaply. He awarded only £25 per week loss of use.
HELD, on the plaintiffs' appeal: There was material before the judge that a reasonable substitute could be hired for £25 per week and he was entitled to reach the conclusion he did. Where as here it was necessary to hire a car for only a short period it was not necessarily right that the defendants had to pay the cost of hiring a car equal in value and prestige to the damaged car.

Martindale v Duncan

[1973] 2 All ER 355, [1973] 1 WLR 574, 117 Sol Jo 168, CA
On 27 November the plaintiff's taxi was damaged. He obtained an estimate of the cost of repair on 1 December and claimed the estimated amount from the defendant. He

did not instruct the repairers to carry out the repairs, not being able to afford them and believing he had to allow the defendant's insurers to inspect the vehicle and also to get permission from his own insurers. It was not until 26 January that the defendant's insurers wrote agreeing the cost of repairs after an engineers' inspection. The plaintiff then instructed the repairers and the repairs were completed by 25 February. Meanwhile the plaintiff had hired a replacement vehicle for ten weeks, starting a month after the accident. The defendant contested payment of the hire charges on the ground that the repairs should have been put in hand immediately after the accident.
HELD: It was not a case like *The Liesbosch*. The plaintiff was seeking to recover his damages from the defendant's insurers and, if that went wrong, to recover from his own insurers. Until he had authorisation to do the work he could not be certain of being in a good position vis-à-vis the insurance company.

HL Motorworks (Willesden) Ltd v Alwahbi

[1977] RTR 276, CA
The plaintiffs were motor repairers. When giving a test run to a customer's car, a Rolls Royce, it was damaged by the defendant's negligence and was off the road 11 days for repairs. The owner hired another Rolls Royce for those 11 days at a cost of £467.55, which the plaintiffs paid. In a claim against the defendant for reimbursement the judge held that it was unnecessary for so great an expense to be incurred and awarded only £160 as being sufficient for hiring a suitable car.
HELD: He should have awarded the whole amount. The owner of the car was entitled to have another Rolls Royce during the 11 days he had been deprived of his own. He was the plaintiffs' customer and it might have been damaging to the relationship to try to cut down the amount of his claim. *Watson Norie Ltd v Shaw* (above) was quite a different case.

Daily Office Cleaning Contractors v Shefford

[1977] RTR 361 (Stabb J)
The plaintiff company supplied its directors with so-called 'prestige' cars for use in their work. One of these, an American-made Rambler car, was damaged in a collision by the defendant's negligent driving. The plaintiffs sent their car to their usual garage by whom it was sent to coachwork repairers who applied to the main suppliers for the necessary parts. Meanwhile the plaintiffs obtained from the garage on hire a Jaguar XJ6 at £75 per week, a concessionary price: the normal price was £100 per week. Because of long delays in obtaining necessary parts repairs were not completed until 25 weeks had elapsed. The plaintiffs claimed 25 weeks' hire at £75 per week. The defendants contended that to hire a Jaguar XJ6 for so long was unreasonable in that a medium-sized car would have sufficed.
HELD: A plaintiff had only to act reasonably when dealing with a situation he finds himself in as a result of the act of a tortfeasor. There was no call for the plaintiffs to shop around to hire a car at a lesser sum from someone with whom they did not normally deal, especially as the Jaguar was supplied at a concessionary rate. Although the repairs took a long time the plaintiffs had pressed the repairers to hasten completion and it would be wrong to blame the plaintiffs for the American Motor Corporation's delay in delivery.

Giles v Thompson, Devlin v Baslington

[1993] 3 All ER 321, HL
The plaintiffs' vehicles were damaged in road traffic accidents for which the defendants were entirely to blame. The plaintiffs hired alternative vehicles until their own vehicles were repaired. The plaintiffs entered into an arrangement with hire car companies whereby the plaintiffs agreed that proceedings for the recovery of these charges could be brought in their names. The plaintiffs were not obliged to make any payments to the hire car company. The defendants argued that the arrangement was champertous, against public policy and, in any event, the plaintiffs had not suffered any loss. The cases were appealed to the House of Lords.
HELD: The law of champerty (which has its origins in medieval times) was designed to prevent the 'wanton and officious intermeddling' in other peoples disputes. There was nothing to indicate that any of the actions of the hire companies had been champertous nor were the arrangements contrary to public policy.

The terms of the arrangements between the plaintiffs and the hire companies were such that the plaintiffs remained liable throughout for the hire charges and therefore they had suffered a recoverable loss.

Per curiam: 'The need for a replacement car is not self-proving . . . there remains ample scope for the defendant in an individual case to displace the inference that might otherwise arise': per Lord Mustill.

REPAIRS COSTING MORE THAN TOTAL LOSS VALUE

O'Grady v Westminster Scaffolding Ltd

[1962] 2 Lloyd's Rep 238 (Edmund Davies J)
The plaintiff claimed for loss and expense he had sustained by the negligence of the defendants in damaging his car on 13 July 1960. The car was a 1937 MG which he had bought in 1947 for £475. It had been maintained by him in exceptionally good condition at considerable expense: in the year before the accident the plaintiff had spent over £300 on a new engine and coachwork. It was doubtful whether a car of the same type in similar condition could be found on the open market. The plaintiff had the car repaired at a price of £253 and claimed this sum plus hire charges of £207 for cars hired whilst the repairs were being carried out. The defendants contended that the pre-accident value of the car was about £180 and the salvage value £35 to £40 and that the plaintiff had acted unreasonably in having the car repaired.
HELD: The pre-accident market value of chattels affords a guide to the measure of compensation when, and only when, a similar chattel can be obtained in the open market. The plaintiff acted reasonably in having the car repaired and in hiring other cars whilst the repairs were being done.

Harbutts Plasticine Ltd v Wayne Tank and Pump Co Ltd

[1970] 1 QB 447, [1970] 1 All ER 225, [1970] 2 WLR 198, 114 Sol Jo 29, CA
Per Widgery LJ: The distinction between those cases in which the measure of damages is the cost of repair of the damaged article and those in which it is the diminution in value of the article is not clearly defined. . . . Each case turns on its own facts, it being remembered, first, that the purpose of the award of damages is to restore the plaintiff to his position before the loss occurred, and second, that the plaintiff must act reasonably to mitigate his loss. If the article damaged is a motor car of popular

make, the plaintiff cannot charge the defendant with the cost of repair when it is cheaper to buy a similar car on the market. On the other hand if no substitute for the damaged article is available and no reasonable alternative can be provided, the plaintiff should be entitled to the cost of repair.

REPAIRS CAUSING LOSS OF VALUE

Payton v Brooks

[1974] RTR 169, [1974] 1 Lloyd's Rep 241, CA
The plaintiff's car, only four weeks old, was damaged by the defendant. He claimed from her not only the cost of repairs but also the sum of £100 being the estimated loss of market value of the car, even after repair, due to its being a repaired car. The judge awarded only the cost of repairs, finding on the evidence that no diminution in market value had been established by the plaintiff.
HELD, ON APPEAL: The judge's finding of fact must be accepted, but obiter, if the judge had found that the diminution in value had been established the plaintiff would have been entitled to an award. The normal measure of damages is the cost of repair but if, despite good repairs, a reduced market value can be proved, compensation for the reduction can be awarded to the plaintiff, the value of his property as a saleable asset having been reduced.

5 MEASURE OF DAMAGES

BETTERMENT

Property

Moss v Christchurch RDC

[1925] 2 KB 750, 95 LJKB 81
A cottage was set on fire as the result of the negligence of the defendants. The fabric was seriously damaged and a quantity of the household effects destroyed. The Official Referee assessed the damage sustained by the owner and tenant as the cost of replacement in each case. The defendants appealed contending the damages were limited to the value of the property at the time it was destroyed.
HELD: The measure of damages is not the cost of replacement but is the value to the owner of the property at the time it was destroyed. The true measure of damage is the difference between the money value of the interest before the damage and the money value of the interest after the damage.

Note—Considered in *Hutchinson v Davidson* 1945 SC 395, where the cost of replacement was awarded.

Hollebone v Midhurst

[1968] 1 Lloyd's Rep 38 (Norman Richards Esq QC, Official Referee)
The plaintiffs' house was damaged by fire caused by the negligence of the second defendants. The cost of making good the damage was £18,991. The difference in

value between the pre-fire value and the value after the fire was £14,850. It was urged on behalf of the defendants that the right measure of damage was the difference in value ie £14,850, not the cost of making good.
HELD: On the authorities there was no firm rule that the diminution in value is the correct measure of damage. In *The Susquehanna* [1926] AC 655 Lord Dunedin said no rigid rule or rules apply and one must consider all the relevant circumstances. These must depend on such matters as the interest which the injured party had in what is damaged, the purpose for which it is used and whether its life is likely to be short or long. In the present case where the property was of a nature that comparable properties were few and far between the cost of repair was the correct measure of damage as providing fair and proper restitution for the damage sustained.

The question remained whether an allowance should be made for 'betterment' on the basis of substitution of new material for old. If an allowance of new for old must always be made this may well prevent a plaintiff from being fairly compensated. It was conceded that the old rafters and floors would have lasted out the life of the house so there could be no betterment for those. In the case of new electrical wiring it had deferred the need for this for 15 to 20 years and there was some benefit to the plaintiffs in this. But it was not a case in which it would be fair to deduct it from the cost of repair.

Hole & Son Ltd v Harrisons

[1973] 1 Lloyd's Rep 345, QBD
The defendants' lorry crashed into a row of three ancient cottages owned by the plaintiff company, causing damage. Two of the cottages were occupied as an office and store by the plaintiffs; the third was occupied by a statutory tenant at a rent of 15s per week and was so badly damaged that she had to move elsewhere, losing her tenancy. The plaintiffs claimed the estimated cost of reinstating all the damaged cottages at a cost of £4,079. At the trial it appeared that the plaintiffs, even before the accident, had intended to demolish the cottages and build new premises in place of them; the departure of the tenant had now enabled them to do this, for which they had obtained planning permission.
HELD: A claim for damage to property was either for cost of reinstatement or diminution in value. The evidence showed that the plaintiffs had no intention of reinstating; the departure of the statutory tenant had increased the value rather than diminished it. The only damages the plaintiffs were entitled to was the cost of a temporary repair already done and an agreed sum for loss of rent.

CR Taylor (Wholesale) Ltd v Hepworths Ltd

[1977] 2 All ER 784, [1977] 1 WLR 659, 121 Sol Jo 15, 242 Estates Gazette 631 (May J)
The plaintiffs owned property consisting of a billiard hall and three shops. The billiard hall had been out of use as such for 30 years and two of the shops were unlet. The plaintiffs had not tried for some time to let or sell; the site was regarded as ripe for redevelopment. By negligence of a servant of the defendants the property caught fire and was damaged. The plaintiffs claimed damages assessed at the amount which it would cost to reinstate the premises, though they were never rebuilt.
HELD: The two basic principles were that (1) damages awarded against a tortfeasor shall be such as will, so far as money can, put the plaintiff in the same position as he would have been had the tort not occurred, but (2) the damages to be awarded are to be reasonable as between the plaintiff on the one hand and the defendant on the other. The plaintiffs had been holding on to the property merely for its development value

which lay in the site itself, not the buildings. It would be totally unrealistic as well as unreasonable as between the plaintiffs and the defendants to award the notional cost of reinstating the premises. The measure of damages was the diminution in the value of the property assessed at £2,500 but as it would have cost the plaintiffs more than that to clear the site for redevelopment they were entitled to nothing in respect of that head of damage.

Farmer Giles Ltd v Wessex Water Authority

[1988] 42 EG 127, QBD
The plaintiffs owned land and a dilapidated mill by a river. The defendants, the water authority and their contractors, negligently caused the collapse of part of the mill during river improvement work. The plaintiffs claimed the cost of rebuilding the mill; the water authority accepted liability in contract and tort, and the contractors only in tort. They disputed quantum, arguing that the proper measure of damage should be the reduction in value of the mill. The Court found that the mill would cost up to £155,000 to rebuild, but that the sale value of the rebuilt building would be then only about £63,000. The market value of the mill at the time it was damaged was £10,000. Refurbishment of the mill before damage would have cost £30,000 and made the building worth £40,000. The site value was £1,000.
HELD: £34,100 should be awarded. The measure of damages, whether in contract or in tort, should put the plaintiffs in the same position as they would have been if they had not suffered the wrong in question. The court could either award damages for the cost of reinstatement, or in respect of the diminution in value but where, as in this case, the cost of rebuilding the structure was unreasonable in proportion to the value of the building, the appropriate measure of damage was the value of the original structure if it had been refurbished, less the estimated cost of such refurbishment and the site value.

Machinery

Bacon v Cooper (Metals) Ltd

[1982] 1 All ER 397 (Cantley J)
In the course of the plaintiff's business as a scrap metal dealer he used a large and expensive machine, called a fragmentiser, for the purpose of reducing scrap metal to fragments. He purchased a consignment of metal from the defendants which, in breach of the contract of sale, contained a large lump of steel. The rotor of the machine was broken by it and had to be replaced by a new one, costing £41,000. No secondhand rotors were available. A rotor lasted seven years; at the time of the damage the plaintiff's rotor had been in use three and a quarter years. The defendants contended that the plaintiff ought to give credit for three and a quarter years' use, reducing the claim to £22,232.
HELD: Not so. Each case should depend on its own facts. There was no certainty that the plaintiff would have needed to buy a new rotor at the end of another three and a quarter years if there had been no damage. After that time the fragmentiser may be out of date or the plaintiff may be using a different process or have died or retired from business. It would be wrong to charge the defendants for the whole cost if the damaged rotor had, say, only three months of the seven years to run, but that was not the case. The plaintiff was entitled to recover the whole cost of the replacement rotor.

Irreplaceable loss

Uctkos v Mazetta

[1956] 1 Lloyd's Rep 209 (Ormerod J)
An Admiral's Barge constructed in America was sold after the war in 1947 by the Admiralty for £600. The owner did work on it and it was moored in the Thames at Isleworth and used for visits at weekends. A painter and decorator known to the owner visited it as a purely social arrangement, and helped to recondition the ship presumably in the hope that he would be allowed some use of it. By his negligence on 2 May 1952 the ship was destroyed. The owner claimed £5,000 as the cost of purchasing another ship or replacing it. The ship was quite an unusual type and was irreplaceable. Evidence was given by an agent for the disposal of craft by the Admiralty after the war of the sale of four other ships of a comparatively similar design and construction and performance, that the value of the ship was about £750.
HELD: The owner was not entitled to damages on the basis of the replacement of his ship, but to the reasonable cost of another craft which reasonably meets his needs and in reasonably the same condition. Judgment for £800 plus £108 for fittings.

Note—See also *O'Grady v Westminster Scaffolding Ltd*, p 356, above.

LOSS OF USE

Note—See also *Watson Norie Ltd v Shaw*, p 354, above.

Private individuals

The Mediana

[1900] AC 113, 69 LJP 35, 82 LT 95
The owner of a chattel who is wrongfully deprived of its use may recover substantial damages for the deprivation, though he may have incurred no out of pocket expenses consequent thereon.

'Nominal damages' is a technical phrase, which means that you have negatived anything like real damage, but that you are affirming by your nominal damages that there is an infraction of a legal right, which, though it gives you no right to any real damages at all, yet gives you a right to the verdict or judgment because your legal right has been infringed. But the term 'nominal damages' does not mean small damages: per Lord Halsbury LC.

Note—See also *The Hebridean Coast*, below.

Caxton Publishing Co v Sutherland Publishing Co

[1939] AC 178, [1938] 4 All ER 389 (Lord Porter)
Even the loss of the use for a time of a chattel which the owner would not have used during that time may give rise to substantial damages, whether in an action for damages or in an action for conversion.

Griffin & Co Ltd v De-La-Haye and De-La-Haye Contractors

[1968] 2 Lloyd's Rep 253 (Paull J)
The plaintiff's vehicle was damaged in an accident by the defendants' negligence on

8 November 1966. The plaintiff's solicitors wrote to the defendants on 15 November saying the vehicle was considered to be a 'write-off' but offering an inspection. The defendants' insurers did not reply but their engineer inspected the vehicle in January 1967: he told them it was a 'write-off'. Despite further letters from the plaintiff's solicitors the insurers made no reply to them until 11 May 1967 when they agreed the vehicle was a total loss. Meanwhile the plaintiff had been hiring a vehicle at £12 per week.
HELD: The question was to decide what was a reasonable time after which the plaintiff ought to have mended his vehicle or bought another. The appropriate date was 8 April even though by then he had not heard from the insurance company. The defendants' insurers could not complain in view of their failure to answer the plaintiff's solicitors' letters.

Dixons (Scholar Green) Ltd v Cooper

[1970] RTR 222, 114 Sol Jo 319, CA
The plaintiffs claimed £589 for loss of use of their 9-ton lorry. This figure comprised £1,189 average deficiency in turnover for 11 weeks during which it was off the road for repair less sums for wear and tear, running costs and wages plus further sums for depreciation etc. The defendants though admitting liability contested the figures. The judge said it was for the plaintiffs to establish their financial loss and they had failed to do so to his satisfaction: he accordingly awarded nominal damages of £2.
HELD, ON APPEAL: This could not be right. This was a valuable vehicle in constant demand and it had been off the road 11 weeks. There were difficulties in arriving at an exact figure but having heard the plaintiffs' evidence (the defendants called none) it was the duty of the judge to make the best he could out of the evidence and choose a figure which was a reasonable estimate of the damage suffered by the plaintiffs. The amount awarded, on examination of the figures, should be £450.

McAll v Brooks

[1984] RTR 99, CA
The plaintiff had a comprehensive insurance policy in respect of his car membership of a scheme whereby for a payment of £5 per annum he would be entitled to the use of a car if his own car was damaged and out of use. In an accident for which the defendant was wholly to blame the plaintiff's car was damaged and, as arranged, he was supplied by the brokers with a car for three weeks. A reasonable hire charge for such a car was £328. In proceedings against the defendant in which he claimed the amount of the excess and £328 as the measure of damages for loss of use the county court judge awarded £50 for the excess but held that he was not entitled to the £328 because (1) he had not lost it; (2) the £5 scheme was insurance business and therefore illegal under the Insurance Companies Act 1974 and there was no right of subrogation; (3) the plaintiff's contract under the scheme was tainted with illegality.
HELD, ON APPEAL: The plaintiff was entitled to recover the sum of £328. It had been accepted that the plaintiff had needed a car when his own was off the road and that £328 was a reasonable hire charge. Following *Donnelly v Joyce* (p 424, below) the plaintiff's need of a car had to be paid for by the wrongdoer and £328 was to cover that need. If the scheme was tainted with illegality and the plaintiff had been a knowing party to that illegality he could not recover, but this was not the case. If there was any taint of illegality on the part of the brokers it was not the concern of the plaintiff. The court was not concerned to consider what the plaintiff was going to do with his money or whether he owed any legal or moral obligation to the brokers or any other third party.

Hatch v Platt

[1988] 1 CLY 1306 (County Court)
The plaintiff, who was a delivery rider, was involved in an accident; his motor-cycle was written-off. He was without use of a motor-cycle for eight weeks, and it was found that it would have cost about £60 a week to hire an alternative. General damages of £480 were awarded for loss of use of the motor-cycle.

Lobb v Everet

[1993] 5 CL 122
The plaintiff's car was written off in an accident. He was without a vehicle for 16 weeks. He was unemployed during this period but would have used the car for domestic purposes, transporting his family and 18 month old daughter around as well as exercising his right of contact to his eight year old son by visiting him every fortnight. The plaintiff had to rely on friends and public transport and described the situation as a 'real aggravation'. The judge awarded damages for loss of use and inconvenience in the sum of £30 per week and commented that this was a head of damage that was often underestimated.

Davies v Tate

[1993] 5 CL 123
The plaintiff was without a vehicle for 20 weeks. The plaintiff worked antisocial hours and had to rely on two trains and a taxi to get to and from work four times a week. Damages for loss of use and inconvenience were assessed in the sum of £1,000 for the 20 week period. The plaintiff was also awarded £1,000 travelling expenses.

Public authorities

The Greta Holme

[1897] AC 596, 66 LJP 166, 77 LT 231, 13 TLR 552, HL
A steam dredger belonging to trustees was damaged and the trustees were deprived of the use of it for some weeks and the dredging works were delayed. The trustees were charged with the duty of maintaining a harbour and waterway, deriving their funds from rates and not entitled to distribute profits.
HELD: Though the trustees were not out of pocket in any definite sum they were entitled to recover damages for the loss of use of the dredger.

Pickfords Ltd v Perma Products Ltd

(1947) 80 Ll L Rep 513 (Hilbery J)
Carriers contracted to carry goods which were dangerous because highly inflammable and the owners of the goods indemnified the carriers against damage arising from the carriage of the goods. In transit the lorry caught fire and because of the inflammable load became a total loss.

The lorry owners claimed under the indemnity for the value of the lorry and for loss of use at £12 per week until the vehicle was replaced a year later under a Ministry of Transport licence. The judge estimated the damage to the lorry if it had not had a dangerous load at £150 and that it would take eight weeks to repair. He allowed the balance of the value of the lorry, and loss of use for the year, less the eight weeks, at

£12 per week, ie £614 claimed, less £96, net £518, plus £200 net for the lorry, total £718.

Birmingham Corpn v Sowsbery

(1969) 113 Sol Jo 877, [1970] RTR 84 (Geoffrey Lane J)
The plaintiff's omnibus was out of use for 69 days for repairs following a collision. They claimed as special damages the cost of maintaining a spare fleet omnibus for 69 days at £4 11s per day.
HELD: (1) If the plaintiffs had hired a replacement vehicle they could have claimed the cost of hire as special damages but as a non-profit making body not needing to hire another vehicle different consideration applied and the claim was one for general not special damage. The maintenance of a stand-by fleet was reasonable and necessary and the whole fleet including the stand-bys must be taken as being in operation at any one time. The plaintiffs had been deprived of the use of a valuable chattel during the relevant period and were entitled to substantial (ie not nominal) general damages for the loss of use. (2) There were two possible methods of arriving at a proper figure to compensate the plaintiffs (a) the cost of maintaining and operating the damaged vehicle (excluding running charges) on the assumption that this figure must represent approximately the value of the vehicle to the operators where the concern is non-profit making, or (b) interest on capital value of the vehicle and depreciation, as in *The Hebridean Coast* [1961] AC 545, [1961] 1 All ER 82, 105 Sol Jo 37, [1960] 2 Lloyd's Rep 423, HL. If the latter method were used a proper rate of interest to take would be 7% on the value of the bus at the material time plus a sum for depreciation. But this method suffers from possible variations in capital value and interest rates. It is important that there should be as much consistency as possible between awards of general damages. In the present case where £4 11s per day was agreed as an accurate estimate of the standing charges of such a vehicle run by a reasonably efficient organisation the first method of assessment was a proper solution of the problem. Judgment for £313 19s being 60 days at £4 11s per day.

Note—In an unreported case, *Manchester Corpn v Campbell* (Oliver J at Manchester Assizes, (27 April 1950, unreported), summarised and discussed in the *Post Magazine* for 31 March 1956, the plaintiffs claimed damages for loss of use of a trolleybus damaged in an accident. The claim was for 90 days at £3 4s 9d per day calculated in accordance with the formula prepared by the Financial Officers' Section of the Municipal Passenger Transport Association. The formula provides for taking the total working expenses of the undertaking and deducting from these the actual cost of running the vehicle on the road. Capital charges in respect of buses and buildings and depreciation of plant and equipment relating to the running of the buses are then added. The total divided by 365 and by the number of buses in the fleet established a figure for the 'charge per day'. This figure multiplied by the number of days' loss of use gives the amount of the claim. The judge accepted the formula and his decision in this respect was not upset on appeal (16 January 1951). The formula is still in use though the amounts are of course now very different.

INCOME TAX

Herring v British Transport Commission

[1958] TR 401, 37 ATC 382 (Donovan J)
A lorry owner sued for loss of use claiming that he lost £12 per week profit on the vehicle whilst it was out of use for seven weeks. The defendants contended that tax should be deducted.

HELD: Income tax is not imposed upon particular items in a business account of profits. The £12 per week is not the profit of a business, but is simply the excess of earnings over expenses attributable to one particular use in a mixed business of haulage, scrap dealing, and dealing in vehicles; and when merged with all the other incomings and outgoings of the entire business, it might increase the profits of that business or it might mitigate the loss on the rest of the business. It is a taxable receipt of the plaintiff's business and the rule in *Gourley*'s case (p 430, below) does not apply.

Diamond v Campbell-Jones

[1961] Ch 22, [1960] 1 All ER 583, [1960] 2 WLR 586, 104 Sol Jo 249, [1960] TR 131, 53 R & IT 502 (Buckley J)
In a case in which a dealer in real property claimed damages for breach of a contract for sale of a house which he intended to convert, it was held that he was entitled to a sum equal to the amount of the profit which he would be likely to have made. The damages he recovered were liable to attract tax as part of the profits or gains of his business: *Gourley's* case was distinguished on the grounds that in that case it was conceded that no part of the sum awarded as damages would be subject to tax.

Pryce v Elwood

(1964) 108 Sol Jo 583 (Fenton Atkinson J)
The plaintiff's car which he used for hire-work, was damaged by the defendant's negligence and was out of use for 30 weeks for repair. He claimed damages including an item for loss of trading profit during the period while his car was being repaired. The defendant claimed that a deduction should be made for tax on the profit lost.
HELD: As the damages for loss of profit must be entered in the plaintiff's profit and loss account he would in due course be assessed to tax on them. It would thus be wrong to deduct the amount of the tax in assessing the damages. *Gourley*'s case was different in that it was agreed that the damages awarded there would not be subject to tax. *Diamond v Campbell-Jones* (above) followed.

London and Thames Haven Oil Wharves Ltd v Attwooll

[1967] Ch 772, [1967] 2 All ER 124, [1967] 2 WLR 743, 110 Sol Jo 979, CA
A jetty was damaged as a result of negligent navigation of a ship. It was out of use 380 days as a result. The jetty owners recovered damages of which £21,000 was in respect of use of the jetty. They were assessed to tax on the £21,000 under case 1 of Schedule D.
HELD, ON APPEAL: They were rightly assessed. If the damages a trader receives from another person pursuant to a legal right (whether in contract or tort) includes a sum to compensate him for losing money, which, if it had been received would have been credited to the amount of profits arising in any year from the trade carried on by him the compensation is to be treated in the same way for tax purposes as that sum of money would have been had it not been lost. The £21,000 was compensation for the loss of amounts the company would have received from customers for use of the jetty less the expenses they would have incurred in earning those sums during the 380 days. Such amounts would have been credited to profits and the £21,000 was to be treated for income tax purposes in the same way.

Note—Applied in *Raja's Commercial College v Gian Singh & Co Ltd* [1977] AC 312, [1976] 2 All ER 801, [1976] 3 WLR 58, 120 Sol Jo 404, PC.

DAMAGES IN FOREIGN CURRENCY

Note—It was formerly the rule that a claim in damages must be made in sterling and the judgment given in sterling. In *Miliangos v George Frank (Textiles) Ltd* [1976] AC 443, [1975] 3 All ER 801 the House of Lords departed from this rule to the extent of holding that in an action for the recovery of money due under a contract (eg the price of goods sold) the court has power to give judgment for payment of the money in a foreign currency. The question whether the same rule should apply to claims for damages for breach of contract or for tort was expressly left open. In an action of tort the question came before the House of Lords in the following case.

The Despina R

[1979] 1 Lloyd's Rep 1, HL
After a collision in which two ships were damaged the owners of one of them incurred expenses of temporary and permanent repairs and other services which had to be paid for in various foreign currencies. All payments were made from a US dollar account in New York; all the expenses incurred in the foreign currencies other than US dollars were met by transferring US dollars from that account. The Court of Appeal, in an action claiming the amount of the expenses from the owners of the negligent vessel, held that the *Miliangos* case entitled the Court to abrogate the former rule and give the money judgment in currency other than sterling.
HELD, ON APPEAL to the House of Lords: An English court had the power to give judgment or make an award in foreign currency. Applying the normal principles in tort of *restitutio in integrum* and reasonable foreseeability of damage, the award should be made in the 'plaintiff's currency', namely, the currency in which the loss was effectively felt by him, having regard to the currency in which he generally operated with which he had the closest connection.

Hoffman v Sofaer

[1982] 1 WLR 1350, 126 Sol Jo 611 (Talbot J)
The plaintiff was an American citizen who was injured by negligent medical treatment when on a visit to England. Damages for pain and suffering were assessed at £19,000. The remainder of the damages comprising special damage and future loss related mainly to loss of earnings and future loss as president of a company in the USA, where he lived.
HELD (applying *The Despina R* (above)): The question was: with what currency was the plaintiff's loss closely linked? All the losses in effect for which damages had been awarded other than for pain and suffering were closely linked with the currency of his country, namely, dollars. To meet his losses he would have to pay in dollars: the judgment would be in US dollars with the exception of the £19,000.

The Texaco Melbourne

[1994] 1 Lloyd's Rep 473, HL
The claim was for breach of contract. There was no agreed currency between the parties in which damages should be paid. It was held that damages could be paid in a different currency if the original currency had depreciated to such an extent as to make the payment of damages in that currency insufficient compensation to the plaintiff.

INTEREST ON DAMAGES

Note—The Law Reform (Miscellaneous Provisions) Act 1934, s 3 empowers the court to award interest on damages for which judgment is given. This section has been superseded as from 1 April 1983, so far as it applied to the High Court and county courts, by respectively the Supreme Court Act 1981, s 35A and the County Courts Act 1959, s 97A (now the County Courts Act 1984, s 69). See pp 442–448, below. Section 3 of the 1934 Act (including the subsections added by the Administration of Justice Act 1969, s 22) remains in force in respect of other courts of record, eg the Court of Appeal. Except in cases where judgment is given for damages for personal injuries or death exceeding £200 the award of interest is not mandatory but is at the discretion of the court. The following cases refer to damage claims. For personal injury cases see pp 442–448, below.

Harbutt's Plasticine v Wayne Tank and Pump Co Ltd

[1970] 1 QB 447, [1970] 1 All ER 225, [1970] 2 WLR 198, 114 Sol Jo 29, CA
The plaintiffs' factory was burned down on 6 February 1963. On 8 November 1968 the defendants were held liable and judgment given against them for £146,581 damages. The plaintiffs applied for interest under the 1934 Act. They had received various payments from time to time before trial totalling £143,658 from their insurers who would not be reimbursed. The judge said that in exercising his power to award interest he could not ignore the fact that the plaintiffs had not been kept of all their money until that date but had had their loss reduced by periodical payments from their insurers. He awarded three years' interest on the whole sum at an agreed rate of 6%.
HELD, ON APPEAL: The judge had applied the right principle but had done so rather unscientifically. The basis of the award of interest is that the defendant has kept the plaintiff out of his money, but this reasoning does not apply when he had in fact been indemnified by an insurance company. The judge should award interest from the date when the defendants should have paid the money but only on the balance remaining after payment had been received from the insurers.

Cousins & Co Ltd v D and C Carriers Ltd

[1971] 2 QB 230, [1971] 1 All ER 55, [1971] 2 WLR 85, 114 Sol Jo 882, [1970] 2 Lloyd's Rep 397, CA
In an action for damages for loss of goods a claim was made for interest. The Master awarded interest from the date when the plaintiffs would have been paid if the goods had not been lost until the date when their insurers paid them in full the amount of their loss. The plaintiffs appealed. The defendants said the point was decided beyond argument by *Harbutt*'s case (above).
HELD: *Harbutt*'s case was decided on the basis, not argued, that the interest would be retained by the plaintiff and not handed over together with the damages to the insurers. In the present case the question had been raised whether interest awarded for the period after the plaintiffs had been indemnified by their insurers could be retained by the plaintiffs or could be claimed by the insurers by subrogation. On the authorities and in particular Brett LJ's wide statement of principle in *Castellain v Preston* [1883] 11 QBD 380, 52 LJQB 366, 49 LT 29, 31 WR 557, CA, any recovery of interest after the date of payment under the policy could be claimed by the insurers. It followed that interest should not be limited to the period up to the date of indemnity.

Vehicle and General Insurance Co Ltd v Christie

[1976] 1 All ER 747, QBD
The plaintiffs claimed from the defendants, insurance brokers, money received for

insurance premiums. After proceedings were started by writ which included a claim for interest the parties agreed in March 1975, that the amounts of premiums due was £314.30. The plaintiffs asked for interest on the agreed amount. The defendants refused saying interest was not payable unless there was a judgment. They paid £314.30 into court. The plaintiffs took the action to trial in October 1975.
HELD: The plaintiffs were entitled to interest and should have the costs of the whole action before and after payment in. Lord Denning had said in *Jefford v Gee* (p 444, below) that a plaintiff who thought the amount paid into court was enough would tell the defendant he was disposed to go to trial to collect the interest. He would not have said this if he thought the plaintiff must necessarily pay all the costs after payment in. The court had discretion as regards costs and where, as here, the parties had come to court on the issue of interest, the amount in court not being in dispute, justice required the discretion to be exercised in the plaintiff's favour.

Note—The claim not comprising damages in respect of personal injuries, the award of interest was not mandatory. See also *Wentworth v Wiltshire County Court* [1993] 2 All ER 256. The issue of interest was dealt with per curiam. In this case the plaintiff was awarded damages for loss of profit, damages for bank interest incurred on his increased overdraft together with interest on both these awards. As the award for interest on the loss of profit claim compensated the plaintiff for delayed payment of these lost profits and his need to borrow money from the bank in the meantime a further award for damages representing the bank interest amounted to double recovery. Furthermore, the award of interest on the award for bank interest amounted to an award of interest on interest which was contrary to s 35A (1) of the Supreme Court Act 1981 which provides that only simple interest may be awarded.

Metal Box Ltd v Currys Ltd and Consolidated Actions

[1988] 1 All ER 341, [1988] 1 WLR 175, 132 Sol Jo 51, [1987] LS Gaz R 3657, QBD
A fire occurred on or about 1 March 1977 destroying stock worth £456,562 belonging to three plaintiffs. Letters before action were sent on behalf of two of the plaintiffs by loss adjusters in April of 1977 and writs were finally issued in those actions in June of 1981. Agreement on quantum was reached in April 1982 and judgment finally given in May 1986, nine years and two months after the fire. The third plaintiffs issued their writ in February 1983, and served it in February 1984. The defendants argued firstly that interest should not be paid because the stock was not income producing until removed from storage and sold so the loss was the value of the goods alone; secondly, that because these were subrogated actions therefore, in reality, interest was of benefit not to the plaintiffs but only to their insurers; thirdly, there had been unjustifiable delay in prosecuting the claim so that interest, if payable, should be for just four years at the most (from service of the writ to judgment was four years seven months in the first two cases and two years three months in the third); and fourthly, that the rate of interest should not be at the commercial rate as this was not a commercial dispute in the strict sense but a dispute between insurers.
HELD: Firstly, there was no authority to say that those who were kept out of the value of a chattel as a result of another's tort were not entitled to interest on that value; secondly, it was plain that in subrogated claims insurers were entitled to reimbursement and interest on the judgment sum; thirdly, there had been unjustifiable delay and the appropriate period for interest in the first two cases was the compromise of seven years but in the third case interest was only payable for the two years and three months from service of the writ; fourthly, the appropriate rate of interest was the commercial rate of 1% over Bank Base Rate.

Note—A claim for interest must be pleaded. RSC Ord 18, r 8 reads: 'A party must plead specifically any claim for interest under section 35A of the Act (Supreme Court Act 1981) or otherwise'. See also CCR Ord 6, r 1(a) and *Ward v Chief Constable of Avon* (1985) 129 Sol Jo 606, CA.

MISCELLANEOUS

Loss of no claims bonus

Ironfield v Eastern Gas Board

[1964] 1 All ER 544, [1964] 1 WLR 1125, 108 Sol Jo 691 (Streatfield J)
The plaintiff was driving his father-in-law's car when it collided with the defendants' lorry due to the defendants' negligence. He was injured and the car was damaged. In a claim for damages for his personal injuries he included a claim for £10 excess insurance and £15 for loss of no-claims bonus.
HELD: (1) The loss of 'no-claims bonus' was a real loss sustained by the assured, the father-in-law, and formed part of the damage which resulted from the accident. He should be put in the same position as if he had not made a claim under the policy at all. (2) Though they were items of loss suffered by the father-in-law and not the plaintiff there was no reason why they should not be dealt with in this action and awarded to the plaintiff on his undertaking to pay them over to his father-in-law.

Baker v Courage

[1989] CLY 2057
The plaintiff and defendant were involved in a motor accident. The defendant was primarily liable but the plaintiff was found 15% contributory negligent. The plaintiff claimed damages for the loss of the no-claims bonus.
HELD: To retain her no-claims bonus the plaintiff had to show to her insurance company that the defendant was 100% to blame for the accident. The plaintiff was 15% to blame and therefore the no claims bonus was lost in any event and so the plaintiff's claim against the defendants for the recovery of this no claims bonus failed.

Loss of premium

Patel v London Transport Executive

[1981] RTR 29, CA
Only a week or so after the plaintiff had paid £222.75 for a year's full comprehensive insurance, his car was damaged beyond repair by negligence of the defendants. He claimed under his policy and his insurers paid him the total loss value of the car. It was a term of the policy that on settlement of a claim on a total loss basis all benefits of the insurance would terminate as from the date of the accident without return of premium. The plaintiff claimed from the defendants £218.47 being the balance of the year's premium from the date of the accident. It was acknowledged by the defendants that the term of the policy was a usual one.
HELD: The plaintiff was entitled to succeed. He had acted reasonably in claiming under his policy instead of incurring the greater delay and expense of claiming for his loss directly against the defendants. The claim on the policy was foreseeable by the defendants; therefore the loss following from that claim was foreseeable. The case

was analogous with *Ironfield v Eastern Gas Board* (above) which was rightly decided.

Proof of damages

Ashcroft v Curtin

[1971] 3 All ER 1208, [1971] 1 WLR 1731, 115 Sol Jo 687, CA
The plaintiff, a self-employed precision engineer, ran his own business which had a staff of six. He received injuries which disabled him permanently for some activities and might well have a damaging effect on the business. There was evidence which pointed to a decline in the profits. The plaintiff had no skill at bookkeeping and his accounts, as the judge found, were rudimentary and unreliable, but he awarded him £10,500 for estimated financial loss. The defendant appealed, contending that as there were no reliable accounts the award for that item should be nil.
HELD: Whilst it was probable that there had been some loss of profitability it was quite impossible to quantify it and make an award for it. But as there was a risk, though slight, that the plaintiff might at some time be thrown on to the labour market and because of his injuries be unable to do the work for which he had been trained an award of £2,500 for that possibility should be substituted for the item of £10,500.

Jackson v Chrysler Acceptances Ltd

[1978] RTR 474, CA
In April the plaintiff took a new car on hire purchase from the defendants. He made it clear to the defendants' agents, who supplied the car, that he intended using it for a four weeks' holiday in France in July with his family. In the course of the first few months' use, including the holiday, the car developed numerous defects, some serious. The plaintiff complained on numerous occasions and work was done by the agents including supplying new parts without charge. During the holiday the engine overheated and lacked acceleration, a sun visor snapped off and there were other faults. The car was in the agents' hands for three weeks for overhaul on its return. In county court proceedings the judge held that the car 'was not fit for its purpose and was not of merchantable quality' but that having used the car for several months the plaintiff could not have the contract rescinded. He awarded £200 damages for the general shortfall in the quality of the car below what was properly to be expected and £75 for the detrimental effect on the plaintiff's holiday in France.
HELD, ON APPEAL: The damages awarded were much too low. To assess damages one had to look to see what would have been the fair market price for that car at the time of the hire-purchase contract if the inherent defects had been known to the vendor and the purchaser. In the case of the holiday the question was one of degree: how much was spoiled? On the facts, substantially greater compensation was called for than the £75 awarded. Without segregating the two elements the award would be increased to £750.

COMMERCIAL VEHICLES

The *Commercial Motor* publishes annually a book of tables of operating costs for all types of commercial vehicle, petrol, oil, steam and electric goods and passenger carrying, based upon prevailing costs. The publishers are Temple Press Limited of Bowling Green Lane, London EC 1.

These tables afford a basis of calculating in claims for loss of use.

Loss of road fund tax

Sandhu v Roberts

[1989] CLY 1291
In addition to the recovery of the pre-accident value of her vehicle, storage and towing charges, the plaintiff was entitled to damages in respect of the unrecovered road fund tax. This was a foreseeable loss.

CHAPTER 13

Damages: Personal Injuries

1 PRINCIPLES

MEASURE OF DAMAGES

H West & Son Ltd v Shephard

[1964] AC 326, [1963] 2 All ER 625, [1963] 2 WLR 1359, 107 Sol Jo 454, HL
The damages which are to be awarded for a tort are those which 'so far as money can compensate, will give the injured party reparation for the wrongful act and for all the natural and direct consequences of the wrongful act' (*Admiralty Comrs v Susquehanna (Owners), The Susquehanna*). The words 'so far as money can compensate' point to the impossibility of equating money with human suffering or personal deprivations. A money award can be calculated so as to make good a financial loss. Money may be awarded so that something tangible may be procured to replace something else of like nature which has been destroyed or lost. But money cannot renew a physical frame that has been battered and shattered. All that judges and courts can do is to award sums which must be regarded as giving reasonable compensation. In the process there must be the endeavour to secure some uniformity in the general method of approach. By common assent awards must be reasonable and must be assessed with moderation. Furthermore, it is eminently desirable that so far as possible comparable injuries should be compensated by comparable awards: per Lord Morris of Borth-y-Gest.

The practice of the courts hitherto has been to treat bodily injury as a deprivation which in itself entitles a plaintiff to substantial damages according to its gravity. In *Phillips v London & South Western Rly Co*, Cockburn CJ, in enumerating the heads of damage which the jury must take into account and in respect of which a plaintiff is entitled to compensation said:

'These are the bodily injury sustained; the pain undergone: the effect on the health of the sufferer according to its degree and its probable duration as likely to be temporary or permanent; the expenses incidental to attempts to effect a cure or to lessen the amount of the injury; the pecuniary loss. . . . '

In *Rose v Ford* Lord Roche said: 'I regard impaired health and vitality not merely as a cause of pain and suffering but as a loss of a good thing in itself.' If a plaintiff has lost a leg, the court approaches the matter on the basis that he had suffered a serious physical deprivation no matter what his condition or temperament or state of mind may be. That deprivation may also create future economic loss which is added to the assessment. Past and prospective pain and discomfort increase the assessment. If there is loss of amenity apart from the obvious and normal loss inherent in the deprivation of the limb—if, for instance, the plaintiff's main interest in life was some sport or hobby from which he will in future be debarred, that too increases the assessment. If there is a particular injury to the nervous system, that also increases the assessment. So too with other personal and subjective matters that fall to be decided in the light of common sense in particular cases. These considerations are not dealt with as separate items but are taken into account by the court in fixing one inclusive sum for general damages: per Lord Pearce.

BREAKDOWN OF DAMAGES

Itemising heads of damages

George v Pinnock

[1973] 1 All ER 926, [1973] 1 WLR 118, 117 Sol Jo 73, CA
Per Sachs LJ: Whatever may have been the differing judicial views up to a few years ago and indeed up to 1970 as to whether a judge should simply award a global sum or whether he should state in his judgment what are the main components in that figure, the modern practice . . . is to adopt the second course. . . . [The] plaintiff and defendant alike are entitled to know what is the sum assessed for each relevant head of damage and thus be able on appeal to challenge any error in the assessments. . . . It is of course always open to a respondent to do something which was not done here; that is, to give a cross-notice [of appeal] that even if one head as awarded by the judge is held to be demonstrably too low, some other head is demonstrably too high and thus seek to produce what is sometimes called a swings and roundabouts position. In other circumstances it seems to me that a court should normally be slow to deal with an appeal on such a basis.

Note—The Court of Appeal considered *George v Pinnock* (above) in the case of *Pritchard v JH Cobden Ltd* [1988] Fam 22 (p 397, below).

Smith v Manchester City Council

(1974) 118 Sol Jo 597, 17 KIR 1, CA
Per Edmund Davies LJ: Now that the assessment of general damages is required to be divided into damages for pain and suffering and loss of amenities on the one hand and future financial loss on the other I think the two matters have to be considered separately. In the result if the award under one head is clearly wrong it should be interfered with even though ultimately there may be no very substantial variation in the global award.

Adding up heads of damage

Fletcher v Autocar and Transporters Ltd

[1968] 2 QB 322, [1968] 1 All ER 726, [1968] 2 WLR 743, 112 Sol Jo 96, CA
The plaintiff, a quantity surveyor aged 56, was seriously injured in a motor accident. Head injuries had so seriously affected his mental capacity that he had little thought or feeling, was incapable of looking after himself and would never be able to work again. He was partly paralysed. He was dependent on his wife for everyday care but in three years or so would have to go into an institution for the rest of his life. His expectation of life was not reduced and was about 16 years. Before the accident he had been leading a very full and active life. He had an income from his profession of £4,000 a year, tax paid, and spent all of it. He had no savings and would have continued at work at least to the age of 69. At trial the judge assessed the following main heads of damage: (1) special damage £10,000; (2) future loss of earnings after allowing for tax and calculating the loss actuarily as a lump sum, £32,000; (3) additional expense (ie expense he would not have incurred but for the accident) in the future comprising the cost of being looked after by his wife for the next three years and then for the rest of his life at an institution, less a saving on food and laundry at

home, £14,000; (4) pain and suffering and loss of amenities £10,000. He added them up and awarded £66,000 damages.
HELD, ON APPEAL: The judge had awarded too much. He was wrong to take each item separately and then just add them up at the end. There is a risk of overlapping if the items are just added up. The plaintiff had spent his income on the pleasures of living and on recreations such as golf, fishing and shooting without saving anything. It was fair to compensate him for the loss of these but not unless account was taken of the fact that he had to pay for them. He should not therefore have been given his full loss of earnings. Another way of looking at it was to say that he should not be given both the cost of his keep at the institution and also his full salary, for that would mean that he would be saving full salary and spending nothing. Award reduced to £51,000.

Harris v Harris

[1973] 1 Lloyd's Rep 445, CA
The plaintiff was 14 when injured in a road accident. The main damage was to her brain: though she had been able after the accident to complete her education and pass GCE examinations she would not be able to take up a career nor do ordinary domestic tasks, such as cooking. She would probably never marry. She was of good middle-class background and might, but for the injuries, have become a solicitor or civil servant. The judge awarded her £20,000 for pain and suffering and loss of amenities including loss of marriage prospects; £22,500 for loss of future earnings (15 years at £1,500 p.a.); and £15,974 for the cost of a housekeeper when she would need a place to live of her own.
HELD, on the defendants' appeal: (1) The award of £20,000 for loss of amenities for life was justified. (2) £22,500 for loss of future earnings was too much. She might have married and not have been able to earn so much; damages for loss of marriage prospects were already compensated for in the first item; in any event she might not have earned for any great length of time. (3) On the third item there was doubt whether she would in fact set up in a flat of her own; having regard to the uncertain prospect and the amounts awarded for the other items the right figure for cost of future support was £6,000. It was very important where a judge was following the modern practice of sub-dividing the claim under various headings to avoid overlapping. There was here a serious overlap between the allowance made for loss of plaintiff's prospects of marriage on the one hand and loss of future earnings and the additional cost of domestic assistance on the other.

Lim Poh Choo v Camden and Islington Area Health Authority

[1980] AC 174, [1979] 2 All ER 910, [1979] 3 WLR 44, HL
The plaintiff, after a minor surgical operation, suffered a cardiac arrest caused by the negligence of an employee of the defendants. Extensive and irremedial brain damage resulted leaving her only intermittently conscious, totally dependent on others and not able to appreciate what had happened to her. She was 36 years of age at the time of the incident; her life expectation was unaffected. The judge at first instance awarded £254,765. The defendants' appeals to the Court of Appeal and the House of Lords were dismissed but with small variations after hearing further evidence. On matters of principle—
HELD: (1) The sheer size of the total award was not a reason for reducing it. The burden on the public through insurance premiums or taxes or the availability of National Health Service care were matters for a legislator, not a judge. (2) The award of general damages for pain and suffering and loss of amenities at £20,000 was not too large,

either on the ground that the plaintiff was unaware of what had happened to her or that she was not suffering any pain. *Wise v Kaye* (p 411, below) and *West v Shephard* (p 411, below) were rightly decided. Those cases drew a distinction between damages for pain and suffering and damages for loss of amenities. The latter are awarded for the fact of deprivation whether the plaintiff is aware of it or not. (3) It is right to award damages for actual and future loss of earnings, even in a catastrophic case, but care should be taken to avoid duplication or overlap with other heads of damage. Two reductions fall to be made, (a) the expenses of earning the income which has been lost and (b) from damages for the cost of caring for the plaintiff, the living expenses she would have incurred had she not been injured (*Shearman v Folland*, p 437, below). (4) Damages for cost of future care are recoverable but must be assessed on the basis that capital as well as income is to be used in meeting the cost. In the present case a multiplier of 12 applied to the annual cost of the plaintiff's care from date of judgment in the House of Lords would be fair. (5) Only in exceptional cases, where justice can be shown to require it, will the risk of future inflation be brought into account in assessing damages for future loss. It would be unrealistic to refuse to take inflation into account at all, but the better course in the great majority of cases is to disregard it. The victims of tort who receive a lump sum award are entitled to no better protection against inflation than others who have to rely on capital for their future support.

Note—In *Re Crowther & Nicholson Ltd* ((1981) 125 Sol Jo 529, Times, 10 June) directors claimed compensation for the balance of their service agreements, which provided for the company to pay inflation-proofed salaries, received annually. The judge said that in *Lim Poh Choo's* case Lord Scarman had said the correct approach was to assess damages without regard to future inflation, but in that case the claimant had no contractual right to protection against inflation. In the present case the service agreements did provide protection and this must be taken into account in assessing compensation.

See also *Housecroft v Burnett* [1986] 1 All ER 332 for a full discussion of catastrophic injury claims and the correct approach to damages.

CALCULATION OF DAMAGES

Actuarial evidence undesirable

Mitchell v Mulholland (No 2)

[1972] 1 QB 65, [1971] 2 All ER 1205, [1971] 2 WLR 1271, 115 Sol Jo 227, [1971] 1 Lloyd's Rep 462, CA

As a result of a road accident the plaintiff aged 32 was so seriously injured that although his life expectation was normal he was totally unemployable and would have to remain permanently in a nursing home or similar institution. Before the accident he was a planning engineer at an aircraft factory earning about £22 per week. The judge awarded a total of £45,757 damages of which £17,570 was in respect of post-trial loss of earnings: he took a figure of £1,325 for the annual loss after allowing something for the prospects of promotion and multiplied by 14. On appeal it was argued that the judge should have fixed the number of years' purchase by actuarial calculation and that he was wrong in excluding evidence on the prospects and likely effect of inflation.

HELD: (1) Actuarial methods were unsatisfactory for assessing future loss since they may ensnare one into treating as virtual certainties what in truth are mere chances. The judge was right in adopting the conventional method of assessing the loss of the individual plaintiff in the light of experience applied to the particular case by seeking out an appropriate multiplier and multiplicand, though actuarial tables might supply a means of cross-checking the calculation. (2) Though it would be wrong to refuse to take inflation into account it does not follow that evidence specifically directed to the prospect of inflation should be admitted. There may be rare cases in which solid evidence regarding a particular plaintiff would justify the court in considering evidence of the likely impact of inflation on his future but this was not one of them. The judge was right in ruling as inadmissible evidence on the rate of inflation of prices and the effect of likely future increases in productivity per head of population.

S v Distillers Co (Biochemicals) Ltd
J v Distillers Co (Biochemicals) Ltd

[1969] 3 All ER 1412, [1970] 1 WLR 114, 113 Sol Jo 672 (Hinchcliffe J)
It may be convenient if the Court should state at this stage how it regards the actuarial calculations introduced into these two cases. It is only comparatively recently that attempts have been made to persuade the courts that pecuniary loss in the future should be itemised under various headings and be based on actuarial calculations. The highwater mark of these cases is *Fletcher v Autocar & Transporters Ltd* (p 373, above) where the court seems to have based its decision on the actuarial tables put before it and in respect of various headings which were then added together, the total of the three headings then being awarded to the plaintiff. This the Court of Appeal said was wrong. Lord Denning stated that the various items were not separate heads of compensation and that the actuarial evidence is only an aid to arriving at fair and reasonable compensation. . . . What this court will do is to look at [the actuarial] tables, use them as a guide, exercising great caution, and will do everything it can to avoid any overlapping. . . . I get the impression that the reformers would like an alteration in the law so that, in assessing damages, pecuniary loss would be itemised and based on actuarial calculations. That time has not yet arrived. In both these cases the court, when assessing the damages, will have regard to the cost of special care, to the loss of earning capacity and the deprivation or loss of amenities suffered by each infant plaintiff. But of course these are not separate heads of compensation. The court will regard them separately because it will assist the court to reach a global sum which is just and reasonable.

Sullivan v West Yorkshire Passenger Transport Executive

[1985] 2 All ER 134, CA
It is for the parties to decide what evidence to call and for the judge to rule as to its admissibility. There was nothing to prevent judges from considering actuarial evidence and it could not be said that such evidence would confuse them.

Note—See *Auty v National Coal Board* [1985] 1 All ER 930, CA where the usefulness of actuarial evidence was questioned.

Objective valuation of injury

Hindmarsh v Henry and Leigh Slater Ltd

(1966) 110 Sol Jo 429, CA
The plaintiff was awarded £22,000 for injuries which included a hideous disfigurement

and a complete change of personality and temperament. He did not himself appreciate his condition. He had a sense of euphoria or well-being, not realising the extent of the disaster which had befallen him or even the extent of his deformity.
HELD, on the defendants' appeal: The fact of the plaintiff's being unaware of his condition was not a ground for reducing the damages. The so-called 'sleeping beauty' cases showed that you must not reduce the damages that would otherwise fall to be awarded to an injured plaintiff by reason of that fact. By parity of reasoning the damages should not be reduced because this unfortunate man was happy and did not realise the awful things that had happened to him.

Falling value of money: inflation

Wooding v Wooding

(1967) Times, 17 October, CA
Per Lord Pearson: While it is important from the point of view of public policy that the general level of damages should be kept moderate rather than extravagant, a judge must keep up with the times and in particular with the decline in the purchasing power of money.

Walker v John McLean & Sons Ltd

[1979] 2 All ER 965, [1979] 1 WLR 760, 123 Sol Jo 354, 374, CA
An award must be reasonable, moderate and 'conventional' in the sense used by Lord Morris in *West v Shephard* (p 411, below) but this did not mean it should not have a relation to the changing value of money. Where there is found to be a steady fall in the value of money the victim of the most serious kind of injury qualifies for protection against it as much as or more than any other economic group in society.

Note—See also *Senior v Barker & Allen Ltd*, p 418, below, and *Mitchell v Mulholland* and *Lim Poh Choo* v *Camden and Islington Area Health Authority*, p 375, above. See also *Auty v National Coal Board* [1985] 1 All ER 930, CA.

Trial by jury

H v Ministry of Defence

[1991] 2 QB 103, [1991] 2 All ER 834, [1991] 2 WLR 1192
The plaintiff was a 27 year old active solider who suffered from Peyronie's Disease causing curvature of the penis. After some minor treatment blistering developed and the plaintiff was advised to have a skin graft. He agreed. However during the operation it became apparent that it was impossible to carry out the skin graft and the infection was such that there was no alternative but to amputate a major part of the penis. The plaintiff suffered considerable psychological trauma. The defendant admitted liability. The plaintiff made an application under RSC Ord 33, r 5(1)(a) that his case be tried by jury. The judge agreed and the defendants appealed.
HELD: Per Lord Donaldson of Lymington MR: 'Trial by jury is normally inappropriate for any personal injury action in so far as the jury is required to assess compensatory damages, because the assessment of such damages must be based upon or have regard to conventional scales of damages. The very fact that no jury trial of a claim for damages for personal injuries appears to have taken place for over 25 years affirms

how exceptional the circumstances would have to be before it was appropriate to order such a trial.'

Per curiam: There may be scope for a jury trial where personal injuries have resulted from conduct on the part of those who were deliberately abusing their authority and there may well be a claim for exemplary damages.

Note—It is common for juries to be involved in a claim being brought against the police for false imprisonment, false arrest and malicious prosecution to assess exemplary damages. For a discussion of exemplary damages, see below.

PLEADING DAMAGES

Special damage must be pleaded

Ilkiw v Samuels

[1963] 2 All ER 879, [1963] 1 WLR 991, 107 Sol Jo 680, CA
The plaintiff was injured in an accident at work in 1958 but his action for damages did not reach trial until 1963. In the Statement of Claim the only loss of earnings claimed as special damage was for four months' absence from work immediately after the accident; this was agreed by the parties at trial at £77. The plaintiff's injuries had reduced his earning capacity, however, and some evidence was admitted to show that he had suffered a loss of earnings since the accident and before trial at about £200 a year. As special damage was agreed no amendment of the Statement of Claim was sought. The judge awarded a sum in general damages which took into account the yearly loss of earnings between the accident and trial.
HELD, ON APPEAL: He should not have done so and the award must be reduced.

Per Diplock LJ: In my view it is plain law—so plain that there appears to be no direct authority, because everyone has accepted it as being the law for the last hundred years—that one can recover in an action only special damage which has been pleaded and, of course, proved. The evidence about the loss of earnings in excess of £77 was admissible, not as proof of special damage (which had not been pleaded) but as a guide to what the future loss of earnings of the plaintiff might be.

Perestrello v United Paint Co Ltd

[1969] 3 All ER 479, [1969] 1 WLR 570, 113 Sol Jo 36, CA
In 1961 the defendants contracted to supply the plaintiffs for a period of five years with information and materials to enable them to make and sell a type of paint in Portugal. In 1963 before they had done anything under the contract they repudiated it and were admittedly in breach. In 1964 the plaintiffs wrote the defendants saying their clients had lost £4,000 in capital and outlay and 'a very considerable sum in respect of net profits'. They issued a specially endorsed writ in July 1964 alleging £4,228 wasted expenditure and ending with the words 'And the plaintiffs claim £4,228 and damages'. No claim was made for loss of profits. In July 1968 the plaintiffs' solicitors wrote the defendants' solicitors saying the claim for damages was in respect of loss of profits, quantifying it at £251,000. A few days before trial they delivered a 51-page document of explanations and figures and at the trial applied to amend the Statement of Claim by adding a claim for £250,000 'loss of profits'. The plaintiffs contended in the alternative that no amendment was necessary as the loss

of profit was general damages sufficiently pleaded by the words 'and damages' in the writ. The judge refused to allow the amendment.

HELD, ON APPEAL: (1) Having regard to the difficulties which such a late amendment would cause the defendants it was rightly refused. (2) The plaintiffs were not entitled without amendment to lead evidence of the loss of profits.

Per Lord Donovan: There is plenty of authority for the proposition that a plaintiff need not plead general damage; but since the expressions 'special damage' and 'special damages' are used in such a wide variety of meaning it is safer to approach this question by considering what a plaintiff *is* required to plead rather than what he is not. . . . If a plaintiff has suffered damage of a kind which is not the necessary and immediate consequence of the wrongful act, he must warn the defendant in the pleadings that the compensation claimed will extend to this damage, thus showing the defendant the case he has to meet and assist him in computing a payment into court. . . . The same principle gives rise to a plaintiff's undoubted obligation to plead and particularise any item of damage which represents out-of-pocket expenses, or loss of earnings, incurred prior to the trial, and which is capable of substantially exact calculation. Such damage is commonly referred to as special damage or special damages but is no more than an example of damage which is 'special' in the sense that fairness to the defendant requires that it be pleaded.

Note—See RSC Ord 18, r 12 and CCR Ord 6, and Chapter 16 generally.

Special circumstances must be pleaded

Domsella v Barr

[1969] 3 All ER 487, [1969] 1 WLR 630, 113 Sol Jo 265, CA

The plaintiff, a steel erector aged 23, sustained head injuries in an accident and was unable to work again as a steel erector, though he was able to do other work. Before the accident he had accepted a contract to work as a steel erector in Nigeria on lucrative terms, and had to give this up. This was pleaded in the Statement of Claim, but at the trial he was permitted also to give evidence of his intention and wish, with help which his father would have given him, to set up in business on his own, if the accident had not occurred, as a steel erector. The judge said that the plaintiff had lost the opportunity of earning very large sums of money and awarded £9,000. The defendants appealed against the amount of the award.

HELD: Where it is proposed to allege that there are any special circumstances which may cause the plaintiff to sustain losses in the future over and above those which in the ordinary ways would reasonably be expected to flow from the accident then those special circumstances should be pleaded. By adverting to the plaintiff's intention to set up business on his own account an entirely new element had been introduced into the case which was not mentioned in the Statement of Claim. The plaintiff had gone outside his pleading and objection might properly have been taken to the leading of such evidence. Lord Donovan's remarks in *Perestrello*'s case (above) quoted with approval. Nevertheless as the evidence had been given it could not be entirely disregarded. Award reduced to £5,750.

WHO CAN RECOVER?

Derivative claims

Note—There is no general principle of English law which entitles a person to recover damages against someone who has caused physical injury to a third person. Thus, for example, a partner cannot recover damages against a person who has caused him financial loss, however direct, by negligently injuring his partner.

There were at common law two exceptions to this: (1) it was a tort actionable at the suit of a husband negligently to do physical harm to his wife whereby the husband was deprived of her society (loss of consortium) or of her services (loss of servitium); (2) it was similarly a tort actionable at the suit of a master (or of a parent suing in respect of a child's services) negligently to cause bodily harm to his servant or child whereby the master or parent was deprived of his services (loss of servitium). The rule in respect of the master and servant relationship was held to be limited to those of the status of domestic servants (*A-G for New South Wales v Perpetual Trustee Co Ltd* [1955] AC 457, [1955] 1 All ER 846, [1955] 2 WLR 707, 119 JP 312, 99 Sol Jo 233, PC).

These exceptional rights of action have been abolished by the Administration of Justice Act 1982, s 2. The section came into force on 1 January 1983, save in respect of causes of action which accrued before that date, and reads as follows:

'**2** No person shall be liable in tort under the law of England and Wales or the law of Northern Ireland—

(a) to a husband on the ground only of his having deprived him of the services or society of his wife;
(b) to a parent (or person standing in the place of a parent) on the ground only of his having deprived him of the services of a child; or
(c) on the ground only—
    (i) of having deprived another of the services of his menial servant;
    (ii) of having deprived another of the services of his female servant by raping or seducing her; or
    (iii) of enticement of a servant or harbouring a servant.'

The following cases should be read in the light of the above. For other cases on loss of consortium and servitium see the 8th edition of this work, pp 414—22.

Husband and wife

HUSBAND'S OWN LOSSES

Kirkham v Boughey

[1958] 2 QB 338, [1957] 3 All ER 153, [1957] 3 WLR 626, 101 Sol Jo 780 (Diplock J)

On 10 September 1955, the plaintiff husband was driving a car with his wife, also a plaintiff, as passenger, when there was a collision with a car driven by defendant, due to the admitted negligence of the defendant. The husband sustained trivial injuries but the wife was severely injured. She was in hospital until 1 February 1956, when she returned home and was then able to do light housework. By August 1956, she was able to do most of the housework except heavy lifting.

With regard to the husband's claim for loss of earnings, he was at the time of the accident on a month's leave from a job in Africa expiring at the end of September 1955. The wife and two children aged four and seven years had remained in England. He did not return to Africa because of his anxiety for his wife and the care of the children. He made no attempt to find work in England until the end of November 1955, when he took a job locally as an electrician at £8 a week.

He claimed difference in earnings up to the £30 per week (his salary in Africa) for so long as the court thought it reasonable for him to refuse to go to Africa because of the anxiety as to the condition of his wife and the problem of looking after the children. The claim was not based on loss of consortium, but on a contention that if the husband acted reasonably, he was entitled to any money loss as if the wrong had not been done to him.

HELD: The argument that a driver owed a duty to members of the family circle of the party injured, eg father or brother, is unsupported by authority and in direct conflict with the dicta, and possibly the *ratio decidendi* in *Best v Samuel Fox & Co*. Such person has no remedy in law against the driver, because he owes no duty to such person. The husband of an injured wife is in no different position except for loss of consortium and there was no claim for loss of consortium. The fact that the husband was present and was himself injured makes no difference. The loss of wages is not recoverable.

The husband also claimed for medical treatment, convalescence, and cost of visiting the wife in hospital. Such damages may be recoverable either as mitigating damages for loss of consortium, or, as stated by Lord Goddard CJ in *Best's* case, lie in the husband's duty to provide proper maintenance and comfort for his wife. The judge preferred the second ground, which applied also to parent and child, which was a legal duty, but would not apply to medical treatment which he was under no legal duty to provide. With regard to the visits to hospital, the cost is frequently awarded to husbands. They may be a factor in recovery and so mitigate damages for loss of consortium, but if the sole justification is comfort or pleasure to the husband, it is not recoverable.

McDonnell v Stevens

(1967) Times, 8 April (Swanwick J)
The plaintiffs, husband and wife, were injured in a road accident. The wife was severely injured and the plaintiffs claimed loss of earnings suffered by the husband by staying at home to look after the wife.

HELD: Neither of the plaintiffs could recover this loss. His looking after her had materially helped her recovery but it was not possible to infer any contractual term that his wife had agreed to recompense him for his loss. There was no principle in law which entitled a plaintiff to recover expenses however properly incurred and however enriching a defendant tortfeasor, in order to compensate a third party for services rendered voluntarily and gratuitously.

Walker v Mullen

(1984) Times, 19 January (Comyn J)
The plaintiff was seriously injured in a road accident. He had two spells in hospital during which his father, who worked in Jordan, stayed in England to be with his wife and son.

HELD: Following Diplock J's decision in *Kirkham v Boughey* (above) the father's loss of earnings was not recoverable because such loss would not reasonably have been within the contemplation of the defendant and as thus too remote.

WIFE HAS NO CAUSE OF ACTION

Best v Samuel Fox & Co Ltd

[1952] AC 716, [1952] 2 All ER 394, 96 Sol Jo 494, HL
The plaintiff's husband, aged 30, suffered serious injuries by the negligence of the defendants. As a result he became impotent. He sued for and recovered substantial damages from the defendants for his own injuries. The plaintiff then sued for damages for loss of consortium by deprivation of normal marital relations.
HELD, ON APPEAL to the House of Lords: She could not succeed. There is no general principle of English law entitling a wife to recover damages for loss of consortium. A husband is entitled to recover damages for loss of consortium against a person who negligently injures his wife but this is an anomaly founded on old authorities from a time when a husband was regarded as having a quasi-proprietary right in his wife.

Note—See now the Administration of Justice Act 1982, s 2, p 380, above.

Lampert v Eastern National Omnibus Co Ltd

[1954] 2 All ER 719, [1954] 1 WLR 1047, 98 Sol Jo 493 (Hilbery J)
A wife disfigured in a motor accident alleged that as a result the husband said he was sick of looking at it and left her, and claimed damages under this head. The judge said it was not a claim for loss of consortium. The question was whether it was damage resulting from the accident. If the facts showed the wife did lose anything of value, it might be consequential damage and recoverable, but in this case it was not the reason but only an excuse for deserting her.

Husband injured: wife's loss of earnings

Janney v Gentry

(1966) 110 Sol Jo 408 (Milmo J)
The plaintiff, a customs employee aged 37 was injured in a road accident to the extent that he was a permanent invalid, unemployable and wholly dependent on the full-time care and assistance of other people for the rest of his life.
HELD: In assessing damages for the wife's loss of earnings as a result of the need to look after the plaintiff *Kirkham v Boughey* (p 380, above) was direct authority against the wife's bringing a claim herself to recover the loss of her earnings. Distinguishing *Schneider v Eisovitch* (p 429, below) it was not possible to see on what principle the plaintiff in the present case could recover that loss. £6,000 should be awarded for future nursing as part of the general damages.

Wattson v Port of London Authority

[1969] 1 Lloyd's Rep 95 (Megaw J)
After an accident the plaintiff was at home for some weeks immobilized by his injuries and unable to work. His wife gave up work to look after him and lost £150 wages. The plaintiff claimed this amount as part of his special damages.
HELD: He was entitled to recover the amount of his wife's loss. *Liffen v Watson* (p 423, below) was an analogous case in showing that it was not necessary to have a binding contract to repay to enable the husband to claim his wife's loss. The position was covered in substance by the judgment in *Schneider v Eisovitch* (p 429, below) except

that in the present case it did not matter that the plaintiff had given no firm undertaking to his wife to repay her.

Note—It does not appear from the report whether *Janney v Gentry* was brought to the attention of the court.

Malcolm v Broadhurst

[1970] 3 All ER 508 (Geoffrey Lane J)
A husband and wife (the plaintiffs) were injured in a road accident for which the defendant was to blame. The husband sustained the more serious injuries and was unable to return to his pre-accident occupation for which his wife had given him some part-time secretarial help. His injuries had made him bad-tempered and difficult to live with. The wife was incapacitated for work due to her own injuries for a year and then had a further six months' incapacity due to the effect of her husband's bad temper on her own unstable temperament. After that she was able to do full-time employment. As her husband was unable to do his old work the part-time secretarial work she had done for him was no longer available and she was not able to find other part-time work which she could fit in with her full-time job.
HELD: (1) She was entitled to recover her loss of wages for the six months when her husband's behaviour was causing the incapacity. The defendant must take her as he finds her; exacerbation of her nervous depression was a readily foreseeable consequence of injuring her. Once damage of a particular kind can be foreseen the fact that it arises or is continued by an unusual complex of events does not avail the defendant (*Hughes v Lord Advocate*, p 3, above). (2) She was not entitled to recover damages for loss of her former part-time earnings as her husband's secretary. The defendant could not reasonably foresee that by injuring the husband he would be depriving the wife of her only means of part-time employment.

NOVUS ACTUS INTERVENIENS

Negligent treatment

Rothwell v Caverswall Stone Co

[1944] 2 All ER 350, 171 LT 289, 113 LJKB 520, 61 TLR 17, CA
A workman met with an accident during employment on 23 March 1943, and suffered a fracture dislocation of his right shoulder. He was treated at the local hospital. His shoulder was not X-rayed and the injury was not correctly diagnosed. If it had been and been correctly treated, he would probably have completely recovered in six to eight weeks. Subsequently, when correctly diagnosed, it was too late for effective treatment and the arm was permanently stiff. On the hearing of an arbitration under the Workmen's Compensation Acts, the county court judge found the then existing incapacity was due to negligent medical treatment and was not the result of the accident.
HELD, ON APPEAL: The workman's condition was due to the negligent treatment and not the accident. No compensation was payable after the date on which he would have recovered if properly treated. The county court judge was bound by authority to come to the conclusion he did on the facts as found by him.

Per du Parcq LJ: In my opinion, the following propositions may be formulated upon the authorities as they stand: first, an existing incapacity 'results from' the original injury if it follows, and is caused by, that injury, and may properly be held so to result even if some supervening cause has aggravated the effects of the original injury and prolonged the period of incapacity. If, however, the existing incapacity ought fairly to be attributed to a new cause which has intervened and ought no longer to be attributed to the original injury, it may properly be held to result from the new cause and not from the original injury, even though, but for the original injury, there would have been no incapacity. Second, negligent or inefficient treatment by a doctor or other person may amount to a new cause and the circumstances may justify a finding of fact that the existing incapacity results from the new cause, and does not result from the original injury. This is so even if the negligence or inefficient treatment consists of an error of omission whereby the original incapacity is prolonged. In such a case, if the arbitrator is satisfied that the incapacity would have wholly ceased but for the omission, a finding of fact that the existing incapacity results from the new cause, and not from the injury will be justified. In stating these propositions I am far from seeking to lay down any new principles of construction. I have sought only to collect, by a process of induction, such general, and necessarily vague, rules as seen to emerge from the decided cases. Such rules do no more than indicate the bounds within which an arbitrator is free to decide—the province of fact. It is constantly being said, and must always be remembered, that the arbitrator is the sole judge of the facts.

Appeal dismissed.

Hogan v Bentinck West Hartley Collieries (Owners) Ltd

[1949] 1 All ER 588, [1949] LJR 865, [1949] WN 109, NL
If a surgeon, by lack of skill or failure in reasonable care, causes additional injury or aggravates an existing injury and so renders himself liable in damages, his intervention is a new cause and the additional injury or aggravation should be attributed to it and not to the original accident. On the other hand, an operation prudently advised and skilfully and carefully carried out should not be treated as a new cause, whatever its consequences may be.

Robinson v Post Office

[1974] 2 All ER 737, [1974] 1 WLR 1176, 117 Sol Jo 915, CA
The plaintiff, a Post Office employee, sustained a wound on his leg when he slipped on an oily rung whilst descending a tower wagon ladder. He visited his doctor who gave him an injection of anti-tetanus serum. A few days later the plaintiff developed symptoms due to an allergy to the serum and eventually suffered serious brain damage. The judge held the doctor was not negligent in administering the serum and that although he was negligent in failing to give a preliminary test dose it would have made no difference if he had. The Post Office admitted that the accident and injury to the plaintiff's leg was caused by negligence on its part but said it was not liable for the serious results of the injection because they were not reasonably foreseeable.

HELD: (1) The injection of serum by the doctor was not a *novus actus interveniens* which broke the chain of causation between the negligence of the Post Office and the plaintiff's disability caused by the injection. Conduct of the doctor falling short of negligence could not amount to a *novus actus* and such negligence as the judge found against him was of no effect in causing the disability. (2) It was foreseeable both that the plaintiff might slip on an oily rung and sustain injury and that if he did he might well require medical treatment. The only unforeseeable result was the terrible extent of the injury caused by the plaintiff's allergy to the serum; in that respect the Post Office must take their victim as they found him. *Smith v Leech Brain & Co* (p 335, above) followed. If a wrongdoer ought reasonably to foresee that as a result of his wrongful act the victim may require medical treatment he is, subject to the principle of *novus actus interveniens*, liable for the consequences of the treatment applied although he could not reasonably foresee those consequences.

Emeh v Kensington & Chelsea & Westminster Area Health Authority

[1985] QB 1012, [1984] 3 All ER 1044, CA
Mrs Emeh underwent an abortion and sterilisation operation at the defendant hospital. Some eight months later she found herself 18—20 weeks pregnant. Mrs Emeh declined an abortion and when her baby was born she was found to be congenitally abnormal. It was held by the trial judge that the defendant had carried out the sterilisation operation negligently but the defendant sought to argue that, by refusing to undergo an abortion, the plaintiff had refused to take reasonable steps to minimise the damage and this constituted a *novus actus interveniens* which eclipsed the negligence of the surgeon. This argument was upheld by Park J. The plaintiff appealed.
HELD: The plaintiff's refusal to have an abortion did not break the chain of causation nor did it constitute a failure to mitigate her damages. Only in the most exceptional circumstances could the court declare it unreasonable for a woman to decline an abortion. In this case, there was no evidence to suggest there was any medical or psychiatric grounds for terminating this pregnancy.

Hotson v East Berkshire Health Authority

[1987] AC 750, [1987] 2 All ER 909, [1987] 3 WLR 232, 131 Sol Jo 975, HL
At 13 the plaintiff fell 12 feet from a tree and suffered an acute traumatic fracture of the left femoral epiphysis and damage to the blood vessels. His injury was not correctly diagnosed nor treated for five days and he suffered avascular necrosis which would result in disability of the hip joint and undoubtedly give rise to osteoarthritis. The judge held that even if there had been no delay, there was a 75% chance that avascular necrosis would have occurred so he awarded £11,500 damages for the loss of the 25% chance of a full recovery. The defendant's appeal was dismissed by the Court of Appeal; they appealed to the House of Lords.
HELD: The appeal would be granted. The plaintiff had to prove on the balance of probabilities that the delay was a material contributory cause of the avascular necrosis before quantification of the claim could be considered. He had not done so. If he had, the defendant would not have been entitled to a discount from the full damages to reflect the chance that the necrosis might well have developed anyway given prompt treatment.

Lord McKay quoted Lord Diplock in *Mallet v McMonagle* (see p 465, below) 'In determining what did happen in the past a court decides on the balance of probabilities. Anything that is more probable than not it treats as certain.'

Note—See also *Ricci Burns Ltd v Toole* [1989] 1 WLR 993, CA.

Refusal to undergo operation

McAuley v London Transport Executive

[1957] 2 Lloyd's Rep 500, CA

It cannot be laid down as a general rule that a plaintiff can disregard the advice given by a doctor examining him, even though the doctor examining him is doing so on behalf of the defendant. The question is one of fact in each particular case. Was the advice, and were the prospects of success of the proposed operation or treatment, clearly put to the plaintiff, so that he, as a reasonable man, would appreciate that he was being advised that this treatment or operation would put him right? If the evidence shows that, the plaintiff, as a reasonable person, ought either to accept that advice, or else go to his own doctor and ask for his advice.

Morgan v T Wallis Ltd

[1974] 1 Lloyd's Rep 165, QBD

Per Browne J: The plaintiff in the present case is not in the slightest degree a malingerer and is a completely honest man who genuinely holds the beliefs about which he has told us in evidence. But in deciding whether the defendants have proved that he had unreasonably refused to have the investigation and operation in question here, it seems to me clear from the authorities to which I have referred [*Steele v Robert George & Co* ([1942] AC 497, [1942] 1 All ER 447), *Marcroft v Scruttons Ltd* ([1954] 1 Lloyd's Rep 395, CA)] that I must apply an objective test, in this sense, would a reasonable man, in all the circumstances, receiving the advice the plaintiff did receive, have refused the operation? I think this question must be considered as at the times when his decision was made and on the basis of the advice he then received. If the plaintiff preferred and prefers to go on as he is rather than have the operation [for removal of a prolapsed intervertebral disc] no one can blame him. But the question I have to consider is not, 'Is the plaintiff to blame for refusing the operation?' but 'Is it fair and reasonable to make the defendants pay for his refusal?'

Subsequent injury/disease

Baker v Willoughby

[1970] AC 467, [1969] 3 All ER 1528, [1970] 2 WLR 50, 114 Sol Jo 15, HL

In September 1964 the plaintiff's left leg was fractured in a road accident caused by the defendant's negligent driving. In a shooting accident in November 1967 the same leg was injured so badly that it had to be amputated. His action for damages for the first injury was heard in February 1968. The judge held that the plaintiff's prospective loss from the defendant's negligence should not be reduced by the fact of the subsequent amputation and awarded damages which included an amount for the prospect of loss of earnings and pain and suffering which the plaintiff would have suffered after 1967 if the amputation had never occurred.

The Court of Appeal said this was wrong. The court must have regard to events which had occurred since the date of the accident and must be guided by those events in so far as they had made certain what would otherwise be uncertain. The award should be restricted to the period up to the shooting incident.

On appeal to the House of Lords the judge's award was restored. Lord Reid said it was not correct that the second injury had submerged or obliterated the effect of the first. A man was not compensated for the physical injury but for the loss he suffered as a result of it. The plaintiff's losses were his inability to lead a full life and earn as much as he used to earn or could have earned if there had been no accident. The second injury did not diminish any of those. Whether injuries received before trial reduced the damages depended on the nature and result of those injuries. If the later injury either reduced the disabilities from the injury for which the defendant was liable or shortened the period during which they would be suffered by the plaintiff the defendant would have to pay less damages. But if the later injuries merely became a concurrent cause of the disabilities caused by the first injury they could not diminish the damages. So far as pain and suffering were concerned if the result of the amputation was that the plaintiff suffered no more pain he could not claim for pain he would never suffer, but the judge's award for pain (as distinct from loss of earnings) subsequent to the amputation was probably only a small part of the award and no deduction from the award should be made for this

Hodgson v General Electricity Co Ltd

[1978] 2 Lloyd's Rep 210 (Latey J)
The plaintiff sustained very serious injuries to his left hand in an accident at work in September 1971. In 1974 liability was agreed at 70%. In mid-1976 a serious heart condition developed making the plaintiff unfit for any work in the future. But for the heart condition his employers would have been able to find him suitable light work. Trial was reached in July 1978. He claimed on the basis of the speeches in *Baker v Willoughby* (above) that he was entitled to compensation for the difference between his pre-accident earnings and the earnings he would have received in such light work during the remainder of his expectation of life. It was accepted that there was no causal connection between the injury to his hand and the heart disease.
HELD: In *Baker*'s case the second injury was tortious; in this case not. If what was said in *Baker*'s case was meant also to apply to cases where the second injury was non-tortious it was *obiter* and not binding. There was no reason in logic or justice why the defendants should compensate the plaintiff for a consequence for which they were not to blame, namely, loss of earnings due to heart disease which came upon him unconnected with anything the defendants did. An award of damages is not the imposition of a fine or penalty but is made to compensate the victim for consequences of the wrongful act of the defendants and nothing else. The defendants were not liable for loss of earnings from mid-1976 onwards.

Jobling v Associated Dairies Ltd

[1982] AC 794, [1981] 2 All ER 752, [1981] 3 WLR 155, 125 Sol Jo 481, HL
In January 1973 the appellant plaintiff slipped and fell at work in circumstances imposing liability for damages in tort on the respondents, his employers. The accident caused injury to his back which kept him off work for a time and on his resuming work his earning capacity was 50% less than before the accident. In 1976 he became totally disabled by myelopathy a disease not brought on by the accident. At the trial of the action in 1979 the judge, following Lord Reid's views in *Baker v Willoughby* (above) awarded the plaintiff damages for loss of earnings for a period after 1976, considering himself 'bound to leave out of account the disability caused to the plaintiff by the myelopathy in assessing the damages resulting from the 1973 incident'. The Court of Appeal reversed the finding.
HELD, by the House of Lords, dismissing the appeal: The appellant was not entitled to damages for loss of earnings after he became disabled by myelopathy. Where the victim of a tort is overtaken before trial by a wholly unconnected and disabling illness

the decision in *Baker v Willoughby* does not apply. No consideration of policy warrant placing liability for loss of earnings on the respondents after the emergence of myelopathy; the onset or emergence of illness is one of the vicissitudes of life relevant to the assessment of damages. Whether the decision in *Baker*'s case was correct on its facts (ie as a case of two successive tortious injuries) must be left open, but Lord Reid's *ratio decidendi* in that case could not be accepted. Per Lord Edmund-Davies: I can formulate no convincing juristic or logical principles supportive of the decision of this House in *Baker v Willoughby*.

2 INTERIM PAYMENTS AND PROVISIONAL DAMAGES

INTERIM PAYMENTS

Supreme Court Act 1981, s 32

The power of the court in actions pending in the High Court to order interim payments of damages is contained in the Supreme Court Act 1981, s 32 which is as follows:

'**32 Orders for interim payment** (1) As regards proceedings pending in the High Court, provision may be made by rules of court for enabling the court, in such circumstances as may be prescribed, to make an order requiring a party to the proceedings to make an interim payment of such amount as may be specified in the order, with provision for the payment to be made to such other party to the proceedings as may be specified or, if the order so provides, by paying it into court.

(2) Any rules of court which make provision in accordance with sub-s (1) may include provision for enabling a party to any proceedings who, in pursuance of such an order, has made an interim payment to recover the whole or part of the amount of the payment in such circumstances, and from such other party to the proceedings, as may be determined in accordance with the rules.

(3) Any rules made by virtue of this section may include such incidental, supplementary and consequential provisions as the rule-making authority may consider necessary or expedient.

(4) Nothing in this section shall be construed as affecting the exercise of any power relating to costs, including any power to make rules of court relating to costs.

(5) In this section "interim payment", in relation to a party to any proceedings, means a payment on account of any damages, debt or other sum (excluding any costs) which that party may be held liable to pay to or for the benefit of another party to the proceedings if a final judgment or order of the court in the proceedings is given or made in favour of that other party.'

For actions in the High Court rules have been made which comprise Part II of Ord 29 (rr 9 to 18). They enable a plaintiff in action for damages for personal injuries to apply for an interim payment of damages at any time after a writ has been served and the time limited for appearance has expired. No order will be made unless the defendant is insured, or is a public authority or is a person whose means and resources are such as to enable him to make the interim payment.

Fryer v London Transport Executive

(1982) Times, 4 December, CA

The plaintiff was seriously injured in a road accident. In an action for damages against the defendants he applied to the court for an interim payment. The master awarded

£20,000, but on appeal the judge awarded £50,000. The defendants appealed against the award on the ground that the plaintiff had disclosed to the master and to the judge that the defendants had already made interim payments and a payment into court. Order 22, r 7 prohibits disclosure to the courts of a payment into court at a trial or hearing. Order 29, r 15 says no communication of an interim payment whether voluntary or pursuant to an order 'shall be made to the Court at the trial or hearing of any . . . issue as to . . . damages until all questions of liability and amount have been determined'.

HELD: (1) Whether or not an interim payment should be made and how much it should be were not questions or issues as to damages but related to what in interlocutory proceedings should be done to meet the justice of the case. (2) The defendants had made their objections too late. The information in question had been before both the master and the judge and the defendants had not objected: it would be wrong to allow them to do so now. Appeal dismissed.

Smith v Glennon

(1990) Times, 26 June, CA

It was held by the Court of Appeal that there was nothing to prevent a High Court judge hearing and determining an application for an interim payment under RSC Ord 29, r 10(1). It was the usual practice for such applications to be made to the Master or district registrar but the Order did not take jurisdiction away from the judge.

Standard of proof

Gibbons v Wall

(1988) Times, 24 February, CA

The standard of proof to be applied by the court when determining whether 'the court is satisfied that, if the action proceeded to trial, the plaintiff would obtain judgment for substantial damages' (Ord 29, r 11(1)) was the normal civil standard of proof, but it was flexible and in the context of an application for an interim payment the standard to be applied was at the high end of the range. The word 'sure' used in *Breeze v McKennon & Son Ltd* (see below) meant merely the ordinary civil standard, not 'satisfied beyond reasonable doubt'.

Two or more defendants

Brian Breeze v R McKennon & Son Ltd

(1985) 130 Sol Jo 16, 32 BLR 41, CA

The plaintiffs, a sports and social club, wanted to convert their basement into a restaurant and bar. The first defendants were the main contractors, the second defendants the specialist subcontractors, the third defendant the borough architect and the fourth defendants the local authority. The architect prepared the plans and specifications which included damp proofing. The design was not criticised but the basement flooded and was unusable. The plaintiffs successfully claimed an interim payment against the local authority. The local authority appealed.

HELD, ON APPEAL: Where two or more defendants were involved the court had to be satisfied under ord 29, r 11(1)(c) that the plaintiffs would recover substantial damages from the defendant against whom the Order was made and not from anyone else (not just from one of the co-defendants). The onus of proof necessary to satisfy the court was high, equivalent to being sure that the plaintiff would recover damages. A mere prima facie case was not enough.

The MIB as defendants

Powney v Coxage

(1988) Times, 8 March, CA

The plaintiff sued for damages as a result of being hit by a motor vehicle which was not insured by the driver or the owner. The MIB was joined as third defendant. An application for an interim payment was made against the defendants which was dismissed by the district registrar. The plaintiff appealed.

HELD, ON APPEAL: The court had no jurisdiction over the MIB to order an interim payment as the plaintiff had no cause of action against the MIB, nor could he obtain judgment against the MIB, which was a party to the action only to enable it to defend the claim on behalf of the other defendants. It would not have a liability to pay any sums until judgment had been unsatisfied. The driver could not be ordered to make an interim payment because he was not 'insured'. Although the MIB would meet a judgment it was not indemnifying him as it expressly reserved rights of action against him for sums paid under the agreement. Further the MIB's assets were not the driver's or owner's and so did not provide the other defendants with the resources to make an interim payment.

Note—See Chapter 19 generally.

PROVISIONAL DAMAGES

Supreme Court Act 1981, s 32A

The Supreme Court Act 1981, s 32A (added by the Administration of Justice Act 1982, s 6) enables a court to make provisional awards of damages, and to award further damages at a later date, in certain types of case. The section is as follows:

'**32A Orders for provisional damages for personal injuries** (1) This section applies to an action for damages for personal injuries in which there is proved or admitted to be a chance that at some definite or indefinite time in the future the injured person will, as a result of the act or omission which gave rise to the cause of action, develop some serious disease or suffer some serious deterioration in his physical or mental condition.

(2) Subject to subsection (4) below, as regards any action for damages to which the section applies in which a judgment is given in the High Court, provision may be made by rules of court for enabling the court, in such circumstances as may be prescribed, to award the injured person—

(a) damages assessed on the assumption that the injured person will not develop the disease or suffer the deterioration in his condition; and

(b) further damages at a future date if he develops the disease or suffers the deterioration.

(3) Any rules made by virtue of this section may include such incidental, supplementary and consequential provisions as the rule-making authority may consider necessary or expedient.

(4) Nothing in this section shall be construed—

(a) as affecting the exercise of any power relating to costs, including any power to make rules of court relating to costs; or

(b) as prejudicing any duty of the court under any enactment or rule of law to reduce or limit the total damages which would have been recoverable apart from any such duty.'

The section was brought into force with effect from 1 July 1985 by SI 1985/846 (Rules of the Supreme Court (Amendment No 2) Order). The rules form rr 7 to 10 of Ord 37. The damages awarded under s 32A(2)(a) are designated 'provisional' damages; those under sub-s (2)(b) as 'further' damages. The court will not award 'provisional' damages unless (1) satisfied that the action is one to which s 32A applies and (2) the claim for 'provisional' damages has been pleaded (see rr 7 and 8). For a detailed examination of the rules reference may usefully be made to 82 LS Gaz 1835 (26 June 1985). See also *Practice Note* [1985] 2 All ER 895.

By the Administration of Justice Act 1982, s 73(2) 'section 6 above [ie containing s 32A of the 1981 Act] . . . shall apply to actions whenever commenced, including actions commenced before the passing of this Act'. By s 6(3) s 32A 'shall have effect in relation to county courts as it has effect in relation to the High Court, as if references in it to rules of court included references to county court rules'.

Practice note

The *Practice Note* [1985] 2 All ER 895, which is worth reproducing in full, states as follows:

A Judgments for provisional damages after trial
The following practice will be followed.

1 *Trial proceedings*
The oral judgment of the judge will specify the disease or type of deterioration: (a) which, for the purpose of the award of immediate damages, has been assumed will not occur; (b) which will entitle the plaintiff to further damages if it occurs at a future date.

2 The material parts of the associate's certificate and the judgment entered pursuant to it will be in the following or similar form with such variations as may be necessary under RSC Ord 37, r 8:

'The judge awarded to the plaintiff by way of immediate damages [*set out the award, differentiating between general and special damage, in the usual way*] on the assumption that the plaintiff would not at a future date as a result of the act or omission giving rise to the cause of action develop the following disease, namely [*specify it*] [*or* suffer deterioration in his physical or mental condition of the following type [*specify it*]].

And the judge further ordered that if the plaintiff at a future date did so develop such disease [*or* did so suffer such deterioration] he should be entitled to apply for further damages.'

3 The judge will normally specify the period within which the application for further damages must be made and this will be set out in the associate's certificate and the judgment.

4 *Documents: case file*
The judge will also direct what documents are to be lodged and preserved as material for any further assessment. These documents are hereinafter called the case file. Subject to his directions the case file will normally include: (a) a copy of the associate's certificate; (b) a copy of the judgment drawn up on it; (c) the pleadings; (d) a transcript of the judge's oral judgment; (e) all medical reports placed before the court; (f) a transcript of such parts of the plaintiff's own evidence as to his physical condition and of the medical evidence as the judge may think necessary.

5 The contents of the case file shall be scheduled to the associate's certificate and to the judgment.

6 The associate shall have overall responsibility for the preparation and transmission of the case file. It shall be a secure file or folder and be clearly marked. The plaintiff's solicitor shall be responsible for procuring any transcripts or other documents directed to be placed on the case file.

7 In every case a judgment shall be drawn up and entered and a copy placed on the case file.

8 *Transmission and preservation*
The associate shall: (1) lodge the case file in the office in which the action is proceeding; (2) forward a copy of the judgment indorsed 'Case file lodged in [name of office] [date].' on to The Officer in Charge, Filing Department, Central Office, Royal Courts of Justice, Strand, London WC2A 2LL.

9 Case files shall be filed and preserved as pleadings after trial.

B Orders without trial
Section 32A of the Supreme Court Act 1981 requires that immediate damages and provisional damages must be the subjects of awards by the court if they are to be enforced under that section. Accordingly the following practice shall be followed in relation to settlements under that section.

10 Application shall be made by summons for leave to enter judgment by consent in the terms of a draft annexed to the summons. If the plaintiff is under a disability, the approval of the court should be asked for in the summons and recited in the draft judgment.

11 The draft shall contain the particulars in paras 1 to 3 hereof. It shall also contain a direction as to the documents to be placed on the case file. These will normally be: (a) a copy of the order made on the summons; (b) a copy of the judgment; (c) pleadings, if any; (d) an agreed statement of the facts; (e) agreed medical reports. The contents of the case file shall be scheduled to the order and to the judgment. The terms of the order and judgment shall be subject to the court's approval.

12 The plaintiff's solicitor shall: (1) prepare the case file, which shall be secure and clearly marked; (2) draw up the order and judgment and place copies on the case file; (3) lodge the case file in the office in which the action is proceeding where it shall be preserved as though it were the pleadings of an action disposed of by trial; (4) forward a copy of the judgment as directed in para 8(2) hereof.

13 *Duties of the Central Office*
The Filing and Record Department of the Central Office shall: (1) file the copy judgments received in order of receipt, giving them file numbers; (2) maintain an index of the judgments under the initial letters of the plaintiffs' surnames and containing file number, action number, date of judgment, period within which application for further damages must be made, plaintiff's name, office where case file lodged.

14 This direction applies to all trial centres and offices of the High Court.

Cases

Willson v Ministry of Defence

[1991] 1 All ER 638, [1991] ICR 595
The plaintiff suffered an injury to his left foot at work. He sued his employers seeking provisional damages on the basis that (i) he would remain prone to further injury as

a result of the weakened ankle; (ii) the ankle would deteriorate over time as it suffered from degeneration and (iii) there was a risk that at some time in the future the plaintiff would not be able to continue with his chosen alternative employment.

Under the Supreme Court Act 1981, s 32A the court is empowered to make an award of provisional damages where, inter alia, there is shown to be: 'a chance that at some time . . . in the future' the plaintiff would 'suffer some serious deterioration in his physical condition' as a result of the defendant's negligence.

HELD: A 'chance' has to be something measurable rather than fanciful. However slim the chances of events numbered (i)-(iii) above occurring they were measurable within the meaning of the section.

'Serious deterioration' within the meaning of s 32A of the 1981 Act meant a clear and severable risk rather than any continuing deterioration. Furthermore, it had to be deterioration that was more than ordinary deterioration. Each case depends on its own facts. On the facts of this case, the risk of arthritis developing and that arthritis necessitating surgery did not constitute 'serious deterioration'. The risk of further injury from a fall and the risk of losing alternative employment was speculative and not a risk that could be equated with 'serious degeneration'.

Note—See also *Hurditch v Sheffield Health Authority* [1989] 2 All ER 869 where an agreement between solicitors was construed by the court as an acceptance of an order for provisional damages under RSC Ord 37, r 9.

Middleton v Elliott Turbo Machinery Limited

(1990) Times, 29 October, CA

A declaration attached to a judgment awarding provisional damages to the effect that if the plaintiff died from a specified disease his dependants would be entitled to recover further damages under the Fatal Accidents Act 1976, was not lawful.

3 STRUCTURED SETTLEMENTS

Structured settlements allow plaintiffs to receive a proportion of their damages in the form of a series of future annual payments which last for the duration of the plaintiff's life or for a minimum number of years if the plaintiff dies early. The remainder of the damages are paid by way of the traditional lump sum.

The amount of money reserved for a structured settlement is used by the compensator (usually an insurance company) to purchase an annuity in order to fund the regular payments that it has to make to the plaintiff.

The advantages to the plaintiff of such a settlement are as follows:

- The plaintiff receives regular payments for life. Furthermore it can be agreed that in the event of an early death the regular payments can be maintained over a certain period to protect dependants.
- The payments are regarded by the Inland Revenue as capital rather than income and are therefore non-taxable.
- The regular payments can be index-linked and varied over the years to take into account the plaintiff's differing social circumstances such as starting a family or moving house.

The advantages to the compensator are as follows:

— Savings on the traditional lump sum figure can be obtained to take into account the tax benefits of a structured settlement.
— The purchase of the annuity can be treated as a reinsurance premium and accordingly treated as a write-off by the compensator as the damages would have been in any event.
— The receipt of the regular annuity is wholly taxable in the hands of the compensator.
— The payment of the gross amount of the debt to the plaintiff can be fully written-off as a tax deductible item by the compensator.

For cases where a structured settlement has been agreed see *Grimsley v Grimsley & Mead* (reported in the Personal & Medical Injuries Law Letter, December 1991, p 66) and *Kelly v Dawes* ((1990) Times, 27 September).

The first structured settlement by a health authority occurred in the case of *Field v Hertfordshire Health Authority* (unreported).

The following practice direction was issued by the Senior Master on 12 February 1992 and reported at [1992] 1 All ER 862:

1 This practice note applies only to proceedings in the Central Office and the Admiralty and Commercial Registry of the High Court. It concerns settlements of claim in respect of personal injury or death where approval of the court is required and which include a structured element. The practice set out below, adapted as indicated, is appropriate whether or not the Court of Protection is involved. It will apply, on an experimental basis, until further notice. If the plaintiff is under mental disability then the additional steps set out in paras 6(viii) and 8 of this practice note should be taken.
2 By this practice note it is intended to establish a practice to overcome the present administrative difficulty caused by the short period over which life offices keep open offers of annuities at a given price. It has proved difficult for plaintiffs' solicitors to do all that is necessary to obtain the approval of the court within the period during which the annuity offer remains open.
3 As from 30 March 1992 all applications for approval in structured settlement cases will be listed for hearing on Friday mornings during term time.
4 After setting down, applications for the fixing of dates for these purposes should be made to the Clerk of the Lists in room 547.
5 Once a hearing date has been obtained, documents should be lodged in room 547 not later than noon on the Thursday immediately before the Friday for which the hearing is fixed.
6 The following are the classes of document which should be lodged in accordance with para 5 above: (i) copies of originating process or pleadings, if any; (ii) an opinion of counsel assessing the value of the claim on a conventional basis (unless approval has already been given) and, if practicable, the opinion of counsel on the structured settlement proposed; (iii) a report of forensic accountants setting out the advantages and disadvantages, if any, of structuring bearing in mind the plaintiff's life expectancy and the anticipated costs of future care; (iv) a draft of the proposed agreement as approved by the Inland Revenue (and by the Treasury where the defendant or other paying party is a health authority); (v) sufficient material to satisfy the court that enough capital is available free of the structure to meet anticipated future capital needs. Particular reference to accommodation and transport needs will usually be helpful in this context; (vi) sufficient material to satisfy the court that the structure is secure and backed by responsible insurers; (vii) evidence of other assets available to the plaintiff beyond the award the subject of the application; (viii) in cases where the plaintiff is under mental disability the consent of the Court of Protection.

The classes of document required to be lodged should be separately bundled and clearly marked so that the presence of the appropriate classes of document (but not the adequacy of their content) may be checked by the clerks in room 547.

7 If the proceedings are in the Admiralty and Commercial Registry application should be made to the Admiralty Registrar in good time for the transfer of the proceedings to the Central Office for the purpose of the application for approval only.
8 In cases where the plaintiff is under mental disability, the documents set out in para 6(i) to (vii) (inclusive) should be lodged in the Enquiries and Acceptances Branch of the Public Trust Office, Stewart House, 24 Kingsway, London WC2B 6JH not later than noon on the Monday immediately before the Friday for which the hearing is fixed. Unless an application has already been made for the appointment of a receiver, there must also be lodged an application for the appointment of a receiver (form CP1 (in duplicate)), a certificate of family and property (form CP5) and a medical certificate (form CP3). (Blank forms are available from the same address.) The Court of Protection's approval, if granted, will be available by 10.30 am on the Thursday immediately before the Friday fixed for the hearing.
9 This practice note is issued with the approval of the Deputy Chief Justice, the judge in charge of the non-jury list, the Admiralty Judge and the Master of the Court of Protection.

The future of structured settlements as well as interim and provisional damages has been considered by the Law Commission whose discussions have been published in Consultation Paper, No 125, 1992.

4 HEADS OF DAMAGES

GENERAL DAMAGES

Epilepsy

Note—The three cases following are of a type to which the procedure under the Supreme Court Act 1981, s 32A would seem now to be appropriate. See below under 'Further disability uncertain'.

Hawkins v New Mendip Engineering Ltd

[1966] 3 All ER 228, [1966] 1 WLR 1341, 110 Sol Jo 633, CA
A fitter aged 27 was struck on the head by a piece of an accumulator which exploded. He was off work seven weeks before resuming his job. There was no fracture of the skull but he developed a minor form of epilepsy. There was a 50—50 chance that he might develop a major epilepsy but it was virtually impossible to tell within five years what the future was likely to be. His present symptoms included headaches, forgetfulness, the feeling known as *déjà vu*, and panosmia. The judge awarded £8,000. The defendants appealed.
HELD: There was no reason to interfere with the judge's award. What had to be quantified was the uncertainty of the future. If major epilepsy did develop it would be a major catastrophe for the plaintiff, virtually ending his working life. The judge was moving in the realm of guesswork and the judge's guess was as good as that of an appellate tribunal.

Prudence v Lewis

(1966) Times, 21 May (Brabin J)
A child of three was struck by a car and sustained a head injury. When trial of his action was reached three years later the doctors said the risk of development of epilepsy was at least 10%. The judge awarded £3,000. The difficulty (he said) in

fixing an award in such a case was that, in the future the award must be wrong, because, if in fact the boy was free from epilepsy, the award would appear to the defendant to have been too high, and if the boy did develop it, the award would appear to him to have been too low. A compromise had to be made in fixing the damages before the medical position became certain.

Jones v Griffith

[1969] 2 All ER 1015, [1969] 1 WLR 795, 113 Sol Jo 309, CA
The plaintiff, aged 21, sustained head injuries in a road accident. One result was a liability to attacks of traumatic epilepsy. She had one major epileptic attack and several further attacks not so serious. With suitable medication she might not have any more fits but there remained a liability to an occasional attack. The trial judge awarded £6,000, of which up to £5,000 was in respect of the epilepsy.
HELD: The question was what were the chances of further attacks of epilepsy of a serious nature. Unlike *Hawkins*' and *Prudence*'s cases (above) the plaintiff had already suffered attacks. One approach was to consider what figure would be appropriate in a case where future serious attacks were virtually certain (say £10,000 to £11,000) and then discount that figure according to the degree of optimism in the medical reports. In the present case the plaintiff's prospects were a little better than 50—50. On that basis it would not be right to interfere with the judge's award.

Joyce v Yeomans

[1981] 2 All ER 21, [1981] 1 WLR 549, 125 Sol Jo 34, CA
The plaintiff, a boy of ten, was hit by a car, sustaining a head injury, ruptured spleen and a fractured clavicle. Some months later he showed symptoms of epilepsy and during three years had four or five grand mal attacks. The judge accepted a doctor's opinion that the boy would have developed epilepsy by the time he was 14 even without the injuries but that they had caused the epilepsy to appear earlier and to be more disabling. The plaintiff had done poorly at school and had been unable to pass any 'O' level examinations. The judge awarded £7,500 inclusive of loss of future earning capacity which he did not assess separately.
HELD, ON APPEAL: The injuries and epilepsy in themselves justified an award of £6,000, which left too little for loss of earning capacity. It was not appropriate to use the multiplier/multiplicand method to calculate this loss because there were so many imponderables but a proper figure in the circumstances would be £7,500, making a total of £13,500 but with interest on the £6,000 only.

Note—See also *Stephenson v Cook* [1975] 1 Lloyd's Rep 495. The above cases have now to be considered in the light of the ability of the courts to award provisional damages.

Personality change

DIVORCE

Jones v Jones

[1985] QB 704, [1984] 3 All ER 1003, CA
The plaintiff was very seriously injured in a road accident, so much that he suffered a personality change and his affairs were administered by the Court of Protection. He was awarded a total of £177,500 damages. At the time of the accident he had a wife

and one child with another expected. As a result of his injuries the marriage broke down; his wife divorced him and lived separately with the two children. It was conceded that the breakdown of the marriage and separation or divorce were reasonably foreseeable by the defendant. The judge at first instance in the light of this concession held there was no reason in principle for refusing to award damages for the extra expense to the plaintiff in maintaining his wife and children in a separate establishment but said at the time of the trial that the plaintiff had not proved any additional loss and expense. After the trial the plaintiff's wife in matrimonial proceedings obtained an order for periodical payments at £2,445 a year and for a lump sum of £25,000 which had been spent on a house for the wife.

HELD: As it was conceded that the particular type of loss was reasonably foreseeable the only issue was quantum (*McLoughlin v O'Brian*, p 401, below). In respect of the periodical payments for maintenance there were so many imponderables it was not proved that such payments were greater than the plaintiff would have had to spend if his wife and family had continued to live with him. But the lump sum payment would not have been necessary if they had continued to live together. On the other hand if she had remained with him he may (or even the Court of Protection on his behalf may) have thought it right to make her a gift for giving up her life to care for him. £10,000 ought to be deducted in respect of this: there should accordingly be an award of a further £15,000 damages additional to the amount awarded in the court below.

Pritchard v JH Cobden Ltd

[1988] Fam 22, [1988] 1 All ER 300, [1987] 2 WLR 627, [1987] 2 FLR 30, CA

In 1976 the plaintiff, aged 30, suffered serious brain damage as a result of a motor accident. He was married with a six-and-a-half-year-old daughter; seven months later his wife gave birth to twins. His injuries meant that he was unemployable; he had suffered a complete change of personality and the marriage did not survive. The defendants did not dispute that the marriage breakdown was a result of the injuries. The judge awarded £53,000 to cover the financial loss arising as a result of the divorce (taking into account the need for separate dwellings, the costs of the divorce and the ancillary relief proceedings). The defendants appealed.

HELD: Appeal allowed. Although the marriage breakdown was caused by the injuries the resultant financial arrangements were a redistribution of the financial assets of the couple, including any damages awarded to the plaintiff for his personal injuries. Any orders under the Matrimonial Causes Act 1973 were therefore not losses to the plaintiff over and above the damages payable and had to be wholly disregarded when calculating compensation. It would also be contrary to public policy and open to abuse to take considerations relevant to matrimonial proceedings into account in personal injury litigation. Damages reduced by the sum of £53,000.

CRIMINAL ACTS: IMPRISONMENT

Meah v McCreamer

[1985] 1 All ER 367 (Woolf J)

The plaintiff sustained a close-head injury to the left frontal lobe of the brain in a road accident. Some years before the accident he had shown a pattern of violent behaviour but no serious crime: he had a number of convictions for offences of dishonesty. After the accident he had become violently and sexually aggressive and was, by the time

of trial, serving two life sentences for crimes of rape and wounding. There was medical evidence that the frontal lobe injury sustained in the accident had removed the inhibitions formerly restraining his aggressiveness. His condition was untreatable and he had to be kept in prison for the protection of society.
HELD: *Jones v Jones* (above) had shown that awards could be made in head injury cases that at first sight seemed surprising. The plaintiff had shown that, on a balance of probabilities, but for the accident he would not have committed the crimes for which he was now in prison. He was entitled to damages for the resulting imprisonment. The right figure in general damages was £60,000 to be reduced by 25% for contributory negligence.

W v Meah and D v Meah

[1986] 1 All ER 935, [1986] NLJ Rep 165, QBD
Two victims that Meah attacked as a result of his injuries referred to in *Meah v McCreamer (No 1)* (above) brought actions against him claiming damages for personal injury and aggravated damages for rape, assault and battery and wounding in one case and assault and battery in another. The sums awarded were assessed on the basis of conventional personal injury actions although a moderate award was nominally included for aggravated damages to take into account the circumstances.

See also *Meah v McCreamer (No 2)*, below for questions of remoteness of damages for criminal acts, and *Smith v Littlewood*, p 346, above.

Note—See also the case of *Stubbings v Webb*, p 513, below.

CRIMINAL ACT—REMOTENESS OF DAMAGE

Meah v McCreamer (No 2)

[1986] 1 All ER 943, [1986] NLJ Rep 235, QBD
Following the judgment in *Meah v McCreamer* two victims of Meah's sexual attacks sued him in damages and were awarded substantial sums, in each case. Meah in the present action sued McCreamer and his insurers to recover the amounts awarded to the two victims.
HELD: The damages were too remote to be recoverable from McCreamer. The plaintiff was seeking to recover, not in respect of his own injuries or damage, but in respect of damage he caused to third parties. Although in deciding what is or is not foreseeable the question is not a pure matter of policy, there is a proper role for the court to play: the right approach is to deal with the matter in a 'robust' manner. On that basis the loss was not recoverable, either from the driver of the car or that driver's insurers. On the question of the liability of the insurers the same approach should be applied as in *Gray v Barr* (above).

Shock

THE RULE

Note—A cause of action in negligence for damages for nervous shock has the same constituents as any other personal injury claim: (1) a duty to the plaintiff to take care, (2) a careless act amounting to a breach of that duty, (3) resultant injury to the plaintiff. The question whether the plaintiff was within that category of persons to whom, in the circumstances, the defendant owed a duty of care was considered in *Hay (or Bourhill) v Young* (p 6, above) and in the following cases.

King v Phillips

[1953] 1 QB 429, [1953] 1 All ER 617, [1953] 2 WLR 526, 97 Sol Jo 171, CA
A boy aged five or six years unaccompanied by any adult, was on his tricycle on the highway at Birstal Road where it joined Greenfield Road. The driver of a taxi-cab stopped at the first house in Greenfield Road beyond the junction with Birstal Road to pick up a passenger. The boy asked the driver if he was going to take someone for a ride and then, so far as the driver saw, disappeared. The passenger entered the cab, and the driver looked round, and thinking the boy had gone some minutes before, began to back the cab. The boy was just behind the cab and was knocked off the tricycle which was pushed a short distance. The driver heard a little shout from behind the cab. He got down and found the tricycle smashed up and the boy running towards his home some 70 or 80 yards distant on the other side of Birstal Road. The boy's mother was in her house looking out of an upstairs window when she heard a scream from the end of the road which she identified as that of her boy. She saw the taxi-cab backing into the tricycle and then saw the tricycle under the taxi but could not see the boy. She ran into the road, met the boy running towards her and took him indoors. She found he was injured but the injuries were very slight and transient. The mother claimed damages for shock.
HELD: *Hay (or Bourhill) v Young* (p 6, above) decided that a driver was not liable for shock unless the injury was within that which he ought to have reasonably contemplated as the area of potential danger which would arise as the result of his negligence. Adopting the expression of 'the reasonable hypothetical observer' in that case, the driver could not reasonably have anticipated that to back the taxi in this way, though negligent vis-à-vis the boy, would cause injury to the boy's mother in her house 70 or 80 yards away. She was wholly outside the area or range of reasonable anticipation. Adopting Lord Wright's language, the line should be drawn where the good sense of the jury or judge decides. It would be contrary to common sense to say that the driver ought reasonably to have contemplated that he might cause injury by shock to a woman in a house some 70 or 80 yards distant on the other side of Birstal Road. Judgment for defendant. [1952] 2 All ER 459, [1952] WN 393, [1952] 2 TLR 277, 96 Sol Jo 513 (McNair J). An appeal was dismissed.

Note—Professor Goodhart (69 LQR 347) points out that the three Lords Justices gave conflicting grounds for their decision. Hodgson LJ said that there was no reasonably foreseeable risk of physical injury to the plaintiff herself. On this view *Hambrook v Stokes* has been overruled for all practical purposes. Singleton LJ said that the defendant could not have anticipated that the plaintiff would see the accident, and this implies that the defendant had far less foresight than in *Haynes v Harwood* (p 00, above), where the plaintiff was injured a quarter of a mile away. Denning LJ said that the test was not foreseeability of physical injury but foreseeability of emotional shock and the defendant could not reasonably have been expected to have foreseen that the plaintiff would suffer from emotional shock and that the shock was too remote to be a head of damage.

He suggests therefore that the case decides (1) the plaintiff in a shock case need not be within the area of physical injury to himself; (2) that the shock need not be based on fear for oneself; fear for the safety of one's child is sufficient; and in the result that a slight alteration in the facts might lead to a different conclusion. See now *Boardman v Sanderson* and *McLoughlin v O'Brian*, p 401, below.

Dooley v Cammell Laird & Co Ltd

[1951] 1 Lloyd's Rep 271 (Donovan J)
A crane driver was lowering a sling when the rope broke and the load fell, and out of sight of the plaintiff dislodged some scaffolding which crashed into the hold where the plaintiff knew fellow workmen were at work. The plaintiff was thereby put into a state of apprehension and acute anxiety and suffered severe nervous shock.

Defendants contended they owed no duty except in the case of impact upon the claimant, his wife or child, or reasonable fear of such impact.
HELD: There is no duty unless physical injury to the person or his relations or friends is reasonably to be expected, or unless shock was reasonably to be expected to him as a result of defendant's negligence. The fear that fellow workmen may have been injured was not baseless or extravagant and was a consequence reasonably to have been foreseen as likely to cause a nervous shock, which fear was not unreasonable in the circumstances and was not too remote.

Galt v British Railways Board

(1983) 133 NLJ 870
The plaintiff, driving a train at 65 mph in conditions of restricted visibility, suddenly saw two men on the track about 30 yards away. He could not stop and thought (mistakenly as it turned out) they had been killed. He suffered nervous shock bringing on a myocardial infarction, to which he was predisposed by a pre-existing symptomless condition.
HELD: He was entitled to damages, no speed limit having been in force. The injury was reasonably foreseeable and the defendants owed him a duty to take reasonable care not to expose him to injury from nervous shock. They were liable for increased damage caused by the pre-existing disease, applying *The Wagon Mound* (p 332, above) and *Jason v Batten (1930) Ltd* [1969] 1 Lloyd's Rep 281.

Boardman v Sanderson

[1964] 1 WLR 1317, 105 Sol Jo 152, CA
The plaintiff and his son, aged eight, went with the defendant to a garage to collect the defendant's car which had been repaired. At the defendant's request the plaintiff went into the office to pay the bill whilst the defendant got into the car a few yards away to back it out of the garage. The boy was standing very near the car when the defendant backed it out and ran on to his foot. The boy screamed and the plaintiff ran out of the office to see what had happened. He saw the wheel of the car on his son's foot and suffered shock.
HELD: He was entitled to damages for the shock. The defendant knew the boy was in the yard and that any carelessness in driving might result in injury to the boy. He knew the father was within earshot and that he was in such a position that if he heard a scream from the boy he was bound to run out. A duty was owed by the defendant not only to the boy but also to the near relatives of the boy who were, as he knew, on the premises within earshot and likely to come upon the scene if any injury or ill befell the boy. *King v Phillips* (above) was distinguishable since in that case it was unknown to the driver that the mother happened to live nearby. He could not reasonably foresee that if he injured the child the mother would be immediately upon the scene of the accident. *Hay (or Bourhill) v Young* (p 6, above) was no authority for saying that if the plaintiff did not actually see the accident (as distinct from the results) he could not succeed. The father's injury by shock was reasonably foreseeable by the defendant.

Chadwick v British Transport Commission

[1967] 2 All ER 945, [1967] 1 WLR 912, 111 Sol Jo 562 (Waller J)
The plaintiff, a window cleaner aged 41, was at home when a serious railway accident occurred about 200 yards away. He did not see it, but went to help. He spent several hours at the scene helping passengers who had serious and horrifying injuries. Afterwards he fell into a condition of depression and nervousness that was eventually diagnosed as an anxiety neurosis caused by his experiences at the scene of the disaster. He claimed damages against the defendants who admitted the railway accident was their fault but denied liability for the plaintiff's condition.
HELD: (1) Shock, other than caused by fear for oneself or children, may be the subject of a claim for damages; (2) it was reasonably foreseeable by the defendants that if trains collided and people were killed some persons who were physically unhurt might suffer from shock; (3) the defendants owed a duty of care to the plaintiff because they could have foreseen that, if passengers were injured by their negligence, somebody might try and rescue the passengers and suffer injury in the process; (4) the fact that the risk run by the rescuer was not precisely that run by the passengers did not deprive the plaintiff of his remedy; it was sufficient that shock was foreseeable and that rescue was foreseeable.

Judgment for the plaintiff.

McLoughlin v O'Brian

[1983] 1 AC 410, [1982] 2 All ER 298, [1982] 2 WLR 982, 126 Sol Jo 347, [1982] RTR 209, HL
The plaintiff's husband and three of her children, George aged 17, Kathleen, 7 and Gillian, 3 were in a car which collided with a lorry. The plaintiff was not present: she was at home two miles away. She was told of the accident by a witness who said he thought George was dying. He drove her to hospital where she was told by her second son (who was not in the car) that Gillian was dead. She saw Kathleen crying and her face cut. She heard George shouting and screaming. She saw her husband, head in hands, covered in mud and oil. As a result she suffered severe shock, organic depression and change of personality, with numerous symptoms of a physiological character. She claimed damages against the defendant lorry drivers and owners responsible for the collision. The judge dismissed her claim on the ground that injury by shock was not reasonably foreseeable in the circumstances. The Court of Appeal dismissed her appeal: the Lords Justices held that injury by shock was reasonably foreseeable but that public policy required a limit to be placed on the extent of the duty of care in such cases: it should be limited to those on or near the highway at or near the time of the accident.
HELD, ON APPEAL, to the House of Lords: The plaintiff was entitled to succeed. When injury from shock was reasonably foreseeable to the plaintiff the duty of care was not to be limited merely by considerations of public policy. A cause of action for injury by shock had developed through a series of cases: (1) without the need for injury to oneself; (2) by injury or fear of it to a near relative (*Hambrook v Stokes Bros* (below), *Boardman v Sanderson* (above)); (3) by coming upon the immediate aftermath (*Boardman*'s case); (4) coming upon the scene as a rescuer (*Chadwick v British Transport Commission* (above)). If the process of logical progression was followed it was hard to see why this plaintiff should not succeed. Her claim may be upon the margin of what the process of logical progression will allow, but the facts being strong and exceptional her case ought to be assimilated to those which have passed the test.

There was no requirement of public policy that the damage to a plaintiff should be on or adjacent to the highway. A defendant's duty of care must depend on reasonable foreseeability and be adjudicated only upon a case-by-case basis.

Note—See also *Baker v Hopkins* (p 49, above) and *Videan v British Transport Commission* (p 50, above).

Attia v British Gas plc

[1988] QB 304, [1987] 3 All ER 455, CA

The defendants were engaged to install central heating. The plaintiff returning home during the afternoon of the installation found smoke coming from the loft of her house. She called the Fire Brigade who took over four hours to control the fire, by which time the house and contents were extensively damaged. The plaintiff sued for nervous shock resulting in a psychiatric or mental illness. The defendants argued that such a reaction was not reasonably foreseeable, and that if it was reasonably foreseeable damages could only in any event be awarded as a matter of law and public policy for injury or death, or fear of such, to a person closely related to the plaintiff. HELD, ON APPEAL: There was no principle that the plaintiff should not recover damages for nervous shock as a result of seeing her house destroyed by fire if this amounted to psychiatric damage or illness and not merely normal grief, sorrow, or emotional distress. Psychiatric damage had, in all the circumstances of the case, to be reasonably foreseeable.

Alcock v Chief Constable of the South Yorkshire Police

[1992] 1 AC 310, [1991] 4 All ER 907

Shortly before the commencement of a football match at the Hillsborough Stadium the police responsible for crowd control permitted too many spectators into a part of the ground already full. As a result 95 spectators were crushed to death and over 400 injured. The disaster was broadcast live on television. None of the depicted scenes showed the suffering or dying of recognisable individuals.

Sixteen relatives, and in one case the fiancee of a person who was in the area, brought actions against the defendant claiming damages for nervous shock, causing psychiatric illness. In the case of 13 of the plaintiffs their relatives and friends were killed. In two other cases relatives and friends were injured and in the case of one plaintiff the relative escaped unhurt.

The defendant admitted liability and negligence but denied it owed a duty of care to the plaintiff. Assuming each plaintiff had suffered nervous shock the question of whether the plaintiffs were entitled to damages was tried as a preliminary issue. Hidden J ([1991] 1 All ER 353) found for 10 of the 16 plaintiffs and against 6. The defendant appealed and the six unsuccessful plaintiffs cross appealed. The Court of Appeal ([1993] 3 All ER 88) allowed the defendant's appeal and dismissed the cross appeals holding that none of the plaintiffs could recover. Ten of the plaintiffs appealed to the House of Lords.

HELD: There are three elements inherent in any claim for shock. The elements to be considered are (i) the class of persons whose claims should be recognised; (ii) the proximity of such persons to the accident in time and space and (iii) the means by which the shock has been caused.

(i) The duty of care could in particular circumstances extend to an innocent bystander if, for example, a petrol tanker careered into a school session and burst into flames.

'I would not be prepared to rule out a potential claim by a passer by so shocked by the scene as to suffer psychiatric illness': per Lord Ackner.

The claims by those in close family relationships referred to by Wilberforce LJ in *McLoughlin v O'Brian* arise from a rebuttable presumption that the intimacy of the relationship should reasonably be contemplated by a defendant. As for more remote relatives Nolan LJ stated:

'For my part, I would accept at once that no general definition is possible. But I see no difficulty in principle in requiring a defendant to contemplate that the person physically injured or threatened by his negligence may have relatives or friends whose love for him is like that of a normal parent or spouse, and who in consequence may similarly be closely and directly affected by nervous shock.... The identification of the particular individual who comes within the category, like that of parent and spouses themselves could only be carried out ex poste facto, and would depend upon evidence of the '"relationship'' in a broad sense which gave rise to the love and affection'.

(ii) 'The proximity to the accident must be close both in time and space. Direct and immediate sight or hearing of the accident is not required... shock can arise through sight or hearing of its immediate aftermath': per Lord Ackner.

Following Wilberforce LJ in *McLoughlin* the plaintiffs in the present case were not in sufficient proximity in time and space to the accident or its immediate aftermath.

(iii) The plaintiffs must suffer nervous shock through seeing or hearing the accident or its immediate aftermath. In the present case the defendant was entitled to suspect that whilst the scenes would be distressing they would not show pictures of suffering by a recognisable individual.

'Although the television pictures certainly gave rise to feelings of deepest anxiety and distress, in the circumstances of this case the simultaneous television broadcasts of what occurred cannot be equated with the "sight or hearing of the event or its immediate aftermath". Accordingly shock sustained by reason of these broadcasts cannot find a claim': per Lord Ackner.

Lord Ackner did recognise that in certain circumstances the simultaneous broadcast of a disaster could satisfy the necessary requirements.

The appeals were dismissed.

Note—The decisions in *Hevican v Ruane* [1991] 3 All ER 65 and in *Ravenscott v Rederiaktiebolaget Transatlantic* [1991] 3 All ER 73 were specifically doubted by Lord Keith and Lord Oliver.

McFarlane v E E Caledonia Ltd

[1994] 2 All ER 1, [1993] NLJR 1367, CA

The plaintiff was employed on the Piper Alpha Oil Rig in the North Sea which exploded and burst into flames causing the deaths of 164 men. The plaintiff was staying on a support vessel some 500 metres from the rig. The support vessel took some part in the rescue operation as a result of which the closest the plaintiff came to the burning oil rig was 100 metres. The plaintiff suffered psychiatric illness arising out of his experiences and claimed damages against the operators of the rig. The question before the court was whether the rig operators owed the plaintiff a duty of care. The judge at first instance held that they did. The defendant appealed.

HELD: The plaintiff's claim failed. The judge considered correctly that the existence of a duty of care depended upon the test of foreseeability of harm and the proximity of relationship between the plaintiff and defendant. However the judge did not go far enough for this test is an objective one ie it is a foreseeability of the reasonable man in the position of the defendants that is material.

The support vessel was never in a position of danger. No one on it sustained any physical injury and there was no evidence that anyone other than the plaintiff suffered psychiatric injury. The circumstances of the plaintiff's movements suggested, and the Court of Appeal accepted, that the plaintiff was not genuinely in fear of his own safety. The plaintiff was not a rescuer having taken no active part in the rescue operation himself. Thus:

'In my judgment it cannot be said that the defendants ought reasonably to have foreseen that the plaintiff or other non essential personnel on board (the support vessel) would suffer such injury': per Stuart Smith LJ.

Furthermore there had to be a sufficiently close tie of love and affection between the plaintiff and the victims to satisfy the test of proximity as confirmed in the Alcock decision above.

'In my judgment both as a matter of principle and policy the court should not extend the duty to those who are mere bystanders or witnesses of horrific events unless there is a sufficient degree of proximity, which requires both nearest in time and place and a close relationship of love and affection between plaintiff and victim': per Stuart Smith LJ.

REMOTENESS OF DAMAGE

Hambrook v Stokes Bros

[1925] 1 KB 141, 94 LJKB 435, 41 TLR 125, CA

Defendants' servant left a motor lorry at the top of a steep and narrow street unattended, with the engine running, and without having taken proper precautions to secure it. The lorry started off by itself and ran violently down the incline. Plaintiff's wife, who had been walking up the street with her children, had just parted from them a little below a point where the street makes a bend, when she saw the lorry rushing round the bend towards her. She became frightened for the safety of her children, who by that time were out of sight round the bend, and who she knew must have met the lorry in its course. She was almost immediately afterwards informed by bystanders that a child answering the description of one of hers had been injured. In consequence of her fright and anxiety she suffered a nervous shock, which eventually caused her death, whereby her husband lost the benefit of her services. In an action by the husband under the Fatal Accidents Acts:

HELD: On the assumption that the shock was caused by what the woman saw with her own eyes as distinguished from what she was told by bystanders, plaintiff was entitled to recover, notwithstanding that the shock was brought about by fear for her children's safety and not by fear for her own safety.

Note—Hambrook v Stokes Bros was discussed in *Hay (or Bourhill) v Young* (p 6, above). Lord Thankerton said he preferred the dissenting judgment of Sargent LJ. Lord Wright said he agreed with that decision.

Owens v Liverpool Corpn

[1939] 1 KB 394, [1938] 4 All ER 727, CA
A funeral procession was passing along a street when a tramcar collided with the hearse, broke its glass side and overturned the coffin, so that there was a danger of its being ejected into the road. The plaintiffs, the relatives of the deceased, were in a carriage following the hearse. One of them actually saw the impact, the others saw its effect immediately after it had happened. Each of the plaintiffs received injury in the nature of shock.
HELD: The right to recover damages for mental shock is not limited to cases in which apprehension as to human safety is involved, but extends to every case where injury by reason of mental shock results from the negligent act of the defendant. The plaintiffs were therefore entitled to recover the damages assessed. Mental or nervous shock, if in fact caused by defendant's negligence, gave a cause of action. The shock was not occasioned by fear for human life, but by the imperilment of the coffin containing the corpse of a near relative. The plaintiffs might be peculiarly susceptible to being disastrously disturbed by the accident, but the idiosyncrasies of the victim did not alter the fact that the injury was the result of the accident.

Note—Owens v Liverpool Corpn was discussed in *Hay (or Bourhill) v Young* (p 6, above). Lord Wright said he would have stopped short of judgement for the plaintiff. Lord Porter said he did not think the driver was in breach of any duty to the plaintiff.

Semble: If the case had been contested on liability instead of remoteness of damage, the judgment would have been for defendants.

Schneider v Eisovitch

[1960] 2 QB 430, [1960] 1 All ER 169, [1960] 2 WLR 169, 104 Sol Jo 89 (Paull J)
The plaintiff was injured and rendered unconscious in a motor accident: her husband was killed. She recovered consciousness in hospital and was then told that her husband was dead. She subsequently suffered from a mental condition resulting from three factors: (1) the shock of the accident itself; (2) the shock of discovering in hospital that her husband had been killed; and (3) the continuing mental strain of having to adjust her life after her husband's death.
HELD: (1) and (2) were allowable in awarding damages: (3) was not. With regard to (2) the shock was a direct consequence of the defendant's negligent act. The fact that owing to the unconsciousness a period of time elapsed before the news was heard makes no difference provided that that news was a consequence which flowed directly from the breach of duty towards the plaintiff. The fact that the defendant by his negligence caused the death of the plaintiff's husband did not give the plaintiff a cause of action for the shock caused to her, but the plaintiff having a cause of action for the negligence of the defendant could add the consequences of shock caused by hearing of her husband's death when estimating the amount recoverable on her cause of action.

Note—This case was decided before the Privy Council decision in *Overseas Tankship (UK) Ltd v Morts Dock and Engineering Co Ltd ('The Wagon Mound')*, p 332, above.

Tregoning v Hill

(1965) Times, 2 March (Paull J)
The plaintiff and her husband were cycling together when they were run into from behind by the defendant's car. Her husband was dragged along and rolled over and

over before being left lying on the road fatally injured. The plaintiff fell off her cycle but did not suffer personal injury. She claimed damages for herself for the shock she suffered at seeing her husband killed in her presence, the depression she suffered as a result of the accident and the loss of her husband's company, especially on cycle tours.

HELD: No damages could at law be awarded for the loss of her husband's company or even for the shock as a result of her husband's death but she was entitled to an amount to cover the difference between the situation where she was at home and heard that her husband had been killed in a cycling accident and the situation where she herself actually witnessed the killing. The fact that she saw him killed did add to her depressed state and £750 was a fair sum for this.

Hinz v Berry

[1970] 2 QB 40, [1970] 1 All ER 1074, [1970] 2 WLR 684, 114 Sol Jo 111, CA
The plaintiff was out for a picnic with her husband and children. Their car was parked and her husband was unloading it when she saw the defendant's car crash into it, killing her husband and injuring the children. She claimed damages for nervous shock. The judge held that the extreme shock of witnessing the exceptionally tragic accident had brought about a morbid state of mind additional to what her condition would have been if she had not witnessed it. He awarded £4,000.

HELD: On the defendant's appeal against the amount of the award, the plaintiff's depressed state arose from five causes: (1) grief and sorrow at losing her husband; (2) anxiety for the welfare of the injured children; (3) financial stress from the loss of the family breadwinner; (4) the need to adjust herself to a new life; (5) shock of witnessing the accident. Only the fifth of these was a proper subject for compensation at law. Was the assessment right for this one factor? There was evidence that the morbid element in her symptoms was due solely to the shock of witnessing the accident and the judge had so found. His figure was high but not so high as to be a wholly erroneous estimate. Appeal dismissed.

Per Lord Denning: Somehow or other the court has to draw a line between sorrow and grief for which damages are not recoverable, and nervous shock and psychiatric illness for which damages are recoverable. The way to do this is to estimate how much the plaintiff would have suffered if, for instance, her husband had been killed in an accident when she was 50 miles away and compare it with what she is now, having suffered all the shock due to being present at the accident.

Note—Referred to and followed in *Allen v Dando* [1977] CLY 738 where the plaintiff was said to be suffering from a morbid depression which was 'a recognisable psychiatric illness' as a result of witnessing the death of his daughter aged 11 in an accident in which he himself sustained slight injuries. He nevertheless at the time of trial four years later had no insomnia, an improved appetite and an active social life; Mrs Hinz's condition was 'far more serious'. Award of damages for nervous shock £2,250. But see *Whitmore v Euroways*, below.

Beecham v Hughes

[1988] 6 WWR 33, British Columbia, CA
The plaintiff and his wife were injured in a car accident. The plaintiff claimed damages for depression which he said had resulted from coping with his wife's brain damage. The judge ruled that damages should not be awarded for the depression because this did not arise from the plaintiff's injuries and did not amount to nervous shock damages. The plaintiff appealed on the basis that the judge should have found

that it was reasonably foreseeable that the defendant's negligence would cause his depression.

HELD: Appeal dismissed: It was clear from the medical evidence that the plaintiff's depression had started so long after the accident that it could not have been caused by the shock of the accident, nor could it be said that the accident caused the depression. A cause could not be reasonably foreseeable if there was insufficient proximity with the end result.

MEANING OF 'SHOCK'

Behrens v Bertram Mills Circus Ltd

[1957] 2 QB 1, [1957] 1 All ER 583, [1957] 2 WLR 404, 101 Sol Jo 208 (Devlin J)
The plaintiff was in a booth at a fun fair which was knocked over by an elephant and the shock must have been considerable. The judge said he was satisfied he could not award damages except to the extremely limited extent that the shock resulted in physical or mental harm. The effect of the authorities is that the word 'shock' is used, not in the sense of a mental reaction but in a medical sense as the equivalent of nervous shock. MacKinnon LJ in *Owens v Liverpool Corpn* [1939] 1 KB 394, [1938] 4 All ER 727, CA, refers to it as being 'ascertainable by the physician' and as 'the form of ill-health known as shock'. The judge appreciated that it is now becoming increasingly difficult to define the boundaries of mental ill-health. Without infringing the general principle embedded in the common law that mental suffering caused by grief, fear, anguish and the like is not assessable, *Owens v Liverpool Corpn* goes as far as any court can go and he could not accept the invitation of counsel for the plaintiff to attempt an extension of what is there said.

Brice v Brown

[1984] 1 All ER 997 (Stuart-Smith J)
The plaintiff, 42 years old at the time of the accident, sustained relatively trivial physical injuries in a road accident. She was a passenger in a hire car with her daughter aged 12, who sustained alarming facial injuries causing the plaintiff both fear and panic. Dating from childhood the plaintiff had a personality disorder which had caused turbulent spells in her married life but it was on the whole well controlled and for a year or so before the accident her home life had been reasonably happy. After the accident and throughout the time to date of trial her behaviour had become wild and disorderly. There were spells when she left home for days or weeks and lived rough; there were several attempts at suicide. At the time of trial she lived in the same house as her husband and family but her conduct was bizarre and she was severely deranged. She was unfit to give evidence. The defendants argued that before the plaintiff could succeed she must prove first that she sustained a psychiatric illness and second that that illness was reasonably foreseeable by the defendants.

HELD: 'Nervous shock' is a convenient phrase to describe mental injury or psychiatric injury to distinguish it from grief and sorrow or from physical or organic injury. The circumstances of the accident had caused or materially contributed to the plaintiff's nervous shock, which was a reasonably foreseeable consequence of the tortfeasor's breach of his duty of care. For this purpose the plaintiff is assumed to be a person of normal disposition—not eg the pursuer in *Hay v Young* (p 6, above) or a person who faints at the sight of a road accident. On establishing these first points the plaintiff is entitled to compensation for nervous shock and for its direct consequences whether or not they were initially reasonably to be foreseen. There is no reason why mental injury should be in a different category from physical: see *Smith v Leech Brian* (p 335, above). The fact that the tortfeasor could not foresee the precise name the psychiatrists were to put on the plaintiff's condition or the precise mental or psychological process that led to that result is immaterial. She was entitled to succeed.

ORDINARY SHOCK

Whitmore v Euroways Express Coaches Ltd

(1984) Times, 4 May
The plaintiff was with her husband in a coach which overturned causing her husband serious injuries. She suffered shock by witnessing him in his injured condition and being with him. It was argued by the defendant that she could not recover damages for the shock without adducing medical or psychiatric evidence.
HELD: The plaintiff was claiming for shock in its everyday meaning, not in a medical or psychiatric sense. It was 'ordinary shock' not susceptible of further definition but it was a concept which everyone understood. Damages could be awarded for it without departing from the law that damages for worry, strain and distress occasioned by the continuing effects of the injury to a spouse were not recoverable. The right figure in the present case was £2,000, bearing in mind that the shock had continued when her husband was in hospital in France and for some weeks afterwards.

Nicholls v Rushton

(1992) Times, 19 June, CA
The plaintiff was involved in a road traffic accident with the defendant. The defendant admitted liability. The plaintiff obtained judgment for £1,151.76 of which £175 was awarded for 'severe shock and shaking up'. The defendant appealed at this part of the award.
HELD: It was conceded that no damages for a nervous reaction could be awarded for an illness unless it resulted from some physical trauma. The plaintiff had suffered no physical trauma nor any recognised psychiatric condition and so she could not recover damages under this head.

Per Parker LJ: Unless there is a physical injury no question of damages for mental suffering, fear, anxiety under this head.

Note—See also *Page v Smith* (1994) Times, 4 May where it was held that in order for a plaintiff to succeed in a claim for nervous shock, he had to show that the psychiatric injury was foreseeable. It would not be foreseeable if a person of ordinary fortitude would not have suffered from it.

Neurosis: hysteria

THE CONDITION

Griffiths v R and H Green and Silley Weir

(1948) 81 Ll L Rep 378 (Birkett J)
A boilermaker, earning £9 per week, aged 32, married, with three young children, was injured in February 1947, the injuries being to the head and causing concussion and resulting in anxiety neurosis. It was agreed by all the medical witnesses that there

were no signs of organic lesion or organic disease, but there was every sign of functional nervous disturbance.

For the plaintiff, the medical evidence was that it was unlikely the plaintiff would ever be able to do his work of a boilermaker again, though he would probably be able to do suitable light work. For the defendants, that the plaintiff's condition had become one of hysteria as a consequence of anxiety neurosis. When the case was settled and that anxiety taken away and he did light work, ultimately all would be well.

The plaintiff had been offered work at his own trade but said he could not do it. He was given a job of watchman but complained he could not do it and gave it up. He later failed to take a job in the stockyard for which he had asked. The employers were still willing to find a job.

HELD, per Birkett J: The field of functional nervous disturbance is difficult for laymen quite to understand. I suppose that there is none of us quite immune from anxiety of one kind and another in these days, but when people speak of anxiety neurosis when a man is not suffering organically but has hysteria, the ordinary sound, healthy man is apt to look upon that with a little disdain or a little suspicion and to treat it rather lightly and to say: 'Well, if you have a little courage or determination you can overcome it. If you have a little will-power to go back to work and confront the difficulty, that would overcome it.' It is comparatively easy for healthy people to think and to speak like that, but people who have undergone an illness frequently look upon small matters as very important and are fearful and nervous and apprehensive. The plaintiff's complaints were genuine and he was really suffering a serious functional disturbance.

The judge allowed full wages to the date of hearing (62 weeks, £558) less £70 received, net £488. He allowed for six months light work with loss of earnings for that period of £4 and £5 per week (£104 to £130); he took into account pain and suffering to the date of trial, and allowance in addition for the condition of anxiety neurosis, he awarded a total sum of £1,500.

Liffen v Watson

[1940] 1 KB 556, [1940] 2 All ER 213, 109 LJKB 367, 162 LT 398, 56 TLR 442, CA (Slesser LJ)

The neurosis may itself prevent the injured person from making the effort necessary to make the disability cease. If the plaintiff can avoid the neurotic pain by not doing certain normal things, then she has been damaged because she cannot do them. Conversely, if she attempts them, and feels pain, the pain causes suffering.

Dupey v T F Maltby and Strick Line

[1955] 2 Lloyd's Rep 645 (Pearce J)

Plaintiff suffered a slight accident at work and afterwards suffered serious post traumatic hysteria.

HELD: The accident produced the hysteria. Defendants could not plead extraneous factors retarding recovery in reduction of damages, but only causes producing or adding to the hysteria caused by the accident.

Love v Port of London Authority

[1959] 2 Lloyd's Rep 541 (Edmund Davies J)

The plaintiff, a lorry driver, sustained a blow on the head from the swinging chains of a crane on 23 July 1955. He received attention for some minor cuts, then drove his

lorry 12 miles to his depot. On 25 July, he had a 'black-out' and was unfit for work to 20 August 1955. Since 1955, however, until trial in November 1959, he had never resumed his pre-accident work. He had done other kinds of work from time to time of a light nature. His incapacity was due to (1) pre-existing heart trouble; (2) neurosis. The neurosis was itself not entirely due to the accident: 70% of the neurosis was due to the heart trouble, 30% to the accident.
HELD: The defendants must take the plaintiff as they find him, that is to say, with his already vulnerable personality. As far as special damages were concerned, if the 30% of the neurosis due to the accident made the difference between working and not working then the defendants would have to recompense the plaintiff for all the special damages arising from the 100% neurosis. Conversely where the interruption in work would have occurred in any event no special damages were recoverable. As to general damages the Court had to try to assess compensation for such precipitation and aggravation in the functional (ie neurotic) condition as was fully attributable to the accident and which would not have developed without it. Award, special damages £825, general damages £850.

Note—See also CCR Ord 17, 11 and Chapter 16 generally.

EFFECT OF DELAY IN LITIGATION

James v Woodall Duckham Construction Co Ltd

[1969] 2 All ER 794, [1969] 1 WLR 903, 113 Sol Jo 225, CA
On 17 March 1962 the plaintiff fell from a ladder and was injured. The physical injuries were not serious: he was in hospital four days and in June 1962 the hospital declared him fit for work. He did not try any work until October 1962 when he worked for three days and then gave up. He did no further work at all. He complained of pains all over his body. The doctors said there was no physical reason for these but he was not a malingerer. The pains were functional or neurotic. On 18 June 1963 a neuro-surgeon reported to the plaintiff's solicitors that the pains would not clear up until his claim for damages was settled and that the longer the functional illness was allowed to continue the more difficult it would be for him to return to work. The claim did not reach trial until 26 June 1968, when the judge awarded £11,267 damages of which £5,000 was for loss of earnings up to date and £2,500 for estimated future loss.
HELD: The plaintiffs solicitors received the report from the neuro-surgeon in June 1963 as agents for the plaintiff. They should at once have issued a writ with the object of bringing the action on for trial. If they had done this and pursued the action with ordinary diligence it would have been heard in 1965 and the plaintiff would soon thereafter have gone back to his old job. Damages should be limited to the amount the plaintiff would have lost if that had been done plus a fair figure for the pain he had suffered. Award reduced from £11,627 to £4,500.

Batchelor v Rederij A and L Polder

[1961] 1 Lloyd's Rep 247 (Megaw J)
The plaintiff was struck on the head by a hawser in an accident at work on 17 October 1957. There was no fracture of the skull or damage to the brain but the plaintiff developed a condition of pseudo dementia which incapacitated him for work and brought about a complete change of personality. Although he had been discharged from the Army in 1946 on account of hysterical amnesia he had recovered and was

living a normal active life before the accident. After the accident he had become completely inactive, unable to walk properly, unable to work and unable to conduct his own affairs. It was a matter of guess-work as to what was likely to happen to him in the future. His average pre-accident earnings were £18 13s 4d per week. What had to be taken into account was what the plaintiff would have earned over the years had he not suffered the accident, what amount, if anything, he was likely to earn in the future and to make various other allowances for mortality or illness which might happen to anyone. It was also necessary to take into account the fact that he had suffered from hysterical amnesia earlier in his career and that had predisposed him to attacks.

Award for future anticipated loss of earnings £7,000.

Award for pain and suffering £1,500.

Unconsciousness

Wise v Kaye

[1962] 1 QB 638, [1962] 1 All ER 257, [1962] 2 WLR 96, 106 Sol Jo 14, CA
The plaintiff, aged 20, received serious brain injuries in a road accident and as a result was in a state of unconsciousness which continued both at the date of the trial and of appeal. She had no purposeful movement of her limbs, had to be fed by tube and was in every way completely helpless. She was kept alive by skilful nursing but complications might easily prove fatal. For all practical purposes the situation was permanent. At assize she was awarded damages amounting to £18,279 comprising (1) £879 special damages (loss of earnings to date of trial); (2) £2,000 general damages for loss of probable future earnings based on her expectation of life before the accident; (3) £400 for loss of expectation of life and £15,000 general damages. On appeal against the award:

HELD: (1) Following *Oliver v Ashman* (p 422, below) the award of £2,000 was made on a wrong principle in so far as it included potential loss over the whole of the plaintiff's expectation of life before the accident and should be reduced to £1,500; (2) the award of £15,000 general damages should stand. Neither the fact that the plaintiff was unaware of her condition nor that the award would in all probability never be used for her personal benefit was relevant. The first element of damages is the physical injury itself, which has always been a head of claim which requires in law an award of damages according to the extent, gravity and duration of the injury.

Note—On damages for loss of future earnings *Oliver v Ashman* was overruled in *Pickett v British Rail Engineering*, p 422, below. In respect of loss of expectation of life see now the Administration of Justice Act 1982, s 1.

H West & Son Ltd v Shephard

[1964] AC 326, [1963] 2 All ER 625, [1963] 2 WLR 1359, 107 Sol Jo 454, HL
The plaintiff, aged 41, sustained severe head injuries when knocked down by the defendant's lorry. As a result she was permanently bedridden, only partly conscious, could not use her limbs (except movements of the right hand) could not speak or eat and required skilled nursing to keep her alive. She appeared to recognise relatives and could respond to some questions by hand movements or show likes and dislikes by facial expression. Her expectation of life was about seven years. In assessing damages the trial judge mentioned *Wise v Kaye* (above) and said this case was worse

because Mrs Shephard must have some realisation of her condition. He awarded general damages of £17,500, ie £2,500 more than was awarded in *Wise v Kaye* for the same head of damage. An appeal against the amount of the award was dismissed both in the Court of Appeal and in the House of Lords. In the House of Lords the majority: HELD: (1) Damages may properly include an element for mental distress, fear or anxiety resulting from realisation of the deprivation of faculty; the fact of unconsciousness will eliminate those heads of damage which can only exist by being felt or thought or experienced. (2) Except for taking into account the expense of future care or treatment the use to which the damages awarded are to be put or whether the plaintiff can or will ever be able to use the money is irrelevant. (3) It is correct for a judge to approach some matters on an objective and some on a subjective basis but he is not required in making his award to segregate the objective and subjective elements. (4) The decision in *Benham v Gambling* as to the level of awards for loss of expectation of life was not intended to affect the assessment of damages for varying degrees of physical deprivation in a living plaintiff.

Andrews v Freeborough

[1967] 1 QB 1, [1966] 2 All ER 721, [1966] 3 WLR 342, 110 Sol Jo 407, CA
On 5 February 1962, a girl aged eight was struck by a car and was rendered instantly unconscious. She remained deeply unconscious until she died on 29 January 1963. As administrator of her estate her father was awarded by the Judge of Assize £31 agreed special damage, and £2,000 for the actual injuries and for the loss of amenities during the year of unconsciousness.
HELD, ON APPEAL: There was no grounds for disturbing the award. The father was entitled to recover such damages for her estate as the child herself could have recovered had an action been brought at the moment immediately preceding her death. The only difference between an action brought before and one brought after death is that in the latter the Court is spared the task of estimating the probable duration of life. *Wise v Kaye* was authority for the principle that unconsciousness and therefore ignorance of the injury suffered was irrelevant except as an element in assessing pain and suffering, and was no ground for reducing damages. *West v Shephard* and *Oliver v Ashman* (p 411, above) were to the same effect. *West v Shephard* being a House of Lords decision was binding on the Court. £2,000 for a year of unconsciousness was in line with the award in *Wise v Kaye*.

Gray v Mid Herts Group Hospital Management Committee

(1974) 118 Sol Jo 501 (Waller J)
A child a year old sustained brain damage in the course of a surgical operation. Thereafter he was blind and deaf and did not react to stimuli of light, heat, sound, cold, hunger, comfort and discomfort. He died aged three years ten months. Damages for loss of amenity were assessed at £5,000.

Cutts v Chumley

[1967] 2 All ER 89, [1967] 1 WLR 742, 111 Sol Jo 458 (Willis J)
Woman aged 28 sustained head injury of 'devastating severity'. Complete personality change, intellectually reduced to level of a child of five, uninhibited in speech, dirty in habits, incontinent, would have to live permanently in a home, charges of which were £1,100 pa. Judge said *West v Shephard* (p 411, above) was not dissimilar but Mrs Cutts had more awareness of her condition than Mrs West and a much longer

expectation of life and was thus entitled to a much higher award for pain and suffering and loss of amenities.

Note—The heads of damage were given in *Roach v Yates* [1938] 1 KB 256 as (1) the actual loss and expenditure; (2) the pecuniary damage which will be incurred; (3) the pain and suffering; (4) the loss of expectation of life; (5) the mental suffering to be undergone; and (6) the physical disabilities.

Hicks v Chief Constable of the South Yorkshire Police

[1992] 2 All ER 65, HL
The two Hicks sisters were killed as a result of overcrowding the Hillsborough Football Stadium. The administrators of the sisters' estates brought a claim against the defendant for damages to compensate for pre death suffering. The sisters suffered from trauma asphyxia caused by the crushing. The judge at first instance accepted medical evidence to the affect that in cases of death by traumatic asphyxia the victim would lose consciousness within a matter of seconds from the crushing of the chest and would die within minutes thereafter. The plaintiff's claims were dismissed by the judge and the Court of Appeal and the plaintiff appealed to the House of Lords.
HELD: The decisions of the preceding courts were upheld. There was no indication that either of the sisters had suffered injuries other than those that had caused the asphyxia and death and as the unconsciousness and death occurred in such a short space of time in reality the asphyxia was part of the death itself. Also: 'It is perfectly clear law that fear by itself, on whatever degree, is a normal human emotion for which no damages can be awarded': per Lord Bridge of Harwich.

Inconvenience and discomfort

Note—The following cases arise from breach of contract.

Hobbs v London and South Western Rly Co

(1875) LR 10 QB 111, 44 LJQB 49, 32 LT 252
Plaintiff and his family were put on the wrong train and so found themselves at Esher late at night instead of at Hampton Court, as a consequence of which they had to suffer the inconvenience of walking home in the rain.
HELD: Damages were recoverable; they could have hired a carriage had one been available and charged the cost as special damage.

Stedman v Swans Tours

(1951) 95 Sol Jo 727, Times, 6 November, CA
Plaintiff contracted with travel agents for transport for a party of six and a fortnight's accommodation at a first-class hotel with superior rooms with a sea view. The rooms were very inferior and had no sea view. The party were unable to obtain accommodation elsewhere. Romer J awarded £13 15s 0d special damages but no general damages.
HELD, ON APPEAL: General damages could be recovered for appreciable inconvenience and discomfort caused by breach of contract assessed at £50 by CA. *Bailey v Bullock* followed.

Jackson v Horizon Holidays Ltd

[1975] 3 All ER 92, [1975] 1 WLR 1468, 119 Sol Jo 759, CA
The plaintiff booked a holiday with the defendants for himself, his wife and their three-year-old twin sons in Ceylon for a month at a cost of £1,450. For the first fortnight they were housed in a hotel which did not fulfil the description given in the defendants' brochure. The judge awarded £1,100 damages for (1) the difference in value between what the plaintiff got and what he bargained for; (2) compensation for distress and disappointment.
HELD, ON APPEAL: The award should stand. The plaintiff was making a contract for the benefit of the whole family. He could recover damages for the discomfort, vexation and upset which the whole family suffered.

Note—In *Woodar Investment Development Ltd v Wimpey Construction (UK) Ltd* ([1980] 1 All ER 571, [1980] 1 WLR 277, 124 Sol Jo 184, HL) Lord Wilberforce referred to *Jackson v Horizon Holidays* and said

'I am not prepared to dissent from the actual decision in that case. It may be supported either as a broad decision on the measure of damages or possibly as an example of a type of contract, examples of which are persons contracting for family holidays, ordering meals in restaurants for a party, hiring a taxi for a group, calling for special treatment . . . [but] I cannot agree with the basis on which Lord Denning MR put his decision in that case.'

Jarvis v Swans Tours Ltd

[1973] QB 233, [1973] 1 All ER 71, [1972] 3 WLR 954, 116 Sol Jo 822, CA
The plaintiff booked a skiing holiday in Switzerland on the strength of the description in the defendants' catalogue promising a houseparty each week, a wide variety of ski runs, hire of skis, sticks and boots and other facilities. On the second week of the holiday he was the only person in the hotel, the skiing was disappointing and there was no satisfactory equipment available. The county court judge awarded as damages only one-half of the cost of the holiday.
HELD, ON APPEAL: This was not the right measure of damages. If the contracting party in a contract for a holiday breaks his contract damages can be given for the disappointment, the distress, the upset and frustration caused by the breach. The damages should be increased to £125.

Ichard v Frangoulis

[1977] 2 All ER 461, [1977] 1 WLR 556, 121 Sol Jo 287 (Peter Pain J)
The plaintiff and defendant were injured when their cars collided on a road in Yugoslavia where both were on holiday. The defendant after hospital treatment continued to Athens where he spent his holiday, though his enjoyment was spoiled by his injuries. The plaintiff conceded he was to blame for the collision.
HELD: On the defendant's counterclaim, the loss of enjoyment was a factor to be taken into account in assessing damages in a claim in tort as it is in contract (eg *Jarvis v Swans Tours* and *Jackson v Horizon Holidays* (above)) provided the damages were foreseeable by the negligent party. Where as here the accident took place in a holiday area much frequented by tourists it was obviously foreseeable.

Damages for loss of job satisfaction

Champion v London Fire and Civil Defence Authority

(1990) Times, 5 July
Mr Champion was employed as a fireman by the defendants. He was injured at work for which the defendants admitted responsibility. As a result of his injury Mr Champion was discharged from the fire service. Prior to trial the figure to compensate Mr Champion's general damages has been agreed. In addition Mr Champion claimed damages for loss of congenial employment/job satisfaction.
HELD: The judge accepted that Mr Champion had suffered a significant loss of job satisfaction. The judge would normally have awarded damages for loss of congenial employment within the award for general damages but as this had been previously agreed the judge made a separate award.

Note—See also *Simkin v City of Liverpool* [1974]) CLY 814, Blamey (16 December 1988, unreported) and *Hardy v Daldorph* (1 February 1990, unreported).

Exemplary damages

AB v South West Water Services Ltd

[1993] QB 507, [1993] 1 All ER 609, [1993] 2 WLR 507, CA
A number of plaintiffs suffered from ill effects due to the defendants' negligent contamination of their water supply. The plaintiffs (of which there were some 180) claimed, inter alia, exemplary and aggravated damages on the basis that the defendant's servants or agents had acted in an arrogant and high handed manner; had wilfully misled their customers about the true state of affairs and had failed to give proper instructions as to the precautions to take to minimise the ill effects of drinking the water. The plaintiffs claimed that they had drunk the water for longer than they would have done had they been properly advised of the dangers.

The defendant sought to strike out the plaintiffs' claim for aggravated and exemplary damages. The judge refused to do so on the basis that it was arguable that the plaintiffs could recover these damages for the tort of nuisance. The defendants appealed.
HELD: The claim for exemplary damages failed. Exemplary damages could not be awarded for a cause of action if they had not been awarded for this cause of action before 1964. There was no reported decision of an award for exemplary damages for the tort of nuisance prior to 1964 and the Court of Appeal was not prepared to extend the remedy to such a case.

Furthermore the plaintiffs would still have to satisfy the two tests set out by Lord Devlin in *Rookes v Barnard* [1964] 1 All ER 367, HL. The defendants were not exercising any executive power derived from the Government nor could it be said that the defendants' conduct had been calculated to make a profit for itself which might exceed the compensation payable.

The claim for aggravated damages was also struck out. This could adequately be dealt with by an increase in the award for general damages.

Also anger and indignation were not a proper subject for compensation. It was neither pain nor suffering.

Note—See also *Alexander v Home Office* [1988] 2 All ER 118, [1988] 1 WLR 968, [1988] ICR 685, *Bradford City Metropolitan Council v Arora* [1991] 2 QB 507 and *Messenger Newspaper Group Ltd v National Graphical Assoc* [1984] IRLR 397.

Infant damages

QUANTUM

Gold v Essex County Council

[1942] 2 KB 293, [1942] 2 All ER 237, 112 LJKB 1, 167 LT 166, 58 TLR 357, 86 Sol Jo 295, CA

Tucker J awarded £125 to an infant aged five, taking into account that the amount would be considerably increased when the time came for it to be handed over. The CA said this was wrong. It held that it ought not to have been taken into account, and awarded £300.

Note—It has been common in the past for a parent to be joined as a plaintiff (other than as next friend) in an infant's action for damages for personal injuries, and to claim separately for loss and expense incurred as a result of the child's injuries. It was always doubtful whether such a claim was maintainable except on the basis of *per quod servitium amisit* even though not expressly pleaded as such: see *Hall v Hollander* (1825) 4 B & C 660. Now that the separate tort has been abolished by the Administration of Justice Act 1982, s 2(b) such a claim ought properly to be made as part of the infant's own case. See eg *Donnelly v Joyce*, p 424, below.

INJURIES TO UNBORN CHILDREN

Note—The Congenital Disabilities (Civil Liability) Act 1976 which came into force on 22 July 1976, provides for children born with a disability to have a remedy in damages in circumstances specified in the Act where the disability can be proved to result from a wrongful act committed by any person. The sections likely to be relevant to motor claims are the following:

'**1 Civil liability to child born disabled** (1) If a child is born disabled as the result of such an occurrence before its birth as is mentioned in subsection (2) below, and a person (other than the child's own mother) is under this section answerable to the child in respect of the occurrence, the child's disabilities are to be regarded as damage resulting from the wrongful act of that person and actionable accordingly at the suit of the child.

(2) An occurrence to which this section applies is one which—

(a) affected either parent of the child in his or her ability to have a normal healthy child; or

(b) affected the mother during her pregnancy, or affected her or the child in the course of its birth, so that the child is born with disabilities which would not otherwise have been present.

(3) Subject to the following subsections, a person (here referred to as "the defendant") is answerable to the child if he was liable in tort to the parent or would, if sued in due time, have been so; and it is no answer that there could not have been such liability because the parent suffered no actionable injury, if there was a breach of legal duty which, accompanied by injury, would have given rise to the liability.

(4) In the case of an occurrence preceding the time of conception, the defendant is not answerable to the child if at that time either or both of the parents knew the risk of their child being born disabled (that is to say, the particular risk created by the occurrence); but should it be the child's father who is the defendant, this subsection does not apply if he knew of the risk and the mother did not. . . .

(6) Liability to the child under this section may be treated as having been excluded or limited by contract made with the parent affected, to the same extent and subject to the same restrictions as liability in the parent's own case; and a contract term which would have been set up by the defendant in an action by the parent, so as to exclude or limit his liability to him or her, operates in the defendant's favour to the same, but no greater, extent in an action under this section by the child.
(7) If in the child's action under this section it is shown that the parent affected shared the responsibility for the child being born disabled, the damages are to be reduced to such extent as the court thinks just and equitable having regard to the extent of the parent's responsibility.

2 Liability of woman driving when pregnant A woman driving a motor vehicle when she knows (or ought reasonably to know) herself to be pregnant is to be regarded as being under the same duty to take care for the safety of her unborn child as the law imposes on her with respect to the safety of other people; and if in consequence of her breach of that duty her child is born with disabilities which would not otherwise have been present, those disabilities are to be regarded as damage resulting from her wrongful act and actionable accordingly at the suit of the child.

4 Interpretation and other supplementary provisions (1) References in this Act to a child being born disabled or with disabilities are to its being born with any deformity, disease or abnormality, including predisposition (whether or not susceptible of immediate prognosis) to physical or mental defect in the future.
(2) In this Act—
(a) "born" means born alive (the moment of a child's birth being when it first has a life separate from its mother), and "birth" has a corresponding meaning; and
(b) "motor vehicle" means a mechanically propelled vehicle intended or adapted for use on roads.
(3) Liability to a child under s 1 or 2 of this Act is to be regarded—
(a) as respects all its incidents and any matters arising or to arise out of it; and
(b) subject to any contrary context or intention for the purpose of construing references in enactments and documents to personal or bodily injuries and cognate matters
as liability for personal injuries sustained by the child immediately after its birth.
(4) No damages shall be recoverable . . . in respect of any loss of expectation of life . . . unless. . . the child lives for at least 48 hours.
(5) This Act applies in respect of births after (but not before) its passing, and in respect of any such birth it replaces any law in force before its passing, whereby a person could be liable to a child in respect of disabilities with which it might be born; but in 1(3) of this Act the expression "liable in tort" does not include any reference to liability by virtue of this Act, or to liability by virtue of any such law.'

The Act binds the Crown and extends to Northern Ireland but not to Scotland.

SPECIAL DAMAGES

Loss of earnings

POTENTIAL LOSS OF EARNINGS

White v Hutton Bros (Stevedores) Ltd

[1960] 1 Lloyd's Rep 524, CA
A stevedore aged 38 suffered injuries to his back which incapacitated him permanently for heavy work. He had taken other employment of a lighter kind in which he earned £5 a week less than in his pre-accident work. He had aching in the back and right leg and was unable to do many of the things he could do before the accident. The judge awarded him £2,250 general damages.

HELD, ON APPEAL: The award was too small. A period of 10 years at £260 per year was the least that could be reasonably taken as a basis for the calculation of prospective earnings. £3,500 was the proper figure to award, the balance above £2,600 being for pain and suffering.

Cook v JL Kier & Co Ltd

[1970] 2 All ER 513, [1970] 1 WLR 774, 114 Sol Jo 207, CA
A foreman of a cable company, 38 years of age, sustained a serious head injury which reduced him permanently to simple factory work at a wage of £14 per week less than his pre-accident work. The judge took eight years as the multiplier of £14 per week.
HELD, ON APPEAL: Eight years was too low and should be increased to ten.

Senior v Barker and Allen Ltd

[1965] 1 All ER 818, [1965] 1 WLR 429, 109 Sol Jo 178, CA
The plaintiff, a Jamaican, was aged 17 when his right hand was severely injured at work. All four fingers were lost except for the proximal phalanx of the index finger, and the dorsum of the hand had to be skin grafted. The thumb was present and there was a reasonable pinch grip between it and the stump of the index finger. The plaintiff had been unable to find work since the injury except by the defendants as a sweeper and he did not want to do that. He was right-handed. Liability was admitted. The judge awarded him £6,500 general damages plus £504 special damage.
HELD, ON APPEAL: The award could not be said to be a wholly erroneous estimate or as being far too high. It was unfortunate that there was no estimate for loss of future earnings: the judge might well have taken it to be £5 to £6 per week. The usual practice was to take a substantial number of years' purchase, especially for a boy. At, say, 15 years' purchase the sum for future loss of earnings might be £4,000. If the figure for loss of the use of the hand were £2,500 the total of £6,500 general damages could not be too high.

Mulvaine v Joseph

(1968) 112 Sol Jo 927 (Thompson J)
The plaintiff was an American club professional golfer. Whilst playing on a European tour he was injured by the negligence of the defendants. As a result he played badly and cut short his tour. He claimed damages.
HELD: The claim was for damages for loss of opportunity of competing in tournaments, the ensuing loss of experience and prestige which might have resulted in his becoming a tournament professional in America, and loss of a chance of winning prize money. The figure was bound to be speculative. £1,000 would be awarded under that head including damages for disappointment felt by the plaintiff through the frustration of his plans.

Note—See also *Jenkins v Richard Thomas and Baldwins Ltd*, p 451, below and *Batchelor v Rederij A & L Polder*, p 410, above.

Larbey v Thurgood

[1993] ICR 66, 136 Sol Jo LB 275
The defendant requested that the plaintiff submit himself to an interview with the defendant's nominated employment consultant. The plaintiff refused and the defendant applied for an order that the action be stayed until the plaintiff agreed to their request.

HELD: An employment consultant may be able to assist the court in establishing the availability of jobs in the area where the plaintiff lived. However issues such as the plaintiff's suitability for work and his willingness and motivation to seek work were issues of fact to be decided by the judge and not an employment consultant. In any event such evidence presented by the employment consultant would be inadmissible.

Blamire v South Cumbria Health Authority

[1993] PIQR Q1, CA
When assessing loss of earnings where there are a number of imponderables, the judge is entitled to reject the multiplier/multiplicand approach and make a global award.

VALUE OF COMPANY CAR

Kennedy v Bryan

(1984) Times, 3 May (Beldam J)
Where the plaintiff had lost the use of a company car the value should be assessed in the range of £750 to £1,000 a year.

Note—Reference should be made to the current AA Guidelines.

LOSS OF EARNING CAPACITY

Smith v Manchester Corpn

(1974) 17 KIR 1, CA
The plaintiff, aged 51, sustained a serious injury to her right elbow in May 1971. She was off work for 14 months. She was then able to resume her work without a drop in earnings and would be able to continue indefinitely, though she was left with severe restriction of movements in the elbow and shoulder which would be permanent. As a result she would be at considerable disability in the competitive labour market should she lose her job, though her employers, the defendants, undertook to continue to employ her so far as they could. The judge awarded £2,000 general damages for pain and disability but only £300 for future financial loss.
HELD, ON APPEAL: The award for future financial loss should be increased to £1,000. An award for loss of future earnings is usually compounded of two elements, (1) actual continuing loss multiplied by the appropriate number of years' purchase, and (2) the weakening of the plaintiff's competitive position in the open labour market; if the plaintiff loses her present employment what are her chances of obtaining comparable employment in the open labour market? If there is a real risk that a plaintiff will lose his or her present employment it calls for real compensation.

Note—See also *Mitchell v Liverpool Area Health Authority* (1985) Times, 17 June, CA.

Moeliker v Reyrolle & Co Ltd

[1977] 1 All ER 9, [1977] 1 WLR 132, 120 Sol Jo 165, CA
In an action for damages for injuries to his left hand sustained at work the plaintiff claimed an award for loss of earning capacity as in *Smith v Manchester Corpn*

(above). He was a skilled man, valued by his employers for whom he had worked for 30 years. He had resumed his pre-accident work after the accident and his employers had no intention of ending his employment with them. If he ever lost his job he would be at a disadvantage in getting an equally well paid job because of the permanent injuries to his left index finger and thumb. The judge awarded £750 for loss of earning capacity.

HELD: The award was sufficient. *Smith v Manchester Corpn* laid down no new principle of law. An award for loss of earning capacity had been made in *Ashcroft v Curtin* [1971] 3 All ER 1208, [1971] 1 WLR 1731, CA three years before *Smith's* case. This head of damage usually arises where a plaintiff is, at the date of trial, in employment but there is a risk of his losing that employment at some time in the future and then because of his injury may be at a disadvantage in getting equally well paid work. It was not correct that whenever a plaintiff establishes a claim under this head the damages must be considerable. Whether and what to award should be considered in two stages: (1) Is there a 'substantial' or 'real' risk that a plaintiff will lose his present job before the end of his working life? (2) If there is (but not otherwise) the court must assess and quantify the present value of the risk of financial damage which the plaintiff will suffer if the risk materialises. A judge must look at all the relevant factors and do the best he can.

Note—In *Page v Enfield & Haringey Area Health Authority* (1986) Times, 7 November the Court of Appeal held that when assessing damages for loss of earning capacity or handicap on the labour market it was not permissible to make a conventional award or to apply any formula, tariff, or marker following previously decided cases. No assistance could be derived, save in the most general sense, from the levels of awards made in other cases as each case was unique.

Clarke v Rotax Aircraft Equipment Ltd

[1975] 3 All ER 794, [1975] 1 WLR 1570, 119 Sol Jo 679, CA

The plaintiff contracted dermatitis of the hands as a result of his work with defendants. After two attacks he had to take work away from the irritant substance, resulting in a loss of £9 a week in wages. In addition to special damage the judge awarded £2,700 for future loss (being £9 per week for six years) and £1,250 for loss of earning capacity.

HELD: (1) It was essential to avoid overlap of the awards for loss of future earnings and for loss of earning capacity. If the plaintiff lost his present lower-paid job he would probably be able to find another at similar wages. In these circumstances £1,250 was too much; a nominal award of £250 was adequate. (2) No interest should be added to the award for loss of earning capacity.

Note—See also *Nicholls v National Coal Board* [1976] ICR 266, CA.

Cook v Consolidated Fisheries Ltd

[1977] ICR 635, CA

Following an accident at work in February the plaintiff resumed his pre-accident work in June but gave it up in December partly because he found the heavy work difficult because of the injury. He decided to become a lorry driver though he was not actually working at the date of the trial. There was persisting disability which might affect his working ability within 10 to 15 years. The judge awarded £3,000 general damages but only £500 for loss of future earning capacity as a total of £3,500 seemed about right.

HELD, ON APPEAL: Loss of future earning capacity should be assessed separately without reference to what was being awarded for general damages. The award of £500 should be increased to £1,500. An award for loss of earning capacity is possible even if the plaintiff is not actually in employment at the time of trial.

Note—See also: *Robson v Liverpool City Council* [1993] PIQR Q78, CA where the plaintiff was awarded £2,500 by way of *Smith v Manchester* damages for the loss of vision in one eye.

CHILD'S LOSS OF EARNING CAPACITY

Cronin v Redbridge London Borough Council

(1987) Times, 20 May, CA
The plaintiff was aged 12 when, during a metal work lesson at school, a fragment of perspex flew into her right eye causing the loss of all useful vision in that eye. Virtually no evidence was called about her future earning capacity save that she had a vague feeling that she would have liked to be an air hostess. Peter Pain J allowed £10,000; the defendants appealed.
HELD, ON APPEAL: Awarding damages to a child still at school for future handicap on the labour market involved much speculation and unsatisfactory guesswork. The plaintiff was an average student and her academic progress had not been hindered to any significant degree. If there was a deterioration she could return under s 32A of the Supreme Court Act 1981 (above). The judge had been excessively generous and a modest sum only was appropriate. The award was reduced to £4,000.

Mitchell v Liverpool Area Health Authority (Teaching)

(1985) Times, 17 June, CA
The plaintiff was barely one month old when, as a result of the defendants' negligence, he suffered damage to the circulation of his right arm necessitating amputation at the elbow level. The judge made no award for loss of earning capacity; to look into so remote a future without having any real guidance 'is inevitably to indulge in such speculation that it would be unfair to the defendants to find that they are liable for an additional sum'. The plaintiff appealed.
HELD: The appeal succeeded; although the court had to allow a heavy discount for the acceleration of the award (the plaintiff was now only two years old) and a further discount because of the large choice of occupations open to the plaintiff. In all the circumstances it was held that the appropriate award was £5,000. Per Lord Justice Purchas: The plaintiff had suffered a substantial disability. It might be that he would find well-paid employment but it was impossible to disregard entirely the risk that he would not do so.

Loss of expectation of life

ADMINISTRATION OF JUSTICE ACT 1982, S 1

Note—For fatal cases, see under 'Law reform damages', p 492, below.

In respect of causes of action accruing on or after 1 January 1983 claims for damages for loss of expectation of life are abolished in part by the Administration of Justice Act 1982, s 1 which is as follows:

'1 Abolition of right to damages for loss of expectation of life (1) In an action under the law of England and Wales or the law of Northern Ireland for damages for personal injuries—
(a) no damages shall be recoverable in respect of any loss of expectation of life caused to the injured person by the injuries; but

(b) if the injured person's expectation of life has been reduced by the injuries, the court, in assessing damages in respect of pain and suffering caused by the injuries, shall take account of any suffering caused or likely to be caused to him by awareness that his expectation of life has been so reduced.

(2) The reference in sub-s (1)(a) above to damages in respect of loss of expectation of life does not include damages in respect of loss of income.'

Sub-section (2) preserves the right to damages for loss of earnings during the 'lost years' for a living plaintiff (but not for the benefit of the estate of a deceased person; see below).

LOSS OF PROSPECTIVE EARNINGS IN 'LOST YEARS'

Oliver v Ashman

[1962] 2 QB 210, [1961] 3 All ER 323, [1961] 3 WLR 669, 105 Sol Jo 608, CA
The plaintiff, a child aged 20 months received very serious head injuries in a road accident. He was aged four years at the time of the trial. As a result of the injuries he had become a low-grade mental defective with a severe traumatic epilepsy. He had ceased to talk and would never be able to earn his living. He would need fairly soon to enter an institution for care and supervision and for such re-education as he was capable of. He would probably spend the rest of his life in a state institution. His expectation of life was reduced from about 60 years to 30 years.

HELD: The matter was concluded by *Benham v Gambling* [1941] AC 157, [1941] 1 All ER 7, 110 LJKB 49, 164 LT 290, 57 TLR 177, 84 Sol Jo 703, HL and the decision of Slade J in *Harris v Bright's Asphalt Contractors* [1953] 1 QB 617, [1953] 1 All ER 395, [1953] 1 WLR 341, 97 Sol Jo 115, 51 LGR 296. There is no authority for distinguishing between the case of a living plaintiff and a dead man's estate. The House of Lords in *Benham v Gambling* showed that the House was intending to settle the problem once and for all, that loss of future wages during the lost years was but an ingredient in the loss of expectation of life and did not fall to be valued as an item on its own.

Pickett v British Rail Engineering Ltd

[1980] AC 136, [1979] 1 All ER 774, [1978] 3 WLR 955, 122 Sol Jo 778, HL
The plaintiff, aged 51, was found to be suffering from mesothelioma caused by the defendants' admitted negligence. His expectation of life was reduced to one year. He claimed damages for loss of expectation of life. The Court of Appeal following *Oliver v Ashman* (above) held that damages for loss of earnings during the 'lost years' were not recoverable.

HELD, ON APPEAL to the House of Lords: *Oliver v Ashman* was wrongly decided. It had been based on a dictum of Lord Simon in *Benham v Gambling* [1941] AC 157: 'No regard must be had to financial losses and gains during the period of which the victim has been deprived.' But in *Benham*'s case no claim for loss of earnings had been made and Lord Simon could not be taken to intend that his words should apply to a case where there was such a claim. Though damages for loss of earnings during the 'lost years' should be assessed with moderation they must not be fixed at a conventional figure because, being damages for pecuniary loss, they can be measured in money. In assessing those damages the plaintiff's own living expenses which the plaintiff would have expended during the lost years should be deducted but whether he had dependants or not or whether he would have looked after them is immaterial. Case remitted for damages to be assessed.

INFANTS

Connolly v Camden and Islington Area Health Authority

[1981] 3 All ER 250 (Comyn J)
When only a few days old the infant plaintiff (four and three-quarters years at the date of trial) suffered serious brain damage when being anaesthetised for a surgical operation. He was left with extensive mental and physical disabilities. His expectation of life, as found by the judge on the evidence, was shortened to 27$^1/_2$ years. Damages were claimed for loss of earnings during the 'lost years'.
HELD: The plaintiff qualified for a 'lost years' payment but the assessment was nil. From *Pickett*'s case (above) and *Gammell*'s case (p 477, below) it was clear that a young or middle-aged man could rightly expect an award for the financial benefit of the years' earnings which he had lost even though it involved a great deal of guesswork, but those cases show that a child is in a different position. No hard and fast rule can be laid down but a child qualifies under this head of damage dependent on the ability to prove the potential loss. As Lord Scarman said in *Gammell*'s case(below) the lost years of earning capacity will ordinarily be so distant that no estimate is possible, though there may be exceptions—eg that of a child television star. Other possible examples are the son of a father who owns a prosperous business or the son of a farmer who is able to leave the estate to his son. But in the present case on the evidence, though there is a claim, the assessment is nil.

Croke v Wiseman

[1981] 3 All ER 852, [1982] 1 WLR 71, CA
The infant plaintiff when 21 months old suffered a cardiac arrest due to negligence of the defendants. He survived but with severe loss of brain function, paralysis of all four limbs and blindness. His expectation of life was limited to 40 years. Damages were claimed for (inter alia) loss of future earnings during life and during the 'lost years' of life expectation.
HELD: Though it is a task of great difficulty to assess an appropriate sum for a young child it has been frequently done eg in the thalidomide cases. Taking a figure of £5,000 per annum for estimated future loss and a maximum working life of 22 years (ie from 18 to 40) the actuarial figure for the multiplier is 8.876. But this makes no allowance for the receipt of a capital sum at least 11 years before earnings would begin nor for the possibility that the child would never have become an earner. The multiplier should be reduced to five years making a total of £25,000 for future loss of earnings. As for earnings during the lost years there are compelling reasons as in *Pickett*'s case (above) for awarding a sum of money to a living plaintiff of mature years which would have been available to spend on his dependants, but in the case of a child there are no dependants and, if the injuries are catastrophic, there never will be any. In such a case the court should refuse to speculate. No sum should be awarded for the lost years.

Board and lodging

Liffen v Watson

[1940] 1 KB 556, [1940] 2 All ER 213, 109 LJKB 367, 162 LT 398, 56 TLR 442, 84 Sol Jo 368, CA
Plaintiff before an accident was a domestic servant receiving a weekly wage of £1

plus board and lodging, which was claimed at 25s. It is for the court to assess the value of the board and lodging, but the loss of the board and lodging is damage equally with the cash. The fact that her father provided board and lodging without payment does not alter the fact that she sustained this loss in kind.

Per Goddard LJ: The right to recover does not depend upon whether or not she made a contract with somebody else to give her board and lodging. She has lost it with the cash wages because she lost her work. It does not matter in the least whether she is taken in by her father or whether she is taken in by a friend. She might say to a friend, 'I cannot make a contract to pay you, but if I get damages I shall pay you something for board and lodging.' These considerations are immaterial. The only consideration is what has she lost. She has lost the value of the board and lodging, just the same as she has lost her wages.

Accommodation costs

Roberts v Johnstone

[1989] QB 878, [1988] 3 WLR 1247, CA
Before the plaintiff's birth her mother had been given a transfusion of an incorrect blood type. This led to the plaintiff contracting haemolytic disease and as a result suffering permanent and serious brain damage. A total award of £334,769.88 was made, including an award for the cost of a suitable bungalow (less the value of property sold) and the cost of conversion of that accommodation (less the value of some improvements) at a total of £28,800. The plaintiff appealed to the Court of Appeal seeking, inter alia, an increase in those damages.
HELD: The plaintiff was not entitled to the capital cost of the new home (approving *George v Pinnock*, p 373) but was entitled to the additional annual cost of purchasing the new property taken at 2% of the difference between the sale price of the old property and the purchase price of the new, after any appropriate deductions, plus the net conversion costs after deduction of that part of the conversion costs which added to the recoverable capital value of the house on resale. The additional annual cost was to be multiplied—here a multiplier of 16 was adopted. The sum of £50,204 was substituted for the award of £28,800.

Care and nursing

Note—In claims based on causes of action accruing on or after 1 January 1983 maintenance of a claimant at public expense is to be taken into account in assessing damages. The Administration of Justice Act 1982, s 5 reads:

'**5 Maintenance at public expense to be taken into account in assessment of damages** In an action under the law of England and Wales or the law of Northern Ireland for damages for personal injuries (including any such action arising out of a contract) any saving to the injured person which is attributable to his maintenance wholly or partly at public expense in a hospital, nursing home or other institution shall be set off against any income lost by him as a result of his injuries.'

Donnelly v Joyce

[1974] QB 454, [1973] 3 All ER 475, [1973] 3 WLR 514, 117 Sol Jo 488, CA
The plaintiff, aged six, received injury to his leg in a road accident. After his discharge from hospital his mother gave up her work for six months to look after him. The judge

awarded the plaintiff £147 in respect of her loss of earnings. On appeal the defendant argued that the time was not claimable by the plaintiff but that his mother might have recovered it had she been a party to the action.
HELD, ON APPEAL: The loss of the mother's wages was rightly claimed by and awarded to the plaintiff. It was his own loss—the existence of the need for nursing services of his mother, valued for the purposes of damages as the proper and reasonable cost of supplying those needs. It does not matter, so far as concerns the defendant, how or by whom the services have been provided nor whether the plaintiff has a legal liability to repay the provider. Nor is the existence of a moral obligation a material factor, nor an agreement between the injured person and the provider of the services to pay for them. On this point *Haggar v de Placido* (above) was wrong. *Roach v Yates* [1938] 1 KB 256 was authority for holding that the plaintiff was entitled to recover damages referable to the past and future financial value of voluntary services rendered to a plaintiff by others. *Liffen v Watson* (p 409, above) embodied the same principle. Contrary to the defendant's 'concession' the plaintiff's mother would not have been entitled to recover the loss herself had she been a party.

Note—See *Housecroft v Burnett* [1986] 1 All ER 332, CA.

Cunningham v Harrison

[1973] QB 942, [1973] 3 All ER 463, [1973] 3 WLR 97, 117 Sol Jo 547, CA
The plaintiff's neck was broken in a motor accident, paralysing him for life in all four limbs and his body. He was entirely dependent on others for dressing, bath, evacuation of bowels and feeding. His wife did everything for him for two years, then committed suicide. Trial of his action for damages came three days afterwards. Because of a difficult personality the plaintiff was considered unsuitable to enter a home and would have to live and be looked after in his own home.
HELD, ON APPEAL: Had the plaintiff's wife continued to look after him the value of her nursing services could have been claimed by the plaintiff without his having to make an agreement with her to pay her for them. On recovering such damages he would hold them on trust for her and pay them over to her; the judge's award for the cost of future nursing was too high. There should be moderation in all things, even in a claim for personal injuries. It was not right that the defendant should have to pay extra because of the plaintiff's difficult personality. Moreover it would be difficult to find people to look after him at home all the time and he would sometimes have to use other and state-provided facilities eg under the Chronically Sick and Disabled Persons Act 1970.

Taylor v Bristol Omnibus Co Ltd

[1975] 2 All ER 1107, [1975] 1 WLR 1054, 119 Sol Jo 476, CA
The plaintiff was three and a half when injured, nine at the date of trial. Very serious head injuries left him unable to control his limbs properly, unable to walk, unable to speak properly, permanently unemployable. The judge awarded £27,500 for pain and suffering and disability, £18,000 for future nursing and care and £16,000 for potential loss of earnings. With some agreed items the total was £63,000.
HELD, ON APPEAL: On particular points, (1) the item for care and nursing should not be any less if the plaintiff is looked after at home instead of in an institution. It is now settled that compensation can be given in money for services rendered by parents. (2) The fact that at the plaintiff's age calculation of future loss of earnings is extremely speculative is no ground for awarding merely a nominal sum. The present practice is

to calculate a likely figure for future loss on present rates of earnings and having regard to the plaintiff's family background.

Rialas v Mitchell

(1984) 128 Sol Jo 704, CA
The plaintiff aged six suffered severe brain damage in a road accident resulting in spastic quadriplegia. He could not speak or feed himself and had to be looked after day and night. Figures for heads of damage if the plaintiff was to be cared for at home were agreed—the cost of a suitable house, future nursing care etc. Evidence was adduced by the defendant that private institutions had homes where the plaintiff could be cared for at substantially less, and that it was unreasonable to compensate him at more than the lower cost.
HELD: Before the accident the plaintiff had been a healthy uninjured child of six living with his parents. He was then in hospital for a year and returned home where he had been looked after for four years. The court was being asked to say that the plaintiff should live in an institution because it would cost less. That was not the true alternative. Once it had been decided by the judge that it was reasonable for the plaintiff to remain at home there was no acceptable reason for saying the defendant should not pay the reasonable cost of caring for him there.

Croke v Wiseman

[1981] 3 All ER 852, [1982] 1 WLR 71, CA
In the case of an infant of nine whose expectation of life was limited to the age of 40, the judge took a multiplier of 16 to 17 years for estimating the cost of future nursing care. On appeal, held, this was too high and should be reduced to 14. The judge's figure made no allowance for the possibility that the infant's life might be ended by accident before reaching the estimated life expectancy.

Davies v Tenby Corpn

[1974] 2 Lloyd's Rep 469, CA
The plaintiff became a quadriplegic as a result of a diving accident. He was completely bedridden and everything had to be done for him by his wife who nursed him with outstanding care and devotion.
HELD: per Lord Denning: In *Cunningham v Harrison* (above) I ventured to say that an award of damages could be made for a wife's services in nursing her injured husband. Even though she had not theretofore been doing paid work, but only domestic duties in the house, nevertheless all extra attendance on him called for compensation. It was not necessary for her to enter into a legal agreement as if she was a paid nurse. Sufficient that she had rendered services which would otherwise have had to be paid for. But I do not think that the award should be as high as that required for outside help. The wife does, after all, fit this extra work into her ordinary household duties and does it out of her wifely duty to keep him in sickness and in health. It is difficult to suggest an appropriate figure but I would suggest £15 a week or £780 a year. . . . His expected life is 10 years from the trial. The present value of this may be taken at £780 multiplied by seven.

Abrams v Cook

(1987) Times, 26 November, CA
In an action for loss of dependency under the Fatal Accidents Act 1976 the plaintiff, a disabled person, sought damages in respect of loss of care and attendance given to her by her husband, the deceased. The Court of Appeal held in substantially dismissing an appeal from the defendants that quantum of damages had to be assessed broadly on the evidence as a whole even if that meant that the quantum so assessed exceeded the cost of employing a nurse or housekeeper to provide similar care and attention.

Note—See also Chapter 13 generally.

Hunt v Severs

[1994] 2 All ER 385, [1994] 2 WLR 602, 138 Sol Jo LB 104, HL
The plaintiff was a pillion passenger on a motorcycle driven by the defendant. An accident occurred as a result of which the plaintiff suffered serious injury. The defendant admitted liability. The defendant regularly visited the plaintiff during her stay in hospital and provided care for her thereafter when she returned home. The plaintiff and defendant later got married. The plaintiff was awarded £77,000 for the cost of past and future care provided by the defendant. The defendant appealed this part of the award on the basis that he was rendering these services voluntarily and was not obliged to compensate the plaintiff by paying damages as well. On appeal, it was held that there was no double recovery for it was accepted that the plaintiff's need for services represented a loss for which she was entitled to be compensated for by the tortfeasor. The defendant appealed to the House of Lords.
HELD, ON APPEAL: The defendant's appeal was upheld. The purpose of an award in respect of voluntary care was compensation for the voluntary carer. In this case, the defendant had gratuitously rendered these services to the plaintiff. There was no ground in public policy, or otherwise, for requiring the tortfeasor to pay to the plaintiff a sum of money in respect of the services which the plaintiff then had to repay to him. Therefore, the award of damages was reduced by the amount awarded for services rendered.

Hospital charges

Section 158 of the Road Traffic Act 1988 applies to emergency medical treatment bills. The driver of a vehicle on a road, which causes bodily injury, must pay the emergency treatment charge which is currently £18.20. This is so irrespective of liability (ie even if the injured person was totally to blame) the sum can be claimed from insurers without any no claims bonus penalty. It can also be recovered from the other side (if proved negligent).

Section 157 of the Road Traffic Act 1988 applies to hospital in and out patient treatment. It only applies if the vehicle owner or insurers have already made a payment out in respect of bodily injury to someone injured in an accident on a road or public place. Currently the amount involved is £2,554 for out-patients and £2,546 for in-patients.

Incapacity for housekeeping

Daly v General Steam Navigation Co Ltd, The Dragon

[1980] 3 All ER 696, [1981] 1 WLR 120, 125 Sol Jo 100, [1980] 2 Lloyd's Rep 415, CA

The plaintiff, seriously injured by the defendants' negligence, claimed damages for, inter alia, her inability to do the heavier kind of housework in her home. She was 34 years of age at the time of the injuries, married and lived with her husband and two children. She was not gainfully occupied before the accident nor did she employ any domestic help. Her incapacity would last for the rest of her life. Trial was reached seven years after the accident. The judge held that: (1) the partial loss of housekeeping capacity should be treated as a separate head of damage and not merely an element in the general damages for loss of amenities; (2) such damages should be assessed by reference to the cost of employing someone else to do the work, even for the period before trial when no one was employed and the plaintiff's husband acted in part as a substitute housekeeper himself; (3) they should be calculated on a basis of ten hours per week at an average of 90p per hour before date of trial and eight hours per week at £1.40 per hour for the future at a multiplier of 15 years: total £11,427.

On appeal the award was varied. In respect of the award for future partial loss of housekeeping capacity in the figure of £8,736, held, the judge was right in assessing it at the estimated cost of employing some third person to come in and do that which the plaintiff was unable to do. It was not requisite that the plaintiff should satisfy the Court that she had a firm intention in any event that such a person should be employed. It was immaterial whether the plaintiff, having received those damages, should choose to alleviate her housekeeping burden by employing someone to do it, or to spend the damages on luxuries she would otherwise be unable to afford. In respect of the award of £2,691 for loss of housekeeping capacity up to date of trial, however, it was wrong to assess it by reference to the cost of employing domestic help which she had not in fact employed but which had been furnished by her husband and daughter. The judge ought instead to have asked himself to what extent the difficulties which the plaintiff had had to contend with in performing her household duties ought to have increased the award for pain and suffering. The Judge's award of £8,000 for pain and suffering should be increased by the sum of £2,691 from which should be deducted the sum of £930, the husband's partial loss of earnings due to his having to help in the home.

5 DEDUCTIONS

CHARITABLE OR VOLUNTARY PAYMENTS

Redpath v Belfast and County Down Rly

[1947] NI 167

A distress fund supported by voluntary contributions from the public was established to assist passengers injured in a railway accident. In an action by a passenger against the railway company claiming damages for negligence, the railway company applied to interrogate the plaintiff as to the amount received by him from the fund.

HELD: The interrogatories were irrelevant. Plaintiff's damages were not to be reduced because plaintiff had received without legal right moneys voluntarily subscribed by third parties.

Dennis v London Passenger Transport Board

[1948] 1 All ER 779, 92 Sol Jo 350 (Denning J)
An injured plaintiff received no wages during disability but the Minister of Pensions and his employers the London County Council paid him approximately the amount of the wages in pension and sick pay. The Minister, without contending there was a legal obligation to refund, said the plaintiff would be expected to refund out of the damages if recovered and the LCC told the plaintiff the same. The plaintiff undertook to repay if he recovered damages.
HELD: The plaintiff was under a moral obligation to repay. A wrongdoer is not to be allowed to reduce damages because other persons have made up the wages. The plaintiff had lost his wages, and prima facie he should be paid them by the wrongdoer. They had been made up to him by other people who expect to be repaid and should be included as damages, subject to the direction that the amounts should be repaid. *Allen v Waters & Co* (see below) followed.

Schneider v Eisovitch

[1960] 2 QB 430, [1960] 1 All ER 169, [1960] 2 WLR 169, 104 Sol Jo 89 (Paull J)
The plaintiff was injured, and her husband killed, in a motor accident in France caused by the defendant's negligence. Immediately after the accident, while the plaintiff was still unconscious, her brother-in-law and his wife flew from England to France to give what help they could. The plaintiff later wished to pay their expenses for so doing and claimed the expenses as part of her special damage.
HELD: She was entitled to recover the expenses from the defendant. Before such a sum can be recovered the plaintiff must (1) show that the services rendered were reasonably necessary as a consequence of the tortfeasor's tort; (2) show that the expenses were reasonable and would have been incurred had the friends not assisted; (3) undertake to pay to those who incurred the expense the amount recovered. *Allen v Waters & Co* [1935] 1 KB 200 (dictum of Goddard J) and *Dennis v LPTB* applied.

Gage v King

[1961] 1 QB 188, [1960] 3 All ER 62, [1960] 3 WLR 460, 104 Sol Jo 644 (Diplock J)
The plaintiffs, husband and wife, were injured in an accident, the wife seriously, the husband less so. In an action by the plaintiffs for damages for personal injuries the defendant was held one-third to blame and the male plaintiff two-thirds. Expenses incurred for the female plaintiff's injuries amounted to £449, most of which had been paid by her husband from a joint bank account on which both were entitled to draw and of which about 4½% of the total came from investments belonging to her, though given to her by her husband. There was no evidence of any agreement between them as to the ownership of the balance in the bank account.
HELD: The question which of the two plaintiffs was entitled to claim the expenses as special damage depended on which of them incurred the legal liabilities to pay them to the persons who had rendered the services. An arrangement between husband and wife for a joint banking account is not intended to have legal consequences while the marriage is still subsisting. On the facts, the expenses were incurred by the husband

and having been found two-thirds to blame, he was entitled only to one-third of the amount claimed.

INCOME TAX

Gourley's case

British Transport Commission v Gourley

[1956] AC 185, [1955] 3 All ER 796, [1956] 2 WLR 41, 100 Sol Jo 12, [1955] 2 Lloyd's Rep 475, HL

The plaintiff was 65 years of age and was a partner in a firm of civil engineers. He was totally disabled for some time and after returning to work his earning capacity was reduced. Pearce J awarded £47,720 being £9,000 pain and suffering, £1,000 out of pocket expenses, £15,220 for actual loss of earnings before the end of 1953 and £22,500 for estimated future loss of earnings. The two latter sums (ie £37,720) did not take income tax or surtax into account. If tax had been, the award would have been £6,695, being £4,945 instead of £15,220 and £1,750 instead of £22,000. The parties agreed that one or other of the two sums fixed by the judge should be awarded.

Per Earl Jowitt: It was agreed by counsel on both sides—and I think rightly agreed—that the respondent would incur no tax liability in respect of the award of £37,720 or alternatively £6,695. The broad principle is an award of such sum of money as will put the injured person in the same position as he would have been if he had not sustained the injuries. The principle of *restitutio in integrum* affords little guidance for pain and suffering and impairment but affords some guidance in assessing financial loss and was referred to by Lord Wright (*The Liesbosch*) as 'the dominant rule of law'. There is no distinction between cases under PAYE where tax is deducted before payment, and cases where tax is paid after the money is received. It is fallacious to consider the problem as though a benefit was being conferred on a wrongdoer. The problem is rather for what damages he is liable. He is liable for such damages as, by reason of his wrongdoing, the plaintiff has sustained. The tax element is not too remote and no sensible person regards his net earnings as equivalent to his available income. The assessment of tax liability need not be elaborate, but an estimate formed on broad lines, even rough and ready. Appeal allowed.

Lyndale Fashion Manufacturers v Rich

[1973] 1 All ER 33, [1973] 1 WLR 73, 117 Sol Jo 54, CA

The defendant was awarded £495 damages on a counterclaim for wrongful dismissal, less tax to be decided by the Court. The defendant had earned £1,343 in the tax year, on which he had paid tax of £23. If he had earned the additional £495 as income he would have paid a total of £160 in tax. The plaintiffs contended that the damages of £495 should be reduced by £137 being the additional tax that would have been attracted by £495 treated as the top slice of his income. The defendant claimed that only the average rate of tax between the £495 and the other income should be deducted.

HELD: The plaintiffs' contention was right. The principle in *Gourley*'s case (above) plainly applied. If a comparison was to be made between a given income and that income with something added, the addition must be treated as the top part of the income; it was the increase in the income which attracted the higher rates of tax.

Hartley v Sandholme Iron Co Ltd

[1975] QB 600, [1974] 3 All ER 475, [1974] 3 WLR 445, 118 Sol Jo 702 (Nield J)
The plaintiff was off work for 19 weeks as a result of injury and claimed loss of earnings for that period calculated on the weekly pre-accident wage after deduction of income tax on a PAYE basis. Afterwards he received a tax rebate of £18.70 due to his not having earned wages during the 19 weeks off work.
HELD: Applying the principles of *Gourley*'s case, his claimed loss should be reduced by the amount of the tax rebate. The saving of tax to the plaintiff was not too remote but stemmed directly from the consequences of the accident; it was not *res inter alios acta* nor completely collateral, and the amount of the saving was not a matter of speculation but was accurately quantified.

Duller v South East Lincs Engineers

[1981] CLY 585, QBD
The plaintiff claimed damages for severe personal injuries sustained in an accident. Before the accident in addition to his full time job he had worked as a part-time barman, but had not disclosed his earnings from the part-time job for income tax purposes.
HELD: He was entitled to be compensated for the loss of the part-time earnings. They did not come from any criminal origin but came lawfully into his hands. His unlawful conduct came later and was only with the Inland Revenue, not with the earnings. He did not base his claim on any unlawful act of his and it was not defeated by being tainted with illegality, but deductions must be made in respect of income tax. *Burns v Edman* (p 471, below) distinguished.

Affect of tax on multiplier for future losses

Thomas v Wignall

[1987] QB 1098, [1987] 1 All ER 1185, [1987] 2 WLR 930, CA
At sixteen and a half the plaintiff (during a routine operation for the removal of her tonsils) suffered severe permanent brain damage leaving her unaware of what had happened. She needed constant care and attention. At the hearing the plaintiff was 27 years old. The judge awarded, inter alia, £435,000 for future care. He had considered the appropriate multiplier to be 14 but in view of the size of the award, increased this to 15 to make allowance for the higher incidence of taxation on the investment income. The defendants appealed arguing that the appropriate multiplier in any event was 13 and that to increase the multiplier as an allowance for the high incidence of tax was wrong in law.
HELD, ON APPEAL, (Lloyd LJ dissenting): High rates of income tax were a fact of life. The larger the income the greater percentage that would be paid in tax. It would be wrong to impose inflexible rigidity and disallow some adjustment to the multiplier to reflect the increased incidence of tax on the income element of the compensation. The original award of 14 was within the range of possible awards and although the adjustment was generous it was not excessive. Appeal dismissed.

Note—But see *Hodgson v Trapp* below.

Hodgson v Trapp

[1988] 3 All ER 870, [1988] 3 WLR 1281, [1989] 2 LS Gaz R 36, HL
At 33 the plaintiff, a wife, mother and woman of many talents and interests suffered catastrophic injuries in a road accident. As a result she became wholly dependent on others and would always remain so. The judge calculated the multiplicand for loss of earnings and chose a multiplier of 11. He then increased this to 12 to take into account the higher tax rates payable on investment income, applying *Thomas v Wignall* (above). He adopted the same approach to nursing care and attendance raising the basic multiplier for that head of damage from 13 to 14. The defendants appealed not on the basis that high tax rates might allow for a multiplier at a higher end of the conventional scale but on the basis that having decided on a multiplier the making of a specific addition to take tax into account as a separate feature was incorrect in law.
HELD, ON APPEAL: Appeal allowed. It was a falsity to assume that higher rates of taxation would not be reduced. Just as inflation is an imponderable and not to be taken into account (see *Cookson v Knowles*, p 463) so (save in exceptional circumstances) income tax should not be used to raise the multiplier for future losses as a separate item.

The dissenting view of Lloyd LJ in *Thomas v Wignall* was correct. Per Lord Oliver: The incidence of taxation in the future should ordinarily be assumed to be satisfactorily taken care of in the conventional assumptions of an interest rate applicable to a stable currency and the selection of a multiplier appropriate to that rate.

PENSIONS

Service pensions

Note—The Ministry of Pensions has declared its practice in relation to reduction of a war pension awarded on account of disablement by reference to damages or other compensation recovered. Of the total amount of damages or other compensation recovered 75% is disregarded altogether. The balance after making this deduction is converted into a weekly sum by assessing the amount of a Government annuity for the life of the pensioner which could be purchased therewith, having regard to the price of consols on the date of payment. The war pension is then reduced by this weekly sum. The reduction operates only from the date of payment of the damages.

Payne v Railway Executive

[1952] 1 KB 26, [1951] 2 All ER 910, [1951] 2 TLR 929, [1951] WN 547, 95 Sol Jo 710, CA
Plaintiff was injured in a railway accident whilst serving in the Royal Navy. He received 100% disability pension of £2 5s per week under the Royal Warrant 1946 (Cmd 6489) because he was injured whilst in the service; later reduced to 90% disability of £2 0s 6d, and increased later when he married by 9s for wife and 6s 9d for child, to £2 16s 3d. The railway executive contended that the pension awarded as a result of the accident should be taken into account in assessing damages for loss of future earnings of £3,000. If it had, the judge would have awarded £750.
HELD: The pension did not operate to reduce the damages. The cases under the Fatal Accidents Acts had no application. The position was similar to that of *Bradburn v Great Western Rly Co* (1874) LR 10 Exch 1, 44 LJ Ex 9, 31 LT 464, where Pigott B in refusing to deduct accident insurance money from damages said:

'there is no reason or justice in setting off what the plaintiff has entitled himself to under a contract with third persons, by which he has bargained for the payment of a sum of money in the event of an accident happening to him. He does not receive that sum of money because of the accident, but because he has made a contract providing for the contingency; an accident must occur to entitle him to it, but it is not the accident, but his contract, which is the cause of his receiving it.'

In *Shearman v Folland* (p 437, below), Asquith LJ quoted from *Mayne on Damages*:

'Matter completely collateral and merely *res inter alios acta*, cannot be used in mitigation of damages. The pension was *res inter alios acta* and would have been paid if defendants had not been liable. No account should be taken of the pension in assessing the loss.'

The defendants appealed. In the Court of Appeal it was pointed out that evidence was given in the court below from the Ministry of Pensions of the present practice that the disability pension was abated by the annuity value of 25% of the damages (less special damages). An opposite conclusion to that of Sellers J would put the Minister in an impossible position. He would not wish to impose a double deduction (a) by the court in assessing damages and (b) by the Minister in adjusting the pension. Appeal dismissed.

Carroll v Hooper

[1964] 1 All ER 845, [1964] 1 WLR 345, 108 Sol Jo 120 (Veale J)
The plaintiff, aged 24, suffered serious injuries including loss of an arm, in a motor cycle accident for which the defendant's husband, who was killed in the accident, was held wholly to blame. At the time of the accident the plaintiff was a National Serviceman in the Royal Corps of Signals. As a result of his injuries he was discharged from the Army and was awarded a service disablement pension of £6 12s 6d per week. The pension was held on the terms of the Pensions Appeal Tribunals Act 1943, s 11 under which the award was subject to the power of the Minister of Pensions to vary, revoke or reduce the award in accordance with any provision of the Royal Warrant. The Royal Warrant of 24 May 1949, art 52(1) provided: 'Where the Minister is satisfied that compensation has been or will be paid to . . . a person to . . . whom a pension . . . is being . . . paid . . . The Minister may take the compensation into account against the pension . . . in such manner or to such extent as he may think fit, and they . . . reduce the pension . . . accordingly.'
HELD: *Browning v War Office* (below), was distinguishable since in that case the service pension was held as of right and could not be taken away. The *ratio decidendi* of Singleton LJ in *Payne v Railway Executive* (above) applied here, that it would be unfair to take the pension into account since as soon as the compensation was awarded by the Court the Minister might cut off or cut down the pension. The pension should be disregarded.

Elstob v Robinson

[1964] 1 All ER 848, [1964] 1 WLR 726, 108 Sol Jo 543 (Elwes J)
The plaintiff, a naval rating aged 18, was seriously injured in a road accident for which the defendant was to blame. As a result of his injuries the plaintiff was discharged from the Royal Navy and was awarded a service disability pension of £5 15s per week under an Order in Council dated 29 September 1949 of which art 52(1) was in the same terms as art 52(1) of the Royal Warrant quoted in *Carroll v Hooper* (above). It

was the current policy of the Minister of Pensions to exercise his discretion to diminish a pension in such a case as this by deducting from the pension an amount equal to the value of a government life annuity which would be produced by one quarter of the damages awarded. In the present case the appropriate figure for general damages was £11,250 so that the Minister would reduce the pension by £3 1s 8d per week being the value of an annuity based on £2,812 10s, one-quarter of the damages recovered. This would leave a pension of £2 13s 4d per week. Ought this to be taken into account in assessing the damages?
HELD: Following *Carroll v Hooper* (above) it should not. The decision in *Payne v Railway Executive* (p 432, above) that the quantum of damages ought not to be reduced by reference to a disability pension which was not payable as a matter of right was binding on the court. Moreover the same rule applied to special damages for loss already sustained. In the present case £1,477 was recoverable for loss of earnings which would be reduced to £740 if the pension were to be taken into account. The vital distinction between a pension received as of right and a pension received at discretion applies equally whether the damages are precisely calculated retrospectively as special damages or assessed for the future as general damages. There should be no deduction from the sum of £1,477 on account of the pension.

Pensions received as of right

Judd v Hammersmith West London and St Mark's Hospitals

[1960] 1 All ER 607, [1960] 1 WLR 328, 104 Sol Jo 270 (Finnemore J)
The plaintiff claimed damages for injuries he received in an accident. He was a local government officer who had contributed compulsorily for 32 years to a superannuation fund maintained by his employer. Because of his injuries he had to retire from his employment earlier than he would otherwise have done and on retirement was awarded a pension of £300 a year from the superannuation fund.
HELD: In assessing damages for loss of earnings due to the injuries he received in the accident the pension should not be taken into account since it was the service of the plaintiff with the borough council and not the accident that gave rise to the pension.

Parry v Cleaver

[1970] AC 1, [1969] 1 All ER 555, [1969] 2 WLR 821, 113 Sol Jo 147, HL
The plaintiff, a policeman, had to leave the police force because of injury caused by the defendant's negligence. He was then aged 36. But for the injury he would not have retired from the force until he was 48 and would then have been entitled as of right to a pension of £10 per week for life. On leaving the force at 36 he became entitled as of right to a pension of £3 per week for life. He had contributed to the fund during his service by payments which were compulsory. The trial judge, following *Judd v Hammersmith Borough Council* (above) held that in assessing damages the pension should be ignored during the period up to age 48, when the plaintiff would have left the force, but should be taken into account thereafter.
HELD, by the Court of Appeal: This was not correct. The general rule is that the injured party should give credit for all sums which he received in diminution of his loss save for exceptional cases such as insurance benefits. The case was indistinguishable from *Browning v War Office* (above) and the pension must be taken into account for the whole period.

The decision of the Court of Appeal was reversed by the House of Lords who by a majority of three to two restored the decision of the trial judge.

Lord Reid drew attention to the two types of payments which are disregarded in assessing damages—benevolent gifts (*Redpath v Belfast and County Down Railway* (p 428, above)) and moneys coming to the plaintiff under a contract of insurance (*Bradburn v Great Western Rly Co*). There was no reason to regard these types of receipt as anomalous. In the case of benevolent payments it would be revolting to a man's sense of justice that the sufferer should have his damages reduced so that he would gain nothing from the benevolence of his friends and relatives. In the case of insurance moneys they are not taken into account because the plaintiff has bought them, and it would be unjust and unreasonable to hold that the benefit from the money he had prudently spent on premiums should ensure to the benefit of the tortfeasor. Why should it make any difference that he insured by arrangement with his employer rather than with an insurance company? If it did not, then a contributory pension, which is a form of insurance, should not be taken into account either. There is no relevant difference between a pension, for which payments are made into a fund to meet future contingencies, and other forms of insurance. The reason the pension was to be taken into account after age 48 was that in the later period it was a comparison of like with like. In the period before age 48 the plaintiff was receiving something different in kind from what he had lost, namely, wages. *Browning v War Office* (above) was wrongly decided.

Smoker v London Fire and Defence Authority, Wood v British Coal Corpn

[1991] 2 AC 502, [1991] 2 All ER 449, HL

Both plaintiffs were injured at work and brought proceedings against their employers for damages. The plaintiffs claimed, inter alia, loss of earnings and the defendants argued that the loss of earnings claimed should be reduced by the amount of ill health pension the plaintiffs had received as a result of suffering the injury.

Mr Smoker had become a member of a firemans' pension scheme from the time that he joined the service and contributed 10.75% of his wages to the scheme. His employers contributed twice that much. Mr Wood was a member of the Mine Workers Pension Scheme and contributed 5.4% of his pay and his employers contributed the same amount.

At first instance, it was held that Mr Smokers' pension would not be deducted and the defendants appealed direct to the House of Lords. Mr Wood's pension was deducted in full at first instance, a decision that was overturned in the Court of Appeal. The defendants appealed to the House of Lords.

HELD: Both plaintiffs had purchased their pensions by way of the contributions they had made to them and, in the words of Lord Reed in *Parry v Cleaver* (p 434, above) these pensions were 'the fruit, through insurance, of all the money which was set aside in the past in respect of his past work'. Therefore the amounts of the ill health pension were not to be deducted from the plaintiffs' damages. It made no difference that the defendants were in the triple position of being employer, tortfeasor and insurer.

Note—See also *Hopkins v Norcros plc* [1994] ICR 11, [1994] IRLR 18, CA where it was held that moneys received by way of a pension arising out of a termination of employment were not to be set off against the damages which an employee was entitled to due to the fact that the termination of his contract of employment was wrongful.

Pension contributions

Dews v National Coal Board

[1988] AC 1, [1987] 2 All ER 545, [1987] 3 WLR 38, [1987] ICR 602, HL
The plaintiff was a miner who was required by his contract of employment to belong to and contribute to a compulsory pension scheme. As a result of an accident at work he was absent on sick leave for 31 weeks. Towards the end of that period he received no pay and so paid no pension contributions. His pension entitlement was not affected. He claimed loss of earnings including the contributions he would have made if he had been earning.
HELD, ON APPEAL: This claim failed; if the plaintiff had not been injured he would not have received his pension contributions as they would have been paid directly into the scheme. As his pension entitlement was not affected, to award him the contributions would have enriched him rather than compensated him. He was not entitled to them as damages for loss of earnings. Per Lord Griffiths: The fundamental principle of English law is that damages for personal injury are compensatory and intended, so far as possible, to put the plaintiff in the same financial position as if the accident had never happened.

PERMANENT HEALTH INSURANCE

Hussain v New Taplow Paper Mills Ltd

[1988] AC 514, [1988] 1 All ER 541, [1988] 2 WLR 266, [1988] ICR 259, HL
The plaintiff was injured at work resulting in the amputation of his left arm below the elbow. He was unable to work but the defendants continued to employ him. Shortly before the hearing the defendants offered him a job as a weighbridge attendant at reduced wages. His contract of employment entitled him to receive full earnings for 13 weeks and then 50% of lost earnings or the difference between present earnings and earnings before incapacity. The payments were financed out of a permanent health insurance scheme which the defendants paid for; the plaintiff's earnings would not have been higher in the absence of such a scheme so he was not contributing to the scheme himself. The judge did not take into account this long-term sickness payment when calculating future losses because it was the benefit of insurance. The defendants appealed successfully to the Court of Appeal and the plaintiff appealed to the House of Lords.
HELD: Appeal dismissed. The sums were payable under the contract of employment to the employee as a partial substitute for loss of earnings. The employee did not contribute to the cost; the fact that the employers had insured themselves against their liability under the contract of employment was irrelevant. The payments should be deducted from the future loss claim.

McCamley v Cammell Laird Shipbuilders Ltd

[1990] 1 All ER 54
Mr McCamley was very badly injured while in the course of his employment with the defendants. The defendants admitted liability. The defendant holding company had taken out personal accident insurance for a certain class of its employee. The plaintiff qualified for a payment under the terms of this policy and was paid the sum of £45,630. The defendant argued that this amount should be deducted from the plaintiff's award of damages. The trial judge held that the proceeds of the insurance

policy were not to be taken into account in assessing the amount of damages. The defendants appealed.

HELD: The existence of a policy was unknown to both the plaintiff and his trade union. The plaintiff made no contribution towards it, it was not paid in substitution for loss of wages and was paid out irrespective of any fault by anybody. Furthermore the sum was quantified before there had been an accident at all when it could not have been foreseen what damages might be sustained when one did take place. Taking all the above points into account the court held that the payment was a payment by way of an act of benevolence even though the means by which this benevolence was achieved was through insurance. The decision of *Hussain v New Taplow Papermills Ltd* (p 436, above) distinguished.

SET OFF

Shearman v Folland

[1950] 2 KB 43, [1950] 1 All ER 976, 66 TLR 853, 94 Sol Jo 336, CA

Plaintiff, lady aged 67, healthy, active and young for her years; one leg amputated at the thigh and the other permanently unstable and in practice largely useless; unable to walk more than 150 yards and that only on a perfectly even surface; unable without assistance to go up and down stairs or to get into or out of a bath or motor car. The special damages included a claim of £12 12s per week for nursing home fees. Before the accident she resided in hotels in London and paid £7 7s per week for board and lodging. Slade J deducted all or most of the £7 7s 0d from the £12 12s and drastically cut down the claim of £12 12s per week on the ground that it was unreasonable and exorbitant.

HELD, ON APPEAL: The £7 7s could not be set off. The precise style in which she would probably or might have lived was a collateral matter. 'Matter completely collateral and merely *res inter alios acta*, cannot be used in mitigation of damages', *Mayne on Damages*. The expenses of a millionaire accustomed to live at a palatial hotel would far exceed the charges of a nursing home. Could a wrongdoer say in such a case that he was entitled to go scot free? A court would not pursue beyond a certain limit what would have been the position if no accident had occurred. Ordinarily a householder or lodger has fixed expenses or charges which continue. Those parts which do not (eg, food) may be difficult to disengage from the total. *Contra* a claim for extra nourishments by implication concedes that the plaintiff is giving credit for the food for which he would have to pay apart from the accident. No such claim to set off had previously been advanced, let alone succeeded. The defendant is entitled to set off living expenses of some amount, and if evidence had been adduced to show what proportion of the £12 12s had been attributable to living expenses, it would have been open to the judge to make a deduction in respect of that.

Berriello v Felixstowe Dock & Rly Co

[1989] 1 WLR 695, CA

The plaintiff was an Italian seaman injured at an English port. He received moneys from an Italian State Seamens Fund on account of future loss of earnings on terms that these monies would be refunded to the extent that damages for loss of earnings were recovered from the defendants. It was held at first instance that the moneys should be deducted from the plaintiff's damages. The plaintiff appealed.

HELD: Since the sums received by the plaintiff were refundable they could not be deducted from the settlement figure. There would be no double recovery since repayment had to be made to the Italian State Seamens Fund.

Note—See also *Hodgson v Trapp*, above.

SOCIAL SECURITY BENEFITS

The principle

On 3 September 1990 new provisions were introduced requiring compensators to deduct from the amount agreed or awarded at trial a sum equivalent to the gross amount of any relevant social security benefits payable to a claimant in respect of the injury or disease. This is regardless of the question of liability and applies to accidents occurred on or after 1 January 1989 and a claim for benefit for a named disease made on or after that date.

For the rules applying to accidents or notified diseases prior to this date see the 9th edition, pp 474–486.

The relevant legislation was set out in s 22 of and Sch 4 to the Social Security Act 1989, supplemented by Sch 1 to the Social Security Act 1990 and is now set out in ss 81–85 of the Social Security Administration Act 1992.

Social Security Administration Act 1992, ss 81–85

81 Interpretation of Part IV (1) In this Part of the Act—

'benefit' means any benefit under the Contributions and Benefits Act except child benefit and, subject to regulations under subsection (2) below, the 'relevant benefits' are such of those benefits as may be prescribed for the purposes of this Part of this Act;

'certificate of deduction' means a certificate given by the compensator specifying the amount which he has deducted and paid to the Secretary of State in pursuance of section 82(1) below;

'certificate of total benefit' means a certificate given by the Secretary of State in accordance with this Part of this Act;

'compensation payment' means any payment falling to be made (whether voluntarily, or in pursuance of a court order or an agreement, or otherwise)—

(a) to or in respect of the victim in consequence of the accident, injury or disease in question, and

(b) either—

 (i) by or on behalf of a person who is, or is alleged to be, liable to any extent in respect of that accident, injury or disease; or

 (ii) in pursuance of a compensation scheme for motor accidents,

 but does not include benefit or an exempt payment or so much of any payment as is referable to costs incurred by any person;

'compensation scheme for motor accidents' means any scheme or arrangement under which funds are available for the payment of compensation in respect of motor accidents caused, or alleged to have been caused, by uninsured or unidentified persons;

'compensator', 'victim' and 'intended recipient' shall be construed in accordance with section 82(1) below;

'payment' means payment in money or money's worth, and cognate expressions shall be construed accordingly;

'relevant deduction' means the deduction required to be made from the compensation payment in question by virtue of this Part of this Act;

'relevant payment' means the payment required to be made to the Secretary of State by virtue of this Part of this Act;

'relevant period' means—

(a) in the case of a disease, the period of 5 years beginning with the date on which the victim first claims a relevant benefit in consequence of the disease; or
(b) in any other case, the period of 5 years immediately following the day on which the accident or injury in question occurred;

but where before the end of that period the compensator makes a compensation payment in final discharge of any claim made by or in respect of the victim and arising out of the accident, injury or disease, the relevant period shall end on the date on which that payment is made; and

'total benefit' means the gross amount referred to in section 82(1)(a) below.

(2) If statutory sick pay is prescribed as a relevant benefit, the amount of that benefit for the purposes of this Part of this Act shall be a reduced amount determined in accordance with regulations by reference to the percentage from time to time specified in section 158(1)(a) of the Contributions and Benefits Act (percentage of statutory sick pay recoverable by employers by deduction from contributions),

(3) For the purposes of this Part of this Act the following are the 'exempt payments'—

(a) any small payment, as defined in section 85 below;
(b) any payment made to or for the victim under section 35 of the Powers of Criminal Courts Act 1973 or section 58 of the Criminal Justice (Scotland) Act 1980;
(c) any payment to the extent that it is made—
  (i) in consequence of an action under the Fatal Accidents Act 1976; or
  (ii) in circumstances where, had an action been brought, it would have been brought under that Act;
(d) (*applies to Scotland only*);
(e) without prejudice to section 6(4) of the Vaccine Damage Payments Act 1979 (which provides for the deduction of any such payment in the assessment of any award of damages), any payment made under that Act to or in respect of the victim;
(f) any award of compensation made to or in respect of the victim by the Criminal Injuries Compensation Board under section 111 of the Criminal Justice Act 1988;
(g) any payment made in the exercise of a discretion out of property held subject to a trust in a case where no more than 50 per cent by value of the capital contributed to the trust was directly or indirectly provided by persons who are, or are alleged to be, liable in respect of—
  (i) the accident, injury or disease suffered by the victim in question; or
  (ii) the same or any connected accident, injury or disease suffered by another;
(h) any payment made out of property held for the purposes of any prescribed trust (whether the payment also falls within paragraph (g) above or not);
(i) any payment made to the victim by an insurance company within the meaning of the Insurance Companies Act 1982 under the terms of any contract of insurance entered into between the victim and the company before—
  (i) the date on which the victim first claims a relevant benefit in consequence of the disease in question; or
  (ii) the occurrence of the accident or injury in question;
(j) any redundancy payment falling to be taken into account in the assessment of damages in respect of an accident, injury or disease.

(4) Regulations may provide that any prescribed payment shall be an exempt payment for the purposes of this Part of this Act.

(5) Except as provided by any other enactment, in the assessment of damages in respect of an accident, injury or disease the amount of any relevant benefits paid or likely to be paid shall be disregarded.

(6) If, after making the relevant deduction from the compensation payment, there would be no balance remaining for payment to the intended recipient, any reference in this Part

to the making of the compensation payment shall be construed in accordance with regulations.

(7) This part of the Act shall apply in relation to any compensation payment made on or after 3rd September 1990 (the date of the coming into force of section 22 of the Social Security Act 1989 which, with Schedule 4 to that Act, made provision corresponding to that made by this Part) to the extent that it is made in respect of—

(a) an accident or injury occurring on or after 1st January 1989; or
(b) a disease, if the victim's first claim for a relevant benefit in consequence of the disease is made on or after that date.

82 Recovery of sums equivalent to benefit from compensation payments in respect of accidents, injuries and diseases (1) A person ('the compensator') making a compensation payment, whether on behalf of himself or another, in consequence of an accident, injury or disease suffered by any other person ('the victim') shall not do so until the Secretary of State has furnished him with a certificate of total benefit and shall then—

(a) deduct from the payment an amount, determined in accordance with the certificate of total benefit, equal to the gross amount of any relevant benefits paid or likely to be paid to or for the victim during the relevant period in respect of that accident, injury or disease;
(b) pay to the Secretary of State an amount equal to that which is required to be so deducted; and
(c) furnish the person to whom the compensation payment is or, apart from this section, would have been made ('the intended recipient') with a certificate of deduction.

(2) Any right of the intended recipient to receive the compensation payment in question shall be regarded as satisfied to the extent of the amount certified in the certificate of deduction.

83 Time for making payment to the Secretary of State The compensator's liability to make the relevant payment arises immediately before the making of the compensation payment, and he shall make the relevant payment before the end of the period of 14 days following the day on which the liability arises.

84 The certificate of total benefit (1) It shall be for the compensator to apply to the Secretary of State for the certificate of total benefit and he may, subject to subsection (5) below, from time to time apply for fresh certificates.

(2) The certificate of total benefit shall specify—

(a) the amount which has been, or is likely to be, paid on or before a specified date by way of any relevant benefit which is capable of forming part of the total benefit;
(b) where applicable—
    (i) the rate of any relevant benefit which is, has been, or is likely to be paid after the date so specified and which would be capable of forming part of the total benefit; and
    (ii) the intervals at which any such benefit is paid and the period for which it is likely to be paid;
(c) the amounts (if any) which, by virtue of this Part of this Act, are to be treated as increasing the total benefit; and
(d) the aggregate amount of any relevant payments made on or before a specified date (reduced by so much of that amount as has been paid by the Secretary of State to the intended recipient before that date in consequence of this Part of this Act).

(3) On issuing a certificate of total benefit, the Secretary of State shall be taken to have certified the total benefit as at every date for which it is possible to calculate an amount that would, on the basis of the information so provided, be the total benefit as at that date, on the assumption that payments of benefit are made on the days on which they first become payable.

(4) The Secretary of State may estimate, in such manner as he thinks fit, any of the amounts, rates or periods specified in the certificate of total benefit.

(5) A certificate of total benefit shall remain in force until such date as may be specified in the certificate for that purpose and no application for a fresh certificate shall be made before that date.

(6) Where a certificate ceases to be in force, the Secretary of State may issue a fresh certificate, whether or not an application has been made to him for such a certificate.

(7) The compensator shall not make the compensation payment at any time when there is no certificate of total benefit in force in respect of the victim, unless his liability to make the relevant deduction and the relevant payment has ceased to be enforceable by virtue of section 96 below.

85 Exemption from deduction in cases involving small payments (1) Regulations may make provision exempting persons from liability to make the relevant deduction or the relevant payment in prescribed cases where the amount of the compensation payment in question, or the aggregate amount of two or more connected compensation payments, does not exceed the prescribed sum.

(2) Regulations may make provision for cases where an amount has been deducted and paid to the Secretary of State which, by virtue of regulations under subsection (1) above, ought not to have been so deducted and paid, and any such regulations may, in particular, provide for him to pay that amount to the intended recipient or the compensator or to pay a prescribed part of it to each of thcm.

(3) The reference in section 81(3)(a) above to a 'small payment' is a reference to a payment from which by virtue of this section no relevant deduction falls to be made.

(4) For the purposes of this section—

(a) two or more compensation payments are 'connected' if each is made to or in respect of the same victim and in respect of the same accident, injury or disease; and
(b) any reference to a compensation payment is a reference to a payment which would be such a payment apart from section 81(3)(a) above.

Small payments

Small payments ie a compensation payment or the aggregate of two or more payments not exceeding £2,500 are exempt. However s 2 of the Law Reform (Personal Injuries) Act 1948 continues to apply to small payments in respect of 'relevant benefits' (s 22 (6)).

Certificate of total benefit

This is issued by the Secretary of State. The 'total benefit' is the gross amount of any relevant benefits paid to the victim. The procedure is to lodge a Form CRU1 with the Compensation Recovery Unit (CRU). The form is acknowledged by the Unit by dispatching to the compensator a Form CRU4. When the compensator is ready to make a compensation payment the Form CRU4 is completed and returned to the Unit and a certificate of total benefit is sent to the compensator within four weeks.

If the compensator makes a payment into court of over £2,500 or settles the claim over £2,500 the CRU benefit is deducted from the compensation payment and paid by the compensator to the Unit.

A copy of the certificate is automatically sent to the victim.

No compensation payment can be made without an up-to-date certificate unless the compensator has applied for the certificate, has received written acknowledgment of receipt but does not receive the certificate within the specified time. The amount may then be recouped by the DSS against subsequent compensation payments.

Relevant benefits

Relevant benefits are prescribed in regulations pursuant to s 22(3) of the 1989 Act. They include:

income support
family credit
attendance allowance
mobility allowance (until 6 April 1992)
severe disablement allowance
disablement benefit
sickness benefit
statutory sick pay
reduced earnings allowance
retirement allowance
disability living allowance
disability working allowance
invalidity benefit
unemployment benefit

Relevant benefits are refundable for the 'relevant period' ie five years following the day the accident or injury occurred. This is with the exception of diseases when the five year period runs from the day the victim first claimed a relevant benefit in consequence of the disease.

Payment into court

The court is not obliged to make any payment to the Secretary of State. The person effecting the payment is not liable to pay the moneys to the Secretary of State until whole or any part of the payment in is paid out.

Appeal

Sections 98 and 99 of the 1992 Act provide for appeals against a certificate of total benefit. An appeal can be brought by the compensator or the victim. An appeal on an amount is dealt with by the Social Security Appeals Tribunal and appeals on causation go to a medical appeal tribunal. An appeal from either of these tribunals is permitted on a point of law only. An appeal may not be brought until the amount due on the certificate of total benefit has been paid. It must be made in writing within three months of the final payment to the Secretary of State.

6 MITIGATION

Waterhouse v H Lange Bell & Co

[1952] 1 Lloyd's Rep 140 (Sellers J)
Amount of loss of earnings, and relative general damages for pain and suffering reduced because the plaintiff could have reduced his claim by taking available work of a lighter nature pending his total recovery.

Barnes v Port of London Authority

[1957] 1 Lloyd's Rep 486 (Byrne J)
A shunter, aged 50, sustained a severe injury to the right foot whereby he lost the outer four toes and a considerable portion of his big toe, and became permanently partially disabled. In February 1956, he was offered work as a night watchman by his employers at a wage which was £2 per week less than his earnings as a shunter, which he refused. At the trial on 28/29 May 1957, the plaintiff said he was now willing to accept the work offered. The judge found that the plaintiff was fit for the work offered in February 1956, and should have accepted the work, and assessed the general damages on that basis.

Luker v Chapman

(1970) 114 Sol Jo 788 (Browne J)
The plaintiff's injuries, caused by the defendant's negligent driving, were such that he was unable to continue his pre-accident job as a telephone engineer. His employers offered him clerical work but he refused it, deciding instead to train as a teacher. He claimed his loss of earnings during the period of his training.
HELD: Though the plaintiff was showing courage in undertaking this training he was under a duty to mitigate his damage and should have accepted the clerical job. The defendant could not be held liable for that loss.

Selvanayagam v University of West Indies

[1983] 1 All ER 824, [1983] 1 WLR 585, 127 Sol Jo 288, PC
The appellant sustained injury to his neck in an accident. There was evidence from a specialist who had treated him that surgical therapy which he had recommended would have reduced his disability and enabled him to resume his professional work. However, the specialist said in evidence that as the appellant was diabetic and knew of the risks of infection it was for him to decide whether to have the operation or not. The judge accepted the appellant's decision not to have the operation as reasonable and awarded damages accordingly.
HELD, ON APPEAL to the Privy Council: The judge was entitled so to decide. The rule that a plaintiff who rejects a medical recommendation of surgery must show that he acted reasonably is based on the principle that a plaintiff is under a duty to act reasonably so as to mitigate his damage. The question is one of fact: whether in all the circumstances, including particularly the medical advice received, the plaintiff acted reasonably in refusing surgery; the burden of reasonableness was on him.

7 INTEREST

Note—The Law Reform (Miscellaneous Provisions) Act 1934, s 3 empowers any court of record (other than the High Court and County Court—see below) to award interest on damages for which judgment is given. Subsection 1 reads as follows:

'(1) In any proceedings tried in any court of record for the recovery of any debt or damages, the court may, if it thinks fit, order that there shall be included in the sum for which judgment is given interest at such rate as it thinks fit on the whole or any part of the debt or damages

for the whole or any part of the period between the date when the cause of action arose and the date of the judgment:
Provided that nothing in this section—
(a) shall authorise the giving of interest upon interest; or
[(b) *and* (c) *inapplicable to actions of tort.*]'

PERSONAL INJURY CASES

Supreme Court Act 1981, s 35A

'**35A Power of High Court to award interest on debts and damages** (1) Subject to rules of court, in proceedings (whenever instituted) before the High Court for the recovery of a debt or damages there may be included in any sum for which judgment is given simple interest, at such rate as the court thinks fit or as rules of court may provide, on all or any part of the debt or damages in respect of which judgment is given, or payment is made before judgment, for all or any part of the period between the date when the cause of action arose and—
(a) in the case of any sum paid before judgment, the date of the payment; and
(b) in the case of the sum for which judgment is given, the date of the judgment.
(2) In relation to a judgment given for damages for personal injuries or death which exceed £200 sub-s (1) shall have effect—
(a) with the substitution of "shall be included" for "may be included"; and
(b) with the addition of "unless the court is satisfied that there are special reasons to the contrary" after "given", where first occurring.
(3) Subject to rules of court, where—
(a) there are proceedings (whenever instituted) before the High Court for the recovery of a debt; and
(b) the defendant pays the whole debt to the plaintiff (otherwise than in pursuance of a judgment in the proceedings),
the defendant shall be liable to pay the plaintiff simple interest at such rate as the court thinks fit or as rules of court may provide on all or any part of the debt for all or any part of the period between the date when the cause of action arose and the date of the payment.
(4) Interest in respect of a debt shall not be awarded under this section for a period during which, for whatever reason, interest on the debt already runs.
(5) Without prejudice to the generality of s 84, rules of court may provide for a rate of interest by reference to the rate specified in the Judgments Act 1838, s 17 as that section has effect from time to time or by reference to a rate for which any other enactment provides.
(6) Interest under this section may be calculated at different rates in respect of different periods.
(7) In this section"plaintiff" means the person seeking the debt or damages and "defendant" means the person from whom the plaintiff seeks the debt or damages and "personal injuries" includes any disease and any impairment of a person's physical or mental condition.
(8) [Bills of Exchange.])'

The County Courts Act 1984, s 69 which repealed and replaced s 97A of the 1959 Act is in similar terms, plus the following sub-s (8) but not including sub-s (5) above:

'(8) In determining whether an amount exceeds—
(a) the county court limit; or
(b) an amount specified in any provision of this Act, no account shall be taken of the provisions of this section or of anything done under it.'

(1) Courts of record other than the High Court and county courts include eg the Court of Appeal when dealing with an appeal in an action for damages. (2) On pleading a claim for

interest see *Practice Direction* 24 February 1983 [1983] 1 All ER 934, [1984] 1 WLR 377, 127 Sol Jo 208. See also Ord 18, r 8(4).

Principles to be applied

Jefford v Gee

[1970] 2 QB 130, [1970] 1 All ER 1202, [1970] 2 WLR 702, 114 Sol Jo 206, CA
The plaintiff sustained severe injuries by accident on the 30 November 1966. At trial on 16 June 1969 the judge awarded special damages (mainly loss of earnings) at £2,131 and general damages at £3,500. On an application for interest under the 1934 Act he allowed no interest on the special damages but awarded 6½% on the general damages from the date of the accident to date of trial.
HELD, ON APPEAL: The principle of the 1934 Act (which is unaltered by the 1969 Act) is that interest should be awarded to a plaintiff for being kept out of money which ought to have been paid to him. In detail the principles to be applied in a case of personal injury are as follows:
(1) *Special damages* should be dealt with on broad lines. Medical expenses and damage to clothing etc. are too small to warrant special calculation. Interest on loss of earnings in principle should be calculated on each week's loss from that week to date of trial but that would mean too much detail. In ordinary cases it would be fair to award interest on the total sum of special damages at half the rate allowed on the other damages.
(2) *Loss of future earnings*: no interest should be awarded.
(3) *Pain and suffering and loss of amenities*: interest should run from the date of service of the writ to the date of trial.
(4) *Fatal Accidents Acts and Law Reform damages*: interest should be awarded from date of service of the writ.
(5) *Rate of interest* should be the rate payable on money in court placed on short term investment account. This rate is fixed from time to time by rules made by the Lord Chancellor. Since 1 March 1970 it has been 7%, but over a period which included lower rates a mean or average of the rate obtainable should be taken: in the present case it should be 6%.
(6) *Tax*: the courts should not concern themselves with deduction of tax but merely award a gross sum of interest. The judgment should state the rate of interest and the period for which it is awarded.
(7) *County courts*: the same principles apply.
(8) *Exceptional cases* (eg where a party has been guilty of gross delay) may require the court to depart from the proposals above either in the rate of interest or the period for which it is allowed.

In the present case interest on special damage awarded at 3% from date of accident, on general damages of £2,500 for pain and suffering at 6% from date of service of the writ, on £1,000 general damages for future loss of earnings no interest.

Note—Income tax is not payable on interest awarded on damages for personal injuries. See pp 448—449, below.

On making payments into court, interest calculated up to date of payments in should be included if appropriate.

In *Cookson v Knowles* ([1977] QB 913, [1977] 2 All ER 820, [1977] 3 WLR 279, 121 Sol Jo 461) Lord Denning in the Court of Appeal said the guideline in *Jefford v Gee* should be changed because of inflation and that no interest should be awarded on the lump sum for pain and suffering and loss of amenities. 'The courts invariably assess the lump sum on the scale for figures current at the date of trial, which is much higher than the figure current at the date of the injury or at the date of the writ. The plaintiff thus stands to gain by the delay in bringing the case to trial. He ought not to gain still more by having interest from the date of service of the writ.' This dictum was disapproved by the House of Lords in *Pickett v British Rail Engineering* (p 422, above). Lord Scarman said it was wrong for two reasons: (1) It was a fallacy to say that because the award at trial was greater than it would have been if assessed at the date of service of the writ therefore it was of greater monetary value; the cash awarded was more but its purchasing power was the same or even less. (2) The Administration of Justice Act 1969, s 22 made the award of interest mandatory in the absence of special reasons why no interest should be given. Inflation was general to society and was not a special reason. However, the Court of Appeal has considered the matter again in the following case:

Birkett v Hayes

[1982] 2 All ER 710, [1982] 1 WLR 816, 126 Sol Jo 399, CA
The plaintiff sustained very serious injury in a road accident on 23 February 1975. She issued a writ for damages on 10 May 1976. On 19 January 1981 the judge assessed her damages for pain and suffering and loss of amenities at £30,000. He added £16,000 interest for the period from service of the writ at the rates available on the short term investment account, reducing the total award by 25% because of her failure to wear a seat belt. The defendant appealed against the amount of interest awarded.
HELD: To award the full rate of interest at the high rates of the STI account on the whole of the award was wrong for the following reasons: (1) the damages were assessed on the value of money at the date of the award, not the date of proceedings; (2) interest on damages was tax free (Finance Act 1971, s 19); (3) there may be good reasons for delay in bringing the action on for trial and the defendant should not be penalised by the rate of interest chosen. Though *Pickett*'s case decided that to award no interest was wrong it was for the Court to award it 'at such rate as it thinks fit' (Law Reform (Miscellaneous Provisions) Act 1934) so as to arrive at a final figure which will be fair to both parties. The appropriate rate here was 2%.

Note—Now see s 329 of the Income and Corporation Taxes Act 1988, below.

Wright v British Railways Board

[1983] 2 AC 773, [1983] 2 All ER 698, [1983] 3 WLR 211, 127 Sol Jo 478 HL
In an action for damages for personal injuries the judge awarded general damages for pain suffering and loss of amenity in the sum of £15,000. In awarding interest on these damages he felt himself bound to follow the guideline in *Birkett v Hayes* (above) and awarded interest at the rate of 2% per annum from the date of service of the writ to the date of judgment. On appeal to the House of Lords under the 'leap-frog' procedure (the Administration of Justice Act 1969, s 13):
HELD: There were no grounds for holding the guideline of 2% wrong during a period when inflation was proceeding at a very rapid rate. That guideline should continue to be followed for the time being.

Dexter v Courtaulds

[1984] 1 All ER 70, [1984] 1 WLR 372, 128 Sol Jo 81, CA
The plaintiff was awarded damages for personal injury he sustained on 22 August 1977. Trial of his action was not reached until May 1982. His damages included sums for loss of wages for four months in 1977 and six weeks in 1978. Interest on these sums was awarded at only half rate from the date of the accident following the method

in *Jefford v Gee*. On appeal it was argued on his behalf that as the whole amount of his loss of wages was ascertained as long ago as 1978 he should have interest at the full rate on the loss calculated from the end of each period.
HELD, dismissing the appeal: This was a straightforward case of personal injuries and the *Jefford v Gee* method of awarding half interest on the wage loss from the date of the accident to date of trial was the right one. There may be special circumstances in which the *Jefford v Gee* method would not be fair but this was not such a case. In the case of a high-earning self-employed man for example, off work for three or four months, whose action does not reach trial for four or five years, or where he has paid for an expensive operation out of his own pocket it may be fair to award interest at the full rate but in the generality of cases *Jefford v Gee* should not be departed from. In special cases the plaintiff claiming full interest should set out the special facts in the claim, so as to enable the defendant to make an appropriate calculation of interest for a payment into court.

Chadwick v Parsons

(1971) 115 Sol Jo 127, [1971] 2 Lloyd's Rep 49; affd [1971] 2 Lloyd's Rep 322, CA (Mars-Jones J)
In *Jefford v Gee* (above) the Court of Appeal did contemplate that interest might be awarded from a date earlier than the service of the writ, namely, the date of the letter before action. It may well be that in exceptional cases it would be right for the Court to award interest on general damages from a date even earlier than that; for example, in cases where the plaintiff has not issued proceedings at an earlier date because he has been suffering under some disability, or where the defendant has fraudulently concealed the facts upon which a cause of action might be based.

Slater v Hughes

[1971] 3 All ER 1287, [1971] 1 WLR 1438, 115 Sol Jo 428, CA
The plaintiff was injured on 23 April 1966. On 7 December 1966 she served a writ on the defendant Hughes who on 29 April 1968 served a third-party notice on Jones. On 31 March 1969 the plaintiff joined Jones as a defendant. At the trial liability was found against the defendants in the proportions 40% to Hughes 60% to Jones. The judge awarded interest on the general damages against both defendants from the date of service of the writ on Hughes. Jones appealed against the award of interest against him from 7 December 1966, as he had no notice of the proceedings until 29 April 1968 when he was served with the third-party notice.
HELD: The principle as established in *Jefford v Gee* was that interest should be paid to a plaintiff from the time when the defendant ought to have paid it. It followed that a party ought not to be treated as liable to pay interest until that party received notice of the claim. Interest should be payable by Jones only from 29 April 1968.

Thomas v Bunn, Wilson v Graham and Lea v British Aerospace plc

[1991] 1 AC 362, [1991] 1 All ER 193, HL
The House of Lords was asked to decide the question whether interest on damages awarded pursuant to s 17 of the Judgments Act 1838 should run from the date of the order or judgment on liability (the liability judgment) or from the date when damages were agreed or assessed and final judgment entered for that figure (the damages judgment).

The argument had arisen out of the decision in *Hunt v R N Douglas (Roofing) Ltd* ([1990] 1 AC 398, [1988] 3 All ER 823) which established the principle that interest

on awards of costs ran from the date upon which judgment was pronounced and not from the date upon which the taxation of costs was completed thereafter.
HELD, Per Lord Ackner: 'I accordingly take the view that the judgment referred to in s 17 of the 1838 Act does not relate to an interlocutory or interim order or judgment establishing any of the defendant's liability. The judgment contemplated by that section is the judgment which quantifies the defendant's liability, the judgment which has been referred to in the course of these appeals as the "damages judgment".'

Interest following acceptance of money in court

Newall v Tunstall

[1970] 3 All ER 465, [1971] 1 WLR 104, 115 Sol Jo 14, [1970] 2 Lloyd's Rep 417 (Ashworth J)
In a personal injury claim the defendant paid £1,300 into court in January. The plaintiff did not then accept but in May she applied to the court for leave to accept £1,300 and asked for interest on that sum under the 1934 and 1969 Acts on the ground that leave to take the money out was an order equivalent to a judgment.
HELD: An order giving leave to take money out of court after the expiry of the 14 days allowed by the rules was not a judgment and no interest was payable.

Note—The same conclusion was reached by Fisher J on an exactly similar application in *Waite v Redpath Dorman Long Ltd* [1971] 1 QB 294, [1971] 1 All ER 513, [1970] 3 WLR 1034. The problem which these two cases presented was overcome by the addition of para (8) to RSC Ord 22, r 1 which provides that the plaintiff's cause of action in respect of damages shall be construed as a cause of action also for such interest as might be included in the judgment if judgment were given at the date of payment in.

Blundell v Rimmer

[1971] 1 All ER 1072, [1971] 1 WLR 123, 115 Sol Jo 15, [1971] 1 Lloyd's Rep 110 (Payne J)
In an action for damages for personal injury the defendant did not dispute negligence and made a payment into court. The plaintiff applied to the district registrar under RSC Ord 27, r 3 and obtained an order that he 'be at liberty to sign interlocutory judgment on admission and that damages be assessed by judge alone'.
HELD, ON APPEAL: The interlocutory judgment would be set aside. This was a further attempt to circumvent the rule in *Jefford v Gee* (above) that on acceptance of money in court the case ended without payment of interest. Even if (contrary to the court's view) Ord 27, r 3 did enable the plaintiff to obtain judgment the court would not exercise its discretion to give leave to sign judgment in the present case: the rights of the parties were governed by Ord 22 which entitled the defendant to make the payment in.

Interest on increased damages on appeal

Cook v JL Kier & Co Ltd

[1970] 2 All ER 513, [1970] 1 WLR 774, 114 Sol Jo 207, CA
After being awarded £9,589 damages the plaintiff appealed. The appeal was reached nearly a year later when the Court of Appeal raised the award to £15,045. The plaintiff asked for interest on the difference since the original judgment.

HELD: Interest should be awarded on the amount by which the award was increased at 5% but credit was to be given against it for 4% which would automatically be running from the date of the judgment under the Judgments Act 1838.

Interest not stopped by adjournment

May v A G Bassett & Sons Ltd

(1970) 114 Sol Jo 269 (Paull J)
The plaintiff's action for damages under the Fatal Accidents Acts was due to be tried on 7 July 1969 but she asked for an adjournment to which the defendants agreed. She died on 6 September. Her administrator was substituted and the action was heard on 20 March 1970. The defendants opposed an award of interest after 7 July 1969 on the ground that the case would have been heard then but for the plaintiff's request for the adjournment.
HELD: Award of interest was in the discretion of the judge. The deciding factor here was that the defendants had had the advantage of keeping the money during the period of the adjournment and had drawn interest on it. The plaintiff should have interest to actual date of trial. There was no principle that interest should cease to be paid because of an adjournment.

Rate of interest

The rate of interest on general damages for pain, suffering and loss of amenities is at 2% per annum.

The rate of interest on special damages is paid at the Court Special Account Rate which varies from time to time. The Court Special Account Rate has been 8% since 1 April 1993 and has been as high as 15%.

The rate of interest for continuing special damages is assessed at half the appropriate Court Special Account Rate.

INCOME TAX AND INTEREST

The Income and Corporation Taxes Act 1988, s 329 provides as follows:

329 Interest on damages for personal injuries (1) The following interest shall not be regarded as income for any income tax purposes—
(a) any interest on damages in respect of personal injuries to a plaintiff or any other person, or in respect of a person's death, which is included in any sum for which judgment is given by virtue of a provision to which this paragraph applies; and
(b) any interest on damages or solatium in respect of personal injuries sustained by a pursuer or by any other person, decree for payment of which is included in any interlocutor by virtue of section 1 of the Interest on Damages (Scotland) Act 1958.
(2) The provisions to which subsection (1)(a) above applies are—
(a) section 3 of the Law Reform (Miscellaneous Provisions) Act 1934;
(b) section 17 of the Law Reform (Miscellaneous Provisions) Act (Northern Ireland) 1937;
(c) section 35A of the Supreme Court Act 1981;
(d) section 69 of the County Courts Act 1984;
(e) section 33A of the Judicature (Northern Ireland) Act 1978; and
(f) Article 45A of the County Courts (Northern Ireland) Order 1980.

(3) A payment in satisfaction of a cause of action, including a payment into court, shall not be regarded as income for any income tax purpose to the extent to which it is in respect of interest which would fall within subsection (1) above if included in a sum for which a judgment is given or if decree for payment of it were included in an interlocutor.
(4) In this section 'personal injuries' includes any disease and any impairment of a person's physical or mental condition.

Mason v Harman

[1972] RTR 1
The Finance Act 1971, s 19 by relieving a plaintiff from tax on interest does not call for a reduction in the rate of interest from that which would have been awarded before the 1971 Act in order to produce the same real net situation as was achieved by the *Jefford v Gee* principles before the relief was granted. There was no reason to suppose that s 19 was not intended by Parliament to benefit the recipient.

Note—See s 329 of the Income and Corporation Taxes Act 1988, above.

8 APPEALS ON AMOUNT

THE RULE

Greenfield v London and North Eastern Rly Co

[1945] KB 89, [1944] 2 All ER 438, 171 LT 337, 61 TLR 44, CA (MacKinnon LJ)
The principle on which the Court of Appeal reviews the assessment of damages, whether too high or too low, is not because the Court of Appeal might have given rather more or rather less, but only (1) if the judge has omitted some relevant consideration or admitted some irrelevant consideration, or (2) if the amount is so excessive, or insufficient, as to be plainly unreasonable.

Flint v Lovell

[1935] 1 KB 354, [1934] All ER Rep 200, 104 LJKB 199, 152 LT 231, 51 TLR 127, 78 Sol Jo 860, CA
Per Greer LJ: I think it right to say that this Court will be disinclined to reverse the finding of a trial judge as to the amount of damages merely because they think that if they had tried the case in the first instance they would have given a lesser sum. In order to justify reversing the trial judge on the question of amount of damages it will generally be necessary that this Court should be convinced either that the judge acted upon some wrong principle of law, or that the amount awarded was so extremely high or so very small as to make it, in the judgment of this court, an entirely erroneous estimate of the damage to which the plaintiff is entitled.

Note—The above statement of the law was adopted by Sir Wilfred Greene MR in *Rook v Fairrie* [1941] 1 KB 507, [1941] 1 All ER 297, 110 LJKB 319, 165 LT 23, 57 TLR 297, 85 Sol Jo 297, CA, by Asquith LJ in *Bull v Vazquez* [1947] 1 All ER 334, [1947] LJR 551, by Lord Wright in *Davies v Powell Duffryn Associated Collieries* [1942] AC 601.

Wilson v Pilley

[1957] 3 All ER 525, [1957] 1 WLR 1138, 101 Sol Jo 868, CA
Per Lord Evershed MR: Again let me emphasise that interference by this court with an award of damages by the trial judge must be a rare thing, and may I say it should be perhaps even rarer in relatively small cases tried in the county court. No one would suggest that, because this court thought that the damages, small in any case, were rather on the low side, this court could consider for a moment slightly raising the figure or adopting the converse course in a different kind of case. In other words, the onus on an appellant seeking to interfere with an award of damages, particularly within this sort of scale, is a heavy one.

Elliott v Preston Corpn

[1971] 2 Lloyd's Rep 328, CA
Per Salmon LJ: Before we can interfere, there has to be (in the phrase which is hallowed, but has now I think a rather archaic ring) a wholly erroneous estimate of damage. That I have always regarded as meaning that the court has to be satisfied that it is very wrong. If you are satisfied that it is wrong, and seriously wrong, then not only is this court entitled to interfere, but it is its duty to interfere. I would agree . . . that you cannot say, if it is wrong by such and such a per cent you do interfere and if it is not you do not. I think each case stands by itself, and a great deal depends upon the amount of the award.

Witten v Robson

(1989) Independent, 2 June, CA
The plaintiff was awarded £50,000 for pain and suffering and loss of amenities. The defendant appealed on the ground that it was excessive.
HELD: Per Lord Justice Parker: A proper approach of the Court of Appeal in this type of case was to ask whether the award was so grossly excessive as to lead it to the conclusion that some error of principle, albeit undemonstrable must have taken place in the judgment, or in a wholly erroneous estimate of the damage suffered (*Pickett v British Rail Engineering Ltd* [1980] AC 136 approved).

The figure of £50,000 was a high one although not sufficiently high to justify interference from the Court of Appeal.

COURT OF APPEAL WILL NOT EXAMINE INJURY

Ellis v Sayers Confectioners Ltd

(1963) 61 LGR 299, CA
The Court of Appeal was invited by counsel to see the appellant's injured leg. The Court declined. Whilst there is no definite rule it is, on the whole, not desirable for the Court of Appeal to see the claimant.

Stevens v William Nash Ltd

[1966] 3 All ER 156, [1966] 1 WLR 1550, 110 Sol Jo 710, CA
The plaintiff's right arm was seriously injured in an accident resulting in permanent weakness and loss of movement both in the arm and in the hand and fingers. At the hearing of his appeal against the amount of an award of damages the Court of Appeal was invited by counsel to see the plaintiff's arm. The Court rejected the invitation.

Per Winn LJ: In general it is probably not wise for this Court to embark on examinations of the physical conditions of appellants—though there may be some cases which call for it. There may be a suggestion of malingering; a man might be tempted to refrain from exerting quite so much movement as he really is capable of. Cases of scarring or shortening are in a different category since they are objective.

JUDGE SHOULD ASSESS DAMAGES

Harrison v National Coal Board

[1950] 1 KB 466, [1950] 1 All ER 171, 66 (pt 1) TLR 300, 94 Sol Jo 145, CA
In cases which involve difficult questions of law and are likely to be taken to appeal, it is always desirable that the trial judge, whether or not he is specifically requested by counsel to do so, should assess the damages provisionally, if his decision is adverse to the plaintiff. Failure to do so frequently results in unnecessary further expense to the parties.

NEW EVIDENCE IN COURT OF APPEAL

Jenkins v Richard Thomas and Baldwins Ltd

[1966] 2 All ER 15, [1966] 1 WLR 476, 110 Sol Jo 111, [1966] 1 Lloyd's Rep 473, CA
The plaintiff was employed by the defendants as a pitman, earning £19 10s per week. He received an eye injury which prevented him from doing the work of a pitman and he was employed instead as a labourer at £11 per week. At the trial of his action for damages the defendants said he could be trained to work as a grinder and in that job would earn £17 per week. The judge awarded £3,040 damages of which £1,040 was in respect of future loss at £2 10s per week. After the trial the plaintiff started working as a grinder but showed no aptitude for it and continued to earn only £11 per week. He appealed against the award. The Court of Appeal allowed fresh evidence to be called including that of two eye surgeons, the plaintiff and a fellow employee.
HELD: The appeal should be allowed. It was only in very special circumstances that the court would hear fresh evidence but here the expectation on which the judge has assessed damages had been entirely falsified by events: the plaintiff had been told he would get £17 per week and only got £11. The general rule in actions of this type is that damages have to be assessed once and for all at the trial. It must not be thought that whenever the assessment of the plaintiff's future earnings turns out to be wrong one or other of the parties can appeal for damages to be increased or reduced. In the present case an exceptional circumstance was that the assessment was based on what the defendants had genuinely but mistakenly said at the trial.

Murphy v Stone-Wallwork Ltd

[1969] 2 All ER 949, [1969] 1 WLR 1023, 113 Sol Jo 546, HL
The plaintiff, aged 54, was injured at work on 17 March 1965. Both the judge at first instance and the Court of Appeal made their awards on the footing that the rest of his working life would probably be spent in the employment of the defendants. Within a fortnight of the Court of Appeal's award the defendants dismissed him from their employment. He appealed within time to the House of Lords.

HELD: The House had a discretion to take evidence of something which had occurred after the date of the decision from which the appeal was brought and which had altered the effect of the order of that Court, especially when as here the appeal was launched within the time allowed. The defendants, though acting in good faith, had falsified the basis of the judgment of the Court of Appeal and it was right that the House should admit the new evidence to enable the damages to be adjusted to the new situation. It was a power which a court should exercise sparingly: *Curwen v James* [1963] 2 All ER 619 was rightly decided but *Jenkins v Richard Thomas & Baldwins* (above) might call for reconsideration, since in that case it was not the defendants who had caused the change of circumstances.

Mulholland v Mitchell

[1971] AC 666, [1971] 1 All ER 307, [1971] 2 WLR 93, 115 Sol Jo 15, HL
At the trial of an action the judge assessed damages for very serious personal injury on the basis that it would be possible for the plaintiff to be looked after at home or alternatively at a nursing home where the charges would be at the rate of £903 a year. The plaintiff appealed and applied for leave to adduce fresh evidence that after the trial it had been found impossible to look after him at home, and that he would have to go to a special nursing home where the charges were £1,827 a year.
HELD: RSC Ord 59, r 10(2) gave the Court of Appeal 'power to receive further evidence on questions of fact . . . but . . . no such further evidence (other than evidence as to matters which have occurred after the date of trial or hearing) shall be admitted except on special grounds'. It is generally undesirable to admit fresh evidence on appeal because there ought to be finality in litigation. The question is largely a matter of degree. Fresh evidence ought not to be admitted when it bears on matters falling within the field or area of uncertainty in which the judge's estimate had previously been made. It may be admitted if some basic assumptions common to both sides have been clearly falsified by subsequent events (particularly if this has happened by the act of the defendant) or when to refuse it would affront common sense or a sense of justice. The situation in the present case was sufficiently exceptional that it could not be said the Court of Appeal had wrongly exercised its discretion in giving leave.

McCann v Sheppard

[1973] 2 All ER 881, [1973] 1 WLR 540, 117 Sol Jo 323, CA
Because of great pain from his injuries, McCann needed a pain-killing drug, palfrium. By the date of the trial of his action for damages in June 1972 he had become reliant on the drug. He was awarded general damages for pain, suffering and loss of amenities, for loss of future earnings and special damage. The defendants lodged notice of appeal in July 1972. On 18 October McCann was convicted in the magistrates' court of procuring drugs by deception. On 22 October 1972, he was found dead from an overdose of drugs. The hearing of the defendant's appeal was begun on 28 February 1973.
HELD, by the Court of Appeal: (1) Evidence of McCann's death should be admitted. Where notice of appeal has been served within the time prescribed by the rules and an event has taken place at a time reasonably proximate to the date of the trial which falsifies the facts on which judgment proceeded the Court of Appeal should not rehear the matter on the basis of the fiction that the event has not taken place. (2) Damages for future loss of earnings must consequently be reduced from 15 years to 20 weeks.

WRONG OR MISTAKEN EVIDENCE

Beaton v Naylors of Plymouth

(1965) 109 Sol Jo 632, CA
The plaintiff gave evidence on the hearing of his action for damages for personal injuries that he had not been able to work since the accident. On that basis his special damage was agreed at £848. The judge awarded him £1,500 general damages in addition. Subsequent to the trial the defendants obtained evidence to show that the plaintiff had done quite a lot of work between the accident and the trial.

The Court of Appeal ordered a new trial. The tests to be applied were (1) that the new evidence could not reasonably have been available at the trial, (2) that it was apparently credible, and (3) that it would have had an important influence on the judge. All these tests were satisfied.

Day v Harland and Wolff Ltd

[1967] 1 Lloyd's Rep 301, CA
At the trial of an action in which the plaintiff alleged he injured his wrist by falling over a pile of dunnage judgment was given in his favour for £1,055. Some days later the defendants received a message that the injury had not been caused in the way alleged but in a fight on the evening of the same day. The defendants' solicitors then obtained statements from a publican and two other men to show that the plaintiff had been injured in a fight at a public house. They applied for a new trial.
HELD: There must be a new trial. The evidence could not have been obtained by reasonable diligence for use at the trial and if given it would have been likely to have had an important influence on the result.

Power v Standard Triumph Motor Co Ltd

(1970) Times, 10 December, CA
The plaintiff sustained a head injury at work which, he said, had changed his whole personality. His life had become a misery, he had lost all sense of taste and smell and could not walk properly. He was awarded £17,648 damages. The defendants appealed and applied to adduce fresh evidence relating to matters both before and after trial which would show that so far from being a cripple the plaintiff could walk up ladders, paint his house, move paving stones and chase vandals.
HELD: The Court clearly had power to admit such evidence under Ord 59. Applying *Ladd v Marshall* (p 681, below) the evidence was apparently credible, could have a material influence on the case, and the defendant's solicitors had acted reasonably. Further if the fresh evidence were true the plaintiff had perpetrated a gross fraud and the court should not allow it to succeed. New trial ordered.

CHAPTER 14

Damages in Fatal Cases

1 THE FATAL ACCIDENTS ACT CLAIMS

BACKGROUND TO FATAL ACCIDENT CLAIMS

Before 1 January 1983 fatal accident claims were regulated by the provisions of the Fatal Accidents Act 1976. The Administration of Justice Act 1982 then brought into effect a number of important changes to both that Act (which itself consolidated the Fatal Accidents Acts 1846 to 1959) and the Law Reform (Miscellaneous Provisions) Act 1934.

Very few claims brought under the old rules remain but cases relevant to those earlier provisions are set out in Appendix A to the 9th edn.

The Fatal Accidents Act 1976 abolished the old common law rule that the death of a person gave no cause of action to others either for mental suffering or material loss. Section 1 gives to a 'dependant' a right of action and an entitlement to recover damages in place of the deceased person provided that the person themselves would have been entitled to pursue an action but for their death.

Similarly, the rule that the wrong done to the deceased himself died with him (*actio personalis moritur cum persona*) was largely overcome by the Law Reform (Miscellaneous Provisions) Act 1934.

The Administration of Justice Act 1982 not only introduced the new ss 1 to 4 of the Fatal Accidents Act 1976, set out below, but also largely overruled the case law which enabled actions to be brought under the Law Reform (Miscellaneous Provisions)

Act 1934 for loss of expectation of life and loss of earnings during the 'lost years. Additionally damages for loss of income for any period after death are no longer claimable by virtue of s 4 of the Administration of Justice Act 1982 substituting s 1(2)(a) of the Law Reform (Miscellaneous Provisions) Act 1934.

The new s 1A of the Fatal Accidents Act 1976 extends the category of 'dependants' and introduces a bereavement award (£7,500 for causes of action accruing after 1 April 1991) for a limited class of claimants. The requirement of s 4 of the Act to ignore 'benefits' accruing to the estate as a result of the death has required interpretation and some of the more important cases are discussed below.

Note—Some cases are referred to in this chapter that are not reproduced in full. These can be found in Appendix A of the 9th edn.

FATAL ACCIDENTS ACT 1976

Fatal Accidents Act 1976, ss 1-4 (as substituted by the Administration of Justice Act 1982, s 3):

1 Right of action for wrongful act causing death (1) If death is caused by any wrongful act, neglect or default which is such as would (if death had not ensued) have entitled the person injured to maintain an action and recover damages in respect thereof, the person who would have been liable if death had not ensued shall be liable to an action for damages, notwithstanding the death of the person injured.
(2) Subject to s 1A(2) below, every such action shall be for the benefit of the dependants of the person ('the deceased') whose death has been so caused.
(3) In this Act 'dependant' means—
(a) the wife or husband or former wife or husband of the deceased;
(b) any person who —
 (i) was living with the deceased in the same household immediately before the date of the death, and
 (ii) had been living with the deceased in the same household for at least two years before that date; and
 (iii) was living during the whole of that period as the husband or wife of the deceased;
(c) any parent or other ascendant of the deceased;
(d) any person who was treated by the deceased as his parent;
(e) any child or other descendant of the deceased;
(f) any person (not being a child of the deceased) who, in the case of any marriage to which the deceased was at any time a party, was treated by the deceased as a child of the family in relation to that marriage;
(g) any person who is, or is the issue of, a brother, sister, uncle or aunt of the deceased.
(4) The reference to the former wife or husband of the deceased in sub-s (3)(a) above includes a reference to a person whose marriage to the deceased has been annulled or declared void as well as a person whose marriage to the deceased has been dissolved.
(5) In deducing any relationship for the purposes of sub-s (3) above —
(a) any relationship by affinity shall be treated as a relationship by consanguinity, any relationship of the half blood as a relationship of the whole blood, and the step-child of any person as his child, and
(b) an illegitimate person shall be treated as the legitimate child of his mother and reputed father.
(6) Any reference in this Act to injury includes any disease and any impairment of a person's physical or mental condition.

1A Bereavement (1) An action under this Act may consist of or include a claim for damages for bereavement.

(2) A claim for damages for bereavement shall only be for the benefit—
(a) of the wife or husband of the deceased; and
(b) where the deceased was a minor who was never married—
  (i) of his parents, if he was legitimate; and
  (ii) of his mother, if he was illegitimate.
(3) Subject to sub-s (5) below, the sum to be awarded as damages under this section shall be £3,500.

Note—£7,500 for causes of action after the 1 April 1991.

(4) Where there is a claim for damages under this section for the benefit of both the parents of the deceased, the sum awarded shall be divided equally between them (subject to any deduction falling to be made in respect of costs not recovered from the defendant).
(5) The Lord Chancellor may by order made by statutory instrument, subject to annulment in pursuance of a resolution of either House of Parliament, amend this section by varying the sum for the time being specified in sub-s (3) above.

2 Persons entitled to bring the action (1) The action shall be brought by and in the name of the executor or administrator of the deceased.
(2) If—
(a) there is no executor or administrator of the deceased, or
(b) no action is brought within six months after the death by and in the name of an executor or administrator of the deceased,
the action may be brought by and in the name of all or any of the persons for whose benefit an executor or administrator could have brought it.
(3) Not more than one action shall lie for and in respect of the same subject matter of complaint.
(4) The plaintiff in the action shall be required to deliver to the defendant or his solicitor full particulars of the persons for whom and on whose behalf the action is brought and of the nature of the claim in respect of which damages are sought to be recovered.

3 Assessment of damages (1) In the action such damages, other than damages for bereavement, may be awarded as are proportioned to the injury resulting from the death to the dependants respectively.
(2) After deducting the costs not recovered from the defendant any amount recovered otherwise than as damages for bereavement shall be divided among the dependants in such shares as may be directed.
(3) In an action under this Act where there fall to be assessed damages payable to a widow in respect of the death of her husband there shall not be taken into account the re-marriage of the widow or her prospects of re-marriage.
(4) In an action under this Act where there fall to be assessed damages payable to a person who is a dependant by virtue of s 1(3)(b) above in respect of the death of the person with whom the dependant was living as husband or wife there shall be taken into account (together with any other matter that appears to the court to be relevant to the action) the fact that the dependant had no enforceable right to financial support by the deceased as a result of their living together.
(5) If the dependants have incurred funeral expenses in respect of the deceased, damages may be awarded in respect of those expenses.
(6) Money paid into court in satisfaction of a cause of action under this Act may be in one sum without specifying any person's share.

4 Assessment of damages: disregard of benefit In assessing damages in respect of a person's death in an action under this Act, benefits which have accrued or will or may accrue to any person from his estate or otherwise as a result of his death shall be disregarded.

WHO HAS A RIGHT OF ACTION?

Liability to the deceased

If the deceased settled his own claim during his lifetime then no cause of action accrues to dependants. In *McCann v Sheppard* (p 452, above) the question was raised whether in the events which happened in that case, the plaintiff's widow could have a cause of action under the Fatal Accidents Acts. Lord Denning and James LJ were of the opinion that the wording of s 1 of the Act ' would appear to put an insuperable obstacle in the path of such proceedings'.

Read v Great Eastern Rly Co

(1868) LR 3 QB 555, 9 B & S 714, 37 LJQB 278, 18 LT 822, 33 JP 199, 16 WR 1040
Declaration by plaintiff as widow of D under Lord Campbell's Act 1846, and Fatal Accidents Act 1864, against a railway company for negligence whereby D, a passenger, was injured, of which injuries he died. Plea, that in the lifetime of D, defendants paid him, and he accepted, a sum of money in full satisfaction and discharge of all the claims and causes of action he had against defendants. Demurrer, on the ground that the accord and satisfaction with D was no accord and satisfaction of the claim arising from his death.
HELD: The cause of action was defendant's negligence, which had been satisfied in deceased's lifetime, and the death of D did not create a fresh cause of action. Nor will there be an award of damages when the deceased obtained Judgment in his lifetime (*Murray v Shuter* [1972] 1 Lloyd's Rep 6, CA.

The Limitation Act 1980, s 12 provides that no action lies under the Fatal Accidents Act where the injured person could no longer maintain an action but otherwise an action is to be brought under the Fatal Accidents Act within three years of the date of death or date of knowledge of the person for whose benefit the action is brought, whichever is the later. Section 33 of the Limitation Act 1980 entitles the court to exercise its discretion in certain circumstances.

Although the common law has allowed a defendant to pursue a defence of *volenti* (*Morris v Murray* [1991] 2 QB 6, [1990] 3 All ER 801 and *Pitts v Hunt* [1990] 3 All ER 344) in road traffic cases such a plea is prevented by virtue of s 149 of the Road Traffic Act 1988 (formerly s 148 of the Road Traffic Act 1972).

An individual right

The Fatal Accidents Act gives a remedy to an individual and the mere fact one dependant of the deceased is precluded from bringing an action has no effect on any other dependant.

Dodds v Dodds

[1978] QB 543, [1978] 2 All ER 539, [1978] 2 WLR 434, 121 Sol Jo 619 (Balcombe J)
The administrators of the estate of the deceased claimed damages under the Fatal Accidents Act 1846 on behalf of his son as a dependant. The defendant was the child's mother, the deceased's wife whose negligent driving was the cause of his death. It was

conceded that she, though also dependent on the deceased, had no claim. The question was raised whether her negligence affected the claim of the child, the other dependant. HELD: The negligence of one dependant does not affect the rights of other dependants. The remedy under the Fatal Accidents Act was given to individuals, not to the dependants as a group.

One action only (s 2(3))

Cooper v Williams

[1963] 2 QB 567, [1963] 2 All ER 282, [1963] 2 WLR 913, 107 Sol Jo 194, CA
In a road accident on 4 December 1959 caused by the negligence of the defendants a man was killed. He left two dependants, (1) his widow (2) an illegitimate daughter aged 10. They instructed separate solicitors to deal with their respective claims under the Fatal Accidents Acts. On 1 March 1960 the daughter by her next friend issued a writ, having reached agreement with the defendants on the amount of damages to be paid to her, subject to the approval of the Court. On 18 May an application to approve the settlement was granted by the District Registrar who made an order by consent staying the proceedings except for such steps as may be necessary to enforce the order. The widow's solicitors had been notified by the daughter's solicitors of the application and the Registrar and the defendants also knew of the widow's existence. By the Fatal Accidents Act 1846, s 3 'not more than one action shall lie for and in respect of the same subject-matter of complaint'. In July 1961 the widow issued proceedings claiming damages under the Fatal Accidents Acts but these were met by the defence that only one action was possible and that the daughter's action had barred any further claim. The widow then applied to intervene in the daughter's action and to have the stay set aside.
HELD: A stay of proceedings is not equivalent to a discontinuance or to a judgment. It can be and may be removed if proper grounds are shown. In the circumstances it would lead to a breach of natural justice to allow the consent order to stand and the Court could and should set aside the order of the district registrar, remove the stay and allow the widow to intervene.

Adopted children (s 1(3))

By virtue of the Adoption Act 1976, s 39(2) which provides that 'an adopted child shall be treated in law as if it were not the child of any person other than the adopters or adopter' (adoption is defined by s 38 of the Act), a right of action accrues to an adopted child as a dependant. When assessing the dependency, account needs to be taken of the adoptive parents' financial standing.

Watson v Willmott

[1991] 1 QB 140, [1991] 1 All ER 473
The mother of Thomas Watson, the infant plaintiff, was killed in a car accident on 9 June 1985. His father committed suicide four months later. Thomas was subsequently adopted by his maternal uncle and his wife who brought proceedings on behalf of Thomas and the estate of his father for damages. The plaintiff's counsel contended that the cause of the action accrued at the time of the parents death and that the adoption should be ignored in entirety. The defendant argued that the young child's

dependency on his parents was extinguished at the date of his adoption, as the Children Act 1975 required him to be treated as if born to the adoptive parents.

Garland J adopting the plaintiff's alternative submission held that the correct approach was to calculate the infant's pecuniary dependency on his natural father and then deduct the dependency on his adoptive father. He further held that the adoptive mother's services had replaced those of the natural mother and that no loss had followed under that head of the claim as from the date of adoption.

Note—Contrast this case with the others under s 4 of the Fatal Accidents Act and the requirement to ignore benefits resulting from death.

Child en ventre sa mere

The absence of case law on this point is presumably because the principle is that a child is entitled to damages. There is only one case in the reports which was decided under the Fatal Accidents Act. See also *Lindley v Sharp*, below.

The George and Richard

(1871) LR 3 A & E 466, 24 LT 717, 20 WR 245, 1 Asp MLC 50
In a suit for limitation of liability, instituted on behalf of the owners of a brig (lost in a collision), an appearance was entered on behalf of a child of one of the drowned men *en ventre sa mere*. The court reserved leave to the child, *en ventre*, if born within due time, to prefer its claim for damages sustained by the death of its father.

Illegitimate child dependant

Kelliher v Ground Explorations

[1955] CLY 741 (Byrne J)
Illegitimate child aged three weeks; mother would probably have obtained a bastardy order of about £1 per week until child 16. Award £500.

Lindley v Sharp

(1973) 4 Fam Law 90, CA
The plaintiff, an illegitimate child born on 18 December 1970, sued by his mother as next friend for Fatal Accident damages for the death of the father, killed in a road accident on 12 August 1970. Paternity was accepted. The deceased was 17 at the time of his death and had not had any steady employment. The judge put a figure of £4 per week on dependency and considered five years' purchase enough.
HELD, ON APPEAL: The question was what would the financial benefit to the plaintiff have been had the father not been killed? Would he have married the mother? Once paternity was established the mother would have been entitled to maintenance whether or not they had married. Five years' purchase was not enough; nine years should have been awarded at £208 a year = £1,872.

WHAT DAMAGES ARE RECOVERABLE (SS 1A AND 3)

Bereavement

Section 1A introduces a new concept of damages for bereavement which, for causes of actions accruing on or after the 1 April 1991, is a fixed award of £7,500 (£3,500 for earlier actions) (SI 1990/2575). This head of damage is intended only to benefit spouses of the deceased or parents (if legitimate or the mother if illegitimate) if the deceased were an unmarried minor.

Doleman v Deakin

(1990) Times, 30 January, CA
The fact the injury resulting in death occurred before the deceased had attained the age of 18, did not entitle the parents to recover damages for bereavement if the actual death occurred when he was of majority and unmarried.

Hicks v Chief Constable of South Yorkshire Police

[1992] 2 All ER 65, 8 BMLR 70, HL
Sarah and Victoria Hicks died from asphyxia when they were crushed in the crowd at the Hillsborough Football Stadium. At the time Victoria was aged 15 and the estate was entitled to the bereavement award of £7,500 (Administration of Justice Act 1982). However, the parents' claim for damages for personal injury had been rejected by the trial judge on the basis that the medical evidence given at trial suggested that death was virtually instantaneous.

The House of Lords, dismissing the parents' appeal, commented that damages for negligence were compensatory and not punitive, and whilst fear of death was an understandable emotion, it did not in itself sound in damages so far as the estate of the deceased was concerned.

Note—See *Wheatley v Cunningham*, p 470, below which illustrates the courts' differing approach where the plaintiff survived the ordeal.

Dependancy—mode of calculation and relevant factors

GENERALLY

Malyon v Plummer

[1964] 1 QB 330, [1963] 2 All ER 344, [1963] 2 WLR 1213, 107 Sol Jo 270, CA
It has been established, first, that the pecuniary loss to the persons for whose benefit the action is brought is the only damage recoverable, and, secondly, that the pecuniary loss recoverable is limited to the loss of a benefit in money or money's-worth which, if the deceased had survived, would have accrued to a person within the defined relationship to the deceased and would have arisen from that relationship and not otherwise.

The pecuniary loss which the court has to assess is a loss which will be sustained in the future. This involves making an estimate of the benefit in money's-worth arising out of the relationship which would have accrued to the person for whom the action is brought from the deceased if the deceased had survived but has been lost by reason of his death.

Because in most cases the most reliable guide as to what would happen in the future if the deceased had lived is what did in fact happen in the past when he was alive, the common and convenient way of making the first estimate where the deceased at the time of his death was the breadwinner of the family is (a) to ascertain what annual benefit in money or money's-worth in fact accrued to the person for whom the action is brought from the deceased and arising out of the relationship before the death of the deceased, (b) to assess the extent (if any) to which that benefit would be likely to have increased or diminished in value in the future if the deceased had lived, (c) to assess the number of years for which that benefit would have been likely to have continued if the deceased had not been killed by the tortious act of the defendant, and (d) to apply to the annual benefit, assessed under (a) and (b) and generally called 'the dependency', the appropriate multiplier derived from (c), allowance being made for the present receipt of a capital sum in respect of annual losses which would be sustained in the future. But the fact that it is convenient to have recourse to the past for guidance as to what would have been likely to happen in a hypothetical future which, owing to the death of the deceased, will never occur, must not blind one to the fact that one is estimating a loss which will be sustained in the future: Per Diplock LJ.

Note—See below for deductibility of 'benefits'.

PERCENTAGE OF NET INCOME

There is now a general tendency to value the dependency by deducting a percentage from the deceased's net income to represent the sums he would have spent on himself.

Harris v Empress Motors Ltd

[1983] 3 All ER 561, [1984] 1 WLR 212, 127 Sol Jo 647, CA

In the course of time the courts have worked out a simple solution to the problem of calculating the net dependency under the Fatal Accidents Acts in cases where the dependants are wife and children. In times past the calculation called for a tedious inquiry into how much housekeeping money was paid to the wife, who paid how much for the children's shoes etc. This has all been swept away and the modern practice is to deduct a percentage from the net income figure to represent what the deceased would have spent exclusively on himself. The percentages have become conventional in the sense that they are used unless there is striking evidence to make the conventional figure inappropriate because there is no departure from the principle that each case must be decided on its own facts. Where the family unit was husband and wife the conventional figure is 33% and the rationale of this is that broadly speaking the net income was spent as to one-third for the benefit of each and one-third for their joint benefit. Clothing is an example of several benefit, rent an example of joint benefit. No deduction is made in respect of the joint portion because one cannot buy or drive half a motor car. Part of the net income may be spent for the benefit of neither husband nor wife. If the facts be, for example, that out of a net income of £8,000 per annum the deceased was paying £2,000 to a charity the percentage would be applied to £6,000 and not £8,000. Where there are children the deduction falls to 25%, as was the agreed figure in the *Harris* case: per O'Connor LJ.

Note—See also *Dodds v Dodds*, p 480, below.

Pevec v Brown

(1964) 108 Sol Jo 219 (Megaw J)
In an action in which damages were claimed under the Fatal Accidents Acts for a child of two whose mother had been killed it was contended that the child had lost the advantage of the loving care of his mother while he was growing up and that it was something in respect of which pecuniary compensation ought to be allowed. The claim was put forward on the analogy of *Preston v Hunting Air Transport Ltd* [1956] 1 QB 454, [1956] 1 All ER 443, [1956] 2 WLR 526, 100 Sol Jo 150, [1956] 1 Lloyd's Rep 45 where Ormerod J had, under the Carriage by Air Act 1932, awarded damages over and above the quantifiable loss by reason of the loss of a mother.
HELD: There could be no claim under the Fatal Accidents Acts. It was clear law that a husband who had lost his wife could not recover anything for loss of companionship of his wife nor a wife for loss of her husband's companionship. There was no distinction in principle in the case of an infant. No damages could be awarded in respect of any element of the boy receiving less care than he would have done had his mother survived. It was financial loss, and financial loss only, which was recoverable.

Note—But see now *Regan v Williamson* and *Mehmet v Perry*, p 483, below. See also, in respect of causes of action occurring on or after 1 January 1983, s 1A of the 1976 Act (above).

MULTIPLIER AND MULTIPLICAND

Cookson v Knowles

[1979] AC 556, [1978] 2 All ER 604, [1978] 2 WLR 978, 122 Sol Jo 386, [1978] 2 Lloyd's Rep 315, HL
The plaintiff's husband, aged 49, was killed in a motor accident on 14 December 1973. He was a woodworker earning £1,820 a year. His wife, aged 45, earned £900 a year as a school cleaner but £300 of this was attributable to the help her husband gave her with certain jobs. Without her husband's help she was unable to do the job and gave it up. At the date of the trial, 27 May 1976, her husband's earnings would, but for his death, have been £2,318 a year and hers £1,056 a year. There were three children aged 16, 13 and 12 at the time of their father's death. The Court of Appeal assessed the damages in two parts: the actual pecuniary loss to date of trial and the future pecuniary loss from the date of the trial onwards. Although the widow could not do her former work she still had an earning capacity which should be taken into account. After allowing for this and adding a notional sum of £200 for services rendered by the husband at home dependency was £1,614 a year at the date of death and £1,980 at date of trial. Actual pecuniary loss to date of trial was thus £4,492 plus interest at 4½% (ie half rate) for 2½ years = £4,997 for the first part. A multiplier of 11 less 2½ (number of years from death to date of trial) = 8½ x £1,980 = £16,830 for the second part with no interest. Total award of Fatal Accidents Act damages £21,827.
HELD, ON APPEAL to the House of Lords: The method adopted by the Court of Appeal was correct: (1) In a normal fatal accidents case the damages should be split into two parts, (a) the pecuniary loss which it is estimated the dependants have already sustained from the date of death up to the date of trial, and (b) the pecuniary loss which it is estimated they will sustain from the trial onwards. (2) The pre-trial loss is the total of the amounts assumed to have been lost by the plaintiffs for each week between the date of death and the trial, though as a matter of practical convenience it is usual to take the median rate of wages as the basis for the multiplicand. (3) Interest on the pre-

trial loss should be awarded at half the short term interest rates current during that period. (4) For calculating future loss the figure for dependency to be multiplied by a number of years' purchase it to be calculated as at the date of trial. (5) The multiplier will be related primarily to the deceased's age and hence to the probable length of his working life at date of death. The figure selected as appropriate is to be reduced by the number of years between the date of death and trial — in this case reducing 11 to 8½. (6) No increase in the award should be made to make allowance for inflation. Though the theory that investment in equities would give protection against inflation has been exploded, the high interest rates available from fixed interest securities will give protection to persons not subject to a high rate of income tax when the courts continue to use about the same multiplicand and multiplier as formerly. (7) No interest should be awarded on post-trial loss. (8) (Per Lord Salmon): In my view it is impossible to lay down any principles of law which will govern the assessment of damages for all time. We can only lay down broad guidelines for assessing damages . . . where economic factors remain similar to those prevailing.

Note—See also *Pidduck v Eastern Scottish Omnibuses Ltd* [1989] 2 All ER 261, [1989] 1 WLR 317, [1989] 10 LS Gaz R 41, QBD.

Graham v Dodds

[1983] 2 All ER 953, [1983] 1 WLR 808, 147 JP 746, HL
The plaintiff claimed damages under the Fatal Accidents (Northern Ireland) Order 1977 for the death of her husband at the age of 41 in a road accident. The Judge suggested to the jury a figure of £14,400 for loss of dependency up to date of trial and that a reasonable multiplier for calculating future loss might be 11 to 14 years. He also suggested a figure of £4,800 as a figure for the annual loss of dependency after the date of trial. The jury awarded £103,000.
HELD, ON APPEAL to the House of Lords: The award implied an excessively high multiplier in the case of a man 41 years old at the date of death. The gross multiplier should be calculated as from the date of death, not trial. It would be wrong to award a sum for loss up to date of trial and then apply a multiplier for the future as if the deceased had survived to trial. The number of years between death and trial should be deducted from the overall figure for the multiplier before applying it to the estimated future loss of dependency per annum. New trial ordered.

Whittome v Coates

[1965] 3 All ER 268, [1965] 1 WLR 1285, 109 Sol Jo 613, CA
The plaintiff was awarded damages under the Fatal Accidents Acts for the death of her husband. At the time of his death he was aged 58, a trade union official earning £1,200 per annum. This salary would have increased at about 6% each year up to retirement at 65, when he would have received a pension. The judge estimated the plaintiff's dependency at £600 a year to the deceased's retirement age and £450 a year after his retirement. The plaintiff was in poor health and her expectation of life was about 12 years. It was assumed that the deceased's was more. The gross dependency over 12 years would be £6,575. Making allowance for the chances and vicissitudes of life and the fact that damages were paid in one sum the judge awarded £5,250. On appeal the defendants pointed out that a little over £4,000, properly invested in 12 years would produce £6,575.
HELD: In a case of this kind the contingencies and circumstances are all uncertain and the Court has to make a reasonable assessment of probabilities. Mathematical

calculations are in no way decisive. Assessments in terms of the price of an annuity were not of much assistance since very few people in his class of life would purchase an annuity. The judge had not erred except in not making sufficient allowance for the fact that the damages would be paid in one immediate payment. Deduction of £1,000 should be made for this.

Higgs v Drinkwater

[1956] CA Transcript 129A
The husband was 25 earning £550 a year as a maintenance assessor with nylon spinners. The wife was 33 earning about £800 a year as a lecturer with the local authority. The parties had only been married a year during which they were both working and building up a home, getting furniture and so forth. The widow hoped not to continue her work indefinitely but in a year or two to start a family. Approximately £150 to £200 of the husband's earnings was being spent yearly for the wife's advantage.
HELD: The figure of loss of earnings to be taken into account was the £150 to £200, and there was to be added his loss of prospects of promotion and the increased benefit from that to her. The contributory pension scheme would enure to her benefit as well as to his.

Gavin v Wilmot Breeden Ltd

[1973] 3 All ER 935, [1973] 1 WLR 1117, 117 Sol Jo 681, [1973] 2 Lloyd's Rep 501, CA
The plaintiff and her husband, both aged 19, were married in 1971. A child was born in November; in December the husband was killed. During the three months or so since the marriage they had lived with his parents, paying £6 for accommodation. The husband had been earning £30 per week of which they had put aside £10 per week in a bank account in her name alone. On an appeal against an award of £16,848 made by the judge using an agreed multiplier of 18, defendants complained that the judge had made no reduction for the £10 weekly savings in determining the widow's dependency at £18 per week.
HELD: If the £10 per week had been spent instead of saved the standard of living of both spouses would have gone up. Some part of the £10 per week, whether saved or spent, should be regarded as likely to have been spent eventually for the benefit of the husband himself. To that extent the loss was not the widow's. The dependency should be reduced by £3 per week to £15.

EFFECT OF INFLATION

There appears to be a degree of inconsistency in the reported cases as to whether future inflation should be taken into consideration when assessing the level of dependency.

Mallett v McMonagle

[1970] AC 166, [1969] 2 All ER 178, [1969] 2 WLR 767, 113 Sol Jo 207, HL
The plaintiff claimed damages under the Fatal Accidents Acts for herself and her three children aged six, four and two. Her husband was aged 25 at his death in 1964. She was 24. He worked as a machine operator at a net wage of £12 per week and had

for six weeks before his death supplemented his earnings by working as a vocalist in a dance band earning £6 to £10 per week. He gave the plaintiff about £10 per week from his wages and about £3 10s per week from his earnings with the band. The plaintiff spent about £3 10s per week on his food leaving a net dependency of about £10 per week. His employers closed down in January 1967 but evidence was given by a man who said he would have employed the deceased as an asphalter at £22 10s per week though this would have called for long hours and much travelling. A jury awarded £21,500 damages.

HELD: By the Court of Appeal in Northern Ireland and by the House of Lords, the award was so excessive that there must be a new trial. The amount awarded, wisely invested, could without resorting to capital produce an income double the rate of dependency at the time of death. This would not necessarily be wrong in the case of a young man with clear prospects of rising high on the ladder of financial prosperity but this was not such a case; there was no evidence that the deceased was likely to rise high on any ladder to success.

Per Lord Diplock: (1) Though sterling has been subject to continuous inflation experience of 20 years of inflation has shown that its effects can be offset to some extent by prudent investment, in buying a home, in growth stock or in short term high interest-bearing securities. The only practicable course for courts to adopt in assessing damages under the Fatal Accidents Acts is to leave out of account the risk of further inflation on the one hand and the high interest rates which reflect the fear of it and capital appreciation of property and equities which are the consequence of it on the other hand. In estimating annual dependency money should be treated as retaining its value, and in calculating the present value of annual payments which would have been received in future years interest rates appropriate to times of stable currency such as 4 to 5% should be adopted. (2) Having regard to the uncertainties that have to be taken into account 16 years would appear to represent a reasonable maximum number of years' purchase where the deceased died in his twenties.

Note—See also *Cookson v Knowles*, p 463, above. In *Doyle v Nicholls* (1978) 122 Sol Jo 386 (below), Bristow J, not following *Mallett v McMonagle* (above), took into consideration in assessing Fatal Accidents Act damages the likelihood of future inflation at not less than 7% per annum.

Young v Percival

[1974] 3 All ER 677, [1974] 1 WLR 17, 119 Sol Jo 33, CA

The deceased, aged 29 at the time of his death, was employed as a sales representative by a travel firm. His annual income net of tax was £1,615 and the dependency of the plaintiff widow and their two children was £1,100. Evidence was given of likely increases in the deceased's earnings. Some of the increases would result from promotion and some would be given to meet the rising cost of living.

HELD: (1) The multiplier of the figure for dependency at death, ie £1,100, should be 14 having regard to all the factors—the ages of the deceased and the plaintiff (both approaching 30), the fact that the deceased had not long been in the job and that it was in a trade of uncertain profitability. (2) By the date of trial, three and a half years after his death, the dependency would probably, but not certainly, have increased to £2,100 per annum on salary increases resulting from promotion. The multiplier for this increased dependency of £1,000 per annum should, because of the imponderable factors, be eight years only. (3) Following *Taylor v O'Connor* (p 467, below) the estimates or forecasts given in evidence of future earnings increases referable solely to anticipations of future inflation must be excluded from the assessment.

Doyle v Nicholls

(1978) 122 Sol Jo 386 (Bristow J)
The plaintiff's claim for damages under the Fatal Accidents Acts was reached in May 1978, six years after her husband's death. His profession had been that of an anaesthetist with a private as well as a National Health Service practice. He was 54 years old.
HELD: There was no uncertainty about the first six years of the ten-year multiplier: for that period the dependency was £32,245. Was future inflation to be taken into account for the remaining four years? On a consideration of *Taylor v O'Connor* (below), *Young v Percival* (above) and *Cookson v Knowles* (p 463, above) the law now seemed to be that, while the court should not use an addition to the multiplier as a means of taking into account the probability of future inflation, if a dependant's situation would be affected by future inflation the court should take it into account as best it could. It was a proper inference that over the next four years inflation would be at least 7% a year. The deceased's salary would have increased accordingly, so the plaintiff's dependency figure must be increased *pari passu*. Award from 1977: £27,872. Loss of pension rights: £26,760.

WIFE'S INCOME

Whilst a wife's private income is not relevant to assessment of dependency, her earned income is and should be deducted unless the widow only goes out to work after the death.

Shiels v Cruickshank

[1953] 1 All ER 874, [1953] 1 WLR 533, 97 Sol Jo 208, HL
Deceased had a salary of £20,000 per annum, of which £17,000 ceased on his death. The widow had a considerable private income.
HELD: The widow's private means could not be taken into account in the assessment of damages.

Taylor v O'Connor

[1971] AC 115, [1970] 1 All ER 365, [1970] 2 WLR 472, 114 Sol Jo 132, [1970] TR 37, 49 ATC 37, HL
The plaintiff's husband was aged 53 at his death, a partner in a firm of architects. In the year before his death his earnings were £14,890 and would have been £21,000 for the next 12 years—about £7,500 per annum after tax. £1,500 of this would have had to be left in the firm for capital and there would have been some savings from the remaining £6,000, he would have spent about £3,000 pa in a manner beneficial to the plaintiff and their daughter. £10,000 came to the plaintiff from the estate. The judge awarded £54,196 damages.
HELD: Though the judge's method of assessment might be varied in some details, his figure was within the reasonable range of possible awards and should be upheld. On individual items: (1) In valuing the dependency the judge's method of allowing for the fact that the widow would receive £10,000 from the husband's estate was to

deduct £200 from the annual value of the dependency to allow for acceleration of her interest in the estate; this was a proper deduction. (2) Although it would be unrealistic to refuse to take inflation into account at all, the judge's method, which was to increase the multiplier of the annual dependency from 10 to 12 was not a valid one. The lump sum of damages should be assessed on the basis that it will be invested with the aim of getting some capital appreciation to offset the probable rise in the cost of living. Having regard to the incidence of tax and surtax and the widow's expectation of life of 21 years, however, 12 was not an unreasonably high multiplier. (3) In taking the incidence of tax into account any private income of the widow's should be ignored.

Davies v Whiteways Cyder Co Ltd

[1975] QB 262, [1974] 3 All ER 168, [1974] 3 WLR 597, 118 Sol Jo 792, [1974] 2 Lloyd's Rep 556, [1974] STC 411 (O'Connor J)
The first plaintiff's husband, a successful businessman, had over the years made various dispositions of his money for her benefit and that of their son. He was killed in a road accident by negligence of the defendant's driver before the period of seven years had elapsed; as a result nearly £40,000 was brought back for estate duty and £17,000 duty was paid.
HELD: In the claim by the widow and son under the Fatal Accidents Acts, the sum of £17,000 (less £500 to cover the small chance of the deceased's not suriving the remainder of the seven years had the accident not happened) was recoverable from the defendants as damages for the death. It was (1) a financial loss which the plaintiffs had suffered and would suffer as a result of death, and (2) arose from the relationship of husband and father, and was accordingly within the words of s 2 of the 1846 Act.

Coward v Comex

(1988) Unreported, CA
Mr Coward worked as a self employed diver. His wife was a midwife. On 5 November 1983 he died as a result of an accident caused by the defendant's negligence. Much evidence was given about the state of the diving industry and Mr Coward's future prospects within it:
(1) Following *Higgs v Drinkwater* [1956] CA Transcript 129A, CA the court refused to assess the plaintiff's dependency at 75% despite her evidence that she would have started a family but for the death of her husband.
(2) Whilst the court had discretion to admit new evidence on appeal, in this instance evidence as to Parliament's intention to change to the tax rules was not something which the court would concern itself with, not least of all because there should be finality in litigation. The calculations made at trial and before the announcement of the tax changes would stand.

FUTURE FINANCIAL PROSPECTS

Where there is likely to be a change in the parties' circumstances the court will adjust the multiplicand to take this into account.

Malone v Rowan

[1984] 3 All ER 402 (Russell J)
The plaintiff's husband was killed in a road accident. She was at the time 25 years old

and he 27. Her earnings were about £60 per week and his £76 which by the date of trial would have risen to £102. At the date of death the plaintiff's dependency was 55% of the deceased's earnings. The plaintiff said in evidence that she had wanted to start a family and would then have given up her job. Her dependency would then have increased (as the judge found) to two-thirds of the deceased's earnings. The judge accepted that she would have become pregnant in the very near future and would have given up her job to look after the children.
HELD: The material facts were indistinguishable from those of *Higgs v Drinkwater* (p 465, above). In that case Denning LJ, said it was not right to increase the figure for pecuniary loss because of the possiblity of the plaintiff having a family. 'She had not suffered any financial loss on that account . . . We can only award damages for financial loss and she has suffered none through not having a family. On the contrary, she had kept at work earning [her] salary'. The judgment was binding in the present case and the fraction for dependency as at the date of death could not be altered.

Mallett v McMonagle

[1970] AC 166, [1969] 2 All ER 178, [1969] 2 WLR 767, 113 Sol Jo 207, HL
See p 465, above.

Hodgson v Trapp

[1989] AC 807, [1988] 3 All ER 870, [1988] 3 WLR 1281, [1989] 2 LS Gaz R 36, HL
At 33 the plaintiff, a wife, mother and woman of many talents and interests suffered catastrophic injuries in a road accident. As a result she became wholly dependent on others and would always remain so. The judge calculated the multiplicand for loss of earnings and chose a multiplier of 11. He then increased this to 12 to take into account the higher tax rates payable on investment income, applying *Thomas v Wignall* (above). He adopted the same approach to nursing care and attendance raising the basic multiplier for that head of damage from 13 to 14. The defendants appealed not on the basis that high tax rates might allow for a multiplier at a higher end of the conventional scale but on the basis that having decided on a multipler the making of a specific addition to take tax into account as a separate feature was incorrect in law.
HELD, ON APPEAL: Appeal allowed. It was a falsity to assume that higher rates of taxation would not be reduced. Just as inflation is an imponderable and not to be taken into account (see *Cookson v Knowles* p 463, above) so (save in exceptional circumstances) income tax should not be used to raise the multiplier for future losses as a separate item. The dissenting view of Lloyd LJ in *Thomas v Wignall* was correct. Per Lord Oliver: The incidence of taxation in the future should ordinarily be assumed to be satisfactorily taken care of in the conventional assumptions of an interest rate applicable to a stable currency and the selection of a multiplier appropriate to that rate.

MARRIAGE BREAKING DOWN

Davies v Taylor

[1974] AC 207, [1972] 3 All ER 836, [1972] 3 WLR 801, 116 Sol Jo 864, HL
The plaintiff and her husband were married in 1955. From December 1966 to February 1968, unknown to her husband she had an adulterous association with a man she met at work. In May 1968 she gave up her job and on the 9 July she left her husband

saying she no longer had any feeling for him. She went to live with her parents. Her husband very much wanted her to return to him and begged her to do so. On 31 July he went to her and asked her to return but she told him of her adulterous affair. On 2 August he instructed solicitors to begin divorce proceedings. On 14 August he met the plaintiff by chance, in the street, told her he had consulted a solicitor but again asked her to return to him; she refused, saying she wanted time to think. Later on the same day he was killed in a motor accident. At the trial of the plaintiff's claim for damages under the Fatal Accidents Acts the judge said that on the question of dependency the test he had to apply was whether the plaintiff had discharged the onus of proving that it was more probable than not that there would have been a reconciliation between her and her husband. He said he was not satisfied there was likely to be a reconciliation and that accordingly the plaintiff had not proved any dependency.
HELD: The judge had applied the wrong test. In this case it had to be decided whether there was a reasonable expectation of a reconciliation, not whether a reconciliation was more likely than not. If, although there was a reasonable expectation, the chance of the reconciliation happening was slight then the damages would be such as would reflect that degree of probability. The plaintiff's damages would be scaled down as the possibility became progressively more remote. But a mere speculative or fanciful possibility of a reconciliation was not sufficient. On the evidence the judge had rightly decided that there was no likelihood of a reconciliation and the plaintiff's claim failed. *Taff Vale Rly Co v Jenkins* (p 477, below) applied.

Wheatley v Cunningham

[1992] PIQR Q100
Paul Wheatley died on the 21 January 1989, six days after a road traffic accident involving the defendant and his wife Jane in whose car he was a passenger. Jane had discovered the day before the accident that she was pregnant, but she subsequently miscarried. She suffered minimal physical injuries in the accident.

Tudor Evans J awarded general damages of £10,000 to reflect the psychiatric problems she had encountered after the accident and the 'terrifying circumstances in which the accident occurred on the issue of nervous shock'. The judge dismissed the statistics on divorce (given as 40% of all marriages failing) as speculative.

Note—See *Martin v Owen* (below) where the court took cognizance of those statistics.

Martin v Owen

(1992) Times, 21 May
The plaintiff widow had twice committed adultery which, in the court's view, tended to suggest that she had little respect for the institution of marriage. The Court of Appeal, taking judicial notice of the statistics of divorce (one in three marriages ending in a decree), reduced the multiplier from 15 to 11 on the basis that the marriage may not have lasted the duration of the joint lives of the plaintiff and the deceased. Section 3(3) of the Fatal Accidents Act 1976 did not prevent the court from so doing, though it could not take into account the prospect of marriage or actual re-marriage of the widow.

DEPENDENCY ON PROCEEDS OF CRIME

Burns v Edman

[1970] 2 QB 541, [1970] 1 All ER 886, [1970] 2 WLR 1005, 114 Sol Jo 356 (Crichton J)
The plaintiff sued for damages for herself and her four children under the Fatal Accidents Acts for the death of her husband. He had had no record of honest employment and no capital assets; he had two convictions for felony. He used to give the plaintiff £20 every Friday. The inference was that such support as he gave came from the proceeds of crime.
HELD: The plaintiff was not entitled to damages. What each dependant was in effect saying was 'I have been deprived of my share of other people's goods brought to me by the deceased dishonestly', and in so far as that was the 'injury' within s 2 of the Acts it was a *turpi causa* and therefore no action in respect of it could be maintained.

DEATH OF PLAINTIFF BEFORE TRIAL

Williamson v John I Thorneycroft & Co

[1940] 2 KB 658, [1940] 4 All ER 61, 110 LJKB 82, CA
An action brought by a widow under the Fatal Accidents and Law Reform Acts. She died before trial. The trial judge ignored the death of the widow before trial.
HELD, by the Court of Appeal: While the damages had to be assessed at the date of the husband's death, the court was entitled to inform its mind of subsequent events throwing light upon the realities of the case, such as the fact that one dependant had only a short tenure of life before her dependence was brought to an end, and that, therefore, only a comparatively small sum ought to have been allowed to the widow under the Fatal Accidents Acts.

DEPENDENCY A QUESTION OF FACT

Peters v Overhead Ltd

(1934) 27 BWCC 190, CA
In 1931, a workman deserted his wife and family, who had to be maintained by the Poor Law Authorities. He was subsequently killed by accident arising out of and in the course of his employment when working under an assumed name. The widow, after learning the facts in 1934, brought a claim on behalf of herself and her children for compensation as dependants. The county court judge held on the facts that there was no dependency or any reasonable probability of dependency and made his award for the employers. The widow appealed.
HELD: The question of dependency was one of fact and could not be presumed from the legal obligation to support. There was evidence to support the finding of fact and no misdirection.

Note—A case under the Workmen's Compensation Acts.

DEATH AS A RESULT OF ACCIDENT

Isitt v Railway Passengers Assurance Co

(1889) 22 QBD 504, 58 LJQB 191, 60 LT 297, 37 WR 477, 5 TLR 194
The assured, under a policy granted by the defendant company against 'death from the effects of injury caused by accident', fell and dislocated his shoulder. He was at once put to bed and died in less than a month from the date of the accident, having been all the time confined to his bedroom. In a case stated in a reference under defendants' special Act the umpire found that the assured died from pneumonia caused by cold, but that he would not have died as and when he did had it not been for the accident; that as a consequence of the accident he suffered from pain and was rendered restless, unable to wear his clothing, weak and unusually susceptible to cold, and that his catching cold and the fatal effects of the cold were both due to the condition of health to which he had been reduced by the accident.
HELD: The death of the assured was due to the 'effects of injury caused by the accident' within the meaning of the policy.

Mardorf v Accident Insurance Co

[1903] 1 KB 584, 72 LJKB 362, 88 LT 330, 19 TLR 274
Under a personal accident policy insurers agreed to pay in case of injury by accidental violence if the injury should be the 'direct and sole cause' of death, excluding 'death caused by or arising wholly or in part from disease or other intervening cause, even although the disease or other intervening cause may either directly or otherwise be brought on or result from accident'.

The assured accidentally scratched his leg, which ten days later became inflamed, and erysipelas set in, followed in three days by septicaemia, and soon afterwards by septic pneumonia, of which in less than a week the insured died.
HELD: The erysipelas, septicaemia, and septic pneumonia were not 'intervening causes' and death was caused directly and solely by the injury.

Re Etherington and Lancashire and Yorkshire Accident Insurance Co

[1909] 1 KB 591, 78 LJKB 684, 110 LT 568, 53 Sol Jo 266, CA
By the terms of a policy an accident insurance company undertook, if, at any time during the continuance of the said policy, the insured should sustain any bodily injury caused by violent, accidental, external, and visible means, then, in case such injury should, within three calendar months from the occurrence of the accident causing such injury, directly cause the death of the insured, to pay to the legal personal representatives of the insured the capital sum of £1,000. The policy contained the following proviso: 'Provided always and it is hereby as the essence of the contract agreed as follows: that this policy only insures against death where accident within the meaning of the policy is the direct or proximate cause thereof, but not where the direct or proximate cause thereof is disease or other intervening cause, even although the disease or other intervening cause may itself have been aggravated by such accident, or have been due to weakness or exhaustion consequent thereon, or the death accelerated thereby.'

The assured, while hunting, had a heavy fall, and, the ground being very wet, he was wetted to the skin. The effect of the shock and the wetting was to lower the vitality of his system, and being obliged to ride home afterwards while wet, still further lowered his vitality. The effect of this lowering of his vitality was to cause the

subsequent development of pneumonia in his lungs, of which he died. The pneumonia was not septic or traumatic, but arose as a direct and natural consequence from the fact that the diminution of vitality caused through the accident, as above-mentioned, allowed the germs called 'pneumococci', which in small numbers are generally present in the respiratory passages, to multiply greatly and attack the lungs.
HELD: The death of the assured was directly caused by accident within the meaning of the policy, and the case did not come within the proviso therein, and the company were consequently liable on the policy.

Jenkins v Lancaster Steam Coal Collieries

(1923) 16 BWCC 11, CA
The foregoing has been accepted in the Court of Appeal as a correct statement of the law.

Smith v Cornhill Insurance Co Ltd

[1938] 3 All ER 145, 54 TLR 869, 82 Sol Jo 625, 61 Lloyd's Rep 122 (Atkinson J)
Policy provided payment for death as the result of bodily injury caused by violent, accidental, external and visible means. Car found badly damaged lying on its side some yards below level of road. A very wavy track which had been forced through bushes near the car, finally led to a river, and there insured was found standing almost upright with the water a few inches over her head. There was an overhanging branch by which she could have pulled herself out. Medical evidence was that she died before or at the moment her face reached the surface of the water. She had suffered severe mental and physical shock as a result of the accident and had wandered aimlessly into the water.
HELD: Death was the result of the accident, as each subsequent event was due to the brain injury resulting from the accident.

Note—For *'Shock, non-fatal'*, p 398, above.

Fuller v Minister of Pensions

(1948) 3 War Pensions Appeal 1623 (Denning J)
The question of causation is always difficult, but suicide is such an overwhelming event in itself that, in the ordinary way, that act is an act of which the cause lies in the man's own individual personality and nothing else. The worries, whether they be personal or whether they be connected with his work are the conditions in which the cause operates and are not a cause at all.

Note—Followed in *Pitt v Minister of Pensions and National Insurance* (1954) Times, 19 January (Ormrod J)

Cavanagh v London Transport Executive

(1956) Times, 23 October (Devlin J)
On 25 September 1953, the plaintiff's husband was injured by an omnibus of the defendants. He sustained a fractured skull and other injuries. Some 16 months later he committed suicide. The deceased was a bookmaker a little over 50 years of age, married with two children, now grown up; he had been married 26 years and appeared to have been successful and happy, both domestically and in business. The injuries were severe including a fracture of the vault of the skull which caused concussion and

immediate loss of consciousness. On 3 February 1954, his doctor signed him off as fit for work and he went back to his business. His bank account appeared to show that from about May or June 1954, the business was going downhill. The plaintiff said he was a changed man after the accident. The kindliness and his fondness for his children disappeared. Before the accident he had been a reserved man who disliked any sort of swearing. After the accident he became abusive and behaved abominably to her and the children and things got worse when he went back to work. On 23 January 1955 he committed suicide.

The defendant's medical evidence was that it was not a characteristic of head injuries that they led to suicide; there was nothing at the examination; the cause was a depressive psychosis, which was the most common cause of suicide in middle-aged men.

The judge said if the head injuries were ruled out, it must have been depressive psychosis and he did not see any evidence of that. It might be that financial worries operating on the state of mind, contributed to it and was perhaps the immediate cause, but the head injuries might have made him incapable of reacting normally to worries.
HELD: There was no *novus actus*; the business losses were likely to result from his decline in business ability. The plaintiff had discharged the burden of proof of causation.

Pigney v Pointers Transport Services Ltd

[1957] 2 All ER 807, [1957] 1 WLR 1121, 101 Sol Jo 851 (Pilcher J)
A workman was injured on 28 July 1955. He brought an action against his employers but on 15 January 1957, before the action had been tried, he committed suicide. His widow and administratrix then commenced proceedings under the Fatal Accidents and Law Reform Acts and the two actions were consolidated.

The injury consisted of a fairly serious cut on the head which had to be stitched and apparently healed perfectly. He was to some extent concussed, was in hospital a few days and made a perfectly good recovery from the physical injury to the scalp. After the accident and up to the time of his death, he suffered from a condition of acute anxiety neurosis with depressive features brought about by the accident. He was not insane under the McNaghten rules. He knew what he was doing and that what he was doing was wrong. He took his life in a fit of depression brought about by a condition of acute anxiety neurosis induced by the accident and injury.
HELD: The case of *Cavanagh v London Transport Executive* (above) and the workmen's cases show that a sane man's death by suicide can in law 'result' from an injury, even though the suicide may not occur until some time after the injury. With regard to the defence of public policy, the last words of s 1 of the Act of 1846 were no doubt introduced so as not to defeat the rights of defendants where no criminal proceedings had been instituted, but the claim, which is a new cause of action created by the Act beyond that which the deceased would have had if he had survived (*Pym v Great Northern Rly Co* (1863) 4 B & S 396, 32 LJQB 377, 8 LT 734), does not depend on that ground but on the ground that the deceased's act did not break the chain of causation. In the case of *Beresford v Royal Insurance Co* (below), it was held to be against public policy to allow a felon by his crime to benefit his own estate. This is not a case of benefit to the estate of the deceased. The defence of public policy was not raised in the *Workmen's Compensation* case nor in *Cavanagh*'s case. The widow is entitled to damages.

Farmer v Rash

[1969] 1 All ER 705, [1969] 1 WLR 160, 113 Sol Jo 57 (Willis J)
The Court was asked to approve a settlement of claims under the Fatal Accidents Acts where £2,100 had been paid into Court and apportion the payment between the claimants and the estate under the Law Reform (Miscellaneous Provisions) Act 1934. The deceased was seriously injured by the defendant's negligent driving on 22 February 1965, sustaining fractures of both legs, broken back and broken hip ramus. He was in hospital only two weeks and was sufficiently recovered to attempt a return to work in the summer. Then he began to suffer from depression which by January was so bad that he was admitted to hospital. On 11 February 1966 he committed suicide. A doctor said he thought the accident was an 'important precipitating factor' in causation of the depression. The dependants under the Fatal Accidents Acts were the deceased's wife, from whom he had been separated for many years, their son and an illegitimate son. By his will the deceased had left everything to a woman with whom he had been living for several years and who was the mother of the illegitimate son. The wife was making application in separate proceedings under the Inheritance (Family Provision) Act 1938.
HELD: The likelihood of the executor recovering anything in a contested claim under the Fatal Accidents Acts was so remote that it would be unrealistic to apportion any part of the sum of £2,100 to that head of claim. The whole sum should go to the estate under the Law Reform Act.

Note—Suicide is relevant in two connections (1) the death benefit under a policy and (2) the result of an accident.

In the case of death by poisoning from the exhaust of a car (asphyxia from carbon monoxide poisoning) this is prima facie an accident in direct connection with the insured car, caused by accidental external and visible means, and the onus is on the insurers to prove the case is suicide within the exception. If it is desired to exclude this risk from the policy, one method is to exclude death by inhalation.

Willis' *Workmen's Compensation* dealt with suicide, as follows:

'When it results from insanity or mental derangement (*Dixon v Sutton Heath and Lea Green Colliery Ltd (No 2)* (1930) 23 BWCC 135, CA) consequent on personal injury by accident, it is rightly held to be death resulting from the injury (*Malone v Cayzer Irvine & Co* 1908 SC 479, 45 SLR 351, 15 SLT 837, 1 BWCC 27; *Graham v Christie* (1916) 10 BWCC 486), but suicide of itself is neither proof nor evidence of insanity (*Grime v Fletcher* [1915] 1 KB 734, 84 LJKB 847, 112 LT 840, 31 TLR 158, 59 Sol Jo 223, 8 BWCC 69, CA).

The onus of proof is on the applicants and they must show not only that the death is due to insanity but that the insanity is the direct result of the injury, and it is not sufficient to show that it is an indirect result, such as that it was caused by brooding over the accident or worrying over the inability to work. *Withers v London Brighton and South Coast Rly Co* [1916] 2 KB 772, 85 LJKB 1673, 115 LT 503, 32 TLR 685, 61 Sol Jo 8, 9 BWCC 616, CA.'

APPEAL ON AMOUNT: PRINCIPLES

Nance v British Columbia Electric Rly Co

[1951] AC 601, [1951] 2 All ER 448, [1951] 2 TLR 137, 95 Sol Jo 543, PC
The principles which apply are not in doubt. Whether the assessment of damages be by a judge or a jury, the appellate court is not justified in substituting a figure of its own for that award below simply because it would have awarded a different figure if it had tried the case at first instance. Even if the tribunal of first instance was a judge

sitting alone, then, before the appellate court can properly intervene, it must be satisfied either that the judge in assessing the damages, applied a wrong principle of law (as by taking into account some irrelevant factor or leaving out of account some relevant one); or, short of this that the amount awarded is either so inordinately low or so inordinately high that it must be a wholly erroneous estimate of the damage (*Flint v Lovell* approved by the House of Lords in *Davies v Powell Duffryn Associated Collieries*). The last named case further shows that when on a proper direction the quantum is ascertained by a jury, the disparity between the figure at which they have arrived and any figure at which they could properly have arrived must, to justify correction by a court of appeal, be even wider than when the figure has been assessed by a judge sitting alone. The figure must be wholly 'out of all proportion': Per Lord Wright in *Davies'* case.

Note—See Chapter 12 on damages generally.

Funeral expenses

STATUTORY PROVISION

If damages are to be awarded in respect of funeral expenses the claim must be for a reasonable sum. Section 3(3) of the Fatal Accidents Act enables a dependant to seek an award of damages in respect of funeral expenses if incurred in respect of the deceased. Section 3(5) of the Act entitles any person to recover damages in respect of funeral expenses which he has incurred even though he has no other claim under the Act, ie, even though he can prove no dependency (*Stanton v Youlden*, below), but those costs must be reasonably proportionate to the deceased's lifestyle.

Schneider v Eisovitch

[1960] 2 QB 430, [1960] 1 All ER 169
The Court of Appeal held that where services were provided to someone as a result of a tortious action, then reasonable expenses were recoverable as an item of special damage. It was irrelevant that those services were provided on a voluntary basis, if the individual to whom help was given agreed to repay those costs, if awarded. Thus the expenses incurred by the plaintiff's brother-in-law and his wife in travelling to France to collect the plaintiff after a road traffic accident were properly included by the plaintiff in her claim and were recoverable against the tort feasor.

Hart v Griffith-Jones

[1948] 2 All ER 729 (Streatfield J)
Funeral expenses of a girl aged four included embalming the body.
HELD: Not unreasonable and allowed as part of the funeral expenses.

By amendment as an afterthought, a claim for £225 was added for a monument over the grave.

Citing *Goldstein v Salvation Army Assurance Society* [1917] 2 KB 291, 86 LJKB 793, 117 LT 63 (per Rowlatt J, that a tombstone was not allowed as a funeral expense for estate duty), the allowance under the Assurance Companies Act 1909, of a stone or tablet on the grave as a reasonable and proper expense in an insurance for funeral expenses including the erection of a tombstone, and the construction of 'funeral expenses' under that Act was irrelevant. The claim for £225 was wholly unreasonable and was disallowed.

INQUEST

The costs of attending an inquest are not damages resulting from the death and were disallowed by Hilbery J in *Gryce v Tuke* at Winchester Assizes on 1 March 1940. However see *Schneider v Eisovitch*, above, for travelling expenses.

GRAVESTONE

Stanton v Ewart F Youlden Ltd

[1960] 1 All ER 429, [1960] 1 WLR 543, 104 Sol Jo 368
A claim for funeral expenses included a sum of £194 15s comprising £155 for a marble memorial erected over the grave six months after the death, synagogue fees £34 10s and £5 5s extra letters on the memorial. The claim also included £5 paid to the minister for attending the funeral, £8 for two additional limousine cars at the funeral, and £5 for removing the body to the house (£18 in all).
HELD: (1) The plaintiff was entitled as executor to recover reasonable expenditure on a gravestone for his wife's grave, and, in the circumstances, an amount of £40 would be included in the damages in respect of the stone. (2) The payments, amounting to £18 as specified would also be included as funeral expenses in the damages recoverable by the plaintiff.

Gammell v Wilson

[1982] AC 27, [1981] 1 All ER 578, [1981] 2 WLR 248, 125 Sol Jo 116, HL
The plaintiff father sought to recover the cost of a gravestone as part of his deceased son's funeral expenses. The trial judge accepted the £595 sum and the Court of Appeal refused to interfere with the award. However, comment was made that this case should be taken to distinguish between a headstone for a grave which was acceptable and a memorial which was not.

Child killed—parents claim

There is little recent authority, but as a general principle damages may be awarded where there is actual financial support being given by a child to his parents or where there is reasonable probability of future pecuniary advantage.

Taff Vale Rly Co v Jenkins

[1913] AC 1, 82 LJKB 49, 107 LT 564, 29 TLR 19, 57 Sol Jo 27, HL
It is not a condition precedent to the maintenance of an action under the Fatal Accidents Act 1846, that the deceased should have been actually earning money or money's worth or contributing to the support of plaintiff at or before the date of the death, provided that plaintiff had a reasonable expectation of pecuniary benefit from the continuance of the life. An action was brought by a father under the Fatal Accidents Act 1846, for damages for the loss of a daughter, aged 16, who was killed by the negligence of defendants and it was proved that at the date of her death the deceased, who lived with her parents, was nearing the completion of her apprenticeship as a dressmaker and was likely in the near future to earn a remuneration which might quickly have become substantial.
HELD: There was evidence of damage upon which the jury could reasonably act.

Wathen v Vernon

[1970] RTR 471, CA
The plaintiff's son aged 17 was killed by negligence of the defendant. He was an apprentice at an engineering works who was paying for his upkeep only £3 pw to his parents out of a wage of £6 10s but who would have probably earned upwards of £19 pw at 21 and £26 per week at 25. The plaintiff, his father, was aged 56: he had suffered a stroke some years earlier and though he had returned to work there was a possibility of a recurrence which would disable him. He had a wife and three other children, two of them grown up. He claimed damages under the Fatal Accidents and Law Reform Acts. The judge, though accepting that the dead boy was a good son who would have helped his parents if there was a recurrence of the plaintiff's illness, held that the deceased would probably have married within about five years and that the possibility of the plaintiff's illness recurring within that time was not sufficiently high to justify an award under the Fatal Accidents Acts.
HELD, on the plaintiff's appeal: *Taff Vale Rly Co v Jenkins* (above) and *Buckland v Guildford Gas Light & Coke Co* (below) were authorities for saying that the court was entitled in proper circumstances to give damages for loss of support where no support had ever been given. Though the chances against the recurrence of the plaintiff's illness within five years were six to one it was right to make some award to cover the possibility. The award under the Fatal Accidents Act should be one of £500 for the deceased's mother, not the plaintiff.

Per Widgery LJ: If we had to decide it on the assumption that the father's health was normal . . . I would not be able to assent that a case had been made out.

Buckland v Guildford Gas Light and Coke Co

[1949] 1 KB 410, [1948] 2 All ER 1086, 93 Sol Jo 41 (Morris J)
Deceased was a bright intelligent girl aged 13 who was competent to look after a younger child aged eight. She assisted her parents in the home and it was anticipated that her gifts would later have enabled her to contribute financially as well as by services to the household, subject to the changes and chances that might have affected her and her parents.
Award: FAA £500.

Barnett v Cohen

[1921] 2 KB 461, 90 LJKB 1307, 125 LT 733, 37 TLR 629 (McCardie J)
In an action under the Fatal Accidents Act 1846, it is not sufficient for plaintiff to prove that he has lost by the death of deceased a mere speculative possibility of pecuniary benefit. In order to succeed it is necessary for him to show that he has lost a reasonable probability of pecuniary advantage.

The deceased child was four years of age. The boy was subject to all the risks of illness, disease, accident and death. His education and upkeep would have been a substantial burden to the plaintiff for many years if he had lived. He might or might not have turned out a useful young man. He would not have earned anything till about 16 years of age. He might never have aided his father at all. He might have proved a mere expense. I cannot adequately speculate one way or the other in any event. He would scarcely have been expected to contribute to his father's income, for the plaintiff even now possesses £1,000 a year by his business and may increase it further, nor could the son have been expected to do any domestic service. The whole matter is beset with doubts, contingencies and uncertainties.

HELD: Upon the facts the plaintiff had not proved damage either actual or prospective. His claim was pressed to extinction by the weight of multiplied contingencies. The action therefore failed.

Croke v Wiseman

[1981] 3 All ER 852, [1982] 1 WLR 71, CA
A 21 month old boy suffered irreparable brain damage as a result of the defendant's negligence following admission to hospital in consequence of an illness. He subsequently required full-time care which was provided at home by his mother who left her teaching career to do so. The trial judge awarded the plaintiff damages for the cost of future care (both professional and parental) and in addition a sum to reflect the loss of his future earnings.

The Court of Appeal reduced the sum awarded for future loss of earnings though they accepted in principle that the judge was entitled to make an award in respect of this loss. By a majority (Denning MR dissenting) they did not consider it relevant that the plaintiff may never personally benefit from those damages, nor did they believe the award to be speculative or incapable of assessment. However, care needed to be taken to ensure that the plaintiff was not doubly compensated; if the total award of damages included the full costs of residential care for his life expectancy, then future loss of earnings would be small as the majority of his needs would have already been met.

The additional allowance of £7,000 to reflect the loss of his mother's pension rights was appropriate as part of the cost of future parental nursing care, even though the mother was not entitled to recover the sum herself.

Dolbey v Goodwin

[1955] 2 All ER 166, [1955] 1 WLR 553, 99 Sol Jo 335, CA
It has been established in *Flint v Lovell* (p 449, above) and other cases that where a judge has not given precise reasons or one cannot see from his judgment exactly what he took into account; whether he took into account something he ought not or omitted something he should, the Court of Appeal can only look at the total amount and consider whether it is excessively high or unreasonably low and so amounts to an erroneous estimate.

Parents killed—child's claim

APPORTIONMENT BETWEEN WIDOW AND CHILD

Kassam v Kampala Aerated Water Co Ltd

[1965] 2 All ER 875, [1965] 1 WLR 668, 109 Sol Jo 291, PC
In an action in Uganda for Fatal Accidents Acts damages the claimants were eight children, aged 3 to 23, of the deceased, a shopkeeper aged about 45. Their mother was also killed in the accident. The judge of first instance awarded £6,000 but did not apportion the sum among the claimants. The Court of Appeal for Eastern Africa reduced the award to £1,795, holding that only four of the children were dependent. The deceased's total annual expenditure on the family had been £572; the Court took four-ninths of this (for the four children) and multiplied by $11^1/_4$ representing the average dependency in years of these four. The Court made deductions to allow for

the advantage of having a capital sum and for the estimated value of the acceleration of the children's interests in their father's estate.

The Privy Council considered the award too low. 'Pure arithmetic does not always . . . lead to a just result where there are so many imponderables. The aim in assessing damages in a case such as the present is to estimate the loss of reasonable expectation of pecuniary benefit. This must in most cases be a matter of speculation and may be conjecture. The more usual method of assessing damages is that adopted by the trial judge of estimating the total dependency as a lump sum and thereafter apportioning it among the various dependants. Another method may be to assess each dependency separately . . . But if the method of assessing the support for each dependant separately leads to a result which is so out of line with what would be a reasonable estimate of the loss of each individual dependant this suggests that some stop in the calculation must be erroneous.' On the evidence there were eight dependants, not four. But the original award of £6,000 was too high because the judge had taken 15 years as the period of dependency, ignoring the fact that not all the children would have been dependant so long. A figure of £3,500 would fairly represent the total loss of dependency among the eight dependants.

Dodds v Dodds

[1978] QB 543, [1978] 2 All ER 539, [1978] 2 WLR 434, 121 Sol Jo 619 (Balcombe J)
The defendant was driving a car with her husband as a passenger when there was an accident in which he was killed and for which she was wholly to blame. It was conceded that she could make no claim for herself under the Fatal Accidents Act; the only other dependant was her son, aged eight and a half. The deceased, aged 29 at death and earning £3,000 a year, could reasonably have expected rapid promotion and increases in his earnings had he lived and might by the date of trial have had take-home pay of £4,720 a year. The defendant had trained as a typist after her husband's death and her take-home pay at the time of the trial was £2,080.
HELD: (1) The way to assess the child's loss was to divide up the family expenditure into four columns—items benefiting the father exclusively, items benefiting the mother exclusively, items which benefited the child exclusively and finally those which benefited the whole family (ie rent or mortgage instalments, rates, repairs and decoration of the family house, heating and lighting, telephone, TV, garden, house insurance etc). The sum of columns three and four was the child's dependency. (2) As at the date of trial the child's estimated dependency was £2,750 a year and the combined family income would have been £6,800 a year. Of this the father's contribution would have been £4,720 so that the child's loss of the benefit of his father's income was £1,908 a year. (3) The multiplier should not be reduced by the number of years which had elapsed from death to trial—the judgment in *Cookson v Knowles* (p 463, above) must be taken to have been given *per incuriam* on this point—and the multiplier at the date of trial, the child being then 12½, was 5. (4) The pecuniary loss from the death to trial, calculated at £7,628, should be added. Total award under Fatal Accidents Act £17,168.

Eifert v Holt's Transport Co Ltd

[1951] 2 All ER 655, 95 Sol Jo 561, CA
Electrical engineer aged 28 earning £659 per annum with excellent prospects; widow aged 23; child aged one year, award £6,400, Fatal Accidents Acts, plus £350 Law Reform; total £6,750.

After hearing counsel for the widow, Barry J apportioned £2,000 to the widow and £4,400 to the child. Defendants appealed and contended the award to the child was excessive and therefore the amount of the total award should be reduced.
HELD: If the total was proper, the defendants were not concerned with the apportionment between widow and child.

Damages for loss of services/wife

Damages are recoverable by a husband who loses the benefit of his wife's services as a mother. The extent of the loss will be variable but comparison may be drawn with the cost of employing a housekeeper or a nanny to care for the children. Having assessed the plaintiff's loss, the judge should then stand back and consider the overall reasonableness of the sums to be awarded, as would a jury, and if appropriate increase or decrease the award. The fact that the husband may have re-married or relatives may have assumed care of the children are benefits within the meaning of s 4 of the Fatal Accidents Act 1976 and must be ignored when calculating the loss, and therefore the damages recoverable by the child.

WIFE

Berry v Humm & Co

[1915] 1 KB 627, 84 LJKB 918, 31 TLR 198
Plaintiff, a workman earning 38s a week, sued defendants to recover damages for the death of his wife, who was knocked down by a motor taxi-cab belonging to defendants and instantly killed. The wife had performed the ordinary household duties of a woman in her position, and in consequence of her death plaintiff had to employ a housekeeper and to incur extra expenses of management by the housekeeper instead of his deceased wife. The jury assessed plaintiff's damages at £50.
HELD: Under Lord Campbell's Act 1846, the damages recoverable in such an action are not limited to the value of money loss, or the money value of things lost, but include the monetary loss incurred by replacing services rendered gratuitously by the deceased where there was a reasonable prospect of their being rendered freely in the future but for the death, and, therefore, plaintiff was entitled to recover the damages assessed by the jury.

Morris v H Rigby (Road Haulage) Ltd

(1966) 110 Sol Jo 834, CA
The husband, a medical officer earning £2,820 a year, claimed damages under the Fatal Accidents Act for the death of his wife. He had five children aged two to fifteen years. He got his wife's sister to come to take care of them and do the domestic duties his wife had done, paying her a gross wage of £20 per week. The judge awarded £8,000.
HELD, ON APPEAL: The award was not too high. The plaintiff was entitled to the reasonable cost of replacing his wife's services — *Berry v Humm* (above). He had acted reasonably in employing his wife's sister at £20 per week.

Burgess v Florence Nightingale Hospital for Gentlewomen

[1955] 1 QB 349, [1955] 1 All ER 511, [1955] 2 WLR 533, 99 Sol Jo 170 (Devlin J)
The deceased became a dancing partner of the plaintiff for amateur purposes in 1942. In July 1948, they started dancing professionally. In 1951 she was divorced by her husband. In September 1952, she married the plaintiff. After the beginning of 1953 they were nearing the peak of professional status. In January 1953, she entered the defendant's hospital and her death resulted from negligent treatment.

The gross income of the plaintiff, who was 38 years of age, was between £1,000 and £1,250 with prospects of increase by £400 or £500. The deceased was 36. The plaintiff was unable to obtain a suitable dancing partner and his estimated income was reduced to £600 per annum. The parties had lived in a flat and the deceased had performed the household duties. After her death the plaintiff had to employ a woman at 25s per week and to have his meals outside. The deceased had contributed towards the household expenses. The rent was £9 13s monthly and there were expenses for gas and electricity. She had also contributed to the school fees of the child of her previous marriage and had spent money on her clothes. The school fees had been reduced by half and the plaintiff paid them. The wife had paid at least £1 weekly to her widowed mother who was 66 years of age.

The joint ability to earn an income greatly exceeded the ability of either of them individually. The joint earnings were shared and so were the living expenses. The loss to the plaintiff of his wife as a dancing partner was assessed at £2,500. The other assessments were £1,000 for the loss as wife (services); £1,000 for loss of wife's contribution; £350 for loss by child of wife's payment and prospective assistance; £300 for loss of wife's payment to her mother.
HELD: As to loss of £2,500 as a dancing partner, it is necessary to read some limitations into the rather wide and general wording of the 1846 Act. The loss would fall within the mere wording but the decisions showed that if, eg a servant lost his employment by the death of his employer or of a departmental manager; or a junior partner lost business by the death of a senior partner; there would be no claim under the Act. It makes no difference that the junior partner was a son. The loss would be *qua* junior partner, not *qua* son. The benefit here was as partner and not as wife. The relationship was superimposed on the partnership. The £2,500 was therefore not recoverable.

Contributions to household expenses: contributions 50 or 100 years ago, where the husband paid all the joint living expenses, and money earnings of the wife were a kind of pin money, do not apply to modern life. The parties were earning equally and contributing equally. No case of mutual dependence of that sort has been cited but there was no difficulty in principle. Where the living expenses are less than twice the expense of each living separately, the benefit which each confers on the other comes within the Act.

Hurt v Murphy

[1971] RTR 186 (Talbot J)
The plaintiff was aged 45, his wife 42. On her death he was left with five children aged from 22 to nine. She had fulfilled all the normal tasks of housewife and mother and also earned £3 pw in part-time work. The plaintiff's house was a council house with only two bedrooms. He had insufficient money to buy a house.
HELD: It would not be proper that the defendant should have to pay for a house big enough to enable the plaintiff to employ a resident housekeeper. Damages should be based on the cost of a daily help. The hours of domestic help needed would reduce as the children grew older. On a multiplier of nine, award £4,118.

MOTHER

Jeffery v Smith

(1970) 114 Sol Jo 268, [1970] RTR 279, CA
The plaintiff's wife was killed in a motor accident caused by the negligence of the defendant. There were three children aged, at the time of the trial, nine, six and three. The plaintiff was 51. His mother-in-law had looked after the children since the wife's death but her bad health prevented her from continuing to do so. The plaintiff called evidence from an employment agency that a housekeeper to look after the children would cost at least £10 per week. The judge took a multiplier of 10 years and awarded £5,200.
HELD, ON APPEAL: The award should stand. There was no evidence.

Regan v Williamson

[1976] 2 All ER 241, [1976] 1 WLR 305, 120 Sol Jo 217 (Watkins J)
At the time of her death the plaintiff's wife was 37 years of age. There were four children of the marriage, all boys, aged 13, 10, 7 and 2. The plaintiff had, after her death, engaged a relative to come in daily, except weekends, to provide meals and look after the boys when he was out at work; he paid her £16 per week and it cost him a further £6.50 per week for her food, journeys to and from home and national insurance stamp. The plaintiff estimated that his wife had cost him £10 per week to clothe and feed.
HELD: Precedent would suggest that the overall figure of dependency for calculation of the plaintiff's damages under the Fatal Accidents Act was £22.50 less £10 per week but this would work an injustice. In valuing the loss of the services of a wife and mother the word 'services' in earlier cases had been too narrowly construed. It should include an acknowledgment that she does not work to set hours nor to rule. She may well during those hours give the children instruction on essential matters or on such things as homework. The figure for dependency should be raised from £12.50 to £20 per week and a further £1.50 per week added for her financial contribution to the home had she eventually gone out to work again. The multiplier should be 11 years.

Bailey v Barking and Havering Area Health Authority

[1979] LS Gaz R 793 (Pain J)
The plaintiff claimed damages under the Fatal Accidents Acts for the death of his wife. Before her death he was employed as a hospital porter but after her death he gave up work and stayed at home to look after his three daughters. He claimed that damages should be assessed on the basis that he had lost a housekeeper; the wages of a housekeeper were more than the wages of a hospital porter.
HELD: Approaching the matter as a juryman would, it was repugnant that a plaintiff should make a profit out of the situation. Commonsense indicated that a husband should be compensated for his actual loss. That was the measure of the damages.

Mehmet v Perry

[1977] 2 All ER 529, QBD
The plaintiff's wife was killed in September 1973 by the negligence of the defendants. There were five children of the marriage aged, at her death, 14, 11, 7, 6 and 3. The two youngest suffered from a serious hereditary blood disease requiring regular medication and frequent visits to hospital. Because of this the plaintiff gave up work

after his wife's death and devoted himself full time to the care of the family. Between September 1973 and trial in October 1976 his net average loss of earnings was £1,500 a year. His future net loss would be at the rate of £2,000 a year. By the date of trial he had received a total of £4,197 supplementary benefit.
HELD: (1) In the particular circumstances, including the illness of the youngest children it was reasonable for the plaintiff to have given up work rather than employ a housekeeper and the proper measure of the loss of the general housekeeping services which his wife had undertaken was his net loss of earnings; (2) for loss of the personal attention of their mother the children were entitled to an additional award (following *Regan v Williamson*, above) but within modest limits because their father was acting as a full-time housekeeper; (3) the plaintiff was entitled to damages for the loss of his wife's services to himself but the sum should be quite small because he was now rendering services to the family unit as a whole as full-time housekeeper and damages were being assessed under (1) by reference to those services; (4) the amount received in supplementary benefit should be deducted from the total. Award for loss of housekeeping services £1,500 x 3 years plus £2,000 x 5 years. £1,500 for children for loss of their mother's care and attention; £3,000 for plaintiff's loss of his wife's care and attention divided as to £1,000 for the first 8 years and £2,000 thereafter. After deduction of supplementary benefit, total award £14,800.

Spittle v Bunney

[1988] 3 All ER 1031, [1988] 1 WLR 847, [1988] Fam Law 433
At the time of her mother's death Kate Hall was aged 3. Kate was also injured in the same accident and proceedings were brought by her maternal aunt for the benefit of the estate and for Kate herself. The natural father was not a beneficiary of the estate and indeed had left the child to the care of the aunt almost immediately following the death of her mother with whom he had lived prior to the accident. The judge awarded damages for personal injury and for loss of the mother's services. He reduced the award of interest on those damages owing to the unjustifiable delay in prosecuting the action. The defendant appealed on quantum.
HELD, ON APPEAL: (1) It was agreed that an acceptable approach to quantification of the loss suffered by a minor as a result of the mother's death was to look at the costs of hiring a notional nanny. Ultimately the test was a jury one and the judge should stand back and look at the matter as would a jury. In this case the jury would have realised that the child's dependency on a nanny decreased with age and would therefore have reduced the multiplicand in the later years so as to arrive at a lower overall figure; (2) the guidelines on rates of interest were well established by the courts and these should be departed from only where there were special reasons particular to the case. In this instance there was nothing to prevent deduction of interest at the full short-term investment rate rather than at a lesser rate where the plaintiff's advisers had been guilty of an unjustifiable delay in prosecuting the action.

Cresswell v Eaton

[1991] 1 All ER 484, [1991] 1 WLR 1113
The three children of the deceased were initially cared for by their grandmother and on her death, by their aunt. The aunt left full time employment to care for the children (and her own two) and she sought to recover her lost earnings. Simon Brown J awarded her that loss on the basis that it had been entirely reasonable for her to leave employment, though discounted it by 15% to reflect the fact that the natural mother had been in part-time employment at the date of her death and therefore had provided

part-time care. The discount also reflected the diminishing needs of the children with age and the loss of the special qualitative factor of maternal care (see *Regan v Williamson* [1976] 2 All ER 241).

Note—The position would be somewhat different if the carer had not lost any income, in which event the notional nanny/housekeeper approach would probably have been followed.

Stanley v Saddique

[1992] QB 1, [1991] 1 All ER 529
The infant plaintiff was brought up by his father and the woman his father married following the death of his natural mother in a road traffic accident when he was aged one. The child enjoyed a stable family life, probably rather more so than had his mother lived. The judge awarded damages having heard evidence about the cost of professional care assistance, though he reduced the overall sum to reflect the decreasing reliance of the child on help and having found that the mother was likely to have returned to part-time employment in any event.

The defendant appealed: (1) on the basis that the court was entitled to take into account the care and support provided by the stepmother which was not a benefit to be disregarded by virtue of s 4 of the Fatal Accidents Act 1976; (2) that in any event the mother was unreliable, the court having heard that she left her first three children to live with the plaintiff's father and that even if she had lived she may not have provided services to the child to the age of 18.
HELD, ON APPEAL: The Court of Appeal accepted the defendant's second contention and using the jury approach it took into account the natural mother's limitations and reduced the award accordingly. However, it was not attracted by the first argument for s 4 was drafted widely enough to require the court to disregard any benefit which may have accrued to the child from the deceased's estate 'or otherwise as a result of the death', both of a pecuniary and non-pecuniary nature.

Spiers v Halliday

(1984) Times, 30 June, QBD
The decision in *Wright v British Railways Board* (p 445, above) has not qualified *Cookson v Knowles* (p 463, above): the court was not to take prevailing interest rates or inflation into account when assessing the appropriate multiplier.

On a preliminary point, held, that the court would not look at 'Actuarial Tables for use in personal injury and fatal accident cases' published by HMSO unless evidence were adduced as to the correctness of the contents.

Corbett v Barking, Havering and Brentwood Health Authority

[1991] 2 QB 408, [1991] 1 All ER 498
The mother of an infant plaintiff died two weeks after giving birth as a result of the negligence of the defendant. The trial of the action took place 11½ years after her death. There was no dispute on liability and the hearing was for the assessment of damages. The court was asked to consider the appropriate multiplier, the multiplicand and to assess interest.
HELD, ON APPEAL: The court would not interfere with the judge's calculation of the multiplicand which had been based on the adjusted net cost of a nanny (following *Spittle v Bunney,* above). Although the starting point was to take the wages of a notional nanny, the assessment of the loss was effectively a jury question and the judge was entitled to stand back and assess the appropriateness of the figures.

By a majority the court held that although the judge was right to calculate the multiplier from the date of the mother's death, he should have adjusted the unexpired portion to take into account that the infant plaintiff may have gone on to tertiary education and to reflect the fact that the delay in bringing the action to trial had resulted in a multiplier of only six month's future loss even though the child was now only aged 11½.

The judge was entitled to reduce the amount of interest recovered to reflect the delays of prosecuting the action.

Butler v Amalgamated Removers and Transport Ltd

(1964) 108 Sol Jo 562, CA
In an action brought by a widow, aged 35, with six children dependency was agreed by counsel at £950 per year. The judge awarded £10,500. On appeal it was argued for the widow that the judge had applied too small a multiplier since £10,500, using both capital and interest, would provide £950 for only 16 years.
HELD: The sum awarded was not erroneous. The judge had taken into account the ages of the parties, the fact that the widow was receiving a capital sum now, all future contingencies and the widow's prospects of remarriage. Counsel had taken a more rigid view of the agreement on dependency and produced tables of interest and of expectation of life. Tables of that sort could not be produced to the court without some technical evidence to support them. This could lead to complications which would greatly lengthen the hearing of fatal accidents cases. It was undesirable to bring in a rigidity which would have the effect of guaranteeing the widow and children the sum of £950 a year over a long period.

Note—Prospects of re-marriage are not now to be taken into account. See p 488, below and Fatal Accidents Act 1976, s 3(3).

Hayden v Hayden

[1992] 4 All ER 681, [1992] 1 WLR 986, [1993] 2 FLR 16
Danielle Hayden's mother was killed in a road traffic accident caused as a result of her father's negligent driving. Danielle, suing by her maternal grandmother, recovered damages for the loss of her mother's services, despite the fact that they were largely replaced by her father, the tortfeasor. The judge awarded £20,000 under s 3(1) of the Fatal Accidents Act 1976. The father appealed and his daughter cross-appealed.
HELD: The services provided by the father were not benefits within s 4, for they did not accrue as a result of the mother's death (the father simply continuing to discharge his parental responsibilities) and the daughter's cross appeal would be dismissed. The child was entitled to be compensated for the loss she had suffered by the deprivation of her mother's services, at least to the extent to which they had not been replaced by the father. The judge's award was not unreasonable and the Court of Appeal would not interfere.

Per Sir David Croom-Johnson: valuing a minor's loss by reference to the cost of employing a notional nanny was inappropriate where it was evident from the facts that a nanny would not have been employed and as quantification of damages was ultimately a jury question, where a tortfeasor had made good the plaintiff's loss, he did not need special protection.

Hay v Hughes

[1975] QB 790, [1975] 1 All ER 257, [1975] 2 WLR 34, 118 Sol Jo 883, [1975] 1 Lloyd's Rep 12, CA
Mr and Mrs Hay, aged 29 and 24, were killed in a road accident. Their children, aged four and a half and two and a half, were then taken by their maternal grandmother, Mrs Toone, into her own home and cared for by her. She did so without thought of being paid and intended to continue to bring them up. Mr Hay was a welder at the time of his death who would, at the date of trial, have been earning £40 per week. Mrs Hay did not work. In assessing damages for the children under the Fatal Accidents Acts the judge adopted a figure of £1,000 per annum as the amount by which they were worse off by the loss of their father and £1,000 per annum by the loss of their mother. The latter figure was based on the assumed cost of providing the housekeeper or nanny. He took a multipler of 8 and, after deducting £2,500 representing the value of the parents' estates, awarded £16,400 damages. On appeal it was argued for the defendant (1) the replacement of the deceased's mother's services not having taken place no award for the pecuniary loss of those services should be made; (2) the services rendered by Mrs Toone in looking after the children for nothing were 'benefits resulting from the death' and should be taken into account.
HELD: The award was right. On (1) the fact that a widower decided to manage for himself after the death of his wife would not disentitle him to sue for and recover damages for the pecuniary loss he had nevertheless sustained. Similarly the fact that the orphaned children had not incurred the expense of a housekeeper did not destroy or diminish their right to be compensated. On (2) it is not possible to discover from the decided cases any established principle to determine whether the benefits conferred by Mrs Toone on the children should be taken into account or not. It was a jury question to which the judge addressed himself and decided in a way which seemed fair, namely, that Mrs Toone's care conferred no benefit which should be taken into account. The principle that the assessed loss of a plaintiff should be reduced by any pecuniary advantage coming to him by reason of the death has been so seriously eroded by legislation that in the light of history the court should hesitate to extend the principle to classes of benefit not directly covered by binding authority.

PERMISSIBLE DEDUCTIONS

Benefits to be disregarded (s 4)

Both pecuniary and non-pecuniary benefits are to be ignored when assessing the level of dependency.

Pidduck v Eastern Scottish Omnibuses Ltd

[1989] 2 All ER 261, [1989] 1 WLR 317, 132 Sol Jo 1593
Upon the death of her husband, two years after retiring from the bank, the plaintiff received a widow's allowance and a lump sum (payable in the event of death within five years of retiring). The defendant argued at trial that these sums should be deducted from her dependency claim as they were simply extensions of the pension paid to the deceased prior to his death. The plaintiff contended that they were 'benefits' and were to be ignored in assessing a loss by virtue of s 4 of the Fatal Accidents Act.

HELD: The allowances and the lump sum were benefits and were therefore to be ignored in any calculation of her dependency claim by virtue of s 4, even though this in effect meant that the plaintiff enjoyed the widow's allowance.

Note—See *Stanley v Saddique* [1992] QB 1, [1991] 1 All ER 529, above.

Wood v Bentall Simplex Ltd

[1992] PIQR P332, CA
Section 4 of the Fatal Accidents Act 1976 (as amended by the Administration of Justice Act 1982) prevented the court from taking into account any benefits accruing to the plaintiffs from the estate irrespective of the source of those benefits. Even if the loss could be compensated for by using another part of the deceased's estate, this was to be ignored. Therefore the deceased's share of the assets of a farming partnership which passed to the widow and the parties children were to be ignored when assessing the loss to the dependants.

RE-MARRIAGE OF WIDOW

The effect of a widow's re-marriage is to be ignored by virtue of s 3(3) of the Fatal Accidents Act 1976.

EFFECT ON CHILDREN'S DAMAGES

Allowance can be made for the financial support offered by the second husband depending upon the particular situation and the duty moral or otherwise to support the child.

Mead v Clarke Chapman & Co Ltd

[1956] 1 All ER 44, [1956] 1 WLR 76, 100 Sol Jo 51, CA
A welder aged 23, earning £8 10s per week was killed on 15 January 1951, leaving a widow aged 19 and a daughter aged four months. On 27 September 1951, the widow re-married a lorry driver earning at the date of trial, 29 June 1955 (four and a half years after the death) the same figure of £8 10s per week. The deceased gave his wife £6 10s per week. It was accepted that the earnings of the second husband were the same as the first husband. A male child was born of the second marriage and the two children were growing up together. The second husband was very fond of his step-daughter and looked after her nicely.

Donovan J assessed the loss of the family at £5 per week and awarded £180 being £5 per week for the 36 weeks between death and re-marriage, as damages under the Fatal Accidents Acts, apportioned £36 to the infant and £144 to the widow, and held there was no financial loss after the remarriage. The plaintiff appealed in respect of the damages awarded to the child.
HELD, ON APPEAL: It should not be assumed that the position will remain the same for all time. The onus is on the defendants to prove that in all reasonable probability the child cannot suffer any pecuniary loss in the future; that she is provided for during the rest of the time for which she might have been dependent on her father. There might be a large family in years to come. The stepfather might be pressed for money. He might not be able to look after the child as well as her own father would have done.

A father can be forced to support his child if he fails to do so, while the stepfather cannot (National Assistance Act 1948, s 42(1)). The father might be willing to assist his own child in education or other ways, which a stepfather might not. The child's claim should be allowed at £200. Appeal allowed accordingly.

Reincke v Gray

[1964] 2 All ER 687, [1964] 1 WLR 832, 108 Sol Jo 461, CA
The plaintiff claimed damages under the Fatal Accidents Acts on behalf of her two children, a boy aged three and a girl aged one, for the death of her husband. He had been in good employment at the time of his death earning £1,800 a year with good prospects. Nine months after his death the plaintiff remarried. Her second husband was a chartered accountant earning £2,500 a year. He had accepted the two children into the family and had agreed to send the boy to public school as his father had intended. On an assessment of damages the master, having regard to *Mead v Chapman Clarke & Co Ltd* (above), awarded £2,000 to the boy and £1,750 to the girl. HELD, ON APPEAL: The awards were excessive. The circumstances in this case were different from those in *Mead*'s case, where the widow of a welder married a lorry driver: in that standard of life the fact that there was only a moral and not a legal duty on her second husband to support the children was not immaterial. Moreover the provisions of the Matrimonial Proceedings (Children) Act 1958, s 1(1) now enabled the High Court to impose a legal obligation to provide for the custody, maintenance and education of the children of one party to the marriage who have been accepted into the family by the other party as if they were the children of both parties. Looking at the evidence and considering the probabilities of the future as to financial loss the court had to consider at what figure the chance of loss should be assessed. The figure of £500 for each child should be substituted for the master's awards.

Thompson v Price

[1973] QB 838, [1973] 2 All ER 846, [1973] 2 WLR 1037, 117 Sol Jo 468 (Boreham J)
As s 4(1) applies to damages 'payable to a widow' the proportion of damages allotted to a child is to be assessed, where the widow had remarried, having regard to that fact.

Deceased 24 years old at death, widow 22, child 18 months. Widow remarried two or three months later, the second husband being in as good a financial position as the deceased would have been. Dependency of widow £9 per week, multiplier 17 years having regard to ages of deceased and widow. Child entitled to two years three months at £3 per week (£337.50) rounded up to £500 to allow for his receiving perhaps less from stepfather than he would from his own and having to compete with children of second marriage.

DAMAGES FOR REDUCED MARRIAGE PROSPECTS

For cases where an injured unmarried female plaintiff has sustained a diminution in marriage prospects see the following cases.

Moriarty v McCarthy

[1978] 2 All ER 213, [1978] 1 WLR 155, 121 Sol Jo 745 (O'Connor J)
In October 1973 the plaintiff sustained spinal injuries which resulted in complete loss of the power to move or feel from the waist down, with no control of bladder and

bowel and no sexual sensation; she would be confined to a wheelchair for the rest of her life. She was then 20 years of age, 24 at the date of assessment for damages, living with her mother and sisters in the Republic of Ireland. Despite some training for sedentary work she had not shown herself capable of any gainful employment.
HELD: Her damages should be assessed under the following heads: (1) Future loss of earnings at a net figure of £1,820 per annum, applying a multiplier of 11 years = £20,000. The multiplier of 11 was taken instead of the 15 years' purchase which would be applicable in the case of a man of the same age so as to allow for the likelihood that the plaintiff would have married and ceased work at least for a number of years. (2) General damages £27,500 plus £7,500 to compensate her for the lost opportunity of marriage and the support of the husband = £35,000. (3) Resident domestic help from someone who would live in, a service that would probably be done many years by her mother, £1,000 per annum at 15 years' purchase = £15,000. (4) The cost of converting or adapting (not buying) an existing house in Ireland, say £8,000. (5) The cost of adapting a suitable car, but not buying one, £70. (6) The cost of future medical expenses in Ireland, £2,500. (7) Telephone on a 15-year multiplier, £820. (8) Agreed special damage, £9,896. The sum of £511 per annum which she was receiving from the Irish State should not be deducted: it was completely non-contributory and a wrongdoer should not have the benefit of it.

Hughes v McKeown

[1985] 3 All ER 284, 1 WLR 963 (Leonard J)
At four and a half years of age in 1973 the plaintiff was struck by the defendant's car and badly injured. Both her prospects of marriage and future earnings were diminished. The case came to trial in December 1984.
HELD: In *Moriarty*'s case (above) O'Connor J applying the decision in *Harris v Harris* (p 374, above) had reduced the multiplier in respect of future earnings but had added a sum equal to that by which the future earnings award had been reduced to compensate for lost marriage prospects. In *Carrick v Camden London Borough Council* (25 July 1979, unreported) he had adopted an approach from *Martin v Scott* (unreported) which was to consider the plaintiff's economic loss. The simplest method of assessing such loss was to use the multiplier applicable to a man and disregard the intervention of marriage altogether. The plaintiff's net annual loss of earnings was £2,812 and the appropriate multiplier, disregarding the possibility of the plaintiff marrying and having children was 17. This figure should be reduced to 14 to take into account the difficulty she would have in the current economic climate in getting employment.

PAYMENTS INTO COURT

It was formerly necessary for a defendant to apportion a payment into court between damages payable under the Fatal Accidents Act and the Law Reform Act (at least without leave of the court) but since 1 January 1964 this has no longer been necessary (RSC Ord 22, r 1(5) and (6)).

PAYMENTS OUT OF COURT

RSC Ord 22, r 4 is as follows:

'(1) Where a plaintiff accepts any sum paid into court and that sum was paid into court in satisfaction either of causes of action arising under the Fatal Accidents Act 1976, and the Law

Reform (Miscellaneous Provisions) Act 1934, or of a cause of action arising under the first mentioned Act where more than one person is entitled to the money then the money in court shall not be paid out except under paragraph (2) or in pursuance of an order of the court, and the order shall deal with the whole costs of the action or of the cause of action to which the payment relates as the case may be.'

Order 80, r 15 provides:

'(2) Where, in an action in which a claim under the Fatal Accidents Act 1976 is made by or on behalf of more than one person, a sum in respect of damages is adjudged or ordered or agreed to be paid in satisfaction of the claim, or a sum of money paid into court under Ord 22, r 1 is accepted in satisfaction of the cause of action under the said Act, then, unless the sum has been apportioned between the persons entitled thereto by a jury, it shall be apportioned between those persons by the court.'

CONTROL OF MONEY IN COURT

Control of money recovered under the Fatal Accidents Act is exercised by the court under RSC Ord 80, r 12. The rule is as follows:

'12(1) Where in any proceedings—
(a) money is recovered by or on behalf of, or adjudged or ordered or agreed to be paid to, or for the benefit of a person under disability, or
(b) money paid into court is accepted by or on behalf of a plaintiff who is a person under disability,
the money shall be dealt with in accordance with directions given by the court, under this rule and not otherwise.

(2) Directions given under this rule may provide that the money shall, as to the whole or any part thereof, be paid into the High Court and invested or otherwise dealt with there.

(3) Without prejudice to the foregoing provisions of this rule, directions given under this rule may include any general or special directions that the court thinks fit to give and, in particular, directions as to how the money is to be applied or dealt with and as to any payment to be made, either directly or out of the amount paid into court and whether before or after the money is transferred to or paid into a county court, to the plaintiff, or to the next friend in respect of money paid or expenses incurred for or on behalf of or for the benefit of the person under disability or for his maintenance or otherwise for his benefit or to the plaintiff's solicitor in respect of costs.

(4) Where in pursuance of directions given under this rule money is paid into the High Court to be invested or otherwise dealt with there, the money (including any interest thereon) shall not be paid out, nor shall any securities in which the money is invested, or the dividends thereon, be sold, transferred or paid out of court, except in accordance with an order of the court.

(5) The foregoing provisions to this rule shall apply in relation to a counterclaim by or on behalf of a person under disability, and a claim made by or on behalf of such a person in an action by any other person for relief under section 504 of the Merchant Shipping Act (1894), as if for references to a plaintiff and a next friend there were substituted references to a defendant and to a guardian ad litem respectively.'

A widow over 18 is not a 'person under disability' and is able to enter into a valid settlement or compromise of her own claim without obtaining the approval of the court under Ord 80, r 11. The Administration of Justice Act 1965, s 19 which formerly enabled the court to control money recovered by a widow under the Fatal Accidents Acts was repealed as from 1 August 1971 by the Law Reform (Miscellaneous Provisions) Act 1971, s 5(1). 'The power of the court to control widows' damages recovered under the Fatal Accidents Act 1976 has been entirely abolished, whether or not the claim is made on behalf of an infant' (Supreme Court Practice 1993, 80/15/4, p 1366).

Jeffrey v Kent County Council

[1958] 3 All ER 155, [1958] 1 WLR 927, 102 Sol Jo 620 (Paull J)
An agreement for a lump sum requires that (1) each of the dependants who is *sui juris* approves, and (2) the court sanctions the agreement as being for the benefit of each of the dependants who are infants. A dependant who is *sui juris* is bound by the administrator's agreement, but the claim of the other dependants remains to be settled by the court, and the court does not consider the amount paid to the settling dependant unless it affects the loss of any of the other dependants. If a settlement by a widow individually is far too small a sum to provide the resources which she would otherwise have had to bring up infant children, the court may give to the infants much larger sums than if the widow had received a proper capital sum.

2 LAW REFORM ACT CLAIMS

LAW REFORM (MISCELLANEOUS PROVISIONS) ACT 1934

'1 Effect of death on certain causes of action (1) Subject to the provisions of this section, on the death of any person after the commencement of this Act all causes of action subsisting against or vested in him shall survive against, or, as the case may be, for the benefit of, his estate. Provided that this subsection shall not apply to causes of action for defamation. [*Remainder of subsection repealed by Law Reform (Miscellaneous Provisions) Act 1970.*]
(1A) The right of a person to claim under section 1A of the Fatal Accidents Act 1976 (bereavement) shall not survive for the benefit of his estate on his death. [*Added by Administration of Justice Act 1982, s 4(1).*]
(2) Where a cause of action survives as aforesaid for the benefit of the estate of a deceased person, the damages recoverable for the benefit of the estate of that person —
(a) shall not include
  (i) any exemplary damages:
  (ii) any damages for loss of income in respect of any period after that person's death; [*subsection (2)(a) substituted by Administration of Justice Act 1982, s 4(2)*]
(b) [*Repealed by Law Reform (Miscellaneous Provisions) Act 1970*];
(c) where the death of that person has been caused by the act or omission which gives rise to the cause of action, shall be calculated without reference to any loss or gain to his estate consequent on his death, except that a sum in respect of funeral expenses may be included.
[*Subsection (3), which required proceedings in tort against a deceased person's estate to be started within six months of the grant of representation, was repealed by the Proceedings Against Estates Act 1970.*]
(4) Where damage has been suffered by reason of any act or omission in respect of which a cause of action would have subsisted against any person if that person had not died before or at the same time as the damage was suffered, there shall be deemed, for the purpose of this Act, to have been subsisting against him before his death such cause of action in respect of that act or omission as would have subsisted if he had died after the damage was suffered.
(5) The rights conferred by this Act for the benefit of the estates of deceased persons shall be in addition to and not in derogation of any rights conferred on the dependants of deceased persons by the Fatal Accidents Acts 1846 to 1908, or the Carriage by Air Act 1932, and so much of this Act as relates to causes of action against the estates of deceased persons shall

apply in relation to causes of action under the said Acts as it applies in relation to other causes of action not expressly excepted from the operation of sub-s (1) of this section.
(6) In the event of insolvency of an estate against which proceedings are maintainable by virtue of this section, any liability in respect of cause of action in respect of which the proceedings are maintainable shall be deemed to be a debt provable in the administration of the estate, notwithstanding that it is in a demand in the nature of unliquidated damages arising otherwise than by a contract, promise or breach of trust.'

[References to Fatal Accidents Acts 1846 to 1908 include a reference to Fatal Accidents Act 1976 — see Sch 1, para 2.] The new s 1(2)(a)(ii) takes effect from 1 January 1983 in respect of causes of action accruing on or after that date.

It will be seen that, taken with the Administration of Justice Act 1982, s 1(1)(a) (p 421, above) these changes abolish the right of an estate, first established in *Rose v Ford* [1937] AC 826, HL to recover damages for loss of expectation of life where personal injury has resulted in death. Subsection 2(a)(ii) also renders obsolete cases such as *Kandalla v British Airways* [1980] 1 All ER 341 and *Gammell v Wilson* (p 477, above) where damages were awarded for loss of earnings during the years lost by the death.

They do not, of course, affect the right of the estate to recover damages for the injury, pain and suffering inflicted on the deceased and suffered by him between the moment of injury and death; eg the award of £2,000 in *Andrews v Freeborough* (p 412, above) or the awards of £20 and £2 in *Rose v Ford* itself.

In *Gammell v Wilson* [1982] AC 27, [1981] 1 All ER 578, [1981] 2 WLR 248, 125 Sol Jo 116, HL it was held, in the House of Lords, that s 1(2)(c) was not intended to deprive the estate of the right to recover damages in respect of losses when the right to recover damages was already vested in the deceased immediately before his death.

Husband and wife

Note—By the Law Reform (Husband and Wife) Act 1962, s 1, an action is maintainable against a spouse by the personal representatives of a deceased spouse for Law Reform damages or by a third party for a contribution.

See *Re Newsham*, p 497, below.

As a surviving spouse is often the executor or administrator of the deceased spouse it should be remembered that a person cannot be plaintiff and defendant in the same action. The Supreme Court Practice cites *Ellis v Kerr* [1910] 1 Ch 529, 79 LJ Ch 291, 102 LT 417, 54 Sol Jo 307, and *Re Phillips* [1931] WN 271, 101 LJ Ch 338, 76 Sol Jo 10. In a case in chambers the driver was killed in an accident, in which the driver's father was injured. The father took out letters of administration to the estate of his deceased son and issued a writ with himself personally as plaintiff and himself as administrator as defendant. The insurers moved to set aside the writ and the Master struck out the action. Plaintiff appealed to the Judge in chambers who upheld the Master and the plaintiff withdrew the action.

Costs—liability of personal representatives

Note—The contention has been put forward in practice that a legal personal representative who brings an unsuccessful action for Law Reform damages is not personally liable for costs but only the estate.

The position is given in *Halsbury's Laws of England* (4th edn) vol 17, para 1562 as follows:

'In ordinary cases an executor or administrator who sues as such and fails, is personally liable for the costs of the action, and unless the defendant has been guilty of some misconduct inducing the plaintiff to bring the action, the judgment against him will be that the defendant recover the costs to be levied *de bonis propriis* (from his own goods). But this will not preclude the personal representative from indemnifying himself out of the estate if he is entitled to such indemnity under the principles previously stated.'

Similarly when the representatives of a deceased plaintiff obtain an order to carry on the proceedings, they become personally liable for all the costs *ab initio* (vol 17, para 1572).

Volume 24 of the *English and Empire Digest* at p 1050, sets out the cases under the heading of 'Personal liability of representative'.

This is subject to the principle that costs are always in the discretion of the court.

PERSONS ENTITLED TO ESTATE ON INTESTACY

Note—The distribution is provided for by the Administration of Estates Act 1925, s 46 as amended by the Intestates' Estates Act 1952 and the Family Provision Act 1966, s 1 and the Family Provisions (Intestate Succession) Orders 1972, 1977, 1981 and 1987 (SIs 1972/916, 1977/415, 1981/255 and 1987/799). See *Tristan & Coote's Probate Practice* (27th edn) pp 188–190 for complete table.

One or more of the same persons is normally entitled to the Grant of Letters of Administration and in the same order.

WHERE THE DECEASED LEFT A SURVIVING SPOUSE

	Intestate leaving	*Distribution*
1	Husband or widow and issue (net estate not exceeding £75,000)	All to husband or widow
2	Husband or widow without issue (net estate not exceeding £125,000)	All to husband or widow
3	Husband or widow and issue (net estate exceeding £75,000)	Husband or widow takes (i) Personal chattels (ii) £75,000 free of costs and duty with interest until payment or appropriation at the rate of 6% (iii) Life interest in half residue with reversion to issue on statutory trusts Issue take the other half of the residue on statutory trusts
4	Husband or widow without issue (net estate exceeding £125,000)	Husband or widow takes (i) Personal chattels (ii) £125,000 free of costs and duty with interest until payment or appropriation at the rate of 6% (iii) One half of the remainder absolutely The other half of the remainder where there are parents then to the parents absolutely; where there are no parents, to the brothers and sisters of the whole blood in equal shares on statutory trusts, the issue of such as have predeceased the intestate taking per stirpes the share to which their parent would have been entitled

5.	Husband or widow without issue, parent, brother or sister of the whole blood or their issue (whatever the amount of the estate)	All to husband or widow

WHERE THE DECEASED LEFT NO SURVIVING SPOUSE

	Intestate leaving	*Distribution*
1	Issue only	On statutory trusts for issue who attain the age of 18 years or marry under that age equally (children of predeceasing children taking their parents' share, per stirpes
2	Father or mother	Father or mother
3	Father and mother	Father and mother in equal shares
4	Brothers and sisters of the whole blood, and issue of such as died in the lifetime of the intestate	On statutory trusts for brothers and sisters of the whole blood in equal shares, the issue of such who have predeceased the intestate taking their parents' share, per stirpes
5	Brothers and sisters of the half blood and issue of such as died in the lifetime of the intestate	On statutory trusts for brothers and sisters of the half blood in equal shares and issue as in 4
6	Grandparents	Grandparents in equal shares
7	Uncles and aunts of the whole blood and issue of such as died in the lifetime of the intestate	On statutory trusts for uncles and aunts of the whole blood and issue as in 4
8	Uncles and aunts of the half blood and issue of such as died in the lifetime of intestate	On statutory trusts for uncles and aunts of the half blood and issue as in 4
9	If no such person as above	The Crown, Duchy of Lancaster or Duchy of Cornwall

Illegitimate children

In the case of death on or after 1 January 1970, but before 4 April 1988, the property rights of illegitimate children and their parents are contained in the Family Law Reform Act 1969 of which s 14 sub-ss (1)–(4) are as follows:

'**14 Right of illegitimate child to succeed on intestacy of parents, and of parents to succeed on intestacy of illegitimate child** (1) Where either parent of an illegitimate child dies intestate as respects all or any of his or her real or personal property, the illegitimate child or, if he is dead, his issue, shall be entitled to take any interest therein to which he or such issue would have been entitled if he had been born legitimate.

(2) Where an illegitimate child dies intestate in respect of all or any of his real or personal property, each of his parents, if surviving, shall be entitled to take any interest therein to which that parent would have been entitled if the child had been born legitimate.

(3) In accordance with the foregoing provisions of this section, Part IV of the Administration of Estates Act 1925 (which deals with the distribution of the estate of an intestate) shall have effect as if—
(a) any reference to the issue of the intestate included a reference to any illegitimate child of his and to the issue of any such child;
(b) any reference to the child or children of the intestate included a reference to any illegitimate child or children of his; and
(c) in relation to an intestate who is an illegitimate child, any reference to the parent, parents, father or mother of the intestate were a reference to his natural parent, parents, father or mother.
(4) For the purposes of sub-s (2) of this section and of the provisions amended by sub-s 3(c) thereof, an illegitimate child shall be presumed not to have been survived by his father unless the contrary is shown.'

Protection is given to personal representatives who have the task of distributing the estate by s 17 of the 1969 Act:

'**17 Protection of trustees and personal representatives** Notwithstanding the foregoing provisions of this Part of this Act, trustees or personal representatives may convey or distribute any real or personal property to or among the persons entitled thereto without having ascertained that there is no person who is or may be entitled to any interest therein by virtue of —
(a) s 14 of this Act so far as it confers any interest on illegitimate children or their issue or on the father of an illegitimate child; or
(b) s 15 or 16 of this Act,
and shall not be liable to any such person of whose claim they have not had notice at the time of the conveyance or distribution; but nothing in this section shall prejudice the right of any such person to follow the property, or any property representing it, into the hands of any person, other than a purchaser, who may have received it.'

In the cases of death on or after 4 April 1988, s 14 of the Family Law Reform Act 1969 has been repealed by s 33(4) of and Schedule 4 to the Family Law Reform Act 1987 but not so as to affect any rights arising out of the intestacy of a person dying before that date. Now, the effect of s 18 of the Family Law Reform Act 1987 is that in determining the right of succession of an illegitimate person or through an illegitimate person illegitimacy is not to be taken into consideration.

Section 17 of the Family Law Reform Act 1969 has been repealed and s 20 of the Family Law Reform Act 1987 provides:

20 No special protection for trustees and personal representatives Section 17 of the Family Law Reform Act 1969 (which enables trustees and personal representatives to distribute property without having ascertained that no person whose parents were not married to each other at the time of his birth, or who claims through such a person, is or may be entitled to an interest in the property) shall cease to have effect.

Adopted children

Note—The status and property rights conferred by adoption are contained in the Adoption Act 1976, s 39. See p 459, above.

Where person entitled may be prejudiced

Re Newshams Estate

[1967] P 230, [1966] 3 All ER 681, [1966] 3 WLR 1207, 110 Sol Jo 621 (Karminski J)
The deceased was killed in a road accident on 25 December 1965 and his wife, who was a passenger in the car he was driving, was injured. She had a claim for damages for her injuries against her husband's estate which was entitled to an indemnity against the claim under a policy of insurance. If the widow became administratrix of the estate her claim might be void against the insurers under the terms of the policy. By virtue of the Supreme Court of Judicature (Consolidation) Act 1925, s 162 as amended by the Administration of Justice Act 1928, the Court had a discretion, where by reason of special circumstances it appeared necessary or expedient, to appoint as administrator some person other than the person by law entitled to the grant. Whilst the Court is slow to pass over the person entitled to the grant, in this case the person so entitled would be prejudiced by such grant and was consenting to being passed over. In these circumstances her stepfather, who was willing to act as administrator, would be so appointed.

Note—For the powers given to the Court by s 162 of the 1925 Act (repealed) see the Supreme Court Act 1981, s 116.

CHAPTER 15

Limitations

1 INTRODUCTION

A general rule for limitation of actions in tort and simple contract requiring such actions to be commenced within six years from the cause of action arising was established by the Statute of Limitation of 1623, which remained in force (with some accretion of exceptions and amendments) until supplanted by the Limitation Act 1939. The six-year period was maintained by s 2 of that Act. A proviso was added to that section by the Law Reform (Limitation of Actions) Act 1954 reducing the limitation period to three years in actions of negligence, nuisance and breach of duty for damages in respect of personal injuries. That Act also helpfully abolished or amended to three years a variety of special periods of limitation contained in particular statutes. The Limitation Act 1963 gave the court power to disapply the limitation period of three years so as to enable a plaintiff to pursue an action for damages for personal injury when material facts 'of a decisive character' were proved to have been outside his knowledge, in effect, when the cause of action arose. The Act also by s 4, prescribed a time limit of two years for contribution proceedings. The Limitation Act 1975 simplified the elaborate provisions of the 1963 Act for disapplying or extending the three-year period and, by ss 2A, 2B and 2C added to the 1939 Act, made rules for determining the date from which time began to run in personal injury and fatal accident cases. A further section inserted as 2D in the 1939 Act provided a new and more liberal rule by which to disapply the three-year period in certain cases. The Limitation Act 1980 (into force 1 May 1981) repeals and re-enacts with some amendments and additions, the surviving provisions of the earlier acts so far as they related to the subject matter of this book.

The Latent Damage Act 1986 (amending the Limitation Act by inserting sections 14A and 14B) added an alternative limitation period in situations where damage could not be discovered until after the ordinary limitation period had expired. These provisions are discussed in more detail below.

As some cases in this Chapter refer to provisions of the Limitation Acts before 1980 the following destination table may be useful:

Limitation Act 1963	Limitation Act 1980
s 4	s 10
Limitation Act 1939	Limitation Act 1980
s 2	s 2 Tort, s 5 Contract
s 2A	s 11, 14
s 2B	s 12, 14
s 2C	s 13
s 2D	s 33

A few cases dealing with the provisions of s 35 of the Limitation Act 1980 have been reported. What guidance has been provided by the courts can be found on pp 528–532, below. Useful general points are as follows:

1 Defendant wishing to rely on the statute of limitation must plead it (RSC Ord 18, r 8(1)).

2 'Damage only' claims have a six-year limitation period (s 2).

3 The day on which the cause of action arose is excluded from the computation of the limitation period.

4 In the case of plaintiffs under age, time does not begin to run until the 18th birthday.

5 The limitation period for trespass to persons is six years.

THE LIMITATION ACT 1980

2 Time limit for actions founded on tort An action founded on tort shall not be brought after the expiration of six years from the date on which the cause of action accrued.

5 Time limit for actions founded on simple contract An action founded on simple contract shall not be brought after the expiration of six years from the date on which the cause of action accrued.

Actions in respect of wrongs causing personal injuries or death

11 Special time limit for actions in respect of personal injuries (1) This section applies to any action for damages for negligence, nuisance or breach of duty (whether the duty exists by virtue of a contract or of provision made by or under a statute or independently of any contract or any such provision) where the damages claimed by the plaintiff for the negligence, nuisance or breach of duty consist of or include damages in respect of personal injuries to the plaintiff or any other person.

(2) None of the time limits given in the preceding provisions of this Act shall apply to an action to which this section applies.

(3) An action to which this section applies shall not be brought after the expiration of the period applicable in accordance with subsection (4) or (5) below.

(4) Except where sub-s (5) below applies, the period applicable is three years from—

(a) the date on which the cause of action accrued; or

(b) the date of knowledge (if later) of the person injured.

(5) If the person injured dies before the expiration of the period mentioned in sub-s (4) above, the period applicable as respects the cause of action surviving for the benefit of his estate by virtue of s 1 of the Law Reform (Miscellaneous Provisions) Act 1934 shall be three years from—

(a) the date of death; or

(b) the date of the personal representative's knowledge;

whichever is the later.

(6) For the purposes of this section 'personal representative' includes any person who is or has been a personal representative of the deceased, including an executor who has not proved the will (whether or not he has renounced probate) but not anyone appointed only as a special personal representative in relation to settled land; and regard shall be had to any knowledge acquired by any such person while a personal representative or previously.

(7) If there is more than one personal representative, and their dates of knowledge are different, sub-s (5)(b) above shall be read as referring to the earliest of those dates.

12 Special time limit for actions under Fatal Accidents legislation (1) An action under the Fatal Accidents Act 1976 shall not be brought if the death occurred when the person injured could no longer maintain an action and recover damages in respect of the injury (whether because of a time limit in this Act or in any other Act, or for any other reason).

Where any such action by the injured person would have been barred by the time limit in s 11 of this Act, no account shall be taken of the possibility of that time limit being overridden under s 33 of this Act.

(2) None of the time limits given in the preceding provisions of this Act shall apply to an action under the Fatal Accidents Act 1976, but no such action shall be brought after the expiration of three years from—

(a) the date of death; or

(b) the date of knowledge of the person for whose benefit the action is brought;

whichever is the later.

(3) An action under the Fatal Accidents Act 1976 shall be one to which ss 28, 33 and 35 of this Act apply, and the application to any such action of the time limit under sub-s (2) above shall be subject to s 39; but otherwise Parts II and III of this Act shall not apply to any such action.

13 Operation of time limit under s 12 in relation to different dependants (1) Where there is more than one person for whose benefit an action under the Fatal Accidents Act 1976 is brought, s 12(2)(b) of this Act shall be applied separately to each of them.
(2) Subject to sub-s (3) below, if by virtue of sub-s (1) above the action would be outside the time limit given by sub-s 12(2) as regards one or more, but not all, of the persons for whose benefit it is brought, the court shall direct that any person as regards whom the action would be outside that time limit shall be excluded from those for whom the action is brought.
(3) The court shall not give such a direction if it is shown that if the action were brought exclusively for the benefit of the person in question it would not be defeated by a defence of limitation (whether in consequence of s 28 of this Act or an agreement between the parties not to raise the defence, or otherwise).

14 Definition of date of knowledge for purposes of ss 11 and 12 (1) In s 11 of this Act references to a person's date of knowledge are references to the date on which he first had knowledge of the following facts—
(a) that the injury in question was significant; and
(b) that the injury was attributable in whole or in part to the act or omission which is alleged to constitute negligence, nuisance or breach of duty; and
(c) the identity of the defendant; and
(d) if it is alleged that the act or omission was that of a person other than the defendant, the identity of that person and the additional facts supporting the bringing of an action against the defendant;
and knowledge that any acts or omissions did or did not, as a matter of law, involve negligence, nuisance or breach of duty is irrelevant.
(2) For the purposes of this section an injury is significant if the person whose date of knowledge is in question would reasonably have considered it sufficiently serious to justify his instituting proceedings for damages against a defendant who did not dispute liability and was able to satisfy a judgment.
(3) For the purposes of this section a person's knowledge includes knowledge which he might reasonably have been expected to acquire—
(a) from facts observable or ascertainable by him; or
(b) from facts ascertainable by him with the help of medical or other appropriate expert advice which it is reasonable for him to seek;
but a person shall not be fixed under this subsection with knowledge of a fact ascertainable only with the help of expert advice so long as he has taken all reasonable steps to obtain (and, where appropriate, to act on) that advice.

14A Special time limit for negligence actions where facts relevant to cause of action are not known at date of accrual (1) This section applies to any action for damages for negligence, other than one to which section 11 of this Act applies, where the starting date for reckoning the period of limitation under subsection (4)(b) below falls after the date on which the cause of action accrued.
(2) Section 2 of this Act shall not apply to an action to which this section applies.
(3) An action to which this section applies shall not be brought after the expiration of the period applicable in accordance with subsection (4) below.
(4) That period is either—
(a) six years from the date on which the cause of action accrued; or
(b) three years from the starting date as defined by subsection (5) below, if that period expires later than the period mentioned in paragraph (a) above.
(5) For the purposes of this section, the starting date for reckoning the period of limitation under subsection (4)(b) above is the earliest date on which the plaintiff or any person in whom the cause of action was vested before him first had both the knowledge required for bringing an action for damages in respect of the relevant damage and a right to bring such an action.
(6) In subsection (5) above 'the knowledge required for bringing an action for damages in respect of the relevant damage' means knowledge both—

(a) of the material facts about the damage in respect of which damages are claimed; and
(b) of the other facts relevant to the current action mentioned in subsection (8) below.

(7) For the purposes of subsection (6)(a) above, the material facts about the damage are such as would lead a reasonable person who had suffered such damage to consider it sufficiently serious to justify his instituting proceedings for damages against a defendant who did not dispute liability and was able to satisfy a judgment.

(8) The other facts referred to in subsection (6)(b) above are—
(a) that the damage was attributable in whole or in part to the act or omission which is alleged to constitute negligence; and
(b) the identity of the defendant; and
(c) if it is alleged that the act or omission was that of a person other than the defendant, the identity of that person and the additional facts supporting the bringing of an action against the defendant.

(9) Knowledge that any acts or omissions did or did not, as a matter of law, involve negligence is irrelevant for the purposes of subsection (5) above.

(10) For the purposes of this section a person's knowledge includes knowledge which he might reasonably have been expected to acquire—
(a) from facts observable or ascertainable by him; or
(b) from facts ascertainable by him with the help of appropriate expert advice which it is reasonable for him to seek;

but a person shall not be taken by virtue of this subsection to have knowledge of a fact ascertainable only with the help of expert advice so long as he has taken all reasonable steps to obtain (and, where appropriate, to act on) that advice.

14B Overriding time limit for negligence actions not involving personal injuries (1) An action for damages for negligence, other than one to which section 11 of this Act applies, shall not be brought after the expiration of fifteen years from the date (or, if more than one, from the last of the dates) on which there occurred any act or omission—
(a) which is alleged to constitute negligence; and
(b) to which the damage in respect of which damages are claimed is alleged to be attributable (in whole or part).

(2) This section bars the right of action in a case to which subsection (1) above applies notwithstanding that—
(a) the cause of action has not yet accrued; or
(b) where section 14A of this Act applies to the action, the date which is for the purposes of that section the starting date for reckoning the period mentioned in subsection (4)(b) of that section has not yet occurred;

before the end of the period of limitation prescribed by this section.

PROCEDURE

The defence of limitation

Ronex Properties v John Laing Construction Ltd

[1983] QB 398, [1982] 3 All ER 961, [1982] 3 WLR 875, 126 Sol Jo 727, CA

A writ or third party notice cannot be struck out as disclosing no cause of action merely because the defendant has a defence under the Limitation Acts. 'Where it is thought to be clear that there is a defence under the Limitation Act, the defendant can either plead that defence and seek the trial of a preliminary issue, or, in a very clear case, seek to strike out the claim on the ground that it is frivolous, vexatious and an abuse of the process of the court. But in no circumstances can he seek to strike out on the ground that no cause of action is disclosed' (per Stephenson LJ).

Arnold v Central Electricity Generating Board

[1988] AC 228, [1987] 3 All ER 694, [1987] 3 WLR 1009, 131 Sol Jo 1487, HL
The plaintiff's husband worked for the Birmingham Corporation between April 1938 and April 1943 in a job which exposed him to asbestos dust. In October 1981 he was diagnosed as suffering from mesothelioma due to that work and he died in May 1982. The widow issued a writ in April 1984. The plaintiff relied upon s 11(4) of the Limitation Act 1980 to establish that for limitation purposes time did not begin to run until a date not earlier than October 1981 which was said to be the 'date of knowledge'. The plaintiff accepted that the cause of action arose during the period of employment and therefore the court was not asked to decide that point.
HELD: Defendants previously entitled to rely on the accrued six-year and one-year time bars under the original 1939 Act were not deprived of them by the Limitation Act 1975. The effect of this is that if the cause of action accrued at least six years prior to the 1954 Act the claim could be statute-barred under the Limitation Acts.

Harris v Newcastle Health Authority

[1989] 2 All ER 273, [1989] 1 WLR 96, 133 Sol Jo 47, CA
The plaintiff, who was born on 30 October 1959, underwent two operations on her left eye in an attempt to correct a squint. The operations in 1961 and 1965 made the condition worse. In February 1987 it was suggested to the plaintiff that she might have a claim for compensation. The plaintiff's solicitors made an application for pre-action discovery on 30 June 1987 which was refused by the district judge and on appeal to the judge. The defendant had made it quite clear that they would be relying on the limitation defence.
HELD, ON APPEAL: If it is plain beyond doubt that a defence of limitation will be raised and will succeed then this is a matter the court may take into account when exercising its discretion whether or not to order pre-action discovery. However, a court can never be so certain in most personal injury cases because of the existence of s 33 of the Limitation Act 1980. On the basis of limited information about limitation issues at such a pre-trial hearing it is difficult for the court to conclude that the proposed action was bound to fail. Therefore, in general, issues relevant to limitation should not be considered at an application for pre-trial discovery.

When to plead limitation

Ketteman v Hansel Properties Ltd

[1987] AC 189, [1988] 1 All ER 38, [1987] 2 WLR 312, HL
The plaintiffs purchased houses built by the first defendants between 1973 and 1975. The foundations were defective and cracking appeared in 1976. The plaintiffs sued the first defendants in 1980. The first defendants joined the architects as third parties, and the architects joined the local authority as fourth parties. In 1982, the plaintiffs obtained leave to join both the architects and the local authority as defendants. Neither party attempted to plead any defence of limitation until the closing stages of the trial, when the effect of a recent judgment might have made such a defence feasible.
HELD, ON APPEAL: The parties' application to amend their defences should be dismissed. Regardless of the existence of new authority, they could have pleaded a defence of limitation if they had chosen long before the hearing had reached its closing stages.

Late amendments should only be allowed if they clarified the issues, rather than giving defendants the opportunity of creating a different defence. A defence of limitation is a procedural bar: it has nothing to do with the merits of the case. In the absence of a plea of limitation the plaintiffs' claims succeeded on the merits.

Judgment or order on limitation—a final order

Dale v British Coal Corpn

[1993] 1 All ER 317, [1992] 1 WLR 964
The plaintiff successfully persuaded the Divisional Court to exercise its discretion to extend the limitation period. Notice of Appeal was then issued by the defendant on the basis that the order of the judge was a final order within the meaning of RSC Ord 59, r 1A. The plaintiff argued that this was not so and the matter went to appeal.
HELD: A judgment or order determining an issue of limitation is to be treated as a final order under RSC Ord 59, r 1A(3) and not an interlocutory order. Therefore leave to appeal was not required and the party had an automatic entitlement to appeal.

SPECIAL TIME LIMITS FOR PERSONAL INJURY ACTIONS (SS 11 AND 14)

Note—In s 38 of the Limitation Act 1980 'personal injuries' includes any disease and any impairment of a person's physical or mental condition, and 'injury' and cognate expressions shall be construed accordingly.

'Damages in respect of personal injuries'

Ackbar v CF Green & Co

[1975] QB 582, [1975] 2 All ER 65, [1975] 2 WLR 773, 119 Sol Jo 219, [1975] 1 Lloyd's Rep 673 (Croom-Johnson J)
The plaintiff instructed the defendants who were insurance brokers to obtain a policy covering the use of his motor lorry including passenger risks. The defendants omitted to ensure that the policy covered claims by passengers. The plaintiff was injured when riding as a passenger in his own lorry but was unable to recover damages from the driver because the policy did not cover him against passenger claims. More than three years but less than six years after the accident the plaintiff issued a writ against the defendants for failing to obtain passenger liability cover. They pleaded that the action was statute-barred as being one where the damages claimed 'consist of or include damages in respect of personal injuries to any person' (Limitation Act 1980, s 11(1)).
HELD: The action was not statute-barred. The question to ask was 'What is the action all about?' The answer was that it was about an alleged breach of contract by the defendants whereby the plaintiff lost the right to recover his loss either from the driver or from his own insurers. The damages for personal injuries which he might have recovered were only the measure of the damages now claimed. The limitation period was thus six years not three.

Note—This claim could not now be brought because of the requirement for compulsory third party insurance (Road Traffic Act 1988).

Howe v David Brown Tractors (Retail) Ltd

[1991] 4 All ER 30, CA
The plaintiff ran a family firm together with his father. On 23 January 1985 the plaintiff was injured as a result of the failure of a piece of farming equipment purchased from the defendant in 1982. The primary limitation period expired on the 22 January 1988 and on the 8 July 1988 the plaintiff issued a writ claiming damages for personal injuries and losses and expenses incurred. The claim was pleaded in tort.

An order was made by consent on 19 December 1988 disapplying the three-year limitation period in respect of the personal injury claim. Thereafter, on the 14 November 1989 the plaintiff applied to amend the writ and statement of claim to add the firm as second plaintiff and to include a claim for damages for breach of contract.

It was necessary for the court to decide (*inter alia*) whether the limitation period for the new contract claim was three or six years, ie whether or not s 11 of the Limitation Act 1980 applied.

HELD: The firm's claim was subject to the statutory provisions of s 11 of the Limitation Act 1980. The supply of dangerous machinery constituted a breach of duty in tort to the plaintiff causing him personal injury. Similarly, the supply of dangerous machinery constituted the breach of contractual duty owed to the firm causing loss.

Per Stuart Smith LJ: The same facts which give rise to the personal injury and breach of statutory duty to the plaintiff gives rise to the breach of duty albeit a different duty, owed to the firm.

Having decided that, it was for the plaintiff to apply under s 33 of the Limitation Act 1980 to disapply the limitation period applicable in respect of the firm's claim before or at the same time as seeking leave under RSC Ord 15, r 6(5)(b) to add the firm as a plaintiff.

Attributable

Guidera v NEI Projects Ltd (India)

(1990) Independent, 19 February, CA
The court considered the definition of 'attributable' in s 14 (1)(b) of the Limitation Act 1980. It was held on appeal that the word 'attributable' meant 'capable of being attributed to'. Thus, the attribution of the injury to the accident need only be a possibility, though a real possibility rather than a fanciful one.

Per Sir David Croom-Johnson: The act or omission of the defendant must be a possible cause as opposed to a probable cause of injury. One is dealing here with knowledge, actual or imputed, and not with proof of liability.

'Knowledge'

Davis v Ministry of Defence

[1985] CA Transcript 413, [1985] LS Gaz R 3265, [1985] CLY 2017, CA
Davis had been employed as a welder by MOD since 1955. In April 1969 he suffered a localised attack of dermatitis. In August 1971 he suffered a generalised outbreak and left MOD's employment. Over ten years later, on 10 November 1981, he sued MOD. Evidence showed that Davis had believed strongly throughout that his dermatitis had been caused by his working conditions and that he had a good claim against MOD. The statement of claim pleaded that before 10 November 1978 he had

been unaware that the general outbreak was 'attributable' to the MOD's negligence and breach.
HELD: The action should not be struck out. Section 14(1)(b) required the court to ask when did Davis first know (not reasonably believe or suspect) that his dermatitis was capable of being attributed to his working conditions. It could not certainly be said that the combined state of mind of Davis and (applying s 14(3)), his doctors and lawyers was such that they knew this, prior to 10 November 1978.

Note—Contrast *Wilkinson v Ancliff (BLT) Ltd*, below.

Wilkinson v Ancliff (BLT) Ltd

[1986] 3 All ER 427, [1986] 1 WLR 1352, 130 Sol Jo 766, [1986] LS Gaz R 3248, CA
The plaintiff was employed as a road-tanker driver based at Felixstowe; the tankers carried Toluene Di-Isocyanate (TDI). In April 1981 he suffered wheezing, coughing and shortness of breath. In August 1981 he stopped work due to ill-health; he claimed DHSS benefit showing his cause of incapacity as 'chest congestion due to inhalation of chemicals'. In November 1981 he was medically examined; the hospital registrar concluded that he had developed bronchial asthma due to sensitisation to TDI. He immediately consulted solicitors about claiming compensation from his employers. On 7 March 1984 a writ was issued stating that he first discovered his asthma was 'attributable to the defendants in November 1981'. In June 1984 a consultant chemist was instructed; his report, in December 1984, made a number of criticisms of the defendants' handling procedures for TDI and concluded that there was little doubt that the plaintiff's asthma had been brought about by his continued exposure to TDI. The writ and statement of claim were served on 29 March 1985. In considering whether the validity of the writ should be extended or that its service be set aside, the court had (applying the principle in *Heaven v Road & Rail Wagons Ltd* [1965] 2 QB 355) to assess whether the defendant might be deprived of a limitation defence. The crucial question for these purposes was—did the plaintiff have the relevant knowledge referred to in s 14 by 6 March 1982 (three years before the writ expired)?
HELD: The service of the writ should be set aside and the action dismissed. On the basis of the plaintiff's own evidence he well knew, after his visit to hospital in November 1981, that his injuries were capable of being attributed to the defendants' failure to provide him with safe working conditions.

Note—Section 14A (added by Latent Damage Act 1986, s 1) which relates only to non-personal injury actions reads, in sub-s (5): 'the starting date for reckoning the period of limitation . . . is the earliest date on which the plaintiff . . . had both the knowledge required for bringing an action for damages in respect of the relevant damage and a right to bring such an action'.

Davis v City and Hackney Health Authority

[1989] 2 Med LR 366, HL
The plaintiff, who suffered from cerebral palsy, was born on 16 June 1963. Immediately before his birth his mother had been given the drug Ergometrine by the defendants. He left home on 3 February 1983. As a result of meeting a helpful law student in August 1985 he instructed solicitors on 13 September 1985. Shortly after receiving an expert's report, on 26 November 1986, the plaintiff was fully informed of his rights of action. A writ was issued on 1 April 1987.

HELD: For the purposes of s 14(1) of the Limitation Act 1980, he acquired relevant knowledge in late November 1986, or alternatively for personal and domestic reasons could not reasonably have been expected to acquire this knowledge before about December 1984. To decide when a plaintiff should have acquired knowledge for the purposes of s 14(3) of the Act, the test was not what a reasonable man would have known, but what an individual of the plaintiff's age, background, intelligence and disabilities would have been expected to have known.

Halford v Brookes

[1991] 3 All ER 559, [1991] 1 WLR 428, CA
The plaintiff was the mother of Lyn Halford who was murdered on 3 April 1978. The second defendant was tried and acquitted of murder though confessed to inflicting injuries on the deceased at the instigation of the first defendant. After the trial further evidence came to light implicating the first defendant but despite a vigorous campaign by the deceased's family the authorities refused to prosecute him.

In July 1985 the plaintiff consulted new solicitors. Counsel advised that a civil action claiming damages on behalf of the estate was feasible and on the 1 April 1987 a writ was issued against both defendants. The defendants pleaded that the action was statute barred.

HELD ON APPEAL: 'Appropriate expert advice' referred to in s 14(3) did not include the legal advice that the plaintiff received from her solicitors in 1985. *Fowell v National Coal Board* [1986] CILL 294, (1986) Times, 28 May followed.

The plaintiff did not require expert advice in order to invest her with the necessary knowledge contemplated by s 14. She was capable of acquiring that knowledge herself and did so at the conclusion of the second defendant's trial in 1978. Whilst the plaintiff's action was statute barred, the Court of Appeal overturned the lower court's refusal to exercise discretion under s 33. The case did not depend on the accuracy of recollection but upon the extent to which it could be discerned whether or not the first and second defendant were telling the truth. The plaintiff's ignorance of her legal rights was also considered by the court to be a relevant consideration exercising discretion under s 33.

Hendy v Milton Keynes Health Authority

[1992] 3 Med LR 114
On 27 February 1985 the plaintiff underwent two operations one of which was a hysterectomy. Complications developed and a further operation was performed on 26 March 1985. The plaintiff met a doctor on 12 November 1986 who explained what had gone wrong during the first operation in February.

The plaintiff's solicitors, instructed in 1987, obtained a favourable expert's report in July 1988. The writ was issued on the 21 November 1988.

HELD: The plaintiff received sufficient information from the doctor on 12 November 1986 to know in general terms that her problem was attributable to the operation in February 1985. It did not matter that she was still unaware of the specific errors. In a relatively straightforward case such as this 'broad knowledge' was sufficient to start time running and therefore the plaintiff's claim was statute barred.

Stephen v Riverside Health Authority

[1990] 1 Med LR 261
The plaintiff underwent a mammography on 11 March 1977. She was aware that the radiographer was not operating the equipment properly. The plaintiff had trained

(though not qualified) as a radiographer in her teens but had not worked in this capacity for the 20 years prior to this mammography. Following the examination the plaintiff suffered from various distressing symptoms for some months but was continually reassured by the defendant that the mammography had been carried out satisfactorily and the symptoms arose from unrelated causes. Despite the assurances and her recovery the plaintiff continued to worry about the possibility that she had received an overdose of radiation which might cause her harm in the future. An expert was instructed in 1980 but was unable to arrive at any reasonably favourable conclusion until further tests had been undertaken. He had attended a conference with counsel on 20 February 1985. The Writ was issued on 15 February 1988.
HELD: The plaintiff's date of knowledge was 20 February 1985. Mere anxiety about an increased risk of cancer founded at most on the plaintiff's suspicion did not amount to knowledge of injury for the purpose of s 14(1)(a). The plaintiff's symptoms after the mammography were not sufficiently serious to justify instituting proceedings for damages. Further, the plaintiff's suspicion or belief that the mammography had been carried out incompetently was not sufficient to impute to her the knowledge that the symptoms could be attributable to excessive exposure to radiation. The plaintiff's past experience in radiography did not make her an expert in this field so as to transform the suspicion or conviction into the knowledge of attributability. Her action was not statute-barred.

Note—See also the cases of *Bentley v Bristol & Western Health Authority* [1991] 2 Med LR 359 and *Broadley v Guy Clapham & Co* (1993) Times, 6 July, CA. In the Bentley case it was held that broad knowledge that the injury was caused by an operation was insufficient to set the limitation running. The limitation period did not arise until the plaintiff had knowledge of an act or omission that could constitute negligence. However, Lord Justice Balcombe in the *Broadley* case expressed the view that *Bentley* had been wrongly decided. In the *Broadley* case it was held that the plaintiff's cause of action in a medical negligence case arose when she could have known with the help of medical advice reasonably obtainable, that her injury had been caused by damage resulting from something done or not done by the surgeon during her operation. Knowledge detailed enough to plead the statement of claim was not required before the time limit began to run.

The Latent Damage Act 1986

The Latent Damage Act 1986 added ss 14A and 14B to the Limitation Act 1980. Section 14A allows a claim to be brought within three years from the date of discovery of a defect subject to the long stop of 15 years from the date of negligence (s 14B). The 1986 Act came into effect on the 18 September 1986. It was intended to remedy the perceived injustice where hidden damage could remain hidden long past the expiry of the relevant limitation period. See the case of *Pirelli General Cable Works v Oscar Faber & Partners* (1983) 2 AC 1 where the House of Lords ruled that the relevant date was not that of discovery or discoverability but that at which the damage actually occurred.

Iron Trade Mutual Insurance Co Ltd v J K Buckenham Ltd

[1990] 1 All ER 808, [1989] 2 Lloyd's Rep 85
In this case it was argued (*inter alia*) that s 14A of the Limitation Act 1980 provided an alternative limitation period for an action framed in contract. It was held that the words 'any action for damages for negligence' set out in s 14A did not apply to an

action for breach of contract founded on an allegation of negligent or careless conduct.

Horbury v Craig Hall & Rutley

[1991] CILL 692

The defendant's surveyor carried out a survey for the plaintiff. The survey was negligently carried out but the errors which first came to the knowledge of the plaintiff were minor and rectified by her without recourse to legal action. More serious errors manifested themselves over three years after the survey was carried out and as a consequence of these the plaintiff commenced proceedings.

HELD: The three-year limitation period under the Latent Damage Act 1986 began to run as soon as the defendant knew (or was taken to have known) that the survey was negligently carried out and so the plaintiff's claim was time barred. The plaintiff did not succeed in arguing that there was a separate limitation period in relation to the other more serious defects which came to light only at a later stage nor was she permitted to abandon her earlier claims in favour of the later claims.

Note—See also *Felton v Gaskill Osborne & Co*, below.

Felton v Gaskill Osborne & Co

[1993] 43 EG 118 (Liverpool County Court)

The plaintiff purchased a house on 6 June 1983 relying on the defendant surveyor's report which despite including the need to remedy dampness, failed to report on three particular defects namely cracking over a bay window, a serious bulge in a gable end and a leaning chimney stack.

The plaintiff was already aware of the leaning chimney stack and remedied this personally. However, it was not until the plaintiff attempted to sell the property in 1989 that he discovered the problems with the bay window and bulging gable end.

The plaintiff originally claimed damages for the problem with the bay window, the bulge in the gable end, the lean in the chimney stack and the damp which had been much more extensive than originally reported.

Following an indication by the defendant that limitation would be an issue, the plaintiff amended his claim to delete reference to problems with the chimney and damp.

HELD per Judge O'Donoghue QC: The judge found for the plaintiff. The wording of s 14A of the Limitation Act 1980 was different from that of s 14. The limitation period for the purposes of s 14A ran from the date when the plaintiff knew of the material facts of the damage giving rise to the claim that is made.

Dobbie v Medway Health Authority

[1994] NLJR 828, CA

In 1973, Margaret Dobbie underwent a mastectomy. The surgeon performing the operation believed that an excision of a lump in her breast was cancerous. He had not conducted any microscopic examination. The growth was subsequently found to be benign. The plaintiff gave evidence to the effect that she knew, within hours, days or months after the operation that it had been carried out unnecessarily. However, at this stage, the plaintiff did not pursue any claim against the Health Authority. It was not until 1988 that she sought legal advice, having been prompted by publicity about a similar case. The writ was served in October 1990.

The judge dismissed the plaintiff's claim, stating that pursuant to s 14(1) of the Limitation Act 1980, time ran from the date of the operation and not from 1988. The judge also refused to exercise his discretion under s 33. The plaintiff appealed.
HELD: It was irrelevant that at the time of the operation, the plaintiff might not have been aware that the act or omission of the defendant was negligent. To start time running, it was only necessary that the plaintiff knew that she had suffered significant injury and that this injury was capable of being attributed to something done or not done by the defendant Authority. This she knew very shortly after the operation. The lack of appreciation that this act or omission was, arguably negligent, did not stop time running. The Court of Appeal also upheld the judge's refusal to exercise his discretion under s 33.

WHEN TIMES BEGINS TO RUN

Pirelli General Cable Works Ltd v Oscar Faber

[1983] 2 AC 1, [1983] 1 All ER 65, [1983] 2 WLR 6, 127 Sol Jo 16, 265 Estates Gazette 979, HL
The defendants were consulting engineers who advised the plaintiffs on the construction of a chimney. It was built in July 1969. The material used was unsuitable and cracks occurred not later than April 1970. The damage was not discovered by the plaintiffs until 1977 and they could not with reasonable diligence have discovered it before October 1972. The writ was issued in October 1978.
HELD, ON APPEAL to the House of Lords: The action was statute-barred. In cases of latent defects to buildings the cause of action will not accrue until damage occurs, which will commonly consist of cracks coming into existence as a result of defect even though the cracks or the defect may be undiscovered and undiscoverable. The principle of the decision, in *Cartledge v E Jopling & Sons Ltd* [1963] AC 758, [1963] 1 All ER 341, [1963] 2 WLR 210, 107 Sol Jo 73, [1963] 1 Lloyd's Rep 1, HL was applicable. It was not correct (as had been held in *Sparham-Souter v Town and Country Planning Developments (Essex) Ltd* [1976] QB 858, [1976] 2 All ER 65, [1976] 2 WLR 493, 120 Sol Jo 216, 74 LGR 355, CA) that a plaintiff suffers damage only when he discovers, or ought with reasonable diligence to have discovered, damage to the buildings.

Dove v Banhams Patent Locks Ltd

[1983] 2 All ER 833, [1983] 1 WLR 1436, 127 Sol Jo 748 (Hodgson J)
In 1967 the defendants, who were specialists in burglary prevention, fixed a security gate to the basement door of a house which in 1976 was purchased by the plaintiff. In 1979 the door was forced by a burglar who effected entry and stole valuable goods. The judge held the defendants to have been negligent in the way in which the gate had been fitted and that they owed the same duty of care to the plaintiff as they had to the owner of the house in 1967 who had employed the defendants to do the work. The defendants pleaded that the plaintiff's claim was statute-barred.
HELD: The claim was not statute-barred. The cause of action did not accrue until physical damage occurred, namely when the gate was forced. It did not accrue at the time when the defective work was done. *Pirelli General Cable Works Ltd v Oscar Faber & Partners* (above) followed.

Note—See also *Kensington & Chelsea v Wettern Composites Ltd* [1985] 1 All ER 346.
These cases now have to be read in the light of the Latent Damage Act 1986.

Bell v Peter Browne & Co (a firm)

[1990] 2 QB 495, [1990] 3 All ER 124, CA
The plaintiff retained the defendant, a firm of solicitors, to act on his behalf in respect of divorce proceedings. An arrangement was agreed between the plaintiff and his wife whereby the matrimonial home would not be sold for the time being but transferred solely into the wife's name and he would receive a sixth share of the proceeds upon sale. The house was transferred into Mrs Bell's name on 1 September 1978 but the defendant failed to register the plaintiff's interest.

In December 1986 the plaintiff learned that his wife had sold the former matrimonial home and had spent all the proceeds. The plaintiff sued the defendant in both contract and tort. The writ was issued on 20 August 1987. The defendant argued that the plaintiff's claim was statute barred.

HELD, ON APPEAL: The plaintiff's claim was dismissed. With respect to the claim in contract the six-year limitation period ran from the date of breach which was when the defendant failed to register the plaintiff's continuing interest in the former matrimonial home. This occurred on or shortly after 1 September 1978 and the failure to make good this breach thereafter did not constitute a further or continuing breach.

The claim in tort was also statute barred. The plaintiff suffered damage when he signed the transfer document over to his wife and at the point when the defendant failed to register his interest in the proceeds of sale within a reasonable time thereafter. The fact that the plaintiff had no knowledge of the damage and would have been able to easily remedy it if he had was irrelevant.

Note—This case now has to be read in the light of the Latent Damage Act 1986.

Nitrigin Eireann Teoranta v Inco Alloys Ltd

[1992] 1 All ER 854, [1992] 1 WLR 498, 135 Sol Jo LB 213
The plaintiff owned a chemical production plant. The defendants supplied alloy tubing pursuant to a contract made in March 1981. This tubing was installed in about August or September 1981. In July 1983 the plaintiff discovered cracking in a section of pipe but despite reasonable investigations no cause was found. The pipe was repaired. In June 1984 the pipe cracked and burst causing damage in the surrounding plant. The writ issued on 21 June 1990 claimed damages for negligence including a claim for the cost of repairs to the plant, the cost of replacing the burst pipe and loss of profit resulting from the shut down of the plant.

The defendant argued that the cause of action arose when the damage to the pipe appeared in 1983 and the loss arising out of the 1984 incident was pure economic loss and was thus irrecoverable. The plaintiff argued that the cause of action arose when the damage was caused by the explosion in 1984, no damage having been caused as a result of the cracking in 1983.

HELD: The cracks appearing in 1983 constituted damage to the pipe only. This was a defect in quality resulting in economic loss which was irrecoverable. Therefore, at this stage no action accrued. The plaintiff was unaware of the extent of the cracking and was therefore not able to sufficiently repair it. However, damage caused by the explosion in 1984 included the damage which did give rise to an action in negligence and therefore the plaintiff's claim was not statute barred (*Pirelli v Oscar Faber* distinguished).

Note—The Latent Damage Act 1986 did not come into force until 18 September 1986 and does not apply to actions already barred or to actions commenced before that date.

Stubbings v Webb

[1993] AC 498, [1993] 1 All ER 322, HL
The plaintiff who alleged she had been sexually abused and raped by the defendants (her adoptive father and brother) as a young girl issued a writ claiming damages for mental illness and psychological disturbance caused by the abuse. The plaintiff was born on 29 January 1957 so she reached her majority 18 years later on 29 January 1975. The writ was issued on 18 August 1987.

The plaintiff argued that she was not aware she had suffered any significant injury attributable to the abuse until she received the advice of a psychiatrist in September 1984.

This view was rejected by the master but accepted on appeal to the judge and by the Court of Appeal. It was previously thought that these actions for trespass to person were actions in respect of personal injuries within s 11(1) of the Limitation Act 1980. The defendants appealed to the House of Lords.
HELD: The House of Lords accepted the defendants' arguments that s 11(1) did not apply to a cause of action based on indecent assault or rape. The plaintiff's cause of action was governed by s 2 of the Act and therefore had a six-year limitation period without any provision for extension. The plaintiff's claim was statute-barred.

Note—The House of Lords derived assistance from the recommendations of the Tucker Committee Report prepared in 1949 which were given effect to by the Law Reform (Limitation of Actions) Act 1954. Hansard was also referred to.

Per Lord Griffiths: The terms in which the Bill had been introduced made it clear beyond peradventure that the intention was to give effect to the Tucker recommendation that the limitation period in respect of trespass to the person was not to be reduced to three years but should remain at six years.

Driscoll-Varley v Parkside Health Authority

[1991] 2 Med LR 346
The plaintiff suffered injuries to her right leg on 18 April 1984. The leg was put in traction for 12 days. It did not heal and throughout the next few years she had to undergo many additional operations. In mid-1985 she was told by her surgeon that there was some dead bone in the leg causing problems. This was removed but it was not possible to obtain a satisfactory union at the fracture site and so the problems and treatment continued.

In late 1986 the plaintiff was becoming profoundly dissatisfied with her treatment and consulted solicitors with a view to commencing proceedings against the defendant. However, she was reluctant to do so fearing that her consultant surgeon, in whom she had confidence, would cease to treat her. In June 1988 expert evidence was obtained which stated that the cause of the plaintiff's problems was the premature removal of her right leg from traction. The writ was issued on 4 May 1989.
HELD: The injury was 'significant' within the meaning of s 14 (1)(a) of the Limitation Act 1980 in September 1985 at the stage when the dead bone was discovered. However, the plaintiff did not have actual knowledge that the failure of her leg to respond to treatment was attributable to the premature removal from traction until June 1988. Neither did the plaintiff have constructive knowledge. The plaintiff's fear that her surgeon might have ceased to treat her was a reasonable one. Thus, it was reasonable for the plaintiff to defer seeking medical assistance until she did.

Marren v Dawson Bentley & Co Ltd

[1961] 2 QB 135, [1961] 2 All ER 270, [1961] 2 WLR 679, 105 Sol Jo 383 (Havers J)
The plaintiff claimed damages for personal injuries received in an accident. The accident occurred at 1.30 pm on 8 November 1954. The writ was issued on 8 November 1957. The defendants contended that as the plaintiff could have issued a writ on 8 November 1954, the last day on which he would be entitled to do so would be 7 November 1957, and that the action was out of time.
HELD: The day on which the cause of action arose was excluded from the computation of the three years and therefore the plaintiff's action was not statute barred.

Young v GLC and Massey

[1987] CLY 2328.
The plaintiff, a fireman, injured his neck in an accident in April 1981. In December 1981 he discovered that he had arthritis in his neck. In May 1984 the plaintiff's doctor decided that he was unfit for work in the fire brigade. In December 1984 the plaintiff realised after a discussion with his superior that he would probably have to retire. In March 1985 the plaintiff issued proceedings for damages in respect of his injury against his employers. The defendants argued that his claim was statute-barred under s 14 of the Limitation Act 1980.
HELD: The date of the plaintiff's knowledge of his injury for the purposes of s 14 of the Limitation Act 1980 was May 1984 and was accordingly not statute-barred.

2 PERSONS UNDER A DISABILITY (S 28)

LIMITATION ACT 1980, S 28

'**28 Extension of limitation period in case of disability** (1) Subject to the following provisions of this section if, on the date when any right of action accrued for which a period of limitation is prescribed by this Act, the person to whom it accrued was under a disability, the action may be brought at any time before the expiration of six years from the date when he ceased to be under a disability or died (whichever first occurred) notwithstanding that the period of limitation has expired.
(2) This section shall not affect any case where the right of action first accrued to some person (not under a disability) through whom the person under a disability claims.
(3) When a right of action which has accrued to a person under a disability accrues, on the death of that person while still under a disability, to another person under a disability, no further extension of time shall be allowed by reason of the disability of the second person.
(4) [Recovery of Land].
(5) If the action is one to which s 10 of this Act applies, sub-s (1) above shall have effect as if for the words "six years" there were substituted the words "two years".
(6) If the action is one to which s 11 or 12(2) of this Act applies, sub-s (1) above shall have effect as if for the words "six years" there were substituted the words "three years".'

'**38 Interpretation** . . . (2) For the purposes of this Act a person shall be treated as under a disability while he is an infant, or of unsound mind.
(3) For the purposes of sub-s (2) above a person is of unsound mind if he is a person who, by reason of mental disorder within the meaning of the Mental Health Act 1959, is incapable of managing and administering his property and affairs.'

Penrose v Mansfield

(1970) Times, 8 October (Waller J); affd (1971) 115 Sol Jo 309, Times, 19 March, CA

The plaintiff was badly injured by negligence of the defendant on 10 November 1965. The writ was issued on 12 December 1968. He claimed that the action was not out of time because due to his injuries, he was not in a fit state to manage his own affairs until after 12 December 1965 and that he was entitled to the protection of s 22 as amended.

HELD: Following *Kirby v Leather* the problem for consideration was whether it had been shown on the probabilities that the plaintiff was for some five weeks or more of unsound mind, that is, 'by reason of mental illness incapable of managing his affairs in relation to the accident as a reasonable man would do.' On the evidence, especially the fact that he had himself on 10 December 1965 signed a consent for operative treatment, he had failed to show that his mental state until after 12 December was such as to bring himself within the terms of s 22. The action was statute-barred.

Note—See also *Kirby v Leather* [1965] 2 QB 367, CA.

Turner v W H Malcolm Ltd

(1992) 136 Sol Jo LB 236, 15 BMLR 40, CA

The plaintiff was involved in an accident on 21 October 1980 which left him of unsound mind within the meaning of s 38(2) and (3) of the Limitation Act 1980 and, thus, under a disability for the purposes of that Act.

A writ was issued on 5 August 1981 and the statement of claim served on 25 November 1981. In December 1988, the defendants made an application to the district judge to strike out the plaintiff's claim for want of prosecution. The district judge dismissed the application and the matter went to an appeal judge who upheld the district judge's decision but on terms disadvantageous to the plaintiff. The plaintiff appealed to the Court of Appeal.

HELD: Sections 28 and 38 of the 1980 Act in effect provided that there was no limitation period for a plaintiff who was under a permanent disability. The effect of striking out this action or imposing any condition on its progress would only extend the period before the plaintiff's claim was finally resolved. The plaintiff's appeal was successful and the plaintiff's claim was allowed to proceed.

Note—See also Chapter 16 generally.

3 FRAUD (S 32)

LIMITATION ACT 1980, S 32

'32 Postponement of limitation period in case of fraud, concealment or mistake

(1) . . . where in the case of any action for which a period of limitation is prescribed by this Act, either—

(a) the action is based upon the fraud of the defendant; or

(b) any fact relevant to the plaintiff's right of action has been deliberately concealed from him by the defendant; . . .

the period of limitation shall not begin to run until the plaintiff has discovered the fraud [or] concealment . . . or could with reasonable diligence have discovered it.'

Kitchen v RAF Association

[1958] 2 All ER 241, [1958] 1 WLR 563, 102 Sol Jo 363, CA

A man serving in the Royal Air Force was on leave and on 22 May 1945, was electrocuted when using some electrical equipment in the kitchen of his home. His widow believed the cause was negligence of the electricity company in the wiring of the installation. A voluntary organisation forwarded particulars of her case to the RAF Association and the RAF Association to a firm of solicitors who had offered to help members of the RAF and their dependants, in November 1945. The solicitors allowed the 12 months' limitation under the Fatal Accidents Act (the limit then in operation) to expire without commencing proceedings. On 3 June 1946, the solicitors endeavoured to persuade the electricity company to make an ex gratia payment, without success. The widow then herself wrote to the company, and as a result a sum of £100 was paid to the RAF Association through the solicitors as a donation from an unknown source on condition that the widow must not know the source. The company did not accept the suggestion of the solicitors that a payment would be taken as a full settlement of all claims. The solicitors had failed to draw any distinction between the claim under the Fatal Accidents Act and the Law Reform Act.

In 1950 the widow obtained legal aid and an action was commenced against the company by another firm of solicitors under the Law Reform Act and settled for £250.

On 30 September 1955, a third firm of solicitors commenced proceedings against the RAF Association and the original solicitors for damages for negligence. The action failed against the Association, and the solicitors denied the negligence alleged and pleaded that the action was statute barred under the Limitation Act 1939, s 2. By her reply the widow pleaded s 26 of the Act.

HELD: The word 'fraud' is not limited to common law fraud or deceit. No degree of moral turpitude is necessary to establish fraud within the section (*Beaman v ARTS Ltd*, p 893 , below). The relationship of solicitor and client existed and negligence was established. The failure of the solicitors to notify the widow of what the company was proposing, which had the effect of throwing away any case she might have had under the Fatal Accidents Acts, is just enough to say that there was concealment by fraud and so to deprive them of the right to set up the Limitation Act 1939. The widow had acted with reasonable diligence. Judgment for the plaintiff.

Johnson v Chief Constable of Surrey

(1992) Times, 23 November, CA

The plaintiff, relying on s 32 of the Limitation Act 1980 brought an action against the defendant long after the limitation period had expired. He alleged that new facts had emerged which had been deliberately concealed by the defendants.

HELD: A distinction had to be drawn between those facts which made the cause of action complete and those facts which improved the plaintiff's chances of success in that action. In this case the new facts were of the latter rather than the former kind and the plaintiff's case was struck out as statute-barred.

Sheldon v RHM Outhwaite (Underwriting Agency) Ltd

[1994] 1 WLR 754

The plaintiff alleged that there had been deliberate concealment by the defendants after the plaintiff's cause of action arose and argued under s 32 of the Limitation Act

1980 that the limitation should be extended accordingly. The defendants argued that s 32 only applied to deliberate concealment at the time that the cause of action arose and not to any later concealment.

HELD: The defendants' arguments were rejected. A deliberate concealment could have the affect of preventing the limitation period from running as provided under s 2 of the Act even when it occurred after the plaintiff's cause of action arose.

4 JUDGE'S DISCRETION

GENERALLY

LIMITATION ACT 1980, S 33

'33 Discretionary exclusion of time limit for actions in respect of personal injuries or death (1) If it appears to the court that it would be equitable to allow an action to proceed having regard to the degree to which—

(a) the provisions of s 11 or 12 of this Act prejudice the plaintiff or any person whom he represents; and

(b) any decision of the court under this subsection would prejudice the defendant or any person whom he represents;

the court may direct that those provisions shall not apply to the action, or shall not apply to any specified cause of action to which the action relates.

(2) The court shall not under this section disapply s 12(1) except where the reason why the person injured could no longer maintain an action was because of the time limit in s 11.

If, for example, the person injured could at his death no longer maintain an action under the Fatal Accidents Act 1976 because of the time limit in Art 29 in Sch 1 to the Carriage by Air Act 1961, the court has no power to direct that s 12(1) shall not apply.

(3) In acting under this section the court shall have regard to all the circumstances of the case and in particular to—

(a) the length of, and the reasons for, the delay on the part of the plaintiff;

(b) the extent to which, having regard to the delay, the evidence adduced or likely to be adduced by the plaintiff or the defendant is or is likely to be less cogent than if the action had been brought within the time allowed by s 11 or (as the case may be) by s 12;

(c) the conduct of the defendant after the cause of action arose, including the extent (if any) to which he responded to requests reasonably made by the plaintiff for information or inspection for the purpose of ascertaining facts which were or might be relevant to the plaintiff's cause of action against the defendant;

(d) the duration of any disability of the plaintiff arising after the date of the accrual of the cause of action;

(e) the extent to which the plaintiff acted promptly and reasonably once he knew whether or not the act or omission of the defendant, to which the injury was attributable, might be capable at that time of giving rise to an action for damages;

(f) the steps, if any, taken by the plaintiff to obtain medical, legal or other expert advice and the nature of any such advice he may have received.

(4) In a case where the person injured died when, because of s 11, he could no longer maintain an action and recover damages in respect of the injury, the court shall have regard in particular to the length of, and the reasons for, the delay on the part of the deceased.

(5) In a case under sub-s (4) above, or any other case where the time limit, or one of the time limits, depends on the date of knowledge of a person other than the plaintiff, sub-s (3) above shall have effect with appropriate modifications, and shall have effect in particular as if references to the plaintiff included references to any person whose date of knowledge is or was relevant in determining a time limit.

(6) A direction by the court disapplying the provisions of s 12(1) shall operate to disapply the provisions to the same effect in s 1(1) of the Fatal Accidents Act 1976.
(7) In this section "the court" means the court in which the action has been brought.
(8) References in this section to s 11 include references to that section as extended by any of the preceding provisions of this Part of this Act or by any other provisions of Part III of this Act.

Conry v Simpson

[1983] 3 All ER 369, CA
On 12 January 1973 the plaintiff was injured by the first defendant's car when standing at the side of the second and third defendants' vehicle. The injury was to his leg. His solicitor failed to issue a writ within three years. He instructed other solicitors who issued a writ against the first solicitor for professional negligence in 1977: that action remained pending. After the decision in *Firman v Ellis* (p 524, below) was reported in February 1978 the plaintiff revived the claim and issued a writ in November 1979 against the potential tortfeasors and applied to the court to disapply s 11 of the 1980 Act. The judge made an order disapplying s 11 as against the first defendant (whose insurers had not denied negligence) but not as against the second and third defendants. The first defendant appealed.
HELD, by the Court of Appeal: The judge had an unfettered discretion, as originally held in *Firman v Ellis*, to disapply s 11 provided he had regard to all the circumstances of the case and in particular to the six circumstances specified in s 33(3). It was not for an appellate court to reverse the discretion of the judge unless he had gone very wrong. The judge had considered all the points in issue and there were no grounds for saying that the judge had fallen into error.

Donovan v Gwentoys Ltd

[1990] 1 All ER 1018, [1990] 1 WLR 472, 134 Sol Jo 910, HL
The plaintiff suffered an injury at work on 3 December 1979 when she was aged 16. She made a claim for four weeks' industrial injury benefit on the basis of an injury to her wrist and returned to work until she left the defendant's employment in 1980 having never indicated her intention to make a claim for damages. The plaintiff consulted solicitors in 1984 who issued the writ on 10 October 1984 some five and a half months after the expiry of the limitation period, her date of birth being 25 April 1963.

The defendant argued that the court should not exercise its discretion under s 33 in favour of the plaintiff in view of the fact that they were unaware of the plaintiff's claim until some five and a half years after the accident and it was not until January of 1986 when the defendant became aware of the circumstances of the alleged accident and the nature of the injuries sustained.

The trial judge exercised his discretion in favour of the plaintiff on the basis that he was confined to consider the prejudice to the defendant caused by the five and a half months delay between the expiration of the limitation period and the issue of the writ. This delay was minimal. The Court of Appeal agreed.
HELD, ON APPEAL to the House of Lords: Section 33 provides the judge with an unfettered discretion to allow an action in respect of personal injuries or death to proceed despite the expiry of the limitation period if he considers it fair and equitable to do so having regard to the prejudice suffered by both the plaintiff and the defendant. This sub-section does not prevent the court from considering other matters which experience has shown need to be evaluated by a judge when exercising his discretion.

In particular an extremely important consideration to take into account is the date on which the claim is first made against the defendant. The judge had misdirected himself by concentrating only on the five and a half months delay after the limitation period had expired. In this case the degree of prejudice suffered by the defendant was greater than that suffered by the plaintiff who would only suffer the slightest prejudice if she was required to pursue her remedy against her solicitors.

Nash v Eli Lilly & Co

[1993] 4 All ER 383, [1993] 1 WLR 782, 14 BMLR 1, CA
The principles to apply when considering s 33 of the Limitation Act 1980 remain the same whether considering an ordinary single case or multi-party litigation.

Per Hidden J: It would not be well for there to be two different sets of principles, one for an ordinary run of the mill case and the other for multi party litigation.

Note—See above for a general discussion of the whole of s 14 of the Limitation Act 1980.

JUDGE'S DISCRETION EXERCISED IN THE PLAINTIFF'S FAVOUR

McCafferty v Metropolitan Police District Receiver

[1977] 2 All ER 756, [1977] 1 WLR 1073, 121 Sol Jo 678, CA
By writ issued in 1974 the plaintiff claimed damages for deafness alleged to be due to his employer's negligence. He had discovered a degree of deafness as a result of an audiogram taken in 1968 but had not then made a claim. He had regarded his deafness at that time merely as 'an irritating nuisance' and had carried on at his work, not thinking of making a claim.
HELD: The discretion of the court could properly be exercised under the Limitation Act 1939, s 2D and his action was not time-barred. The plaintiff had known by 1968 what had happened to his hearing and it was not a case to be dealt with under s 2A. It could be inferred that the plaintiff had carried on in 1968 without making a claim because he did not consider the 'irritating nuisance' to be worth the risk of losing his job by litigating with his employers. That was commendable and could be taken into consideration by the court in considering s 2D.

Wood v SKF (UK) Ltd

(7 April 1982, unreported) (Cantley J) (taken from transcript supplied)
The plaintiff when working as a machine operator in the defendants' employment sustained a burn to his right eyelid from a piece of hot swarf on an occasion in 1936. The injury was treated in the first-aid room; the plaintiff did not cease work and made no kind of claim. For some years the scar at the site of the burn was only a slight nuisance due to occasional throbbing, but became more troublesome in the 1950s. From 1955 to 1957 he received medical treatment including x-ray therapy to a cell carcinoma on the eyelid resulting from the burn. The x-ray treatment cured the carcinoma but caused a hardening of the inner surface of the eyelid and changes in the eye itself, giving rise to ulceration. The plaintiff continued at work throughout but in June 1978 to prevent further trouble the eyelids of his right eye were sewn together permanently, causing him the permanent loss of use of the eye. He consulted solicitors through his trade-union and a writ was issued on 12

November 1980 claiming damages. The defendants pleaded that the action was statute-barred.

HELD: (1) The plaintiff could not reasonably have considered the injury sufficiently serious to justify instituting proceedings for damages during the six years from the injury to the end of the then limitation period, but the situation was different by 1957: by that date he had knowledge that his injury was significant as defined in s 2A of the Limitation Act 1939 as amended by the 1975 Act. The claim was barred by s 2A unless it would be equitable to direct under s 2D that 2A should not apply. (2) The delay which fell to be considered was the period after 1957, though until the 1975 Act any action brought would have been that the action was statute barred. When the plaintiff did take advice in 1978 he acted promptly and reasonably on it. As to the defendants, they pleaded prejudice from the long delay by depriving them of evidence of the system of work in 1936 but they had not challenged some of the evidence or countered the evidence of the plaintiff and his three witnesses who were working in the factory in 1936. Taking all the circumstances into consideration as required by s 2D, s 2A should not apply to this action.

Note—The action proceeded and the plaintiff was awarded damages. The gap of 44 years from cause of action to institution of proceedings in an ultimately successful accident claim would seem to be much the longest on record.

Hartley v Birmingham City District Council

[1992] 2 All ER 213, [1992] 1 WLR 968, CA

The plaintiff suffered an accident on 10 December 1986. The limitation period expired on 11 December 1989 due to the fact that 9 December was a Saturday. The plaintiff's solicitor did not manage to issue the writ until the morning of 12 December. The plaintiff applied to the District Registry for the time-limit on s 11 of the Limitation Act 1980 to be disapplied. The plaintiff's application failed and on appeal to the judge. The plaintiff appealed to the Court of Appeal.

HELD: The court exercised its discretion under s 33 in the plaintiff's favour. A judge had to take into account all the circumstances of the case as well as the specific matters mentioned in s 33 (3).

Per Parker LJ: If in this case the discretion is not to be exercised in favour of the plaintiff I find it difficult to envisage circumstances in which it could ever be so exercised.

Note—Parker LJ reviewed the law and held that recent cases of *Thompson v Brown and Donovan v Gwentoys Ltd* affirmed most of what was said in *Firman v Ellis* (see p 524, below). Thus, if there is a short delay which is not due to the plaintiff but to a slip on the part of his solicitor, which did not affect the ability of the defendants to defend the claim because of earlier notification, the exercise of discretion in favour of the plaintiff will be justified even if the plaintiff, if not allowed to proceed, had a cast iron action against his solicitor.

See also the case of *Ramsden v Lee* [1992] 2 All ER 204, CA where it was held that although it was highly relevant that a plaintiff had a case against his solicitors, it would be contrary to the requirements of s 33(3) of the 1980 Act to discount entirely the fact that the plaintiff would suffer some prejudice in pursuing that claim.

Jeffrey v Bolton Textile Mill Co

[1990] CLY 2944

The deceased, a mule spinner, died in 1959 having been forced to give up work in a cotton mill in 1957 allegedly because of byssinosis. The mill closed in 1959.

HELD: The judge applied s 33 in the plaintiff's favour and disapplied the normal limitation period on the basis that there was still evidence available to describe conditions in the mill during the 1950s.

Ward v Foss, Heathcote v Foss

(1993) Times, 29 November, CA
The plaintiff brought a claim on behalf of the deceased's estate arising out of a fatal accident that occurred in July 1982. The writ was issued in November 1989 and the plaintiffs sought to rely on s 33 of the Limitation Act 1980 to disapply the limitation period. Part of the plaintiff's claim was for damages for lost years, a head of damage which had been abolished by the Administration of Justice Act 1982 which applied to causes of action accruing after 1 January 1983. The Act provided that no claims might be brought on behalf of the deceased's estate for loss of income in respect of any period of the deceased's death.

The defendants argued that it was inequitable to disapply the limitation period when it would have the affect of allowing the plaintiff to pursue a claim which had been abolished. The plaintiff succeeded at first instance and the defendants appealed.
HELD: The defendants' appeal was dismissed. The Court of Appeal accepted that a claim for lost years could result in the plaintiff benefiting from double recovery and that it was specifically this element of over compensation that the 1982 Act was designed to avoid. However, s 33 did not require the court to look at the fairness or otherwise of the laws of England at the time that the cause of action arose. The court had to consider whether or not it was equitable to disapply the limitation period by reference to the specific criteria mentioned in the section. Looking at the case from this point of view the defendants' arguments were unconvincing.

JUDGE'S DISCRETION EXERCISED IN THE DEFENDANT'S FAVOUR

Davies v British Insulated Callender's Cables Ltd

(1977) 121 Sol Jo 203 (Thesiger J)
In November 1970 the plaintiff sustained a back injury when at work. No report of the accident was made nor any statements taken. Though he obtained Social Security benefit he made no claim for damages until 1975. A writ was issued in 1976.
HELD: The court's discretion to allow the action to proceed should not be exercised, since 'the evidence adduced or likely to be adduced [would be] less cogent than if the action had been brought within the time allowed by s 2A.' It would be extremely difficult for anyone to remember what had happened at the time of the accident.

Davis v Saltenpar

(1983) 133 NLJ 720 (Hobhouse J)
On 10 October 1977 the plaintiff was struck and injured by a car driven by the defendant, who was uninsured. The claim was notified to the Motor Insurers' Bureau who appointed an insurance company as investigating office. After a good deal of correspondence the plaintiff's solicitors issued a writ on 3 November 1980. The defendant pleaded the action was out of time. As a preliminary point the plaintiff asked the court to disapply the Limitation Act 1939, s 2A (now s 11 of the 1980 Act) under the provisions of s 2D of the 1939 Act (now s 33 of the 1980 Act).
HELD: Section 2D(3) required the court to have regard to all the circumstances of the case. The application must be refused since (a) the balance of advantage to the

plaintiff was that he should sue his solicitors for negligence; (b) the defendant would be prejudiced by continuing to be involved in the action; it was legitimate and appropriate for the court to take into account the position of the Motor Insurers' Bureau since it was a composite unit with the defendant; and (c) a trial was never going to be satisfactory because of the defendant's character and the plaintiff's injuries (including amnesia).

Dale v British Coal Corpn

[1993] 1 All ER 317, [1992] 1 WLR 964, 136 Sol Jo LB 197, CA
On 25 June 1972, a spark entered the plaintiff's boot. The injury this caused eventually led to the plaintiff's left leg being amputated. The local Mineworkers Union helped the plaintiff to obtain £500 compensation from the Medical Tribunal but did not support the plaintiff's claim for further compensation.

In November 1975 the plaintiff wrote to the Union's President who advised him to pursue a claim at common law and to contact his branch secretary immediately. The plaintiff did not. The colliery closed in 1981. The plaintiff lost his right leg in September 1985 and consulted solicitors on 3 September 1987 who then served a writ and statement of claim. The defendant pleaded that the plaintiff's claim was statute-barred. The judge allowed the plaintiff's claim to proceed and the defendant appealed.
HELD: Where the existence of a claim and sufficient particulars are given so late that it is virtually impossible for the defendant to investigate, the defendant is gravely prejudiced and it requires exceptional circumstances for the court to disapply s 11 of the 1980 Act.

As to the reasonableness of the plaintiff's conduct the judge had applied a subjective test which was wrong. The test is an objective one: what would a reasonable man in the position of the plaintiff have done? A reasonable man would have followed Union advice.

The court is also entitled to take into account the plaintiff's prospects of success in considering whether the limitation period should be disapplied.

The plaintiff's application to disapply the limitation period failed.

OTHER S 33 CASES

Co-defendant liable

Liff v Peasley

[1980] 1 All ER 623, [1980] 1 WLR 781, 124 Sol Jo 360, CA
The plaintiff was injured in a road accident on 25 October 1973 by the negligence of the defendant Peasley. He issued a writ against him on 14 August 1975. In 1978 he was required by MIB (Peasley being uninsured) to join another defendant Spinks. The Statement of Claim was amended for this purpose by order of 5 October 1978 and a copy of the amended writ was sent to Spinks's solicitors. They entered unconditional appearance and served a defence which pleaded that the action against Spinks was statute-barred. They then applied for an order under Ord 15, r 6 that Spinks should cease to be a party in that he was joined after the expiry of the limitation period.
HELD: (1) There were no grounds for exercising the discretion of the Court under the Limitation Act 1939, s 2D in favour of the plaintiff since he was not disadvantaged by s 2A: he already had a cast iron case against Peasley; (2) it was an established rule

of practice that the court will not allow a person to be added as a defendant to an existing action if the claim sought to be made against him is already statute-barred and he relies on it as a defence; (3) the preferable basis, both on the rules of the court and on the decided cases, on which the rule can be justified is that the action against the added party is deemed to begin against him on the date of the amendment of the writ, not the date of the original writ; (4) Spinks was not precluded from obtaining an order that he cease to be a party by his solicitors having entered unconditional appearance. When it became apparent that he intended to rely on the claim being statute-barred he became a party who had been improperly added, or who had ceased to be a proper party, within the meaning of Ord 15, r 6(2)(a).

Note—Note from the *Supreme Court Practice* 1988, p 349, Ord 20/5-8/2:

'In relation to an action to which the Limitation Act 1939 applies (this will of course be progressively more rare), an amendment to add a defendant takes effect, not by way of relating back to the date of the original writ but on the date on which he is effectively joined as a party, ie the date of the service of the amended writ on him or serving his own defence (*Ketteman v Hansel Properties Ltd* [1988] 1 All ER 38, HL approving the dictum of Brandon LJ in *Liff v Peasley* [1980] 1 All ER 623, [1980] 1 WLR 781, and see *Gawthrop v Boulton* [1978] 3 All ER 615, [1979] 1 WLR 268).

On the other hand, in actions to which the Limitation Act 1980 applies, the relation back theory of amendment is expressly provided for by statute. By s 35(1), it is provided that any new claim made in the course of the action will be deemed to be a separate action and except in the case of third party proceedings will be deemed to have been commenced on the same date as the original action and for this purpose s 35(2) provides that 'a new claim' means any claim by way of set-off or counteraction and any claim involving either (a) the addition or substitution of a new cause of action or (b) the addition or substitution of a new party (see Vol 2, Limitation Act 1980, para 6160).'

Prejudice as to costs

Lye v Marks & Spencer plc

(1988) Times, 15 February, CA

The plaintiff sought leave under s 33 of the Limitation Act 1980 to allow her action against the defendants to proceed out of time. She was legally aided and her application was refused. She appealed.

HELD, ON APPEAL: The fact that the plaintiff was legally aided and thus unlikely to meet the defendants' costs had to be considered when weighing the prejudice which the defendants might suffer if the action was allowed to continue out of time but it was not an overriding factor. The appeal was dismissed.

Name of defendant unknown

Simpson v Norwest Holst Southern Ltd

[1980] 2 All ER 471, [1980] 1 WLR 968, 124 Sol Jo 313, CA

The plaintiff was employed on a building site as a carpenter; the memorandum given to him under the Contracts of Employment Act gave the employers' name as 'Norwest Holst Group', which was not a legal entity. He was injured at work on 4 August 1976. He claimed damages but was unable to tell his solicitors which company in the group employed him, nor did letters from the employers' insurers

reveal it until, in reply to a direct inquiry from his solicitors, they wrote on 4 July 1979 giving the defendant company's name. The solicitors issued a county court summons on 17 August 1979. The defendants applied to dismiss the action as being out of time. The court refused the application, exercising its discretion under the Limitation Act 1939, s 2D to disapply s 2A.
HELD, dismissing appeal: (1) As the identity of an employer against whom proceedings could be taken was not known to the plaintiff until the insurers' letter of 4 July 1979 time did not run until he had that 'knowledge' for the purposes of s 2A(4)(b) and the action was not out of time. (2) Section 2D should not be read in any restrictive sense so as to apply only to exceptional cases (following *Firman v Ellis* (below), on this point). (3) It was not correct, as the defendants maintained, that the plaintiff was prejudiced only by his solicitors' delay and not by s 2A. By 4 August 1979 his claim was likely to be barred by a limitation plea and this was due to s 2A not to his solicitors' delays. The defendants were not prejudiced, as they were in no worse position to defend the claim on 17 August 1979 than on the 3rd. There was ample evidence on which the county court judge could properly exercise his discretion under s 2D.

Note—Section 2A(4)(b) has now become the Limitation Act 1980, s 11(4)(b).

Starting second action out of time

Firman v Ellis
Down v Harvey
Pheasant v Smith (Tyres) Ltd

[1978] QB 886, [1978] 2 All ER 851, [1978] 2 WLR 1, 122 Sol Jo 147, CA
The plaintiffs claimed damages for injuries received in a road accident. In each case no issue arose on liability: the only issue was the amount of damages to be awarded when the plaintiffs should be sufficiently recovered to enable this to be done. In each case the plaintiffs' solicitors issued writs but allowed them by inadvertence to expire before service. When three years had elapsed the defendants' insurers refused to entertain the claims because they had become statute-barred. The plaintiffs began new actions by issuing writs out of time and applied under the Limitation Act 1939, s 2D that the limitation period in s 2A should not apply.
HELD: The court could properly exercise its discretion under s 2D in favour of the plaintiffs. Section 2D was not limited to exceptional cases: it gave a discretion to extend time in all cases where the three-year limitation had expired before the issue of the writ. The solicitors' slip had not prejudiced the defendants at all. On subsidiary points: (1) under the 1975 Act the negligence of the plaintiff's solicitor was an admissible consideration; it might tip the scale where the defendant had been substantially prejudiced by the delay; (2) the words 'the plaintiff' in s 2D(3) included his solicitor or agent except where the context confined it to the plaintiff personally; (3) 'the court' in sub-s (2) meant a judge hearing an application as a preliminary issue, but not a master in the High Court or a registrar in the county court.

Note—But see below, *Walkley v Precision Forgings Ltd.*

Walkley v Precision Forgings Ltd

[1979] 2 All ER 548, [1979] 1 WLR 606, 123 Sol Jo 354, HL
In 1966 the plaintiff found himself to be suffering from Reynaud's disease, possibly

caused by vibration of machine tools at work. He issued a writ in October 1971 and served it. The employers' solicitors entered appearance. Nothing more was done because the plaintiff's solicitors advised him that he did not have a good claim. A second firm of solicitors revived the claim in 1973 but the defendants' solicitors wrote saying that if the plaintiff intended to proceed with the action they would apply to dismiss it for want of prosecution. Nothing more was done in the action. In December 1976 a third firm of solicitors issued a new writ for the plaintiff and served it with a statement of claim. The defendants' solicitors applied for the second action to be struck out under Ord 18, r 19 as an abuse of the process of the court. It was conceded by the plaintiff that the first action would be likely to have been dismissed for want of prosecution. On appeal from the master, the judge declined to strike out the second action on the plaintiff's undertaking to discontinue the first action. The Court of Appeal said the judge was right and that the plaintiff was entitled to have the question whether his second action should be allowed to proceed tested under the Limitation Act 1939, s 2D by reference to the criteria there set out.

HELD, on the defendants' appeal to the House of Lords: The second action should be struck out. The affidavit of the defendants' solicitor had been directed to the issue under s 2D and the plaintiff had not answered it; no answer was possible for on the facts before the court it was clear that since the plaintiff had begun an action within the period limited by s 2A he had not been prejudiced by it. *Birkett v James* (p 636, below) had no relevance; all that case decided was that when a plaintiff had allowed an action to go to sleep it would be an improper exercise of the court's discretion to dismiss it for want of prosecution before the expiry of the limitation period: it had no application to a personal injury action after the primary limitation period had expired.

Per Lord Diplock: Once a plaintiff has started an action (the first action) within the primary limitation period it is only in the most exceptional circumstances that he would be able to bring himself within s 2D in respect of a second action brought to enforce the same cause of action. If the first action is still in existence . . . he has not been prevented from starting his action by s 2A or s 2B at all, so the provisions of those sections cannot have caused him any prejudice. Does it make any difference that the first action is no longer in existence at the time of the application under s 2D either because it has been struck out for want of prosecution or because it has been discontinued by the plaintiff of his own volition? In my view it does not. The only exception . . . where is might be proper to give a direction under s 2D . . . would be a case in which the plaintiff had been induced to discontinue by a misrepresentation or other improper conduct by the defendant.

Note—The *Firman v Ellis* cases (p 524 above) were not cited.

Thompson v Brown Construction Ltd

[1981] 2 All ER 296, [1981] 1 WLR 744, 125 Sol Jo 377, HL

The plaintiff was injured at work by the collapse of a scaffold. He claimed damages from the second defendants, a scaffolding company, who did not dispute liability. The plaintiff's solicitors negotiated for a time and then lost the file. By the time they found it more than three years had elapsed. The writ was issued 37 days out of time. The defendants pleaded the Limitation Act 1939 and denied that it would be equitable to allow the action to proceed under s 2D. The judge considered himself bound by the decision in *Browes*'s case (1979) 123 Sol Jo 489, CA to hold as a matter of law that the plaintiff was not prejudiced by the provisions of s 2A because he had a cast iron claim in negligence against his solicitors. He refused to make a direction under s 2D.

HELD: *Browes*'s case should not be treated as authority for the proposition of law for which the judge treated it. In deciding whether discretion should be exercised under s 2D a court must have regard not only to the provisions of s 2D(1) but also those of s 2D(3). The onus of showing that in the particular circumstances of the case it would be equitable to make an exception lies on the plaintiff; but subject to that the court's discretion to make or refuse an order is unfettered. The conduct of the parties as well as the prejudice one or other will suffer if the court does or does not make an order are all to be put into the balance. What was said about the nature of the discretion in *Firman v Ellis* (above) was right though the actual decision in that case must be regarded as having been overruled by *Walkley*'s case (above). The judge in the present case had not exercised his discretion and the issue must be remitted to him for a decision.

Deerness v John R Keeble & Son (Brantham) Ltd

[1983] 2 Lloyd's Rep 260, 133 NLJ 641, [1983] Com LR 221, HL
On 7 October 1977 the plaintiff was very seriously injured in a road accident. The defendants were to blame. Their insurers embarked on negotiations for settlement of the claim. The plaintiff's solicitors issued a writ on 23 August 1979 but did not serve it. On 4 August 1980 the insurers paid by agreement the sum of £5,000 as an interim payment. A few days still remained for service of the writ but it was not served, the plaintiff's solicitors apparently regarding the interim payment as an admission of liability and believing the limitation period would date from that payment. Later, appreciating their error, the solicitors issued a second writ on 23 April 1981 and served it on 12 May: they applied for an order under the Limitation Act 1980, s 33 that the action should be allowed to proceed notwithstanding s 11 of the Act.
HELD: The action could not proceed. The decision in *Walkley v Precision Forgings Ltd* (above) was binding on the court. No waiver or agreement that the limitation period would not be insisted upon could be made out of the fact that an interim payment had been made. An appeal to the House of Lords was dismissed. The fatal obstacle to the application under s 33 of the Limitation Act 1980 was the fact that the plaintiff's solicitors did cause a writ to be issued within the primary limitation period. The plaintiff had not been prejudiced by s 11 of the Act. She had brought the first action within the normal limitation period; if she suffered any prejudice it was by her own solicitors' inaction and not by operation of the Act.

White v Glass

(1989) Times, 18 February, CA
The plaintiff suffered an injury on 7 April 1984. The writ was issued on 16 February 1987. The defendant was incorrectly sued as Corby Hazeltree Football Club. This error could have been corrected in a number of ways but instead on 8 September 1987 the plaintiff's solicitors consented to have the writ set aside on the grounds that the pleadings were improperly constituted and ineffective. A fresh writ naming the correct defendant was issued on 23 September 1987. The question for the court was whether the plaintiff was entitled to rely on s 33 of the Limitation Act 1980 to have the three-year limitation period disapplied in view of the decision in *Walkley v Precision Forgings Ltd* (above).
HELD: Although in the *Walkley* case the only exception was where there has been improper conduct on the part of the defendant, this was not the only circumstance and each case has to be looked at on its facts. In the *Walkley* case there was a subsisting properly constituted action against the same defendants as in the first writ. However,

in this case the defendant sued in the second action was not the same as that sued in the first. The defendant in the first action was non-existent. There was no action in being against the defendant in the second writ at the time that the limitation period expired. Therefore, the plaintiff was prejudiced by s 11 and could avail themselves of s 33. It was irrelevant that the initial error could have been remedied by other means.

Restoration of a defendant company to the Company Register

Workvale Limited (No 2)

[1992] 2 All ER 627, [1992] BCLC 544, CA

The plaintiff was injured on 27 September 1983 and notice was given to his employers, a company, that a claim would be made against them. The employer company went into liquidation in 1984 and was dissolved in July 1986. The plaintiff commenced his action against the company just over three weeks before the expiry of the limitation period. The action then proceeded normally and by September 1988 the case was nearly ready for trial. However, at that stage the defendant's solicitors informed the plaintiff's solicitors that the defendant company had been dissolved and in 1990 the defendant's solicitors managed to strike out the plaintiff's claim on the basis that the defendant company no longer existed.

In the meantime, the plaintiff died and his widow pursued the claim by seeking a declaration that the dissolution of the company was void and a direction under s 651(5) of the Companies Act 1985 that the company be restored to the register and that the period between the dissolution of a company and its restoration on a register be disregarded pursuant to s 651(6). The plaintiff succeeded before the judge and the defendant's insurers appealed.

The insurers of the defendant company argued that on the true construction of s 651(5) of the Companies Act 1985, s 33 of the Limitation Act 1980 was to be disregarded. Secondly, if s 33 was not to be disregarded, the court was required to consider whether at trial s 33 was likely to be invoked and on the present facts this was not so.

HELD: It was necessary to look at the entirety of the Limitation Act 1980 when considering whether the plaintiff's application under s 651(5) should succeed. This consideration included the consideration of s 33. It was enough for the widow to satisfy the court that there was an arguable case that s 33 would be used to disapply the limitation period.

As these proceedings had been commenced within the limitation period the necessity of a s 33 application could be avoided by seeking a declaration under s 651(6) of the Companies Act 1985 that the period between the dissolution of the company and the making of the order shall not count.

5 SECTION 35

NEW CLAIMS IN PENDING ACTION—RULES OF COURT

LIMITATION ACT 1980, S 35

'**35 New claims in pending actions: rules of court** (1) For the purposes of this Act, any new claim made in the course of any action shall be deemed to be a separate action and to have been commenced—

(a) in the case of a new claim made in or by way of third party proceedings, on the date on which those proceedings were commenced; and

(b) in the case of any other new claim, on the same date as the original action.

(2) In this section a new claim means any claim by way of set-off or counterclaim, and any claim involving either—

(a) the addition or substitution of a new cause of action; or

(b) the addition or substitution of a new party;

and 'third party proceedings' means any proceedings brought in the course of any action by any party to the action against a person not previously a party to the action, other than proceedings brought by joining any such person as defendant to any claim already made in the original action by the party bringing the proceedings.

(3) Except as provided by s 33 of this Act or by rules of court, neither the High Court nor any county court shall allow a new claim within sub-s (1)(b) above, other than an original set-off or counterclaim, to be made in the course of any action after the expiry of any time limit under this Act which would affect a new action to enforce that claim.

For the purposes of this subsection, a claim is an original set-off or an original counterclaim if it is a claim by way of set-off or (as the case may be) by way of counterclaim by a party who has not previously made any claim in the action.

(4) Rules of court may provide for allowing a new claim to which subsection (3) above applies to be made as there mentioned, but only if the conditions specified in subsection (5) below are satisfied, and subject to any further restrictions the rules may impose.

(5) The conditions referred to in subsection (4) above are the following—

(a) in the case of a claim involving a new cause of action, if the new cause of action arises out of the same facts or substantially the same facts as are already in issue on any claim previously made in the original action; and

(b) in the case of a claim involving a new party, if the addition or substitution of the new party is necessary for the determination of the original action.

(6) The addition or substitution of a new party shall not be regarded for the purposes of subsection (5)(b) above as necessary for the determination of the original action unless either—

(a) the new party is substituted for a party whose name was given in any claim made in the original action in mistake for the new party's name; or

(b) any claim already made in the original action cannot be maintained by or against an existing party unless the new party is joined or substituted as plaintiff or defendant in that action.

(7) Subject to subsection (4) above, rules of court may provide for allowing a party to any action to claim relief in a new capacity in respect of a new cause of action notwithstanding that he had no title to make that claim at the date of the commencement of the action. This subsection shall not be taken as prejudicing the power of rules of court to provide for allowing a party to claim relief in a new capacity without adding or substituting a new cause of action.

(8) Subsections (3) to (7) above shall apply in relation to a new claim made in the course of third party proceedings as if those proceedings were the original action, and subject to such other modifications as may be prescribed by rules of court in any case or class of case.'

Note—See Rules of the Supreme Court 1993, Part 2, notes at paragraphs 6161—6168.

Kennett v Brown

[1988] 2 All ER 600, [1988] 1 WLR 582, 132 Sol Jo 752, CA

The plaintiff, a pillion passenger on Mr Brown's motor-cycle, was injured in a collision with Mr Teagle's motor-cycle. The plaintiff sued Brown who in turn blamed Teagle, who was subsequently joined as second defendant. Teagle served a contribution notice on Brown; after the three-year limitation period had passed, Brown also served a contribution notice in which he sought both an indemnity against the plaintiff's claim and damages for his own personal injuries. The District Registrar (relying upon s 35 of the Limitation Act 1980) held that Brown's claim for his own injuries could not be considered until he had made an application under s 33 to set aside the limitation period. Brown appealed and it was held that before an application under s 33 was necessary, Teagle had to plead the limitation point. Teagle then appealed to the Court of Appeal.

HELD: Brown's claims were both new claims made in the course of the action and not new claims by way of third party proceedings. The effect of s 35(1) was to relate these back to the date of the original action so it was for Teagle to plead s 35(3), whereupon s 33 could be considered and the court's discretion exercised.

Leicester Wholesale Fruit Market Ltd v Grundy

[1990] 1 All ER 442, [1990] 1 WLR 107, CA

The plaintiff issued a writ on 5 December 1984 against six defendants claiming damages for negligence or breach of statutory duty arising out of the construction of a fruit market. On 28 February 1985 and before the writ was served it was amended to include the seventh defendant. The seventh defendant argued that it should not be a party to the action on the basis that the writ was amended to add them after the limitation period of six years had expired.

HELD: The effect of s 35(1) of the Limitation Act 1980 was that after the amendment of the writ, the proceedings against the seventh defendant were deemed to have commenced on the date when the writ was initially issued (ie 5 December 1984). However, if the seventh defendant could have availed himself of a limitation defence if a new writ had been issued at the time of amendment then they should not be joined as a defendant because it would have been deprived of this defence. In this case time ran for the seventh defendant from early 1982 so the case against this defendant was not statute-barred at the time of the original writ or amendment.

Per Glydewell LJ: In my judgment the proper approach in the circumstances such as these is for the court to ask itself: if at the time when the writ was amended the plaintiff had instead issued a fresh writ against the said defendant, could that defendant have successfully applied to strike out the action on the grounds that the limitation period had expired and the action was thus an abuse of the process of the court? If the answer to that question is 'no' then I can see no reason why exactly the same result should not be achieved by amending the writ to add the defendant as a defendant instead of issuing a new piece of paper.

Note—See also *Holland v Yates Building Co Ltd* (1989) Times, 5 December, CA.

Balfour Beatty Construction Ltd v Parsons Brown & Newton Ltd

(1991) 7 Const LJ 205, (1990) Financial Times, 7 November
The plaintiff's writ and statement of claim claimed damages for breach of contract and negligence arising out of an agreement that came into effect in about mid-1982. In January and May 1990 the plaintiff applied for leave to amend the writ and statement of claim to include breaches of contract and negligence arising out of a prior agreement entered into by the parties in 1981.
HELD: The effect of s 35 was to allow a new cause of action which would otherwise be statute-barred to be raised in an existing action provided, in the first instance, that it 'arises out of the same facts or substantially the same facts as or are already in issue in any claim previously made in the original action' (see s 35 (5)(a)). If this condition is not satisfied then the plaintiff's pleadings cannot be amended.

On the facts of this case the allegations raised in the original writ and statement of claim could not be read to extend to cover the earlier period. The new allegations did not arise out of the same facts or substantially the same facts as were already in issue in the original proceedings. As there was no jurisdiction to allow the amendments under s 35 the judge did not examine the appropriate rules of the court (RSC Ord 20, r 5) or consider whether it would be proper to allow the amendments.

Note—In *Steamship Mutual Underwriting Association Ltd v Trollope & Collis Ltd* (1985) 6 Con LR 11, 2 Const LJ 75; affd (1986) 33 BLR 77, 6 Con LR 11, 2 Const LJ 224, CA, the Court of Appeal refused to allow a re-amendment of the statement of claim to add a new cause of action because this was not based on substantially the same facts. For the purposes of s 35 of the Limitation Act 1980 the question to be asked was whether an amendment amounted to an addition of a new cause of action. This required an assessment of the issues raised in the statement of claim and the proposed amendment 'avoiding unnecessary subtleties'.

Hancock Shipping Co Ltd v Kawasaki Heavy Industries Ltd, The Casper Trader

[1991] 2 Lloyd's Rep 237, CA
The defendant carried out repairs to the plaintiff's ship between 5 May and 15 May 1984. On 24 May a fire occurred in the engine room killing three of the crew and rendering the vessel a constructive loss. The writ was issued on 22 April 1987 and the points of claim were served on 3 October 1987. In October 1990 the plaintiff sought leave under RSC Ord 20, r 5 to amend. It was agreed between the parties that the proposed amendments introduced new causes of action which would have been time barred if raised in a new action at the time of the application. The judge refused leave to make the amendments. The defendants appealed.
HELD: Ord 20, r 5(5) was satisfied as the new causes of action arose out of substantially the same facts as the original action.

Ord 20, r 5(2) was only satisfied in respect of one amendment. Once the limitation period had expired a defendant is entitled to raise any prejudice that he has suffered by reason of the fact that the new claim was not included in the original pleadings. When considering an application under this sub-section, the court must take into account the fact that if the amendment is allowed, the defendants will be deprived of an accrued defence.

Bank of America National Trust & Savings Association v Chrismas, The Kyriaki

[1993] 1 Lloyd's Rep 137
The plaintiffs obtained an order granting them leave to amend the writ to join six new defendants outside the limitation period. The defendants sought an order setting aside the amended writ on the grounds that pursuant to s 35(3) of the Limitation Act 1980 the court was debarred from allowing a new claim involving the additional substitution of a new party to be made after the expiry of the relevant limitation period.
HELD: The defendant was successful. Section 35(3) precluded the court from allowing any amendment to be made at a date after the expiry of the limitation period. An order which permitted service on a new defendant outside the limitation period was wrong. It was unjust to join a new party as a defendant when the effect of the amendment would be to deprive the defendant of a limitation defence.

PRE-1980 CASES

Weait v Jayanbee Joinery Ltd

[1963] 1 QB 239, [1962] 2 All ER 568, [1962] 3 WLR 323, 106 Sol Jo 369, CA; appeal to House of Lords [1962] 1 WLR 1083, HL
The infant plaintiff was injured in an accident at work and sued his employers. Their insurers had medical examinations by two doctors before proceedings, neither of whom criticised the treatment received by the plaintiff. The writ was issued two and a quarter years after the accident. After proceedings were begun the defendants asked for an examination by a neuro-surgeon. The plaintiff agreed but owing to some delay which was not the fault of the defendants the examination did not take place until three and a half years after the accident. The neuro-surgeon reported that part of the plaintiff's disability was due to negligent medical treatment. The defendants applied to amend the defence to plead this, though the plaintiff would no longer be able to sue those responsible for the treatment because the limitation period had expired.
HELD: The defendants should be allowed to amend. The question was what was the proper amount of damages for the defendants to pay. It was a misfortune if some fact which was not ascertained before the limitation period expired showed that the damages recoverable against the defendants were only part of the loss and that the remainder could have been recovered from a third party had it been known in time; but that misfortune could not be put on the defendants when they had been free from fault.

Turner v Ford Motor Co Ltd

[1965] 2 All ER 583, [1965] 1 WLR 948, 109 Sol Jo 354, CA
The plaintiff, working on a building site, was injured when a brick dropped on his head. He sued two defendants, neither of whom was his employer, alleging that the brick was dropped by a servant of one or the other. Both defendants denied negligence. Discovery in the action was not completed until after the expiration of the limitation period. On information appearing in a document disclosed by one of the defendants the other applied to amend his defence to allege negligence on the part of the plaintiff in not wearing a safety helmet provided by his employers. The plaintiff opposed the amendment on the ground that if he had known within the limitation period that this point was to be taken he would have joined his employers as

defendants, a course which was not now open to him, and that he would thus be prejudiced by the amendment.
HELD: In *Weait v Jayanbee Joinery Ltd* (above) the question was discussed whether leave to amend should be granted after the statutory period when the proposed amendment sought to cast blame on some third party. In such a case there was a great deal to be said for refusing leave to amend. This case was different as the proposed amendment sought only to put blame on the plaintiff. It did nothing to encourage the plaintiff to do anything he could not have done within the three years. He must know whether he was issued with a helmet and wore it and it had always been open to him to proceed against his employers if he had wished. There was no good reason for refusing the amendment.

6 THIRD PARTY CASES

Note—The Limitation Act 1963, s 4(1) as substituted by the Civil Liability (Contribution) Act 1978, s 9(1) appears now in the Limitation Act 1980, s 10(1)—(5) as follows:

'**10 Special time limit for claiming contribution** (1) Where under s 1 of the Civil Liability (Contribution) Act 1978 any person becomes entitled to a right to recover contribution in respect of any damage from any other person, no action to recover contribution by virtue of that right shall be brought after the expiration of two years from the date on which that right accrued.
(2) For the purposes of this section the date on which a right to recover contribution in respect of any damage accrues to any person (referred to below in this section as 'the relevant date') shall be ascertained as provided in sub-ss (3) and (4) below.
(3) If the person in question is held liable in respect of that damage—
(a) by a judgment given in any civil proceedings; or
(b) by an award made on any arbitration;
the relevant date shall be the date on which the judgment is given, or the date of the award (as the case may be).

For the purposes of this subsection no account shall be taken of any judgment or award given or made on appeal in so far as it varies the amount of damages awarded against the person in question.
(4) If, in any case not within sub-s (3) above, the person in question makes or agrees to make any payment to one or more persons in compensation for that damage (whether he admits any liability in respect of the damage or not), the relevant date shall be the earliest date on which the amount to be paid by him is agreed between him (or his representative) and the person (or each of the persons, as the case may be) to whom the payment is to be made.
(5) An action to recover contribution shall be one to which ss 28, 32 and 35 of this Act apply, but otherwise Parts II and III of this Act (except ss 34, 37 and 38) shall not apply for the purposes of this section.'

George Wimpey & Co Ltd v BOAC

[1955] AC 169, [1954] 3 All ER 661, [1954] 3 WLR 932, 98 Sol Jo 686, HL
Littlewood was employed by BOAC and on 28 July 1949, was injured by a motor vehicle of Wimpeys. Writ was issued against both defendants on 26 April 1951. Third-party notice was issued by Wimpeys against BOAC on 8 June 1951. BOAC pleaded in their defence that action was not brought within 12 months (as the law then required), and was barred. This defence succeeded.

With regard to the third-party proceedings, Parker J held that Wimpeys must show that the BOAC was a tortfeasor who is or would if sued have been liable in respect of the damage. The word 'liable' in the Law Reform (Married Women and Tortfeasors) Act 1935, s 6(1)(c) (now replaced by the Civil Liability (Contribution) Act 1978, s 1) means 'held liable', ie successfully sued to judgment. Recovery can also be made against him if he has not been sued but if he had been sued to judgment he would have been held liable. In this case BOAC had been sued and held not liable. The claim for contribution failed.

An appeal to the House of Lords was dismissed.

Per Viscount Simonds and Lord Tucker: The right conferred by s 6(1)(c) to recover contribution from a joint tortfeasor who would, if sued, have been liable, does not extend to a joint tortfeasor who has been sued and held not to be liable. Where the language of a statute is not calculated to deal with a situation to which it has to be applied and the arguments are fairly evenly balanced, that which causes the least alteration in the law should be chosen.

Note—The words 'who would, if sued, have been held liable' do not appear in s 1 of the Civil Liability (Contribution) Act 1978. The single word 'liable' is used, but sub-s (3) excludes liability to contribute where a person has 'ceased to be liable by virtue of the expiry of a period of limitation', thus preserving the effect of the above case.

See also *Southern Water Authority v Carey* [1985] 2 All ER 1077 and *Harper v Gray and Walker* [1985] 2 All ER 507, [1985] 1 WLR 1196.

Nottingham Health Authority v Nottingham City Council

[1988] 1 WLR 903, 132 Sol Jo 899, CA

A warehouse and office building was designed and built in 1967; cracks were noticed in 1971 and serious cracking had developed by 1975. Proceedings were issued in 1981 against four defendants including the local authority, contractors and architects. On 8 December 1983 the action against the contractor was dismissed as frivolous and vexatious and an abuse of the Court; the claim against the architect was dismissed as merely frivolous and vexatious. This left the local authority as the only defendants; on 17 July 1985 they served third party notices on the contractors and architects.

HELD, ON APPEAL: The District Registrar, when dismissing the actions, whilst strongly critical of the plaintiff's approach as 'irresponsible inept and unhappy' did not make an express finding on limitation—merely that the point was 'a proper one'. In the absence of a clear final judgment on limitation the contractors and architects had not been sued to judgment and third party proceedings could continue to enable contribution to be recovered, in respect of damage occurring before 1 January 1979. Per curiam: if any damage had occurred after 1 January 1979, no available limitation defence would be relevant to the local authority's claim for contribution.

Note—See also *Harper v Gray & Walker* [1985] 2 All ER 507, [1985] 1 WLR 1196.

7 MISCELLANEOUS

ENDORSEMENT DEFECTIVE

Collins v Hertfordshire County Council

[1947] KB 598, [1947] 1 All ER 633, [1947] LJR 789, 176 LT 456, 111 JP 272, 63 TLR 317, 45 LGR 263 (Hilbery J)
In an action for negligence against a hospital, the statement of claim alleged (inter alia) the negligence of a house surgeon as a servant of the hospital.

More than 12 months (which was then the limitation period) after the cause of action, an amendment was applied for alleging the negligence of a pharmacist also as a servant of the hospital.
HELD: Not a new cause of action; it was only particulars of the cause of action for negligence of the hospital.

Pathak v James Nourse Ltd

(1961) 105 Sol Jo 1106, [1961] 2 Lloyd's Rep 467, CA
The plaintiff was injured when working as a seaman on the defendant's vessel. He was struck by a rope when the operation of winding the vessel away from the quay was being attempted. The endorsement on the writ claimed damages for 'personal injuries caused by the negligence of the defendants their servants or agents sustained by the plaintiff. . . .' The case reached trial after the limitation period had expired, the statement of claim having alleged that the accident was due to a defective stopper rope. At the trial it soon appeared that this case was false. The judge expressed the view that the accident was due to the negligent way in which those in charge of the ship were conducting the operation. The plaintiff applied and was permitted to amend the statement of claim to allege this negligence. The trial was continued several months later and the defendants held liable to the plaintiff on the grounds set out in the amendment.
HELD: The endorsement on the writ was sufficient to cover the new allegation in the amended statement of claim which did not amount to a new cause of action.

Dornan v J W Ellis & Co Ltd

[1962] 1 QB 583, [1962] 1 All ER 303, [1962] 2 WLR 250, 105 Sol Jo 1083, CA
On 10 April 1957 the plaintiff sustained an eye injury from a piece of a drill which broke when being used by a fellow-servant of the defendants. He claimed damages by a writ the endorsement of which alleged 'breach of statutory duty and/or negligence of the defendants, their servants or agents'. The statement of claim contained no allegation against the fellow-workman. On 21 October 1961 (after the limitation period had expired), the plaintiff applied to amend the statement of claim to allege negligence against the fellow-workman.
HELD: The amendment should be allowed. The fresh allegations did not introduce a new cause of action nor a new set of ideas. It must be a question of degree in each case on its particular facts.

Fannon v Backhouse

(1987) Times, 22 August, CA
In 1978 the defendant and his father were in partnership as farmers; in June 1979 probate of his father's estate was granted to him. The plaintiffs, building contractors,

issued a writ against the defendant alone in October 1981 in which they alleged that they had agreed in 1978 with the partnership to construct a barn, in consideration for which the partnership would convey land and pay money. By March 1986 it was clear that the defendant, who had in the meantime been convicted and imprisoned for murder, would not be able to meet any judgment for the sums which still remained outstanding. On 27 March 1986 the plaintiffs obtained leave to amend their statement of claim to add a claim against the defendant in his capacity as executor of his father's will. The plaintiffs' claim had become statute-barred against the estate on 15 August 1984, six years after the date they alleged the works were complete. The plaintiffs could only amend to join the defendant as executor if s 35 of the Limitation Act 1980 was satisfied, by showing that the new cause of action against him arose out of the same or substantially the same facts as were already in issue or that the addition or substitution of a new party was necessary for the determination of the original claim.
HELD: On appeal, 'in issue' means 'material' and neither the death of the father nor the grant of probate was material to the claim already made against the defendant personally. The addition of a new party was not necessary to the determination of the original action. It would be extraordinary if an action had been maintainable against the estate simply because the defendant was an executor.

MISNOMER OF DEFENDANT AND WRONG DEFENDANT

Whittam v W J Daniel & Co Ltd

[1962] 1 QB 271, [1961] 3 All ER 796, [1961] 3 WLR 1123, 105 Sol Jo 886, CA
The plaintiff was injured in an accident at work on 10 September 1957 when in the employment of W J Daniel & Co Ltd. On 9 September 1960, she issued a writ against 'W J Daniel and Company (a firm)'. On 12 October 1960 (after the limitation period had expired) she amended the description of the defendants in the writ by master's fiat to 'W J Daniel & Co Ltd'. After service of the writ the defendants sought to have it set aside on the ground that nobody was sued within the period of limitation and that they were made defendants for the first time on 12 October 1960. The defendants were incorporated on 6 October 1931 taking over a business run by Walter James Daniel which ceased to be carried on with effect from 10 November 1931.
HELD: It was a case of mere misnomer and the amendment was properly allowed. The defendants could be in no doubt from the original description of the defendants in the writ that it was intended for them. The word 'Limited' was not an essential part of the name of a company and its omission did not mean that nobody was sued when the writ was issued.

Rodriguez v Parker

[1967] 1 QB 116, [1966] 2 All ER 349, [1966] 3 WLR 546 (Nield J)
On 30 October 1961, the plaintiff was injured when knocked down by a van owned by R J Parker and driven by his son R S Parker. On 20 April 1962, solicitors on behalf of the plaintiff wrote to R S Parker claiming damages for 'your negligent driving'. An insurance company replied acknowledging the letter 'addressed to our insured', their own letter being headed 'R J Parker'. Negotiations for settlement were eventually broken off and the solicitors ceased to act. On 28 August 1963, the plaintiff's trade union on his behalf wrote the insurers a letter headed 'Your insured — R S Parker' renewing the claim and in November 1963 fresh solicitors were instructed by or on behalf of the plaintiff. These solicitors obtained an offer which the plaintiff refused

and on 11 June 1964, they issued a writ against 'R J Parker (male)': the endorsement claimed damages for the 'negligent driving of the defendant'. On 4 January 1965, they served the writ on R J Parker. His insurers instructed solicitors who entered appearance. On 14 June 1965, the statement of claim was served alleging 'negligent driving of the defendant'. The insurers' solicitors served a defence denying that the 'defendant was . . . driving any motor vehicle at the time and place alleged'. The plaintiff's solicitors then realised they had sued the wrong defendant and applied to amend the writ to substitute 'R S Parker' for 'R J Parker' and to extend the validity of the writ.
HELD: They were entitled to the order asked for. RSC Ord 20, r 5 allowed the Court to amend a writ so as to correct the name of a party even if the effect was to substitute a new party where the Court was satisfied that the mistake was genuine and not misleading. It was not necessary to show that it was a case of mere misnomer. The mistake was genuine on the part of the plaintiff's solicitors and was not misleading to the insurers or their solicitors because: (1) the letter before the action of 20 April 1962; (2) the union's letter of 28 August 1963, and (3) the references to the defendant's negligent driving in the writ and statement of claim all made it clear that R. S. Parker was the person intended to be sued. It was just to allow the amendment as the claim was first made within six months of the accident and the intended defendant had ample time and opportunity to prepare his case. The amendment being allowed it followed that the validity of the writ should be extended.

Mitchell v Harris Engineering Co Ltd

[1967] 2 QB 703, [1967] 2 All ER 682, [1967] 3 WLR 447, 111 Sol Jo 355, CA
The plaintiff claimed damages from his employers, Harris Engineering Co Ltd, for injury sustained at their works at Tunbridge Wells. The company was registered in Northern Ireland. The plaintiff's solicitors, unaware of this, issued the writ against an associated company Harris Engineering Co (Leeds) Ltd which was registered in England and which they assumed was the correct defendant. The writ was not served until after the limitation period had expired. When the company secretary (who was secretary of both companies) received the writ he sent it to the employers' insurers who told the plaintiff's solicitors they had sued the wrong company. The plaintiff applied to amend writ by substituting Harris Engineering Co Ltd for Harris Engineering Co (Leeds) Ltd.
HELD, ON APPEAL: They could have leave to do so. Order 20, r 5 was not ultra vires the rules committee merely because it might have the effect of depriving a defendant of the benefit of a statute of limitations. Whenever a writ has been issued within the permitted time but is found to be defective the defendant has no 'right' to have it remain so. The court can permit the defect to be cured by amendment. The circumstances in which a litigant may amend existing proceedings, for example by adding or substituting defendants, are essentially a matter of practice or procedure. Whether it is proper to allow the amendment is a matter for the discretion of the court within the language of the rule. There was a genuine mistake on the part of the plaintiff's solicitors: it did not mislead the defendants since the secretary could tell from the writ that the accident occurred at the Irish company's works.

Evans Constructions Co Ltd v Charrington & Co Ltd

[1983] QB 810, [1983] 1 All ER 310, [1983] 2 WLR 117, 126 Sol Jo 658, 264 Estates Gazette 347, CA
The defendants having served notice on the plaintiffs under the Landlord and Tenant

Act 1954 'as agents for Bass Holdings Ltd' to terminate the plaintiffs' tenancy the plaintiffs' solicitors issued an originating application against the defendants in the county court for grant of a new lease. They did so mistakenly believing the defendants to be the landlords. The defendants applied to the court to strike out the application on the ground that they were not the plaintiffs' landlords. The plaintiffs sought to have Bass Holdings joined as defendants.
HELD, in the Court of Appeal: Bass Holdings should be substituted as defendants under Ord 20, r 5(3) and the plaintiffs have 14 days to serve them, the time under the Act having expired. It was important to bear in mind the distinction between suing A in the mistaken belief that he is the party responsible for the matters complained of and seeking to sue B but mistakenly naming him as A. Order 20, r 5(3) is designed to correct the latter and not the former category of mistake. But the party applying must also satisfy the court that the mistake was genuine, the error in the name not misleading and that it is just to allow the correction. In the present case all the criteria were met.

WRONG DATE

Hay v London Brick Co Ltd

(1981) 131 NLJ 657, [1981] LS Gaz R 974, Times, 12 May, CA
The plaintiff sustained injury in an accident at work. He began proceedings giving 18 November 1974 as the date of the accident. In February 1980 the defendants disclosed documents showing that the date of the accident was in fact 3 December 1975. The plaintiff applied to amend the pleadings to substitute 3 December 1975 for 18 November 1974. The judge refused the amendment on the ground that it introduced a new cause of action.
HELD: Order 20, r 5(5) did not permit an amendment made after expiry of the limitation period if the effect would be to add or substitute a new cause of action, unless it arose out of substantially the same facts. The date of the cause of action was of importance on the question whether the action was statute-barred but that was a procedural matter, not one of substance. The date also affected the special damage but that went only on the measure of damages, not the cause of action. A plaintiff could prove his cause of action without being able to prove its precise date. The proposed amendment did not create a new cause of action: the court therefore had a discretion to allow the amendment and should do so. Appeal allowed.

RENEWAL OF WRIT AFTER LIMITATION OPERATIVE

Heaven v Road and Rail Wagons Ltd

[1965] 2 QB 355, [1965] 2 All ER 409, [1965] 2 WLR 1249, 109 Sol Jo 335 (Megaw J)
In a personal injury claim the cause of action arose on 31 March 1961. A writ was issued on 20 December 1963, but not served. Negotiations were in progress between the parties but had broken down by 15 September 1964. The writ expired on 19 December 1964 but on an ex parte application on 26 January 1965, the master renewed it for three months. It was served on 29 January 1965: the defendants applied for the writ to be set aside and service declared invalid.

HELD: It was not correct that the new Ord 6, r 8 (in effect from January 1964) had widened the discretion of the Court to renew a writ after the period allowed for service had expired. The decisions in *Battersby v Anglo-American Oil Co Ltd* ([1945] 1 KB 23) and *Sheldon v Brown Bayley's Steel Works Ltd* ([1953] 2 QB 393) are still binding on the court. The rule is that leave will not be given to extend the validity of a writ when application is made retrospectively after the period of 12 months prescribed by the rules has expired if the effect of so doing would be to deprive the defendant of a defence which he would have had under the relevant statute of limitation had leave to extend not been given and the plaintiff had to serve a fresh writ. To justify the exercise of the discretion there must be exceptional circumstances, eg agreement between the parties to defer service or where the defendant had evaded service. A technical slip by the plaintiff's solicitors is not sufficient. The writ here must be set aside.

Note—In *Brickfield Properties v Newton* [1971] 3 All ER 328, [1971] 1 WLR 862, 115 Sol Jo 307, CA Sachs LJ said that if it was intended to convey in *Heaven*'s case that the courts were not in process of liberalising, insofar as they have a discretion, their view as to what constituted the justice of the case as between the parties he would not agree. Since *Pontin v Wood* [1962] 1 QB 594, CA there had been a progressive development to a broader approach which had been encouraged by the amendments of the rules embodied in RSC Ord 20, r 5.

Hay-Kellie v Michaelides

(1969) 113 Sol Jo 902, CA
Accident 4 June 1964 causing plaintiff serious injuries. Writ issued 1 November 1965, served on second defendant 2 February 1966. Not served on first defendant who was said to have gone to Greece in October 1964. Next friend appointed 8 May 1969, the plaintiff's mental state being such that he was unable to conduct his own affairs. An application was made for leave to renew the writ as against the first defendant.
HELD: It was a doubtful point whether under Ord 6, r 8(2) once the writ had been served on one defendant it might be good. In all the circumstances including the fact that both defendants were covered by the same insurance policy, leave should be given to renew the writ for 12 months and to serve it out of the jurisdiction.

Chappell v Cooper

[1980] 2 All ER 463, [1980] 1 WLR 958, 124 Sol Jo 544, CA
On an application to extend the validity of a writ which had expired it was argued that since 1975, because of the provisions of s 2D of the Limitation Act 1939, there was no longer valid reason for refusing an extension on the ground that it would deprive the defendant of the benefit of a limitation period which had accrued, since the plaintiff can apply to have the limitation period disapplied.
HELD: Not so. Had *Firman v Ellis* (p 524, above) remained good law it might have been otherwise, but having regard to the restrictive interpretation of the relevant provisions of the 1975 Act by the House of Lords in *Walkley v Precision Forgings* (p 524, above) the principles which have long existed upon which extensions of time to serve a writ which had not been timeously served as determined remain unaffected.

Siksnys v Hanley

(1982) Times, 26 May, CA
The plaintiff was badly injured in a road accident by the negligent driving of the defendant on 30 April 1977. His solicitor issued a writ on 25 January 1980. Despite

efforts by the plaintiff and his solicitors the defendant could not be found and his whereabouts were unknown. In February 1981 the writ having expired unserved the plaintiff applied to the Court for an extension and an order for substituted service at the address of the defendant's insurers. The validity of the writ was extended under Ord 6, r 8 on the ground that there were exceptional circumstances. On appeal the defendant argued that exceptional circumstances did not exist: the plaintiff should have applied for an order for substituted service at the insurer's address (as Lord Diplock had recommended in *Gurtner v Circuit* (p 776, below)) before the writ had expired.
HELD: The order should stand. The way in which the defendant had kept out of the way did make the case one of exceptional circumstances.

The Gaz Foundation

[1987] 2 Lloyd's Rep 151, QBD
Two vessels collided on 2 January 1982; negotiations for settlement of the resultant claims began in March 1982. Extensions of time for the issue of a writ were obtained on 2 November 1983, 29 November 1984, 19 December 1986. A writ was issued on behalf of the plaintiffs on 14 January 1987, without the extension having been renewed; this was admitted to be due to 'an unfortunate oversight'. The extensions of time had been obtained as a matter of course, despite the plaintiff's own anxiety to obtain settlement.
HELD: The writ should be struck out. In the exercise of the court's discretion to extend time, it is not a sufficient 'exceptional circumstance' to argue that the failure to issue the writ was due to an oversight. That is the usual circumstance.

Kleinwort Benson Ltd v Barbrak Ltd, The Myrto (No 3)

[1987] AC 597, [1987] 2 All ER 289, [1987] 2 WLR 1053, 131 Sol Jo 594, HL
In 1977 The Myrto was arrested and unloaded by the plaintiff mortgagee. After the failure of attempts to reach settlement with the cargo owners for the unloading costs, the plaintiffs decided to try to avoid the huge legal costs of suing most or all of the cargo owners by proceedings against only the owner of the largest amount of cargo, to seek to establish a claim against all the owners. The plaintiff sued the owner of the most cargo in June 1980. On 4 November 1982 the plaintiff issued an omnibus writ against the other owners, their insurers and guarantors, naming a total of 162 defendants but this writ was not served because the first action could not be heard until January 1984. The omnibus writ was extended twice (in October 1983 and 1984) ex parte, on the clear grounds of saving unnecessary legal costs. When the omnibus writ was finally served, on 24 January 1985, the mortgagee having succeeded in the first action, four of the defendants applied to set aside the two extensions of the writ. The Court of Appeal (reversing decisions in lower courts) did so on the grounds that the real purpose of granting extensions was to deal with difficulties of service, and not simply to enable a plaintiff to deal with matters in a slightly cheaper way. The fundamental and paramount principle was that no extension would be granted if there were no exceptional circumstances. The plaintiffs appealed.
HELD: This was incorrect. Per Lord Brandon: 'It has been unhelpful to put the condition for extension as high as "exceptional circumstances", an expression which conveys to my mind at any rate a large degree of stringency. (Ord 6, r 8) should be interpreted as requiring "good reason" and no more.' Good reason must depend upon the circumstances; here it was 'the saving of unnecessary proceedings and costs achieved without any prejudice to the respondents'. Here the Admiralty judge had

exercised his discretion properly, weighing the balance of hardship between the parties, by upholding the extensions.

Waddon v Whitecroft-Scovell Ltd

[1988] 1 All ER 996, [1988] 1 WLR 309, 132 Sol Jo 263, [1988] 11 LS Gaz R 43, HL
The plaintiff contracted dermatitis towards the end of 1979. He first consulted solicitors in June 1982. Limited legal aid was granted in October 1982 to avoid the expiry of the limitation period. This was done on Counsel's advice; he also advised that an expert's report should be obtained. Legal aid to cover the issue but not service of the writ had been obtained on 26 November 1982. Investigations proceeded slowly but November 1983 proved to be crucial. On the 9th the plaintiff's solicitors applied ex parte to extend the validity of the writ; on the 18th their expert advised favourably and on the 24th the plaintiff's solicitors heard that their application had been granted; but for this, the validity of the writ would have expired on 28 November 1983. On 1 December Counsel advised that the case could proceed, so on the 6th the plaintiff's solicitors applied to have the remaining limitations removed on the legal aid certificate; this was granted on the 7th. The writ was served (as it appeared to have been lost at the District Registry) on 16 April 1984. On 3 May 1984 the defendant's solicitors applied to set aside the extension. The judge held, on all the facts of the case, that the plaintiff had not shown good and sufficient reason for an extension. The Court of Appeal agreed. The plaintiff appealed.
HELD: Appeal dismissed. Per Lord Brandon: In *Kleinwort Benson Ltd v Barbrak* (above) the House of Lords had set out the principles for the exercise of the court's discretion on applications for extensions of the validity of a writ where questions of limitation are involved: (i) on the true construction of Ord 6, r 8 the power to extend the validity of a writ should only be exercised for good reason; (ii) the question of whether such good reason exists in any particular case depends on all the circumstances of that case. The difficulty in effecting service of the writ may well constitute good reason but it is not the only matter which is capable of doing so; (iii) the balance of hardship between the parties can be a relevant matter to be taken into account in the exercise of the discretion; and (iv) the discretion is that of the judge and his exercise of it should not be interfered with by an appellate court except on special grounds the nature of which is well established. One factor to consider is the effect of delays due to the legal aid system. In this case the existence of the legal aid restriction, although part of the background, was not the cause of the failure to serve the writ within the original 12-month period. The real cause was the plaintiff's failure to take the necessary steps and to serve the writ in the 10 days between the receipt of their expert's report on 18 November and the expiry of the writ on 28 November.

Doble v Haymills (Contractors) Ltd

(1988) 132 Sol Jo 1063, CA
The plaintiff's solicitor mistakenly transposed vital dates, and thus failed to serve the writ in time. The judge held that although the confusion that led to this transposition of dates constituted a good reason, he was not prepared to exercise his discretion under Ord 6, r 8 and extend the validity of the writ. The plaintiff appealed.
HELD: Appeal dismissed. The reasons given for the failure to serve the writ and thus the need to extend the validity of the writ were not persuasive. In cases which are delayed, solicitors should act quickly, but the plaintiff's solicitor had not done so and should have taken action long before the final date.

FAILURE TO PERFECT AMENDMENT IN TIME

Braniff v Holland Hannen and Cubitts (Southern) Ltd

[1969] 3 All ER 959, [1969] 1 WLR 1533, 113 Sol Jo 836, CA
In an action for damages for personal injuries the accident occurred on 24 October 1965 and the writ was issued against the first defendants on 25 October 1966. On 24 July 1968, the plaintiff, wishing to join the second defendants, obtained an order for amendment of the writ and statement of claim. By an oversight he failed to amend and reseal the writ within 14 days as required by Ord 15, r 8(4). On 23 October 1968 (after expiry of the limitation period), he obtained an extension of time for making the amendment. When the writ was served the second defendants applied to set aside the writ and service and obtained an order from the judge in chambers to that effect.
HELD, ON APPEAL: The judge rightly exercised his discretion in so ordering. By Ord 15, r 8(4) the added defendant is not to be a party to the action until the amendment is duly completed in accordance with the rule. Thus there was no writ available against the second defendant at all until the amendment was made. To permit the plaintiff an extension of time beyond the expiry of the limitation period deprived the added party of a defence under the Limitation Acts and put the case in the category of those where a plaintiff seeks to renew an expired writ, as in *Heaven v Road and Rail Wagons Ltd* (p 537, above). The fact that under Ord 20, r 5 certain amendments were permitted although the statutory period had run did not mean that in general there had been any relaxation in the principle formerly applying in *Weldon v Neal* (1887) 19 QBD 394.

RENEWAL BY MASTER UNASKED

Bugden v Ministry of Defence

[1972] 1 All ER 1, [1972] 1 WLR 27, 115 Sol Jo 811, CA
The plaintiffs, passengers injured in a motor accident, sued for damages. They were bound to succeed against one or other of the defendants. Negotiations took a long time. A writ was issued on 23 September 1969, just within the limitation period. On 7 September 1970, they applied to the master for issue of a concurrent writ so that it could be served on the third defendant in Scotland. The master made the order and added, without being asked, 'Liberty to renew for three months'. The plaintiff's solicitors accepted the renewal and did not serve the writ until December 1970. The third defendant then applied to have the renewal set aside.
HELD: The renewal of the writ was valid. Although no application had been made to the master for renewal as required by Ord 6, r 8(2) there were in existence at the time of the master's order good and sufficient grounds for renewing the writ—there was no issue on liability, there was a difficult medical position and negotiations were proceeding—plus the fact that only 12 days remained at the time in which to serve it in Scotland. The plaintiffs' solicitors would have been acting reasonably if they had applied for the extension which was in fact given. The order should stand.

WAIVER OF LIMITATION DEFENCE

Lubovsky v Snelling

[1944] KB 44, [1943] 2 All ER 577, 113 LJKB 14, 170 LT 2, 60 TLR 52, CA
A defence that the action is statute-barred can be waived by agreement or conduct.

In a claim under the Fatal Accidents Acts, the defendants' insurers agreed with the claimant's solicitors before the limitation period expired (1) that they had no defence, and that the negotiations should proceed 'on the basis of admission of liability', but (2) that 'a writ would have to be issued in any event because whether they agreed about the quantum of damages or not, the court would have to approve and apportion it.' This amounted to a contract not to plead the Fatal Accidents Act 1846, s 3.

Appeal from Tucker J (reported 75 Ll L Rep 165) allowed.

Note—The practical result of this decision seems to be that an insurer should never admit liability as distinct from admitting negligence. It was cited and distinguished in the following case, where it was pointed out that in *Lubovsky*'s case it was an essential part of the bargain made between the parties that liability for the cause of action was definitely accepted and that the defendants were thereafter precluded from putting forward any defence whatever which would impeach that liability and was a contract not to plead the statute of limitations. They were debarred from raising the point.

The Sauria and the Trent

[1957] 1 Lloyd's Rep 396, CA

The plaintiff's motor vessel was lying moored at a wharf when it was struck and damaged by a barge which was being towed by a tug. Correspondence took place between solicitors of the parties and eventually the solicitors for defendants admitted liability. Attempts were then made to arrange an arbitration to fix the amount of damages, but agreement was not reached, and in January 1957, the plaintiffs began an action. The collision took place on 16 June 1953; the admission of liability was by letter dated 19 January 1955. The defendants took a preliminary objection that the claim was barred by the Maritime Conventions Act 1911, s 8 which required proceedings within two years from the date of damage. Judge Block in the City of London Court held that the action was barred. The plaintiff submitted the admission was qualified and not absolute; while the matter was still under discussion the admission was withdrawn. The plaintiffs appealed.

HELD: There was an admission of liability but there was no undertaking to waive the right of defendants to rely on the section. The case of *Lubovsky v Snelling* was distinguishable on its facts. There was no ground for exercising the discretion given to the court by the proviso to the section. Appeal dismissed.

Re Chittenden, Chittenden v Doe

[1970] 3 All ER 562, [1970] 1 WLR 1618, 114 Sol Jo 954 (Ungoed-Thomas J)

The plaintiff issued an originating summons within the time allowed by the Inheritance (Family Provision) Act 1938 but at the suggestion of the executors, who were the defendant, did not serve it while negotiations were pending. More than 12 months later the plaintiff obtained an order ex parte extending the time for service of the summons. It was then served and the defendant entered unconditional appearance. More than a year later the defendant applied to set aside the order and service.

HELD: It would be unjust to refuse to exercise discretion in the plaintiff's favour on the ground that to do so would deprive the defendant of the benefit of a statute of limitation where the defendant is himself a party to the withholding of service of the originating process whether by asking or agreeing to it or otherwise.

The Owenbawn

[1973] 1 Lloyd's Rep 56 (Brandon J)
Collision between two vessels 28 August 1969. Negotiations for settlement of claims begun between solicitors 10 September 1970 still continuing on 2 July 1971 when plaintiffs' solicitors issued writ and notified defendants' solicitors it was 'to protect the two year time limit which would otherwise expire in August'. Further discussions took place at long intervals. On 3 August 1972 the writ having expired and the latest offer from the defendants being still outstanding, the plaintiffs' solicitors applied ex parte for, and were granted, a renewal to 27 August 1972. The defendants applied for renewal to be set aside.
HELD: On the facts, there was an agreement that service of the plaintiffs' writ should be deferred so long as negotiations were continuing and the writ was rightly renewed. *Re Chittenden* (above) applied.

Hare v Personal Representatives of Malik

(1980) 124 Sol Jo 328, CA
The plaintiff was injured in July 1976 as a passenger in a car accident in which the driver was killed. His solicitors notified the deceased's insurers of the intended claim in July 1976. The parties negotiated. In September 1978 the plaintiff's solicitors issued a writ naming the defendants as 'the personal representatives of the estate' of the deceased. The insurers nominated solicitors who continued to negotiate. There was delay whilst the insurers' solicitors tried to find personal representatives. When in September 1979 the plaintiff's solicitors made application to proceed under Ord 15, r 6A it was pointed out that the writ had expired. An application to renew was refused by the judge on the ground that there were no exceptional circumstances.
HELD, allowing an appeal: There were exceptional circumstances in that negotiations had continued on the basis that both parties agreed that the case should proceed and neither should take technical points against the other. The fact that the plaintiff's solicitors were at fault did not in itself mean that the situation was not exceptional.

CHAPTER 16

Evidence

1 ADMISSIBILITY: HEARSAY EVIDENCE

THE RULE

Note—Rules of the Supreme Court, Ord 38, r 1 reads: 'Subject to the provisions of these rules and of the Civil Evidence Act 1968 and the Civil Evidence Act 1972, and any other enactment relating to evidence, any fact required to be proved at the trial of any action begun by writ by the evidence of witnesses shall be proved by the examination of the witnesses orally and in open court.'

Nicholls v Williams

(1983) Times, 21 May (Mann J)
RSC Ord 25, r 8(1)(d) (which provides that '. . . the contents of any police accident report book shall be receivable in evidence at the trial . . .') does not make hearsay statements recorded in a police officer's notebook admissible in evidence unless the rules of court made under the Civil Evidence Act 1968 and contained in RSC Ord 38 are complied with. It could not have been intended that Ord 25, r 8(1)(d) should afford an exception to the Ord 38 rules.

Greenaway v Homelea Fittings (London) Ltd

[1985] 1 WLR 234, 129 Sol Jo 49, QBD
The plaintiff was injured when unloading one of the defendants' vans. He claimed damages and applied for an order that certain statements of the van driver should be admissible in evidence at the trial without calling the driver as a witness. The Master made an order under RSC Ord 38, r 9(2).
HELD, ON APPEAL: The order should not have been made. The Master had reasoned that if the driver had been joined as a defendant his statement would have been admissible. But in that event it would have been admissible only against himself and not against the other defendant. In spite of the Civil Evidence Act 1968 the best evidence rule should apply unless there were compelling reasons why not. There was no reason why the driver should not be called.

Note—The Civil Evidence Act 1968 provides for the admissibility of hearsay evidence (whether oral or written) in civil proceedings. It is important in motor claims cases in providing the means by which evidence from the following sources can be conveniently brought before the court whether or not the person making the statement is called as a witness:
1 statements made by parties or witnesses to police officers and recorded in the police report;
2 evidence given orally in proceedings in the magistrates' courts;
3 evidence given at an inquest and recorded by the coroner;
4 statements of fact contained in hospital notes and records.

The machinery for adducing hearsay evidence in the High Court is contained in RSC Ord 38, rr 20 to 34 made in pursuance of s 8 of the Act.

The Civil Evidence Act 1972 makes hearsay statements of opinion admissible in evidence in civil proceedings to substantially the same extent as are hearsay statements of fact under the 1968 Act.

R v Coventry Justices, ex p Bullard

(1992) 136 Sol Jo LB 96, [1992] RA 79, 95 Cr App Rep 175
Mr and Mrs Bullard were prosecuted for the non-payment of community charge. The local authority obtained a liability order against the Bullards. The amount of the

community charge was proved by reference to a computer print out produced by the local authority. Mr and Mrs Bullard submitted that the computer print out was inadmissible as evidence on the grounds that it was hearsay.
HELD: Subject to the Evidence Act of 1938 and its own exceptions the hearsay rule remained fully applicable in civil proceedings in the magistrates' court. The critical input on the computer had been of information wholly or in part implanted by humans. Thus this input was hearsay and inadmissible as evidence either as to the amount which the applicant was liable to pay or the amount which was unpaid.

CIVIL EVIDENCE ACT 1968

1 Hearsay evidence to be admissible only by virtue of this Act and other statutory provisions, or by agreement (1) In any civil proceedings a statement other than one made by a person while giving oral evidence in those proceedings shall be admissible as evidence of any fact stated therein to the extent that it is so admissible by virtue of any provision of this Part of this Act or by virtue of any other statutory provision or by agreement of the parties, but not otherwise.
(2) In this section 'statutory provision' means any provision contained in, or in an instrument made under, this or any other Act, including any Act passed after this Act.

2 Admissibility of out-of-court statements as evidence of facts stated (1) In any civil proceedings a statement made, whether orally or in a document or otherwise, by any person, whether called as a witness in those proceedings or not, shall, subject to this section and to rules of court, be admissible as evidence of any fact stated therein of which direct oral evidence by him would be admissible.
(2) Where in any civil proceedings a party desiring to give a statement in evidence by virtue of this section has called or intends to call as a witness in the proceedings the person by whom the statement was made, the statement—
(a) shall not be given in evidence by virtue of this section on behalf of that party without the leave of the court; and
(b) without prejudice to paragraph (a) above, shall not be given in evidence by virtue of this section on behalf of that party before the conclusion of the examination-in-chief of the person by whom it was made, except—
  (i) where before that person is called the court allows evidence of the making of the statement to be given on behalf of that party by some other person; or
  (ii) in so far as the court allows the person by whom the statement was made to narrate it in the course of his examination-in-chief on the ground that to prevent him from doing so would adversely affect the intelligibility of his evidence.
(3) Where in any civil proceedings a statement which was made otherwise than in a document is admissible by virtue of this section, no evidence other than direct oral evidence by the person who made the statement or any person who heard or otherwise perceived it being made shall be admissible for the purpose of proving it:
Provided that if the statement in question was made by a person while giving oral evidence in some other legal proceedings (whether civil or criminal), it may be proved in any manner authorised by the court.

[*Section 3 provides for a witness's previous statement, if proved, to be evidence of any facts stated therein of which direct oral evidence by him would be admissible.*]

4 Admissibility of certain records as evidence of facts stated (1) Without prejudice to section 5 of this Act, in any civil proceedings a statement contained in a document shall, subject to this section and to rules of court, be admissible as evidence of any fact stated therein of which direct oral evidence would be admissible, if the document is, or forms part of, a record compiled by a person acting under a duty from information which was supplied by a person (whether acting under a duty or not) who had, or may reasonably be supposed to have had, personal knowledge of the matters dealt with in that information and which, if not supplied by that person to the compiler of the record directly, was supplied by him to the compiler of the record indirectly through one or more intermediaries each acting under a duty.

(2) Where in any civil proceedings a party desiring to give a statement in evidence by virtue of this section has called or intends to call as a witness in the proceedings the person who originally supplied the information from which the record containing the statement was compiled, the statement—

(a) shall not be given in evidence by virtue of this section on behalf of that party without the leave of the court; and

(b) without prejudice to paragraph (a) above, shall not without the leave of the court be given in evidence by virtue of this section on behalf of that party before the conclusion of the examination-in-chief of the person who originally supplied the said information.

(3) Any reference in this section to a person acting under a duty includes a reference to a person acting in the course of any trade, business, profession or other occupation in which he is engaged or employed or for the purposes of any paid or unpaid office held by him.

[*Section 5 deals with statements produced by computers.*]

6 Provisions supplementary to ss 2 to 5 (1) Where in any civil proceedings a statement contained in a document is proposed to be given in evidence by virtue of s 2, 4 or 5 of this Act it may, subject to any rules of court, be proved by the production of that document or (whether or not that document is still in existence) by the production of a copy of that document, or of the material part thereof, authenticated in such manner as the court may approve.

(2) For the purpose of deciding whether or not a statement is admissible in evidence by virtue of s 2, 4 or 5 of this Act, the court may draw any reasonable inference from the circumstances in which the statement was made or otherwise came into being or from any other circumstances, including, in the case of a statement contained in a document, the form and contents of that document.

(3) In estimating the weight, if any, to be attached to a statement admissible in evidence by virtue of s 2, 3, 4 or 5 of this Act regard shall be had to all the circumstances from which any inference can reasonably be drawn as to the accuracy or otherwise of the statement and, in particular—

(a) in the case of a statement falling within s 2(1) or 3(1) or (2) of this Act, to the question whether or not the statement was made contemporaneously with the occurrence or existence of facts stated, and to the question whether or not the maker of the statement had any incentive to conceal or misrepresent the facts;

(b) in the case of a statement falling within s 4(1) of this Act, to the question whether or not the person who originally supplied the information from which the record containing the statement was compiled did so contemporaneously with the occurrence or existence of the facts dealt within that information, and to the question whether or not that person, or any person concerned with compiling or keeping the record containing the statement, had any incentive to conceal or misrepresent the facts.

7 (1) Subject to rules of court, where in any civil proceedings a statement made by a person who is not called as a witness in those proceedings is given in evidence by virtue of s 2 of this Act—

(a) any evidence which, if that person had been so called, would be admissible for the purpose of destroying or supporting his credibility as a witness shall be admissible for that purpose in those proceedings; and

(b) evidence tending to prove that, whether before or after he made that statement that person made (whether orally or in a document or otherwise) another statement inconsistent therewith shall be admissible for the purpose of showing that that person has contradicted himself:

Provided that nothing in this subsection shall enable evidence to be given of any matter of which, if the person in question had been called as a witness and had denied that matter in cross-examination, evidence could not have been adduced by the cross-examining party.

NOTICE OF INTENTION TO ADDUCE HEARSAY EVIDENCE

Note—Order 38, r 21 requires any party who wishes to adduce hearsay evidence at the trial to serve notice of his intention to do so on every other party. A party who is served with notice under r 21 may, if he wishes, serve a counter-notice requiring a person mentioned in the notice to be called as a witness. The object is to avoid a party being taken by surprise at the trial. The following cases refer to this procedure.

Ford v Lewis

[1971] 2 All ER 983, [1971] 1 WLR 623, 115 Sol Jo 145, CA

A plaintiff, aged five, was struck and injured by the defendant's vehicle when crossing the road with her parents. At the trial, ten years later, the defendant through mental illness was not available to give evidence. His counsel sought to put in evidence under s 2 of the Civil Evidence Act 1968 a written statement made by the defendant shortly after the accident of which no notice had been served on the plaintiff as required by Ord 38, r 21. The judge, purporting to exercise his discretion under s 8(3)(a) of that Act and Ord 38, r 29, admitted the statement in evidence and found the defendant not liable. At the hearing of the plaintiff's appeal counsel for the defendant said he himself had advised against disclosing the statement before the trial because he thought the plaintiff's parents might in some way adjust or trim their evidence so as to meet and destroy it if they knew of the statement in advance.

HELD: The judge had been left ignorant of the vital fact that non-compliance by the defendant with the statutory requirement was due, not to inability, inadvertence or slackness on the part of his advisers, but to a deliberate decision not to comply. There could be no valid exercise of the discretion given to the court by r 29 where there has been a deliberate withholding from the court of the reason for non-compliance. Even if the judge had known of the reason he would not be acting judicially if he had exercised his discretion in favour of the defendant and thus enabled him to adopt tactics of surprise which the rules as to notice were designed to prevent. There must be a new trial.

Rasool v West Midlands Transport Executive

[1974] 3 All ER 638 (Finer J)

The defendants, sued for damages for injuries sustained by the plaintiff when knocked down by a bus, sought to put in evidence a written statement from a witness highly prejudicial to the plaintiff's case. The defendants served a notice on the plaintiff under RSC Ord 38, rr 21 and 22(3) asserting that the witness could not be called because 'She has left her former address number 225 Charles Road Small Heath Birmingham and cannot at present be found. It is understood that she is now beyond the seas and is probably resident in Jamaica.' The defendants had made extensive inquiries in the Birmingham area to find the witness and had received information from two people that she had gone to Jamaica but they had made no inquiries in Jamaica to find her. The plaintiff served a counter-notice under r 25(2) and claimed the defendants had not shown reasonable diligence in trying to find the witness.

HELD: (1) Of the five reasons given in the Civil Evidence Act 1968, s 8(2)(b) the defendants' notice really invoked only the assertion that the witness could not be found, but the evidence of their inquiries was sufficient to show a probability that she was in fact beyond the seas; (2) the reason given in s 8(2)(b) was disjunctive: if the maker of the statement is beyond the seas it does not have to be proved also that she cannot by reasonable diligence be found: (3) if the court is satisfied on any of the five specified reasons it has no residuary discretion to exclude the statement by reference to other circumstances; (4) the defendants' notice was out of order: it should have read simply 'because she is beyond the seas'. Order made accordingly.

Note—Approved in *Piernay Shipping Co SA v Chester* [1978] 1 All ER 1233, [1978] 1 WLR 411, 121 Sol Jo 795, CA. 'I agree in its entirety with the reasoning of the judgment of Finer J': per Megaw LJ. See also *Rover International Ltd v Cannon Films Sales Ltd (No 2)* [1987] 3 All ER 986, [1987] 1 WLR 1597. Reference to RSC Ord 38, r 25(2) has now been replaced by Ord 38, r 26.

THE OPERATION OF S 2 AND S 4

Taylor v Taylor

[1970] 2 All ER 609, [1970] 1 WLR 1148, 114 Sol Jo 415, CA
The shorthand writer's transcript of the evidence given in a criminal trial is admissible in evidence in civil proceedings both under the Civil Evidence Act 1968, s 2(1) and under s 4(1) of that Act. The summing-up of the judge might not be admissible under s 2(1) but would probably be under s 4(1) since it is a record compiled by the shorthand writer in his capacity as such.

H v Schering Chemicals Ltd

[1983] 1 All ER 849, [1983] 1 WLR 143, 127 Sol Jo 88 (Bingham J)
The plaintiffs wished to put in evidence as records under the Civil Evidence Act 1968, s 4 articles from medical journals, documents summarising research and letters from medical journals for the purpose of showing that the administering of a drug caused certain injuries.
HELD: The documents were not records within the meaning of s 4. The intention of that section is to admit in evidence documents which either give effect to a transaction itself or which contain a contemporaneous register of information supplied by those with direct knowledge of the facts. The documents in the present case were not records nor primary or original sources. They were a digest or analysis of records which must exist or have existed but were not themselves records. Nor was RSC Ord 38, r 3 intended to permit the adducing on an issue crucial to the outcome of an action of material which does not rank as evidence even for the purposes of the Act of 1968.

Note—Applied in *Savings and Investment Bank Ltd v Gasco Investments* [1984] 1 All ER 296, [1984] 1 WLR 271, 128 Sol Jo 115, [1984] BCLC 179.

Garsin v Amerindo Investment Advisers Ltd

[1991] 4 All ER 655, [1991] 1 WLR 1140
The plaintiffs alleged that a crucial document was a forgery. A witness residing in New York was required to give evidence in relation to the making of the document. The witness was unwilling to travel to London to give the evidence. The defendant suggested that arrangements could be made for the witness to be examined on oath by a New York judge but this would have necessitated an adjournment of the trial for some three to four months.

The plaintiff suggested that this evidence should be received via video conferencing. The defendant objected on the basis that the court had no jurisdiction to make an order allowing evidence to be given in this manner.

HELD: Per Mr Justice Morritt: The first question to decide was whether the evidence given by this means was admissible. The evidence would be admissible under s 2 of the Civil Evidence Act 1968 if proved by a person who heard it. Similarly a video tape of the examination and cross-examination would be admissible as a document in which the statement was made so long as both parties and the witness co-operated. Furthermore evidence obtained in this manner would be of greater weight than a Civil Evidence Act statement because the judge would have the benefit of seeing the witness cross examined.

Having adjudged the evidence admissible it was held that its transmission to the court by means of the television linkage was a manner of presenting evidence which fell squarely within the words of RSC Ord 38, r 3. Therefore the court had jurisdiction to order that the evidence could be presented in this manner.

Ventouris v Mountain (No 2), The Italia Express

[1992] 3 All ER 414, [1992] 1 WLR 887, [1992] 2 Lloyd's Rep 216, CA

The Ro-Ro ferry boat, *Italia Express*, was undergoing repairs just outside the Port of Piraeus. On the 24 March 1988 the vessel was damaged by a number of explosions and rendered a total loss. The plaintiff, the owner of the vessel, claimed under his marine policy under which the vessel was insured, loss by explosion being one of the perils insured against. The defendant underwriters rejected the claim on the basis that the explosions were caused or connived at by the plaintiffs. The defendant relied heavily on evidence from the plaintiff's cousin, George Dimitrios Ventouris (GDV) who had been involved in a prior conspiracy (subsequently abandoned) to blow up the *Italia Express*. GDV had made tape recordings of conversations between himself and those alleged to have been involved in the conspiracy (the interlocutors). GDV had provided the tapes but was unable to be present at trial. The Court of Appeal decided on four issues arising out of the Civil Evidence Act 1968:

(1) Were the tapes admissible as evidence of facts stated by the interlocutors other than GDV? As the interlocutors were wholly unaware that their statements were being taped (or if aware of it could do nothing about it) they were making statements orally. Thus s 2(3) applied so the statements could only be proved by direct oral evidence by the person who made each statement or someone who heard it made. This could not be done and so the tapes were inadmissible as evidence of the facts stated by the interlocutors.

(2) Were the tapes admissible as evidence of facts stated by GDV? GDV knew the conversations were being taped and so he was making statements both orally and in a document. Therefore the statements made by GDV were admissible as evidence of the facts so stated.

(3) Could an 'out of court statement' contained in a document be proved by another out of court statement introduced into evidence under the provisions as the 1968 Act? Yes. Admissible statements made by GDV stating that he had recorded the conversations could prove that the tapes were the record which he had made of conversations between himself and the interlocutors.

(4) GDV deposited tapes with a judge in Greece and made a statement under oath in which he identified the interlocutors involved in the conversations on the tapes. The question arose: were the tapes admissible under s 4 as forming part of the

record? No. The tapes did not form part of the record. The record only confirmed that the tapes had been deposited with the judge.

2 CONVICTIONS

PROOF OF CONVICTION AND ACQUITTALS

(1) Where in any proceedings the fact that a person has in the United Kingdom been convicted or acquitted of an offence otherwise than by a Service court is admissible in evidence, it may be proved by producing a certificate of conviction or, as the case may be, of acquittal relating to that offence, and proving that the person named in the certificate as having been convicted or acquitted of the offence is the person whose conviction or acquittal of the offence is to be proved.
(2) For the purposes of this section a certificate of conviction or of acquittal—
(*a*) shall, as regards a conviction or acquittal on indictment, consist of a certificate, signed by the clerk of the court where the conviction or acquittal took place, giving the substance and effect (omitting the formal parts) of the indictment and of the conviction or acquittal; and
(*b*) shall, as regards a conviction or acquittal on a summary trial, consist of a copy of the conviction or of the dismissal of the information, signed by the clerk of the court where the conviction or acquittal took place or by the clerk of the court, if any, to which a memorandum of the conviction or acquittal was sent;
and a document purporting to be a duly signed certificate of conviction or acquittal under this section shall be taken to be such a certificate unless the contrary is proved.
(3) References in this section to the clerk of a court include references to his deputy and to any other person having the custody of the court record.

ADMISSIBILITY IN CIVIL PROCEEDINGS

Note—It was formerly the rule (propounded in *Hollington v Hewthorn* [1943] KB 587) that evidence of conviction for a motoring offence was inadmissible in subsequent civil proceedings. The opinion of the criminal court was held to be irrelevant.

The rule was abolished by the Civil Evidence Act 1968, Part II (ss 11 to 19). The relevant subsections of s 11 are as follows:

'**11 Convictions as evidence in civil proceedings** (1) In any civil proceedings the fact that a person had been convicted of an offence by or before any court in the United Kingdom or by a court-martial there or elsewhere shall (subject to sub-s (3) below) be admissible in evidence for the purpose of proving, where to do so is relevant to any issue in those proceedings, that he committed that offence, whether he was so convicted upon a plea of guilty or otherwise and whether or not he is party to the civil proceedings; but no conviction other than a subsisting one shall be admissible in evidence by virtue of this section.
(2) In any civil proceedings in which by virtue of this section a person is proven to have been convicted of an offence by or before any court in the United Kingdom by a court-martial there or elsewhere—
(a) he shall be taken to have committed that offence unless the contrary is proved; and
(b) without prejudice to the reception of any other admissible evidence for the purpose of identifying the facts on which the conviction was based, the contents of any document which is admissible as evidence of the conviction, and the contents of the information, complaint, indictment or charge-sheet on which the person in question was convicted, shall be admissible in evidence for that purpose.
(3) Where in any civil proceedings the contents of any document are admissible in evidence by virtue of sub-s (2) above, a copy of that document, or of the material part thereof,

purporting to be certified or otherwise authenticated by or on behalf of the court or authority having custody of that document shall be admissible in evidence and shall be taken to be a true copy of that document or part unless the contrary is shown.'

Wauchope v Mordecai

[1970] 1 All ER 417, [1970] 1 WLR 317, 113 Sol Jo 941, CA
The plaintiff was injured when the defendant opened a car door and knocked him off his bicycle. The defendant admitted to the police that he opened the car door: he was charged with the offence and convicted. The plaintiff's action for damages was tried after the Civil Evidence Act 1968, s 11 had come into force. The judge was told of the conviction but said he would ignore it. He found for the defendant.
HELD, ON APPEAL: Section 11(1) of the 1968 Act made the conviction admissible as evidence to prove, where it was relevant, that the offence was committed. When the judge gave judgment he put his decision on the burden of proof; but under s 11(2) the defendant was to be taken to have committed the offence unless the contrary was proved. It was for the defendant to prove he had not opened the car door. If the judge had had the Act in mind he must have found for the plaintiff. Appeal allowed.

Stupple v Royal Insurance Co Ltd

[1970] 1 QB 50, [1970] 3 All ER 230, [1970] 3 WLR 217, 114 Sol Jo 551, CA
Per Lord Denning MR: The Act does not merely shift the evidential burden, as it is called. It shifts the *legal* burden of proof. . . . Take a running down case where a plaintiff claims damages for negligent driving by the defendant. If the defendant had not been convicted, the legal burden is on the plaintiff throughout. But if the defendant has been convicted of careless driving the legal burden is shifted. It is on the defendant himself. At the end of the day, if the judge is left in doubt the defendant fails because the defendant had not discharged the legal burden which is on him. The burden is, no doubt, the civil burden: he must show, on the balance of probabilities, that he was not negligent.

Conviction must be pleaded

Note—Rule 7A to RSC Ord 18 requires any party who, in pursuance of s 11 or s 12 of the 1968 Act, wishes to rely on a previous conviction to include in his pleading the particulars if it specified in the rule. A party who wishes to deny the conviction or its relevance to the proceedings must do so in his pleading.

PRODUCTION OF RESULTS OF CRIMINAL INVESTIGATIONS

Marcel v Metropolitan Police Comr

[1992] Ch 225, [1992] 1 All ER 72, [1992] 2 WLR 50, CA
The plaintiffs had been arrested and documents in their possession seized pursuant to the Police and Criminal Evidence Act 1984. Subsequently charges of conspiracy to defraud a Mr Jaggard had been made against the plaintiffs. These charges were dropped. Thereafter the plaintiffs brought proceedings against Mr Jaggard. Mr Jaggard's solicitor issued a *subpoena duces tecum* against the officer in charge of the criminal investigation to produce the seized documents at the civil trial. The plaintiffs objected and commenced another action against the police to decide the issues.

HELD: There was no reason why the police should not produce documents seized pursuant to the 1984 Act for use in criminal proceedings in obedience to a *subpoena duces tecum* if the original owner of the documents could have been required to produce them under such an order if they were still in his possession.

The plaintiff's objection to the production of documents subject to legal professional privilege was upheld.

There were other acceptable grounds for limiting the production of documents in this way, such as privilege against self incrimination, but they were not available to the plaintiffs in this case.

Note—See also the case of *Istel (AT&T) Limited v Tully* [1993] AC 45, [1992] 3 All ER 523, HL in which it was held that a party in a civil case could be ordered to disclose information which would incriminate him in criminal proceedings as long as a court could ensure that the material disclosed would not be used against him in a criminal court. It would be necessary to obtain agreement from the prosecuting authorities not to make use of the material disclosed.

3 MEDICAL EVIDENCE

EXCHANGE OF MEDICAL EVIDENCE (RSC ORD 38, RR 36–39)

Worrall v Reich

[1955] 1 QB 296, [1955] 1 All ER 363, [1955] 2 WLR 338, 99 Sol Jo 109, CA
In an action for damages for personal injuries, there is no power under what is now Ord 25, r 6(3) to order the parties to exchange medical reports. Such a report is a document privileged from disclosure and so is excluded by para (4). The order should be that a medical report be agreed, if possible, and if not, the medical evidence be limited to (two) witnesses for each party. It should follow the printed form of summons. It is a matter of agreement and not the subject of an order.

Dalton v Clark & Fenn Ltd

(1963) 107 Sol Jo 595 (Glyn-Jones J)
In an action for damages for personal injuries where liability had been admitted the defendants declined to agree medical reports and the parties had not exchanged reports. The judge said he strongly deprecated the keeping back of medical reports. The proper course was for the plaintiff to hand over his medical reports on the terms that, if they were not agreed, he should be entitled to know why by seeing the defendant's reports.

Note—See also *McGuinness v Fairbairn Lawson Ltd*, below.

McGuinness v Fairbairn Lawson Ltd

(1966) 110 Sol Jo 870, CA
On a summons for directions an order was made that a medical report be agreed if possible and, if not agreed, medical help should be limited to two witnesses for each side. The plaintiff's solicitors suggested mutual simultaneous exchange of medical reports by posting them the same day but the defendants merely sent copies of two reports and asked for the plaintiff's reports in exchange. The plaintiff sent only one

and the defendants obtained an order from the judge in chambers requiring the plaintiff to produce the other.
HELD, ON APPEAL: The order should not have been made. A doctor's report was protected by legal professional privilege and the other side was not entitled as of right to see it. Only if there was an agreement to produce it could production be enforced and, on the facts, there was no agreement here. A party was not bound to produce an unfavourable report.

Causton v Mann Egerton (Johnsons) Ltd

[1974] 1 All ER 453, [1974] 1 WLR 162, [1974] 1 Lloyd's Rep 197, CA
In the course of a claim against them for damages for personal injuries the defendants asked for medical examinations of the plaintiff and were granted them by the plaintiff's solicitors 'on the usual terms' which was taken to mean merely on payment of the plaintiff's expenses. The plaintiff's solicitors obtained medical reports separately from time to time. The order for directions in the action ordered that a medical report be agreed upon if possible, and if not, medical evidence be limited to two witnesses for each party. The defendants' solicitors asked the plaintiff's solicitors for copies of all the reports they had obtained and were sent them. They then agreed the plaintiff's reports and refused to disclose their own. On the plaintiff's application for disclosure—
HELD: As was clear from *Worrall v Reich* above a medical report was a privileged document and the Court had no power under Ord 5, r 6 to order its disclosure. There was nothing in the correspondence in the present case from which an agreement to exchange reports could be inferred, nor anything amounting to a waiver by the defendants of their privilege. The plaintiff's solicitors could have attached conditions to production of their reports but they did not. An agreement to disclosure was not implied in the phrase 'usual terms': the plaintiff's solicitor should have told the defendants what agreement they were seeking or making so that no dispute could arise.

Kirkup v British Railways Engineering Ltd

[1983] 3 All ER 147, [1983] 1 WLR 1165, 127 Sol Jo 447, CA
Although in many personal injury cases it was convenient and just for there to be simultaneous disclosure of experts' reports because the area of inquiry and possible disagreement was comparatively limited it was different where the case was such that until the defendants knew what the plaintiff was going to say they could not start to prepare their expert evidence. Order that the plaintiff should disclose reports by his experts within 28 days of setting down for trial and reports by the defendants' experts be disclosed within 42 days thereafter confirmed.

Turner v Carlisle City Council

[1989] CLY 2964
The plaintiff had obtained a medical report upon which he intended to rely. The defendant had not had the plaintiff medically examined. The plaintiff sought an order that the defendant state in writing that it either did not intend to obtain any medical evidence or would undertake to disclose any medical evidence they subsequently obtained. The plaintiff relied on RSC Ord 25, r 8 arguing that each party had to obtain medical evidence so that there could be mutual exchange.
HELD: It was not appropriate to make the order that the plaintiff sought. As the defendant had not obtained its own medical evidence RSC Ord 25, r 8 did not apply.

It was for the plaintiff to comply with Ord 25, r 8 (1) (b) being the party who intended to rely on medical evidence at trial.

Guinness Peat Properties Ltd v Fitzroy Robinson Partnership

[1987] 2 All ER 716, [1987] 1 WLR 1027, 131 Sol Jo 807, CA
The plaintiffs were building developers who commenced proceedings against the defendant architects for damages. The plaintiffs alleged that the defendants were responsible for a deficiency in the design of an atrium within the plaintiffs' building. The defendants inadvertently included a document in their list of documents for which they had intended to claim privilege. The document was a letter written by an employee of the defendants to the defendants' insurance company notifying the insurers of the claim and expressing the view that the design error was the defendants' responsibility.

On inspection the plaintiffs' representative obtained a copy of the letter and passed it on to the plaintiffs' expert who referred to it in his report. On seeing the report the defendants' solicitor, realising his mistake, sought an injunction restraining the plaintiff from using the letter during the course of the litigation and demanding the return of all copies. At first instance it was held that the letter was privileged and an injunction was granted. The plaintiffs appealed.

HELD: The appeal was dismissed. The court had to consider the following questions: (1) was the letter a privileged document; and (2) had that privilege been lost by reason of the letter's disclosure.

(1) In deciding whether a document is privileged the court must look at the dominant purpose for which that letter was brought into existence. The 'dominant purpose' must be looked at objectively in view of the whole of the evidence. On the facts of this case the letter was written ' in order to obtain legal advice or to conduct or aid in the conduct of litigation which was at the time of its production in reasonable prospect: per Slade LJ at p 1037.
(2) The plaintiffs' solicitors were, by their conduct, seeking to take advantage of what they must have known to have been an obvious error. The general rule is that once a party has inspected a document it is too late for the other party to claim privilege to remedy that mistake by way of an injunction. However if 'the other party or his solicitor either (a) has procured inspection of the relevant document by fraud, or (b) by inspection, realises that he has been permitted to see the document only by reason of an obvious mistake, the court has the power to intervene for the protection of the mistaken party by the grant of an injunction in the exercise of the equitable jurisdiction illustrated by [the case law]: per Slade LJ at p 1045.

Pizzey v Ford Motor Co Ltd

[1993] 17 LS Gaz R 46, CA
The plaintiff's solicitors arranged for their client to be examined by a senior surgeon. This surgeon produced two reports which were adverse to the plaintiff's case. The surgeon died shortly afterwards.

During the course of the procedures an order for discovery was made against the plaintiff pursuant to s 34(2) of the Supreme Court Act 1981. Medical records were disclosed by the plaintiff's solicitors who inadvertently included the two adverse medical reports. The plaintiff's solicitors sought an injunction restraining the defendants from using the reports. The judge refused to grant an injunction. The plaintiff appealed.

HELD: The court considered the judgment of Slade LJ in *Guinness Peat Properties Ltd v Fitzroy Robinson Partnership* (above). Cases of mistake were confined to those where the mistake was obvious ie evidence to the recipient of the documents. In this case the defendants' solicitors had sworn an affidavit that she genuinely believed the reports had been disclosed pursuant to the order for discovery. Although the reports had the appearance of being privileged the court was satisfied that on the balance of probabilities a reasonable solicitor could not have realised that the privilege of the two documents had not been waived.

AGREEING MEDICAL EVIDENCE

Proctor v Peebles (Papermakers) Ltd

[1941] 2 All ER 80, 57 TLR 375, 85 Sol Jo 281, CA
Order on Summons for Directions that medical reports be agreed and dispensing with the attendance of doctors as witnesses should not be made as a matter of form.

Harrison v Liverpool Corpn

[1943] 2 All ER 449, 60 TLR 14, CA
The summons for directions makes provision for an agreed medical report. In order that a report may be an agreed medical report for this purpose it must contain a statement of facts and opinions on which the doctors on both sides who make it are in agreement, or, where the parties agree to accept a report from one doctor, the facts and opinions stated and given by that doctor. Independent reports made by doctors on each side without agreement as to the facts and opinions appearing in them are not agreed medical reports within the meaning of the form.

In future orders should refer not to 'medical reports', but to 'a medical report'. This will not preclude the making of more than one agreed report where different doctors on each side deal with different aspects of the case eg where two different kinds of injury are dealt with by different specialists.

Where doctors are instructed with a view to obtaining an agreed medical report it is desirable that the parties should agree on a statement of any relevant matters to which it is desired that the attention of the doctors should be directed. For example, in claims at common law or for breath of statutory duty the doctors should be instructed that general disability as well as disability in respect of earning capacity is a relevant matter (*Practice Direction* [1943] WN 221).

Devine v British Transport Commission

[1954] 1 All ER 1025, [1954] 1 WLR 686, 98 Sol Jo 287 (Denning LJ, sitting in QB)
The common form order for directions that unless a medical report be agreed medical evidence be limited to two witnesses on each side does not impose any legal duty to attempt to agree. Mutual disclosure is a matter of arrangement. If the defendant invites the plaintiff's reports, there is an implied understanding to reciprocate. The agreed report should be confined to the medical issues strictly so called. Agreement in most cases is desirable to save costs and the time of medical men but in a serious case the court may be greatly helped by the attendance of medical men.

Gravatt v Card

[1957] 1 Lloyd's Rep 19 (Gorman J)
The judge said the amount of damages had given some anxiety because while it was right to agree medical reports, it was not right to agree them where so much was left to guess and conjecture which could be solved either by asking questions about the reports or by arranging for a doctor to attend. There was no evidence whether the man was fit to undergo an operation or evidence that the operation would be successful or otherwise. The parties would not agree to the calling of the doctor; they stood by their agreement that the medical reports should be read. I mention that because it is putting the court in the position in which a court should not have to be put when one is concerned to do complete justice to the parties.

Peters v Harding

(1963) 107 Sol Jo 852, CA (Willmer LJ)
The judge said some difficulty had been caused by a statement in one of the medical reports: 'as is well known, there was a well-defined history of psychological trouble before the accident'. The doctor who wrote that report had clearly derived that from another doctor's report, but the court knew nothing about it. It would be useful when a medical report was being prepared for the purpose of agreement with the other side if a doctor who drew on information obtained from some other doctor were to annexe an extract from that other doctor's report or state in some greater detail what the view expressed by that other doctor was.

Constanti v Papageorgiou (Practice Note)

(1963) 107 Sol Jo 596 (Havers J)
In an action for personal injuries the plaintiff's medical report was not given to the defendant and the plaintiff called a surgeon to give evidence. The defendant would have agreed his report. The hearing lasted several days. Judgment was given for the plaintiff but on a submission from the defendant that he should not be required to pay the surgeon's fees for attending Court it was ordered that the question whether the plaintiff was entitled to recover the costs of calling the surgeon was to be determined by the taxing master.

Kaiser v Carlswood Glassworks Ltd

(1965) 109 Sol Jo 537, CA
On the hearing of an appeal by the defendants against an award of £3,500 for head injuries Sellers LJ pointed out that there were two medical reports only, the second of which was 12 months old at the date of hearing in the court below. The judge was entitled to have up-to-date reports otherwise it was more difficult for him to assess developments one way or the other.

Vose v Barr

[1966] 2 All ER 226n (Lyell J)
The plaintiff was injured in a road accident on 23 April 1964. Liability was not in issue. His solicitor obtained a medical report on 12 June 1965, and issued a writ on 17 June. On 2 July, the defendant's solicitors asked for a copy of the medical report so that they could make an offer in settlement. The plaintiff's solicitor replied enclosing the statement of claim and said he would consider the request for a copy of

the medical report when the defence had been served. When the defence was served the plaintiff's solicitor still withheld the medical report in spite of several requests from the defendant's solicitors, who could make no offer without it. The medical report was not disclosed until shortly before trial, several months later, when an immediate settlement resulted.
HELD: On the defendant's application, it was a proper case in which to deprive the plaintiff of part of his costs. There was an omission on the part of the plaintiff's solicitor within the provisions of Ord 62, r 7 to do something which would have been calculated to save costs. Judgment for the plaintiff with costs against the defendant down to 12 July 1965, but not beyond.

Note—The judge made it clear that this is not a decision that a refusal to disclose a medical report is in every case an omission which should affect the order as to costs. It was a decision on the facts. The plaintiff had fully recovered and the medical evidence was entirely contained in the medical report of 12 June 1965. See also *Chetland v Babcock and Wilcox Ltd*, p 660, below.

Mullard v Ben Line Steamers Ltd

[1971] 2 All ER 424, [1970] 1 WLR 1414, 114 Sol Jo 570. CA
Per Sachs LJ: Where serious damages are in issue and where above all things what purport to be agreed medical reports do not in fact agree, it is essential for oral medical evidence to be adduced before the court. . . . Parties who do not take the trouble to bring their medical witnesses to court have only themselves to blame for the results of such difficulties; but I would add that in my view an obligation lies on the trial judge to insist in serious cases that he have oral evidence before he makes an assessment.

Hambridge v Harrison

[1973] 1 Lloyd's Rep 572, CA
Per Edmund Davis LJ: It is thoroughly undesirable, and indeed irregular, for the Court to be called upon to make its own choice between so-called agreed medical reports which are, in fact, in conflict. . . . It is therefore well to sound a note of warning that the day may come when the court, confronted with so-called agreed medical reports which in fact disagree with each other in a material respect, will have no alternative but to send the matter back for a further hearing.

MALINGERING

Stojalowski v Imperial Smelting Corpn (NSC) Ltd

(1976) 121 Sol Jo 118, CA
The defendants were the plaintiff's employers from whom he claimed damages for injury sustained at work. They alleged he was malingering. There was a conflict of medical evidence. The judge accepted the written evidence of a hospital registrar in deciding the plaintiff was a malingerer.
HELD, ON APPEAL: The judge was wrong to treat the registrar's written evidence as proof of his views. An allegation of malingering was a charge of fraud and any positive evidence from the defendants should be put to the witness. Damages increased from £4,000 to £37,328.

Joyce v Yeomans

[1981] 2 All ER 21, [1981] 1 WLR 549, 125 Sol Jo 34, CA
It is not correct that where expert (ie medical) witnesses are concerned the trial judge has no significant advantage over an appellate court in forming a correct judgment between conflicting views: *Stojalowski v Imperial Smelting Corpn* (above) was not intended to go as far as that. Even when dealing with expert witnesses, a trial judge has an advantage over an appellate court in assessing the value, the reliability and impressiveness of the evidence given by experts called on either side.

Khan v Armaguard Ltd

(1994) Times, 4 March, CA
The defendants obtained video evidence which they claimed demonstrated that the plaintiff was deliberately malingering. The defendants made an application to the district judge pursuant to RSC Ord 38, r 5 for an order that there be pre-trial non-disclosure of the video evidence. The defendants relied upon the judgment in *McGuinness v Kellogg Co of Great Britain Ltd* ([1988] 1 WLR 913), arguing that non disclosure was in the interests of justice between the parties when it was the defendants' intention to uncover the plaintiff's deceit. The district judge refused to make the order and the defendants appealed.
HELD: Three changes had occurred in the conduct of personal injury actions since the decision in the *McGuinness* case. There were now provisions for the pre-trial exchange of witness statements, discovery in personal injury accidents was automatic and the 'cards on the table' approach to this sort of litigation had continued to develop. The interests of the parties would be best served by an early settlement of the plaintiff's action and this would be facilitated by the pre trial disclosure of the video evidence. It would only be in the most exceptional circumstances that an order for non-disclosure pursuant to RSC Ord 38, r 5 would be justified.

MISCELLANEOUS

National insurance doctor

Ward v Shell Mex and BP Ltd

[1952] 1 KB 280, [1951] 2 All ER 904, [1951] 2 TLR 976, 95 Sol Jo 686 (Streatfield J)
Plaintiff sought to call as a witness a doctor who was a member of a medical board under the National Insurance (Industrial Injuries) Act 1946, s 38(1), to testify as to the plaintiff's condition at the time he examined the plaintiff as such member and his own conclusions as to the cause of that condition.
HELD: The evidence was not admissible. He was a member of a statutory body rather than an individual expert. His position was judicial or quasi-judicial somewhere between that of an arbitrator and that of a judge. He was a competent witness to prove matters material to the issue but his evidence was limited to what took place at the hearing before him, what issues were raised, but not competent, nor was it relevant for him to explain, and still less vary, the award he had given. That award must stand on its own footing. He could not give evidence as to the reasons which prompted him to the conclusion which resulted in the certificate granted. The certificate stands on its own footing and cannot be contradicted or explained or varied by a member of that tribunal. The evidence of this witness ought not to be received.

Too much medical evidence

Re Yeomans (minors)

[1985] Fam Law 121, CA
At a hearing concerning the future management of children a senior psychiatric consultant and two colleagues of the same team working at the same hospital were called to give evidence. The evidence of all three witnesses overlapped considerably.
HELD: It had been unnecessary for all three witnesses to be called: the expenditure of both time and money was wholly unjustified. The senior consultant, or his deputy, could have dealt with the matter alone. Solicitors should consider such matters as part of their duty to public funds and to the Legal Aid Fund in particular. The circumstances in which members of the same medical team are justifiably called as witnesses should be rare and exceptional. Penalties as to costs could be ordered in the future in similar circumstances.

Warner v Jones

(1993) Times, 22 March
At a trial of a personal injury action the judge was presented with 15 medical reports totalling more than 50 pages. Many points in the medical evidence were repeated.
HELD: It would be beneficial if notice could be taken that it would be a great benefit to all the parties and a very great benefit for the court if medical evidence could be agreed rather than run in parallel.

Dunn v British Coal Corpn

[1993] ICR 591, [1993] IRLR 396, 137 Sol Jo LB 81, CA
The plaintiff, aged 53, suffered an injury to his neck at work and claimed that he was unable to resume his employment. He claimed, inter alia, damages for loss of earnings until retirement. The defendant arranged to have the plaintiff medically examined and sought disclosure of all hospital records and GP notes to their nominated expert. The plaintiff refused to consent to full disclosure and this refusal was upheld by the district judge and on appeal to the judge who considered that the defendant was embarking on a 'fishing expedition' in an attempt to discover something in the plaintiff's medical records that might reduce the plaintiff's loss of earnings claim. The defendant appealed to the Court of Appeal.
HELD: Per Stuart-Smith LJ: The court had to decide on the level of the plaintiff's financial loss arising from the accident. The plaintiff's financial loss could be affected by the existence of any pre-existing symptoms in his neck and any unrelated condition which might affect the plaintiff's working capacity as well as the effects of the accident itself. The documents requested by the defendant were relevant to this issue.

Alternatively, as it was not disputed that these documents contained some relevant material, the parties could wait until the trial when the defendant would serve a *subpoena duces tecum* on relevant persons who would be obliged to bring all notes and records to court. However this was not in the interest of justice. The current trend for a cards on the table approach demanded that early disclosure of this information was made.

There was concern about the possibility of some embarrassing unrelated medical fact being disclosed. This concern was dealt with by limiting disclosure to the defendant's medical advisers who would respect the confidentiality of the information if it was not related to the issues in the case.

Lacey v Harrison

(1992) 11 BMLR 75
The plaintiff and defendant were involved in an accident. The defendant was the only defence witness. The plaintiff sought an order that the defendant should undergo a medical examination to investigate whether or not he was capable of remembering the accident. The judge refused to make an order that the defence be struck out unless the defendant underwent a medical examination by a doctor selected by the plaintiff. The plaintiff appealed.
HELD: The plaintiff's appeal was successful. The question of fact to decide was whether the defendant could remember the accident and this was something that could be tested by a medical examination. The court had discretion to order that the defence to a personal injury action should be struck out unless the defendant agreed to undergo the medical examination.

4 EVIDENCE AT TRIAL

WITNESS STATEMENTS—EXCHANGE, LODGMENT AND ADMISSIBILITY

Mercer and Holden v Chief Constable of the Lancashire Constabulary

[1991] 2 All ER 504, [1991] 1 WLR 367, CA
Both Mercer and Holden brought proceedings against the defendant for wrongful arrest and false imprisonment. The defendant appealed an order directing that there be:
1 simultaneous exchange of written statement of the oral evidence each side intended to adduce at trial (RSC Ord 38, r 2A); and
2 exchanged witness statements of fact were to be served as evidence in chief at the trial of the action (RSC Ord 38, r 2A (5)(b)).
HELD: (1) There had been many changes to the conduct of litigation over the last quarter of a century, the most important of which was the requirement that, save in exceptional circumstances, witness statements were to be exchanged before trial. The modern approach to litigation required the earliest possible identification of both the real issues of a case and its strengths and weaknesses to reduce the length of trial and more importantly, to facilitate settlement. No exceptions could be made in the case of jury trials. The normal rule is that witness statements should be exchanged simultaneously.
(2) When considering whether a witness statement should stand as evidence in chief at the trial, a judge must consider the nature of the witness (whether expert or of fact): the nature of the trial (by jury or judge alone) and, most importantly the extent to which the evidence of a particular witness is likely to be controversial and his credibility in issue. RSC Ord 38, r 2A(5)(b) is not intended to empower the judge at the directions hearing to fetter the trial judge's discretion in any way.

Ahmed v Brumfitt

(1967) 112 Sol Jo 32, CA
The plaintiff claimed damages for the injuries he received when he was struck by the defendant's car when crossing the road. At the trial a witness for the defendant was

cross-examined about a report of the accident he had given and which was inconsistent with his evidence-in-chief. In re-examination he was allowed by the judge to give evidence of a statement he had given to the police a week after the accident. The plaintiff was held 60% to blame for the accident. He appealed, contending that the judge should not have allowed the earlier statement to be put in.
HELD: There was nothing wrong in admitting the statement. When in cross-examination a statement is put to a witness which was said to conflict with his examination-in-chief it is always admissible to put to him in re-examination an earlier statement consistent with it for the purpose of rehabilitating his credit respect of the evidence he had given.

DRIVER NOT AGENT TO ADMIT NEGLIGENCE

Tustin v Arnold

(1915) 84 LJKB 2214, 113 LT 95, 31 TLR 368
An admission by the driver of a vehicle of his liability for a collision is not admissible against his employer, unless he had the express authority of his employer to make admissions, or the admissions were part of the *res gestae*. Words, even spoken words, are not part of the *res gestae* unless made at the time and the natural consequence of the accident, springing spontaneously out of the accident, and germane to it.

Note—And see *Burr v Ware RDC*, p 619, below.

Glasgow Corpn v Muir

[1943] AC 448, [1943] 2 All ER 44, 112 LJPC 1, 169 LT 53, 59 TLR 266, 87 Sol Jo 182, HL
At a church picnic party in a public park of the defendants the manageress of the tea room gave permission for the party to have their tea in the tea room at the park. Two members of the party were carrying a tea urn when hot water was spilled on children. The defendants were sued for the alleged negligence of the manageress who should have anticipated such a risk. The manageress admitted that if she had been told of the arrival of the men with the urn, she 'certainly would have got the children away from the entrance to the doorway'.
HELD: By Lord Macmillan, not an admission binding on the defendants.

NON-STOP MOTORIST IDENTIFICATION

Grew v Cubitt

[1951] 2 TLR 305, 95 Sol Jo 452, Div CT
A lorry driver was convicted of driving without due care, failing to stop after an accident, and failing to report it, arising out of an alleged collision between the lorry and a car. The car driver could not describe the lorry at all or identify it; his recollection was that it was a browny-red. An eye-witness said the lorry had a little red on it and that he observed its index number and caused his wife to write it down but he did not remember the number himself. The defendant admitted to the police he was the owner of a lorry of that number; that he was driving the lorry on that day at the place concerned, but he denied any accident. The constable did not give any description of the lorry in evidence.

HELD: There was no evidence on which the defendant could be convicted. The wife should have been called or the piece of paper produced. There was no evidence that the lorry involved was the defendant's lorry.

Jones v Metcalfe

[1967] 3 All ER 205, [1967] 1 WLR 1286, 131 JP 494, 111 Sol Jo 563, Div CT
The defendant was charged with driving a lorry without due care and attention on the evidence of a witness who said he saw an accident caused by the driving of a lorry which did not stop. He had taken the registration number of the lorry and reported it to the police. In a statement to the police the defendant admitted he had driven a lorry of that number on that day. At court the witness could not remember the number. The defendant was convicted.
HELD, ON APPEAL: The conviction must be quashed. There was no admissible evidence identifying a lorry bearing the number reported to the police since the independent witness had been unable to testify to the number in court and the police evidence as to the number was merely hearsay.

R v McLean

(1967) 111 Sol Jo 925, 52 Cr App Rep 80, CA
A man who was attacked and robbed made a mental note of the number of the car used by his attackers and dictated it three minutes later to another man who wrote it down. The car bearing that number had been hired under a false name by the defendant, who was convicted of the robbery. The man who had been robbed was unable in evidence to say that the number written by the other man (who had given evidence of it) was right since he had not been shown it at the time.
HELD: The conviction could not stand. Following *Jones v Metcalfe* (above) the evidence of the number of the car contravened the hearsay rule.

Hampson v Powell

[1970] 1 All ER 929, 134 JP 321, [1970] RTR 293, Div CT
On a charge of careless driving against the driver of a lorry which did not stop a witness said he stopped his car at traffic lights and felt a bump at the back from a lorry which came out of a side street. He took the number of the lorry but did not say in evidence what it was. He said the collision caused the boot of his car to fly open. Another witness said he saw a lorry come out of a side street and hit a car and the boot lid flew open. He did not know the number of the lorry. A police officer gave evidence of tracing a lorry number HXJ 604 F and of interviewing the defendant who admitted he was driving a lorry HXJ 604 F at the place and time of the accident but said he knew nothing of the collision. The defendant gave no evidence. The magistrates found that the defendant was the driver of the lorry involved in the accident because there was evidence that a lorry collided with the car and also evidence that the defendant was the driver of a lorry at the precise time and place of the accident.
HELD: The magistrates' decision should stand. In *Jones v Metcalfe* (above) the conviction had been quashed because the magistrates had accepted inadmissible evidence. In the present case they had simply accepted that as the lorry driven by the defendant was at the precise spot at the precise time the accident occurred and there was no evidence of any other lorry being present there was sufficient proof that the defendant was the driver concerned.

EXPERT EVIDENCE

Expert evidence not needed/permitted

Hinds v London Transport Executive

[1979] RTR 103, CA
The plaintiff was injured in a collision with the defendants' bus. His solicitors obtained a report from a consulting engineer giving arguments in favour of the plaintiff on the issues of negligence and causation. They sent a copy to the defendants and applied under Ord 38, r 40 on summons for directions. The master refused leave for the report to be given in evidence.
HELD, ON APPEAL: Leave was rightly refused. The report was not expert evidence at all and even if it were it should not be called; it was a case where expert evidence was not needed.

Note—RSC Ord 38, r 40 was revoked by SI 1980/1010.

Croft v Jewell

(1993) PIQR 270, CA
The plaintiff sued the defendant for injuries arising out of a road traffic accident. The plaintiff obtained expert evidence from an accident reconstruction expert and disclosed the report to the defendant's solicitors. The defendant stated that they would not be relying on any expert evidence. The matter was sent down for trial for 4 May 1993 and on 1 April, the defendant's solicitors stated that they would be seeking leave to obtain their own expert evidence. The judge granted leave and the plaintiff appealed.
HELD: The plaintiff's appeal succeeded. There was no good reason shown for the defendant's change of mind and the plaintiff had been prejudiced by sequential, rather than simultaneous exchange of expert evidence.

Kenning v Eve Construction Ltd

[1989] 1 WLR 1189
Paul Kenning claimed damages for personal injuries arising out of an accident at work. The defendant's solicitors obtained an expert's report from a firm of consulting engineers which concluded that the defendant would have little difficulty defending the allegations of negligence pleaded against it in the Statement of Claim. However the expert wrote a covering letter drawing attention to two points not raised in the Statement of Claim or his report which were not favourable to the defendant.

The expert's report was disclosed to the plaintiff's solicitors in accordance with RSC Ord 25, r 8 but inadvertently a copy of the covering letter was sent with the report. The defendant sought to bar the plaintiff from relying upon the content of the covering letter.
HELD: The covering letter was a privileged document but once the defendant made the decision to rely on the evidence of the expert at trial, the evidence of that expert had to be disclosed under RSC Ord 25, r 8. This included not only evidence to be given in examination in chief but also matters that could arise in cross-examination. The defendant was obliged to waive the privilege attached to the covering letter and disclose it with the report. The only way of retaining the privilege of the covering letter was not to call the expert to evidence.

Derby & Co Ltd v Weldon (No 8)

[1990] 3 All ER 762, [1991] 1 WLR 73, 135 Sol Jo 84, CA
The defendant disclosed experts' reports dealing with one issue alleged by the plaintiff. These reports expressly stated that they did not deal and did not intend to deal with an alternative allegation which the plaintiffs had recently amended the Statement of Claim to include. Subsequently the defendant decided that he would not put in any report dealing with the alternative allegation.
HELD: Per Dillon LJ: The rules permit a party to choose whether or not to call his expert and until that expert's report is disclosed it is privileged. When disclosed it loses its privilege but that waiving of privilege does not extend to the thoughts of an expert on a topic that the expert has expressly stated he is not dealing with. The court has no jurisdiction to order production and disclosure of a report covering these thoughts. To this extent *Kenning v Eve Construction Ltd* was endorsed as in this case the defendant was not committed to using the experts report and letter for they could withdraw the expert's evidence altogether. But, per Staughton LJ: It is the evidence which a party proposes to adduce as part of his case that Ord 38 is dealing with, and that is the substance of the evidence which has to be disclosed pursuant to a direction under Ord 38, r 37. If and insofar as the case of *Kenning v Eve Construction Ltd* reached a different conclusion, then in my opinion it was wrongly decided. . . . . I do not think that an expert witness, or any other witness, obliges himself to volunteer his views on every issue in the whole case when he takes an oath to tell the whole truth. What he does oblige himself to do is to tell the whole truth about those matters which he is asked about.

Webster v James Chapman & Co (a firm)

[1989] 3 All ER 939
The plaintiff's solicitors were pursuing a personal injury claim on behalf of their client. The plaintiff's solicitors commissioned an expert's report from a firm of engineers to comment on the plaintiff's case. The engineer's report contained a number of conclusions adverse to the plaintiff's case but was inadvertently disclosed to the defendant's solicitors. The defendant's solicitors refused to return the report and refused to make an undertaking that they would make no use of it. The plaintiff brought an action against the defendant's solicitors and others seeking the return of all copies of the adverse engineer's report and restraining them from making use of it in the proceedings.
HELD: Once a privileged document or a copy of that document passes into the hands of some other party then, prima facie, the benefit of that privilege is lost. However, since this document was a confidential document it retained its eligibility for protection. It was a matter for the discretion of the court, taking into account all the circumstances of the case, whether or not the report lost or retained its privilege. The court had to balance the interest of the plaintiff in seeking to keep the confidential report suppressed with the interest of the defendant who wished to make sure of the information. It was relevant to consider the manner in which the document came into the defendant's possession, the issues in the action and the relevance of the document to those issues and whether or not the document should have been disclosed anyway by reason of the rules of the Supreme Court. In the circumstances the justice of this case demanded that the relief sought by the plaintiff should be refused.

Duties of expert witnesses

National Justice Compania Naviera SA v Prudential Assurance Co Ltd

[1993] 2 Lloyd's Rep 68

Mr Justice Cresswell listed the duties and responsibilities of expert witnesses in civil cases as follows:

(1) Expert evidence presented to the court should be, and should be seen to be, the independent product of the expert uninfluenced as to form or content by the exigencies of litigation: see *Whitehouse v Jordan* [1981] 1 WLR 246, per Lord Wilberforce.

(2) Independent assistance should be provided to the court by way of objective unbiased opinion regarding matter within the expertise of the expert witness; see *Polivitte Ltd v Commercial Union Assurance Co plc* [1987] 1 Lloyd's Rep 379, 386, per Mr Justice Garland, and *Re J* [1991] FCR 193, per Mr Justice Cazalet. An expert witness in the High Court should never assume the role of advocate.

(3) Facts or assumptions upon which the opinion was based should be stated together with material facts which could detract from the concluded opinion.

(4) An expert witness should make it clear when a question or issue fell outside his expertise.

(5) If the opinion was not properly researched because it was considered that insufficient data was available then that had to be stated with an indication that the opinion was provisional (see *Re J*). If the witness could not assert that the report contained the truth, the whole truth and nothing but the truth then that qualification should be stated on the report: see *Derby & Co Ltd v Weldon (No 9)* [1991] 2 All ER 901 per Lord Justice Staughton.

(6) If, after exchange of reports, an expert witness changed his mind on a material matter then the change of view should be communicated to the other side through legal representatives without delay and, when appropriate, to the court.

(7) Photographs, plans, survey reports and other documents referred to in the expert evidence had to be provided to the other side at the same time as the exchange of reports.

Note—See also: *Winchester Cigarette Machinery Ltd v Payne* (1993) Times, 19 October, CA where it was held that the court had inherent jurisdiction to refuse an application by a litigant for leave to adduce expert evidence brought by a summons under Order 38, rule 36 of the Rules of the Supreme Court.

POLICE REPORTS

Note—In the case of *Taylor v Young* heard at the Reading County Court on 11 June 1992 in front of HH Judge Oppenheimer the effect of CCR Ord 17, r 11 (3)(c) was considered. The rules state that in an action for personal injuries the contents of any police accident book shall be receivable in evidence at trial and shall be agreed if possible. A police report is, therefore, admissible as to the truth of its contents and this is so whether or not the content is agreed or not and whether any of its content would, irrespective of Ord 17, r 11, amount to hearsay or inadmissible opinion. The amount of weight to attach to the content is at the discretion of the judge. If a party wishes to prevent the police report being receivable in evidence that party must make an application to vary the automatic directions.

This Order was considered further in the case of *Sealey v Gibbons*, below.

Sealy v Gibbons

(26 February 1993, unreported) Haywards Heath County Court, HH Judge Coltfart
The defendant agreed the authenticity of the police report but did not agree its contents. The plaintiff was unable to call a police witness to attend the trial and relied on Ord 17, 11(3)(c) of the County Court Rules 1981. This states that 'photographs and sketch plans and, in an action for personal injuries, the contents of any police accident report book shall be receivable in evidence at the trial and shall be agreed if possible'.
HELD: According to the wording of this Order once the authenticity of the police report was agreed it was receivable in evidence at the trial and the judge was bound to admit it. However, in the absence of agreement of its contents and in the absence of the police officer to give the disputed evidence, little weight was to be attached to the evidence in the report.

MISCELLANEOUS

Inconsistent with pleadings

Roberts v Dorman Long & Co Ltd

[1953] 2 All ER 428, [1953] 1 WLR 942, 97 Sol Jo 487, 51 LGR 476, CA
Evidence given which is at variance with further and better particulars of the defence ought not to be admitted even though the opposing party does not take objection.

Motor car log book (vehicle registration document)

R v Sealby

[1965] 1 All ER 701, Liverpool Crown Court (Chapman J)
A motor car log book is not admissible evidence of its contents, in particular of the chassis number and engine number. It is merely hearsay evidence of its contents and is not a 'public document' so as to bring it within the exception in favour of public documents to the rule against hearsay evidence. Although it contains an extract from the registration particulars in the register kept by the county council (which is a public document) it is a private document issued to the owner of the car.

View by judge

Buckingham v Daily News Ltd

[1956] 2 QB 534, [1956] 2 All ER 904, [1956] 3 WLR 375, 100 Sol Jo 528, CA
A workman was injured by the blade or plate of a rotary machine and sued the employers alleging a failure to provide a safe system of work. The judge, with consent of the parties, inspected the machine before the evidence. The defendants called no evidence. Judgment was given for the defendants. The plaintiff appealed, contending that what the judge did was something forbidden by law.

A note in the *County Court Practice* says: 'A view is merely for the purpose of enabling the tribunal to understand the questions raised and to follow and apply the evidence, and must not be used to supply or take the place of evidence.'
HELD: The view was a matter of evidence and not of opinion. Where the matter is one of ordinary common sense, the judge is entitled to rely on the real evidence of a view, just as much as on the oral evidence of witnesses.

Note—72 LQR 470 points out that models are frequently brought into court and are regarded as evidence on which a conclusion can be based. The judge was acting on the evidence which he had seen with his own eyes. It is surprising that there should have been any doubt on this point, as the introduction of real evidence is a commonplace, and it cannot make any difference whether the evidence is produced in court, or at the site of the accident.

Salsbury v Woodland

[1970] 1 QB 324, [1969] 3 All ER 863, [1969] 3 WLR 29, 113 Sol Jo 327, CA
In a case where there was a question whether a driver should have seen a telephone wire which had fallen across a road the trial judge visited the scene in his own car without telling the parties. He had been doubtful before doing so whether the driver could have been expected to see the wire but after making his view came to the conclusion the driver ought to have seen it in time to slow down. On appeal it was suggested that the judge should not have done this and there should be a new trial.
HELD: In general a view is something which should be conducted by the judge by appointment in the presence of representatives of both sides, but where it is merely a case of a judge visiting a public place to see what it looks like there is nothing wrong in it, provided he makes sure there have been no material changes in the locality.

Witness called by judge

The following note appears in the Supreme Court Practice 1993, p 640:

38/1/6 Witness called by Judge—The Judge may call a witness whom neither party proposes to call, and may examine him himself; but since such witness is not the witness of either party, neither has the right to cross-examine him, though the Judge would usually allow either, or (possibly) both parties to do so (*Fallon v Calvert* [1960] 2 QB 201; [1960] 1 All ER 281, CA; *Re Enoch and Zaretzky, Boch & Co's Arbitration* [1910] 1 KB 327, CA limiting dictum of Esher MR in *Coulson v Disborough* [1894] 2 QB 316, CA).

Disclosure of witness details

Cahalin v West Yorkshire Bus Co

(11 August 1989, unreported) Harrogate County Court, HH Judge Barker
The plaintiff and defendant were involved in a road traffic accident. Prior to the commencement of proceedings the defendant's insurers had disclosed to the plaintiff's solicitors copies of witness questionnaires. The names and addresses of the witnesses were not disclosed. After the plaintiff had commenced proceedings for personal injuries the defendant's insurers refused to reveal the witnesses' names and addresses. The plaintiff made an application to the Registrar for an order that this information be disclosed. The Registrar refused to make an order and the plaintiff appealed to the judge.
HELD: It was obvious that the defendant's insurers had disclosed the witness statements in an attempt to dissuade the plaintiff from commencing proceedings. This practice was not to be encouraged but if it was done it was essential that the names and addresses of the witnesses were also disclosed (HH Judge Barker).

5 WITHOUT PREJUDICE

THE RULE

Paddock v Forrester

(1842) 3 Man & G 903, 3 Scott NR 715
Where a letter written by one of the parties to a dispute to the other, is expressed to be 'without prejudice', neither that letter nor the answer to it can be given in evidence on the part of the writer of the first letter, although the answer is not expressed to be 'without prejudice'.

Hoghton v Hoghton

(1852) 15 Beav 278, 21 LJ Ch 482, 17 Jur 99
Where letters are written 'without prejudice' with a view to a compromise, they cannot be given in evidence.

Re Harris, ex p Harris

(1875) 10 Ch App 264, 44 LJ Bcy 33, 32 LT 417, 23 WR 531
Where a negotiation for a compromise is commenced by one letter written 'without prejudice', the whole is protected.

Walker v Wilsher

(1889) 23 QBD 335, 58 LJQB 501, 54 JP 213, 37 WR 723, 5 TLR 649, CA
I think the words 'without prejudice' mean without prejudice to the position of the writer of the letter. If the terms proposed in the letter are accepted, a complete contract is established, and the letter, although written without prejudice, operates to alter the position of affairs and to establish a contract. Supposing a letter is written without prejudice, it is taken, according both to authority and good sense, that the answer should also be without prejudice.

India Rubber, Gutta Percha and Telegraph Works Ltd v Chapman

(1926) 20 BWCC 184, CA
Letters following a letter written 'without prejudice' should be treated as being also inadmissible unless there is a clear break in the chain of correspondence to indicate that the ensuing letters are open.

Rabin v Mendoza & Co

[1954] 1 All ER 247, [1954] 1 WLR 271, 98 Sol Jo 92, CA
Plaintiff instructed surveyors to advise on the purchase of a house. He claimed from them damages for negligence. Before action was taken, the parties met to discuss a settlement without prejudice. The parties agreed that the report of another surveyor should be obtained by defendants. Later on action was commenced.
HELD: The report was made solely for the purpose of 'without prejudice' negotiations and as the result of an express or tacit agreement that it would not be used to the prejudice of either party and was privileged from production.

Tomlin v Standard Telephones and Cables Ltd

[1969] 3 All ER 201, [1969] 1 WLR 1378, 113 Sol Jo 641, CA
In dealing with a claim for damages for personal injury the defendants' insurers wrote the plaintiff's solicitor a letter marked 'Without Prejudice' saying 'We are only prepared to deal with the case on a 50-50 basis.' The solicitor replied 'my client had instructed me to say that he will agree to settle his case on a 50-50 basis as you propose and accordingly this leaves only the question of quantum to be disposed of. 'In subsequent letters the insurers referred to 'the agreement come to between us' and eventually wrote 'It has already been agreed that this is a 50-50 case and accordingly we are prepared to pay £625 in settlement.' All the insurers' letters were marked 'Without Prejudice'. The plaintiff rejected the offer and sued for damages to be assessed, on the basis that there was a concluded agreement to pay him one-half.
HELD: There was a binding agreement. The court was entitled to look at letters marked 'Without Prejudice' to see if an agreement had been reached. There was a concluded agreement on the issue of liability leaving over for further negotiation the separate and severable question of quantum of damages.

Rush & Tompkins Ltd v Greater London Council

[1989] AC 1280, [1988] 3 All ER 737, HL
The plaintiff started proceedings against the first and second defendants for monies owed under a building contract. The plaintiff settled its claim against the first defendants. The second defendant made a counterclaim against the plaintiff and sought discovery of the without prejudice correspondence passing between the plaintiff and the first defendant which led to the settlement. The plaintiff conceded that this correspondence might be relevant to the valuation of the second defendant's counterclaim but objected to discovery on the grounds that it was privileged.
HELD: The underlying purpose of the 'without prejudice' rule is to protect a litigant from being embarrassed by any admissions made purely in an attempt to achieve settlement. The privilege remains in force even after the compromise has been reached. Any admissions made on a without prejudice basis were protected from discovery by other parties to the same litigation and remained privileged for any subsequent litigation connected with the same subject matter. Thus it followed that the second defendant was not entitled to discovery of without prejudice correspondence which passed between the plaintiff and the first defendant.

Cheddar Valley Engineering v Chaddlewood Homes

[1992] 4 All ER 942, [1992] 1 WLR 820
Where one party wishes to change the basis of discussions from 'without prejudice' to 'open' then the burden is on him to bring this to the attention of the other parties. The test is whether a reasonable man would realise that there had been a change in the basis of how the negotiations were being carried out. The use of the word 'open' during a telephone conversation was not sufficient.

Dixon Stores Group Ltd v Thames Television plc

[1993] 1 All ER 349
The plaintiffs commenced proceedings against the defendants alleging that a television programme broadcast by the defendants was defamatory to the plaintiff. The writ was issued on 11 July 1991 and between February and June 1992 the parties exchanged

'without prejudice' correspondence in an attempt to negotiate a settlement. The negotiations came to nothing.

On 1 and 9 July the defendants wrote two letters to the plaintiffs offering a settlement. The first was not marked 'without prejudice' and the second was marked 'open letter'. At the trial of the action the defendants sought to refer to the terms of these two letters and the plaintiffs objected on the basis that the letters were privileged.

HELD: It was clear that the two letters written in July 1992 were written with the intention that they should be referred to at the trial of the action. The letters were not written as part of continuing without prejudice negotiations. Without prejudice negotiations had occurred between February and June 1992 and had come to nothing and were at an end. A letter containing an offer to settle may be written as an open letter with the intention that it is referred to at trial providing that it is relevant to the issues. The letters were not privileged.

Per Drake J: The policy of the law is clearly to encourage settlement of actions and I think it is quite clear that the modern tendency has been to enlarge the cloak under which negotiations may be conducted without prejudice.

Note—See also *Parry v Newsgroup Newspapers* [1990] NLJR 1719, CA. The parties had held a without prejudice telephone conversation. It was held that the note recording this conversation was not a privileged document.

LOSS OF PRIVILEGE

Black & Decker Group Inc v Flymo Ltd

[1991] 3 All ER 158, [1991] 1 WLR 753, [1991] FSR 93
The defendant sought specific discovery of documents mentioned in the plaintiff's witness statements disclosed pursuant to an order given under RSC Ord 38, r 2A. The plaintiff contended that the defendant could not rely upon the contents of the witness statement in support of its motion for specific discovery because that statement was a privileged document.

HELD: Once the statement has been disclosed pursuant to Ord 38, r 2A the statement is no longer privileged. It is not possible to assert a right to refuse to disclose in respect of a document which has already been disclosed. Therefore once disclosed a witness statement is admissible for the purposes of an application for specific discovery.

Note—This can be taken a step further under Ord 38, r 2A(4). This deals with the circumstances in which a party other than the party serving the witness statement may or may not make use of it. A court has the discretion to allow one party to adduce under the Civil Evidence Act 1968 a statement that the other party has exchanged. See *Youell v Bland Welch & Co Ltd (No 3)* [1991] 1 WLR 122 (Phillips J).

Alizadeh v Nibkin

(1993) Times, 19 March, CA
The general rule was that admissions made in the course of negotiations for settlement should not be admitted in evidence. (see *Rush & Tompkins Ltd v Greater London Council*, p 571, above). However a tape recording of a without prejudice negotiation could become admissible if there was an unambiguous admission of impropriety during the course of the recorded discussion.

USE OF WITHOUT PREJUDICE CORRESPONDENCE IN INTERLOCUTORY APPLICATIONS

Family Housing Association (Manchester) Ltd v Michael Hyde & Partners

[1993] 2 All ER 567, [1993] 1 WLR 354, CA

The plaintiff brought proceedings against a number of defendants claiming loss and damage arising out of alleged defects in the construction and design of the plaintiff's premises. The first and third defendants applied for an order striking out the plaintiff's claim for want of prosecution. In response the plaintiff's solicitor filed an affidavit referring to and setting out the nature and content of without prejudice discussions which had taken place between 1986 and 1991. The defendants acknowledged that the plaintiff could refer to the fact without prejudice negotiations had taken place and the period of the negotiations but argued that the plaintiff was not permitted to refer to the details of what was offered. They argued that this was privileged information, inadmissible without the consent of the parties. The defendants brought an application to have the plaintiff's solicitor's affidavit struck out. The judge sitting as Official Referee refused to do so and the defendants appealed.

HELD: The defendants' application failed. There was nothing in reported authorities which excluded the use of without prejudice correspondence in applications of this kind. The unreported authorities did recognise a practice of allowing without prejudice correspondence to be admitted in applications of this kind. There was also evidence of a convention permitting the use of such documents for this purpose. As to public policy, there was a public policy consideration in favour of admitting the evidence in these sorts of applications.

Per Hirst LJ: I am unable to see how exposure of the course of negotiations in this narrow context is in any way harmful to either side. If the application succeeds, the action will be at an end. If it fails, and the case proceeds to trial, the material will not be available to the trial judge and he will not be in any way embarrassed.

6 DISCOVERY : CROWN PRIVILEGE

THE RULE

Re Grosvenor Hotel London

[1964] Ch 464, [1964] 1 All ER 92, [1964] 2 WLR 184, 107 Sol Jo 1002, CA (Cross J)

It has been clear law since the decision of the House of Lords in *Duncan v Cammell Laird & Co Ltd* that an objection to production properly taken by a public department on the ground that to produce the document would be injurious to the public interest is conclusive. Viscount Simon said in *Duncan*'s case:

'The essential matter is that the decision to object should be taken by the minister who is the political head of the department and that he should have seen and considered the contents of the documents and himself have formed the view that on grounds of public interest they ought not to be produced either because of their actual contents or because of the class of documents, eg departmental minutes to which they belong.'

When an objection to production is supported by a minister's affidavit the affidavit must (1) contain evidence from which the court can judge whether the minister came to a fresh decision of his own on the question whether the documents should be withheld, without any regard to a previous decision taken by his subordinates, and (2) specify the class of documents to which those for which he claims privilege belong. It is important that the public should know the principles on which ministers purport to act on these cases.

Note—The whole subject of Crown privilege on discovery of documents was exhaustively considered in proceedings reported as *Re Grosvenor Hotel London (No 2)* [1965] Ch 1210, [1964] 3 All ER 354, [1964] 3 WLR 992, 108 Sol Jo 674. The Court of Appeal (Lord Denning MR, Harman LJ and Salmon LJ) reached the following conclusions:
1 If Crown privilege is to be successfully claimed the objection must be taken in proper form, in the ordinary way by the minister himself after considering the documents himself.
2 A document may be privileged either because of its contents or because it is one of a class of documents privileged, apart from their contents, by the source from which they proceed.
3 There is a residual power in the courts to override the executive in cases where Crown privilege is unreasonably claimed for a class of document, eg comprising routine communications between civil servants, and the court may ask to see the documents to make a decision.
4 Where a minister is objecting to production of all documents in a particular class which is not privileged by reason of the contents he must justify his objection with reasons, describing the nature of the class and the reason why the documents should not be disclosed.

The subject of Crown privilege was further considered by the House of Lords in *Conway v Rimmer*.

Conway v Rimmer

[1968] AC 910, [1968] 1 All ER 874, [1968] 2 WLR 998, 112 Sol Jo 191, HL
A probationary constable claimed damages from a police superintendent for malicious prosecution. On discovery of documents the defendant claimed privilege for reports submitted to his superior officer on the ground that they were of a class of documents which it was contrary to the public interest to disclose. The plaintiff submitted that where the objection was to production of a document because of the class to which it belonged as opposed to its own contents the court might examine the document and, if satisfied that the interests of justice so demanded, overrule the Crown objection. He relied on *Merricks v Nott-Bower* [1965] 1 QB 57, [1964] 1 All ER 717, [1964] 2 WLR 702, 128 JP 267, 108 Sol Jo 116, CA; *Re Grosvenor Hotel* (above) and *Wednesbury Corpn v Ministry of Housing* [1965] 1 All ER 186, [1965] 1 WLR 261, 129 JP 123, 108 Sol Jo 1012.
HELD, in the House of Lords: *Duncan v Cammell Laird* is not an authority for saying that in all cases where privilege is claimed for a document on the grounds that it is one of a class which must be withheld from production for reasons of public interest the certificate of the minister must, as a matter of law, be treated as conclusive. The court has an inherent right to decide for itself on the information supplied, or if necessary, by inspection of the document itself, whether it comes within a class of document which must as a class be withheld from production.

Note—For the considerations that ought to influence judges in deciding whether to order inspection see *Air Canada v Secretary of State for Trade (No 2)* [1983] 2 AC 394, [1983] 1 All ER 910, [1983] 2 WLR 494, 127 Sol Jo 205, HL.

Sharples v Halford

(1991) Times, 9 October, EAT
Police disciplinary files, documents relating to the private lives of chief police officers and positive vetting documentation in the files of the association of chief police officers were privileged on the grounds of public interest immunity.

ORAL EVIDENCE NOT PRIVILEGED

Broome v Broome

[1955] P 190, [1955] 1 All ER 201, [1955] 2 WLR 401, 99 Sol Jo 114, CA
In a divorce suit a wife petitioner issued a *subpoena ad test* to be served on a representative of the Soldiers', Sailors' and Airmen's Families' Association in Hong Kong, and a *subpoena duces tecum* on the Secretary of State for War to produce documents of the Association. The Secretary of State gave a certificate that it was not in the public interest that the documents should be produced or the evidence of the representative given orally.
HELD: Crown privilege could attach to all documents from or to a servant or agent of the Crown, but it was wrong to attempt to prevent the witness giving evidence of any sort. Application to set aside the *subpoena* failed.

WRITTEN EVIDENCE NOT PRIVILEGED

Parks v Tayside Regional Council

1989 SLT 345 (Scottish Outer House)
The plaintiff claimed that she had contracted hepatitis from a child which the defendants had placed in her care. She claimed that the defendants had failed to protect her safety and sought an order for inspection of the defendants' records relating to the child and its mother, to ascertain whether the defendants had been negligent. The defendants argued that the records were confidential and subject to public interest privilege.
HELD: Disclosure was ordered. The possible breach of a person's interest in his own privacy, which was of public interest, had to be set against the necessity that a litigant should be enabled to present his case properly, which was also a matter of public interest. In this case, the latter consideration prevailed, particularly in view of the fact that the disclosure of the records sought was of a limited nature.

CHAPTER 17

Practice and Procedure

GENERALLY

An action for personal injuries means an action in which there is a claim for damages in respect of personal injuries to the plaintiff or any other or in respect of a person's death, and 'personal injuries' includes any disease, any impairment of a person's physical or mental condition (RSC Ord, r 3).

Whether such an action is brought in the High Court or in the county court, depends upon its value, and it is now necessary to include a certificate of value when issuing proceedings in accordance with art 7(3) of the High Court and County Courts Jurisdiction Order 1991, SI 1991/724. If it does not exceed the sum specified in art 7(3) or has no quantifiable value, then the action must fall within the criteria mentioned in art 7(5) of the Order before it is deemed to be suitable for determination in the High Court (see RSC Ord 1, r 4 generally).

County Court Rules

As a majority of personal injury actions are now likely to proceed in the county court, the rules relevant to that jurisdiction have been detailed, though the rules for the Supreme Court are mentioned in the summary of an action set out below. Reference should be made of course to the Green Book or the White Book in the event of recent amendments. All references in this chapter are to the 1993 editions.

SUMMARY OF HIGH COURT ACTION AND COUNTY COURT RULES

Note—The page numbers refer to places in this book where relevant case material may be found: the references do not purport to be exhaustive.

(1) Letter before action: it should contain the date, time and place of the accident and sufficient information to identify the event together with the name(s) of the claimant(s). Detailed particulars of the alleged negligence are not requisite. A request to pass the letter to insurers is advisable.

(2) If no reply is received from any insurers in claims for personal injuries, details of insurance should be sought before proceeding further. There are the following possible sources or methods:

(a) a police report—write to the appropriate force;

(b) if no police report can be supplied yet, the police may notify insurance details by letter on request;

(c) a letter to the person against whom the claim is being made, drawing attention to the Road Traffic Act 1988, s 154 (p 763, below) and requiring disclosure of the particulars.

(3) If and when the identity of the insurers is known but no letter or other acknowledgement has been received from them write them with a copy of the letter before action. If no insurer can be traced, write to the Motor Insurers' Bureau (see pp 765–790, below).

(4) If necessary or desirable, apply for legal aid certificate.

(5) Issue of proceedings by writ or summons: necessary points to note:

(a) jurisdiction for personal actions (see RSC Ords 5 and 6 and in particular Ord 6, r 2 (23));

(b) time-limits for commencement of proceedings (see Ch 15, above, especially those sections of the Limitation Act 1980 dealing with personal injury claims, pp 501–502).

(c) in fatal cases representation of the deceased's estate by probate or letters of administration is needed unless the case is one to which the Fatal Accidents Act 1976, s 2(2) can conveniently apply (p 457, above);

(d) notice must be given to the insurer of the issue, or intended issue of proceedings (pp 755–759, below) or to the Motor Insurers' Bureau where there is no traceable insurer (cl 5(1)(a) of the Uninsured Drivers' Agreement, p 766, below) within seven days after the commencement of proceedings;

(e) ensure endorsement to writ identifies cause of action (pp 534–535, above) and see RSC Ord 6 generally) and that CCR Ords 4 and 5 (venue) have been complied with;

(f) ensure correctness of names of parties and capacity in which they sue or are sued (pp 535–537, above); next friend for plaintiff under age see RSC Ord 6, r 3 and CCR Ord 5;

(g) in proceedings against the Crown, refer to the requirements of Crown Proceedings Act (p 595, below).

(6) If the writ is not served within four months of issue, (RSC Ord 6, r 8, CCR Ord 7, r 20) renew before expiry and before expiry of limitation period (pp 537–543, above).

(7) Service of the writ or summons may be effected by:

(a) personal service on individual defendant (see RSC Ord 10, r 1 and Ord 65 and CCR Ord 7, r 9);

(b) ordinary post at defendant's usual or last known address;

(c) insertion through defendant's letter box;

(d) leaving writ at or posting it to the registered office of limited company.

In case of a defendant abroad, see RSC Ord 11 and CCR Ord 8. For service on corporate bodies other than limited companies, see RSC Ord 65, r 3 and CCR Ord 7, r 14. For service on partnerships, see RSC Ord 81, r 3 and CCR Ord 7, r 13. For service by post on solicitors, see RSC Ord 10, r 4 and CCR Ord 7, r 10(a) for authority to accept service of proceedings in personal injury actions;

(e) substituted service by order of the court when the defendant cannot be found (RSC Ord 65, r 4 and CCR Ord 7, r 8): if insured by post, at insurer's address; if not insured by post, at the address of the Motor Insurers' Bureau, or otherwise (for untraced motorist see the MIB agreement at p 766, below).

(8) Once service has been effected in accordance with RSC Ord 10 or CCR Ord 7, r 10(3), the date of service shall be the seventh day after the date the copy was sent or put through the letter box (RSC Ord 10, r 3, though see Ord 10 generally where other methods of service have been employed).

(9) The defendant's acknowledgment of service and notice of intention to defend are due within 14 days of service (RSC Ord 12, r 5) and in the form prescribed (see Ord 12 generally),

and in the county court the defence must be served within 14 days after the service of the summons (CCR Ord 9, r 6) if he intends to defend the proceedings:

(a) a defendant applying to set aside the writ or service must issue his application within 14 days of filing the acknowledgment of service (if the writ is served with the statement of claim) or within the time limited for service of the defence (RSC Ord 12, r 8 and see CCR Ord 37 for setting aside);

(b) the acknowledgment and notice can be validly filed at any time before the plaintiff signs judgment in default.

(10) The plaintiff's statement of claim may be endorsed on the writ or may be served with it. If not, then it should be served within 14 days after the defendant gives notice of intention to defend (RSC Ord 18, r 1). In the county court, as a general rule the plaintiff shall, at the time of commencing an action file particulars of his claim specifying his cause of action and the relief or remedy sought. He should also state the material facts on which he relies. For exceptions to the rule see CCR Ord 6, r 1. Note:

(a) any special damage claimed must be pleaded and, in any personal injury action, a medical report must be served with the statement of claim (RSC Ord 18, r 12(1)(a) and CCR Ord 6, r 1(5)) unless leave is given (RSC Ord 18, r 12(1)(b) and CCR Ord 6, r 1(6));

(b) a claim for interest must be pleaded (RSC Ord 18, r 8(4) and CCR Ord 6, r 1(a); see p 368, above);

(c) provisional damages may be claimed (RSC Ord 37, Part 2, CCR Ord 22, r 6A, p 390, above);

(d) possible difficulties in amending out of time (pp 528–532, above).

(11) If no acknowledgment of service of the writ with notice of intention to defend is filed by the defendant within 14 days of service, or, after service of the Statement of Claim no defence is served within 14 days, interlocutory judgment can be signed by the plaintiff (RSC Ord 13, r 2) unless the defendant has obtained an extension of time by consent or by order of the court on a time summons. The defendant may apply to set aside the judgment (see p 604, below) or contest the claim on assessment of damages only. Contributory negligence (eg failure by the plaintiff to wear a seat belt) is not an issue which can be contested on a mere assessment of damages following interlocutory judgment: it is an issue on liability which must be pleaded in a defence.

If the action is proceeding in the county court, the application for interlocutory judgment should be made pursuant to CCR Ord 9, r 6.

(12) The defence must be served within 14 days of the time limited for acknowledgment of service or service of the Statement of Claim (or Particulars of Claim in the county court), whichever is the later. Note:

(a) the court will not normally order further and better particulars of the Statement of Claim before service of the defence (pp 616–617, below and RSC Ord 18, r 12(5) and CCR Ord 6, r 7(2));

(b) circumstances in which the court will set aside a default judgment (p 604, below and RSC Ord 13, r 9 and CCR Ord 37);

(c) limitation period for counter-claim (see Ch 15);

(d) service of defence on every other party to action including other defendants (RSC Ord 18, r 2);

(e) admissions and denials in pleadings (RSC Ord 18, r 13 and Ord 27 and CCR Ord 9).

(13) The plaintiff may serve a reply (if appropriate) and a defence to a counterclaim within 14 days of defence.

(14) Third-party proceedings may be started by the defendant before service of defence without leave (RSC Ord 16, r 1(2)); but after defence served leave of the court is required, obtained usually ex parte on affidavit evidence (pp 615–616, below). Note:

(a) between defendant tortfeasers no specific contribution proceedings are needed merely to establish proportions of liability (*Croston v Vaughan*, p 615, below);

(b) new rules on limitations are established in the Limitation Act 1980, s 35 (p 528, above).

(c) third party and contribution proceedings have 'a life of their own' (p 615, below and see the Civil Liability (Contribution) Act 1978).

In the county court third-party proceedings can be issued without leave (CCR Ord 12, r 1(2)) provided that in a default action no day has been fixed under Ord 9, r 3 (or 5) for the hearing of a pre-trial review of the action or if automatic directions apply by virtue of CCR Ord 17, r 11, then leave is required after pleadings are deemed to be closed in accordance with Ord 17, r 11(a).

(15) Application for interim payment of damages (see pp 388–390, above and RSC Ord 29, rr 9—18). Note:
(a) application may be made at any time after service of writ and expiry of time limited for acknowledgment of service (RSC Ord 29, rr 9—18);
(b) interim payments must not be disclosed to the court at trial (p 388, above).

(16) Automatic directions in personal injury actions. RSC Ord 25, r 8, CCR Ord 17, r 11 and 11(3) which came into force on the 16 November 1992 requires service of witness statements within ten weeks (County Court (Amendment) (No 2) Rules 1992, SI 1992/1965) of close of pleadings. All automatic directions take effect when pleadings are closed. They deal with discovery (see below) expert evidence, expert witness, photographs, sketch plan and police report, setting down and place of trial. See Chapter 16, above (evidence).

(17) Consolidate actions in which common questions of law or fact arise (p 596, below and RSC Ord 4, r 9 and CCR Ord 13, r 9).

(18) Discovery and interrogatories:
(a) discovery is to be given within 14 days of close of pleadings by list of documents (RSC Ord 24, r 2 and see Ord 24 generally, CCR Ord 14);
(b) defendant in an action arising from a collision or apprehended collision involving vehicle is not required to make discovery to the plaintiff;
(c) legal professional privilege (p 620, below);
(d) Crown privilege—public policy (p 573, above);
(e) interrogatories can now be served twice on a party without leave (RSC Ord 26, r 3 and CCR Ord 14, r 11) though a party may apply within 14 days for them to be withdrawn or varied (RSC Ord 26, r 3(2) and CCR Ord 14, r 11).

(19) Payment into court (see RSC Ord 22 generally). Note:
(a) addition of interest (RSC Ord 22, r 13(8), CCR Ord 11, r 1(8));
(b) effect on costs (see RSC Ord 62, r 5 regarding costs, CCR Ord 38, r 1 where payment in);
(c) payment out (RSC Ord 22, r 10 and CCR Ord 11, r 4).

(20) Settlement of action. Note possible points arising:
(a) inadequate settlements (pp 676–679, below);
(b) 'without prejudice' letters (pp 570–573, above);
(c) binding receipt (RSC Ord 80, r 11, CCR Ord 10, r 10);
(d) court approval (RSC Ord 80, r 11).

(21) Transfer of proceedings: proceedings having been commenced in the High Court, the court will consider on setting down or earlier perhaps on an interlocutory application, the transfer of the action to the county court. The criteria is set out in art 7(5) of the High Court and County Courts Jurisdiction Order 1991, SI 1991/724 and see *Practice Direction*, 26 June 1991 by the Lord Chief Justice reproduced in [1991] 3 All ER 349, [1991] 1 WLR 643 and s 40 of the County Courts Act 1984 (as substituted by s 3 of the Courts and Legal Services Act 1990) and see notes to CCR Ord 16, r 6 in the *Green Book* for a summary.

(22) Trials: all actions will be automatically struck out after 15 months if there has been no application for a trial date in a county court action (CCR Ord 17, r 11(9)). There will be an automatic reference to arbitration for all claims limited to £1,000 (CCR Ord 19, r 3). Note:
(a) solicitors to supply calculation (*Practice Note,* 1 August 1984, LS Gaz R 2742);
(b) if and when by jury (RSC Ord 33, r 5, CCR Ord 13, r 10);
(c) adjournments (RSC Ord 35, r 3, CCR Ord 13, r 3);

(d) medical evidence to have been disclosed in accordance with automatic directions and see RSC Ord 38, r 4, CCR Ord 20, r 27 for restrictions on adducing expert evidence;
(e) assessment of damages by judge (RSC Ord 37, CCR Ord 22, r 16);
(f) provisional damages (RSC Ord 37, Part 2, CCR Ord 22, r 6A);
(g) award of interest on damages (pp 442–449, above);
(h) unassisted defendant; award of costs (pp 692–695, below).

(23) Appeal:
(a) new evidence (pp 681–682, below) see RSC Ord 59, r 12 for Court of Appeal; see RSC Ord 58 for appeals from Masters, district judges and judges;
(b) unassisted party—costs from Legal Aid Fund (pp 696–697, below);
(c) appeal from jury (above);
(d) appeals on amount—principles (pp 449–451, above).

(24) Judgment:
(a) effect—res judicata (pp 608–612, below);
(b) interest on judgment debt (RSC Ord 42, r 1(12) on costs, CCR Ord 9, r 8. See *Supreme Court Practice* 1993 p 709 for RSC Ord 42, r 1(12)—(13).

Note—See also *Hunt v RM Douglas (Roofing) Ltd* [1988] 3 All ER 823, HL.

(25) Costs:
(a) Bullock and Sanderson orders (RSC Ord 63, CCR Ord 38 and pp 656–659, below);
(b) effect of payment into court (pp 666–669, below);
(c) claim and counter-claim (pp 664–665, below);
(d) on infant's settlement (RSC Ord 62, r 16 and p 666, below)
(e) party and party and common fund (p 662, below).

(26) Dismissal for want of prosecution:
(a) principles (pp 635–645, below);
(b) special cases (pp 645–651, below).

CONSIDERATIONS IN A TYPICAL ACTION

Jurisdiction

THE HIGH COURT

Note—All personal injury actions brought in the High Court must include a certificate to the effect that the value of the claim exceeds £50,000 and, therefore, is not one by which, virtue of art 5 of the High Court and County Courts Jurisdiction Order 1991, must be commenced in a county court (RSC Ord 6, r 2(1)(f)). This is for all actions commenced after the 1 July 1991 (see generally High Court and County Courts Jurisdiction Order 1991, SI 1991/724 and arts 5, 9 and 10 thereof and also *Practice Direction (personal injury actions: endorsement on writ)* [1991] 3 All ER 352, [1991] 1 WLR 642. The endorsement should be in the following form:

'This writ includes a claim for personal injury, but may be commenced in the High Court because the value of the action for the purposes of article 5 of the High Court and County Courts Jurisdiction Order 1991 exceeds £50,000.'

The endorsement is to be signed by the plaintiff (if he acts in person) or his solicitor. In the event there is no endorsement, proceedings must be commenced in the county court.

TRANSFER FROM THE HIGH COURT TO THE COUNTY COURT

Note—See art 7(5) of the High Court and County Courts Jurisdiction Order 1991, SI 1991/724 (see note to CCR Ord 16, r 6 in the *Green Book*).

THE COUNTY COURT

Financial limits

Note—Unless the action has been certified as likely to exceed £50,000 (or the current limit), all personal injury actions must now be commenced in the county court which has concurrent jurisdiction with the High Court (SI 1991/724, art 2). By virtue of CCR Ord 21, r 5 the district judge (formerly the Registrar) has power to hear and determine actions or matters, the value of which do not exceed £5,000. In an action for an unliquidated sum, the value of the plaintiff's claim shall, for the purposes of CCR Ord 21, r 5 be limited to £5,000 unless otherwise stated (Ord 6, r 1A). All claims below £1,000 (ignoring the counter claim) shall stand referred for arbitration though the court has power to rescind that reference (CCR Ord 19, r 2(4)) but not without notice to the parties (CCR Ord 19, r 2(4A)).

Residence of the parties

Note—CCR Ord 4, r 2(1) provides that an action may be commenced:

(a) in the court where the defendant resides;
(b) where the cause of action arose wholly or in part;
(c) for default actions in any county court.

However, the court has full discretion for ordering the transfer of actions (see CCR Ord 16, rr 1 and 2) and in liquidated claims where a defence has been filed will automatically transfer the action to the defendants' home court if the action was not commenced there (CCR Ord 9, r 2(8)).

Application to transfer from the county court to the High Court

Forey v London Buses Ltd

[1991] 2 All ER 936, [1991] 1 WLR 327, [1992] PIQR P48, CA
Once a matter has been transferred to the county court for hearing (by virtue of s 40 of the County Courts Act 1984) the county court judge has the power to award costs on the High Court scale, if he considers it appropriate (County Courts Act 1984, s 45(1); CCR Ord 38, r 1(2)). See CCR Ord 16, r 9 and the *Practice Direction* (*county court transfer of actions*) [1991] 3 All ER 349, [1991] 1WLR 643. An application may be made stating the grounds by reference to art 7(1) of the High Court and County Courts Jurisdiction Order 1991 and a statement is to be included stating whether or not the value of the action exceeds the sum specified in art 7(3) of the Order. Actions worth less than £25,000 must normally be tried in the county court and above £50,000 in the High Court with those in between being determined on the basis of the criteria set out in art 7(5).

Note—The county courts are now empowered to deal with provisional damages and *Kennedy v Bowater* [1991] 1 All ER 669 is no longer relevant on an application to transfer down pursuant to s 40 of the County Courts Act 1984. Rules 5 and 6 of the County Courts (Amendment No 4) Rules 1989, SI 1989/2426 grant the county court power to make such an award in a personal injury claim.

El Buka v Quinn

[1993] 2 Ch 397
Even though the accident occurred in Birmingham and the defendant's insurers were based there, the circuit judge refused to transfer the action from Birkenhead County Court as this was convenient to the plaintiff and his advisers. The judge took into

account the fact that the matter was only listed for assessment of damages and that the defendant would not be in attendance when deciding upon the balance of convenience.

Restick v Crickmore

[1994] 2 All ER 112, [1994] 1 WLR 420, 138 Sol Jo LB 4
The Court of Appeal held that there was discretion to the court to transfer actions wrongly commenced in the High Court, to the county court. Although there may be a costs sanction against the plaintiff, it would not be appropriate to remove his cause of action simply as a result of a procedural error on the part of his advisers.

Azfal v Ford Motor Co Ltd

(1994) Times, 6 July, (1994) Independent, 16 June, CA
The Court of Appeal considered provisions for the automatic reference to arbitration of small claims in the county court. The relevant points were summarised as follows

(a) If a plaintiff does not expect his claim to exceed £1,000 then his claim can be limited to that amount. If he considers the case should not proceed to arbitration then objection can be raised on the appropriate county court form.
(b) If the claim is not limited to £1,000 then the defendant can indicate in his defence that he thinks it should be and ask for the claim to be referred to arbitration.
(c) The defendant can specify the value of the claim in his defence, if he so wishes.
(d) In the event of a dispute between the parties the district judge will determine whether the matter should proceed to arbitration, or he may hear the parties at his own discretion.
(e) If a claim is overstated or the defence without merit then parties are at risk as to costs under Ord 19, r 4(2)(c).

Note—This is an important decision concerning the conduct of litigation of small claims and demonstrates the court's willingness to use its powers where the parties abuse the process.

ARBITRATION

Note—
(a) automatic reference under CCR Ord 19, r 2(3);
(b) that reference may be rescinded on application or of the court's own motion (CCR Ord 19, r 2(4));
(c) notice to be given to the parties by the court if they intend to rescind the reference (CCR Ord 19, r 2(4)(a));
(d) the fact the parties are legally represented is not of itself a sufficient reason for directing a trial in court rather than in arbitration.

The question of recoverability of costs for actions settled at below the arbitration limit is of increasing significance in view of the large numbers of minor accident claims which fall below the £1,000 limit.

Russell v Wilson

(1989) Times, 26 May, CA
The availability of insurance cover in respect of legal fees is of no relevance and does not justify an action proceedings in the county court rather than by way of arbitration if CCR Ord 19 is otherwise appropriate.

Pepper v Healey

(1982) 126 Sol Jo 497, [1982] RTR 411, CA
Following a collision between their cars the plaintiff began proceedings against the defendant in the county court for an amount not exceeding £200. The defendant, represented by solicitors instructed by her insurers, denied liability. Both parties proposed to call expert and other witnesses at the trial and have legal representation. The plaintiff applied to the registrar for an order rescinding automatic reference of the claim to arbitration under Ord 19, r 1(4) on the grounds provided by Ord 19, r 1(5)(d) 'that it would be unreasonable for the claim to proceed to arbitration having regard to . . . the circumstances of the parties'. The registrar made the order as asked and was upheld by the judge.
HELD, ON APPEAL: There was no reason to suggest that the judge had applied his discretion wrongly. The contest between the parties was unequal as the defendant had the protection of an insurance company and the plaintiff had not. If there was an arbitration no solicitors' charges would be allowed as between party and party. If, on the other hand, the case was tried in the county court and the plaintiff won she would recover her costs; as she needed representation the judge was entitled to conclude that the case should be tried by the county court.

Note—No solicitors' charges are allowed as between party and party in respect of any proceedings referred to arbitration under CCR Ord 19, r 2(3) except:
(a) the costs of the summons;
(b) the costs of enforcing the award;
(c) such further costs as the arbitrator may direct where there has been unreasonable conduct on the part of the opposing party in relation to the proceedings or the claim there in (see generally CCR Ord 19, r 6).

Newland v Boardwell

[1983] 3 All ER 179, [1984] 1 WLR 1453, 127 Sol Jo 580, CA
The County Court Rules 1936, Ord 19, r 1(4) provides that when the amount claimed in proceedings does not exceed £500 the action shall on receipt of a defence of the claim be referred for arbitration by the registrar. Order 19, r 1(11) provides that no solicitors' costs shall be allowed in respect of any proceedings referred to arbitration unless certified by the registrar to have been incurred through the unreasonable conduct of the opposite party.

In an action arising from a collision of two vehicles the defendant in his defence admitted negligence but expressly did not admit the plaintiff's alleged injuries, loss and damage. The claim being limited to £500 the registrar referred it for arbitration, since the refusal to admit the injuries, loss and damage amounted to a defence on the issue of causation. The plaintiff having later accepted a payment into court the registrar gave a certificate that her costs should be paid by the defendant by reason of his 'unreasonable conduct' in defending the action. If the defendant had submitted to interlocutory judgment for damages to be assessed he could have called evidence and been heard on quantum of damages but would have been liable to an order for costs against him.
HELD, in the Court of Appeal: The denial of liability in the defence was a device to take advantage of Ord 19, r 1(4) and avoid an order for costs. It was a misuse of the pleading process and justified the registrar's certificate under r 1(11)(c). But the words 'through the unreasonable conduct of the opposite party' could not affect costs incurred before the unreasonable conduct. When the plaintiff knew from the defence

that the case would have to be referred for arbitration she could have withdrawn her retainer to her solicitors and incurred no more costs. Thus her liability for costs after the defence was not the result of the defendant's 'unreasonable conduct' but of her own failure to protect herself. She was entitled against the defendant only to the costs on the summons (ie her costs up to the filing of the defence).

Note—Order 19 of the County Court Rules 1936 is now contained in Ord 19 of the 1993 Rules.

Kirk-Smith v Richardson

[1992] 12 CL 458
Proceedings were commenced in the county court for a claim limited to £1,000, following the breakdown in negotiations. The defendant's insurers made three payments in to achieve the total sum claimed by the plaintiff. However, they refused to pay his costs.

The district judge held that the defendant's conduct had been unreasonable in circumstances where they were prepared to pay the entirety of the claim if necessary. Looking at their conduct objectively, he accepted the plaintiff's contentions and awarded him the costs. That decision was upheld on appeal.

Note—*Newland v Boardwell* distinguished and *Bloomfield v Roberts* [1989] CLY 2948 confirmed.

Barrowclough v British Gas Corpn

[1986] 10 CL 34
A plaintiff who inflates his claim in order to increase his claim beyond the limit in CCR Ord 19, r 2(3) above may be penalised in costs.

Amranari v Shaikh

[1993] 5 CL 328
If the plaintiff inflates his claim to avoid the provisions of CCR Ord 19 then his costs would in any event be limited to those set out in Ord 19, r 6 even though he had accepted a payment into court (CCR Ord 11, r 3(5) is not therefore relevant).

Smith v Springer

[1987] 3 All ER 252, [1987] 1 WLR 1720, 131 Sol Jo 1248, CA
The defendant drove into the rear of the plaintiff's stationary car; although liability was not admitted, it was not denied. The plaintiff's solicitors wrote claiming £86.32 uninsured losses and £23 costs from the defendant's insurers. The insurers paid £86.32 but refused to pay costs as the claim was for less than £500. The plaintiff's solicitors refused the payment and commenced proceedings which were in a slightly different form, with an additional head of damage and with the claim for loss of use unparticularised. The defendant applied to have the plaintiff's case struck out as an abuse of the court process; the plaintiff applied for interlocutory judgment with damages to be assessed.
HELD: The court had sympathy with insurers who were prepared to settle claims in full but did not want to pay legal costs as the price of avoiding litigation, but decided that as this was an unliquidated claim it was not possible to decide what would have been recovered by the plaintiff. The proper course of action was to enter interlocutory

judgment for the plaintiff ordering damages to be assessed following which the county court registrar could exercise his discretion as to costs.

Snape v O'Reilly

[1992] 9 CL 91

Where proceedings are commenced purely with the intention of recovering costs which would not otherwise be payable as the claim was within the arbitration limit, the action should be struck out as an abuse of the process.

Daly v Ford Motor Co

[1992] CLY 3438

When considering whether a claim for damages should be limited to the £1,000 arbitration limit, a court should look to see whether there was a 'reasonable and genuine' expectation that the claims had a potential in excess of the automatic referral limit. If they did not, they should be referred to arbitration and costs would not be recoverable if the actions were commenced in the county court.

Motley v Courtaulds

[1990] 12 LS Gaz R 39, CA

Even though the defendant did not apply for a reference to arbitration, the plaintiff's costs should be limited to those allowed under CCR Ord 19, r 6 if the claim was obviously valued at less than £500.

Arbitrations generally—Arbitration Act 1950

Note—The Arbitration Acts 1889 to 1934 were repealed and consolidated without any substantial alteration by the Arbitration Act 1950 (14 Geo 6, c 27), which came into force on 1 September 1950. Important reforms in the law and practice of arbitrations were made by the Arbitration Act 1979.

The application of a condition in insurance policies requiring any dispute to be referred to arbitration has become of less importance in view of the decision of insurers not to require compliance with such condition except on a dispute relating to amount when liability is not in issue.

Abandonment of arbitration

Note—The following statement was issued in January 1957:

'The British Insurance Association and *Lloyd's* announce that their members have entered into an agreement in respect of United Kingdom business, the general effect of which is to allow an assured who prefers to have questions of liability, as distinct from amount, determined by the Courts, to do so notwithstanding that the policy contains an Arbitration Clause.

The insurers have defined their intentions as follows:

'If in dispute arising under a contract of insurance made in the United Kingdom the assured brings an action in any Court in the United Kingdom, the insurers will, notwithstanding that the contract contains an arbitration clause, not apply to the Court for a stay of action on that ground unless—

(1) the whole of the dispute relates to the amount of the claim, liability being admitted; or

(2) the dispute relates partly to liability and partly to amount and the assured refuses to give an undertaking that, in the event of the insurer being found liable, he will agree to any dispute as to amount being determined in the manner provided in the arbitration clause.

Nothing in the foregoing shall apply—
(a) to a contract of reinsurance; or
(b) to a contract of marine insurance; or
(c) to a contract which is an insurance of all or any of the following risks relating to aviation, namely, loss of or damage to aircraft liability of the assured to third parties or to passengers, and loss of or damage to, or liability in respect of, cargo consigned by air; or
(d) to a contract of credit insurance; or
(e) where the terms of the insurance are set out in a contract or policy which is specially negotiated and in which an arbitration clause has been specifically agreed.'''

FOREIGN TORTS

Actionable

Note—It is well established that actions for personal wrongs arising in foreign countries may be brought in an English court. However, once a litigant has submitted to the jurisdiction of a foreign court, all proceedings are subject to that jurisdiction, even interlocutory orders which may have been made before the jurisdiction was invoked. See *Marc Rich & Co AG v Societa Italiana Impianti* (1992) Financial Times, 24 January.

Hart v Gumpach

(1873) LR 4 PC 439, 9 Moo PCCNS 241, 42 LJPC 25, 21 WR 365
By the law of England actions for personal wrongs arising in foreign countries may be brought in an English court.

Phillips v Eyre

(1870) LR 6 QB 1, 10 B & S 1004, 40 LJQB 28, 22 LT 869, Ex Ch
An act committed abroad, if valid and unquestionable by the law of the place cannot, so far as civil liability is concerned, be drawn in question elsewhere. As a general rule, in order to found a suit in England for a wrong alleged to have been committed abroad, two conditions must be fulfilled. (1) The wrong must be of such a character that it would have been actionable if committed in England; (2) the act must not have been justifiable by the law of the place where it was done.

Carr v Fracis Times & Co

[1902] AC 176, 71 LJKB 361, 85 LT 144, 50 WR 257, 17 TLR 657, HL
A tort that has been committed abroad is not actionable in the English courts unless two conditions are satisfied. In the first place, the wrong must be of such a character that it would have been actionable if committed in England; and secondly, the act must not have been justifiable by the law of the place where it was committed.

Kohnke v Karger

[1951] 2 KB 670, [1951] 2 All ER 179, [1951] 2 TLR 40
The plaintiff was a passenger in a car driven by the defendant in France when there was a collision with a lorry and she was injured. A French court awarded her £1,400 damages in correctional proceedings against the lorry driver, which were paid. The defendant was held one-third to blame in those proceedings, and reimbursed the lorry driver in that proportion. The plaintiff considering herself inadequately recompensed began proceedings against the defendant in the present action in England undertaking to give credit for the amount already recovered. The defendant contended that as she

had already recovered from the lorry driver in France she could not have damages against the defendant.
HELD: If the plaintiff obtains abroad a judgment which is satisfied against a defendant and then sues him in this country for the same debt or damages the plaintiff cannot succeed: *Barber v Lamb* (1860) 8 CBNS 95, 29 LJCP 234, 2 LT 238, 6 Jur NS 981, 8 WR 461 but it may be different if there are separate causes of action against different defendants for the same damage. On the evidence the plaintiff was not adequately compensated by the award of £1,400. The award of an amount against the lorry driver in France could not avail the present defendant except to the extent that the damages were in part satisfied by the lorry driver. Award £2,200 less the £1,400 recovered from the lorry driver.

Note—This case is discussed at p 309 of 101 LJ (8 June 1951), that it is well settled that if a foreign judgment has been satisfied the creditor will be considered to have elected to take it in discharge of the whole cause of action, and will be debarred from suing in this country on the original cause ofaction, even if, owing to a difference between the laws of the two countries, the amount of the foreign judgment is less than he might have recovered if the action had been brought in this country: *Barber v Lamb* (1860) 8 CBNS 95, 29 LJCP 234, 2 LT 238, 6 Jur NS 981, 8 WR 461; *Taylor v Hollard* [1902] 1 KB 676, 71 LJKB 278, 86 LT 228, 50 WR 558, 18 TLR 287.

Damages

Chaplin v Boys

[1971] AC 356, [1969] 2 All ER 1085, [1969] 3 WLR 322, 113 Sol Jo 608, HL
The defendant was injured in a road accident in Malta. The defendant admitted negligence. Maltese law limits damages for personal injuries to actual financial loss and allows no damages for pain and suffering. Both parties were British servicemen and the plaintiff brought this action in England. The defendant claimed that questions of remoteness of damage fell to be decided by the *lex loci delicti*, ie Maltese law, and that the plaintiff was entitled only to his special damage.
HELD: Following *Machado v Fontes* ([1897] 2 QB 231, 66 LJQB 542, 76 LT 588), when there is a right of action in this country for a tort committed abroad the question what damages are to be awarded falls to be decided by English law just as if the tort had been committed in this country. The plaintiff was entitled to recover both the general damages of £2,250 and the special damage of £53.

Appeals to the Court of Appeal and to the House of Lords were dismissed. All the Law Lords were agreed in dismissing the appeal but differed on the reasons for doing so.

Lord Hodson: The right to damages for pain and suffering is a substantive right. Controlling effect in determining the questions between the parties should be given to the law of that jurisdiction which because of its relationship with the occurrence and the parties has the greater concern with the issue raised in the litigation. The law of England is applicable since even though the occurrence took place in Malta this was overshadowed by the identity and circumstances of the parties, British subjects temporarily serving in Malta.

Lord Guest: To justify an action in England for a tort committed abroad the conduct must be actionable by English law and by the laws of the country in which the conduct occurred. Whatever relates to the remedy to be enforced must be determined by the *lex fori* but there is a distinction between the kind of damage for which a remedy will be given and the method of compensating the plaintiff for his loss. The kind of damage is a matter of substantive law to be decided by the *lex loci delicti* but the method of compensation is a procedural matter to be determined by the *lex fori*. Damages for pain and suffering were merely an element in the quantification of the total compensation and therefore a matter for the *lex fori*, ie English law.

Lord Donovan: I am content with the rule enunciated by Willes J in *Phillips v Eyre* (p 587, above) and would leave it alone. I would not substitute 'actionable' for 'not justifiable'. An English court was competent to entertain this action under the rule in *Phillips v Eyre* and once it had done so it was right that it should award its own remedies.

Lord Wilberforce: The broad principle should be that a person should not be permitted to claim in England in respect of a matter for which civil liability does not exist, or is excluded, under the law of the place where the wrong was committed. Provisions of the *lex delicti* denying or limiting recovery of some head of damage (such as pain and suffering) should be given effect to but some qualification of the rule is required in certain individual cases. The principle to be applied is whether with respect to a particular issue some other jurisdiction has a significant relationship with the occurrence and the parties. In the present action between two British subjects the question of damages for pain and suffering must be segregated and when this is done it is seen that an English court should apply its own rules.

Lord Pearson: The English authorities show that the Willes formula (in *Phillips v Eyre*) has been accepted. The first of his conditions gives the predominant role to English substantive law and the second of his conditions does not require actionability by the law of the place where the act was committed. I can see no reason for discarding this established rule and it was right for the trial judge in accordance with it to apply the English substantive law, the *lex fori*.

University of Glasgow v The Economist

(1990) Times, 13 July

Per Popplewell J: The plaintiff need only set out that (the tort) is actionable by the law of the foreign country and then say there is the presumption. If he chooses to do that, it is for the defendant to raise the issue that the foreign law is different from English law.

Parties to the action

PLAINTIFF

Husband and wife

Note—With effect from 1 August 1962, the common law rule by which spouses were precluded from suing each other in tort was abolished. This is the effect of the Law Reform (Husband and Wife) Act 1962, s 1 of which is as follows:

'1 Actions in tort between husband and wife (1) Subject to the provisions of this section each of the parties to a marriage shall have the like right of action in tort against the other as if they were not married.

(2) Where an action in tort is brought by one of the parties to a marriage against the other during the subsistence of the marriage, the court may stay the action if it appears—

(a) that no substantial benefit would accrue to either party from the continuation of the proceedings; or

(b) that the question or questions in issue could more conveniently be disposed of on an application made under s 17 of the Married Women's Property Act 1882 (determination of questions between husband and wife as to the title to or possession of property);

and without prejudice to para (b) of this subsection the court may, in such an action, either exercise any power which could be exercised on an application under the said section seventeen, or give such directions as it thinks fit for the disposal under that section of any question arising in the proceedings.'

When dealing with such an action reference should be made to RSC Ord 89, r 2 for the special rules relating to such actions in tort.

By s 3(3) of the Act 'parties to a marriage' includes parties to a marriage which has been dissolved.

See also the Family Proceedings Rules 1991, SI 1991/1247.

Age

Note—No action can be commenced by an individual who has not attained the age of majority.

Next friend

Note—Form of authority required, and solicitor's certificate if an infant.

Company

Note—Action to be brought in the registered name and served at the registered office (see p 602, below).

Administrators

Note—It has been contended that a claim by a legal personal representative suing in a representative capacity cannot be joined in the same action with a claim by the same person in a personal capacity. It now seems established that this is not the case.

Littlechild v Holt

[1950] 1 KB 1, [1949] 1 All ER 933, [1949] LJR 1299, 65 TLR 270, 93 Sol Jo 387, CA

Per Lord Goddard CJ: It is always the case that a claim by an executor or administrator, as executor or administrator, can be joined with a claim by the executor or administrator personally. So, too, if there is a claim by the executor personally, it can be joined with a claim by him or her as executor. It is open to a person who obtains an order to continue proceedings as administrator or executor to join a claim by himself or herself in his or her personal capacity with the claim that is made in the representative capacity. At any rate, it is within the discretion of the court to allow those two claims to be made at the same time. Where the two claims are of a very similar nature, I see no reason at all why they should not be joined.

DEFENDANT

Liquidated company

Note—The Companies Act 1985, s 651(1)–(3), which has replaced s 352 of the Companies Act 1948 reads as follows:

651 Power of court to declare dissolution of company void (1) Where a company has been dissolved, the court may at any time within 2 years of the date of the dissolution, on an application made for the purpose by the liquidator of the company or by any other person appearing to the court to be interested, make an order, on such terms as the court thinks fit, declaring the dissolution to have been void.
(2) Thereupon such proceedings may be taken as might have been taken if the company had not been dissolved.
(3) It is the duty of the person on whose application the order was made, within 7 days after its making (or such further time as the court may allow), to deliver to the registrar of companies for registration an office copy of the order.

If the person fails to do so, he is liable to a fine and, for continued contravention, to a daily default fine.

Re Roehampton Swimming Pool Ltd

[1968] 3 All ER 661, [1968] 1 WLR 1693, 112 Sol Jo 670 (Megarry J)
On 30 August 1965 an infant sustained injury when diving into a swimming pool in the occupation of a limited company. In July 1967 the company went into voluntary liquidation and on 12 April 1968, the company was deemed to have been dissolved. No writ had been issued against the company. In August 1968 the infant's solicitor applied in her own name to resuscitate the company under s 352 so that it could be sued.
HELD: If the application had been made by the claimant himself there would have been no difficulty in granting it since he, with a claim for damages against the company, plainly fell within the words 'any other person who appears to the court to be interested'. But the solicitor was not a 'person . . . interested', since those words mean a person having a pecuniary or proprietary interest.

Re BBH (Middletons) Ltd

(1970) 114 Sol Jo 431 (Plowman J)
31 December 1965: company passed special resolution for voluntary winding-up; 15 February 1966: applicant, an employee of the company, injured in road accident when driving company's van; 21 March 1968: company dissolved; 14 February 1969: applicant issued writ against company for damages for personal injury; 19 March 1970: applicant began proceedings to have company's dissolution declared void under s 352(1).
HELD: Assuming time under the Limitation Acts was running in favour of the company during the period until the dissolution it could not have continued to run after 21 March 1968, because the company had been dissolved and there was no one in whose favour it could have run. As the claim was not necessarily statute-barred, or would be barred if an order were made under the section, the dissolution should be declared void but without prejudicing any defence the company cared to put forward in any further action the applicant might bring against it.

Note—The Companies Act 1948, s 353(6) has been replaced by the Companies Act 1985, s 653 which reads as follows:

653 Objection to striking off by person aggrieved (1) The following applies if a company or any member or creditor of it feels aggrieved by the company having been struck off the register.
(2) The court, on an application by the company or the member or creditor made before the expiration of 20 years from publication in the Gazette of notice under section 652, may, if satisfied that the company was at the time of the striking off carrying on business or in

operation, or otherwise that it is just that the company be restored to the register, order the company's name to be restored.
(3) On an office copy of the order being delivered to the registrar of companies for registration the company is deemed to have continued in existence as if its name had not been struck off; and the court may by the order give such directions and make such provisions as seem just for placing the company and all other persons in the same position (as nearly as may be) as if the company's name had not been struck off.

Re Harvest Lane Motor Bodies Ltd

[1969] 1 Ch 457, [1968] 2 All ER 1012, [1968] 3 WLR 220, 112 Sol Jo 518 (Megarry J)
The widow of a man killed in a road accident on 16 July 1961 issued a writ on 26 April 1963 claiming damages under the Fatal Accidents and Law Reform Acts against the limited company whose servant she alleged was to blame. In June 1965 whilst the action was still proceeding the company's name was struck off the register under the Companies Act, s 353 as being a defunct company.
HELD: She was for the purpose of s 353(6) a 'creditor' and entitled to apply. The subsection is concerned with a grievance on the part of some person whether a company, a member or a creditor. The petitioner had an action in being when the company was struck off. The Act could not have intended to differentiate between those creditors whose debts are fixed and ascertained and those whose debts are contingent and prospective. The company's name should be restored to the register.

Note—It is not necessary that there should be an action in being against a company at the date of its being struck off for an application under s 353(6) to succeed. In *Re Regent Insulation Co Ltd* ((1981) Times, 4 November) the company was struck off the register in May 1976 for non-compliance with provisions of the Companies Act. A former employee who had worked for the company from November 1964 to January 1967 using asbestos was found in 1976 to be suffering from asbestosis. He applied in January 1981 that the company be restored to the register to enable him to institute proceedings against it. The registrar made an order in February 1981 restoring the company to the register and directing that the period between its being struck off in 1976 and its restoration should not be counted for the purposes of any Statute of Limitation. An appeal in the name of the company by its insurers was dismissed.

It is not necessary that there should be an action in being against a company at the date of its being struck off for an application under s 353(6) to succeed. In *Re Regent Insulation Co Ltd* ((1981) Times, 4 November) the company was struck off the register in May 1976 for non-compliance with provisions of the Companies Act. A former employee who had worked for the company from November 1964 to January 1967 using asbestos was found in 1976 to be suffering from asbestosis. He applied in January 1967 that the company be restored to the register to enable him to institute proceedings against it. The registrar made an order in February 1981 restoring the company to the register and directing that the period between its being struck off in 1976 and its restoration should not be counted for the purposes of any Statute of Limitation. An appeal in the name of the company by its insurers was dismissed.

Bankrupt

Employer/employee

Note—In most circumstances an employer will be vicariously liable for his employees' negligence, however, this will not be so if the employee was not acting in the course of his employment.

Estate of deceased tortfeasor

Note—Under the Supreme Court Act 1981, s 87(2) (replacing the Proceedings against Estates Act 1970, s 2) the court has power to make rules to enable proceedings to be commenced against the estate of a deceased person where no grant of probate or letters of administration had been made, or to enable an action started against an estate to be maintained against personal representatives to whom a grant had been made or a person appointed by the court to represent the estate. The rules are contained in RSC Ord 15, r 6A to which reference should be made for details of the appropriate procedures. Proceedings can be started before the issue of a grant. An application must then be made for an order appointing a person to represent the deceased's estate for the purpose of the proceedings. The defendants can be named as 'the personal representatives of A B deceased'.

Pratt v London Passenger Transport Board

[1937] 1 All ER 473, 156 LT 265, 53 TLR 355, 81 Sol Jo 79, CA
The plaintiff applied in a pending action to add the Official Solicitor under Ord XVI, r 46 (now RSC Ord 15, r 15(3)) without the consent of the Official Solicitor.
HELD: An order could not be made without his consent.

Re Amirteymour

[1978] 3 All ER 637, [1979] 1 WLR 63, 122 Sol Jo 525, CA
An Iranian died indebted to the plaintiff bank. The bank issued a writ against the estate described as 'The personal representatives of' the deceased. There had been no grant of probate or letters of administration in this country. With the consent of the Official Solicitor the plaintiffs obtained an order from the court under Ord 15, r 6A appointing him as representative of the estate limited to accepting service of the writ. He refused consent to an order which extended to his taking any further step in the proceedings. He accepted service of the writ. The bank signed judgment in default of appearance and sought to enforce it by garnishee proceedings.
HELD: Proceedings against the estate of a deceased person were actions *in personam*. In all such actions there had to be a natural or artificial person whom the law could recognise as a defendant against whom steps in the action could be taken. The appointment of the Official Solicitor to act as defendant was strictly limited and lapsed as soon as he had accepted service of the writ. No one else had been appointed to take his place and the judgment was a nullity.

Note—Where a person dies intestate, his real and personal estate, until administration is granted, shall vest in the President of the Family Division of the High Court in the same manner and to the same extent as formerly in the case of personal estate it vested in the Ordinary.

Watts v Official Solicitor

[1936] 1 All ER 249, 80 Sol Jo 204, CA
Plaintiff issued writ on 11 May 1935, against two defendants. On 5 June 1935 one defendant died. The deceased was insured. Plaintiff required judgment against deceased's estate to sue insurers under the Road Traffic Act 1934, s 10 (now the Road Traffic Act 1988, s 151). The Official Solicitor consented to act and was appointed representative of deceased's estate under Ord XVI, r 46 (now Ord 15, r 15), plaintiff undertaking to pay his costs. Insurer's solicitors had appeared for deceased before his death. The Official Solicitor nominated his own solicitors and served notice of change. Insurers' solicitors objected, and although the Official Solicitor offered to

employ them, they contended under the policy the Official Solicitor was bound to do so and notice of change was unnecessary.

Atkinson J ordered the notice of change to be removed from the file and that insurers' solicitors should remain on the record.

HELD, ON APPEAL: Insurers had no *locus standi* and could not be heard. The Official Solicitor was entitled to conduct and to select his own solicitors.

Note—Now the Road Traffic Act 1988, s 151.

Lean v Alston

[1947] KB 467, [1947] 1 All ER 261, [1947] LJR 559, CA

A pillion passenger was injured in a collision between a motor cycle and a car. The motor cyclist was killed in the collision. The pillion passenger issued a writ against the car owner, who wished to serve a third-party notice on the deceased's representative, but no administrator had been appointed and the widow declined to act. Defendant applied under Ord XVI, r 46 (now Ord 15, r 15), to appoint a representative of deceased's estate, who could be made a third party in the action, and the master made the appointment. Denning J allowed an appeal, taking the view that there was no power to make the order or if he had a discretion he ought not to make the appointment.

HELD, ON APPEAL: per Morton LJ: If the judge exercised his discretion because he thought the widow, being a person beneficially interested in the estate, should not have this representation imposed on her, the discretion was exercised on a wrong principle. Granting the application would possibly save the estate the expense of an application to the Probate Division to appoint a personal representative. The court understanding that the person appointed was to be indemnified for costs by the defendant, there was power to make the order and in the exercise of the discretion it was obviously right to do so because the defendant had a right to claim contribution and it would save the expense of a second trial and unfairness to the defendant if a material witness died in the interval.

The Crown

Note—Before the Crown Proceedings Act 1947, the Crown was in general immune from legal process, and the principle that the King could do no wrong was a defence to any government department or official, other than the actual driver, to a claim for damage or injury caused by a government vehicle. The Treasury Solicitor as a matter of grace defended proceedings against the driver and the Treasury met any judgment against him. The Act reversed both rules, that the Crown could not be sued in its own courts, and that 'the Crown could do no wrong'.

The Act and the Rules are set out in the *Supreme Court Practice* and the *County Court Practice*. Sections 2, 4 and 10 of the Act are set out below, together with a short note of other relevant sections to assist reference.

In the High Court the Rules are in Ord 77.

In the county court they are Ord 42.

CROWN PROCEEDINGS ACT 1947
(10 & 11 Geo 6, c 44)

2 Liability of the Crown in tort (1) Subject to the provisions of this Act, the Crown shall be subject to all those liabilities in tort to which, if it were a private person of full age and capacity, it would be subject:

(a) in respect of torts committed by its servants or agents;
(b) in respect of any breach of those duties which a person owes to his servants or agents at common law by reason of being their employer; and
(c) in respect of any breach of the duties attaching at common law to the ownership, occupation, possession or control of property:

Provided that no proceedings shall lie against the Crown by virtue of para (a) of this subsection in respect of any act or omission of a servant or agent of the Crown unless the act or omission would apart from the provisions of this Act have given rise to a cause of action in tort against that servant or agent of his estate.

(2) Where the Crown is bound by a statutory duty which is binding also upon persons other than the Crown and its officers, then subject to the provisions of this Act, the Crown shall, in respect of a failure to comply with that duty, be subject to all those liabilities in tort (if any) to which it would be so subject if it were a private person of full age and capacity.

(3) Where any functions are conferred or imposed upon an officer of the Crown as such either by any rule of the common law or by statute, and that officer commits a tort while performing or purporting to perform those functions, the liabilities of the Crown in respect of the tort shall be such as they would have been if those functions had been conferred or imposed solely by virtue of instructions lawfully given by the Crown.

(4) Any enactment which negatives or limits the amount of the liability of any Government department or officer of the Crown in respect of any tort committed by that department or officer shall, in the case of proceedings against the Crown under this section in respect of a tort committed by that department or officer, apply in relation to the Crown as it would have applied in relation to that department or officer if the proceedings against the Crown had been proceedings against the department or officer.

(5) No proceedings shall lie against the Crown by virtue of this section in respect of anything done or omitted to be done by any person while discharging or purporting to discharge any responsibilities which he has in connection with the execution of judicial process.

(6) No proceedings shall lie against the Crown by virtue of this section in respect of any act, neglect or default of any officer of the Crown, unless that officer has been directly or indirectly appointed by the Crown wholly out of the Consolidated Fund of the United Kingdom, moneys provided by Parliament, the Road Fund, or any other Fund certified by the Treasury for the purposes of this subsection or was at the material time holding an office in respect of which the Treasury certify that the holder thereof would normally be so paid.

4 Application of law as to indemnity, contribution, joint and several tortfeasors, and contributory negligence (1) Where the Crown is subject to any liability by virtue of this Part of this Act, the law relating to indemnity and contribution shall be so enforceable by or against the Crown in respect of the liability to which it is so subject as if the Crown were a private person of full age and capacity.

(2) [Repealed by Civil Liability (Contribution) Act 1978, s 9(2) and Sch 2.]

(3) Without prejudice to the general effect of s 1 of this Act, the Law Reform (Contributory Negligence) Act 1945 (which amends the law in relation to contributory negligence) shall bind the Crown.

[Section 5 of the Civil Liability (Contribution) Act 1978 reads:

'Without prejudice to s 4(1) of the Crown Proceedings Act 1947 (indemnity and contribution), this Act shall bind the Crown, but nothing in this Act shall be construed as in any way affecting Her Majesty in Her private capacity (including in right of Her Duchy of Lancaster) or the Duchy of Cornwall.']

10 Provisions relating to the armed forces
[This section was repealed by the Crown Proceedings (Armed Forces) Act 1987.] In limited circumstances actions may now be brought against the Crown.

List of Government Departments and Solicitors
Reference should be made to the latest edition in the Supreme Court Practice for the up-to-date list of authorised government departments and solicitors and the addresses for service.

Diplomatic privilege

Dickinson v Del Solar

[1930] 1 KB 376, [1929] All ER Rep 139, 99 LKJB 162, 142 LT 66, 45 TLR 637 (Lord Hewart CJ)
The defendant was First Secretary of the Peruvian Legation, an appointment entitling him to immunity from legal process. The plaintiff obtained a judgment against him for damages for personal injury caused by the defendant's negligent driving. He had not claimed diplomatic immunity because the Minister of the Peruvian Legation had instructed him not to do so, the accident having happened when he was not on official business. The defendant's insurers refused to indemnify him because their policy covered him only against 'legal liability' and he was, they said, under no legal liability.
HELD: The insurers were wrong. Diplomatic agents are not immune from legal liability for wrongful acts. More accurately, they are not liable to be sued in English courts unless they submit to the jurisdiction. Diplomatic privilege does not import immunity from legal liability but only exemption from local jurisdiction. In the present case the privilege was waived. The judgment created a legal liability against the defendant which the insurance company must meet.

Note—Subsequently the Foreign Office obtained from all authorised motor insurers doing business in the UK an assurance, still effective, that they will not attempt to rely on the privileged positions of their diplomatic clients.

Consolidation of proceedings

Note—See RSC Ord 4, r 9.

Healey v A Waddington & Sons Ltd

[1954] 1 All ER 861, [1954] 1 WLR 688, 98 Sol Jo 286, CA
Arising out of one accident, eight actions were brought against three defendants. Before delivery of pleadings, the three defendants applied to consolidate the actions. The master ordered the actions to be consolidated and tried together; one statement of claim to be delivered to include the special damage of each plaintiff and separate issues as to damages.

The judge in chambers set this order aside and ordered one action to be tried as a test action and the other actions stayed.
HELD, ON APPEAL: The actions should be consolidated up to determination of issue of liability, any issue peculiar to one plaintiff to be separately dealt with; separate particulars of damage and issues of damages separately dealt with; order in terms agreed between counsel.

COSTS WHERE TWO ACTIONS ARE TRIED TOGETHER

John Fairfax & Sons Pty Ltd v E C De Witt & Co Pty Ltd

[1958] 1 QB 323, [1957] 3 All ER 410, [1957] 3 WLR 877, 101 Sol Jo 901, CA
The order that two actions be listed and tried together does not make them anything else than two actions. The discretion as to costs of either action must be confined to the parties to that action. A cannot be ordered to pay the costs of B incurred in proceedings to which A was not a party. The order does not have the effect of turning separate proceedings into one set of proceedings. Appeal from the decision of the trial judge that he had no jurisdiction to make such an order, dismissed.

DEDUCTION OF COSTS WHERE ONE OF TWO DEFENDANTS SETTLES

Banque Keyser Ullman SA v Skandia (UK) Insurance Co Ltd (No 2)

[1988] 2 All ER 880, [1988] NLJR 31
The plaintiffs, who were unable to recover under insurance policies because of fraud, sued two insurance brokers, Notcutt and Skandia. On the first day of the trial Notcutt settled, paying a sum to include claims for costs; the plaintiffs continued with their action against Skandia and established liability against them. In giving credit to Skandia for the sum received from Notcutt in the settlement, were the plaintiffs entitled first to deduct their costs of the action against Notcutt?
HELD: They were, because the legal costs of the action against Notcutt was a separate, additional claim against them. Thus these costs should be deducted from the amount paid by Notcutt before allowing credit to Skandia in calculating the amount they should now pay.

Joinder of parties

AFTER AMENDMENT OF DEFENCE

Brittain v Martin

(1965) 109 Sol Jo 76, Times, 14 January, CA
The plaintiff was struck and injured by a rear wheel of the defendants' lorry which had broken away from the lorry as a result of the rear axle fracturing. The statement of claim pleaded *res ipsa loquitur*. In the defence it was pleaded, on the basis of expert advice, that the fracture was due to metal fatigue which the defendants could not have discovered. At the trial the defendants' expert made it clear he had abandoned the theory of metal fatigue and was now attributing the fracture to a hair-line crack arising from the way in which the axle had been manufactured. After hearing other expert evidence the judge allowed an amendment of the defence to give effect to the new evidence but refused an application by the plaintiff to add the manufacturers of the lorry as defendants.
HELD, ON APPEAL: There was no good ground why the judge, once having admitted the evidence of the defendants' experts and granted leave to amend the defence, could resist the application. The evidence criticised, whether consciously or not, the method of manufacture of the axle casing. The plaintiff must be entitled to join any defendant on whom the original defendant sought to cast responsibility, even though she may have no means of her own of determining where the fault lay.

Issue and service of proceedings

PRE-ACTION DISCOVERY

Note—The Administration of Justice Act 1970, s 31 gave the court power to order discovery and production of documents before proceedings against 'a person who appears to the court to be likely to be a party to the proceedings in which a claim in respect of personal injuries is likely to be made.' The Section now appears as the Supreme Court Act 1981, s 33(2) as follows:

'(2) On the application, in accordance with rules of court, of a person who appears to the High Court to be likely to be a party to subsequent proceedings in that court in which a claim in respect of personal injuries to a person, or in respect of a person's death, is likely to be made, the High Court shall, in such circumstances as may be specified in the rules, have power to order a person who appears to the court to be likely to be a party to the proceedings and to be likely to have or to have had in his possession, custody or power any documents which are relevant to an issue arising or likely to arise out of that claim—

(a) to disclose whether those documents are in his possession, custody or power; and
(b) to produce such of those documents as are in his possession, custody or power to the applicant or, on such conditions as may be specified in the order—
    (i) to the applicant's legal advisers; or
    (ii) to the applicant's legal advisers and any medical or other professional adviser of the applicant; or
    (iii) if the applicant has no legal adviser, to any medical or other professional adviser of the applicant.'

Dunning v United Liverpool Hospital's Board of Governors

[1973] 2 All ER 454, [1973] 1 WLR 586, 117 Sol Jo 167, CA

A patient who entered hospital for investigations became gravely ill and her family suspected a wrong diagnosis and treatment. She obtained a legal aid certificate to get a medical opinion. She was examined by a specialist who said the hospital was probably not at fault but that his assessment of the medical aspect was probably hampered by the absence of the hospital notes, and that he ought to see them. The hospital board refused to disclose them.

HELD: The claimant was entitled to an order for disclosure of the notes. 'Likely to be made' in the Act means 'may well be made' dependent on the outcome of the discovery. The fact that the only basis for saying that a claim is not 'likely' is the absence of the documents for which discovery is sought does not preclude the court from ordering their production; but the applicant must disclose the nature of the claim and show there is a reasonable basis for making it.

Shaw v Vauxhall Motors Ltd

[1974] 2 All ER 1185, [1974] 1 WLR 1035, 118 Sol Jo 347, CA

A factory worker was injured when a fork lift truck failed to stop, as it should, when he took his foot off the pedal. He applied to the court for an order against his employers under the Administration of Justice Act 1970, s 31 for discovery of maintenance reports on the machine. The judge in chambers refused an order, considering discovery should be made in the ordinary course of action, if brought.

HELD: Allowing the appeal, one of the objects of s 31 is to enable a plaintiff to find out before he starts proceedings whether he has a good cause of action or not. That object would be defeated if he had to show in advance that he already had a good cause of action. He should set out the substance of his case in an open letter or other document which could if necessary be used at the subsequent trial, if any. An important aspect of the matter was that legal aid should not, in the public interest, continue beyond the point at which it is reasonably clear that the plaintiff had no prospect of success. Counsel in the present case had conceded that if the reports showed nothing wrong the applicant could not succeed in an action and litigation would be avoided.

Deistung v South Western Metropolitan Regional Hospital Board

[1975] 1 All ER 573, [1975] 1 WLR 213, 119 Sol Jo 13, CA
When an order is made under s 31 against a hospital for production of the hospital notes and records to the plaintiff's medical adviser only, the plaintiff is not bound by his report but can write him for further advice or have him seen by counsel in conference as an expert witness.

Note—See RSC Ord 24, r 7(c) at p 457 of the *Supreme Court Practice 1993.*

SETTING ASIDE SERVICE OF THE WRIT

Lawson v Midland Travellers Ltd

[1993] 1 All ER 989, [1993] 1 WLR 735, CA
A writ was issued on 31 August 1990 for damages. The limitation period for the plaintiff pursuing the claim expired on 25 September 1990 and the writ was not served within the four months prescribed by the rules. Upon the eventual service of the writ, the defendants filed an acknowledgment of service and the plaintiffs extended time for serving the defence generally determinable upon 14 days after service of their schedule of special damage which they had failed to serve with the Statement of Claim in accordance with Ord 18, r 12(1)(a). The defendant applied to set aside service of the writ.
HELD, ON APPEAL: An extension of time for serving the defence automatically extended time for an application to set aside the writ under Ord 12, r 8(1). As the Statement of Claim was defective, for it failed to have served with it the schedule of special damage, the defendant had not waived their entitlement to make the application and in the circumstances service of the writ would be set aside.

Sage v Double A Hydraulics Ltd

[1992] CLY 3630, CA
If service of a writ was to be challenged, then no steps should be taken by the defendant save for acknowledging service and issuing a summons to set aside.

SERVICE GENERALLY

Katzenstein Adler Ltd v Boraland Lines Industries (1975) Ltd

[1988] 2 Lloyd's Rep 274
An amendment to a typographical error relating to the plaintiff's name would be allowed after expiry of the limitation period but before service of a writ, as would a change to the plaintiff's nationality and place of business provided no-one had been misled by the error.

Bank of America National Trust v Chrismas, The Kyriaki

[1994] 1 All ER 401, [1993] 1 Lloyd's Rep 137
A writ amended to include a new defendant must be served before the expiry of the limitation period.

Foster v Turnbull

(1990) Times, 22 May, CA
Following the death of her husband in a road traffic accident in May 1983, Mrs Foster brought proceedings against the motorcyclist and his pillion passenger who were the other party to the accident and both of whom died as a result of the injuries they sustained. The motorcyclist was uninsured and Norwich Union were appointed by the Motor Insurers Bureau to handle the claim on their behalf. Upon appointment of new solicitors by Norwich Union some time after expiry of the limitation period, an application was made to strike out the proceedings for failing to comply with Ord 15, r 6A. The plaintiff should have applied for the appointment of a representative of the deceased's estate to have the conduct of the proceedings.

The Court of Appeal, upholding the deputy district registrar, struck out the plaintiff's claim as the writ had never validly been served. There was no issue of estoppel as all steps after the issue of the writ in the proceedings were a nullity.

Note—The Court of Appeal expressed the view that they hoped Norwich Union would meet this undisputed claim, and would not seek to rely upon procedural irregularities.

Service by post: on manager

Willmott v Berry Bros (a firm)

(1981) 126 Sol Jo 209, [1982] LS Gaz R 536, CA
The defendants, a firm, became a limited company in 1979 without any change in the business carried on or the principal place of business. The change of status was not publicised. The plaintiffs, alleging negligence between 1973 and 1976 began proceedings against 'Berry Bros (a firm)' and served the writ by giving it to a manager, employed since March 1980, at the principal place of business in August 1980 in accordance with Ord 81, r 3(1)(b).
HELD: The plaintiffs had acted reasonably under Ord 18, r 1 in using on the writ the name 'Berry Bros' since the business was generally known by that name. 'Business of the partnership' in r 3(1)(b) included a business which was a partnership at the time the cause of action accrued, the ownership of which had changed by the time of service of the writ, if identifiable as the same business. The person having control or management for the purpose of service did not have to be one who had been a servant of the partners at the date of accrual of the cause of action. The writ had been validly served.

County court

White v Weston

[1968] 2 QB 647, [1968] 2 All ER 842, [1968] 2 WLR 1459, 112 Sol Jo 217, CA
After a motor accident the plaintiff and defendant exchanged addresses. Subsequently the plaintiff claimed for the damage to his car and had correspondence with the

defendant's insurers. Some months later the plaintiff issued a summons in the county court. By this time the defendant had moved to a different address. The bailiff was unable to serve the defendant but as he thought him to be still at the old address the registrar ordered service at that address by post. The summons did not reach the defendant who was quite unaware of it when the plaintiff obtained judgment. When he did learn of it the defendant applied to set aside the judgment. The judge made an order setting aside the judgment but made the costs of the first hearing to be costs in the cause.
HELD, ON APPEAL: This was not correct. As the summons had not been served on the defendant (since he no longer lived at the address to which it was sent) he was *ex debito justitiae* entitled to have the judgment set aside without terms being imposed.

Deemed service of writ

Abu Dhabi Helicopters Ltd v International Aeradio plc

[1986] 1 All ER 395, [1986] 1 WLR 312, 130 Sol Jo 130, [1986] LS Gaz R 617, CA
Two helicopters collided in Abu Dhabi on 29 May 1983; the plaintiffs proposed to sue four defendants, only one of whom was English. To avoid possible complications with the Abu Dhabi two-year limitation period the plaintiffs issued a writ against the English defendants on 22 May 1985, endorsed in very general terms. In the course of discussions between solicitors, the plaintiffs' solicitors sent a photocopy of the writ to the defendants' solicitors stating in the clearest terms that this was for information only; neither party believed that this amounted to proper service. The defendants nevertheless voluntarily acknowledged service and required the plaintiffs to serve a statement of claim under the terms of RSC Ord 18, r 1. Should the writ be deemed to be served under Ord 10, r 1(5)?
HELD: No; the terms of Ord 10 allow for a writ to be deemed to have been served on the date of the acknowledgment of service, even if the writ has not been duly served 'unless the contrary is shown'. Here the contrary clearly was shown; the plaintiffs informally sent a copy of the writ to help the defendants' solicitors.

By solicitor

Note—CCR Ord 3, r 3(1A) entitles a solicitor to serve a county court summons by post in an action for damages for personal injury.

Summons not received

Cooper v Scott-Farnell

[1969] 1 All ER 178, [1969] 1 WLR 120, 112 Sol Jo 945, CA
The plaintiff issued a county court summons on 24 April, which, by the procedures for service set out in Ord 8, r 8(2), was sent by post to the defendant's address. But the defendant had gone abroad on holiday on 31 March and did not return until 22 June. Meanwhile the plaintiff had obtained judgment against him. It was set aside because obtained without his knowledge but the judge made the costs of the abortive hearing costs in the cause.
HELD, ON APPEAL, against the order as to costs: *White v Weston* (above) was not an authority for saying that there could be no service where the defendant had not received the summons. In *White*'s case the summons was wrongly addressed and

therefore not served. In the present case the summons was properly served by post in accordance with the code for service of documents contained in Ord 8. The judge therefore had a discretion as to costs and had exercised it properly.

Note—The County Court Rules, Ord 8, r 8 has been replaced by Ord 7, rr 9 and 10 of the 1981 Rules.

Service on a company

Note—The County Court (Amendment) Rules 1985, r 3 (SI 1985/566) entitles a plaintiff to serve a court summons at any local office of the company if that company is registered in England or Wales. However, it is necessary for the local office or branch to have a real connection with the claim being pursued and not just purely out of convenience to the plaintiff. If the position is at all unclear proceedings should continue to be served on the registered office.

Effect of technical service error

Bondy v Lloyds Bank plc

(1991) 135 Sol Jo 412, CA
Even though the plaintiff's solicitors had failed to comply with Ord 10, r 1(6) in that no acknowledgment of service accompanied the writ, this caused no prejudice to the defendants' solicitors and in view of the expiry of the limitation period it would be unjust to prevent the plaintiff from pursuing his claim because of this sort of technicality.

Towers v Morley

[1992] 2 All ER 762, [1992] 1 WLR 511, 136 Sol Jo LB 88, CA
The act of filing an acknowledgment of service did not make good a writ that had not been properly served. If the defendant wished to make a payment into court he could do so at any time, even before the writ was served.

Service personally

Barclays Bank of Swaziland v Hahn

[1989] 2 All ER 398, [1989] 1 WLR 506
Provided the defendant can satisfy the court in his opinion that proceedings served within a jurisdiction in accordance with RSC Ord 10, r 1(3) will come to the attention of the defendant within seven days, there is no necessity for the defendant to be physically present within the jurisdiction at the time the writ is posted through his letter box.

Rolph v Zolan

[1993] 4 All ER 202, [1993] 1 WLR 1305
A defendant could be validly served even though he was not physically in the jurisdiction at the time, provided the summons comes to his attention in accordance with CCR Ord 7.

Service on a partner

Marsden v Kingswell Watts

[1992] 2 All ER 239, CA
RSC Ord 81, r 3 required a writ to be placed through the letterbox of a person's 'usual or last known address' ie his place of residence and not his place of business. Once posted through the letterbox, the writ would be deemed served seven days later unless the plaintiff could show that the writ came to the attention of the partner within that period, in which event that would be the relevant date of service.

Kenneth Allison Ltd v AE Limehouse & Co

[1990] 2 QB 527, [1990] 2 All ER 723, CA
Although there were express rules governing service of a writ, these did not prohibit separate arrangements between the parties. Therefore, proceedings handed to an individual nominated by a partner of a firm, and who expressed herself to have authority to accept service, was validly served.

Date of expiry of the writ

Trow v Ind Coope (West Midlands) Ltd

[1967] 2 QB 899, [1967] 2 All ER 900, [1967] 3 WLR 633, 111 Sol Jo 375, CA
Accident 11 September 1962; writ issued 10 September 1965; writ served on 10 September 1966 though earlier in the day than when the writ was issued a year before. The defendants applied to set aside service on the ground that the writ had not been served within '12 months beginning with the date of its issue' (Ord 6, r 8(1)).
HELD: (1) 'Date' means the whole day of the date of issue. The time of day of issue or service is immaterial. (2) The words 'beginning *with* the date of its issue' means that the day of the date of issue is to be included in the period of 12 months: the words must be taken to have been used to avoid the application of the general rule which might otherwise have applied that the first day of a specified period should be excluded in determining whether the period has elapsed. The period having begun with 10 September 1965 expired at the end of 9 September 1966. Service on the following day was bad and should be set aside.

Note—Contrast *Marren v Dawson Bentley & Co* (p 514, above) where the operative words were 'The following actions shall not be brought after the expiration of three years from the date on which the cause of action accrued' (Limitation Act 1939, s 2(1) as amended: now the Limitation Act 1980, s 2).

Pritam Kaur v S Russell & Sons Ltd

[1973] QB 336. [1973] 1 All ER 617, [1973] 2 WLR 147, 117 Sol Jo 91, CA
The plaintiff's husband was killed at work on 4 September 1967. She issued a writ on 7 September 1970. 5 and 6 September 1970, were a Saturday and Sunday when the court office was closed for business.
HELD: (1) Following *Marren v Dawson Bentley & Co Ltd* (p 514, above) the computation on which the cause of action arose was to be excluded from the computation of the three years limitation period. (2) When a time is prescribed by statute for doing any act which can only be done if the court office is open on the day when the time expires then if that day is a Sunday or other *dies non* the time is

extended to the next day on which the court office is open. Thus by issuing on 7 September 1970 the plaintiff was in time.

Note—Applied in *The Clifford Maersk* [1982] 3 All ER 905, [1982] 1 WLR 1292, 126 Sol Jo 446, [1982] 2 Lloyd's Rep 251.

Service by fax

Ralux NV/SA v Spencer Mason

(1989) Times, 18 May, CA
Service by fax was effective if the party can demonstrate that a legible copy was received by the individual or organisation to be served.

Note—Confirmed *Hastie & Jenkerson v McMahon* [1991] 1 All ER 255, [1990] 1 WLR 1575.

TWO DEFENDANTS

Jones v Jones

[1970] 2 QB 576, [1970] 3 All ER 47, [1970] 3 WLR 20, 114 Sol Jo 374, CA
On 19 July 1965 the plaintiff was a passenger in one of two cars which collided. He was injured. A writ was issued on 13 June 1968 against both drivers. The first was served with the writ on 12 June 1969. The second was served on 3 July 1969. He applied to the court to set aside service on the ground that the writ had expired. The plaintiff's solicitor, who had relied on Ord 6, r 8 as meaning that after service on one defendant the writ did not need renewal, consulted the practice master, who expressed the same view. When the second defendant's application came before another master he ordered service to be set aside. On the plaintiff's appealing to the judge he merely exercised his discretion to extend the time for service and the writ was re-served on the second defendant, who then appealed to the Court of Appeal.
HELD: (1) Order 6, r 8(2) did not and could not be taken to mean that if one defendant had been properly served the writ remains valid for service after 12 months from the date of issue without renewal; (2) in the present case the judge was justified in using his discretion to extend the writ, because the plaintiff's solicitor was not unreasonable in his interpretation of the rule as was evidenced by the fact that the practice master had taken the same view; (3) nevertheless that view was mistaken and in the unlikely event of a solicitor making the same mistake again it will be no sufficient reason for renewing the writ.

Judgment

SETTING ASIDE

Burns v Kondel

[1971] 1 Lloyd's Rep 554, CA
The plaintiff was injured in a traffic collision with the defendant, who was then charged by the police with careless driving and pleaded guilty. The plaintiff's solicitors issued a writ and served it on the defendants personally on 21 October. On 29 October, they wrote to the defendant saying that unless appearance was entered

within four days they would sign judgment. The defendant replied that he handed the writ to his insurers. His letter reached the solicitors on 3 November just after they had signed judgment. The insurers applied to set aside the judgment.
HELD: The court does not set aside a judgment in default unless there is an affidavit showing a defence on the merits, but that does not mean the defendant must show a good defence. He need only show a defence which discloses an arguable or triable issue. In an accident case it is sufficient if he shows that there is a triable issue of contributory negligence.The insurers, who are the people who have to pay should not be shut out altogether from having contributory negligence investigated.

COSTS ON SETTING ASIDE

Peter Cox v Thirwell

(1981) 125 Sol Jo 481 (Forbes J)
The plaintiff served a writ on the defendant by post pursuant to Ord 10, r 1(2)(a). The defendant was abroad and did not receive it; the plaintiff signed judgment in default. The master on the defendant's application set aside the judgment but ordered that he pay the plaintiff's costs in any event. On the defendant's appeal on the question of costs:
HELD: The previous practice on setting aside a regular judgment of giving the plaintiff his costs in any event was not appropriate where neither party was at fault. In such a case the correct order was costs in cause.

SUMMARY JUDGMENT

Dummer v Brown

[1953] 1 QB 710, [1953] 1 All ER 1158, [1953] 2 WLR 984, 97 Sol Jo 331, CA
A judge has a discretion to permit this procedure though the suitable cases must be very small indeed. In this case the defendants had not filed any answer to the affidavit of the plaintiff reciting a plea of guilty to dangerous driving by the driver and alleging there was no defence.
SEMBLE: If the defendants by affidavit had given even a slight indication of some real defence, the judge's decision might have been different.

Rankine v Garton Sons & Co Ltd

[1979] 2 All ER 1185, 123 Sol Jo 305, CA
RSC Ord 27, r 3 says: 'Where admissions of fact are made by a party to a cause or matter either by his pleadings or otherwise, any other party . . . may apply to the court for such judgment or order as upon those admissions he may be entitled to without waiting for the determination of any other question . . . and the court may give such judgment . . . as it thinks just.' The plaintiff claimed damages from the defendants for injury alleged to have been sustained when he slipped on a pool of glucose at the defendants' premises. In their defence the defendants denied the incident alleged, denied the negligence alleged and denied that any negligence resulted in damage. In a letter to the plaintiff's solicitors, however, the defendants' solicitors admitted that the incident resulted from the defendants' negligence and said that the allegations of contributory negligence would not be pursued, the intention being 'to explore the

possibilities of amicably terminating the proceedings'. The plaintiff applied under Ord 27, r 3 for judgment for damages to be assessed. The master gave leave for judgment to be entered. The judge in chambers dismissed the defendants' appeal.
HELD, by the Court of Appeal: The judgment should be set aside. Approving Payne J's decision in *Blundell v Rimmer* (below) and following Lord Reading's statement of the law in *Munday v LCC* [1916] 2 KB 331, two elements were needed for the cause of action (1) the breach of duty, ie negligence, and (2) damage suffered by the plaintiff. The letter from the defendants' solicitors did not in terms admit liability but only negligence, and had preserved the defendants' right to question the causal connection between the plaintiff's injuries and the accident. The admission of negligence did not necessarily involve an admission that some damage had resulted. Appeal allowed.

Defence

ADMISSION OF NEGLIGENCE AND DAMAGE

Note—Two elements are needed in an admission:
(a) an admission of negligence;
(b) an admission of damage.

Heggarty v Murray

[1993] 11 CL 446 (2 June 1993, Southend County Court)
The plaintiff and defendant were involved in a motor traffic accident. Before obtaining a copy of the police report, the defendant insurers admitted liability. The plaintiff's solicitors commenced proceedings and the defendant's solicitors entered a defence denying liability, having now had an opportunity of reading the police report. The plaintiff applied for summary judgment, relying on the insurer's admission.
HELD: The defendant was permitted to 'resile' from the admission. The admission had not prejudiced the plaintiff. The plaintiff's solicitors had not discontinued investigations as a result of the admission and had commenced proceedings in the normal way without relying on the admission.

Bird v Birds Eye Walls

(1987) Times, 24 July, CA
In an action for damages in negligence the defendants denied liability but later wrote a letter to the plaintiffs' solicitors saying liability was no longer disputed. They did not amend the defence. Eighteen months later when the action had been set down for trial the defendants wrote to say they had changed their attitude and would contest liability. The county court judge treated the issue as one of estoppel and held that the plaintiffs had not been so prejudiced as to prevent the defendants from resiling from their letter.
HELD: This was not right. The answer to the case lay in the requirement of leave to amend the defence. The defendants had not amended the original defence since it would have been a waste of time to do so, the letter admitting liability being equivalent to an admission on the pleadings. The court had to exercise its discretion whether to give leave to the defendants to contest liability by withdrawing the admission. The right test was to have regard to the interests of both sides. There was some risk of damage to the plaintiffs' case if they had to start investigating after the delay which had occurred. The defendants' only explanation was that the admission

had been made by their insurers without their parent company's knowledge. It did not justify the granting of leave.

Blundell v Rimmer

[1971] 1 All ER 1072, [1971] 1 WLR 123, 115 Sol Jo 15, [1971] 1 Lloyd's Rep 110 (Payne J)
The plaintiff was a passenger in a car when he was injured in a collision with a car driven by the defendant. In his defence the defendant denied the negligence alleged against him, denied the damage alleged and blamed the driver of the car in which the plaintiff was travelling. Later the defendant's solicitors made a payment into court and sent a letter to the plaintiff's solicitors admitting the defendant's negligence and, though admitting that the plaintiff would be entitled to damages which flowed in law from the negligence, denying that the plaintiff had suffered any damage. The plaintiff applied for interlocutory judgment under RSC Ord 27, r 3; the registrar made the order asked.
HELD, ON APPEAL: The order should not have been made. The letter from the defendant's solicitors was an admission only of negligence and was a denial of damage. Until damage was proved by evidence the plaintiff was not entitled to judgment on the admission because no claim against the defendant had been established; no admissions of fact had been made upon which he became entitled to judgment in pursuance of Ord 27, r 3. The case should be distinguished from judgments in default of appearance or defence or where part of a liquidated claim had been admitted.

Rankine v Garton Sons & Co Ltd

[1979] 2 All ER 1185, 123 Sol Jo 305, CA
RSC Ord 27, r 3 says: 'Where admissions of fact are made by a party to a cause or matter either by his pleadings or otherwise, any other party . . . may apply to the court for such judgment or order as upon those admissions he may be entitled to without waiting for the determination of any other question . . . and the court may give such judgment . . . as it thinks just.' The plaintiff claimed damages from the defendants for injury alleged to have been sustained when he slipped on a pool of glucose at the defendants' premises. In their defence the defendants denied the incident alleged, denied the negligence alleged and denied that any negligence resulted in damage. In a letter to the plaintiff's solicitors, however, the defendants' solicitors admitted that the incident resulted from the defendants' negligence and said that the allegations of contributory negligence would not be pursued, the intention being 'to explore the possibilities of amicably terminating the proceedings'. The plaintiff applied under Ord 27, r 3 for judgment for damages to be assessed. The master gave leave for judgment to be entered. The judge in chambers dismissed the defendants' appeal.
HELD, by the Court of Appeal: The judgment should be set aside. Approving Payne J's decision in *Blundell v Rimmer* (above) and following Lord Reading's statement of the law in *Munday v LCC* [1916] 2 KB 331, two elements were needed for the cause of action (1) the breach of duty, ie negligence, and (2) damage suffered by the plaintiff. The letter from the defendants' solicitors did not in terms admit liability but only negligence, and had preserved the defendants' right to question the causal connection between the plaintiffs' injuries and the accident. The admission of negligence did not necessarily involve an admission that some damage had resulted. Appeal allowed.

CONTRIBUTORY NEGLIGENCE

Note—See *Fookes v Slaytor* [1979] 1 All ER 137. All allegations of contributory negligence should be pleaded.

See RSC Ord 18, r 18.

COUNTER-CLAIM

Note—See RSC Ord 15, r 2 generally and CCR Ord 9.

RES JUDICATA

Brunsden v Humphrey

(1884) 14 QBD 141, [1881–5] All ER Rep 357, 53 LJQB 476, 51 LT 529, 49 JP 4, 32 WR 944, CA

The rule of the ancient common law is that where one is barred in any action real or personal by judgment, demurrer, confession or verdict, he is barred as to that or the like action of the like nature for the same thing for ever. It is a well settled rule of law that damages resulting from one and the same cause of action must be assessed and recovered once for all. One wrong was damage to property. A further wrong was injury to the person.

Note—See also *Sanders v Hamilton*, p 685, below.

Two actions, same accident

Marginson v Blackburn Borough Council

[1939] 2 KB 426, [1939] 1 All ER 273, 108 LJKB 563, 160 LT 234, 55 TLR 389, 83 Sol Jo 212, CA

Car of A driven by A's wife, with A and his daughter as passengers, collided with bus of B and as a result there was damage to property of C. C sued A and B in the county court. B served third-party notice on A and counter-claimed against A for damage to bus. A served third-party notice on B. The judge found A and B equally to blame. Afterwards A sued B in the High Court for damages for injury to himself, his daughter and death of his wife.

HELD: The plaintiff was estopped from proceeding with his personal claims but not with claims in representative capacity as it had been necessary to decide in the first action the question of negligence as between the parties to the second action.

Townsend v Bishop

[1939] 1 All ER 805, 160 LT 296, 55 TLR 433, 83 Sol Jo 240 (Lewis J)

A motor car was driven by the son as servant of the owner and collided with a lorry. The father brought an action in the High Court against the lorry owner for the father's damage in negligence, which was sent to the county court. The judge found the son was negligent and the action failed. The son then brought an action in the High Court against the lorry owner for the son's own damage.

HELD: No *res judicata*. The defendant had failed to prove that the matter now in issue was the same as that previously litigated and between the same parties. The son was not a party, but an agent, in the previous litigation.

Johnson v Cartledge and Matthews

[1939] 3 All ER 654 (Cassels J)
A was a passenger in car of B which collided with taxi cab of C. C brought a county court action against B, and C was held by the county court judge alone to blame. Afterwards, A sued B and C in High Court and Cassels J found B alone to blame. B had issued third-party proceedings against C in the action. B contended issue of negligence between B and C was *res judicata* and he was entitled to indemnity on this ground.
HELD. Per Cassels J: C had been found in the High Court proceedings not to be a tortfeasor, and B could not therefore recover indemnity or contribution from C. Furthermore this was not a case of *res judicata*, as the damage in the two cases was different. For the doctrine of *res judicata* to apply the parties must be the same, and the damage must be the same, and the issues of law and of fact must be the same. (*Marginson v Blackburn Borough Council* (above) distinguished.)

The action in the county court was for damage to property; in the High Court for personal injuries and in the third-party proceedings the claim would not have been possible before the Law Reform (Married Women and Tortfeasors) Act 1935.

Bell v Holmes

[1956] 3 All ER 449, [1956] 1 WLR 1359, 100 Sol Jo 801 (McNair J)
A motor car driven by A collided with a motor car driven by B which had a passenger X on 26 March 1955. A issued a writ against B for personal injuries and B counter-claimed for his own personal injuries. On 7 October 1955, X issued a summons against both A and B as defendants in the county court. The pleadings in the two actions were substantially identical. In the county court action each defendant blamed the other and adopted the allegations made by the plaintiff against the other. No formal notice of contribution was filed by either defendant against the other but the judge was requested by both defendants to deal with the matter of apportionment between the defendants. On 17 February 1956, the judge found against both defendants and held A five-sixths to blame and B one-sixth. Both judgments were satisfied and the time for appeal had long expired when the action between A and B came on for hearing. By his amended defence B pleaded A was bound by the county court judgment and A by his reply denied that he was so bound. McNair J directed this issue be tried as a preliminary issue.
HELD: (1) It was plain on the authorities, and was common practice, that the court as to apportionment had power to determine the question of contribution between defendants without any formal notice of contribution; (2) as to *res judicata*, this was a matter of evidence, and included a case where judgment had been given after the issue of the writ, and was a good plea in this case; (3) as to the plea that the issues were not the same, the issues of fact were identically the same and the fact that they were technically different was immaterial; (4) as to the contention that a plea of estoppel by record could only be proved by production of the record under the County Court Rules 1936, Ord 24 [now Ord 22 of the 1981 Rules] whilst not satisfied that this was necessary. A had waived this form of proof by his pleadings. The apportionment was *res judicata*.

Randolph v Tuck

[1962] 1 QB 175, [1961] 1 All ER 814, [1961] 2 WLR 855, 105 Sol Jo 157 (Lawton J)
The plaintiff received injuries on 19 July 1957, when riding in a car owned and driven by the first defendant which collided with a car owned by the second defendants and driven by their servant the third defendant. In a county court action heard on 13 July 1958, in which the first defendant had sued the second and third defendants for damages for his own personal injuries he was found wholly to blame. The plaintiff issued her writ on 15 October 1959 and on 1 January 1960 the second and third defendants by third-party notice claimed indemnity from the first defendant in the event of their being found liable to pay damages to the plaintiff. The claim was based on the Law Reform (Married Women and Tortfeasors) Act 1935. They pleaded that the issue between them and the first defendant had been determined by the county court judge and that his decision was binding on the first defendant. The plaintiff's action was heard on 6 February 1961, when Lawton J held that the damage suffered by the plaintiff was caused by the negligence of both the first and third defendants and that they were equally to blame.
HELD, in the third-party proceedings: (1) The second and third defendants were not entitled to claim indemnity as persons entitled to be indemnified under the Law Reform (Married Women and Tortfeasors) Act 1935, s 6(1)(c) since to do so would be to base a cause of action on an estoppel by record. At common law this cannot be done and s 6(1)(c) does not allow that which common law would not. (2) The first defendant was not estopped by the judgment in the county court from denying his own sole responsibility for the damage suffered by the plaintiff, since the precise issue decided in the county court was not the same as in the plaintiff's action. In the county court the issue decided was that the damage suffered by the first defendant was caused, not by any breach of duty owed him by the third defendant, but by his own failure to take proper care for his own safety. In the present action the issue decided was whether the damage suffered by the plaintiff had been caused by breach ofduty owed to her by the first or the third defendant or either of them. These duties were similar but nevertheless separate and distinct (*Hay (or Bourhill) v Young*, p 6, above). Moreover the extent of the respective responsibilities of the first and third defendants for the damage suffered by the plaintiff, ie blameworthiness as distinct from causation, had never been before the county court. (3) *Marginson v Blackburn Borough Council* (p 608, above) was distinguished on the ground that in that case the county court judge had made a separate decision in the damage claim between Marginson and the bus company. *Bell v Holmes* (above) not followed.

Note—For the Law Reform (Married Women & Tortfeasors) Act 1935 s 6(1)(c) see now Civil Liability (Contribution) Act 1978, p 17, above.

Wood v Luscombe

[1966] 1 QB 169, [1964] 3 All ER 972, [1965] 3 WLR 996, 109 Sol Jo 833 (Streatfield J)
L and W, both riding motor cycles, collided. L was injured and so also was W's father who was riding pillion on W's machine. L sued W for damages: at the trial of the action Phillimore J held them both to blame equally for L's injuries. W's father then sued L for damages for his own injuries and L joined W as third party, claiming a contribution. L contended that, as Phillimore J in the previous action had held L and

W equally to blame, W was estopped from denying in the present proceedings that they were equally to blame.
HELD: The contention was correct. W's father being an innocent passenger the thing actually in dispute, namely, who was to blame for the damage done in the accident had already been determined by Phillimore J and was *res judicata*. The issue was precisely the same in both actions and the same evidence would support both. *Bell v Holmes* followed: *Randolph v Tuck* not followed. *Marginson v Blackburn Borough Council* not applicable because the facts were different.

Scope of doctrine

Greenhalgh v Mallard

[1947] 2 All ER 255, CA
Res judicata is not confined to the issues which the court is actually asked to decide, but covers issues of facts which are so clearly part of the subject matter of the litigation and so clearly could have been raised that it would be an abuse of the process of the court to allow a new proceedings to be started in respect of them. In *Green v Weatherill* [1992] 2 Ch 213 at 221, Maugham J quoted some observations by Wigram VC in *Henderson v Henderson* (1843) 3 Hare 100 at 114:

'I believe I state the rule of the court correctly when I say, that, where a given matter becomes the subject of litigation in, and of adjudication by, a court of competent jurisdiction, the court requires the parties to that litigation to bring forward their whole case, and will not (except under special circumstances) permit the same parties to open the same subject of litigation in respect of matter which might have been brought forward as part of the subject in contest, but which was not brought forward only because they have, from negligence, inadvertence, or even accident, omitted part of their case. The plea of *res judicata* applies, except in special cases, not only to points upon which the court was actually required by the parties to form an opinion and pronounce a judgment, but to every point which properly belonged to the subject of litigation and which the parties, exercising reasonable diligence, might have brought forward at the time.'

Re Waring, Westminster Bank Ltd v Burton-Butler

[1948] Ch 221, [1948] 1 All ER 257, [1948] LJR 705, 64 TLR 147 (Jenkins J)
Where a decision of the Court of Appeal is overruled by a later case in the House of Lords, a person who was a party to the proceedings in the Court of Appeal is bound by the decision of the Court of Appeal on the principle of *res judicata*, but a person who was not a party is not bound and is entitled to take advantage of the decision of the House of Lords.

Wright v Bennett

[1948] 1 All ER 227, 92 Sol Jo 95, CA
The issues need not be identified. The plea will succeed if the issues and facts are in substance the same.

Winnan v Winnan

[1949] P 174, [1948] 2 All ER 862, [1949] LJR 345, 65 TLR 22, 92 Sol Jo 688, 47 LGR 10, CA
The observations by Wigram VC in *Henderson v Henderson* quoted on p 611, above were also quoted by Lord Shaw in *Hoysted v Taxation Comr* [1926] AC 155, 95 LJPC 79, 134 LT 354, 42 TLR 207, PC and adopted in this case.

ESTOPPEL

Note—In *Mills v Cooper* [1967] 2 QB 459 at 468 Diplock LJ said the doctrine of issue estoppel so far as it affects civil proceedings may be stated thus: a party to civil proceedings is not entitled to make, as against the other party, an assertion, whether of fact or of the legal consequences of facts, the correctness of which is an essential element in his cause of action or defence, if the same assertion was an essential element in his previous cause of action or defence in previous civil proceedings between the parties or their predecessors in title and was found by a court of competent jurisdiction in such previous civil proceedings to be incorrect, unless further material which is relevant to the correctness or incorrectness of the assertion and could not by reasonable diligence have been adduced by that party in the previous proceedings has since become available to him.

Miller v British Railways Board

(1968) 112 Sol Jo 595 (Browne J)
The plaintiff, a railway passenger, lost the tip of a finger in the door of a carriage after an altercation with the station manager. He was charged by a police constable of British Railways under byelaw 14(1) and (3) with opening the carriage door and entering the train when it was in motion, and convicted. He sued British Railways for damages for slamming the door on his finger when the train was stationary. Without pleading it the defendants contended at trial that the conviction raised an issue estoppel which prevented the plaintiff from giving evidence that the train was not in motion when he entered it.
HELD: The prosecution could not be regarded as being between the same parties as the action as the constable was not the same party as the defendants. The principle stated in *Mills v Cooper* was limited to a finding in civil proceedings. A finding in previous criminal proceedings did not give rise to issue estoppel in subsequent civil proceedings.

Note—The final sentence in the above case may call for reconsideration; see *McIlkenny v Chief Constable of the West Midlands* [1980] QB 283, [1980] 2 All ER 227, [1980] 2 WLR 689, 144 JP 291, CA. *Miller's* case was not cited there but Sir George Baker said of *Mills v Cooper* that it was not an 'authority for the proposition that an issue of fact affirmatively decided in a criminal case cannot be used as conclusive, that is, as an issue estoppel, in a subsequent civil case'.

Hayler v Chapman

[1989] 1 Lloyd's Rep 490, CA
In 1984, the plaintiff's and the defendant's cars collided. The plaintiff's insurers paid out the written-off value of the car, and in April 1985 claimed that amount and the plaintiff's uninsured losses from the defendant's insurers, who denied liability. Meanwhile, the plaintiff claimed the uninsured loss from the defendant's insurers in May 1985, and on receiving a denial of liability, commenced proceedings in June 1985. He obtained an arbitrator's award in August 1985, which the defendant's

insurers satisfied. The plaintiff's insurers were unaware that the plaintiff had obtained the award and in May 1987 issued proceedings in the plaintiff's name against the defendant for the written-off value of the car. The defendant's insurers applied successfully to the court for an order that the second action should be struck out as an abuse of process, since two actions could not be brought in respect of the same cause of action. The court refused the plaintiff's insurer's application to have the arbitrator's award set aside. The plaintiff's insurers appealed against the refusal. HELD, dismissing the appeal: The judge was entitled to exercise his discretion not to set aside the award. There was no evidence that it would have been unjust or inequitable for it to stand. The plaintiff had been compensated, and if the insurer had kept in closer contact with the insured,the issue would have been avoided altogether.

Wall v Radford

[1991] 2 All ER 741
A passenger in Miss Wall's car established liability against her to the extent of 50% with the balance being recovered against the defendant, Mr Radford. Subsequent to determination of that claim, Miss Wall instituted her own proceedings against Radford for damages for the personal injury she had suffered. Radford successfully argued that Miss Wall's claim was barred by issue estoppel.

Note—Affirmed *Talbot v Berkshire County Council.*

Talbot v Berkshire County Council

[1993] 4 All ER 9, [1993] 3 WLR 708, [1993] RTR 406
The plaintiff's action for damages for personal injury he suffered in a road traffic accident caused partly as a result of the defendant's negligence could not be pursued where the issues of liability had already been tried in an action brought against Mr Talbot by his passenger. The doctrine of *res judicata* was to be applied in the absence of special circumstances which would have precluded its operation.

Third party proceedings

WITHOUT LEAVE

Note—No leave is required in an action commenced by writ if the third party notice is served before the defence is served (RSC Ord 16, r 1) or pleadings have closed in the county court (CCR Ord 12, r 1).

WITH LEAVE

Note—Leave is required if action commenced by fixed date summons or defence served.

NECESSITY AS BETWEEN CO-DEFENDANT TORTFEASORS

Clayson v Rolls Royce Ltd

[1951] 1 KB 746, [1950] 2 All ER 884, 66 (pt 2) TLR 827, 94 Sol Jo 741, CA
If one defendant wishes to obtain particulars, or discovery of documents, or interrogatories from his co-defendant, he is entitled to do so under the principle of

Croston v Vaughan that there is a right of contribution without formal proceedings. He must first issue and serve a notice under Ord XVIA, r 12(1) (now Ord 16, r 8(1)) and issue a summons for directions pursuant to para (2) (now r 4), so that the issues may be clearly defined.

SUMMONS FOR DIRECTIONS

Note—A summons must be served upon receipt of notice of intention to defend (RSC Ord 16, r 4) and in the county court, a date will automatically be supplied to the parties.

CONTINUATION AFTER SETTLEMENT OF MAIN ACTION

Stott v West Yorkshire Road Car Co Ltd

[1971] 2 QB 651, [1971] 3 All ER 534, [1971] 3 WLR 282, 115 Sol Jo 568, CA
The defendants' bus collided with the plaintiff on his motor cycle when passing a parked vehicle. He was seriously injured. They brought third-party proceedings against the owners of the parked vehicle for a contribution to any damages awarded to the plaintiff. Before the action reached trial the defendants settled the plaintiff's claim by a payment of £10,000 made expressly 'without any admission of liability whatsoever by' the defendants. On an appeal from a summons for third-party directions the judge held that the third-party proceedings could not continue because (1) the original action being dead there was nothing on which the third-party proceedings could bite, and (2) as they had made the payment to the plaintiff without admission of liability the defendants had no right to contribution at all.
HELD, by the Court of Appeal: This was wrong. (1) Once an action is settled the third-party proceedings can proceed as if they had been started by separate action—RSC Ord 16, r 4(3)(b). (2) It was not necessary that the defendants should have admitted liability to the plaintiff or been held liable to him; it was only in third-party proceedings that they had to show that they would have been held responsible in law to the plaintiff and liable to pay him damages.

Note—See now Civil Liability (Contribution) Act 1978, s 1(4) p 17, above.

Harper v Gray & Walker (a firm)

[1985] 2 All ER 507, [1985] 1 WLR 1196, 129 Sol Jo 777, QBD
Architects, contractors and engineers were sued by a veterinary surgeon in connection with the building in 1973 to 1974 of an animal hospital complex. On 12 April 1984 the architects learned that the plaintiff was negotiating with the contractor and engineer so, on 19 April, they wrote to both the contractor and engineer stating that, if negligence was proved, they would apply for an apportionment of blame. On 23 May settlements were reached between the plaintiff, engineer and contractor. On 8 June 1984 the architects served contribution notices under RSC Ord 16, r 8 on the engineers and contractors and on 18 June applied for discovery in the contribution proceedings. The plaintiff discontinued his proceedings against the engineers and contractors on 27 June. Was the contribution notice effective? If necessary, could the architects now serve third party notices or were they prevented because the engineers and contractors could not now be held liable to contribute because of the settlement?

HELD: The contribution notice was valid and remained effective; the plaintiff had not discontinued against the contractors and architects when the notices were served and the action continued even after they had ceased to be parties to the main action. If (despite this finding) the architects now needed leave to serve a third party notice, such leave would be granted because a settlement is not tantamount to a judgment.

Note—Followed in *R A Lister & Co Ltd v E G Thomson (Shipping) Ltd, The Benarty (No 2)* [1987] 1 WLR 1614. See also *Nottingham Health Authority v Nottingham City Council.*

R A Lister & Co Ltd v E G Thomson (Shipping) Ltd, The Benarty (No 2)

[1987] 3 All ER 1032, [1987] 1 WLR 1614
A defendant remained a party and capable of issuing contribution proceedings until an action was struck out; the mere staying of proceedings did not affect his capacity under RSC Ord 16.

Contribution proceedings

THIRD-PARTY PROCEDURE—HIGH COURT

Note—The procedure is contained in RSC Ord 16.

Order 16, r 10 enables a written offer of contribution by a third party or one of two or more tortfeasors to be treated as a payment into court without any order to that effect, such offer to be taken into account by the judge at the trial in exercising his discretion as to costs.

The form of letter may be as follows:

'Please take notice that the defendant . . . hereby makes a written offer to contribution of . . . per cent (or 1/4, 1/3, 1/2) of the liability of the defendants to the plaintiff and reserves the right for the purposes of Ord 62, r 9(1)(a) to bring this offer to the attention of the judge at the trial. Please acknowledge receipt of this letter.'

BETWEEN CO-DEFENDANTS

Croston v Vaughan

[1938] 1 KB 540, [1937] 4 All ER 249, 107 LJKB 182, 158 LT 221, 102 JP 11, 54 TLR 54, 81 Sol Jo 882, 36 LGR 1, CA
The court can apportion damages between two defendants in the action brought by the original plaintiffs against those defendants without the necessity of any fresh or further proceedings.

Note—Order 16, r 8, provides for service by one defendant upon another of notice of claim for contribution.

C E Heath Ltd v Ceram Holding Co

[1989] 1 All ER 203, [1988] 1 WLR 1219, 132 Sol Jo 1299, [1988] NLJR 280, CA
The plaintiffs claimed the sum of £6.2m from the first defendants, who alleged that the moneys had never been paid to them by the second defendants. The second defendants counterclaimed against both the plaintiffs and the first defendants and issued a summons for judgment against only the first defendants.
HELD, ON APPEAL: If a defendant wishes to obtain summary judgment against a co-defendant, the correct procedure is to join the co-defendants as a third party under Ord

16 and make the application for judgment under Ord 16, r 4(3) at the summons for directions stage. It was not possible to achieve a similar result by serving a contribution notice and applying to the court for relief under Ord 16, r 8(1), because Ord 16, r 8(2) provided that the third party procedure should always be used where there was or could be a counterclaim. Since the second defendants had served a counterclaim on the first defendants, but not joined them as third parties, they could not obtain judgment through contribution proceedings under Ord 16, r 8. Per Neill LJ: The effect of the rules was anomalous and merited the attention of the Supreme Court Procedure Committee.

Pride of Derby and Derby Angling Association Ltd v British Celanese Ltd

[1952] 1 All ER 1326, [1952] WN 227, [1952] 1 TLR 1013, 96 Sol Jo 263 (Harman J)
Plaintiffs as riparian owners obtained an injunction restraining three defendants from allowing effluent to pass into the River Derwent so as to interfere with the plaintiffs' right of fishing, and an inquiry into damages. The defendants were not joint tortfeasors but were severally liable. They applied to the judge to apportion the damages, when certified as the result of the inquiry, in proportions agreed between the three defendants.
HELD: The court had jurisdiction to make the order: *Croston v Vaughan* followed.

OFFER BETWEEN

Note—See RSC Ord 16, r 10 and CCR Ord 12, r 7.

Interlocutory proceedings

NOTICES TO ADMIT

Note—See RSC Ord 27, r 2 and CCR Ord 20, r 2.

REQUEST FOR FURTHER AND BETTER PARTICULARS

Monk v Redwing Aircraft Co Ltd

[1942] 1 KB 182, [1942] 1 All ER 133, 111 LJKB 277, 166 LT 42, 58 TLR 94, CA
Order XIX, r 7(b) provided that further and better particulars of the statement of claim shall not be ordered before defence unless necessary or desirable to enable the defendant to plead or for any special reason. The defendant is entitled to particulars of special damage before defence to enable him to decide whether or not to make a payment into court, and if so, the amount.

Note—Order XIX, r 7, is now replaced by Ord 18, r 12. Paragraph (5) of r 12 provides that the court shall not order particulars 'before service of the defence unless, in the opinion of the court, the order is necessary or desirable to enable the defendant to plead or for some other special reason'.

Tarbox v St Pancras Borough Council

[1952] 1 All ER 1306. [1952] WN 254, [1952] 1 TLR 1293, 96 Sol Jo 360, CA
Plaintiff alleged that whilst walking on the footpath a servant of the defendants swept rubbish, including a tin lid, into his path and under his feet so that he slipped and fell and was injured. The master ordered particulars of the place where the plaintiff was walking; the position of the defendants' servant when sweeping and the position of the plaintiff when he fell and that the particulars should be marked on a scale plan. The judge in chambers affirmed the order. Plaintiff's appeal was dismissed.
HELD: There was discretion to make the order. It was a reasonable method to adopt in the circumstances of the case.

An article by Sir William Ball in the *Law Times* of 10 June 1949 calls attention shortly to some general principles including the following. The court will not sanction an attempt to deliver interrogatories under the guise of seeking particulars: *Lister v Thompson* (1890) 7 TLR 107. A summons for particulars will be dismissed if it appears that the application is a mere attempt to ascertain the names of witnesses: *Temperton v Russell* (1893) 9 TLR 321, CA. But particulars in a proper case may be ordered although they involve disclosure of evidence which will be relied on at the trial: *Marriott v Chamberlain* (1886) 17 QBD 154, 55 LJQB 448, 54 LT 714, 34 WR 783, 2 TLR 640, CA and although the applicant must know the true facts better than his opponent, because he is entitled to know the case that opponent intends to set up: *Harbord v Monk* (1878) 38 LT 411.

In an action for damages for personal injuries caused by negligence, it is now common form to give particulars of the negligence alleged.

'Special damage' must always be particularised. Care should be taken to avoid extravagance as the special damage may have to be proved. The plaintiff should not omit to give particulars of anything to which he is justly entitled as the plaintiff may be held bound by his particulars, and the point is also important if defendant makes a payment into court. An extravagant claim in an item of special damage may discredit the plaintiff at the trial.

Phipps v Orthodox Unit Trusts Ltd

[1958] 1 QB 314, [1957] 3 All ER 305, [1957] 3 WLR 856, [1957] TR 277, CA
The plaintiff brought an action for damages for wrongful dismissal from his position of sole managing director. The defendant company applied for further and better particulars as follows: 'Of the alleged damage stating whether the plaintiff received any taxable income in any of the tax years from 1948—9 onwards, and if so then (1) the amount of such income from every source in each of such years; (2) the amount of any and all assessments to income tax and surtax respectively in each of such years showing how such amounts are made up; and in any event giving full particulars of any facts which entitled or would have entitled the plaintiff to tax allowances in respect of each of the said years.'
HELD: Applying the principles established in the case of *British Transport Commission v Gourley* (p 430, above) and applying the decision in *Monk v Redwing Aircraft Co* (p 616, above), the particulars must be supplied.

Per Jenkins LJ: Our decision, unless applied with caution and common sense, may well result in a great waste of time and expense. Particulars should be limited to what is really reasonably necessary to enable the party seeking them to know what case he has to meet.

Per Parker LJ: Particulars should generally be confined to the broad facts, such as 'The plaintiff is a married man', 'He is entitled to an allowance in respect of two children', 'His unearned income is £100 a year', matters of that sort, and in the ordinary case that can give rise to no difficulties.

INTERROGATORIES

Note—See RSC Ord 26, r 3.

Potter v Metropolitan District Rly Co

(1873) 28 LT 231, 37 JP 696
A passenger on the railway of defendants having been hurt by a train, was accompanied to her home by two of their servants under the direction of a third, an inspector. Subsequently bringing an action for damages in respect of the injury received, she sought to administer certain interrogatories to defendants.
HELD: They might be interrogated as to the names of their inspector, of their other servants who accompanied plaintiff home and of the driver of the engine driving the train by which she was a passenger, but might not be asked whether any of the servants of the company witnessed the accident, and, if so, what were their names.

Marskell v Metropolitan District Rly Co

(1890) 7 TLR 49, CA
In an action for personal injuries against a railway company, an interrogatory was disallowed which was directed to ascertaining which of the company's servants saw plaintiff at the time of the accident and what plaintiff's position then was.

Note—The *Law Times Journal* of 13 September 1947, p 142, cites this case as authority for the statement that 'An interrogatory in an action for personal injuries as to the number and names of the defendants' witnesses of the accident will not be allowed.'

Griebart v Morris

[1920] 1 KB 659, 89 LJKB 397, 122 LT 736, 64 Sol Jo 275, CA
The plaintiff was seriously injured when hit by the defendant's car and had little recollection of the accident, nor were there any witnesses. She sought leave to interrogate the defendant on the positions of the vehicles at the moment of the accident.
HELD: She was entitled to interrogate. There was no rule of practice in running-down cases not to allow interrogatories. There is a right to interrogate in order to obtain an admission if necessary for disposing fairly of the action, subject to two limitations (1) interrogatories are not permissible if of a 'fishing' nature nor (2) if they seek to obtain the names of the opponents' witnesses.

Maxiplus v Lunn

(1992) Times, 28 February
The court had the power to refuse interrogatories served without leave, even though there had been no application to withdraw or vary those interrogatories pursuant to Ord 26, r 3(2).

Legal professional privilege

Conlon v Conlons Ltd

[1952] 2 All ER 462, [1952] WN 403, [1952] 2 TLR 343, 96 Sol Jo 547, CA
Plaintiff claimed damages for personal injuries from defendants. His solicitors wrote to defendants' insurers without prejudice offering terms of settlement. Later plaintiff

issued a writ. Defendants pleaded that terms of settlement had been agreed and that the plaintiff's claim had been compromised by way of accord and satisfaction. Plaintiff in his reply denied any agreement to compromise and pleaded that if any agreement had been entered into, his solicitors had no authority to enter into it.

Defendants administered interrogatories asking—

1 Were the solicitors at the dates of the letters acting on his behalf?

2 Had he not authorised the solicitors to negotiate or to hold themselves out as having authority to do so.

3 Had he not authorised the solicitors to make the offers?

4 At what date were their instructions withdrawn.

The Court of Appeal suggested it would be legitimate and proper to put a question—Did you authorise your solicitors to accept £1,000 and costs, or to settle the case for £1,000 and costs?

The plaintiff declined to answer on the ground that they related to communications between him and his solicitors confidentially and in their professional character, and were privileged.

HELD: Citing *Welsh v Roe* (1918) 87 LJKB 520, [1918–19] All ER Rep 620, 118 LT 529, 34 TLR 187, 62 Sol Jo 269 after issue of writ a solicitor had implied general authority to settle the action which could not be limited unless brought to the notice of the other side; and *Macauley v Polley* [1897] 2 QB 122, 66 LJQB 665, 76 LT 643, 45 WR 681, CA that a solicitor could not compromise before writ issued where actual authority must be proved; the rule as to privilege did not extend to communications which the client instructed the solicitor to repeat to the other party. Such communications were not confidential. Order to answer the interrogatories upheld.

Note—As to interrogatories between co-defendants in a contribution case, see *Clayson v Rolls Royce Ltd* p 613, above. For interrogatories in an action calling for leave under the Limitation Act 1980, s 33, see *Jones v Searle*, p 624, below.

Fatal case

Sloan v Hanson

[1939] 1 All ER 333, 55 TLR 417, 83 Sol Jo 174, [1939] WN 28, CA
'Did you at an inquest held by Dr Lord, one of His Majesty's coroners for the County of Surrey, at the Guildhall, Kingston, in the said county, on 4 and 11 April 1938 (in answer to questions or otherwise), make any and if so which of the statements contained in the document served herewith?' A copy of the deposition of the defendant at the inquest on Adam Sloan was served with the interrogatory. Interrogatory allowed.

Burr v Ware RDC

[1939] 2 All ER 688, CA
An interrogatory will not be allowed in a fatal case asking for the admission of the statement of the driver at the inquest, where the driver is the defendant's servant, and there was no proof that the driver was an agent with authority to made admissions.

Note—And see *Tustin v Arnold*, above. The Civil Evidence Act 1968 has largely eliminated the need for interrogatories of this kind.

SUMMONS FOR DIRECTIONS

Note—The rules provide for automatic directions in personal injury actions: see RSC Ord 25, r 8 and CCR Ord 17, r 11.

DISCOVERY

Legal professional privilege

Note—RSC Ord 24, r 1, provides that after close of pleadings in an action begun by writ there shall be discovery by the parties of documents relating to matters in question in the action. By r 2(2) of the Order a defendant to an action arising out of an accident on land due to a collision or apprehended collision involving a vehicle shall not make any discovery unless the court otherwise orders. Thus in respect of motor claims discovery against the defendant can generally be obtained only by order of the court. Where an order has been obtained the question may arise whether a claim form and correspondence with insurers must be produced to the plaintiff's solicitor.

The Hopper No 13

[1925] P 52, 94 LJP 45, 132 LT 736, 41 TLR 189, Div Ct

The Port of London Authority issued general instructions to masters of their craft to report in triplicate on the form provided 'immediately after every casualty'. The report was made on a printed form headed 'Confidential report furnished for the information of the Authority's solicitor in view of anticipated litigation, in respect of a casualty occurring between the Authority's . . . and the . . .'. The report was sent to a firm of solicitors who invariably acted for the Authority on the instructions of underwriters. In practice the report was sent to the dredging superintendent, who passed it on to the chief harbour master, who in turn passed it on to the manager of the Authority's insurance department, and in every case of collision he sent the report to the solicitors.

The owners of a vessel in collision with a dredger of the Authority, relying on the decision of *Birmingham and Midland Motor Omnibus Co v London and North Western Rly Co* [1913] 3 KB 850, 83 LJKB 474, 109 LT 64, 57 Sol Jo 752, CA that it was necessary in any large business organisation for written records to be regularly made, and to hold such documents privileged merely because the proprietors of the business organisation had in mind their utility in case of litigation, feared, threatened, or commenced, would be unsound in principle and disastrous in practice, contended the report was not privileged.

HELD: The document was furnished for the information of the solicitors and made bona fide for the purpose of being used by the solicitors in anticipated litigation. There was the almost inevitable certainty of litigation where there is a collision between craft; in default of settlement litigation must inevitably follow. The report was made for the purpose of being submitted to solicitors. The document was obtained for the solicitors in the sense of being procured as materials upon which professional advice should be given in proceedings pending, or threatened, or anticipated. The document was prepared in such a way that it is useful in the case of a claim, and it gives the very information which an experienced person would look for if a claim were to be made.

The document was privileged from production.

Westminster Airways Ltd v Kuwait Oil Co Ltd

[1951] 1 KB 13, [1950] 2 All ER 596, 66 TLR 281, 94 Sol Jo 551, 84 Ll L Rep 297, CA

A motor lorry belonging to defendants ran into an aircraft belonging to the plaintiffs which had been forced to land on a road in Kuwait. The accident occurred on 25 November 1947. Formal notice of a claim for damages was given by the plaintiffs to the defendants on 29 December 1947.

Pursuant to an order for discovery of documents, the defendants made an affidavit which included the following paragraph:

'The defendant company object to produce any of the documents set forth in the schedule hereto upon the ground that they came into existence and were made after litigation was in contemplation and in view of such litigation for the purpose of obtaining and furnishing to the solicitors of the defendants' company evidence and information as to the evidence which could be obtained and otherwise for the use of the solicitors to enable them to conduct the defence in this action and to advice the defendants.'

The defendants disclosed (inter alia) the following documents:
(1) a letter from defendants' representative at Kuwait to the defendants in London dated 27 November 1947;
(2) a similar letter dated 3 December 1947;
(3) a letter from the defendants' insurance brokers to the defendants' insurers dated 19 December 1947, which enclosed document 2.

The defendants claimed privilege for documents which included letters from their insurers to their brokers of 22 and 23 December 1947, and from the defendants to the brokers of 31 December 1947.

HELD: The letter of 3 December made it quite clear that there was more than a probability of litigation at that time. It gave details of the accident and stated that the pilot of the aircraft had made a statement of his evidence which resulted in the driver of the motor lorry being found guilty of driving without due care and attention in the political agents' court. It was obvious from the nature of the accident and the letter of 31 December that litigation was anticipated before the actual claim (29 December) was received.

Per Jenkins LJ: Insurers are concerned in the matter only because they have agreed by the contract of insurance to indemnify their assured against claims of the character in question. That being so, the very fact that the insurance company is communicated with at all indicates that a claim is anticipated.

Seabrook v British Transport Commission

[1959] 2 All ER 15, [1959] 1 WLR 509, 103 Sol Jo 351 (Havers J)

The plaintiff was the widow of a workman employed by the defendants who was killed whilst at work. She sued for damages alleging negligence and breach of statutory duty. The summons for directions ordered a list of documents. The defendants claimed privilege for some documents including correspondence between and reports made by the defendants' officers and servants.

The plaintiff called for particulars of the 'reports' and in particular whether they included a statement by James Munro with whom the deceased was working. The defendants replied as follows: 'the reports are accident reports and reports by the defendants' officers and servants on their enquiries into this accident, which reports include a statement of James Munro, with whom the deceased was working.'

HELD: A party may ask the judge to look at the documents but it is entirely a matter for the judge to exercise his discretion on the facts of any particular case. It is not necessary in this case to look at them. The claim for privilege has been established. Appeal dismissed.

Note—The Editorial Note in the All England Report points out that this decision must be considered with that of *Longthorn v British Transport Commission*, below. The *Supreme Court Practice 1993* says the scope of Seabrook and the correctness of *Westminster Airways* and the practice based upon them 'will need reconsideration'.

Longthorn v British Transport Commission

[1959] 2 All ER 32, [1959] 1 WLR 530, 103 Sol Jo 352 (Diplock J)
Plaintiff was injured by accident whilst in the employ of the defendants, and shortly after the defendants held a private inquiry into the cause of the accident, which occurred on 21 January 1955, and the inquiry was in March 1955. At the inquiry, in which the plaintiff took part, the object of the inquiry as set out in the defendant's affidavit of documents was as follows:

'It was then explained to the injured man the purpose of the inquiry, that it was not so much convened to establish guilt or attach blame to either himself or any other person who may have been concerned, but rather to ascertain the cause of the accident with a view to safeguarding against any possible similar happening in the future. Longthorn's co-operation was invited to this end, this being willingly promised by him.'

At the time of the inquiry, the defendants did not know that the plaintiff intended to bring the action and first became aware of it by a letter of 5 July 1955. Writ was issued on 29 February 1956. In the proceedings the defendants first filed a list of documents, also claiming privilege, on the same grounds as in *Seabrook*'s case, subject to the wording of these documents. In *Seabrook*'s case the affidavit said that the documents were prepared 'wholly or mainly' for the purpose of being furnished to the solicitor. In *Longthorn*'s case there was no such claim.The list of documents used the words 'inter alia' for the appropriate purpose. The judge said he agreed with every word of the judgment of Havers J in *Seabrook*'s case. The judge decided to look at the documents and held that the claim for privilege was not established on the ground put forward in the affidavit.
HELD: The document nor any part of it is not privileged, because the inquiry was not to any appreciable extent for the purpose of safeguarding against a similar occurrence.

If this ground is wrong, I think the defendants are estopped from claiming privilege in respect of that part of the document which contains the plaintiff's evidence. Appeal dismissed.

'Dominant purpose'

Waugh v British Railways Board

[1980] AC 521, [1979] 2 All ER 1169, [1979] 3 WLR 150, [1979] IRLR 364, 123 Sol Jo 506, HL
The plaintiff's husband, an engine driver, was killed when two locomotives collided. She claimed damages under the Fatal Accidents Acts. Soon after the accident a joint internal report on it was prepared by two officers of the defendant board as was the

board's normal practice after an accident. Its objects were to assist in establishing the cause of the accident and equally for the purpose of providing the board's solicitor with material on which he could advise the board in any proceedings arising out of the accident. Proceedings were to be anticipated in the present case. The report was headed 'For the information of the board's solicitor . . . for the purpose of enabling him to advise the BRB in relation thereto'. The plaintiff sought discovery of the report; the defendants refused on the ground of legal professional privilege.
HELD: Reversing the decision of the Court of Appeal, the report should be disclosed. Unless the purpose of submission to the legal adviser is at least the *dominant* (but not necessarily the sole) purpose for which the relevant document was prepared the reasons which require privilege to be extended to it cannot apply. Here the two purposes for which the report was prepared were of equal rank or weight.

Neilson v Laugharne

[1981] QB 736, [1981] 1 All ER 829, [1981] 2 WLR 537, 125 Sol Jo 202, CA
In an action against the police for, inter alia, damage to property and wrongful arrest the plaintiff sought discovery of statements taken by the police for the purposes of an inquiry under the Police Act 1964, s 49 into a complaint made by the plaintiff arising from the same incidents. The defendants claimed legal professional privilege against disclosure.
HELD, following *Waugh v British Railways Board* (above): The dominant purpose of the police in taking the statements was to carry out the statutory duty to investigate required by s 49 and there was no legal professional privilege in respect of those statements.

Note—Applied in *Hehir v Metropolitan Police Comr* [1982] 2 All ER 335, [1982] 1 WLR 715, 126 Sol Jo 330, CA.

Re Highgrade Traders Ltd

[1984] BCLC 151, CA
Following a fire at the premises of Highgrade Traders Ltd in suspicious circumstances the fire insurers obtained reports from loss adjusters, accountants and fire investigators at the instance of their solicitors. As a result the insurers refused to meet a claim. The company later went into liquidation. The liquidators applied to the court under the Companies Act 1948, s 268(3) for an order that the insurers' claims officer should produce the reports.
HELD, ON APPEAL: No orders should be made. Applying the test in *Waugh v British Railways Board* (above) the dominant purpose of the reports was to discover the cause of the fire so as to ascertain if there had been a fraud. It was clear that if a claim was persisted in there would be litigation. The judge's view that finding the cause of the fire was the main purpose and legal advice only a secondary purpose was a misinterpretation of the relevant authorities. Knowing the cause of the fire was of no use on its own: the insurers had formed a view early on in the dispute that litigation was probable. The documents were privileged.

Note—The Companies Act 1948 is now repealed. Comparable provisions to s 268(3) of this Act can be found in the Insolvency Act 1986, s 236 and supplementary provisions under the Insolvency Rules 1986.

Plaintiff's statement

Britten v F H Pilcher & Sons

[1969] 1 All ER 491 (Thesiger J)
The plaintiff suffered injury when in the defendant's employment. Three weeks after the accident he gave a statement to the defendants' insurers, and signed it, describing the accident. Later he sued for damages and in the statement of claim gave a different version of the accident. At the trial he was confronted with his signed statement and lost the action. The statement was headed 'This statement is intended for the use of the company's legal advisers in connection with litigation already commenced or anticipated'. It had not been disclosed by the defendants on discovery. The plaintiff opposed the defendants' application for costs on the ground that the statement should have been disclosed and that if it had the action might have been abandoned at an early stage.
HELD: The defendants were not under a duty to disclose it. As Havers J said in *Seabrook v British Transport Commission* (above) the practice on discovery is a reconciliation of two opposing principles, (1) the need to protect professional legal assistance and advice, and (2) the requirement that in the interests of justice and in order that the parties should not be taken by surprise, all relevant documents should be before the court. In the present case as the statement was admissible against the plaintiff and was in the possession of the defendants there was no risk that it would not be brought to the attention of the court. The plaintiff must have known he had made the statement and could not be taken by surprise by it. It had never been previously suggested that documents under the heading that this document had should be disclosed in advance to plaintiffs so as to enable them to trim their evidence to suit.

Interrogatory

Jones v G D Searle & Co

[1978] 3 All ER 654, [1979] 1 WLR 101, 122 Sol Jo 435, CA
In an action for damages for alleged medical negligence the plaintiff asked for the discretion of the court to be exercised in her favour under the Limitation Act 1939, s 2D (now the Limitation Act 1980, s 33). She revealed that she had taken counsel's opinion. The defendants sought to interrogate whether the opinion had been favourable or not. The plaintiff refused to answer on the ground of legal professional privilege.
HELD: Section 2D(3)(f) required the court to have regard to the steps taken by the plaintiff to obtain 'medical legal or other expert advice and the nature of any such advice'. As the court is under a duty to consider the advice it must be able to demand evidence as to what the nature of the advice was. The defendants were entitled to have the interrogatory answered.

Birmingham v Kelly

(26 April 1979, unreported) (Jupp J in chambers)
The plaintiff alleged he was injured in a motor accident on 8 June 1973. As the proposed defendants' whereabouts could not be ascertained, the plaintiff's solicitors notified his claim to the Motor Insurers' Bureau on 22 May 1975. The Motor Insurers' Bureau appointed an insurance office to investigate the claim who communicated with the plaintiff's solicitors. On 17 August 1977 the investigating office denied

liability on the Motor Insurers' behalf as no writ had been issued. The plaintiff instructed new solicitors who issued a writ and applied in due course for specific discovery of correspondence and recorded notes of telephone conversations between the Motor Insurers' Bureau and the investigating office from 22 May 1975 to 24 February 1978.
HELD: The documents were privileged: although the Motor Insurers' Bureau had not instructed solicitors during the period in question everything they did was to prepare the case for settlement or defence, whichever would prove appropriate. The Limitation Act 1939, s 2D did not justify overriding the privilege. Prejudice to the defendants had not been averred and *Jones v Searle* (above) which dealt with interrogators, did not apply.

Note—The Limitation Act 1939, s 2D has now become the Limitation Act 1980, s 33.

See against third party

Paterson v Chadwick

[1974] 2 All ER 772, [1974] 1 WLR 890, 118 Sol Jo 169 (Boreham J)
The plaintiff issued proceedings against solicitors claiming damages for professional negligence in failing to bring proceedings within the limitation period against a hospital where, she alleged, she had suffered personal injury during medical treatment. In the action against the solicitors she applied under the Administration of Justice Act 1970, s 32(1) (now the Supreme Court Act 1981, s 34) for an order against the hospital management committee for discovery of the hospital records of her treatment. The committee opposed the application on the ground that her claim against the solicitors was not 'in respect of personal injuries'.
HELD: An order for discovery should be made. 'In respect of' conveys some connection or relation between the claim and the personal injuries. The nature and extent of her personal injuries formed an essential ingredient in the proof of her claim; unless she could prove the injuries she would fail. The connection was clear.

Gibbons v Wall

(1988) Times, 24 February, CA
The standard of proof to be applied by the court when determining whether 'the court is satisfied that, if the action proceeded to trial, the plaintiff would obtain judgment for substantial damages' (Ord 29, r 11(1)) was the normal civil standard of proof, but it was flexible and in the context of an application for an interim payment the standard to be applied was at the high end of the range. The word 'sure' used in *Breeze v McKennon & Sons Ltd* (see below) meant merely the ordinary civil standard, not 'satisfied beyond reasonable doubt'.

O'Driscoll v Sleigh

[1985] CA Transcript 510, CA
The plaintiff was injured when the omnibus she was travelling in braked sharply so as to avoid a wheel which had become detached from the first defendant's vehicle. The first defendant appealed an order to make an interim payment. The first defendant's insurers had indicated to their insured that they intended to avoid the policy for late notification and because he was driving a defective vehicle. Counsel argued that the application against the first defendant should fail as the plaintiff could

not satisfy Ord 29, 11(2) in that the motorist did not have the means to satisfy any order.

Having considered the effects of s 145 of the Road Traffic Act 1988 and satisfied themselves that any order would have to be met by the first defendant's insurers in the first instance (subject to the right to recovery against their insured) the Court of Appeal dismissed the first defendant's appeal.

Schott Kem Ltd v Bentley

[1991] 1 QB 61, [1990] 3 All ER 850
It was not necessary for a plaintiff to show on an application for an interim payment either need or prejudice if he did not obtain one, and the court's discretion to make an award was wide.

INTERIM PAYMENTS

Note—See RSC Ord 29, r 10 and CCR Ord 13, r 12.

Stringman v McArdle

(1993) Times, 19 November, CA
Provided the plaintiff satisfied the criteria set down in RSC Ord 29, r 11, it was not necessary for the court to inquire as to the use for which any interim award of damages was intended.

SCHEDULE OF SPECIAL DAMAGE

Note—In personal injury actions the schedule must be served with the Statement of Claim—see RSC Ord 18, rr 12—32.

MEDICAL EVIDENCE

Privilege from discovery

Schneider v Leigh

[1955] 2 QB 195, [1955] 2 All ER 173, [1955] 2 WLR 904, 99 Sol Jo 276, CA
The doctor examined a plaintiff claiming damages for personal injuries sustained in a motor accident on the instructions of the defendants' solicitors and reported to the solicitors, who wrote to the plaintiff's solicitors and in their letter quoted two paragraphs of the report. The plaintiff's solicitors showed the letter to the plaintiff. The plaintiff by the same solicitors, whilst the action for personal injuries was still pending, issued a writ against the doctor claiming damages for libel alleging the two paragraphs were defamatory and that the doctor was guilty of malice. In his defence in the libel action the doctor pleaded privilege. The plaintiff applied in the libel action for discovery of the whole report and of the other documents passing between the doctor and the defendants' solicitors in the first action. Plaintiff by his counsel contended that an order for inspection should take effect only after the first action had been disposed of.

HELD: By Hodson and Romer LJJ, Singleton LJ dissenting, the documents were not privileged in the libel action.

Per Romer LJ. The privilege which exists in the first action is that of the company and of no one else; and the company can at any time waive the privilege without the defendant's consent. ['The company' were the defendants in the first action.]

Note—71 LQR 316 points out that the person making the report must take the risk that it may thereafter be disclosed and subject him to an action for libel. Whether he can protect himself by obtaining from his employers a guarantee that the report will be kept secret in all circumstances is uncertain (cf *Weld-Blundell v Stephens* [1920] AC 956, [1920] All ER Rep 32, 89 LJKB 705, 123 LT 593, 36 TLR 640, 64 Sol Jo 529, HL).

Patch v United Bristol Hospitals Board

[1959] 3 All ER 876, [1959] 1 WLR 955, 103 Sol Jo 833 (Streatfield J)
The plaintiff had an operation to his hand at the defendants' hospital, and following the operation he developed an infection. Pursuant to the recommendation in a circular issued by the Ministry of Health, and before the plaintiff had intimated any intention of making a claim, written statements were made by the consulting surgeon, the senior registrar, house surgeons and nurses at the hospital, and were sent to the solicitors to the hospital. Subsequently the plaintiff commenced proceedings against the hospital. The hospital claimed that the statements were privileged. The judge ruled that although no action had been commenced, the statements were not made in the ordinary course of hospital treatment, but in order to provide the legal adviser of the hospital with the necessary material to advise, if such a claim should be made.

Watson v Cammell Laird & Co

[1959] 2 All ER 757, [1959] 1 WLR 702, 103 Sol Jo 470, [1959] 2 Lloyd's Rep 175, CA
Plaintiff's affidavit of documents contained a document described as 'Copy of Birkenhead Hospital Management Committee Case Notes' relating to the plaintiff.
HELD: Although it was no more than a verbatim copy of a document which was itself not privileged, it was entitled to legal professional protection as the copy had been prepared by the plaintiff's solicitors for the purposes of the action.

Kenning v Eve Construction Ltd

[1989] 1 WLR 1189, QBD
The plaintiff was injured by a winch belonging to the defendants. In the course of the action, experts' reports were disclosed under RSC Ord 25, r 8. The defendants' solicitors disclosed a report to the plaintiff's solicitors, which dealt with the pleaded allegations and favoured the defendants. They also inadvertently disclosed a covering letter with the report which pointed out other matters which would cause problems to the defendants if alleged by the plaintiff. The defendants applied to have the plaintiff debarred from using the letter as a basis for an amendment to his statement of claim or cross-examination.
HELD: The practice of preparing experts' reports in two parts, one for disclosure, and one with confidential comments, was to be condemned. (See *Ollett v Bristol Aerojet* [1979] 1 WLR 1197.) Although the letter was privileged, it was admissible, because under RSC Ord 25, r 8, disclosure should be made of the full substance of the evidence, good and bad, if the witness was to be called in evidence at trial.

Supplying copy of medical report

Clarke v Martlew

[1973] QB 58, [1972] 3 All ER 764, [1972] 3 WLR 653, 116 Sol Jo 618, CA
The second defendant asked for a medical examination of the plaintiff by two named doctors. The plaintiff agreed subject to her solicitors being supplied with copies of the reports. The second defendant objected to this requirement and applied for a stay until the plaintiff should grant facilities for the examination.
HELD: The plaintiff's stipulation was fair. It was reasonable and just as a condition of being granted a medical examination that the defendant should make available the doctor's report to the plaintiff. If and when the plaintiff got further reports on her own she must reciprocate and show those to the defendant.

Megarity v D J Ryan & Sons Ltd

[1980] 2 All ER 832, [1980] 1 WLR 1237, 124 Sol Jo 498, CA
The defendants, against whom the plaintiff claimed damages for personal injury, applied for an order that the action be stayed until the plaintiff submitted to medical examination by the defendants' medical adviser. The district registrar refused an order except on condition that the defendants supplied a copy of the report to the plaintiff as required by *Clarke v Martlew* (above). An appeal to the judge in chambers succeeded.
HELD, by the Court of Appeal: The judge was right. When *Clarke v Martlew* was decided RSC Ord 38, rr 36 and 37 did not exist. Those rules established a complete code dealing with the conditions which attach to the adducing of expert evidence at the trial. The 'fairness' which Lord Denning required in *Clarke's* case was secured by the new rules. A condition calling for disclosure of the defendant's report should not be imposed.

McGinley v Burke

[1973] 2 All ER 1010, [1973] 1 WLR 990, 117 Sol Jo 488, [1973] 2 Lloyd's Rep 508
In an action for damages for personal injuries the defendant's solicitors asked permission to have the plaintiff medically examined. The plaintiff's solicitors stipulated that they must be supplied with a copy of the report. Defendant's solicitors were agreeable to this provided the plaintiff's solicitors applied for a stay of the action.
HELD: The plaintiff must at least offer reciprocity. If the plaintiff's solicitors require to see a copy of the defendant's medical report immediately they must be prepared to offer an equivalent report of their own in exchange but they are not obliged to disclose all their reports. The court is only concerned with those on which the plaintiff intends to rely at the trial. As an alternative to immediate disclosure the parties can agree to eventual exchange before trial.

Note—Present-day practice under RSC Ord 25, r 8 (automatic directions) requires parties to disclose the substance of any medical or other expert evidence as a condition of being allowed to call such evidence.

Booth v Warrington Health Authority

[1992] PIQR P137, [1993] CLY 3230
The medical report disclosed by the defendants made reference to the number of witness statements. That reference did not in itself amount to a waiver of privilege and the plaintiff could not insist upon their disclosure.

Owen v Grimsby & Cleethorpes Transport

[1992] PIQR Q27, (1991) Times, 14 February, CA
Updated medical opinion did not require a plaintiff to amend his pleadings in personal injury actions.

Pizzey v Ford Motor Company Limited

[1993] 17 LS Gaz R 46, CA
The plaintiff's solicitors disclosed unfavourable medical reports by mistake. The defendants were entitled to rely upon them at trial.

ENGINEER'S REPORT

Mechanical defects—reports of earlier complaints

Blakebrough v British Motor Corpn Ltd

(1969) 113 Sol Jo 366, CA
The plaintiffs claimed damages for injuries received when an 1100 car made by the defendants overturned. They alleged that the car was dangerous and that other 1100 cars made by the defendants had crashed in circumstances suggesting the existence of manufacturing defects. On an application for discovery of documents relating to reports, investigations and complaints of uncontrollability for unknown causes in 1100 cars it was held by the Court of Appeal the plaintiffs should have an order to include all complaints relating to sudden uncontrollability of steering for unknown causes in the defendants' 1100 cars. A party was entitled to discovery of every document relating to the matters in question in the action containing information which might directly or indirectly enable him to advance his own case or damage his adversary's.

OTHER STATEMENTS/REPORTS

Cross-examination of witness

Burnell v British Transport Commission

[1956] 1 QB 187, [1955] 3 All ER 822, [1956] 2 WLR 61, 100 Sol Jo 33, [1955] 2 Lloyd's Rep 549, CA
A witness made and signed a statement to defendants and at the trial was called by the plaintiff. With the statement in his hands, defendants' counsel asked the witness whether he had not given a statement and made certain statements in it.
HELD: Plaintiff's counsel was entitled to call for production of the whole document.

Although the defendants might have been entitled to claim privilege at one stage not to produce the document, having used it in part and waived privilege as to part, it is waived as to the whole.

Note—See also *General Accident Assurance v Tanter, The Zephyr* [1984] 1 All ER 35. All reports to be lodged even if not agreed (*Press v West Cumbria Health Authority* reported in Current Law).

Kirkup v British Railways Engineering Ltd

[1983] 1 All ER 855, [1983] 1 WLR 190, 126 Sol Jo 730; affd [1983] 3 All ER 147, [1983] 1 WLR 1165
On a summons for directions in a personal injury action the master ordered disclosure of the plaintiff's experts' reports within 28 days after setting down and of the defendants' experts' reports within 42 days thereafter. The plaintiff appealed against the order.
HELD: The basic rule was that experts' reports obtained for the purpose of the litigation were privileged. Ord 25, r 8(1)(b) provided for disclosure by mutual exchange. On applications relating to calling expert evidence Ord 38, r 37(2) required the court to order disclosure unless it considered there was 'sufficient reason for not doing so'. The question in issue was the extent of the court's discretion. The instances given in Ord 38, r 37(3) and (4) were guidelines but not the only circumstances in which disclosure may be withheld. Mutuality, and fairness were not the only matters to be considered; there were also the saving of costs, the avoidance of surprise and the need to avoid amendments at trial. It would not be unreasonable in appropriate circumstances to require the plaintiff to show his hand by sending his experts' report first so that the defendant might consider the issues raised in it. Appeal dismissed.

Exchange

Black & Decker v Flymo

[1991] 3 All ER 158, [1991] 1 WLR 753, [1991] FSR 93
A witness statement was not privileged once it had been disclosed in accordance with Ord 38, r 2A(2).

Employment consultants

Larby v Thurgood

[1993] 3 CL 350, [1993] 1 CLR 66
It was for the trial judge to consider the plaintiff's suitability and motivation for any proposed employment, and evidence from an employment consultant on that point was not relevant. It was therefore inappropriate to stay an action until a plaintiff submitted to an interview by a nominated consultant.

MEDICAL EXAMINATIONS

Note—Halsbury's Laws (4th edn) vol 30, para 38, p 34 says:

'A medical practitioner who examines a person against his will and without statutory authority to do so, and a surgeon who performs an operation without his patient's express or implied consent, are each liable in trespass.'

Beven on *Negligence in Law* (3rd edn), p 997, says:

'Outside this enactment (Regulation of Railways Act 1868) there appears to be no power to order an examination of a person injured and whose injuries are the subject of legal proceedings, though the strong comment that a refusal to submit to examination would elicit at the trial is a considerable safeguard against the want of such a power working practical injustice.'

McDowell v Strannix

[1951] NI 57, [1952] CLY 2768
Plaintiff's advisers refused medical examination except upon terms that evidence limited to damage and no evidence given to statements made by plaintiff to defendant's doctor as to liability.
HELD: Terms reasonable.

Pickett v Bristol Aeroplane Co Ltd

[1961] CLY 7183, (1961) Times, 17 March, CA
In an action for damages for dermatitis the plaintiff was examined by doctors instructed by the defendants. One of the doctors having died the defendants asked for a further examination by a dermatologist. The plaintiffs refused. On an interlocutory application by the defendants for an order that the action be stayed until the plaintiff submitted to examination:
HELD: The court has an inherent jurisdiction to make such an order, but this was not a case in which it ought to be exercised. The defendants could have no possible right to a direct order compelling the plaintiff to submit to examination and to order a stay until he submitted to examination would be an indirect method of achieving the same result. Such an order would be an improper interference with the plaintiff's civil liberty and with his right to present his case in his own way.

Per Donovan LJ: It would be wrong to shut out a plaintiff from the Seat of Justice even if he refused any examination at all, still less where, as in the present case, he had refused to be examined only by one particular doctor.

Note—See *Starr v National Coal Board* and *Lane v Willis*, pp 632–633, below.

Edmeades v Thames Board Mills Ltd

[1969] 1 QB 67, [1969] 2 All ER 127, [1969] 2 WLR 668, 113 Sol Jo 88, [1969] 1 Lloyd's Rep 221, CA
In an action for damages for personal injuries the defendants were given facilities for a medical examination of the plaintiff by Dr A. When reports were exchanged the defendants saw that the plaintiff's doctor was saying that there was a condition of osteoarthritis not alleged in the statement of claim and therefore not considered by Dr A. They asked for a new examination by a specialist, naming six specialists from whom the plaintiff could choose. The plaintiff's solicitors refused to grant any facilities for a further examination except by Dr A who was not one of the six. The defendants applied to the court for an order that the action be stayed unless the plaintiff submit to examination by one of the six.
HELD: The court had ample jurisdiction to grant a stay whenever it was just and reasonable so to do. The request of the defendants was reasonable and if not granted would result in the court being unable to do justice to their case. *Pickett's* case (above) was different in that only one name was put forward. The defendants were entitled to the order sought.

Murphy v Ford Motor Co Ltd

(1970) 114 Sol Jo 886, CA
In an action for damages for pneumoconiosis the defendants asked for a medical examination by a named doctor. The plaintiff's solicitors refused on the ground that the doctor made reports only for insurance companies. This allegation was shown to be untrue and the plaintiff's solicitors withdrew it but still declined to agree to the examination. The defendants sought a stay as in *Edmeades*'s case.
HELD: They were entitled to have a stay. If the defendants in a personal injury case make a reasonable request for the plaintiff to be medically examine by a doctor whom the defendants have chosen, then the plaintiff should accede to such a request unless he has a reasonable ground for objecting to that particular doctor. If the plaintiff has any reasons he should give them so that the court can see what they are: a mere refusal does not put the onus on the defendant to show that his choice was justified. Having nominated a fit and proper person the defendants were entitled to the examination.

Starr v National Coal Board

[1977] 1 All ER 243, [1977] 1 WLR 63, 120 Sol Jo 720, CA
The plaintiff claimed damages for injury to the elbows by ulnar nerve compression alleged to have been sustained over a period of time at work. After receiving an indeterminate report from a surgeon the defendants asked for an examination by Dr X a neurologist. The plaintiff's solicitors refused, saying, in effect: 'Any consultant neurologist other than Dr X, but under no circumstances Dr X.' The defendants applied for a stay unless and until the plaintiff submitted to examination by Dr X.
HELD: They were entitled to a stay. In exercising its discretion the court must have regard to the fundamental right of the plaintiff to personal liberty but also of the defendant to defend himself in litigation as he and his advisers think fit. The principles to be followed were those indicated in *Edmeades*'s and *Murphy*'s case (above), *Pickett*'s case (p 631, above) cannot stand against those two cases. The court's discretion cannot be exercised unless each party exposes the reason for his action. The plaintiff had sought to prove that he and his advisers entertained a reasonable apprehension that Dr X might produce a misleading report which might make a just determination of the cause more difficult. On the evidence adduced he had failed to do this.

Hall v Avon Health Authority

[1980] 1 All ER 516, [1980] 1 WLR 481, 124 Sol Jo 293, CA
The defendants to an action for damages for personal injury asked for a medical examination of the plaintiff to be carried out by their specialist medical adviser. The plaintiff's solicitors had no personal objections to the specialist but asked as a term of agreement to the examination that a doctor nominated by them on behalf of the plaintiff should be present.
HELD: The term could not be insisted upon. The court ought to have good and substantial reasons put before it if it is to impose conditions of this kind on a reasonable request for a medical examination. It was not an adequate reason to say that the plaintiff was a woman of 52, or that in other cases plaintiffs had been upset by the way in which they had been examined by other doctors for other defendants. An FRCS of good standing should be given credit for being fair and considerate in his examination and report on an opposite party.

Lane v Willis

[1972] 1 All ER 430, [1972] 1 WLR 326, 116 Sol Jo 102, CA

The plaintiff received injuries in a road accident in 1968. In the statement of claim they were given as 'bruising of chest, contusion of left knee, nervous shock and depressive anxiety state'. In February 1971 these particulars were considerably extended by amendment to include severe depression requiring treatment in a sanatorium and possibly early retirement. The defendants had two examinations by a neurologist after the amendment and then asked the plaintiff's solicitors for examination by a psychiatrist. The request was refused. They applied for a stay of the action unless the plaintiff should submit to examination by a named psychiatrist.

HELD: The defendants were entitled to the order asked. In *Pickett*'s case (above) Lord Donovan had expressed doubt whether the court had jurisdiction to make the order but the real point there was that the defendants were insisting on examination by one doctor to whom the plaintiff objected. In the present case there was no objection to the particular doctor nominated but to any further examination. The correct test was that laid down in *Edmeades*'s case, that the court had jurisdiction to grant a stay whenever it was just and reasonable so to do and could do so where the plaintiff's refusal was such as to prevent the just determination of the cause.

Per Sachs LJ: There was a heavy onus on the defendant to show why a further examination was needed. In future cases medical evidence should be produced to show that the further examination was required in the interests of justice.

Aspinall v Sterling Mansell Ltd

[1981] 3 All ER 866 (Hodgson J)

The plaintiff claimed damages for industrial dermatitis allegedly contracted in the defendants' employment. They asked for a medical examination at which their doctor would administer a patch test. She refused to undergo an examination which would include a patch test. The defendants applied for an order that the action be stayed unless and until the plaintiff submitted to such examination.

HELD: No stay would be granted. There was a slight risk of a major recrudescence of dermatitis from a patch test. There is a difference not of degree but of kind between an ordinary examination and one which includes such procedures as patch testing. It is not the reasonableness of the defendants' request which is in question but the reasonableness of the plaintiff's refusal. It cannot ever be unreasonable for a plaintiff to refuse to undergo a procedure which carries with it a risk, however slight, of serious injury.

Prescott v Bulldog Tools Ltd

[1981] 3 All ER 869 (Webster J)

The plaintiff claimed damages for alleged industrial deafness contracted in the defendants' employment. He underwent a number of medical examinations from some of which it appeared that the deafness was in part due to causes other than his employment. The defendants asked for a further examination by a specialist who intended to carry out a caloric test, x-ray photographs and an electrocochleography. The plaintiff refused to undergo the tests. The defendants applied for a stay unless and until the plaintiff submitted to the examination and tests. There was evidence that the caloric test induces a degree of discomfort and the electrocochleography involves risk and discomfort.

HELD: In cases of this kind the court should examine objectively the weight of reasonableness of the defendant's request as seen by the defendant and the weight of the reasonableness of the plaintiff's objections as seen by him and balance the one against the other. Although it is extremely unlikely that a court would hold it unreasonable for the plaintiff to refuse a test which carried a risk of serious injury the court should (despite the view expressed in *Aspinall*'s case (above)) consider the matter without introducing any presumption one way or the other. In the present case the reasonableness of the plaintiff's objections to the electrocochleography and x-rays outweighed the reasonableness of the defendant's request, but as the plaintiff had already undergone a caloric test by his own expert the reasonableness of the defendants' request for that test outweighed the reasonableness of his refusal.

FATAL ACCIDENTS CLAIM

Baugh v Delta Water Fittings Ltd

[1971] 3 All ER 258, [1971] 1 WLR 1295, 115 Sol Jo 485 (Lawson J)
The plaintiff, aged 54, was the widow of a man killed in an accident at work. She claimed damages as administratrix of her husband's estate under the Law Reform (Miscellaneous Provisions) Act 1934 and for herself as his dependant under the Fatal Accidents Acts. The defendants required her to be medically examined: she refused. The defendants applied for a stay of the action as in *Edmeades*'s case (p 631, above). They had no reason to believe her health was other than normal.
HELD: (1) The plaintiff's expectation of life was irrelevant to the claim under the Law Reform (Miscellaneous Provisions) Act 1934 and there could be no grounds for a stay of proceedings under that Act. (2) Even if the view of the Court of Appeal in *Edmeades*'s case was right that the court can order a stay when an injured plaintiff refuses an examination, the same considerations do not apply when the plaintiff is a dependant suing under the Fatal Accidents Acts. In such a case no order should be made unless the defendant can show substantial grounds for making the application, eg that the widow has a grave disease. That was not the case here and there was no reason to compel her to submit to examination.

PLAINTIFF'S DOCTOR'S FEE

Bram v Ponsford and Devenish

[1953] CLY 3463, Mayor's Court
Defendants' solicitors requested a medical examination of plaintiff and by letter agreed that it should take place 'on the usual terms'.
HELD: The solicitors were liable for the attendance fee of the plaintiff's specialist but not for any sum referable to his travelling expenses in the absence of express subsequent agreement.

Note—On presence of plaintiff's doctor at examination see *Hall v Avon Health Authority* (above, p 632).

Striking out

DISMISSAL FOR WANT OF PROSECUTION

Note—Before 1967 orders to dismiss for want of prosecution were rarely made on a first application without giving the plaintiff an opportunity of keeping the action in being. The successful applications to dismiss in *Reggentin*'s and *Fitzpatrick*'s cases (below) led to a flood of similar applications. Three were dealt with together after full argument and are reported under the title of *Allen v Sir Alfred McAlpine & Sons Ltd* at [1968] 2 QB 229. The Court of Appeal made the following general observations:

1 The court will do all in its power to enforce expedition, if need be by striking out actions when there has been excessive delay.

2 There is no rule or practice that the court should never on first application dismiss the action. When the delay is prolonged and inexcusable and is such as to do grave injustice the court may in its discretion dismiss the action straightaway, leaving the plaintiff to his remedy against his own solicitors.

3 Mere inactivity on the part of the defendant will not amount to acquiescence in delay and prejudice his application to dismiss but he cannot rely on delay for which he has been responsible, eg in failing to comply with a procedural step.

4 The court must consider whether the plaintiff will himself be prejudiced by the dismissal when he is not personally to blame for the delay, ie whether his solicitors (if they were the cause of the delay) are good for the damages. But see *Rowe v Tregaskes* and *Martin v Turner*, p 638, below.

In *Bremer Vulkan v South India Shipping* [1981] AC 909 [1979] 3 All ER 194, [1979] 3 WLR 471, 123 Sol Jo 504) Donaldson J after commenting that the law had developed considerably in the past 12 years summarised the guidelines as follows:

1 The power to dismiss for want of prosecution should be exercised only where the court is satisfied that either: (a) the default has been intentional and contumelious, eg disobedience to a peremptory order of the court or conduct amounting to an abuse of the process of the court; or (b)(i) there has been inordinate and inexcusable delay on the part of the plaintiff or his lawyers, and (ii) such delay (1) either will give rise to a substantial risk that it is not possible to have a fair trial of the issues in the action, or (2) is such as is likely to cause or to have caused serious prejudice to the defendants either as between themselves and the plaintiff or between each other or between them and a third party.

2 Only in exceptional cases should an action be dismissed before the relevant limitation period has expired, at least if it is likely that the plaintiff will issue a new writ.

3 The action of a plaintiff in delaying for almost all or any part of the limitation period cannot be relied on as constituting inordinate or inexcusable delay, but such delay is far from being irrelevant. It will have an important bearing on the degree of expedition required of the plaintiff once the proceedings have been instituted; delay which would be acceptable if the proceedings had begun promptly may become inordinate and inexcusable after a late start, and the degree of prejudice to the defendant may be greatly heightened.

4 Prejudice to the defendant may take many forms; witnesses may die, become untraceable or their recollections may dim. More than that, the very fact of having a large unquantified claim hanging over the defendant's head for a long period may itself be highly prejudicial.

5 The defendant will lose his right to have the action dismissed if he induces in the plaintiff a reasonable belief that, notwithstanding the delay, he is willing for the action to proceed, and the plaintiff does work or incurs further expenses as a result.

Acquiescence in delay is not a permanent bar to obtaining a dismissal after further delay. Each case will have to be considered in the light of its own particular facts.
6 Mere inactivity on the part of the defendant is not to be construed as acquiescence in delay by the plaintiff.

Illustrations of the 'guidelines' are to be found in the following cases:

Generally

Birkett v James

[1978] AC 297, [1977] 2 All ER 801, [1977] 3 WLR 45, 121 Sol Jo 444, HL
In a claim for payment of a sum of money alleged to be due from the defendant under an oral agreement made in 1969 the plaintiff issued a writ in July 1972. The action proceeded at a reasonable pace until July 1973 when an order was made to set down within 28 days. This was not done and for reasons relating to costs and legal aid nothing further was done until new solicitors gave notice to proceed in July 1975. The defendant applied to dismiss for want of prosecution. The limitation period did not expire until March 1976.
HELD, ON APPEAL, to the House of Lords: (1) Non-expiry of the limitation period is generally a conclusive reason for not dismissing an action that is already pending. Insofar as *Spring Grove Services v Deane* (p 647, below) is an authority for saying that a second writ asserting the same claim can be struck out as an abuse of the process it was wrong. (2) As the time elapsed before the issue of a writ within the limitation period cannot of itself constitute inordinate delay the delay relied on by the defendant as prejudicial must relate to the time which the plaintiff allows to elapse unnecessarily after the writ has been issued. *William Parker Ltd v Ham & Son Ltd* (p 643, below) was rightly decided despite later comments on it by the Court of Appeal. The additional prejudice resulting from delay after issue of the writ need not be great but it must be more than minimal. If the delay is not excusable after proceedings are launched but does worsen the position of the defendant then it is not a case for dismissing for want of prosecution. (3) Whether or not the plaintiff may have an action for negligence against his solicitor responsible for the delay is irrelevant. *Martin v Turner* (p 638, below) approved.

Wright v Morris

(1988) Times, 31 October
On 19 November 1984 the plaintiffs, all members of the pop group Paper Lace, issued a writ alleging passing off. Since 1963 the defendants have been performing many of the songs written by the original group and had used the same name. An interlocutory injunction was granted pending trial, but no further steps were taken by the plaintiffs. The defendants sought to strike out the action by way of application heard in November 1987.

Distinguishing *Birkett v James* (above) in part, on its facts, Millet J struck out the plaintiffs' action even though the primary limitation period had not expired. The court had a residual discretion in these matters and this was a situation where it would be appropriate to exercise it.

Hornagold v Fairclough Building Ltd

(1993) 137 Sol Jo LB 153, [1993] 27 LS Gaz R 35, CA
To succeed in an application to strike out a plaintiff's claim for want of prosecution, it was not enough for the defendants to make general assertions that the plaintiff's

conduct had prejudiced the defence or created a substantial risk that there could not be a fair trial. What was required was something additional and specific. For example, the defendant had to show that a particular witness was no longer available or was too old to give reliable evidence.

In this case, the defendants did not identify particular witnesses, nor particular respects in which their evidence had been impaired and, therefore, their affidavit evidence could not justify striking out the plaintiff's claim for want of prosecution.

Granted

Reggentin v Beecholme Bakeries Ltd

[1968] 2 QB 276n, [1968] 1 All ER 566n, CA
Accident October 1961. Claim made: medical examination January 1963. Widow issued writ January 1964. Order for Directions June 1964. Interrogatories November 1964. Inspection of *locus in quo* August 1965. Nothing then done until November 1966 when plaintiff applied for further interrogatories and defendants applied to dismiss for want of prosecution.
HELD: The action should be dismissed. It was the duty of the plaintiff's solicitors to get on with the action and when it went to sleep for 13 months the defendants were entitled to apply for dismissal. Public policy demanded that actions should be brought on speedily.

Fitzpatrick v Batger & Co Ltd

[1967] 2 All ER 657, [1967] 1 WLR 706, 111 Sol Jo 276, CA
Accident 13 December 1961. Legal aid certificate October 1962. Writ issued 7 February 1963. Defence served 19 April 1963. In June 1963 defendants offered £300 in settlement which was refused. Nothing more was done until February 1965 when further negotiations took place ending without result in May 1965. Nothing more happened until February 1967 when the plaintiff's solicitors wrote seeking to revive the claim. The defendants thereupon applied to dismiss for want of prosecution. The master and the judge in chambers allowed the plaintiff to continue on payment of £30 into court as security for costs.
HELD, ON APPEAL: The action should be dismissed forthwith. Public policy demands that the business of the courts should be conducted with expedition. It is impossible to have a fair trial six years after the accident. It was immaterial that the defendants could have taken out an application to dismiss earlier: they were justified in letting sleeping dogs lie. The plaintiff would have his remedy against his solicitors in negligence.

Allen v Sir Alfred McAlpine & Sons Ltd

[1968] 2 QB 229, [1968] 1 All ER 543, [1968] 2 WLR 366, 112 Sol Jo 49, CA
Accident February 1959. Writ 13 July 1960. Pleadings closed January 1961. Discovery 1965. February 1967 plaintiff's solicitors wrote saying they were ready to proceed. April 1967 defendants applied to dismiss. Only two witnesses out of six could still be traced.
HELD: Impossible to have fair trial.

Clough v Clough

[1968] 1 All ER 1179, [1968] 1 WLR 525, 112 Sol Jo 154, CA
Accident 7 October 1961. Writ 2 October 1964. No statement of claim served until defendants issued summons to dismiss on 1 September 1967. Before summons was heard plaintiffs served statement of claim.
HELD: Delay prolonged and inexcusable. Under Ord 19, r 1 court had a discretion to dismiss for failure to serve statement of claim even if it was served before hearing of summons.

Gloria v Sokoloff

[1969] 1 All ER 204, 112 Sol Jo 422, CA
Accident 8 November 1961. Writ 6 November 1964. Statement of claim next day. Defences January 1965. August 1966 issue of liability disposed of between defendants, who asked for particulars of special damage but did not get them. April 1967 defendants issued summons for directions and got order for particulars which were not delivered until December 1967 and even then were hopelessly vague and imprecise. January 1968 defendants applied to dismiss.
HELD: Delay inexcusable. Having regard to plaintiff's complaints of anxiety, depression, etc and of a continuing loss of £40 per week earnings defendants were seriously prejudiced by it and fair trial was impossible.

Rowe v Tregaskes

[1968] 3 All ER 447, [1968] 1 WLR 1475, 112 Sol Jo 764, CA
Accident 23 November 1962. Plaintiff reported it to his trade union who made no claim until March 1965. Writ September 1965. Defendant's insurers denied liability March 1966. Trade union instructed solicitors to carry on. They served writ August 1966 and did a great deal of work on investigation. They were just about to serve statement of claim in March 1968 when defendant applied to dismiss.
HELD: Delay had made it impossible to have a fair trial. The fact that the plaintiff may not be able to prove negligence against the solicitors was not sufficient reason for refusing order to dismiss.

Martin v Turner

[1970] 1 All ER 256, [1970] 1 WLR 82, 113 Sol Jo 817, CA
Accident 29 May 1960. Liability not in dispute. Writ issued 25 April 1963, served 2 April 1964. Plaintiff's solicitors were unable to get from him the information they required to deal with his claim. Surgeons had said in February 1964 that he was fit for work but he insisted he was not fit and could never work again. A psychiatrist reported that he had become neurotically obsessed about the consequences of the accident.
HELD: The action should be dismissed for want of prosecution even though the solicitors were not to blame and it meant the plaintiff would get nothing from anyone. The defendants had been prejudiced by the delay. The test of the plaintiff's conduct was an objective one: he had acted unreasonably and the delay was therefore inexcusable.

Samuel Butler & Co Ltd v Mills Scaffold Co Ltd

(1970) 114 Sol Jo 912, CA
Accident February 1959 in which four men were killed in the course of building a bridge. Thorough inquest in March 1959 for which an expert made a full report. Evidence of a witness taken on commission in early 1960. In 1962 the plaintiffs who were subcontractors for the erection of heavy steel girders, settled the claims of the widows of the four men. In April 1963 the plaintiffs issued a writ against the defendants, who were scaffolders, for damages for negligent design or erection of scaffolding towers. After two extensions writ served in March 1966: statement of claim for £58,000 damages served March 1967. Defence and counter-claim for £6,000 served October 1967: reply and defence to counter-claim February 1968. March 1970 defendants applied to strike out for want of prosecution. The plaintiffs conceded there had been inordinate and inexcusable delay but contended a fair trial was still possible because of the full inquest and contemporaneous reports.
HELD: The action should be struck out and the counter-claim too. Such an action could not be tried by reading the evidence of witnesses at an inquest or the reports of experts. It was impossible to have a fair trial after 12 years.

Paxton v Allsopp

[1971] 3 All ER 370, [1971] 1 WLR 1310, 115 Sol Jo 446, CA
Plaintiff, 20, injured February 1957. Writ issued October 1957 and statement of claim served. November 1957 defence served. After medical examinations and negotiations, offer of £2,050 made in May 1960 to plaintiff's solicitors which they reported to the plaintiff's father who did not tell the plaintiff and did not answer the letter or reminders. 1964, plaintiff's father died; she found letter of 1960 reporting offer but did nothing about it until 1967. She then consulted solicitors who obtained some information from plaintiff's doctor but did not communicate with defendant's insurers until March 1970. Insurers said if any attempt was made to revive action they would apply to dismiss, but later offered £500. Plaintiff refused on counsel's advice. May 1970 plaintiff served notice of intention to proceed. Defendant applied to dismiss for want of prosecution. There was a hysterical element in the plaintiff's condition due partly to the accident. To avoid prejudice to defendant by delay plaintiff's counsel offered to limit damages to £2,050.
HELD: (1) The action should be dismissed. Though negligence was admitted and contemporaneous medical records were available the defendant was prejudiced because oral examination of medical witnesses was no longer possible to deal with hysterical element in the case. (2) It was not practicable to limit the claim to £2,050. (3) Per Davies LJ: the question whether the plaintiff would have a claim in negligence against her solicitors was irrelevant. *Martin v Turner* (above) approved.

Mordi v LEC Refrigeration Ltd

(1971) 115 Sol Jo 812, CA
Accident (cause of action) 28 January 1966. Writ 22 March 1968. Pleadings closed July 1968. Application to dismiss in default of summons for directions October 1970 when master further short period for summons for directions and setting down. Summons heard 11 November 1970 but action not set down. On 20 April 1971 action dismissed for want of prosecution.
HELD: Master's order upheld. All the delay had to be looked at, not merely the period from November 1970 to second application.

Vaughan v Parnham Ltd

[1972] 1 Lloyd's Rep 519, CA
Accident August 1964 causing plaintiff very serious injuries. Writ issued, statement of claim served November 1966; defence and request for particulars January 1967. Then nothing until plaintiff changed to other solicitors in September 1970. Application for legal aid: from November 1970 to April 1971 plaintiff's solicitors were obtaining statements: wrote to defendants' solicitors showing active steps being taken; in August 1971 they delivered the particulars asked for in 1967. Defendants' solicitors acknowledged their letters and said they looked forward to receiving a plan referred to in the particulars. In November 1971 they applied to dismiss for want of prosecution. The judge in chambers ordered dismissal.
HELD, ON APPEAL: The order was rightly made. The defendants' attitude in merely acknowledging letters and doing nothing did not amount to conduct conducing to the delay or acquiescing in it. Following *Allen v McAlpine* (p 637, above) to sit quiet and do nothing was not a waiver of rights which had accrued.

Note—See also *Steamship Mutual Underwriting Association Ltd v Trollope & Colls Ltd* (1985) 6 Con LR 11, 2 Const LJ 75; affd (1986) 33 BLR 77, 6 Con LR 11, 2 Const LJ 224, CA where May LJ criticised the practice of issuing a groundless writ as an abuse of the process of the court. He commented that no plaintiff should be surprised if a defendant took no steps to put an end to inanimate litigation, so that if a defendant, having received such a writ, did nothing to procure service of a statement of claim, 'the last vestige of life left the litigation's moribund carcass'.

Hayes v Bowman

[1989] 2 All ER 293, [1989] 1 WLR 456, 133 Sol Jo 569, [1989] 18 LS Gaz R 36, CA
The plaintiff was injured in a motor accident in August 1981. The writ was issued two and a half years later; liability was admitted but negotiations failed. On the defendant's eventual application, the district registrar struck out the case for want of prosecution in April 1987. The plaintiff successfully appealed; though the judge held that the plaintiff's advisers had been guilty of inordinate and inexcusable delay, the defendant had failed to show a sufficient degree of prejudice. The defendants appealed.
HELD: There was no justification for interfering with the exercise of the judge's discretion, but if the defendant had argued financial prejudice, as a result of the multiplicand being much larger in net terms in 1988 than in 1985 when the case should have been heard, because wages had increased at a faster rate than inflation, the court might have allowed the appeal, although the degree of financial prejudice varied from case to case and would usually be difficult to prove.

Note—See also *Newman v Hopkins* (1988) Times, 28 December, CA where an increase of 75% was held not to amount to serious prejudice.

Harwood v Courtaulds Ltd

(1993) 137 Sol Jo LB 52, 82, [1993] 12 LS Gaz R 32, CA
If a defendant acquiesced in the plaintiff's delay in prosecuting an action, he would be estopped from making an application to strike out notwithstanding the plaintiff's delay was inordinate and inexcusable.

Dismissed

Bostic v Bermondsey Management Committee

[1968] 2 QB 229, [1968] 1 All ER 543, [1968] 2 WLR 366, 112 Sol Jo 49, CA
Accident 25 September 1958. Solicitors instructed November 1958. Writ 21 February 1961. Statement of claim July 1961. Defendants asked for further and better particulars but did not deliver a defence. Plaintiff's solicitor struck off roll October 1962, but the plaintiff did not find out until August 1965 when she instructed another solicitor who pressed defendants for a defence. They asked for extensions but had still not delivered one when they applied to dismiss for want of prosecution in 1967.
HELD: The defendants' own conduct in not serving a defence and in inducing the plaintiff to incur costs in providing particulars was such as to debar them from being granted a dismissal of the action. Justice was not impossible because they still had all the records.

Hood v Concrete (Midlands) Ltd

(1968) 112 Sol Jo 844, CA
Accident 11 May 1963. Claim August 1964. Writ 5 April 1966. Defendants' insurers repeatedly answered plaintiff's inquiries by saying their inquiries were not yet complete. A technical report was not revealed by them to plaintiff's expert until 1967. Application to dismiss October 1968.
HELD: The insurers should have got on with the case. It did not lie in their mouths to apply for the action to be struck out.

Spriggs v Norrard Trawlers Ltd

[1969] 2 Lloyd's Rep 627, CA
Per Harman LJ: The overriding question is always whether justice can still be done despite delay in prosecuting a claim. There have been a great number of such cases in the past year or so and it is a pity they have got into the Law Reports, for each depends on its own particular facts. It is impossible to have a calender, so to say, and rule that 18 months is inordinate delay and 15 months is not. Except in very general terms no one case is an authority for another.

Akhtar v Harbottle (Mercantile) Ltd

(1982) 126 Sol Jo 643, Times, 4 August, CA
Writ for breach of contract issued and served March 1976. Plaintiff arrested and imprisoned in Burma April 1977. Case listed for hearing on 2 April 1979 but taken out of list on plaintiff's application and adjourned generally as he was still in prison. Application to dismiss July 1980 adjourned twice and heard on 20 April 1982 when plaintiff still in prison awaiting trial. Judge held defendants prejudiced and delay inexcusable.
HELD, ON APPEAL: The delay was not inexcusable as the plaintiff had given a complete excuse for it and the trial could not proceed without his evidence.

Dutton v Spink and Beeching (Sales) Ltd

[1977] 1 All ER 287, 120 Sol Jo 488, CA
Per Stamp LJ: The law, as I understand it, is this: The court in the exercise of its inherent jurisdiction, may dismiss an action on the ground of the plaintiff's delay in prosecuting it but will not do so unless the delay is inordinate, inexcusable and

prejudicial to a fair trial . . . but it does not follow because those conditions are satisfied the jurisdiction ought to be exercised as a matter of course. If one finds that, as the result of the passage of time, the recollection of witnesses is likely to be so dimmed that a fair trial of the action is likely to be prejudiced the temptation to dismiss the action is, I think, rather greater . . . but the court does not strike out an action merely on the ground that there has been such delay that the recollection of witnesses has become impaired. If it were so a multitude of actions would not be tried.

Sayle v Cooksey

[1969] 2 Lloyd's Rep 618, CA
Plaintiff injured January 1960. Defendant and his insurers then began an arbitration to determine whether the insurers were entitled to refuse indemnity. The plaintiff's solicitors, knowing of the dispute, waited to see the outcome. The award was not made until January 1966 and was in favour of the defendant whose insurers now said they were prepared to handle the claim. After some negotiations the plaintiff's solicitors did nothing from December 1966 to November 1967. In January 1968 they obtained counsel's opinion who advised a new medical examination. The doctor instructed did not produce a report until May 1969. Meanwhile in April 1969 the District Registrar made an order to dismiss for want of prosecution.
HELD, ON APPEAL: The action should not be dismissed. The delay from 1961 to 1966 while waiting for the defendant's arbitration to be decided was excusable. The delay from January 1968 was due to the doctor. The delay from December 1966 to November 1967 was inexcusable but had not given rise to any substantial risk that it would make a fair trial of the issues impossible nor would cause serious prejudice to the defendant.

STEP FATAL TO STRIKING OUT

Simpson v Smith

(1989) Times, 19 January, CA
The infant plaintiff was injured on 7 June 1976. A writ was issued on 21 September 1982 but little more was done until October 1987, when the plaintiff's new firm of solicitors served notice of intention to proceed, and pushed the action forward, setting it down for trial on 23 November 1987. The defendants' solicitors applied for a fixed date on 7 December 1987; on 17 March 1988, they issued a summons to dismiss the action because of inordinate and inexcusable delay. The limitation period expired on 1 June 1988. The defendants' solicitors served their summons to dismiss on 27 June.
HELD, ON APPEAL: The application failed. As a matter of principle, an attempt to strike out within the limitation period would have failed; the step taken, within that period, by the defendants' solicitors, in applying for a fixture, would have given the plaintiff the impression that the defendants were prepared to allow the action to proceed, Otherwise, the plaintiff would have issued a fresh writ within the limitation period. The timing of the application to strike out, coupled with the application to fix, meant that the defendants were not entitled to their order.

Reynolds v British Leyland Ltd

[1991] 2 All ER 243, [1991] 1 WLR 675, CA
The plaintiff's Statement of Claim for damages for personal injury was served in February 1985. The alleged incident occurred on 6 May 1981. On 21 July 1989 the

defendants applied to strike out the claim despite their opposition to and attendance at the plaintiff's summons to inspect the scene of the accident. On the facts the claim would be struck out, but as a general rule where the defendants' conduct was such that the plaintiff held a reasonable belief that the matter was to proceed to trial, the court had no discretion.

County and District Properties Ltd v Lyell

[1991] 1 WLR 683, CA
Although a plaintiff may be guilty of inordinate and inexcusable delay, the action will not be struck out, if the defendant's actions cause the plaintiff to incur further costs by proceedings on the assumption that the defendant intended to pursue the matter to trial.

Note—See also *Roche v Church* (1992) Times, 23 December, CA.

OR NOT FATAL

Armstrong v Glofield Properties

(1992) Independent, 17 January
The mere fact the plaintiff was put to expense in answering a request for further and better particulars served by the defendants did not in itself prevent the defendants from then seeking to strike out the claim for want of prosecution. It was for the plaintiff to show that their actions had given rise on his part to a reasonable belief that they acquiesced in the delay and anticipated the matter would proceed to trial.

Draper v Ferrymasters Ltd

(1993) Times, 10 February, CA
Even though the defendant had been a party to settlement negotiations and had made a payment into court, he was not prevented from applying to strike out.

Roebuck v Mungovin

[1994] 1 All ER 568, [1994] 2 WLR 290, [1994] 1 Lloyd's Rep 481
Even though the defendant had entered into further correspondence with the plaintiff's solicitors following a prolonged period of silence, it did not necessarily amount to acquiescence in the delay nor did it provide an absolute bar to any application to strike out for want of prosecution. It was one factor to be considered by the judge when exercising his discretion.

EFFECT OF DELAY BEFORE ISSUE OF WRIT

William Parker Ltd v Ham & Son Ltd

[1972] 3 All ER 1051, [1972] 1 WLR 1583, 116 Sol Jo 903, CA
Cause of action (breach of contract) April 1963. Writ issued December 1967. Pleadings closed December 1968; then no step by plaintiffs until notice of intention to proceed in February 1972.
HELD: Inordinate and inexcusable delay after issue of writ but no prejudice to the defendants by this delay because their situation from the point of view of getting information had not deteriorated since about 1969.

Per Buckley LJ: Delay before the issue of the writ in an action or before the action once commenced ceases to be actively or timeously pursued, may have a bearing on whether delay which follows thereafter is to be regarded as inordinate and inexcusable but cannot itself be inordinate or inexcusable delay. If the facts are such that no additional prejudice to the defendant has arisen as the result of delay after the end of that period in which delay can be said to be excusable it cannot be right in my judgment, for the court to dismiss the action.

Note—But see the following cases and *Birkett v James*, p 636, above.

Department of Transport v Chris Smaller (Transport) Ltd

[1989] AC 1197, [1989] 1 All ER 897, [1989] 2 WLR 578, 133 Sol Jo 361, HL
The defendant's lorry hit and damaged the plaintiff's motorway bridge in December 1978. A claim was made in writing in June 1982 and a writ issued in May 1984. The statement of claim was served in September 1985, but the plaintiff did little more, so the defendant issued the summons for directions in June 1986 and applied to strike out the action for want of prosecution in April 1987.
HELD, on the defendant's appeal: The application failed. Applying *Birkett v James* (p 636), the defendant had to show prejudice in the period since the writ was issued but here they could show only minimal prejudice because of the additional 13 months' delay. There could still be a fair trial and an order to strike out, simply as a disciplinary measure, would do no good. Per Lord Griffiths: A far more radical approach was required to tackle the problems of delay, including an overhaul of the whole civil procedural process and the introduction of court-controlled case management techniques to ensure compliance with a prescribed timetable.

Tabata v Hetherington

(1983) Times, 15 December, CA
'Inordinate' delay means a period of time which has elapsed which is materially longer than the time usually regarded by the courts and the profession as an acceptable period of time.

President of India and Union of India v John Shaw & Sons (Salford) Ltd

(1977) 121 Sol Jo 795, CA
Actions for damages were begun by writs in 1971 and 1972 on contracts alleged to have been breached several years earlier. Statements of claim were served in January 1972 but did not quantify the claim. Only in a postscript to a letter of 7 March 1974 did the plaintiffs' solicitors mention that the claim was 'in the region of £1m'. In October 1974 the plaintiffs said the action would proceed but on their giving notice of intention to proceed in May 1976 the defendants applied to dismiss.
HELD: They were entitled to have the action dismissed. *Birkett v James* (p 636, above) had made the decisive delay that which arose after the issue of the writ to cause prejudice but defective memory was only one cause of prejudice to be taken into account. It was a matter of great prejudice to a commercial concern like the defendants to have such unquantified claims hanging over their heads. Additional prejudice had been created by the delay since issue of the writs.

Abouchalache v Hilton International Hotels (UK) Ltd

(1982) 126 Sol Jo 857, Times, 15 November, CA
The plaintiff was badly injured in a bomb explosion at the Hilton Hotel, London, in 1975. He issued a writ but discontinued in 1976 so as to begin proceedings against the defendant's parent company in New York where damages would be higher. After three years of those proceedings, however, it was decided that England was the *forum conveniens* and the action was dismissed on the terms that the defendants would not plead the Limitation Act if an action was started before 12 December 1979. A writ was then issued in England before that date, but nothing more was done for two years. The defendants applied to have the action dismissed for want of prosecution.
HELD: The action should not be dismissed. The defendants, unlike those in the *Biss* case were part of a large international undertaking whose servants were not fearful of the outcome of the litigation. No records had been destroyed and there was no prejudice additional to any present at the time when the writ was issued within the agreed time limit.

Costellow v Somerset County Council

[1993] 1 All ER 952, [1993] 1 WLR 256, CA
Proceedings were issued by the plaintiff on 14 September 1990, one day before the expiry of the limitation period. The writ was served on the local authority claiming damages for personal injury on the 11 January 1991 just within the four months allowed by the rules. In the absence of the Statement of Claim, the defendants issued a summons to strike out on 24 May 1991. The application was granted by the district judge and upheld on appeal.

Reinstating the action, the Court of Appeal, could find no real risk of prejudice to the defendants. If, however, there had been procedural abuse, questionable tactics or other special circumstances, the court would take a rather different view. So too there was no justification for considering an application to strike out before a cross application to extend time for service of the defence and the proper approach would be to consider them together.

THIRD PARTY PROCEEDINGS

Hart v Hall and Pickles Ltd

[1969] 1 QB 405, [1968] 3 All ER 291, [1968] 3 WLR 744, 112 Sol Jo 786, CA
The plaintiff was injured in 1962 when unloading a lorry. He sued his employers who blamed haulage contractors and joined them as third parties. The plaintiff then joined the haulage contractors as second defendants. These steps were completed by July 1965. Nothing more was done and in March 1968 the second defendants successfully applied for an order dismissing the action against them for want of prosecution. The first defendants then made a similar application but it was refused. The action went on to trial where the third parties (formerly second defendants) claimed to be dismissed from the action on the ground that there could no longer be a claim against them for contribution under the Law Reform (Married Women and Tortfeasors) Act 1935 as they were parties who had been sued but were not liable, the action against them having been dismissed for want of prosecution.
HELD: The third parties were not entitled to be dismissed from the action. The words in s 6(1) 'who is, or would if sued have been, liable' mean sued to judgment. To be

exempted from contribution a person must have been sued to judgment and found not to be liable. When an action has been dismissed for want of prosecution the defendant has not been sued to judgment. It is only an interlocutory order, a matter of procedure, which does not affect substantive rights. The case as between the defendant and third parties must be tried as if there had been no dismissal at all.

Note—See also Civil Liability (Contribution) Act 1978, s 1(3).

CLAIM AND COUNTERCLAIM

Zimmer Orthopaedic Ltd v Zimmer Manufacturing Co

[1968] 2 All ER 309, [1968] 1 WLR 852, 112 Sol Jo 335 (Cross J)
In an action relating to trade marks and passing off neither party did anything for nearly five years after close of pleadings. Then the defendants applied to dismiss: the plaintiffs applied to dismiss the counter-claim.
HELD: It is for the plaintiff and his advisers to get on with the action and the defendant is normally under no duty to stimulate him into action, but in the circumstances of the present case the defendants having done nothing to secure that the counter-claim should be heard as soon as possible should not have an order to dismiss the claim unless they submitted to a similar order dismissing the counterclaim.

Janata Bank v Noor

(1983) Times, 18 November, CA
Although a defendant is in the same position in respect of pursuing a counter-claim as the plaintiff is in pursuing the main action he is not precluded thereby from applying to strike out the main action. *Zimmer*'s action (above) was not authority for precluding a counter-claiming defendant from applying to dismiss the main action for want of prosecution, though the plaintiff might equally succeed in an application to dismiss the counter-claim on the same grounds.

City of Westminster v Clifford Culpin & Partners and J Jarvis & Sons Ltd

[1987] NLJ Rep 736, CA
The plaintiffs engaged the first defendants, Culpin, as architects and the second defendants, Jarvis, as builders to erect two blocks of flats and an office block. On 28 September 1979 (the last day before the limitation period expired), the plaintiffs issued a writ against both Culpin and Jarvis. In December 1981 the statement of claim was served; Culpin served a defence in July 1982 and Jarvis in September 1982. Jarvis counterclaimed and also issued third party proceedings against Culpin. In December 1985 the plaintiffs served notice of intention to proceed. During January and February 1986 Culpin and Jarvis respectively issued summonses to strike out for want of prosecution. In July of 1987 the plaintiffs' claim against the defendants was struck out but they were given leave to issue third party proceedings against Culpin in Jarvis' surviving counterclaim. The plaintiffs appealed.
HELD: Appeal dismissed. Each defendant was entitled to have his position considered individually under the principles in *Birkett v James* (p 636). A claim and counterclaim did not necessarily stand or fall together in a striking out application. Culpin and Jarvis had been prejudiced by the death of a witness and had not caused nor contributed to the delay. The counterclaim was allowed to continue.

LIMITATION PERIOD NOT EXPIRED

Spring Grove Services Ltd v Deane

(1972) 116 Sol Jo 844, CA
Writ issued 7 October 1969 claiming £1,564 for hire of linen. After unsuccessful application for judgment under Ord 14 plaintiffs took no further step. October 1971 on defendant's application action dismissed for want of prosecution, defendant saying on affidavit that he had been told claim had been abandoned. November 1971 plaintiffs issued new writ for £1,564; defendant applied to strike out writ as an abuse of the court.
HELD: The second action should be struck out. Though a new action could be started on the same cause of action it was always subject to the inherent jurisdiction to dismiss it as an abuse of the court. In the present case the plaintiffs had given no explanation for the new claim; it was an attempt to resurrect something that was dead and buried.

Department of Health and Social Security v Ereira

[1973] 3 All ER 421, CA
The plaintiffs sued the defendant for £9,000 arrears of National Insurance contributions by writ issued 15 November 1967. Nothing more was done until April 1972 when the plaintiffs gave notice of intention to proceed. On defendant's application the action was struck out for want of prosecution. Plaintiffs then issued a new writ on 27 July 1972 for the proportion of the £9,000 not already statute-barred. Defendant applied to strike out second action as an abuse of the court.
HELD: It should not be struck out. *Spring Grove Services v Deane* did not mean that a second action would automatically be struck out. In that case there were good reasons for doing so. In the present case in which the defence was of the thinnest possible character and the defendant was not prejudiced in his defence there were not.

Note—In *Maxwell v Raeburn* (1973) 117 Sol Jo 527 in the Chancery Division, where the facts were somewhat similar to *Ereira*'s case, the second action was likewise allowed to continue. No reference was apparently made to either *Spring Grove Services v Deane* or *Ereira*'s case.

Janov v Morris

[1981] 3 All ER 780, [1981] 1 WLR 1389, 125 Sol Jo 641, CA
An action for breach of contract was dismissed for want of prosecution when the plaintiff failed, without giving any reason, to comply with a peremptory order of the court to issue a summons for directions. There were still four years of the limitation period remaining. He issued a new writ based on the same cause of action as the first.
HELD: Where an action had been struck out for failure to obey a peremptory order of the court, the court had a discretion to strike out the second action as being an abuse of the process of the court order under Ord 18, r 19(1)(d). Order accordingly.

Note—In *Palmer v Birks* [1985] NLJ Rep 1256 (where the plaintiff's claim was struck out in default of the master's order that the statement of claim should be served within seven days), the plaintiff issued a second writ within the limitation period, serving it after this period had expired but within the 12 months of its issue. The Court of Appeal struck out the second action as an abuse of the process because of the deliberate flouting of the peremptory order.

Bailey v Bailey

[1983] 3 All ER 495, [1983] 1 WLR 1129, 127 Sol Jo 551, CA
The plaintiff was injured in a motor accident on 28 September 1973 by her husband's negligent driving. She dealt personally with his insurers claiming damages for her injuries and accepted £325 in settlement, a sum substantially less than the value of her claim. Later she instructed solicitors who issued a writ against her husband on the 24 September 1976 for damages for his negligence. A defence was served pleading accord and satisfaction. The statement of claim was amended to allege fraudulent misrepresentation on the part of her husband's insurers in letters sent to her before the settlement. Some delay followed and in April 1980 the defendant issued an application to strike out for want of prosecution. The hearing being adjourned until August the plaintiff issued a new writ in July 1980 four days before the limitation period expired, against her husband and the insurers for fraudulent misrepresentation. On the 12 August 1980 the registrar dismissed the first action for want of prosecution. The defendants applied to strike out the second action as being an abuse of process.
HELD, by the Court of Appeal: There is a distinction in principle between a situation in which an action has been struck out for disobedience of an order of the court (as in *Janov v Morris*, above) and where an action has been dismissed for want of prosecution. The plaintiff may have failed in the first action to obey the rules of the court but she had issued her second writ quite lawfully within the limitation period. It was impossible to say that the second action constituted abuse of the process of the court. *Birkett v James* (p 636, above) and *Tolley v Morris* (below) applied. *Janov v Morris* distinguished.

Tolley v Morris

[1979] 2 All ER 561, [1979] 1 WLR 592, 123 Sol Jo 353, HL
The plaintiff was born on 12 November 1961; injured in an accident 21 May 1964. Writ issued 3 May 1967, served 20 April 1968; then nothing more done until notice of intention to proceed followed by statement of claim 19 August 1977. The defendant applied to have the action dismissed.
HELD: The Limitation Act 1939, s 22 as amended by the Limitation Act 1975 enabled the plaintiff to bring an action for personal injuries until 3 years after her eighteenth birthday, ie until 12 November 1982. The facts brought the case within the rule laid down in *Birkett v James* (p 636, above). If the action were dismissed the plaintiff could bring a fresh action and the defendant would be even more seriously prejudiced. *Biss v Lambeth* was distinguishable; in that case the court was dealing with cases (eg under the Limitation Act, s 2D) where the plaintiff had only a defeasible, not an absolute, right to begin a fresh action. The action should go on.

COUNTY COURT

Kirkpatrick v Salvation Army Trustee Co

[1969] 1 All ER 388, [1969] 1 WLR 1955, 112 Sol Jo 823, CA
In a personal injury action in the county court the defendant applied to the registrar to dismiss for want of prosecution. The registrar made an order accordingly but on appeal the judge held that though the registrar has power to strike out an action under

Ord 13, r 4(4) (now the County Court Rules 1981, Ord 13, r 3) there was no power in the county court to strike out an action for want of prosecution on an application by the defendants.
HELD, by the Court of Appeal: This was not right. There was no reason for thinking that because the court has power to act on its own motion to strike out an action the defendant should be deprived of making an application himself to dismiss for want of prosecution.

Kerr v National Carriers Ltd

[1974] 1 Lloyd's Rep 365, CA
Road accident July 1968. Letter before action June 1970, particulars of claim filed November 1970, defence three days later than action adjourned generally to allow defendant to join a third party. January 1971, leave to join third party then further adjournment. Hearing fixed by court for June 1972, but further adjournment when third party died; his executors were joined November 1972. Court gave notice in June 1973 of intention to strike out unless hearing date applied for. Hearing fixed for 9 August 1973 but adjournment again applied for by parties' consent on 2 August. On 9 August judge struck it out of his own motion.
HELD: Dismissing plaintiff's application for leave to appeal out of time from the judge's order, the delay had been quite shocking. In running down actions the memory of witnesses of matters which frequently happen in seconds deteriorates with the passing years. The rules of the court are there to be observed and parties cannot by mutual cordiality agree to prolong the trial by agreeing to adjournments in the interlocutory stage. There is a supervising duty vested in the court of scrutinising cases such as the present.

Rastin v British Steel plc

[1994] 2 All ER 641, [1994] 1 WLR 732, CA
The Court of Appeal was asked to decide whether the county court had jurisdiction to reinstate actions that had been automatically struck out under Ord 17, r 11 (9) of the County Court Rules 1981 due to the plaintiff's failure to request a trial date.
HELD: The court did have discretion to reinstate the plaintiff's action. To be successful, the plaintiff first had to establish that, apart from failure to comply with this rule, the case had been conducted with diligence. If that test was satisfied, then the court could consider the interests of justice generally including any prejudice to the defendant.

FOLLOWING INTERLOCUTORY COSTS ORDER

Teheran-Europe Co Ltd v S T Belton (Tractors) Ltd (No 2)

[1971] 2 QB 491, [1971] 2 All ER 1121, [1971] 2 WLR 1113, 115 Sol Jo 207, CA
In an action begun in 1959 preliminary issues were ordered to be tried and in 1967 were decided in favour of the plaintiffs, with costs ordered against the defendants. In 1968 an order was made for discovery. The plaintiffs then did nothing more and in 1969 the action was dismissed for want of prosecution. The defendants claimed that the plaintiffs were not entitled to tax the costs awarded to them in the interlocutory proceedings because (1) the dismissal of the action precluded any further step in the

action and taxation of costs was a step, and (2) loss of the costs was a part of the sanction against undue delay.

HELD: Neither contention could be accepted. There was no rule or authority that on dismissal of an action a party should be prohibited from taking any further step. Though dismissal was a sanction it was a heavy sanction in itself and there was no cause to add to it a forfeiture of an existing order for costs.

FAILURE TO COMPLY WITH ORDER

Pryer v Smith

[1977] 1 All ER 218, [1977] 1 WLR 425, 120 Sol Jo 839, CA

Accident 16 August 1971. Claim made 24 March 1972 by solicitors who, after some correspondence with defendant's insurers, ceased to act. The plaintiff then acted in person, issuing a writ on 8 August 1974 and serving statement of claim on 14 January 1975. Further and better particulars delivered 12 April 1975, defence served 18 June 1975. Order for directions 6 October 1975 required action to be set down in 56 days but it was not. Plaintiff instructed other solicitors on 31 December 1975 who came on the record in March 1976. Defendant issued summons to dismiss for want of prosecution on 23 March 1976; heard by district registrar on 20 April 1976 and order made to dismiss. Plaintiff's appeal to judge in chambers on 7 May 1976 was allowed, but conditionally upon the plaintiff setting action down for trial within 10 days and taking certain other steps within specified time limits, otherwise action dismissed. None of the steps ordered were complied with in time. On 25 May the defendant drew up the order dismissing the action. The plaintiff appealed to the judge on 2 July for extension of time limits but the judge held he had no jurisdiction to do so. The plaintiff appealed to the Court of Appeal against orders of 7 May and 2 July.

HELD: Even assuming the judge was wrong in holding he had no jurisdiction to extend time after the order of 7 May had been drawn up, he had correctly exercised his discretion on 7 May to dismiss the action if the time limits set down were not complied with. It was not correct, as the plaintiff maintained, that the judge must be satisfied before making such an order that there has been, not merely inordinate and inexcusable delay, but also the likelihood of serious prejudice to the defendant. The judge has jurisdiction in an application to dismiss for want of prosecution, if the circumstances in his view warrant it, to make an order which prescribes time conditions and to provide that on failure to take those further steps within the time limits the action shall be dismissed, even though he is not satisfied at that moment of time that there is a likelihood of serious prejudice to the defendant.

Re Jokai Tea Holdings Ltd

[1993] 1 All ER 630, [1992] 1 WLR 1196n, CA

If a party can show that there was no deliberate intention to ignore a pre-emptory order and that there were good reasons for their failure to do so, then the court would not seek to strike out the claim. If, however, the failure was intentional and contumacious there will be no relief granted.

Grand Metropolitan Nominee (No 2) Co Ltd v Evans (Practice Note)

[1993] 1 All ER 642, [1992] 1 WLR 1191
An action should not automatically be struck out where a party was in breach of an order. It was still necessary to show that the failure was intentional and contumelious.

Trial

SETTING DOWN

Note—See new RSC Ord 34, r 3(1) and CCR Ord 17, r 2.

BUNDLES

Note—See RSC Ord 34, r 10.

PLAN

Davey v Harrow Corpn

[1958] 1 QB 60, [1957] 2 All ER 305, [1957] 2 WLR 941, 101 Sol Jo 405, CA
Judicial notice may be taken of a practice of the Ordnance Survey.

Note—The order for directions in a motor accident case usually contains an order for a plan or sketch plan, which is usually agreed. In view of the above case, it seems possible that an ordnance map may be put in without evidence, but the practice will probably remain of submitting to the opponents for agreement. An ordnance map to scale of 50 inches to the mile is suitable for most cases. Such maps can be obtained from Edward Stansford Ltd, 12 Long Acre, London WC 2.

JUDGMENT

Note—See RSC Ord 35, r 2 for the effect of death of a party before judgment is given.

ADJOURNMENT

Green v Northern General Transport

(1970) 115 Sol Jo 59, CA
When a personal injury action was listed for hearing at assizes the judge refused an application by the defendants for the case to be stood out; they said a material witness was not then available. The action was heard and judgment was given for the plaintiff. HELD, ON APPEAL: If there was a material witness who was not available and whose presence was desirable the judge should grant an adjournment, where injustice would otherwise be done, provided that any injustice to the other party could be compensated in costs. There should be a new trial.

Renge v Collins

(1966) 110 Sol Jo 724, 116 NLJ 1061, CA
The plaintiff, who had a legal aid certificate with a nil contribution, sued in the county court for damages for personal injury alleged to have been sustained on the defendant's premises. On the day fixed for the hearing she could not face going to court and went to see her doctor. He gave her a certificate that she was suffering from nervous debility and was unable to attend court. She took it to her solicitors and then went off. At court where the defendant was ready with his witnesses to contest the case, the plaintiff's counsel produced the certificate and asked for an adjournment. The judge sent for the doctor, who gave evidence that the plaintiff was physically able to come to court but was unbalanced emotionally and might be just the same next time. On appeal it was said for the plaintiff that the judge should have granted either an adjournment or a non-suit.
HELD: The judge had rightly exercised his discretion in not adjourning the case, the defendant being present with all his witnesses. On the question of granting a non-suit, which would have enabled the plaintiff to reinstate the case on paying all the costs, it was for her counsel to elect to have a non-suit if she wanted it. She had a right to non-suit as was shown by *Clack v Arthur's Engineering Ltd* [1959] 2 QB 211. As her counsel had not exercised her right to make the election she could not now come to the Court of Appeal to seek an alteration of the order dismissing the action.

Joyce v King

(1987) Times, 13 July, CA
The plaintiffs alleged that damp was penetrating their property from the defendant's adjoining property. The defendant required legal aid to cover the fees of her expert witness, a surveyor, otherwise he would not attend court. He was crucial to her defence.The first hearing was adjourned; at the second, of which the defendant had known for some weeks, she had still not obtained legal aid. The recorder, who had set aside a full day for the hearing, dismissed the defendant's late application for an adjournment. She appealed.
HELD: The case should be remitted for a fresh hearing. Once an adjournment was refused there was no possibility of justice being done but if an adjournment had been granted the plaintiff's claim would remain. Questions of adjournment were essentially a matter of discretion for the judge, and the Court of Appeal should only interfere if the judge was wholly wrong. When an adjournment was required for justice to be done, it was to be granted even though it was highly inconvenient to do so.

SPLIT TRIAL

Coenen v Payne

[1974] 2 All ER 1109, [1974] 1 WLR 984, 118 Sol Jo 499, CA
Cars driven by the plaintiff and defendant collided head-on, injuring both. The plaintiff, a German veterinary surgeon, claimed heavy damages including large sums for potential loss of earnings. Trial would be likely to be extended by four days by the evidence on damages.The defendant counter-claimed in respect of his own injuries and applied for separate trials in the issues of liability and damages. The judge refused separate trials on the ground that the plaintiff was entitled to choose the normal method of trying liability and quantum at the same time.

HELD, ON APPEAL: This was not right. The Winn Committee had recommended a less restrictive approach to separate trials. Winn LJ himself had alluded to separate trials in *Hawkins*'s case. RSC Ord 33, r 4(2) gives the courts power to grant separate trials and they should be ready to do so wherever it is just and convenient. In the present case much time and expense in trying the issue of damages would be wasted if the plaintiff were to fail on the issue of liability. The plaintiff could not claim the right to choose merely by agreeing to pay for the extra expense. Appeal allowed.

JURY

Hope v Great Western Rly Co

[1937] 2 KB 130, [1937] 1 All ER 625, 106 LJKB 563, 156 LT 331, 53 TLR 399, 81 Sol Jo 198, CA
It is completely within the discretion of the judge to order an action to be tried with or without a jury.

Pease v George

[1960] 1 All ER 709n, [1960] 1 WLR 427, 104 Sol Jo 328, CA
An infant plaintiff claimed damages for injuries received in a road accident which he alleged was due to the defendant's negligence. In his summons for directions the plaintiff asked for an order that the trial should be with a jury. His injuries, according to the statement of claim, were such that he was a total invalid and would remain so mentally and physically for the rest of his life. The master ordered trial by judge alone and, on appeal, the judge in chambers upheld the master's order.
HELD, by the Court of Appeal: There might be much to be said for having a jury in so serious a case, but under RSC Ord 36, r 1(3) it is in the discretion of the Court or the judge to decide one way or the other and that is an absolute discretion. The master and judge in chambers had each refused a jury and there were no grounds for interfering. *Hope v Great Western Rly Co* followed.

Note—The present rule for determining the mode of trial is Ord 33, r 4. It omits para (3) of the former Ord 36, r 1, but the Court still has a discretion in making an order for mode of trial and the following cases are still effective. See Supreme Court Act 1981, s 69(3) and notes to Ord 33, r 5 in the *Supreme Court Practice*.

Hennell v Ranaboldo

[1963] 3 All ER 684, [1963] 1 WLR 1391, 107 Sol Jo 829, CA
The plaintiff claimed damages for injuries to his right leg including a fracture, a dislocation of the knee and amputation of two toes. He was off work six months but had made quite a good recovery. On the summons for directions the master made an order for trial by a jury: on appeal to the judge the order was upheld.

The Court of Appeal ordered trial by judge alone. It was an ordinary case of personal injuries. Though the matter was completely in the discretion of the judge (*Hope v Great Western Rly Co*, above) he had not properly exercised it, having indicated that he thought it desirable to have a case tried by jury occasionally as a sample. The court could therefore exercise its own discretion. Trial by judge alone has the advantages (1) that judges know the sort of scale of damages which are awarded in these cases: this secures uniformity and (2) that if a judge makes an award wholly out of proportion it can be corrected in the Court of Appeal; it could not be done so easily in the case of a jury award. Trial by jury causes costs for the parties and extra work for the public and was not warranted in these circumstances.

Sims v William Howard & Son Ltd

[1964] 2 QB 409, [1964] 1 All ER 918, [1964] 2 WLR 794, 108 Sol Jo 174, CA
The plaintiff suffered injury to his spinal cord in a factory accident as a result of which he was confined to a wheelchair. He applied for trial by jury and on appeal from the master the judge in chambers so ordered.
HELD, ON APPEAL: It was not correct that cases of serious injury were particularly suitable for trial by jury. In personal injury cases there should be some degree of uniformity. The judges have evolved a scale of awards which is well known, but it can never be applied by a jury since they cannot be told of it. *Hope v Great Western Rly Co* (above) did not mean that the discretion of the judge was so absolute that no appeal lay from it. It can be reviewed on appeal if he fails to take into account what ought to be taken into account. The principle of uniformity is so important that it is a relevant consideration for the judge to take into account: he must have failed to do so in this case and trial should be by judge alone.

Watts v Manning

[1964] 2 All ER 267, [1964] 1 WLR 623, 108 Sol Jo 257, CA
The plaintiff was injured when she was struck by a scooter ridden by the defendant. She began an action for damages for personal injuries. Her husband began a separate action for loss of consortium. The plaintiff's most serious injury was to her pelvis, causing, she alleged, inability to have sexual intercourse or conceive a child. On her application the master ordered trial by jury: in her husband's action he ordered trial by judge alone. On appeal in the plaintiff's action the judge in chambers decided it should also be tried by judge alone since the defendant ought to be entitled to consolidate the two actions and this would not be possible if there were different modes of trial; he also said there was a complicated medical issue fit for a judge alone. The plaintiff appealed. Immediately before the hearing of the appeal the husband discontinued his action.
HELD: The judge's decision should not be disturbed. In exercising the discretion there should, in fairness to both plaintiffs and defendants, be some accepted maxims which should be applied. In order to achieve uniformity, even in a case of serious injury, there should be trial by judge alone. The main disadvantages of jury trial are (1) extra time and expense; (2) impossibility of securing uniformity of awards; (3) no reference can be made to awards in similar cases; (4) difficulty in putting right a jury award on appeal; (5) unsuitability of jury for dealing with complicated issues. These factors should be borne in mind when a decision is to be made whether or not jury trial is to be ordered.

Ward v James

[1966] 1 QB 273, [1965] 1 All ER 563, [1965] 2 WLR 455, 109 Sol Jo 111, [1965] 1 Lloyd's Rep 145, CA
As a result of a road accident for which he alleged the defendant was to blame the plaintiff was a permanent quadriplegic, both arms and legs being paralysed. In July 1963 the master and, on appeal the judge in chambers, ordered trial by jury. In October 1964, following the reported decisions in *Sims v Howard* and *Watts v Manning* (above), the defendant applied for leave to appeal against the order out of time. The

Court of Appeal gave leave to appeal and decided that the appeal should be heard by the full court, the point not having been considered by a full court since *Hope v Great Western Rly Co* (p 653, above).

Judgment was delivered in the appeal by Lord Denning MR (the other members of the court concurring) dealing with the following matters:

Hope's case decided that the mode of trial was in the discretion of the court of a judge without being fettered by a *presumption of law* in favour of or against a jury.

The Court of Appeal can and will interfere with the discretion of the judge if it can see that the judge has given no weight (or not sufficient weight) to those considerations which ought to have weighed with him. Even if he has given no reasons, the court may infer he has gone wrong and reverse his decision.

In the great majority of personal injury cases trial by judge alone is acceptable to the parties. The judges set the standard for awards and thus there is uniformity of decision. If a party asks for a jury it is often because he has a weak case or desires to appeal to sympathy. Serious injuries have been said in the past to afford a good reason for ordering trial by jury but recent experience has led to doubts on this score. In very serious cases scales and conventional figures have been worked out by the judges which juries do not know of and cannot be told.

The lessons of recent cases are that three things are desirable: (a) assessability, ie, the award in very serious cases must basically be a conventional figure: (b) uniformity: unless similar decisions are given in similar cases there is dissatisfaction with and criticism of the administration of justice; (c) predictability: if awards are predictable with some measure of accuracy settlements are encouraged. None of these desiderata is achieved when damages are left at large to the jury.

The Court of Appeal can interfere with a jury award if it is 'out of all proportion to the circumstances of the case' and with a judge's award if it is 'a wholly erroneous estimate of the damage suffered'. In practice the court has been much less willing to interfere with a jury award than with a judge's. In future the court will not feel the same hesitation as it formerly did. If it is 'out of all proportion' it will be set aside and the court may order a new trial by judge alone, or, by consent of the parties, substitute its own figure.

Hodges v Harland and Wolff Ltd

[1965] 1 All ER 1086, [1965] 1 WLR 523, 109 Sol Jo 178, [1965] 1 Lloyd's Rep 181, CA

The plaintiff's injuries in an accident at work included the tearing off of the penis and of the scrotal skin. He applied for trial by jury but the master felt himself bound by authority to order trial by judge alone. On appeal the judge in chambers considered the cases and the principle of uniformity but nevertheless thought it was a case for a jury and so ordered. On appeal to the Court of Appeal, held, the judge had taken into account all the considerations he ought to bear in mind and none that he should not, there was no ground for disturbing this exercise of his discretion.

Per Lord Denning MR: It is a mistake to suppose *Ward v James* took away the right to trial by jury . . . What *Ward v James* did do was this: it laid down the considerations which should be borne in mind by a judge when exercising his discretion, and it is apparent that, on those considerations, the result will ordinarily be trial by judge alone. It will not result in trial by jury save in exceptional circumstances . . . I think the judge was well entitled to take the view that this was an exceptional case.

Note—See *H v Ministry of Defence* [1991] 2 All ER 834 where the Court of Appeal expressed the view that juries were not generally to be used in personal injury actions.

SHORTHAND NOTE

Theocharides v Joannou

[1953] 2 All ER 52, [1955] 1 WLR 296, 99 Sol Jo 205 (Roxburgh J)
A judge has a right to require a shorthand note which is unlettered subject to appeal to the Court of Appeal. His discretion is not affected by the Legal Aid (General) Regulations, reg 14(3). Case adjourned until transcript available.

Dixon v City Veneering Mills Ltd

[1953] 2 All ER 1112 n, [1953] 1 WLR 1369, 97 Sol Jo 780, CA
It is the duty of parties to consider whether it is enough for part only of the transcript of the shorthand note of the evidence to be copied and not the whole. Certain of the costs may be disallowed.

Costs

WHERE THERE ARE CO-DEFENDANTS

Bullock Order

Bullock v London General Omnibus Co

[1907] 1 KB 264, 76 LJKB 127, 95 LT 905, 23 TLR 62, 50 Sol Jo 66, CA
Where the plaintiff claims damages for personal injuries against two companies for their joint negligence or alternatively against each of them for its negligence, there is jurisdiction to order the plaintiff to pay the costs of the successful defendant and recoupment to the plaintiff by the unsuccessful defendant.

Note—The note to RSC Ord 62, r 2 in the *Supreme Court Practice 1988,* p 934, 62/4/46 includes the following:

Co-defendants
Where a plaintiff sues two defendants, making his claim against them in the alternative, and succeeds only against one of them, the court in its discretion may order the unsuccessful defendant to pay the successful defendant's costs. This may be done either by an order that the unsuccessful defendant pay the successful defendant's costs direct to him (known as a 'Sanderson Order' from *Sanderson v Blyth Theatre Co* [1903] 2 KB 533, CA) or by an order that the plaintiff pay the successful defendant's costs to him and recover them from the unsuccessful defendant as part of the plaintiff's costs of the action (known as a 'Bullock Order' from *Bullock v London General Omnibus Co* [1907] 1 KB 264, CA). The form of order is in the discretion of the Court (*Meyer v Harte* [1960] 2 All ER 840, [1960] 1 WLR 770) and the term 'Bullock Order' has often been used to describe both forms of order. A Sanderson order has been considered to be appropriate where the plaintiff was likely to be insolvent, per Jessel MR in *Rudow v Great Britain Mutual Life Assurance Soc* (1881) 17 Ch D 600, at 608.

Mayer v Harte

[1960] 2 All ER 840, [1960] 1 WLR 770, 104 Sol Jo 603, CA
The plaintiff brought an action for damages against two defendants of whom one paid into court £15. The plaintiff did not accept the payment and later joined a third defendant who, unknown to her, was an undischarged bankrupt. At the trial she obtained judgment for £20 10s against the third defendant, the first and second

defendants succeeding in their defence. The judge awarded the first and second defendants' costs against the plaintiff, such costs to be added to the plaintiff's costs recoverable from the third defendant (a Bullock Order). He refused to order the first and second defendants' costs to be paid by the third defendant direct (a Sanderson Order).

HELD, by the Court of Appeal. There was no principle which required that the judge must necessarily order that the successful defendants should recover their costs direct from the unsuccessful defendant. The matter was one for the discretion of the court provided that the discretion was judicially exercised.

Besterman v British Motor Cab Co Ltd

[1914] 3 KB 181, 83 LJKB 1014, 110 LT 754, 30 TLR 319, 58 Sol Jo 319, CA
Plaintiff was injured as a result of a collision between a motor cab and an omnibus. He sued and recovered against the cab company and failed against the bus company. The cab company before trial had notified the bus company, but not the plaintiff, that they blamed the bus company; they did not blame them in their defence, but did at the trial.

HELD: The plaintiff was entitled to a Bullock Order. The fact that there were two people and either might have been liable makes it reasonable for a plaintiff to join both defendants. A defendant should not be joined unreasonably. If it is reasonable to be in a state of uncertainty and to join both defendants, the costs of both defendants are costs in the action. The test is whether there are reasonable grounds for suing both defendants.

Wickens v Associated Portland Cement Manufacturers Ltd

[1951] 1 Lloyd's Rep 162 (Cassels J)
The test is whether plaintiff was reasonable in issuing a writ against both defendants.

QBE Insurance (UK) Ltd v Mediterranean Insurance

[1992] 1 All ER 12, [1992] 1 WLR 573, [1992] 1 Lloyd's Rep 435
Where a payment into court by one defendant is accepted by the plaintiff pursuant to Ord 62, r 5(4), the costs recoverable by the plaintiff are limited to those incurred in pursuing that defendant and there is no automatic entitlement to the costs of pursuing the other defendants.

Sanderson Order

Rudow v Great Britain Mutual Life Assurance Society

(1881) 17 Ch D 600, 50 LJCh 504, 44 LT 688, CA
Under the Judicature Acts it is no longer necessary to order a plaintiff to pay the costs of a defendant and have them over against another defendant so that if the second defendant is insolvent the plaintiff loses them. The proper form of order now is to order defendant who is liable to them as between himself and his co-defendant to pay them to the co-defendant.

Sanderson v Blyth Theatre Co

[1903] 2 KB 533, 72 LJKB 761, 89 LT 159, 52 WR 33, 19 TLR 660, CA (Stirling LJ)
The proper form of order was laid down in *Rudow*'s case. I think this practice ought to be adhered to wherever it is practicable to do so.

Ryan v T F Maltby Ltd

[1954] 1 Lloyd's Rep 196 (Hilbery J)
The courts have adopted the procedure of the *Sanderson* case and not the Bullock Order. The successful defendant then has a right to be heard on taxation of their costs and this is not left to the plaintiff.

No Bullock Order

Won Kwok Hong v A and R Brown Ltd

[1948] 1 KB 515, [1948] 1 All ER 185, 64 TLR 132, 92 Sol Jo 124, CA
The plaintiff acting on the old Ord XVI, r 7 (now revoked), that where a plaintiff is in doubt whom to sue, he may sue two or more defendants, sued two defendants. The judge found for the plaintiff against one defendant but in favour of the other defendant. He awarded plaintiff costs against the unsuccessful defendant, and the successful defendant costs against the plaintiff but did not order the unsuccessful defendant to pay the costs of the successful defendant to the plaintiff. In the case of *Besterman v British Motor Cab Co Ltd* (p 657, above), the unsuccessful defendant had contended in the correspondence that the successful defendant was partly to blame although the plaintiff had not been told of the contention, and the judge made a Bullock Order.

By the Supreme Court of Judicature (Consolidation) Act 1925, s 31, there is no right of appeal on a matter of costs only without the leave of the court or a judge. The judge did not give leave.

The plaintiff contended he had a right of appeal without leave on the ground that costs are a matter of discretion and the discretion had not been really exercised, (1) due to the failure to act as a judge should act, ie judicially, or (2) there were no materials on which he could exercise discretion.
HELD: *Besterman*'s case did not entitle a plaintiff in this position as of right to a Bullock Order. Order XVI, r 7, had nothing to do with costs, and acting on it did not entitle the plaintiff to any special order as to costs. It only decided that the judge had a discretion. There was no failure to act judicially and there was material on which to exercise discretion. The appeal failed for want of leave to appeal.

Note—The Supreme Court of Judicature (Consolidation) Act 1925 has been repealed.

Partial order

Keating v Channel Shipping Ltd

[1961] 1 Lloyd's Rep 264 (Winn J)
The plaintiff issued proceedings against the first defendants for damages for personal injuries. The first defendants denied liability and blamed Astridge & Sons. The plaintiff joined the latter as second defendants only two and a half months before the three-year limitation period expired. The plaintiff failed against the first defendants but succeeded against the second, who in their defence had not blamed the first. He was ordered to bear the first defendants' costs up to joinder of the second defendants, thereafter a Bullock Order for the recovery of the first defendants' costs from the second defendants.

Bankamerica Finance Ltd v Nock

[1988] AC 1002, [1988] 1 All ER 81, [1987] 3 WLR 1191, 131 Sol Jo 1699, HL
The first defendant was the hirer of a car from the plaintiffs, a finance company, under a hire-purchase agreement. The plaintiffs had bought the car from dealers, the second defendants. After some months the car was discovered to have been stolen from the original owners and was repossessed by the police. The plaintiffs sued for the balance of the hire charges; the first defendant pleaded in defence that the plaintiffs had no title to the car and counterclaimed for return of the hire payments already made. The dealers had meanwhile gone into liquidation and did not appear. The plaintiffs' claim failed against the first defendant but succeeded against the second defendants: the first defendant succeeded in his counterclaim against the plaintiffs. The effect of this was that the first defendant would receive £8,000 damages from the plaintiffs who, because the second defendants were insolvent, would be unable to obtain the £23,000 awarded to them.

On costs the judge made a Sanderson Order, ie no order as to costs as between the plaintiffs and the first defendant but an order that the second defendants should pay all the costs of both the plaintiffs and first defendant. Thus as the second defendants were insolvent the plaintiffs and first defendant could recover no costs at all. The first defendant sought leave to appeal against the order for costs on the ground that the judge had not exercised judicially his discretion as to costs. The Court of Appeal refused to entertain the application on the ground that the decision was within the judge's discretion and therefore an appeal was precluded by s 18(1)(f) of the Supreme Court Act 1981. The first defendant appealed against this refusal to the House of Lords.

HELD, ON APPEAL: On applying the principles derived from the authorities by the Court of Appeal in *Scherer v Counting Instruments Ltd* [1986] 2 All ER 529 and having regard to the relative hardships to the plaintiffs and first defendant of respectively a Bullock or a Sanderson Order it could not be said that the judge did not exercise his discretion judicially in making a Sanderson Order.

HIGH COURT/COUNTY CONSEQUENCES OF CHOSING WRONG JURISDICTION

High Court costs refused

Finch v Telegraph Construction and Maintenance Co

[1949] 1 All ER 452, 65 TLR 153, [1949] WN 57, 93 Sol Jo 219 (Devlin J)
A workman sustained an injury to his eye. Two months later the eye became inflamed and painful, and a medical report to his solicitors said it was obviously a very serious matter. The plaintiff recovered £10.

HELD: No 'sufficient reason' for bringing action in High Court to justify costs on High Court scale under the County Courts Act 1934, s 47(3)(a). Costs awarded on county court scale.

Matarazzo v Kent Area Health Authority

(1983) 127 Sol Jo 393, CA
When a minimum award of damages to entitle costs on the High Court scale was £1,200 the plaintiff was awarded £1,000 damages plus interest agreed at £225. He claimed costs on the High Court scale.

HELD: The Law Reform (Miscellaneous Provisions) Act 1934, s 3(1C) as added by the Administration of Justice Act 1969, s 22 showed that interest should be disregarded. The plaintiff was not entitled to High Court costs.

Note—In respect of county court cases the Law Reform (Miscellaneous Provisions) Act 1934 s 3(1C) was replaced by the County Courts Act 1959, s 97A, added by the Administration of Justice Act 1982. Subsection (8) retained the effect of s 3(1C) of the 1934 Act. The County Courts Act 1959, s 97A has been replaced without amendment by the County Courts Act 1984, s 69.

When High Court costs recoverable

Hopkins v Rees and Kirby Ltd

[1959] 2 All ER 352, [1959] 1 WLR 740, 103 Sol Jo 509 (Glyn-Jones J)
Plaintiff, a steel erector, sued his employers for damages for negligence in respect of an accident at work on 20 November 1955. Writ was issued on 6 May 1957. The defence included a contention of contributory negligence. On 25 November 1957, trial was ordered at Glamorgan. In March 1958 defendants paid into court £250 and plaintiff served notice of acceptance within the prescribed time. The plaintiff applied for costs on the High Court scale.
HELD: The question is, is the court satisfied that at the time the writ was issued it was then obvious that it was a county court action, or was it an action which, when tried by one judge, rather than another, and leaving out any question of contributory negligence, might have resulted in an award exceeding £400. Looking at the medical evidence and no more, I am unable to say that it should have been quite clear to the plaintiff as a reasonable man that no judge would award more than £400 for that injury.

I do not accept the contention of the defendants that regard should be had to all matters that were in dispute in the action, including medical evidence and the circumstances in which the accident happened.

UNSATISFACTORY CONDUCT OF ACTION

Chetland v Babcock and Wilcox Ltd

(1966) 110 Sol Jo 430 (Blain J)
The plaintiff was injured at work and claimed damages against the defendants. In correspondence the plaintiff's solicitors alleged that the hospital notes supported the diagnosis of their client's doctor, but on being asked by the defendant's solicitors to grant access to those notes they refused. On the issue of liability the plaintiff's solicitors had statements about the accident from witnesses who would not give statements to the defendants, being prevented, it was said, by the shop steward of the plaintiff's trade union. The defendants denied liability and made no payment into court. At the hearing the witnesses gave evidence about the accident and the defendants then admitted liability. The hospital notes only partially supported the doctor's diagnosis. The plaintiff was awarded £455 but the defendants opposed his application for costs of the whole action.
HELD: He should have only 75% of his costs. The combination of circumstances on the medical aspects and the question of proof of liability in this case was very unsatisfactory. It was wrong that litigation should be conducted as warfare, since it made a mockery of the opportunity to use the machinery of payment into court. That

machinery was a way not only of saving costs but often a good method of ensuring that an unfortunate injured plaintiff received a fair sum of money very much sooner than by a hearing.

Note—See also *Vose v Barr* p 558, above.

H A (Harold) v Pack (David) & Sons

[1993] CLY 3191 (Kettering County Court)
The plaintiff brought proceedings against the defendant for damages arising out of a motor traffic accident. The case was referred to arbitration. After the commencement of proceedings, the defendant served on the plaintiff a statement from an independent witness which supported the defendant's case. Ten days before the hearing, the plaintiff served a Notice of Discontinuance. The defendant applied to the court for costs on the basis that the plaintiff had discontinued late in the day and had commenced proceedings which had no prospects of success.
HELD: The defendant's claim for costs was dismissed. The plaintiff's solicitors had acted sensibly in discontinuing the proceedings before the hearing. Time had to be allowed for instructions and advice taken on the contents of the defendant's independent witness statement. The test whether a person acted unreasonably in commencing proceedings was based on knowledge at the time that proceedings were commenced. At that time, the plaintiff was unaware of the independent witnesses' evidence.

ORDER AGAINST SOLICITOR PERSONALLY

Sinclair-Jones v Kay

[1988] 2 All ER 611, [1989] 1 WLR 114, 133 Sol Jo 220, CA
The plaintiff sued in the Liverpool County Court on 27 January 1987; proceedings were served by post on the defendant's solicitors on 29 January, with a notice that the plaintiff was legally aided. On 3 March the plaintiff signed judgment in default of defence and 1 May was fixed for the assessment of damages. On 29 April the defendant's solicitors stated that they were seeking to set aside the judgment and that the defendant had obtained legal aid, although the issue of a legal aid certificate had been notified to them on 13 March. On 1 May the application to set aside judgment failed and judgment was entered for the plaintiff. The usual order for costs on the judgment and for those thrown away on the unsuccessful application could not be made because the defendant was legally aided. The plaintiff therefore sought an order that her costs be paid by the defendant's solicitors personally under RSC Ord 62, r 11.
HELD: The defendant's solicitors should pay. To make such an order no longer requires a finding of gross misconduct. Order 62, r 11 of the Rules of the Supreme Court refers to payment of costs incurred unreasonably or improperly or wasted by the failure to conduct proceedings with reasonable competence and expedition. What is reasonable depends on the circumstances of each case but here the defendant's solicitors' failure to apply promptly to set aside the judgment and to tell the plaintiff's solicitors, in mid-March, that legal aid had been granted, resulted in the waste of the costs of the hearing on 1 May, which they should pay.

Note—See RSC Ord 62, rr 10 and 11 generally.

COSTS BASIS

Standard basis

Indemnity basis

Note—The rules for taxation of costs have been entirely revised, so that since 1986 neither party and party nor common fund bases exist. Now, costs are taxed on either a standard basis (which means a reasonable amount in respect of all costs reasonably incurred and any doubts (as to the question of reasonableness) shall be resolved in favour of the paying party) or an indemnity basis (which means all costs except insofar as they are of an unreasonable amount or have been unreasonably incurred and any doubts (as to questions of reasonableness) shall be resolved in favour of the receiving party). Neither is broadly comparable to the previous categories; both seem likely to reduce the proportion of irrecoverable costs. As the names imply, standard basis will apply unless there is a specific order or agreement for indemnity basis costs (although indemnity basis will almost always apply between a client and his solicitor, whose costs the client is taxing). A wholly new RSC Ord 62 has been implemented by SI 1986/632. The relevant rule is r 12, to be found at p 967 of vol I of the *Supreme Court Practice 1988*.

Old rules

Layzell v British Portland Cement Manufacturers Ltd

[1961] 1 All ER 244, [1961] 1 WLR 557, 105 Sol Jo 322
In a case in which he was asked to exercise his discretion under sub-rule (3) Paull J dealt with the meaning of 'common fund basis' as follows:

'A query which arises under para (4) of r 28 is whether that means that costs which are taxed on a common fund basis are taxed on what used to be known as solicitor and client basis, or on what used to be known as solicitor and own client basis. As far as I can see and understand the matter, it seems to me that that rule lays down that if costs are taxed on a common fund basis, they should be taxed on the same basis as costs were taxed before the rule came into force if the order made was that costs should be taxed on a solicitor and client basis. Although there is talk of common fund, and although submission has been made that it may be that the use of those words would entail taxation on a solicitor and own client basis. I do not so read the rules. I cannot govern the taxing master, but I think that I ought to indicate that in my judgment, under para (4) of r 28, taxation on the common fund basis is really the same as taxation on the old solicitor and client basis.'

EMI Records Ltd v Ian Cameron Wallace Ltd

[1983] Ch 59, [1982] 2 All ER 980, [1982] 3 WLR 245, 126 Sol Jo 465
On an application for a review of costs on an indemnity basis, the court's conclusions included the following:
1 The Judicature Act 1925, s 50(1) gave the court a wide discretionary power over costs which had not been cut down by Ord 62, r 28 so as to confine the court to making orders only on a party and party basis or the common fund basis and no other basis.
2 The court had power to order the payment of costs on an indemnity basis, the result being that all the costs incurred would be allowed except those unreasonably incurred or of an unreasonable amount, and is applying those exceptions, the receiving party would be given the benefit of the doubt.

Taxation

Zaniewski v Scales

(1969) 113 Sol Jo 525, Times, 28 June (Chapman J)
An agreement by an insurance company with solicitors to pay 'your reasonable costs' is an agreement to pay 'your costs to be taxed if not agreed'.

Hosie v Malcolm

[1966] LS Gaz R 404 (McNair J)
In an action arising from a road accident the second defendants, a bus company, briefed leading counsel. The first defendant was man of straw. The second defendants were successful and were awarded costs to be taxed as between party and party. The taxing master allowed the costs of briefing leading counsel on the ground that the plaintiff had only to establish a scintilla of negligence against the second defendants to saddle them with all the damages and all the costs, a liability running well into four figures, with only a worthless remedy over against the first defendant.
HELD, on a review by the judge: It was not a case which justified allowing the fee of leading counsel on a party and party taxation. The taxing master's grounds were not apposite because if the second defendants had been sued alone they would have been exposed to exactly the same risk. There was no complex problem in the case and it was the kind of case commonly dealt with by junior counsel. Appeal allowed.

Interest on costs

Note—In *Hunt v RM Douglas (Roofing) Ltd* [1988] 3 All ER 823 the House of Lords held that a litigant who has been awarded costs is entitled to interest on those costs from the date of judgment or order (the incipitur rule) rather than from the date of issue of the taxing master's certificate (the allocatur rule). The House of Lords so held when finding that the cases of *K v K* (divorce costs: interest) [1977] Fam 39 and *Erven Warnink BV v J Townend & Sons (Hull) Ltd (No 2)* [1982] 3 All ER 312 were wrongly decided, being based upon a misunderstanding of the nature of an amendment to the Rules of the Supreme Court in 1965. It followed that *Boswell v Coaks* (1887) 57 LJ Ch 101, CA was correct.

See also *Pauls Agriculture Ltd v Smith*: [1993] 3 All ER 122 if there is a lengthy delay in lodging a bill for taxation part of the costs can be disallowed, the effect of which may be to deprive the successful party of interest (RSC Ord 62, r 28(4)(b)(ii)).

DISCLOSURE TO COURT DURING TRIAL OF INSURANCE POLICY

Gowar v Hales

[1928] 1 KB 191, [1927] All ER Rep 631, 96 LJKB 1088, 137 LT 580, CA
It is an established rule of practice that, in an action for personal injuries, the fact that the defendant is insured should not be disclosed to the jury, and it is within the discretion of the judge to discharge the jury and order the plaintiff to pay costs.

Note—See also *Askew v Grimmer* (1927) 43 TLR 354; *Wright v Hearson* [1916] WN 216; *Grinham v Davies* [1929] 2 KB 249, 98 LJKB 703, 139 LT 379, 44 TLR 523, 72 Sol Jo 303, Div Ct; *Jones v Birch Bros Ltd* [1933] 2 KB 597, [1933] All ER Rep 251, 102 LJKB 746, 149 LT 507, 49 TLR 586, CA. As appears from the following cases the 'established rule of practice' is virtually a dead letter, even in those rare cases tried before a jury.

Morey v Woodfield

(1961) Times, 12 July, [1961] CLY 2333
The plaintiff, a child of nine, suffered a dislocation of the cervical vertebrae causing complete paralysis of her body and legs and almost complete paralysis of her arms. Little improvement could be expected in her condition. Her injuries were received in a motor accident for which the defendant admitted liability. Her action for damages was tried by a judge sitting with a jury who awarded her £50,000. In his summing-up the judge (Glyn-Jones J) said: 'I am not going to be bound by the old-fashioned rule which has long out-lived its usefulness and pretend these damages are going to be paid by the defendant. They are not and you all know it.'

Harman v Crilly

[1943] KB 168, [1943] 1 All ER 140, 112 LJKB 224, 168 LT 42, 59 TLR 96, 87 Sol Jo 76, CA
The plaintiff brought an action against the driver Crilly, and the owners, A W Robey Ltd, of a motor vehicle for damages for personal injuries. Both defendants issued a third-party notice claiming indemnity against the insurers of the motor vehicle. The insurers contended the policy was issued to A W Robey, who had assigned his business, including the vehicle, to the limited company, and therefore the policy was not available to the defendants. The insurers contended that the disclosure of the insurance would prejudice or embarrass the fair trial of the action.
HELD: The rule of practice of non-disclosure of insurance to a jury (*Gowar v Hales* [1928] 1 KB 191; *Jones v Birch Bros Ltd* [1933] 2 KB 597; and *Carpenter v Ebblewhite* [1939] 1 KB 347, [1938] 4 All ER 41, 108 LJKB 110, 159 LT 564, 55 TLR 17, 82 Sol Jo 889, CA) does not apply to trial by judge alone. It was left open whether it still applies in jury trials of motor cases since the Road Traffic Acts.

Note—See *Morey v Woodfield*, above.

Murfin v Ashbridge and Martin

[1941] 1 All ER 231, CA
Although the insurers have control over the proceedings, they are not parties to the action and cannot therefore make an application in their own name.

Note—And see *Semtex Ltd v Gladstone* [1954] 2 All ER 206, [1954] 1 WLR 945, 98 Sol Jo 438.

SCALE OF COSTS

Note—See County Court (Amendment) (No 3) Rules 1991, SI 1991/1328 brought into force from the 1 July 1991.

CLAIM AND COUNTERCLAIM

Medway Oil and Storage Co Ltd v Continental Contractors Ltd

[1929] AC 88, 98 LJKB 148, 140 LT 98, 45 TLR 20, HL
When a claim and counter-claim are both dismissed with costs, upon the taxation of the costs, the true rule is that the claim should be treated as if it stood alone, and the

counter-claim should bear only the amount by which the costs of the proceedings have been increased by it. No costs not incurred by reason of the counter-claim can be costs of the counter-claim. In the absence of special directions by the court there should be not apportionment. The same principle applies where both the claim and the counter-claim have succeeded.

Note—In motor accident cases where there is injury or damage suffered by both parties and liability is in dispute it may be important on the question of costs to choose whether to proceed by way of claim or counter-claim.

Cinema Press Ltd v Pictures and Pleasures Ltd

[1945] KB 356, [1945] 1 All ER 440, 172 LT 295, 61 TLR 282, CA
Defendants paid into court £25, with denial of liability. Plaintiffs recovered £5. The judge awarded costs to the plaintiffs and gave defendants costs on the issue of damages after payment in.

The taxing master allowed nothing to defendants on the ground that there is no apportionment in issue cases.
HELD: The principles of costs of claim and counter-claim laid down in *Medway Oil & Storage Co v Continental Contractors* (above) applied. There is no apportionment, but a division of some items common to the issue of negligence and the issue of damages, eg brief fee, instructions for brief, discovery and correspondence. There is jurisdiction to award to one side such proportion of the costs as the judge thinks fair. This is the simplest way and simplicity is desirable.

Lowther v Lewin

(1964) 109 Sol Jo 33 (Sachs J)
In an action arising from a road accident the plaintiff was found 30% to blame and awarded £1,323; the defendant was found 70% to blame and on his counter-claim was awarded £103. Each party was insured against third-party risks. The plaintiff supported by the defendant applied to the Court not to exercise its discretion under Ord 15, r 2(4) to give judgment for the plaintiff for the balance of £1,220 but to give judgment for both parties with appropriate costs so as to avoid difficulties in apportioning costs between the insurance companies.

The judge said he saw no objection: judgment for the plaintiff for £1,323 with costs of the action save in so far as they were increased by the counter-claim; judgment for the defendant for £103 with such costs as were solely referable to the counter-claim.

COSTS ON DISMISSAL OF APPEAL AND CROSS APPEAL

The Stentor

[1934] P 133, [1934] All ER Rep 545, 103 LJP 105, 152 LT 450, 18 Asp MLC 490, CA
When an appeal and cross-appeal are dismissed with costs, the principle of no apportionment laid down as to claim and counter-claim in the Medway case is applicable.

Per Scrutton LJ: The matter is not to be dealt with by apportionment. Only those extra costs which are occasioned by the cross-appeal are the subject-matter of the order for costs on the cross-appeal.

EXERCISE OF JUDGE'S DISCRETION

Jones v McKie and Mersey Docks and Harbour Board

[1964] 2 All ER 842, [1964] 1 WLR 960, 108 Sol Jo 442, CA
The plaintiff's vehicle was damaged by the second defendant's vehicle owing to the negligent driving of the first defendant, a servant of the second defendants, whose defence was that he was not acting in the scope of his employment at the time of the collision. The action was brought in the Liverpool Court of Passage. The evidence at the trial showed that when the accident occurred the first defendant had been using his employers' vehicle to return home for his house key which he would need when he had finished work. He gave evidence that the second defendants did not forbid drivers to take their vehicles when going home to dinner and that he and other drivers did so. The judge held that the first defendant was not acting in the scope of his employment at the time of the accident and gave judgment for the second defendants against the plaintiff. He refused to award them costs against the plaintiff on the ground that they exercised no proper control over the use of their vehicles by the drivers. On appeal, held, an appeal on costs was permissible only on the same principle as is provided by the Supreme Court of Judicature (Consolidation) Act 1925, s 31(1)(h), namely, that the Court of Appeal must be able to say that the judge in the court below, however much he may have been purporting to exercise his discretion, has not really exercised his discretion at all, that is, by taking into consideration wholly extraneous and irrelevant matters. It was impossible to say in the present case that, in thinking the second defendants' failure to control their transport was reprehensible, the judge proceeded on grounds which were wholly unconnected with the cause of action. He did exercise his discretion, however wrongly, and it was not open to the Court of Appeal to interfere.

INFANT'S COSTS—TAXATION

Note—This is now dealt with in the note to RSC Ord 80, 12 (16) in the *Supreme Court Practice 1993* p 1364.

TAXATION

Marks v King's College Hospital Medical School

(10 May 1991, unreported)
An application to extend time for lodging a bill of costs for taxation would only be refused if there had been inordinate, inexcusable and prejudicial delay.

PAYMENT INTO COURT

Corby District Council v Holst & Co Ltd

[1985] 1 All ER 321, [1985] 1 WLR 427, 129 Sol Jo 172, CA
The defendants wrote a letter headed 'Without prejudice' to the plaintiffs offering a sum of money in full and final settlement of the action and sought an interlocutory order that the offer be treated for all purposes as a payment into Court pursuant to RSC Ord 22, r 1. The Official Referee declined to make an order.

HELD, ON APPEAL: It was questionable whether the court had any jurisdiction to make such an order but even if it had, the Official Referee was right to refuse to make an order. Costs were by statute left to the discretion of the judge which had to be exercised in accordance with the rules. Whether such an offer as the one in the present case was to be treated as a payment into court was itself a matter for the trial judge and could not be legislated for in advance in interlocutory proceedings.

Note—The Rules of the Supreme Court, Ord 62, provide by r 5 'The court in exercising its discretion as to costs shall, to such extent, if any, as may be appropriate in the circumstances take into account . . . any payment of money into court and the amount of such payment.'

Findlay v Railway Executive

[1950] 2 All ER 969, [1969] WN 570, 66 (pt 2) TLR 836, 94 Sol Jo 778, CA
An accident causing personal injury occurred on 24 October 1947, and before February 1948, the defendants in correspondence admitted liability. Defence was delivered on 23 March 1948, and admitted negligence, leaving the only issue of quantum of damages. Medical examination took place in March 1949, and in June 1949 defendants paid £920 into court, which was not accepted. Trial took place on 27 April 1950. Special damages were agreed at £117 5s 1d and the judge awarded £750 as general damages making £867 5s 1d in all. The judge awarded the plaintiff the costs of the action, and gave leave to appeal on the question of costs.
HELD, ON APPEAL: per Somervell LJ: Order LXV, r 6 [now revoked but see RSC Ord 62, r 5] provides that the judge in exercising his discretion as to costs takes into account both the fact that money has been paid into court and the amount of such payment. In *Donald Campbell & Co v Pollak* [1927] AC 732, 96 LJKB 1132, 137 LT 656, 43 TLR 495, 787 it was stated that there was a settled practice of the courts or reasonable expectation that in the absence of special circumstances a successful litigant should receive his costs and that it was necessary to show some grounds for exercising discretion to refuse such costs. The discretion was absolute and unfettered but must be exercised judicially and a discretion exercised on no grounds could not be judicial nor should it be exercised except for some reason connected with the case. The defendant was a successful litigant and there were no circumstances entitling the judge to deprive him of costs.

Hultquist v Universal Pattern and Precision Engineering Co Ltd

[1960] 2 QB 467, [1960] 2 All ER 266, [1960] 2 WLR 886, CA
The defendants denied liability but paid a sum of money into court in satisfaction of the plaintiff's claim. At the trial the plaintiff succeeded on the issue of liability but was awarded less damages than the amount in court. The plaintiff asked for the costs of the issue of liability.
HELD, ON APPEAL: The matter was one for the discretion of the judge but it is very rare that a plaintiff in such a case and in such circumstances is awarded the costs of the issue of liability. The action of tort consists of wrong-doing and damage resulting therefrom and the plaintiff must prove both to obtain judgment. On the face of it there can be no complaint and no ground for an order for costs on the issue of liability where the plaintiff has been called upon to prove a case to establish his right to damages and has failed to get more than the amount in court.

Wagman v Vare Motors Ltd

[1959] 3 All ER 326, [1959] 1 WLR 853, 103 Sol Jo 600, CA
The plaintiff commenced an action for damages. The defendants paid a sum of money into court. The plaintiff did not accept it. The case proceeded and the only issue was damage. The amount awarded by the judge was the exact sum paid into court. The defendants applied for costs from the payment in, when the amount was disclosed. The plaintiff asked the judge to exercise the discussion given to him by the rule. The judge awarded the plaintiff his costs up to the date of payment in, but ordered that there should be no order as to costs thereafter, on the ground that he had been inclined at one time to give a larger sum than he had finally awarded. The defendants appealed.

The Court of Appeal held that the discretion had not been really exercised at all, and therefore the exercise of discretion did not arise. The fact that the judge had at one time thought of giving a larger sum did not constitute any material on which his discretion could be exercised. The Court of Appeal decided that the judge's decision must be disturbed and the costs after the date of payment in should be the defendants'.

McGuckin v Cammell Laird & Co

(1962) 106 Sol Jo 547, [1962] 1 Lloyd's Rep 635, CA
In an action under the Fatal Accidents Acts in which the defendants admitted liability, the judge awarded the plaintiff £4,548 damages. He arrived at this sum by multiplying the figure of weekly loss by the number of years' purchase, making a total of £4,004; increased this to £4,500 by estimating and allowing for a sum in respect of the deceased's probable increase of earnings, and finally added the funeral expenses of £48. The defendants had made a payment into court earlier in the action of exactly the same sum. The judge declined to give the defendant costs against the plaintiff after payment in on the ground that he had reached the figure of £4,500 merely as a round sum and that it was not a precise valuation. He made no order as to costs after date of payment in.
HELD, ON APPEAL (following *Wagman v Vare Motors*, above): There was no material on which the judge could exercise his discretion in this way. The defendants were entitled to costs after the date of payment in.

Bettaney v Five Towns Demolitions Co Ltd

(1971) 115 Sol Jo 710, CA
The defendants paid into court £50 on 28 January, £21 on 29 January, and £30 on 1 February. On 1 February the defendants' solicitor telephoned the plaintiffs' solicitors and told him there was £101 in court: he replied that the least his clients would accept was £150 and the action continued. Trial began on 2 February, continued on 16 March, and finished on 23 March. The plaintiffs recovered only £76. On costs the judge said that his discretion was unfettered because the prescribed notice of the third payment in could not have been received by the plaintiffs' solicitors before 2 February. He awarded the costs to the plaintiffs.
HELD: On the defendants' appeal, the judge had founded himself on the language of Ord 11, r 9 of the County Court Rules [now Ord 11, r 3 of the 1981 Rules] and had apparently concluded that the plaintiffs had been prejudiced because they could not give notice of acceptance of the payment in before the trial began. But all r 9 meant was that unless the plaintiff gave notice of acceptance as specified the action would not be automatically stayed. The plaintiffs had known of the payment in of £101 by 1 February, and had elected to go on. The judge was bound to take the payment into

Court into account and, if he had, could not have deprived the defendants of their costs as from the date of the final payment in.

King v Weston-Howell

[1989] 2 All ER 375, [1989] 1 WLR 579, 133 Sol Jo 750, CA
RSC Ord 22, r 1 entitled a defendant to make a payment into court at any time. The mere fact it is made less than 21 days before trial does not necessarily make it ineffective in protecting him against costs and the court will consider the surrounding circumstances. If the plaintiff's delay prevents the defendant from making an effective payment in before the 21 days, then prima facie the defendant is entitled to his costs from the date of the payment in, if the plaintiff does not beat it at trial.

Nominal damages recovered

Alltrans Express Ltd v CVA Holdings Ltd

[1984] 1 All ER 685, [1984] 1 WLR 394, 128 Sol Jo 47, CA
The plaintiffs obtained judgment under Ord 14, the defendants contesting only the amount of the plaintiffs' loss. The action was transferred to the Official Referee for assessment of damages. He held the plaintiffs had not proved any loss and awarded £2 nominal damages. He awarded the costs of the trial to the plaintiffs on the ground that they had been awarded £2 assessed damages and there was no payment in court by the defendants.
HELD: This was not right. The judge had attached far too much weight to the absence of any payment into court. If the defendants had paid in £2 it would not have been accepted. The truth was that it was the defendants who were the successful party. Costs of the trial to the defendants.

Gupta v Klito

(1989) Times, 23 November, CA
If a party recovers more than nominal damages he can usually expect an order for costs in his favour.

Claim increased at trial

Cheeseman v Bowaters (UK) Paper Mills Ltd

[1971] 3 All ER 513, [1971] 1 WLR 1773, 115 Sol Jo 931, CA
As pleaded in the statement of claim the plaintiff's claim was for damages for a back injury and loss of earnings for three periods off work. The defendants paid £750 into court three weeks before trial. At court the plaintiff claimed a further sum for a fourth period off work and damages for accelerated retirement caused by his injury. The judge awarded damages for both these items. Without them the award would have been less than the amount in court.
HELD, by the Court of Appeal: As the additional award which brought the total above the amount in court was on a new case calling for amendments to the statement of claim at the trial the defendants should have their costs from the date of payments in ie the standard order when the plaintiff fails to recover as much as the amount in court.

Interest

Note—RSC Ord 22, r 1(8) says: 'For the purposes of this rule, the plaintiff's cause of action in respect of a debt or damages shall be construed as a cause of action, also, of such interest as might be included in the judgment, whether under s 35A of the Act or otherwise, if judgment were given at the date of the payment into court'. Thus a payment into court should also include interest on the damages up to the date of payment in.

Causes of action

The Talamba

[1965] P 433, [1965] 2 All ER 775, [1965] 3 WLR 562, 109 Sol Jo 631, [1965] 2 Lloyd's Rep 128 (Hewson J)
The plaintiffs were the owners, masters and crews of nine tugs, four of which rendered salvage services to the *Talamba* and the others to the *Troll*. The *Talamba* and the *Troll* were both owned by the defendants who paid into court a sum of money in respect of the services to each vessel. On an application to apportion the sums as between each tug.
HELD: The owners, masters and crews had a separate cause of action in respect of each tug. Under the new rule if a plaintiff was embarrassed by the defendants' payment the court might order apportionment. Embarrassment meant being put in a difficulty. The plaintiffs were in difficulty until they knew how the services of each tug were regarded by the defendants in terms of money. The overall amount offered to each tug in respect of the services should be designated in such a case as this.

Tingay v Harris

[1967] 2 QB 327, [1967] 1 All ER 385, [1967] 2 WLR 577, 110 Sol Jo 926, CA
The plaintiff, an architect, sued the defendant in the county court for fees which he put at £166 for work done, including preparing plans. The defendant paid into court £75 in satisfaction of the amount claimed. The plaintiff did not accept it. Subsequently the plaintiff obtained leave of the court to add another defendant and claimed damages against both for conversion of the plans. At the trial the judge awarded the plaintiff £75 for fees and £2 nominal damages for the conversion. The case against the second defendant was dismissed. He awarded the plaintiff the costs of the action against the first defendant, purporting to apply Ord 11, r 3 and Ord 15, r 1 of the County Court Rules [now Ord 11, r 1 and Ord 15, r 1 of the 1981 Rules]. The defendant appealed against the award of costs.
HELD: The judge was wrong. The payment into court of £75 had been made before the plaintiff added the further cause of action and he could not have been in any doubt as to the cause of action in respect of which it was paid in, namely, the claim for the fees. As only £75 was awarded for that claim the defendant was the successful party and entitled to costs after date of payment in. The award of £2 for the conversion being de minimis should not carry any costs for the plaintiff.

Payment in by one of two defendants

Parkes v Knowles

[1957] 3 All ER 600, [1957] 1 WLR 1040, 101 Sol Jo 816 (Lynskey J)
Plaintiff was injured whilst a passenger in the car driven by the first defendant which collided with the omnibus of the second defendants. Plaintiff commenced proceedings

in the High Court against both defendants, and each defendant in his defence blamed the other for the cause of the accident. The first defendant paid £100 into court under RSC Ord 22, r 1. Plaintiff gave notice of acceptance and thereupon, as provided by r 4(3) (now r 3(4)) all further proceedings were stayed, and the money could not be paid out except pursuant to an order dealing with the whole costs of the action. Plaintiff applied for an order under r 4(3) to deal with the amount in court, and contended it was not money recovered in the action under the County Courts Act 1955, s 1(2) [now the County Courts Act 1984, s 1(2)] which provides that where an action is commenced in the High Court which could have been commenced in the county court, if the plaintiff recovers a sum of less than £300 unless there was reasonable ground for supposing the amount of the plaintiff's claim would exceed the amount recoverable in the county court.
HELD: (1) It was money recovered in the action under the County Courts Act 1955, s 1(2) [now the County Courts Act 1984, s 1(2)]. (2) As to costs, the acceptance of the £100 showed that the plaintiff thought the amount was fair and there were no reasonable grounds for supposing the claim would exceed the county court limit. The plaintiff was only entitled to recover from the first defendant costs on scale 3 of the county court. So far as the second defendant was concerned, there was no further issue to be tried, and he was entitled to judgment against the plaintiff with costs on the High Court scale. On the question whether the plaintiff was entitled to add in his costs against the first defendant the costs he had to pay the second defendant: from the very start the car driver blamed the bus driver and in view of a letter written to the plaintiff, and the allegations in the pleadings, the plaintiff was reasonable in suing both defendants and in fact was bound to do so. He was entitled to recover from the first defendant the costs which he has to pay to the second defendants. A Bullock Order would involve double taxation and the proper order is, first defendant to pay plaintiff's costs on scale 3 of the county court, and the first defendant to pay the second defendant's costs on the High Court scale.

Note—For limitation of recoverable costs of action in contract and tort see now the County Courts Act 1984, ss 19 and 20.

Scania (GB) Ltd v Andrews

[1992] 3 All ER 143, [1992] 1 WLR 578, CA
The acceptance of a payment into court made by a defendant sued jointly and severally, results in an automatic stay of the action against the other defendant. Leave is required if the plaintiff wishes to continue those proceedings and the court will have to consider the question of costs. If he intends to accept the payment in in satisfaction of all his causes of action against both defendants, he is entitled to the money in court provided the non paying defendant consents to the action against them being discontinued. See RSC Ord 22, rr 3 and 4.

Hodgson v Guardall Ltd

[1991] 3 All ER 823
The court had the discretion to allow the plaintiff's costs in pursuing all of the defendants against the one defendant who had made a payment into court which he had accepted: Ord 62, r 5(4).

Note—This rule also entitles a plaintiff to recover all of his costs of the action even where the payment in is made in respect of one cause of action and he subsequently abandons all of the others. See *Hudson v Elmbridge Borough Council* [1991] 1 WLR 880.

Two plaintiffs

Smith v Schilling

[1928] 1 KB 429, 97 LJKB 276, 138 LT 475, 44 TLR 109, CA
If there are two plaintiffs, such as an infant and his father, a payment into court must be divided and appropriated to the cause of action of each plaintiff or the payment in is bad.

Note—Followed in *Emcee Ltd v Sunday Pictorial Newspaper (1920) Ltd* [1939] 2 All ER 384, 83 Sol Jo 456 (Singleton J).

Walker v Turpin

[1993] 4 All ER 865, [1994] 1 WLR 196, CA
Pursuant to RSC Ord 22, r 1(1), a defendant was permitted to make a payment into court unapportioned between two plaintiffs. However, r 1 (5) enabled the court to direct that the payment in be apportioned if the plaintiffs were embarrassed.

Wrong amount paid in

H v L

(1982) Times, 1 July, QBD (McCullough J)
In an action for damages the defendants made a payment into court which the plaintiff accepted by the usual notice to the defendants' solicitors. All proceedings were consequently stayed. A month later the defendants issued a summons for an order removing the stay and for repayment of the money accepted on the ground that the payment into court had been made in error. It was not alleged that the plaintiff or his solicitors realised that any mistake had been made.
HELD: The court had an inherent jurisdiction to set aside a stay and to order repayment of money paid out of court if proper grounds were shown. It was not restricted to cases of fraud or mistake. The existence of the power was evidenced by such authorities as *Derrick v Williams* (p 678, below), *Cooper v Williams* (p 459, above) and *Lambert v Mainland Deliveries* (p 684, below). It was a matter of discretion for the court. In the present case the plaintiff had done nothing wrong and the defendants had made a careless mistake. The plaintiff was an old man and some anxiety would be imposed by ordering repayment. Order refused.

Discretion to alter judgment

Millensted v Grosvenor House (Park Lane) Ltd

[1937] 1 KB 717, [1937] 1 All ER 736, 106 LJKB 221, 156 LT 383, CA
Judge of High Court gave judgment for £50 with costs on county court scale. He was then informed that £20 had been paid into court. Next day he altered the damage to £35 and by formal judgment ordered payment of £35 and county court costs.
HELD: Judge had discretion to allow case to proceed after being told of sum in court, and to alter his judgment at any time before it was drawn up and perfected.

Withdrawal of money paid in

Garner v Cleggs

[1983] 2 All ER 398, [1983] 1 WLR 862, 127 Sol Jo 347, CA

In an action for damages for professional negligence the defendants paid into court £25,655 and served notice of payment in on the 11 August. The plaintiff did not serve notice of acceptance within 21 days or at all. Having obtained some evidence which they considered showed a change of circumstance the defendants applied to the court to be allowed to take the money out of court: an order to that effect was made on the 26 February. Trial began on 16 March and lasted eight days. Judgment was given for the plaintiff for less than the sum that was originally in court. The judge gave the plaintiff all his costs against the defendants on the ground that at the date of the trial there was no money in court which he could take to avoid the trial. The defendants appealed against the order claiming all the costs of the action from the date of payment in.

HELD: As the defendants had applied simply for all the costs from date of payment in and no other apportionment had been sought from the judge he was entitled to exercise his discretion in the way he had. Nevertheless it would have been wrong to disregard altogether the fact that a payment into court had been made. From the expiry of the 21 days after payment in until the notice of payment in was withdrawn by the defendants the plaintiff was at risk as to costs and the costs incurred during that period should ordinarily be borne by him.

Manku v Seehra

[1986] NLJ Rep 236

The plaintiff sued the defendant for the balance of his account covering building works at the defendant's premises. The defendant denied liability and counterclaimed for breach of contract. He paid money into court on 18 November but, after consulting another surveyor, applied on 25 November to withdraw the payment in because it was based upon incorrect expert advice. The defendant's summons was served on the 28th but later that day the plaintiff gave notice of acceptance of the payment in.

HELD: The court could allow withdrawal of a notice of payment in within the period allowed for acceptance, even if the plaintiff had sought to accept the payment in, because acceptance merely stayed proceedings and this stay can be notionally removed for the subsequent application. In this case though the defendant's application was based upon a last-minute review of existing evidence which was not 'good reason' to withdraw the sum in court as envisaged by the Court of Appeal in *Cumper v Pothecary* (p 674, below).

No mention in notice of appeal

Phillips v Gordon

(1966) 110 Sol Jo 189, CA

Per Davies LJ: Whatever the rights and wrongs of the Court of Appeal knowing that there was money paid into court, and how much it was, it was undesirable that that should be underlined in being mentioned in the notice of appeal.

Thornton v Swan Hunter (Shipbuilders) Ltd

[1971] 3 All ER 1248, [1971] 1 WLR 1759, 115 Sol Jo 832, CA
In an appeal by the defendants against the amount of damages it was ordered by the Court of Appeal, on the defendants' application, that in the transcript of the evidence and judgment in the court below (1) the discussion after the award (which included references to the amount paid into court by the defendants) should be deleted, but (2) a passage in the evidence which showed that an offer had been made, and a reference in the judgment to a payment into court without mentioning the amount, should not be deleted.

Note—Followed in *Beaumont v British Uralite Ltd* (1973) 117 Sol Jo 914, CA.

PAYMENT OUT OF COURT

Cumper v Pothecary

[1941] 2 KB 58, [1941] 2 All ER 516, 110 LJKB 577, 165 LT 243, 57 TLR 503, CA
A defendant who has paid money into court is not entitled as of right to have it paid out to him if not accepted in the time allowed. The court has a discretion for good reasons, eg the discovery of a complete defence (*Frazer and Haws v Burns* (1934) 49 Ll L Rep 216, *Williams v Boag* [1941] 1 KB 1, [1940] 4 All ER 246, 109 LJKB 913, 165 LT 56, CA), or the change caused by the decision of the House of Lords in *Benham v Gambling* [1941] AC 157, [1941] 1 All ER 7, 110 LJKB 49, 164 LT 290, HL. The proper procedure is to apply to withdraw the notice of payment in and for payment out, or to substitute a notice for a reduced amount and payment out of the difference.

Note—For effect of withdrawal see *Garner v Cleggs*, p 673, above.

During trial

Gaskins v British Aluminium Co Ltd

[1976] QB 524, [1976] 1 All ER 208, [1976] 2 WLR 6, 119 Sol Jo 848, CA
The plaintiff claimed damages for an injury at work. A writ was issued in December 1973. The defendants paid into court £5,500 on 23 January 1975. The trial began on 24 March 1975. The plaintiff's case did not go well and on the following morning he applied under Ord 22, r 5 to take the £5,500 out of court. The defendant opposed the application. The judge refused the plaintiff's application and adjourned the case to be heard by another judge.
HELD, dismissing the plaintiff's appeal: (1) An application to take money out of court during a trial should not be granted when the defendant opposes it. (2) It would also be right to refuse the application if, on the facts, the position had altered since the money was paid in. (3) RSC Ord 22, r 7 forbidding disclosure to the trial judge that money has been paid into court is directory, not compulsive. If he is made aware of the payment in by inadvertence or otherwise, the judge has a discretion to decide whether to continue to hear the case or not. Leave was given to apply to the judge to continue the hearing.

County court

Gold v Introductions Ltd

[1963] 2 All ER 279, [1963] 1 WLR 517, 107 Sol Jo 252, CA
In an action for £307 commission due to the plaintiff the defendant made payments into Court amounting to £83, the last of these on 2 October. On 29 November, ie more than the four days limited by Ord 11, r 9(a) [now Ord 11, r 3 of the 1981 Rules] of the County Court rules the plaintiff gave notice of acceptance. The judge refused to award the plaintiff his costs up to the date of payment in on the ground that Ord 11, r 11 [now Ord 11, r 5 of the 1981 Rules] of the County Court Rules did not empower him to do so.
HELD: Rules 7 and 9 should be read with r 11. The plaintiff was entitled to his costs up to the date of payment in but the money was not to be paid out without an order of the court, which could order the plaintiff to pay any costs reasonably incurred by the defendant after date of payment in.

Note—See also *Seacroft Hotel (Teignmouth) Ltd v Goble* [1984] 3 All ER 116, [1984] 1 WLR 939, 128 Sol Jo 499, CA on late notice of acceptance and limits of judge's discretion on costs.

White v Harding

(1976) 120 Sol Jo 590, CA
In an action for damages in the county court in which the hearing date was 17 October, the defendant paid an amount into court on 9 October. Notice was given by the registrar to the plaintiff on the 10th, so that the plaintiff had until the 17th to accept. On the 17th before the hearing began she agreed to accept but the defendant would not agree to payment out unless his costs were paid after the 9th. The trial then proceeded but the plaintiff was awarded only the same amount as was in court, with costs up to the 9th.
HELD, ON APPEAL: The operative notice of the payment in was that of the registrar and by RSC Ord 11, r 9 [now Ord 11, r 3 of the 1981 Rules] she could accept on the 17th before the hearing; but the rule also provided that notice had to be given to the registrar and every defendant. As no such notice had been given the costs were within the judge's discretion and he had exercised it correctly. Appeal dismissed.

Infant's damages

Note—RSC Ord 80, r 12, gives to the court control of money paid into court for an infant whether under a settlement or judgment. (For the text of the rule see p 491, above).

By the Family Law Reform Act 1969, s 1 a person on and after 1 January 1970 attains full age at 18 instead of 21. He may be called a minor (s 12) until of full age.

M v Lester

[1966] 1 All ER 207, [1966] 1 WLR 134, 110 Sol Jo 53 (Lawton J)
As a result of a brain injury received in a road accident the infant plaintiff would be unable to work and would require constant care and supervision, though his condition was not such that he would need to be detained in hospital. After the court had approved a settlement of his claim at £15,000 an application was made to decide how the money should be dealt with.

The judge ordered that the money be transferred to the Court of Protection. In the ordinary way the Court of Protection was not concerned with looking after the affairs of infants but in some cases, such as this, it would do so. It has full powers of investment, expert investment advice available and long experience in dealing with people who are incapable of looking after themselves. It would do the job better than trustees, and would provide continuity.

Morey v Woodfield (No 2)

[1964] 1 QB 1, [1963] 3 All ER 584, [1963] 3 WLR 486, 107 Sol Jo 651 (Megaw J)
Costs incurred in the preparation and approval of a trust deed settling £50,000 damages awarded to an infant for personal injuries were not chargeable to the defendants under the Supreme Court Rules 1959, r 28(2) (ie on a taxation on a party and party basis); they were not incurred for the attainment of justice between the plaintiff and defendant. They were costs incurred, perfectly properly, in providing for the disposition of damages paid by the defendant.

Note—This decision was accepted by the Court of Appeal as 'obviously right' in the similar case of *Warren v King* [1964] 1 WLR 122n, 108 Sol Jo 114, CA. The rule is now Ord 62, r 28.

Settlement of action

BY CONSENT

Martin v Bannister

(1933) 47 Ll L Rep 270, CA
To constitute a binding settlement the mind of the claimant must go with the apparent settlement.

An injured man whilst in hospital settled his claim through a solicitor acting on his behalf with an insurance company for £100 and 35 guineas costs without proceedings. Later the man instructed a fresh solicitor who issued a writ. The company in the name of their assured applied to stay the action on the ground that the cause of action had been settled.

HELD, by the Court of Appeal: As on the face of the receipt no mention was made of the 35 guineas costs and it was doubtful whether plaintiff had assented to a compromise whereby the solicitor was to receive what was relatively such a large sum for costs, the action must proceed and the stay was refused.

Note—See also *Taylor v Walker*, p 678, below.

Roberts v Eastern Counties Rly Co

(1859) 1 F & F 460
Plaintiff accepted £2 for damage to clothes, not supposing he had sustained any serious injury.

HELD: Not an accord and satisfaction for a patent and severe injury.

Ellen v Great Northern Rly Co

(1901) 17 TLR 453, CA
Plaintiff signed receipt for money paid by defendants as compensation for accident in full settlement for all claims. His eyesight soon began to fail and he became totally

blind as a result of the accident. He brought an action and defendant pleaded action not maintainable.

HELD: Action maintainable, it being a question for the jury.

Saunders v Ford Motor Co

[1970] 1 Lloyd's Rep 379 (Paull J)

On 10 April 1964 the plaintiff suffered a severe injury to his eye at work. On his return to work he was sent by his employers to see E, a representative of their insurers who had an office at the works, to settle a claim for compensation. The plaintiff accepted an offer of £200, believing from the conversation that it was for pain and suffering and loss of wages only and that if the eye got worse he could go back for more. He signed a receipt for the £200 'in settlement of all claims, whether now or hereafter to become manifest, arising directly or indirectly from the accident. He could not read the receipt because of bad sight; it was filled in by E. When asked at court what 'manifest' meant the plaintiff did not know.

HELD: He was not bound by the receipt. There was attached to the payment of £200 an understanding that if his eye deteriorated he could come back; alternatively the parties were not *ad idem* because he signed the receipt believing he would be able to come back. The form of receipt used should not be used between employers and a workman who had no professional advice. The receipt ought to make it clear in simple language that whatever happens to him he can receive no more money.

Horry v Tate & Lyle Refineries Ltd

[1982] 2 Lloyd's Rep 416 (Pain J)

The plaintiff sustained a hernia by accident at work; there was a 15% chance of recurrence. He accepted £1,000 in settlement of his claim for damages. The employers' insurers negotiated the settlement; the plaintiff was not professionally represented nor independently advised. He signed what purported to be a final discharge. Later, following a recurrence, he sought advice and in proceedings based on the original accident the employers by their insurers pleaded a release by way of accord and satisfaction based on the settlement.

HELD: The plaintiff was not bound by the settlement. He had relied on the insurers' advice and they knew it. They had a fiduciary duty of care which they could have discharged by asking him to obtain independent advice. There was a duty on them to specify what deduction was made for contributory negligence. They should have supplied him with a copy of the medical report and ensured he understood that no further claim could be made. Their interest conflicted with his. The relationship imposed on them a fiduciary duty. *Lloyd's Bank Ltd v Bundy* ([1975] QB 326, [1974] 3 All ER 757, [1974] 3 WLR 501, CA) and *Saunders v Ford Motor Co* (above) applied.

Arrale v Costain Civil Engineering Ltd

(1975) 119 Sol Jo 527, [1976] 1 Lloyds Rep 98, CA

The plaintiff, an Arab labourer working in Dubai for the defendants, sustained a serious injury at work resulting in the loss of his left arm. The law of Dubai provides for payment of compensation to a workman by the employer on a fixed scale. The amount due for the plaintiff's injury was £490. The defendants paid to him this amount and he signed a receipt which referred to the compensation law and continued with the same words as were used in the receipt in *Saunders v Ford Motor Co* (above).

Later the plaintiff came to England and sued the defendant for damages at common law. They pleaded that all liability had been discharged by the receipt.
HELD: (1) As the plaintiff was entitled to the payment of compensation of £490 there was nothing else the receipt could apply to; (2) there was no true accord and satisfaction — no one had told the plaintiff when he signed the receipt that he might have a claim at common law. He was not prevented by the receipt from proceeding with the claim.

Rideal v Great Western Rly Co

(1859) 1 F & F 706
If the mind of the plaintiff went with the terms of settlement and he understood their effect when he assented to them, agreement binding.

Lee v Lancashire and Yorkshire Rly Co

(1871) 6 Ch App 527, 25 LT 77, 35 JP 726, 19 WR 729
A mere receipt in writing is simply an acknowledgment of money paid, and may be impeached or explained by parol evidence.

Lovell v Williams

(1938) 62 Ll L Rep 249, CA
Plaintiff brought an action in the county court and accepted £35 in full settlement and the action was withdrawn. He afterwards discovered he had sustained a fractured skull and was permanently disabled. He issued writ and defendant applied to stay the action as being frivolous and vexatious and an abuse of the process of the court.
HELD: Not a case for a stay. The question whether there had been a settlement of all future claims must be decided in the action.

Taylor v Walker

[1958] 1 Lloyd's Rep 490 (Havers J)
The plaintiff was crossing the road when he was struck and injured by a motor cycle ridden by W. He was introduced by a so-called claims service to a claims assessor B, who made a claim against W. B did not fully investigate the facts and did not obtain a medical report, though he saw one obtained by W's insurers. He received an offer of £300 from the insurers and asked them for 40 guineas costs. He strongly recommended the plaintiff to accept, saying nothing about the fee, and the plaintiff did so. The insurers paid the fee of 40 guineas to B by a separate cheque from the damages. Later the plaintiff by a next friend sought to rescind the settlement.
HELD: He was entitled to do so. As an agent B had to act in good faith in the interest of his principal. In obtaining payment of 40 guineas for himself without telling the plaintiff he had not so acted. It was not necessary for the plaintiff to prove a corrupt motive on the part of the insurers in paying the 40 guineas. On the facts the payment was a bribe since it was a payment to B himself without disclosure to B's principal, the plaintiff. The settlement was therefore voidable by plaintiff.

Derrick v Williams

[1939] 2 All ER 559, 160 LT 589, 55 TLR 676, 83 Sol Jo 397, CA
On 26 July 1935 the infant child of the respondent was killed by a motor lorry belonging to the appellant. The respondent, as the personal representative of the

infant, thereupon brought an action claiming damages under the Law Reform (Miscellaneous Provisions) Act 1934, and in October 1935 the appellant, as defendant in that action, paid into court £50 with a denial of liability, and that sum was taken out by the respondent. At the time, in reliance upon the decision of the Court of Appeal in *Rose v Ford* it was thought that damages could not be recovered in respect of loss of expectation of life, but that decision was in 1937 reversed in the House of Lords. The respondent on 27 September 1938, brought the present action, based upon the same facts as the previous action, and claimed damages for loss of expectation of life. The appellant took the preliminary point that the acceptance of the sum paid into court in the previous action was a bar to the present proceedings. The court decided this point in favour of the appellant but gave the respondent leave to amend his statement of claim in the first action, without, however, defining the terms of the amendment. The respondent in his amended statement of claim, claimed to be entitled to withdraw his acceptance of the sum of £50 or, alternatively, to have the agreement by which he accepted the sum set aside, on the ground that it was made under a mistake of fact or a mistake of law. The appellant appealed against the order so far as it allowed an amendment of the statement of claim.
HELD: (1) As the effect of the acceptance of the money paid into court was to stay the proceedings the respondent's proper course was to apply in the action to have the stay removed and to have liberty to withdraw his consent. This was not, however, a case in which such an application would have been granted. (2) A litigant whose claim has been satisfied by money paid into court cannot afterwards contend that that money was accepted under a mistake in law, on the ground that the law was not as then laid down by the Court of Appeal, but as subsequently enunciated by the House of Lords. (3) Where leave to amend is asked for, the actual amendment should be formulated before leave is given.

FORM OF ORDER

Note—See RSC Ord 42 generally and CCR Ord 22.

INFANT CASES

Note—See RSC Ord 80 generally and CCR Ord 10.

Appeals

PRINCIPLE IN RUNNING DOWN ACTION

Lofthouse v Leicester Corpn

(1948) 64 TLR 604, CA
Deceased cyclist was killed in collision with a motor omnibus. Oliver J held deceased alone to blame.
HELD, ON APPEAL: The Court of Appeal had a wider power on appeal from a judge than a jury and can reverse the judge on the facts. The judge sees and hears the witnesses and obtains the atmosphere. Although not exhaustive, the Court of Appeal ought not to interfere on a pure question of fact unless the judge did not take all the circumstances and evidence into account, or misapprehended certain of the evidence, or that he had

drawn an inference which there is no evidence to support. The judge must decide the case on the evidence given, not on how he thought the accident probably happened.

Lincoln v Hayman

[1982] 2 All ER 819, [1982] 1 WLR 488, [1982] RTR 336, CA
Two lorries collided on a country lane too narrow for them to pass without one or both going on to the grass verge. Immediately after the accident police officers and a press photographer arrived: photographs were taken and a sketch plan made showing the positions of the vehicles and of certain wheel marks on the road and the grass verges. The accounts of the accident from the two drivers differed very widely.
HELD, ON APPEAL: Where, as here, the judge's reasoning was based on inferences from plans and photographs (and not from the demeanour of the witnesses) the Court of Appeal was in as good a position as the judge to draw its own inferences from the undisputed primary material. Judge's finding of blame wholly on the defendant altered to two-thirds on the plaintiff, one-third on the defendant.

INCONSISTENT FINDINGS OF TWO JUDGES

Baker v Market Harborough Industrial Co-operative Society
Wallace v Richards (Leicester) Ltd

[1953] 1 WLR 1472, 97 Sol Jo 861, CA
Two vehicles proceeding in opposite directions collided and both drivers were killed. An action by widow of driver A was dismissed by Mr Justice X on the ground that there was no proof of negligence of driver B. An action by the widow of driver B was afterwards heard and Mr Justice Y held both drivers equally to blame. The Court of Appeal granted leave to appeal out of time in the A action. Facts and references at p 31, above, *res ipsa loquitur*.

Kemshead v British Transport Commission

[1958] 1 All ER 119, [1958] 1 WLR 173, 102 Sol Jo 122, CA
On 6 December 1952, a motor car collided with a train at an accommodation level crossing. One passenger in the car named Bland was killed and another passenger named Kemshead was injured. Bland's widow sued the British Transport Commission and on 4 February 1954, Stable J gave judgment for her. The Commission did not appeal.

Kemshead also sued the Commission and on 10 May 1956 Stable J gave judgment for him. The Commission appealed and the appeal was allowed.

Per Denning LJ: It is very unfortunate that in regard to two different plaintiffs there should be different results in the courts of law. The parties ought to have taken a different course. They ought all to have been plaintiffs in one action or should have agreed on one action being a test action.

The defendants not having appealed and having paid the damages in the first action was a direct encouragement to the second plaintiff and were therefore refused costs.

Note—See below and Ch 13, pp 371–453, above.

FRESH EVIDENCE ON APPEAL

Ladd v Marshall

[1954] 3 All ER 745, [1954] 1 WLR 1489, 98 Sol Jo 870, CA
Per Denning LJ: In order to justify the reception of fresh evidence [on appeal] or a new trial, three conditions must be fulfilled: first, it must be shown that the evidence could not have been obtained with reasonable diligence for use at the trial; second, the evidence must be such that, if given, it would probably have an important influence on the result of the case, although it need not be decisive; third, the evidence must be such as is presumably to be believed, or in other words, it must be apparently credible, although it need not be incontrovertible.

Note—See also pp 451–453, above.

House v Haughton Bros (Worcester Ltd)

[1967] 1 All ER 39, [1967] 1 WLR 148, 110 Sol Jo 891, CA
In the plaintiff's claim for damages for injury received at work an important issue was the number of scaffold boards available to him at the time of the accident. The judge accepted the evidence of the defendants' main witness that no further boards had been provided after the accident before the factory inspector's visit; he dismissed the action. Afterwards three men tendered statements that additional boards had been delivered in the interval before the factory inspector's visit. These men had all been present at the trial and two had given evidence for the plaintiff but had not been asked any question in that issue.
HELD: The plaintiff was entitled to have a new trial. The requirements in *Ladd v Marshall* (above) that the new evidence could not have been obtained with reasonable diligence for use at the trial can be amplified by saying that where the situation is that although a witness is called at the trial and gives evidence on other matters but had not told the plaintiff's solicitors what he was able to say on that issue then if the solicitors are now shown to have been negligent or dilatory in the way in which they had interviewed him his evidence 'could not have been obtained with reasonable diligence'. Insofar as the evidence he could have given was not known to them then *quoad* such evidence neither he nor that evidence was available.

Roe v Robert MacGregor & Sons Ltd

[1968] 2 All ER 636, [1968] 1 WLR 925, 112 Sol Jo 235, CA
At 1 am Roe was driving a van with his wife and others as passengers. They were going home from an RAF mess function. Roe failed to see a 'road closed' sign, crashed through a barrier and went over an embankment. He and his wife were injured. They sued contractors who were doing the road works and who, he alleged, had not lighted the obstacle. At the trial Roe said he had drunk only three half-pints of beer during the evening. The judge treated him as having been quite sober and awarded him damages. On hearing of the case and the result another passenger told the contractors' solicitor that to his knowledge Roe had been hopelessly drunk and that that was the cause of the accident. The solicitor also found a publican who said (contrary to what Roe had said in evidence) that Roe and other members of his party had been drinking heavily before they went to the RAF mess. The contractors appealed and applied for leave to adduce further evidence.

HELD: (1) It would be hopelessly inconvenient merely to allow the new evidence to be adduced: the only course, if the Court was to do anything was to order a new trial, since evidence in rebuttal must also be admitted. (2) The three conditions required by *Ladd v Marshall* (above) were duly satisfied. The defendants' solicitor could not reasonably have sought the evidence from the passenger before the trial since he might himself have had a claim. The evidence would certainly have a most important effect on the judge's view of contributory negligence. It could not be said it was not credible: the word 'credible' in this connection means that on the face of it the evidence was not worthy of any credence. In the present case one could not go as far as that. New trial ordered.

Delaney v Douglas

[1969] 3 All ER 1454n, CA
At an early stage in the investigation of a road accident claim the question arose whether or not a car had been parked opposite a public house at the material time. The plaintiff's solicitor had evidence from some witnesses that a car was so parked but did not inquire at the public house itself until a considerable time after the accident: by that time the licensee had moved and could not be found. At the trial the judge held there was no car there. The former licensee was then found and was prepared to say that there was a parked car. The plaintiff sought leave to adduce this evidence on an appeal.
HELD: Leave must be refused. Reasonable and due diligence on the part of the plaintiff's solicitor should require him when the story was being originally investigated to inquire at the house immediately opposite the relevant scene. This was not done until too late.

TRANSFER TO DIFFERENT JUDGE

Birch v County Motor and Engineering Co Ltd

[1958] 3 All ER 175, [1958] 1 WLR 980, 102 Sol Jo 632, CA
A was a pillion rider on a motor cycle driven by B which collided with a car driven by C. Both A and B sustained injuries. B brought an action against C in the county court. The only witnesses were B and A. The judge accepted the evidence of C on the only disputed evidence of fact, and found both B and C negligent in the proportions of three-fourths blame to B and one-fourth to C. Later A brought an action in the same court against C, who joined B as third party. C applied under Ord 16, r 1(1) to transfer the action to another county court on the ground that the judge having made up his mind that C was in some degree to blame, the probable result was that A would recover his damages from C, as A was not affected by the apportionment in the former action, and B might not be worth powder and shot. C appealed.
HELD: The question is clearly a matter for the discretion of the judge, and he had not taken into account matters not relevant to the proper exercise of that discretion. It was not a case where the judge formed a very unfavourable view of a witness or his credibility. The grounds stated by the judge for his refusal of the application were not entirely satisfactory, and it must be a real trial. Application to transfer to another court rejected, but the judge must try the second case fairly and fully, listening to the evidence and making a note.

LEAVE IN THE COUNTY COURT

Note—The County Court Appeals Order 1981, SI 1981/1749, requires leave to be obtained to appeal from a county court where the claim (or counter-claim, if larger) is for an amount not exceeding one-half of the loss of the limit of the jurisdiction of a county court under the County Courts Act 1984, s 15 (at present £5,000).

Splitting the cause of action

Note—A plaintiff may bring two separate actions in respect of the very same circumstances provided there are two causes of action, ie (1) personal injuries, (2) damage to property.

Brunsden v Humphrey

(1884) 14 QBD 141, 53 LJQB 476, 51 LT 529, 49 JP 4, 32 WR 944, CA
Damage to goods and injury to the person give rise to distinct causes of action, although occasioned by the same wrongful act.

The plaintiff brought an action against the defendant in the county court for damage to his goods (in that case a cab) and recovered the amount he claimed. He later brought an action in the High Court against the same defendant in respect of the same act of negligence for personal injuries.

HELD: The action was maintainable and was not barred by the previous proceedings in the county court.

The test is not whether he had the opportunity of recovering in the first action what he claims in the second, but whether he sought to do so.

Per Bowen LJ: Two separate kinds of injury were in fact inflicted and two wrongs done. . . . One wrong was done as soon as the plaintiff's enjoyment of his property was substantially interfered with. A further wrong arose as soon as the driving also caused injury to the plaintiff's person. . . . The wrong consists in the damage done without lawful excuse, not the act of driving, which (if no damage had ensued) would have been legally unimportant.

Note—The relevance of this point is that damage to vehicle and loss of use are parts of the same cause of action.

In *Buckland v Palmer* (p 685, below) Griffiths LJ said 'I take it to be settled by the decision of this court in *Brunsden v Humphrey* that if as a result of a car accident a plaintiff suffers both personal injury and damage to his car he has two distinct causes of action, one for his personal injuries and the other for damage to his property. I confess that I have always had difficulty in following the reasoning of the majority in *Brunsden v Humphrey* and I observe that it has not been followed in either the United States or Canada.'

Taylor v O Wray & Co Ltd

[1971] 1 Lloyd's Rep 497, CA
The plaintiff when driving his car collided with the defendants' lorry. He sustained some personal injury and through his own solicitors claimed damages. They issued a county court summons and included in the claim the £10 excess under the plaintiff's comprehensive policy. Meanwhile his insurers had written to the defendants' insurers notifying a claim for the balance of the cost of repairs to the car amounting to about £180. In the plaintiff's action the defendants paid into court £30 which the plaintiff after further negotiations accepted 'in full settlement of his claims in this action'. His insurers then instituted fresh proceedings in his name to recover the balance of the costs of repairs to his car. The defendants pleaded that as the plaintiff

had already claimed in respect of the cause of action for damage to the car (by claiming his £10 excess) disposal of that claim had *ipso facto* put an end to that cause of action and barred all further proceedings.
HELD: The defence was a technical one of no merit. The principle underlying *Brunsden v Humphrey* (above) was that if a party prosecutes a cause of action to judgment he cannot start all over again and sue for further relief in respect of that same cause of action; but notwithstanding that decision the same cause of action can in certain circumstances be the subject of more than one set of proceedings. In the present case the plaintiff's solicitors had made it clear that acceptance of the £30 was in settlement only for the claims in the first action. Moreover the defendants' insurers already knew that the plaintiff's insurers were claiming from them the balance of the repair charges. The cogency of the maxims *Nemo bis debet vexari* and *Interest reipublicae ut sit finis litium* depends on the facts: the plaintiff and his insurers had not acted vexatiously or oppressively in pursuing the present claim nor were they prevented from doing so.

Note—See also *Haigh v Lawford,* above.

Lambert v Mainland Market Deliveries Ltd

[1977] 2 All ER 826, [1977] 1 WLR 825, 121 Sol Jo 477, [1978] 1 Lloyd's Rep 245, CA
The plaintiff's parked car was struck by a vehicle driven by the defendant's driver and damaged beyond repair. There was no knock-for-knock agreement between the respective insurers. The plaintiff's insurers paid him £982.37 for the total loss value of his car less his £30 excess. They claimed the amount of their outlay from the defendants' insurers who, pleading inevitable accident, offered 50%. Meanwhile the plaintiff acting in person issued a summons in the county court for his uninsured losses of £72.80 including the £30 excess. On service of the summons the defendants' insurers immediately paid into court the £72.80 plus costs on the summons and wrote the plaintiff's insurers withdrawing the offer of 50% of the claim. The county court paid out the £72.80 to the plaintiff, the action being thereby stayed under the County Court Rules Ord 11, r 7(2): 'Where the amount paid into court is the whole amount of the claim together with the costs stated on the summons the action shall be stayed.' The plaintiff's insurers in the name of the plaintiff applied for a removal of the stay to enable them to continue with the action for recovery of their own outlay. The county court judge held that he had a discretion to remove the stay but that it was not a case in which he should do so.
HELD, ON APPEAL: (1) The court had jurisdiction in a proper case to remove a stay which has resulted from the operation of Ord 11, r 7(2), though it is a jurisdiction which should be exercised with very great care. When an action is stayed it does not come to an end but loses its inherent ability to go forward; but it can be started up again by order of the court. Dicta in *Derrick v Williams* (p 678, above) and *Cooper v Williams* (p 459, above) adopted. (2) This was one of the probably few and rare cases in which a stay ought to be set aside. The defendants' insurers, at the time when they made the payment into court, were well aware that the plaintiff's claim was only a small part of the whole claim which was intended to be prosecuted against them. They were seeking to take advantage of the procedure to bar any further claim against them.

Note—It was accepted by the plaintiff's insurers that they could not start a fresh action in the plaintiff's name for the amount of their claim. *Taylor v Wray*, above, is not mentioned in the judgments. The County Court Rules, Ord 11, r 7 has been replaced by Ord 11, rr 2, 3 and 4 of the 1988 Rules.

Buckland v Palmer

[1984] 3 All ER 554, [1984] 1 WLR 1109, 128 Sol Jo 565, CA
After a damaging collision between her car and the defendant's the plaintiff issued a summons against him in the county court for £50 being the excess not covered by her policy. He paid the whole amount into court, though denying liability, and she accepted it. The action was thereby automatically stayed by operation of Ord 11, r 3(3) of the then County Court Rules. Subsequently her insurers began proceedings in her name against the defendant for the balance of the cost of repairs which they had paid for. The defendant applied to the court that the second action be struck out on the ground that it was an abuse of the process of the court. The county court judge, relying on *Taylor v O Wray & Co Ltd* (above) refused to strike out the action.
HELD, on the defendant's appeal: *Taylor*'s case was distinguishable and out of line with the general stream of authority. It was in the public interest that there should be finality in litigation. On principle and on the authorities (including *Derrick v Williams* (p 678, above) and *Lambert v Mainland Market Deliveries* (above)) (1) it is an abuse on the process of the court to bring two actions in respect of the same cause of action, and (2) where there has been no judgment in the first action it can, when appropriate, be revived and amended to include the whole claim. The second action should be struck out without prejudice to an application to remove the stay on the first action and amend the particulars of claim in that action.

Note—John Donaldson MR said the decision left open the problem of what is to happen if the first action has proceeded to judgment, but he said he would expect the courts to reappraise the circumstances in which a judgment could be set aside if justice so required.

Steamship Mutual Underwriting v Trollope & Colls Ltd

(1985) 6 Con LR 11, 2 Const LJ 75; affd (1986) 33 BLR 77, 6 Con LR 11, 2 Const LJ 224, CA
The Court of Appeal, adopting the definition of a cause of action in *Letang v Cooper* as a factual situation the existence of which entitled one person to obtain from the court a remedy against another, rejected the suggestion that all damage caused by breach of the same duty by the same party under the same contract gave rise to a single cause of action. Such an approach would deprive the plaintiffs of any right to sue for later damage once they had obtained judgment for the first.

Vines v Arnold
(1849) 8 CB 632, 7 Dow & L, 277, Rob L & W 180, Cox M & H 320

Adkin v Friend
(1878) 38 LJCP 277, 38 LT 393
'It shall not be lawful for any plaintiff to divide any cause of action for the purpose of bringing two or more actions in one or more of the county courts.'

It would seem that if a plaintiff divides his causes of action, and sues for part of his claim, and the defendant does not raise the objection at the trial of the first action, the plaintiff can afterwards sue for the rest of his claim, and the defendant is not protected by the above section.

Sanders v Hamilton

(1907) 96 LT 679, 23 TLR 389
But where the plaintiff by mistake claims too small a sum and the defendant admitting

liability pays that amount into court, and it is taken out by the plaintiff, the plaintiff cannot, when leave to amend his claim has been refused, maintain a new action for the larger amount both on the principle of *res judicata* and by reason of the provisions of this section.

In an action in detinue in the county court, plaintiff by mistake claimed too small a sum. Defendant paid into court the amount claimed without denial of liability and it was taken out by plaintiff. Upon discovering his mistake, plaintiff asked leave to amend his particulars, which was refused, and judgment was given in the action for defendant. Plaintiff then began a new action for the larger amount, giving credit to defendant for the sum previously paid into court.
HELD: The matter was *res judicata*, and the action was not maintainable.

Poulett v Hill

[1893] 1 Ch 277, 62 LJ Ch 466, 68 LT 476, 41 WR 503, CA
If two actions are commenced, the second asking for relief which might have been obtained in the first, the second is prima facie vexatious, and may be stayed.

Alfred Rowntree & Sons Ltd v Frederick Allen & Sons

(1935) 41 Com Cas 90
Plaintiff cannot bring two actions for different parts of damage arising from the same breach.

CHAPTER 18

Legal Aid*

ASSISTED PERSON'S COSTS

Legal aid

Note—The Legal Aid Acts 1974, 1979 and 1982 have been repealed and replaced by the Legal Aid Act 1988 with effect from 1 April 1989. The chief administrative effect of the Act is to transfer administration of the Legal Aid Scheme from the Law Society to the Legal Aid Board, members of which are appointed by the Lord Chancellor. The current regulations under the Act include the Civil Legal Aid (General) Regulations 1989, the Legal Advice and Assistance Regulations 1989 and the Civil Legal Aid (Assessment of Resources) Regulations 1989, all of which came into force on 1 April 1989.

Right of assisted person to costs from Fund

Page v Page, Metcalf v Wells

[1953] Ch 320, [1953] 1 All ER 626, [1953] 2 WLR 432, 97 Sol Jo 150, CA
A party who has been granted a legal aid certificate is entitled as of right to an order for taxation of his costs under the Act. There is no discretion in the court to withhold an order, although no order is made as to the costs of the proceedings.

Legal Aid Fund charge

LAW SOCIETY'S GAZETTE, FEBRUARY 1959, P 95

At page 19 of the Annual Statement of the General Council of the Bar for 1954, the attention of members of the Bar was drawn to s 3(4) of the Legal Aid and Advice Act 1949 [now s 16(6) of the 1988 Act] and to the case of *R v Judge Fraser Harrison, ex p Law Society* [1955] 1 QB 287, [1955] 1 All ER 270, [1955] 2 WLR 220, 99 Sol Jo

* This chapter has been written by David Lawton.

79. It was there stated that when settling actions, counsel are reminded that s 3(4) of the Act creates a charge for the benefit of the Legal Aid Fund on any property recovered or preserved for the assisted person and on any damages recovered to the extent of any unpaid costs of the proceedings and that this charge operates even where the assisted person's contribution is nil.

The Bar Council are aware that there were at one time exceptional cases in which this charge had been waived. They are also aware that there have been cases in which counsel for parties to a settlement have sought and obtained the approval of the judge to the settlement subject to a recommendation by the judge that those responsible should consider refraining from enforcing the statutory charge.

The Bar Council have now been informed that as the statute creating the charge provides no exception, the Law Society cannot obtain any waiver of the charge in future cases.

In these circumstances the Bar Council have issued a circular to the Bar drawing attention to the position of counsel acting for an assisted plaintiff who is offered some sum by way of settlement on behalf of the defendant. Unless such an offer contains a provision to pay an adequate sum to the assisted plaintiff by way of costs the charge will reduce and may exceed the sum offered.

Particular attention is drawn to the effect of the charge where there has been a payment into court and advice is sought upon the question of acceptance.

The Bar Council are of the opinion that in such circumstances counsel are bound to draw the attention of the assisted person and of the instructing solicitor to these matters and should themselves clearly appreciate that any recommendation from the Bench which may have been sought or volunteered is incapable of effecting any waiver of this statutory charge.

DEFENDANT'S COSTS AGAINST ASSISTED PERSON

Deduction from damages

Nolan v C and C Marshall

[1954] 2 QB 42, [1954] 1 All ER 328, [1954] 2 WLR 285, 98 Sol Jo 108, CA
Defendants paid £763 into court. Plaintiff awarded £504 1s 11d at trial. Disposable capital and contribution assessed at nil.

ORDER: Plaintiff to recover costs up to payment in; defendants to recover their costs after payment in; defendants to deduct excess of their costs over plaintiff's costs from damages (McNair J).

HELD, ON APPEAL: Section 4(3) of the 1949 Act (now reg 4 of the Civil Legal Aid (Assessment of Resources) Regulations 1989) deals with contribution by the assisted person. When the award was made, the case had passed that stage. There is nothing in the Act or Regulations to show that the costs could not be deducted from damages.

Bloomfield v British Transport Commission

[1960] 2 QB 86, [1960] 2 All ER 54n, [1960] 2 WLR 693, 104 Sol Jo 329, CA
The plaintiff appealed against an award of £1,500 damages on the ground that it was insufficient. The appeal was dismissed. The defendants asked for the costs of the appeal though the plaintiff was an assisted person under the Legal Aid and Advice Act 1949.

HELD: There was no ground why the full costs of the appeal should not be awarded and they would have to come out of the damages. They would be assessed at £75.

Cook v S

[1967] 1 All ER 299, [1967] 1 WLR 457, 110 Sol Jo 964, CA
In an action for negligence against a solicitor the defendant paid into court £1,500. At trial the plaintiff, who was legally aided, was awarded only £1,110. The defendant's costs after payment in amounted to £1,400 but the judge gave him only £200 costs.
HELD, ON APPEAL: As the Legal Aid Fund had a charge on the damages for the plaintiff's costs (*Bloomfield v British Transport Commission*, above) and as the balance of the damages (£910) would be wholly absorbed by the plaintiff's costs the contest was between the defendant and the Legal Aid Fund. As the Legal Aid Fund was maintaining the plaintiff's action and as the defendant had made a successful payment into court he should have all his costs, at least up to £1,110, but the plaintiff should not be ordered personally to pay any of the excess. Appeal allowed.

Lockley v National Blood Transfusion Service

[1992] 2 All ER 589, [1992] 1 WLR 492, CA
A legally aided plaintiff was ordered to pay the costs of the defendant's interlocutory application not to be enforced without leave of the court save as to set-off against the plaintiff's damages and costs.
HELD, ON APPEAL: It is permissible to direct that the costs with an interlocutory order made against a legally-aided party in favour of an unassisted party be set-off against damages or costs to which the legally aided party may in the future become entitled in the action, since the provision in s 16(8) of the Legal Aid Act 1988 that the Legal Aid Board's charge under s 16(6) of that Act over property recovered or reserved for an assisted party in proceedings is not to prevent a court allowing damages or costs subject to that charge to be set-off against other damages or costs, does not create any new right of set-off but specifically preserves as against the legally-aided party the rights of set-off available under general law and protects such rights against the charge. *Cook v S*, above, followed.

Order for costs against assisted person

Blatcher v Heaysman

[1960] 2 All ER 721, [1960] 1 WLR 663, 104 Sol Jo 545, CA
The plaintiffs were successful in an action against the defendants for fraudulent misrepresentation and were awarded £350 damages. On finding that both parties were legally aided, the judge refused to make an order for costs against the defendants.
HELD, ON APPEAL: An order for costs should be made against the defendants since if no parties had been legally aided the defendants would have been ordered to pay costs. An award of costs was to be made subject to the provisions of the Legal Aid and Advice Act 1949, s 2(2) (now s 12(1) of the 1988 Act) that the amount should be reasonable 'having regard to all the circumstances'. The duty of considering who is to pay must be fulfilled in accordance with the same principles of which discretion is normally exercised.

Mercantile Credit Co v Cross

[1965] 2 QB 205, [1965] 1 All ER 577, [1965] 2 WLR 687, 109 Sol Jo 47, CA
The plaintiff, an assisted person with nil contribution, failed in his action against the defendants. The county court judge ordered him to pay the whole of the defendant's costs.

HELD: Section 2(2) of the 1949 Act (now s 12(1) of the 1988 Act) requires the judge to award not more than an amount which is a reasonable one for the assisted person to pay. As against a defendant with a nil contribution the order made here was a wholly unreasonable one and one which did not amount to a proper exercise of the judge's discretion. The contribution would be restricted to £25.

Barling v British Transport Commission

[1955] 2 Lloyd's Rep 393 (Devlin J)
I think the same amount as the plaintiff is asked to contribute to her costs should be the same amount towards the costs of the defendant if the defendant is successful. Order £35 10s payable by the same instalments.

THE MOTOR INSURERS' BUREAU DEFENDING

Godfrey v Smith

[1955] 2 All ER 520, [1955] 1 WLR 692, 99 Sol Jo 419 (Donovan J)
A motor cyclist with a pillion passenger collided with another motor cyclist, who was uninsured. The two first named, who were not legally assisted, sued the uninsured motor cyclist, who obtained legal aid. The action succeeded and the usual order for costs was made against the defendant. At that time the legal aid certificate was not available, but was later obtained, and application was made on his behalf for the costs to be assessed in accordance with the certificate.

The judge said that, apart from the fact that the defendant was represented by the Motor Insurers' Bureau, he would have made an order for £50 costs by instalments. It was largely a matter of discretion whether a court took the Motor Insurers' Bureau Agreement into account. It would be unjust that the plaintiff should be out of pocket because the defendant was legally aided and could not pay the costs. The Motor Insurers' Bureau Agreement was relevant on the question of a full order for costs, and the judge ordered payment of the taxed costs in the ordinary way.

Limited certificate

Dugon v Williamson

[1964] Ch 59, [1963] 3 All ER 25, [1963] 3 WLR 477, 107 Sol Jo 572, CA
After judgment against him in the High Court the defendant served notice of appeal. He then obtained a legal aid certificate for the appeal limited to obtaining a transcript of the judgment and obtaining counsel's opinion on the prospects of the appeal. While the appeal was in the warned list the legal aid committee discharged the certificate after considering counsel's opinion. The defendant continued the appeal of his own resources and lost. On an application by the plaintiff for costs it was held that whilst the certificate was in force even though for a limited purpose the defendant was an 'assisted person' so that his liability for costs during that period was not to exceed an amount which was reasonable in the circumstances (the Legal Aid and Advice Act 1949, s 2(2)(e)). In the present case the amount was nil.

Note—Section 2(2)(e) of the 1949 Act is re-enacted as s 12(1) of the 1988 Act.

Impecunious defendant submitting to judgment

Ranson v Burns

(1964) 108 Sol Jo 676 (Sachs J)
The plaintiff was awarded £800 damages for personal injuries, the defendant having admitted negligence. After judgment given counsel for the defendant applied for a stay of execution: the defendant was not insured against this claim, had no means and had a legal aid certificate limited to defending on the amount of damages only. The plaintiff and her advisers knew this before trial.

The judge said that where a legally-aided defendant was not in a position to pay money into court he was nonetheless in a position to submit to judgment for some specific sum. For an impecunious defendant to take advantage of legal aid to proceed without making some offer to submit to judgment was certainly wrong. He ordered the defendant to pay the costs of the action.

Security for costs—foreign plaintiff

Jackson v John Dickinson & Co (Bolton) Ltd

[1952] 1 All ER 104, [1952] WN 9, CA
Plaintiff, an assisted person, was ordinarily resident in Dublin. Defendants applied for security for costs under Ord LXV, r 6 (now Ord 23, r 1), on the ground of residence abroad. The district registrar took into consideration the fact that the plaintiff was an assisted person and made an order fixing the security at £25. His order was reversed by the commission of assize.
HELD, ON APPEAL: Security is ordered as a matter of course under Ord XLV, r 6, against a plaintiff out of the jurisdiction because an order for costs may be ineffective unless he had property within the jurisdiction, and this applies to an assisted person although a full order for costs will probably not be made against the plaintiff. The order for security was right, and there was no reason to interfere with the sum fixed. *Conway v George Wimpey* (above) did not apply.

Note—Security for costs against an assisted person is now covered by s 17(1) of the Legal Aid Act 1988 and reg 123 of the Civil Legal Aid (General) Regulations 1989. These provide that where in any proceedings an assisted person is required to give security for costs the amount of such security shall not exceed the amount which is a reasonable one for him to pay having regard to all circumstances including the financial resources of all the parties and their conduct in connection with the dispute.

Wyld v Silver

[1963] 1 QB 169, [1962] 2 All ER 809, [1962] 1 WLR 863, 106 Sol Jo 409, CA
Although the court will not ordinarily make an order to give security for costs of an appeal against a legally-aided person (*Conway v George Wimpey*, above) it has jurisdiction to do so. The defendant had disposable capital of £323 and his contribution to the Legal Aid Fund was £207. He was required to give security for £100 before prosecuting an appeal.

DEFENDANT'S COSTS FROM LEGAL AID FUND

Payment of costs to unassisted opponents

Note—The Legal Aid Act 1964 provided for the payment out of the Legal Aid Fund of costs incurred by successful opponents of legally-aided litigants. The legislation is now contained in the Legal Aid Act 1988, s 18. The court may make an order for payment of such costs provided the following requirements are satisfied:

1 The successful party is unassisted in the sense that he does not have legal aid when he incurred the costs in the proceedings which he seeks to recover (s 18(1)(c)) and see *Re H (Minors) (Abduction: Custody Rights) No 2,* below.

2 The proceedings must be 'finally decided' in favour of the unassisted party. They are to be treated as finally decided:
   (a) if no appeal lies against the decision;
   (b) if an appeal lies with leave and the time for applying for leave has expired without leave being granted;
   (c) if no leave is required, or leave to appeal has been granted and no appeal is brought within the time limited for appeal.

3 The court must be satisfied that it is just and equitable in all the circumstances that the costs should be paid out of public funds (s 18(4)(c)).

4 The Court must in every case first consider what order should be made for costs against the party who has legal aid and for determining his liability in respect of the cost under s 17.

5 As respect the costs incurred in a court of first instance, those proceedings were instituted by the assisted party and the court is satisfied that the unassisted party will suffer severe financial hardship unless the order is made (s 18(4)(b).

6 Proceedings are not such that, apart from the Act, no order would be made for payment of the unassisted party's costs (s 18(4)(a)).

Only the court by which the proceedings are 'finally decided' can make the order. Costs means party and party costs but includes the costs of applying for the order. Appeal against an order lies only on a point of law.

See also the Legal Aid (General) Regulations 1989, regs 134-147.

Nowotnik v Nowotnik

[1967] P 83, [1965] 3 All ER 167, [1965] 3 WLR 920, 109 Sol Jo 632, CA
In a case in which a wife who had a legal aid certificate unsuccessfully sued for divorce from her husband who had not, the Court of Appeal decided that no order could be made for payment of the husband's costs from the Legal Aid Fund for three reasons:

1 Apart from the Act no order would have been made for costs against the wife, since it had not been the practice in the Divorce Court even before 1949 to make an order for costs against a wife without means. (See requirement 6 above.)

2 The husband would not suffer 'severe financial hardship' if no order were made. He earned about £1,200 a year and had about £10 in hand per week after paying ordinary living expenses.

3 It was not 'just and equitable' to make an order: even if the husband had earned £500 a year less and had thus qualified for a legal aid certificate himself if his contribution would have exceeded the amount of his costs and the Legal Aid Fund would have paid nothing. He could not be allowed to be better off by having no legal aid certificate.

Note—Held wrongly decided in next case.

Hanning v Maitland (No 2)

[1970] 1 QB 580, [1970] 1 All ER 812, [1970] 2 WLR 151, 114 Sol Jo 14, CA
In a dark lane at night the plaintiff, a cyclist, collided with the defendant, a pedestrian, and was injured. He succeeded in getting a legal aid certificate to sue for damages. The defendant was aged 54; his net wage was about £18 per week but he was thrifty and had saved about £2,700 with which he hoped to buy a house. He did not apply for legal aid and would not have got it if he had because of his savings. The action was fought and the plaintiff's claim was dismissed. When the defendant applied for payment of his costs out of the Legal Aid Fund under the 1964 Act the trial judge said the litigation was a waste of time and it would be a wicked thing if the defendant had to pay anything. Despite this the taxing master refused any payment; on appeal the judge (not the trial judge) also refused, considering himself bound by *Nowotnik v Nowotnik* (above).
HELD, ON APPEAL to the Court of Appeal: *Nowotnik*'s case was wrongly decided in giving emphasis to 'severe' in the phrase 'severe financial hardship'. The word should be construed to exclude insurance companies, commercial organisations and wealthy folk who can meet the costs without feeling it. It should not be construed to exclude people like the defendant of modest income or capital who would find it hard to bear his own costs of £325 out of his hard-earned savings. *Nowotnik*'s case was also wrong in holding that an unassisted person would not get more out of the Legal Aid Fund than he would if he were an assisted person. If the legally-aided plaintiff loses his case it is 'just and equitable' that the Fund should pay every penny of his taxed costs. Appeal allowed.

Co-defendants' costs from Legal Aid Fund

Landau v Purvis

(1986) Times, 12 August, CA
Mr Warrener was an accountant who prepared accounts at the request of Mr and Mrs Purvis for submission to the Inland Revenue. Mr and Mrs Purvis sold parts of an estate agency business to the plaintiffs; in doing so they produced Mr Warrener's accounts, without his knowledge. When the plaintiffs sued Mr and Mrs Purvis for misrepresentation they also sued Mr Warrener for a breach of the duty he allegedly owed the plaintiffs properly to prepare the accounts. All the parties except Mr Warrener received legal aid. The plaintiffs succeeded in their action against Mr and Mrs Purvis but lost against Mr Warrener. No order for costs was made in Mr Warrener's favour against the plaintiffs but Mr and Mrs Purvis were ordered to pay his costs, subject to their liability for these being determined under the terms of the Legal Aid Act 1974.
HELD: To come within s 13 of the 1974 Act (now s 18 of the 1988 Act), costs had to have been awarded against the legally-aided party who had instituted the proceedings. This had not happened here. Thus there was no jurisdiction under s 13 of the 1974 Act to grant payment of Mr Warrener's costs from the Legal Aid Fund, so, despite his clearly suffering severe financial hardship, no payment could be made.

Jones v Zahedi

[1993] 4 All ER 909, [1993] 1 WLR 1445, CA
The unassisted defendant applied for costs against the Legal Aid Board under s 18 of the 1988 Act. He filed an affidavit but the judge held the defendant had not discharged

the burden on him showing that he would suffer severe financial hardship if the costs order was not made and dismissed the application.

HELD, ON APPEAL: The court could not make an order in favour of an unassisted party applying for payment of his costs by the Legal Aid Board in s 18 of the 1988 Act on the grounds of severe financial hardship if the applicant's affidavit of costs and resources failed to comply with the requirements of Sch 2 to the 1989 Regulations in a significant respect of which the Legal Aid Board complained unless the applicant could show that he could not in all the circumstances comply with Sch 2. The defendant's affidavit was defective in that it gave no estimate of his inter partes costs, it contained no statement as to his financial resources of every kind during the three year period specified in para 2 of Sch 2, ie three years prior to the application for costs, nor of his estimated future financial resources and expectations, it did not exhibit any supporting evidence. The defendant's failure to comply with the Schedule was of such significance that an order in his favour could not properly have been made. The appeal was therefore dismissed.

Kelly v London Transport Executive

[1982] 2 All ER 842, [1982] 1 WLR 1055, 126 Sol Jo 262, CA

On 21 October 1974 the plaintiff sustained a trivial injury in the defendant's employment. He returned to work but gave up work in March 1975 complaining of depression, eye trouble and deafness. He consulted solicitors in March 1977 who got opinions from two counsel, obtained a legal aid certificate and from time to time amassed 19 medical reports. They also with counsel's opinions obtained unlimited leave from the legal aid committee to go on with the action. The defendants engaged five medical specialists. They paid £750 into court on 28 July 1980 which was not accepted and offered £4,000 on 24 September 1980 because they would be unable to recover costs from the legally aided plaintiff. This was also refused on the advice of counsel. At trial in October 1980 the judge rejected the claim as bogus: the symptoms complained of were due to chronic alcoholism. He awarded £75 for the original small injury. The defendants applied under the Legal Aid Act 1974, s 13(1) (now s 18 of the 1988 Act) to recover their costs of £8,000.

HELD: No order could be made because they could not show 'severe financial hardship'. They were a huge corporation 'hopelessly and continuously' in deficit almost to £175m, supported by a grant from the GLC. It would not be 'severe financial hardship' for them to meet a bill for £8,000. They could (per Lord Denning) proceed against the solicitors and counsel personally.

Adams v Riley

[1988] QB 372, [1988] 1 All ER 89 (Hutchison J)

A legally-aided plaintiff brought an unsuccessful action for damages for alleged professional negligence against the defendant architect. The defendants sought an order that his costs estimated to be £12,600 be paid by the Legal Aid Fund pursuant to s 18 of the 1988 Act. The defendant's wife worked and had cash savings. It was held that the capital and income of a successful unassisted party were not to be aggregated with those of his spouse in determining whether he would suffer severe financial hardship. However, the spouse's means were relevant to the extent that she was able to support herself and therefore relieve the defendant of the necessity of providing day-to-day maintenance and financial support to her. It was further held that were a successful unassisted party to establish that he would suffer severe financial hardship he was not necessarily entitled to the payment of the whole of his costs, but only to payment of that amount which would cause such hardship. An order was made that the defendant recover from the Fund his costs over and above the sum of £4,500.

Re H (minors) (Abduction: Custody Rights) (No 2)

[1992] 2 AC 303, [1992] 3 All ER 380, HL
The House of Lords had jurisdiction under s 18 of the 1988 Act to order payment by the Legal Aid Board of a legally-assisted successful defendant's costs incurred before the issue of his legal aid certificate. The plaintiff had been legally aided throughout. The defendant initially bore his own costs, but was legally aided before the conclusion of the proceedings at first instance until the disposal of the appeal by the House. Lord Bridge held in construing sub-s 1 of s 18 of the 1988 Act that the mere conjunction of the words 'finally decided' and 'unassisted party' in the single phrase afforded no ground to link required status of the party with the moment of the final decision. What matters is the status of the party as unassisted at the time when he incurred the costs in the proceedings which he sought to recover.

CLAIM AND COUNTER-CLAIM

Millican v Tucker

[1980] 1 All ER 1083, [1980] 1 WLR 640, 124 Sol Jo 276, CA
The plaintiffs, unassisted litigants, claimed against legally-aided defendants who counter-claimed on substantially the same issues. The action was settled at the hearing on terms which amounted to a total surrender by the defendants. The plaintiffs applied for an order for payment of their costs out of the Legal Aid Fund under the Legal Aid Act 1974, s 13 (now s 18 of the 1988 Act). The judge ordered payment by the Fund of the plaintiffs' costs of the counter-claim and directed that in taxing those costs the costs on issues common to both claim and counter-claim should be divided equally between the costs of the claim and those of the counter-claim. The Legal Aid Fund appealed.
HELD: The judge had no jurisdiction to make such an order. If it had been made inter partes it would have been well within the judge's discretion, but as it was made pursuant to a statutory power only and against the Legal Aid Fund, which was not a party, the judge had no power to do it.

Where a court orders that claim and counter-claim be dismissed, or allowed, with costs, and the rule of taxation is that the claim should be treated as if it stood alone and the counter-claim should bear only the amount by which the costs of the proceedings had been increased by it. A judge had a wide discretion to make a special order inter partes if he thinks fit, and can make such order as he likes, but however the costs may be dealt with by the judge's order, costs incurred in connection with the claim can never be appropriated to the counter-claim so as to become part of the costs of the counter-claim.

Note—See also *R & T Thew Ltd v Reeves* [1982] QB 172, [1981] 2 All ER 964, [1981] 3 WLR 190, 125 Sol Jo 358, CA.

Costs of appealing

Parker v Thompson

[1966] 3 All ER 766n, [1967] 1 WLR 28, 110 Sol Jo 772, CA

The requirement of 'severe financial hardship' does not apply to costs in the Court of Appeal.

The defendant successfully contested an action for damages against him at assizes, incurring costs of £271 in so doing. An appeal failed completely, the defendant incurring costs of £120 in fighting it. He was uninsured but could not show severe financial hardship. The plaintiffs were legally aided. An order was made to pay the defendant £120 out of the Legal Aid Fund to meet the costs of the appeal since it was 'just and equitable in all the circumstances'.

Saunders v Anglia Building Society

[1971] AC 1004, [1970] 3 All ER 961, [1970] 3 WLR 1078, 114 Sol Jo 885, 22 P & CR 300, HL

In an action against a building society the assisted person succeeded in the court of first instance but failed in the Court of Appeal and in the House of Lords. On the society's application for costs to be paid out of the Legal Aid Fund under the Legal Aid Act 1964—

HELD: (1) The court must first be 'satisfied that it is just and equitable in all the circumstances' that the unassisted party should get relief. The phrase was a composite phrase conveying one idea and it would be useless and might be misleading to seek to split it up. (2) A distinction had to be drawn between costs in the court of first instance, where the means of the unassisted person had to be considered, and costs in an appeal, where there was no means test. (3) The society had not been taken to the Court of Appeal by the assisted litigant: there was no sufficient reason why they should recover from public funds costs which they themselves chose to incur. But it was right that they should have their costs in the House of Lords from the Legal Aid Fund, the assisted litigant having obtained legal aid to appeal to the House.

Note—See also *General Accident Fire and Life Assurance Ltd v Foster* [1973] QB 50, [1972] 3 All ER 877, [1972] 3 WLR 657, [1972] 2 Lloyd's Rep 288, CA.

Clifford v Walker

[1972] 2 All ER 806, [1972] 1 WLR 274, 116 Sol Jo 275, CA

Saunders's case did not decide that an unassisted litigant who appeals to the Court of Appeal and wins is barred from recovering costs from the Legal Aid Fund. He can recover his costs against the Legal Aid Fund if it is just and equitable for him to do so, even though it was he who was the appellant. The fact that the unassisted party is of relatively limited means is a consideration that may be sufficient to justify an order.

Note—But see *Davies v Taylor (No 2)*, below.

Lewis v Averay (No 2)

[1973] 2 All ER 229, [1973] 1 WLR 510, 117 Sol Jo 188, CA

In the county court both parties had legal aid, but in the Court of Appeal the appellant Averay was unable to get legal aid and was supported by the Automobile Association whose solicitors acted for him. He applied under s 1(2) of the 1964 Act for his costs to be paid out of the Legal Aid Fund.

HELD: An order should be made to that effect. Averay was the litigant and the costs were 'incurred by him'. It was just and equitable that he should have them because he was a member of the AA and was in honour bound to reimburse the AA so far as he recovered the costs against the other side.

Davies v Taylor (No 2)

[1974] AC 225, [1973] 1 All ER 959, [1973] 2 WLR 610, 117 Sol Jo 246, HL
The respondent, successful in both the Court of Appeal and the House of Lords (in both of which the appellant was legally aided) applied for an order under s 1(1) of the 1964 Act that his costs on the appeal should be paid out of the Legal Aid Fund (see *Davies v Taylor*, above). He was insured under a motor policy and his insurers would pay his costs.
HELD: An order should be made. The costs were 'incurred by him in the proceedings' within s 1(1) even though the insurers agreed to pay them, unless there was an agreement between him and his solicitors that he would not pay their costs; it had not been proved there was. The fact that the order would benefit the insurers did not prevent it from being 'just and equitable'. The court had a very wide discretion under the Act; success in the appeal alone (contrary to the view expressed by the Court of Appeal in *Clifford v Walker* [1972] 2 All ER 806 (above)) could be a sufficient justification for an order. But the court should not usually give its reasons.

Note—See also two applications similarly dealt with on the same occasion: *Shiloh Spinners Ltd v Harding (No 2)* and *O'Brien v Robinson (No 2)* [1973] 1 All ER 966 and 969n. For s 1(1) of the 1964 Act see now s 18 of the 1988 Act.

Megarity v Law Society

[1982] AC 81, [1981] 1 All ER 641, [1981] 2 WLR 335, 125 Sol Jo 167, HL
The plaintiff made an unsuccessful interlocutory appeal (see *Megarity v Ryan*, above) and the Court of Appeal ordered the unassisted defendants costs of the appeal to be paid out of the Legal Aid Fund. The Law Society objected that 'proceedings' meant the whole action and that the court had no power to award costs of an interlocutory appeal since the action was not yet 'finally decided'.

DUTIES OF LEGAL ADVISORS

Duty of solicitor to client

The solicitor has a professional duty to consider whether or not a client will benefit from legal aid and to advise the client accordingly. This applies whether or not the solicitor does legal aid work.

Duty of solicitor and counsel to the Legal Aid Board

The 1988 Act has increased the obligations upon solicitors and counsel to report to the Legal Aid Board. The principal obligations include the following:

1 A duty to report abuse of legal aid either by an assisted party requiring a case to be conducted unreasonably or by an assisted party failing to provide information to the Legal Aid Board or making a false statement to the Board (reg 67).
2 A duty to report his reasons for refusing to act or for giving up a case for an assisted party (reg 69).

3 A duty to report the progress of proceedings including:
   (i) reporting when the assisted person declines to accept a reasonable offer of settlement or a payment into court;
   (ii) notify the Area Director where a legal aid certificate is issued to another party to the proceedings (reg 70).

4 A solicitor who has acted or is acting for an assisted person shall on becoming aware that this person:
   (a) has died or;
   (b) has had a bankruptcy order made against him report that fact to the Area Director (reg 71).

5 All moneys payable to an assisted person shall be paid to the solicitor of the assisted person or, if he is no longer represented by a solicitor, to the Board and only the solicitor or the Board shall be capable of giving a good discharge for moneys so payable. This duty therefore extends to an opposing party's solicitor and where the assisted person's solicitor has reason to believe that an attempt may be made to circumvent the provisions of this regulation he shall inform the Board (reg 87).

Hopeless cases—penalty in costs

Edwards v Edwards

[1958] P 235, [1958] 2 All ER 179, [1958] 2 WLR 956, 102 Sol Jo 402 (Sachs J)
A wife obtained legal aid and commenced proceedings for wilful neglect to maintain. In the proceedings it became clear that the chances of success did not really exist at all. The husband's solicitors wrote with information to the area committee and sent a copy to the wife's solicitor, who attended before the committee; the certificate was not revoked, and the case proceeded to trial. The husband applied for an order that the wife's solicitor should personally bear the costs incurred by him.
HELD: The court has inherent powers over solicitors in their capacity as officers of the court. The duty is to conduct litigation with due propriety and is due to the court and to all those against whom they are concerned. It is not enough to invoke the jurisdiction that the case failed, or error or judgment even of an order equivalent to negligence. It must be serious dereliction of duty but need not amount to *mala fides* or other obliquity. Unreasonably to initiate or continue an action when it has no or substantially no chance of success may give jurisdiction. The fact that the solicitor is acting under a legal aid certificate does not affect the position. Section 1(7)(b) of the 1949 Act (now s 31(1)(b) of the 1988 Act) preserves the rights of other parties.

Order for payment by the solicitors personally of all costs from and after the issue by them of the summons for directions.

Kyle v Mason

(1963) Times, 3 July, CA
An order to pay costs personally was made by the Court of Appeal in a case in which the plaintiff's appeal, for which he had obtained a legal aid certificate, was dismissed. The court said there were no grounds at all for the appeal, which arose from a claim for damages for injuries received in a road accident. The certificate had been granted on the basis of a letter from the plaintiff's solicitor and on seeing the letter the court required the solicitor to show cause why he should not personally pay the costs.

Through counsel the solicitor agreed that the letter was misleading though written under an honest mistake as to the effect of the evidence. He agreed to pay all the costs himself and an order was made accordingly.

Per Ormerod LJ: This case underlined the care which must be taken when supplying information to legal aid committees. Misleading information made their task difficult if not impossible. The information given by the solicitor was misleading and therefore the court felt impelled to take the course which it had adopted.

Holmes v National Benzole Co Ltd

(1965) 109 Sol Jo 971, (1965) Times, 30 November (Lyell J)
In an action for damages in which the plaintiff was legally aided all the claims were abandoned in the course of the trial in February 1964 and the action withdrawn. The taxing master reported after an inquiry that there was evidence of costs having been incurred without reasonable cause. On an application for the plaintiff's costs to be taxed under the Third Schedule of the Legal Aid and Advice Act 1949 the judge refused any costs to the plaintiff's solicitor after 1 March 1962. It was implicit (he said) from the judgment of Lord Maugham in *Myers v Elman* [1940] AC 282, [1939] 4 All ER 484, 109 LJKB 105, 162 LT 113, 56 TLR 177, 84 Sol Jo 184, HL that a solicitor who without any investigation of his client's claim allowed or encouraged a client to pursue a claim which proper investigation would at an early stage have shown to be a hopeless one was in breach of his duty to his client for he would be causing his client to incur costs without reasonable cause. Where the client was legally aided the sanction of the client's displeasure where money was spent on fruitless litigation was not so present as in the case of a private client but the absence of that sanction would not be an excuse to exercise a lesser degree of care. There was a heavy duty on counsel and solicitors to test their client's case with the same anxious care as they would bring to one where they looked to their clients for the costs.

Note—Regulation 102 of the 1989 Regulations provides that where an assisted person's solicitor fails to comply with any provision of the regulations and, as a result, the Fund incurs loss, the Area Committee may defer payment for all or part of the profit costs and may refer the conduct of the solicitor to the Solicitors' Disciplinary Tribunal. Regulation 109 provides that any costs wasted by failure to conduct the proceedings with reasonable competence and expedition shall be disallowed or reduced and where the solicitor has without good reason delayed putting his bill for taxation the whole of the costs may be disallowed or reduced.

MISCELLANEOUS

Costs of winding up proceedings

Re Peretz Co Ltd

[1965] Ch 200, [1964] 3 All ER 633, [1964] 3 WLR 1159, 108 Sol Jo 840 (Buckley J)
The petitioner's legal aid certificate authorised him to prosecute an action against a company for damages for trespass and nuisance and included enforcement proceedings in respect of any order or judgment obtained in the action. It was held that the certificate was effective to cover winding-up proceedings founded on a judgment debt.

Sharing counsel with unassisted party

Howson v M A Forte

(1965) 109 Sol Jo 702, CA
Two plaintiffs, one legally aided, the other not, brought a joint action against the defendants for breach of contract. They came to the trial represented by separate counsel. The defendants objected and the judge upheld the objection, applying the ordinary rule that there should be only one representation. They appealed. The grounds on which they applied for separate representation were that the plaintiff who had legal aid had a certificate for leading counsel; if the other plaintiff's name appeared on leading counsel's brief he might be liable for half the fee, which he could not afford.
HELD: This was no ground for granting the application. If neither party had been legally aided they would have had to make their own financial arrangements; the fact that one of them was legally aided did not make any difference.

Contribution computation—money received by litigant

R v Legal Aid Board, ex p Clark

(1992) Times, 25th November (MacPherson J)
Money received by a litigant in connection with the incident giving rise to the legal dispute in respect of which a legal aid application had been made was not to be taken into account in assessing the litigant's means for computing the amount of our contribution. The DSS erred in taking into account receipt of a lump sum retiring allowance of £13,107 where the retirement was on medical grounds as a result of the injury complained of in the dispute in respect of which he was legally aided (Civil Legal Aid (Assessment of Resources) Regulations 1989, Sch 3, para 14(b)).

Advice and assistance provided by specialist in welfare law

R v Legal Aid Board, ex p Bruce

[1992] 1 All ER 133, [1991] 1 WLR 1231, CA
Mrs Bruce was not a solicitor but had become an acknowledged expert on welfare law when employed in a solicitor's firm. She set up a business to provide advice to solicitors on their client's entitlement to welfare benefits.
HELD, ON APPEAL: Under s 2(6) of the 1988 Act a charge for advice on English law could only be made under that Act if it was made by a barrister or solicitor. Fees charged by an expert who was a specialist in a particular field of law who was neither a barrister nor solicitor could not be recovered from the Legal Aid Board by a solicitor retaining such a specialist as a disbursement under the Green Form Scheme.

CHAPTER 19

Third Party Insurance

INTRODUCTION

Since 1930 it has been compulsory for any person having control of a motor vehicle to insure against liability for personal injury to a third party arising out of the use of the vehicle. The obligation to insure was extended to cover passengers in 1971, and the legislation consolidated in the Road Traffic Act 1972 is now contained in the Road Traffic Act 1988.

An obligation is also imposed on insurers to meet a judgment against their insured, subject to a right of recovery against him personally. In addition, there is a remedy against an uninsured or an untraceable driver by virtue of the agreements between the Motor Insurers' Bureau and the Department of Transport (see Ch 20 generally).

Note—The statutory provisions relating to compulsory insurance against third party risks are contained in Part VI of the Road Traffic Act 1988 incorporating provisions of the Motor Vehicles (Compulsory Insurance) Regulations 1987 which made amendments to ss 145 and 149 of the Road Traffic Act 1972. The 1988 Act came into force on 15 May 1989. The 1972 Act is repealed, though remaining in force in respect of matters arising before that date. Repeals and consequential amendments are made by the Road Traffic (Consequential Provisions) Act 1988 which came into force on the same date.

ROAD TRAFFIC ACT 1988, SS 143, 144

143 (1) Subject to the provisions of this Part of this Act—

(a) a person must not use a motor vehicle on a road unless there is in force in relation to the use of the vehicle by that person such a policy of insurance or such a security in respect of third party risks as complies with the requirements of this Part of this Act, and

(b) a person must not cause or permit any other person to use a motor vehicle on a road unless there is in force in relation to the use of the vehicle by that other person such a policy of insurance or such a security in respect of third party risks as complies with the requirements of this Part of this Act.

(2) If a person acts in contravention of subsection (1) above he is guilty of an offence.

(3) A person charged with using a motor vehicle in contravention of this section shall not be convicted if he proves—

(a) that the vehicle did not belong to him and was not in his possession under a contract of hiring or of loan,

(b) that he was using the vehicle in the course of his employment, and

(c) that he neither knew nor had reason to believe that there was not in force in relation to the vehicle such a policy of insurance or security as is mentioned in subsection (1) above.

(4) This Part of this Act does not apply to invalid carriages.

144 (1) Section 143 of this Act does not apply to a vehicle owned by a person who has deposited and keeps deposited with the Accountant General of the Supreme Court the sum of £15,000, at a time when the vehicle is being driven under the owner's control.

(2) Section 143 does not apply—

(a) to a vehicle owned—

  (i) by the council of a county or county district in England and Wales, the Common Council of the City of London, the council of a London borough, the Inner London Education Authority, or a joint authority (other than a police authority) established by Part IV of the Local Government Act 1985;

  (ii) by a regional, islands or district council in Scotland, or

  (iii) by a joint board or committee in England or Wales, or joint committee in Scotland, which is so constituted as to include among its members representatives of any such council,

  at a time when the vehicle is being driven under the owner's control;

(b) to a vehicle owned by a police authority or the Receiver for the Metropolitan Police district, at a time when it is being driven under the owner's control, or to a vehicle at a time when it is being driven for police purposes by or under the direction of a constable, or by a person employed by a police authority, or employed by the Receiver, or

(c) to a vehicle at a time when it is being driven on a journey to or from any place undertaken for salvage purposes pursuant to Part IX of the Merchant Shipping Act 1894;

(d) to the use of a vehicle for the purpose of its being provided in pursuance of a direction under section 166(2)(b) of the Army Act 1955 or under the corresponding provision of the Air Force Act 1955;

(e) to a vehicle which is made available by the Secretary of State to any person, body or local authority in pursuance of section 23 or 26 of the National Health Service Act 1977 at a time when it is being used in accordance with the terms on which it is so made available;

(f) to a vehicle which is made available by the Secretary of State to any local authority, education authority or voluntary organisation in Scotland in pursuance of section 15 or 16 of the National Health Service (Scotland) Act 1978 at a time when it is being used in accordance with the terms on which it is so made available.

Note—Part VI of the 1972 Act is replaced by Part VI of the 1988 Act; by s 193 of and Sch 4 to the 1988 Act, tramcars and trolley vehicles are excluded from Part VI of the 1988 Act (ss 143–162).

MOTOR VEHICLE

Note—The Road Traffic Act 1988, s 185(1) and the Road Traffic Regulation Act 1984, s 136(1) define 'motor vehicle' as a mechanically propelled vehicle intended or adapted for use on roads.

Lawrence v Howlett

[1952] 2 All ER 74, 116 JP 391, [1952] WN 308, [1952] 1 TLR 1476, 96 Sol Jo 397, 50 LGR 531, [1952] 1 Lloyd's Rep 483, Div Ct
A bicycle was fitted with an auxiliary engine but could be used as an ordinary pedal cycle. The auxiliary motor was not in working condition, the cylinder, piston, and connecting rod having been removed, and it was being used as a pedal cycle. The rider was charged with using a motor vehicle without insurance and convicted.
HELD, ON APPEAL: It could not be mechanically propelled. A motor car is designed so that it has only a mechanical means of propulsion and would therefore be classified whether in working order or not as a mechanically propelled vehicle, but a dual-purpose machine may depend on its working condition and purpose of use. It was not at the material time a 'motor vehicle' and did not require third party insurance.

It was an exceptional case not to be extended beyond its particular facts.

Floyd v Bush

[1953] 1 All ER 265, [1953] 1 WLR 242, 117 JP 88, 97 Sol Jo 80, 51 LGR 162, [1953] 1 Lloyd's Rep 64, Div Ct
A pedal cycle with an auxiliary motor the engine of which is in working order is a mechanically propelled vehicle within s 1 of the 1930 Act although the driver pedals the cycle without using the engine, and requires an insurance policy; distinguishing *Lawrence v Howlett* where the engine had been dismantled. *Shimmell v Fisher* [1951] 2 All ER 672, 115 JP 526, [1951] 2 TLR 753, 95 Sol Jo 625, 49 LGR 813, 35 Cr App Rep 100 followed.

R v Tahsin

[1970] RTR 88, Div Ct
The defendant was riding a moped by using the pedals as on an ordinary bicycle. The engine was not working and he said a temporary defect had prevented him from starting it.
HELD: Even if a moped was to be treated as falling within a different class from that of cars and lorries a temporary defect which prevented the engine from being started did not exclude it from being a 'mechanically propelled vehicle' within the meaning of the Road Traffic Act 1960, s 253(1) and therefore a 'motor vehicle' for the purposes of the 1960 Act. *Floyd v Bush* applied; *Lawrence v Howlett* distinguished.

Note—Section 253(1) of the 1960 Act was in the same terms as s 185 of the Road Traffic Act 1988.

McEachran v Hurst

[1978] RTR 462, [1978] Crim LR 499, Div Ct
The defendant was riding a moped on a public road by pedalling it. The engine was not in working order and there was no petrol in the tank. The defendant had bought it for £5 and had never used the engine. He was taking it to a friend to be repaired.
HELD: Following *R v Tahsin* (above) the test is whether the vehicle is constructed so that it can be mechanically propelled, not whether it has an engine in working order at the relevant time. There must be a conviction.

Newberry v Simmonds

[1961] 2 QB 345, [1961] 2 All ER 318, [1961] 2 WLR 675, 125 JP 409, 105 Sol Jo 324, 59 LGR 309, Div Ct QBD
The respondent's car was parked on a public road for a month without a road fund licence in force. The outward appearance of the car was normal but at the material time it had no engine. A charge under the Vehicles (Excise) Act 1949, s 15 of using on a public road a mechanically propelled vehicle for which no licence under the Act was in force was dismissed by the justices on the ground that if there were no engine in the car it was not a mechanically propelled vehicle.
HELD: On a case stated, there must be a conviction. The words 'mechanically propelled vehicle' have the same meaning in the Vehicles (Excise) Act 1949, as in the Road Traffic Act 1930, and the same decisions are relevant to both Acts. Following *Floyd v Bush* (above) and *Lawrence v Howlett* (above) a motor car does not cease to be a mechanically propelled vehicle on the mere removal of the engine if the evidence admits the possibility that the engine may shortly be replaced and the motive power restored.

Note—The Vehicles (Excise) Act 1949, s 15, is now replaced by the Vehicles (Excise) Act 1971, s 8. 'Mechanically propelled vehicle' is not defined in either Act.

Smart v Allan

[1963] 1 QB 291, [1962] 3 All ER 893, [1962] 3 WLR 1325, 127 JP 35, 106 Sol Jo 881, 60 LGR 548, Div Ct QBD
The defendant bought a Rover car for £2 for scrap and left it parked on a public highway. The engine was incomplete and did not work. It had no gearbox, one tyre was missing and the other flat; it had no battery and could be moved only by towing on two wheels. It could have been put in running order only at a cost out of all proportion to its value. It was not taxed or insured and the defendant was charged with using the car on the road within the meaning of the Road Traffic Act 1960, s 201 (now the Road Traffic Act 1988, s 143), when not insured.
HELD: Some limit must be put and some stage reached when one says of a vehicle. 'This is so immobile that it has ceased to be a mechanically propelled vehicle.' In the present case, unlike *Newberry v Simmonds* (above) there was no reasonable prospect of the vehicle ever being made mobile again. It had ceased to be 'a mechanically propelled vehicle' within the meaning of the Road Traffic Act 1960, s 253(1) (which was in the same terms as the Road Traffic Act 1972, s 190(1)), and was therefore not a 'motor vehicle' for the purposes of s 201.

McNeill v Ritchie

1967 SLT (Sh Ct) 68
The accused's car, parked on a public road, had the gear-box removed together with the overdrive and propeller shaft which he sold as scrap. It would have cost more to replace these parts than the car was worth. He had no intention of putting the car in running order and was hoping to find someone to buy it for spares. He was charged with using it without insurance and a test certificate. He contended it was not a 'motor vehicle' within the meaning of the Road Traffic Act 1960, s 253 (now ss 185 and 186 of the 1988 Act).
HELD: The test was whether the car had reached the stage where there was no reasonable prospect of ever making it mobile again. The facts that it was uneconomic to restore the missing parts and that the accused was only keeping it for spares raised sufficient doubt as to remove the car from the class of 'mechanically propelled vehicles'.

Law v Thomas

(1964) 108 Sol Jo 158, 62 LGR 195, Div Ct
The defendant's car was left standing in the roadway for three months untaxed and uninsured. It could not be driven because of a defect which the defendant thought was a cracked cylinder block. When the car was inspected it was found that the fault was merely a blown core plug. When the plug was replaced the car was in working order. On a charge against the owner of using a vehicle on a road when uninsured contrary to s 201 of the 1960 Act (now the Road Traffic Act 1988, s 143) the justices, having been referred to *Smart v Allan* (above) held that the car was not 'a mechanically propelled vehicle intended or adapted for use on the roads' and dismissed the charge.
HELD, ON APPEAL: *Smart v Allan* was an extreme case. In the present case the car could be made mobile in a matter of minutes. It was at all times a mechanically propelled vehicle which the owner was using on a road without the necessary insurance cover. There must be a conviction.

Note—Followed and applied in *Binks v Department of Environment* [1975] RTR 318 (an excise case).

Intended or adapted

Burns v Currell

[1963] 2 QB 433, [1963] 2 All ER 297, [1963] 2 WLR 1106, 127 JP 397, 107 Sol Jo 272, 61 LGR 356, Div Ct
The appellant drove a 'go-kart' on one occasion on a road to which the public had access. He was convicted by justices of unlawfully using a motor car contrary to the Road Traffic Act 1960, s 201 (now the Road Traffic Act 1988, s 143) and the Motor Vehicles (Construction and Use) Regulations 1955. The go-kart had a tubular frame on four small wheels, an engine, single seat and steering column. It had no horn, springs, parking brake, driving mirror or wings and had rear wheel brakes only. There was no policy of insurance in force.
HELD, ON APPEAL: The real question was whether the go-kart was a motor vehicle within the meaning of the Road Traffic Act 1960, s 253(1) (now the Road Traffic Act 1988, ss 185(1) and 186(1)), ie 'a mechanically propelled vehicle intended or adapted for

use on the roads'. 'Intended' does not mean intended by the manufacturer or retailer or by the user at the moment of the offence. The test is whether a reasonable person looking at the vehicle would say that one of its uses would be some general use on the road. There was no evidence before the justices to satisfy this test. 'Adapted' means 'fit and apt' for use on the road and the go-kart was not. Appeal allowed.

Chief Constable of Avon v Fleming

[1987] 1 All ER 318, [1987] RTR 378, 84 Cr App Rep 345, QBD
Mr Fleming was stopped when pushing a motor-cycle on a public road. To adapt it for scrambling, its registration plate, reflectors, lights and speedometer had been removed, although the police description of the vehicle was vague and unsatisfactory. At least partly because of this, the court concluded that the police had failed to prove that the motor cycle was a motor vehicle for the purposes of s 190 of the Road Traffic Act 1972 (s 185 of the 1988 Act). The test in *Burns v Currell* (above) was applied; the police had not satisfied it.

Note—In *Reader v Bunyard* [1987] RTR 406, a vehicle which lacked engine and gear box, but the future of which was uncertain (whether to be scrapped or repaired) was judged not to be a 'motor vehicle' for the purposes of s 190(1) of the 1972 Act (now s 185 of the 1988 Act). This was, though, largely because the evidence was unsatisfactory. *Burns v Currell* (above) was cited.

In *Motorists Mutual Insurance Co v Co-op* F Supp 1033 (1988) a child's motorised minibike was held to be 'a motor vehicle' but this was under an extended definition of that phrase set out in an insurance policy.

Chalgray Ltd v Apsley

(1965) 109 Sol Jo 394, Div Ct
The defendants were the owner and driver of a 15 cwt dumper. On a number of occasions it was driven along the pavement and roadway of a public highway for distances up to 100 yards for the purposes of carrying building materials for work being carried on at an adjoining building site. The defendants were charged with using a motor vehicle on a road when not covered by insurance contrary to the Road Traffic Act 1960, s 201.
HELD: On a case stated, the sole issue was whether the dumper was a motor vehicle within s 253(1). The present case fell within the ambit of those cases where there was only occasional use of the dumper on the highway as part of the construction plant. *Burns v Currell* (above) showed that the real test was whether some general use on the road was intended. The mere intention of the driver to use the plant on the highway could not without further evidence turn the dumper as a whole by way of general use into a motor vehicle. There was no evidence of that type of general use which would justify a conviction. There were many pieces of plant used for constructional work that were self-propelled and yet were not motor vehicles merely because they might, from time to time, emerge on the highway.

Note—Section 201 of the 1960 Act was effectively the same as s 143 of the Road Traffic Act 1988 set out at p 702, above.

Brown v Abbott

(1965) 109 Sol Jo 437, Div Ct
The defendant steered along a road a Ford car which was being towed by another car. He was charged with using the Ford on a road whilst uninsured. The Ford had been

adapted for racing by substitution of a different engine, removal of front and rear passenger seats and replacement of glass by perspex. There was no silencer and no number plates; the lights did not operate and the battery and propeller shaft had been removed. The justices, applying *Burns v Currell* (above), held that it was not 'intended or adapted for use on roads' and thus not within s 201 (now the Road Traffic Act 1988, s 143).

HELD, on a case stated: The justices' decision should stand.

Per Lord Parker CJ: Counsel for the prosecutor sought to say that, although the justices had applied the latest test in *Burns v Currell* they must have misdirected themselves. Although he might have come to a different conclusion if he had heard the case, and thought it was not a piece of building plant or equipment nor a go-kart, and it might well have been said that the vehicle still remained a vehicle for use on the road notwithstanding the alteration, that was not the test. It could not be said, bearing in mind the onus of proof on the prosecution, that the justices could not as a reasonable tribunal be satisfied that the car had not at the material time been intended or adapted for use on the roads.

Nichol v Leach

[1972] RTR 476, Div Ct

The defendants were prosecuted for using a motor vehicle on a road without insurance. The vehicle was a mini which the defendants had bought as scrap and had rebuilt for autocross racing, removing the windows, passenger seat and number plates and substituting a rev. counter for the speedometer. They towed it on public roads to a meeting, one defendant driving the towing vehicle and the other steering the mini. They contested the charge on the ground that the mini was not 'intended or adapted for use on roads' within s 253(1) of the 1960 Act (now ss 185(1) and 186(1) of the Road Traffic Act 1988), since they had no intention of using it on roads nor had they adapted it for that purpose.

HELD: A car does not cease to be a vehicle intended for use on roads merely because its present owner sees no prospect of driving it on a road under its own power. The mini had retained its character as a motor car intended to run on roads and was within s 253(1).

Note—Burns v Currell, p 705, above, and *Brown v Abbott*, above, were not cited.

'USING' A MOTOR VEHICLE

Brown v Roberts

[1965] 1 QB 1, [1963] 2 All ER 263, [1963] 3 WLR 75, 107 Sol Jo 666, [1963] 1 Lloyd's Rep 314 (Megaw J)

A van owned and driven by the defendant was drawing up at the kerb when the passenger, to whom he was giving a lift, opened the nearside door. It struck and injured the plaintiff who was on the pavement. She claimed damages against the defendant on the grounds that the passenger was 'using' the vehicle within the meaning of the Road Traffic Act 1930, s 35(1) (which was in similar terms to s 143 of the 1988 Act) and that, as the defendant's policy did not cover negligence of a passenger, he was in breach of the statutory duty as in *Monk v Warbey* (p 713, below).

HELD: The passenger thought negligent was not 'using' the vehicle within the meaning of the section and the defendant was not under a duty to provide insurance against that negligence. Although there may be more than one person 'using' a vehicle at any given time and though the element of driving the vehicle is not an essential element of 'using' (*Elliott v Grey*, p 710, below) a person, does not 'use a motor vehicle on the road' for the purposes of s 35(1) of the 1930 Act unless there is present in the person alleged to be the user an element of controlling, managing or operating the vehicle at the relevant time. The mere relationship of a passenger to a motor vehicle or to a particular part of a motor vehicle is not 'use' for the purposes of the Act.

Note—See also *Thomas v Hooper* (1985) Times, 25 October.

Leathley v Tatton

[1980] RTR 21, Div Ct
The defendant went to an address with two friends intending to look at a car with a view to buying it. The owner did not turn up. One of the friends had a key which fitted the car. The car would not start so one of the friends got into the driving seat and the defendant pushed the car: when it started he jumped into the passenger seat. He took no part in the driving of the car. He was charged with using the car when uninsured contrary to s 143 of the 1972 Act.
HELD: There was a case to answer. It was a clear situation in which the defendant and his friend were acting in concert, a joint enterprise for the purpose of setting the car in motion and to see how the car functioned. The defendant was 'using' it, and the fact that someone else was driving it was irrelevant.

Note—*Brown v Roberts* (above) was cited but distinguished on the ground that it was a case which concerned civil liability and did not reflect on the meaning of 'use' in the present case.

B v Knight

[1981] RTR 136, QBD
O'Nion took a van without the owner's consent. He drove it to a place where he met the defendant, B, a minor. B got into the van and O'Nion drove off. During the journey, but not before, B learned that O'Nion had taken the van without the owner's consent. He did not ask to be allowed to get out as he 'did not fancy the idea of walking home'. He was convicted of using the van uninsured contrary to s 143 of the RTA 1972.
HELD, allowing his appeal: He was not 'using' the vehicle. A passenger merely letting himself be driven where there is no element of joint enterprise does not 'use' the vehicle. B was simply getting a lift from O'Nion in the course of O'Nion's 'use'.

Cobb v Williams

[1973] RTR 113, [1973] Crim LR 243, Div Ct
The defendant was being brought home from work in his own car driven by a woman who was not his servant when an accident occurred. Neither of them was insured. The defendant was charged with 'using' his car when not insured, contrary to the Road Traffic Act 1960, s 201 (now s 143 of the 1988 Act). The magistrates dismissed the charge on the ground that the meaning of 'use' should not be extended beyond driving and that the charge should have been one of 'permitting'.
HELD: This was not right. The word 'use' is wider than 'drive'. The defendant was using his own car for his own purposes and in person in being driven home, though the driver was somebody else.

Bennett v Richardson

[1980] RTR 358, QBD
The defendant, a registered blind person, was charged with, inter alia, using a motor vehicle without insurance in force contrary to the Road Traffic Act 1972, s 143. At the time in question he was a passenger sitting in the back of an ice cream van driven by his partner. The van was hired, the two partners being equally liable under the hire terms. The defendant's job in the business was cleaning the van and helping to serve ice cream. It was being used on partnership business. The justices applied Lord Parker's principle in *Windle v Dunning* (p 728, below) and dismissed the charge.
HELD, on the prosecutor's appeal: The justices' decision was right. Per Lord Widgery: I would be anxious to see that [the] principle was adhered to and not easily jettisoned for some alternative. The principle to which I refer is this. A man cannot be convicted for using a motor vehicle which he is not personally driving unless he is the employer of the driver. If the owner is driving the vehicle then, good enough, he can be charged with using it. If the owner's employee, in the strict sense of the master-servant relationship, is driving the vehicle, again the employer can be regarded as vicariously being responsible. . . . But if the relationship between driver and would-be defendant is any other than those on which I have referred, then it is not possible to convict the person not driving of these offences. . . . The fact that [the defendant] was blind was quite irrelevant . . . the fact that the driver and the defendant were partners is also irrelevant because there is authority which shows that the mere relationship of partnership between driver and the would-be driver or passenger is not enough. *Cobb v Williams* (above) distinguished.

Garrett v Hooper

[1973] RTR 1, [1973] Crim LR 61, Div Ct
A co-partner does not 'use' a vehicle merely because it is driven by his partner on partnership business.

Passmoor v Gibbons

[1979] RTR 53, [1978] Crim LR 498, QBD
On the other hand a partner who did not take part in the day-to-day running of the company nonetheless 'uses' a vehicle when it is being driven by an employee in the course of his business on behalf of the company.

Jones v Chief Constable of Bedfordshire

[1987] RTR 332, QBD
Mr Jones, a police officer, drove his own car, which was uninsured, while on duty and taking part in a murder inquiry. Taking a commonsense view of the meaning of ss 143 and 144 of the 1972 Act, the justices concluded that it could not mean that policemen did not have to insure their own vehicles.
HELD, ON APPEAL: The meaning of s 144(2)(b) of the 1972 Act, now s 144(2)(b) of the 1988 Act, was clear. Section 143 did not apply to a vehicle when it was being driven for police purposes by a constable, so the conviction should be quashed.

Servant driving

Mickleborough v BRS (Contracts) Ltd

[1977] RTR 389, [1977] Crim LR 568
The defendants were owners of a vehicle hired out with driver for five years to a hirer who alone decided what journeys to do and what loads to carry. Having found the vehicle overloaded a traffic examiner prosecuted the defendants for 'using' the vehicle when overloaded. The loading had been done by the hirers. The justices held the defendants were not 'using' the vehicle since the hirers had control of the vehicle.
HELD: This was not right. Citing Lord Parker, in *Windle v Dunning* (p 729, below) where there is an alternative of 'causing or permitting' then 'using' has a restricted meaning. It is not to be extended to cover persons other than the owner and the driver, provided the driver is his servant and engaged at the material time on his employer's business. The driver was driving on his employer's, the defendant's, business of hiring out motor lorries and therefore the defendants were 'using' the vehicle at the material time.

Richardson v Baker

[1976] RTR 56, [1976] Crim LR 76
An employee of the defendant without the defendant's knowledge and without his express or implied authority took a tractor unit on to a road to convey a load for the purposes of the defendant's business as a haulage contractor.
HELD: The defendant was guilty of 'using' the vehicle in contravention of the Vehicles (Excise) Act 1971. Even if 'using' was limited to the narrow meaning given when there was an alternative of 'causing or permitting' then prima facie a vehicle was being used by a master when it was on a road driven by his servant about his master's business. Absence of any authority from him for such use made no difference.

Vehicle not being driven

Elliott v Grey

[1960] 1 QB 367, [1959] 3 All ER 733, [1959] 3 WLR 956, 124 JP 58, 103 Sol Jo 921, 57 LGR 357
Defendant's car broke down on 20 December 1958, and defendant placed it outside his house in the road. Before 7 February 1959 he had jacked up the wheels, removed the battery and terminated his insurance cover. On 7 February 1959 he had unjacked the wheels, cleaned the car, and sent its battery to be recharged, but the car could not be mechanically propelled because the engine would not work. He had no intention of driving it on 7 February 1959, or of removing it from its position in the road. He was convicted of using the car whilst uninsured contrary to the Road Traffic Act 1930, s 35(1). The defendant appealed.
HELD: The words 'to use' meant 'to have the use of a motor vehicle on a road' and, as the car could be moved on 7 February 1959, even though it could not be driven, the appellant had the use of it on a road, within the meaning of s 35(1). Appeal dismissed.

Note—The Road Traffic Act 1930, s 35(1) was in similar terms to s 143 of the 1972 Act.

Napthen v Place

[1970] RTR 248, Div Ct
A motor car was bought at an auction and subsequently stood on the roadway outside the defendant's premises for several weeks untaxed and uninsured. He was charged with using a vehicle on a road uninsured and unlicensed. The prosecution sought to prove that he was the owner but justices did not accept that he was and dismissed the charges.
HELD: On a case stated, it is not essential for either of the charges that the person charged should have been the owner or proved to be the owner of the vehicle in question.

Gosling v Howard

[1975] RTR 429, Div Ct
The defendant's car was parked on a grass verge of a rural road well off the carriageway and had not been moved for three months. The justices dismissed summonses against him for 'using' a vehicle on a road uninsured and without a test certificate.
HELD, on the prosecutor's appeal: This was wrong. There was no evidence that the car was not in running order and as in *Elliott v Grey* (above) the defendant had the use of the vehicle.

Williams v Jones

[1975] RTR 433, Div Ct
The defendant used his employer's trade plates to bring a vehicle back to his premises to do it up for sale. On the way it broke down and the defendant left it on a part of the highway that was no longer used because of road improvements. He removed the trade plates and abandoned the vehicle. He was charged with using the vehicle on a road uninsured, his employer's policy being effective only when the trade plates were on. The justices dismissed the charge, holding there had been no use of the vehicle after removal of the trade plates.
HELD: Following *Elliott v Grey* (above) that notwithstanding that the vehicle was abandoned and the trade plates removed, the defendant was thereafter 'using' the vehicle within the meaning of the Road Traffic Act 1960, s 201 (now the Road Traffic Act 1988, s 143).

Eden v Mitchell

[1975] RTR 425, [1975] Crim LR 467, Div Ct
The defendant was charged with using his car on a road with tyres which did not comply with the Motor Vehicles (Construction and Use) Regulations. It was parked outside his house but he had not driven it for some time and had no intention of doing so having been ill. The justices accepted that his sickness and intention not to drive was as sufficient as if the vehicle itself had been immobilised and dismissed the charge.
HELD, on the prosecutor's appeal: This was the wrong test. The intention of the defendant was immaterial. The true test was whether or not such steps had been taken as to make it impossible for anyone to use the vehicle.

Local authority — s 144(2)(a)

R v Urmston UDC and Jones

(1953) Times, 29 July
An urban district council were summoned for permitting the use of an uninsured motor lorry and the driver for using the uninsured lorry. The lorry was drawing a trailer and the certificate of insurance did not cover the use of the lorry with a trailer. The Manchester county magistrates dismissed the summonses. Local authorities need not insure their motor vehicles when they were being driven by council employees in the course of their employment. The insurance of their vehicles by a local authority was quite voluntary.

Disabled vehicle

Police v Turton

(1953) Post Magazine, 2 May, 488
A haulage contractor towed a lorry belonging to a friend to a garage. The towed lorry had had the engine removed and the tow was for a new engine to be fitted. The policy did not cover the drawing of a trailer other than a disabled mechanically propelled vehicle. He was prosecuted for having no effective insurance. The police relied on *Lawrence v Howlett* (p 703, above). Insurers gave evidence that they would regard the towed vehicle as being mechanically disabled and they would have accepted liability for an accident.

The magistrates (Holmfirth) convicted.

Note—See also *Elliott v Grey*, p 710, above.

Trailers attached

Leggate v Brown

[1950] 2 All ER 564, 114 JP 454, [1950] WN 379, 66 (pt 2) TLR 281, 94 Sol Jo 567, 49 LGR 27, 84 Ll L Rep 395, Div Ct
The defendant's motor policy covered a tractor with an endorsement which enabled the tractor to be used with two trailers. The defendant used the tractor on a road towing two laden trailers. The Road Traffic Act 1930, s 18(1) made it an offence for a tractor to draw two laden trailers. The defendant was prosecuted for driving uninsured, and the prosecution contended that as the defendant was using the tractor in an illegal manner, the policy was void because an indemnity against the consequences of an illegal act was void as being against public policy. The magistrates convicted the defendant.
HELD, ON APPEAL: The policy insured the defendant, as the Act required, against the consequences of the negligent driving of the tractor. It said nothing about laden trailers. It simply allowed the vehicle to be used with two trailers. If the policy had insured the defendant against using the tractor illegally, to that extent it would have been ineffective, but that had nothing to do with injury to third persons. The policy was an insurance against the consequences of negligent driving of the vehicle, because a third party can only claim if there has been negligent driving. If there has been negligent driving, it does not matter whether there were two trailers or none. If

the tractor was driven negligently, an injured person has a right to compensation, and this policy indemnified against negligent driving. Conviction quashed.

Kerridge v Rush

[1952] 2 Lloyd's Rep 305, Div Ct
The policy of insurance on an agricultural motor tractor excluded indemnity when the vehicle was drawing a greater number of trailers in all than permitted by law. The Road Traffic Act 1930, s 18(1) provided that a motor tractor shall not draw on the highway more than one laden trailer or two if unladen. The tractor was drawing a four-wheel laden trailer and a tumbril, constructed and intended to be drawn by a horse, laden with a horse-hoe frame.
HELD: The tumbril was a trailer. The tractor was drawing a greater number of trailers than was permitted by law and was not insured.

BREACH OF STATUTORY DUTY TO INSURE

Note—In the case of *Monk v Warbey* it was held s 143 imposes a statutory duty similar to that recognised in the case of unfenced machinery in the decision of *Groves v Lord Wimborne* [1898] 2 QB 402, 67 LJQB 862, 79 LT 284, 14 TLR 493, 34 Dig 218. *Monk v Warbey* was followed in *Richards v Port of Manchester* (1934) 152 LT 413, 50 Ll L Rep 132, CA. If, therefore, the owner of a car insured owner-driver only permits another person to drive his car, and that person being so uninsured has not the means to meet a third-party claim the owner is liable for damages for personal injury sustained by a third party.

Monk v Warbey

[1935] 1 KB 75, 104 LJKB 153, 152 LT 194, 51 TLR 77, 78 Sol Jo 783, 50 Ll L Rep 33, CA
The owner of a motor car who, in contravention of the Road Traffic Act 1930, s 35(1) (now replaced by s 143 of the 1988 Act), permits his car to be used by a person who is not insured against third-party risks is liable in damages to a third party who has been injured by the negligent driving of the uninsured person. In such a case the object and purview of the Act show that the penalties prescribed by s 35(2) were not intended to be the sole remedy for the breach of the owner's statutory duty. Where a person uninsured against third-party risks is permitted by the owner to use a car, and injury is caused by his negligent driving to a third party the latter may, where the uninsured person is without means, sue the owner of the car directly for damages for breach of statutory duty and need not first sue the uninsured person.

Gregory v Ford

[1951] 1 All ER 121 (Byrne J)
A lorry owned by the first defendant was driven by their servant, the second defendant, and injured the plaintiff, a motor cyclist. The plaintiff obtained judgment against both defendants.

The lorry at the time was uninsured. The first defendant claimed indemnity from the second defendant on the ground of his negligence. The second defendant claimed indemnity from the first defendant on the ground that it was an implied term of the employment that the servant should not be required to do an unlawful act.

The judge referred to the observation of Singleton J in *Blows v Chapman* [1947] 2 All ER 576, 112 JP 8, 63 TLR 575, 46 LGR 13 Div Ct: 'It is not, I think, the duty of a workman to ask his employer each day, is this vehicle insured.'

HELD: The second defendant was entitled to indemnity from the first defendant on this ground. The first defendant was not entitled to indemnity from the second defendant because, although the servant was negligent, it was owing to the breach of statutory duty of the first defendant that the damages fell upon him.

Lister v Romford Ice and Cold Storage Co Ltd

[1957] AC 555, [1957] 1 All ER 125, [1957] 2 WLR 158, 121 JP 98, 101 Sol Jo 106, [1956] 2 Lloyd's Rep 505, HL
Per Lord Morton of Henryton, speaking of *Gregory v Ford*: I agree that it was an implied term of the employment that the servant should not be required to do an unlawful act but there is no implied term that the driver is entitled to be personally indemnified by a policy.

Note—For references see p 155, above.

Implied indemnity

Road Transport and General Insurance Co v Adams

[1955] Crim LR 377
The defendant had hired a car from the third party and had asked whether it was insured, to which the third party answered in the affirmative. In fact the car was not covered if the defendant drove it. After a collision, he was convicted of driving uninsured. In the present action the plaintiffs obtained judgment against both the defendant and the third party for the amount expended by the insurers in settling claims arising from the accident. The defendant claimed indemnity from the third party who pleaded that as the damages the defendant had had to pay arose out of a crime the court should not grant relief.
HELD: The defendant was entitled to be indemnified by the third party, as he had been led by him to believe in the existence of a fact, which, if it had been true, would have been an answer to any imputation of illegality (applying *Burrows v Rhodes* [1899] 1 QB 816, 68 LJQB 545, 80 LT 591, 63 JP 532, 48 WR 13, 15 TLR 286).

Policy avoided

Goodbarne v Buck

[1940] 1 KB 771, [1940] 1 All ER 613, 109 LJKB 837, 162 LT 259, 56 TLR 433, 84 Sol Jo 380, CA
The fact that a policy is avoided by insurers does not bring into operation the principle of *Monk v Warbey*.

Motor Insurers' Bureau not a defence

Corfield v Groves

[1950] 1 All ER 488, [1950] WN 116, 66 (pt 1) TLR 627, 94 Sol Jo 225 (Hilbery J)
A third party was fatally injured by an uninsured car. The driver was not the servant or agent of the owner. The administratrix, who was the widow and the only dependant, sued the driver for negligence and the owner for breach of statutory duty

under *Monk v Warbey*, alleging that the driver was without means to satisfy any judgment against him. A witness from the Motor Insurers' Bureau expressed the opinion that under the Motor Insurers' Bureau Agreement the Bureau would satisfy any judgment against the driver. The owner pleaded that as the Bureau would pay the damages, the plaintiff would suffer no loss by reason of the lack of means of the driver or her breach of statutory duty. The driver was found guilty of negligence.
HELD: The breach of statutory duty was a continuing breach operative at the time of the accident (the time of the tortious act), and the cause of action arose at the moment of the tortious act. On the death the widow's right of action under the Fatal Accidents Acts immediately accrued and an enforceable claim against the owner for any damages which she then sustained by reason of the breach of statutory duty which existed at the time of the tortious act. The damage accrued because at the time the driver was uninsured and financially nothing was obtainable from him even by bankruptcy proceedings. Greer LJ in *Monk v Warbey* pointed out that it does not matter, even if it were the fact, that at the time of the tort her damages could not be quantified. In theory, of course, her damages are quantified as on the day of the accruing of her complete cause of action. If the judgment was satisfied by the Bureau, no difficulty arises, because the damages cannot be taken twice by the plaintiff. Judgment against both defendants.

Note—Apparently the point dealt with in *Fleming v McGillivray*, below, was not taken.

Fleming v McGillivray

1945 SLT 301 (Lord Mackintosh)
An action under *Monk v Warbey* is not competent against the owner of the car until it is known that the wrongdoer cannot pay and there is no effective policy. It must be established—

1 that the driver could not pay; and
2 that the insurers could not be made to pay.

Note—See also *Martin v Dean*, below.

Damage not result of breach

Daniels v Vaux

[1938] 2 KB 203, [1938] 2 All ER 271, 107 LJKB 494, 159 LT 459, 54 TLR 621, 82 Sol Jo 335 (Humphreys J)
Defendant bought car and allowed her son to use it, though not insured. About 21 June 1934, plaintiff injured. On 29 December 1936, the son died. No action had then been commenced. The son had substantial means.
HELD: (1) The son was not servant or agent; (2) the defendant was guilty of breach of statutory duty; (3) no legal damage from breach. The damage was due to the delay in commencing the action and not to the defendant's breach of her duty to insure.

Note—The limitation in the Law Reform (MP) Act 1934, that an action is not maintainable unless the cause of action arose not earlier than six months before the death was repealed by the Law Reform (Limitation of Actions) Act 1954, s 4.

Driver unable to meet judgment

Martin v Dean

[1971] 2 QB 208, [1971] 3 All ER 279, [1971] 2 WLR 1159, 115 Sol Jo 369, [1971] RTR 280 (John Stephenson J)
Dean lent his motor cycle to Kirby, who was not insured for riding it. The plaintiff was knocked down and injured as a result of Kirby's negligence. He sued both Kirby and Dean, alleging against the latter a breach of s 201 of the 1960 Act. He alleged he had suffered loss by the breach in that Kirby might be impecunious and unable to satisfy a judgment promptly or at all. Kirby was a single man, a bus driver earning £23 per week, and had no savings.
HELD: The plaintiff had to show not only that Dean had committed a breach of s 201 but that the breach had caused him loss. It was right that the plaintiff should sue both defendants in the same action so that the rights of the defendants *inter se* could be disposed of but if it was shown that the borrowing driver could pay in full there would be no liability on the owner except for nominal damages. If the borrowing driver could pay some of the damages the lending owner could be liable only for the remainder. The question was how much the borrower could pay, not over a long period or after being made bankrupt, but within a few weeks of judgment. In the present case the amount Kirby could pay was minimal and there should be judgment against both defendants for the whole sum awarded.

Note—Section 201 was in the same terms as s 143 of the 1972 Act (see now 1988 Act).

DRIVER: WHETHER POLICY EFFECTIVE

Servant driving

Sutch v Burns

[1943] 2 All ER 441, 60 TLR 1, 87 Sol Jo 406, 76 Ll L Rep 203 (Atkinson J)
A lorry driver delivered goods to a customer. The customer asked the driver to carry some goods of the customer across the road to another branch of the customer's works. The driver agreed. The customer's goods were loaded on to the lorry, and the customer's workmen got on the lorry. The driver turned to the left where the road was wide enough to turn. In turning, some goods were dislodged and knocked one of the workmen off the lorry, and he was killed. The widow brought proceedings against the lorry owner and the driver and obtained judgment against the driver but not the owner. The widow sued insurers under s 10 of the 1934 Act (now the Road Traffic Act 1988, ss 151 and 152).

Insurers conceded that the policy was to be treated as one which complied with s 35(1) of the 1930 Act. It was admitted that deceased was a passenger by reason of or in pursuance of a contract of service with the customer. Insurers contended that the legal obligation of the section only arose where there was liability of the policy holder, and that the driver was only indemnified where his employer was liable. The third party contended that the policy must cover any permitted driver and that there was no limitation on the use of the vehicle.
HELD: The section did not limit use by a permitted driver to the authority given by the employer. The policy must insure against any liability incurred by the driver to third parties. A person giving permission must insure against all claims of third parties

arising out of the user on a road. A policy which purported to insure the employer or the driver to a less extent did not comply with the Act.

Note—In the Court of Appeal the judgment was set aside on the ground that a decision had been sought on a hypothetical policy and a court had no jurisdiction to do this.

The Divisional Court disagreed with the decision of Atkinson J in the following case.

John T Ellis Ltd v Hinds

[1947] KB 475, [1947] 1 All ER 337, [1947] LJR 488, 176 LT 424, 63 TLR 181, 91 Sol Jo 68, 45 LGR 118, 80 LI L Rep 231, Div Ct

A company owned a motor vehicle which was driven by a lad of 17 who was not himself entitled to be treated as insured under the policy. The facts are set out at p 831, below.

HELD: The company was not in breach of the section. The section refers to the use of the vehicle and says nothing about driving. The statute uses the word 'Drive' in ss 5, 9 and 15.

If the car is being driven by a servant on the employer's business so that the owner is liable to a third person, and the liability of the owner is covered by insurance, there is in force in relation to the use of the vehicle whether by the owner or driver a policy of insurance.

We cannot agree with the decision of *Sutch v Burns*. An owner is bound to take out a policy which covers the use of the vehicle by his servant but only whilst on his business. If a servant is driving without authority, his master has not caused or permitted the use of the vehicle. The owner of a car is not bound to cover the liability of his chauffeur on a 'joy ride', or in circumstances which absolve the master from liability. There was no obligation on the facts in *Sutch v Burns* for the employer of the driver to have a policy which would cover the driver when he was not driving on the employer's business.

Note—In *Sutch v Burns* in the Court of Appeal the case was argued on its merits, and the court took time to consider its verdict. Meanwhile the case of *Sun Life Assurance of Canada v Jervis* [1944] AC 111 had been decided in the House of Lords, and in consequence of that decision, it became unnecessary to deal with the arguments.

It was pointed out in argument that if, eg an owner of a motor car insured for pleasure purposes but not for carriage of goods lent his car to a friend for pleasure use, and the friend used it for the carriage of goods, this could not mean that insurers were liable under the policy, nor that the owner was liable on the principle of *Monk v Warbey*.

The point has now been settled by *Ellis v Hinds*, above.

Lees v Motor Insurers' Bureau

[1952] 2 All ER 511, [1952] WN 409, [1952] 2 TLR 356, 96 Sol Jo 548, [1952] Lloyd's Rep 210 (Lord Goddard CJ)

The owner of a motor lorry had a policy which indemnified him but did not indemnify the driver personally. The policy excluded liability where the accident to the third party arose out of and in the course of his employment by the owner. On 5 May 1948, a servant of the owner was killed by the negligence of the driver in an accident which arose out of and in the course of the employment of the deceased by the owner. The widow sued the driver and obtained a judgment by default against him. She then sued the Motor Insurers' Bureau contending that the judgment was in respect of a liability required to be covered by s 35(1) and s 36(1)(b) of the 1930 Act (now s 143 of the 1988 Act), being a liability incurred by the driver caused by the use by the driver of a vehicle

on a road: that the Act required the policy to cover the driver personally and that the Bureau had incurred a liability to satisfy the judgment under the terms of the Agreement.
HELD: On a special case stated by an arbitrator, the contention that the policy was required to insure the driver personally is exactly what was held in *Sutch v Burns* which was overruled in *John T Ellis Ltd v Hinds*. Section 35(1) required a person to insure because he is the owner, the person who uses or permits the use. What has to be covered is the use of the vehicle not the person using the vehicle. *Ellis v Hinds* (above) and *Marsh v Moores* (p 718, below). In *Richards v Cox* [1943] 1 KB 139, [1942] 2 All ER 624, 112 LJKB 135, 168 LT 313, 59 TLR 123, 87 Sol Jo 92, CA following *Digby*'s case (p 854, below) there were in effect two policies in one document, a policy insuring the owner and a policy insuring the driver. There was no such term in this policy. The policy complied with the Act and covered all the persons whom the Act required to be covered. It excluded employees of the insured in cases arising out of and in the course of the employment, and underwriters are entitled to exclude that liability under the Act. A policy had been taken out by the owner to cover the use of the vehicle and therefore the vehicle was an insured vehicle and the liability which was incurred was not one which was required to be covered by insurance. The respondents were under no liability to the claimant.

Note—The accident occurred before the abolition of common employment on 5 July 1948. After that date a third party would presumably sue the employers without reference to a motor policy or to the Bureau.

Driver retaining control when teaching

Marsh v Moores

[1949] 2 KB 208, [1949] 2 All ER 27, [1949] LJR 1313, 113 JP 346, 65 TLR 318, 93 Sol Jo 450, 47 LGR 418, Div Ct
A policy issued to a limited company covered the company against third-party risks for social, domestic and business purposes. There was an exception from liability if the car with the company's consent was being driven by a person who to the knowledge of the company was a disqualified person or had never been licensed. A servant of the company who was the son of the managing director on the latter's instructions was making a journey in the car. As a servant of the company he was entrusted by the company with the control, driving and management of the vehicle. He had as passenger his cousin, a girl of 17 who to the son's knowledge had not and never had had a licence. The son allowed the cousin to take over the wheel, whilst he himself retained control of the hand-brake.
HELD: There was an effective policy. The test whether the car was being used uninsured was not whether the son or cousin was insured in respect of his or her personal liability, but whether the company would have been liable to a third party. The son still remained the driver; in allowing his cousin to take the wheel he was still acting within the scope of his employment although in an unauthorised and improper way, and the company would have been liable to a third party. The only person driving with the general consent of the company was the son, who held a licence; the cousin was not driving with the company's consent or knowledge. The policy complied with the requirements of s 35(1) (s 143 of the 1988 Act), which does not require a policy covering the driver's personal liability. *Ellis v Hinds* followed.

Langman v Valentine

[1952] 2 All ER 803, 116 JP 576, [1952] WN 475, [1952] 2 TLR 731, 96 Sol Jo 712, 50 LGR 685, Div Ct

The owner of a motor car had a policy which covered him and also any person driving with his permission who had or had held and was not disqualified from holding a licence. The owner was teaching a passenger to drive on a road. The passenger had not and had never had a licence. The passenger was sitting in the driver's seat and was steering the car under the guidance of the owner and using the accelerator and the footbrake. The owner was in the passenger's seat with his left hand on the steering wheel and his right hand on the handbrake. He was able to steer the car, stop it and start it, the ignition switch being within his reach and the hand-brake under his control. The passenger was summoned for using a motor car uninsured and for driving without a licence. The owner was summonsed for permitting the former and abetting the latter. The justices held the owner was the driver and dismissed the summonses. HELD ON APPEAL, Lord Goddard CJ and Finnemore J: (1) The passenger was a driver and should have been convicted for driving without a licence; (2) there was no evidence that the owner knew the passenger did not have a licence; (3) though not 'the driver' the owner was 'a driver' and an injured person could have brought an action against him and he would have been liable as a driver and there was therefore an effective policy. There could be two drivers at the same time.

Per McNair J dissenting: The passenger was a user of the car and there was no effective policy in relation to her.

Ellis v Hinds and *Marsh v Moores* followed.

Note—The case of *Rubie v Faulkner* (p 59, above) is not mentioned in the reports, nor *Sampton v Aitchison* (p 58, above).

Evans v Walkden

[1956] 3 All ER 64, [1956] 1 WLR 1019, 120 JP 495, 100 Sol Jo 587, 54 LGR 467, Div Ct

A son 15 years old and therefore unlicensed was in the driving seat and his father was seated with him. The car was being driven in bottom gear at not more than 4 or 5 mph for a total distance of about 200 yards. The father was in a position to control the driving of the son and was doing so and could have stopped the car immediately. The steering wheel was within the father's reach and also the brake and clutch pedals, the ignition key and the gear handle on the steering wheel. The handbrake was on the right-hand side of the driver and was not accessible to the father. The father's policy excluded liability whilst driven by an unlicensed driver. The justices found that the father was at the same time a driver of the car and dismissed summonses against the son and father for driving without insurance and for permitting respectively. HELD: There was no evidence to support the finding that the father was in control of the car or that he was a driver of the car. The insurance policy permitted use for tuition provided — 'There shall be present in the insured car as a tutor a person under whose supervision the holder of a provisional licence would be entitled to drive.' This did not affect the exclusion of liability if driven by an unlicensed driver. *Langman v Valentine* (above) distinguished. Case remitted to justices to convict.

Tyler v Whatmore

[1976] RTR 83, [1976] Crim LR 315, Div Ct
The defendant was charged with 'actually driving a motor vehicle' when in such a position that she could not have proper control. She was sitting beside a man who was in the driving seat operating the pedals. She had both hands on the steering wheel; he made no attempt to steer and his hands were not on the wheel.
HELD: Following *Langman v Valentine* (above) she was 'driving'. It was a question of fact. Both were driving, since he was able to control the propulsion and she was controlling the steering.

Note—See also *R v Wilkins*, p 833, below.

Paid driver

Bryan v Forrow

[1950] 1 All ER 294, 114 JP 158, 48 LGR 347, sub nom *Forrow v Bryan* [1950] WN 91, 94 Sol Jo 194, Div Ct
The owner of a motor lorry was insured by a cover note, under which the person or persons allowed to drive were—
1 the above-named proposer only;
2 the above-named proposer or his paid driver;
3 the above-named proposer or his paid employee or any friend or relative of the proposer driving with his unremunerated permission provided such person holds a licence to drive such motor vehicle or had held and is not disqualified by order of a court of law from holding or obtaining such licence.

The lorry owner contracted with a customer to transport goods of the customer. The lorry owner was ill and arranged for the lorry to be driven by a driver in the regular employ of the customer.

The owner was prosecuted for permitting the use of the lorry without an effective policy of insurance. It was contended that the customer's driver was not the paid driver of the owner.
HELD: The contrast was between the professional and the non-professional driver — the paid driver and the paid employee. The words 'paid driver' are capable of two constructions: (1) the driver paid by the owner; (2) a driver driving for the owner who is a paid driver. The latter construction is right and the cover note was effective to cover third-party risks and insurers would be liable under it.

Disqualified driver

Saycell v Bool

[1948] 2 All ER 83, 112 JP 341, 64 TLR 421, 92 Sol Jo 311, 46 LGR 447, Div Ct
Respondent was the owner of a motor van and was disqualified from holding a licence. The van was standing in a road outside his premises which was on an incline. His garage was 100 yards lower down. He pushed the van down the incline and when in motion, got into the driving seat and steered it towards the garage. There was no petrol in the tank and the engine was not running.
HELD: Respondent was 'driving' the van, and being disqualified there was no third party insurance in force.

Note—And see *Floyd v Bush*, p 703, above. See also *R v MacDonagh* and *Blayney v Knight*, pp 833, 834 below.

Driver not in employ

Lyons v May

[1948] 2 All ER 1062, 113 JP 42, [1948] WN 483, 65 TLR 51, 93 Sol Jo 59, Div Ct
A garage proprietor who had repaired a motor lorry drove it at the owner's request to the owner's premises. The owner's policy covered only the owner or 'any duly authorised person in his employ'. The policy of the garage proprietor did not cover the risk. The justices held the garage proprietor was temporarily in the owner's employ for the purpose of delivering the lorry.
HELD: (1) The garage proprietor was not in the owner's employment. (*Burton*'s case, p 827, below, is not mentioned in the report.) (2) The owner had given 'permission'. He had not asked the garage proprietor if he had an effective policy.

Ballance v Brown

[1955] Crim LR 384, [1955] CLY 2451, Div Ct
A policy provided that the company would 'treat as though he were the insured any person in the insured's employ who is driving such a vehicle on the insured's order or with his permission for the purpose of the business of the insured'. The insured, who from time to time bought scrap from the defendant, instructed him to take the insured's car to the defendant's house and to pick him up the next morning to go on a business trip; he also told him to do any business he could.
HELD: The car was insured while being driven by the defendant. *Lyons v May* (above) distinguished.

Tapsell v Maslen

(1966) 110 Sol Jo 853, [1967] Crim LR 53 Div Ct
The respondent allowed Williams to use his motor scooter when there was no policy of insurance in force. When he lent the scooter to Williams he honestly believed Williams had an insurance certificate. The justices dismissed a charge of permitting the use of the scooter when there was no policy in force.
HELD, ON APPEAL: The justices must convict. Section 201 (s 143 of the 1988 Act) was expressed in terms whereby all the prosecution had to do was to show first that permission to use had been given and next that there was no insurance cover. *Lyons v May* (above) and *Morris v Williams* (p 724, below) were binding authorities for this.

Named driver

Goodwin v Leckey

[1946] NI 40, (1946) LR Dig 118 (MacDermott J)
A taxi was insured under a policy which indemnified only when driven by the insured or two named drivers. A driver not named was driving with the permission of and in the course of the employment of the insured.
HELD: The policy was inoperative. A policy complies with the Northern Ireland Act although it does not cover any driver with permission. *Sutch v Burns* (p 716, above) not followed.

No heavy goods vehicle licence

Police v Hepper

[1978] CLY 2591, Knightsbridge Crown Ct
The defendant was charged with driving a heavy goods vehicle when not insured. There was a policy in force allowing any person to drive who 'holds a licence to drive the vehicle or has held and is not disqualified from holding or obtaining such a licence'. The defendant had held and was not disqualified from holding an ordinary driving licence but had never held a heavy goods vehicle licence.
HELD: The policy did not cover him.

Hired vehicle

Sands v O'Connell

[1981] RTR 42, QBD
The defendant was aged 20. Anticipating difficulty in hiring a car to drive whilst under 21 she induced a friend aged 23 to hire a car for her. He did so by a contract of hire which stipulated 'Drivers must be aged between 21 and 70 years'. He also completed a 'supplementary proposal form' for insurance declaring 'I am not under 21 or over 70 years of age', and that 'the above declaration applies also in respect of all persons who will drive'. The insurance policy covering the vehicle was issued to the company hiring out the vehicle and extended to indemnify any person driving the vehicle 'on the order or with the permission of the policyholder'. The friend lent the vehicle during the hire period to the defendant who drove it for herself. She was charged with driving whilst uninsured.
HELD: (1) The contract of hire by referring to 'drivers' authorised the friend to permit other persons to drive limited to those between 21 and 70; but (2) the defendant was not driving on the order or with the permission of the policyholder since she had no direct permission from them and the friend's authority was limited to drivers between 21 and 70; (3) though by an unusual indorsement the policy extended to treat a person driving the vehicle as if he or she was in the employment of the policyholder under a contract of service the defendant did not receive authority from the friend within the scope of his employment and such decisions as *Marsh v Moores* (p 718, above) were not applicable. Her appeal against conviction was dismissed.

Crown servant—private use

Salt v MacKnight

1947 JC 99, 1947 SLT 327, High Ct of Justiciary
The Road Traffic Act 1930, s 121(2) (which provides that Parts I and III of the Act shall apply to the Crown) is no warrant for the suggestion that Part III of the Act (in which falls s 35) does not apply to servants of the Crown irrespective of what they are doing nor to Crown vehicles irrespective of the purpose for which they are being used, and consequently a departmental official who is using a Crown vehicle for his own business is not immune from prosecution under s 35 (which requires a third-party insurance to be in force).

Note—The equivalent provisions to s 121(2) of the 1930 Act is s 183(1) of the 1988 Act which reads:

(1) Subject to the provisions of this section—
(a) Part I of this Act,
(b) Part II of this Act, except ss 68 to 74 and 77,
(c) Part III of this Act, except s 103(3)
(d) Part IV of this Act and,
(e) in this part, ss 163, 164, 168, 169, 170(1) to (4), 177, 178, 181 and 182,
apply to vehicles and persons in the public service of the Crown.

CAUSE OR PERMIT

Note—For s 35(1) of the 1930 Act see now the Road Traffic Act 1988, s 143, p 702, above.

McLeod v Buchanan

[1940] 2 All ER 179, 84 Sol Jo 452, 1940 SC (HL) 17, 1940 SN 20, 1940 SLT 232
A solicitor owned a poultry farm which was managed by his brother. A private car owned by the solicitor was registered and insured in the name of the brother for private and business use of the brother. The solicitor knew that his brother used the car for his private purposes. This car was replaced by a van which was registered and insured in the name of the solicitor for commercial use only. The certificate was sent from the solicitor's office to the brother without any comment, and the brother did not notice that it was limited to commercial use. The solicitor never gave the brother any permission to use the van for private purposes and did not know of this use, nor did he tell the brother that the insurance was restricted or make any conditions as to the use of the van. The brother used it for private purposes.
HELD: The solicitor had permitted the brother to use an uninsured vehicle and was liable on the principle of *Monk v Warbey*.

Per Lord Wright: To 'cause' involves some express or positive mandate, or some authority. To 'permit' is a looser and vaguer term. It may denote an express permission, general or particular, as distinguished from a mandate. The other person is not told to use the vehicle in the particular way, but he is told that he may do so if he desires. It includes cases where permission is merely inferred. If the other person is given control of the vehicle, permission may be inferred if the vehicle is left at the other person's disposal in such circumstances as to carry with it a reasonable implication of a discretion or liberty to use it in the manner in which it was used.

In order to prove permission, it is not necessary to show knowledge of similar use in the past, or actual notice that the vehicle might be, or was likely to be, so used, or that the accused was guilty of a reckless disregard of the probabilities of the case, or a wilful closing of his eyes. He may not have thought of his duties under the section. The sending of the insurance certificate without any further intimation was not sufficient notice to his brother of the change. . . . In my opinion the necessary permission is established.

Watkins v O'Shaughnessy

[1939] 1 All ER 385, 161 LT 144, 83 Sol Jo 215, CA
At a public auction held by the second defendants, the first defendant bought a motor car. He drove it away, although, to the knowledge of the servants of the second defendants, the car was uninsured and unlicensed. In fact, the servants of the second

defendant lent the first defendant the company's trade number plates for the purpose, and supplied him with a slip, referring to a different car, but altered by them to appear to refer to the car in question, and assured him that such a proceeding was quite in order. The plaintiff was injured by the alleged negligent driving of the first defendant, but, as a judgment against him would be useless, the plaintiff did not ask for judgment against him, but did ask for judgment against the second defendants, alleging that they had caused or permitted the first defendant to use a motor vehicle in respect of which there was not in existence a policy of insurance in accordance with the Road Traffic Act 1930, s 35.

HELD: As the sale had been completed before the driving of the car by the first defendant, the second defendants had no control over him, and could not, therefore, be said to have 'caused or permitted' him to drive, and, in any event, the acts of the servants of the second defendant were quite unauthorised by them.

For A to permit B to do anything, the relation between A and B must be such that it is not open for B lawfully to do the thing in question without such permission. It must be open for A to withhold that permission without which B cannot lawfully do the thing in question. Permission to do that thing must be necessary for the thing's performance.

Goodbarne v Buck

[1940] 1 KB 771, [1940] 1 All ER 613, 109 LJKB 837, 162 LT 259, 56 TLR 433, 84 Sol Jo 380, CA

Cause or permit are two different verbs. To make a person liable for 'permitting' another person to use, he must be in a position to forbid the other person to use the vehicle, ie where he is the owner of the car. The fact that one person assisted another to get a worthless piece of paper in place of an effective policy, did not 'cause' him to use the vehicle on the road without an effective policy.

Note—See also *Thompson v Lodwick* p 60, above.

Lloyd v Singleton

[1953] 1 QB 357, [1953] 1 All ER 291, [1953] 2 WLR 278, 117 JP 97, 97 Sol Jo 98, 51 LGR 165, Div Ct

A company owned a motor car which was insured in the name of the managing director of the company and covered who had his permission to drive. The respondent, the assistant general manager of the company, had full discretion himself to use the vehicle for his work or to allow other employees of the company to use it in the course of the company's business. The respondent permitted his brother, who was not an employee of the company, to drive, and was charged with permitting the use without insurance. The justices dismissed the charge on the dictum of MacKinnon LJ in *Goodbarne v Buck* (above).

HELD: The part of that judgment which stated that the person permitting must be in a position to forbid the other person to use, followed. The court was unable to agree with the further statement that the only person who could forbid was the owner, which must have been *per incuriam*.

Morris v Williams

(1951) 50 LGR 308, Div Ct

A company owned four vehicles, one of which was a van which was uninsured. The manager of the company instructed an employee to go by car. The employee used the

van. The manager was summonsed for permitting a vehicle to be used when uninsured. The magistrates convicted.
HELD, ON APPEAL: The employee was permitted by the manager to use the van. There was implied, if not express, authorisation. Conviction upheld.

Note—See also *Kelly v Cornhill Insurance Co Ltd*, p 829, below.

Newbury v Davis

(1974) 118 Sol Jo 222, [1974] RTR 367, Div Ct
The defendant gave permission to Jarvis to borrow his car and use it provided he insured it. Jarvis failed to insure it and was convicted of using the car without insurance. The defendant was charged with 'permitting' Jarvis to use the car uninsured.
HELD: He was not guilty. Permission given subject to a condition which is unfulfilled is no permission at all.

Baugh v Crago

[1976] 1 Lloyd's Rep 563, [1975] RTR 453, Div Ct
The policy of insurance covering the defendant's vehicle was effective only when the driver held a driving licence. He allowed a man to drive who had no licence, though he thought he had.
HELD: The defendant was guilty of a breach of the Road Traffic Act 1972, s 143. It was not the same as in *Newbury v Davis* (above). A distinction must be drawn between a case where the owner of a car grants permission to another to drive believing that the other is covered by insurance when he is not and a case where a person allows another to drive making it a condition that he shall not drive unless and until he is covered by insurance.

Clydebank Co-op Society v Binnie

1937 JC 17
A business firm kept cars for hire. A customer hired a car for 13s and arranged with five friends to pay 2s 6d each. Defendant's manager knew other passengers were to be carried, but did not know of the separate payments. The passengers were joining together to make frequent journeys, picked up at different places. Defendants were put on their guard and had a duty to inquire.
HELD: Defendants guilty of 'permitting'.

Churchill v Norris

(1938) 158 LT 255, 82 Sol Jo 114, 31 Cox CC 1
Defendant told his driver not to drive with too heavy a load, put instructions in the cabin of his vehicle, and instructed driver if in doubt to weigh the laden vehicle. Defendant knew the weight of timber was by custom measured in a rough and ready way by size, which might be erroneous. He had not ordered his servants specifically never to start a journey without weighing. Having knowledge of the prevailing method, he had connived at conduct which might well lead to commission of the offence, and had therefore 'permitted'. 'Permit' may mean no more than a failure to take proper steps to prevent.

DPP v Fisher

(1991) Crim LR 787, Div Ct
The defendant lent his car to A on condition that he find someone to drive it who was insured. A asked B to drive, both A and B assuming that B was properly insured to drive. In fact B was not properly insured. The defendant submitted, relying on *Newbury v Davis*, that as he had imposed a condition on the loan, he had discharged his responsibilities and taken all reasonable precautions. The justices dismissed the information and the prosecutor appealed by way of case stated.
HELD, allowing the appeal and remitting the case with a direction to convict: That the principle in *Newbury v Davis* was to be very strictly limited to exceptional cases. Here the defendant had no idea who A would ask to drive, and there was no communication at all between the defendant and B.

Sidcup Building Estates Ltd v Sidery

(1936) 24 Ry & Can Tr Cas 164
Defendants had threatened drivers with instant dismissal if they worked more than the legal number of hours. They did not dismiss a driver who disobeyed.
HELD: Guilty of 'permitting'.

Note—And see *Cox & Son Ltd v Sidery* (1935) 24 Ry & Can Tr Cas 69.

Grays Haulage Co Ltd v Arnold

[1966] 1 All ER 896, [1966] 1 WLR 534, 130 JP 196, 110 Sol Jo 122, Div Ct
The defendants were convicted by magistrates of 'permitting' their driver to drive for continuous periods amounting in the aggregate to more than 11 hours contrary to the Road Traffic Act 1960, s 73. He had driven their vehicle from Carlisle to London from 10 am to 10.30 pm with only one hour's rest. They had failed to take steps which would or might have prevented the driver doing as he did such as providing a recorder on the vehicle or making arrangements for the driver to telephone them during the journey by reversing the charges.
HELD, ON APPEAL to the Divisional Court: This was not 'permitting'. In *James & Son Ltd v Smee* (p 728, below) it had been pointed out that knowledge is of two kinds, actual knowledge, and knowledge which consists of shutting one's eyes to the obvious, that is, failing to do something or doing something not caring whether contravention takes place or not. Here there was no question of actual knowledge nor was it a case of shutting one's eyes to the obvious. There was no evidence that the defendants had any knowledge of circumstances which they had allowed to go on without caring whether an offence had been committed or not. Knowledge is not imputed by mere negligence. Conviction quashed.

Fransman v Sexton

[1965] Crim LR 556, Div Ct QBD
The defendant, who operated a self-drive car hire service, was held not guilty of 'permitting' the use of a car with an inadequate braking system where one of the rear brakes was defective and did not work but where new parts had been provided about a year before and the defendant did not know the brake was inoperative. Knowledge is an essential element in 'permitting' something. It is not to be imputed by mere negligence, but by something more, such as recklessly sending out a car not caring what would happen.

Goldsmith v Deakin

(1933) 150 LT 157, 98 JP 4, [1933] WN 255, 50 TLR 73, 31 LGR 420, 30 Cox CC 32.
The dictionary definition of 'to permit' is to give lead to; allow; to afford means. The offence of 'permitting use' arises where, to quote the words of Lawrence J: 'Although the respondent may not have known affirmatively the way in which the vehicle was being used, if in fact he allowed it to be used, and did not care whether it was being used in contravention of the statute or not, he did, in my view, permit its use under Road Traffic Act 1930.'

Note—Distinguished in next case.

Evans v Dell

[1937] 1 All ER 349, 156 LT 240, 101 JP 149, 53 TLR 310, 81 Sol Jo 100, 35 LGR 105, Div Ct
A vehicle was hired by the organisers of a dance to take persons attending the dance from A to C. This intention had been advertised in a newspaper without the respondent's knowledge. At the dance it was announced that passengers must take tickets and contribute not less than sixpence. A number bought tickets which were collected in the coach. Neither the respondent nor his driver knew of the payments.
HELD: That as the respondent had no knowledge of the advertisement or the payments, and had not deliberately shut his eyes to what was being done, he had not 'permitted'.

Per Goddard J: Mens rea is an essential ingredient in offences under the Road Traffic Acts.

Shave v Rosner

[1954] 2 QB 113, [1954] 2 All ER 280, [1954] 2 WLR 1057, 18 JP 364, 98 Sol Jo 355, Div Ct
A motor car repairer reshoed the brakes of a motor van and drove it to the owner, who drove the repairer back to his garage, testing the brakes himself. A little later the same day the owner was driving the van when a wheel came off and injured a pedestrian. The wheel came off because the repairer's servants had not properly fastened the hub nuts. The repairer was prosecuted for 'using or causing or permitting to be used' a vehicle 'causing or likely to cause danger to any person'.
HELD: In one sense it might be said the repairer 'caused' the van to be used by delivering it in a dangerous condition and the owner unwittingly using it. He did not 'use' it himself; he did not 'permit' because he could not give permission to the owner to use his own car. When 'causes or permits' are found in contrast, 'permits' means giving leave and licence to somebody to use the car, and 'causes' means ordering or directing someone to use it. The repairer had ceased to have control or dominion over the van, and had not caused its use, and was not criminally liable under the Regulations.

Note—70 LQR 453 points out that the words 'cause' and 'causation' have various meanings depending on the circumstances and that it is clear in a civil action for injuries to the passer-by the defendant would have been liable on the ground that he had caused the accident as it was his negligence which had caused the wheel to break off from the car.

Windle v Dunning & Son Ltd

[1968] 2 All ER 46, [1968] 1 WLR 552, 132 JP 264, 112 Sol Jo 196, 66 LGR 516, Div Ct

Lorries hired to the respondents but loaded by them were found by an inspector of weights and measures to be overloaded. The respondents were convicted of 'using' the lorries on a road carrying loads exceeding that allowed by the Construction and Use Regulations, contrary to the Road Traffic Act 1960, s 64(2) (now ss 68—73 of the 1988 Act). The drivers were not the respondents' servants but were hired with the lorries.

HELD, ON APPEAL: The respondents were not 'using' the lorries.

Per Lord Parker: 'Using' when used in connection with causing and permitting has a restricted meaning. It certainly covers the driver; it may also cover the driver's employer if he, the driver, is about his master's business, but beyond that I find it very difficult to conceive that any other person could be said to be using the vehicle as opposed to causing it to be used.

Swan v MacNab

[1977] JC 57, High Ct of Justiciary

A vehicle driven by an employee was found to have a defective braking system. His employers were charged with 'using' the vehicle when it did not comply with the Road Traffic Act 1972, s 40(5). They contended that they could not be convicted of 'using' but only of 'causing or permitting' the use of the vehicle.

HELD: The offence of 'using' a vehicle could be committed both by the driver of the vehicle and by the company on behalf of whom the vehicle was being driven.

Note—See also *Carmichael & Sons Ltd v Cottle* (1971) 114 Sol Jo 867, [1971] RTR 11 and *Crawford v Haughton* [1972] 1 All ER 535, [1972] 1 WLR 572, 116 Sol Jo 125, [1972] RTR 125. Also *Balfour Beatty v Grindey* [1975] RTR 156 and *Howard v G T Jones & Co Ltd* [1975] RTR 150.

James & Son v Smee

[1955] 1 QB 78, [1954] 3 All ER 273, [1954] 3 WLR 631, 118 JP 536, 98 Sol Jo 771, 52 LGR 545, Div Ct

A motor lorry and trailer left the owner's premises with the brakes complying with the regulations. At the premises of third parties, the driver with a boy assistant, uncoupled the trailer to enable loading. After loading, the driver left the boy to couple the trailer to the lorry. The boy failed to connect the brakes of the trailer properly and the driver took no steps to check the connections. The owners were prosecuted for 'permitting'.

HELD: They had not permitted; conviction quashed. The question should be: 'Has the permitter authorised the very thing which happened?' If so, or if he had more than a very shrewd idea of what would happen, then he should be found guilty. If not, no case has been proved against him. A permission to use it is not, unless more is proved, a permission to use in contravention.

LF Dove Ltd v Tarvin

(1964) 108 Sol Jo 404, Div Ct

A firm of motor engineers lent one of their cars to a customer to use whilst they were repairing his own. He drove it to London and as a result a charge was brought against

the motor engineers that they did unlawfully use the car all the tyres of which were not maintained in safe condition contrary to the Motor Vehicles (Construction and Use) Regulations 1955, reg 78. The defendants contended that as they had parted with possession and control of the car to the customer for his use, they were not using it at the time of the offence.
HELD: The point was a good one. The defendant had not been charged with causing or permitting the use of the car. The word 'use' was found in many regulations and there was a clear distinction between 'use' for oneself by oneself or a servant or agent and causing or permitting someone not a servant or agent to use. Here the defendants had not used the car at the time of the offence.

ROAD

Note—'Road' is defined in s 192(1) of the Road Traffic Act 1988 as any highway and any other road to which the public has access, and includes bridges over which a road passes.

The definition in the Road Traffic Act 1930, s 121, the Road Traffic Act 1960, s 257(1) and s 196(1) of the Road Traffic Act 1972 was in similar terms.

Purves v Muir

1948 JC 122, SLT 529, 98 LJ 413, High Ct of Jus, Scot
A courtyard not on the same level as the adjoining road which could be used for turning or parking vehicles only and was not a means of vehicle communication and not a road in the ordinary sense, although the public had access to it, is not a 'road' within the meaning of the section.

Bugge v Taylor

[1941] 1 KB 198, 110 LJKB 710, 164 LT 312, 104 JP 467, 85 Sol Jo 82, 39 LGR 100, Div Ct
The forecourt of a hotel was the private property of the owners. It was about 60 ft long and varied in width from 20 ft to 10 ft and was bounded on the west side by an island public pavement but open to the street at both ends. There was no obstruction to prevent the public, on foot or vehicles, from going over the forecourt, or to separate it from the street, and the public used it without let or hindrance to reach the hotel and to cut the corner. On occasions, public service and other vehicles had been over and through it.
HELD: It was a road within the Act.

R v Shaw

[1974] RTR 225, [1974] Crim LR 672, CA
An alley 8 ft 6 in wide led to a path 10 ft wide. Together they joined two public roads, and though contained within council property, were used by pedestrians as a short cut between the two roads. The Council did not object to people using it in this way.
HELD: The evidence was quite sufficient to entitle the jury to make the finding that the public had access and that the alley and path were a 'road'.

O'Brien v Trafalgar Insurance Co

(1945) 109 JP 107, 61 TLR 225, 78 Ll L Rep 223, CA
A road in a fenced-in factory within a protected area is not a road within the Road Traffic Act 1930, s 121(1). There was no access and it was not open to the public.

R v Lynn

[1963] 1 QB 164, [1963] 3 All ER 659, [1963] 3 WLR 946, 128 JP 48, 107 Sol Jo 833, CCA
The appellant was charged with driving a vehicle on a road in a manner dangerous contrary to the Road Traffic Act 1960, s 2(1) (now s 6 of the 1988 Act). The incident giving rise to the charge occurred in the Tuesday Market Place, King's Lynn, which was laid out as a car park with Herring-Bone markings.
HELD: The particular issue whether the place where the car was driven was a road was essentially one of fact for the jury and they must have been satisfied that the place was a road within the meaning of the Road Traffic Act 1960. Appeal dismissed.

Harrison v Hill

1932 JC 13, Scot
A road was part of a farm and led only to the farmhouse, where it terminated. It had no other houses on it, and it was not maintained by any public authority but by the farm tenant in terms of his lease. There was no gate at the entrance to it, and no intimation that it was not open to the public; and except at times in summer, when the farmer placed a pole across it to prevent the straying of cattle, there was no obstacle to prevent the public having access to it. The road was used by the public as an access to the farm, and members of the public not having business there also frequently walked on it. They had, on several occasions, been turned off by the farmer when there were growing crops in the adjoining fields.
HELD: The road was a road to which the public had access within the Road Traffic Act 1930, s 121(1).

Note—See also p 731, below.

Harrison v Co-operative Insurance Co Ltd

(1968) 118 NLJ 910 (Hinchcliffe J)
The plaintiff was injured in a collision between his motor cycle and a car on a private roadway within factory premises. The insurers of the car refused to meet a judgment for damages the plaintiff obtained against the car driver on the ground that the place was not a 'road' within the meaning of s 203. The road was used by members of the general public as well as by vehicles having no business at the factory to gain access to a weighbridge and to avoid other congested highways. There had once been a 'private road' sign at the entrance to the road but it had been removed a considerable time before the date of the accident from causes unknown.
HELD: It was a question of fact whether the road was 'a highway . . . to which the public had access'. The absence of the 'private road' sign was important; the public had access to adjacent roads and in the absence of any prohibition express or implied or any obstruction would not have any reason to suppose that access to the particular road in question was restricted in any way. The plaintiff was entitled to succeed.

Note—Section 203 — see now the Road Traffic Act 1988, s 145.

R v Beaumont

[1964] Crim LR 665, CCA
B was charged with being in charge of a motor vehicle on a road when unfit to drive through drink. The road in question was an occupation road leading to a farm and to

part of the farmer's land occupied by 200—250 caravans in one of which B lived. The road also led to a river and by leave of the farmer was used by anglers and picnickers. At the entrance to the road was a gate (always kept open), and two notices which read: 'Trespassers will be prosecuted' and '10 mph'. B contended there was not sufficient evidence that the road came within the definition in the Road Traffic Act 1960, s 257. The prosecution relied on the number of people using the road; the persons living in the caravans, their visitors, anglers, etc.
HELD: There was no evidence that the general public used the road. The court was unable to accept the contention that where a particular class of persons uses a road the number of persons in the class makes the road one to which the public has access. *Harrison v Hill* (above) applied.

Thomas v Dando

[1951] 2 KB 620, [1951] 1 All ER 1010, 115 JP 344, [1951] 1 TLR 1067, 49 LGR 793, Div Ct
Respondent occupied a shop with a forecourt and unpaved area between the pavement and kerbstone of the highway and the garden attached to the shop. The forecourt and unpaved area were his private property. There was no physical interruption between the surface of the unpaved area and that of the road, but the only people who used the unpaved area were respondent's customers going to the shop. Respondent left his car unlighted at night on the unpaved area. He was prosecuted for having an unlighted vehicle on a road contrary to the Road Transport Lighting Act 1927, s 1(1).
HELD: The statement in *Harrison v Hill*, below, that the class of road in s 121 of the Road Traffic Act 1930 is wider than the class of public roads to which the public has access in virtue of a positive right belonging to the public, and flowing either from statute or from prescriptive user, was held by Lord Caldecote CJ in *Bugge v Taylor* (p 729, above) to be applicable to the definition of 'road' in the 1927 Act. This was not a 'road' within the 1927 Act. *Bugge v Taylor* distinguished.

Note—The Road Transport Lighting Act 1927, s 15 is now repealed and replaced by the Road Traffic Act 1988 which in s 192 defines 'road' as set out on p 729, above.

The cases of *Bugge v Taylor* and *Thomas v Dando* are decisions under the 1927 Act but, as mentioned in those cases, are applicable in the 1960 Act.

The following quotations from the judgment in *Harrison v Hill* (below) were quoted by McNair J in the case of *Buchanan v Motor Insurers' Bureau* [1955] 1 All ER 607, [1955] 1 WLR 488, 119 JP 227, [1954] 2 Lloyd's Rep 519. He said that they seemed to him to give very clear guidance as to the proper way of approaching the question.

Harrison v Hill

1932 JC 13, Scot
Per Lord Clyde: It is plain, from the terms of the definition, that the class of road intended is wider than the class of public roads to which the public has access in virtue of a positive right belonging to the public, and flowing either from statute or from prescriptive user. A road may therefore be within the definition (1) although it belongs to the class of private roads, and (2) although all that can be said with regard to its availability to the public is that the public 'has access' to it. I think that, when the statute speaks of 'the Public' in this connection, what is meant is the public generally, and not the special class of members of the public who have occasion for business or social purposes to go to the farmhouse or to any part of the farm itself; were it otherwise, the definition might just as well have included all private roads as

well as all public highways. I think also that, when the statute speaks of the public having 'access' to the road, what is meant is neither (at one extreme) that the public has a positive right of its own to access, nor (at the other extreme) that there exists no physical obstruction, of greater or less impenetrability, against physical access by the public; but that the public actually and legally enjoys access to it. It is, I think, a certain state of use or possession that is pointed to. There must be, as matter of fact, walking or driving by the public on the road, and such walking or driving must be lawfully performed—that is to say, must be permitted or allowed, either expressly or implicitly, by the person to whom the road belongs. I include in permission or allowance the state of matters known in right of way cases as the tolerance of a proprietor.

Per Lord Sands: In my view, any road may be regarded as a road to which the public have access upon which members of the public are to be found who have not obtained access either by overcoming a physical obstruction or in defiance of prohibition express or implied.

Kreft v Rawcliffe

(1984) Times, 12 May, QBD
The defendant was charged with offences on a 'road' as defined in s 196(1). The only evidence that members of the public had access to the road was that of a farmer of the land on which the road ran, that in 55 years he had seen members of the public on the land very rarely. A police constable patrolling the road, merchants and postmen visiting the farms down the road, the borough engineer realigning footpaths near the road and customers to a wholesaler fronting the road were not members of the public for the purposes of the statute.
HELD: Not a 'road'.

Knaggs v Elson

(1965) 109 Sol Jo 596, Div Ct
The defendant parked his car without lights in a private road the ownership of which was vested in trustees. It was a cul-de-sac having 36 houses: there were no gates or other barriers but there was a notice 'Private Road — No Parking'. The trustees had taken steps to try to prevent parking. A police officer gave evidence of driving his car into the road, turning and reversing without restriction. The prosecution contended it was a 'road to which the public has access'.
HELD: It had been long held, deriving from *Harrison v Hill* (above) that the public might have access to a road, whether or not they had the right of access, if their presence was tolerated by the owners, but not if they entered by overcoming an obstruction or in defiance of a prohibition expressed or implied. Here there was a sign which on the face of it prohibited members of the public from entering; but it was not conclusive that their presence was not tolerated. Steps had been taken to prevent parking and no member of the public was likely to enter it for any other purpose; the police officer's evidence did not prove otherwise. No doubt the road was used by the inhabitants and their visitors but they were a limited class. Applying *R v Beaumont* (above) and *R v Waters* (1963) 107 Sol Jo 275, 47 Cr App Rep 149 (which showed that if only a restricted class was admitted the road would be private but if a restricted class was excluded the road would be public) this was not a 'road to which the public had access'.

Deacon v A T (a minor)

[1976] RTR 244, Civ Ct
The defendant aged 15 was driving a car on a road within a housing estate the property of the Greater London Council. There were gates to the estate normally kept open and no signs either restricting or permitting the public or any class of the public from entering the estate on foot. The justices found that the roads of the estate were used by residents on the estate and visitors to them.
HELD: Without any evidence that members of the public in the wide sense, that is to say, persons who were not residents and were not visitors to residents, used the road of this estate it was not a 'road' as defined in the Road Traffic Act 1972, s 196(1).

Note—In *Cox v White* [1976] RTR 248, Lord Widgery CJ said 'I would invite . . . justices charged with this same question (whether a road on an industrial estate was within the definition in s 196(1) to look at the very brief statement of Lords Sands in *Harrison v Hill* (quoted at p 732, above) . . . I think that in 99 cases out of 100 that direction is all the justices need to decide whether a road is a"road" for current purposes.'

Adams v Metropolitan Police Comr

[1980] RTR 289 (Jupp J)
The plaintiffs were residents in houses in Aberdeen Park, Highbury, London, a private estate built in Victorian times. The estate road was originally gated at both points of access and there was no access to the public except on business. In the course of time one of the gates disappeared but notices remained saying access was limited to residents and their authorised callers only. Nevertheless the road was in regular daily use by persons entering the estate to pass through to places on the other side. Motorists and motor cyclists used the road as a kind of free race track or as a car park. The police refused to prosecute for offences under the Road Traffic Acts because they were advised the road was not one to which the public had access within the meaning of s 196 because of the notices. In November 1970 the notices forbidding access to unauthorised persons were removed by the estate company. The plaintiffs sued for a declaration that the road was one to which the public had access within the meaning of the section.
HELD: There was ample evidence that the public had access, especially by the pedestrians from properties outside the estate who passed through it to shops and a public open space on the other side. They had access without 'either by overcoming a physical obstruction or in defiance of prohibition express or implied' following Lord Sands's test in *Harrison v Hill* (p 731, above). The public use of Aberdeen Park, notwithstanding the signs, was tolerated by the owners of the road. The road was therefore one coming within s 196(1). Even so it was not a case for making a declaration the notices having now been removed and the police acknowledging that they would accept the view of the court.

Kellett v Daisy

[1977] RTR 396, Div Ct
The justices found that the defendant had driven without due care and attention on Elles Road, Farnborough, a road to which the public had access but which was a Crown road as defined by the Transport Act 1968, s 149(5)(b). The defendant maintained that he could not be convicted because the prosecution had not shown that the Road Traffic Act 1972 bound the road.

HELD: That approach was false. The question was not whether the road was bound by the Act but whether the defendant was. He was driving without due care on a road as defined by the Road Traffic Act 1972, s 196 and he was bound by the Act.

Chapman v Parlby

(1963) 108 Sol Jo 35, 62 LGR 150, Div Ct
A cyclist was struck by the defendant's car when riding along a road connecting a public highway with a War Department depot. The road was 49 feet long and had a solid white line across it half-way along. The cyclist was between the highway and the white line when struck. Justices dismissed a charge of careless driving on the grounds that the road was not a 'road' within the Road Traffic Act 1960, s 3 (now s 3 of the 1988 Act).
HELD: Following *Harrison v Hill* the road was a 'road' for the purposes of the section as it was one on which members of the public were to be found and which had no obstacle to prevent them from using it. A member of the public would meet with no physical obstruction and would meet with no prohibition express or implied until he reached the solid white lines.

Houghton v Schofield

[1973] RTR 239, [1973] Crim LR 126, Div Ct
A local authority made a traffic control order prohibiting waiting in a road giving access to a car park. There was an adjoining loading area and a cul-de-sac, not separated from the road by any physical barrier: the double yellow lines on the road included the area and cul-de-sac. The defendants were lessees of a shop from the authority on terms which gave them some right over the cul-de-sac but not a right to exclude the public. The defendants parked a vehicle in the cul-de-sac and were prosecuted for contravening the traffic order. They contended that the cul-de-sac was not a 'road'.
HELD: Following *Buchanan v MIB* (above p 731) the test was whether there was any physical obstruction for the public to overcome or any prohibition express or implied to public access. The magistrates were justified in holding on the evidence that the cul-de-sac was a road.

Lorry crossing pavement

Randall v Motor Insurers' Bureau

[1969] 1 All ER 21, [1968] 1 WLR 1900, 112 Sol Jo 553, [1968] 2 Lloyd's Rep 553 (Megaw J)
The plaintiff in the course of his duty tried to prevent a lorry from leaving a building site. The lorry ran him down at the entrance to the site, the rear wheel passing over his leg and severely injuring it. He was just inside the boundary when this occurred; the front of the lorry was crossing the pavement of the street which the site adjoined. The plaintiff obtained judgment against the driver for damages which was not satisfied. He sued the Motor Insurers' Bureau for satisfaction of the judgment. They resisted the claim on the ground that the lorry was not being used 'on a road' within the meaning of the Road Traffic Act 1960, s 203(3)(a) (now s 145 of the 1988 Act).
HELD: The fact that the plaintiff was still on private property and therefore not 'on a road' at the time of the injury was immaterial. The defendants did not deny that the

pavement was a part of the road. At the time when the lorry wheel ran over the plaintiff's leg the greater part of the lorry was on the road and the lorry was using the road. It was the use of the lorry on the road—the fact that it was being driven further on to the road in order to drive away along the road—which caused the injury.

Quayside

Walton v Newcastle-upon-Tyne Corpn

[1957] 1 Lloyd's Rep 412, Div Ct
A quayside road was vested in the defendants under various local statutes that all public rights of way or passage over the road were extinguished. The road joined a public highway at each end. There was no hindrance or obstruction to prevent members of the public walking or proceeding along it and no notice boards or other indication to the public that they did not use it as of right. It was distinguished from the highway by marks on the road and was private property not repaired or maintained by any highway authority. In fact many motor vehicles, both motor cars and lorries, frequently proceeded in either direction and members of the public were free to walk or motor along the roadway in either direction and did so. It was used by the public just in the same way as any other road.
HELD: The road was within the definition of 'road' in s 121(1) of the 1930 Act (now in the Road Traffic Act 1988, s 192).

Dock roads

Note—Roads on dock property are not normally within the definition in s 192(1) since they are not places to which the general public has access as a matter of legal right (*Buchanan v Motor Insurers' Bureau* [1955] 1 All ER 607, [1955] 1 WLR 488, 119 JP 227, 99 Sol Jo 319 [1954] 2 Lloyd's Rep 519). But the Port of London Act 1968, s 199, as substituted by the Port of London Act 1982, s 4 extends many of the provisions of the Road Traffic Acts to 'dock roads', including the requirements of ss 143 and 144 of the Road Traffic Act 1988. Section 199 has the following definitions:

'dock road' means any road, pier, wharf, quay, bridge or other work which, or any land which is:

(1) vested in or the property of the Port Authority; and
(2) situate within the customs wall or fence bounding any dock of the Port Authority; and
(3) accessible to motor vehicles;

'motor vehicle' has the same meaning as in the Road Traffic Act 1988.

In respect of docks of the British Transport Docks Board see the British Transport Commission Act 1961, s 26(2) (as amended): 'The Road Traffic Act 1972 shall have effect as if, in the provisions thereof referred to in this section, the expression "road" included a dock road.' Section 143 of the 1972 Act is one of the provisions referred to. By s 26(1) a 'dock road' means 'any road, pier, wharf, quay, bridge, works or land which is situate within any dock or harbour premises of the Docks Board (not being a road as defined by the Road Traffic Act 1972, s 196) . . . '

Section 2(4) of the Road Traffic (Consequential Provisions) Act 1988 provides that references to the Road Traffic Act 1972 and other enactments repealed by the Road Traffic Act 1988 are to be read as a reference to the corresponding provision of the Road Traffic Act 1988 in so far as the nature of the reference permits.

Aerodromes

Note—The Airports Act 1986, s 65(1) applies the road traffic enactments to roads within a designated aerodrome to which the public does not have access to the same extent as they apply in relation to roads which the public has access.

Car park

Griffin v Squires

[1958] 3 All ER 468, [1958] 1 WLR 1106, 123 JP 40, 102 Sol Jo 828, 56 LGR 442, Div Ct
A car park owned and maintained by the urban district at the public expense, had a frontage to the main road of 123 ft and a depth of 80 ft. The south side abutted on the pavement of the main road, with two entrances each 11 ft wide; the east wide was bounded by a wall; the west side by railings and a privet hedge; and the north side by a fence. At the north-west corner there was an opening 15 ft wide abutting on a private footpath leading to a bowling club and council allotments. The allotment users had to cross the car park to get to their gardens.

An unlicensed and uninsured woman driver drove a car from a stationary position in the car park for a distance of 10 yards, in the course of which the car crossed through the privet hedge and came to rest on a lawn outside the council buildings. She was prosecuted under the Road Traffic Act 1930, ss 4(1) and 55.
HELD: The question whether the car park as a part of the footpath was a 'road' was a question of fact for the magistrates, and so was the question whether the car park was a road. It is not enough alone that the public have access, but that it is a road. There was evidence to justify the finding that it was not a road. Appeal dismissed.

Note—The provisions of s 4(1) of the Road Traffic Act 1930 are now contained in the Road Traffic Act 1988, ss 87(1) and (2); those of s 35 of the 1930 Act in s 143 of the 1988 Act.

Oxford v Austin

[1981] RTR 416, QBD
In determining whether a car park can be a road within the Road Traffic Act 1972, s 196(1) there is a well established process founded on findings of fact. The first question to be asked is whether there is in the ordinary understanding of the word a road, ie a definable way between two points over which vehicles can pass, a way of communication ordinarily to be thought of as a road. The second question is whether or not the public or a section of the public has access to that which has the appearance of a definable way. If one or two members of the public demonstrate as a fact that the public has a right of access it is irrelevant that the area is privately owned. Even a private car park may be one to which the public has access. If both questions can be answered affirmatively then there is a road for the purposes of the various Road Traffic Acts and Regulations.

Note—See also *R v Lynn*, p 730, above.

Paterson v Ogilvy

1957 SLT 354, [1957] CLY 3147, High Ct of Justiciary
A field, used as a parking place at an agricultural show, held a 'place' within the Road Traffic Act 1930, s 15.

Note—The relevant provisions of the Road Traffic Act 1930, s 15 are now contained in the Road Traffic Act 1988, s 4.

Private property

Norton v Hayward

(1968) 112 Sol Jo 767, Div Ct QB

An area of ground consisting partly of an entrance to a passageway giving access to the rear of business premises and a street was designated a 'double yellow line' road under the Road Traffic Act 1960, s 26 (now s 2 of the Road Traffic Regulation Act 1984). Part of it was demised to the defendant whose business premises adjoined it. He parked his car in the area and was prosecuted.

HELD: Although part of the relevant area was private land in the sense of forming part of the demise that did not prevent it from being a 'road' within s 257 of the Act.

Note—The Road Traffic Act 1960, s 26 has been replaced by the Road Traffic Regulation Act 1984, s 2. In that Act 'road' is defined as in the Road Traffic Acts 1960 and 1972.

REQUIREMENTS OF POLICY

Road Traffic Act 1988, s 145

145 (1) In order to comply with the requirements of this Part of this Act, a policy of insurance must satisfy the following conditions.

(2) The policy must be issued by an authorised insurer.

(3) Subject to subsection (4) below, the policy—

(a) must insure such person, persons or classes of persons as may be specified in the policy in respect of any liability which may be incurred by him or them in respect of the death of or bodily injury to any person or damage to property caused by, or arising out of, the use of the vehicle on a road in Great Britain, and

(b) must insure him or them in respect of any liability which may be incurred by him or them in respect of the use of the vehicle and of any trailer, whether or not coupled, in the territory other than Great Britain and Gibraltar of each of the member States of the Communities according to the law on compulsory insurance against civil liability in respect of the use of vehicles of the State where the liability may be incurred, and

(c) must also insure him or them in respect of any liability which may be incurred by him or them under the provisions of this Part of this Act relating to payment for emergency treatment.

(4) The policy shall not, by virtue of subsection (3)(a) above, be required—

(a) to cover liability in respect of the death, arising out of and in the course of his employment, of a person in the employment of a person insured by the policy or of bodily injury sustained by such a person arising out of and in the course of his employment, or

(b) to provide insurance of more than £250,000 in respect of all such liabilities as may be incurred in respect of damage to property caused by, or arising out of, any one accident involving the vehicle, or

(c) to cover liability in respect of damage to the vehicle, or

(d) to cover liability in respect of damage to goods carried for hire or reward in or on the vehicle or in or on any trailer (whether or not coupled) drawn by the vehicle, or

(e) to cover any liability of a person in respect of damage to property in his custody or under his control, or

(f) to cover any contractual liability.

SUBSECTION (3)(A): 'ANY PERSON'

Cooper v Motor Insurers' Bureau

[1985] QB 575, [1985] 1 All ER 449, [1985] 2 WLR 248, 129 Sol Jo 32, CA
Killacky bought an old motor cycle and took it to Cooper, who he knew had expert knowledge of motor cycles, to try it out. Cooper mounted the machine and rode off. On approaching a major road he applied the brakes and they failed to operate. He collided with a car and was seriously injured. He sued Killacky in negligence for failing to warn him that the brakes were defective and obtained judgment for £214,207. Killacky was not insured and unable to satisfy the judgment. Cooper sued the Motor Insurers' Bureau, claiming that Killacky's liability was a 'relevant liability' within the definition in cl 1 of the Motor Insurers' Bureau Uninsured Driver's Agreement 'a liability in respect of which a policy of insurance must insure a person in order to comply with Part VI of the Road Traffic Act 1972'. It was argued on his behalf that 'any person' in s 145(3)(a) of the 1972 Act included the plaintiff even though he was driving. For the Bureau it was argued that s 143 was vital and that it was the use of the vehicle causing damage to others which was the only liability to be covered. The judge held the Motor Insurers' Bureau not liable. Section 143 spoke first of a person using and second of one who caused or permitted the use; the section was not intended to insure against personal injury to the person actually using the vehicle.
HELD, ON APPEAL: The judge was right. Section 145(3)(a) was not the end of the story. Consideration had to be given to s 143(1). The obligation imposed by that subsection is an obligation to abstain from using, or from causing or permitting any other person to use, a motor vehicle on the road unless there is in force in relation to the use of the vehicle by that person or that other person a policy of insurance complying with the requirements of Part VI of the Act. A policy covering him 'in respect of third-party risks' clearly does not include the actual driver of the vehicle at the time of the use of the vehicle which gives rise to the damage. The scope of the phrase 'any person' in s 145(3)(a) is limited by s 143(1) so as to exclude the driver of the vehicle.

SUBSECTION (4)(A): 'ARISING OUT OF AND IN THE COURSE OF'

Vandyke v Fender

[1970] 2 QB 292, [1970] 2 All ER 335, [1970] 2 WLR 929, 134 JP 487, 114 Sol Jo 205, CA
Vandyke and Fender were moulders employed by the second defendants at a foundry 30 miles from their homes. The second defendants arranged with Fender to lend him a car in which he could drive to work, bringing Vandyke and two other employees. Although the arrangements for providing the car and paying him an allowance for petrol was part of Fender's contract of service neither he nor Vandyke was obliged to use the car if they did not wish to do so. It was not a term of their contract of service that they must use it. When riding as a passenger in the car on the way to work Vandyke was injured in an accident for which Fender was held to blame.
HELD: Vandyke was in the vehicle 'by reason of . . . a contract of employment' but not 'in the course of' his employment. The test whether Vandyke was in the car 'in the course of' his employment was the same as in the leading cases under the Workmen's Compensation Acts, namely, whether he was under an obligation as a term of his employment to travel in the car, and he was not. The words injury 'arising out of and in the course of his employment' were used in the old Workmen's Compensation Acts

from 1897 to 1945. The selfsame words have been used in the Road Traffic Acts 1930 and 1960. They have also been used in employers' liability policies. In my opinion they should receive the same interpretation in all three places, for they are all so closely connected that they ought, as matter of commonsense, to receive the same interpretation in each. The words were construed and applied in thousands of cases under the Workmen's Compensation Acts: and I think we should follow those cases. The two leading cases, most apposite for present purposes are *St Helens Colliery Co Ltd v Hewitson* [1924] AC 59, 93 LJKB 177, 130 LT 291, 40 TLR 125, 68 Sol Jo 163 and *Weaver v Tredegar Iron and Coal Co Ltd* [1940] AC 955. They show, to my mind, quite conclusively that when a man is going to or coming from work, along a public road, as a passenger in a vehicle provided by his employer, he is not then in the course of his employment—unless he is obliged by the terms of his employment to travel in that vehicle. It is not enough that he should have the right to travel in the vehicle, or be permitted to travel in it. He must have an obligation to travel in it. Else he is not in the course of his employment. That distinction must be maintained; for otherwise there would be no certainty in this branch of the law: per Lord Denning.

St Helens Colliery Co v Hewitson

[1924] AC 59, 93 LJKB 177, 130 LT 291, 40 TLR 125, 68 Sol Jo 163, 16 BWCC 230, HL
A workman employed at a colliery travelled by a special train provided by an agreement between his employers and a railway company. The employers paid the railway company and the workman agreed to a deduction from his wages of half the fare paid by his employers and to waive all claims against the railway company.
HELD: The workman was under no obligation or duty to be there, he was not doing something in discharge or performance of a duty to his employers directly or indirectly imposed upon him by or arising out of his contract of service. There was only a right and not an obligation. Not 'arising out of and in the course of his employment'.

Note—Hewitson's case was distinguished (except by Viscount Maugham who considered it indistinguishable) in the following case.

Weaver v Tredegar Iron and Coal Co Ltd

[1940] AC 955, [1940] 3 All ER 157, 109 LJKB 621, 164 LT 231, 56 TLR 813, 84 Sol Jo 584, HL
A railway line passed through the premises of a colliery company. There was a halt station used only by the colliery workmen. The access to the station was the property of the railway company. Workmen obtained tickets from the colliery company, who arranged with the railway company for the trains. The workmen were not compelled to use the trains, but practically all did so. A workman was injured on the platform.
HELD: The employment continued whilst the workman was on any private exist which he was only entitled to use by reason of his status of a workman. The accident arose out of and in the course of the employment.

Craw v Forrest

1931 SC 634, 24 BWCC Supp 67, Ct of Sess
A girl accepted employment as a weeder and picker on a fruit farm on condition that the employer conveyed her a distance of eight miles each day to her work. The time

occupied in this conveyance was not paid for as working time. The workman was neither expressly bound by her contract, nor ordered by her employer or by anyone on his behalf, to use the means of conveyance provided, which was a motor lorry belonging to the employer and under the control of his son. The lorry was the only practicable means by which the workman could get to her work in time to start at the prescribed hours, and but for the offer of the conveyance to her work the workman would not have accepted the employment.
HELD: The workman was neither bound by her contract of service nor ordered by her employer to use the means of transport provided. Not 'arising out of and in the course of'.

Black v Aitkenhead

(1938) 31 BWCC Supp 73, Ct of Sess
A labourer, while engaged on work at a distance from his home, was conveyed over part of the distance on a motor lorry which was provided by his employers. There was no express contract between the workman and his employers for the use of this conveyance; but, before accepting the job, the workman knew that the lorry would be provided free of cost, and he would not have accepted the offer of employment if it had not been available. This free conveyance was entirely optional, but it was used by employees who resided at a distance from the work. There was no direct transport connection between the workman's home and place of work, and travel by the ordinary route would have materially increased both the cost and the time of the journey. While being conveyed to his work, the workman fell from the lorry and was killed.
HELD: As the workman was not under any contractual obligation to use the lorry, his death while he was proceeding to his work on that conveyance was not the result of an accident arising in the course of his employment within the Workmen's Compensation Act 1925, s 1(1).

Netherton v Coles

[1945] 1 All ER 227, 37 BWCC 165, CA
A workman was employed at a job 11 miles from his home. He had travelling allowances and free travelling facilities by voucher or otherwise. He left the place of work on a motor cycle and met with an accident on the public road.
HELD: Not 'out of'; the workman outside working hours was at liberty to choose his own time and method of transport.

Allen v Siddons

(1932) 25 BWCC 350
A foreman was employed at a fixed weekly wage of £3 and his hours of work were from 7 am–5 pm. On one job he had to be at work at 7.30 am. He left home at 7 am on his motor cycle and met with an accident on his way to work. The employer argued that he was not concerned with what the man did before 7.30 am. The county court judge held the accident arose out of and in the course of. The Court of Appeal said that although the employer might have had the right to give orders to the workman at any time after 7 am he did not on this occasion exercise that right, and the workman's employment in fact began at 7.30 am. The accident having happened merely when the workman was going to work, it did not arise out of and in the course of.

Alderman v Great Western Rly Co

[1938] AC 454, 30 BWCC 64, HL
A travelling ticket collector signed on for duty at Oxford in the morning, travelled by train to Paddington and there joined a train to Swansea where he signed off duty for the night. The next morning he had to sign on at Swansea and return via Paddington to Oxford where his duties ended. Whilst spending the night at Swansea, he was under an obligation to lodge within a reasonable distance of the station and to leave his address in case of emergency. He was injured on his way from his lodgings to sign on for duty at Swansea station. The House of Lords held that the accident did not arise out of and in the course of the employment.

Blee v London and North Eastern Rly Co

[1938] AC 126, [1937] 4 All ER 270, 107 LJKB 62, 158 LT 185, 54 TLR 71, 81 Sol Jo 941, 30 BWCC 364, HL
A platelayer was liable to be called on at any time for emergency work for which he received overtime commencing from the time he left his home. At 10.30 pm after retiring to bed, he was called up on an emergency. On his way from his home to the railway siding, he met with an accident. The House of Lords held that the employment commenced at the time he left home and the accident arose out of and in the course of his employment.

Dunn v AG Lockwood & Co

[1947] 1 All ER 446, 40 BWCC 60, CA
A workman who lived at Whitstable was employed as a plasterer by a firm of builders at Margate. Work began each day at 8 am but the workman was permitted to catch the 7.40 am train from Whitstable arriving at Margate at 8.15 am and was paid from 8 am. He was permitted to take the train on condition that he started work as soon as possible after he arrived at Margate station. On his way from the station to his work he met with an accident. The Court of Appeal held that the permission to the workman to take a train which caused him to be late for work placed upon him the contractual duty to go from the station to his place of work as quickly as possible. It was in performing this duty to his employers that the accident happened and it accordingly arose out of and in the course of his employment.

Paterson v Costain and Press (Overseas) Ltd

(1979) 123 Sol Jo 142, [1979] 2 Lloyd's Rep 204, CA
The defendants were carrying out constructional work at Bid Boland 170 km from Abadan in Persia. They provided transport in their own vehicles for their employees, of whom the plaintiff was one, from Abadan to Bid Boland where the plaintiff both worked and was housed. The only other way of making the journey was by taxi, very rarely done because expensive. After a short holiday in Kuwait the plaintiff returned to Abadan to make the remainder of the journey by road to Bid Boland; the defendants had arranged for a Landrover to be available. On the journey to Bid Boland he was injured in an accident. If the accident arose 'in the course of' his employment the defendants would be indemnified by their employers' liability insurers; if not, then by their public liability insurers.
HELD: Applying *St Helens Colliery v Hewitson* (p 739, above) the accident arose 'in the course of' the employment. There had to be on the part of the plaintiff an obligation and not merely a right to use the transport provided but on the facts there

was an obligation. It was not a case of a man going from his home to his place of work. It was part of the sphere of his employment to travel on the employer's vehicle from Abadan to the site of his work and his home 170 km away at Bid Boland: [1978] 1 Lloyd's Rep 86 (Talbot J).

An appeal was dismissed. The accident had occurred in Iran; the contract showed that virtually from the time of getting off the aircraft at Abadan the plaintiff was in the defendants' employment. It was clearly distinguishable from the English cases.

Nancollas v Insurance Officer

[1985] 1 All ER 833, CA
The plaintiff worked for the Department of Employment. He was based at Worthing but his job involved calling at other Job Centres and visiting disabled people. One morning, he set out from home to conduct an interview in Aldershot without first calling in to his office. He was involved in a collision and suffered personal injury. The Commissioners held he was not driving in the course of his employment for the purposes of s 50(1) of the Social Security Act 1975, as he was travelling to and from work.
HELD, ON APPEAL: He was acting in the course of his employment. The principal issue was whether this was a journey to work or whether the journey itself was part of his work. As he was an itinerant officer the journey was part of his work. The court must look at the whole factual picture. No one factor is conclusive. The dictum of Lord Denning MR in *Vandyke v Fender* was doubted; dicta in *St Helens Colliery Co v Hewitson* applied.

Smith v Stages

[1989] AC 928, [1989] 1 All ER 833, [1989] 2 WLR 529, HL
An employee who is paid for travelling from his residence to the site at work is not taken outside the course of his employment simply by reason of his having a discretion as to mode of travel.

Hutton v West Cork Rly Co

(1883) 23 Ch D 654, 52 LJ Ch 689, 49 LT 420, 31 WR 827, CA
Nor, as such, is he a servant of the company.

R v Stuart

[1894] 1 QB 310, 63 LJMC 63, 58 JP 299, 42 WR 303
He may, however, be employed as a servant.

Trussed Steel Concrete Co v Green

[1946] Ch 115, 115 LJ Ch 123, 174 LT 122, 110 JP 144
And a managing director with a contract of service may be an employee of the company.

Lee v Lee's Air Farming Ltd

[1961] AC 12, [1960] 3 All ER 420, [1960] 3 WLR 758, 104 Sol Jo 969, PC
In 1954 the appellant's husband formed a company for the purpose of conducting an aerial top-dressing business. The nominal capital was 3,000 shares of £1 each of which he held 2,999. He was governing director. By the articles of the company it was

provided that the company should employ him as the chief pilot and that the relationship of master and servant should apply. In 1956 he was piloting the company's aircraft on top-dressing operations when it crashed and he was killed. HELD: He was a 'person who has entered into or works under a contract of service with an employer' for the purposes of the New Zealand Workers Compensation Act 1922. The contractual obligations in the articles were not invalidated by the circumstance that the deceased was the sole governing director in whom was vested the full government and control of the respondent company.

Road Transport Industry Training Board v Readers Garage Ltd

(1969) 113 Sol Jo 125, 6 KIR 137, Div Ct
The managing director of a garage company having seven employees held 99½% of the shares and drew £1,450 pa from the business, in which he took an active part. HELD: The fact that he held the overwhelming majority of the shares, decided what was to be done and who was to do it and how much money he could draw out on his own account did not preclude him from being also an employee of the company. If his main work was that of a director and he only occasionally stepped into the shoes of his workmen that was one thing. But if he spent many hours in the filling station or in the garage for repairs with only short periods on director's duties a tribunal might come to a different decision. It was a question of fact whether a contract of service could be implied.

PASSENGER INSURANCE

Note—Neither the Road Traffic Act 1960 nor its predecessor the 1930 Act required users of motor vehicles to be insured in respect of liability for death or bodily injury to passengers in the vehicle being used except a vehicle in which passengers were carried for hire or reward or by reason of or in pursuance of a contract of employment. However, under the Road Traffic Acts 1972 and now 1988 such insurance is now compulsory save that insurance against claims by passengers arising out of and in the course of their employment is still not required (1988 Act, s 145(4)(a)).

Insurance certificate

ROAD TRAFFIC ACT 1988, S 147

From 15 May 1989 the Road Traffic Act 1972, s 147 has been replaced by the Road Traffic Act 1988, s 147 which reads as follows:

147 (1) A policy of insurance shall be of no effect for the purposes of this Part of this Act unless and until there is delivered by the insurer to the person by whom the policy is effected a certificate (in this Part of this Act referred to as a 'certificate of insurance') in the prescribed form and containing such particulars of any conditions subject to which the policy is issued and of any other matters as may be prescribed.
(2) A security shall be of no effect for the purposes of this Part of this Act unless and until there is delivered by the person giving the security to the person to whom it is given a certificate (in this Part of this Act referred to as a 'certificate of security') in the prescribed form and containing such particulars of any conditions subject to which the security is issued and of any other matters as may be prescribed.
(3) Different forms and different particulars may be prescribed for the purposes of subsection (1) or (2) above in relation to different cases or circumstances.

(4) Where a certificate has been delivered under this section and the policy or security to which it relates is cancelled by mutual consent or by virtue of any provision in the policy or security, the person to whom the certificate was delivered must, within seven days from the taking effect of the cancellation—

(a) surrender the certificate to the person by whom the policy was issued or the security was given, or

(b) if the certificate has been lost or destroyed, make a statutory declaration to that effect.

(5) A person who fails to comply with subsection (4) above is guilty of an offence.

Starkey v Hall

[1936] 2 All ER 18, 80 Sol Jo 347, 55 Ll L Rep 24, Div Ct

A policy is not in force until delivery of the certificate to the assured and delivery of the certificate to a hire purchase company is not delivery to the assured and the assured is liable for an offence under s 35(1).

Note—Section 35, ie of the 1930 Act. See s 143 of the 1988 Act.

Egan v Bower

(1939) 63 Ll L Rep 266, Div Ct

A certificate contained limitation of use to policy holder's business under C licence not covering carrying passengers for hire or reward. Policy holder was carrying his wife and children not on business. Insurers wrote to the police that they would indemnify for private pleasure purposes.

HELD: The policy did not cover the risk and the policy holder had committed an offence under s 35(1).

Carnill v Rowland

[1953] 1 All ER 486, [1953] 1 WLR 380, 117 JP 127, 97 Sol Jo 134, 51 LGR 180, [1953] 1 Lloyd's Rep 99, Div Ct

A proposal form for motor cycle insurance restricted the cover to use when a sidecar or box carrier was permanently attached. A cover note with temporary certificate was issued restricted to use of the motor cycle to which a sidecar was permanently attached. The permanent certificate would have contained the words 'use of the cycle is only permitted when a sidecar or box carrier is attached'. The insured removed the sidecar body and drove with only the sidecar chassis and the wheel, and was summoned for driving uninsured. The insurers gave evidence that for the purposes of the policy they regarded what was attached as a sidecar and would have held covered.

HELD: The meaning of the cover note may be a question of doubt. The construction put on it by the insurers was not impossible and the justices were entitled to accept the insurers' construction.

A decision by justices or on appeal of a Divisional Court does not bind the insurer or the insured and the fact that justices have to decide a question of insurance law in the absence of the insurers, who are the parties most interested, makes it desirable to make use of an arrangement that has been entered into with the approval of the appropriate authorities for consultation between the police and insurance companies whether insurers hold covered. If a respectable insurance company consider themselves on risk, the mischief aimed at by the Act does not arise.

Note—The existence of such an 'arrangement' is a matter of doubt. See *Boss v Kingston*, p 837, below.

Certificate does not enlarge policy

Note—A question which was for some time unsettled was whether a certificate of insurance which contains terms which are different from the terms of the policy has any legal effect at all as regards third parties, or between the insurer and the assured, or whether the conditions of the policy are the only test. It has now been settled in *Spraggon*'s case, below.

In *Gray v Blackmore* [1934] 1 KB 95, 103 LJKB 145, 150 LT 99, 50 TLR 23, 47 Ll L Rep 69 a policy excluded use for any purpose in connection with the motor trade, and the certificate contained a similar limitation. The argument for the insurers was that there was no estoppel by the certificate because it stated on its face the limitations to which it was subject.

Per Branson J: It is obvious from s 36(5) relating to the certificate of insurance that the policy may contain conditions the nature of which is left completely open. So it clearly contemplates conditions, and unless they are to be conditions limiting the liability of the underwriter, what possible reason can there be for their inclusion in the certificate, the object of which is to make clear to whom it may concern the conditions, if any, subject to which the policy has been issued.

McCormick v National Motor Accident Insurance

(1934) 50 TLR 528, 78 Sol Jo 633, 40 Com Cas 76, 49 Ll L Rep 361, CA
Insurers discovered just before the trial of an action brought by a third party against their assured that they were entitled to avoid the policy for false statement in the proposal form. It was contended for the third party that the issue of the certificate prevented insurers from asserting that the policy was avoided.
Per Greer LJ: The effect and need of the certificate is this, that it enables the assured to say: 'Here is my certificate of insurance, and I am not liable as long as I have got an insurance.' It is not a document which is supposed to be addressed to all the world, including people who have never seen it and may never have heard—and a great many people never have heard—either of the Act of Parliament or of the certificate. It is only issued for the purpose of enabling the assured to produce that document when he is on the road, which will show that he has complied with the Act to the extent of getting a policy of insurance; but it is not intended to be a representation that the policy which he has got will in any event become a policy on which he will be entitled in the event of an accident happening and damages resulting.

Per Slesser LJ: The certificate is merely giving the means of enabling a man to drive a motor car. It has no greater effect than that.

Note—For s 36(5) see now s 147 of the Road Traffic Act 1988.

Spraggon v Dominion Insurance Co Ltd

(1940) 67 Ll L Rep 529 (Stable J); on appeal (1941) 69 Ll L Rep 1, CA
Tomrley hired a car from Warnes. Insurers had issued a policy to Warnes providing indemnity to drivers hiring cars unless within the category of excluded drivers. Excluded drivers included any who had not (1) satisfied the insured (Warnes) by an actual driving test, (2) completed a proposal form, (3) a current driving licence for 12 months free from endorsements, (4) forwarded the proposal form immediately after the driving test to insurers by registered post. Insurers had issued a certificate to Warnes insuring any driver who holds a licence and is not disqualified. Tomrley held a licence and was not disqualified. He was therefore within the wording of the certificate. He had a provisional licence from 25 November 1937 to 22 February 1938, and thereafter an annual licence, which was indorsed with a conviction for speed on 24 March 1938. He did not post the proposal form he signed to insurers. He never had a driving test.

He was therefore not within the wording of the policy. Warnes assured Tomrley that he was covered. An action was brought by a third party against the insurers.
HELD: Insurers were not liable, because it is only where there is a policy of insurance in respect of which the certificate has been issued that the third party had a cause of action against insurers. The accident was not covered by the policy, and the certificate was therefore of no effect: Per Stable J.
HELD, ON APPEAL: Tomrley was not insured by the policy; the CA made no reference to the certificate.

Note—It follows that the opinion previously widely held by insurers that the insurer is bound by the wording of the certificate as distinct from the policy is without foundation. It is now made perfectly plain that the policy is the only document which creates any liability on insurers, and the certificate is (in this respect) merely a piece of paper to produce to the police to show that there is a policy in existence, without affecting in any way the limitation contained in the policy.

Some policies expressly incorporate the certificate in the policy, and in that case different consideration may arise as between insurers and the assured.

Biddle v Johnston

(1965) 109 Sol Jo 395, [1965] 2 Lloyd's Rep 121, Div Ct
A policy of insurance insured C Ltd and four other named associated companies in respect of the use of a motor vehicle owned by C Ltd, but did not insure R Ltd, a company some of whose shareholders were directors of C Ltd. There had been some co-operation between C Ltd and R Ltd until a receiver of C Ltd was appointed when it largely ceased. The certificate issued under the policy was expressed to cover use by C Ltd 'and/or associated companies', without naming them, in connection with the policyholder's business. The appellant, a director of R Ltd, caused an employee of R Ltd, to drive the vehicle on an occasion after the appointment of the receiver of C Ltd. He was charged with causing him to use the vehicle when uninsured contrary to the Road Traffic Act 1960, s 201 (now s 143 of the 1988 Act). He contended that R Ltd was 'an associated company' covered by the certificate. The justices convicted on the ground that since the appointment of the receiver, who had control of C Ltd, R Ltd and C Ltd were no longer associated companies.
HELD: On a case stated, there was evidence to support the justices' finding. Apart from this, under s 201 of the 1960 Act there must be an enforceable contract of insurance; a cover note referred to in s 216(1) was such a contract, but a certificate, which was not in itself a contract at all, could not comply with the requirements of the Act. By s 205(1) a policy of insurance was of no effect unless and until a certificate were delivered, but that did not affect the position. The difficulty here was that the policy and certificates did not agree with each other.

SPECIMEN CERTIFICATE OF INSURANCE FOR PRIVATE CAR

Note—This certificate complies with the provisions of the Road Traffic Act 1988 and the Motor Vehicles (Third Party Risks) Regulations 1972.

1 Index Mark and Registration Number of Vehicle
2 Name of Policyholder
3 Effective date of the Commencement of Insurance for the purposes of the Act
4 Date of Expiry of Insurance
5 Persons or Classes of Persons entitled to drive*
(a) The Policyholder

The Policyholder may also drive a Motor Car (or Motor Cycle) not belonging to him and not hired to him under a hire purchase agreement.

(b) Any other person who is driving on the Policyholder's order or with his permission. Provided that the person driving holds a licence to drive the vehicle or has held and is not disqualified for holding or obtaining such a licence.

6 Limitations as to use*

Use only for social, domestic and pleasure purposes and by the Policyholder in person in connection with his business or profession. The Policy does not cover use for hiring, racing, pace-making, speed testing, commercial travelling, the carriage of goods or samples in connection with any trade or business or use for any purpose in connection with the Motor Trade.

The towing (not for reward) of one disabled mechanically propelled vehicle is covered.

I Hereby Certify that the Policy to which this Certificate relates is issued in accordance with the provisions of Part VI of the Road Traffic Act 1988

Authorised Insurers

* Limitations rendered inoperative by the Road Traffic Act 1988, s 148, are not to be included under this heading.

An 'open' certificate is one which in place of the index mark and registration number of the insured vehicle specifies 'any motor car the property of the policy holder or hired to him under a hire purchase agreement'. The certificate remains effective when the insured changes his vehicle but the cover provided by the policy is limited to Road Traffic Act liability until particulars of the replacement vehicle have been accepted by the insurer.

SPECIMEN FORM OF RENEWAL NOTICE AND TEMPORARY CERTIFICATE

The renewal premiums on the above Insurance Policy fall due on the renewal date above-mentioned and the Company will issue to the insured after the payment of the premium a new Certificate of Insurance as prescribed by the Road Traffic Act 1988. As the certificate cannot be issued until the premium has been received, payment should be made in time to allow of the certificate being in the hands of the Insured not later than the renewal date of the policy.

The object of the covering note on the reverse side of this renewal notice is to protect you under the above Acts should the new permanent Certificate of Insurance not reach you by the renewal date. It is, therefore, most important that you should retain this notice until the permanent certificate reaches you.

You are reminded that it is an offence to use a motor vehicle on a road without a certificate of insurance.

The cover referred to in the Covering Note hereon which is given solely to enable the policyholder to comply with the provisions of the Road Traffic Acts operates only if and when such Acts require the issue of a certificate to the policyholder.

TEMPORARY COVER NOTE

Insurance is hereby granted in terms of the policy referred to in this notice until and including the fifteenth day from the renewal date referred to in this notice, but only in respect of such insurance as is necessary to comply with the requirements of the Road Traffic Act 1988, Part VI, subject otherwise to the terms and conditions and exceptions of the said policy and in accordance with the particulars of the certificate of insurance relating to the said policy current on the said renewal date and provided that an insurance covering the aforesaid liability has not been effected with any other Authorised Insurers.

I Hereby Certify that this Covering Note is issued in accordance with the provisions of Part VI of the Road Traffic Act 1988.

Authorised Insurers

Taylor v Allon

[1966] 1 QB 304, [1965] 1 All ER 557, [1965] 2 WLR 598, 109 Sol Jo 78, [1965] 1 Lloyd's Rep 155, Div Ct
The defendant's car was insured under a policy which expired on 6 April. The insurance company had sent him the usual renewal notice on the back of which was printed a 'temporary cover note' giving third-party cover for 15 days from the date of expiry. This was expressed to be for the purpose of protecting the policyholder on renewal until his new certificate arrived. In fact the plaintiff had no intention of renewing the policy as he proposed to change his insurance to another company. He did not become insured by the new company until 16 April though he used his car on the 15th. He was charged with using his car on that day when not insured, contrary the Road Traffic Act 1960, s 201. He produced the temporary cover note sent him by the old company, whose representative gave evidence that they considered themselves liable and in the case of an accident would have paid.
HELD: (1) In the definitions in s 216 of the Act 'insurance' means insurance pursuant to an enforceable contract and therefore 'covering note' must mean a cover-note enforceable as a contract; (2) the evidence of the insurance company's representative could not help the court when the issue was whether there was an enforceable contract; (3) if there was any contract embodied in the temporary cover note it could arise only by offer and acceptance. As there was no provision in the policy for an extension of the cover the temporary cover note must be an offer to insure for the future which could be accepted by paying the renewal premium. Even if the policyholder did not communicate his acceptance in this way there might be an implied acceptance from conduct if he took his car out in reliance on the temporary cover, and there would then be liability on him to pay the renewal premium or a premium for the period of cover. But this was not the position in the present case. The defendant had no intention of renewing the policy and had not given evidence that he was relying on the temporary cover note at the time of the offence. The magistrates were right in convicting him.

Note—For section numbers see note following *Biddle*'s case, p 746, above.

COVER NOTE

Roberts v Warne

[1973] RTR 217, Div Ct
Roberts, a hire-car driver, made an agreement with Davies, who ran a hire-car booking office, that he would drive Davies's car when required on bookings provided by Davies, who would ensure that Roberts was covered by Davies's insurance. As the car, when the agreement was made, was insured only for named drivers of whom Roberts was not one, they went to the insurance brokers through whom Davies's insurance was placed, where Davies in Roberts's presence asked the brokers that the policy should be varied to cover any driver. The brokers telephoned the insurers who specifically authorised them to give insurance cover for any driver of the car. The brokers thereupon issued a 60-day cover note to Davies providing for such cover. The

insurers later decided not to provide 'any driver' cover but their letters to the brokers on the subject were delayed by a postal strike and did not reach them. More than 60 days after the issue of the cover-note Roberts was stopped and charged with driving when uninsured.
HELD, ON APPEAL by case stated: Roberts was rightly convicted. The Road Traffic Act 1960, s 201, requires that there shall be a policy of insurance in force in relation to the persons using the vehicle. The cover note was in itself a policy of insurance (though an insurance certificate is not) albeit a temporary one and there was a certificate printed on it; but the policy had not been amended when the cover note expired and did not cover Roberts. The telephone conversation between brokers and insurers did not amount to an oral variation of the existing written policy. The fact that the insurers might in the circumstances have been estopped as against Roberts from denying that he was entitled to be indemnified did not make up for the lack of a policy on the relevant date so far as s 201 was concerned, since a policy is something which has to be in writing and requires stamping, and no amendment to include Roberts expressly had been done when the cover note expired.

Note—Section 201 of 1960 Act now s 143 of 1988 Act.

Cartwright v MacCormack

[1963] 1 All ER 11, [1963] 1 WLR 18, 106 Sol Jo 957, [1962] 2 Lloyd's Rep 328, CA
The defendant claimed to be indemnified by the third party, an insurance company, against damages awarded to the plaintiff for injuries sustained in a road accident. The cover note was on the third party's printed form with some entries in handwriting. It contained the words 'This cover note is only valid for 15 days from the commencement date of risk'. The 'effective time and date of commencement of risk' was entered at '11.45 am' and '2.12.59'. The accident giving rise to the claim occurred at 5.45 pm on 17 December 1959. The third party claimed that the cover note had expired before the accident happened.
HELD: 'Time' and 'date' were used on the cover note as separate terms and the duration of the insurance company's liability was expressed as 15 days from the commencement date. The commencement date was 2 December and the policy therefore expired 15 days from 2 December. On the ordinary rules of construction these words excluded the first date and began at midnight on that date: the defendant was still insured when the accident happened.

Note—A cover note cannot be ante-dated or the certificate is false in a material particular. At the Huddersfield Police Court on 23 March 1939 the Prudential Assurance Co were fined £30 and £10 10s 0d costs for issuing, and the agent Sam Whitehead £3 for aiding and abetting, a cover note which was ante-dated ((1939) Times, 24 March).

London and Scottish Assurance Corpn Ltd v Ridd

(1940) 65 Ll L Rep 46, Div Ct
The issue of cover notes, even though £3 is paid on account of premium of £37, does not require insurers to issue a certificate for 12 months, and they cannot be convicted of failing to issue a certificate of insurance under the Motor Vehicle (TP Risks) Regulations 1933.

Neil v South East Lancashire Insurance Co

1932 SLT 29
'Subject to the usual terms of the company's policy' referred only to the general conditions and did not incorporate the warranty contained in the proposal form.

Broad v Waland

(1942) 73 Ll L Rep 263 (Atkinson J)
But if the cover note is granted on the faith of a statement in the proposal form, which is a material misrepresentation or non-disclosure, the policy contained in the cover note can be set aside in a declaration action.

INEFFECTIVE RESTRICTIONS IN POLICY

ROAD TRAFFIC ACT 1988, S 148(1)–(4)

148 (1) Where a certificate of insurance or certificate of security has been delivered under section 147 of this Act to the person by whom a policy has been effected or to whom a security has been given, so much of the policy or security as purports to restrict—
(a) the insurance of the persons insured by the policy, or
(b) the operating of the security,
(as the case may be) by reference to any of the matters mentioned in subsection (2) below shall, as respects such liabilities, as are required to be covered by a policy under section 145 of this Act, be of no effect.
(2) Those matters are—
(a) the age or physical or mental condition of persons driving the vehicle,
(b) the condition of the vehicle,
(c) the number of persons that the vehicle carries,
(d) the weight or physical characteristics of the goods that the vehicle carries,
(e) the time at which or the areas within which the vehicle is used,
(f) the horsepower or cylinder capacity or value of the vehicle,
(g) the carrying on the vehicle of any particular apparatus, or
(h) the carrying on the vehicle of any particular means of identification other than any means of identification required to be carried by or under the Vehicles (Excise) Act 1971.
(3) Nothing in subsection (1) above requires an insurer or the giver of a security to pay any sum in respect of the liability of any person otherwise than in or towards the discharge of that liability.
(4) Any sum paid by an insurer or the giver of a security in or towards the discharge of any liability of any person which is covered by the policy or security by virtue only of subsection (1) above is recoverable by the insurer or giver of the security from that person.

Passengers

Note—Under s 149 of the Road Traffic Act 1988 any agreement between a passenger and driver made before liability arises, and which purports to negative or restrict the driver's liability, is of no effect. However it is uncertain whether, where the assured is himself being carried as a passenger by another driver, the protection of compulsory insurance extends to him. Public policy may prevent a passenger from recovering in circumstances where he would otherwise recover.

Ashton v Turner

[1981] QB 137, [1980] 3 All ER 870
The court refused to allow the passenger in a 'getaway' vehicle to sue the driver who was his accomplice in the bank raid.

Note—The following case deals with the situation where a passenger accepts a lift in circumstances he knows to be highly dangerous.

Pitts v Hunt

[1991] 1 QB 24, [1990] 3 All ER 344
The defendant and the plaintiff, having drunk too much, drove home on the defendant's motor cycle for which he had neither a licence nor insurance. The defendant drove erratically and dangerously and in the inevitable accident, the plaintiff was injured. The plaintiff could recover under the MIB Scheme only if he could establish the defendant's liability to him.
HELD, by the Court of Appeal: That although the defence based on voluntary assumption of risk was now renowned by s 149(3) of the Road Traffic Act 1988 this section does not effect public policy considerations. The plaintiff had participated in criminal activity and had encouraged the defendant to drive in a dangerous fashion and so under the doctrine *ex turpi causa non oritur actio* the plaintiff was unable to establish the defendant's liability.

BREACH OF CONDITION AFTER ACCIDENT

ROAD TRAFFIC ACT 1988, S 148

(5) A condition in a policy or security issued or given for the purposes of this Part of this Act providing—
(a) that no liability shall arise under the policy or security, or
(b) that any liability so arising shall cease,
in the event of some specified thing being done or omitted to be done after the happening of the event giving rise to a claim under the policy or security, shall be of no effect in connection with such liabilities as are required to be covered by a policy under section 145 of this Act.
(6) Nothing in subsection (5) above shall be taken to render void any provision in a policy or security requiring the person insured or secured to pay to the insurer or the giver of the security any sums which the latter may have become liable to pay under the policy or security and which have been applied to the satisfaction of the claims of third parties.

Note—This section relates to breach of policy conditions after accident, such as failure to report an accident, but does not affect breaches before or at the time, such as not having a driving licence in force.

Bright v Ashfold

[1932] 2 KB 153, 101 LJKB 318, 147 LT 74, 96 JP 182, 48 TLR 357, 76 Sol Jo 344, Div Ct
A motor cycle policy contained a condition exempting from liability if carrying a passenger unless a sidecar was attached. The assured drove the motor cycle with a pillion passenger without a sidecar, and was charged with driving without an effective policy.

HELD: Section 38 only applied to a breach of condition after accident, whereas in this case the condition circumscribed the operation of the policy from the beginning. Therefore there was no policy in force.

Note—Section 38 of the 1930 Act is now s 148 of the 1988 Act.

There is nothing in the Road Traffic Act, apart from s 148(5) to prevent an underwriter and an insured from agreeing that a motor car policy against third-party risks shall contain any conditions when they think fit. If the insured uses the car on the road without complying with the Act he will be liable to a penalty, but this cannot lay a greater burden on the underwriter. The object of s 148(5) is that where at the time when an accident happened, the person using the car was properly insured, so that the liability of the underwriter arose when the accident happened, the underwriter should not be allowed to escape from that liability owing to something which the insured did or omitted to do after the happening of the accident.

ROAD TRAFFIC ACT 1988, S 148(7)

148 (7) Notwithstanding anything in any enactment, a person issuing a policy of insurance under section 145 of this Act shall be liable to indemnify the persons or classes of persons specified in the policy in respect of any liability which the policy purports to cover in the case of those persons or classes of persons.

Note—The question whether this subsection operates in a case other than of compulsory insurance has been a matter of discussion among insurers since the Act was passed.

The history of the subsection begins with the case of *Williams v Baltic Insurance Association* [1924] 2 KB 282, 93 LJKB 819, 131 LT 671 (Roche J), where the policy was issued to Williams, and his sister, who was not named in the policy, was driving the car. The insurance company took the point that the Life Assurance Act 1774, required the insured to be named in the policy or it was void as a gaming transaction. The court held against the company on two grounds: (1) That it was an insurance of goods, and (2) alternatively, the policy holder was trustee for his sister.

In a case in the Privy Council of *Vandepitte v Preferred Accident* [1933] AC 70, 102 LJ PC 21, 148 LT 169, 49 TLR 90, the suggestion that the policyholder was a trustee was disapproved.

Until the case of *Austin v Zurich Insurance Co* (p 845, below), this point does not seem to have been the subject of express decision. The point arose in *Digby v General Accident* (p 854, below), but was not taken. Insurers generally have probably taken the view that it would be inequitable to say in the policy that they indemnify the driver, though not named, and when a claim arises that they are not bound to do so because he is not named.

Tucker J in *Austin*'s case (1944) held that the subsection applies to all cases and is not limited to cases where indemnity is compulsory. The Court of Appeal was not required to deal with the point but expressed no dissent from the judge's view:

'The position and interest of a person not named in an indemnity policy has been considered in *Mark Rowlands Ltd v Berni Inns Ltd* [1985] 3 All ER 473, by the Court of Appeal. A tenant was held to have an insurable interest (although he had correctly conceded he was not a co-insured) where he leased part of a building and, by his lease, agreed to pay the relevant proportion of the fire insurance premium to the landlord, who then insured the building in his name only. The lease required the landlord to apply any insurance payment, if there was a fire, to re-instating the premises. Thus the landlord's insurance enured for the benefit of the tenant. When the building was destroyed by a fire caused by the tenant's negligence, the fact that the landlord had been indemnified by his insurers meant that, though the tenant's negligence was covered by the policy, the landlord had no further claim in negligence against the tenant (otherwise he would receive a double indemnity), and neither could the landlord's insurers as they had no relevant rights of subrogation. In so deciding, Kerr LJ stated that s 2 of the Life

Assurance Act 1774 'was not intended to apply, and does not apply, to indemnity insurance, but only to insurances which provide for the payment of a specified sum on the happening of an insured event'.

ROAD TRAFFIC ACT 1988, S 150

150 (1) To the extent that a policy or security issued or given for the purposes of this Part of this Act—

(a) restricts the insurance of the persons insured by the policy or the operation of the security (as the case may be) to use of the vehicle for specified purposes (for example, social, domestic and pleasure purposes) of a non-commercial character, or

(b) excludes from that insurance or the operation of the security (as the case may be)—

  (i) use of the vehicle for hire or reward, or

  (ii) business or commercial use of the vehicle, or

  (iii) use of the vehicle for specified purposes of a business or commercial character,

then, for the purposes of that policy or security so far as it relates to such liabilities as are required to be covered by a policy under section 145 of this Act, the use of a vehicle on a journey in the course of which one or more passengers are carried at separate fares shall, if the conditions specified in subsection (2) below are satisfied, be treated as falling within that restriction or as not falling within that exclusion (as the case may be).

(2) The conditions referred to in subsection (1) above are—

(a) the vehicle is not adapted to carry more than eight passengers and is not a motor cycle,

(b) the far or aggregate of the fares paid in respect of the journey does not exceed the amount of the running costs of the vehicle for the journey (which for the purposes of this paragraph shall be taken to include an appropriate amount in respect of depreciation and general wear), and

(c) the arrangements for the payment of fares by the passenger or passengers carried at separate fares were made before the journey began.

(3) Subsections (1) and (2) above apply however the restrictions or exclusions described in subsection (1) are framed or worded.

(4) In subsections (1) and (2) above 'fare' and 'separate fares' have the same meaning as in section 1(4) of the Public Passenger Vehicles Act 1981.

DUTY OF INSURERS TO SATISFY JUDGMENTS

ROAD TRAFFIC ACT 1988, SS 151 AND 152

151 (1) This section applies where, after a certificate of insurance or certificate of security has been delivered under section 147 of this Act to the person by whom a policy has been effected or to whom a security has been given, a judgment to which this subsection applies is obtained.

(2) Subsection (1) above applies to judgments relating to a liability with respect to any matter where liability with respect to that matter is required to be covered by a policy of insurance under section 145 of this Act and either—

(a) it is a liability covered by the terms of the policy or security to which the certificate relates, and the judgment is obtained against any person who is insured by the policy or whose liability is covered by the security, as the case may be, or

(b) it is a liability, other than an excluded liability, which would be so covered if the policy insured all persons or, as the case may be, the security covered the liability of all persons, and the judgment is obtained against any person other than one who is insured by the policy or, as the case may be, whose liability is covered by the security.

(3) In deciding for the purposes of subsection (2) above whether a liability is or would be covered by the terms of a policy or security, so much of the policy or security as purports to restrict, as the case may be, the insurance of the persons insured by the policy or the operation

of the security by reference to the holding by the driver of the vehicle of a licence authorising him to drive it shall be treated as of no effect.

(4) In subsection (2)(b) above 'excluded liability' means a liability in respect of the death of, or bodily injury to, or damage to the property of, any person who, at the time of the use which gave rise to the liability, was allowing himself to be carried in or upon the vehicle and knew or had reason to believe that the vehicle had been stolen or unlawfully taken, not being a person who—

(a) did not know and had no reason to believe that the vehicle had been stolen or unlawfully taken until after the commencement of his journey, and
(b) could not reasonably have been expected to have alighted from the vehicle.

In this subsection the reference to a person being carried in or upon a vehicle includes a reference to a person entering or getting on to, or alighting from, the vehicle.

(5) Notwithstanding that the insurer may be entitled to avoid or cancel, or may have avoided or cancelled, the policy or security, he must, subject to the provisions of this section, pay to the persons entitled to the benefit of the judgment—

(a) as regards liability in respect of death or bodily injury, any sum payable under the judgment in respect of the liability, together with any sum which, by virtue of any enactment relating to interest on judgments, is payable in respect of interest on that sum,
(b) as regards liability in respect of damage to property, any sum required to be paid under subsection (6) below, and
(c) any amount payable in respect of costs.

(6) This subsection requires—

(a) where the total of any amounts paid, payable or likely to be payable under the policy or security in respect of damage to property caused by, or arising out of, the accident in question does not exceed £250,000, the payment of any sum payable under the judgment in respect of the liability, together with any sum which, by virtue of any enactment relating to interest on judgments, is payable in respect of interest on that sum,
(b) where that total exceeds £250,000, the payment of either—
    (i) such proportion of any sum payable under the judgment in respect of the liability as £250,000 bears to that total, together with the same proportion of any sum which, by virtue of any enactment relating to interest on judgments, is payable in respect of interest on that sum, or
    (ii) the difference between the total of any amounts already paid under the policy or security in respect of such damage and £250,000, together with such proportion of any sum which, by virtue of any enactment relating to interest on judgments, is payable in respect of interest on any sum payable under the judgment in respect of the liability as the difference bears to that sum,

whichever is the less, unless not less than £250,000 has already been paid under the policy or security in respect of such damage (in which case nothing is payable).

(7) Where an insurer becomes liable under this section to pay an amount in respect of a liability of a person who is insured by a policy or whose liability is covered by a security, he is entitled to recover from that person—

(a) that amount, in a case where he became liable to pay it by virtue only of subsection (3) above, or
(b) in a case where that amount exceeds the amount for which he would, apart from the provisions of this section, be liable under the policy or security in respect of that liability, the excess.

(8) Where an insurer becomes liable under this section to pay an amount in respect of a liability of a person who is not insured by a policy or whose liability is not covered by a security, he is entitled to recover the amount from that person or from any person who—

(a) is insured by the policy, or whose liability is covered by the security, by the terms of which the liability would be covered if the policy insured all persons or, as the case may be, the security covered the liability of all persons, and
(b) caused or permitted the use of the vehicle which gave rise to the liability.

(9) In this section—

(a) 'insurer' includes a person giving a security,
(b) 'material' means of such a nature as to influence the judgment of a prudent insurer in determining whether he will take the risk and, if so, at what premium and on what conditions, and
(c) 'liability covered by the terms of the policy or security' means a liability which is covered by the policy or security or which would be so covered but for the fact that the insurer is entitled to avoid or cancel, or has avoided or cancelled, the policy or security.

(10) In the application of this section to Scotland, the words 'by virtue of any enactment relating to interest on judgments' in subsections (5) and (6) (in each place where they appear) shall be omitted.

152 (1) No sum is payable by an insurer under section 151 of this Act—
(a) in respect of any judgment unless, before or within seven days after the commencement of the proceedings in which the judgment was given, the insurer had notice of the bringing of the proceedings, or
(b) in respect of any judgment so long as execution on the judgment is stayed pending an appeal, or
(c) in connection with any liability if, before the happening of the event which was the cause of the death or bodily injury or damage to property giving rise to the liability, the policy or security was cancelled by mutual consent or by virtue of any provision contained in it, and also—
   (i) before the happening of that event the certificate was surrendered to the insurer, or the person to whom the certificate was delivered made a statutory declaration stating that the certificate had been lost or destroyed, or
   (ii) after the happening of that event, but before the expiration of a period of fourteen days from the taking effect of the cancellation of the policy or security, the certificate was surrendered to the insurer, or the person to whom it was delivered made a statutory declaration stating that the certificate had been lost or destroyed, or
   (iii) either before or after the happening of that event, but within that period of fourteen days, the insurer has commenced proceedings under this Act in respect of the failure to surrender the certificate.

(2) Subject to subsection (3) below, no sum is payable by an insurer under section 151 of this Act if, in an action commenced before or within three months after, the commencement of the proceedings in which the judgment was given, he has obtained a declaration—
(a) that, apart from any provision contained in the policy of security, he is entitled to avoid it on the ground that it was obtained—
   (i) by the non-disclosure of a material fact, or
   (ii) by a representation of fact which was false in some material particular, or
(b) if he has avoided the policy or security on that ground, that he was entitled so to do apart from any provision contained in it.

(3) An insurer who has obtained such a declaration as is mentioned in subsection (2) above in an action does not by reason of that become entitled to the benefit of that subsection as respects any judgment obtained in proceedings commenced before the commencement of that action unless before, or within seven days after, the commencement of that action he has given notice of it to the person who is the plaintiff (or in Scotland pursuer) in those proceedings specifying the non-disclosure or false representation on which he proposes to rely.

(4) A person to whom notice of such an action is so given is entitled, if he thinks fit, to be made a party to it.

NOTICE TO INSURERS— S 152(1)(A)

Note—Pursuant to sub-s (1)(a) of s 152 a plaintiff's solicitor should give formal notice to the insurer of the commencement of proceedings. The subsection speaks of commencement of proceedings, not the service of the writ. Presumably it is intended to protect the insurers where an insured fails to send on the writ to insurers and judgment is signed in default, rendering the insurers liable without having had the opportunity to defend.

Similar notice is required to achieve for the plaintiff the protection of the MIB Uninsured Drivers Agreement:

Formal notice necessary

Herbert v Railway Passengers Assurance Co

[1938] 1 All ER 650, 158 LT 417, 60 Ll L Rep 143 (Porter J)
Notice under sub-s (1)(a) must be something more formal than a casual mention of the proceedings in a conversation. There must be something which indicates that notice is being given.

Weldrick v Essex and Suffolk Equitable Insurance Society

(1949) 83 Ll L Rep 91, erratum p 477 (Birkett J)
On 11 July 1947 solicitors acting for a passenger wrote to the insurers of the car as follows: 'We have been consulted by Mrs Eva Weldrick of 42a High Street, King's Lynn, who is a partner in the business of a drapery peddling carried on by Mr Jan Mahomed, who, we are advised, sustained injuries as a result of an accident which occurred as long ago as 11 March 1947 as a result of Mahomed's car, in which she was travelling in connection with the said business, coming into collision with a stationary lorry. We understand your Society has repudiated liability, and we shall be grateful to have your confirmation thereof in writing, because you will appreciate, we shall have to take proceedings as against Mahomed, and as against the owner of the other vehicle, and at the same time give notice to the Motor Insurers' Bureau of your repudiation of liability.'

The insurers replied on 18 July as follows: 'We are in receipt of your letter of the 11th inst, and in reply have to confirm that we have repudiated liability in respect of the unfortunate accident.'

HELD: The insurers had notice that proceedings would almost inevitably be brought but that was not sufficient to satisfy the requirements of s 10(2)(a) of the 1934 Act (now s 152 of the 1988 Act). Adopting Porter J in *Herbert v Railway Passengers Assurance Co* (above) formality was necessary for such a notice and a statutory requirement of this kind must be pretty strictly fulfilled. There was no evidence that defendants had notice of the proceedings either before or within seven days after they had been brought. What they did have was an intimation that in certain circumstances proceedings might be brought, but not necessarily that they would be brought. The requirements of s 10 had not been fulfilled. Insurers did not have notice of the bringing of the action. Judgment for insurers.

Ceylon Motor Insurance Association v Thambugala

[1953] AC 584, [1953] 2 All ER 870, [1953] 1 Lloyd's Rep 289, PC
The Motor Car Ordinance of Ceylon contains provisions in the same terms as s 152 of the Road Traffic Act 1988.

On 21 May 1946 claimant's solicitors wrote to insurers that they were instructed to file an action on behalf of T of (address) for the recovery of damages against K of (address) caused by car No X 4851 on 1 September 1945; that the claim was Rs 15,000; that they understood the car was insured with insurers, and that unless the

claim was settled on or before the 31st inst, they were instructed to file action against the owner of the car.
HELD: The notice was sufficient. The name of the court was not required, and the words 'unless the claim is settled' did not affect the notice. *Weldrick*'s case not relevant.

Note—For a further illustration of this point, see *Harrington v Link Motor Policies at Lloyd's* [1989] 2 Lloyd's Rep 310, CA.

Counter-claim: notice

Cross v British Oak Insurance Co Ltd

[1938] 2 KB 167, [1938] 1 All ER 383, 107 LJKB 577, 159 LT 286, 60 Ll L Rep 46 (du Parcq J)
Fowler, insured by defendants, was driving a motor vehicle on 7 January 1936, and injured Cross and Baker. In March 1936, Baker commenced an action against Fowler in the county court. Fowlerbrought in Cross on a third-party notice. Cross filed a counter-claim in county court against Fowler. Cross recovered £90 damages and £28 9s 9d costs against Fowler. The company were served with notice of the third-party proceedings but not of the counter-claim.
HELD: The counter-claim was the commencement of separate proceedings, and notice of those proceedings, not having been given within seven days the company was not liable on the certificate. Proceedings means the proceedings begun by a person who may for this purpose be regarded as a plaintiff, which results in the judgment upon which reliance is placed as against the insurers.

No notice must be pleaded

Baker v Provident Accident and White Cross Insurance Co Ltd

[1939] 2 All ER 690, 83 Sol Jo 565, 64 Ll L Rep 14 (Cassels J)
Absence of notice, if relied on, should be pleaded by insurers.

Setting aside default judgment

Windsor v Chalcraft

[1939] 1 KB 279, [1938] 2 All ER 751, 107 LJKB 609, 159 LT 104, 54 TLR 834, 82 Sol Jo 432, 61 Ll L Rep 69, CA
Third party issued writ against assured and gave notice to insurers under s 10 (now s 152 of the 1988 Act). The writ was served and assured did not inform insurers and allowed judgment to go by default. Damages were assessed by a master. Third party sued insurers on the certificate. No notice was given by third party to insurers that writ served or case set down.
HELD: (Slesser LJ dissenting): Insurers were entitled under Ord XXVII, r 15 (now Ord 13, r 9), which empowers the court to set aside a judgment by default on terms, to have the judgment set aside on the ground that they had an actual interest by reason of the liability imposed by statute and were injuriously affected by it. (*Jacques v Harrison* (1884) 12 QBD 136 followed.)

Cancellation

JH Moore & Co v Crowe

[1972] 2 Lloyd's Rep 563, Mayor's and City of London Court
The plaintiffs' fleet of 82 vehicles was insured under a policy issued by the defendant underwriters containing a provision that they were entitled to cancel the policy on seven days' notice and in such event they would refund a proportion of the premium on surrender of the insurance certificate. The defendants supplied the plaintiffs with six copies of the certificate all identical except for the numbers. After receiving notice of cancellation the plaintiffs returned three of the copies but could not find the others. The defendants refused to make a refund of premium until all should be returned.
HELD: The plaintiffs were entitled to a refund. The defendants had not issued six certificates but one only with five additional copies. By returning the certificate numbered 1 the plaintiff had complied with the terms of the policy. The provisions of the Road Traffic Act (ie ss 147 and 152 of the 1988 Act) were irrelevant.

Note—Notice of cancellation given by Lloyd's Underwriters to brokers. A summons was issued and defendant refused to surrender certificate on the ground that the necessary notice had not been served upon him.

Defence upheld, Lord Mayor, at Mansion House, *City Press*, 3 June 1938.

Form of statutory declaration

I, . . . (name) of. . . (address) in the County of . . . (occupation) DO SOLEMNLY AND SINCERELY DECLARE that the certificate of insurance delivered to me by . . . (Insurers) under s 147(1) of the Road Traffic Act 1988, pursuant to Policy No . . . in respect of . . . (make) motor car registration number . . . (which policy has been cancelled) has been lost or destroyed.

AND I MAKE THIS SOLEMN DECLARATION conscientiously believing the same to be true and by virtue of the provisions of the Statutory Declarations Act 1835. DECLARED at . . . in the County of . . . this day of 19. . . Before me,

A Commissioner for Oaths

Form of summons for failure to surrender certificate

In the City of London

To   of

Information has been laid this day by . . . for and on behalf of . . . solicitor to the . . . Insurance Co Ltd for that you on the . . . day of . . . 19 . . at . . . (address of insurers) in the said City being a person to whom a certificate of insurance had been delivered under s 147(1) of the Road Traffic Act 1988, and the Policy in relation to such certificate having been cancelled on and from the . . . 19 . . by virtue of a provision therein, did unlawfully fail within seven days to surrender the certificate to the insurers, to wit, the . . . Insurance Co Ltd or, if it had been lost or destroyed, to make a statutory declaration to that effect. Contrary to s 147(4) of the Road Traffic Act 1988.

You are therefore hereby summoned to appear before the Court of Summary Jurisdiction, sitting at . . . in the . . . on the . . . day of . . . at the hour of eleven in the forenoon to answer to the said information.

Dated the . . . day of . . . 19 . .

ACTION FOR DECLARATION

Note—An action under s 152 for a declaration is still essential for an insurer in cases where liability arises under s 151 and where it is sought to make the insurers of a potential co-defendant who is only fractionally to blame entirely liable for the judgment by operation of the provisions of the MIB Domestic Agreement.

Indorsement of writ for declaration

The plaintiffs claim—

1 A declaration that they were entitled to avoid a policy of insurance, dated . . . No . . . issued by them to the defendant, apart from any provision contained in the said policy on the ground that it was obtained by non-disclosure of a material fact or facts and/or representations of fact which were false in some material particular or particulars.

2 Further or other relief.

3 Costs.

Notice to third party

As solicitors for and on behalf of (insurers) we hereby give you notice in pursuance of sub-s (3) of s 152 of the Road Traffic Act 1988, that the said . . . (*insurers*) as the Insurers under PolicyNo . . . , dated . . . issued by them to one . . . (*assured*) have commenced an action (19) No . . in the Queen's Bench Division of the High Court of Justice on the . . . day of . . . against the said . . . (*assured*) for a declaration in pursuance of sub-s(3) of s 152 of the Road Traffic Act 1988, that the said . . . (*insurers*) were entitled to avoid the said policy on the ground that it was obtained by the said . . . (*assured*) by non-disclosure of material facts and/or representations of fact which were false in material particulars, and that they propose to rely on the following representations and non-disclosure.

Representations

By a written proposal, dated . . . the said . . . (*assured*) represented (1) that . . . when in truth it was . . . and (2) . . .

Non-disclosure

The said . . . (*assured*) failed to disclose that . . . Dated . . .

To . . . (*third party*).

Declaration action before third party action

Zurich General Accident and Liability Insurance Co v Livingston

1938 SC 582, 1938 SLT 441, Scot
Insurers brought proceedings for a declaration and third parties, who had not commenced proceedings against the assured before the commencement of the action for a declaration, applied for leave to be joined as defendants.
HELD: That the third parties were entitled to be added as defendants, in respect that while they had not a statutory title by virtue of the proviso to s 10(3) they had at common law a title to defend an action which might deprive them of the statutory right conferred upon them by s 10(1).

Note—For s 10(1) and s 10(3) of the 1934 Act, see now the Road Traffic Act 1988 s 152 (p 755, above).

Rights limited to notice

Contigency Insurance Co v Lyons

(1939) 65 Ll L Rep 53, CA
Insurers issued writ for declaration and served notice on third party on the ground that the car, insured for private pleasure, was being used for hiring. In the statement of claim they added grounds, not mentioned in the notice, of non-disclosure of material facts in the proposal form. The third party applied to strike out the additional grounds from the statement of claim.

The Court of Appeal declined to strike out and held the questions should be dealt with at the trial.
SEMBLE (per MacKinnon LJ): It is doubtful if grounds not stated in the notice are open to the insurer.

Note—This point was afterwards decided in the following case.

Zurich General Accident and Liability Insurance Co v Morrison

[1942] 2 KB 53, [1942] 1 All ER 529, 111 LJKB 601, 167 LT 183, 58 TLR 217, CA
A declaration cannot be made against a third party on grounds not stated in the notice. The court cannot vary the section of the Act.

Per MacKinnon LJ: The grounds are limited to those specified in the notice.

Delay in declaration action

Trafalgar Insurance Co Ltd v McGregor

[1942] 1 KB 275, 111 LJKB 193, 166 LT 213, 71 Ll L Rep 107, CA
Insurers on 4 October 1939, issued a writ for a declaration for non-disclosure of all motoring convictions. On 11 March 1940 the third party wrote for particulars. On 15 March 1940, on motion by insurers for judgment in default against assured. Charles J adjourned the motion until trial and ordered the particulars. The assured disappeared and insurers were unable to obtain the information required for the particulars. After 18 months the third party applied for dismissal of the action for non-compliance with the order for particulars.

ORDERED: That insurers be precluded at the trial from giving evidence in support of certain parts of the statement of claim. The judge at the trial has discretion to admit evidence on terms.

Declaration action: position of MIB

Note—See *Fire Auto and Marine Insurance Co Ltd v Greene*, p 781, below.

Discovery of documents

Merchants' and Manufacturers' Insurance Co v Davies

[1938] 1 KB 196, [1937] 2 All ER 767, 106 LJKB 423, 156 LT 524, 53 TLR 717, 81 Sol Jo 457, 58 Ll L Rep 61, CA
In a declaration action by motor insurers to avoid a policy for non-disclosure of convictions the defendant applied for discovery of documents against the insurers to show cases where non-disclosure of convictions had not been relied on as a ground for refusing cover. The application was refused.

Agreement in lieu of action

Note—It is frequently desirable to deal with a case whilst denying liability under the policy to avoid the expense of declaration. In such a case a written authority should be taken.

To . . . (*insurers*)
I hereby authorise and request you to instruct a solicitor on my behalf to defend the action brought against me by . . . and I agree that your so doing is entirely without prejudice to all questions under the policy issued by you to me and without prejudice to your right to apply for a declaration under s 152 of the Road Traffic Act 1988, and that the repudiation of all liability under the policy by you remains in full force and effect.

Liability covered by the terms of the policy

Campbell v McFarland and Armagh UDC

[1972] NI 31
In a collision between McFarland's car and a refuse lorry a dustman was injured. He sued McFarland and his own employers, the owners of the lorry, and obtained judgment for £12,500 against both. The judgment allocated 25% blame to McFarland and gave a right to contribution as between the defendants. McFarland's insurers had refused to indemnify him under their policy on the ground of misrepresentation and took no part in the action. The plaintiff demanded that his employers should satisfy the whole of the judgment and they did so. They then applied to the Court to order direct reimbursement to them from McFarland's insurers of one-quarter of the damages by virtue of the Motor Vehicles and Road Traffic Act (Northern Ireland) 1934, s 18 (which was similar in effect to s 207 of the Road Traffic Act 1960 (now s 152 of the Road Traffic Act 1988)).
HELD: The application failed. The question was whether a policy issued for the purposes of that part of the Act requiring compulsory insurance against third-party

risks is required to cover liability under an order for contribution. There were two distinct liabilities facing McFarland (1) his liability at common law to the plaintiff for which he was obliged to have compulsory insurance, and (2) his liability under the Law Reform (Miscellaneous Provisions) Act (Northern Ireland) 1937, s 16 (which was to the same effect as the Law Reform (Married Women and Tortfeasors) Act 1935, s 6, p 17, above). The first was a liability to meet in full a judgment obtained against him by the plaintiff, and he was bound by statute to insure against it; but the second was a separate liability created by the Law Reform Act. Though the policy did give cover against the liability to contribute it was not a liability the policy was required to cover by the compulsory insurance provisions of the Road Traffic Act. Following *Lockerbie*'s case (below) a liability which was covered by the policy but which was not required to be covered did not come within the scope of s 18 of the 1934 Act.

Lockerbie v Eagle Star Insurance Co

(20 March 1936 unreported) (Lord Jamieson)
The pursuer was a passenger (not within the category of passengers required to be covered) in a motor car belonging to one Lee and was injured in an accident to the car. She obtained a judgment for damages against Lee and then sued Lee's insurers under s 10(1) of the Road Traffic Act 1934 (now s 152 of the 1988 Act).

The words 'being a liability covered by the terms of the policy' did not apply. That would bring within the scope of the section any liability covered by the policy whether required to be covered or not. That is clearly not the meaning of the section. It is limited to cases in which liability is required to be covered. The words quoted are necessary to protect insurers who are not liable unless the liability is in fact covered by the policy.

WR Chown & Co Ltd v Herbert

(1950) 100 LJo 597, Wandsworth Cty Ct (Judge Hodgson)
The Trafalgar insured the defendant under a motor policy containing the condition 'the insured shall repay to the company all sums paid by the company in discharge satisfaction or settlement of the liability' required by the Road Traffic Act to be covered by insurance 'incurred to a third party by the insured . . . which the company would not have been liable to pay but for the provisions of the Act'. After a collision between the insured's car and a cab the Trafalgar refused indemnity because of a mis-statement in the proposal form but settled the cab driver's claim for damages for personal injury at £75 and also paid the hospital charges of £15. The plaintiffs sued the defendant for damage to the cab; the defendant joined the Trafalgar as third parties in the action, claiming indemnity and the Trafalgar counterclaimed for the £90 they had paid to the cab driver. The judge held that the Trafalgar were entitled to refuse indemnity because of the mis-statement, but on the counterclaim:
HELD: The Trafalgar could not recover the £75 paid to the cab driver from the defendant. The liability to pay the cab driver under the Road Traffic Act 1934, s 10 (now s 152 of the 1988 Act) did not arise until there was a judgment and there had been no judgment. The condition in the policy covered an existing liability only, not a contingent one. The payment of hospital charges was a statutory liability, however, and the Trafalgar were entitled to be repaid the £15 by the defendant under the terms of the condition.

Intentional injury

Note—See *Hardy v MIB*, p 779, and *Gardner v Moore*, p 780, below.

BANKRUPTCY OF INSURED

ROAD TRAFFIC ACT 1988, S 153

153 (1) Where, after a certificate of insurance or certificate of security has been delivered under section 147 of this Act to the person by whom a policy has been effected or to whom a security has been given, any of the events mentioned in subsection (2) below happens, the happening of that event shall, notwithstanding anything in the Third Parties (Rights Against Insurers) Act 1930, not affect any such liability of that person as is required to be covered by a policy of insurance under section 145 of this Act.
(2) In the case of the person by whom the policy was effected or to whom the security was given, the events referred to in subsection (1) above are—
(a) that he becomes bankrupt or makes a composition or arrangement with his creditors or that his estate is sequestrated or he grants a trust deed for his creditors,
(b) that he dies and—
  (i) his estate falls to be administered in accordance with an order under section 421 of the Insolvency Act 1986,
  (ii) an award of sequestration of his estate is made, or
  (iii) a judicial factor is appointed to administer his estate under section 11A of the Judicial Factors (Scotland) Act 1889,
(c) that if that person is a company—
  (i) a winding-up order or an administration order is made with respect to the company,
  (ii) a resolution for a voluntary winding-up is passed with respect to the company,
  (iii) a receiver or manager of the company's business or undertaking is duly appointed, or
  (iv) possession is taken, by or on behalf of the holders of any debentures secured by a floating charge, of a property comprised in or subject to the charge.
(3) Nothing in subsection (1) above affects any rights conferred the Third Parties (Rights Against Insurers) Act 1930 on the person to whom the liability was incurred, being rights so conferred against the person by whom the policy was issued or the security was given.

DUTY TO GIVE PARTICULARS OF INSURANCE

ROAD TRAFFIC ACT 1988, S 154

154 (1) A person against whom a claim is made in respect of any such liability as is required to be covered by a policy of insurance under section 145 of this Act must, on demand by or on behalf of the person making the claim—
(a) state whether or not, in respect of that liability—
  (i) he was insured by a policy having effect for the purposes of this Part of this Act or had in force a security having effect for those purposes, or
  (ii) he would have been so insured or would have had in force such a security if the insurer or, as the case may be, the giver of the security had not avoided or cancelled the policy or security, and
(b) if he was or would have been so insured, or had or would have had in force such a security—
  (i) give such particulars with respect to that policy or security as were specified in any certificate of insurance or security delivered in respect of that policy or security, as the case may be, under section 147 of this Act, or

(ii) where no such certificate was delivered under that section, give the following particulars, that is to say, the registration mark or other identifying particulars of the vehicle concerned, the number or other identifying particulars of the insurance policy issued in respect of the vehicle, the name of the insurer and the period of the insurance cover.

(2) If without reasonable excuse, a person fails to comply with the provisions of subsection (1) above, or wilfully makes a false statement in reply to any such demand as is referred to in that subsection, he is guilty of an offence.

ROAD TRAFFIC ACT 1988, S 157

Note—See 'Hospital charges', p 427, above.

EMERGENCY MEDICAL TREATMENT

ROAD TRAFFIC ACT 1988, S 158

158 (1) Subsection (2) below applies where—

(a) medical or surgical treatment or examination is immediately required as a result of bodily injury (including fatal injury) to a person caused by, or arising out of, the use of a motor vehicle on a road, and

(b) the treatment or examination so required (in this Part of this Act referred to as 'emergency treatment') is effected by a legally qualified medical practitioner.

(2) The person who was using the vehicle at the time of the event out of which the bodily injury arose must, on a claim being made in accordance with the provisions of section 159 of this Act, pay to the practitioner (or, where emergency treatment is effected by more than one practitioner, to the practitioner by whom it is first effected)—

(a) a fee of £15.00 in respect of each person in whose case the emergency treatment is effected by him, and

(b) a sum, in respect of any distance in excess of two miles which he must cover in order—

(i) to proceed from the place from which he is summoned to the place where the emergency treatment is carried out by him, and

(ii) to return to the first mentioned place.

equal to 29 pence for every complete mile and additional part of a mile of that distance.

(3) Where emergency treatment is first effected in a hospital, the provisions of subsections (1) and (2) above with respect to payment of a fee shall, so far as applicable, but subject (as regards the recipient of a payment) to the provisions of section 159 of this Act, have effect with the substitution of references to the hospital for references to a legally qualified medical practitioner.

(4) Liability incurred under this section by the person using a vehicle shall, where the event out of which it arose was caused by the wrongful act of another person, be treated for the purposes of any claim to recover damage by reason of that wrongful act as damage sustained by the person using the vehicle.

Note—The fee of £15 and the mileage allowance of 29p is implemented by the Road Traffic Accidents (Payment for Treatment) Order 1987, SI 1987/353, in respect of accidents occurring on or after 1 April 1987.

In respect of accidents occurring on or after 1 August 1981 £10.00 is substituted for £1.25 and 18 pence for 2½ pence by the Road Traffic Accidents (Payments for Treatment) (England and Wales) Order 1981, SI 1981/929. SI 1982/1194 increases £10.00 to £10.90 as from 20 September 1982. The Road Traffic Act 1988, s 159 contains supplementary provisions as to payments for treatment.

CHAPTER 20

Motor Insurers' Bureau

HISTORICAL NOTE

The Third Parties (Rights Against Insurers) Act 1930 and the Road Traffic Acts 1930 and 1934 enable persons injured in road accidents to enforce against motor insurers judgments obtained against motorists who were in breach of policy conditions or whose policies were voidable. This still left effectively uncompensated persons injured by motorists who had no insurance at all. In 1937 the Cassel Committee recommended that a Central Fund should be set up from which victims of motor accidents caused by uninsured motorists could obtain compensation. The Second World War having intervened it was not until 1946 that such a fund was set up by the motor insurance market, including Lloyd's. It was done by forming a company, limited by guarantee, known as the Motor Insurers' Bureau to hold and administer the Central Fund, which was and is funded by the motor insurers themselves. Most motor insurers and Lloyd's motor syndicates became members of the Bureau. Since 1974 all authorised insurers as defined in the Road Traffic Act 1972, s 145 are required to be members of the Bureau (Road Traffic Act 1988, s 145). The Bureau is not itself an insurance company. The means by which uninsured claims were to be satisfied were laid down in an agreement with the Minister of Transport of 17 June 1946. This was replaced from time to time by similar agreements. The current Uninsured Drivers Agreement is that of 21 December 1988 (below), entered into between the Bureau and the Secretary of State for Transport.

The MIB's involvement in claims involving uninsured motorists has decreased following the enactment of s 151 of the Road Traffic Act 1988 which has extended the scope of an insurer's liability.

The 1946 Agreement still left uncompensated the victim of a 'hit-and-run' driver, ie a driver whose identity was unknown, except that by note 6 of the agreement the Bureau undertook to give 'sympathetic consideration to the making of an ex gratia payment to the victim'. This loose arrangement was replaced in 1969 by an Untraced

Drivers Agreement establishing a detailed procedure by which to deal with such cases. The current Untraced Drivers Agreement, dated 22 November 1972 is set out below.

The Bureau deals also with personal injury claims

1 against foreign motorists visiting Britain (p 796, below), and
2 where the user of the vehicle was insured but the insurer has become insolvent.

THE UNINSURED DRIVERS AGREEMENT

Note—In respect of accidents occurring on or after 31 December 1988 the Agreement of 22 November 1972 is replaced by an Agreement of 21 December 1988 set out below. The new Agreement became necessary as a result of the amendments of s 145 of the Road Traffic Act 1972 made by the Motor Vehicles (Compulsory Insurance) Regulations 1987—principally the requirement of insurance against liability for property damage. The new Agreement will continue in effect in respect of accidents occurring on or after 15 May 1988 when the Road Traffic Act 1972 is replaced by the Road Traffic Act 1988 (see the second paragraph to the notes of the Agreement, p 770, below).

The Agreement and the notes is an official publication and is Crown copyright. It is reproduced by permission of the Controller of HM Stationery Office, from which copies can be bought.

The parties to the Agreement dated 22 November 1972 are the Motor Insurers' Bureau and the Secretary of State for the Environment. The parties to the Agreement dated 21 December 1988 are the Secretary of State for Transport and the Motor Insurers' Bureau. There is thus no privity of contract between the Bureau and a claimant, nor between the Bureau and the uninsured driver. Nevertheless the Bureau allows itself to be sued if a breach of the terms of the Agreement is alleged (see p 777, below). The whole of the Bureau's duties and liabilities in respect of a claim against an uninsured driver arise from the agreement. Thus the first essential for anyone conducting such a claim is to READ THE AGREEMENT and the notes appended to it.

Agreement dated 22 November 1972

Text of an Agreement dated 22 November 1972 between the Secretary of State for the Environment and the Motor Insurers' Bureau together with some notes on its scope and purpose.

In accordance with the Agreement made on 31 December 1945 between the Minister of War Transport and insurers transacting compulsory motor vehicle insurance business in Great Britain (published by the Stationery Office under the title 'Motor Vehicle Insurance Fund') a corporation called the 'Motor Insurers' Bureau' entered into an agreement on 17 June 1946 with the Minister of Transport to give effect from 1 July 1946 to the principle recommended in July 1937 by the Departmental Committee under Sir Felix Cassel (Cmd 5528), to secure compensation to third party victims of road accidents in cases where, notwithstanding the provisions of the Road Traffic Acts relating to compulsory insurance, the victim is deprived of compensation by the absence of insurance, or of effective insurance. That Agreement was replaced by an Agreement which operated in respect of accidents occurring on or after 1 March 1971. The Agreement of 1971 has now been replaced by a new Agreement which operates in respect of accidents occurring on or after 1 December 1972.

The text of the new Agreement is as follows—

MEMORANDUM OF AGREEMENT made the 22nd day of November 1972 between the Secretary of State for the Environment and the Motor Insurers' Bureau, whose registered office is at Aldermary House, Queen Street, London, EC4N 1TR (hereinafter referred to as

'MIB') SUPPLEMENTAL to an Agreement (hereinafter called 'the Principal Agreement') made the 31st day of December 1945 between the Minister of War Transport and the insurers transacting compulsory motor vehicle insurance business in Great Britain by or on behalf of whom the said Agreement was signed in pursuance of paragraph 1 of which MIB was incorporated.

IT IS HEREBY AGREED AS FOLLOWS—

DEFINITIONS

1 In this Agreement—

'contract of insurance' means a policy of insurance of a security,

'insurer' includes the giver of a security;

'relevant liability' means a liability in respect of which a policy of insurance must insure a person in order to comply with Part VI of the Road Traffic Act 1972.

Note—For Part VI of the Road Traffic Act 1988 see pp 702 to 764 above, especially ss 143 and 145; for a relevant decision see *Cooper v MIB*, p 738 above. It is also a necessary factor that the accident should have occurred on a 'road' within the definition in s 192(1) and (2) of the 1988 Act, pp 729 to 737 above.

SATISFACTION OF CLAIMS BY MIB

2 If judgments in respect of any relevant liability is obtained against any person or persons in any court in Great Britain whether or not such a person or persons be in fact covered by a contract of insurance and any such judgment is not satisfied in full within seven days from the date upon which the person or persons in whose favour the judgment was given became entitled to enforce it then MIB will, subject to the provisions of Clauses 4n 5 and 6 hereof, pay or satisfy or cause to be paid or satisfied to or to the satisfaction of the person or persons in whose favour the judgment was given any sum payable or remaining payable thereunder in respect of the relevant liability including any sum awarded by the Court in respect of interest on that sum and any taxed costs or any costs awarded by the Court without taxation (or such proportion thereof as is attributable to the relevant liability) whatever may be the cause of the failure of the judgment debtor to satisfy the judgment.

Note—See notes 2 and 3 appended to the Agreement (p 770, below). As there is no privity of contract between a claimant and the Bureau the claimant has, at law, no cause of action but in practice the Bureau submits to being sued without taking the point. See p 777, below. 'Enforcing judgment: proceedings against the Motor Insurers' Bureau'.

PERIOD OF AGREEMENT

3 This Agreement shall be determinable by the Secretary of State at any time or by MIB on twelve months' notice without prejudice to the continued operation of the Agreement in respect of accidents occurring before the date of termination.

RECOVERIES

4 Nothing in this Agreement shall prevent insurers from providing by conditions in their contracts of insurance that all sums paid by them or by MIB by virtue of the Principal Agreement or this Agreement in or towards the discharge of the liability of their assured shall be recoverable by them or by MIB from the assured or from any other person.

Note—This clause relates to recovery of sums paid to a claimant by or on behalf of an 'insurer concerned' (see p 780, below). A usual form of words in a policy is 'The insured shall repay to the Company all sums paid by the Company which the Company would not have been liable to pay but for the provisions of the law of any territory in which the policy operates.'

CONDITIONS PRECEDENT TO MIB'S LIABILITY

5 (1) MIB shall not incur any liability under Clause 2 of this Agreement unless—

Notice of proceedings

(a) notice of the bringing of the proceedings is given before or within seven days after the commencement of the proceedings—

(i) to MIB in the case of proceedings in respect of a relevant liablity which is either not covered by a contract of insurance or covered by a contract of insurance with an insurer whose identity cannot be ascertained, or
(ii) to the insurer in the case of proceedings in respect of a relevant liablity which is covered by a contract of insurance with an insurer whose identity can be ascertained.

Note—'Notice'. See note 4 at the end of the agreement. The requirement of notice is in similar terms to that of notice to insurers in the Road Traffic Act 1988, s 152(1)(a) and the cases under the Act (p 750, above) would seem equally applicable to cl 5(1)(a) of the Motor Insurers' Bureau Agreement.

It should be observed that this condition, like the others in cl 5, is a condition precedent to the Bureau's liability. Any failure to comply precludes ab initio enforcement against the Bureau of an unsatisfied judgment obtained against a tortfeasor.

Supply of information
(b) such information relating to the proceedings as MIB may reasonably require is supplied to MIB by the person bringing the proceedings;

Judgment against all persons liable
(c) if so required by MIB and subject to full indemnity from MIB as to costs the person bringing the proceedings has taken all reasonable steps to obtain judgment against all the persons liable in respect of the injury or death of the third party and, in the event of such a person being a servant or agent, against his principal;

Note—Another tortfeasor liable. As the Bureau is required by the agreement only to meet unsatisfied judgments it will not meet or contribute to any judgment which another tortfeasor is liable for and is able to satisfy. This is so even where the uninsured driver is partly to blame. If some degree of blame might conceivably be attached to another driver who is insured then a claimant can be required under cl 5(1)(c) to join the insured driver as a defendant and pursue the claim against him. However, the requirement should be properly worded so as to make clear that cl 5(1)(c) is being referred to and the indemnity for costs mentioned. If the insurer of the other tortfeasor is a motor insurer and therefore a party to the Domestic Agreement (see p 783, below) then the liability of the insurer to the Bureau is provided for by that agreement. If the other tortfeasor is not insured (eg a highway authority) or is insured in respect of a liability other than vehicle insurance then, it is submitted, a contribution judgment obtained by such a party against the uninsured driver cannot be enforced against the Bureau in separate proceedings or otherwise (see *Campbell v McFarland*, p 761, above for an analogous situation under the Road Traffic legislation). As to costs on a full indemnity basis see *EMI Records Ltd v Ian Cameron Wallace Ltd*, p 662, above).

Assignment of judgment
(d) the judgment referred to in Clause 2 of this Agreement and any judgment referred to in paragraph (c) of this Clause which has been obtained (whether or not either judgment includes an amount in respect of a liability other than a relevant liability) and any order for costs are assigned to MIB or their nominee.

Note—This condition (which must be fulfilled by the claimant on request as a condition precedent to any payment by the Bureau or an unsatisfied judgment) is to enable the Bureau to execute the judgment against the uninsured driver. It also may, it is submitted, operate to give the Bureau (or a Domestic Regulations Insurer) the rights of a judgment creditor under the Road Traffic Act 1988, s 152 against the insurer of the judgment debtor under a driver-other-vehicles extension who has declined to meet the judgment for breach of a condition which is void or of no effect under s 148.

(2) In the event of any dispute as to the reasonableness of a requirement by MIB for the supply of information or that any particular step should be taken to obtain judgment against other persons it may be referred to the Secretary of State whose decision shall be final.

(3) Where a judgment which includes an amount in respect of a liability other than a relevant liability has been assigned to MIB or their nominee in pursuance of para (1)(d) of this Clause MIB shall apportion any moneys received in pursuance of the judgment according to the proportion which the damages in respect of the relevant liability bear to the damages in respect of the other liabilities and shall account to the person in whose favour the judgment was given in respect of such moneys received properly apportionable to the other liabilities. Where an order for costs in respect of such a judgment has been so assigned moneys received pursuant to the order shall be dealt with in the same manner.

EXEMPTIONS

6 (1) MIB shall not incur any liability under Clause 2 of this Agreement in a case where—

(a) the claim arises out of the use of a vehicle owned by or in the possession of the Crown, except where any other person has undertaken responsibility for the existence of a contract of insurance under Part VI of the Road Traffic Act 1972 (whether or not the person or persons liable be in fact covered by a contract of insurance) or where the liability is in fact covered by a contract of insurance;

(b) the claim arises out of the use of a vehicle the use of which is not required to be covered by a contract of insurance by virtue of s 144 of the Road Traffic Act 1972, unless the use is in fact covered by such a contract;

(c) at the time of the accident the person suffering death or bodily injury in respect of which the claim is made was allowing himself to be carried in a vehicle and —

  (i) knew or had reason to believe that the vehicle had been taken without the consent of the owner or other lawful authority except in a case where—

    (A) he believed or had reason to believe that he had lawful authority to be carried or that he would have had the owner's consent if the owner had known of his being carried and the circumstances of his carriage; or

    (B) he had learned of the circumstances of the taking of the vehicle since the commencement of the journey and it would be unreasonable to expect him to have alighted from the vehicle; or

  (ii) being the owner of or being a person using the vehicle, he was using or causing or permitting the vehicle to be used without there being in force in relation to such use a contract of insurance as would comply with Part VI of the Road Traffic Act 1972, knowing or having reason to believe that no such contract was in force.

Note—'Knowing or having reason to believe' (Clause 6(1)(c)(ii)). See *Porter v Addo, Porter v Motor Insurers' Bureau*, p 778, below.

(2) The exemption specified in sub-para (1)(c) of this Clause shall apply only in a case where the judgment in respect of which the claim against MIB is made was obtained in respect of a relevant liability incurred by the owner or a person using the vehicle in which the person who suffered death or bodily injury was being carried.

(3) For the purposes of these exemptions—

(a) a vehicle which has been unlawfully removed from the possession of the Crown shall be taken to continue in that possession whilst it is kept so removed;

(b) references to a person being carried in a vehicle include reference to his being carried in or upon or entering or getting on to or alighting from the vehicle.

(c) 'owner' in relation to a vehicle which is the subject of a hiring agreement or a hire-purchase agreement, means the person in possession of the vehicle under that agreement.

AGENTS

7 Nothing in this Agreement shall prevent MIB performing their obligations under this Agreement by Agents.

Note—See note 4 appended to the Agreement. Where there is no policy or the identity of the insurer is unknown the Bureau for the purpose of investigation appoints an insurance office, the 'investigating member' to make inquiries and, where appropriate, negotiate settlement. This function does not, of course, mean that the office in question is a 'Domestic Regulations Insurer', as to which see p 783, below. This should be self-evident, but the mistake is often made.

OPERATION

8 This agreement shall come into operation on the first day of December 1972 in relation to accidents occurring on or after that date. The agreement made on 1 February 1971 between the Secretary of State and MIB shall cease and determine except in relation to claims arising out of accidents occurring before the first day of December 1972.

IN WITNESS etc

NOTES

The following notes are for the guidance of those who may have a claim on the Motor Insurers' Bureau under the Agreement, and of their legal advisers, but they must not be taken as rendering unnecessary a careful study of the Agreement itself. Communications on any matter connected with the Agreement should be addressed to the Motor Insurers' Bureau whose address is 152 Silbury Boulevard, Central Milton Keynes, MK9 1NB.

1 The agreement, which operates from 1 December 1972, supersedes earlier agreements made on 17 June 1946 (which was operative from 1 July 1946) and on 1 February 1971 (which was operative from 1 March 1971) in relation to claims arising out of accidents occurring on or after 1 December 1972.

2 If damages are awarded by a court in respect of death or personal injury arising out of the use of a motor vehicle on a road in circumstances where the liability is one which was, at the time the accident occurred, required to be covered by insurance and such damages, or any part of them, remain unpaid seven days after the judgment becomes enforceable, the Bureau will, subject to the exceptions in Clause 6 of the Agreement, pay the unrecovered amount (including any interest awarded by the court and costs) to the person in whose favour the judgment has been given against an assignment of the judgment debt. This applies whether the judgment debtor is a British resident or a foreign visitor.

3 Nothing in the Agreement affects the position at law of the parties to an action for damages arising out of the driving of a motor vehicle. The Bureau's liability under the Agreement can only arise when the plaintiff has successfully established his case against the person or persons liable in the usual manner and judgment has been given in his favour. There is, of course, nothing to exclude the acceptance of compensation by the plaintiff under a settlement negotiated between the plaintiff and the alleged person liable or the Bureau.

4 WHERE THERE IS A POLICY In cases where it is ascertained that there is in existence a policy issued in compliance with the Road Traffic Act 1972, the insurer concerned will normally act as the agent of the Bureau and, subject to notice being given as provided for in Clause 5(1)(a)(ii), will handle claims within the terms of the Agreement. This will apply even if the use of the vehicle at the time of the accident was outside the terms of the policy or the insurer is entitled to repudiate liability under the policy for any other reason. (In the latter connection, victims and those acting on their behalf are reminded of the requirements as to the giving of notice to the insurer if the protection afforded to third parties by s 149 of the Road Traffic Act is sought.) This arrangement is, of course, without prejudice to any rights insurers may have against their policy holders and, to avoid any possible misapprehension, it is emphasised that there is nothing in this Agreement affecting any obligations imposed on a policy holder by his policy. Policy holders are not released from their contractual obligations to their insurers, although the scheme protects THIRD PARTY VICTIMS from the consequences of failure to observe them. For example, the failure of a policy holder to notify claims to his insurers as required by his policy, although not affecting a victim's right to benefit under the scheme, may leave the policy holder liable to his insurers.

WHERE THERE IS NO POLICY OR THE IDENTITY OF THE INSURER CANNOT BE ASCERTAINED In cases where there is no policy, or for any reason the existence of a policy is in doubt or where there is a policy but the identity of the insurer cannot be ascertained, the victim or those acting on his behalf must notify the Bureau of the claim. It is a condition of the Bureau's liability that they should receive notification before or within 7 days after the commencement of proceedings against the alleged person liable. In practice, however, it will be preferable to notify the Bureau in all cases where the name of the insurer is not speedily forthcoming.

5 Claims arising out of the use of uninsured vehicles owned by or in the possession of the Crown will in the majority of cases be outside the scope of the Bureau's liability (see Clause 6 of the Agreement). In such cases the approach should be made to the responsible authority in the usual way. The same benefits in respect of compensation will be afforded by the Crown to the victim in such cases as they would receive were the accident caused by a private vehicle except where the victim is a serviceman or servicewoman whose death or injury gives rise to an entitlement to a pension or other compensation from public funds.

6 The Bureau have no liability UNDER THIS AGREEMENT to pay compensation in respect of any person who may suffer personal injuries or death resulting from the use on a road of a vehicle, the owner or driver of which cannot be traced. However, in relation to accidents occurring ON OR AFTER 1 May 1969 and before 1 December 1972, an Agreement dated 21 April 1969 between the Minister of Transport (now the Secretary of State for the Environment) and the Bureau for the Compensation of Victims of Untraced Drivers applies. In relation to accidents occurring on or after 1 December 1972, an Agreement dated 22 November 1972 between the Secretary of State and the Bureau applies.

Agreement dated 21 December 1988

Note—In accordance with the Agreement made on 31 December 1945 between the Minister of War Transport and insurers transacting compulsory motor vehicle insurance business in Great Britain (published by HMSO under the title 'Motor Vehicle Insurance Fund') a corporation called the 'Motor Insurers' Bureau' entered into an Agreement on 17 June 1946 to the principle recommended in July 1937 by the Departmental Committee under Sir Felix Cassel (Cmnd 5528); to secure compensation to third party victims of road accidents in cases where, notwithstanding the provisions of the Road Traffic Acts relating to compulsory insurance, the victim is deprived of compensation by the absence of insurance, or of effective insurance. That Agreement was replaced by an Agreement which operated in respect of accidents occurring on or after 1 March 1971 which in turn was replaced by a new Agreement which operated in respect of accidents occurring on or after 1 December 1972. The Agreement of 1972 has now been replaced by a new Agreement which operates in respect of accidents occurring on or after 31 December 1988.

The text of the new Agreement is as follows—

MEMORANDUM OF AGREEMENT made the 21st day of December 1988 between the Secretary of State for Transport and the Motor Insurers Bureau, whose registered office is at New Garden House, 78 Hatton Garden, London EC1N 8JQ (hereinafter referred to as 'MIB') SUPPLEMENTAL to an Agreement (hereinafter called the 'Principal Agreement') made the 31st Day of December 1945 between the Minister of War Transport and the insurers transacting compulsory motor insurance business in Great Britain by or on behalf of whom the said Agreement was signed and in pursuance of paragraph 1 of which MIB was incorporated.

Note—The MIB's registered office is now 152 Silbury Boulevard, Central Milton Keynes, MK9 1NB (DX 84753 MILTON KEYNES).

IT IS HEREBY AGREED AS FOLLOWS

DEFINITIONS

1 In this Agreement—

'contract of insurance' means a policy of insurance or a security;

'insurer' includes the giver of a security;

'relevant liability' means a liability in respect of which a policy of insurance must insure a person in order to comply with Part VI of the Road Traffic Act 1972;

and references to the Road Traffic Act 1972 are references to that Act as amended by the Motor Vehicles (Compulsory Insurance) Regulations 1987 (SI 1987/2171).

Note—For Part VI of the Road Traffic Act 1988, especially ss 143 and 145 of the Road Traffic Act 1988 (formerly 143 and 145 of the Road Traffic Act 1972) see *Cooper v MIB*, p 738, above. It is also a necessary factor that the accident should have occurred on a 'road' within the definition of s 192(1) of the 1988 Act (s 196(1) of the 1972 Act).

Part VI of the Road Traffic Act 1972 has been replaced by Part VI of the Road Traffic Act 1988.

SATISFACTION OF CLAIMS BY MIB

2(1) If judgment in respect of any relevant liability is obtained against any person or persons in any court in Great Britain whether or not such a person or persons be in fact covered by a contract of insurance and any such judgment is not satisfied in full within seven days from the date upon which the person or persons in whose favour the judgment was given became entitled to enforce it then MIB will, subject to the provisions of paragraphs (2), (3) and (4) below and to Clauses 4, 5 and 6 hereof, pay or satisfy or cause to be paid or satisfied to or to the satisfaction of the person or persons in whose favour the judgment given any sum payable or remaining payable thereunder in respect of the relevant liability including any sum awarded by the court in respect of interest on that sum and any taxed costs or any costs awarded by the court without taxation (or such proportion thereof as is attributable to the relevant liability) whatever may be the cause of the failure of the judgment debtor to satisfy the judgment.

Note—As there is no privity of contract between a claimant and the Bureau, the Claimant has, at law, no cause of action but in practice the Bureau submits to being sued without taking the point. See p 777, below; 'Enforcing judgment: proceedings against the Motor Insurers' Bureau'.

(2) Subject to paragraphs (3) and (4) below and to Clauses 4, 5 and 6 hereof, the MIB shall incur liability under paragraph (1) above in respect of any sum awarded under such a judgment in respect of property damage not exceeding £250,000 or in respect of the first £250,000 of any sum so awarded exceeding that amount.

(3) Where a person in whose favour a judgment in respect of relevant liability which includes liability in respect of damage to property has been given, has received or is entitled to receive in consequence of a claim he has made, compensation from any source in respect of that damage, MIB may deduct from the sum payable or remaining payable under paragraph (1) above an amount equal to the amount of that compensation in addition to the deduction of £175 by virtue of paragraph (4) below. The reference to compensation includes compensation under insurance arrangements.

(4) MIB shall not incur liability under paragraph (1) above in respect of any amount payable or remaining payable under the judgment in respect of property damage liability where the total of such amounts is more than £175, in respect of the first £175 of such total.

PERIOD OF AGREEMENT

3 This Agreement shall be determinable by the Secretary of State at any time or by MIB on twelve months notice without prejudice to the continued operation of the Agreement in respect of accidents occurring before the date of termination.

RECOVERIES

4 Nothing in this Agreement shall prevent insurers from providing by conditions in their contracts of insurance that all sums paid by them or by MIB by virtue of the Principal Agreement or this Agreement in or towards the discharge of the liability of their insured shall be recoverable by them or by MIB from the insured or from any other person.

Note—This clause relates to recovery of sums paid to a claimant by or on behalf of a Domestic Regulation Insurer (p 783, below). A usual form of words in a policy is 'the insured shall repay to the company all sums paid by the company which the company would not have been liable to pay but for the provisions of the law of any territory in which the policy operates'.

CONDITIONS PRECEDENT TO MIB's LIABILITY

5 (1) MIB shall not incur any liability under Clause 2 of this Agreement unless—

(a) notice in writing of the bringing of the proceedings is given within seven days after the commencement of the proceedings—
  (i) to MIB in the case of proceedings in respect of a relevant liability which is either not covered by a contract of insurance or covered by a contract of insurance with an insurer whose identity cannot be ascertained, or
  (ii) to the insurer in the case of proceedings in respect of a relevant liability which is covered by a contract of insurance with an insurer whose identity can be ascertained;

Such notice shall be accompanied by a copy of the writ, summons or other document initiating the proceedings;

Note—'Notice' the requirement of notice is in similar terms to that of notice to insurers in the Road Traffic Act 1988, s 152(1)(a) (formerly s 149(2)(a) of the Road Traffic Act 1972) and the cases under the Act (p 702, above) would seem equally applicable to cl 5(1)(a) of the Motor Insurers' Bureau Agreement.

It should be observed that this condition, like the others in cl 5, is a condition precedent to the Bureau's liability. Any failure to comply precludes ab initio enforcement against the Bureau of an unsatisfied judgment obtained against a tortfeasor.

(b) the person bringing the proceedings furnishes to MIB—
  (i) such information (in such form as MIB may specify) in relation thereto as MIB may reasonably require; and
  (ii) such information (in such form as MIB may specify) as to any insurance covering any damage to property to which the claim or proceedings relate and any claim made in respect of the damage under the insurance or otherwise and any report which may have been made or notification which may have been given to any person in respect of that damage or the use of the vehicle giving rise thereto, as MIB may reasonably require;

(c) the person bringing the proceedings has demanded the information and, where appropriate, the particulars specified in section 151 of the Road Traffic Act 1972 in accordance with that section or, if so required by MIB, has authorised MIB to do so on his behalf;

(d) if so required by MIB and subject to full indemnity from MIB as to costs the person bringing the proceedings has taken all reasonable steps to obtain judgment against all the persons liable in respect of the injury or death or damage to property and, in the event of any such person being a servant or agent, against his principal; and

Note—Another tortfeasor liable. As the Bureau is required by the Agreement only to meet unsatisfied judgments it will not meet or contribute to any judgment which another tortfeasor is liable for and is able to satisfy. This is so even where the uninsured driver is partly to blame. If some degree of blame might conceivably be attached to another driver who is insured then a claimant can be required under cl 5(1)(c) to join the insured driver as a defendant and pursue the claim against him. However, the requirement should be properly worded so as to make clear that cl 5(1)(c) is being referred to and the indemnity for costs mentioned. If the insurer of the other tortfeasor is a motor insurer and therefore a party to the Domestic Regulations (see p 783, below) then the liability of the insurer to the Bureau is provided for by that agreement. If the other tortfeasor is not insured (eg a highway authority) or is insured in respect of a liability other than vehicle insurance then, it is submitted, a contribution judgment obtained by such a party against the insured driver cannot be enforced against the Bureau in separate proceedings or otherwise (see *Campbell v McFarland*, p 761, below for an analogous situation under the Road Traffic legislation). As to costs on a full indemnity basis see *EMI Records Ltd v Ian Cameron Wallace Ltd*, p 662, above).

(e) the judgment referred to in Clause 2 of this Agreement and any judgment referred to in paragraph (d) of the Clause which has been obtained (whether or not either judgment includes an amount in respect of a liability other than a relevant liability) and any order for costs are assigned to MIB or their nominee.

Note—This condition (which must be fulfilled by the claimant on request as a condition precedent to any payment by the Bureau of an unsatisfied judgment) is to enable the Bureau to execute the judgment against the uninsured driver. It also may, it is submitted, operate to give the Bureau (or a Domestic Regulations Insurer) the rights of a judgment creditor under the Road Traffic Act 1988, s 152 (formerly s 149 of the Road Traffic Act 1972) against the insurer of the judgment debtor under a driving-other-vehicles extension who has declined to meet the judgment for breach of a condition which is void or of no effect under s 148.

(2) In the event of any dispute as to the reasonableness of a requirement by MIB for the supply of information or that any particular step should be taken to obtain judgment against other persons it may be referred to the Secretary of State whose decision shall be final.

(3) Where a judgment which includes an amount in respect of a liability other than a relevant liability has been assigned to MIB or their nominee in pursuance of paragraph (1)(e) of the Clause MIB shall apportion any moneys received in pursuance of the judgment according to the proportion which the damages in respect of the relevant liability bear to the damages in respect of the other liabilities and shall account to the person in whose favour the judgment was given in respect of such moneys received properly apportionable to the other liabilities. Where an order for costs in respect of such a judgment has been so assigned moneys received pursuant to the order shall be dealt with in the same manner.

EXCEPTIONS

6 (1) MIB shall not incur any liability under Clause 2 of this Agreement in a case where—

(a) the claim arises out of the use of a vehicle owned by or in the possession of the Crown, except where any other person has undertaken responsibility for the existence of a contract of insurance under Part VI of the Road Traffic Act 1972 (whether or not the person or persons liable be in fact covered by a contract of insurance) or where the liability is in fact covered by a contract of insurance;

(b) the claim arises out of the use of a vehicle the use of which is not required to be covered by a contract of insurance by virtue of s 144 of the Road Traffic Act 1972, unless the use is in fact covered by such a contract;

(c) the claim is in respect of a judgment or any part thereof which has been obtained by virtue of the exercise of a right of subrogation by any person;

(d) the claim is in respect of damage to property which consists of damage to a motor vehicle or losses arising therefrom if at the time of the use giving rise to the damage to the motor vehicle there was not in force in relation to the use of that vehicle when the damage to it was sustained such a policy of insurance as is required by Part VI of the Road Traffic Act 1972 and the person or persons claiming in respect of the loss or damage either knew or ought to have known that that was the case;

(e) at the time of the use which gave rise to the liability the person suffering death or bodily injury or damage to property was allowing himself to be carried in or upon the vehicle and either before the commencement of his journey in the vehicle or after such commencement if he could reasonably be expected to have alighted from the vehicle he—

   (i) knew or ought to have known that the vehicle had been stolen or unlawfully taken, or

   (ii) knew or ought to have known that the vehicle was being used without there being in force in relation to its use such a contract of insurance as would comply with Part VI of the Road Traffic Act 1972.

Note—Now Part VI of the Road Traffic Act 1988.

'Knowing or having reason to believe' (Clause 6(1)(e)(ii)). See *Porter v Addo, Porter v Motor Insurers' Bureau*, p 778, below.

Stinton v Stinton (1992) Times, 5 August, decided on 6(1)(a) 1972 agreement, p 778, below.
(2) The exception specified in sub-paragraph (1)(e) of the Clause shall apply only in a case where judgment in respect of which the claim against MIB is made was obtained in respect of a relevant liability incurred by the owner or a person using the vehicle in which the person who suffered death or bodily injury or sustained damage to property was being carried.
(3) For the purposes of these exceptions—
(a) a vehicle which has been unlawfully removed from the possession of the Crown shall be taken to continue in that possession whilst it is kept so removed;
(b) references to a person being carried in a vehicle include references to his being carried in or upon or entering or getting onto or alighting from the vehicle; and
(c) 'owner' in relation to a vehicle which is the subject of a hiring agreement or a hire-purchase agreement, means the person in possession of the vehicle under that agreement.

AGENTS

7 Nothing in the Agreement shall prevent MIB performing their obligations under this Agreement by agents.

Note—Where there is no policy or the identity of the insurer is unknown the Bureau for the purpose of investigation appoints an insurance office, the 'investigating member' to make inquiries, and, where appropriate, negotiate settlement. This function does not of course mean that the office is a 'Domestic Regulations Insurer' as to which see p 783, below. This should be self evident, but the mistake is often made.

OPERATION

8 This Agreement shall come into operation on the 31st day of December 1988 in relation to accidents occurring on or after that date. The Agreement made on 22nd November 1972 between the Secretary of State and MIB shall cease and determine except in relation to claims arising out of accidents occurring before the 31st day of December 1988.

IN WITNESS etc.

LIABILITY TO CLAIMANTS

Where there is a policy

Note—Where there is a policy in force on a vehicle even though the policy was not effective to cover the driver at the time of the accident, or was voidable or for some reason unenforceable, the insurer who issued the policy (the 'Domestic Regulations Insurer': see p 783, below) will deal with the claim. In such cases Motor Insurers' Bureau itself is not normally concerned with the claim at all, unless there is a disagreement with the Domestic Regulations Insurer whether the claim comes within the Agreement. See p 777, below, 'Enforcing judgment' and see generally s 151(2)(b) of the Road Traffic Act 1988 which extends liability of insurers.

Defendant disappeared—substituted service

Claims against a driver whose identity has never been established (ie a hit-and-run driver) are not within the Agreement set out above but come within the Agreement on untraced drivers, p 784, below. But a driver whose identity is known but who has disappeared is not an 'untraced' driver and judgment must be obtained to create liability on the Bureau. In such a case substituted service of proceedings can be effected at the address of the Bureau as in *Gurtner*'s case (below) and set out in the Supreme Court Practice in the note 65/4/6 to Ord 65, r 4. An affidavit to be sworn in support of the application showing what efforts have been made to trace the defendant.

The plaintiff's solicitors sometimes attempt to serve a disappeared defendant by posting the writ to his 'last known address' (RSC Ord 10, r 1(2)), and then proceed to sign judgment in default of notice of intention to defend. It would seem that if it can be shown that, at the time of posting, the address in question was no longer the defendant's address and that the writ could not have reached him there service is bad and the judgment will be set aside. See *White v Weston* (p 600, above).

Gurtner v Circuit

[1968] 2 QB 587, [1968] 1 All ER 328, [1968] 2 WLR 668, 112 Sol Jo 73, [1968] 1 Lloyd's Rep 171, CA

The plaintiff's solicitors issued a writ against the defendant but were unable to serve it personally because he had gone to Canada and could not be traced. Although it appeared from the policy report that the defendant had produced a valid insurance certificate after the accident the insurers could not be identified. The plaintiff's solicitors applied to the Motor Insurers' Bureau who instructed the Royal Insurance Company to investigate. The solicitors obtained an order for substituted service of the writ on the defendant by sending it to the Royal Insurance Company by ordinary prepaid post.

HELD, ON APPEAL: It was obviously wrong to order service on the defendant at the address of the Royal Insurance Company, since the affidavit did not show that the writ was likely to reach the defendant or come to his notice. The order could be set aside if it would serve any useful purpose. If there was any possibility of tracing the defendant in Canada, substituted service should be ordered by advertisement but that seemed useless in the present case and the order should be allowed to stand. Where it is not possible to ascertain the insurers an order might be made for service at the address of the Bureau but such an order should not be made except on evidence that all reasonable efforts have been made by the plaintiff to trace the defendant and effect personal service.

Clarke v Vedel

[1979] RTR 26, CA

The plaintiffs were injured in a collision with a motor cycle. The motor cyclist gave his name as David Vedel. He disappeared after the accident and could not be traced. The address he gave turned out to be false; he produced no insurance or other documents to the police. The motor cycle, bearing false number plates, had been stolen from its lawful owner some months earlier. The records of the Registrar of Births and Deaths showed no entry for any person named David Vedel at the time of the date of birth he gave. The plaintiffs issued a writ against 'David Vedel' and obtained an order for substituted service at the address of the Motor Insurers' Bureau. The 'insurers concerned' under the Domestic Agreement applied in the name of the Bureau to set aside the order.

HELD: The order should be set aside. *Gurtner v Circuit* (above) was not an authority for saying that it is proper in every case where the Bureau may be involved to make an order for substituted service on the defendant at the address of the Bureau. The order could not possibly bring the proceedings to the notice of whoever was the motor cyclist. It was an Untraced Drivers Agreement case and should be dealt with under that Agreement.

Per Stevenson LJ: This court recognises that there may be cases where a defendant who cannot be traced and, therefore, is unlikely to be reached by any form of substituted service, can nevertheless be ordered to be served at the address of the insurers or the Bureau in a road accident case. But . . . I am not satisfied that it applies to this case.

Enforcing judgment: proceedings against the Motor Insurers' Bureau

Cases can, and do, arise where the Motor Insurers' Bureau or the 'Domestic Regulations Insurer' (see p 783, below) dispute their liability under the Agreement on the ground that the case is outside the Road Traffic Act, eg that the place of the accident was not a 'road' or (in cases arising before 1 December 1972) that the claimant was a passenger not carried for reward or by reason of or in pursuance of a contract of employment. In such cases where a judgment had already been obtained against the uninsured motorist and is unsatisfied proceedings can be taken against the Bureau. The Bureau is a corporation and therefore a legal persona capable of being sued in its own name. Theoretically the claimant cannot claim the benefit of the Motor Insurers' Bureau Agreements because he is not a party, but in practice the Bureau does not take the point by way of defence. Lord Donovan mentioned the point in *Albert v Motor Insurers' Bureau* [1972] AC 301, [1971] 2 All ER 1345:

'The question immediately suggests itself as to how the appellant as a third party can claim the benefit of this Agreement. The point was looked at in *Hardy v Motor Insurers' Bureau* (p 779, below) where Lord Denning remarks that the agreement is on the face of it a contract between two parties for the benefit of a third, and that no point was taken by the Bureau that the Agreement was not enforceable by the third person. Diplock LJ also considered the matter in *Gurtner v Circuit* (p 776, above) saying that on a number of occasions the court had turned a blind eye to the position; and that unless the point were specifically raised the court was "entitled to proceed on the assumption that the Bureau has, before action is brought, contracted for good consideration with the plaintiff to perform the obligations specified in its contract with the Minister or has by its conduct raised an estoppel which would bar it from relying on absence of privity of contract". In the present case the Bureau has likewise raised no point . . . and in the circumstances I say no more on the matter.'

For examples of cases in which the Bureau has been sued, see the cases of *Lees* (p 717, above) and *Hardy* (p 779, below). For cases where the Bureau's right to be joined was considered see p 781, below.

When suing an uninsured driver plaintiffs sometimes add MIB as second defendants for a declaration of liability under the Uninsured Drivers Agreement even where no issue on the applicability of the agreement has been raised. As the following decision shows this is not a maintainable nor permissible procedure.

Carpenter v Ebblewhite

[1939] 1 KB 347, [1938] 4 All ER 41, 108 LJKB 110, 159 LT 564, CA

The plaintiffs, injured in a road accident by a car driven by B, sued E as being vicariously liable for B's negligence. They also joined E's insurers for a declaration that they were liable to meet a judgment against E. E's defence was that he had sold the car to B, who was not his servant or agent. The insurers applied to strike out the claim against them on the ground that it disclosed no reasonable cause of action.

HELD: The insurers were entitled to be struck out of the action. They were not saying E was not entitled to indemnity under the policy if he was found liable. In an action by a plaintiff against a defendant there cannot be a claim by the plaintiff for a declaration of liability against a third person for the relief claimed in the action where no dispute has yet arisen between the plaintiff and that person.

Per Greer LJ: The claim against the insurance company was frivolous and vexatious, as there could not be any claim for a declaration in view of the fact that there was not at the time any dispute between the plaintiffs and the insurance company.

Note—This decision, though arising from an insurance policy is equally relevant to the Uninsured Drivers Agreement.

Passenger claims

Porter v Addo: Porter v Motor Insurers' Bureau

(1978) 122 Sol Jo 418, [1978] 2 Lloyd's Rep 463, [1978] RTR 503 (Forbes J)
Mrs Porter bought a car in Holland and brought it to England. She was told by the Customs she must not drive the car because it was not insured. She told Mr Addo, a television engineer who she knew used a car in the course of his work, about her difficulties and he offered to drive the car for her from Harwich to London. She did not ask him if he was insured to drive but as she had told him the Customs had said she must get an insured driver to drive it she assumed his insurance policy covered him to drive other people's cars including hers. On the journey an accident occurred caused by his negligence and she was injured. He was not in fact insured to drive her car. She sued Addo for damages and the Motor Insurers' Bureau for a declaration that the Bureau should pay an unsatisfied judgment against Addo. The Bureau relied on cl 6(1)(c)(ii) of the 1972 Agreement, saying that as owner she was permitting the vehicle to be used 'having reason to believe' there was no contract of insurance in force.
HELD: She was entitled to a declaration. 'Having reason to believe' is not the same as 'having reasonable belief' nor as 'having no reason to believe' a contract was in force. 'Having reason to believe' is a reference to a rational process of thought. It placed the onus quite differently. What reason could Mrs Porter have to believe no contract was in force? On the facts as found she could have none.

Stinton v Stinton

(1992) Times, 5 August
Christopher Stinton brought an action for damages against his brother Leslie following a road traffic accident caused by his negligent driving. At the time Leslie was uninsured and this was known to Christopher. For the MIB to rely upon Clause 6(1)(c) of the 1972 Agreement it was necessary to show that the plaintiff was 'using the vehicle'.

Simon Brown J found that the plaintiff knew he was going to be carried in the uninsured vehicle during the course of the evening's drinking. Clause 6(1)(c) exempted the MIB from liability where the plaintiff allowed himself to be carried in a vehicle which he was using or causing or permitting to be used without there being in force in relation to such use a contract of insurance, and in those circumstances the claim against the MIB failed.

Note—See p 766, for the Agreement.

Claims against liquidated insurance companies

As the Uninsured Drivers Agreement requires the Motor Insurers' Bureau to meet any judgment obtained in a Road Traffic Act claim if it has not been satisfied within seven days the obligation extends to judgments obtained against motorists who were insured at the time of the accident but whose insurers have subsequently gone into liquidation. In dealing with such claims the Bureau does not attempt to recover from policy holders.

In respect of liquidations by resolution or presentation of a winding-up petition after 29 October 1974, the Policyholders Protection Act 1975, s 7 provides for payment by the Policyholders Protection Board of the full amount of a sum payable to a person entitled to the benefit of judgment under the Road Traffic Act 1988, ss 151 and 152 (formerly s 149 Road Traffic Act 1972) as soon as reasonably practicable after the beginning of the liquidation.

Wilful injury

Hardy v Motor Insurers' Bureau

[1964] 2 QB 745, [1964] 2 All ER 742, [1964] 3 WLR 433, 108 Sol Jo 422, [1964] 1 Lloyd's Rep 397, CA
The plaintiff was chief security officer at a large metal works. Having seen a stolen road fund licence in a van belonging to a fitter named Phillips he waited at the place where the private road leading from the works joined the main road and stopped the van as it came out. He put his head in at the window and asked Phillips to pull in to the nearside. Instead Phillips drove foward at a fast rate on to the main road dragging the plaintiff along and injuring him. The plaintiff obtained judgment against Phillips for £300 damages but the judgment was unsatisfied. Phillips was uninsured and the plaintiff, having given notice of the proceedings against Phillips to the Motor Insurers' Bureau began this action against the Bureau for the amount of the unsatisfied judgment. It was argued for the defendants that liability for a criminal act was not a liability which the Road Traffic Act 1960 required or could require to be covered by insurance.
HELD: Applying the test in *DPP v Smith* [1961] AC 290, [1960] 3 All ER 161, [1960] 3 WLR 546, 124 JP 473, 104 Sol Jo 683 Phillips must be taken to have intended to injure the plaintiff and was guilty of a felony under the Offences against the Person Act 1861, s 18. The Road Traffic Act 1960, s 203(3)(a) required Phillips to be covered by a policy of insurance 'in respect of any liability which may be incurred by him in respect of the death of or bodily injury to any person caused by, or arising out of, the use of a vehicle on a road'. This included any use by him of the vehicle, be it an innocent use or a criminal use, or be it a murderous use or a playful use. Such a policy would be good in its inception but the question arises whether the motorist can enforce it when he had made criminal use of the vehicle. Clearly he could not, since no person can claim reparation or indemnity for the consequences of a criminal offence of which his own wicked intent is an essential ingredient—*Beresford v Royal Insurance Co Ltd* (below). There is a broad rule of public policy that no person can claim reparation or indemnity for his own wilful and culpable crime. Thus if Phillips had himself met the plaintiff's judgment he would have been unable to claim indemnity from an insurer if he had been insured. But this rule of public policy

affected only the wrongdoer and would not prevent an innocent third party from claiming the benefit of such a policy against an insurer. Part VI of the Act gave a third party a direct right of action under s 207 against insurers where there was a liability against which the statute required a motorist to insure. It followed that where, as here, the motorist was not insured the liability was one which the plaintiff could require the defendants to meet under the Motor Insurers' Bureau Agreements.

Gardner v Moore

[1984] AC 548, [1984] 1 All ER 1100, [1984] 2 WLR 714, 128 Sol Jo 282, [1984] 2 Lloyd's Rep 135, HL

The defendant Moore, when driving his car without any insurance cover, deliberately drove on to the pavement, striking and injuring the plaintiff. It was an intentionally criminal act for which Moore was convicted and sentenced to imprisonment. Gardner sued Moore for damages in an action in which Moore took no part. Judgment was given against him for £15,526 damages. The Motor Insurers' Bureau (joined as second defendants) denied liability to meet the judgment, maintaining that *Hardy*'s case (above) was wrongly decided.

HELD: *Hardy*'s case had been correctly decided and the Bureau was liable to satisfy the judgment. The general principle that no person can claim indemnity for his own wilful and culpable crime cannot be invoked against an innocent third party whose claim is not through that of the wrongdoer. The Motor Insurers' Bureau Agreement was intended to protect an innocent third party where the wrongdoer was not covered by a relevant policy of insurance; for the Bureau to invoke the doctrine of public policy that a man may not profit by the consequences of his own wrong doing was contrary both to the object and grammatical sense of the Agreement.

MOTOR INSURERS' BUREAU'S AUTHORITY TO ACT FOR UNINSURED DRIVER

As the Bureau is not an insurer and has no contractual relationship with the uninsured driver it cannot file acknowledgment of service of a writ on behalf on an uninsured driver without express authority. In this respect a Domestic Regulations Insurer is in the same position as MIB. When the uninsured driver is available he may, and often does, give an authority coupled with an agreement to indemnify the Bureau. A suitable form of authority and indemnity is the following:

'I . . . (name) consent to Motor Insurers' Bureau taking over and conducting in my name the defence of the plaintiff's claim against me in this action arising from the accident of the . . . (date).

It is understood that the cost of the defence of the plaintiff's claim will be borne by Motor Insurers' Bureau. I hereby give Motor Insurers' Bureau full authority to effect a settlement of the plaintiff's claim on my behalf and I hereby agree to indemnify them against and to repay to them all sums paid by them in respect of such settlement, including the costs of the plaintiff.

I undertake to give Motor Insurers' Bureau all information and assistance in my power.

This agreement is determinable at any time by Motor Insurers' Bureau or myself by notice in writing and I agree that after such determination by either of us Motor

Insurers' Bureau will have no obligation to conduct my defence and will not be responsible for any costs incurred after such determination.
Dated this . . . day of . . . 19 . .
Signed . . . .'

With such authority the Bureau can then file acknowledgment of service and conduct a defence in the name of the defendant. If a judgment is obtained against a driver and it remains unsatisfied the member must ensure that the original judgment is endorsed with the following words. In a proportion of cases, however, the uninsured driver either cannot be found by the time a claim falls to be dealt with or refuses to sign an authority. In such cases the Bureau may, when proceedings have been instituted against the uninsured driver, apply to the court under RSC Ord 15 r 6 (2)(b) to be joined as a defendant in the action with liberty to exercise the rights of the uninsured defendant. This procedure evolves from the following case.

When Motor Insurers' Bureau entitled to be joined as defendant

Gurtner v Circuit

[1968] 2 QB 587, [1968] 1 All ER 328, [1968] 2 WLR 668, 112 Sol Jo 73, [1968] 1 Lloyd's Rep 171, CA
The plaintiff was struck and injured by a motor cyclist in 1961. The police took particulars of the accident, including the motor cyclist's name and address and the number of his insurance certificate but no writ was issued against him by the plaintiff until 1964. By that time he had gone to Canada and could not be traced. The particulars of his insurance certificate in the police report did not enable the insurers to be identified. After two renewals of the writ the plaintiff in June 1966 obtained an order for substituted service on the motor cyclist at the office of the insurance company handling the matter for the Bureau. As the motor cyclist could not be found no appearance could be entered for him. The Bureau then applied to be joined as defendants in the action.
HELD: They were entitled to be joined as defendants. Order 15, r 6 provides that the court may order any person to be added as a party 'whose presence before the court is necessary to ensure that all matters in dispute . . . may be completely and effectively determined and adjudicated upon'. When two parties were in dispute in an action and the determination of that dispute would directly affect a third person in his legal rights or in his pocket the court had a discretion to allow him to be added as a party on such terms as it thought fit. The Bureau were directly affected not only in their legal rights but also in their pocket. They ought to be allowed to come in as defendants.

Declaration action: position of the Motor Insurers' Bureau

Fire Auto and Marine Insurance Co Ltd v Greene

[1964] 2 QB 687, [1964] 2 All ER 761, [1964] 3 WLR 319, 108 Sol Jo 603, [1964] 2 Lloyd's Rep 72 (John Stevenson J)
The plaintiff company were motor insurers but were not members of the Motor Insurers' Bureau. After an accident from which claims arose by injured persons against a policyholder the plaintiffs began this action against him under the Road Traffic Act 1960, s 207(3) for a declaration that they were entitled to avoid the policy on the ground of non-disclosure of a material fact. The Motor Insurers' Bureau

applied under RSC Ord 15, r 6 to be added as a defendant in the action, since they would be required under Bureau Agreements to meet any judgment obtained by an injured party against the policyholder if the plaintiffs succeeded in obtaining the declaration. Order 15, r 6 provides that the court may order any person to be joined as party whose presence before the court is necessary to ensure that all matters in dispute in the cause or matter may be effectually and completely determined and adjudicated upon.
HELD: The Bureau were not entitled to be joined as a party. A person who applies for an order under Ord 15, r 6 to be added as a defendant must at least be able to show that some legal right enforceable by him against one of the parties to the action or some legal duty enforceable against him by one of the parties to the action will be affected by the result of the action. These plaintiffs were not parties to the domestic agreement. Moreover, even if the Bureau were legally liable to satisfy an injured claimant's judgment against the policy-holder it would be liable to the Minister, not to the injured person himself. Its liability is not statutory but contractual and its agreement with the Minister confers no rights except on him. The fact that Bureau has never taken this point against a claimant makes no difference and did not prevent the plaintiffs in this action from taking the point against them.

Note—The Road Traffic Act 1988, s 31 now requires all authorised insurers as defined in s 145(2) and (5) of the 1988 Act to be members of the Motor Insurers' Bureau. In any event the basis of that decision must be regarded as inconsistent with, and superseded by, the decision in *Gurtner v Circuit* (above).

Costs where the Motor Insurers' Bureau defend—legal aid

See *Godfrey v Smith*, p 690, above. In essence the court is entitled to take into account the fact the defendant has the MIB behind it, when considering whether to make an order for costs in favour of the plaintiff. See also *Lamb v Budd* (1988) LEXIS Enggen Library, cases file.

Interim payments

The MIB has no liability to make an interim payment.

Powney v Coxage

(1988) Times, 8 March
The plaintiff failed in his appeal from the district judge who had refused to order the MIB to make an interim payment in respect of damages for personal injury. The 1972 Agreement between the Secretary of State for Transport and the Bureau only required it to meet judgments against uninsured motorists after the expiry of a seven day period (subject to the conditions set out in the Agreement). At the time of this application the plaintiff did not have a judgment capable of assignment nor did he fall within the criteria set out in RSC Ord 29, r 9. The MIB was not a defendant who had admitted liability and the uninsured motorist could not be considered as 'insured' by the Bureau or in any sense fall within rule 11(2)(a).

Note—(1) The Agreement is set out at p 766, above.

(2) Order 29 rule 11(1) reads as follows:

'11 (1) If, on the hearing of an application under rule 10 in an action for damages, the court is satisfied—

(a) that the defendant against whom the order is sought (in this paragraph referred to as "the respondent") has admitted liability for the plaintiff's damages, or
(b) that the plaintiff has obtained judgment against the respondent for damages to be assessed, or
(c) that, if the action proceeded to trial, the plaintiff would obtain judgment for substantial damages against the respondent or, where there are two or more defendants, against any of them,

the court may, if it thinks fit and subject to paragraph (2), order the respondent to make an interim payment of such amount as it thinks just, not exceeding a reasonable proportion of the damages which in the opinion of the court are likely to be recovered by the plaintiff after taking into account any relevant contributory negligence and any set-off, cross-claim or counterclaim on which the respondent may be entitled to rely.'

THE DOMESTIC REGULATIONS BETWEEN THE MOTOR INSURERS' BUREAU AND INSURERS

The 'Domestic Regulations' is an agreement between the Motor Insurers' Bureau and its members, namely those insurance companies and members of underwriting syndicates at Lloyd's transacting compulsory motor vehicle insurance business in the UK. The purpose of the agreement is financial: to establish and maintain a central fund from which payments can be made when there is no 'Domestic Regulations Insurer' and secondly to determine when a liability falls to be met by a member as 'Domestic Regulations Insurer'.

The general principle established by the agreement is that if there is a policy in existence in respect of the vehicle being used at the time of the relevant accident, even though the tortfeasor is not himself insured by it, the insurer issuing the policy will meet the claim. In cases where there is no such policy the cliam will be met from the Bureau's central fund. The definition of 'Domestic Regulations Insurer' is thus of importance and is as follows:

'Domestic Regulations Insurer'

Domestic Regulations Insurer means the insurer who at the time of the accident which gave rise to the Road Traffic Act liability was providing any insurance against such liability in respect of the vehicle arising out of the use of which the liability of the judgment debtor was incurred. An insurer is concerned within the meaning of this Agreement notwithstanding that:

(i) the insurance has been obtained by fraud, misrepresentation, non-disclosure of material facts or mistake; or
(ii) some term, description, limitation, exception or condition (whether express or implied) of the insurance or of the proposal form on which it is based expressly or by implication excludes that Insurer's liability whether generally or in the particular circumstances in which the judgment debtor's liability was incurred; or
(iii) the judgment debtor was in unauthorised possession of the vehicle arising out of the use of which the liability of the judgment debtor was incurred,

and only ceases so to be concerned:

(i) in the case of an insurance expressed to be for a term of twelve months at least, after the expiry of fifteen days from the date on which the insurance by its terms lapsed;
(ii) in the case of an insurance expressed to be for a term of twelve months or more, but which by provision in the policy or by notice in writing by either party is not intended to be renewed, from the date on which the insurance by its terms lapsed.
(iii) in the case of an insurance for a term of less than twelve months, when the term thereof expires;
(iv) when the insurance has been cancelled before the date on which the Road Traffic Act liability was incurred by agreement of the parties to the insurance or under a power of cancellation contained therein;
(v) when the insurance has ceased to operate by reason of a transfer of interest in the vehicle which the insurance purports to cover;
(vi) when before the date on which the Road Traffic Act liability was incurred the Insurer has obtained a declaration from a court of competent jurisdiction that the insurance is void or unenforceable.

When a driver or users of a vehicle are not covered by the policy issued in respect of the vehicle and the insurer deals with the claim only as 'Domestic Regulations Insurer' under the Domestic Agreement then the insurer cannot claim the benefit of any of the terms of the policy (eg in defending the action in the name of the defendant driver) but is in precisely the same position as MIB would be if there were not policy at all; the insurer cannot file notice of acceptance of service of the writ without obtaining the defendant's express authority or by application to the court under Ord 15, r 6 in the name of the Motor Insurers' Bureau (see p 781, above). On the other hand the 'Domestic Regulations Insurer' has the protection of the Bureau Agreement, eg under cll 5 and 6 (see pp 773–775, above).

It will be seen from the definition of 'Domestic Regulations Insurer' that the insurance has to be in respect of the vehicle involved. Thus an insurer cannot become a 'Domestic Regulations Insurer' by reason of a 'driving other cars' clause in a policy covering another vehicle.

THE UNTRACED MOTORISTS

Note—Under an Agreement with the Minister of Transport dated 21 April 1969 the Motor Insurers' Bureau undertook to make payments of compensation to persons injured by motor vehicles when the owner or driver could not be traced. This Agreement has been replaced by an agreement of 22 November 1972.

An 'untraced' driver is one whose identity is unknown and has not been established; hence proceedings against him in a court of law are not possible. But a driver whose name and address or other necessary details sufficient to establish his identity and enable a writ or summons to be issued against him are known does not become an 'untraced' driver merely because he has disappeared or cannot be found when a claim is made. However, a driver who, having given fictitious particulars at the time of the accident, cannot be traced is 'untraced'; see *Clarke v Vedel*.

Motor Insurers' Bureau (compensation of victims of untraced drivers)

Text of an Agreement dated 22 November 1972, between the Secretary of State for the Environment and the Motor Insurers' Bureau together with some notes on its scope and purpose.

On 21 April 1969 the Minister of Transport and the Motor Insurers' Bureau entered into an agreement to secure compensation for third party victims of road accidents when the driver responsible for the accident could not be traced. That agreement has now been replaced by a new agreement which operates in respect of accidents occurring on or after 1 December 1972. The text of the new agreement is as follows.

AN AGREEMENT made on 22 November 1972 between the Secretary of State for the Environment and the Motor Insurers' Bureau, whose registered office is at Aldermary house, Queen Street, London, EC4N 1TR (hereinafter referred to as 'MIB').

IT IS HEREBY AGREED as follows: —

1 (1) Subject to paragraph (2) of this clause, this agreement applies to any case in which an application is made to MIB for a payment in respect of the death of or bodily injury to any person caused by or arising out of the use of a motor vehicle on a road in Great Britain and the case is one in which the following conditions are fulfilled, that is to say, — (a) the event giving rise to the death or injury occurred on or after 1 December 1972; (b) the applicant for the payment either — (i) is unable to trace any person responsible for the death or injury, or (ii) in a case to which clause 5 hereof applies where more than one person was so responsible, is unable to trace one of those persons; (any person so untraced is hereby referred to as 'the untraced person'); (c) the death or injury was caused in such circumstances that on the balance of probabilities the untraced person would be liable to pay damages to the applicant in respect of the death or injury; (d) the liability of the untraced person to pay damages to the applicant is one which is required to be covered by insurance or security under Part VI of the Road Traffic Act 1972, it being assumed for this purpose, in the absence of evidence to the contrary, that the vehicle was being used in circumstances in which the user was required by the said Part VI to be insured or secured against third party risks; (e) the death or injury was not caused by the use of the vehicle by the untraced person as a weapon, that is to say, in a deliberate attempt to run the deceased or injured person down; (f) the application is made in writing within three years from the date of the event giving rise to the death or injury.

(2) This agreement does not apply to a case in which — (a) the death or bodily injury in respect of which such application is made was caused by or arose out of the use of a motor vehicle which at the time of the event giving rise to the death or bodily injury was owned by or in the possession of the Crown, unless the case is one in which some other person has undertaken responsibility for the existence of a contract of insurance under Part VI of the Road Traffic Act 1972; (b) at the time of the accident the person suffering death or bodily injury in respect of which the application is made was allowing himself to be carried in a vehicle and — (i) knew or had reason to believe that the vehicle had been taken without the consent of the owner or other lawful authority, except in a case where — (A) he believed or had reason to believe that he had lawful authority to be carried or that he would have the owner's consent if the owner had known of his being carried and the circumstances of his carriage; or (B) he had learned of the circumstances of the taking of the vehicle since the commencement of the journey and it would be unreasonable to expect him to have alighted from the vehicle; or (ii) being the owner of or being a person using the vehicle he was using or causing or permitting the vehicle to be used without there being in force in relation to such use a policy of insurance or such security as would comply with Part VI of the Road Traffic Act 1972, knowing or having reason to believe that no such policy or security was in force.

(3) The exemption from the application of this agreement specified in sub-para (2)(b) of this clause shall apply only in a case where the application is made to MIB in respect of a liability arising out of the use of the vehicle in which the person who suffered death or bodily injury was being carried.

(4) For the purpose of para (2) of this clause — (a) a vehicle which has been unlawfully removed from the possession of the Crown shall be taken to continue in that possession whilst it is kept so removed; (b) references to a person being carried in a vehicle include references to his being carried in or upon, or entering or getting on to or alighting from the vehicle; (c) 'owner' in relation to a vehicle which is the subject of a hiring agreement or a hire purchase agreement means the person in possession of the vehicle under that agreement.

2 (1) An application to MIB for a payment in respect of the death of or bodily injury to any person may be made either by the person for whose benefit that payment is to be made (hereinafter called 'the applicant') or by any solicitor acting for the applicant or by any other person whom MIB may be prepared to accept as acting for the applicant.
(2) Any decision, award or payment given or made or other thing done in accordance with this agreement to or by a person acting as aforesaid on behalf of the applicant, or in relation to an application made by such a person, shall, whatever may be the age, or the circumstances affecting the capacity, of the applicant, be treated as having the same effect as if it had been done to or by, or in relation to an application made by, an applicant of full age and capacity.
3 Subject to the following provisions of this agreement, MIB shall, on any application made to them in a case to which this agreement applies, award to the applicant in respect of the death or injury in respect of which the application is made a payment of an amount which shall be assessed in like manner as a court, applying English law in a case where the event giving rise to the death or injury occurred in England or Wales or applying the law of Scotland in a case where that event occurred in Scotland, would assess the damages which the applicant would have been entitled to recover from the untraced person in respect of that death or injury if proceedings to enforce a claim for damages in respect thereof were successfully brought by the applicant against the untraced person.
4 In making an award in accordance with clause 3 hereof — (a) MIB shall not be required to include in the payment awarded any amount in respect of any damages for loss of expectation of life or for pain or suffering which the applicant might have had a right to claim under the Law Reform (Miscellaneous Provisions) Act 1934, or, as the case may be, under any corresponding rule of law in force in Scotland nor, in a case where the application is made in respect of a death, shall MIB be required to include in the payment awarded any amount in respect of solatium for the grief of any relative of the deceased which the applicant might have had a right to claim under any enactment or rule of law in force in Scotland; and (b) in assessing the amount to which the applicant is entitled in respect of loss of earnings if the applicant has received his wages or salary in full or in part from his employer, whether or not upon an undertaking given by the applicant to reimburse his employer if he recovers damages, he shall be not to the extent of the amount so received be regarded as having sustained a loss of earnings.
5 (1) This clause applies to any case to which this agreement applies where the death or bodily injury in respect of which an application has been made to MIB under this agreement (hereinafter in this clause referred to as 'the relevant death or injury') was caused partly by the untraced person and partly either by an identified person, or by identified persons, or by some other untraced person or persons whose master or principal can be identified and was so caused in circumstances making the identified person or persons or any such master or principal as aforesaid liable to the applicant in respect of the relevant death or injury.
(2) If in a case to which this clause applies one or other of the conditions specified in the next following paragraph is satisfied, the amount to be awarded by MIB to the applicant in respect of the relevant death or injury shall be determined in accordance with the provisions of para (4) of this clause and their liability to the applicant shall be subject also to the provisions of para (7) of this clause and to clause 6 hereof.
(3) The conditions referred to in the last foregoing paragraph are — (a) that the applicant has obtained a judgment in respect of the relevant death or injury against the identified person or against one or more of the identified persons or against any person liable as their master or principal or the master or principal of any other person which has not been satisfied in full within three months from the date on which the applicant became entitled to enforce it; or (b) that the applicant — (i) has not obtained and has not been required by MIB to obtain a judgment in respect of the relevant death or injury against the identified person or persons or against any person liable as the master or principal of any such identified person or persons or as the master or principal of any other person, and (ii) has not received any payment by way of compensation from any such person or persons.
(4) The amount to be awarded by MIB to the applicant in a case to which this clause applies shall be determined as follows: (a) if the condition specified in para (3)(a) of this clause is

satisfied and the judgment mentioned in that paragraph is wholly unsatisfied within the period of three months therein referred to, the amount to be awarded shall be an amount equal to the untraced person's contribution to a full award; (b) if the condition specified in para 3(a) of this clause is satisfied but the judgment mentioned in that paragraph is satisfied in part only within the period of three months therein referred to, the amount to be awarded — (i) if the unsatisfied part of the said judgment is less than the untraced person's contribution to a full award, shall be an amount equal to that unsatisfied part, or (ii) if the unsatisfied part of the said judgment is equal to or greater than the amount of the untraced person's contribution to a full award, shall be an amount equal to the untraced person's said contribution; (c) if the condition specified in para (3)(b) of this clause is satisfied, the amount to be awarded shall be an amount equal to the untraced person's contribution to a full award.

(5) The following provisions of this paragraph shall have effect in any case in which an appeal from or any proceeding to set aside any such judgment as is specified in para (3)(a) of this clause (hereinafter in this clause referred to as 'the original judgment') is commenced within a period of three months beginning on the date on which the applicant became entitled to enforce the original judgment: (a) until the said appeal or proceeding is disposed of the foregoing provisions of this clause shall have effect as if for the period of three months referred to in the said para (3)(a) there were substituted a period expiring on the date when the said appeal or proceeding is disposed of; (b) if as a result of the said appeal or proceeding the applicant ceases to be entitled to receive any payment in respect of the relevant death or injury from any of the persons against whom he has obtained any such judgment as is specified in the said para (3)(a), the foregoing provisions of this clause shall have effect as if he had neither obtained nor been required by MIB to obtain a judgment against any person or persons; (c) if as a result of the said appeal or proceeding, the applicant becomes entitled to recover an amount which differs from that which he was entitled to recover under the original judgment, the foregoing provisions of this clause shall have effect as if for the reference in the said para (3)(a) to the original judgment there were substituted a reference to the judgment under which the applicant became entitled to the said different amount; (d) if as a result of the said appeal or proceeding the applicant remains entitled to enforce the original judgment the foregoing provisions of this clause shall have effect as if for the period of three months referred to in the said para (3)(a) there were substituted a period of three months beginning on the date on which the appeal or other proceeding was disposed of. The foregoing provisions of this paragraph shall apply also in any case where any judgment given upon any such appeal or proceeding is itself the subject of a further appeal or similar proceeding and shall apply in such a case in relation to that further appeal or proceeding in the same manner as they apply in relation to the first mentioned appeal or proceeding.

(6) In this clause — (a) 'full award' means the amount which would have fallen to be awarded to the applicant under clause 3 thereof in respect of the relevant death or injury if the untraced person had been wholly responsible for that death or injury; and (b) 'untraced person's contribution' means that proportion of a full award which on the balance of probabilities would have been apportioned by a court as the share to be borne by the untraced person in the responsibility for the event giving rise to the relevant death or injury if proceedings to recover damages in respect of that death or injury had been brought by the applicant against the untraced person and all other persons having a share in that responsibility.

(7) MIB shall not be under any liability in respect of the relevant death or injury if the applicant is entitled to receive compensation from MIB in respect of that death or injury under the agreement providing for the compensation of victims of uninsured drivers entered into between the Secretary of State and MIB on 22 November 1972.

6 (1) The following shall be conditions precedent to any liability falling upon MIB upon an application made to them under this agreement in respect of any death or injury, that is to say, — (a) the applicant shall give all such assistance as may reasonably be required by or on behalf of MIB to enable any investigation to be carried out under this agreement, including, in particular, the furnishing of statements and information either in writing, or, if so required, orally at an interview between the applicant and any person acting on behalf of MIB; (b) if so required by MIB at any time before MIB have communicated their decision upon the

application to the applicant, the applicant shall, subject to the following provisions of their liability to the applicant in respect of the death or injury as having caused or contributed to that death or injury as being the master or principal of any person who has caused or contributed to that injury; (c) if so required by MIB the applicant shall assign to MIB or to their nominee any judgment obtained by him (whether or not obtained in pursuance of a requirement under sub-paragraph (b) of this paragraph) in respect of the death or injury to which his application to MIB relates upon such terms as will secure that MIB or their nominee shall be accountable to the applicant for any amount by which the aggregate of all sums recovered by MIB or their nominee under the said judgment (after deducting all reasonable expenses incurred in effecting such recovery) exceeds the amount payable by MIB to the applicant under this agreement in respect of that death or injury.

(2) If MIB require the applicant to bring proceedings against any specified person or persons: (a) MIB shall indemnify the applicant against all costs reasonably incurred by the applicant in complying with that requirement unless the result of those proceedings materially contributes to establish that the untraced person did not cause or contribute to the relevant death or injury; and (b) the applicant shall, if so required by MIB and at their expense; furnish MIB with a transcript of any official shorthand note taken in those proceedings of any evidence given or judgment delivered therein.

(3) In the event of a dispute arising between the applicant and MIB as to the reasonableness of any requirement by MIB under para (1)(b) of this clause, or as to whether any such costs as are referred to in para (2)(a) of this clause were reasonably incurred, that dispute shall be referred to the Secretary of State whose decision thereon shall be final. Provided that any dispute arising between the applicant and MIB as to whether MIB are required to indemnify the applicant under para (2)(a) of this clause shall, in so far as it depends on the question whether the result of any proceedings which MIB have required the applicant to bring against any specified person or persons have or have not materially contributed to establish that the untraced person did not cause or contribute to the relevant death or injury, be referred to the arbitrator in accordance with the following provisions of this agreement, whose decision on that question shall be final.

7 MIB shall cause any application made to them for a payment under this agreement to be investigated and, unless MIB decide that the application should be rejected because a preliminary investigation has disclosed that the case is not one to which this agreement applies, they shall cause a report to be made on the application and on the basis of that report MIB shall decide whether to make an award and, if so, the amount of the award which shall be calculated in accordance with the foregoing provisions of this agreement.

8 MIB may before coming to a decision on any application made to them under this agreement request the applicant to furnish them with a statutory declaration to be made by the applicant, setting out to the best of his knowledge, information and belief the facts and circumstances upon which his claim to an award under this agreement is based, or such of those facts and circumstances as may be specified by MIB.

9 (1) MIB shall notify their decision to the applicant and when so doing shall (a) if the application is rejected because a preliminary investigation has disclosed that it is not one made in a case to which this agreement applies, give their reasons for the rejection; or (b) if the application has been fully investigated furnish him with a statement setting out (i) the circumstances in which the death or injury occurred and the evidence bearing thereon, (ii) the circumstances relevant to the assessment of the amount to be awarded to the applicant under this agreement and the evidence bearing thereon, and (iii) if they refuse to make an award their reasons for that refusal; and (c) in a case to which clause 5 of this agreement applies specify the way in which the amount of that award has been computed and its relation to those provisions of clause 5 which are relevant to its computation.

(2) Where MIB have decided that they will not indemnify the applicant against the costs of any proceedings which they have under clause 6(1)(b) hereof required the applicant to bring against any specified person or persons on the ground that those proceedings have materially contributed to establish that the untraced person did not cause or contribute to the relevant death or injury, they shall give notice to the applicant of that decision and when doing so they

shall give their reasons for it and furnish the applicant with a copy of any such transcript of any evidence given or judgment delivered in those proceedings as is mentioned in clause 6(2)(b) hereof which they regard as relevant to that decision.

10 Subject to the provisions of this agreement MIB shall, (a) on being notified by the applicant that MIB's award is accepted; or (b) if at the expiration of the period during which the applicant may give notice of an appeal under clause 11 hereof there has not been given to MIB either any such notification as aforesaid of the acceptance of MIB's award or a notice of an appeal under the said clause 11, pay the applicant the amount of that award, and such payment shall discharge MIB from all liability under this agreement in respect of the death or injury in respect of which that award has been made.

11 The applicant shall have a right of appeal to an arbitrator against any decision notified to him under clause 9 hereof on any of the following grounds, that is to say (a) that the case is one to which this agreement applies and that his application should be fully investigated by MIB with a view to their deciding whether to make an award to the applicant and, if so, the amount of that award; or (b) where the application has been fully investigated (i) that MIB were wrong in refusing to make an award, or (ii) that the amount they have awarded to the applicant is insufficient; or (c) in a case where a decision not to indemnify the applicant against the costs of any proceedings has been notified under clause 9(2) hereof, that that decision was wrong, if within six weeks from the date when notice of the decision against which he wishes to appeal was given him, the applicant, not having previously notified MIB that their decision is accepted, gives notice to MIB that he wishes to appeal against their decision.

12 A notice of appeal under clause 11 hereof shall state the grounds of the appeal and shall be accompanied by an undertaking to be given by the applicant or by the person acting on his behalf as provided in clause 2 hereof, that (a) the applicant will accept the decision of the arbitrator; and (b) the arbitrator's fee shall be paid to MIB by the applicant or by the person giving the said undertaking in any case where MIB are entitled to reimbursement of that fee under the provisions of clause 22 hereof.

13 The applicant may, when giving notice of his appeal or at any time before doing so, make comments to MIB on their decision and may supply them with such particulars as the applicant may think fit of any other evidence not contained in the written statement supplied to the applicant by MIB which he considers is relevant to the application and MIB may, before submitting the applicant's appeal to the arbitrator, cause an investigation to be made into this further evidence and shall report to the applicant the result of that investigation and of any change in their decision which may result from it. The applicant may, within six weeks from the date on which this report was sent to him, unless he withdraws the appeal, make such comments thereon as he may desire to have submitted to the arbitrator.

14 (1) In a case where MIB receive from the applicant a notice of appeal in which the only ground of appeal which is stated is that the amount awarded to the applicant is insufficient MIB may before submitting that appeal to the arbitrator give notice to the applicant that if the appeal proceeds they will request the arbitrator to decide whether the case is one in which MIB should make an award at all and if they do so they shall at the same time furnish the applicant with a statement setting out such comments as they may consider relevant to the decision which the arbitrator should come to on that question.

(2) Where MIB give a notice under para (1) of this clause, the applicant may within six weeks from the date on which that notice is given make such comments to MIB and supply them with such particulars of other evidence not contained in any written statement furnished to him by MIB as he may consider relevant to the question which the arbitrator is by the notice requested to decide, and clause 13 hereof shall apply in relation to any comments made or particulars supplied by the applicant under this paragraph as it applies in relation to any comments made or particulars supplied under the said clause 13.

15 MIB shall, where they receive notice of an appeal from the applicant under the foregoing provisions of this agreement, unless the appeal is previously withdrawn, submit that appeal (but in a case where they cause such an investigation to be made as is mentioned in clause 13 hereof, not until the expiration of six weeks from the date on which they sent the applicant a

report as to the result of that investigation and, in a case where they gave such notice to the applicant as is mentioned in clause 14(1) hereof, not until the expiration of six weeks from the date on which they gave that notice and, if they have caused an investigation to be made into any evidence supplied under clause 14(2) hereof, not until the expiration of six weeks from the date on which they sent the applicant a report as to the result of that investigation) to an arbitrator for a decision, sending to the arbitrator for that purpose the application made by the applicant, a copy of their decision thereon as notified to the applicant and of all statements, declarations, notices, undertakings, comments, transcripts, particulars or reports furnished, given or sent under this agreement either by the applicant or any person acting for him to MIB or by MIB to the applicant or a person so acting.

16 On any such appeal (a) if the appeal is against a decision by MIB rejecting an application because a preliminary investigation has disclosed that the case is not one to which this agreement applies, the arbitrator shall decide whether the case is or is not one to which this agreement applies and, if he decides that it is such a case, shall remit the application to MIB for full investigation and for a decision by MIB in accordance with the foregoing provisions of this agreement; (b) if the appeal is against a decision by MIB given after an application has been fully investigated by MIB (whether before the appeal or in consequence of its being remitted for such investigation under para (a) of this clause), the arbitrator shall decide, as may be appropriate, having regard to the grounds stated in the notice of appeal and to any notice given by MIB to the applicant under clause 14 thereof, whether MIB should make an award under this agreement to the applicant and, if so, the amount which MIB should award to the applicant under the foregoing provisions of this agreement; (c) if the appeal relates to a dispute which has arisen between the applicant and MIB which is required by the proviso to clause 6(3) hereof to be referred to the arbitrator, the arbitrator shall also give his decision on that dispute.

17 The arbitrator shall decide the appeal on the documents submitted to him as set out in clause 15 hereof and no further evidence shall be produced to him: Provided that — (a) the arbitrator shall be entitled to ask MIB to make any further investigation which he considers desirable and to submit a written report of their findings to him for his consideration; and (b) MIB shall send a copy of any such report to the applicant who shall be entitled to submit written comments on it to MIB within four weeks of the date on which that copy is sent to him; and (c) MIB shall transmit those comments to the arbitrator for his consideration.

18 The arbitrator by whom any such appeal as aforesaid shall be decided shall be an arbitrator to be selected by the Secretary of State from two panels of Queen's Counsel appointed respectively by the Lord Chancellor and the Lord Advocate for the purpose of determining appeals under this agreement, the arbitrator to be selected from the panel appointed by the Lord Chancellor in cases where the event giving rise to the death or injury occurred in England or Wales and from the panel appointed by the Lord Advocate where that event occurred in Scotland.

19 The arbitrator shall notify his decision on any appeal under this agreement to MIB and MIB shall forthwith send a copy of the arbitrator's decision to the applicant.

20 Subject to the provisions of this agreement, MIB shall pay the applicant any amount which the arbitrator has decided shall be awarded to the applicant, and such payment shall discharge MIB from all liability under this agreement in respect of the death or injury in respect of which that decision has been given.

21 Each party to the appeal will bear his own costs.

22 MIB shall pay the arbitrator a fee approved by the Lord Chancellor or the Lord Advocate, as the case may be, after consultation with MIB: Provided that the arbitrator may in his discretion, in any case where it appears to him that there were no reasonable grounds for the appeal, decide that his fee ought to be paid by the applicant and, where the arbitrator so decides, the person giving the undertaking required by clause 12 hereof shall be liable to reimburse MIB the amount of the fee paid by them to the arbitrator except in so far as that amount is deducted by MIB from any amount which they are liable to pay to the applicant in consequence of the decision of the arbitrator.

23 If in any case it appears to MIB that by reason of the applicant being under the age of majority or of any other circumstances affecting his capacity to manage his affairs it would be in the interest of the applicant that all or some part of the amount which would otherwise be payable to him under an award made under this agreement should be administered for him by the Family Welfare Association or by some other body or person under a trust MIB may establish for that purpose a trust of the whole or part of the said amount to take effect for such period and subject to such provisions as may appear to MIB appropriate in the circumstances of the case.

24 This agreement may be determined at any time by the Secretary of State or by MIB by either of them giving to the other not less than 12 months previous notice in writing: Provided that this agreement shall continue to have effect in respect of any case where the event giving rise to the death or injury occurred before the date on which this agreement terminates in accordance with any notice so given.

25 This agreement shall come into operation on 1 December 1972 in relation to accidents occurring on or after that date, and the agreement made on 21 April 1969 between the Secretary of State and MIB shall cease and determine except in relation to applications arising out of accidents which occurred on or after 1 May 1969 and before the said 1 December 1972.

IN WITNESS etc.

NOTES

The following notes are for the guidance of those who may wish to make application to the Motor Insurers' Bureau for payment under the agreement, and for the guidance of their legal advisers, but they must not be taken as rendering unnecessary a careful study of the agreement itself. Communications connected with the agreement should be addressed to the Motor Insurers' Bureau, whose address is Aldermary House, Queen Street, London, EC4N 1TR.

1 This agreement replaces a previous one dated 21 April 1969 which put on a formal basis the arrangements which have existed since 1946 under which the Bureau have made ex gratia payments in respect of death or personal injuries resulting from the use of a motor vehicle the owner or driver of which cannot be traced. Provision is made for an appeal against the Bureau's decision in such cases.

2 The agreement dated 21 April 1969 applies to a death or bodily injury arising out of an accident occurring on a road in Great Britain on or after 1 May 1969, and before 1 December 1972. This agreement applies in relation to accidents occurring on or after 1 December 1972.

3 Subject to the terms of the agreement, the Bureau will accept applications for a payment in respect of the death of, or bodily injury to, any person resulting from the use of a motor vehicle on a road in Great Britain in any case in which (a) the applicant for the payment cannot trace any person responsible for the death or injury (or, in certain circumstances, a person partly responsible) (clause 1(1)(b)); and (b) the death or injury was caused in such circumstances that the untraced person would be liable to pay damages to the applicant in respect of the death or injury (clause 1(1)(c)); and (c) the untraced persons' liability to the applicant is one which at the time the accident occurred, was required to be covered by insurance or security (clause 1(1)(d)). The Bureau will not, however, deal with deliberate 'running down' cases (clause 1(1)(e)) nor with certain other cases relating to Crown vehicles and certain categories of 'voluntary' passenger (clause 1(2)-(4)).

4 Application for a payment under the agreement must be made in writing to the Bureau within three years of the date of the accident giving rise to the death or injury (clause 1(1)(f)).

5 Under clause 3, the amount which the Bureau will award will (except for the exclusions of those elements of damages mentioned in clause 4) be assessed in the same way as a court would have assessed the amount of damages payable by the untraced person had the applicant been able to bring a successful claim for damages against him.

6 Clause 5 relates to cases where an untraced person and an identified person are each partly responsible for a death or injury, and defines the conditions under which the Bureau will in such cases make a contribution in respect of the responsibility of the untraced person.

7 Under clause 6(1)(b), the Bureau may require the applicant to bring proceedings against any identified person who may be responsible for the death or injury, subject to indemnifying the applicant as to his costs as provided in clause 6(2) and (3).
8 On receipt of an application, the Bureau will, if satisfied that the application comes within the terms of the agreement, investigate the circumstances and, when this has been done, decide whether to make a payment and, if so, how much (clause 7).
9 The Bureau may request the applicant to make a statutory declaration setting out all, or some, of the facts on which his application is based (clause 8).
10 The Bureau will notify the applicant of their decision, setting out the circumstances of the case and the evidence on which they base their decision and, if they refuse to make a payment, the reasons for that refusal (clause 9).
11 If the applicant does not exercise his right to appeal against the Bureau's decision, the Bureau's decision will be final and the applicant will be entitled to be paid the amount awarded by the Bureau (clause 10).
12 If the applicant wishes to appeal against the decision on the grounds specified in clause 11, he must notify the Bureau within six weeks of being notified of the decision, and give the undertakings set out in clause 12.
13 The Bureau may, as a result of comments made by the applicant on their decision, investigate the application further, and if so they will communicate with the applicant again. In such a case, the applicant will have six weeks from the date of that further communication in which to decide whether or not to go on with his appeal (clause 13).
14 Where the applicant appeals only on the grounds that the amount awarded to him is too low, the Bureau may give him notice that if the matter proceeds to appeal, they will ask the arbitrator to decide also the issue of the Bureau's liability to make any payment. The applicant will have six weeks from the date of any such notice in which to comment to the Bureau on this intention (clause 14).
15 Appeals will be decided by an arbitrator who will be a Queen's Counsel selected by the Minister of Transport from one of two panels to be appointed by the Lord Chancellor and the Lord Advocate respectively (clause 18).
16 All appeals will be decided by the arbitrator on the basis of the relevant documents (as set out in clause 15) which will be sent to him by the Bureau. If the arbitrator asks the Bureau to make a further investigation, the applicant will have an opportunity to comment on the result of that investigation (clause 17).
17 The arbitrator may, at his decision, award the cost of his fee against the applicant if he considers the appeal unreasonable; otherwise, each party to the appeal will bear their own costs, the Bureau paying the arbitrator's fee (clauses 21 and 22).
In certain circumstances, the Bureau may establish a trust for the benefit of an applicant of the whole or part of any award (clause 23).

[Reproduced by permission of the Controller of HM Stationery Office.]

Note—The agreement provides a complete code of practice for such applications. So long as MIB complies with the procedure provided by the agreement its decisions cannot be the subject of litigation.

Persson v London Country Buses

[1974] 1 All ER 1251, [1974] 1 WLR 569, 118 Sol Jo 134, [1974] 1 Lloyd's Rep 415, CA

The plaintiff, a bus conductor, was injured when the bus pulled up sharply. He claimed damages from his employers on the ground that the driver was negligent, but they denied liability; they said the accident was caused by the negligence of a motorist who could not be identified or traced. The plaintiff applied to the Motor Insurers' Bureau for an award under the 1969 (untraced drivers) agreement. After investigation the Bureau decided that no award should be made because the plaintiff had not satisfied cl 1(1)(c). He then began proceedings in the county court against his employers and the Bureau, alleging a failure by the Bureau to compensate him in accordance with the 1969 agreement. The county court judge ordered the claim against the Bureau to be struck out on the grounds that it disclosed no cause of action. HELD, ON APPEAL: The judge was right. The agreement is enforceable by the Minister and (by consent of the Bureau) by an applicant, but only in accordance with the terms of the agreement. An award under cl 3 in favour of an applicant is expressly made subject to the provisions of the following clauses, including cl 7, which prescribes what the Bureau has to do and, when done, requiring the Bureau to decide whether to make an award. The process under cl 7 is subject to a right of appeal under cl 11, but if there is no award there is no right to payment. The Bureau's decision to reject the application was in fulfilment of the terms of the agreement and not a repudiation of it. An applicant cannot bring an action against the Bureau alleging breach of the agreement upon a basis of fact which is reserved by the agreement for the Bureau's decision.

Elizabeth v Motor Insurers' Bureau

[1981] RTR 405, CA
The appellant was injured when riding his motor-cycle behind a van. The van braked and the appellant ran into it. The van did not stop and was not traced. In an appeal under the Motor Insurers' Bureau Untraced Drivers Agreement the arbitrator said he found it impossible to say that the appellant had proved on the balance of probabilities that the van driver did anything negligent.
HELD, on appeal from the decision of a judge refusing to remit the case to an arbitrator: The burden of proof in the circumstances was not on the appellant. Having regard to the fact that all the evidence was contained in documents a judge should be ready to inquire closely into the proceedings before the arbitrator. The decision in *Gussman v Gratton-Storey*, p 34, above was relevant and was worthy of consideration. Award remitted.

Suing possible joint tortfeasor—cl 6(a)(b)

White v London Transport Executive

[1971] 2 QB 721, [1971] 3 All ER 1, [1971] 3 WLR 169, 115 Sol Jo, [1971] RTR 326, CA
The plaintiff was in a bus when it pulled up sharply and she was injured. The bus driver said the accident was due to the negligence of the driver of a vehicle which had not stopped and could not be traced. The plaintiff applied to the Motor Insurers' Bureau under the 1969 agreement. The Bureau then required the plaintiff under para 6(1)(b) of the agreement to take proceedings against the bus driver and his employers the LTE. When she did so the Bureau applied under Ord 15, r 6(2)(b) to be joined as a party.
HELD: The application should be rejected. The 1969 agreement gave the Bureau considerable powers of control over the litigation which it required the plaintiff to conduct, eg cll 6(1)(a) and (b), 6(2) and 8. Since the plaintiff was bringing this action on the direction of the Bureau she was bound to pursue it with all the vigilance and skill to make the defendants liable, so that all matters in the claim against the LTE would be properly and fully investigated without joining the Bureau. Joinder of the Bureau was not 'necessary' within the opening words of Ord 15, r 6(2)(b).

Note—The 1969 Untraced Drivers Agreement has been replaced by the 1972 Agreement. See p 784, above.

Supplementary Agreement

A Supplemental Agreement dated 7 December 1977 has been made the object of which is to provide for speedier disposal of certain types of application. It enables the Bureau at its discretion to offer an award in a specified sum furnishing the applicant with particulars of the circumstances and of the evidence on which the offer is based. The applicant can accept the offer at that stage foregoing the right of appeal and discharging the Bureau from all liability. The agreement relates to applications on or after 3 January 1978. There is an upper limit for the operation of the accelerated procedure. As from 19 July 1982 the limit is £20,000. Before that date the limit was £10,000.

Supplemental Agreement between the Secretary of State for Transport and the Motor Insurers' Bureau

Text of an Agreement dated 7 December 1977, between the Secretary of State for Transport and the Motor Insurers' Bureau together with some notes on its scope and purpose.
AN AGREEMENT made 7 December 1977 between the Secretary of State for Transport and the Motor Insurers' Bureau, whose registered office is Aldermary House, Queen Street, London, EC4N 1TR (hereinafter referred to as 'MIB') SUPPLEMENTAL to an agreement (hereinafter referred to as the 'Principal Agreement') relating to compensation of victims of untraced drivers and made 22 November 1972 between the Secretary of State for the Environment and MIB.
IT IS HEREBY AGREED as follows:
1 (1) In any case in which an application has been made to MIB in pursuance of clause 2(1) of the principal agreement on or after the 3 January 1978 and in which a preliminary investigation in pursuance of clause 7 thereof has disclosed that the case is one to which that agreement, but not clause 5 thereof, applies MIB may, instead of causing a report to be made on the application as provided by the said clause 7, make, or cause to be made, to the applicant an offer to settle his application in a specified sum, assessed in accordance with clause 3 of the principal agreement. (2) Where an offer is made in pursuance of paragraph (1) above, there shall be furnished to the applicant (at the same time) in writing particulars of (i) the circumstances in which the death or injury occurred and the evidence bearing thereon, and (ii) the circumstances relevant to the assessment of the amount to be awarded to the applicant and the evidence bearing thereon.
2 On receipt by MIB or its agent of an acceptance of the offer referred to in the foregoing clause, in the form specified in the Schedule hereto and duly completed by the applicant: (a) the principal agreement shall have effect in relation to the application as if in clause 7 the words 'and unless MIB decide' to the end of that clause, and clauses 9 to 22 inclusive were omitted; and (b) MIB shall pay to the applicant the amount specified in the offer, and such payment shall discharge MIB from all liability under this and the principal agreement in respect of the death or injury in relation to which the payment has been made.
3 In clause 4(a) of the principal agreement after the words 'solatium for the grief of any relative of the deceased' there shall be inserted the words 'or a loss of society award to a member of the immediate family of the deceased under s 1(4) of the Damages (Scotland) Act 1976'.
4 In clause 16 of the principal agreement there shall be added at the end the following proviso: 'Provided that where the arbitrator has dealt with an appeal under paragraph (a) of this clause all the foregoing provisions of this agreement shall apply as if the case were an application to which this agreement applies upon which MIB had not communicated a decision'.

5 This agreement shall be construed as one with the principal agreement and, without prejudice to the operation of clause 6 thereof, shall cease to have effect on the date that that agreement terminates in accordance with clause 24 thereof, and subject to the proviso there mentioned.

6 Clauses 1 and 2 of this agreement may be determined at any time by the Secretary of State or by MIB, by either of them giving to the other not less than 12 months previous notice in writing: Provided that the said clauses shall continue to have effect in respect of any case where the event giving rise to the death or injury occurred before the date on which those clauses terminate in accordance with any notice so given.

SCHEDULE (referred to in clause 2)

Form of Acceptance (under Supplemental Agreement dated 7 December 1977) I, [*full name of applicant*] of [*address*] HEREBY ACCEPT the sum of £ . . . . offered, in pursuance of clause 1 of an agreement made between the Secretary of State for Transport and the Motor Insurers' Bureau (hereinafter called 'MIB') and dated 7 December 1977, by or on behalf of MIB in settlement of the application made by me or on my behalf on [*date*] to MIB in pursuance of clause 2(a) of an agreement made between the Secretary of State for the Environment and MIB and dated 22 November 1972 relating to compensation of victims of untraced drivers in respect of: [*particulars of, and circumstances giving rise to, injuries*] AND UNDERSTAND that payment of that sum will discharge MIB from all liability under the aforementioned agreements, and that I shall have no further rights under those agreements (in particular any right of appeal to an arbitrator under clause 11 of the agreement of 22 November 1972).

Name and address and description of witness Date: Signature of applicant:

IN WITNESS etc.

NOTES

1 This agreement supplements the agreement dated 22 November 1972 concerning compensation for personal injuries suffered by victims of untraced drivers.

2 The following notes are for guidance only and must not be taken as rendering unnecessary a careful study of this supplemental agreement itself together with the main agreement to which it relates. Communications concerning these agreements should be addressed to the Motor Insurers' Bureau, whose address is Aldermary House, Queen Street, London EC4N 1TR.

3 Clause 1 of the supplemental agreement provides for the use of a shorter form of procedure than that stipulated in the main agreement with the object of securing speedier disposal of certain applications to the Bureau. Except in a case where both an untraced person and an identified person may each partly be responsible for the injuries giving rise to an application, the Bureau may, at its discretion, make an offer of an award in a specified sum furnishing the applicant at the same time with particulars of the circumstances of the case and of the evidence on which the offer is based. If the applicant is prepared to accept the offer and undertake, on payment by the Bureau, to discharge them from all liability and forgo any right of appeal to an arbitrator the Bureau will pay the sum offered forthwith. If the offer is not acceptable the application will thereafter be dealt with in accordance with the full procedure as set out in the main agreement.

4 The purpose of clause 4 of the supplemental agreement is to make clear that the Bureau remain entitled to require any applicant to take proceedings against a known person in accordance with clause 6(1)(b) of the main agreement, notwithstanding that the applicant had successfully appealed against a decision by the Bureau to reject the application after a preliminary investigation.

Note —The MIB is now based at 152 Silbury Boulevard, Central Milton Keynes, MK9 1NB (DX 84753 MILTON KEYNES 3).

FOREIGN MOTORISTS IN ENGLAND

THE MOTOR VEHICLES (INTERNATIONAL MOTOR INSURANCE CARD) REGULATIONS 1971, SI 1971/792.

1 Regulations come into operation 10 June 1971.
2 Revokes the Motor Vehicles (International Insurance Card) Regulations 1969, SI 1969/668.
3 Interpretation 'British Bureau' is the MIB. 'Foreign Bureau' is a central organisation set up by motor insurers in any country abroad (ie outside the UK the Isle of Man and the Channel Islands) having an agreement with the British Bureau for third-party insurance of motorist. Description and meaning of 'insurance card'.
4 Sets out requirements for the validity of the insurance card.
5 As respects the use of a motor vehicle specified in a valid insurance card s 201 of the Road Traffic Act 1960 shall have effect as though the said card were a policy of insurance.
6(1) The insurance card shall have the effect of an insurance certificate. Duty to give information as to insurance under s 209(1) of the Road Traffic Act 1960 to be fulfilled by giving particulars of serial number, name of Bureau and name and address of person specified on card as the insured.
(2) Person making a claim shall give notice in writing to British Bureau as soon as practicable after the accident, specifying the nature of the claim and against whom it is made.
(3) When an accident occurs and the insurance card is produced to a police constable he may detach the duplicate page from the card for the purposes of recording the insurance particulars.
7 Holder of insurance card may produce it on application for motor vehicle licence for purposes of reg 9 of Motor Vehicles (Third Party Risks) Regs 1961.*
8 Special provision for motor vehicles from Northern Ireland — effective policy and certificate required.

* Now replaced by the Motor Vehicles (Third Party Risks) Regulations 1972, SI 1972/ 1217. Sections 201 and 209(1) of the Road Traffic Act 1960 are now replaced by ss 143 and 154 respectively of the Road Traffic Act 1988.

CHAPTER 21

Motor Policies

Note—The legal principles and remedies discussed throughout this chapter should be considered when dealing with policyholders in their private capacity in the light of the Statement of General Insurance Practice issued by the Association of British Insurers.

1 THE DUTY TO DISCLOSE MATERIAL FACTS

THE GENERAL PRINCIPLE

A contract of insurance is a contract *uberrima fides*, that is one of the utmost good faith. This means that the proposer is obliged to disclose to the insurer of all material information affecting the risk the insurer is taking on. The duty of utmost good faith is mutual.

The principle is long established. Lord Mansfield's judgment in *Carter v Boehm* (1766) 3 Burr 1905 at 1909 is the classic exposition. He stated:

'The special facts, upon which the contingent chance is to be computed, lie more commonly in the knowledge of the insured only; the underwriter trusts to his representation and proceeds upon confidence that he does not keep back any circumstance in his knowledge, to mislead the underwriter into a belief that the circumstance does not exist, to induce him to estimate the risque as if it did not exist. Keeping back such a circumstance is a fraud, and, therefore the policy is void.'

The duty of utmost good faith is not an implied contractual term. In *Bank of Nova Scotia v Hellenic Mutual War Risks Association (Bermuda); The Good Luck* [1989] 3 All ER 628 held that the obligation of utmost good faith in a contract of insurance arises by operation of law and not from any implied contractual term and was incapable of supporting a claim to damages.

MATERIALITY—GENERAL DEFINITION

The meaning of materiality was recently considered by the House of Lords in *Pan Atlantic Insurance Co Ltd v Pine Top Insurance Co Ltd* [1994] 3 All ER 581. The case concerned the meaning of s 18 of the Marine Insurance Act 1906. Section 18(1) of that Act provides that 'every material circumstance' must be disclosed. Section 18(2) reads 'every circumstance is material' which would effect the judgment of a prudent insurer in fixing the premium or determining whether he will take the risk.

HELD: (1) The test of materiality of disclosure was, on the natural and ordinary meaning of s 18(2), whether the relevant circumstance would have had an effect on the mind of a prudent insurer in weighing up the risk, not whether had it been fully and accurately disclosed it would have had a decisive effect on the prudent underwriter's decision whether to accept the risk and if so, at what premium. That test accorded with the duty of the assured to disclose all matters which would be taken into account by the underwriter when assessing the risk which he was consenting to assume. (2) For an insurer to be entitled to avoid a policy for misrepresentation or non-disclosure, not only does the misrepresentation or non-disclosure have to be material but in addition it has to have induced the making of the policy on the relevant terms. Accordingly, an underwriter who was not induced by the misrepresentation or non-disclosure of a material fact to make the contract cannot rely on the misrepresentation or non-disclosure to avoid the contract.

EFFECTS OF NON DISCLOSURE—VOID OR VOIDABLE

The effect of misrepresentation/material non-disclosure is to allow the aggrieved party to elect either to carry on with the contract or not. If that party does not choose to continue the contract then it becomes void *ab initio* by operation of law.

Durrant v Maclaren

[1956] 2 Lloyd's Rep 70, Div Ct
The defendant obtained insurance to drive a hired car by giving replies in a proposal form which were untrue and which would have entitled the insurer to avoid the policy *ab initio*.

He was prosecuted for driving an uninsured car, the argument being put that if the policy can be avoided *ab initio* then it is not a policy in force.
HELD: The argument could not succeed. The Road Traffic Act 1934, s 10 (now ss 151 and 152 of the Road Traffic Act 1988) provides that the insurer must pay if judgment is obtained in respect of an accident unless proceedings are taken under sub-s (2). No such proceedings having been taken the insurance was in force at the time when the alleged offence occurred.

Adams v Dunne

[1978] RTR 281, [1978] Crim LR 365, Div Ct
The defendant obtained a cover note from insurers by concealing the fact that he was disqualified from driving. He was prosecuted for driving uninsured; on the relevant date the insurers had not taken any steps to avoid the contract although they would not have given cover had they known he was disqualified. The prosecution conceded that if the contract was merely voidable the case would be covered by *Durrant v Maclaren* (above) but argued that as the contract was void *ab initio* the case was different; a contract of insurance purporting to insure a disqualified driver was an illegal contract.
HELD: The insurers had been misled and had not, with open eyes, entered into a contract to insure a disqualified driver. Until the insurers took steps to avoid it the contract remained a contract of insurance for the purposes of the Road Traffic Act 1972, s 143 (now the Road Traffic Act 1988, s 143).

Note—See also *Evans v Lewis*, p 835, below.

THE PROPOSAL FORM

Obligation to disclose material facts not limited to questions on form

Note—The insured's duty is not limited to answering truthfully questions put to him but extends to disclosing additional facts which are material to the risk.

Glicksman v Lancashire and General Assurance Co

[1927] AC 139, 136 LT 263, 43 TLR 46, 70 Sol Jo 1111, 26 Ll L Rep 69, HL
Two partners, the plaintiff and another, wanted to insure the stock in trade of their tailor business. They completed proposal form. One question was: has any company declined to accept, or refused to renew, your burglary insurance? If so, state the name of the company. Answer: Lancashire accepted, but proposers refused. The court found as a fact that the plaintiff had been declined insurance whilst trading by himself

form the same business premises. There was criticism of the wording of the proposal but nonetheless the court held that the fact that this had not been disclosed was a material fact entitling insurers to avoid the policy.

Schoolman v Hall

[1951] 1 Lloyd's Rep 139
The plaintiff suffered a burglary at his jewellery business. Insurers sought to avoid the policy on grounds of non-disclosure of his criminal record. The latest entry on the record being in relation to a conviction 15 years prior to the inception of the policy. The proposal comprised 15 questions, generally restricted to trade matters within one year and previous losses within five years. References were also required and there was a question as to whether insurance had previously been refused. None of these questions asked about previous convictions. The answers to the questions were made the basis of the contract.
HELD: The basic clause relating to the answers to the 15 specific questions had the effect of preventing any argument as to materiality of those questions but it did not relieve the proposer of his general obligation at common law to disclose any material which might affect the risk being run or the mind of the insurer as to whether or not he should issue the policy. The jury found the conviction to be material notwithstanding the fact that other questions were only concerned with a five-year history.

Arterial Caravans Ltd v Yorkshire Insurance Co Ltd

[1973] 1 Lloyd's Rep 169
Insurers sought to avoid property insurance on the grounds of non-disclosure of a pre-inception fire. The judge referred to a passage of Lord Justice Bankes' judgment in *Mann MacNeal & Sleeves Ltd v Capital & Counties Insurance Co Ltd* [1921] 2 KB 300, 309 quoting Lord Esher :
'It is not necessary to disclose minutely every material fact; assuming that there is a material fact which he is bound to disclose, the rule is satisfied if he discloses sufficient to call the attention of the underwriter in such a manner that they can see that they ought to ask for it.'

The trial judge stated :
'In other words, if you give some indication, for example, about a fire, then it is for the underwriters, if they feel inclined, to go into it further . . . here, they were kept in total ignorance of there ever having been a fire in the history of the business; and the fact that they did not ask questions does not seem to me to amount to a waiver or an estoppel.'

Note—See also *Holt's Motors Ltd v South East Lancashire Insurance Co Ltd*, p 808, below and *Trustees of GH Mundy (a Bankrupt) v Blackmore*, p 807, below.

Circumstances where materiality is waived by scope of questions

Note—The failure to ask a specific question on a proposal form would increase the chances of a court determining that the matters that would have been revealed by that question were immaterial.

Jester-Barnes v Licenses and General Insurance Co

(1934) 49 Ll L Rep 231
Per MacKinnon J: If they had asked him the question 'have you or your driver during the past five years been convicted of any offence' and he had said 'no' and that was true, I should have come without hesitation to the conclusion that they were not entitled after asking that question and receiving that answer to take it to mean that he had failed to disclose that he had been convicted eight years ago and that it was a material fact.

Revell v London General Insurance Co Ltd

(1934) 152 LT 258, 50 LI L Rep 114

Note—See p 810, below.

Taylor v Eagle Star Insurance Co Ltd

(1940) 67 Ll L Rep 136

Note—See p 811, below.

Hair v Prudential Insurance Co Ltd

[1983] 2 Lloyd's Rep 667
Insurers sought to avoid liability following a fire at a private property on the grounds of material non-disclosure. The plaintiff, in answer to questions on the proposal form, had stated that the buildings were kept in a good state of repair, were occupied by his son and left unattended regularly for eight hours daily. The judge found that at the time of the fire the son was not in occupation and that the building was unoccupied and uninhabitable. Woolfe J stated:
'It seems to me that the proper way to regard the questions and answers is to treat them as being an indication of the state of affairs which existed at the time that the answers were given . . . and was going to continue so far as the insured was concerned for the period of the policy, but they did not amount to a warranty that no change would occur. To regard them as a continuing obligation to have a named individual in occupation throughout the period seems to me to be putting an unreasonable interpretation upon the effect of the questions and answers there appearing.'

Roberts v Plaisted

[1989] 2 Lloyd's Rep 341, CA
Insurers sought to repudiate liability following a fire for non-disclosure. The insured owned a hotel which operated an occasional discotheque. The proposal form asked a number of specific questions as to the uses which the hotel or parts of it were put. The Court of Appeal upheld the judge's finding that by failing to ask specific questions as to whether there was a disco (as they had done, for example, as to a casino) the insurers had waived any right to repudiate for non-disclosure.

Effect of warranty

Note—The effect of a warranty on a proposal form of the truth of its contents and/or a statement that it forms the basis of the contract is that even a non-material non-disclosure or misrepresentation is sufficient to enable an insurer to avoid liability under the policy.

Dawson Ltd v Bonnin

[1922] 2 AC 413, 91 LJPC 210, 218 LT 1, 38 TLR 836, 11 Ll L Rep 57, 12 Ll L Rep 237, HL
A firm of contractors in Glasgow insured a motor lorry at Lloyds against damage by fire and third-party risks. The policy recited that the proposal should be the basis of the contract and be held as incorporated in the policy, and it was expressed to be granted subject to the conditions at the back thereof. By the fourth condition 'material mis-statement or concealment of any circumstances by the insured material to assessing the premium herein, or in connection with any claim, shall render the policy void'. In reply to a question in the proposal form, 'State full address at which the vehicle will usually be garaged', the answer given was 'Above address', meaning thereby the firm's ordinary place of business in Glasgow. This was not true, as the lorry was usually garaged at a farm on the outskirts of Glasgow. The inaccurate answer in the proposal was given by inadvertence. The lorry having been destroyed by fire at the garage, the insured claimed payment under the policy.
HELD: (1) This mis-statement in the proposal was not material within the meaning of condition 4. (2) The recital in the policy that the proposal should be the basis of the contract made the truth of the statements contained in the proposal, apart from the question of materiality, a condition of the liability for the insurers; the effect of this recital was not cut down by the special conditions on the back of the policy; and the claim failed.

Condogianis v Guardian Assurance Co

[1921] 2 AC 125, 90 LJPC 168, 125 LT 610, 37 TLR 685, 3 Ll L Rep 40, PC
Appellant sued respondents upon a policy issued by them insuring certain laundry premises against fire. A proposal form filled up by appellant when applying for the policy contained the following question: 'Has proponent ever been a claimant on a fire insurance company in respect of the property now proposed, or any other property? If so, state when and name of company.' Appellant's answer was, 'Yes. 1917. Ocean.' That answer was literally true, as in 1917 he had claims against the Ocean Insurance Co in respect of the burning of a motor car, but in 1912 he had made a claim against another company in respect of a similar loss. The proposal form stated that it was the basis of the policy, and that the particulars given by appellant were to be express warranties. The policy contained a condition that if there was any misrepresentation as to any fact material to be known in estimating the risk, respondents were not to be liable upon the policy.
HELD: (1) The answer was untrue, since the question could not reasonably be read as being intended to have the limited scope which would render the answer true. (2) There was a breach of warranty, whether or not the misrepresentation was as to a material fact. (3) Applicant could not recover on the policy.

Kelsall v Allstate Insurance Co

(1987) Times, 20 March
A warranty in a proposal form of 'no known adverse facts' only requires a policy holder to disclose facts that the reasonable man would recognise as adverse and not to disclose facts not so recognised but which subsequently turn out to be adverse.

CASE EXAMPLES ON MATERIALITY

Age of driver/proposer

Merchants' and Manufacturers' Insurance Co Ltd v Hunt

[1940] 4 All ER 205, 57 TLR 32, 84 Sol Jo 670
A proposal form which had the usual declaration and warranty contained the following questions: 'Q. Have you or any person who to your knowledge will drive the car ever been convicted of an offence in connection with a motor vehicle or motor cycle, or is any prosecution pending? A. No.' The proposer knew that his son was likely to drive the car, and the son had been convicted of three motoring offences.
HELD: The representation of fact is material. The answer of an unqualified negative is an assertion (1) that the proposer has the knowledge which he purports to impart, and (2) that that knowledge is what he is imparting. The answer does not mean 'No, to the best of my knowledge and belief.'

'*Q*. Will the car be driven by any person under twenty-one? *A*. No.'

The proposer knew that the car would be driven quite frequently by his son, who was 17. The question of age is 'material'. Although each representation was innocent, the information was in fact false.

Note—In the Court of Appeal the case was decided on a different point but Scott LJ agreed with the construction of the questions and answers in the proposal form.

Broad v Waland

(1942) 73 Ll L Rep 263
A cover note was issued on the faith of proposal that proposer was 21 years of age. The brokers had clear and definite instruction not to issue a cover note to any person under 21. The proposer was 19 years 6 months and 2 weeks.
HELD, in an action for a declaration: (1) The misrepresentation was material; (2) the policy had been 'obtained' by the misrepresentation. The declaration was granted.

Physical condition of driver

James v British General Insurance Co

[1927] 2 KB 311, 27 Ll L Rep 328
In this case the judge held that as a matter of fact that the plaintiff's response in the negative to a question in the proposal form as to whether he was free from physical defects and infirmities was in fact correct. He had some years before suffered a slight hernia, some giddiness and some functional heart trouble but these disabilities had ceased by the time the declaration was made.

Note—The physical condition of a driver will certainly be material insofar as it affects his capabilities as a driver.

Occupation of proposer

Holmes v Cornhill Insurance Co Ltd

(1949) 82 Ll L Rep 575
Proposer orally asked an insurance company for insurance of a motor car for use in his business as a commission agent. The company told him they did not insure

bookmakers. Proposer stated he was not a bookmaker but was a commission agent dealing in furniture. He had had a furniture shop for a short time three or four years before but for two years had no shop, warehouse or business premises in connection with furniture dealing and kept no books or records of any such dealing. His main occupation was that of a bookmaker and not that of a dealer. He signed a proposal form stating his occupation as dealer. The proposal form contained the usual declaration and warranty.

The arbitrator made his award in the form of a special case. His findings were:

1 The description of dealer was untrue.
2 The failure to disclose that he was a bookmaker was material.
3 That (1) and (2) each constituted a breach of the warranty which was made the basis of the policy.
4 The policy was induced by the false representation that he was not a bookmaker.

The arbitrator found the company not liable. The finding was upheld.

McNealy v The Pennine Insurance Co

[1978] 2 Lloyd's Rep 18
The plaintiff was a property repairer and a part-time musician. He effected low premium motor insurance through brokers. The brokers were aware that full and part time musicians were an unacceptable risk to the insurers. The brokers had asked the plaintiff for his occupation and had recorded the answer 'property repairer' on the proposal form.
HELD: Insurers were entitled to avoid for material non-disclosure but the plaintiff had a remedy against the broker.

Proposer an alien

Horne v Poland

[1922] 2 KB 364, 91 LJKB 718, 127 LT 242, 38 TLR 357, 66 Sol Jo 368, 10 Ll L Rep 175, 275
The plaintiff was born in Rumania and was brought to England at the age of 12. He assumed an English name but was not naturalised and was registered as an alien under the war legislation. He took out burglary insurance 22 years after arriving in England. None of these facts were disclosed on the proposal form. This was held to be a material non-disclosure. The judge said that the circumstances of each case must be considered and in this case it was relevant that the plaintiff came from Eastern Europe and that he and his parents were subjects of a state whose habits and traditions underwriters will naturally know nothing and furthermore that the plaintiff had lived in that country until he was 12 years old.

Owner not proposer

Guardian Assurance Co Ltd v Sutherland

[1939] 2 All ER 246, 55 TLR 576, 83 Sol Jo 398, 63 Ll L, Rep 220
On 17 March 1938, Sutherland signed a proposal form for Mercedes Benz BXD 1 and plaintiffs issued cover notes until policy issued on 26 May 1938. On 20 May 1938, Sutherland telegraphed to plaintiffs to transfer to a Lancia car, confirmed on 10 June

by application form signed by Sutherland for substitution, and policy endorsed accordingly. On 17 June 1938, at request of Sutherland an employee of Green Park Motors Ltd telegraphed to insurers 'Please cover me on Mercedes EYT 114 as well as Lancia, and insurers issued cover note. On 20 June 1938, Sutherland signed a form that EYT 114 should be substituted for the Lancia and stating Sutherland was the owner of EYT 114 and that it was registered in his name. On 20 June 1938, before the form signed on 20 June by Sutherland had reached insurers car EYT 114 driven by one Sidebotham was involved in an accident causing personal injuries to third parties. EYT 114 was the property of Green Park Motors. Sidebotham introduced one Chang, a Chinese, as purchaser, and on 17 June Chang agreed to purchase. Chang, owning to his foreign nationality, could not get cover without delay. Sidebotham had a policy from 15 August 1937, to 15 August 1938, but he had not revealed in his proposal form a number of convictions for dangerous driving and driving without due care, and some of his previous accidents, and had mis-stated his age as over 21 when in fact it was nineteen and a half and his policy was avoided in October 1938. Sutherland had no interest in EYT 114.

HELD: It was all one contract and was obtained by mis-statement and concealment. If the cover note for EYT 114 was a new contract it was obtained by material misrepresentation. The telegram represented that EYT 114 was Sutherland's property. It was material for insurers to know that Sutherland had nothing to do with the car, but that it was sold to Chang and about to be driven by Sidebotham with his bad record of offences and accidents. A policy obtained by misrepresentation insures no one and is not a policy within s 36(4) of the 1930 Act: (1) the opening words of the subsection were inserted to get rid of the difficulty created by the Life Assurance Act 1774; (2) the function of the subsection was to get over the difficulty that nobody who was not a party to a contract could sue upon it (compare *Vanderpitte v Preferred Accident* (p 752, above)).

Sidebotham was not driving EYT 114 on the assured's order or with his permission. Sutherland had no interest whatever in EYT 114 and had no right to give or refuse permission. Application for declaration granted.

Note—For a recent view of the application of s 2 of the Life Assurance Act 1774, see *Mark Rowlands Ltd v Berni Inns* [1985] 3 All ER 473 (p 752, above). Section 148 (7) of the Road Traffic Act 1988 has replaced s 36 (4) of the 1930 Act.

Zurich General Accident and Liability Insurance Co Ltd v Buck

(1939) 64 Ll L Rep 115

A, a greengrocer carrying on business at No 56 Brewery Road on 1 September 1936, took out a policy, and two subsequent policies, with the X Co, each of which policies lapsed for non-payment of premium. On 4 October 1937, A took out a policy with plaintiffs subject to termination if hire-purchase agreement terminated except if due to purchase by A. On 9 December 1938, A was fined for speeding. On 15 March 1938, the hire-purchase agreement terminated and the policy was cancelled. Judgment was obtained against A by the motor trader and was unsatisfied.

On 15 March 1938, B, the brother of A, who had a butcher's business next door to A, bought a motor van and lent it to A for use in A's business. It was registered in B's name. Plaintiffs' agent received proposal forms and issued cover notes. A informed the agent that the van belonged to A but he wished it to be insured in the name of B, but A would use it in his business and it would be driven by A only. The proposal stated that the proposer was B; that B's business was at No 56 and was a greengrocery business; that no person who would drive had been convicted of a motoring offence; that proposer had been insured with the Co-operative; that no company had cancelled his policy. A had been insured with the Employers' Liability and the plaintiffs.

HELD: Cancelled or refused to renew does not mean allowed to lapse by non-payment. The conviction and some of the mis-statements taken by themselves were not very material, but the proposal as a whole quite obviously did not in the least represent a true state of the facts, and some of the mis-statements would have led an underwriter to consider whether to accept the proposal or at least to make further inquiries. B had nothing to do with A's use of the van, and a third party could have no possible claim against B and B had no insurable interest and the policy was valueless. Application for declaration granted.

Goodbarne v Buck

[1940] 1 KB 771, [1940] 1 All ER 613, 109 LJKB 837, 162 LT 259, 56 TLR 433, 84 Sol Jo 380, CA

The third party in the previous case afterwards sued B on the principle of *Monk v Warbey*.

HELD: B was never the owner of the van and could not prevent A, who was the owner, from driving it. The policy was voidable, not void; it was valid and subsisting unless and until insurers elected to avoid it. This did not mean that for all purposes of s 35 of the 1930 Act the policy must be regarded as never having been in existence at all. There was a policy in force at the time which satisfied the section and the fact that it was subsequently avoided did not prevent there having been a policy in force at the material time.

Accident record

Dent v Blackmore

(1927) 29 Ll L Rep 9

Insurers avoided on the grounds of material non-disclosure. On the proposal was the question 'what accidents have occurred in connection with your motor car during the past two years, including costs?' the plaintiff replied: damaged wings. In fact the plaintiff had had six accidents with his car all resulting in damage to wings. The judge held that the answer conveyed clear impression that the plaintiff had suffered one accident only and that the plaintiff was guilty of a material non-disclosure entitling the insurers to avoid the policy.

Dunn v Ocean Accident

(1933) 47 Ll L Rep 129, CA

The plaintiff completed a proposal form using her maiden name, although she was in fact married. Her husband was killed whilst driving the car. The facts are unusual in that they had married secretly and lived apart. The husband had bought the car on hire-purchase and 'gave' it to the plaintiff as a present. The husband had use of the vehicle during week days and the plaintiff used it at weekends. The husband was prone to driving at great speed and had had several accidents to the plaintiff's knowledge and had been refused insurance cover. The plaintiff completed a proposal form and answered 'no' to the following questions:

(1) Have you or your driver during the past five years been convicted of any offence in connection with the driving of a motor vehicle?
(2) Has a company or underwriter declined your proposal or required you to carry the first portion of any loss?
HELD: The plaintiff's failure to disclose her marital status and the material fact that her husband had been involved in accidents amounted to a material non-disclosure entitling the insurers to avoid the policy. The judge considered it to be of significance that the husband had filled in parts of the proposal form himself.

Trustees of GH Mundy (a bankrupt) v Blackmore

(1928) 32 Ll L Rep 150
Mundy took out motor insurance. The insurers asserted that by a proposal incorporated into the contract Mundy had warranted:
(1) that during the past two years with eight cars insured the only accidents were minor accidents; also ran off the road in France owing to tyre bursting; and
(2) that he had not previously been refused insurance.
In fact the insured's Bugatti had been involved in an accident costing between £130 and £140 to repair. It was a head-on collision and the car had both axles bent, and its gear box thrown out of line. It was argued that if an insurance company accepts a disclosure of a minor accident it cannot afterwards say that we do not think this was a minor accident and you should have mentioned it specifically. The judge found that no reasonably fair minded man could have called the accident minor and so insurers were entitled to repudiate notwithstanding the failure to inquire further. It was also held that the failure to disclose the previous refusal was material.

Where vehicle garaged/standard of garage

Dawsons Ltd v Bonnin

[1922] 2 AC 413, 91 LJPC 210, 128 LTI, 38 TLR 836, 11 LI L Rep 57, 12 LI L Rep 237, HL

Note—See p 802, above.

Johnson & Perrott Ltd v Holmes

(1925) 21 Ll L Rep 330
The plaintiffs had a garage business and insured against riots and civil commotion. In 1922 the garage was raided and a Cadillac taken away during the Irish disturbances. The insurers alleged that there had been a breach of the terms of the policy in that the plaintiffs had assisted in the disturbances by repairing and supplying motor cars to the irregular forces before the recognition of the Irish Free State. The actual loss occurred after the confirmation by Parliament of the Treaty. The garage was raided by armed men and the vehicle removed. It was suggested that a material fact had been concealed from underwriters—namely that the garage had previously been used by the IRA before their official recognition. The judge held that nothing material was concealed on the basis that if cars were taken by the IRA then claims would be made against the compensation fund rather than against insurers and that 'a gentleman who has a garage which is patronised by the IRA whose taking of a car would not create a loss on the policy, is in a better position than a person who has a private car hidden away which the IRA officially might never have heard of or have had any interest in at all'.

Declinature of previous insurers/increased premium

Holt's Motors Ltd v South East Lancashire Insurance Co Ltd

[1930] 36 Ll L Rep 17 (Horridge J); on appeal 35 Com Cas 281, 37 Ll L Rep 1, CA
An intimation by a previous insurer that they would not invite renewal is a material fact which should be disclosed by a proposer.

Cornhill Insurance Co Ltd v L & B Assenheim

(1937) 58 Ll L Rep 27
Insurers sought a declaration that they were entitled to avoid on grounds of material non disclosure of the fact that previous underwriters had refused to renew. A proposal had been signed on the 3 April 1935 with the answer 'no' to the question whether any underwriter had refused to renew. Subsequently, in September other insurers declined to renew in respect of other vehicles. At later dates various additions and substitutions were made to the vehicles covered by the policy. The defendant signed proposals in relation to these various alterations which included a declaration that that proposal and the proposal signed on the 3 April 1935 formed the basis of the contract.
HELD: The failure to disclose the letter received in September 1935 from other insurers refusing to renew was a material non-disclosure.

Mackay v London General Insurance Co Ltd

(1935) 51 Ll L Rep 201
The plaintiff answered 'no' to questions as to whether he had ever had to pay an increased premium or been convicted. The answers were made the basis of the contract. In fact some three years earlier the plaintiff had had to take on an excess of two pounds ten shillings to insure his motorbike. This was the insurer's standard practice for minors. He had also been fined ten shillings some considerable time earlier for having a loose nut on the brake of his motorbike. The judge held that both these matters were quite immaterial. He expressed sympathy for the plaintiff but said that nonetheless the answers formed the basis of the contract and the insurers were therefore entitled to avoid.

Purchase price—part exchange

Brewtnall v Cornhill Insurance Co Ltd

(1931) 40 Ll L Rep 166
An insured car was destroyed by fire. A claim was made, the defence being that there had been a concealment of a material fact in the proposal form. The question was: '*Q.* Cost price to proposer. *A.* £145.'

There was evidence that proposer gave £45 and another car (agreed price £100) in part exchange—should exchange of car have been disclosed?
HELD: The defence of concealment failed. Judgment for assured.

Driving 12 months regularly; provisional licence

Zurich General Accident and Liability Insurance Co Ltd v Morrison

[1942] 2 KB 53, [1942] 1 All ER 529, 111 LJKB 601, 167 LT 183, 58 TLR 217, 86 Sol Jo 267, 72 Ll L Rep 167, CA

A question in a proposal form for motor insurance asked 'Have you driven cars regularly and continuously in the UK during the past 12 months?'

HELD: The question was most embarrassing and if taken literally no one could answer it other than in the negative. If the insurers want to know how long a man has driven on the road or for how long he had held a licence they should ask the questions in plain terms. The proposer had done some driving on a provisional licence and some on works roads during the 12 months preceding the proposal and it could not be said his answer to the question, 'Yes', was untrue. The failure to reveal that he had only a provisional licence to drive and had failed one driving test was not a material non-disclosure since there was no evidence that the insurers would not have issued a policy on the same terms had those matters been disclosed. In a case of this kind the insurers must establish two propositions in order to avoid the policy: (1) that the matter relied on was 'material' in the sense that the mind of a prudent insurer would be affected by it, and (2) that in fact the underwriter's mind was so affected and the policy thereby obtained. The insurers had not established these propositions.

Note—Followed by Atkinson J in *Broad v Waland* (1942) 73 Ll L Rep 263 at 628 and 679.

Previous convictions—motor offences

Jester-Barnes v Licences and General Insurance Co

(1934) 49 Ll L Rep 231

Note—See p 801, above.

Mackay v London General Insurance Co

(1935) 51 Ll L Rep 201 (Swift J)

Note—See p 808, above.

Bond v Commercial Assurance Co

(1930) 35 Com Cas 171, 36 Ll L Rep 107

Appellant took out with respondents a motor car policy of insurance in respect of a car of which he was the owner. Appellant employed more than one driver in the course of his business and at the time when the insurance was effected the agent of respondents told him that if he paid an extra premium the policy would protect him whoever might be driving the car, and appellant paid the extra premium accordingly. During the currency of the policy the car, while being driven by a son of appellant, came into collision with a cyclist. The cyclist brought an action against appellant for damages, and appellant referred the claim to respondents, who repudiated liability on the ground that at the time when the policy was taken out appellant had failed to disclose a material fact. It appeared that before the insurance was effected appellant's son had been convicted several times of motoring offences, chiefly in relation to a motor cycle, and respondents contended that this was a material fact which ought to have been disclosed by appellant. Before the policy was issued appellant had received a proposal form from respondents and had answered all the questions in that form fully and truthfully and he did not know that any further information

was required. At that time he had not his son in mind. Appellant's claim against respondents was referred to arbitration as required by the policy and the arbitrator awarded in favour of respondents on the ground that a material fact had not been disclosed. Appellant now appealed to the Divisional Court to have the award set aside.
HELD: The arbitrator had decided rightly and the award must be confirmed.

Butcher v Dowlen

(1980) 124 Sol Jo 883, [1981] RTR 24, 1 Lloyd's Rep 310, CA
The plaintiff claimed money due under a policy of motor insurance issued by the defendant to her husband who had been killed in an accident. The defendant served a defence denying liability under the policy on the ground that her husband had failed to disclose criminal charges and a conviction in the proposal form. The plaintiff, who said she had no knowledge of any conviction, obtained an order for further and better particulars specifying the alleged offences and charges with dates and other details. The defendant was unable to say more in reply than that the deceased had 'been convicted of offences on several occasions' without any details. The plaintiff applied to strike out the defence for failure to supply the particulars ordered.
HELD, dismissing an appeal from a judge: The defence should be struck out. It was not good enough for the defendant to say the action should go to trial so that a police officer could produce evidence from the Criminal Records Office which at present the defendant did not have. The burden of proof was on the defendant and there was not enough to justify the allegations made in the defence going to trial.

Note—But see the contrasting decision in *Revell v London General Insurance Co Ltd.*

Revell v London General Insurance Co Ltd

(1934) 152 LT 258, 50 Ll L Rep 114 (MacKinnon)
A proposal form contained the following question: 'Q. Have you or any of your drivers ever been convicted of any offence in connection with the driving of any motor vehicle? A. No.'

Driver in fact previously convicted: (1) of unlawfully driving a car without a suitable reflecting mirror; (2) of unlawfully using a car without having in force an insurance policy covering third party risks.
HELD: Question might reasonably mean carefulness of driver and answer was not untrue.

Previous convictions—non motor/moral hazard

Note—The following cases must be considered in conjunction with the meaning of materiality as defined in *Pan Atlantic Insurance Co Ltd v Pine Top Insurance Co Ltd* (see p 798, above).

Locker and Woolfe Ltd v Western Australian Insurance Co Ltd

[1936] 1 KB 408, 105 LJKB 444, 154 LT 667, 52 TLR 293, 80 Sol Jo 185, CA
Per Slesser JL: It is elementary that one of the matters to be considered by an insurance company in entering into contractual relations with a proposed insured is the question of the moral integrity of the proposer—what has been called the moral hazard.

Cleland v London General Insurance Co Ltd

(1935) 51 Ll L Rep 156 CA
The defendants repudiated liability on the ground of the non-disclosure of material facts on the proposal form. They relied upon the following statement in the proposal

form: 'I have withheld no information which would tend to increase the risk or influence the acceptance of this proposal'. It was said that the insured had answered 'No' to the question on the proposal form: 'Have you or your driver ever been convicted or had a motor licence indorsed?' when in fact there were convictions against him as follows: 10 January 1922: Breaking and entering a garage and stealing a motor cycle and sidecar. Released on recognisances. 17 July 1922: Forging a cheque. Five months' imprisonment. 26 September 1922: Breach of recognisances. Nine months' imprisonment. 19 July 1926: Breaking and entering shop and stealing parcels and other articles. Eighteen months' imprisonment with hard labour. Stealing a fur stole and other articles to the value of £1,000. Three years' penal servitude.

It was submitted that the insured had accurately and truthfully answered the question on the proposal form, because the convictions had no relation to motor car offences. Counsel also contended the insured was under no common law liability to disclose to the London General his past bad character except so far as that character was material to the subject matter of the policy.

HELD, in the Court of Appeal (affirming Horridge J): A person entering into such a contract was bound to disclose the fact that he had been convicted although those convictions had nothing at all to do with motor offences, and therefore the insurance company were entitled to repudiate liability.

Taylor v Eagle Star Insurance Co Ltd

(1940) 67 Ll L Rep 136 (MacNaghten J)

A question in a proposal form was as follows: '*Q*. Have you or has your driver been convicted of any offence in connection with the driving of any motor vehicle? *A*. No'.

An accident occurred on 20 April 1937. The assured had been convicted of the following offences. 7 June 1927: Drunk and disorderly; fined £2. Assaulting the police; one month imprisonment. Throwing a glass bottle to the public danger; fined £2. 23 October 1931: Permitting use of uninsured car; fined £2. 27 March 1933: Driving car without road fund licence; fined 10s. 13 June 1933: Drunk on licensed premises; fined 10s. 7 December 1935: Drinking during prohibited hours; fined 15s.

Following *Revell*'s case, the answer in respect of the motoring offences was not untrue, but the other convictions were facts material to be known to insurers and not having been disclosed, insurers were not liable on the ground of non-disclosure.

Note—Other cases illustrating the principle of moral hazard in context other than in motor insurance are set out below.

Roselodge Ltd v Castle

(1966) 110 Sol Jo 705, [1966] 2 Lloyd's Rep 113 (McNair J)

The plaintiffs, diamond merchants, insured their diamonds against all risks with defendant underwriters. The proposal form did not contain any question about previous convictions of employees. The plaintiffs did not disclose: (1) that in 1946 their managing director (the effective principal of the company) had been convicted of giving a bribe of five shillings to a police officer and had been fined £75; (2) that their sales manager had in 1956 (before entering the plaintiff's employment) been convicted of smuggling diamonds into the USA. On 31 January 1965 in Hatton Garden the managing director was robbed of diamonds worth £300,000. The plaintiffs claimed to be indemnified under the policy. The defendants refused to pay, claiming that the policy was void for non-disclosure of material facts known to the plaintiffs, namely, the two convictions. On the evidence the judge found that the

robbery had actually occurred as alleged and that there was no suggestion that the sales manager had anything to do with it.
HELD: The defendants were entitled to repudiate on the grounds of material non-disclosure. Expert evidence of materiality may be given by underwriters but the issue as to disclosability was still one to be determined by the view of reasonable men. On the facts of the present case the managing director's offence and conviction were not material and need not have been disclosed, but the sales manager's conviction was different. He had been a party to a dishonest transaction and a reasonable man would appreciate that he remained or might remain a security risk. His conviction was a material fact which ought to have been disclosed.

Regina Fur Co v Bossom

[1957] 2 Lloyd's Rep 466 (Pearson J)
Burglary claim by limited company; directors Waxman and Freeman. The company failed to disclose that Waxman had been convicted 20 years before of receiving a quantity of fur skins knowing the same to have been stolen.
HELD: The test was that disclosure must be of all that a proposer ought to have realised to be material. A first impression would naturally be that an isolated conviction more than 20 years old must be too ancient and too remote. When the first policy was issued Waxman held a predominant position in the company. Evidence is admissible on the point whether the conviction affected the moral hazard to such an extent as to be material (*Yorke v Yorkshire Insurance Co Ltd* [1918] 1 KB 662 at 670). Expert evidence that it was was given by two underwriters, and a witness for the plaintiff was unable to say that it was not. On the special facts of this case, and not based on any decision in any other case, the court found it was material.

Note—An appeal was dismissed [1958] 2 Lloyd's Rep 425.

March Cabaret Club and Casino Ltd v London Assurance

[1975] 1 Lloyd's Rep 169 (May J)
The plaintiff company owned and ran a club and casino and was itself controlled and directed by S and his wife. In 1967 the defendant insurers issued a policy covering the contents against fire risks, extended on renewal to cover the company's buildings. On 14 June 1969 S was arrested on a charge of handling stolen goods and on 28 November 1969 was committed for trial. The policy fell due for renewal on 20 April 1970; when renewing S did not disclose his arrest and committal to the insurers. On 22 June 1970, he was convicted and fined £2,000. On 14 September 1970 there was a fire at the club premises causing £27,024 damage. The insurers, after investigation in which they learned of S's prosecution and conviction declared the policy void on the ground of material non-disclosure when the policy was renewed in April 1970.
HELD: There had been a material non-disclosure entitling the insurers to avoid the policy. The duty to disclose material facts arises outside the contract of insurance and not by way of implied term. The test of materiality was whether the facts would, on a fair consideration of the evidence, influence a reasonable insurer to decline the risk. Whether a particular circumstance is material or not is a question of fact in which the moral integrity of the proposer is important. S should, before renewal in April 1970, have disclosed that he had committed the crime referred to; even if he had subsequently been acquitted he ought to have disclosed the fact of his arrest, charge and committal, but not if he had been acquitted before the renewal.

Note—In *Reynolds and Anderson v Phoenix Assurance Co Ltd* [1978] 2 Lloyd's Rep 440 (noted at p 813, below), another fire insurance case. Forbes J disagreed with a comment by May J that the fact of the arrest, charge and committal should have been disclosed even though in truth S was innocent. He said the most relevant circumstance for disclosure is that the proposer had actually committed an offence of a character which would in fact influence the insurer's judgment; the material circumstance is the commission of the offence.

Inversions Maria SA v Sphere Drake Insurance Co Plc, The Dora

[1989] 1 Lloyd's Rep 69

A yacht was insured which subsequently sustained a fire. Insurers sought to avoid on a number of grounds including the fact that the skipper and the insured's representative both had criminal records. The representative's conviction was for failing to keep proper books of account under the Italian Bankruptcy Code. The skipper had been convicted on seven charges of issuing cheques not backed by funds.

By the time the contract of insurance was placed the representative had ceased to have anything to do with *The Dora* so the judge found there was no obligation to disclose her record and so didn't decide as to whether the record would otherwise have been material. So far as the skipper is concerned, the judge held that the plaintiff had entrusted the management of *The Dora*, including the placing of insurance to a Mr Lionello and that if he had made appropriate inquiries he would have discovered the skipper's conviction.

Per Philips J: The role of the skipper of a yacht is well recognised and involves overall responsibility for the vessel. Financial competence and probity is an essential requirement. I have no doubt that any underwriter would consider it material to be told that the skipper was only competent to look after the navigational aspects of the running of the yacht and that his crew would be responsible for other aspects of the operation of the vessel. For the reasons I hold that the defendants made out their right to avoid the contract for non-disclosure of (the skipper's) criminal record.

Note—The effect of the Rehabilitation of Offenders Act 1974 is set out in the cases below.

Reynolds v Phoenix Assurance Co Ltd

(1978) 122 Sol Jo 161, [1978] 2 Lloyd's Rep 22, CA

The plaintiffs sued the defendant insurers under a fire policy for payment of a loss caused by a fire at the insured property. In the course of the proceedings the defendants learned that one of the insured plaintiffs had been convicted of an offence 16 years earlier. They applied to amend the defence to plead that the conviction should have been disclosed when proposing for the policy and that the non-disclosure was material.

HELD, ON APPEAL: Though the Rehabilitation of Offenders Act 1974, s 4 excluded the possibility of bringing evidence of a spent conviction it was subject to s 7(3) which enabled a judge to admit evidence of such a conviction if satisfied 'that justice cannot be done in the case except by admitting' the evidence. The amendment should be allowed so that the issue could be brought before the court, when the judge could hear evidence and decide whether the conviction was a material matter without evidence of which justice could not be done.

Note—At the subsequent trial of the action Forbes J held that evidence of the conviction should be admitted. Injustice would otherwise be done to the defendant insurers since they would be prevented from avoiding a policy which on the evidence it would be the universal practice of insurers to avoid: [1978] 2 Lloyd's Rep 440.

WAIVER OF MATERIALITY: APPROBATING POLICY/DEALING WITH CLAIM

Insurers may expressly elect to waive a breach and the contract will continue. They may also be deemed to have waived a breach by conducting themselves in a manner inconsistent with the continuance of their right to rely on the breach.

Note—See also *Greenwoods v Martins Bank*, p 877, below.

West v National Motor & Accident Insurance Union Ltd

[1954] 2 Lloyd's Rep 461
In a household contents insurance proposal the plaintiff had declared full value of the contents at £500. The proposal required the value of jewellery to be stated if it exceeded one-third of the declared value. The declaration was expressed to be the basis of the contract. A burglary occurred and goods estimated to be worth more than £500 were stolen. The insurers did not repudiate the policy but sought to repudiate the claim. The plaintiff then limited his claim to comply with the policy declaration.
HELD: Having approved the policy insurers could not then repudiate the claim but were liable to pay the amount due under the terms of the policy.

McCormick v National Motor and Accident Insurance Union Ltd

(1934) 50 TLR 528, 78 Sol Jo 633, 40 Com Cas 76, 49 Ll L Rep 361, CA
During the course of the trial of an action between a third party and the assured, it came out in evidence that the assured had been previously convicted for dangerous driving. He had stated on the proposal form that he had not been convicted. Insurers continued to defend the action, and five days later repudiated liability under the policy.
HELD: This did not amount to waiver. The insurers were entitled to continue to defend the action.

Whether you treat it as an election or whether you treat it as a ratification or whether you treat it as a decision simply to act on the knowledge you have acquired, the duty to take action does not arise (1) unless you know all the facts—being put on inquiry is not sufficient; you must know the facts—and (2) unless you have a reasonable time to make up your mind. You are not bound the moment the statement is made to you to make up your mind at once; you are entitled to a reasonable time to consider—to a reasonable time to make inquiries: Per Scrutton LJ.

There must be an irresistible inference that the parties intended to adopt one of two courses open to them and to discard or waive the other and in such a manner as to represent to other persons definitely and unequivocally that he has taken that view whereby it may act to their detriment: Per Slesser LJ.

Evans v Employers' Mutual Insurance Association Ltd

[1936] 1 KB 505, 105 LJKB 141, 154 LT 137, 52 Ll L Rep 51, CA
If it is established by evidence that the duty of investigating and ascertaining facts has been delegated in the ordinary course of a company's business to a subordinate official, the company will, in law, be bound by his knowledge in the same way as it

is affected by the knowledge of the board of directors. The claimant said in the proposal form that he had been driving for five years, which was untrue. An accident occurred and in the claim form he stated he had been driving six weeks. The claim form and proposal form were handed to the respondents' claims superintendent, who was authorised to deal with such matters, and was passed on by him in accordance with the practice of the office to a clerk for the purpose of checking the statements they contained and noting any discrepancies therein. The clerk noticed the discrepancy, but did not call attention to it, considering it of no importance. Thereafter the respondents paid for damage to car and medical expenses, and negotiated claims by third parties. Before settling those claims the claims superintendent became aware of the untrue statement, whereupon the respondents repudiated liability.
HELD: The respondents had waived their right to repudiate liability.

Locker and Woolf Ltd v Western Australian Insurance Co Ltd

[1936] 1 KB 408, 105 LJKB 444, 154 LT 667, 52 TLR 293, 80 Sol Jo 185 (Swift J)
On a fire loss the company's assessors sold the salvage. The policy contained a condition that the company may, without thereby incurring any liability and without diminishing the rights of the company to rely on conditions of this policy, take possession of the property insured and deal with it for all reasonable purposes and in any reasonable manner.
HELD: There was no waiver.

Stone v Licences and General Insurance Co Ltd

(1942) 71 Ll L Rep 256 (Birkett J)
16 May, 4 am: accident involving lorry carrying load in breach of policy condition. 8 am: driver telephoned assured who informed insurers. 6.30 pm: branch manager of insurers visited accident and saw the unauthorised load. 17 May: driver made full disclosure at insurer's office. Insurers then had full knowledge of all material facts. 23 May: Branch manager gave instructions to remove debris and sell it for £1. The assured was not consulted. 7 June: Insurers wrote repudiating liability under policy and sent their own cheque for £1 to assured who refused to accept the cheque.
HELD: The breach of condition had been waived.

Lickiss v Milestone Motor Policies at Lloyd's

[1966] 2 All ER 972, [1966] 1 WLR 1334, 110 Sol Jo 600, [1966] 2 Lloyd's Rep 1
Davies and Lickess were involved in a motor accident. Davies sought to recover the cost of repairing damage to his vehicle from Lickess. It was a condition precedent of Lickess' insurance policy that full particulars would be given to insurers of any accident and that any notice of intended prosecution, writ etc would be sent immediately to insurers. The accident occurred on 17 May 1964 and Lickess advised insurers on 25 May. By that time insurers had already been made aware of the accident by Davies' solicitors. The insurers sent Lickess a claim form for completion. The insured subsequently received notice of intended prosecution and a summons but did not forward these to insurers. The insurers learned of these proceedings from the police before the return date of the summons. The insurers subsequently repudiated liability stating that their position had been prejudiced.
HELD: The insured was in breach of the condition precedent but by writing to the insured enclosing a claim form that breach had been waived.

MUTUAL MISTAKE

Magee v Pennine Insurance Co Ltd

[1969] 2 QB 507, [1969] 2 All ER 891, [1969] 2 WLR 1278, 113 Sol Jo 303, [1969] 2 Lloyd's Rep 378, CA
The plaintiff took out a motor insurance policy with the defendants in 1961. There were serious misstatements of fact in the proposal which would entitle the defendants to repudiate liability under the policy or declare it void. In 1964 the car was damaged in an accident. After an inspection by an engineer the defendants wrote to the plaintiff saying it was damaged beyond repair, that its value according to the engineer was (after salvage) £385 and offering him that amount 'in settlement of your claim'. The plaintiff accepted but the insurers then discovered the inaccuracy of the statements in the proposal form and refused to pay. The county court judge found that the plaintiff had not been fraudulent and that the defendants' letter was a binding offer which had been accepted.
HELD: There had been a common mistake of fact, namely, that there was a valid policy of insurance. Accepting that the agreement to pay £385 was a separate contract the defendants were entitled to avoid it on the ground of mutual mistake in a fundamental and vital matter.

Note—The facts of this case must be contrasted with situations where there has been a mistake of law rather than of fact. In those circumstances moneys paid will be irrecoverable.

EFFECT OF PROPOSAL THROUGH AGENT

Agent is agent of proposer

Newsholme Bros v Road Transport and General Insurance Co Ltd

[1929] 2 KB 356, 98 LJKB 751, 141 LT 570, 45 TLR 573, 73 Sol Jo 465, CA
With regard to mis-statements in a proposal form the insurance agent is the agent of the assured and not of the insurer. A proposal form for the insurance of a motor-bus was signed by the person wishing to effect the insurance, but the answers to the questions therein, which were warranted to be true and to form the basis of the contract, were filled in by the insurance company's agent, who, although told the true facts, wrote, for some unexplained reason, answers which were untrue in a material respect. The agent was not authorised by the insurance company to fill in proposal forms and it did not appear that the company knew that he had in fact done so. His duties were to procure persons to effect insurance and to see, so far as he could, that proposal forms were correctly filled up; he was not authorised to give a cover note or to enter into a policy of insurance. A policy was issued to the person who had signed the proposal form and during its currency he made a claim under it, but the insurance company repudiated liability on the ground of the untrue statements in the proposal form.
HELD: The agent of the insurance company in filling in the proposal form was merely the *amanuensis* of the proposer, that the knowledge of the true facts by the agent could not be imputed to the insurance company, and, therefore, that the insurance company was entitled to repudiate liability on the ground of the untrue statements in the proposal form.

Facer v Vehicle and General Insurance Co Ltd

[1965] 1 Lloyd's Rep 113 (Marshall J)
The plaintiff signed a proposal form which was filled in for him by a Mr Bonham, a sub-agent or servant of Mr Braun, who was an agent of the defendants. The answer 'No' was written on the proposal form to the question 'Do you suffer from any defective vision or hearing or from any physical infirmity?' though the plaintiff had disclosed to Bonham that he had only one eye. The proposal form ended 'I agree that this proposal and declaration shall be the basis of the contract between the company and myself, and also said 'If this proposal is written by another it shall be deemed he shall be my agent and not an agent of the company.'
HELD: The vital question was whether Bonham, when he inaccurately answered the question about defective vision by putting in the word 'No' was the agent of the plaintiff in filling in the form or the agent of the defendants. The case was governed by *Newsholme Bros v Road Transport & General Insurance Co Ltd* (above) with this further strengthening factor that in the present case there was an express declaration in the proposal that the person filling in the form was to be deemed the agent of the proposer and not of the company. The defendants were entitled to avoid the policy.

Note—But contrast with *Stone v Reliance Mutual Insurance Society Ltd*, below.

Stone v Reliance Mutual Insurance Society Ltd

[1972] 1 Lloyd's Rep 469, CA
In 1966 the plaintiff insured his house with the defendants under a fire and theft policy. In 1967 there was a fire and the defendants paid him £280. The policy then lapsed. In 1968 the defendants' district inspector called with a view to getting the plaintiff to take out a new policy. He called only on people who had previously held policies and it was the company's practice that for the proposal form he should put the question orally and write down the answers himself. He filled in a proposal form without asking any questions and plaintiff's wife signed it without reading it. The form contained a declaration by the proposer that the person writing down the answers did so as the proposer's agent. Two of the answers filled in by the inspector were to the effect that the plaintiff had not previously held a policy with the defendants and that he had not previously made any claims in respect of the risks proposed. Later a burglary took place for which the plaintiff claimed, disclosing on the claim form the earlier fire claim. The defendants refused to indemnify on the ground of non-disclosure of the fire claim in the proposal form.
HELD: Though the proposal form was expressed to be filled in by the inspector as the plaintiff's agent his express evidence had been that it was company practice that he should put the questions and write down the answers. The proper inference was that it was his duty, owed to his employers, to take proper care. It was quite different from *Newsholme*'s case (above); it was far more like *Bawden*'s case (referred to below). The inspector knew of the earlier policy and of the fire claim: it was his mistake and not the proposer's. The company could not rely on it to avoid the policy.

Note—An insured will not generally be responsible for the agents failure to pass on relevant information. Knowledge of such information is to be imputed to insurers. The insured may still be liable in contract.

Magee v Pennine Insurance Co Ltd

[1969] 2 QB 507, [1969] 2 All ER 891, [1969] 2 WLR 1278, 113 Sol Jo 303, [1969] 2 Lloyd's Rep 378, CA

Note—See further, p 816, above.

Bawden v London Edinburgh & Glasgow Assurance Co

[1892] 2 QB 534, CA
Bawden was an illiterate man and had lost the sight of one eye. Quinn, the insurer's local agent, was aware of this. Quinn prepared a proposal form for accident insurance and completed this to Bawden's dictation. The answers included a statement that Bawden was in good health, free from disease, not ruptured and had no physical infirmity. Quinn did not inform the company that Bawden had only one eye. An accident occurred and Bawden claimed on the policy. The insurers refused to indemnify.
HELD: Quinn was an agent of the company to negotiate the terms of the proposal and to induce a person who wished to insure to make the proposal.

Per Lord Esher MR: He was not merely the agent to take the piece of paper containing the proposal to the company. The company could not alter the proposal. He must accept it or decline it. Quinn, then, having authority to negotiate and settle the terms of a proposal, what happened? He went to a man who had one eye, and persuaded him to make a proposal to the company, which the company might either accept or reject. He saw that the man only had one eye. The proposal must be construed as having been negotiated and settled by the agent with a one eyed man. In that sense the knowledge of the agent was the knowledge of the company.

Holdsworth v Lancashire and Yorkshire Insurance Company

(1907) 23 TLR 521
The plaintiff was a joiner and builder. He effected insurance in respect of his liability to his workmen under the Workmen's Compensation Act 1897. The insurer's agent knew that the plaintiff was a joiner and builder. The agent filled in a proposal form which was stated to be the basis of the contract in which the plaintiff was described as a joiner. When the plaintiff got the policy he objected to being so described and the agent got sanction from the insurer's branch office to insert the words 'and builder', no communication of this was made to Head Office. A workman was injured and insurers sought to avoid liability.
HELD: (1) By receiving premiums the insurers were precluded from denying the agent's authority to contract and in those circumstances the knowledge of the agent was the knowledge of the company; (2) even if the policy hadn't been altered the company would have been liable because the contract must be treated as having been negotiated by the agent with a joiner and builder, and the knowledge of the agent must be treated as the knowledge of the company.

The brokers implied authority to bind insurers

Stockton v Mason

[1978] 2 Lloyd's Rep 430, CA
The policy holder had a policy covering a Ford Anglia car. He exchanged the car for an MG. His wife telephoned the brokers on 8 April and told them; she asked that the

MG be substituted for the Anglia as the car insured under the policy. The broker said 'Yes, that will be all right. We will see to that.' On 18 April at 3.30 pm the plaintiff was seriously injured when travelling as a passenger in the MG driven by the policy holder's son. The policy covered driving by any authorised driver. At 5.15 pm on the 18th the policy holder received a letter from the brokers written on the 17th saying cover for the MG was limited to himself only. The judge held that the brokers' remark was merely a statement that they would seek to negotiate a contract of insurance on the MG; the insurers were not liable and the brokers were liable in negligence to the policy holder's son for failing to notify the policy holder of their failure to get insurance on the desired terms.
HELD, ON APPEAL: There was a valid contract of interim insurance. A broker had implied authority to issue on behalf of the insurer or enter into as agent for the insurer contracts of interim insurance normally recorded in cover notes. In making the remark quoted the brokers were acting as agents for the insurers and not for the person wishing to be insured. Such an interim contract of insurance can be made orally and in informal colloquial language. The insurers were liable.

2 LIMITS OF COVER

Note—There is nothing in the compulsory insurance sections of the Road Traffic Act 1988 to make an insurer liable when the vehicle is being used outside the limits of the policy. But the insurer may be 'the insurer concerned' for the purposes of the Motor Insurers' Bureau Agreements (see p 783, above).

USE TO WHICH VEHICLE PUT

Sale of business to new company

Levinger v Licences and General Insurance Co Ltd

(1936) 54 Ll L Rep 68 (Eve J)
Proposer insured car to cover use in her business of milliner. Her business was taken over by a limited company of which she was chief shareholder.
HELD: Car at time of accident was on the business of the company, which had no interest in the policy. The company was not insured, nor its business.

Description of use clause

Passmore v Vulcan Boiler and General Insurance Co Ltd

(1935) 154 LT 258, 52 TLR 193, 64 Ll L Rep 92, 80 Sol Jo 167 (du Parcq J)
Policy covered assured whilst using car for the purpose of her business. Exception not liable if used otherwise than in 'description of use' clause, ie business of assured of representative and no other. Assured and another representative both employed by same company were using car on employer's business. The car was not being used for the business of the assured alone, but also the business of other employee.
HELD: Policy covered business use of assured only, and insurers not liable when used for business of any other person whether also used for business of assured or not. The

business of the other person might have been of a different kind and insurers were entitled to know exactly what business risk they were covering and the extent of the risk they were undertaking.

If the policy holder extended a courtesy to a friend or acquaintance or stranger who was carrying on some business and was assisted in carrying on that business by the use of the car, and the assured gave a lift as a matter of kindness, courtesy or charity, I think the proper view would be that the car was being used for a social purpose.

Note—See also *D H R Moody Ltd v Iron Trades*, p 826 below. In *Seddon v Binions* (below) the passage in du Parcq J's judgment summarised in the second paragraph above was considered and explained by all three members of the court. Roskill L J said that nothing in his judgment in *Seddon*'s case was intended to cast any doubt upon the applicability of that passage to a case to which it is appropriate.

Browning v Phoenix Assurance Co Ltd

[1960] 2 Lloyd's Rep 360 (Pilcher J)
The owner of a car asked the plaintiff, a garage foreman, to take his car for a long run to get the back axle oil well warmed so that it could be drained and changed: he said that if the plaintiff cared to do this on a Sunday and take his wife and family with him, he had no objection. The owner's insurance policy covered any other person who drove with his permission provided that such person should be subject to the exceptions and conditions of the policy as if he were the insured. A general exception excluded liability of the insurers while the vehicle was being used otherwise than in accordance with the 'description of use'. The latter was set out in a schedule and excluded 'use for any purpose in connection with the Motor Trade'. After the oil had been changed in the back axle the plaintiff took the car out with his brother and brother-in-law as passengers partly, as he alleged, for the pleasure of the ride and partly to check the car for any defects. Whilst on this run there was a collision with another vehicle due to his admitted negligence. The defendant company refused to indemnify him.
HELD: On the facts the plaintiff was not driving with the owner's permission since the long run which the owner asked him to make was for the purpose of draining the oil from the back axle, and that had already been done. But even if the plaintiff had been driving with the owner's permission the policy would not have covered him: he was driving for two purposes (1) the permitted purpose of taking his family for a ride, (2) a second purpose which would have been a purpose in connection with the motor trade. The plaintiff's user would thus have been for a permitted purpose and a specifically excluded purpose. In these circumstances, following *Passmore v Vulcan Boiler and General Insurance Co Ltd* the plaintiff would not be entitled to recover from the defendant.

Seddon v Binions

(1977) 122 Sol Jo 34, [1978] 1 Lloyd's Rep 381, [1978] RTR 163, CA
The defendants were father and son. The son carried on the business of carpet layer. The father helped the son in the business but was not his employee. The son had an employee named Hale. When the son was working on a job some miles from home the father brought Hale in the son's van. Hale claimed he had toothache and wanted to go home at lunchtime. It was the son's normal practice to take Hale to and from jobs. The father intended going home for lunch so it was arranged that he would take Hale in the son's Triumph car. On the journey there was a collision with another

vehicle in which the plaintiff was injured. The father had a policy on a car of his own covering him when driving other cars, restricted to use for social, domestic and pleasure purposes or in connection with his own business.
HELD: He was not covered by his policy at the time of the accident. He was driving his son's car for two purposes—his own social and domestic purposes and, in driving Hale home, for purposes of his son's business. An alternative test to apply was to look for the primary purpose, or essential character, of the journey; and in the present case it was to take the son's employee home and was not social, domestic or pleasure.

Per Megaw LJ: If there be such a primary purpose, or essential character, then the courts should not be meticulous to find some possible secondary purpose, or some in essential character, the result of which could be suggested to be that the use of the car fell outside the proper use for the purposes of which cover was given by the insurance company. If, however, there are cases in which there are, in the proper sense of the word, two 'purposes', as was the case in *Passmore v Vulcan Boiler and General Insurance Co Ltd* (above) on the finding of the arbitrator, then I have no reason to disagree in any way with the conclusion in that case as to the results that would follow.

Pailor v Co-operative Insurance Society Ltd

(1930) 38 Ll L Rep 237, CA
Car driven by employee of insured's friend on friend's business—'The Society will also similarly indemnify any relations or friend of the insured . . . whilst driving . . . with the insured's knowledge and consent.' 'The Society shall not be liable while the car is being used for other than private pleasure or professional purposes or for driving to and from the insured's place of business or for making personal business calls (excluding commercial travelling) or personal visits to the scene of his business operations.'
CONSTRUCTION: Arbitrator's finding of fact that employee was a friend of the insured.
HELD: That a 'general knowledge and consent' was sufficient to bring the friend within the ambit of the policy, but that the friend's use of the car on his own employer's business did not come within the exception to the exception clause, and that the company were therefore not liable. Appeal and cross-appeal dismissed.

Singh v Rathour, Northern Star Insurance Co Ltd, third party

[1988] 2 All ER 16, [1988] 1 WLR 422
The defendant borrowed a minibus from an association of which he was a member. The association's representative who gave permission believed the defendant wanted to use it for the purposes of the association. In fact the defendant used it to drive a party of friends to a wedding. The plaintiff, a passenger, was killed in a crash. The defendant's insurance covered him for any car provided he had the consent of the owner. Insurers sought to repudiate on the grounds that he didn't have the consent of the owner of the minibus. The trial judge's finding that the user was outside the consent given was upheld and insurers were entitled to refuse indemnity.

Jones v Welsh Insurance Corpn Ltd

[1937] 4 All ER 149, 157 LT 483, 54 TLR 22, 81 Sol Jo 886, 59 Ll L Rep 13 (Goddard J)
Assured was a motor mechanic who earned £2 14s per week. He ceased work at 5 pm. He bought five sheep and rented two acres to keep them. He had a private car policy excepting liability if used otherwise than in accordance with 'description of use'

clause, ie private purposes and use by assured in person in connection with his business . . . of motor engineer and no other . . . excluding use for carriage of goods in connection with any trade or business. Assured's brother took car and brought two sheep and two lambs to the father's house.
HELD: Assured was not keeping sheep for pleasure or for food for himself and family, but was a sheep farmer in a small way as a sideline, and it was a business, and the car was being used for carriage of goods in connection with business of sheep farming. It was not a case of physical characteristics of the goods under s 12(d) but the use of the car for business purposes and carriage of goods in connection with a business.

Farr v Motor Traders' Mutual Insurance Society

[1920] 3 KB 669, 90 LJKB 215, 123 LT 765, 36 TLR 711, CA
Plaintiff was the owner of two taxicabs which he insured with defendants in February 1918, for one year against damage caused to either of them by accidental external means. In the proposal for the policy plaintiff, in answer to a question, stated that each cab was to be driven in one shift per 24 hours. At the foot of the proposal form plaintiff stated that the above statement was true, and the policy provided that the statements in the proposal were to be the basis of the contract, and to be considered as incorporated therein. In August 1918, while one of the cabs was undergoing repair, the other cab was driven in two shifts per 24 hours for a very short time, and from that time until the accident hereinafter mentioned happened, the two cabs were driven in one shift only. In November 1918, the cab which had been driven in two shifts in August was damaged by an accident. It was at that time being driven in one shift only. In an action on the policy to recover in respect of the damage so caused, defendants contended that the statement in the proposal that the cab was to be driven in one shift per 24 hours was a warranty, and upon breach thereof the insurance came to an end.
HELD: The statement was not a warranty, but was merely descriptive of the risk, indicating that the cab, whilst being driven in more than one shift per 24 hours, would cease to be covered by the policy, but would be covered whilst being driven in one shift; and defendants were liable.

Roberts v Anglo-Saxon Insurance Association

(1927) 27 Ll L Rep 313, CA
The policy contained the following words: 'Warranted used only for the following purposes—commercial travelling'.

Per Lord Justice Banks: It does not follow at all that because it is not used on some one occasion, or on more than one occasion, for other than the described use, the policy is avoided. If the proper construction, on its language, is a description of the limitation of the liability, then the effect would be that the vehicle would be off cover during the period during which it was not being used for the warranted purpose but would come again on the cover when the vehicle was again used for the warranted purpose.

A fire broke out in the car when it was not being used for commercial purposes. The judge held that he did not attach undue importance to the word 'warranted' but when used in conjunction with 'only' then there was a condition that the vehicle should only be used for that purpose and therefore insurers were entitled to refuse indemnity.

Note—Contrast this case with *Provincial Insurance Co Ltd v Morgan*, below.

Provincial Insurance Co Ltd v Morgan

[1933] AC 240, 102 LJKB 164, 49 TLR 179, 44 Ll L Rep 275, 38 Com Cas 92, Sub nom **Morgan v Provincial Insurance Co Ltd** (1932) 148 LT 385, HL
A proposal form contained the following questions and answers. 'Q. State the nature of the goods to be carried. A. (a) The delivery of coal; (b) coal.' The vehicle was used for carrying a load of timber and 5 cwt of coal.
HELD: The questions and answers were intended to ascertain the intentions of the assured with regard to the user of the lorry and the goods to be carried therein and the answers were true, correct and complete, and there was no breach of warranty or of any condition precedent to liability.

Piddington v Co-operative Insurance Society Ltd

[1934] 2 KB 236, 103 LJKB 370, 151 LT 399, 50 TLR 311, 78 Sol Jo 278 (Lawrence J)
The insurance of a private car excluded liability when used for other than private pleasure: or for conveying goods other than personal luggage. The insured was a designer for a firm of brassworkers, and drove home from work at noon with two laths, 12 or 14 feet long, fastened lengthwise on top of the car, intended for the repair of some trellis work in his garden. The same afternoon, without removing the laths, he went on a pleasure run, and met with an accident causing fatal injuries to a pedestrian. Insurers declined liability under the policy, contending that the use was otherwise than 'solely for private purposes' as set out in the proposal form, and was 'conveying goods other than personal luggage'.
HELD: The word 'pleasure' was in contradistinction to 'business' and 'personal luggage' to 'merchandise' and the insured's garden was his pleasure and not his business, and the laths were personal luggage and not merchandise.

Lee v Poole

[1954] Crim LR 942, [1954] CLY 2948 Div Ct
Insured carried some furniture for a friend without payment.
HELD: Within the policy cover.

Note—These cases also illustrate the principle that if a car is being used for two purposes neither of which is predominant and one use is excluded then the insurer will be able to repudiate liability but the contract will not be void ab initio unless the insured warranted that it would only be put to one use (see *Provincial Insurance Co Ltd v Morgan*, above).

Use for hire or reward

Wyatt v Guildhall Insurance Co Ltd

[1937] 1 KB 653, [1937] 1 All ER 792, 106 LJKB 421, 156 LT 292, 53 TLR 389, 81 Sol Jo 358, 57 Ll L Rep 90 (Branson J)
A motor policy described the permitted use as 'for social, domestic and pleasure purposes' and excluded use for 'hiring'. The plaintiff and another were passengers in a car belonging to Wilcox. All three were going to London on the same business, the passengers had arranged to travel by train but agreed they would travel up in Wilcox's car and each pay a sum equivalent to the train fare. It was accepted that this was an

isolated incident and that Wilcox was not in the habit of using his car in this way. An accident occurred and Wyatt was injured.
HELD: The car was being used for hiring and outside the permitted use.

Bonham v Zurich General Accident and Liability Insurance Co Ltd

[1945] KB 292, [1945] 1 All ER 427, 114 LJKB 273, 172 LT 201, 61 TLR 271, 78 Ll L Rep 245
A proposal form contained the question 'Will passengers be carried for hire or reward?' and the answer was 'No'. The answers in the proposal were made the basis of the contract. The policy excluded use for hiring.

The assured habitually and regularly carried three passengers who worked at the same place. Two passengers paid 1s 2d or 1s 3d per return journey calculated on the cost of railway fares. The other never did pay.

The assured never asked the passengers for payment but the two passengers voluntarily offered him the money. He would have carried them if they had not paid anything. The assured paid for petrol, oil, tyres, insurance and other expenses of the car. The assured would have made the journeys if there were no passengers. An accident occurred and one of the passengers was killed.
HELD, ON APPEAL, per du Parcq LJ and Uthwatt J (MacKinnon LJ dissenting): Insurers were not liable. A distinction is to be drawn between 'hire' and 'reward' or the words 'or reward' would not be necessary. The assured intended to accept from the passengers a payment which he expected to be tendered and which they intended to tender. He took from them each day a sum which they never failed to pay and which he expected to receive. This was carrying passengers for reward.

The reward need not be payable under an agreement enforceable at law. 'Hire' imports an obligation to pay. 'Reward' included cases where there is no obligation to pay. All the judges in the Court of Appeal agreed the car was not being used for hire.

Note—See now s 150(1) and (2) of the Road Traffic Act 1988.

McCarthy v British Oak Insurance Co Ltd

[1938] 3 All ER 1, 159 LT 215, 82 Sol Jo 568, 61 Ll L Rep 194 (Atkinson J)
Assured, a garage proprietor, without receiving any payment, lent a car for the evening to a driver (who had at times driven a coach for him and done odd jobs for him as a mechanic) for private purposes excluding use for hire. The driver paid the assured 10s or 12s for the petrol and oil but nothing more, and the driver took two friends as passengers, and the passengers paid the driver what he had paid for the petrol and oil, and for two quarts of beer which was for the use of the driver and passengers.
HELD: Hire meant a genuine business contract for a stipulated reward. In *Wyatt*'s case the passenger agreed to pay for conveyance and the money was clear profit for the assured. Here the driver did not make anything for himself and there was nothing to constitute a legal contract for hire, and the insurers were liable.

Note—See now s 150(1) and (2) of the Road Traffic Act 1988.

Since 1975 the insurance industry has as a matter of practice regarded contributions to petrol costs alone as not falling within the scope of the 'hire or reward' exclusion. Following consultations with the Government who sought to facilitate car sharing within the terms of the

Transport Act 1980 motor insurers agreed, in 1978, to widen the previous interpretation and issued an undertaking in the following terms:
'The receipt of contributions as part of a car sharing arrangement for social or other similar purposes in respect of the carriage of passengers on a journey in a vehicle insured under a private car policy will not be regarded as constituting the carriage of passengers for hire or reward (or the use of the vehicle for hiring) provided that:
(a) the vehicle is not constructed or adapted to carry more than seven passengers (excluding the driver);
(b) the passengers are not being carried in the course of a business of carrying passengers;
(c) the total contributions received for the journey concerned do not involve an element of profit.'

Private hire

Lyons v Denscombe

[1949] 1 All ER 977, 113 JP 305, [1949] WN 257, 93 Sol Jo 389, 47 LGR 412, Div Ct
A mineworker drove his car to the colliery each morning and in the evening drove home four fellow workmen under an agreement or contract with one of them to pay 8s per week (2s each) whether they used the car or not. The car was licensed for private hire and hackney purposes. The insurance policy did not cover use for hire or reward other than private hire; which was defined as the 'letting of the vehicle supplied direct from the policy holder's garage'. He was prosecuted for (1) not being insured, (2) not holding a licence for an express carriage, and (3) not holding a road service licence. The justices found there was one contract for one fare of 8s paid weekly and not four contracts for 2s each.
HELD: The car was not used as an express carriage under s 61(1) of the 1930 Act and did not require a public service vehicle licence under s 67(1) or a road service licence under s 72(1).

Per Lord Goddard CJ: It is said that the letting of the vehicle was not direct from the policy holder's garage because it was driven to the colliery in the morning and the four men only travelled in the evening. Private hire is distinct, in my opinion, from plying for trade, that is to say, using the car as a taxi cab . . . if I wanted a car to meet me at a railway station, it has to come to the station from the garage where it is kept. If it does so it is supplied direct from the garage. It is not plying for hire. Can it make any difference for the purpose of insurance that the car is driven to the place where the hirers are going to get into it some hours before they do get into it? Admittedly, if the car came straight out of the garage to the colliery and picked up the men there, it would be letting direct from the garage. Why does it cease to be a letting direct from the garage if it gets to the colliery five minutes before the men get into it? If not, does it cease to be such a letting after half an hour or an hour elapses? Obviously not. For these reasons I think the policy was in force.

Note—The sections referred to above are all now repealed.

Social, domestic and pleasure purposes

Wood v General Accident Fire and Life Assurance Corpn Ltd

[1948] WN 430, 65 TLR 53, 92 Sol Jo 720, 82 Ll L Rep 77 (Morris J)
A Daimler car was insured for 'social, domestic and pleasure purposes'. The insured, a garage proprietor, used the car for a journey to interview a firm with the object of negotiating a contract in connection with his garage business. He was 67 years old and it was more convenient to travel in his own Daimler which was immediately available than a hired car.

The arbitrator found it was a more comfortable, pleasurable and restful way of making the journey than in a hired car, but held it was not covered by the policy.

On appeal by special case stated, the insured argued that the test was the reason for the use of the journey and not what might happen at the end, and the reason was use in a comfortable and pleasurable way.

HELD: The words were well known and well used, and in their natural, ordinary, normal and reasonable meaning, did not cover the journey. Appeal dismissed.

Orr v Trafalgar Insurance Co Ltd

(1948) 82 Ll L Rep 1, CA
The insurance policy on a motor car indemnified whilst being used solely for the purposes in the schedule—the schedule stated 'Private purposes only'. The policy defined 'Private purposes' as social, domestic and pleasure purposes and use by the insured in person travelling to and from his permanent place of business. The policy excluded liability if being used for private or public hire.

The insured was in the house of one Gallagher who carried on a private hire business when Gallagher received a telephone request for a hire. Gallagher asked the insured to do the job for him. Whilst doing so the insured's car met with an accident. The insured telephoned Gallagher who went in his car and finished the journey. The passenger asked what the charge would be and Gallagher did not make a charge because the accident caused the passenger to miss his train.

Pritchard J held that he should draw the inference that there was an implied obligation on the passenger to pay; that the use was private hire and insurers were not liable.

Upheld in Court of Appeal.

DHR Moody (Chemists) Ltd v Iron Trades Mutual Insurance Co Ltd

(1970) 115 Sol Jo 16, 69 LGR 232, [1971] 1 Lloyd's Rep 386, [1971] RTR 120 (Wrangham J)
The defendants insured the plaintiff's vehicles, the description of use under the policy being 'for social, domestic and pleasure purposes and use for the business of the insured including carriage of goods'. One of the plaintiff's employees was the Chairman of the Town Twinning Committee of Clacton Urban District Council and had borrowed a car from his employers, with their permission, to drive a delegation from a French town back to London airport. The insurers denied liability on the grounds that the vehicle was not being used for a social purpose but rather in connection with duties to the Council, ie for 'business purposes'. The judge found that the French visitors were not in England on commercial or industrial business but rather to promote the twinning of their town with Clacton the object being that their respective towns inhabitants would get to know one another and compete against each

other in games or sport. The judge considered that to be a social activity. He did not accept the contention that no activities of a local authority could be termed social. He stated: 'It seems to me that just as the activities of an individual can be divided into those which he pursues because he must in order to earn a living, which we call business, and those which he pursues of his own free will, such as social, domestic or pleasure activities, so the activities of a local authority can be either the official duties which they are by statute or convention compelled to carry out, or voluntary activities which may be, and often will be of a social character.'

In the circumstances the insurers were found liable to indemnify the plaintiff.

Whitehead v Unwins (Yorks)

(1962) Times, 1 March, [1962] Crim LR 323
A vehicle was used for carrying food for consumption by cows. The policy covered use for 'social and domestic' purposes. The justices dismissed a charge under the Road Traffic Act 1960, s 201, of using the vehicle when not covered by insurance.
HELD: On a case stated, there must be a conviction. The argument that as cows are domestic animals the carrying of food for cows is a domestic use is a complete fallacy. The fact that the vehicle was lent did not itself make the use social.

Note—See also *Seddon v Binnions*, p 820, above.

Towing/drawing a trailer

JRM (Plant) Ltd v Hodgson

[1960] 1 Lloyd's Rep 538
A motor lorry was engaged in carting rubble from a contractor's site. The contractor's foreman asked the driver as a favour to tow a cement mixer a short distance to another site along a public road. The policy had a provision excluding cover when the lorry was used for drawing a trailer 'except the towing of any one disabled mechanically propelled vehicle or any farm implement or machine not constructed or adapted for the conveyance of goods'.
HELD: 'Farm implement or machine' meant 'farm implement or farm machine' and since the cement mixer was neither the policy did not cover the use of the lorry when towing the mixer.

DRIVER NOT WITHIN POLICY

Driver in 'insured's employ'

Burton v Road Transport and General Insurance Co Ltd

(1939) 63 Ll L Rep 253 (Branson J)
Cross, a motor dealer, was insured under a Motor Traders' policy which covered, as if he were the insured, 'any person in the insured's employ'. Cross had a car to sell; in pursuance of a pre-existing arrangement between them Westwood told Cross of a possible purchaser, Goulding. Cross then commissioned Westwood to take Goulding on a demonstration run. Westwood would be, and was, paid £1 by Cross for doing the demonstration for him, whether or not he succeeded in selling the car. During the run

there was a collision in which the plaintiff, a motor cyclist, was injured. Cross's insurers refused to pay damages awarded against Westwood on the ground that he was not in Cross's employment.
HELD: It was not necessary in order to give a business effect to the policy, to restrict the meaning of 'employment' to employment under a contract of service. Cross was using Westwood to try to sell the car to someone introduced by him: in so doing he was 'employing' him. The insurers were liable under s 10 of the 1934 Act (now the Road Traffic Act 1988, ss 151 and 152).

Driving 'with consent'

Paget v Poland

(1947) 80 Ll L Rep 283 (Lewis J)
The daughter of the owner of a car working for the Ministry of Information had to drive a van of the Ministry from St Albans to Cambridge and obtained the loan of her mother's car to enable her to return. This required that a driver should take the car to Cambridge. The daughter suggested a friend Miss P, but the mother refused to allow her car to be driven by Miss P, and the mother suggested Miss M, a friend of the mother. Miss M started as driver and on the way changed places with Miss P. An accident occurred while Miss P was driving and Miss M was injured.

Miss M recovered judgment against the daughter and Miss P. Presumably the daughter was liable because Miss P was treated as her agent.

Section 1 of the policy on the mother's car read: The underwriters will indemnify under this section any licensed driver personally driving with the insured's consent any motor vehicle hereby insured.
HELD: In an action against underwriters, Miss P was not personally driving with the consent of the insured, and underwriters were not liable on the policy.

Herbert v Railway Passengers Assurance Co

[1938] 1 All ER 650, 158 LT 417, 60 Ll L Rep 143 (Porter J)
Insured (OOD) with friend in sidecar, fell ill, and allowed friend to drive. Company not liable.

Bankers and Traders Insurance Co Ltd v National Insurance Co Ltd

[1985] 1 WLR 734, 129 Sol Jo 381, [1985] 2 Lloyd's Rep 195, PC
In 1969, two pedestrians were knocked down and injured on a road in Malaysia by a car owned by Mr Kwang, which was being driven with his consent by Mr Ko. Kwang was insured by Bankers and Traders Insurance Co Ltd under a policy which provided indemnity cover to any driver authorised by the owner, provided that the driver was not indemnified under another policy. Ko was insured by National Insurance Co Ltd under a policy which provided that he would be indemnified while driving a private car which did not belong to him. The question arose as to which insurance company was on risk under the Malaysian Road Traffic Ordinance of 1958, s 80.
HELD, on appeal to the Privy Council: It was clear that Ko was the authorised driver and entitled to an indemnity under his own policy. Kwang's insurers were not on risk. It was not a case of double insurance. Ko's insurers were therefore responsible for indemnifying him against his liability to the pedestrians.

Note—See also *Sing v Rathour, Northern Star Insurance Co (Third Party)*, p 821, above.

Driving 'with permission'

Kelly v Cornhill Insurance Co Ltd

[1964] 1 All ER 321, [1964] 1 WLR 158, 108 Sol Jo 94, [1964] 1 Lloyd's Rep 1, HL (Sc)
On 11 April 1958 Michael Kelly proposed for insurance to the Cornhill Insurance Co Ltd in respect of his own car. In the proposal form he said the car would be driven by his son Kevin Kelly and that he himself had no licence to drive and did not intend having one. Insurance was granted on 26 April 1958 and was renewed for a further year on 26 April 1959. On 2 June 1959 Michael Kelly died. Neither his executrix nor anyone else told the insurers of his death until after 4 February 1960, on which date damage was caused to the car and other property in an accident whilst Kevin Kelly was driving. The latter claimed indemnity under the policy as a person 'driving the insured car . . . with the permission of the insured'. It was admitted that whilst Michael Kelly was alive Kevin had permission from him to drive the car without limitation.
HELD: The question for decision was simply whether Kevin Kelly was driving on 4 February 1960 with the permission of his father who had died on 2 June 1959: did a permission to use the car which could at any time be revoked lapse on the death of the person giving it? It had been argued for the respondents that permission necessarily involved a continuing power of control but it could not be said that continuing opportunity or ability to control was necessary, because prolonged absence or illness might negative that. In the absence of any express provision in the policy there was no reason to hold as a matter of law that a permission should automatically lapse on death of the permittor. The son was entitled to the benefit of the policy on 4 February 1960.

Disqualification of driver

General Accident Assurance Corpn v Shuttleworth

(1938) 60 Ll L Rep 301 (Humphreys J)
The condition in a policy that the assured shall not be disqualified or the company will not be liable is a limitation of the insurance cover and is outside the purview of the policy or certificate. The insured signed a proposal on 10 June 1936, and declared he had not been convicted of a motoring offence. On 5 August 1936, the assured was convicted of driving a motor cycle without an insurance certificate and disqualified for 12 months. On 11 August 1936, the assured applied to transfer the insurance to another car and signed a declaration that he had not been convicted of a motoring offence. On 5 September 1936, the company issued a cover note and insurance certificate for 14 days, instead of a certificate for 12 months as a means of obtaining payment of the additional premium of £4, in terms of the company's usual form of policy. On 16 September 1936, a third party was injured.
HELD: Risk was outside policy.
SEMBLE: (1) A motor car covers a motor cycle; (2) the false declaration invalidated the cover note.

Edwards v Griffiths

[1953] 2 All ER 874, [1953] 1 WLR 1199, 117 JP 514, 97 Sol Jo 595, 51 LGR 549, [1953] 2 Lloyd's Rep 269, Div Ct
The respondent had passed a driving test and obtained a driving licence for motor

cycles and tractors in October 1951. In 1952 he was informed by the licensing authority that as he was under supervision under the Mental Deficiencies Act, he must not drive a motor cycle. The respondent's application for renewal of driving licence was refused. His employer's certificate of insurance provided for use by any person driving with permission provided such person held a licence or had held and was not disqualified from holding or obtaining a licence.
HELD: 'Disqualified' in the certificate meant disqualified by an order of the court and not prohibited from obtaining a licence by mental or physical disability.

Mumford v Hardy

[1956] 1 All ER 337, [1956] 1 WLR 163, 100 Sol Jo 132, 54 LGR 150, [1956] 1 Lloyd's Rep 173, Div Ct
A youth born on 7 June 1939 (ie under 16) obtained a provisional licence to drive a car on 13 April 1955, expiring 12 July 1955, by falsely stating that he was born on 22 January 1938. His father permitted him to drive a car which was insured to indemnify any driver with consent holding a licence to drive such a car. The son was charged with driving uninsured on 23 April 1955, and 1 June 1955. The father was charged with permitting on 1 June 1955.

The insurers told the justices they would have considered themselves liable by reason of *Edwards v Griffiths* (above). The justices accordingly dismissed the informations.

By the Road Traffic Act 1930, s 9(2) a person under 17 years of age is prohibited from driving a car; by s 9(5) such a person shall be deemed disqualified for holding or obtaining such a licence; s 7(4) provides that a licence obtained by a disqualified person shall be of no effect.
HELD: An offence was proved on each of the three informations.

Note—Destination Table:

1930 Act	*1972 Act*	*1988 Act*
s 9(2)	s 4(1) repealed 1976	–
s 9(5)	s 96	s 101
s 7(4)	s 98(2)	s 103(2)

Unaccompanied provisional licence holder

Rendlesham v Dunne

[1964] 1 Lloyd's Rep 192, CC (Herbert J)
Dunne, who held only a provisional licence to drive, was driving Griffin's car with his permission. He was unaccompanied and the car was without 'L' plates. Griffin's insurance policy was expressed to indemnify any person driving with his permission provided that 'such person holds a licence to drive' the car. An accident having occurred, the insurers refused to indemnify Dunne.
HELD: They were bound to indemnify him. (1) It was impossible to construe the policy so as to restrict the meaning of the word 'licence' to that of a full licence. The Road Traffic Act 1960 uses the word 'licence' to include both types of licence. It cannot be said that a man has not got a licence to drive a car on the road merely because he has failed to comply with a condition upon which he has been granted a licence. (2) A condition of the policy requiring the insured to take all reasonable steps to

safeguard the car from loss and damage was not broken by allowing Dunne to drive. That condition was concerned with the physical condition of the car and did not cover damage caused by negligent driving or driving by somebody in contravention of the terms of his licence.

Unqualified employee of limited company

John T Ellis Ltd v Hinds

[1947] KB 475, [1947] 1 All ER 337, [1947] LJR 488, 176 LT 424, 63 TLR 181, 91 Sol Jo 68, 45 LGR 118, 80 Ll L Rep 231, Div Ct
A company owned a motor vehicle which was driven by a lad under 17 years of age who did not hold and never had held a driving licence and by reason of his age was not qualified to obtain one. The company had no express knowledge of these facts. The driver told the company that he held a licence and that he had already driven for several firms including one that he named. A request to the driver to produce his licence and an investigation would have disclosed the facts and the company recklessly omitted to make these inquiries.

The policy exempted from liability if a person driving with consent did not to the knowledge of the insured or his representative who gave consent hold a licence unless he had held and was not disqualified from obtaining one.
HELD: If a man deliberately shuts his eyes to the obvious, he had as much knowledge as if he were expressly told the facts to which he had closed his eyes, but it is quite another thing to say that because a man has means of knowledge of which he does not avail himself, therefore he has knowledge. If he does not know of something which it is his duty to know, and which, therefore, ought to have known, he cannot plead lack of knowledge, but knowledge and means of knowledge are not the same thing. This is an exception clause which is construed strictly. It would be for insurers to prove that the company knew the driver was unlicensed. It does not impose a duty to make inquiries. In the circumstances the policy was effective.

Note—Contrast this case with *Lester Bros (Coal Merchants) Ltd v Avon Insurance Co Ltd*, below.

Lester Bros (Coal Merchants) Ltd v Avon Insurance Co Ltd

(1942) 72 Ll L Rep 109 (Atkinson J)
The plaintiffs took out a commercial motor vehicle policy. An employee had an accident whilst driving one of the plaintiff's lorries. The employee had, to the plaintiff's knowledge, applied for a driving licence. The licence had not been received at the time of the accident. The arbitrator was not satisfied that the plaintiff knew that the licence hadn't been obtained but held that they could easily have ascertained this by enquiry of the driver. The policy excluded liability if the vehicle was:

'(b) being driven by the insured unless he (i) holds a licence to drive such vehicle or (ii) has held and is not disqualified from holding or obtaining such a licence;
(c) being driven with the general consent of the insured or his representative by any person who to the knowledge of the insured or such representative does not hold a licence to drive such a vehicle unless such a person has held and is not disqualified from holding or obtaining such a licence.'

The court held that 'being driven by the insured' in this context meant 'being driven by or on behalf of the insured'. The court also rejected the suggestion that the driver would be covered under (c) above unless the plaintiffs knew as a fact that their driver did not hold a licence. Atkinson J stated: 'The result of that from a commercial point of view would be rather startling—they have only to take good care not to make enquiry as to the driver of their lorries, and if an accident happens and it turns out the driver is not licensed, they can say: "I am very sorry, but it did not occur to me that a man would come to drive a lorry who had not got a licence and never had one; at any rate I did not know that he never had one".'

Repairer driving

Samuelson v National Insurance and Guarantee Corpn Ltd

[1984] 3 All ER 107, QBD
The motor policy issued by the defendants to the plaintiff gave indemnity against theft. The 'limitations as to use' were 'social, domestic and pleasure' only, though by General Exception 1(a)(i) 'the exclusion of use for any purpose in connection with the Motor Trade' was not to prejudice the indemnity whilst the car was 'in the custody or control of a member of the Motor Trade' for repair. General exception 1(c) excluded indemnity when the car was 'being driven by or for the purpose of being driven' in charge of any person other than the authorised driver. By reference to the certificate of insurance the only authorised driver was 'the policy holder'. A repairer who had the car for some necessary work on it drove it to the manufacturers' agents for some spare parts. He needed to take the car to the agents to ensure that the parts did fit. He parked it nearby but whilst he was away for a few minutes getting the parts the car was stolen and was never recovered. The plaintiff claimed under the policy for the loss.

The judge held that he was not entitled to indemnity. Paragraph 1(a)(i) simply declared that the limitation of use was not breached by delivering it into the custody or control of a member of the motor trade for repair. The exception 1(c) related to driving and was not affected by this. At the time of the theft the car was, for the purpose of being driven, in the charge of a person other than the authorised driver.
HELD, ON APPEAL: The judge was right in saying that clause 1(c) was not cut down by 1(a). But on the facts of this case, namely, that the repairer needed to take the car to the agents to ensure that the new parts would fit, it was, at the moment it was stolen, in the repairer's charge for the purpose of repair and not for the purpose of driving, and the indemnity was restored by General Exception 1(a)(i). Appeal allowed.

Note—See also *Browning v Phoenix*, p 820, above.

Definition of driver/more than one driver

By s 192(1) of the Road Traffic Act 1988 it is possible for more than one person to be the 'driver' of a vehicle. If one of such drivers holds a licence to drive, the exceptions clause in the insurance policy providing that the insurers shall not be liable if the insured vehicle is driven by a person not holding a driving licence does not apply, then the vehicle remains insured under the policy.

R v Wilkins

(1951) 115 JP 443, [1951] CLY 9109 Berkshire Quarter Sessions
Section 121(1) of the Road Traffic Act 1930 provided:
'"Driver", where a separate person acts as steersman of a motor vehicle, includes that person as well as any other person engaged in the driving of the vehicle and the expression "drive" shall be construed accordingly.'

There may, therefore, be more than one driver of a vehicle. If one of such drivers holds a licence to drive, the exceptions clause in the insurance policy providing that the insurers shall not be liable if the insured vehicle is driven by a person not holding a driving licence, does not apply, and the vehicle remains insured under the policy.

The appellants, brother and sister, were on a public road on a tractor. The sister, who had no driving licence, was seated in the driving seat. The brother, who had a licence, was standing behind her. Both were charged and convicted of driving a vehicle which was uninsured by reason of the fact that it was being driven by a person who did not hold a driving licence.
HELD: There were two drivers, and since one held a licence, the exceptions clause did not apply and the vehicle was insured.

Note—The definition of 'driver' is now contained in s 192(1) of the 1988 Act but is similar to the definition in s 121(1) of the 1930 Act.

R v MacDonagh

[1974] QB 448, [1974] 2 All ER 257, [1974] 2 WLR 529, 118 Sol Jo 222, CA
A motorist pushing his car with his shoulder against the door pillar and both feet on the road, controlling movement by his hand on the steering wheel, is not 'driving' within the meaning of the Road Traffic Act 1972.

McQuaid v Anderton

[1980] 3 All ER 540, [1981] 1 WLR 154, 144 JP 456, 125 Sol Jo 101, [1980] RTR 371, Div Ct
A motor vehicle was being towed by another vehicle by means of a tow rope. The appellant was sitting in the driver's seat of the towed vehicle steering by means of the steering wheel and able to operate the brakes.
HELD: He was 'driving' the vehicle within the meaning of the Road Traffic Act 1972, s 99.

Note—Section 103(1) of the 1988 Act has replaced s 99 of the 1972 Act.

Caise v Wright, Fox v Wright

[1981] RTR 49, QBD
Caise was driving a car which was towing another car of which Fox was in the driver's seat able to slow, stop and steer it to a limited extent.
HELD, following *McQuaid v Anderton* (above): Fox was 'driving' the towed car.

Burgoyne v Phillips

(1983) 147 JP 375, [1983] RTR 49, [1983] Crim LR 265, QBD, Div CT
The defendant was sitting at the wheel of his car after dropping a friend off. Assuming the ignition key was still in the ignition lock he released the handbrake and let the car

roll forward preparatory to driving away. He then realised he had no keys. The steering was locked and the engine not running. He hastily applied the brakes but the car collided with a vehicle in front, having rolled forward about 30 feet.
HELD: He was 'driving' the car. The essence of driving is the use of the driver's control to direct the movement of the car however produced. An important factor was that he had himself deliberately set the vehicle in motion.

Jones v Pratt

[1983] RTR 54, QBD
A front seat passenger, seeing a small animal run across the road, grabbed the steering wheel causing the car to go off the road and crash.
HELD: He was not 'driving' the car.

Blayney v Knight

(1975) 60 Cr App Rep 269, [1975] RTR 279, [1975] Crim LR 237, Div Ct
A taxi driver drove his car to a club to pick up a fare. He got out of the car leaving the engine running and the driver's door open; the automatic transmission lever was in 'drive' but the handbrake was on. He went to the door of the club to speak to his fare and, on turning round, saw the defendant sitting in the driver's seat talking to two men who had got into the rear seat. He went to the car and tried to pull the defendant out of the driver's seat. There was a struggle and the car moved forward along the road. The driver fell off on to the road and the rear wheel passed over his legs. The defendant was charged with various offences including careless driving and driving when not insured. The justices accepted the defendant's evidence that he had not intended to drive and that his foot must accidentally have pressed the accelerator.
HELD, ON APPEAL: He was not 'driving'. Following the test applied in *R v MacDonagh* (above) an activity was not 'driving' if it was not driving in any ordinary sense of the word. It was not a case where a person was consciously seeking the movement of the car in some way and it was thus not 'driving'.

Car hirers policy

Haworth v Dawson

(1946) 80 Ll L Rep 19 (Lewis J)
Insurers issued a policy to G & K Hire, indemnifying them and any person hiring a car who completed a proposal form which was the basis of the contract and who was not an excluded hirer. A hirer was excluded unless (1) he was a person whom G & K Hire had satisfied themselves by an actual driving test was a qualified, careful and competent driver; (2) he had completed a proposal form; (3) he held a current driving licence which was continuous for at least 12 months and free from any endorsements. The proposal form required that the hirer should never have been prosecuted under the Motor Car or Road Traffic Acts for any offence thereunder; had never had a licence endorsed or suspended; had not been involved in any motor accidents of any kind whatever during the prior 12 months; and had never been refused insurance nor the renewal of any policy issued. The proposal form required G & K Hire to warrant that (1) they had tested the hirer and satisfied themselves of his capability to drive by causing him to drive the car on the highway in their presence; (2) to examine the hirer's driving licence and warrant it had been issued for more than twelve months

and was free from endorsements; and (3) that the car was in sound condition and working order. One Dawson hired a car from G & K Hire, and injured a third party, who sued Dawson and G & K Hire. Judgment was given against Dawson and the action was adjourned to join the insurers as defendants. It was admitted Dawson was a man of straw, and G & K Hire admitted they were liable under *Monk v Warbey*. Dawson's licence was endorsed for speeding in 1937 and again in 1938; he had had two accidents; G & K Hire did not give him any test.

Insurers denied that Dawson or G & K Hire were covered by the policy and that s 10 of the 1934 Act therefore did not apply.

HELD: Dawson was an excluded hirer and insurers were not liable.

On the question of costs, G & K Hire contended that the insurers had been wrongly joined, as there could have been no cause of action against them at the date of the writ, and the plaintiff ought to have issued a fresh writ, but the court held they had been party to the proceedings without raising any objection, and made an order in the Sanderson form that G & K Hire pay the costs of insurers.

Note—Section 10 of the 1934 Act is now effectively replaced by ss 151 and 152 of the 1988 Act.

Evans v Lewis

(1964) 108 Sol Jo 259, [1964] 1 Lloyd's Rep 258, Div Ct

The defendant was charged with using a motor vehicle on a road without there being in force a policy of insurance in respect of third party risks contrary to the Road Traffic Act 1960, s 201 (now s 143 of the 1988 Act). At the time of the offence he was driving a car hired from a car-hire garage. There was a policy in force issued by insurers to the garage to cover their vehicles when out on hire. It included the words 'This policy is only to cover any vehicle . . . subject . . . to the following conditions (a) that the insured shall verify . . . that the hirer is not among the excluded persons enumerated below . . . (b) publicans . . . (c) the Company's form of proposal for hirer driving insurance shall be completed and signed by each hirer'. The defendant was a publican but declared in the proposal form that he was a printer. Relying on *Durrant v MacLaren*, (p 799, above) he claimed that he was insured by virtue of s 207 of the Act (ss 151 and 152 of the 1988 Act) until proceedings had been taken under the section by the insurer and this had not been done.

HELD, ON APPEAL from a dismissal of the charge: This case was not the same as *Durrant*'s. Here there was no contract of insurance between the defendant and the insurance company and the document he completed was wrongly called a proposal form. The defendant was never covered by the insurance policy, for it specifically excluded publicans: in such circumstances s 207 did not apply.

SALE OF VEHICLE

Vehicle sold

Rogerson v Scottish Automobile and General Insurance Co Ltd

(1931) 146 LT 26, 48 TLR 17, 75 Sol Jo 724, 41 Ll L Rep 1, HL

The appellant effected motor insurance on a Lancia car. Shortly afterwards he exchanged the car for another of a similar type. He had an accident in the new car and sought an indemnity. The contract included the following clause: 'This insurance shall cover legal liability as aforesaid of the assured in respect of the use by the insured of any motor car, provided that such car is at the time of the accident being used instead of "the insured car".'

Per Lord Buckmaster: To me this policy depends upon the hypothesis that there is, in fact, an insured car. When once the car which is the subject of the policy is sold, the owner's rights in respect of it ceases as the policy so far as the car is concerned is at an end.

Tattersall v Drysdale

[1935] 2 KB 174, 104 LJKB 511, 153 LT 75, 51 TLR 405, 79 Sol Jo 418, 52 Ll L Rep 21 (Goddard J)
A policy (third party) contained the following clause: 'Subject to the terms and conditions of this policy, this section is extended to cover: The insured whilst personally driving for private purposes any other private motor car not belonging to the insured in respect of which no indemnity is afforded the insured by any other insurances applying to such car, provided always that the car or cars hereby insured shall not be in use at the same time.'

The insured sold the car referred to in the policy, and after the sale had an accident whilst driving a car lent to him.
HELD: The policy was in respect of the ownership and use of a particular car, and the clause was expressly stated to be an extension clause; the insured had ceased to be interested in the subject matter of the insurance and the extension fell with the rest of the policy.

Wilkinson v General Accident Insurance Corpn Ltd

[1967] 2 Lloyd's Rep 182, Manchester Assizes
Middleton, a motor dealer, acted as agent of the defendants to procure insurance business. He had authority to issue cover notes; insurance certificates and policies would be issued by the defendants themselves. The plaintiff had a car insured under a policy issued by the defendants through Middleton's agency. The policy had the usual extension to cover the holder when driving a car not owned by him. In October 1961 he sold the car and Middleton witnessed the hire purchase agreement. In December 1961 Middleton told the plaintiff that his policy would expire if a further premium was not paid. Thereupon the plaintiff paid a year's premium and received in due course a new certificate, which referred to the car which he had sold in October. He did not buy another car but occasionally used his brother-in-law's car. In September 1962 he had an accident whilst doing so. He claimed indemnity under the policy. In this action his counsel conceded that in the ordinary way where an insured parts with the car insured the policy ceases to have effect (*Tattersall v Drysdale*), but he contended that as Middleton, the defendants' agent, had known of the sale of the car and yet had invited renewal some weeks later the defendants were estopped from denying that the plaintiff was covered.
HELD: This was not correct. Middleton had obtained knowledge of the sale of the car in his capacity as a motor dealer, not insurance agent, and his knowledge so obtained was not to be imputed to the defendants. Once the car was sold the policy was void: the plaintiff knew Middleton's authority was limited to issuing cover notes and receiving premiums. It would not be possible for such an agent to effect so fundamental a change in the policy as to give general cover to the plaintiff when driving cars belonging to others after he had disposed of his own.

Boss v Kingston

[1963] 1 All ER 177, [1963] 1 WLR 99, 106 Sol Jo 1053, 61 LGR 109, Div Ct, QBD
Boss was driving Hansford's motor cycle with Hansford on the pillion. Hansford's insurance was effective only when Hansford was driving. Boss had a policy in respect of a Triumph motor cycle which he had sold a fortnight before. This policy afforded cover to Boss when riding 'any motor cycle described in the schedule' and also whilst riding any other motor cycle 'not belonging to him . . . as though such motor cycle were a motor cycle described in the schedule'. The schedule contained particulars of the Triumph motor cycle only. They were charged with using a motor cycle on a road when there was not in force a policy of insurance in relation to the user of that vehicle contrary to the Road Traffic Act 1960, s 201 (now s 143 of the 1988 Act). The justices convicted on the ground that Boss's policy lapsed when he sold the Triumph because he then ceased to have an insurable interest in the vehicle to which the policy related.
HELD: On a case stated: (1) As Boss's policy, unlike those considered in *Rogerson v Scottish Automobile* (p 835, above) and *Tattersall v Drysdale* (p 836, above), was in respect of third-party risks only there was no need for him to have an insurable interest in the vehicle and the justices' reasoning was wrong. (2) The decisive question was whether the policy provided two wholly independent indemnities, ie one when riding the Triumph and the other when riding another motor cycle, or whether the second was dependent on the first and lapsed with it. For three reasons the policy could not be construed as providing two separate indemnities: (a) the premium was fixed by reference to the named vehicle; (b) the natural interpretation of the second indemnity was to effect temporary cover whilst the named vehicle was out of use; (c) condition 5 of the policy requiring the insured to keep the Triumph in efficient condition was a condition precedent to liability. (3) Section 201 requires the driver of a motor vehicle to have a legally binding policy of insurance in force. It was no defence to bring evidence, as was done in this case, that the insurers would have met any claim. The conviction was right though for the wrong reasons.

Peters v General Accident Fire and Life Assurance Corpn Ltd

[1938] 2 All ER 267, 158 LT 476, 54 TLR 663, 82 Sol Jo 294, 36 LGR 583, 60 Ll L Rep 311, CA
A sold his van to B and handed over the insurance policy which covered any person driving with assured's consent or permission. Plaintiff obtained judgment against B and took proceedings against insurers under s 10. Part of the purchase price remained owing on sale.
HELD: (1) Purchaser was not driving with consent or permission of assured, as the van was purchaser's own property. (2) Assured was not entitled to assign the policy. It is a contract of personal indemnity and insurers cannot be compelled to accept responsibility of a person who may be quite unknown to them. The policy was one in which there was inherent a personal element of such a character as to make it quite impossible to say that it was assignable at the volition of the assured.

The risk that A is going to incur liability by driving his motor car, or persons authorised by A, is one thing. The risk that B will incur or persons authorised by B may be a totally different thing. Insurers made inquiries as to the driving record of proposer. A good record may be accepted. A bad record may be refused, or a higher premium required.

Smith v Ralph

[1963] 2 Lloyd's Rep 439, Div Ct
On 15 March 1963 the respondent bought a car from Davies, who handed him a certificate of insurance issued by motor insurers to Davies valid from 25 February 1963 to 24 February 1964. The respondent was charged with using the car on 13 April 1963 when uninsured. He produced the certificate issued to Davies which was expressed to cover not only the policy holder but any other person who was driving on the policy holder's order or with his permission.
HELD: Any permission or authority given by the policy holder Davies could not extend beyond the time of the sale when he ceased to be a policy holder in the sense of having any insurable interest. The respondent was not covered and there must be a conviction.

Vehicle bought on approval

Bullock v Bellamy

(1940) 67 Ll L Rep 392 (Cassels J)
The plaintiff had obtained judgment against a Mr Borrett in an action arising from a collision caused by Mr Borrett's negligent driving. The plaintiff sought to recover the judgment sum against Borrett's insurers. Borrett had insurance in respect of a Morris and his insurance extended to any vehicle personally belonging to him. The policy also covered him whilst personally driving for pleasure purposes any other motor car not belonging to him and not hired to him under any hire-purchase agreement. At the time of the accident he was driving a Chrysler. Borrett maintained that he was driving this car on approval and that he had paid the seller £10 by way of security. The seller said that the purchase had been completed and the £10 was a deposit. The judge accepted that at the time of the accident Borrett had not purchased the vehicle and therefore the vehicle was covered by the 'any other car' provision.

3 BREACH OF CONDITION

ONUS OF APPROVING BREACH OF CONDITION

Note—The burden of proving that a condition has been broken lies on the insurers and will only be shifted to the insured if clear words are used.

Bond Air Services Ltd v Hill

[1955] 2 QB 417, [1955] 2 All ER 476, [1955] 2 WLR 1194, 99 Sol Jo 370, [1955] 1 Lloyd's Rep 488 (Lord Goddard CJ)
An aircraft insurance policy contained the following general conditions:
General Condition 8: The observance and performance by the insured of the conditions of this policy as far as they contain anything to be observed or performed by the insured are of the essence of the contract and are conditions precedent to the insured's right to recover hereunder.
Condition 7: The insured and all persons in his employment or for whom he is responsible shall duly observe the statutory orders, regulations and directions relating to air navigation for the time being in force.

An aeroplane insured under the policy crashed and the insures contended that as the policy provides that the observance of the conditions is a condition precedent to the insured's right to recover it is for the insured to prove observance so that the onus is shifted.

Per Lord Goddard CJ: I do not think it can be doubted that, ordinarily, it is for the underwriter to prove a breach of condition, at least where he is not contending that the policy is void on the ground that there has been a breach of a condition precedent to the formation of the policy. So, too, it is for him to prove an exception. The difference between a condition and an exception is that the former places some duty or responsibility on the assured, while the latter restricts the scope of the policy.

As to the insurers' contention he deemed this decided by the decision in *Stebbing v Liverpool and London Globe Insurance Co Ltd* [1917] 2 KB 433. In that case there was also a provision that compliance with the conditions should be a condition precedent to any liability on the part of the insurer and the court decided that the burden of proving the falsity of an answer which amounted to a breach of warranty was on the insurer.

Per Lord Goddard CJ: The parties to a policy can use words which will relieve insurers of the onus and cast it on the assured, as they may with regard to any other matter affecting an insurer's liability. But, in my opinion, much clearer words than are used here would be necessary to change what I think, certainly for a century and probably for much longer, has always been regarded as a fundamental principle of insurance law, namely, that it is for the insurers who wish to rely on a breach of condition to prove it.

CONDITION OF VEHICLE

Damaged or unsafe condition/efficient condition/safeguarding from loss or damage

Barrett v London General Insurance Co

[1935] 1 KB 238, 104 LJKB 15, 152 LT 256, 51 TLR 97, 78 Sol Jo 898, 50 Ll L Rep 99 (Goddard J)
By a policy of motor car insurance the defendants agreed to indemnify the assured against third party risks, 'liability in respect of any accident while driving the car in an unsafe or unroadworthy condition' being excluded.
HELD: Applying the principle of marine insurance that there is an implied warranty that a ship is seaworthy at the time of sailing, but no warranty that she shall continue seaworthy throughout the voyage, the policy must be taken to mean that, for the assured to be covered by it, the car must be roadworthy when it set out on its journey but need not continue to be roadworthy throughout the journey. An assignee of the assured was, therefore, entitled to recover in an action against the defendants on the policy where the defendants (on whom lay the onus of proving unroadworthiness) failed to prove that the car was unroadworthy when it began its journey and only showed that, by reason of a defective brake, it was unroadworthy at the time of the accident.

Note—But the reasoning of Goddard J was disapproved in *Trickett v Queensland Insurance Co Ltd*, below.

Trickett v Queensland Insurance Co Ltd

[1936] AC 159, 105 LJPC 38, 154 LT 228, 52 TLR 164, 80 Sol Jo 74, 53 Ll L Rep 255, PC

A general exceptions clause in a private motor vehicle insurance policy provided that: 'No liability shall attach to the company under this policy in respect of . . . any personal accident to the insured occurring: (1) While any motor vehicle in connection with which indemnity is granted under this policy is: (c) Being driven in a damaged or unsafe condition.'

The insured, while driving at night a motor car covered by the policy, was involved in a collision with another motor car and was killed. At and about the time of the accident the lights of his motor car were not shining. On a claim under the policy by the insured's daughter as assignee of the rights under the policy from the legal personal representative of the insured:

HELD: At the time of the accident the motor car driven by the insured was in a damaged or unsafe condition within the meaning of the exceptions clause, and that the insurance company was accordingly relieved from liability under the policy irrespective of whether or not the insured was aware at the time of the accident of the damaged or unsafe condition of the car. The terms of the exceptions clause were unambiguous and plain, and there was no justification for supplementing them by adding 'to the knowledge of the driver', or for reforming the contract into which the insured had entered.

The position of a motor car on land cannot be assimilated to that of a ship at sea and the same code of law rigidly applied to both cases so as to make the exceptions clause to the policy only applicable where the motor vehicle was in a damaged or unsafe condition at the beginning of its journey. Such an argument based on the identity of the conditions which govern the seaworthiness of a ship at sea and the roadworthiness of a motor car on land is unsound.

Reasoning of Goddard J to the contrary in *Barrett v London General Insurance Co Ltd* [1935] 1 KB 238 disapproved. Judgment of the Court of Appeal of New Zealand (1932) NZLR 1727 affirmed.

Liverpool Corpn v T and H R Roberts

[1964] 3 All ER 56, [1965] 1 WLR 938, 109 Sol Jo 510, [1964] 2 Lloyd's Rep 219 (Cumming-Bruce J)

The defendant firm, who were motor coach proprietors and operators, were insured against third-party risks under a policy containing the following condition: 'The insured shall take all due and reasonable precautions to safeguard the property insured and to keep it in a good state of repair. The underwriters shall not be liable for damage or injury caused through driving the motor vehicle in an unsafe condition either before or after the accident.' An accident occurred due to the brakes of the defendants' motor coach failing to stop the vehicle within a reasonable distance. A motor engineer inspected the vehicle and found the brake linings worn and the servo mechanism defective due to neglect over a period of months. The firm's business was managed by T. Roberts who relied on a qualified mechanic G. Roberts to deal with maintenance. The firm had no system of written reports on maintenance and no instructions were given for periodical inspection or overhaul of braking systems.

HELD: (1) The two sentences of the condition were not separate obligations so as to create an absolute obligation by the second sentence to keep the vehicle in safe condition. The second sentence was merely an expression of the consequences of a failure to fulfil the duty imposed by the first sentence. The wording of the condition in *Trickett v Queensland Insurance Co* (above) was quite different. In the present case the fact that the vehicle was objectively in an unsafe condition irrespective of knowledge or want of precautions on the part of the insured would not be enough to constitute a breach. (2) Applying *Woolfall and Rimmer v Moyle* (below) the duty under the policy to keep the vehicle in a good state of repair was personal to the defendants and a casual act of neglect by an employee would not amount to a breach of it: but on the facts the defective condition of the vehicle was due to the failure of T. Roberts to impose or exercise any system for periodical inspection and the condition had been broken.

Brown v Zurich Accident and Liability Insurance Co

[1954] 2 Lloyd's Rep 243 (Sellers J)
The claimant was the owner of a Fordson van insured with the respondents under a comprehensive motor car policy. The van was involved in a collision in December 1950. The tyres of both front wheels were completely devoid of tread though not worn down to the canvas at any point. The collision was due to the van going into an uncontrollable skid on an icy road. The tyres were inspected by the police after the accident but no proceedings were taken by the police under reg 71 of the 1947 regulations.The skid might have occurred even if the front tyres had adequate treads. The respondents contended that the claimant was in breach of the condition requiring him to maintain the vehicle in an efficient condition and was therefore not entitled to recover. Fulfilment of the policy condition was a condition precedent to liability. The arbitrator held that the policy requirement was to take all reasonable steps to safeguard from loss or damage and maintain the vehicle in efficient condition; that the smooth state of the front tyres made the vehicle inefficient and the claimant had failed to take reasonable steps to maintain in efficient condition.
HELD: 'Efficient condition' meant 'roadworthy'. The finding of fact by the arbitrator that the tyres were dangerous and made the vehicle unsafe and inefficient in condition, could not be disturbed by the court. 'Vehicle' includes tyres. *Woolfall and Rimmer v Moyle* (p 847, below) not applicable. Award for respondents upheld.

Conn v Westminster Insurance Association Ltd

[1966] 1 Lloyd's Rep 407, CA
The plaintiff was driver and owner of a taxicab for the use of which the defendants issued an insurance policy covering third-party claims and damage. Condition 5 of the policy said 'The Policy holder shall take all reasonable steps to safeguard from loss or damage and maintain in efficient condition the vehicle' insured. Condition 1 made the due observance and fulfilment of the conditions of the policy a condition precedent to the insurers' liability under the policy. The plaintiff was driving the cab when it veered off the roadway into some railings and was damaged beyond repair. After the accident the police found both front tyres were bare of tread and one brake shoe was worn down to the metal. The defendants refused to meet claims under the policy, relying on condition 5. The cause of the accident was not established but there was no evidence that it was due to the condition of the brakes or tyres.
HELD: (1) The words 'efficient condition' in the context of condition 5 meant 'roadworthy condition'. (2) On the plaintiff's evidence that he noticed no symptoms of wear in the brakes, and bearing in mind that the actual state of the brakes could not be ascertained without dismantling them, the defendants had not shown a failure on the part of the plaintiff to take all reasonable steps to maintain his brakes. (3) Unlike

the brakes the state of the tyres was plain for anyone to see: having no tread they were unroadworthy and the plaintiff was in breach of condition 5. (4) It was irrelevant whether any breach of condition 5 caused the accident. The only question was whether there was a breach of the condition. There was a breach and the plaintiff could not succeed.

Jones and James v Provincial Insurance Co Ltd

(1929) 46 TLR 71, 35 Ll L Rep 135 (Rowlatt J)
The policy contained a condition that 'the assured shall take all reasonable steps to maintain such vehicle in efficient condition', and it provided that the observance of the conditions should be a condition precedent to the liability of the insurers. The claimants removed the foot-brake from the vehicle, leaving only a hand-brake, and in this state of affairs the vehicle caused damage, and was itself damaged, in an accident, but the exact cause of the accident could not be ascertained.
HELD: The condition was a condition precedent and as it had been broken, the insurers were not liable on the policy.

New India Assurance Co Ltd v Yeo Beng Chow

[1972] 3 All ER 293, [1972] 1 WLR 786, 116 Sol Jo 373, [1972] 1 Lloyd's Rep 479, [1972] RTR 356, PC
Insurers issued a motor policy to the respondent insured. It was in the form of a comprehensive policy, but cover was restricted to third party liability only by deleting section I of the policy which indemnified against loss of or damage to the insured vehicle. The remaining section indemnified against liability in respect of personal injury to any person or damage to property of third parties. The policy contained conditions of which condition 3 required the insured to 'take all reasonable steps to safeguard the vehicle from loss or damage and to maintain the vehicle in efficient condition . . . '. After a collision in which a motor cyclist was killed the insured's vehicle was found by a vehicle examiner not to have been kept in an efficient and roadworthy condition. The insurers, in conformity with the compulsory insurance legislation, paid the damages and costs awarded against the insured for the death of the motor cyclist and then claimed these sums from the insured for breach of condition 3. It was argued on his behalf, and accepted by the Federal Court of Malaysia, that, section I of the policy having been deleted, condition 3 could not survive unaffected; that as loss or damage was not covered by the policy, so much of the condition as required the insured to safeguard the vehicle from loss or damage could have no application and that the condition had been 'mutilated'.
HELD: This was not right. It did not follow from a limitation of the cover provided by the policy that any alteration was to be implied in the conditions precedent contained in the policy. Insurance companies can insert such conditions as they choose and if the conditions inserted are accepted by the insured, they are binding on him. There is no obligation on an insurance company to relate the conditions to particular aspects of the policy.

Overloading—passengers

Clarke v National Insurance and Guarantee Corpn Ltd

[1964] 1 QB 199, [1963] 3 All ER 375, [1963] 3 WLR 710, 107 Sol Jo 573, [1963] 2 Lloyd's Rep 35, CA

The plaintiff was the owner of a Ford Anglia four-seater car for which a motor policy was issued to him by the defendants, an insurance company. A term of the policy excluded liability whilst the car was 'being driven in an unsafe or unroadworthy condition'. The plaintiff was driving the car with eight adult passengers in it when it collided with another car whilst descending a steep hill. The judge found that by reason of the overloading the steering, braking and control of the car were seriously impaired. The defendants refused to meet claims arising from the accident.

HELD, ON APPEAL: The defendants were not liable under the policy. Maritime cases dealing with the warranty of seaworthiness, though by no means governing the matter, are of some assistance; in such cases it has been held that overloading or bad stowage can render a vessel unseaworthy. At the time of the accident the vehicle was unroadworthy through being overloaded and the exception clause applied.

Per Harman LJ: I think that one must regard the car as it was as it proceeded along the road, not look at it empty before it was loaded up and say: This was a safe and mechanically sound car. The words which are important for this purpose are 'being driven' and, when it was being driven it was, by reason of overloading, just as in the ship cases, rendered unsafe and unroadworthy.

Houghton v Trafalgar Insurance Co Ltd

[1954] 1 QB 247, [1953] 2 All ER 1409, [1953] 3 WLR 985, 97 Sol Jo 831, [1953] 2 Lloyd's Rep 503, CA

On 10 March 1951, plaintiff bought a 1939 Morris private saloon car. He signed a proposal form which contained a marginal note that 'All policies exclude legal liability to passengers', and obtained a cover note containing the words 'Full comprehensive' which incorporated the proposal form and was subject to the terms and conditions of the company's policy of insurance. The car had two bucket seats at the front. The back seat was for two passengers but had a centre arm which could be raised to make room for a further passenger. An accident occurred on 18 March 1951, involving damage to car, damage to property of third parties and injury to passengers. At the time of the accident there were five passengers and the driver. The policy was issued on 9 April 1951, and excluded passenger liability. Insurers contended (1) that the car was conveying a load in excess of that for which it was constructed, in which case liability was excluded by the policy; and (2) the insurance did not cover liability to passengers. There was no evidence from the makers of the load the car was constructed to carry. The car had a boot but was not carrying any luggage. The weight of the six persons in the car was 62 stones 4 lb.

HELD: As to (1) the words were inapt for a private car or in relation to passengers. Overloading was not the same thing as overcrowding. The dictionary meanings of 'load' are—'weight, carriage, act of loading, that which is laid on either a person on an animal to be carried'. The load is not in excess of the load for which the car was constructed unless the load carried, whether it be passengers, luggage or both, is in excess of the total load for which the car is constructed. Here it is not. Verdict for plaintiff on this point.

As to (2), the marginal words were part of the proposal form and the cover note incorporated the proposal form and the proposal was for an insurance excluding legal liability to passengers. Defendants succeeded on this point. Plaintiff was entitled to indemnity in respect of damage to car and to the building but not passenger liability: [1953] 2 Lloyd's Rep 18 (Gorman J).

The company appealed on the first point. Appeal dismissed.

Per Somervill LJ: It would need the plainest possible words if it were desired to exclude the insurance cover by reason of the fact that there was at the back one passenger more than the seating accommodation. I hope any company will print their definition in red ink when the policy is inapplicable when an extra passenger is carried.

Per Denning LJ: If the clause had the meaning contended for, I would regard it was almost a trap.

Per Romer LJ: If this provision is applied to a private motor car, I have not the least idea what it means.

DUTY TO NOTIFY INSURERS

'Detailed particulars'

Cox v Orion Insurance Co Ltd

[1982] RTR 1, CA

The plaintiff was issued with a motor insurance policy by the defendants whereby it was a condition precedent to their liability that he should give notice and deliver detailed particulars of any accident, loss and damage. Whilst the plaintiff was driving the car it collided with another vehicle and was damaged. He claimed under the policy but declared that someone else was driving the car at the time of the collision. Later he made a claim for theft in respect of the same incident. The defendants repudiated liability under the policy. The plaintiff had been convicted of various road traffic offences as being the driver at the time of the collision.

HELD: The defendants were entitled to repudiate. The plaintiff was in breach of the condition precedent in that they had not been given detailed particulars of the collision. *Lickiss v Milestone Motor Policies* (above) distinguished.

Note—See also *Lickiss v Milestone Motor Policies* at Lloyd's, p 815, above.

'As soon as possible'

Verelst's Administratrix Motor Union Insurance Co Ltd

[1925] 2 KB 137, 94 LJKB 659, 133 LT 364, 41 TLR 343, 69 Sol Jo 412 (Roche J)

A policy of insurance covering (inter alia) the death of the insured by accident, contained the following condition: 'In the case of any accident, injury, damage or loss . . . the insured or the insured's representative for the time being shall give notice . . . in writing to the head office of the company of such accident, injury, damage or loss as soon as possible after it has come to the knowledge of the insured or of the insured's representative for the time being.'

During the currency of the policy namely, on 14 January 1923, the insured was killed in a motor accident in India. Knowledge of her death reached her personal representative in England within a month, but the personal representative did not know of the existence of the policy of insurance until January 1924. Notice was given to the insurance company as soon as possible thereafter. The insurance company repudiated liability on the ground that notice was not given 'as soon as possible' within the meaning of the condition.

HELD: In considering whether notice was given 'as soon as possible' within the meaning of the condition, all existing circumstances must be taken into account, including the available means of knowledge of the insured's personal representative of the existence of the policy and the identity of the insurance company; and the arbitrator, to whom the dispute had been submitted, was entitled to find that notice had been given 'as soon as possible'.

Allen v Robles

[1969] 3 All ER 154, [1969] 1 WLR 1193, 113 Sol Jo 484, [1969] 2 Lloyd's Rep 61, CA

The defendant took out an insurance policy with the third party, a French insurance company, for the use of his motor car. On 9 April he collided with the plaintiff's house, causing damage. The policy contained a condition which relieved the company of liability to the insured if he failed to give notice within five days of having knowledge of a claim. The defendant received a letter from the plaintiff on 18 April claiming damages, but he did not report the claim to the company until some date in August. The company's solicitors wrote the defendant's solicitors on 10 August, saying their clients reserved their position under the policy. Shortly afterwards they wrote the plaintiff's solicitors that the company was not indemnifying the defendant but did not write the defendant's solicitors to this effect until 29 November.

HELD: There was a breach of condition and the insurers had not lost their right to rely on it merely by their delay in notifying the defendant. The position was that when the insurers discovered in August (1) that there was a claim and (2) that the defendant was in breach of his condition they were in a position then either to elect whether to repudiate or accept liability or it was open to them to delay their decision particularly in view of the letter of 10 August. Mere lapse of time would only operate against them if the insured was thereby prejudiced or if rights of third parties intervened or the delay was so long as to be evidence that they had accepted liability. None of these possibilities arose in the present case.

Note—See also *Pioneer Concrete (UK) Ltd v National Employers Mutual Insurance Association Ltd* [1985] 2 All ER 395.

Condition will also bind a driver who is not the policyholder.

Austin v Zurich General Accident and Liability Insurance Co Ltd

[1945] KB 250, [1945] 1 All ER 316, 114 LJKB 340, 172 LT 174, 61 TLR 214, 78 Ll L Rep 185, CA

The plaintiff, Austin, was insured with the Bell Assurance Association, and was driving a car belonging to Aldridge, who was insured with the Zurich Insurance Co. Aldridge and one Nicholson were passengers in the car which met with an accident. Aldridge was killed and Nicholson injured. The accident occurred on 23 May 1938. By two informations dated 22 June 1938, Austin was charged with dangerous driving and careless driving. The summonses were returnable on 20 July. Austin gave no notice to the Zurich Co of these impending prosecutions.

The Bell settled a claim by Aldridge's executors for £4,000 and costs and a claim by Nicholson for £305 and costs. The Bell in the name of Austin as plaintiff sued the Zurich for these sums, claiming in right of subrogation.

The Zurich policy provided indemnity to any person driving the vehicle with the insured's (ie Aldridge's) permission subject to the terms of the policy. It was a condition of the policy that notice should be given to the insurers as soon as possible after an accident or of an impending prosecution.

HELD: (1) There was a right to sue in subrogation, apart from the right of one insurer to claim in contribution from another. (2) Austin was entitled to sue the Zurich though not named in their policy. Subsection (4) of s 36 of the 1930 Act applied. This subsection did not include the words 'in respect of a liability required to be covered by a policy issued under this section', which appear in s 10 of the 1934 Act, and is not confined to a liability required to be covered by s 36. (3) Each insurer (subject to (5) below) was liable for 50%. (4) The Zurich cover was subject to the fulfilment of the policy conditions by Austin, and one condition required notice in writing immediately if the insured shall have knowledge of any impending prosecution. Austin could have obtained information of the provisions of the Zurich policy, and he had not fulfilled the condition. On this ground only, judgment was for the Zurich with one-third of the costs: [1944] 2 All ER 243, 77 Ll L Rep 409 (Tucker J).

ON APPEAL: As to subrogation and double insurance: the plaintiff having been completely indemnified by one insurer, was not entitled to claim on the principle of subrogation. The claim would be by and in the name of that insurer against the other insurer for contribution on the principle of double insurance.

As to s 36(4): the subsection gave Austin a right to sue the Zurich company but in so doing he was claiming a benefit under a document to which he was not a party. A person who claims the benefit of a document in that way is bound to take it as he finds it. He cannot claim the benefit of anything which the document gives him without complying with its terms.

Note—Section 36(4) of the 1930 Act is now s 148(7) of the Road Traffic Act 1988; s 10 of the 1934 Act is ss 151 and 152 of the 1988 Act; and s 36 is now s 145 of the 1988 Act.

Impossibility of compliance

Re Coleman's Depositories v Life and Health Assurance Association

[1907] 2 KB 798, 76 LJKB 865, 97 LT 420, 23 TLR 638, CA

On 28 December 1904, the assured signed a proposal form for an Employer's Liability policy and a cover note was issued which did not contain any conditions. On 3 January 1905 a policy was issued and delivered to the assured on 9 January 1905, in force from 1 January. The policy contained a condition requiring immediate notice of accident which was of the essence of the contract. On 2 January 1905, an accident occurred to a workman which was believed slight, and no notice given. Dangerous symptoms supervened. Notice was given on 14 March, and the workman died on 15 March.

HELD: The assured did not know and had no opportunity of knowing of the existence of the condition at the date of the accident, the condition was one with which it was impossible to comply, and the policy did not impose a condition on the assured in respect of this accident, and the assured was entitled to indemnity.

Note—It is now common practice for the cover note to contain a statement that it is issued subject to the conditions of the policy.

REPUGNANCY OF CONDITIONS

Woolfall and Rimmer Ltd v Moyle

[1942] 1 KB 66, [1941] 3 All ER 304, 111 LJKB 122, 166 LT 49, 58 TLR 28, 86 Sol Jo 63, CA

An employer's liability policy issued to a limited company contained the condition: 'The assured shall take reasonable precautions to prevent accidents and to comply with all statutory obligations.'

The purchase and supply of timber for scaffolding was left entirely to the foreman, who was competent and skilled. Scaffolding was erected and a ledger broke, injuring workmen. The foreman admitted he had no suitable timber available.

HELD, in the Court of Appeal: The assured had taken reasonable precautions by employing a competent foreman. Insurers could not say, I will insure you against negligence on condition that you are not negligent. They could not grant an indemnity with one hand and take it away with the other, but could say the assured should not carry on business in a reckless manner. The contention that the condition applied to the negligence of the foreman was a complete misconception. The condition was not a warranty that everybody employed by the assured, or in fact anybody except the assured, would take reasonable precautions. In appointing the foreman the assured were not delegating their duty under the condition, but performing it.

Maltby (TF) Ltd v Pelton Steamship Co Ltd

[1951] 2 All ER 954n, [1951] WN 531, 95 Sol Jo 834, [1951] 2 Lloyd's Rep 332 (Devlin J)

Shipowners indemnified stevedores against claims by workmen arising from use of gear, provided they took reasonable precautions to prevent accidents and to comply with statutory requirements, and that their gear was regularly and properly tested, and did not use improper or inadequate gear. On a claim by stevedores for indemnity under the contract, the court found the foreman of the stevedores was negligent.

HELD: The decision in *Woolfall*'s case made it impossible to contend that the negligence of the foreman brought them within the first part of the stipulations.

With regard to the gear, the words must be construed as meaning 'You the owner of the business shall not use improper or inadequate gear.' It did not mean 'You through your foreman, shall not use improper or inadequate gear.' The claim for indemnity succeeded.

Fraser v BN Furman (Production) Ltd

[1967] 3 All ER 57, [1967] 1 WLR 898, 111 Sol Jo 471, [1967] 2 Lloyd's Rep 1, CA

The defendants were found liable in damages to the plaintiff, their employee, for negligence and breach of statutory duty in failing to guard a welding machine in which she sustained injury. It had originally had a guard but they had removed it. They sued insurance brokers in third-party proceedings for an indemnity against these damages for breach of contract in having failed to insure them against the plaintiff's claim. The policy which it had been intended to obtain for the defendants was an Eagle Star employers' liability policy which contained the condition 'The insured shall take reasonable precautions to prevent accidents'. The brokers denied liability on the ground that if the policy had been issued the insurers would have been entitled to repudiate liability under it for breach of the condition.

HELD: (1) Following *Woolfall and Rimmer v Moyle* (above) the obligation to take precautions is on the insured personally: failure by an employee to do so would not be a breach of the condition. (2) 'Reasonable precautions' means reasonable as between insurer and insured, without being repugnant to the commercial purpose of the contract. By this test what is reasonable is that the insured must not deliberately court a danger by taking measures which he knows are inadequate to avert it. It is not enough that his omission to take some precaution is negligent: it must be reckless, not caring, though aware of the danger, whether it is averted or not. The purpose of the condition is to ensure that the insured will not refrain from taking precautions simply because he is covered. That was not the case here: the defendants had not appreciated the risk to which they were exposing the plaintiff. (3) It was not a defence to show merely that the insurers would have been entitled to repudiate. It must be shown that they would in fact have done so. The good repute of the company in question and the absence of any evidence that they would have sought to rely on the alleged breach of condition made it impossible to hold that they would have done so. The brokers were liable to indemnify the defendants.

W and J Lane v Spratt

[1970] 2 QB 480, [1970] 1 All ER 162, [1969] 3 WLR 950, 113 Sol Jo 920, [1969] 2 Lloyd's Rep 229 (Roskill J)
The plaintiffs, haulage contractors, were insured under a goods in transit policy issued by the defendant, an underwriter at Lloyd's. It contained the condition 'the Insured shall take all reasonable precautions for the protection and safeguarding of the goods . . .'. The plaintiffs engaged a driver after interviewing him and after making one abortive attempt to follow up a reference by telephone. On his first day at work he drove off with a lorry load of merchandise and was not seen again. The defendant refused to indemnify the plaintiffs on the ground that there had been a breach of condition.
HELD: In failing to take up references the plaintiffs had failed to take the elementary precautions which were usual in the trade and if the only duty was to take reasonable care they had failed in that duty. But that did not put them in breach of the condition. Following *Fraser v BN Furman (Production) Ltd* (above) it is not enough that the omission to take a particular precaution should be negligent, it must be at least reckless, not caring whether the danger was averted or not. That was not true of these plaintiffs and they were entitled to indemnity.

Devco Holder Ltd v Legal and General Assurance Society Ltd

[1993] 2 Ll L Rep 567, CA
A Ferrari motor car was stolen from a station car park. The insured's driver had left the car unlocked with the key in the ignition. The car was stolen whilst he was in his office on a road opposite the station.

The insurance policy included the following condition: 'You may take all reasonable steps to protect your car against loss or damage and to maintain it in a safe and efficient condition.'

The court found that the keys had been left in the car deliberately and not inadvertently.

Per Slade LJ: (Counsel on behalf of the insurers) submitted that the judge in applying what I may call the 'deliberate courting the danger' test, adopted too high a test of negligence for the relevant purpose. He pointed out that, as Diplock LJ himself had made clear in *Fraser v B N Furman (Production) Ltd*, a condition, such as general condition 2, has to be construed in the context of the particular policy in which it appears, and in the context of the commercial purpose of that policy. He submitted that, where a claim is asserted under the theft provisions of a policy of motor insurance rather than under a policy of employers liability insurance (such as that dealt with by Diplock LJ in *Fraser*) a condition obliging the insured to take all reasonable steps to protect his car is not limited in its effect to precluding a deliberate courting of recognised risks by the insured, but extends to ordinary negligence. He submits that to give it a broader ambit in this way would not involve any repugnancy with the operative provisions of the policy giving insurance cover. Beyond saying that I see some force in those submissions, I do not find it necessary to deal with them.

CHAPTER 22

Other Insurance Points

INTERPRETATION OF POLICY

Contra proferentes

Thomson v Weems

(1884) 9 App Cas 671, HL (Lord Watson)
The question must be interpreted according to the ordinary and natural meaning of the words used, if their meaning be plain and unequivocal, and there is nothing in the context to qualify it. On the other hand, if the words used are ambiguous, they must be construed *contra proferentes*, and in favour of the assured.

Cornish v Accident Insurance Co

(1889) 23 QBD 453, 58 LJQB 591, 54 JP 262, 38 WR 139, 5 TLR 733 (Lindley LJ)
In a case on the line, in a case of real doubt, the policy ought to be construed most strongly against the insurers; they frame the policy and insert the exceptions. But this principle ought only to be applied for the purpose of removing doubt, not for the purpose of creating a doubt or magnifying an ambiguity when the circumstances of the case raise no real difficulty.

Ejusdem generis

Sun Fire Office v Hart

(1889) 14 App Cas 98, 58 LJPC 69, 60 LT 337, 53 JP 548, 37 WR 561, 5 TLR 289, PC
Per Lord Watson: It is well-known canon of construction, that when a particular enumeration is followed by such words as 'or other', the latter expression ought, if not enlarged by the context, to be limited to matters *ejusdem generis* with those

specially enumerated. The canon is attended with no difficulty, except in its application. Whether it applies at all, and if so, what effect should be given to it, must in every case depend upon the clause under construction.

Note—The phrase is chiefly used in cases where general words have a meaning attributed to them less comprehensive than they would otherwise bear, by reason of particular words preceding them.

One line of authority is to give all the words their common meaning unless it is reasonably plain on the face of the document itself that they are not used with that meaning.

The other line of authority is that the general words which follow particular and specific words of the same nature as themselves take their meaning from them and are presumed to be restricted to the same genus as those words.

The phrase was considered by Devlin J in the following case citing *Scrutton on Charterparties* (15th edn) p 239:

'It must be remembered that the question is whether a particular thing is within the genus that comprises the specified things. It is not a question (though the point is often so put in argument), whether the particular thing is like one or other of the specified things.'

Chandris v Isbrandtsen-Moller Co Inc

[1951] 1 KB 240, [1950] 1 All ER 768, 66 (pt 1) TLR 971, 94 Sol Jo 303, 83 Lloyd's Rep 385 (Devlin J)
The rule is merely, as I think, an aid to ascertaining the intentions of the parties.

If there is something to show that the literal meaning of the words is too wide, then they will be given such other meaning as seems best to consort with the intention of the parties. In some cases it may be that they will seem to indicate a genus; in others that they perform the simpler office of expanding the meaning of each enumerated item. If a genus cannot be found, doubtless that is one factor indicating that the parties do not intend to restrict the meaning of the words. But I do not take it to be universally true that whenever a genus cannot be found the words must have been intended to have their literal meaning, whatever other indications there may be to the contrary. I see no reason why, if it accords with the apparent intention of the parties, the words should not be treated, as suggested by Lord Macnaghten in *Thames and Mersey Marine Insurance Co Ltd v Hamilton Fraser & Co* ((1887) 12 App Cas 484 at 501), as being 'inserted in order to prevent disputes founded on nice distinctions' and 'to cover in terms whatever may be within the spirit of the cases previously enumerated'.

Continuing warranty

Note—The theory that answers in a proposal form import a warranty which continues during the insurance did not receive any support in the case of *Woolfall and Rimmer Ltd v Moyle*.

Woolfall and Rimmer Ltd v Moyle

[1942] 1 KB 66, [1942] 3 All ER 304, 111 LJKB 122, 166 LT 49, 58 TLR 28, 86 Sol Jo 63, CA
A proposal form for Employers' Liability contained the question: 'Are your machinery, plant and ways properly fenced and guarded and otherwise in good order and condition?' The answer was 'Yes.' It was contended by insurers that the question was not limited to the date of the proposal form but continued during the currency of the policy. The Court of Appeal said that it was to enable insurers to find out the character

of the risk. There was not a particle of justification for reading into it any element of futurity whatsoever.

Sweeney v Kennedy

(1948) 82 Ll L Rep 294, Eire Div Ct
A proposal dated 4 March 1946, for insurance of a motor lorry contained the question: 'Are any of your drivers under 21 years of age or with less than 12 months' driving experience?' and was answered 'No.'

The policy was issued on 18 March 1946. At that date the answer was true and the assured had no intention of employing a driver under 21. A son of the assured was first employed as a driver on 17 June 1946, and occasionally employed as driver until 2 February 1947, after which date he was regularly so employed. On 7 October 1947, an accident occurred when the son, who was under 21, was driving.

The declaration in the proposal form was stated to be 'promissory and so form the basis of the contract'.
HELD: (1) No such alteration of risk as to avoid policy. (2) No continuing warranty that no driver under 21 would be employed. (3) 'Promissory' read with the following words, did not refer to the future. It signified a positive declaration: 'I promise you that it is so.' Underwriters held liable.

Kirkbride v Donner

[1974] 1 Lloyd's Rep 549, Mayor's and City of London Court
Miss Kirkbride filled in a proposal form for insurance of her car. In answer to the question 'Will the car to your knowledge be driven by any person under 25 years of age?' she put merely 'Yes, self.' She signed the usual declaration at the end of the form containing the words 'this declaration signed by me is promissory'. The policy when issued provided that the underwriters would not be liable in respect of loss whilst the car was 'being driven by or in charge for the purpose of any person in whose record there is to the knowledge of the policy holder a prejudice existing such as would amount to material information to be known to the underwriters'. On an occasion when she intended to visit a theatre club she allowed her younger brother to drive there in her car on an arrangement that she would use it to drive him back at the end of the visit. Her brother drove the car there, parked it and handed her the keys. During the evening the car was stolen and not recovered. The underwriters refused to meet the loss.
HELD: They were not entitled to decline liability under the policy, because (1) on the facts Miss Kirkbride's brother was not in charge of the car when it was stolen, since the purpose for which he had driven the car had come to an end and Miss Kirkbride was herself at the club; (2) the use of the word 'promissory' in the declaration did not mean that she was warranting that the situation implied or expressed in the proposal form would continue into the future: all it meant was, 'At the time of signing the form those are my intentions.' When she signed the proposal form Miss Kirkbride did not intend that the car would be driven by anyone under the age of 25 other than herself.

Assured as a third party

Note—There was formerly a difference of opinion on the question whether an assured of a policy could claim against insurers under the policy for personal injury caused to him whilst a passenger in his own car driven by his own servant, or other person driving on his order or with his permission.

The point was the subject of an award by Lord Robertson in an arbitration under the Scottish procedure. The policyholder was injured whilst a passenger in her own car driven by a person with permission. It was admitted the driver was entitled to indemnity if there was a liability to 'Third Parties', but denied that the policyholder was a third party. The section in the policy was headed 'Liability to Third Parties'. Lord Robertson held that the policyholder was not a third party within the meaning of the policy and there was no liability under it (reported 73 Lloyd's Rep 189). The same question came before the courts in *Digby v General Accident Fire and Life Assurance Corpn Ltd*, where in the House of Lords, a conclusion was reached to the contrary.

Digby v General Accident Fire and Life Assurance Corpn

[1943] AC 121, [1942] 2 All ER 319, 111 LJKB 628, 167 LT 222, 58 TLR 375, 87 Sol Jo 29, 73 Ll L Rep 175, HL

The policyholder was a passenger in her own car, driven by her servant owing to his negligent driving she was injured and awarded damages against him (*Thompson v Bundy* (1938) Times, 5 May). He then brought an action against her insurers, claiming indemnity. The judge (Atkinson J) held that the driver was entitled to be indemnified ([1940] 1 All ER 514, 66 Ll L Rep 89). In the Court of Appeal his decision was reversed ([1940] 2 KB 226, [1940] 3 All ER 190, 109 LJKB 740, 163 LT 366).

HELD, ON APPEAL to the House of Lords (Lord Atkin, Lord Wright and Lord Porter, Viscount Simon LC and Viscount Maugham dissenting): The insurers were liable to indemnify the driver against the claim of the assured.

The policy contained six sections of which section 2 (described in the margin as dealing with 'Third-party liability') gave the assured indemnity against '(1) all sums which the policy-holder shall become legally liable to pay in respect of any claim by any person (including passengers in the automobile) for loss of life or accidental bodily injury . . . caused by, through, or in connexion with such automobile . . .'. The same section further provided '(3) The insurance under this section shall also extend to indemnify in like manner any person whilst driving [the car] on the order or with the permission of the policy-holder, provided . . . that such person shall as though he were the policy-holder observe, fulfil and be subject to the terms, exceptions and conditions of this policy in so far as they can apply'.

Per Lord Atkin: There was no justification for transferring the words from the margin to the body of the document and saying that 'any claim by any person' must be read as 'any claim by any third party'. 'Any person' means any member of the public. In section 2(1) 'any person' cannot include the policy holder because he cannot be liable to pay himself, but in section 2(3) which begins anew with a fresh promise of indemnity the driver is to be indemnified 'in like manner', and on this occasion the policy holder is plainly 'any person'.

Per Lord Wright: By section 2(3) the insurers undertake in favour of the driver a separate insurance against third-party liability so that he becomes the assured whilst the policyholder becomes *pro hac vice* the third party. There is no warrant for extending the meaning of 'any person' in section 2(1) to 'any person other than the policy-holder' when the words are brought over into section 2(3).

Per Lord Porter: 'Third-party' is merely a useful description of a particular type of insurance and does not mean that 'any claim by any person' must be confined to a third person who is not a party to the contract. In a policy such as this there is not one contract of insurance only; there is one with the policy holder and one also with each person driving on her order and with her permission. For the purposes of a claim made by her against him, he is the assured, the company are the insurers and she is the third party.

Goods in trust

Engel v Lancashire and General Assurance Co Ltd

(1925) 41 TLR 408, 69 Sol Jo 447, 30 Com Cas 202, 21 Ll L Rep 327
Applicants insured claimant, who was a furrier, against burglary, the policy covering not only goods belonging to claimant but goods which were on his premises and were in his possession on trust or on commission and for which he was 'responsible'. A burglary took place, and claimant lost both goods of his own and goods which were in his custody as a bailee. Claimant had not been guilty of any negligence as a bailer, and so was not liable to the owners of the bailed goods for their loss.
HELD: 'Responsibility' in such a connection meant legal liability only, and therefore, claimant could not recover on the policy in respect of the bailed goods.

John Rigby (Haulage) Ltd v Reliance Marine Insurance Co Ltd

[1956] 2 QB 468, [1956] 3 All ER 1, [1956] 3 WLR 407, 100 Sol Jo 528, [1956] 2 Lloyd's Rep 10, CA
Plaintiffs, road transport contractors, conducted business through subcontractors. They agreed with customers to carry goods lying at a Liverpool dock to Birmingham. A man driving a lorry called on plaintiffs and stated he was employed by and the lorry belonged to sub-contractors on the plaintiffs' list. He was given a collection order for the goods. He was not a servant of the sub-contractors and the lorry did not belong to them. Neither he nor the goods were ever heard of again. Plaintiffs' insurance policy covered 'goods belonging to the assured or held by the assured in trust for which the assured are themselves responsible'.
HELD: The words 'in trust' were not used in a policy in a strict technical sense, and should be construed according to their ordinary meaning. The collection order was as between the plaintiffs and the man wholly invalid, but as between the plaintiffs and the owners of the goods it was an offer to undertake the carriage of their goods if they would deliver them to the person holding the collection order. The plaintiffs were entrusted with the goods, and liable for their loss, and were entitled to indemnity under their policy.

Hepburn v A Tomlinson (Hauliers) Ltd

[1966] AC 451, [1966] All ER 418, [1966] 2 WLR 453, 110 Sol Jo 86, [1966] 1 Lloyd's Rep 309, HL
The plaintiffs were road hauliers who regularly carried cigarettes for the Imperial Tobacco Co. The goods carried were insured by the plaintiffs under a policy binding the underwriters 'to pay or make good to the assured . . . or to indemnify them against . . . all risks of loss or damage however arising'. The goods covered included 'Tobacco . . . the property of the Imperial Tobacco Co'. The goods were stolen whilst in the plaintiffs' lorry, though in circumstances which did not make the plaintiffs liable to the owners for the loss. The plaintiffs claimed against the underwriters under the policy for the value of the goods lost. The underwriters refused to pay on the grounds that the policy was a contract of indemnity and the plaintiffs had suffered no loss.
HELD: The plaintiffs were entitled to succeed. A bailee has an insurable interest beyond his own personal loss if the goods are destroyed. This has never been regarded

as in any way inconsistent with the overriding principle that insurance of goods is a contract of indemnity. The question is whether the bailee has insured his whole insurable interest—a goods policy—or whether he has only insured against personal loss—a personal liability policy. The policy wording in this case was appropriate to a goods policy and the underwriters must pay the full value of the goods to the plaintiffs, who must account to the owners for the money so recovered. The intention of the assured at the time of entering into the policy is irrelevant.
Per Lord Reid: The principle preventing *jus quaesitum tertio* has been firmly established for at least half a century, but I do not think we are bound to be astute to extend it on a logical basis so as to cut down an exception, if it be an exception, which has stood unchallenged since the decision of *Waters*' case more than a century ago.

Non-compliance with condition

Walker v Pennine Insurance Co Ltd

[1979] 2 Lloyd's Rep 139 (Sheen J); affd [1980] 2 Lloyd's Rep 156, CA
On 5 August 1970 Miss W, a passenger in the plaintiff's car, was seriously injured in an accident. The plaintiff was insured under a policy issued by the defendants indemnifying him against liability at law for damages in respect of bodily injury to any person. The policy contained a condition. 'If the company shall disclaim liability to the insured for any claim hereunder and if within 12 calendar months from the date of such disclaimer legal proceedings have not been instituted . . . in respect thereof by the insured . . . then the claim shall for all purposes be deemed to have been abandoned . . .'. In November 1970 Miss W's solicitors wrote the plaintiff claiming damages for her but he did not reply nor tell the defendants. The solicitors then wrote notifying the claim to the defendants themselves who on making investigations decided not to indemnify the plaintiff because, they maintained, he was in breach of a policy condition as to the roadworthiness of the car at the time of the accident. They notified him through the brokers on 3 February 1971 that they would not meet the claim. On 17 February 1971 the plaintiff's solicitors wrote the defendants denying the alleged breach of condition and saying the plaintiff expected to be indemnified. The defendants replied on 22 March 1971 maintaining their refusal. They nominated solicitors to accept service of proceedings against themselves but the plaintiff took no further step to enforce indemnity for nearly four years. Meanwhile Miss W took proceedings against the plaintiff who did nothing about them until she had obtained judgment in default of appearance and in 1975 was about to have damages assessed. In July 1975 the plaintiff's solicitors wrote the defendants seeking to revive the claim for indemnity. The defendants denied liability on the ground that he had not instituted proceedings against them within one year of their refusal to indemnify.
HELD: (1) The defendants' letter of 22 March 1971 quite clearly disclaimed liability under the policy and no proceedings had been started against them within a year thereafter. It was not a breach of the contract. The refusal to indemnify was on the terms of the contract. (2) It was not necessary that the amount of the claim should be known before it constituted a claim under the policy. The defendants were not liable. An appeal was dismissed. 'I would be content in this case wholly to adopt the judgment of the Learned Judge upon which . . . I could not hope to improve' (per Roskill LJ).

False representation

Brown, Jenkinson & Co Ltd v Percy Dalton (London) Ltd

[1957] 2 QB 621, [1957] 2 All ER 844, [1957] 3 WLR 403, 101 Sol Jo 610, [1957] 2 Lloyd's Rep 1, CA
Shipowners, at request of owners of goods shipped on their vessel and on a promise by owners to indemnify, issued bills of lading stating the goods were shipped in apparently good order and condition. Both parties knew that statement was false. Shipowners had to pay a loss to consignees and sued owners for indemnity.
HELD: By Morris and Pearce LJJ, Lord Evershed MR dissenting: Although shipowners did not desire or intend that anyone should be defrauded, they had made a representation of fact which they knew to be false with intent that it should be acted on, and had committed the tort of deceit, and the indemnity was unenforceable.

Admission in breach of policy condition

Terry v Trafalgar Insurance Co

[1970] 1 Lloyd's Rep 524, Mayor's and City of London Court
The defendants issued to the plaintiff a policy of motor insurance containing the condition 'No liability shall be admitted nor any offer, promise or payment made to third parties without the company's written consent'. After a collision between his car and another he wrote to the other driver later on the same day. 'As damage to your vehicle was not severe I will pay for the making good. Technically the blame for the accident falls on me . . .'. Afterwards, the third party's damage proving more severe than he had thought, the plaintiff claimed indemnity from the defendants, who refused cover on the ground that there had been a breach of the condition.
HELD: The letter was an admission of liability; judgment for the defendants.

Written words in printed document

Note—Where an instrument is in a printed form with written additions or alterations, the written words (subject always to be governed in point of construction by the language and terms with which they are accompanied) are entitled, in case of reasonable doubt as to the meaning of the whole, to have a greater effect attributed to them than the printed words: *Halsbury's Laws of England* (2nd edn) vol 10, p 279. Cited in *Addis v Burrows* [1948] 1 KB 444, [1948] 1 All ER 177, [1948] LJR 1033, 64 TLR 169, 92 Sol Jo 124, CA.

WORDS AND PHRASES COMMONLY FOUND IN POLICIES

Age of insured

Lloyds Bank Ltd v Eagle Star Insurance Co Ltd

[1951] 1 All ER 914, [1951] 1 TLR 803, [1951] 1 Lloyd's Rep 385 (Jones J)
A proviso in a policy allowed a company to avoid liability if 'under the age of 16 years or over the age of 65 years'.
HELD: The proviso means a person who has reached his 65th birthday and applies to anyone who has lived beyond the attainment of the 65th birthday.

Meaning of 'garage'

Barnett and Block v National Parcels Insurance Co

[1942] 1 All ER 221, 166 LT 147, 58 TLR 144, 86 Sol Jo 140 (Atkinson J); affd [1942] 1 All ER 55n, 58 TLR 270, 86 Sol Jo 233, 73 Ll L Rep 17, CA
Policy insured against theft from van 'whilst left in a garage'. It was in a yard at the back of a private hotel; there were two gates to the yard, both fastened by bolts on the inner side; it was completely enclosed, partly by buildings and partly by a wall over 12 feet high, but there was no roof.
HELD: Applying the test of plaintiff's counsel 'a garage is a place where one can get reasonable protection and shelter for a car' the yard was not a garage. 'Garage' means a building with a roof and is not applicable to an unroofed yard.

Affirmed in CA.

It is a pure question of fact. If the arbitrator had found the other way, I do not think we should have interfered with his finding: Per Goddard LJ in the Court of Appeal.

Civil commotion—riot

Levy v Assicurazioni Generali

[1940] AC 791, [1940] 3 All ER 427, 56 TLR 851, 84 Sol Jo 633, 67 Ll L Rep 174, PC
The court approved the definition of 'Civil commotion' in *Welford & Otter v Barry's Fire Insurance*—as follows:

This phrase is used to indicate a state between a riot and civil war. It has been defined to mean an insurrection of the people for general purposes, though not amounting to rebellion; but it is probably not capable of any very precise definition. The element of turbulence or tumult is essential; an organised conspiracy to commit criminal acts, where there is no tumult or disturbance until after the acts, does not amount to civil commotion. It is not, however, necessary to show the existence of any outside organisation at whose instigation the acts were done.

Influence of intoxicating liquor

Louden v British Merchants Insurance Co Ltd

[1961] 1 All ER 705, [1961] 1 WLR 798, 105 Sol Jo 209, [1961] 1 Lloyd's Rep 154 (Lawton J)
A private motor car policy issued by the defendants provided that they would pay compensation for injury or death caused to the policyholder whilst travelling in a motor car not belonging to him, subject to the provisos that the defendants should not be liable for injury sustained by him 'whilst under the influence of drugs or intoxicating liquor'. The plaintiff's husband, the holder of the policy, was killed whilst travelling in a car owned and driven by someone else. The alcohol content of his blood was found to be such as would cause some degree of incoordination of movement and a tendency to stagger.
HELD: (1) Following the test in *Mair v Railway Passengers Assurance Co Ltd* (1877) 37 LT 356 the words 'under the influence of intoxicating liquor' meant such influence as would disturb 'the quiet, calm, intelligent exercise of his faculties' and, on the facts, the defendants had proved such influence. (2) The word 'whilst' had a temporal,

not a causative, meaning. The exemption clause did not call for any causal connection between the bodily injury sustained and the influence of intoxicating liquor. The defendants were not liable under the policy.

Kennedy v Smith

1976 SLT 110
After drinking a pint and a half of lager with friends the defender gave them a lift in his car. On a straight section of a dual carriageway road the car crossed the central intersection and collided with a sign. The two passengers were killed. The defender's motor policy contained a condition exempting the insurers from liability for any claim arising when the insured was driving and was under the influence of intoxicating liquor. The defender had signed a declaration when proposing for insurance that he was a total abstainer from birth and would notify the insurers if this ceased to apply.
HELD, ON APPEAL: (1) The phrase 'under the influence of intoxicating liquor' meant under such influence as to disturb the balance of the mind; on the evidence this was not the case here. (2) The declaration of abstinence was not an undertaking by the defendant as to future conduct and the insurers were not excepted from liability by a breach of the declaration.

'Loss or damage' unauthorised driver

Greenleaf Associated Ltd v Monksfield

[1972] RTR 451, [1972] 2 Lloyd's Rep 79
A policy issued by the defendant underwriter to the plaintiff indemnified against 'loss of or damage to the insured car'. A general exception excluded liability in respect of 'any accident, injury, loss, damage or liability . . . caused sustained or incurred while (the car) is being driven by any person' not specified in the statutory certificate 'which is deemed to be incorporated herein'. The only persons specified in the certificate were Mr and Mrs B. The car was damaged when being driven by a mechanic who had taken it on a joy ride without the insured's consent.
HELD: The plaintiffs were not entitled to indemnity for the damage to the car. It had been argued that if the car was being driven without the insured's consent the exception did not apply because the words 'with the consent of the insured' ought to be read into it; but there was no reason for inserting in the policy words that were not there. There was no ambiguity in regard to 'loss' while the vehicle was being driven by an unauthorised person even though the policy covered theft, since there could be no 'loss' by theft in the way of damage to the vehicle because the theft occurred at the moment of taking: 'loss' meant physical not financial loss.

Lorry—includes removed engine

Seaton v London General Insurance Co Ltd

(1932) 48 TLR 574, 76 Sol Jo 527, 43 Ll L Rep 398 (du Parcq J)
Assured removed the engine of his motor lorry to his carpenter's shop 150 yards away for repair, and while there it was destroyed by fire. The proposal form stated the lorry would be garaged on assured's own premises.
HELD: Insurer liable. The engine and the rest of the lorry together were still the lorry insured.

Motor car

Laurence v Davies

[1972] 2 Lloyd's Rep 231 (Dunn J)
The defendant was insured for use of his motor car by a policy which extended cover to him additionally against third-party claims arising from accidents caused by or in connection with 'the driving by the insured of any motor car . . . not belonging to him . . .'. He was driving a Ford Transit van not belonging to him when there was an accident in which the plaintiff was injured. The defendant's insurers refused to indemnify him on the ground that the van was not a 'motor car'. The defendant relied on the definition in the Road Traffic Act 1960, s 253(2) (now s 185(1) of the 1988 Act) '"motor car" means a mechanically propelled vehicle, not being a motor cycle or invalid carriage, which is constructed itself to carry a load or passengers and the weight of which unladen . . . does not exceed three tons'.
HELD: The van was a motor car. The words had to be considered in the context of motor insurance. If motor insurers wished to put some meaning on words like 'motor car' other than those contained in the Road Traffic Act they should make it abundantly clear in the policy; if they failed to do so the words would be deemed to have the statutory meanings.

Personal luggage

Buckland v R

[1933] 1 KB 329, 49 TLR 39, 76 Sol Jo 850 (McCardie J); affd [1933] 1 KB 767, 102 LJKB 404, 148 LT 557, 49 TLR 244, CA
There is no distinction between 'ordinary luggage' and 'passenger luggage' and 'personal luggage'.

The court called attention to various decisions which are difficult to reconcile as follows:

Held to be personal luggage: All articles of apparel, whether for use or ornament, the gun case or fishing apparatus of the sportsman, the easel of the artist on a sketching tour, the books of the student, officer's revolver and binoculars.

Held not to be personal luggage: Title deeds carried by a solicitor; truck containing six pairs of sheets, six pairs of blankets, and six quilts; violin-cello carried for professional purposes; the pencil sketches of an artist; hamper containing professional costumes and property of a comedian; sewing machine; invalid chair, bicycle.

The definition adopted by the court was 'articles intended for the traveller's personal use and convenience as distinct from merchandise carried for purposes of business'.

DOUBLE INSURANCE

Note—The right of contribution in a case of double insurance is a part of the equity of contribution, which is most prominent in the law of guaranty. The right of contribution does not depend on contract but on principles of equity and natural justice (see *Godin v London Assurance Co* (1758) 1 Burr 489).

Pro rata contribution clause

Note—If at the time of loss or damage happening to any property insured by this policy, there be any other subsisting insurance or insurances, whether effected by the insured, or by any other person, covering the same property or any part thereof, this policy shall not be liable to pay or contribute in respect of such loss or damage more than its rateable proportion of the aggregate liability under all the insurances covering such property.

Non-contribution clause

Note—This insurance does not cover any loss or damage which at the time of the happening of such loss or damage is insured by or would, but for the existence of this policy, be insured by any other existing policy or policies except in respect of any excess beyond the amount which would have been payable under such other policy or policies had this insurance not been effected.

Gale v Motor Union Insurance Co Ltd
Loyst v General Accident Fire and Life Assurance Corpn Ltd

[1928] 1 KB 359, 96 LJKB 199, 38 LT 712, 43 TLR 15, 70 Sol Jo 1140, 26 Ll L Rep 65 (Roche J)
G took with the M Co a motor car insurance policy covering himself and any friend driving with G's consent and providing as follows: 'Condition 6. The extension of the indemnity to friends or relatives of the insured is conditional upon such friend or relative being a licensed and competent driver and not being insured under any other policy. Condition 10. If at the happening of any accident, injury, damage or loss covered by this policy there shall be subsisting any other insurance or indemnity of any nature whatever covering same, whether effected by insured or by any other person, then the company shall not be liable to pay or contribute towards any such damages or loss more than a rateable proportion of any sum payable in respect thereof for compensation.' L, G's brother-in-law, took out with the G Co a similar policy, providing that 'insured will also be indemnified hereunder while personally driving a car not belonging to him provided that there is no other insurance in respect of such other car whereby insured may be indemnified', and that 'if at the time of the occurrence of any accident, loss or damage, there shall be any other indemnity or insurance subsisting, whether effected by insured or by any other person, the corporation shall not be liable to pay or contribute more than a rateable proportion of any sums payable in respect of such accident, loss or damage'. While L was driving G's car with G's consent it had a collision and L had to pay damages. G, as trustee for L, claimed against the M Co and L, on his own behalf, claimed against the G Co. HELD: In each policy the provision as to rateable contribution qualified the preceding clause, and each company was liable to pay claimants half the amount claimed.

Portavon Cinema Co v Price and Century Insurance Co Ltd

[1939] 4 All ER 601, 161 LT 417, 84 Sol Jo 152, 65 Ll L Rep 161 (Branson J)
This clause (non-contribution) should be applied only to cases which are strictly cases of double insurance.

Weddell v Road Transport and General Insurance Co Ltd

[1932] 2 KB 563, 101 LJKB 620, 146 LT 162, 48 TLR 59, 75 Sol Jo 852, 41 Ll L Rep 69 (Rowlatt J)
A motor car accident policy issued by the respondent company to JRW extended the insurance to a relative driving the car provided that the latter was not entitled to indemnity for the same risk under another policy. LWW, a relative of JRW, while driving the car, injured a third party, who claimed damages. LWW was himself insured with the C insurance company against claims for injuries caused by him while driving a car not belonging to him, provided that he was not entitled to an indemnity in respect thereof from another company. The respondents denied liability on the ground of the proviso in their policy exempting them where the claimant was entitled to indemnity under another policy.
HELD: On the proper construction of the policies, the insurance clause in each policy expressed to be cancelled by the co-existence of a similar clause in the other policy should be excluded from the category of co-existing cover, and that therefore the respondents, not being protected by their proviso, were liable.

Note—Weddell's case and *Gale*'s case (above) were approved in *Steelclad Ltd v Iron Trades Mutual Insurance Co Ltd* 1984 SLT 304.

National Employers Mutual General Insurance Association Ltd v Hayden

[1979] 2 Lloyd's Rep 235 (Lloyd J); revsd [1980] 2 Lloyd's Rep 149, CA
A firm of solicitors were covered, in respect of a claim against them for professional negligence, by two policies of insurance. The first, issued by the plaintiff company, contained a clause: 'This policy does not indemnify the insured in respect of any claim made against him for which the insured is or would but for the existence of this policy be entitled to indemnity under any other policy except in respect of any excess beyond the amount payable by such other policy.' The second had a provision: 'This insurance shall not indemnify the assured in respect of any loss arising out of any claim in respect of any circumstance or occurrence which has been notified under any other insurance.'
HELD: There was dual insurance. Both clauses were exceptions clauses even though one was narrower than the other, but even if they were not exclusion clauses in the strict sense but clauses restricting cover, it would still be impossible to distinguish between them. By giving effect to both clauses neither policy would pay. In those circumstances the principle in *Weddell*'s case (above) should be applied: if each policy would cover but for the existence of the other then the exclusions are treated as cancelling each other out. The plaintiffs were entitled to contribution.

Note—The defendant appealed and the appeal was allowed. The principle of *Weddell*'s case, said the court, was not in doubt but it could only apply where an insured is covered by both policies, were it not for the excluding clauses. On the construction of the policies in the present case, however, there was no co-existing cover. The two policies were not concurrent but consecutive. The NEM were alone liable ([1980] 2 Lloyd's Rep 149, CA).

See also the decision of Tucker J on this point in *Austin v Zurich Insurance Co*, p 845, above.

A case in practice arose where the assured had failed to give notice of the loss to one insurer and that insurer was in consequence not liable to the assured. The question was whether that insurer was nevertheless liable on the principle of dual insurance.

The case went to arbitration. The arbitrator held there does not appear to be any direct authority and considered the question to be 'Is the right of contribution an independent right arising as between insurers or merely a benefit accruing to the insurer who pays by subrogation?' The principle does not seem to have been dealt with since *Newby v Reed* (1763) 1 Wm BL 416, and *Rogers v Davis* (1777) 2 Park *Marine Insces* 8th edn, 601. He considered that the principle of natural justice as between co-insurers was the principle to be applied and not subrogation, and that the right of contribution is an independent right of the insurers against his co-insurer which arises as a contingent right when the loss occurs though not enforceable until payment is made. This view is supported by the Marine Insurance Act 1906, s 80. Being an independent right, the failure of the assured to comply with a policy condition cannot take away that right. On the basis of apportionment, he referred to *American Surety Co of New York v Wrighton* (1910) 103 LT 663, 27 TLR 91, 16 Com Cas 37. But see next case.

Breach of condition of one policy—effect

Monksfield v Vehicle and General Insurance Co Ltd

[1971] 1 Lloyd's Rep 139, Mayor's and City of London Court

P was involved in an accident when driving a car belonging to W. He was insured under a policy issued to himself by the plaintiff, a member of Lloyds, who dealt with and paid the third party claim. W had a policy issued by the defendants which extended to cover P but neither P nor W reported the claim to them nor claimed indemnity under that policy. Each policy had a term excluding cover if the driver was entitled to indemnity under any other policy, so that, other considerations apart, there was dual insurance as in *Weddell*'s case (above). A condition in W's policy required the insured to give notice in writing to the company as soon as possible after the occurrence of any accident, but the defendants did not hear of the accident until eight months later.

HELD: The fact that there had been a breach of condition of their policy by failing to report the accident relieved the defendants of the liability to make contribution. They would clearly have been in a position to repudiate a claim by W; it could not be an equitable result that insurers who had no notice of the accident and had no say in the handling of the claim should be called upon to make a contribution when they would have been entitled to repudiate if the claim had been brought under the terms of their own policy.

Legal and General v Drake Insurance

[1992] QB 887, [1992] 1 All ER 283

On facts very similar to those in *Monksfield*, whether *Monksfield* was correctly decided. In fact, the Court of Appeal decided that *Monksfield* had been wrongly decided.

Per Lloyd J: The fact that a co-obligor has 'no say' in the handling of the claim has never been an answer to a contribution, whether in the field of insurance or in any other field in which the equitable doctrine prevails. As to the right to repudiate, this would, as I have said, have been a good defence to a claim for contribution if the assured had been in breach of condition prior to the loss and a breach of condition subsequent to the loss by failing to give notice in time vitiates, if I may respectfully say so, the learned judge's conclusion. So I would hold that *Monksfield*'s case was wrongly decided.

INSURER, INSURED AND THIRD PARTIES

Excess clause

Beacon Insurance Co Ltd v Langdale

[1939] 4 All ER 204, 83 Sol Jo 908, 65 Ll L Rep 57, CA

A motor policy covering third party risks contained a condition that the company should be entitled, if it so desired, to take over and conduct in the name of the assured the defence or settlement of any claim and should have full discretion in the settlement of any claim. The policy was subject to a £5 excess.

The company settled a third-party claim by a cyclist without the express sanction of the assured and also against his view of the rights of the matter, as he wished to claim against the third party. The company made what they believed to be, in his interest and theirs, an advantageous settlement, and they were at pains to show that the settlement should be made with a denial of liability, so that no one could say that they had admitted any culpability whatever on his behalf. The assured contended that the company were not entitled to settle the claim without notice to him and that they had not acted reasonably in the exercise of their authority.

HELD (distinguishing *Groom v Crocker*, p 883, below): The policy gave the company power to settle the claim without consulting the assured, and the assured was liable to pay the company the £5 excess.

Knock for knock agreement

Morley v Moore

[1936] 2 KB 359, [1936] 2 All ER 79, 105 LJKB 421, 154 LT 646, 52 TLR 510, 80 Sol Jo 424, 55 Ll L Rep 10, CA

The plaintiff was insured for damage to his car bearing a £5 excess. The car damage was £33 2s 8d, and his insurers paid the £28 2s 8d. Plaintiff sued for £33 2s 8d. Defendants pleaded the 'knock for knock' agreement and that plaintiff only entitled to receive £5.

HELD: Plaintiff entitled to recover £33 2s 8, but he would hold £28 2s 8d as trustee for his insurers, they being subrogated in his rights. The 'knock for knock' agreement does not prevent a plaintiff who has been paid for damage to his car by his own insurers from suing the negligent party for such damage in spite of a direction from his own insurers that they do not want him to claim it. The insurers are entitled to be subrogated but had no right to forbid the assured from exercising his common law right against the wrongdoer.

Bourne v Stanbridge

[1965] 1 All ER 241, [1965] 1 WLR 189, 108 Sol Jo 991, CA

In an action in the county court the plaintiff claimed £230 being the cost of repairs to his car, damaged in a collision with the defendant's car. His driver being found two-thirds to blame he recovered only £76 being one-third of the amount claimed. When the judge was considering costs, counsel for the defendant revealed that, as the plaintiff knew before proceedings, there was a knock for knock agreement between the plaintiff's and defendant's insurers and that the only sum in respect of repairs for which the plaintiff was liable was his excess of £10. The judge then awarded the plaintiff his costs only on Scale 2 and not on Scale 3.

HELD: Though the judge had a discretion under the County Court Rules, Ord 47, r 1 he had not exercised it on a right principle. The plaintiff was quite entitled to bring an action for the whole amount of the damage as *Morley v Moore* (above) shows; the knock for knock agreement between insurers was not a matter which he should have considered as of any relevance in respect of the award of costs.

Note—But see next case.

Hobbs v Marlowe

[1978] AC 16, [1977] 2 All ER 241, [1977] 2 WLR 777, 121 Sol Jo 272, [1977] RTR 253, HL

The plaintiff's car was damaged in a collision for which the defendant was wholly to blame. The cost of repairs at £237.59 (less the excess) was paid by the plaintiff's insurers, who were parties to a knock for knock agreement with the defendant's insurers. The plaintiff's uninsured loss amounted to £73.53 which was not enough under the County Court Rules to entitle him to an award of costs (except the court fee) in an action against the defendant. His solicitors, solely to obtain an award of their costs, sued on his behalf for the whole of the cost of the repairs and uninsured losses, ie £301.12. On payment of a judgment for the whole amount the defendant's insurers would be entitled under the knock for knock agreement to payment of £227.59 from the plaintiff's insurers who would then recover that sum from the plaintiff. In county court proceedings the defendant (by his insurers) admitted liability and paid into court £73.53. The judge, following *Morley v Moore* (above) gave judgment for the whole amount claimed but in awarding costs held that the inflation of the claim solely for costs was an abuse of the process of the court and awarded only the costs appropriate to an award of £73.53, ie the court fee of £7.50.

HELD, ON APPEAL to the House of Lords: (1) *Morley v Moore* was rightly decided and the plaintiff was not precluded from suing for the full amount of the damages by reason of the fact that he had already received a large part of that sum from his insurers. (2) The judge's exercise of his discretion on the award of costs was a proper one and there were no grounds for an appellate court to interfere with it. *Bourne v Stanbridge* (above) should be regarded as wrongly decided.

Note—If a policy indemnity is limited to a named figure, and litigation is begun, and the damages are likely to exceed the indemnity, the business plan is to pay over the limit, otherwise the costs of litigation must also be paid.

Allen v London Guarantee and Accident Co Ltd

(1912) 28 TLR 254

By a policy of insurance, defendants insured the assured in respect of accidents caused by his employees when in charge of his horse-drawn vehicle. The total liability of defendants was limited to £300 for all claims for compensation and costs, charges and expenses, paid or payable in respect of or arising out of any accident or occurrence, and defendants were to be entitled, in the name and on behalf of the assured, to take over and have the absolute control of all negotiations and proceedings which might arise in respect of any accidents or claim. There was a further provision that defendants might pay the maximum to the assured in the case of any one accident or occurrence or occurrences and thereupon their liability in respect of that accident or occurrence should cease; but if the assured wished defendants to continue the defence he should pay and make good all costs and expenses incurred thereby. Two

persons who had been injured by an accident caused by a cart belonging to the assured brought actions against him claiming damages. The assured gave notice thereof to defendants, and they defended the actions, the assured, not being consulted having nothing to say as to the advisability of defending the actions. The actions resulted in verdicts against the assured for £200 and £175, respectively. The costs in these actions recoverable by two plaintiffs against the assured amounted to £218; and as he did not pay those costs an execution was levied on his goods and to get rid of this he had to pay the £218, which he now claimed from the defendants.
HELD: Although there were two accidents there was only one 'occurrence' within the meaning of the policy, and therefore defendants' limit of £300 applied; but defendants having defended the action in the name of the assured without his consent they incurred a common law liability for the costs, and were therefore liable to repay £218, which the assured had been compelled to pay.

Knight v Hosken

(1943) 75 Ll L Rep 74
Underwriters issued to an estate agent a policy indemnifying against negligence limited to £2,000. An action was brought against the assured claiming £3,700. Underwriters by their solicitors defended the action, and invited the assured to contribute seventeen-thirty-sevenths of the costs of defence. The assured agreed to contribute towards the costs of defence in the event of damages being awarded in excess of £2,000 which event happened.
HELD, by Atkinson J (72 Ll L Rep 206) and upheld in the Court of Appeal: There was no promise for a consideration and the assured was under no liability to contribute. Underwriters defended the action primarily for their own benefit.

Burnand v Rodocanachi
(1882) 7 App Cas 333, 51 LJQB 548, 47 LT 277, 31 WR 65, 4 Asp MLC 576, HL

Castellain v Preston

(1883) 11 QBD 380, 52 LJQB 366, 49 LT 29, 31 WR 557, CA
The general rule of law is that when there is a contract of indemnity and a loss happens, anything which reduces or diminishes that loss reduces or diminishes the amount which the indemnifier is bound to pay, and if the indemnifier has already paid it then if anything which diminishes the loss comes into the hands of the person to whom he has paid it, it becomes an equity that the person who has already paid the full indemnity is entitled to be recouped by having that amount back.

John Edwards & Co v Motor Union Insurance Co

[1922] 2 KB 249, 91 LJKB 921, 128 LT 276, 38 TLR 690, 16 Asp MLC 89, 27 Com Cas 367
McCardie J said: The doctrine of subrogation was derived by our English courts from the system of Roman law, and has been widely applied in our English body of law, eg to sureties and to matters of ultra vires as well as to insurance. In connection with insurance it was recognised ere the beginning of the eighteenth century. In *Randal v Cockran* (1748) 1 Ves Sen 98, it was held that the plaintiffs' insurers after making satisfaction stood in the place of the assured as to goods, salvage, and restitution in proportion for what they paid. As the Lord Chancellor (Lord Hardwicke) said: 'The plaintiffs had the plainest equity that could be.'

It is curious to observe how this doctrine of subrogative equity gradually entered into the substance of insurance law and at length became a recognised part of several branches of the general common law. In *Mason v Sainsbury* (1782) 3 Doug KB 61 at 64 Lord Mansfield said: 'Every day the insurer is put in the place of the insured', and Buller J, in the same case, in approving judgment for the plaintiff insurer, said: 'Whether this case be considered on strict legal principles, or upon the more liberal principles of insurance law, the plaintiff is entitled to recover.' These more liberal principles were based on equitable considerations, and in the well-known case of *Burnand v Rodocanachi* (1882) 7 App Cas 333 at 339, Lord Blackburn said in reference to a marine policy: 'If the indemnifier has already paid it, then, if anything which diminishes the loss comes into the hands of the person to whom he has paid it, it becomes an equity that the person who has already paid the full indemnity is entitled to be recouped by having that amount back.' This equity springs I conceive solely from the fact that the ordinary and valid contract of marine insurance is a contract of indemnity only. The point was put most clearly by Brett LJ in *Castellain v Preston* (1883) 11 QBD 380 at 386, when he said: 'The very foundation, in my opinion, of every rule which has been applied to insurance law is this, namely, that the contract of insurance contained in a marine or fire policy is a contract of indemnity, and of indemnity only.' That is the principle embodied in the Marine Insurance Act 1906, s 79.

If then subrogation is based on indemnity it is well to consider the features flowing from subrogation. This matter is neatly stated in *Porter on Insurance* (6th edn) p 236, as follow: 'This right rests upon the ground that the insurer's contract is in the nature of a contract of indemnity, and that he is therefore entitled, upon paying a sum for which others are primarily liable to the assured, to be proportionably subrogated to the right of action of the assured against them.' See, too, *Arnould on Marine Insurance* (10th edn) vol ii, s 1226, and *MacGillivray on Insurance* p 733. If once the claim be paid then as a matter of equity the rights to recover against third persons pass from the assured to the insurer although the legal right to compensation remains in the assured and although actions at law must be brought in the name of the assured and not of the insurer: see *London Assurance Co v Sainsbury* (1783) 3 Doug KB 245 at 254; *King v Victoria Insurance Co* [1896] AC 250, 65 LJPC 38, 74 LT 206, 44 WR 592, 12 TLR 285. As pointed out in *MacGillivray* p 740, it follows from this equity that if the assured upon tender of a proper indemnity as to costs refuse the use of his name the insurer can by proceedings in equity compel him to give the use of his name. This has long been settled law.

Scottish Union and National Insurance Co v Davis

[1970] 1 Lloyd's Rep 1, CA

The plaintiffs insured the defendant's car under a comprehensive policy. It was damaged by a third party and was sent to coachbuilders for repair. They did not do the work well and the defendant twice returned the car for them to make good the repair without the job being done satisfactorily. An engineer advised that the work done was so bad that it would cost more to put right than the original estimate. The defendant complained several times to the plaintiffs' branch representative and did not sign a satisfaction note. Despite this the plaintiffs paid the repairer's bill of £409. Later the defendant recovered £350 from a third party in respect of the original damage. The plaintiffs claimed this sum on the principle of subrogation.

HELD: The only basis on which the alleged subrogation could be put forward was that the plaintiffs had fully indemnified the defendant; but they had done nothing of the kind. The attempts to repair the car had been quite valueless and the payment of £409 by the plaintiffs to the repairers was not a payment for the successful doing of the repairs under the policy at all. Even if it was unreasonable of the defendant not to allow the repairers to make yet another effort to make good their work (and it could not be held that he was) it was irrelevant to the right of subrogation. Judgment for the defendant.

Yorkshire Insurance Co Ltd v Nisbet Shipping Co Ltd

[1962] 2 QB 330, [1961] 2 All ER 487, [1961] 2 WLR 1043, 105 Sol Jo 367, [1961] 1 Lloyd's Rep 479 (Diplock J)
The 'Blairnevis' became a total loss after a collision with the 'Orkney' in 1945. The insurers paid the owners the agreed value of £72,000 for a total loss. The owners then sued the owners of the 'Orkney, in Canada and recovered $336,000 being the value of the 'Blairnevis' in 1945 at $4.45 to the £1 sterling which was the rate of exchange at that time. The sum was paid to the owners in Canada in 1958 and when transmitted to England realised £127,000 at the current rate of exchange. The insurers claimed to be entitled to the whole sum of £127,000 from the owners and not merely to the £72,000 they had paid under the policy.
HELD: The insurers were entitled to the amount they had paid under the policy and no more.

Meacock v Bryant

[1942] 2 All ER 661, 167 LT 371, 59 TLR 51, 74 Ll L Rep 53 (Atkinson J)
The question whether a contingency policy was one of indemnity or not was contested and it was held that subrogation applied.

Note—And see decision of Tucker J in *Austin v Zurich Insurance Co*, p 845, above. The insurer is not usually subrogated to the rights of the innocent insured against the co-insured who caused the loss.

Motor repairs—insurer not agent of insured

Godfrey Davis Ltd v Culling and Hecht

(1962) 106 Sol Jo 918, [1962] 2 Lloyd's Rep 349, CA
The defendants, insured by the Brandaris Insurance Company, sustained damage to their car. They delivered the car to the plaintiffs, motor repairers, who sent them an estimate for repairs costing £160 and invited instructions from them or their insurers. The defendants sent the estimate to the Brandaris who instructed assessors to inspect the damage. The assessors wrote the plaintiffs saying they would make an examination 'on behalf of [the defendants'] insurers' and after inspection wrote the plaintiffs confirming that it would be in order for them to proceed with the repairs to the Brandaris. When the repairs were done the defendants collected the car from the plaintiffs who charged them only the £10 excess under the policy and an agreed payment for a new tyre. The Brandaris went into liquidation and the plaintiffs received no payment from that company for the work done. They then sought in this action to make the defendants liable for the whole cost of the repairs.
HELD: An insurer is not by necessary implication an agent of the insured to arranging for repairs to be done. On the letters which passed in this case it was clear that the insurers had themselves made a contract with the plaintiffs to do the repairs. There

was no holding out and no circumstances from which an agency could be implied. There is no general rule of law that when an insured person surrenders or subrogates to the insurer all his rights and liabilities over a particular accident giving rise to a claim that what the insurer thereafter does he does as agent of the insured person: that depends entirely on the terms of the policy or some express or ostensible authority. The defendants were not liable.

Cooter and Green Ltd v Tyrrell

[1962] 2 Lloyd's Rep 377, CA
The defendant's car was damaged in an accident. His father asked the plaintiffs, who were motor repairers, for an estimate of the cost of the repairs. The plaintiffs sent a provisional estimate which was sent on to the defendant's insurers. The plaintiffs knew the estimate was required for the insurers, who instructed assessors to inspect the car. As a result and at the request of the assessors, a revised estimate was prepared and sent to them by the plaintiffs. The assessors wrote in reply confirming their inspection on behalf of the insurers, approving the estimate, and confirming that repairs might proceed accordingly. The letter asked the insurers to collect the excess of £15 from the defendant and said the insurers' net liability would be £241: they asked for a satisfaction note and account to be forwarded to them. The repairs were shortly afterwards completed: they had been started before the assessors' letter was received because the plaintiffs knew the defendant and his father personally and the defendant had frequently telephoned asking them to expedite the work. He eventually signed the satisfaction note after trying the car. The insurers shortly afterwards became insolvent and failed to pay the plaintiffs' account for the repairs. The plaintiffs then sued the defendant for the whole cost of the repairs. The policy contained a provision: 'The company may at its own option repair . . . such motor car . . . or may pay in cash the amount of loss or damage . . .'.
HELD: The defendant was not liable. The letter from the assessors was an offer which was accepted by the conduct of the plaintiffs in completing the repairs and complying with the request for the satisfaction note and account to be sent to the assessors. There was a binding contract between the plaintiffs and the insurers and no one else. The insurers had exercised their choice under the policy by electing to place their own contract for the repairs. The father's request for an estimate was not the same as an order for the work: the final estimate was not discussed with the defendant at all and his telephone calls gave rise to no inference which could affect the contract.

Brown and Davis Ltd v Galbraith

[1972] 3 All ER 31, [1972] 1 WLR 997, 116 Sol Jo 545, [1972] 2 Lloyd's Rep 1, [1972] RTR 523, CA
The owner of a car damaged in an accident took it to repairers telling them it was comprehensively insured and asking for an estimate of the cost of repair. The estimate was sent to him a few days later. He also notified his insurers who sent their assessor to see the repairers. Agreement was reached between assessor and insurer on the cost of repairs and a printed form was filled in by the assessor which inter alia notified the repairers of the need for them to collect the £25 excess from the owner. The repairs were then carried out and an invoice sent by the repairers to the insurers, though without a signed satisfaction note from the owner, as he was not satisfied with the work done. He had some work done to the car elsewhere (the cost of which he deducted from the excess) and then took the signed satisfaction note to the repairers.

By that time the insurers had gone into liquidation and the repairers were not paid. They sued the owner for the whole cost of the repairs.
HELD: There were two contracts involved, one between the repairers and the insurers whereby the insurers undertook to pay for the repairs and one between the owner and repairers (to be implied from his having taken the vehicle to them for repair) by which the repairers undertook to carry out the work expeditiously (as in *Charnock v Liverpool Corpn*, p 871, below). But there was nothing from which in the contract between the owner and repairers a term could be implied that the owner had a liability to pay for the repairs beyond the amount of the excess. The facts of the case were clearly parallel with those in *Godfrey Davis Ltd v Culling and Hecht* (p 868, above) and *Cooter and Green v Tyrrell* (above) and there was nothing in the judgments in *Charnock*'s case to controvert the principles applied in either of those cases.

Indemnity or insurance

Solicitors' and General Life Assurance Society v Lamb
(1864) 2 De GJ & Sm 251, 4 New Rep 313, 33 LJ Ch 426, 10 LT 702

Dane v Mortgage Insurance Corpn Ltd
[1894] 1 QB 54, 63 LJQB 144, 70 LT 83, 10 TLR 86
The principle operates when there is a contract of indemnity but does not apply to insurances which are not contracts of indemnity.

Kirkland's Garage (Kinrose) Ltd v Clark

1967 SLT (Sh Ct) 60
The pursuers carried out repairs to the defender's car on the instructions of insurance assessors after the defender had filled in a claim form from his insurers. He signed a satisfaction note and collected the car. The insurers did not pay for the repairs and subsequently went into liquidation. The pursuers claimed that as the defender's name appeared on documents passing between them, the assessors and the insurers, it proved that the insurers were acting as the defender's agents in ordering the repairs.
HELD: So far as the documents went the defender's name appeared only as a reference; the insurers appeared to be acting as principals and made no disclosure that they were to be treated as agents of the defender. That being so the pursuers could not succeed unless there was a general rule of law that insurers are always acting as agents for the insured in instructing repairs. *Godfrey Davis Ltd v Culling* and *Hecht and Cooter and Green v Tyrrell* (above) show that there is no such rule.

A contrary decision

Martin v Stannard

[1964] CLY 585, Cty Ct (Judge Dow)
The plaintiff carried out repairs to the defendant's motor vehicle at the defendant's request after his insurance company had sent an assessor to inspect the damage and had intimated by telephone through the defendant's insurance brokers, that the work could proceed on the plaintiff's estimate of £138. After carrying out the work the plaintiff released the vehicle to the defendant on receiving an assurance over the telephone from the insurance brokers that if the defendant signed a satisfaction note

the insurance company would pay. On the insurers becoming insolvent without paying, the plaintiff claimed the £138 from the defendant.
HELD: The contract for the repairs was between the plaintiff and the defendant (who had received the benefit of them), the insurance company being merely in the position of a guarantor. The plaintiff was entitled to recover the £138 from the defendant.

Charnock v Liverpool Corpn

[1968] 3 All ER 473, [1968] 1 WLR 1498, 112 Sol Jo 781, [1968] 2 Lloyd's Rep 113, CA
The plaintiff's car was damaged in an accident by negligence of the first defendant's servant. He took the car to a garage where he wanted the repairs done and by arrangement met his insurer's assessor there. The repairers prepared an estimate and eventually the insurers wrote them: 'We confirm it is in order to proceed with the repairs as per your estimate . . . Please forward your final account to this office on completion, together with a signed satisfaction note.' A reasonable period for doing the repairs was five weeks but the repairers took eight. The plaintiff hired a car for the whole of the eight weeks and sued the first defendants and the repairers for the costs. The first defendants were admittedly liable for five weeks' hire charges: the judge held the repairers liable for the other three on the grounds that they had impliedly contracted with the plaintiff to do the repairs within a reasonable time and were in breach of that contract.
HELD, ON APPEAL by the repairers: The judge was right. The decisions in *Cooter and Green v Tyrrell* and *Godfrey Davis Ltd v Culling and Hecht* (above) did not decide that there was no contract of any sort between the owner and repairer. In those cases the question was whether the contract to pay for the repairs was made between the insurers and the repairers or between the owner and repairers. In the present case there was a clear contract to be inferred from the facts between the repairers and the plaintiff that in consideration of his leaving his car with them for repair they would carry out the repairs with reasonable expedition and care and that they would be paid by the insurance company. The repairers were in breach of this contract.

Davidson v Guardian Royal Exchange Assurance

[1979] 1 Lloyd's Rep 406, Ct of Sess
Insurers issued a comprehensive motor policy covering 'loss of or damage to the vehicle' and containing a provision in the case of damage: 'The company may at its own option repair the vehicle.' There was an exemption from liability to pay for 'loss of use'. The insured's car was damaged by fire; the insurers elected to repair it and sent it away for this purpose. It was not returned repaired until 40 weeks had elapsed. A reasonable time for repair would have been eight weeks. The insured claimed damages for loss of use of the car.
HELD: (1) Having undertaken to repair the car the insurers were bound to do so within a reasonable time. There was a breach of this implied term for the period beyond the eighth week. (2) If there was any ambiguity in the policy the construction had to be *contra proferentum*. (3) The insured's claim in this action was based on breach of contract; the policy was not concerned with breach of contract and the exemption clause did not apply.

Total loss

Page v Scottish Insurance Corpn

(1929) (Scrutton J), 98 LJKB 308, 140 LT 571, 45 TLR 250, 73 Sol Jo 236, 33 Ll L Rep 134, CA

A condition of the assured's right to claim as for total loss is his obligation to surrender the subject matter of the insured risk to his insurers.

On abandonment the property and all its incidents pass to the underwriter to whom it is abandoned. I have known cases myself in my own practice where underwriters have made an extremely good thing by accepting abandonment because they have got something more than the amount they had to pay.

The Third Parties (Rights against Insurers) Act 1930

Note—This Act has been amended by the Insolvency Act 1985, s 235(1), Sch 8, para 7(2), and by the Insolvency Act 1986, s 439(2) and Sch 14, and in respect of Scotland by the Bankruptcy (Scotland) Act 1985, s 75(1), and Sch 7 Pt I.

The effect of the two decisions in *Re Harrington Motor Co Ltd, ex p Chaplin* [1928] Ch 105, 97 LJ Ch 55, 138 LT 185, 44 TLR 58, and *Hood's Trustees v Southern Union General Insurance Co of Australasia* [1928] Ch 793, 97 LJCh 467, 139 LT 536, [1928] B & CR 95, CA was that the right of indemnity contained in a policy was property of the assured and passed to the liquidator or trustee on liquidation or bankruptcy. A third party who obtained a verdict from the assured did not obtain his damages, but the liquidator or trustee collected the money from the insurer and it was assets for distribution between all the creditors, and the third party had to share his claim with the other creditors.

These decisions resulted in the Third Parties (Rights against Insurers) Act 1930, as follows:

'**1 Rights of third parties against insurers on bankruptcy, etc, of the insured** (1) Where under any contract of insurance a person (hereinafter referred to as the insured) is insured against liabilities to third parties which he may incur, then—

(a) in the event of the insured becoming bankrupt or making a composition or arrangement with his creditors; or
(b) in the case of the insured being a company, in the event of a winding-up order [or an administration order] being made, or a resolution for a voluntary winding-up being passed, with respect to the company, or of a receiver or manager of the company's business or undertaking being duly appointed, or of possession being taken, by or on behalf of the holders of any debentures secured by a floating charge, of any property comprised in or subject to the charge [or of [a voluntary arrangement proposed for the purposes of Part I of the Insolvency Act 1986 being approved under that Part]];

if, either before or after that event, any such liability as aforesaid is incurred by the insured, his rights against the insurer under the contract in respect of the liability shall, notwithstanding anything in any Act or rule of law to the contrary, be transferred to and vest in the third party to whom the liability was so incurred.

(2) Where [the estate of any person falls to be administered in accordance with an order under section [421 of the Insolvency Act 1986]], then, if any debt provable in bankruptcy [(in Scotland, any claim accepted in the sequestration)] is owing by the deceased in respect of a liability against which he was insured under a contract of insurance as being a liability to a third party, the deceased debtor's rights against the insurer under the contract in respect of that liability shall, notwithstanding anything in [any such order], be transferred to and vest in the person to whom the debt is owing.

(3) In so far as any contract of insurance made after the commencement of this Act in respect of any liability of the insured to third parties purports, whether directly or indirectly, to avoid the contract or to alter the rights of the parties thereunder upon the happening to the insured of any of the events specified in paragraph (a) or paragraph (b) of subsection (1) of this section

or upon the [estate of any person falling to be administered in accordance with an order under section [421 of the Insolvency Act 1986]], the contract shall be of no effect.

(4) Upon a transfer under subsection (1) or subsection (2) of this section, the insurer shall, subject to the provisions of section three of this Act, be under the same liability to the third party as he would have been under to the insured, but—

(a) if the liability of the insurer to the insured exceeds the liability of the insured to the third party, nothing in this Act shall affect the rights of the insured against the insurer in respect of the excess; and

(b) if the liability of the insurer to the insured is less than the liability of the insured to the third party, nothing in this Act shall affect the rights of the third party against the insured in respect of the balance.

(5) For the purposes of this Act, the expression ''liabilities to third parties'', in relation to a person insured under any contract of insurance, shall not include any liability of that person in the capacity of insurer under some other contract of insurance.

(6) This Act shall not apply—

(a) where a company is wound up voluntarily merely for the purposes of reconstruction or of amalgamation with another company; or

(b) to any case to which subsections (1) and (2) of section seven of the Workmen's Compensation Act 1925 applies.

2 Duty to give necessary information to third parties (1) In the event of any person becoming bankrupt or making a composition or arrangement with his creditors, or in the event of [the estate of any person falling to be administered in accordance with an order under section [421 of the Insolvency Act 1986]], or in the event of a winding-up order [or an administration order] being made, or a resolution for a voluntary winding-up being passed, with respect to any company or of a receiver or manager of the company's business or undertaking being duly appointed or of possession being taken by or on behalf of the holders of any debentures secured by a floating charge of any property comprised in or subject to the charge it shall be the duty of the bankrupt, debtor, personal representative of the deceased debtor or company, and, as the case may be, of the trustee in bankruptcy, trustee, liquidator, [administrator,] receiver, or manager, or person in possession of the property to give at the request of any person claiming that the bankrupt, debtor, deceased debtor, or company is under a liability to him such information as may reasonably be required by him for the purpose of ascertaining whether any rights have been transferred to and vested in him by this Act and for the purpose of enforcing such rights, if any, and any contract of insurance, in so far as it purports, whether directly or indirectly, to avoid the contract or to alter the rights of the parties thereunder upon the giving of any such information in the events aforesaid or otherwise to prohibit or prevent the giving thereof in the said events shall be of no effect.

[(1A) The reference in subsection (1) of this section to a trustee includes a reference to the supervisor of a [voluntary arrangement proposed for the purposes of, and approved under, Part I or Part VIII of the Insolvency Act 1986].]

(2) If the information given to any person in pursuance of subsection (1) of this section discloses reasonable ground for supposing that there have or may have been transferred to him under this Act rights against any particular insurer, that insurer shall be subject to the same duty as is imposed by the said subsection on the persons therein mentioned.

(3) The duty to give information imposed by this section shall include a duty to allow all contracts of insurance, receipts for premiums, and other relevant documents in the possession or power of the person on whom the duty is so imposed to be inspected and copies thereof to be taken.

3 Settlement between insurers and insured persons Where the insured has become bankrupt or where in the case of the insured being a company, a winding-up order [or an administration order] has been made or a resolution for a voluntary winding-up has been passed, with respect to the company, no agreement made between the insurer and the insured after liability has been incurred to a third party and after the commencement of the bankruptcy or winding-up [or the day of the making of the administration order], as the case may be, nor any waiver, assignment, or other disposition made by, or payment made to the insured after the commencement [or day] aforesaid shall be effective to defeat or affect the rights transferred to the third party under this Act, but those rights shall be the same as if no such agreement, waiver, assignment, disposition or payment had been made.

4 (*Applies to Scotland only.*)

5 Short title This Act may be cited as the Third Parties (Rights against Insurers) Act 1930.'

Note—An infant cannot be made bankrupt. A married woman formerly could not, but can now.

It is to be noted that this Act is not limited to motor accidents but is general in its application, and that only the rights which the assured possesses against the insurer pass to the third party. The third party is therefore bound by the policy conditions, except as is mentioned later. If, therefore, there is an arbitration clause in the policy, this binds the third party. A similar position arose under the Workmen's Compensation Acts, and this point was decided in the case of *King v Phoenix Assurance Co* [1910] 2 KB 666, 80 LJKB 44, 103 LT 53, 3 BWCC 442, CA. The same point has been decided in motor cases.

In the case of *Firma C-Trade SA v Newcastle Protection, The Fanti* [1991] 2 AC 1, [1990] 2 All ER 705 the House of Lords reiterated the principle that where the answer had a good defence to a claim by the insured before the statutory transfer of the insurance rights, the insurer would have the same defence to a claim by the third party.

Post Office v Norwich Union Fire Insurance Society Ltd

[1967] 2 QB 363, [1967] 1 All ER 577, [1967] 2 WLR 709, 111 Sol Jo 71, [1967] 1 Lloyd's Rep 216, CA

Contractors carrying out drainage works damaged a buried telephone cable. The Post Office claimed from them the cost of making good the damage. The contractors did not pay, alleging that the damage was due to wrong information given to them by a Post Office engineer. A year after the incident and before any proceedings had been started they went into liquidation. The Post Office thereupon sued their insurers (the defendants) claiming that under the Third Parties (Rights against Insurers) Act 1930, s 1 they were entitled to recover the amount of the damage.

HELD: The Post Office could not claim against the insurers until it had first obtained a judgment against the contractors. The Act transfers to the third party the wrongdoer's rights against the insurers under the policy. In the present case those rights were to be indemnified 'against all sums which the insured shall become legally liable to pay as compensation in respect of loss of or damage to property'. The right to indemnity would not arise until the insured's liability to pay the third party had been ascertained and brought into existence by a judgment of the court or by agreement. It was not open to the plaintiff to establish its right to damages from the contractors in the present proceedings against the insurers: the liability must first be established by a judgment in a separate action against the contractors.

Doris Bradley v Eagle Star Insurance Co Ltd

[1988] 2 Lloyd's Rep 233, CA; affd [1989] 1 All ER 961, [1989] 2 WLR 568, 133 Sol Jo 359, HL

The plaintiff was employed in a cotton mill during various periods until 1970, when she was certified by the Pneumoconiosis Panel to be suffering from byssinosis, a lung disease of cotton workers. In 1976 the limited company by whom she had been so employed was voluntarily wound up and dissolved. In 1987 by originating summons she applied under s 33(2) of the Supreme Court Act 1981 for an order that the

defendants, an insurance company, disclose all contracts issued by them to the employers in respect of personal injuries sustained at work.
HELD: She was not entitled to the order sought. Her object was to proceed against the defendant insurers under the Third Parties (Rights against Insurers) Act 1930. An order would enable her to proceed against the defendant insurers only if she could first establish liability against the employers either by judgment of the court or by award in arbitration or by agreement (*Post Office v Norwich Union Fire Insurance Society Ltd* (p 874, above)).
An appeal to the House of Lords was dismissed ((1989) Times, 3 March). *Post Office v Norwich Union Fire Insurance Society* was rightly decided and as the company employing the appellant no longer existed and was incapable by any means of being restored to existence, liability could not be established by action, arbitration or agreement. The 1930 Act was passed to remedy the injustice apparent in *Re Harrington Motor Co and Hoods Trustees v Southern Union* (p 872, above) and not to remedy any injustice arising from the dissolution of a company making it impossible to establish the liability of such a company to a third party. As the employers had been dissolved and could not be restored to the register under s 651 of the Companies Act 1985 any contingent right to claim against the insurers could not be established and there was no point in making the order sought.

Freshwater v Western Australian Assurance Co Ltd

[1933] 1 KB 515, 102 LJKB 75, 148 LT 275, 49 TLR 131, 76 Sol Jo 888, 44 Ll L Rep 282, CA
Plaintiff was injured in a motor accident and recovered judgment against C & H for £300 damages for negligence. He subsequently became bankrupt. At the time of the accident H was insured with defendant company against third-party risks. The policy of insurance contained the usual arbitration clause making an award a condition precedent to bringing an action on the policy. Plaintiff issued a writ against defendant company contending that under the Third Parties (Rights against Insurers) Act 1930, s 1, and the Road Traffic Act 1930, s 36(4) (now replaced by the Road Traffic Act 1988, s 148(7), they were accountable to him for the amount of the judgment. The defendant company thereupon took out a summons to stay the action on the ground that under the arbitration clause the obtaining of an award was a condition precedent to bringing the action.
HELD: The rights of the defendant company under the policy were not affected by either of the Acts of 1930 and it was therefore entitled to rely on the arbitration clause, which made it a condition precedent to bringing an action that an award should first be obtained.

Hassett v Legal and General Assurance Society Ltd

(1939) 63 Ll L Rep 278 (Atkinson J)
The third party served a writ on the assured company by registered post. The company had ceased to exist and the writ was ignored. The third party signed judgment in default and damages were assessed at £1,050.

The assured had failed to fulfil the policy condition requiring them to give notice to insurers of the commencement of proceedings. No notice of the claim was given to insurers. The assured company were to blame and (*semble*) the third party's solicitors, who had not informed insurers of plaintiff's claim against assured. The third party had no greater rights than the assured would have had. Insurers not liable.

Farrell v Federated Employers Insurance Association Ltd

[1970] 3 All ER 632, [1970] 1 WLR 1400, 114 Sol Jo 719, [1970] 2 Lloyd's Rep 170, DA

The plaintiff was injured in November 1962. He claimed damages against the employers who were insured by the defendants. In September 1964 a receiver was appointed by the employers' secured creditors. In September 1965 the plaintiff issued a writ against the employers and served it by registered post at their registered office on 6 January 1966. There was no one there to deal with it, the employers having ceased to trade. The plaintiff's solicitors signed judgment in default of appearance on 28 February 1966. On 2 March 1966 they notified the defendant insurers of the judgment: this was the first the defendants knew of the issue and service of proceedings. They refused to satisfy the judgment on the ground that there had been a breach of a condition of the policy requiring the insured to notify and forward any writ immediately on receipt. The plaintiff accepted that for the purposes of the Third Parties (Rights against Insurers) Act 1930 he stood in the shoes of the employer as against the insurers but claimed (1) the burden of proof was on the insurers, to show that the condition was binding on the employers, (2) that he had complied with the condition, (3) that if there was a breach the insurers had not been prejudiced.

HELD: (1) On the case as pleaded the burden of proof was not on the insurers but even if it was they had discharged it by showing that in the usual course of business the employers would have received the policy document; (2) notification of the service of the writ eight weeks later and after signing judgment was not 'immediately on receipt'; (3) the insurers had been prejudiced by signing judgment before notifying them. They were not liable to meet the judgment.

Pioneer Concrete (UK) Ltd v National Employers Mutual Insurance

[1985] 2 All ER 395, [1985] 1 Lloyd's Rep 274, QBD

Contractors carried out work on the plaintiffs' plant. Seven months later the plant collapsed, causing the plaintiffs substantial loss and damage. The contractors were insured against public liability claims under a policy issued by the defendants (NEM) containing a condition requiring the contractors to give NEM written notice of 'any accident or claim or proceedings immediately the same shall have come to the knowledge of the insured or his representative'. The plaintiffs' solicitors notified a claim to NEM immediately after the accident and pressed them in correspondence. Eventually, the contractors having meanwhile gone into liquidation, the plaintiffs' solicitors issued a Writ against the contractors without notifying NEM and served it on the liquidator. No appearance having been entered they signed judgment for damages to be assessed and then notified NEM's solicitors. NEM refused to indemnify the contractors under the policy on the ground of breach of condition in that no written notice of proceedings had been given. The plaintiffs issued proceedings against NEM under the Third Parties (Rights against Insurers) Act 1930.

HELD: The claim failed: (1) though it did not matter for compliance with the condition whether notification came from the contractors or the plaintiffs (following *Lickiss v Milestone Motor Policies* (p 815) there had been a failure to comply with the condition as to notice of proceedings. 'Any action or claim or proceedings' meant any accident and any claim and any proceedings. Notification of the claim alone was not sufficient; (2) it is not necessary for an insurer to show he has been prejudiced by the breach of condition in the policy before he can rely on it but if it were necessary then in the present case there was sufficient prejudice from the breach in that their position had been somewhat weakened after judgment had been entered without prior notice. *Farrell v Federated Employers Insurance Association Ltd* (p 876) applied.

Murray v Legal and General Assurance Society Ltd

[1970] 2 QB 495, [1969] 3 All ER 794, [1970] 2 WLR 465, 113 Sol Jo 720, [1969] 2 Lloyd's Rep 405 (Cumming-Bruce J)
The plaintiff was injured at work in March 1963. In July 1963 his employers went into voluntary liquidation. They were insured against liability to employers by the defendants to whom they owed £1,708 in respect of adjusted premiums. The plaintiff obtained judgment against his employers in 1966 for £1,750. He claimed against the defendants under the Third Parties (Rights against Insurers) Act 1930 for payment of this amount. The insurers claimed to set off against the amount of the judgment the sum owed for premiums on the ground that the 1930 Act vested in the plaintiff a statutory right of subrogation whereby he was in no better position than the person whose rights he had acquired.
HELD: They could not do so. It is not all the rights and liabilities of the insured under the contract of insurance which are transferred to the third party but only those in respect of the liability incurred by the insured to the third party. There is no express transfer of liabilities of the insured to the insurer in the Act, but if there is under the policy a defence by way of condition available against the insured (as in *Hassett*'s case) that defence would be available against the third party. Rights which were not referable to the particular liability of the insured to the particular third party were not transferred.

Lefevre v White

[1990] 1 Lloyd's Rep 569
For the purposes, inter alia, of limitation the third party's cause of action accrues against the insurer when the cause of action of the insured accrues. The third party cause of action does not accrue or arise out of the bankrupting of the insured.

MISCELLANEOUS CASES

Estoppel

Greenwood v Martins Bank Ltd

[1933] AC 51, 101 LJKB 623, 147 LT 441, 48 TLR 601, 75 Sol Jo 544, HL (Lord Tomlin)
The essential factors giving rise to an estoppel are, I think:
1 A representation or conduct amounting to a representation intended to induce a course of conduct on the part of the person to whom the representation is made.
2 An act or omission resulting from the representation whether actual or by conduct by the person to whom the representation is made.
3 Detriment to such person as a consequence of the act or omission.

Mere silence cannot amount to a representation, but when there is a duty to disclose deliberate silence may become significant and amount to a representation.

Insurance Companies Act 1958

Department of Trade and Industry v St Christopher Motorists Association Ltd

[1974] 1 All ER 395, [1974] 1 WLR 99, 117 Sol Jo 873, [1974] 1 Lloyd's Rep 17, ChD
The defendant company ran an association to protect the interests of motorists. Members could pay an annual sum and, subject to the decision of a committee could be provided with a chauffeur if they became legally unable to drive because of, eg becoming disqualified on conviction of a road traffic offence. The decision of the committee was final and an applicant had to satisfy certain requirements but the committee's discretion was not absolute: if the member fulfilled the requirements he was entitled to the services offered by the association.
HELD: Contracts of insurance were not confined to contracts for payment of a sum of money but included contracts for some benefit corresponding to the payment of a sum of money. The defendants were an insurance company to which the Insurance Companies Act 1958 applied.

Note—The Insurance Companies Act 1958 has been repealed and replaced by the Insurance Companies Act 1974 (consolidated in the Insurance Companies Act 1982), which, though it does not reproduce the 1958 Act, fulfils the same function.

Public policy

Beresford v Royal Insurance Co Ltd

[1938] AC 586, [1938] 2 All ER 602, 107 LJKB 464, 158 LT 459, 54 TLR 789, 82 Sol Jo 431, HL
A man who had insured his life for £50,000 shot himself. He did so to enable his creditors to have some benefit from the proceeds of the policies.
HELD: A man is not to be allowed to have recourse to a court of justice to claim a benefit of his crime whether under a contract or a gift. Deliberate suicide, *felo de se*, has always been regarded in English law as a crime. It is contrary to public policy for a court of law to enforce a contract to pay a sum of money to a person's representatives in the event of his committing *felo de se*. His administrator claims as his representative and as such falls under the same ban.

Euro-Diam Ltd v Bathurst

[1988] 2 All ER 23, [1988] 2 WLR 517, 132 Sol Jo 372, [1987] 1 Lloyd's Rep 228, CA
The plaintiffs, a UK company, sent a quantity of diamonds to a German company on sale or return and dispatched them to West Germany. At the request of the intending purchaser the value of the diamonds was invoiced at a figure substantially less than the true price. The object of this, as the plaintiff's representative well knew, was to reduce the duty payable by the purchasers to West German Customs, a criminal offence in that country. The diamonds were insured under a policy issued by the defendant underwriter. When in a warehouse in Germany and still the property of the plaintiffs the diamonds were stolen. The insurers refused to indemnify the plaintiffs on the ground that their transaction relating to the dispatch of the diamonds was 'tainted with illegality'; by reason of the plaintiffs' understated invoice: *ex turpi causa non oritur actio*.

HELD: The *ex turpi causa* defence failed. Though the issue of a false invoice by the plaintiffs' representative was reprehensible and was criminal under German law he did not issue the invoice for his own or the plaintiffs' purposes. The understated invoice had no bearing on the loss of the diamonds nor did it deceive the insurers since the true value was recorded in the plaintiffs' register and the correct premium paid. The mere fact that the understated invoice might prove an embarrassment to the insurers in any subrogation proceedings was not sufficient to tip the scales of public policy in their favour.

Ashmore, Benson, Pease & Co Ltd v AV Dawson Ltd

[1973] 2 All ER 856, [1973] 1 WLR 828, 117 Sol Jo 203, [1973] 2 Lloyd's Rep 21, [1973] RTR 473, CA
The plaintiffs arranged with the defendants, who were hauliers, to carry two pieces of machinery each weighing 25 tons from Stockton to Hull. The defendants sent two articulated lorries each of 10 tons laden weight to collect the machinery which was loaded on the lorries in the presence of the plaintiffs' transport manager, who knew that when loaded each vehicle would weigh 35 tons. He was aware of the regulation in the Motor Vehicles (Construction and Use) Regulations 1966 limiting the permissible loaded weight of an articulated lorry to 30 tons. On the journey one of the lorries overturned damaging the machinery.
HELD: The plaintiffs were barred from suing the defendants for the damage. Even if the contract was lawful when made (in that it could have been performed by using the right kind of vehicle) the performance of it was illegal. The plaintiffs' transport manager who knew the weight of the two loads and the regulations failed to stop the loading when he went to watch it being done: he was a participator in the illegality.

Bedford Insurance Co v Instituto de Resseguros do Brasil

[1984] 3 All ER 766, [1984] 3 WLR 726, 128 Sol Jo 701, [1984] 1 Lloyd's Rep 210 (Parker J)
By the Insurance Companies Act 1974, s 2 no person might carry on in Great Britain business of a class listed in s 1 without authorisation from the Secretary of State. The plaintiffs were an insurance company operating through brokers in London who entered into insurance contracts of a specified class listed in s 1 in respect of which they obtained reinsurance cover from the defendants. The plaintiffs had no authorisation from the Secretary of State. Any person carrying on business in contravention of the Act was guilty of an offence punishable by fine or imprisonment. The plaintiffs sued the defendants under the reinsurance contract for amounts due under the primary contracts.
HELD: What was prohibited was both the making and performance of any contract of insurance of the relevant class by way of business. Though it was the insurer who committed the offence, not the insured, no enforceable right under the prohibited contract was acquired by the insured, for under the Act it would be an offence for the insurer to pay him. The contracts written by the plaintiffs' agents were null and void. Quoting Denning LJ in *Marles v Philip Frant* ([1954] 1 QB 29, [1953] 1 All ER 645, [1953] 2 WLR 564, 97 Sol Jo 189, CA) 'if the plaintiff requires any aid from an illegal transaction to establish his cause of action, then he shall not have any aid from the court'. The plaintiffs were not entitled to recover under the reinsurance contract because the primary contracts were unenforceable.

Stewart v Oriental Fire & Marine Insurance Co

[1984] 3 All ER 777, [1984] 3 WLR 741, 128 Sol Jo 645, [1984] 2 Lloyd's Rep 109 (Leggatt J)
The plaintiffs were underwriters at Lloyd's claiming sums due on risks reinsured by the defendants, a foreign company doing insurance business in London through sub-agents. The defendants were not authorised for any relevant business by the Department of Trade under the Insurance Companies Act 1974 (see *Bedford Insurance Co v Instituto de Resseguros do Brasil*, above). If the *Bedford* case were rightly decided the plaintiffs could not recover under the reinsurance contract. It was submitted that what the Act rendered illegal was business of effecting and carrying out particular classes of contracts of insurance, not individual contracts.
HELD: It was important to consider the purpose of the statute: it was principally designed to protect the public by ensuring the financial soundness of insurers. To render individual contracts of insurance void would be repugnant to the policy of the Act. There was no express prohibition of contracts of insurance in the Act; it deliberately maintained a distinction between carrying on insurance business and making individual contracts of insurance. It did not intend to go further and prohibit contracts of insurance, the effecting and carrying out of which constituted the carrying on of insurance business. Judgment for the plaintiffs. *Bedford Insurance Co v Instituto de Resseguros do Brasil* (above) not followed.

Criminal negligence

James v British General Insurance Co Ltd
[1927] 2 KB 311, 96 LJKB 729, 137 LT 156, 43 TLR 354, 71 Sol Jo 273, 27 Ll L Rep 328 (Roche J)

Tinline v White Cross Association Insurance Co
[1921] 3 KB 327, 90 LJKB 118, 125 LT 632, 37 TLR 733 (Bailhache J)
Insurers are liable even though the assured is guilty of criminal negligence amounting to manslaughter. A policy covered liability of the assured for accidental injury caused by his negligence, even though gross and attended by criminal consequences; the policy, by covering these liabilities, was not void as against public policy, and the assured was entitled to the indemnity which he claimed.

Note—Both these decisions were cases of motor car manslaughter, and policies against third party liability were enforceable

These cases were questioned in *Haseldine v Hosken* [1933] 1 KB 822, 102 LJKB 441, 148 LT 510, 49 TLR 254, 45 Ll L Rep 59, CA (insurance against solicitor's negligence, where solicitor guilty of champerty).

Alexander v Rayson

[1936] 1 KB 169, 105 LJKB 148, 154 LT 205, 52 TLR 131, 80 Sol Jo 15, CA
The court will not enforce transactions tainted with fraudulent or immoral purposes or objects.

Note—Untrue statement of rent in lease to avoid stamp duty.

Applied in *Edler v Auerbach* [1950] 1 KB 359, [1949] 2 All ER 692, 65 TLR 645, 93 Sol Jo 727 (Devlin J).

Beresford v Royal Insurance Co Ltd

[1938] AC 586, [1938] 2 All ER 602, 107 LJKB 464, 158 LT 459, 54 TLR 789, 82 Sol Jo 431, HL
But in the case of a crime, such as *felo de se*, which is a deliberate felony akin to murder, the court will not allow the criminal or his representatives to recover.

Note—See p 878, above. But by the Suicide Act 1961, s 1 suicide is no longer a crime.

Gray v Barr

[1971] 2 QB 554, [1971] 2 All ER 949, [1971] 2 WLR 1334, 115 Sol Jo 364, [1971] 2 Lloyd's Rep 1, CA
The defendant was insured against liability to pay 'damages in respect of . . . bodily injury to any person . . . caused by accidents'. Being suspicious one night that his wife was at the house of a neighbour, Gray, with whom she was having an affair he went to find her and took with him a loaded shotgun. In Gray's house he fired a shot at the ceiling to frighten him; the other barrel then discharged accidentally, killing him. Gray's widow sued for damages under the Fatal Accidents Acts; the defendant in third party proceedings claimed to be covered by the policy.
HELD, ON APPEAL: (1) The policy did not cover, because the events leading to Gray's death were not an 'accident' but arose from the defendant's deliberate act in taking a loaded gun to enforce his search; (2) the further question arose of public policy. In *Tinline*'s and *Jame*'s cases (p 880, above) the act indemnified was one intended by the law that people should insure against; so far as manslaughter on the road by gross negligence is concerned public policy does not prevent the enforcement of an indemnity. The present case, in which the person seeking indemnity was guilty of deliberate, intentional and unlawful violence or threats of violence, was not of that type. As in *Beresford*'s case (above) the rule of public policy applied that no person can claim indemnity for his own wilful and culpable crime. The defendant was not entitled to indemnity under the policy.

Marcel Beller Ltd v Hayden

[1978] QB 694, [1978] 3 All ER 111, [1979] 2 WLR 845, 122 Sol Jo 279, [1978] 1 Lloyd's Rep 472, [1978] RTR 344 (Judge Edgar Fay QC)
The plaintiffs took out a personal accident policy on the life of their employee John McCredie issued by the defendant. Compensation was payable under the policy if Mr McCredie sustained 'accidental bodily injury which shall solely and independently of any other cause . . . result in his death'. McCredie was killed when the car he was driving at high speed crashed out of control on a bend. His blood alcohol content at the time was 261 milligrammes per 100 millilitres. Liability under the policy was excluded if death resulted from 'deliberate exposure to exceptional danger . . . or the insured person's own criminal act'.
HELD: (1) McCredie's death was accidental; (2) driving the car knowing he had consumed an excessive amount of alcohol, though negligent, was not deliberately exposing himself to exceptional danger; (3) the offences of dangerous driving and driving under the influence of drink were sufficiently serious to qualify as criminal acts within the meaning of the exemption. Judgment for the defendant.

'Though the court will rectify an instrument which fails through some mistake of the draftsman in point of law to carry out the real agreement between the parties, it is not sufficient in order to create an equity for rectification that there has been a mistake as to the legal construction or the legal consequences of an instrument.'

Quoting Turner LJ in *Stone v Godfrey* (5 De G M & G 76 at 90):
'I assume . . . that this court has power (as I feel no doubt that it has) to relieve against mistakes in law as well as against mistakes in fact.'
ON APPEAL, per Evershed MR: I do not read that passage as meaning that if the mistake made is in using language to perfect an agreement which in law has some result different from the common intention, that is not a case in which there can be rectification. I think that would be too wide. I think it may well be that if the mistake has arisen from the legal effect of the language used that may provide a ground for the exercise of the court's reforming power. Subject, however, to that qualification, I think that the passage cited is correct.

As has been said, this discretionary remedy of rectification must be cautiously watched and jealously exercised.

George Cohen Sons & Co v Docks and Inland Waterways Executive

(1950) 84 Ll L Rep 97, CA
The defendants cannot be heard to say that they misapprehend their own document; still less to say that they did not misapprehend it, but sought to gain an advantage over the plaintiffs by getting past the plaintiffs without them being made aware of it a change in the obligation as to repairs.

Citing Lord Chelmsford LC in *Fowler v Fowler* (1859) 4 De G & J 250:
'The power which the court possesses of reforming written agreements where there has been an omission or insertion of stipulations contrary to the intention of the parties and under a mutual mistake, is one which has been frequently and most usefully exercised. But it is also one which should be used with extreme care and caution. To substitute a new agreement for one which the parties have deliberately subscribed ought only to be permitted upon evidence of a different insertion of the clearest and most satisfactory description.'

Lloyd's slip part of contract

Note—The contract is made on the issue of the policy and the policy is not therefore a memorandum of an antecedent contract. In *MacKenzie v Coulson* (1869) LR 8 Eq 368, James VC at 375: 'Courts of Equity do not rectify contracts; they may and do rectify instruments purporting to have been made in pursuance of the terms of contracts. But it is always necessary for a plaintiff to show that there was an actual concluded contract antecedent to the instrument which is sought to be rectified; and that such contract is inaccurately represented in the instrument.' *MacKenzie v Coulson* was concerned with an attempt to rectify a policy of insurance to accord with the terms of a 'slip'.

The nature of the cover is defined in the contract of insurance with the assured. There are two documents: the policy itself and the brokers' 'slip'. The 'slip' identifies briefly the type of cover required and the parties to the contract. It is addressed from the brokers to the underwriters; and for this purpose the broker is treated as the agent of the assured. It may be suggested the 'slip' is in the nature of a proposal and to have a similar effect.

The policy on the other hand, is a contracted document and is presumed to embody the terms agreed by the parties. Lord Wright in *Izzards* case ([1937] AC 773) dealing with a proposal and the policy said: Though the warranties and conditions expressed in the proposal are declared to be the basic conditions of the policy, that must be subject to their being overridden by any express terms to the contrary effect in the actual policy. The documents must be read together and reconciled so that every part of the contract may receive effect, but if there is a final and direct inconsistency, the positive and express terms of the policy must prevail. The 'slip' should therefore be admissible in any consideration of the effect of the policy.

Renewal—implied warranty

Re Wilson and Scottish Insurance Corpn

[1920] 2 Ch 28, 89 LJCh 329, 123 LT 404, 36 TLR 545, 64 Sol Jo 514 (Astbury J)
It may be very material to the insurer on renewal to know of any change in the extent of the risk to enable them to determine whether or not they will continue the insurance, and that if on the renewal the assured had informed the insurers of the alteration, the premium would have been increased or the renewal refused.

Express declaration on renewal

Note—I declare that the particulars given above are true and that the motor car is and shall be kept in good condition, and I also declare that since the issue of the above-numbered policy neither I nor any other person who will ordinarily drive the car has been declined insurance by any other insurance company or association, nor has any stipulation been made that I or such other person should bear the first portion of any loss. I further declare that neither I nor such other person has developed a physical infirmity, defective vision or hearing or been convicted of any offence in connection with the driving of any motor car: *Re Wilson and Scottish Insurance Corpn* [1920] 2 Ch 28, 89 LJCh 329, 123 LT 404, 36 TLR 545, 64 Sol Jo 514.

In *Law Accident Insurance Society v Boyd* 1942 SC 384, a proposal was made and policy issued in 1935. It was renewed, and the last renewal was in February 1940. In July 1939 the assured was convicted of an offence under the Road Traffic Act 1930, s 15. He did not disclose this conviction on renewal in February 1940. Insurers took proceedings for a declaration. The defendants moved the court for a ruling that there was no prima facie case. Lord Stephenson negatived the motion. Defendants appealed. The appeal was dismissed.

The Lord Justice Clerk said that on each renewal there at once arose an obligation on the insured to make such disclosure or correct any statement in his original proposal form which may be material to the risk for which he seeks cover during the year still to come. He considered the rule stated on p 429 of *Macgillivray* (2nd edn) as follows, to be true:

'In fire policies and similar risks where the insurers may decline to renew a policy at the expiration of the original period each renewal is made on the faith of the continued truth of the original representations and if there has been any material change adverse to the interests of the insurers which has not been disclosed on or before payment of the renewal premium the insurers may repudiate liability or limit their liability to the amount for which they would have been liable if there had been no change.'

I think it is quite clear that there was a duty upon the proposer for renewal to disclose all the material facts in exactly the same way as at the date when the policy was originally taken up: Per Lord Wark, Lord Mackay and Lord Jamieson concurring.

And see 'Continuing warranty', pp 852–853, above.

Solicitor's duty to insured

Groom v Crocker

[1939] 1 KB 194, [1938] 2 All ER 394, 108 LJKB 296, 158 LT 477, 54 TLR 861, 82 Sol Jo 374, 60 Ll L Rep 393, CA
A passenger in a car belonging to his brother was injured in a collision with a lorry. The lorry driver was convicted of dangerous driving. The car owner took proceedings against the lorry owner, whose insurers paid £100 into court with denial which was accepted. The passenger brought proceedings against the lorry owner and, at the request of the lorry owner, joined his brother as defendant. Insurers of the car

instructed solicitors who advised that the car owner was not negligent. The two insurers agreed to share the passenger claim. Negligence was admitted on behalf of the car owner in the defence and the action dropped against the lorry owner. The car owner's solicitors wrote a letter to the passenger's solicitors that the car owner admitted negligence. The insurer's branch office wrote a letter to the agent discussing this admission. The policy gave insurers absolute conduct and control of proceedings, and contained the *Scott v Avery* (1856) 5 HL Cas 811, 25 LJ Ex 308, 28 LTOS 207) clause.

The car owner sued insurers and solicitors for negligence and/or breach of duty and libel. The car owner alleged the letters were written without his consent; that he had not been negligent; that the letters were defamatory; that he had suffered damage because he would not be able to obtain insurance at normal rates; that it was an implied term of the policy and also the duty of insurers that insurers would act as plaintiff's agent with due regard to his interests; that the admission of negligence was a device to reduce damages which would not be assessed so high against a brother as against a stranger. The jury found for the plaintiff on all points.

HELD: As against insurers—there was a relationship of solicitor and client following *Walsh v Julius White and Bywaters* (1927) Times, 13 July and in *Re Crocker Re Taxation of Costs* [1936] Ch 696, [1936] 2 All ER 899, 105 LJ Ch 276, 155 LT 344, [1936] WN 192, 52 TLR 565. £1,000 damages for negligence awarded. The letter was defamatory, and plea of privilege failed because there was malice, ie indirect motive. £1,000 damages for libel awarded.

HELD, ON APPEAL: Insurers cannot in terms admit that the assured has been negligent contrary to the fact without their solicitor incurring a liability for breach of duty and possibly also the insurers, unless the assured consents. The right given to the insurers is to have control of proceedings in which they and the assured have a common interest because he is the defendant and the insurers because they are contractually bound to indemnify him. Each is interested in seeing that any judgment to be recovered against the assured shall be for a small a sum as possible.

The assured is not entitled to complain of anything the insurers require the assured to submit to provided it falls within the policy, properly construed. Insurers have the right to decide upon the proper tactics to pursue in the conduct of the action, provided it is in what they bona fide consider to be the common interest of themselves and the assured, but not to be influenced by matters altogether outside the litigation with which the assured has no concern. The policy is subject to the implied term that the solicitor shall act reasonably in the interests of both the assured and the insurers.

Note—See also *Meah v McCreamer*, p 180, above.

Although the relationship of solicitor and client exists between the insurer's solicitor and the insured, the solicitor must not say he is instructed by the insured or call him his client, or he may find the insured and his personal solicitor protesting it is not the fact. The personal solicitor may, as has happened, report the insurer's solicitor to the Law Society, who will uphold his protest. Insurer's solicitor should say they are instructed 'on behalf of'.

Re Crocker

[1936] WN 192

An insured is entitled to production and inspection of the documents in the possession of his insurers' solicitors relating to the defence of his action by the insurers.

Note—Where it is impracticable to obtain the permission of the assured to the admission of negligence, a form of defence designed to avoid the incurring of costs on the issue of negligence; as distinct from damage, is the following. It is useful where the insurers of two defendants have a sharing agreement.

DRAFT DEFENCE

Note—1 The defendants admit that subject to proof of the alleged injury, loss and damage the plaintiff is entitled to damages against one or other or both of them in this action, and do not contest the issue of liability.
2 The defendants do not admit the alleged or any personal injury, loss or damage.

ALTERNATIVE SHORT FORM WITH ASSURED'S CONSENT

Note—The defendants, for the purposes of this action only and not further or otherwise and reserving all rights between themselves, jointly admit negligence.

Brokers' negligence

Osman v Ralph Moss Ltd

[1970] 1 Lloyd's Rep 313, CA
The plaintiff, a Turk having only a limited knowledge of English asked the defendants, insurance brokers, to provide him with motor insurance. They recommended a policy underwritten by a company which they knew was of doubtful stability. The plaintiff accepted their recommendation and paid a year's premium. Shortly afterwards the insurers went into liquidation and the plaintiff was uninsured. He did not realise this. A letter the defendants sent him was misleading and inadequate to warn him. A few weeks later he had an accident as a result of which he was prosecuted for having no insurance, fined £25 and incurred 30 guineas costs. In addition he was sued by the other party in the accident and judgment given against him for £207 and £37 costs which, being uninsured, he had to meet himself.
HELD: The defendants were liable for negligence in failing properly to acquaint him that he was uninsured. He was entitled to be repaid the amount of the premium and (1) the damages he had to pay plus £5 of the costs, (2) the amount of the fine and the costs in the magistrate's court. It was foreseeable that by reason of the defendant's breach of duty and negligence he might incur liability for damages but he should have mitigated the loss of costs by submitting to judgment when the claim was made. It was not against public policy that he should be indemnified against the fine because there had been no mens rea and no personal negligence.

Bromley London Borough Council v Ellis

(1970) 114 Sol Jo 906, [1971] 1 Lloyd's Rep 97, CA
In July Mrs D sold a car to E and agreed to have insurance transferred to him. E asked her brokers to do this and they agreed. They filled up a proposal form, which he signed, but failed to send it off until November. The insurers wrote asking a question which the brokers did not answer. The insurers wrote in December saying that in the absence of a reply within seven days the insurance would be cancelled. The brokers did nothing and did not tell E. The insurers cancelled the policy. In February E collided with the plaintiff's car and was found liable for £805 damage and loss. Only after the accident did he discover he was not insured. He claimed indemnity from the brokers.

HELD: The brokers, though agents for the insurance company and not for E, were under a duty of care to look after his interests. They had failed to use reasonable care and were liable to indemnify him.

Warren v Henry Sutton & Co Ltd

[1976] 2 Lloyd's Rep 276, CA
The plaintiff, about to go abroad with his car, telephoned his insurers and asked for his insurance to be extended to cover a friend whom he knew to have a bad driving record. He gave his insurers the name of his broker; the insurers telephoned the broker for details and were told by him that the plaintiff's friend had 'no accidents, no conviction and no disabilities'. A bad accident occurred whilst the friend was driving and on discovering his bad record the insurers refused indemnity to the plaintiff, who then sued the broker.
HELD: It was the duty of the broker when obtaining extension of the cover to make such inquiries about the friend's record as would enable him to make a truthful statement to the insurers. His recklessness in making the statement he did was the cause of the insurers' repudiation and he was liable to the plaintiff in damages.

McNealy v Pennine Insurance Co Ltd

(1978) 122 Sol Jo 229, [1978] 2 Lloyd's Rep 18, [1978] RTR 285, CA
The plaintiff's main occupation was the repair of property, but he was also an expert guitarist and sometimes played in a band. Before going abroad with a band he went to brokers to get insurance for his car. The policy suggested by the brokers excluded cover for part-time musicians and they knew this. They asked the plaintiff what his occupation was and he said 'property repairer'. A policy was issued. When an accident occurred the insurers refused indemnity; it was conceded they were entitled so to do. The plaintiff sued the brokers.
HELD: The plaintiff was entitled to succeed. It was the duty of the brokers to use all reasonable care to see that the assured was properly covered. They should have gone through the list of excluded categories and asked the plaintiff if he was or had been a part-time musician. It was their duty to ensure as far as possible that he came within the list of categories acceptable to the insurance company. They were in breach of their duty of care.

T O'Donoghue Ltd v Harding and Hamilton & Carter Ltd

[1988] 2 Lloyd's Rep 281, QBD
The plaintiffs were jewellers who employed Mr Collins as a travelling salesman. Following the usual practice of the trade, he carried a valuable stock case of jewellery with him which he kept under close attention. On 6 November 1984 the stock case, containing jewellery worth £145,000, was stolen whilst he was paying for petrol at a garage. The plaintiffs claimed against the insurers, the first defendants, who denied liability by relying on an exclusion clause in the policy which provided that cover would not be available in respect of thefts from unattended road vehicles. The plaintiffs also claimed against their brokers, the second defendants, who had stated orally in January 1984 that the policy would cover loss in the specific circumstances mentioned above.
HELD: Mr Collins had behaved in a perfectly responsible manner and, according to the evidence, had kept the car and the case under observation as much as possible. The crime had probably been committed by a skilled gang of thieves. Accordingly, there

was no negligence on the part of the plaintiffs and the insurers could not claim the benefit of the exclusion clause. Per curiam: if the circumstances of the theft had been different, and the court had found on the evidence that the car had not been attended, the advice of the brokers could have rendered them liable in negligence to the plaintiffs.

Broker not liable to insured

O'Connor v BDB Kirby & Co

[1972] 1 QB 90, [1971] 2 All ER 1415, [1971] 2 WLR 1233, 115 Sol Jo 267, [1971] 1 Lloyd's Rep 454, [1971] RTR 440, CA

The plaintiff having bought a car went to the defendant, an insurance broker, to take out an insurance policy. The broker filled in a proposal form for him for the T company. He told the plaintiff the premium would be higher if he did not have a garage for the car, and he also told the plaintiff to check the proposal form to see if it was correct before signing it. On the form the broker had shown incorrectly that the car would be kept in a private garage. The plaintiff signed the form and in due course a policy was issued. Subsequently the insurers on finding that the car was parked in the street refused to indemnify the plaintiff against a loss he sustained. The plaintiff claimed damages against the broker alleging breach of a contractual duty to fill in the form properly.

HELD: It was the duty of a proposer for insurance to see and make sure that the information in the proposal form was accurate and he cannot be heard to say that he did not read it properly or was not fully appraised of its contents. The plaintiff should have read the form: he signed it and if he was so careless as not to read it properly he had only himself to blame. Judgment for the defendant.

CHAPTER 23

Conversion

INTRODUCTION

Note

The majority of motor policies indemnify in respect of the loss of or damage to the car insured, without any qualification or limitation, so that they are somewhat similar to an all risks policy in this respect. Other policies limit the indemnity, so far as conversion is concerned to loss by theft.

A common cause of claims for loss of car arises where the insured takes a cheque in payment on the sale of the car and the cheque is dishonoured on presentation. In the absence of circumstances such as in the cases of *Cundy* and *Pearson*, this is a case of loss of the proceeds of sale and not of loss of the car.

Where insurers are liable and have paid the loss, they are subrogated to the rights of the insured in respect of recovery of the car or of damages, and this involves tracing the property, as distinct from the possession, in the car. It is therefore necessary to consider the subjects of theft, sale of goods and hire purchase.

Where the car is in the possession of the police, there is a right to proceed in the magistrates' court for its return (below).

If the car is not in police possession, the proceedings are in the civil court for delivery up of the car or payment of its value and damages for detention. There is also the right to claim damages for conversion against any intermediate purchaser. The question is whether the title has passed to a subsequent purchaser.

Definition of conversion

Lancashire and Yorkshire Rly Co v MacNicoll

(1918) 88 LJKB 601, 118 LT 596, 34 TLR 280, 62 Sol Jo 365
Dealing with goods in a manner inconsistent with the right of the true owner amounts to a conversion, provided that it is also established that there is an intention on the part of the defendant in so doing to deny the owners' right or to assert a right which is inconsistent with the owner's right.

Note—Approved in *Oakley v Lyster* [1931] 1 KB 148, 100 LJKB 177, 144 LT 363.

Meaning of 'loss'

Holmes v Payne

[1930] 2 KB 301, 99 LJKB 441, 143 LT 349, 46 TLR 413, 37 Ll L Rep 41
Jewellery was missed on 24 November; reported as a loss to insurers the following day; on 4 December an agreement for replacement was suggested, and in December and the following February articles in replacement were selected. On 27 February the jewellery was found. Underwriters were held bound by the agreement, and, *semble*, there was a loss within the meaning of the policy.

Per Roche J: 'Uncertainty as to recovery of the thing insured is, in my opinion, in non-marine matters the main consideration on the question of loss. In this connection it is, of course, true that a thing may be mislaid and yet not lost, but, in my opinion, if a thing has been mislaid and is missing or has disappeared and a reasonable time has elapsed to allow of diligent search and of recovery and such diligent search has been made and has been fruitless, then the thing may properly be said to be lost. The recovery of the thing is at least uncertain and, I should say, unlikely.

Subsequent discovery or recovery of the thing assured is, of course, of itself no disproof of the loss.

British and Foreign Marine Insurance Co v Gaunt

[1921] 2 AC 41, 90 LJKB 801, 125 LT 491, 37 TLR 632, 65 Sol Jo 551
There are, of course, limits to 'all risks'. They are risks, and risks insured against. The expression does not cover inherent vice or mere wear and tear. It covers a risk, not a certainty. It does not cover a loss which the insured brings about by his own act, for then he has injured them himself.

Note—Quoted in *London and Provincial Leather Processes v Hudson* [1939] 2 KB 724, [1939] 3 All ER 857, 109 LJKB 100, 62 LT 140, 55 TLR 1047, 83 Sol Jo 733 (Goddard LJ).

Webster v General Accident Assurance Corpn

[1953] 1 QB 520, [1953] 1 All ER 663, [1953] 2 WLR 491, 97 Sol Jo 155, [1953] 1 Lloyd's Rep 123, (Parker J)
A comprehensive policy on a motor car included the following words: 'Section 1 Loss of or damage to the insured motor car. The corporation will indemnify the policyholder against loss of . . . any motor car described in the schedule hereto.'

The car owner entered his car for sale with a reserve of £325, which was not reached. He was about to collect his car, when Taylor (who had arranged the auction) said to him—'Don't go' and told him he had an offer to buy the car privately for £335.

The owner then left the car with Taylor on the understanding that it would be sold as soon as Taylor had communicated to the private buyer that his offer was accepted. There was no such buyer. Taylor sent the car to another auction sale the car was sold to A at auction and afterwards by A to B. Taylor sent cheques for varying amounts in purported payment, all of which were dishonoured, and the last returned 'account closed'. The arbitrator found that there was no larceny by a trick nor larceny by a bailee, but that the owner had been swindled out of the car by the fraud and false pretences of Taylor. The arbitrator found that the purchaser had acquired a good title and it was not unreasonable for the owner to refrain from attempting to claim the car from the purchaser. He considered that 'loss' could be fairly defined as 'an effective deprivation in circumstances making recovery uncertain'.

If a chattel is handed over to an agent, whether or not as a result of a fraudulent misrepresentation, and the agent then proceeds to deal with the chattel in a way which amounts to a conversion of the chattel, there may be a loss. The claimant had taken all reasonable steps to recover his car and recovery was, to say the least, uncertain. There was a loss within the meaning of the policy.

The judge declined the argument that the loss was of the proceeds of sale and not the loss of the chattel. Following *London and Provincial Leather Processes Ltd v Hudson* (p 890, above), award affirmed.

Note—69 LQR 163 points out that the fact that the plaintiff had voluntarily handed the car to T did not mean that a loss could not be established. If the owner of a chattel hands it over to X for sale, X having honestly represented that he has a buyer, and the chattel is duly sold by X who misappropriates the proceeds, there would not be a loss of the chattel but a loss of the proceeds of sale. Here, however, the loss occurred when T sent it to the auction for sale, for at that moment he deprived the plaintiff of his title without authority.

Eisinger v General Accident Fire and Life Assurance Corpn Ltd

[1955] 2 All ER 897, [1955] 1 WLR 869, 99 Sol Jo 511, [1955] 2 Lloyd's Rep 95 (Lord Goddard CJ)

The owner of a motor car agreed to sell the car to a purchaser and accepted a cheque in payment and parted with the car and the log book. The purchaser never had any intention of paying for the car and the cheque was worthless. The car was insured against loss or damage and the owner claimed from insurers for a loss of the car.

HELD: The car had been obtained by false pretences and the property in the car had passed to the purchaser. The consent of the owner was real consent induced by fraud and not an appearance of consent induced by fraud produced by a trick. The transaction amounted to obtaining a car by false pretences and not that of larceny by a trick. The loss was the value of the cheque and not the loss of the car. Parting with the property as well as the possession distinguished it from Webster's case (above). The owner had not lost the car. He had lost the proceeds of sale. There was no loss within the meaning of the policy.

Infant defendant

Ballett v Mingay

[1943] KB 281, [1943] 1 All ER 143, 112 LJKB 193, 168 LT 34, CA

The plaintiff loaned goods to an infant who agreed to pay a weekly sum for the loan. Plaintiff demanded the return of the goods. Defendant had meanwhile parted with

possession of the goods. Plaintiff sued the infant in detinue, ie in tort. The infant pleaded that the claim was for breach of contract and infancy was a defence.
HELD: The terms of the bailment did not permit the infant to part with the possession of the goods. The action of the infant in parting with the goods fell outside the contract altogether. The act was one of tort, distinct from the contract, and the infant was liable in tort.

LIMITATIONS

The six-year limitation period applied

RB Policies at Lloyd's v Butler

[1950] 1 KB 76, [1949] 2 All ER 226, [1949] WN 229, 65 TLR 436, 93 Sol Jo 553, 82 Ll L Rep 841 (Streatfield J)
A motor car registration number JD 6412 was stolen by some person unknown on 27 June 1940. In January 1947 the car, bearing the registration number ALN 765 was found in the possession of the defendant, having passed to him through a line of intermediate purchasers during the previous seven years. Insurers had paid for loss by theft and acquired the title and sued for possession. The defendant pleaded the statute of limitations.

The Limitation Act 1939, s 2(1) provides that no action shall be brought after the expiration of six years from the date on which the cause of action accrued. The defendant was an innocent purchaser for good consideration in good faith.

Section 3(1) provides: 'Where any cause of action in respect of the conversion or wrongful detention of a chattel has accrued to any person and, before he recovers possession of the chattel, a further conversion or wrongful detention takes place, no action shall be brought in respect of the further conversion or detention after the expiration of six years from the accrual of the cause of action in respect of the original conversion or detention.'

Section 3(2) provides: 'Where any such cause of action has accrued to any person and the period prescribed for bringing that action and for bringing any action in respect of such a further conversion or wrongful detention as aforesaid has expired and he has not during that period recovered possession of chattel, the title of that person to the chattel shall be extinguished.'

Halsbury's Laws of England (2nd edn) vol 20, p 618, said (cf 4th edn, vol 28, p 279): 'A cause of action cannot accrue unless there be a person in existence capable of suing and another person in existence who can be sued.'
HELD: The fact that a person is not traceable or is not known, does not mean that he is not in existence and cannot be sued. The fact that the plaintiffs could not find a defendant whose name they could insert in a writ does not mean that there is not in existence a person who can be sued. The provision that the period of limitation shall not 'begin to run' under s 26 until discovery in the case of fraud shows that time runs even though a plaintiff is ignorant that he has a cause of action. The cause of action 'accrued' in 1940 when the car was stolen. The plaintiffs' claim was therefore barred by the statute.

Note—The subsections referred to have been repealed and substantially re-enacted by the Limitation Act 1980, ss 2 and 3. In s 3 the words 'or wrongful detention' and 'or detention' have been omitted wherever they appeared in s 3(1) and (2) of the 1939 Act, the tort of detinue having been abolished.

See also Ch 14 generally and s 40 of the Limitation Act 1980 which enables owners from whom goods are stolen to sue the thief without limit of time.

Fraudulent concealment

Beaman v ARTS Ltd

[1949] 1 KB 550, [1949] 1 All ER 465, 65 TLR 389, 93 Sol Jo 236, CA

The Limitation Act 1939, s 26 provides that where the right of action has been concealed by fraud the period of limitation shall not begin to run until the plaintiff has or could with reasonable diligence have discovered it. In 1935 the plaintiff, who was going abroad, deposited four packages with the defendant company, and paid storage charges on them until 1938. In January 1940 she wrote to the company from Turkey to send the packages to her at Athens where she would go to collect them but this was not possible owing to war conditions. Six months later the company desiring to close down their business and being of opinion that the contents of the packages were worthless, gave the packages to the Salvation Army. No communication was sent to the plaintiff, and it was not until her return to England towards the end of 1946 that she was informed of the position. She thereupon brought proceedings against the company more than six years after the date of the conversion.

HELD: The plaintiff had placed confidence in the company, who had disposed of the packages in its own interest and made no attempt to communicate with the plaintiff and kept no adequate record of what had been done with the goods. These acts were calculated to keep the plaintiff in ignorance of the wrong that had been committed and amounted to a fraudulent concealment of the cause of action.

Note—The Limitation Act 1939, s 26 has been replaced by s 32 of the 1980 Act without relevant alteration.

See also Ch 14.

REMEDIES OF OWNER

THE TORTS (INTERFERENCE WITH GOODS) ACT 1977, S 3

Note—The Torts (Interference with Goods) Act 1977, provides by s 3:

'3 Form of judgment when goods are detained (1) In proceedings for wrongful interference against a person who is in possession or in control of the goods relief may be given in accordance with this section, so far as appropriate.

(2) The relief is—

(a) an order for delivery of the goods, and for payment of any consequential damages, or

(b) an order for delivery of the goods, but giving the defendant the alternative of paying damages by reference to the value of the goods, together in either alternative with payment of any consequential damages, or

(c) damages.

(3) Subject to rule of court—

(a) relief shall be given under only one of paras (a), (b) and (c) of sub-s (2),

(b) relief under para (a) of sub-s (2) is at the discretion of the court, and the claimant may choose between the others.

(4) If it is shown to the satisfaction of the court that an order under sub-s (2)(a) has not been complied with, the court may—

(a) revoke the order, or the relevant part of it, and

(b) make an order for payment of damages by reference to the value of the goods.

(5) Where an order is made under sub-s (2)(b) the defendant may satisfy the order by returning the goods at any time before execution of judgment, but without prejudice to liability to pay any consequential damages.
(6) An order for delivery of the goods under sub-s (2)(a) or (b) may impose such conditions as may be determined by the court, or pursuant to rules of court, and in particular, where damages by reference to the value of the goods would not be the whole of the value of the goods, may require an allowance to be made by the claimant to reflect the difference.

For example, a bailor's action against the bailee may be one in which the measure of damages is not the full value of the goods, and then the court may order delivery of the goods, but require the bailor to pay the bailee a sum reflecting the difference.
(7) Where under sub-s (1) or sub-s (2) of s 6 an allowance is to be made in respect of an improvement of the goods, and an order is made under sub-s (2)(a) or (b), the court may assess the allowance to be made in respect of the improvements, and by the order require, as a condition for delivery of the goods, that allowance to be made by the claimant.
(8) This section is without prejudice—
(a) to the remedies afforded by s 133 of the Consumer Credit Act 1974, or
(b) to the remedies afforded by ss 35, 42 and 44 of the Hire-Purchase Act 1965, or to those sections of the Hire-Purchase Act (Northern Ireland) 1966 (so long as those sections respectively remain in force), or
(c) to any jurisdiction to afford ancillary or incidental relief.

For rules of court see RSC Ord 13, r 3.

Reclaiming possession

Note—An owner can lawfully reclaim and take possession of a car wrongfully detained wherever he happens to find it, so long as it is not in a riotous manner or attended with breach of the peace, and may even justify an assault to recapture the car if the person in possession refuses to return it (*Blades v Higgs* (1861) 10 CBNS 713 at p 720 per Erle CJ). In that event it seems that if the person wrongfully in possession has spent money on improving the car, this money might not be recoverable from the owner.

See *Greenwood v Bennett* (p 902, below) and the Torts (Interference with Goods) Act 1977, s 6 (p 901, below).

In the report of the next case the following abbreviations are used: HP—Bowmaker Ltd. R—Rudolph, 5th party. K—Kennedy, 4th party. H—Hayton, 3rd party, M—Kingsway Motors defendants. B—Butterworth, plaintiff.

Butterworth v Kingsway Motors

[1954] 2 All ER 694, [1954] 1 WLR 1286, 98 Sol Jo 717 (Pearson J).
A hire-purchase company as owners hired a car to R on a usual hire-purchase agreement on 3 January 1951. Before R had paid all the instalments or exercised the option to purchase, she purported on 1 August 1951 to sell the car to a motor dealer, K, for £350 cash and a car valued at £650. On 11 August 1951 K sold the car to H for £1,015. The same day H sold it to M for £1,030. On 15 August 1951, M sold it to B for £550 cash and a car valued at £725 (£1,275). B continued to use the car until but not after 16 July 1952. R meanwhile continued to pay the instalments until she learned she had no right to sell and she then informed the HP company of the position. On 15 July 1952, the HP company wrote to B stating that the car was their property and calling for its delivery up, adding without prejudice, that they would accept £175 14s 2d to validate the title. On 17 July 1952, B's solicitors wrote to K claiming the return of the money paid for the car, and to the HP company for a copy of the HP agreement. On 23 July 1952 the HP company's solicitors wrote to B's solicitors that they had received a cheque from R which when met would discharge their interest. The cheque

was met on 25 July. On 9 August B's solicitors wrote to M for the return of the purchase price of £1,275 and for instructions with regard to the return of the car. On 14 August the HP company wrote to B's solicitors that their interests had been completed and on 18 August M's solicitors wrote to the same effect to B's solicitors, who on 22 August wrote to B's solicitors referring to their letter of 17 July. The reply was on 22 August that they had nothing to add to their letter of 18 August. On 12 September 1952 a specially indorsed writ was issued claiming £1,275.

M issued a third-party notice against H; H issued a fourth-party notice against K; and K issued a fifth-party notice against R.

HELD: B had effectually rescinded the contract of sale and was entitled to recover £1,250: *Rowland v Divall* [1923] 2 KB 500, 92 LJKB 1041, 129 LT 757, 67 Sol Jo 703. On 25 July 1952 R had acquired a good title and this fed the previously defective title of the subsequent buyers. *Whitehorn Bros v Davison* [1911] 1 KB 463, 80 LJKB 425, 104 LT 234. CA, *Blundell-Leigh v Attenborough* [1921] 3 KB 235, 90 LJKB 1005, 125 LT 356, 37 TLR 567, 65 Sol Jo 474, CA, *Robin and Rambler Coaches v Turner* (p 919, below). M was entitled to damages from H assessed on the value of the car in July 1952, assessed by the court at £800; judgment for £475. H was entitled to £475 from K and K to £475 from R.

Recovery over

Rowland v Divall

[1923] 2 KB 500, 92 LJKB 1041, 129 LT 757, 67 Sol Jo 703, CA
If the person wrongfully in possession has purchased the car from a third party, he can recover his full loss from the third party.

Mason v Burningham

[1949] 2 KB 545, [1949] 2 All ER 134, [1949] LJR 1430, 65 TLR 466, 93 Sol Jo 496, CA
This would be limited to money expended in the ordinary course of events and not fancy expenditure at the buyer's whim.

Note—See p 893, above.

If the owner sues for delivery up, but the court does not order the return of the car and awards damages, then on recovery over from a third party, of all the damage suffered, the car would of course become the property of the third party. See the Torts (Interference with Goods) Act 1977, s 5(1):

'**5 Extinction of title on satisfaction of claim for damages** (1) Where damages for wrongful interference are, or would fail to be, assessed on the footing that the claimant is being compensated—

(a) for the whole of his interest in the goods, or
(b) for the whole of his interest in the goods subject to a reduction for contributory negligence, payment of the assessed damages (under all heads), or as the case may be settlement of a claim for damages for the wrong (under all heads), extinguishes the claimant's title to that interest.'

Sale by sheriff

Curtis v Maloney

[1951] 1 KB 736, [1950] 2 All ER 982, [1950] WN 525, 66 (pt 2) TLR 869, 94 Sol Jo 761, CA

The owner of a motor cabin cruiser left it in the care of a firm of boatwrights. In execution of a writ of *fieri facias* against the boatwrights, the sheriff seized the boat and sold it by public auction. The sale was advertised, and no claim was made to the sheriff in respect of the boat before the sale. The owner sued the purchaser for the return of the boat or its value and damages for detention.

The Bankruptcy and Deeds of Arrangement Act 1913, s 15 provides:

'Where any goods in the possession of an execution debtor at the time of seizure by a sheriff, high bailiff, or other officer charged with the enforcement of a writ, warrant, or other process of execution, are sold by such sheriff, high bailiff, or other officer, without any claim having been made to the same, the purchaser of the goods so sold shall acquire a good title to the goods so sold, and no person shall be entitled to recover against the sheriff, high bailiff, or other officer, or anyone lawfully acting under the authority of either of them, except as provided by the Bankruptcy Acts 1883 and 1890, for any sale of such goods or for paying over the proceeds thereof, prior to the receipt of a claim to the said goods unless it is proved that the person from whom recovery is sought had notice, or might be making reasonable inquiry have ascertained that the goods were not the property of the execution debtor. Provided that nothing in this section contained shall affect the right of any claimant who may prove that at the time of sale he had a title to any goods so seized and sold to any remedy to which he may be entitled against any person other than such sheriff, high bailiff, or other officer as aforesaid.'

The plaintiff contended that as he had a title to the goods at the time of the sale and as the purchaser was a person other than such sheriff, high bailiff, or other officer, the proviso preserved the plaintiff's rights.

The defendant contended that the first part of the section gave a good title to the purchaser, and the proviso reserved the rights against the execution creditor.

HELD: By Finnemore J [1950] 2 All ER 201, 66 (Pt. 2) TLR 147, the purchaser acquired a good title and the action failed.

The decision was upheld on appeal.

Per Somervell LJ: A good title means a good title against everybody. The proviso cannot be read so as to contradict and make these express words meaningless by excluding from them the true owner at the time of the sale.

Per Cohen LJ: The proviso preserves the true owner's rights against the execution creditor, and removes any doubts as to the right of the true owner to sue the execution creditor for money he had received.

Per Denning LJ: The proviso preserves the rights of the original owner against the execution creditor or any wrongdoer who had converted the goods prior to the sale.

Note—Approved in *Dyal Singh v Kenyan Insurance Ltd* [1954] AC 287, [1954] 1 All ER 847, [1954] 2 WLR 607, 98 Sol Jo 231, PC. On 'notice' and 'reasonable inquiry' see *Observer Ltd v Gordon* [1983] 2 All ER 945, [1983] 1 WLR 1008, 127 Sol Jo 324.

Servant or agent

Re Samuel (No 2)

[1945] 2 All ER 71 (Evershed J)
Jewellery was handed to a solicitor acting for an undischarged bankrupt with a letter of authority from the bankrupt to place the same at a bank in the name of Mrs M. Later some of the jewellery was handed to the bankrupt, the rest remaining with the bank. It was contended the solicitor was liable for conversion.
HELD: The cases such as *Hollins v Fowler* (1875) LR 7 HL 757, 44 LJQB 169, 33 LT 73, 40 JP 53; *Salmond* (9th edn) pp 302, and 313; *Bowstead on Agency* (10th edn) pp 269, 270, show that provided certain conditions are fulfilled an innocent agent is liable, eg auctioneers as in *Consolidated Co v Curtis & Son* [1892] 1 QB 495, 61 LJQB 325, 56 JP 565, 40 WR 426, 8 TLR 403. But where one deals with goods at the request of the person who has the actual custody in the bona fide belief that the custodier is the true owner, or has his authority, he should not be held liable.

If the act of the agent is purely ministerial it would not amount to conversion, eg a servant transferring goods from one place to another, or from one servant to another on the same premises. In the case of auctioneers they disposed of the property altogether by selling and delivering it, which could not be called ministerial, nor excused if done by the authority of a person merely entrusted with custody. The solicitor had received them as agent or minister for the bankrupt. His act was ministerial and did not amount to a conversion by him.

An appeal was dismissed, [1945] 1 Ch 408.

Waiver

United Australia Ltd v Barclays Bank Ltd

[1941] AC 1, [1940] 4 All ER 20, 109 LJKB 919, 164 LT 139, 57 TLR 13, 46 Com Cas 1, HL
A party who sues one tortfeasor for conversion does not waive his rights against another tortfeasor unless he has obtained judgment and satisfaction.

DAMAGES

Measure of damages

Caxton Publishing Co v Sutherland Publishing Co

[1939] AC 178, [1938] 4 All ER 389, 108 LJCh 5, 160 LT 17, 55 TLR 123, 82 Sol Jo 1047, HL
Per Lord Roche: The measure of damages for conversion is the value of the thing converted at the date of conversion. In *Reid v Fairbanks* (1853) 13 CB 692, 43 Dig 509, there was a list of value available, because the true owner had contracted to sell a ship under construction for £x. It was held, or rather, agreed (because the actual decision was on another point) that the damage was £x-£y representing the cost of finishing the construction. I entirely accept the view that expenses incurred after the conversion should come off [the damages]. As the appellants in fact used the material, the proper inquiry is as to its fair value.

Per Lord Porter: Damages to the full value of the property converted may be given against two persons for successive conversions of the same chattel, and, until payment in full of the sum awarded is made by one of the defendants, the judgment remains in force against the other. In neither case, however, would the plaintiff be permitted to recover more than the sum awarded for the injuries received or the value of the chattel, as the case might be, because the law will not permit any greater sum to be recovered than that representing the actual damage suffered. Mere possession of the property of others is not conversion, since, by a fiction, the original possession is regarded as lawful.

The Mediana

[1900] AC 113, 69 LJP 35, 82 LT 98, 48 WR 398, HL
Even the loss of the use for a time of a chattel which the owner would not have used during that time may give rise to substantial damages, whether in an action for damages or in an action for conversion.

Sachs v Miklos

[1948] 2 KB 23, [1948] 1 All ER 67, [1948] LJR 1012, 64 TLR 118, CA
While the measure of damages for conversion is usually the value of the goods at the date of judgment, if the bailor knew or ought to have known at an earlier date that the conversion had taken place or was about to take place and took immediate steps to recover the goods, the measure of damages was the value of the goods at the date of his knowledge or supposed knowledge.

Note—The Torts (Interference with Goods) Act 1977, s 2 (which came into force on the 1 June 1978) states as follows:

'2 Abolition of detinue (1) Detinue is abolished.
(2)An action lies in conversion for loss or destruction of goods which a bailee has allowed to happen in breach of his duty to his bailor (that is to say it lies in a case which is not otherwise conversion, but would have been detinue before detinue was abolished).'

London and Provincial Motor and Tractor Co Ltd v Boundary Garage

[1948] WN 267, 92 Sol Jo 499 (Birkett J)
B bought A a motor car for £350 on the faith of statements made with utter recklessness and without any inquiry whether they were true or false and therefore fraudulent. B entered into a hire-purchase agreement with C. The car was a stolen car and had to be returned to the true owner.
HELD, in an action by B against A: B was entitled to recover the £350 from A and a declaration (following *Household Machines Ltd v Cosmos Exporters Ltd* [1947] KB 217, [1946] 2 All ER 622, [1947] LJR 578, 176 LT 49, 62 TLR 757) that the plaintiffs are entitled to recover from the defendants such damages as the plaintiffs may be held liable to pay and/or may reasonably pay to C in consequence of any breach by plaintiffs of the hire purchase agreement with C, in so far as such breaches are attributable to the breach of contract or tortious acts found in the judgment in the action.

Strand Electric Co v Brisford Entertainments Ltd

[1952] 2 QB 246, [1952] 1 All ER 796, [1952] 1 TLR 939, 96 Sol Jo 260, CA
Defendants, the owners of a theatre, allowed possession to a prospective purchaser, who obtained lighting equipment from the plaintiffs on hire at £9 6s 8d per week. The

prospective purchaser was unable to complete and notified the plaintiffs to collect the equipment. Defendants refused to allow plaintiffs to take possession of the goods. The judge assessed damages on the prospective receipts from hire if the goods had been returned.

HELD, ON APPEAL: The defendants had used the goods for their own benefit and were liable for the payments payable under the hire agreement.

Per Denning LJ: If a car used in business is detained, and the owner has to hire another car at an increased rate, he can recover the cost of the substitute, ie the actual loss. If a car is put out of action during repair, the wrongdoer is only liable for the loss suffered by the plaintiff.

Hillesden Securities Ltd v Ryjak Ltd

[1983] 2 All ER 184, [1983] 1 WLR 959, 127 Sol Jo 521, [1983] RTR 491 (Parker J)

R, the owner of a Rolls Royce car, leased it on the 11 June 1979 to V for a term of 36 months. On 13 September 1980 V purported to sell the car to E and a company of which E was a director and shareholder. V paid no leasing instalments after October 1980 and R accordingly sought the return of the car. Having failed he assigned his rights in the car to the plaintiffs who began proceedings against E and his company. On 11 March 1982 E ceased to be a director or shareholder in the company. The action came on for trial on 30 November 1982. The car was returned to the plaintiffs on 3 December 1982. On the issue of damages it was argued on behalf of E that s 3 of the Act had no application as he had not been in possession and control of the car after 11 March 1982.

HELD: E plainly converted the car on the 13 September 1980 and was liable for conversion. The parties had agreed that a proper figure for the use of the car which the defendants had enjoyed was £115 per week. Section 3 of the 1977 Act referred to relief which may be given 'in proceedings . . . against a person who is in possession or control of the goods'. This meant persons who were in possession and control of the goods when the proceedings were launched. Following the decision in *Strand Electric Co v Brisford Entertainments* (above), in the case of a profit-earning chattel which a defendant has used for his own benefit the owner can recover by way of damages a hire charge plus either the return of the chattel or, if there has been a subsequent conversion by disposal, the value of the chattel at the date of such conversion. The plaintiffs had lost the use of the car over the whole period from the original conversion to the 3 December 1982. Though E had ceased to have any connection with the company on the 11 March 1982 he could not be heard to say that by putting it out of his power to return the car he terminated his liability. Judgment against both defendants for the hire charge at the agreed weekly figure for the whole period to 3 December 1982, namely, £13,280, plus interest from 23 February 1981 the date when R first made a written demand for return of the car.

IBL Ltd v Coussens

[1991] 2 All ER 133, CA

The plaintiff company purchased two vehicles for the defendants' use in his capacity as chairman and managing director of the company. Subsequently, the defendant was dismissed. The plaintiff company gave the defendant the option of returning the two vehicles or purchasing them for a total cost of £62,000. The defendant neither returned the vehicles nor took up the option to purchase and the plaintiff brought proceedings against him seeking the delivery of the vehicles and damages for conversion. The Master, giving judgment for the plaintiff, ordered that the vehicles be returned to the plaintiff without the option to purchase. On appeal to the deputy High Court judge the defendant managed to vary the order to allow him the option of purchasing the vehicles for the original sum of £62,000.

The plaintiff appealed. The plaintiff did not seek an order returning the vehicles but argued that: firstly, the offer to sell at £62,000 was only valid at the time that it was made and this offer was refused; secondly, the value of the vehicles had increased since the time that the offer was made and, thirdly, there was a continuing conversion of the vehicles by the defendant and, thus, damages should be assessed on the basis of the value of the vehicles at the time of judgment rather than original conversion.

The defendant argued that the vehicle had been converted at the time the offer to sell at £62,000 was made and so this was the value to be taken for the purposes of the assessment of damages.

HELD: Although the tort of detinue had been abolished by s 2(1) of the Torts (Interference with Goods) Act 1977 the remedies available for detinue subsisted. There were many competing considerations to be taken into account when considering the provisions of the 1977 Act thus 'if one takes account of all these considerations and the fact that several different remedies are available under s 3 of the 1977 Act it is not possible, or indeed appropriate, to attempt to lay down any rule which is intended to be of universal application as to the date by reference to which the value of goods is to be assessed. The method of valuation and the date of valuation will depend on the circumstances' (per Neill LJ).

On the facts of the case it was held that the damages were to be assessed by reference to the value of the vehicles at the date of judgment and not at the date of the initial conversion. The case was referred back to the Master for the assessment of damages.

Note—But contrast *BBMB Finance (Hong Kong) Ltd v Eda Holdings Ltd*, below.

BBMB Finance (Hong Kong) Ltd v Eda Holdings Ltd

[1991] 2 All ER 129, [1990] 1 WLR 409

The defendant received a share certificate to be held on trust for the plaintiffs. Subsequently the defendants disposed of the shares (and handed over the share certificate) to a third party for a value of $5.75 per share receiving a cheque in return which was never presented for payment. About six months later the defendants replaced these shares by purchasing an equivalent number on the open market at a price of $2.40 per share. The plaintiffs sued the defendants for conversion and were awarded damages equivalent to the difference between the value of the shares at the time ofconversion and the value of the replacement shares. The defendants appealed to the Privy Council.

HELD: Per Lord Templeman: The general rule is that a plaintiff whose property is irreversibly converted has vested in him a right to damages for conversion measured by the value of the property at the date of conversion.

The defendant had sold and irreversibly converted the plaintiffs' shares and at that stage the plaintiffs became entitled to damages for conversion equal to the market price. It was irrelevant that the defendant had failed to present the cheque from the third party.

Allowance for improvement of goods

Note—The Torts (Interference with Goods) Act 1977 provides by s 6:

'**6 Allowance for improvement of the goods** (1) If in proceedings for wrongful interference against a person (the "improver") who has improved the goods, it is shown that the improver acted in the mistaken but honest belief that he had a good title to them, an allowance shall be made for the extent to which, at the time at which the goods fall to be valued in assessing damages, the value of the goods is attributable to the improvement.
(2) If, in proceedings for wrongful interference against a person "the purchaser") who has purported to purchase the goods—
(a) from the improver, or
(b) where after such a purported sale the goods passed by a further purported sale on one or more occasions, or any such occasion,
it is shown that the purchaser acted in good faith, an allowance shall be made on the principle set out in sub-s (1).

For example, where a person in good faith buys a stolen car from the improver and is sued in conversion by the true owner the damages may be reduced to reflect the improvement, but if the person who bought the stolen car from the improver sues the improver for failure of consideration, and the improver acted in good faith, sub-s (3) below will ordinarily make a comparable reduction in the damages he recovers from the improver.
(3) If in a case within sub-s (2) the person purporting to sell the goods acted in good faith, then in proceedings by the purchaser for recovery of the purchase price because of failure of consideration, or in any other proceedings founded on that failure of consideration, an allowance shall, where appropriate, be made on the principles set out in sub-s (1).
(4) This section applies, with the necessary modifications, to a purported bailment or other disposition of goods as it applies to a purported sale of goods.'

For rules of court see RSC Ord 42, r 1A.

Munro v Willmott

[1949] 1 KB 295, [1948] 2 All ER 983, [1949] LJR 471, 64 TLR 627, 92 Sol Jo 662 (Lynskey J)
Defendant allowed plaintiff to leave her car in the yard of the premises of which he was licensee without charge in 1942. In 1945 he wanted the car moved. He tried but failed to get in touch with the plaintiff. The car was not roadworthy and he had it repaired at a cost of £85, and sold it by auction for £105. In 1946 the plaintiff sued for the full value of the car without any allowance for the £85 spent on repairs.
HELD: The defendant was not an agent of necessity and was liable. He was entitled to credit, not because he had made the payment, but to ascertain the true value of the property which the plaintiff had lost. If the car had not been repaired, it would at the time of the judgment have realised something in the nature of £25 as scrap. Judgment for £35, being value of car, £120, crediting the £85.

Wilson v Lombank Ltd

[1963] 1 All ER 740, [1963] 1 WLR 1294 (Hinchcliffe J)
The plaintiff, a dealer, bought a car and took it for repairs to a garage where he had a monthly account. After the repairs were done the garage staff put the car on the forecourt to await collection. A representative of the defendants, a finance company, saw it there and took it away. Both parties thought themselves to have a good title to the car but neither in fact was the owner: it really belonged to another finance company to whom the defendants delivered it when satisfied that this was so. The plaintiff sued for damages for trespass on the ground that he had possession of the car and the defendants had no right to take it away.
HELD: The plaintiff was entitled to immediate possession of the car at the time when it was on the forecourt since he could at any moment demand its return. The garage

had no lien for the costs of repairs having regard to the course of dealing, ie the monthly account. The plaintiff having never lost possession of the car the defendants had wrongfully taken it and must pay damages. Delivery to the true owner did not defeat the plaintiff's claim. The measure of damages was the full value of the car at the time the tort was committed, namely, the price the plaintiff paid for the car plus the cost of repairs.

Wickham Holdings Ltd v Brooke House Motors Ltd

[1967] 1 All ER 117, [1967] 1 WLR 295, CA
When a finance company sues in conversion (eg when the hirer under a hire-purchase agreement wrongfully sells the goods or the benefit of the agreement) it can recover its actual loss and no more. It does not recover the full value of the goods but only the balance outstanding on the hire-purchase price.

Note—Followed in *Belvoir Finance Co Ltd v Stapleton* [1971] 1 QB 210, [1970] 3 All ER 664, [1970] 3 WLR 530, 114 Sol Jo 719, CA. Both *Wickham* and *Belvoir* were considered in *Chubb Cash Ltd v John Crilley & Son* [1983] 2 All ER 294, [1983] 1 WLR 599, 127 Sol Jo 153, CA. Per Bush J: These cases decided that the measure of damages was the market value of the goods, or the amount still owing under the hire-purchase agreement, whichever was the lower as at the date of the conversion. It was a limited decision, not a decision which entitled the plaintiffs, if the amount outstanding on the hire-purchase agreement was greater than the value of the goods, to claim that.

Greenwood v Bennett

[1973] QB 195, [1972] 3 All ER 586, [1972] 2 WLR 691, [1972] RTR 535, CA
Bennett wishing to have some work done to a car to prepare it for sale entrusted it to Searle to do the work. Searle used the car for his own purposes and in doing so damaged it. He wrongfully 'sold' it in its damaged state to Harper who in good faith paid him £75 for it. Harper spent £226 on it to put it in good order and then sold it for £450 to a finance company. When Searle's misdealing with the car was discovered the police seized the car and brought interpleader proceedings to determine the ownership. The judge ordered the car to be delivered up to Bennett and held that Harper was not entitled to be paid by Bennett for the £226 worth of work done to the car.
HELD: The judge should have required Bennett to pay Harper the £226 as a condition of being given delivery of the car. The principle that lay to hand to meet the case was derived from the law of restitution—that the owners should not be allowed to enrich themselves at the expense of a person who has done work to a property of which he honestly believes himself to be the owner.

OWNER'S RIGHTS AGAINST PURCHASERS IN GOOD FAITH

Statute law

THE FACTORS ACT 1889

1 Definitions For the purposes of this Act—
(1) The expression 'mercantile agent' shall mean a mercantile agent having in the customary course of his business as such agent authority either to sell goods, or to consign goods for the purpose of sale, or to buy goods, or to raise money on the security of goods.

(2) A person shall be deemed to be in possession of goods or of the documents of title to goods, where the goods or documents are in his actual custody or are held by any other person subject to his control or for him or on his behalf.
(3) The expression 'goods' shall include wares and merchandise.
(4) The expression 'document of title' shall include any bill of lading, dock warrant, warehouse-keeper's certificate, and warrant or order for the delivery of goods, and any other document used in the ordinary course of business as proof of the possession or control of goods, or authorising or purporting to authorise, either by endorsement or by delivery, the possessor of the document to transfer or receive goods thereby represented.
(5) The expression 'pledge' shall include any contract pledging, or giving a lien or security on, goods, whether in consideration of an original advance or of any further or continuing advance or of any pecuniary liability.
(6) The expression 'person' shall include any body of persons corporate or unincorporate.
2 Powers of mercantile agent with respect to disposition of goods (1) Where a mercantile agent is, with the consent of the owner, in possession of goods or of the documents of title to goods, any sale, pledge, or other disposition of the goods, made by him when acting in the ordinary course of business of a mercantile agent, shall, subject to the provisions of this Act, be as valid as if he were expressly authorised by the owner of the goods to make the same; provided that the person taking under the disposition acts in good faith, and has not at the time of the disposition notice that the person making the disposition has not authority to make the same.
(2) Where a mercantile agent has, with the consent of the owner, been in possession of goods or of the documents of title to goods, any sale, pledge, or other disposition, which would have been valid if the consent had continued, shall be valid notwithstanding the determination of the consent: provided that the person taking under the disposition has not at the time thereof notice that the consent has been determined.
(3) Where a mercantile agent has obtained possession of any documents of title to goods by reason of his being or having been, with the consent of the owner, in possession of the goods represented thereby, or of any other documents of title to the goods, his possession of the first-mentioned documents shall, for the purposes of this Act, be deemed to be with the consent of the owner.
(4) For the purposes of this Act the consent of the owner shall be presumed in the absence of evidence to the contrary.

Pearson v Rose and Young Ltd

[1951] 1 KB 275, [1950] 2 All ER 1027, 66 (pt 2) TLR 886, 94 Sol Jo 778, CA
The plaintiff on 15 March 1949 was told by a mercantile agent that the agent could obtain a new motor car for the plaintiff for £467 in six months, but required a deposit of £100. Three days later plaintiff saw the agent and discussed whether the plaintiff could sell his car because of the covenant against resale, and to clear up this point the plaintiff produced his log book and handed it to the agent. Whilst the agent had it, he asked the plaintiff to accompany the agent's wife to hospital, which the plaintiff did and forgot about the log book. Later the same day the agent sold the plaintiff's car and handed the log book to the purchaser. The purchaser sold the car, and his purchaser in turn also sold it. The agent was afterwards convicted of fraud in connection with this and other cars. The plaintiff sued the ultimate purchaser for damages for conversion.

Devlin J held the agent was in possession of the car with the consent of the plaintiff, that the agent had tricked the plaintiff out of possession of the log book, and dismissed the plaintiff's claim.

HELD, ON APPEAL: On the sale of a second-hand car the purchaser would ordinarily require delivery of the log book. Cars could be sold without a log book but the price would be substantially reduced, and the sale of a car without a log book was not a sale in the ordinary course of business. The sale of a car with its log book is a more valuable subject matter than a car without its log book. The agent was never in possession of the log book with the consent of the plaintiff.

Appeal allowed with costs.

Stadium Finance Ltd v Robbins

[1962] 2 QB 664, [1962] 2 All ER 633, [1962] 3 WLR 453, 106 Sol Jo 369, CA
The defendant was the owner of a car which he wished to sell. He took it to a dealer who agreed to put it in his showroom and to report any inquiries. The defendant kept the ignition key but, probably by accident, left the log book locked in the glove box. The dealer obtained an ignition key and also opened the glove box, finding the log book. He arranged for his salesman to take the car on hire-purchase and sold it to the plaintiffs, a hire-purchase company. The salesman failed to make the first monthly payment and the plaintiffs sought to take possession of the car. They found that the defendant had already seized it as his property. They claimed the return of the car or its value and damages.
HELD: The plaintiffs could succeed only if they could show that the sale of the car to them by the dealer was made by him when acting in the ordinary course of business of a mercantile agent, ie within the terms of the Factors Act 1889, s 2(1). The car, with or without the ignition key and the log book, was 'goods' within the meaning of the Act but the dealer was not acting in the ordinary course of his business as a mercantile agent. The car had been put in possession of the dealer with no key and no registration book easily available: a dealer who sells motor cars in the ordinary course of his business sells those which are in a condition to be used as cars and the sale of a car deficient both of log book and ignition key could not be in the ordinary course of business of a mercantile agent. The provision in s 2(4) of the Act that consent of the owner shall be presumed in the absence of evidence to the contrary did not affect the case because the defendant's retention of the key was evidence of his intention to control the sale.

Lambert v G and C Finance Corpn Ltd

(1963) 107 Sol Jo 666 (Havers J)
The plaintiff advertised his car for sale. E agreed to buy it and offered a cheque in payment of the price. The plaintiff was unwilling to let E have the car except for cash but eventually agreed to let E take the car away in exchange for the cheque on the terms that he, the plaintiff, retained the log book, which he would send on when the cheque was cleared. In fact the cheque was dishonoured and the plaintiff reported the matter to the police. The car was subsequently sold by a dealer to the defendants, a hire-purchase company. The plaintiff sued for damages for its conversion. The defendants contended that he was not the owner, having sold it to E.
HELD: The Sale of Goods Act 1893, s 18(1) provides that unless a different intention appears the property in specific goods passes when the contract is made. Section 25(2) provides that where a person agrees to buy goods and is given possession of them by the owner he has the same power to give a good title as a mercantile agent under the Factors Act 1889 (see above). In the present case a different intention was shown for the purposes of s 18(1) by the plaintiff's retaining the log book. The defendants could not rely on s 25(2) because a sale of a car without a log book is not a sale in the ordinary course of business. The plaintiff was still the owner and was entitled to damages.

Note—The Sale of Goods Act 1893, s 18(1) is repeated in the Sale of Goods Act 1979, s 18(1) and s 25(2) of the 1893 Act in s 25(1) of the 1979 Act.

Newtons of Wembley Ltd v Williams

[1965] 1 QB 560, [1964] 3 All ER 532, [1964] 3 WLR 888, 108 Sol Jo 619, CA
On 15 June the plaintiffs sold a car to Andrew who gave them a cheque for £735 for it. He drove it away and registered it in his name on the same day. On 18 June the plaintiffs heard from the bank that the cheque would not be met. They at once made extensive though unsuccessful enquiries to find Andrew, sent a 'Stop' notice to the Hire-Purchase Information Bureau and informed the police. On 6 July in Warren Street, London, Andrew sold the car to Biss, a dealer, for £550 cash. Biss took the car to Wincanton and on 12 July sold it to the defendant for £505, which was all the defendant would give him for it. Later in July as a result of an effort by the defendant to sell the car, the Hire-Purchase Information Bureau became aware of its whereabouts and told the plaintiffs. On 14 September Andrew pleaded guilty at Middlesex Sessions to a charge of obtaining a car by false pretences. The plaintiffs claimed the return of the car or its value on the ground that like the defendant in *Car and Universal Finance Co v Caldwell* (p 913, below) they had rescinded the contract before the car was sold by the fraudulent party who could thus pass no title to it.
HELD: The unequivocal acts of the plaintiffs on finding that the cheque would not be met were effective to rescind the contract as in *Caldwell*'s case so that after 20 June at latest Andrew had at common law no title to pass. But the Factors Act 1889, s 9 provided that when a buyer of goods obtained possession of them with the seller's consent delivery of the goods on sale to any person acting in good faith without notice of the original seller's rights in respect of them had the same effect as if the person making the delivery were a mercantile agent in possession of the goods with the consent of the owner. Section 2 of the Act provides that a sale of goods by a mercantile agent in possession of the goods with the consent of the owner (which has not, to the knowledge of the person taking under the sale, been determined) shall be valid if made when acting in the ordinary course of business of a mercantile agent. Biss took the car in good faith without notice of the plaintiffs' rights. Andrew was acting in the ordinary course of business of a mercantile agent in that the sale to Biss was made at the well-known kerbside market for cash dealing in second hand cars in Warren Street. Accordingly Biss received a valid title to the car which he later passed to the defendant.

George v Revis

(1966) 111 Sol Jo 51 (Megaw J)
The plaintiff advertised his car for sale. A man named Robinson called and agreed to buy it, subject to a satisfactory engineer's report. He was allowed by the plaintiff to take the car away for an engineer's inspection. After he had gone the plaintiff discovered he had taken the log book also, though the plaintiff had not consented to his having possession of it. Robinson did not return and a month later sold the car to the defendant, who bought in good faith.
HELD: The Factors Act 1889 protected an innocent purchaser if (1) there had been an agreement by the owner to sell; (2) the original purchaser (here Robinson) had obtained the goods with the consent of the seller; (3) the ultimate purchaser (the defendant) had acted in good faith and without notice of any rights of the original seller. Conditions (1) and (3) were fulfilled. Condition (2) was fulfilled as far as the car alone was concerned if the facts as to the log book were disregarded, but the log

book was of vital significance in the sale of a car. *Pearson v Rose & Young* (above) was clear authority for this and was sufficient to decide the case. The plaintiff had not consented to Robinson having possession of the log book: he was entitled to a return of the car or damages.

Note—See also *Bentworth Finance Ltd v Lubert*, p 922, below.

SALE OF GOODS ACT 1979

11 When condition to be treated as warranty (1) (*Applies to Scotland only.*)
(2) Where a contract of sale is subject to a condition to be fulfilled by the seller, the buyer may waive the condition, or may elect to treat the breach of the condition as a breach of warranty and not as a ground for treating the contract as repudiated.
(3) Whether a stipulation in a contract of sale is a condition, the breach of which may give rise to treat the contract as repudiated, or a warranty, the breach of which may give rise to a claim for damages but not to a right to reject the goods and treat the contract as repudiated, depends in each case on the construction of the contract; and a stipulation may be a condition, though called a warranty in the contract.
(4) Where a contract of sale is not severable and the buyer has accepted the goods or part of them, the breach of a condition to be fulfilled by the seller can only be treated as a breach of warranty, and not as a ground for rejecting the goods and treating the contract as repudiated, unless there is an express or implied term of the contract to that effect.
(5) (*Applies to Scotland only.*)
(6) Nothing in this section affects a condition or warranty whose fulfilment is excused by law by reason of impossibility or otherwise.

21 Sale by person not the owner (1) Subject to this Act, where goods are sold by a person who is not their owner, and who does not sell them under the authority or with the consent of the owner, the buyer acquires no better title to the goods than the seller had unless the owner of the goods is by his conduct precluded from denying the seller's authority to sell.
(2) Nothing in this Act affects—
(a) the provisions of the Factors Acts, or any enactment enabling the apparent owner of the goods to dispose of them as if he were their true owner;
(b) the validity of any contract of sale under any special common law or statutory power of sale, or under the order of a court of competent jurisdiction.

22 Market overt (1) Where goods are sold in market overt, according to the usage of the market, the buyer acquires a good title to the goods, provided he buys them in good faith and without notice of any defect or want of title on the part of the seller.

23 Sale under voidable title When the seller of goods has a voidable title to them, but his title has not been avoided at the time of the sale, the buyer acquires a good title to the goods, provided he buys them in good faith and without notice of the seller's defect of title.

24 Seller in possession after sale Where a person, having sold goods, continues or is in possession of the goods, or of the documents of title to the goods the delivery or transfer by that person, or by a mercantile agent acting for him, of the goods or documents of title under any sale, pledge, or other disposition thereof, to any person receiving the same in good faith and without notice of the previous sale, has the same effect as if the person making the delivery or transfer were expressly authorised by the owner of the goods to make the same.

25 Buyer in possession after sale (1) Where a person, having bought or agreed to buy goods, obtains, with the consent of the seller, possession of the goods or the documents of title to the goods, the delivery or transfer by that person, or by a mercantile agent acting for him, of the goods or documents of title, under any sale, pledge or other disposition thereof, to any person receiving the same in good faith and without notice of any lien or other right of the original seller in respect of the goods, has the same effect as if the person making the delivery or transfer were a mercantile agent in possession of the goods or documents of title with the consent of the owner.

26 Supplementary to section 24 and 25 In ss 24 and 25 above 'mercantile agent' means a mercantile agent having in the customary course of business as such agent authority either—
(a) to sell goods, or
(b) to consign goods for the purpose of sale, or
(c) to buy goods, or
(d) to raise money on the security of goods.

Note—See *Lambert v G and C Finance Ltd* and *Newtons of Wembley Ltd v Williams* (pp 904–905, above).

29 Rules about delivery (1) Whether it is for the buyer to take possession of the goods or for the seller to send them to the buyer is a question depending in each case on the contract, express or implied, between the parties.
(2) Apart from any such contract, express or implied, the place of delivery is the seller's place of business if he has one, and if not, his residence; except that, if the contract is for the sale of specific goods, which to the knowledge of the parties when the contract is made are in some other place, then that place is the place of delivery.
(3) Where under the contract of sale the seller is bound to send the goods to the buyer, but no time for sending them is fixed, the seller is bound to send them within a reasonable time.
(4) Where the goods at the time of sale are in the possession of a third person, there is no delivery by seller to buyer unless and until the third person acknowledges to the buyer that he holds the goods on his behalf; but nothing in this section affects the operation of the issue or transfer of any document of title to goods.
(5) Demand or tender of delivery may be treated as ineffectual unless made at a reasonable hour; and what is a reasonable hour is a question of fact.
(6) Unless otherwise agreed, the expenses of and incidental to putting the goods into a deliverable state must be borne by the seller.

Shaw v Metropolitan Police Comr (Natalegawa, claimant)

[1987] 3 All ER 405, [1987] 1 WLR 1332, 131 Sol Jo 1357, [1987] LS Gaz R 3011, CA

The claimant, Mr Natalegawa was a student from Indonesia who acquired a red Porsche in December 1982 for £16,750. In March 1984 he decided to return to Indonesia and advertised the car for sale. On 15 April a man called London contacted Mr Natalegawa who let London have the car on 16 April, and on 1 May gave him a letter purporting to certify that he had no further legal responsibility connected with the car. London gave a post-dated cheque which proved to have no value.

On 1 May London agreed to sell the car to the plaintiffs.

The plaintiffs gave London a draft for the purchase price, but when London's bank refused to cash it, London disappeared. The car was left with the plaintiffs, who subsequently commenced proceedings against the police claiming that the car belonged to them. Mr Natalegawa discovered the location of the car, and also claimed it. The police issued an interpleader summons to determine who was entitled to the vehicle. The plaintiffs submitted that the property in the car had passed to them firstly because London had bought or agreed to buy the car from Mr Natalegawa and secondly in reliance on s 25 of the Sale of Goods Act 1979.

HELD, ON APPEAL: The case was most unusual because if the plaintiffs succeeded, they would have obtained a car without having had to pay for it. However, since it was found as a fact at first instance that there was no purported sale between Mr Natalegawa and London, s 25 did not apply. Section 25 could only apply when there had been an actual sale or agreement to sell the goods. Therefore, London could not pass good title to the plaintiffs. Further, although s 21 of the Sale of Goods Act 1979 provided that the buyer acquires no better title to goods than the seller had, unless the owner of the goods is by his conduct precluded from denying the seller's authority to sell, this section could not apply, again because there had been no proper sale or agreement to sell. Indeed, nothing in ss 21 to 26 of the 1979 Act, or the general law of estoppel could alter the simple fact that London never purported to transfer the property in the car on the evidence before the court.

National Employers Mutual General Insurance Association Ltd v Jones

[1988] 2 All ER 425, [1988] 2 WLR 952, 132 Sol Jo 658, [1988] RTR 289, HL
On 3 February 1983, a Ford Fiesta was stolen from Miss H who later assigned her rights in the car to the plaintiffs, her insurers, in return for a cash payment. After the theft the car had passed through a number of hands before it was sold to the defendant, who purchased it in good faith. The plaintiffs claimed from the defendant the return of the car or its monetary value, plus damages for its detention. The defendant claimed that he was entitled to retain possession of the car under s 9 of the Factors Act 1889. (Section 25(1) of the Sale of Goods Act 1979 is in the same terms.) The plaintiff maintained in reply that s 9 of the 1889 Act had no application to the purported purchase by the defendant of the car. The judge at first instance and the Court of Appeal gave judgment for the plaintiff.

HELD, on appeal to the House of Lords by the defendants: The terms 'owner' and 'seller' in s 9 should not be equated. On a historical view of the Factors Act, there was no indication that the legislature had ever intended to depart from the basic principle of '*nemo dat quod non habet*' to enable a factor or agent, entrusted with goods from a thief or a purchaser from a thief, to give title to a bona fide purchaser and override the title of the true owner. The proper approach was to go back along the chain of transactions until the initial defect in title was located, ie the thief who sold the car to the first innocent purchaser. This was not a sale under the Factors Act since there had been no transfer of title. The first purchaser from the thief did not get a good title to the car, and could not pass one on. Appeal dismissed.

THEFT ACT 1968, S 31(2)

'(2) Notwithstanding any enactment to the contrary where property has been stolen or obtained by fraud or other wrongful means, the title to that or any other property shall not be affected by reason only of the conviction of the offender.'

Market overt

Bishopsgate Motor Finance Corpn Ltd v Transport Brakes Ltd

[1948] 1 All ER 408, [1948] LJR 1000, 64 TLR 163, 92 Sol Jo 246 (Humphreys J); affd [1949] 1 KB 322, [1949] 1 All ER 37, [1949] LJR 741, 65 TLR 66, 93 Sol Jo 71, CA
A obtained a car from plaintiffs under a hire-purchase agreement under which the property in the car remained in the plaintiffs. A instructed a firm of auctioneers to

offer the car in their auction sale at Maidstone market, where under statutory powers a cattle and general market, which was a long established public market, is held every Tuesday. The auctioneers paid on behalf of A the toll of 1s (which was repaid by A) payable on every vehicle put up for sale. The car was put up in its turn at the auction, which was held about 11.45 am, but did not reach the reserve price and later with a lower reserve, which again was not reached, and was withdrawn. B was in the market at the auction but did not bid. Later in the day B was looking at the car and was approached by A, and after negotiation A sold the car to B about 2.30 pm.

B at a later date sold the car to C.

HELD: The sale was in market overt and B acquired a good title under the Sale of Goods Act 1893, s 22 (now replaced by s 22 of the 1979 Act). The test laid down by Blackburn J in *Crane v London Dock Co* ((1864) 5 B & S 313, 4 New Rep 94, 33 LJQB 224, 10 LT 372, 28 JP 565, 10 Jur NS 984, 12 WR 745), applied, that the vendor must buy the goods under circumstances such as would induce him to think the sale was a good sale in the market overt: namely, he must buy a thing which is openly exposed in market overt under such circumstances that he might say to himself no person but the owner would dare expose them for sale here, and therefore I have a right to assume that the shopkeeper has a right to sell them. The goods must be corporeally present and exposed in the market.

ON APPEAL: It was contended (1) market overt could only rest upon a grant, and not upon a statute; (2) a toll, if payable, must be paid by the person who affects the sale; (3) the goods must be put up for sale by a trader in the market; and (4) a sale by private treaty was not a sale according to the usage of the market.

HELD: As to (1) market overt extended to markets established by statute; there was no authority for the proposition; as to (2) A had paid the 1s toll by the auctioneers to the corporation's collector; as to (3) it was not necessary that goods must be put up for sale by a trader in the market; the sale could be made by the possessor himself; and as to (4) there was no proof of usage that a car could only be sold in the market by public auction. Appeal dismissed.

Reid v Metropolitan Police Comr

[1973] QB 551, [1973] 2 All ER 97, [1973] 2 WLR 576, 117 Sol Jo 244, [1973] Lloyd's Rep 518, CA

At 7 in the morning of 13 February Cocks bought a silver candelabra from a stall-holder who was just erecting his stall in the New Caledonian Market, Bermondsey. The candelabra had been stolen from the plaintiff by a person unknown.

HELD: Cocks did not obtain a good title. Though the market overt rule extended to statutory markets such as the New Caledonian a sale which would give a good title against the true owner must be made 'between the rising of the sun and the going down of the same' (Coke, 2 Inst 713). Sunrise being at 8.19 am on 13 February, the sale was not one made in market overt.

The *Post Magazine* of 31 January 1948 (p 735), reports the case of a stolen car entered in an auction sale of motor vehicles in the market place of a county town where it was eventually purchased by the garage proprietor who ran the sale. He sold the car to A, who sold it to B, who applied for registration. It then transpired that the registration plates of the vehicle had been changed. The true owner claimed from B. The thief could not be prosecuted to conviction for lack of evidence. The garage proprietor pleaded market overt.

An old grant in Latin in the town's museum from the Lord of the Manor had constituted the market on the appointed day of the week (Wednesday). The auction was on Monday.
HELD: Not market overt.

Long v Jones

[1991] TLR 113
'A portrait of a gentleman', a painting attributed to John Brewster and painted in Philadelphia in 1819, was purchased by Mr Long in 1982. It was displayed in his office until it disappeared in 1985. The portrait was later sold for £140 by Mr Little to a Mr Skinner who ran a market stall in a disused garage forecourt adjacent to the Bermondsey and New Caledonia market. Mr Jones purchased the portrait from Mr Skinner for £180 and then put it up for sale at Christies.

Mr Long brought proceedings to reclaim the picture. Mr Jones argued that he had purchased the picture in a 'market overt' and thus good title had passed to him under the Sale of Goods Act 1979.
HELD: Mr Long retained good title. The court rejected Mr Jones arguments that over the years the Bermondsey and New Caledonia market had spilled over to include Mr Skinner's stall. Mr Skinner rented the garage forecourt on a casual basis from a man who in turn rented it from the owner. The court was satisfied that Mr Skinner knew that his part of the market was a private market.

Furthermore there were none of the features present which defined the market where the portrait was purchased as a market overt as defined in s 22 of the Sale of Goods Act 1893. 'The essence of a market was its regularity, its conduct in accordance with established usage and the fact that it must be shown to have been established in one of the ways recognised by law—that is, by charter, by statute, by long continual user, either immemorial user or by prescription or by the principle of lost modern grant' (per Waterhouse J).

Note—Market Overt is abolished by the Sale of Goods (Amendment) Bill which will come into force two months after Royal Assent, expected after the Summer recess 1994.

Contract

THE LAW

Nanka-Bruce v Commonwealth Trust

[1926] AC 77, 94 LJPC 169, 134 LT 35, PC
The law upon this branch of the contract of sale is thus expressed by Lord Cairns LC in *Cundy v Lindsay* [1878] 3 App Cas 459, 47 LJQB 481, 38 LT 573, 42 JP 483, 26 WR 406, HL:

'Now, with regard to the title of personal property, the settled and well-known rules of law may, I take it, be thus expressed: by the law of our country the purchaser of a chattel takes the chattel as a general rule subject to what may turn out to be certain infirmities in the title. If he purchases the chattel in market overt, he obtains a title which is good against all the world: but if he does not purchase the chattel in market overt, and if it turns out that the chattel has been found by the person who professed to sell it, the purchaser will not obtain a title against the real owner. If it turns out that the chattel has been stolen by the person who professed to sell it, the purchaser will not obtain a title. If it turns out that the chattel has come into the hands of the person who professes to sell it by a de facto contract, that is to say, a contract which has purported to pass the property to him from the owner of the property, there the purchaser will obtain a good title, even although afterwards it should appear that there were circumstances connected with that contract, which would enable the original owner of the goods to reduce it, and to set it aside, because these circumstances so enabling the original owner of the goods, or of the chattel, to reduce the contract and to set it aside, will not be allowed to interfere with a title for valuable consideration obtained by some third party during the interval while the contract remained unreduced.'

NO CONTRACT/VOIDABLE CONTRACT

Ingram v Little

[1961] 1 QB 31, [1960] 3 All ER 332, [1960] 3 WLR 504, 104 Sol Jo 704, CA
The plaintiffs were the owners of a car which they advertised for sale. A swindler called on them and made them an offer which they were willing to accept, but on its appearing that he intended to pay by cheque the plaintiffs said that they would accept only cash. The swindler then said he was a Mr P G M Hutchinson of Stanstead Road, Caterham. Whilst the matter was being discussed, one of the plaintiffs went to the Post Office nearby and found that there was Mr P G M Hutchinson at the address mentioned. She returned and told the co-plaintiff and as a result the plaintiffs agreed to accept a cheque. The swindler took the car away in exchange for the cheque and sold it to the defendants. He was not P G M Hutchinson of Caterham and the cheque was dishonoured.
HELD: There was no contract for sale between the plaintiffs and the swindler and the property in the car had not passed to him. The plaintiffs were the offerors and the swindler was the offeree. In making their offer to sell the car not for cash but for a cheque the plaintiffs were under the belief that they were dealing with, and therefore making their offer to, the honest Mr P G M Hutchinson of Caterham. The swindler knew what was in the minds of the plaintiffs for he had put it there and he knew that their offer was intended for Mr P G M Hutchinson of Caterham and not for him. There was no offer which he (the swindler) could accept and therefore there was no contract.

Milford Mutual Facilities Ltd v HW Hidson Ltd

(1962) Guardian, 7 December
The defendants were motor dealers. A man came to them with a Ford car and asked to exchange it for an Austin which was in their showroom. He said he was R Ashworth of Cheadle. He produced a log book for the car in that name and a driving licence in the same name. He was allowed to take away the Austin and collected the log book of that car four days later. The defendants sold the Ford but it was later found to be a stolen car and the defendants had to reimburse the purchaser. Meanwhile the man had offered the Austin for sale to a Mr Wright. As the latter required hire-purchase facilities both he and the man (who was still representing himself to be R Ashworth of Cheadle) went in person to the office of the plaintiffs, a hire-purchase company. The log book of the Austin showed the defendants as owners and the man produced a receipt showing the exchange for the Ford. The plaintiffs then bought the Austin for £480, entering into a hire-purchase agreement with Wright. The defendants, having found that the Ford was stolen traced the Austin to Wright and repossessed themselves of it by driving it away from outside his house. In this action the plaintiffs claimed its return and damages for detinue and conversion. The defendants contended that the car was not the property of the plaintiffs as there had been no contract of sale: the plaintiffs had intended to contract with R Ashworth of Cheadle and not with the man

who had brought the car for sale. There was a real R Ashworth of Cheadle but he was entirely unconnected with the transactions.
HELD: The court was bound by *Ingram v Little* (above) which had to be applied to this case. When parties contracted in each others' presence there was a presumption that the offeror intended to contract with the person physically before him and it was a difficult presumption to rebut. The vital question was whether the persons contracted with the man or with the real Mr Ashworth. Did the physical presence in their offices preponderate over the personality of the real person who was fraudulently misrepresented? On the facts of this case they were contracting with the person present before them: not a man who represented himself to be Mr R Ashworth but a man who represented himself as owner of the car. There was accordingly a voidable, not a void, contract and the property passed. The plaintiffs were entitled to succeed.

Lewis v Averay

[1972] 1 QB 198, [1971] 3 All ER 907, [1971] 3 WLR 603, 115 Sol Jo 755, CA
The plaintiff advertised his car for sale. A man came to see it: he said he was Richard Green and led the plaintiff to believe he was a well-known film actor of that name. Eventually he said he would like to buy the car and proffered a cheque for the price. The plaintiff agreed to sell but was unwilling to let the man take the car until the cheque had been cleared. He asked if he had anything to prove he was Richard Green. The man produced a pass of admission to a film studio bearing his photograph and the name 'R A Green'. The plaintiff was satisfied and let the man take the car and log book in exchange for the cheque. On presentation the cheque was found to be from a stolen cheque book and was worthless. A day or two later the man, under the name of the plaintiff, sold the car to the defendant who bought it in good faith. The plaintiff, on discovering what had happened, sued the defendant for a return of the car and damages for its retention.
HELD: The plaintiff could not succeed. The facts were very similar to those in *Ingram v Little* (above) and *Phillips v Brooks* (p 913, below) but those two cases could not be reconciled with one another. The true principle is that when two parties have come to what appears to be a contract the fact that one party is mistaken as to the identity of the other does not mean that there is no contract, but merely that the contract is voidable and liable to be set aside provided it is done before a third party has in good faith acquired rights under it. The plaintiff had made a contract with the man who was before him: the misrepresentations as to his identity merely made the contract voidable and it had not been avoided when the defendant acquired the car.

Note—Megaw LJ said he found it 'difficult to understand the basis, either in logic or in practical considerations, of the test laid down by the majority of the court in *Ingram v Little*' by which the validity of the offer 'is made to depend on the view which some rogue should have formed . . . as to the state of mind of the opposite party . . . who does not know that he is dealing with a rogue'.

See also *Dennant v Skinner*, p 914, below.

Four Point Garage Ltd v Carter

[1985] 3 All ER 12, QBD
On 2 October 1984 the defendant agreed with a garage called Freeway to purchase a new Ford Escort XR3i. On 8 October he posted the contract sum to Freeway, who agreed to deliver the car to him on 10 October. Freeway did not have the car in stock, and ordered it from the plaintiffs, who sold it to Freeway but delivered it direct to the

defendant. The defendant was unaware that it was not Freeway who had delivered the car to him. The plaintiffs, for their part, were under the impression that Freeway were intending to lease the car to the defendant, not to sell it. On 13 October the plaintiffs discovered that Freeway were insolvent and going into liquidation. Soon afterwards, they took proceedings against the defendant for the return of the car, which was subject to a reservation of title (Romalpa) clause as between the plaintiffs and Freeway.

HELD: (1) The defendant could rely on s 25 of the Sale of Goods Act 1979 (see pp 906–907, above). There was no difference between a seller delivering the goods directly to the sub-purchaser, and the seller delivering the goods to the purchaser for on-sale to the sub-purchaser. In both circumstances the sub-purchaser received good title under s 25 of the Act.

(2) There was also an implied term in the contract between the plaintiff and Freeway that the car could be sub-sold to the defendant. The wording of the retention of title clause was sufficient to rebut this term. The fact that the plaintiff believed that he was delivering the car to the defendant for leasing purposes was irrelevant and the title to the car had validly passed to the defendant.

CONTRACT MUST BE DIS-AFFIRMED

Phillips v Brooks Ltd

[1919] 2 KB 243, 88 LJKB 953, 121 LT 249, 35 TLR 470, 24 Com Cas 263

If A, fraudulently assuming the name of a person of credit and stability, buys, in person, and obtains delivery of, goods from B, the property in the goods passes to A, and he can therefore give a good title thereto to a third party who, acting bona fide and without notice, has given value therefor, unless in the meantime B has taken steps to dis-affirm the contract with A.

Note—See *Lewis v Averay*, p 912, above and *Ingram v Little*, p 911, above.

REPUDIATION OF SALE BY CONTRACT

Car and Universal Finance Co Ltd v Caldwell

[1965] 1 QB 525, [1964] 1 All ER 290, [1964] 2 WLR 600, 108 Sol Jo 15, CA

On 12 January the defendant sold his car to a swindler Norris, accepting for it a cheque for £975. On the following day he presented the cheque to the bank and was told it was worthless. He at once went to the police so as to recover the car and telephoned the AA for the same purpose. On 20 January the police found the car in the possession of Motobella Ltd, who claimed to have bought it in good faith and to have sold it on 15 January to G & C Finance Corpn Ltd, a finance company. On 29 January Norris was arrested and pleaded guilty to obtaining the car by false pretences. On 13 August the car was transferred from G & C Finance to the plaintiffs, another finance company. After the defendant had obtained judgment against Motobella Ltd by default for the return of the car the plaintiffs claimed in this action that the title in the car was vested in them.

HELD: The question was whether G & C Finance obtained a good title to the car from Norris. The sale to Norris was voidable by the defendant: could he avoid it without communicating his rescission to Norris? Normally the rule is that an election to avoid a contract is not complete until the decision has been communicated to the other party, but in the circumstances of the present case where a fraudulent rogue would know that the defendant would want his car back as soon as he discovered the fraud it would not be right to hold that such a man could claim to have the rescission communicated to him. The position has to be viewed as between Norris and the defendant, who could not have made his position plainer. In circumstances such as the present case the innocent party may evince his intention to disaffirm the contract by overt means falling short of communication or repossession. The plaintiffs had not obtained any title to the car as against the defendant.

Auction

Dennant v Skinner and Collom

[1948] 2 KB 164, [1948] 2 All ER 29, [1948] LJR 1576 (Hallet J)
The plaintiff carried on business as the South London Motor Auctions and was a certified auctioneer. He held an auction sale of 35 vehicles and knocked down six vehicles to a man named King. When the first vehicle, a Commer van, was knocked down, the plaintiff asked the buyer his name. The man said it was King; that he was from King's Motors of Oxford and the son of the proprietor. This firm was known to the plaintiff as of high repute. A later vehicle was a Standard car. When King went to the plaintiff's office after the sale, plaintiff asked how he meant to pay, and King said he would like to pay by cheque. Plaintiff said he did not accept cheques from people he did not know. King was in possession of trade plates and had drivers there to drive away the vehicles. He repeated that he was the son of the proprietor of King's of Oxford and said he was running the Portsmouth branch and produced a cheque book showing by the counterfoils he had been paying large sums to other auctioneers. Plaintiff believed these representations and accepted the cheque on King signing a form certifying that the cheque would be met on presentation and agreeing that the ownership of the vehicles would not pass until the cheque was met. The cheque was dishonoured and King was convicted of obtaining the vehicles by false pretences and with intent to defraud.

King had meanwhile sold the Standard car to Collom, who sold it to Skinner. Plaintiff sued Skinner for possession of the car on the ground that the transaction was larceny by a trick. Skinner brought in Collom as third party.
HELD: The sale was complete on the fall of the hammer (Sale of Goods Act 1893, s 58(2)). The property passed on the sale (s 18, r 1). It was not a case of larceny by a trick but obtaining goods by false pretences. The distinction stated in *Archbold* is that in larceny the owner does not intend to part with the property but only the possession; in false pretences he intends to part with the property. Citing Lord Haldane in *Lake v Simmons* [1927] AC 487 at 501, HL adopting Fry J in *Smith v Wheatcroft* (1878) 9 Ch D 223, 47 LJ Ch 745, 39 LT 103, 27 WR 42 when consideration of the person is an element in the contract, error with regard to the person destroys consent and annuls the contract, but where it does not and the vendor is willing to sell to any person, the contract stands. Here the sale was irrespective of the identity of the buyer. Plaintiff did not sell to King because of the false statements. The car was sold before King's identity was mentioned. The case was indistinguishable from *Phillips v Brooks Ltd* (p 913, above). In *Lake v Simmons* the goods were handed to the swindler as bailee and the vendor did not intend to enter into any contract of

sale. In *Heap v Motorists Advisory Agency Ltd* [1923] 1 KB 577, 92 LJKB 553, 129 LT 146, 39 TLR 150, 67 Sol Jo 300, the plaintiff never intended to part with the property to the fraudulent person but merely the custody to sell to a person who was imaginary.

By parting with the property, the plaintiff lost his rights of lien or re-sale (the Sale of Goods Act 1893, s 39(1)(a) and (c), but the property had already passed. The signed agreement that the property would not pass could not affect the fact that the property had already passed. It did not divest King of the property and re-vest it in the plaintiff.

The defendant was acting reasonably in joining the third party.

Judgment for the defendant, and for the third party against the defendant with costs: defendant's costs against plaintiff to include all costs of third-party proceedings.

Note—See also *Lewis v Averay*, p 912, above. The Sale of Goods Act 1893, s 58(2) has been replaced in the same terms by the Sale of Goods Act 1979, s 57(2) and s 18 of the 1893 Act by s 18 of the 1979 Act. Section 39(1)(a) and (c) of the 1893 Act was repeated in s 39(1)(a) and (c) of the 1979 Act.

RH Willis & Son v British Car Auctions Ltd

[1978] 2 All ER 392, [1978] 1 WLR 438, 122 Sol Jo 62, [1978] RTR 244, 246 Estates Gazette 134, CA
Where goods are sold by the intervention of an auctioneer, under the hammer or as a result of a provisional bid, then if the seller has no title, the auctioneer is liable in conversion to the true owner.

Sale by intermediaries

Jerome v Bentley & Co

[1952] 2 All ER 114, [1952] WN 357, [1952] 2 TLR 58, 96 Sol Jo 463 (Donovan J)
Plaintiff handed to T a diamond ring on approval to try and sell the ring and if sold to pay the plaintiff £550, and if not sold within seven days to return it to the plaintiff. After the seven days T representing himself as owner, sold the ring to defendants. T shortly afterwards sent a cheque for £50 to the plaintiff, which was dishonoured. T was charged with larceny as a bailee and pleaded guilty and was convicted. Plaintiff sued defendants for damages for conversion.
HELD: At the time of sale T had no authority to deal with the ring at all. it was not a case of a servant as in *Farquharson v King* [1902] AC 325, HL but of a person without authority to deal with the thing except for safe custody (*Mercantile Bank of India v Central Bank of India* [1938] AC 287, [1938] 1 All ER 52, 107 LJPC 25, 158 LT 269, PC). T became a thief of the ring as in *R v Henderson* (1871) 23 LT 628, 35 JP 325, 11 Cox CC 593. There was no representation as agent with authority to sell. In *Commonwealth Trust v Akotey* [1926] AC 72, 94 LJPC 167, 134 LT 33, 41 TLR 641, PC, the owner sent the goods and the consignment note to L, and so had permitted L to be in possession of all the insignia of possession and apparent title, and L passed them on to the purchaser from L. The owner could not contend the title had not passed. In the dictum in *Lickbarrow v Mason* (1787), cited in *Akotey*'s case, that the loss falls on the person who has 'enabled' a third party to occasion the loss, 'enabled' means doing something by one of the innocent parties which misled the other.

Judgment for plaintiff for the value of the ring. *Akotey*'s case not followed.

Eastern Distributors Ltd v Goldring (Murphy, third party)

[1957] 2 QB 600, [1957] 2 All ER 525, [1957] 3 WLR 237,101 Sol Jo 553, CA
The owner of a motor van authorised a motor dealer to sell the van to a hire-purchase finance company, to obtain an agreement by the company to sell it to him on hire-purchase terms and to apply the proceeds of sale in paying the deposits on the van and on a car which he desired to purchase from the dealer. He signed in blank a proposal form and memorandum of hire-purchase agreement in respect of both vehicles and gave them to the dealer to complete. The dealer certified in the proposal form that the van was his (the dealer's) absolute property. The dealer sold the van to the plaintiffs, a hire-purchase finance company, who accepted the owner's proposal and sent him a counterpart of the agreement. The hire-purchase transaction in respect of the car was not implemented and the dealer told the owner that the whole transaction was cancelled. The owner afterwards sold the van, believing it to be his own property, to a third party who bought it in good faith and without knowledge of the dealer's action. The owner made no payments under the hire-purchase agreement to the plaintiffs, who terminated the agreement and claimed the van or its value from the third party. HELD: The plaintiffs were entitled to recover (1) The owner had clothed the dealer with apparent authority to sell and was precluded from denying authority within the Sale of Goods Act 1893, s 21(1); (2) although the agreement had not been 'made and signed by the hirer' as required by the Hire-Purchase Act 1938, s 2(2)(a), neither that section nor s 17 of that Act took away their rights against any person other than the hirer; (3) the judge assumed the owner to be the seller under s 25(1) of the 1893 Act and he had not remained in possession; the hire-purchase agreement was effective to change his possession as seller to possession as bailee.

Note—For sections of Sale of Goods Act see note above.

HIRE PURCHASE

'Sale' by hirer

North Central (or General) Wagon and Finance Co v Graham

[1950] 2 KB 7, [1950] 1 All ER 780, 66 (pt 1) TLR 707, CA
The plaintiffs, a hire-purchase company, let a motor car on hire purchase under an agreement which contained obligation on the hirer:
1 not to do anything prejudicially to affect the ownership or financial position of the owner;
2 not to attempt to sell or otherwise dispose of the car;
3 (a) if the hirer shall fail to pay any sum due or to observe or perform any stipulation on his part herein contained the owner may terminate the hiring; (b) if this hiring be terminated for any reason the owner may by written notice put an end to the hiring under any other agreement between the parties;
4 this agreement is only a contract of bailment.

The hirer instructed an auctioneer to sell the car, and the auctioneer sold it. Plaintiffs sued the auctioneer for damages for conversion.

Lewis J dismissed the action, being influenced by the absence of a clause that breach ipso facto put an end to the agreement. He held the plaintiffs were not entitled to possession at the time of sale.
HELD, ON APPEAL: It was essential for the plaintiffs to show that they were entitled at the time of the sale to immediate possession. The case was similar to *Jelks v Hayward*

[1905] 2 KB 460, 74 LJKB 717, 92 LT 692, 53 WR 686, except that the right to determine the hiring and take possession did not include the words 'without previous notice'. There could be no implied term requiring notice, because such notice was required in the case of other agreements. There is, apparently, no direct authority on the construction of the words 'may terminate the hiring', and it is a little startling that there should not be because it is the commonest form of expression in hire-purchase agreements. The plaintiffs could terminate the hiring without notice, and the moment a breach occurred the owner had the right to immediate possession. The plaintiffs therefore had the right to terminate the hiring at will the moment after the breach occurred. They therefore had an immediate right to possession and could sue the defendant in conversion.

The general principle of law is that a bailee who does something inconsistent with the terms of the contract, or any act or disposition which is wholly repugnant to or an absolute disclaimer of the holding as bailee, terminates the bailment and re-vests the bailor's right to possession. Here that general law does not apply because the contract makes special provision.

Appeal allowed.

United Dominion Trust (Commercial) Ltd v Parkway Motors

[1955] 2 All ER 557, [1955] 1 WLR 719, 99 Sol Jo 436 (McNair J)
On 8 October 1952, a hire-purchase company hired a van to Williams by an agreement which contained a condition that the hirer should keep the van in his possession and should not sell, offer for sale, assign or charge the van or the benefit of the agreement; a further condition provided that default in payment of an instalment or any breach or act which in the opinion bona fide formed of the hire-purchase company would jeopardise their rights, gave them the right by notice forthwith to terminate the agreement and retake possession; and a further clause after all payments had been made and provided the hirer had not committed any breach of agreement, the hirer had the option to purchase for 10s.

On 8 December 1953, the instalment was not paid. On 23 December 1953, Williams advertised the van for sale and the following day sold the van to Trotter for £410. Two days after this, Trotter sold the van to Parkway Motors for £410 10s 0d, Trotter undertaking to see that £96 the balance due under the agreement and the 10s option money, was paid to the hire-purchase company. Trotter's cheque to Williams was not met, and Williams on 28 December 1953, reported the position to the hire-purchase company and paid the instalment due on 8 December. On 4 January 1954, the hire-purchase company served Williams with a notice terminating the agreement. On the same day Parkway Motors tendered to the hire-purchase company by cheque, and on 12 January in cash, £96 10s the balance of hire and the 10s option money. The hire-purchase company refused to accept either the cheque or cash and sued for the return of the van.

HELD: Williams was prohibited from assigning and therefore unable to pass any rights. Parkway Motors had no rights to cut down the hire-purchase company's prima facie right to recover the van. The case of a pledge of goods is irrelevant. Earlier decisions differed because there was an assignable interest. Judgments for the hire-purchase company for the return of the van or £350 its value.

Note—The Hire-Purchase Act 1964 provides protection for private purchasers of motor vehicles which are subject to hire-purchase contracts. Part III of the Act (substituted by the Consumer Credit Act 1974 as from 19 May 1985) provides that where a hirer of a motor vehicle under a hire-purchase agreement disposes of that vehicle to a private purchaser who buys in good faith and without notice of the hire-purchase agreement the disposition shall have effect as if the title of the owner to the vehicle had been vested in the hirer immediately before that disposition, ie the purchaser gets a good title. Where a hirer disposes of the vehicle to a trade or finance purchaser who disposes of it to a private purchaser in good faith without notice the same result follows. Where the 'first private purchaser' takes the vehicle under a new hire-purchase agreement from the original purchaser in good faith and without notice of the original hire-purchase agreement he still gets a good title under the provisions of the agreement (eg when he has paid all the instalments) even though by that time he can no longer satisfy the requirement of taking in good faith without notice of the original agreement. The Act has effect notwithstanding anything in the Sale of Goods Act 1979, s 21 or the Factors Acts. It does not exonerate the hirer from any liability, civil or criminal, to which he would otherwise be subject nor does it protect any trade or finance purchaser who takes from the hirer or from another trade or finance purchaser who is not claiming under the 'first private purchaser's' title. The Act applies to dispositions made on or after 1 January 1965. For a detailed account of the provisions of the Act see *Halsbury's Laws of England* (4th edn) paras 121, 122, 268 and 269 and the extensive notes to those paragraphs.

A 'trade or finance purchaser' within the meaning of the Acts (s 29(2)) does not receive the protection of a 'private purchaser' under s 27 merely because in a particular transaction he buys a car for his own private use: *Stevenson v Beverley Bentinck Ltd* [1976] 2 All ER 606, [1976] 1 WLR 483, 120 Sol Jo 197, [1976] RTR 543, CA

Moorgate Mercantile Co Ltd v Finch

[1962] 1 QB 701, [1962] 2 All ER 467, [1962] 3 WLR 110, 106 Sol Jo 284, CA

The plaintiffs were a finance company who let a car on hire purchase to the first defendant. At a time when he was in arrear with payments under the agreement he lent the car to the second defendant at his request though without knowing for what purpose it was required. The second defendant loaded the car with uncustomed watches and was subsequently caught by Customs men with the watches in the car. As a result he was convicted and the car was forfeited to the Customs authorities under the relevant statutory provisions. The plaintiffs claimed damages for conversion of the car by the second defendant. The hire-purchase agreement contained the words 'in case of any and every breach of any term or condition hereof the owners shall forthwith without notice or demand become entitled immediately to recover possession of the vehicle'.

HELD: (1) The second defendant knew that forfeiture of the car was a natural and probable consequence of his conduct and there was a conversion of the car. (2) As the first defendant was in arrear with payments under the hire-purchase agreement this was a breach which entitled the plaintiffs to immediate possession (following *North Central Wagon & Finance Co v Graham*, above) and the second defendant was therefore liable to the plaintiffs for conversion of the vehicle.

Union Transport Finance v British Car Auctions Ltd

[1978] 2 All ER 385, 246 Estates Gazette 131, CA

Smith took a car on hire-purchase from the plaintiffs. The contract gave the plaintiffs the right at any time to declare the hiring terminated on breach of its terms or default in rental payments on notice given to the hirer at his last known address. Smith took the car to the defendant auctioneers without disclosing the hire-purchase contract and they sold it at auction to an innocent purchaser. The plaintiffs sued the defendants in conversion for damages. The defendants contended that the plaintiffs had no right to immediate possession of the car at the time of the sale, not having served notice, and could not sue in conversion. It was not disputed that for a bailor or lessor on hire purchase to sue in conversion he must show that he is entitled at the time of the sale to immediate possession of the goods.

HELD: The defendants could not succeed. At common law a bailor becomes entitled at once to bring the contract to an end and acquire the right to immediate possession if the bailee acts in a way which destroys the basis of the contract. The express term of the contract enabling the plaintiffs to terminate the hiring by notice did not oust the common law rule and deprive the plaintiffs of their rights at common law. Smith had torn up the contract of bailment by fraudulently selling the car through an auctioneer to an innocent third party. It would require very clear language to deprive the bailor of his common law rights in such circumstances and the language used in the present contract was nothing like strong enough. *North Central Wagon Co v Graham* (above) applied.

Car on hire purchase in part exchange

Robin and Rambler Coaches Ltd v Turner

[1947] 2 All ER 284 (Hilbery J)

B obtained a Hillman car on hire purchase from W, paying £200 deposit. He paid one instalment of £40 10s.

B sold the Hillman car to plaintiffs for £275 cash and a Jaguar car in part exchange.

B sold the Jaguar car to defendants for £525. Defendants sold it to F for £550.

W claimed the Hillman car from plaintiffs, and plaintiffs paid to W the balance due under the hire-purchase agreement, and costs, to obtain the title to the Hillman.

Plaintiffs claimed the Jaguar car from defendants.

HELD: The contract was voidable by the fraud of B but was not void; and was not avoided before the sale to defendants; defendants bought in good faith and the property in the Jaguar car passed to the defendants.

Finance company with no title

Warman v Southern Counties Car Finance Corpn

[1949] 2 KB 576, [1949] 1 All ER 711, [1949] LJR 1182, 93 Sol Jo 319 (Finnemore J)

In September 1947, a hirer entered into a hire-purchase agreement, paying £155 down and agreeing to pay £9 18s 'rent' each month. After paying the instalments the hirer was to have the option of purchasing the car for 1s. In January, February and March 1948, the hirer received letters from a company claiming that the car was their property, which he ignored, but did not inform the hire-purchase company of the claim. He made the final payment of rent in April 1948, and on the same day was served with a writ by the owner of the car. The hirer handed over the car to the true owners and claimed damages from the hire-purchase company.

HELD: The hirer was entitled to rely on the warranty of ownership, which became effective at the date of the agreement and not when the final payment was made. The plaintiff was entitled to recover. The hire-purchase company were not entitled to any counterclaim or set off for the use of the car.

Hirer's duty on termination of hire

Capital Finance Co Ltd v Bray

[1964] 1 All ER 603, [1946] 1 WLR 323, 108 Sol Jo 95, CA
The defendant hired a car from the plaintiffs under a hire-purchase agreement. He fell behind with his instalments and the plaintiffs repossessed themselves of the car by taking it from outside his house in the middle of the night. This was unlawful since the contract was one within the Hire-Purchase Act 1938 and the defendant had paid more than one-third of the hire-purchase price. Perhaps realising the error the plaintiffs returned the car on the following day. The defendant paid no further instalments though there was evidence that he made some use of the car. The plaintiffs wrote the defendants requiring him to return the car by delivering it to one of three specified addresses. The defendant did not do so: the plaintiffs then sued him for instalments due and for damages in detinue for the period subsequent to their letter demanding a return of the car.
HELD: (1) The hire-purchase agreement was determined by the illegal retaking of the car and was not revived by returning it, since this was merely an implied offer to revive it which the defendant had not accepted. (2) The defendant's failure to return the car, following the plaintiff's requiring him to deliver it to one of the specified addresses, did not give them any cause of action in detinue. He was not bound to take the car to them but only to let them have it if they came for it. No one, except by contract, is under a duty to take a chattel to its owner. In this case the contract, that is, the hire-purchase agreement, was already at an end.

HP Information Limited

Moorgate Mercantile Co Ltd v Twitchings

[1977] AC 890, [1976] 2 All ER 641, [1976] 3 WLR 66, 120 Sol Jo 470, HL
In about 1938 a number of finance companies set up an organisation called HP Information Ltd to obtain and register details of hire-purchase contracts and supply it to dealers and finance houses who were concerned to know whether a vehicle was the subject matter of a hire-purchase agreement. By 1971 98% of all such agreements were registered with HPI. The plaintiff company was a member and the defendant, a motor dealer, was an associate member. The plaintiffs let a vehicle on hire purchase to McLorg but negligently failed to register the transaction with HPI. McLorg offered the car for sale to the defendant who inquired of HPI whether there was any hire-purchase agreement and was told that no hire-purchase agreement was registered in relation to that car. The defendant then bought the car from McLorg and resold it. When the plaintiffs heard of it they sued the defendant for damages for conversion.
HELD: They were entitled to succeed. The plaintiffs were not estopped from claiming title to the car by reason of their failure to register the agreement because (1) the reply given by HPI to the defendant's inquiry was not a representation that no hire-purchase agreement existed but only that no such agreement had been communicated to them. Moreover, their reply was not made as agents for the plaintiffs. (2) There was no legal duty of care owed by the plaintiffs to the defendant to register the agreement with HPI and estoppel by negligence could not arise in the absence of a duty of care.

Note—See also *Debs v Sibec Developments Ltd* [1990] RTR 91.

Loan on security

Polsky v S and A Services Ltd

[1951] 1 All ER 185 (Lord Goddard CJ): appeal dismissed [1951] 1 All ER 1062n, [1951] WN 256, 95 Sol Jo 414, CA
Plaintiff purchased a motor car from a dealer for £895 and paid by cheque. Next day, to obtain £400 to pay into his bank to meet the cheque, he arranged with defendants, a hire-purchase company, to advance £400. By the documents defendants purported to buy from plaintiff the car and let it to him on hire purchase. The value of the car was stated to be £895; that an initial payment of £495 had been made, leaving £400, plus £50 for charges, as 'balance of hire' payable by instalments. Plaintiff signed a receipt saying 'Received cheque £400 payment for the car', and a document that he clearly understood he was selling the car to defendants.
HELD: Not a genuine sale and re-hire, but a loan of £400 on the security of the car and void for non-registration as a bill of sale.

R v Deller

(1952) 36 Cr App Rep 184, CCA
Defendant entered into a transaction with a hire-purchase company which purported to buy the defendant's car and to let the car back to him on hire-purchase terms. The documents were not registered as a bill of sale. Before he had paid all the instalments, he exchanged the car with C for the car of C, representing to C that he, the defendant, was the owner of the first car free from incumbrances and that there was no money owing on it. He was prosecuted for obtaining the car of C by false pretences.
HELD: It is a question of fact for the jury whether it was a genuine sale and re-hiring or a transaction of loan on the security of the car. If the latter, and void for non-registration as a bill of sale, the first car remained the property of the defendant and he was not guilty of any false pretence. *Polsky*'s case followed.

REGISTRATION DOCUMENT (LOG BOOK)

Not a document of title

Joblin v Watkins and Roseveare (Motors) Ltd

[1949] 1 All ER 47, 64 TLR 464 (Croom-Johnson J)
Plaintiff entered into an agreement on 4 November 1945, with one Smith whereby plaintiff purchased from Smith a second-hand motor car for £275 with option to Smith to re-purchase for £300 on or before 6 December 1945. Smith handed plaintiff the registration book of the car and a cheque post-dated to 6 December 1945, for £300. The registration book showed one Adams as the last owner. The plaintiff never saw the car and never took delivery. Earlier in 1945 the defendants had employed Smith as an agent to buy cars in their name, but had ceased to do so in April 1945. The car had been bought by defendants from Adams but remained in Adams' possession for repairs for defendants. The cheque was dishonoured on presentation, and plaintiff was unable to obtain the money or the car from Smith. He sued defendants alleging Smith was a mercantile agent of defendants in possession of the document of title to goods under the Factors Act 1889, s 2(1).

By s 1(4) document of title includes any document authorising or purporting to authorise the possessor of the document to transfer the goods.

The Road Vehicles (Registration and Licensing) Regulations 1949, reg 9(1) (now reg 12(1) of the 1971 Regulations), provides that on sale of a car the then owner shall deliver the registration book to the new owner and forthwith notify the change to the authority.
HELD: The true transaction was a loan; it was not a disposition under the 1889 Act.
OBITER: (1) Smith was not a mercantile agent. (2) The registration book was not a document of title. The primary object was to show who was liable to pay the tax. It might indicate the right of the seller to be dealing with the vehicle, when the licence fell due, and the position generally, and that it was duly registered. It showed Adams as the owner.

Bishopsgate Motor Finance Corpn Ltd v Transport Brakes Ltd

[1949] 1 KB 322, [1949] 1 All ER 37, [1949] LJR 741, 65 TLR 66, 93 Sol Jo 71, CA
Per Denning LJ: Whilst the log book was not a document of title, it was the best evidence of title and a transfer was open to suspicion if the log book was not handed over. If not produced, or containing the wrong name, or if obviously tampered with, the buyer was put on enquiry, and purchased at his own risk. The plaintiffs here did not keep the log book in their own hands or in their own name. They were a finance company who allowed the hirer to have the car and take the log book in his own name. By reason of that fact, he was able to dispose of the car to an innocent purchaser.

Note—Also noted at p 908, above, 'Market overt'.

These observations do not seem to have regard to the Road Traffic Act 1930, s 121, which provides that 'owner' in relation to a vehicle which is the subject of a hire agreement or a hire-purchase agreement, means the person in possession of the vehicle under that agreement. This section is now replaced by the Road Traffic Act 1988, s 192, in which 'owner' is defined in the same terms. The vehicle registration document contains a warning notice: 'The Registered Keeper is not necessarily the legal owner'.

Car/car and log book

Bentworth Finance Ltd v Lubert

[1968] 1 QB 680, [1967] 2 All ER 810, [1967] 3 WLR 378, 111 Sol Jo 272, CA
The defendant signed a hire-purchase agreement with the plaintiffs, a finance company for a car. The car was delivered to her house but not a log book. She did not use the car, not being able to tax it, and did not pay any instalments. The plaintiffs took possession of the car and sued for arrears of instalments.
HELD: There was an implied condition that there should be a log book and as no log book had been supplied the contract of hire purchase had never come into effect and the plaintiffs could not sue on it.

Per Lord Denning MR: It is the common understanding of people that, if a car is bought or is taken on hire purchase, the log book will be provided. There is a great difference between the price of a car *with* the log book and the price of a car *without* the log book. The absence of it gives rise to the suspicion that the seller has a doubtful title. In short, the log book, though not a document of title, is very good evidence of title.

Owner parting with log book

Central Newbury Car Auction Ltd v Unity Finance Ltd

[1957] 1 QB 371, [1956] 3 All ER 905, [1956] 3 WLR 1068, 100 Sol Jo 927, CA
In July 1947, a new car was registered with the index number CFX805 and a registration book issued. In October 1948, a change of ownership was registered which continued until 23 January 1955, when the car was bought by one Ashley and registered in his name but he did not sign the book. In September 1955, the car was sold at an auction to the plaintiffs, motor dealers, who did not register as owners. On 4 November 1955, a man giving the name of Cullis agreed with plaintiffs to take the car on hire purchase and left a Hillman car in part purchase. Cullis signed the forms for a hire-purchase agreement giving a fictitious address and a fictitious name and address as his employers. Plaintiffs recommended Cullis to the hire-purchase company as a suitable and responsible person. Without waiting for the completion of the hire-purchase agreement, plaintiffs allowed Cullis to take the car and the registration book. The next day the finance company declined the proposed agreement because of these fictitious statements. Plaintiffs then made inquiries about the Hillman car and found it was on hire purchase and paid £100 to the finance company concerned to validate their title. On 7 November 1955, a man who was probably Cullis but gave the name of Ashley, the name in the book, sold the Morris car to dealers in a distant town for £200, and these dealers sold it to the first defendant. Plaintiffs sued both defendants for damages for conversion. The county court judge dismissed the action, holding that the plaintiffs were estopped by conduct. The plaintiffs appealed.

HELD, per Hodson LJ: It was a case of larceny by a trick by Cullis. The plaintiffs were not estopped by their negligent conduct from claiming as true owners. The case fell to be determined, not on a consideration of negligence, but on what is the nature of the representation made by the delivery of the registration book. The book itself is not a document of title: its terms negative ownership.

Per Morris LJ: By parting with the car and registration book the plaintiffs did not give an authority to sell. The registration book does not prove legal ownership. It proclaims a clear warning and intimation that it does not. Plaintiffs made the mistake of being deceived by a plausible trickster but the case does not depend on their carelessness in parting with the car and the book, but on the effect of their so acting. The plaintiffs are not estopped by their negligent conduct.

Appeal allowed by a majority; judgment against both defendants for damages agreed at £240.

Note—'Larceny': see Theft Act 1968, p 908, above.

J Sargent (Garages) Ltd v Motor Auctions (West Bromwich) Ltd

[1977] RTR 121, CA
The plaintiffs, father and son, were car dealers. They bought a Jaguar E-type car for eventual resale but, pending sale, the son used it himself. A business acquaintance, Spencer, had become friendly with the plaintiffs. He owned and ran a business for providing special registration numbers. He suggested that he might get a special number for the car: the son agreed and gave him the log book for that purpose. A few days later, having sold a car of his own to the plaintiffs, Spencer asked to borrow the Jaguar for a couple of days. The plaintiffs rather reluctantly agreed. Spencer took the car and did not return. He took it a few days later to the first defendants who were

auctioneers and it was sold at auction to the second defendant. The plaintiffs sued for damages for conversion.
HELD: The plaintiffs were not estopped from denying Spencer's authority to sell by their conduct in allowing Spencer to have both the car and log book. *Central Newbury Car Auctions Ltd v Unity Finance* (p 923, above) was still good law. The log book was not a document of title. The plaintiffs, on the facts, had not been negligent but even if they had it would not have created an estoppel because they owed no duty of care to the general public.

Owner giving possession of log book

Du Jardin v Beadman Bros Ltd

[1952] 2 QB 712, [1952] 2 All ER 160, [1952] 1 TLR 1601, 96 Sol Jo 414 (Sellers J)
On 12 May 1951, G obtained possession from the defendants of a Standard car on payment of £10 and a cheque for £700 leaving a Hillman car as security for the cheque, stating he wanted to take the car right away to show to a prospective buyer. Defendants handed him the registration book and receipt. Shortly afterwards, G or another man, in the absence of defendants, drove the Hillman car away. On 15 May 1951, plaintiff purchased the Standard car from G. The cheque for £700 was worthless and subsequently the police took possession of the Standard car from the plaintiff. G was convicted of obtaining the car by false pretences, and the Standard car returned to the defendants.
HELD: Though G had obtained possession of the car by larceny by a trick, he had possession with consent. The fact that there was only an agreement for sale and not a sale was immaterial. *Pearson*'s case followed: *Lake*'s case not followed. There was no inconsistency in *Pearson*'s case. The question was whether possession was with consent and this depended on the knowledge of the owner or seller. The defendants consented to possession. Order for car to be returned to plaintiff.

Note—See also *Pearson v Rose & Young Ltd* (p 903, above), *George v Revis* (p 905, above), *Stadium Finance Ltd v Robbins* (p 904, above).

Index